LEARNING FROM FAILURE

Operations Profile: Lessons Learned stories spark classroom discussions of companies that have made significant supply chain or operations mistakes and had to deal with the negative consequences of these decisions.

OPERATIONS PROFILE: LESSONS LEARNED
Apple Puts All Its Eggs in One (Very Expensive) Basket

The 2014 release of the Apple iPhone 6 was, as are all Apple Inc.'s (Cupertino, CA) product release announcements, one that was greatly anticipated. In addition to its desire to maintain a technological lead in the highly competitive smartphone industry, Apple knows that product release announcements have a direct impact on its stock price and the valuation of the corporation. As a result, nothing is left to chance. All technology is carefully verified, products must be available on the announced delivery date, and all suppliers have been certified and the quality of their materials checked and rechecked.

It came as a huge surprise to Apple's executives when GT Advanced Technologies (Merrimack, NH), the chief supplier of one of the iPhone's most technologically advanced features, called them to say that it was going out of business. GT was Apple's sole supplier of the super-hard sapphire smartphone screen that Apple was counting on to give them a notable advantage over their chief competitors, such as Samsung (Ridgefield Park, NJ). The sapphire screen, a crystalized form of aluminum oxide, was scratch resistant and could withstand shocks and accidental drops better than the standard Gorilla Glass (Corning Inc., Corning, NY) used by other phone makers. Sapphire screens are expensive—more than five times the cost of regular glass. Apple was so set on this technology that it had just entered a joint venture with GT to build a US$1 billion manufacturing plant in Arizona to provide 30 times as many sapphire screens as any other plant in the world.

Problems with quality control plagued the GT manufacturing process from the beginning. GT had never mass-produced sapphire glass, and early test batches were flawed and unusable. Meanwhile, GT had hired workers too quickly, and hundreds of them ended up cleaning floors or sitting around and waiting while the company got [...] any's executives blamed [...] had turned them into a [...] and costs under Apple's

Cole Bennetts/Getty Images News/Getty Images

restrictive contracts. Apple, in turn, put the blame squarely on GT's management, arguing that they over-promised on their ability to supply the new iPhone's screen when they were still working out the flaws in their production systems and were still developing the huge furnaces needed to produce sapphire glass. Meanwhile, the quality of the product failed to improve as GT got further and further behind on its commitments for quality and delivery schedules. Apple was forced to offer GT more than US$100 million in loans to keep it in business throughout these development problems. Finally, GT company officials realized they would not be able to honor their supplier commitments to Apple and in August 2014 sought bankruptcy protection.

Apple's only logical response to this disaster has been to use the standard glass screen for the iPhone release. Apple continues to investigate the possibility of sapphire glass for future model releases, but it has learned a hard lesson about using a sole-source supplier for such a critical product.[15]

OPERATIONS PROFILE: Zara: Bringing Speed to Fashion Through Supply Chain Management

"Fashion doesn't sleep." Miss a new trend or fail to capitalize on an emerging opportunity in the fast-paced, frenetic fashion industry, and it is usually gone for good. As a result, the fashion industry and its retailers spend thousands of hours studying the latest styles and trying to anticipate hot new trends. The Spanish firm Zara has taken a bold new approach to fashion by pioneering an innovative technique for fashion retailing through the clever design of its supply chain. On average, it takes Zara three weeks to spot, design, manufacture, and ship one of the 300,000 different pieces of clothing it sells to stores each year. In doing so, Zara can beat the high-end fashion houses to the market with similar designs, made from cheaper materials, and costing much less than haute couture. A new PRADA (PRADA Group, Milan, Italy) handbag costs US$500, but Zara sells the same design for US$109.

Zara has initiated Z-days at its stores, which take place twice a month, when new shipments of styles are delivered to the shops. The promotion attracts shoppers who know that if they hesitate, the style will be gone. Zara thrives on creating immediate but only temporary buzz for any of its fashions. Unlike other retailers, Zara is not concerned about products being out of stock. Instead, they count on shoppers being attracted by styles in limited supply. Speed to market, rapid turnaround, and the equally rapid introduction of new styles keep Zara store shoppers motivated to return constantly just to find out what's new.

The secret to Zara's success is a well-developed supply chain that includes the firm's own retail stores, distribution centers, a design and manufacturing center, and textile-milling factories. Thus, the retailer does not have to depend on any other firm in the chain, allowing the company to move quickly. A second advantage Zara has is that, because it controls the entire supply chain, it can make limited runs of clothing and accessories. That is, the company does not depend on another manufacturer that will insist on producing large, lengthy runs to maximize efficiency. Zara can spot a fashion trend in one region or country and create items for just that opportunity without having to inundate all its regions with similar designs.

Zara is able to develop, change, or drop clothing styles in a matter of days; in fact, in time for the next Z-day at its stores. The firm also makes it easy on its retailers near the end of the chain because Zara presses, wraps, and tags all clothing, even hanging it on hangers, at their distribution centers. Retail shops only have to open the boxes and transfer the goods directly to their shelves and displays, with no delays in getting the goods in front of customers. By paying careful attention to supply chain management, Zara has managed to stay ahead in the fashion industry and create a unique niche for itself.[14]

WORKPLACE EXPOSURE

Operation Profiles in every chapter demonstrate key concepts to students by aligning success stories of operations and supply chain management with corresponding concepts in the chapter.

D0151256

INSTRUCTORS: WE MAKE IT EASY FOR YOU TO BRING YOUR CLASSROOM TO LIFE!

The book is just the beginning! A robust suite of online resources is available with this text to help bring operations management to life for your students and make your job easier.

SAGE PREMIUM VIDEO:

SAGE Premium Video is assignable, tied to learning objectives, and produced exclusively for this text to bring concepts to life and appeal to different learning styles, featuring:

- **Corresponding multimedia assessment options** that automatically feed to your gradebook

- **Engaging video case studies** that feature exclusive interviews at companies including Rolls Royce and the Rockefeller Gastropub that highlight how effective operations management can lead to a firm's success

- **Animated problem-solving videos** that show students step by step how to use equations in the text to solve problems

$SAGE coursepacks

OUR CONTENT TAILORED TO YOUR LMS

SAGE coursepacks makes it easy to import our quality instructor and student resource content into your school's learning management system (LMS). Intuitive and simple to use, SAGE coursepacks allows you to customize course content to meet your students' needs.

SAGE coursepacks include

- Intuitive, simple format that makes it easy to integrate the material into your course with minimal effort

- Test banks, pre-tests, and post-tests built on AACSB standards, Bloom's taxonomy, and chapter learning objectives

- Additional homework problems that are autograded and feed to your gradebook

- Assignable SAGE Premium Video (available via the Interactive eBook, linked through SAGE coursepacks)

- Multimedia assessment

- Additional video and multimedia resources

- A comprehensive Media Guide

- PowerPoint slides

- Lecture notes

- Case notes

- A solutions manual for problems in the book

- Sample answers to questions in the text

- Excel® templates for formulas

- Suggested class activities

- Sample course syllabi

- Integrated links to the Interactive eBook

- Tables and figures from the book

ONLINE SIMULATIONS

Your students can practice what they learn through a fun, hands-on simulation. Select chapters of the book include interactive assignments that ask students to manage **Littlefield Labs'** daily operations to test their understanding of operations and supply chain concepts. You have the flexibility to make the simulation experience as short as a one-hour assignment for use in class or as homework, or as involved as a two-week-long, out-of-class, small-group project. Instructor resources are available at **edge.sagepub.com/venkataraman**.

Contact your SAGE sales rep for a demo!

Demonstrate your understanding of **demand management** at Littlefield Labs.

Littlefield Laboratories is a highly automated, state-of-the-art blood testing facility for clinics and hospitals. The lab will operate 24 hours a day for a total of 210 days. You're asked to step in as the operations manager on Day 30, and are tasked with managing the lab's demand by setting prices and by limiting the number of jobs allowed in the lab at one time. You are also tasked with managing the lab's capacity to meet demand. Based on historic data you must manage demand and capacity to maximize the lab's profits.

Compete against your classmates to prove your understanding of the chapter concepts:

- LO 12-1: Explain the importance of demand management for organizations, and identify factors that affect it.

- LO 12-2: Describe the challenges of global demand management and the strategies that can be used to address them.

- LO 12-3: Identify the unique nature of service demand management, and discuss the risks from excess and insufficient capacity.

The team with the most cash in hand at the end of the 210-day time frame wins!

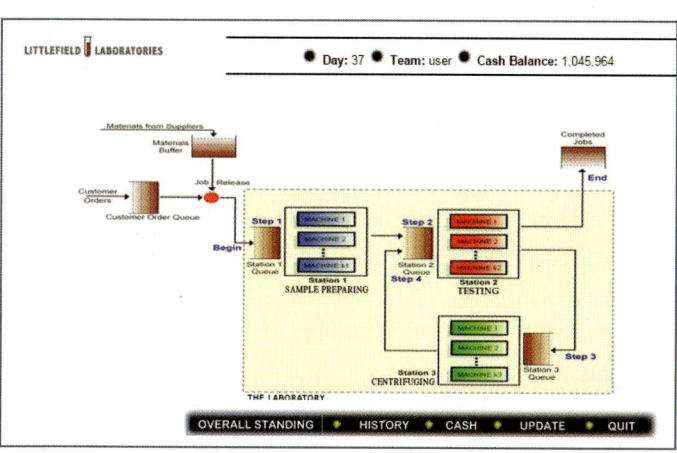

SAGE GIVES YOU OPTIONS

To make it even easier to integrate this dynamic online content, consider adopting the **Interactive eBook!** The **IEB** includes interactive icons that link to multimedia resources and notetaking tools. Use the following ISBN to give your students the print book and accompanying Interactive eBook: **978-1-5063-5677-8.**

 video resources

 example videos

 audio resources

 web content

Order the loose-leaf version of this text and save! **ISBN 978-1-5063-7763-6**

SAGE PUBLISHING: OUR STORY

We believe in creating fresh, innovative content to help you prepare your students to compete in the modern business world and be the global leaders of tomorrow. Founded in 1965, SAGE continues to make research accessible and remains focused on fostering **strategic and analytical thinking**.

- By partnering with **top business authors** with just the right balance of research, teaching, and industry experience, we bring you the most current and applied content.

- As a **student-friendly publisher**, we keep our prices affordable and provide multiple formats of our textbooks so your students can choose the option that works best for them.

- We are majority-owned by our founder who has ensured we will remain permanently **independent** and fiercely committed to publishing the highest-quality resources for you and your students.

STUDENTS: GET A BETTER GRADE IN THIS COURSE!

Pssst, want to know the secret to getting a better grade in this class? Use the learning and study tools that accompany this book! Access your instructor's online course site and visit **edge.sagepub.com/ venkataraman** for open access to these great resources, designed just for you.

- **Learning objectives and chapter outlines** for each chapter make it clear what topics to focus on when studying.

- **Online Excel® templates** are included to help you with assignments.

- **Practice quizzes and digital flashcards** for each chapter help you do better on the test!

- **Additional web resources** like videos and articles show how real companies manage their operations.

To my loving wife, Uma, for her patience and unwavering support without which this project would not have been possible; to my daughters, Vidhya and Aruna, for the joy they bring to my life; to my sister and brother-in-law, Radha and Jambunathan, for their encouragement in every venture of my life; and finally, to my late parents, Rajam and Ramanathan, for their selfless love and dedication to the well-being and success of their children.

–Ray

For Mary Beth, Emily, Josh, Adrian (AJ), and Joe, whose presence in my life continually reminds me that family is what counts.

–Jeff

OPERATIONS MANAGEMENT

Managing Global Supply Chains

RAY R. VENKATARAMAN
Penn State Erie, The Behrend College

JEFFREY K. PINTO
Penn State Erie, The Behrend College

Los Angeles | London | New Delhi
Singapore | Washington DC | Melbourne

FOR INFORMATION:

SAGE Publications, Inc.
2455 Teller Road
Thousand Oaks, California 91320
E-mail: order@sagepub.com

SAGE Publications Ltd.
1 Oliver's Yard
55 City Road
London EC1Y 1SP
United Kingdom

SAGE Publications India Pvt. Ltd.
B 1/I 1 Mohan Cooperative Industrial Area
Mathura Road, New Delhi 110 044
India

SAGE Publications Asia-Pacific Pte. Ltd.
3 Church Street
#10-04 Samsung Hub
Singapore 049483

Acquisitions Editor: Maggie Stanley
Development Editor: Abbie Rickard
eLearning Editor: Katie Ancheta
Editorial Assistant: Neda Dallal
Production Editor: David C. Felts
Copy Editor: Sheree Van Vreede
Typesetter: C&M Digitals (P) Ltd.
Proofreaders: Lawrence W. Baker,
        Sally Jaskold, Liann Lech,
        Alison Syring
Indexer: Naomi Linzer
Cover Designer: Scott Van Atta
Marketing Manager: Ashlee Blunk

Copyright © 2018 by SAGE Publications, Inc.

Printed in Canada

Library of Congress Cataloging-in-Publication Data

Names: Venkataraman, Ray R., author. | Pinto, Jeffrey K., author.

Title: Operations management : managing global supply chains / Ray R. Venkataraman, Penn State University, Erie, USA, Jeffrey K. Pinto, Penn State University, Erie, USA.

Description: First Edition. | Thousand Oaks : SAGE Publications, 2018. | Includes bibliographical references and index.

Identifiers: LCCN 2016041356 | ISBN 978-1-5063-0293-5 (hardcover : alk. paper)

Subjects: LCSH: Business logistics. | Project management.

Classification: LCC HD38.5 .V46 2017 | DDC 658.5—dc23 LC record available at https://lccn.loc.gov/2016041356

This book is printed on acid-free paper.

17 18 19 20 21 10 9 8 7 6 5 4 3 2 1

BRIEF CONTENTS

PART V: OPERATIONAL DECISIONS

PART VI: QUANTITATIVE MODULES

DETAILED CONTENTS

PART V: OPERATIONAL DECISIONS

Chapter 18: Master Scheduling and Material Requirements Planning, 640

Chapter 18 Supplement: Capacity Requirements Planning, MRP II, ERP, and DRP, 684

Module D: Simulation, 840

Module E: Learning Curves, 862

Module F: Decision-Making Tools, 878

Operations and supply chain management are among the most critical components of modern organizations. Effectively managing complex and often far-flung supply chains, coordinating vendor and customer relationships, and developing supply chain and operations strategies are the hallmarks of successful for-profit and non-profit organizations worldwide. Whether organizations operate in service or manufacturing settings, they must actively utilize the myriad opportunities and challenges their supply chain strategies identify. In modern business enterprises, operations and supply chain management integrate directly into the broader context of organizational activities, and the current global economy dictates that companies take an international perspective on these topics. Marketing, new product or service development, and retail strategies all directly depend on a firm's ability to successfully manage both its operations and supply chain activities in efficient and effective ways. Decisions about opening new facilities in foreign countries and finding global sources for supplies are elements in operations and supply chain management that directly contribute to an organization's bottom line. In short, operations and supply chains are not issues that can be addressed—or taught—separately from each other. They must be combined into a fully integrated package, bringing attention to both concepts simultaneously from a global perspective. Our motivation is to write a textbook that adopts a joint supply chain/operations focus for each chapter, highlighting how these concepts must integrate for companies to be successful in the global marketplace.

Approach

At one time, the primary focus of the operations function was to streamline costs and improve internal efficiency. As we have noted here, through the joint pressures of global competition and the need to manage supply chains, a broadening of our understanding of the meaning of "operations," along with the requirement for ethical and sustainable practices, the operations and supply discipline in many ways bears a faint resemblance to the manner in which previous generations of business students learned and practiced this functional discipline. Modern operations and supply chain management is an exciting career opportunity that rewards creativity, technical mastery, and the desire to think globally. This textbook supports and represents the broader—and ultimately, we believe, a far more interesting—perspective, recognizing several critical and simultaneously occurring elements: supply chain management, global operations, sustainability and business ethics, and a focus on the service industry.

Supply Chain Management

Operations managers must recognize the inextricable links to the larger supply chain. Looking at the internal operations of the organization, in either service or production settings, is one important but limited perspective that successful firms must address. Today, effective organizations are characterized by their outward-looking focus, linking internal operations to external suppliers, customers, and delivery systems. Firms that master the management of their supply chains tend to become leaders in their respective industries.

Global Operations

The business setting we operate within is truly world-wide; an international focus is not a distraction but a necessity when considering how best to manage operations and supply chains. As its starting point, this text takes this global perspective. Examples used throughout the text employ international settings, showing the ways in which manufacturing or strategic decisions taken in China, for example, have far-reaching implications for economic and commercial outcomes in the European Union or North America.

Sustainability and Business Ethics

Because we live in a world defined by scarce resources, operations managers must take a sustainability perspective when identifying and exploiting resources, raw materials, and methods for transporting and disposing of goods. This text deliberately addresses sustainability within each chapter, showing that sustainable operations and supply chain practices are not only attainable but critical and often profitable practices for organizations to undertake. In tandem with the focus on sustainability, an additional point of emphasis in this text is the use of a business ethics mindset. It is beneficial to recognize that many operations and supply chain challenges also carry ethical considerations with them. Thus, while we advocate for better operations and supply chain management techniques throughout this text, we also lay the foundation for students to recognize that in managing operation and global supply chains, it is possible to "do well by doing good." Operations and supply chain management offers a number of critical lessons for businesses that are adopting sustainable practices. We have included these important issues within every chapter and have added some cases and critical thinking exercises focusing on sustainability and ethical business practices. Our goal is to highlight the ways in which global operations and supply chain management challenges must be considered within the broader context of managing for sustainable and ethical standards.

The Service Industry

It is critical to recognize that the business environment we live in today is characterized by an explosion in service firms; in fact, service industries continue to out-pace more traditional manufacturing in the number of new start-ups, revenue generated, and jobs created. As a result, this text deliberately adopts a joint focus of manufacturing and service operations throughout the chapters. We demonstrate the application of important techniques and methods for production organizations while also spotlighting the manner in which these methods can be employed in service settings, making this text more relevant to the job environment our readers will enter.

This text takes a holistic, integrated approach to managing operations and supply chains, exploring both technical and managerial challenges. It not only emphasizes specific operations methods and current practices, focusing on managing the wide variety of challenges operations professionals face, but throughout, we emphasize the strategic implications of many of these activities on their companies' supply chains, showing that supply chain and operations decisions have important implications for wider organization success.

Organization of the Book

This textbook is organized to address the subject matter of operations management from a global supply chain perspective. The book provides treatment of operations and supply chain management in a hierarchical framework of strategic, integrative and tactical, and operational decisions. The book is organized into five major sections:

- **Part I: Introduction** provides an overview of the field of operations management in a supply chain framework and its strategic importance to businesses in both the manufacturing and service sectors.
- **Part II: Strategic Decisions** discusses the strategic operations and supply chain decisions that guide a company's subsequent activities in its operations and supply chain. This section examines strategic concepts such as product and service design, quality, supply chain design, process design, and layout planning.
- **Part III: Integrative Decisions** deals with integrative decisions such as supplier management, logistics management, and demand management and forecasting that cut across strategic, tactical, and operational decision levels.
- **Part IV: Tactical Decisions** addresses the important tactical planning decisions such as lean operations and supply chains, sales and operations planning, and inventory mangement.
- **Part V: Operational Decisions** examines key operational decision topics such as master scheduling, material and capacity requirements planning, and scheduling.
- **Part VI: Quantitative Modules** with the vast and varied audience of operations management instructors in mind, we deliberately separate the majority of the quantitative material from the "managerial" or theoretical topics associated with each of these chapters into chapter supplements and end-of-book modules. This allows instructors the flexibility to decide which chapters and topics they would prefer to treat from a broader perspective and which they require their students to delve into in a more quantitative manner. Moreover, within the quantitative chapters and supplements themselves, we offer a comprehensive treatment of this material, allowing instructors to decide which of the various models and methods they choose to apply to the subject at hand. We have found that from a pedagogical perspective, separating the theory from the more in-depth quantitative solutions allows faculty to teach this material in ways that can be best tailored to their audience, as well as their own comfort level.

Features
In-Chapter Features

OPERATIONS PROFILE

This textbook employs a managerial, business-oriented approach to the management of operations and supply chains. To demonstrate these concepts in real-world settings, we have integrated *Operations Profiles* into the text. Each chapter contains one or more of these features to highlight current examples of operations and/or supply chain management in action. Some reflect on significant achievements; others detail important examples of operations challenges. Because they cover service operations, manufacturing, successes, and failures, there will be at least one profile per chapter that is meaningful to the class's focus. These stories of success and failure align with the chapters to which they are attached. For example, as we study supplier management in Chapter 10, it is useful to consider the tragic implications of poor supervision and corruption that contribute to the incidence of factory fires in third world countries like Bangladesh.

OPERATIONS MANAGEMENT: LESSONS LEARNED

A unique feature of this text is the inclusion of a feature box titled "Operations Management: Lessons Learned." The purpose of this feature is to highlight companies that have made significant supply chain or operations mistakes and, as a result are discovering the negative consequences of these decisions. One of the benefits of these examples is to help students understand the critical cause-and-effect relationships between decisions made (or not made) and subsequent problems resulting from these choices. These boxes are placed within the chapters to coincide with important topics and can serve as an excellent source of in-class discussion or as a means to get students to explore the topics in more detail.

EXAMPLES WITH MS EXCEL®

An additional feature of the text is the inclusion within several chapters of sample problems and activities that require students to generate MS Excel output files. Excel is a very useful device for solving a variety of operations problems and we deliberately used it throughout the text to highlight its usefulness. It is the purpose of this text to not fully develop these skills but rather to plant the seeds for future application.

CONSIDER THIS

"Consider This" feature boxes discuss examples, both successful and unsuccessful, of companies addressing various challenges with their operations and supply chain management. "Consider This" boxes help personalize the content for students and convert the theory found in the chapters into practice. These up-to-date examples demonstrate the many ways in which companies are addressing various challenges in managing their service or product operations and supply chains.

End-of-Chapter Features

DISCUSSION AND REVIEW QUESTIONS

Discussion questions serve as a means to review just-completed chapter content and are intended to help students better understand the content they have read by posing some thoughtful questions for classroom discussion. Many of the discussion questions offer opportunities for instructors to frame the discussion in the form of debates, as students examine the pros and cons of specific operations and supply chain challenges.

SOLVED PROBLEMS

Each chapter includes a number of Solved Problems as a means for students to have actual examples that can guide them as they answer many of the quantitative problems they will solve in the chapters and supplements.

PROBLEMS

We have included over 500 practice problems in this text to give students as many opportunities as possible to practice and apply chapter concepts. Although many of these problems are quantitative and follow standard formats to allow students to practice what they have learned in the book, we have also included a number of qualitative problems that require critical thinking and reflection. As a result, most chapters contain a combination of qualitative and quantitative problems that give good practice opportunities to demonstrate the mastery of the subject matter.

CASE STUDIES

This text blends operations and supply chain management within the context of any successful organization, whether publicly held, private, or not-for-profit. Further, the discussion is deliberately global, highlighting operations challenges across the widest possible spectrum. The modern business student must become familiar with and comfortable dealing with supply chain issues whether their origin is North or South America, Asia, Europe, or Africa. We illustrate this through the use of within-chapter and end-of-chapter cases. At the end of each chapter are case studies that take specific examples of the material covered in the chapter and apply them in a narrative format. Some of the cases are fictitious, but the majority of them are based on real situations. These cases include discussion questions to evoke recollection, understanding, critical thinking, and application for the reader that can be used either for homework or to facilitate classroom discussions.

CRITICAL THINKING EXERCISES

Each chapter contains a set of critical thinking exercises that require students to reflect on the main points of the chapter and apply them to other, equally important problems, as a result of expanding on either theory or practical implications. These critical thinking exercises may require students to use Internet search engines to come up with solutions, or they may be broader, allowing students to work in teams to formulate possible solutions for the challenges posed.

AACSB Statement

The Association to Advance Collegiate Schools of Business (AACSB) is a global association that provides business schools with accreditation standards for the advancement of management education. Dr. Venkataraman, Dr. Pinto, and SAGE Publishing understand the value of these accreditation standards to the success of business students and have tied test bank questions that accompany *Operations Management: Managing Global Supply Chains* to the general knowledge and skill areas identified by AACSB.

SAGE edge and Online Resources

Additional resources for instructors are available on a password-protected website at **edge.sagepub.com/venkataraman**. These materials include a test bank with over 100 questions per chapter, a solutions manual for the practice problems in the book, additional auto-gradable practice problems to assign as homework, PowerPoint slides, lecture notes, case notes, sample answers to the questions in the book, class activities, a sample syllabus, tables and figures from the book, Excel templates for selected formulas, and video and multimedia resources.

SAGE coursepacks, available for download at edge.sagepub.com/venkataraman, are available for a variety of learning management systems. The SAGE coursepacks for *Operations Management* include a video case study for each chapter, demonstrating what operations management looks like in real organizations, with quiz questions accompanying each video. The SAGE coursepacks also feature additional assessment questions for each chapter, supplement, and module, as well as video walkthroughs of solved problems in the book.

Online resources for students are open-access and free at **edge.sagepub.com/venkataraman**. These include, for each chapter, an action plan checklist, learning objectives with summaries, a downloadable chapter outline to assist with note-taking, mobile-friendly practice quizzes and eflashcards, Excel templates that can be used with practice problems, and numerous multimedia resources to keep students engaged and better able to see operations management concepts from multiple perspectives.

In acknowledging the contributions of past and present colleagues to the creation of this text, we must first convey our deepest thanks and appreciation to Dr. Jay Nathan of St. John's University, C. S. Gopala Krishnan of Hyundai Motor India, V. Krishna Kumar of Maruti-Suzuki India, Capt. Muralidharan of Asean Aromatics India, N. Bala Baskar I.A.S. former Secretary of Auroville India, and Mr. Venkatesh of Elite Shipping India. We would also like to thank the numerous colleagues, scholars, and friends who have had an impact on our professional careers. Of particular note are the late Brother Leo V. Ryan C. S. V., Dr. Harold Welsch and the late Dr. Gemma Welsch, Dr. Helen Lavan, Dr. Michael J. Brusco, Dr. William J. Tallon, Dr. John Lilley, and Dr. John Magneau III. Please know that you have our gratitude and best wishes always.

We are indebted to the editorial and marketing reviewers of this text whose numerous suggestions and critiques have been an invaluable aid in shaping its content. Among them, we would like to especially thank the following:

Henry Aigbedo, Oakland University

Shahid Ali, Rockhurst University

A. D. Amar, Seton Hall University

Antonio Arreola-Risa, Texas A&M University

Leslie Bobb, Baruch College—CUNY

Salem Boumediene, Montana State University Billings

Robert H. Buckham, Whitworth University

Kevin Caskey, State University of New York at New Paltz

Janice Cerveny, Florida Atlantic University

Greg DeYong, Southern Illinois University

Terence Egan, University of Texas at Dallas

Jared Everett, Boise State University

Robert Flores, South Florida State College

Rick Gibson, American University

Mohan Gopalakrishnan, Arizona State University

Christian Grandzol, Bloomsburg University of Pennsylvania

Haresh Gurnani, University of Miami

David O. Hartman, Quinnipiac University

Jose Humberto Ablanedo Rosas, University of Texas at El Paso

Faizal Huq, Ohio University

David W. Hwang, Shippensburg University of Pennsylvania

Joseph Ingles, Lynn University

Xin James He, Fairfield University

Jian-yu Ke, California State University, Dominguez Hills

Sunder Kekre, Carnegie Mellon University

Burcu B. Keskin, The University of Alabama

Beate Klingenberg, Marist College

Patrick Lee, Fairfield University

Anita Lee-Post, The University of Kentucky

Yulong Li, Simmons College

Lloyd W. Lunde, Southeast Tech

William A. Maligie, California State University, Chico

Chris McCart, Roanoke College

Philip Musa, The University of Alabama at Birmingham

Seong-Hyun Nam, University of North Dakota

Ravi Narayanaswamy, University of South Carolina Aiken

Anthony Narsing, Middle Georgia State University

Penina Orenstein, Seton Hall University

Leyla Ozsen, San Francisco State University

Abirami Radhakrishnan, Morgan State University

Kannan Ramanathan, The University of Texas at Dallas

Pedro M. Reyes, Baylor University

Liz Ross, University of Alaska Fairbanks

Vafa Saboori, Dominican University of California

Samia Siha, Kennesaw State University

Ernest A. Silver, Curry College

Roger Solano, Slippery Rock University

Stan Solomon, Sam Houston State University

Mahesh Srinivasan, University of Akron

Harm-Jan Steenhuis, Eastern Washington University

Feng Tian, Governors State University

Rajendra Tibrewala, New York Institute of Technology

Geoff Willis, University of Central Oklahoma

Xiaowei Zhu, West Chester University of Pennsylvania

Zhiwei Zhu, University of Louisiana at Lafayette

Zhiwei Zhu, University of Louisiana at Lafayette

We would also like to thank our colleagues in the Samuel Black School of Business at Penn State, the Behrend College. Additionally, Anita Lee-Post, David Cadden, Terrence Egan, Elkanah Faux, Ravi Narayanaswamy, Kannan Ramanathan, Vafa Saboori, and Geoff Willis helped prepare the online resources that accompany this text, for which we thank them.

Finally, we wish to extend our sincere thanks to the people at SAGE Publishing for their support for the text during its development, including acquisitions editor Maggie Stanley, development editor Abbie Rickard, editorial assistant Neda Dallal, eLearning editor Katie Ancheta, production editor David Felts, designer Scott Van Atta, and Amy Ray.

Feedback

We and the textbook team would appreciate hearing from you. Let us know what you think about this textbook by writing to orders@sagepub.com. Please include "Feedback about Venkataraman and Pinto" in the subject line.

Ray Venkataraman, PhD
Professor and Chair of Project and Supply Chain Management, Sam and Irene Black School of Business, Penn State Erie, The Behrend College, rrv2@psu.edu

Jeffrey K. Pinto, PhD
Andrew Morrow and Elizabeth Lee Black Chair in the Management of Technology, Sam and Irene Black School of Business, Penn State Erie, The Behrend College, jkp4@psu.edu

Dr. Ray R. Venkataraman is a Professor of Project and Supply Chain Management at the Sam and Irene Black School of Business at Penn State Erie, The Behrend College. He has a PhD in Management Science from Illinois Institute of Technology and has over thirty years of teaching experience. He has taught a variety of courses including Operations Planning and Control, Supply Chain Management, Operations Strategy, Purchasing, Business Statistics and Project Management. He has received the Ideal Industries Award for Excellence in Business Teaching at Northern Illinois University. He currently teaches online courses in Planning and Resource Management in Projects, and Cost and Value Management in projects at the Masters level. Dr. Venkataraman has several research publications in top-tier Operations Management journals. He has published in journals such as *The International Journal of Production Research, Omega, International Journal of Operations and Production Management, Production and Operations Management (POMS), Production and Inventory Management, Production Planning and Control, The International Journal of Quality and Reliability Management,* and *Interfaces.* In addition, he has coauthored books titled *Cost and Value Management in Projects* and *Decision Making in Project Management.* His current research interests is in the area of sustainability integration in project and supply chain management. As an Assistant Manager with a multinational bank in India, Dr. Venkataraman has several years of industry experience in the financial services industry. He has served on the editorial review boards of *Production and Operations Management (POMS)* and *IEEE Transactions on Engineering Management* journals.

Dr. Jeffrey K. Pinto is the Andrew Morrow and Elizabeth Lee Black Chair in the Management of Technology in the Sam and Irene Black School of Business at Penn State Erie, The Behrend College. Dr. Pinto held previous academic appointments at the University of Cincinnati and University of Maine. In 2016 he was a visiting scholar at the Kemmy School of Business, University of Limerick, Ireland. He is the lead faculty member for Penn State's Master of Project Management program. The author or editor of 26 books and over 150 scientific papers that have appeared in a variety of academic and practitioner journals, books, conference proceedings, video lessons, and technical reports, Dr. Pinto's work has been translated into nine languages. He served as Editor of the *Project Management Journal* from 1990 to 1996, is past-Department Editor for R&D and engineering projects with *IEEE Transactions on Engineering Management,* and serves on several other journal editorial boards. With over 25 years' experience in the field of project management, Dr. Pinto is a two-time recipient of the Distinguished Contribution Award from the Project Management Institute for outstanding service to the project management profession. He received PMI's Research Achievement Award in 2009 for outstanding contributions to project management research.

Dr. Pinto has taught and consulted widely in the United States and Europe on a variety of topics, including project management, supply chain management, new product development, information system implementation, organization development, leadership, and conflict resolution.

CHAPTER 1

Introduction to Managing Global Operations and Supply Chains

LEARNING OBJECTIVES

After studying this chapter, you should be able to:

1. Explain how globalization has influenced the management of supply chains and their operations.

2. Describe the role of operations management within a company and in society.

3. Trace the path of a raw material from the start of the supply chain to the final consumer.

4. Explain why it is important to have an integrated view of operations from a larger supply chain framework.

5. Describe the evolution of operations and supply chain management from the Industrial Revolution to the present.

6. Identify some of the current and emerging trends in operations and supply chain management.

OPERATIONS PROFILE: Intel Uses Quality Control to Achieve World Domination

Intel Corporation (Santa Clara, CA) is the world's largest manufacturer of microprocessor chips. Having captured 80% of its market, the company's microprocessors power personal computers (PCs), servers, and smartphones manufactured worldwide. Staying on top of the fast-paced microprocessor-chip industry, however, is complicated.

The development and manufacture of computer chips is a fantastic and complex global voyage: Chips start out as single crystals and are grown into large ingots of silicon by Toshiba Ceramics Co., Ltd (Tokyo, Japan). Toshiba Ceramics then slices the ingots into thin wafers, which are flown across the Pacific Ocean to one of Intel's semiconductor fabricating plants in Arizona or Oregon. At the fabricating facilities, hundreds of integrated circuits are etched and layered on each wafer, forming individual dies on the wafers. The finished wafers are then packed and flown *back* across the Pacific to Intel's Assembly and Test Operations in Malaysia, where they are treated and cut, and the dies are sealed in ceramic packages. The packages are then placed in shipping trays that are put into Intel boxes and packed again for shipment back across the Pacific to Intel's warehouses in Arizona.

Having traveled across the Pacific three times, the chips are then shipped to computer manufacturers around the globe. Dell Inc. (Round Rock, TX), for example, has factories in Texas, Tennessee, Ireland, Brazil, Malaysia, and China. HP Inc.'s (formerly Hewlett-Packard, Palo Alto, CA) factories operate in South Africa, Saudi Arabia, Vietnam, Russia, China, and Taiwan. The journey ends when the product ships from the PC manufacturer to the customer's home or office anywhere in the world.

Quality control practices ensure that Intel's chips are nearly identical and of the highest possible quality. Achieving this level of quality is difficult. No other mass-produced item in the history of humankind is as complicated or as challenging to make as a computer chip. The average size of a typical transistor that goes on the chips, for instance, is 22 nanometers, or less than one thousandth the size of the period at the end of this sentence. Moreover, each chip has more than 2 *billion* transistors connected to one another by several layers of stacked copper wiring. How difficult is it to achieve superior quality control when you are making intricate products that are microscopic in size? Very.

How does Intel manage the task? It does so by isolating and controlling the phenomenal number of tiny inputs required to produce the ever-shrinking chip. Everything from dust to water purity is carefully controlled. In developing this process, Intel created one perfect plant and one ideal chip-making

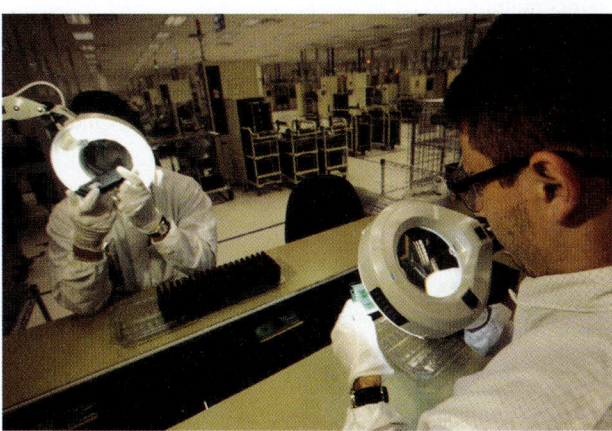

Note the sterile suits worn by all employees at this Intel chip manufacturing center as a further guard against any contamination of the manufacturing process. Intel doesn't apologize about its near-obsessive quality-control efforts; it believes they have helped make it the most advanced manufacturer in its business.

Gilles Mingasson/Hulton Archive/Getty Images

process, and then it copied everything. Whether its chips are made in Arizona, New Mexico, Ireland, or any of its 10 other factories, they are made the same way, with the same equipment, with workers performing the same tasks in the same order.

What sets Intel apart from other manufacturers is its devotion to this process, even copying what may seem to be random elements in its manufacturing centers. For example, if a pipe that delivers chemicals to one of the chip-making machines is 20 feet longer in one factory than in another, Intel will make it match (and it will even match the number of bends in the pipe). If the water quality is different among the factories, then a purification system is used to eliminate the differences. Intel spent two years developing one of its newest chips in a plant in Oregon. Before transferring the chip-making process to its New Mexico plant, the company noticed that the barometric pressure differed between the sites and it adjusted the plant's internal heating, ventilation, and air conditioning (HVAC) system to replicate the pressure of the Oregon facility.

1.1

Explain how globalization has influenced the management of supply chains and their operations.

1.1 Supply Chains and Operations Management in the Global Economy

We live in an interconnected world. To a greater degree than ever before, companies can sell their products and services internationally. Likewise, customers are better able to purchase products or services from firms, regardless of where they are located. Today, consumers living in the far corners of the world can watch MTV (Viacom Media Networks, New York, NY), wear Levi's (Levi Strauss & Co., San Francisco, CA), or eat at McDonald's (Oak Brook, IL) or Pizza Hut (Dallas, TX). The rapid advancements in information technology (IT) and the elimination of trade barriers between countries are the primary reasons for this accelerated pace of global interaction. These changes have helped customers and companies transcend cultural and language boundaries and interact in real time.

Currently, more than two thirds of businesses operate in global markets. Even small businesses that typically lack resources can now cater to the needs of consumers in other countries. This all happened as a result of the globalization of markets. Globalization means that a business can sell in a foreign country, manufacture products in a foreign land, buy materials from an overseas supplier, operate as franchises, or partner with a foreign company.

> **Why** *Managing Global Operations and Supply Chains* **Matters**

Conducting business internationally presents many unique challenges; companies that perform in the competitive global marketplace must understand how to manage their internal operations to anticipate and navigate these challenges. Viewing operations decisions in the context of a global supply chain allows companies to see how one affects the other.

Offshoring and Outsourcing

Two prominent phenomena have accompanied the globalization of business—offshoring and outsourcing. **Offshoring** refers to sourcing from overseas or getting work done in a foreign country. For example, China has now become the preeminent source of low-cost offshore manufacturing. Chinese exports had been low and stable until 1990 and then rose dramatically from 1991 to 2005, particularly after China joined the World Trade Organization. The benefits of offshoring include being able to tap a larger pool of skilled people, get work done faster, and lower a company's labor costs. Risks of offshoring include transfer of jobs to other countries, geopolitical risk, language differences, and poor communication.

Figure 1.1 compares the average hourly compensation costs in U.S. dollars for manufacturing employees in 25 countries. The hourly amount includes the payments made directly to workers, as well as employers' expenditures on benefits and social insurance.[1]

Offshoring: sourcing from overseas or getting work done in a foreign country

Outsourcing: contracting with a third party or an external company to manufacture a good or deliver a service

Charges of defective electrical systems and sticking accelerators were thought to be the result of Toyota's decision to outsource the production of some of the critical components of its cars. As a result, the Japanese automaker was forced to recall and repair millions of vehicles beginning in 2009.

Justin Sullivan/Getty Images News/ Getty Images

Figure 1.1 shows why many of the manufacturing jobs are outsourced to countries such as China, India, and Sri Lanka. The hourly employee compensation is less than US$2 in these countries. By contrast, a U.S. manufacturing worker's average hourly compensation is about the weekly average compensation for a Sri Lankan manufacturing worker.

Outsourcing refers to contracting with a third party or an external company to manufacture a good or deliver a service. The external

FIGURE 1.1: Average Hourly Compensation Costs for Manufacturing Employees in 25 Countries, 2012 (in U.S. dollars)

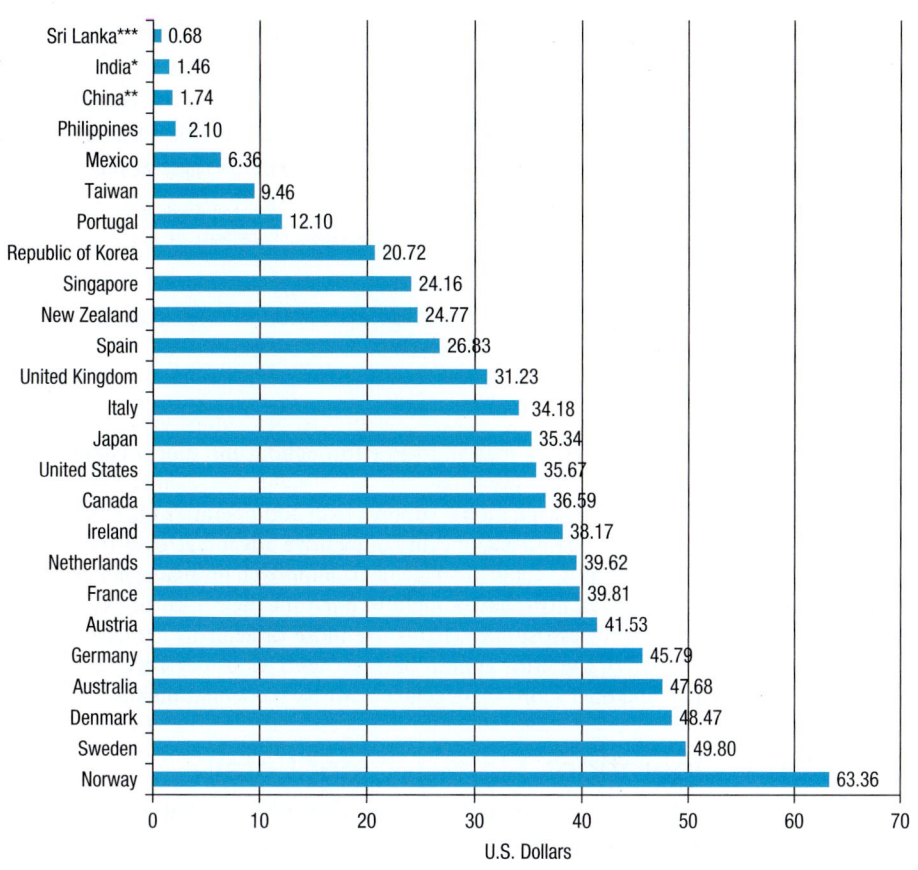

* 2010 data.
** 2009 data.
*** 2008 data.

SOURCE: Adapted from the U.S. Bureau of Labor Statistics, International Comparisons of Hourly Compensation in Manufacturing, August 9, 2013.

company may or may not be a foreign company. India has now become the hotspot for outsourcing many business processes, such as accounting, data entry, customer service, and research and development. GE Transportation (Chicago, IL) is one of the many U.S. companies that have outsourced some of their business processes to India. This company has outsourced all of its design work on locomotives to Bangalore, India. A company usually outsources work to take advantage of specialized skills, cost efficiencies, or operational flexibility that they may lack. Risks of outsourcing include conflicting interests of the company and the third-party provider, excessive reliance on third parties, and lack of in-house knowledge of critical business operations.

Because of the continuing offshoring and outsourcing, manufacturing in United States has declined from nearly 30% of the gross domestic product (GDP) after World War II to just 10% by 2008. Despite this decline, Western manufacturers remain competitive because of their higher productivity. Globally, productivity rates continue to remain the highest in North America.

Globalization, Supply Chains, and Operations Management

Offshoring and outsourcing have had a huge impact not only on trade but also on supply chains and operations management—which is, of course, the subject of this book. A supply chain is a sequence of interconnected organizations that help develop, produce, distribute, and sell a product to the final consumer. The supply chain also includes organizations that help consumers return products as well as dispose of them. Each organization adds value in some way to the product as it moves along the supply chain toward its destination to the final consumer and beyond. For this reason, a supply chain is often called a value chain. Global supply chains are a global network of organizations involved in these activities. Operations management (OM) is the process of managing the system of designing,

Supply chain: a sequence of interconnected organizations that helps develop, produce, distribute, and sell a product to the final consumer

Value chain: See **supply chain**

Operations management (OM): the process of managing the system of designing, producing, and delivering goods or services that add value throughout the supply chain and benefit the final consumer

Consider This 1.1
Is American Manufacturing Dead?

Can American manufacturers survive the onslaught of offshoring and outsourcing? A study conducted by the Boston Logistics Group (Wellesley, MA), a global supply chain research and consulting company, found that American manufacturers have a better chance of success if they adhere to the following principles:[2]

1. Build technologies that cannot be duplicated. Developing cutting-edge technologies that cannot be readily copied and reproduced by firms in other regions can help a company maintain a manufacturing advantage.

2. Bundle value-added services along with manufactured products. Including add-on services such as technical support and special design engineering can increase the appeal of manufactured goods.

3. Manufacture high-quality, high-priced goods in-house, and outsource low-profit and labor-intensive work. That is, do not attempt to compete on the basis of the volume of output, but instead focus on producing those goods that require special skills and can be priced at a premium.

Global Supply Chains

producing, and delivering goods or services that add value throughout the supply chain and benefit the final consumer.

The good news is that, because managing global supply chain and operations is challenging, people and companies that do it well can gain a significant competitive advantage over their rivals. This advantage is particularly true for supply chain management. Supply chain management is the next great competitive frontier. For decades, firms have sought to fine-tune their operations and have done so. Supply chains are next. Nevertheless, supply chains are more difficult to manage because they involve not just your firm, but all of the firms you do business with. Consider This 1.2 describes the exciting kinds of supply chain and operations management careers you might pursue.

1.2 What Does Operations Management Entail?

1.2 Describe the role of operations management within a company and in society.

Each organization in a supply chain has internal operations that it has to manage effectively. When run well, these internal operations create and enhance the value of products and services by lowering costs to the consumer (adding economic value), by improving quality of goods and services produced (adding functional value), and by improving its appearance and desirability (adding aesthetic value). Managing operations within each company in a supply chain requires planning, organizing, and executing both long-term and short-term tasks. Effectively managing operations requires cross-functional cooperation not only within your own company but also with other businesses, or partners, in the supply chain.

Operations management plays a pivotal role in our lives. The food that we eat in restaurants, the movies that we watch at home or in theaters, the modes of travel that we use, and our shopping needs in retail and grocery stores are all made possible by people working in the operations functions of these businesses and their managers. There are operation functions in the traditional manufacturing or goods producing industry and in service industries such as banks, hospitals, food service, communications, and government. Let's now look at how the two types of outputs—goods or services—and the operations related to them differ.

A good is a tangible physical entity such as a car, camera, or a television set. Services are intangible in the sense that they are a set of benefits that may or may not be accompanied by a tangible good. A pure service is a set of benefits with no accompanying physical good. For example, when you visit a hair stylist, you receive a service—ideally, an enhancement in your looks. Table 1.2 compares goods and services.

The operation functions of most businesses provide a mixture of both goods and services. Figure 1.2 illustrates the degree to which different products are considered to be either a good or a service. Some organizations, however, such as sugar and oil refineries, predominantly produce goods. Other entities, such as hospitals, law offices, and educational institutions, predominantly focus on the delivery of services. There are also key structural differences in the operational processes required to design a service system as opposed to a system required to design a tangible product. We will discuss these differences in Chapter 4 on product and service design.

The second major difference between goods and services is that goods can be produced and stored in inventory until they are sold to end customers. The inventory serves as a buffer to bridge the gap between the demand for the product by customers and a firm's operational, or production, capacity.

Consider This 1.2
Why You Should Consider a Career in Operations and Supply Chain Management

Managing operations and supply chains has become the focus of every senior executive and is at the top of the corporate agenda. In 2009, American firms spent $970 billion (10.5% of the nation's GDP) on just the logistical activities of wrapping, bundling, loading, unloading, sorting, reloading, and transporting goods. In the face of increasing global competition, streamlining operations and supply chain activities have become incredibly important for improving bottom-line profitability as well as for enhancing a firm's reputation for reliability. Therefore, operations and supply chain management professionals are in high demand.[3]

Career opportunities in operations and supply chain management (SCM) exist in every sector, whether they are manufacturing and service industries, governmental organizations, educational institutions, or retail industries. In particular, the phenomenal rate of growth in the service sector has expanded the opportunities for operations and supply chain professionals. According to the U.S. Bureau of Labor Statistics, a significant percentage of jobs in the operations area in the foreseeable future will be in the service industry. Graduates with specialization in service operations will be hired to work in areas such as data services, IT, telecommunications, freight and courier services, transport, aviation, consulting, entertainment, hospitality, environmental services, design of service facilities, management of service quality, and management of day-to-day operations.[4]

People who work in operations or supply chain management typically start out as college graduates and then become line associates reporting to a supply chain or plant manager. Their specific job titles may vary from being a purchasing associate, quality control associate, or monitoring warehouse inventory levels to vendor management and shift supervision. For those with quantitative skills, it is possible to work on more rigorous, mathematical applications, such as scheduling in the airline industry. All operations and supply chain jobs require people management skills, quantitative skills, problem-solving skills, and familiarity with IT.[5]

An undergraduate degree in operations or supply chain management is good preparation for entry-level positions. There are many career opportunities in a variety of organizations for people with these credentials. Those who have proven themselves in the field become senior operations managers and product managers, and some cross over into more general corporate positions, such as vice president of procurement, operations, or logistics, chief financial officer (CFO), industrial relations manager, or even chief executive officer (CEO). According to PayScale.com, as of January 2016, a U.S. operations manager earns an average salary of US$60,572. Note, however, that these salary ranges vary from one geographic region to another. In addition to securing a degree in operations or supply chain management, you can enhance your education and career opportunities by joining professional organizations that offer certifications. Some of these professional organizations are:

- APICS, Association for Operations Management (www.apics.org)
- ISM, Institute for Supply Management (www.ism.ws)
- ASQ, American Society for Quality (www.asq.org)
- Council of Supply Chain Management Professionals (www.cscmp.org)
- PMI, Project Management Institute (www.pmi.org)

You may be hired by traditional manufacturers, retailers, supply chain specialists such as consulting firms, or transportation services providers. Table 1.1 shows some common career positions available to those with operations and supply chain management credentials.

For example, manufacturers produce toys throughout the year and store them so that they don't run out of stock during the holiday shopping season.

 What is Operations Management?

Unlike goods, services can't be stored. Instead, their production and consumption occurs concurrently. Firms that provide services must maintain enough capacity to meet peak-demand periods or they will face a physical backlog of customers. In the case of air travel, if you fly during peak periods, you will join a queue of fellow passengers waiting in line to check their luggage. To reduce the backlog, most service delivery systems use reservations and appointments. Services are *time perishable*. An empty seat at a theater or an empty hotel room will never be available again for that particular play or for that specific night, which demonstrates why services cannot be inventoried and stored for later use. Services cannot be transferred or reused but must be sold directly to a customer.

Third, in the case of services, customers are directly involved and interact in the production and consumption of those services. In a classroom, both the teacher and the student are directly involved in the transfer of knowledge of specific subject matter. Likewise, if you were to consult with an attorney, the attorney produces a service (legal advice) that you consume immediately. By contrast, goods-producing firms such as a petrochemical company have very little interaction or contact with the final users of their products.

TABLE 1.1: Careers in Operations and Supply Chain Management[6]

JOB TITLE	RESPONSIBILITIES
Chief Operating Officer (COO)	A top-level executive of a company. Responsible for the entire company's operations and makes sure that the company is profitable.
Operations or Supply Chain Manager	Supervises and manages the work environment, vendor selection process, supply chains, real estate, and budgets.
Materials Manager	Supervises and manages product storage through all phases from production to finished goods, shipping between departments, transportation to distribution centers, warehouses, and customers. Ensures that the company has the right goods and services at the right time, at the right place, and for the right price. Responsibilities for service firms include ordering, receiving, storing, and distributing any resources required to perform the service. Other titles for this job are traffic manager, warehouse manager, and logistics manager.
Purchasing Manager	Supervises and manages the purchase of goods and services, including raw materials and supplies required by the firm for its operation. Responsibilities include coordinating the quantity, quality, price, and timing of the delivery of appropriate materials for the firm's needs. Other related jobs in this area are expediter, buyer, and purchasing agent.
Industrial Production Manager	Supervises and manages the activities of production of goods. Responsibilities include production scheduling, staffing, quality control, equipment operation and maintenance, inventory control, and interfacing and coordinating the production activities with those of other departments. Other related jobs in this area are line supervisor, manufacturing manager, and production planner.
Operations Research Analyst	Ensures that resources of the firm such as time, money, people, space, and raw materials are allocated most efficiently. Analysts also select from competing research projects and choose those that perform best in terms of time, results, and cost, given the constraints of resource availability.
Quality Assurance Manager	Responsible for the elimination of product defects through prevention, detection, and correction to ensure preestablished quality standards are met. The quality assurance manager is an integral part of a firm's total quality management strategic initiatives.
Facilities Coordinator	Responsible for designing the physical environment of a company, such as building design, furniture, and related equipment.
Logistics Manager	Responsible for the accurate and efficient transportation and storage of goods and materials both for the outbound and inbound areas of the supply chain.
Warehouse Operations Manager	Responsible for the efficient and cost-effective operation of commercial or industrial distribution centers or warehousing facilities. Manages inbound activities related to the receipt and storage of goods, inventory management, and claims. Oversees the outbound activities related to filling orders, replenishing stock, and shipping. Responsible for budgeting, customer service, facility and equipment operations. Administers overall inventory management, productivity, accuracy, and loss prevention programs to ensure that customer requirements are met. Related positions are director of logistics, distribution supervisor, distribution center manager, warehouse manager, warehouse and delivery manager, and director of warehouse operations.

Fourth, most goods-producing businesses have capital-intensive equipment. Equipment of this type is expensive and requires a major investment. By contrast, services are often labor intensive. Many goods-producing organizations have computer systems and machinery that reduce their labor costs. For example, Anheuser Busch InBev's (Leuven, Belgium) automated production lines control the entire sterilization, filling, and storage process for beer kegs with minimal need for workers. This type of automation is not possible in service organizations, such as restaurants. If you want a beverage at a restaurant, you depend on your server to get it for you quickly.

Some industries, such as the airline industry, are both capital and labor intensive. Airline companies invest heavily in planes and other flight equipment, but they also invest in labor. Airlines require pilots, flight attendants, mechanics, and support staff to keep their businesses running.[7]

Finally, it is easy to measure and control the quality of a good because standards can be set before manufacturing to ensure the good performs its function. During production, these quality levels can be monitored using quality control tools. Potato chip consumers are aware that the quality of a potato chip depends on its crunchiness and salt content. A company such as Frito-Lay, Inc. (Plano, TX) has

TABLE 1.2: Differences Between Goods and Services

GOODS	SERVICES
Tangible physical entity	Intangible bundle of benefits
Can be stored for future use	Cannot be stored—the service is produced and consumed simultaneously
Often capital intensive	Often labor intensive
Low level of customer contact	High level of customer contact
Quality assurance and control are relatively easy	Quality assurance and control relatively more difficult
Physical transformation of materials	Physical or psychological transformation of customer

preestablished standards to measure the crunchiness of its chips and monitor their salt content during the production process.

Measuring and monitoring the quality of a service is much more difficult because the view of what constitutes good quality in a service is much more subjective. Consider times when you shopped at a high-end department store. At some stores, a salesperson will greet you immediately, whereas in other stores, employees are advised not to intrude on you too quickly as it might seem invasive and pushy. Clearly, in the case of services, no uniform standard of quality can be applied to all individuals.

Operations management is a system that transforms inputs into outputs. As Figure 1.3 shows, the inputs may be raw materials, machines, labor, management, capital, or energy. Such inputs are transformed into outputs to produce the desired products and services. Value is created in the transformation process. In an automobile factory, sheets of steel transformed into different shapes and sizes are assembled together with thousands of component parts and are then painted and finished to create a brand new automobile. In a bakery, flour, yeast, and other ingredients are converted into dough and baked to produce a loaf of bread. In service operations, such as hospitals, doctors help restore sick patients to health through diagnosis, medication, and surgical procedures. In each situation, the transformation process of the operations system creates value—a new automobile, a loaf of bread, or a healthy person.

FIGURE 1.2: Goods-Services Continuum

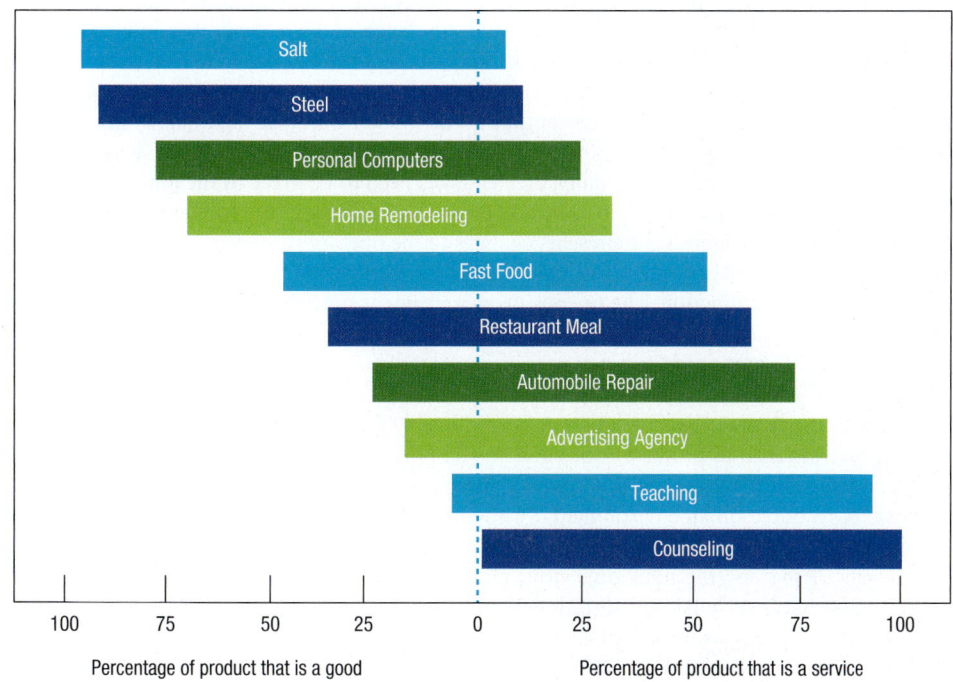

SOURCE: Adapted from Economypedia.com. Retrieved June 16, 2015, from http://www.economypedia.com/wiki/index.php?title=Goods_and_services

(Left) Inside a toy manufacturing plant in China.

(Right) Zhu Zhu Pets were the runaway hit of the 2009 Christmas holiday season—and also in short supply. The shortage occurred even though Russell Hornsby, the CEO of St. Louis–based Cepia, the maker of the pets, spent two months in China prior to Christmas convincing four plants the company had under contract to increase their production of Zhu Zhus from 70,000 pieces to 120,000 per day.

The transformation and value creation of operations systems can take many different forms. The transformation process can be:[8]

- *physical*, as in manufacturing operations
- *locational*, as in transportation and warehouse operations
- *transactional*, as in banking and retail operations
- *physiological*, as in health care
- *psychological*, as in entertainment
- *informational*, as in teaching and communication

In any operations management system, certain inputs are expected to produce certain outputs and the outputs produced should meet preestablished standards (such as high quality or low cost) for that system. If the output does not meet the standards, then changes need to be made to the transformation process, the inputs, or both. In an educational system, such as a college or university, the students and faculty, among others, would be inputs. The output of this system would be high-quality graduating students who have acquired the necessary knowledge in their major fields. If the output does not measure up to this preestablished standard of quality, then changes need to be made to the inputs (recruit better students or faculty) or to the transformation process (make changes in the teaching approaches). The feedback control loop in Figure 1.3 represents changes to the operations management system.

From the perspective of both an individual firm and its supply chain, several key points describe the operations management function. The operations management function has some key characteristics:

Operations Management and Value Creation

- The operations management function transforms inputs such as materials, energy, information, and capital and labor to produce goods and services, thereby creating value.
- The operations management function is responsible for designing, operating, and improving the processes used to produce goods and services that the final consumer values.
- The operations management function is concerned with the acquisition, efficient use, and disposal of resources in an environmentally and a socially responsible manner.
- In the context of a global supply chain, the operations management function brings together five sets of players: the individual firm, global suppliers, logistics providers (companies that provide services such as transportation, warehousing, and distribution), global customers, and stakeholders (persons, groups, or companies that have an impact on an organization or are affected by the organization's actions).
- To be effective, the goals and objectives of the operations function of each business in the supply chain should align, not only with the strategic goals of the individual firm, but also with the overall goals of the firm's supply chain strategy.

Consider This 1.3
Service Operations in India

China is a giant in international trade and global supply chain management (see Case Study 1.1). But it's not the only developing country that is making great economic strides. Although India is not a major manufacturer, it is the world's leading service provider. In the past 20 years, there has been a dramatic increase in the global sourcing of services. The global sourcing of services that initially began with routine office work such as accounting, claims processing, and computer programming has expanded to include more advanced work in IT, call centers, financial analysis, brokerage firms, research and development, medical diagnosis, engineering, and architectural design. India has a large pool of highly skilled and technically trained workers, talented engineers, and scientists whose services are available at less than half the cost of similar workers in more developed countries. Many Indian companies such as Tata Consultancy Services (TCS, Mumbai, India), WIPRO Limited (Bangalore, India), Infosys Limited (Bengaluru,

India), and Tech Mahindra Limited (Mumbai, India) are global leaders in software development and business processes. These companies are continuing to expand not only in India but also in many of their client countries, including the United States and United Kingdom. In IT services alone, India exported US$47 billion in 2009, and by 2020, this figure is expected to be around US$200 billion. Many multinational companies such as Microsoft Corporation (Redmond, WA), IBM (International Business Machines Corporation, Armonk, NY), PepsiCo Inc. (Purchase, NY), The Coca-Cola Company (Atlanta, GA), Siemens AG (Munich, Germany), BP plc (aka British Petroleum, London, U.K.), Nike, Inc. (Beaverton, OR), and Nestlé S.A. (Vevey, Switzerland) have established operations in India to take advantage of India's low-cost services. For example, PepsiCo established its business operations in India in 1989 and is now the fourth largest consumer products company in India, having invested more than US$1 billion in its operations. PepsiCo provides direct and indirect employment to 150,000 people in India and has more than 36 bottling plants. In addition, it has three state-of-the-art food plants in the Indian states of Punjab, Maharashtra, and West Bengal.[9]

- The operations management function must be dynamic to respond to continual changes in customers' demands, technology, competition, and resources.

Operations management is a multifaceted and complex field of study. Anyone pursuing a career in business, whether interested in marketing, finance, accounting, IT, or human resources, should have a thorough grounding in the fundamental concepts and challenges of managing operations. Decisions made in any functional areas have an impact on operations, and vice versa. This is how typical functions, or departments, interface with operations:[10]

- *Finance* provides funding that allows a firm's operations group to produce products and invest in new production equipment.
- *Marketing* gathers market intelligence and can provide the operations group with meaningful ideas for product-improvement programs.
- *IT* provides the operations group with technical information support.
- *Human resources* (HR) provides the recruitment, hiring, and training of operations personnel as well as health-and-safety compliance training and advice related to current environmental and regulatory issues.
- *Research and development* develops product and service ideas for the operations group to pursue.

FIGURE 1.3: Operations as a Transformation System

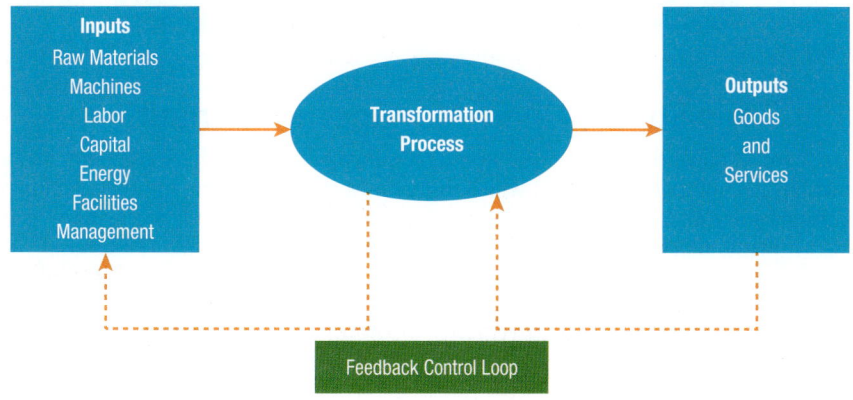

FIGURE 1.4: Operations Management Internal Interfaces

```
                              Finance
                                ↕
  • Production and inventory data          • Budgets
  • Capital budgeting requests             • Cost analysis
  • Capacity expansion                     • Capital investments
  • Technology plans                       • Stockholder needs

  Human                                                    Accounting
  Resources  ←→        Operations         ←→
                                ↕
  • Hiring and firing                      • Production and service availability
  • Training                               • Lead time estimates
  • Legal requirements                     • Order delivery status
  • Union contract negotiations            • Schedules
  • Personnel needs                        • Customer orders
  • Skill sets                             • Customer feedback
  • Performance evaluation     Marketing   • Returns
  • Job design                             • Promotions
  • Work measurement
```

SOURCE: Adapted from Russell, R.S., and Taylor III, B.W., (2011) *Operations Management: Creating Value along the Supply Chain*, 7th Ed., John Wiley and Sons, Hoboken, NJ, page 4.

Figure 1.4 shows the internal interfaces between operations and the four primary functional areas of finance, accounting, marketing, and human resources.[11]

The operations function also interfaces with groups and organizations outside of the firm:[12]

- External suppliers who provide the components and materials used by the operations group
- In the case of services, the customer during the delivery of the service
- Competitors so as to monitor their activities and improve the development of new products and processes that lower the firm's costs
- External agencies such as regulators and trade associations to ensure the firm complies with current laws and codes of practice

Figure 1.5 shows some external interfaces with the operations function.

FIGURE 1.5: Operations Management External Interfaces

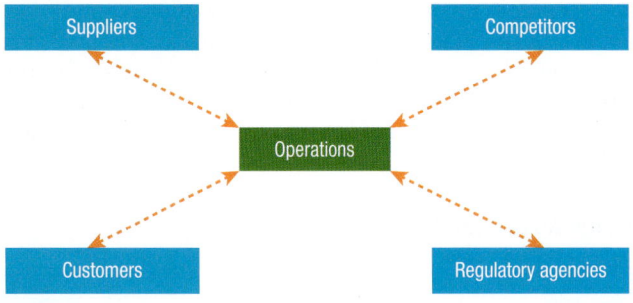

1.3 What Does Supply Chain Management Entail?

1.3

Trace the path of a raw material from the start of the supply chain to the final consumer.

Firms have many challenges when managing their supply chains globally. A company has to decide which functions it should outsource and which functions it should perform in-house. Companies that choose to locate their manufacturing facilities overseas face such logistical problems as deciding on the number of plants that will be needed and where they should be located. These companies must also examine these issues from the perspective of the global supply chain. For example, if a company uses several raw material suppliers around Dacca, Bangladesh, then it also might want to locate its manufacturing facilities in or around Dacca to avoid shipping the materials to other production facilities.

The recent financial turmoil and economic turbulence have made the job of managing supply chains even more complex. One vice president of supply chain management summed up today's issues this way: "We seem to have every issue coming at us at once. We have supplier insolvency, supply disruptions, port closings, volatile commodity prices, quality issues. My second e-mail this morning was about a supplier that literally caught on fire. They'll be out of business for a year. How many different risks can you handle at once?"[13] The following Operations Profile shows how the clothing company Zara (Coruña, Spain) has not only managed its supply chain risks but also used its supply chain to gain a competitive advantage.

Supply Chain Structures and Partners

Figure 1.6 illustrates a typical global supply chain for a manufacturing company. Each organization's supply chain has inbound and outbound elements. The inbound portion can consist of local or foreign suppliers of product ideas, designs, basic raw materials and components, transportation links, and warehouses. It ends with the internal operations of the company.

The outbound portion begins when the organization delivers its output to its immediate customers in the supply chain. This portion of the supply chain might include globally dispersed wholesalers, retailers, distribution centers, and transportation companies, the consumer, and companies that facilitate the return of products or their disposal. Many online businesses often contract with other companies to handle the return of products purchased online by their customers.

Let us consider each element in the supply chain to understand better their characteristics and how they relate to each other.

The Crest SpinBrush quickly became the best-selling electric toothbrush in the world after it hit the marketplace. But Proctor & Gamble (P&G), the maker of Crest, didn't actually invent the device. Instead, the company purchased the design from Nottingham Spirk, an external product development company. It is a supply chain practice that P&G has begun to use more frequently to remain competitive.

©iStockphoto.com/matsou

First-Tier Suppliers

First-tier suppliers provide components, systems, or finished goods and services to the primary firm, which can be a manufacturing, retail, or service organization. For example, L.L. Bean, Inc. (Freeport, ME) contracts with shirt makers worldwide to produce the company's wide assortment of shirts for men and women. These shirt manufacturers represent first-tier suppliers for L.L. Bean, while they

FIGURE 1.6: Standard Global Supply Chain Model

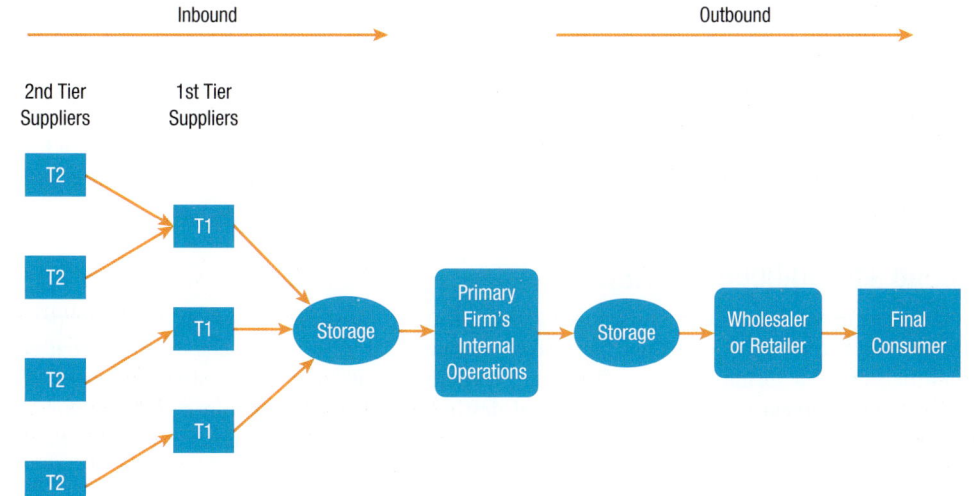

Inbound portion: elements of a supply chain that consist of local or foreign suppliers of product ideas, designs, basic raw materials and components, transportation links, and warehouses that end with the internal operations of the company

OPERATIONS PROFILE: Zara: Bringing Speed to Fashion Through Supply Chain Management

"Fashion doesn't sleep." Miss a new trend or fail to capitalize on an emerging opportunity in the fast-paced, frenetic fashion industry, and it is usually gone for good. As a result, the fashion industry and its retailers spend thousands of hours studying the latest styles and trying to anticipate hot new trends. The Spanish firm Zara has taken a bold new approach to fashion by pioneering an innovative technique for fashion retailing through the clever design of its supply chain. On average, it takes Zara three weeks to spot, design, manufacture, and ship one of the 300,000 different pieces of clothing it sells to stores each year. In doing so, Zara can beat the high-end fashion houses to the market with similar designs, made from cheaper materials, and costing much less than haute couture. A new PRADA (PRADA Group, Milan, Italy) handbag costs US$500, but Zara sells the same design for US$109.

Zara has initiated Z-days at its stores, which take place twice a month, when new shipments of styles are delivered to the shops. The promotion attracts shoppers who know that if they hesitate, the style will be gone. Zara thrives on creating immediate but only temporary buzz for any of its fashions. Unlike other retailers, Zara is not concerned about products being out of stock. Instead, they count on shoppers being attracted by styles in limited supply. Speed to market, rapid turnaround, and the equally rapid introduction of new styles keep Zara store shoppers motivated to return constantly just to find out what's new.

The secret to Zara's success is a well-developed supply chain that includes the firm's own retail stores, distribution centers, a design and manufacturing center, and textile-milling factories. Thus, the retailer does not have to depend on any other firm in the chain, allowing the company to move quickly. A second advantage Zara has is that, because it controls the entire supply chain, it can make limited runs of clothing and accessories. That is, the company does not depend on another manufacturer that will insist on producing large, lengthy runs to maximize efficiency. Zara can spot a fashion trend in one region or country and create items for just that opportunity without having to inundate all its regions with similar designs.

Zara is able to develop, change, or drop clothing styles in a matter of days; in fact, in time for the next Z-day at its stores. The firm also makes it easy on its retailers near the end of the chain because Zara presses, wraps, and tags all clothing, even hanging it on hangers, at their distribution centers. Retail shops only have to open the boxes and transfer the goods directly to their shelves and displays, with no delays in getting the goods in front of customers. By paying careful attention to supply chain management, Zara has managed to stay ahead in the fashion industry and create a unique niche for itself.[14]

themselves depend on a wide assortment of second-tier suppliers at textile mills, cotton plantations, and so on. In short, although the first-tier suppliers are directly connected to the production or service organization, they too represent just another link in the delivery chain by playing an important role in moving the products forward that can be sold as goods or services.

Second-Tier Suppliers

Outbound portion: elements of a supply chain that begin when the organization delivers its output to its immediate customers in the supply chain and may consist of globally dispersed wholesalers, retailers, distribution centers, and transportation companies, the consumer, and companies that facilitate the return of products or their disposal

Second-tier suppliers are firms that provide raw materials, basic services, or manufacturing components for the primary firm's manufacturing or service production processes. Because these items can often be unfinished or raw goods, they are acquired at the source. For example, raw palladium, which is used in automobile catalytic converters, is mined in South Africa and Russia. It is shipped as a raw material to the first-tier supplier's processing centers to be converted into a useful commodity for the automotive industry. Second-tier suppliers typically link to their own supply chains and pass their commodities, services, or components along to first tier-suppliers.

Inbound and Outbound Storage

Storage refers to the warehousing function that organizations must use to varying degrees, depending on the products they sell. Companies often store inbound materials to prevent shortages that could curtail their manufacturing activities. Outbound warehousing is common for storing finished goods prior to their shipment to a wholesale or retail destination. Note that within a supply chain there could be multiple storage facilities, such as warehouses and distribution centers, on both the inbound and the outbound side.

OPERATIONS PROFILE: LESSONS LEARNED
Apple Puts All Its Eggs in One (Very Expensive) Basket

The 2014 release of the Apple iPhone 6 was, as are all Apple Inc.'s (Cupertino, CA) product release announcements, one that was greatly anticipated. In addition to its desire to maintain a technological lead in the highly competitive smartphone industry, Apple knows that product release announcements have a direct impact on its stock price and the valuation of the corporation. As a result, nothing is left to chance. All technology is carefully verified, products must be available on the announced delivery date, and all suppliers have been certified and the quality of their materials checked and rechecked.

It came as a huge surprise to Apple's executives when GT Advanced Technologies (Merrimack, NH), the chief supplier of one of the iPhone's most technologically advanced features, called them to say that it was going out of business. GT was Apple's sole supplier of the super-hard sapphire smartphone screen that Apple was counting on to give them a notable advantage over their chief competitors, such as Samsung (Ridgefield Park, NJ). The sapphire screen, a crystalized form of aluminum oxide, was scratch resistant and could withstand shocks and accidental drops better than the standard Gorilla Glass (Corning Inc., Corning, NY) used by other phone makers. Sapphire screens are expensive—more than five times the cost of regular glass. Apple was so set on this technology that it had just entered a joint venture with GT to build a US$1 billion manufacturing plant in Arizona to provide 30 times as many sapphire screens as any other plant in the world.

Problems with quality control plagued the GT manufacturing process from the beginning. GT had never mass-produced sapphire glass, and early test batches were flawed and unusable. Meanwhile, GT had hired workers too quickly, and hundreds of them ended up cleaning floors or sitting around and waiting while the company got the manufacturing process right. The company's executives blamed Apple for their problems, arguing that Apple had turned them into a captive supplier, required to bear all risks and costs under Apple's

Cole Bennetts/Getty Images News/Getty Images

restrictive contracts. Apple, in turn, put the blame squarely on GT's management, arguing that they over-promised on their ability to supply the new iPhone's screen when they were still working out the flaws in their production systems and were still developing the huge furnaces needed to produce sapphire glass. Meanwhile, the quality of the product failed to improve as GT got further and further behind on its commitments for quality and delivery schedules. Apple was forced to offer GT more than US$100 million in loans to keep it in business throughout these development problems. Finally, GT company officials realized they would not be able to honor their supplier commitments to Apple and in August 2014 sought bankruptcy protection.

Apple's only logical response to this disaster has been to use the standard glass screen for the iPhone release. Apple continues to investigate the possibility of sapphire glass for future model releases, but it has learned a hard lesson about using a sole-source supplier for such a critical product.[15]

Wholesalers and Retailers

Wholesalers receive goods directly from an organization and are responsible for providing the goods to end-point retailers, who sell directly to consumers. Note that the outbound portion of a company's supply chain could have many wholesalers and retailers. Sometimes a firm will use wholesalers, and sometimes it will sell directly to retail establishments. Some firms bypass retailers altogether and sell their products directly to customers.

Managing a Supply Chain

Final Consumers

The people and firms that consume the good produced by the organization are the final consumers or end users of the product. The organization is responsible for producing a product that gives customers value. A product's value is determined by the end user, not by the manufacturer. Thus, if BlackBerry Limited (formerly Research in Motion Ltd., Waterloo, Ontario, Canada) manufactures a new model BlackBerry smartphone that customers find difficult to use, although it may be high quality, its value is diminished in the eyes of customers.

Explain why it is important to have an integrated view of operations from a larger supply chain framework.

1.4 An Integrated Perspective on Operations and Supply Chain Management

In Section 1.2, we examined operations management, and we described it as managing a set of processes required to design, produce, and deliver products or services that add value throughout the supply chain and, ultimately, to the final consumer. Then in Section 1.3, we saw that successful supply chain management requires the firm to manage its business processes, relationships, and *flows* of materials, information, money, and people, with the ultimate goal of creating value to customers and stakeholders. Both operations management and supply chain management have the same goal of producing and delivering products or services that create value for customers. Firms integrate the two, and we describe how that is done for firms producing products and firms producing services. First, however, we start with an overview of the kinds of decisions firms must make in managing their operations and supply chains.

Decisions in Operations and Supply Chain Management

Operations and Decision Making

There are three general types of decisions in operations and supply chain management: the *strategic decisions*, *tactical decisions*, and *operational decisions*. These types of decisions fall into a hierarchy, as shown in Figure 1.7. The decisions at a higher level in the pyramid will set the constraints for lower level decisions. Strategic decisions have a long-term impact on the firm, whereas tactical decisions are made for the medium term and operational decisions are short-term, day-to-day decisions.

Here are some examples of tasks that fall into each decision category:

Strategic Decisions: Product and service design, process design, plant and warehouse location, layout planning, supplier selection, outsourcing and offshoring, choosing transportation modes, and quality management.

Tactical Decisions: Sales and operations planning, inventory management, master production scheduling, material requirements planning, distribution, and transportation planning.

Operational Decisions: Inventory control, quality control, production scheduling, supplier evaluation, performance measurement, and customer relations management.

FIGURE 1.7: Hierarchy of Supply Chain and Operations Decisions

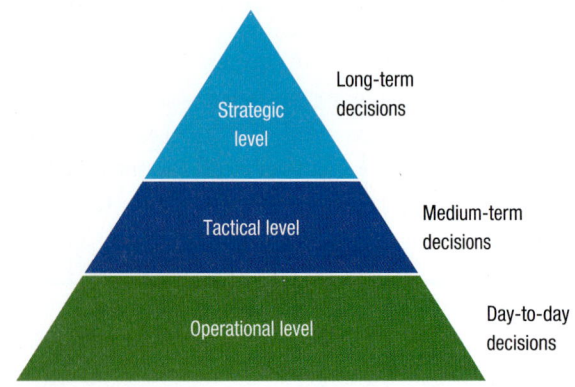

SOURCE: Enterprise Integration Laboratory (EIL). (n.d.). *Supply chain management.* Toronto, Ontario, Canada: University of Toronto. Retrieved from http://www.eil.utoronto.ca/profiles/rune/node5.html

The tasks in this list are not all inclusive. In addition, decisions about these tasks as indicated in Figure 1.7 are not as sharply delineated as the illustration implies. Strategic decisions may be interrelated. For example, the strategic decisions of choosing a transportation mode such as rail, water, truck, or air depend on the strategic decision of choosing a location for manufacturing plants.

In addition, there is no clear separation between tactical and operational decisions. Although managing customer relations is a day-to-day ongoing activity, customer relationship planning is often a tactical decision. Thus, decisions in the hierarchy can subsequently affect other decisions.

Decisions at the strategic, tactical, and operational levels need to be aligned. That is, tactical and operational decisions have to conform to their higher order, strategic choices. The decision hierarchy requires that choices be naturally linked and internally coherent.

Operations Interfaces in a Product Supply Chain

Figure 1.8, which expands Figure 1.6, shows a detailed view of the interrelationship between operations and supply chain activities with operations at the core of a business. Three interfaces, or relationships, need to be managed effectively:

- *Upstream Interfaces: Supplier Management.* Upstream interfaces typically include suppliers that provide raw materials, components, and parts required in the downstream operations process. The management activities in this interface include prequalifying suppliers, selecting and negotiating contracts with them, and materials storage and planning—that is, purchasing the materials, managing their inbound transportation, and inspecting and warehousing them.

FIGURE 1.8: Expanded Supply Chain Model with Operations Interfaces

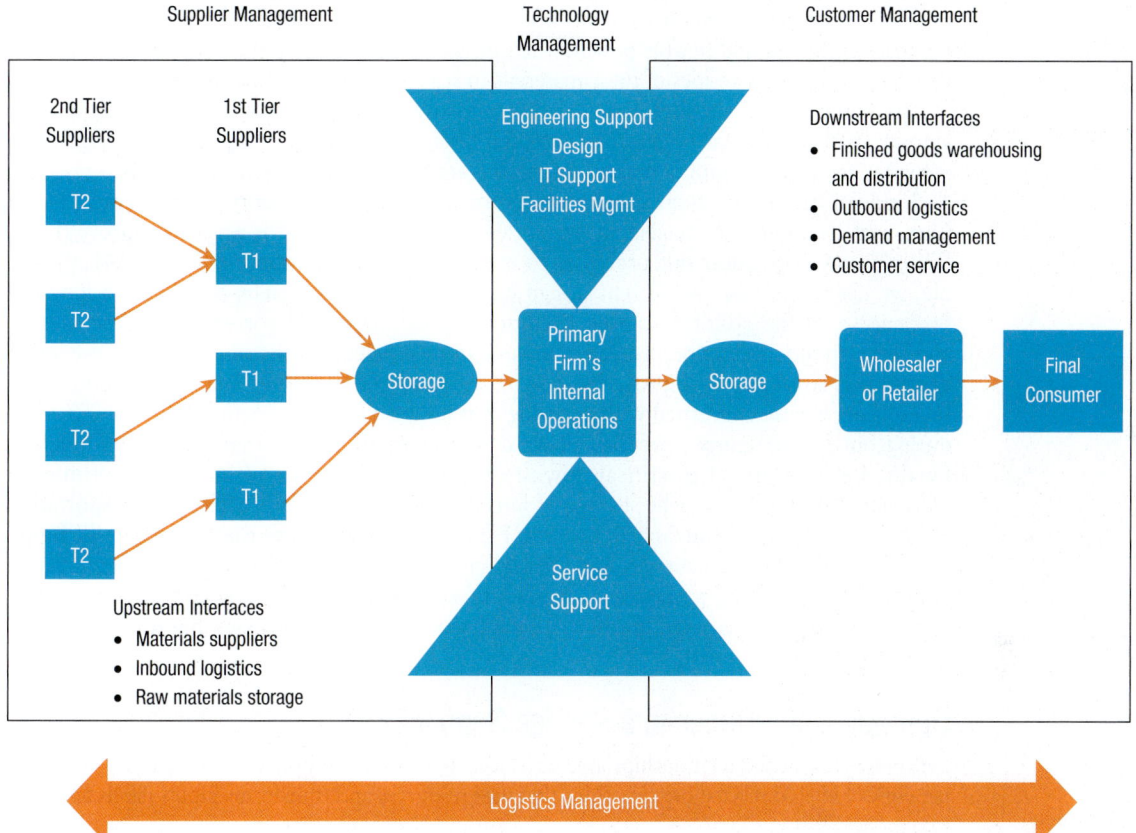

- *Downstream Interfaces: Customer Management.* Interfaces downstream include individuals or companies that buy and use the finished products. These customers could be internal to the firm, external intermediate customers, or the final consumer of the firm's product. Consider, Sony, a manufacturer of electronic products. For the television sets manufactured by Sony Corporation (Tokyo, Japan), the distribution center owned by Sony is an internal customer, whereas a retail Best Buy (Richfield, MN) store is an external intermediate customer; you, as the potential buyer of that TV set, are the final consumer. Although each of these consumer groups is important, the operations group of a firm has to identify which consumer groups are critical and pay closest attention to these groups because they have the greatest impact on the firm's sales, product designs, and future growth. This process is part of **demand management** used to anticipate and manage customer demand for a product or service. See the Lessons Learned box, which shows how Apple failed to manage the demand for its iPhone. In addition, the operation management function interacts with the firm's external partners that provide additional downstream services such as outbound transportation, packaging, warehousing, and storage of the company's products.

- *Vertical Interfaces: Technology Management and Service Support.* An operations management group interfaces vertically with suppliers that provide the technology and the skilled labor needed to design products, processes, and other services. If the firm contracts with other firms to supply it with IT services, engineering or design services, or facility management, this would be an example of vertical interfaces. Operation management's vertical interfaces also include interacting with suppliers that provide the company with support such as equipment maintenance, recycling, disposal, and repair services.

Consider a practical example of the operational interfaces in a product supply chain. Suppose a company was part of an organization that specialized in the manufacturing of marble countertops and sinks for residential bathrooms. The company requires raw materials, such as rosin, marble powder, assorted chemicals, molds, pouring equipment, and grinding, sanding, and finishing equipment to maintain its

Integrating Operations and the Supply Chain

....

Demand management: the process of anticipating and managing customer demand for a product or service

production levels and meet the demand of building contractors. To avoid bottlenecks or delayed deliveries, it is critical that the company creates and maintains a supply chain that ensures the timely arrival of all these materials when the company needs them. Therefore, it might contract with first-tier suppliers for these chemicals and marble powder that, in turn, would contact their suppliers to make sure that they had sufficient quantities of these materials to sell to the company when needed.

All of the critical supplies arrive at the company's warehouse for storage. They store a certain amount of them to guard against unexpected disruptions in their suppliers' deliveries. All of these activities are part of supplier management and are focused on upstream processes.

Inside of the factory, technology management and service support functions must be managed. First, with technology management, we are continuously looking for ways to improve the design of facilities and to engineer our processes to make our production more efficient. Perhaps, for example, we determine that the current design of the factory is inefficient and leads to long delays, or bottlenecks, at the grinding station. Facilities engineering would correct these process deficiencies and redesign the production process to make it more efficient. At the same time, we use logistics and distribution strategies to improve the flow of inbound and outbound materials and finished goods. In addition, we are concerned with ensuring that no critical shortages in production materials occur during our manufacturing process, so we design a supply system that ensures on-time deliveries. Finally, we must attend to critical downstream processes as part of our customer management, including warehousing for the storage of finished goods until orders arrive or transportation to the construction site can be arranged. Overall, Figure 1.8 demonstrates the complexity of supply chain and operations management through identifying the variety of critical interfaces organizations must address. These challenges range from horizontal supply chain issues related to upstream and downstream activities, as well as to the more fully integrated, vertical processes that form a critical element in operations management.

Operations Interfaces in a Service Supply Chain

Let's now look at the relationships and interfaces in a services supply chain. A service supply chain is a network of interconnected organizations that uses resources and transforms inputs (skills and knowledge) into services.[16]

Figure 1.9 represents a service supply chain, showing the interfaces and relationships for an operations service delivery system. The interfaces and activities such as supplier relationship management, demand management, and customer relationship management are identical to those that exist in a product supply chain. The only significant differences are the overlapping ovals that indicate direct interaction between the service provider and the customer because the service is provided and consumed simultaneously. An electrical power service provider's supply chain might look like the one shown in Figure 1.9. The electrical service provider would purchase fuel (coal, oil, or natural gas) from a supplier of fuel sources. The company would then convert the fuel energy into electric power for transmission to the consumer.

Service businesses are a rapidly growing (and, indeed, dominant) sector of many western European and North American economies. Throughout this text, we describe their operations and incorporate service firms into our discussions of operations management and supply chains.

Supplier management: a business process that enables a company to identify and select the best possible suppliers and negotiate the best possible prices for the resources it purchases from them

Technology management: the process of continuously looking for ways to improve the design of facilities and engineering of processes to make production more efficient

Service support: the process of interfacing with suppliers that provide the company with support

Customer management: the process of interfacing with individuals or companies that buy and use finished products

FIGURE 1.9: Standard Service Supply Chain Model

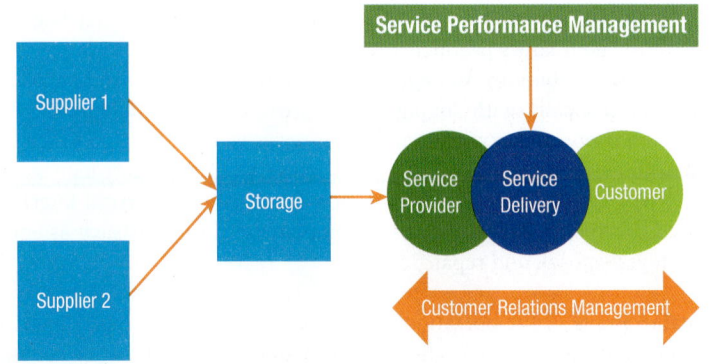

SOURCE: Baltacioglu, T., Ada, E., Kaplan, M., Yurt, O., & Kaplan C. (2007). A new framework for service supply chains. *Services Industry Journal, 27.*

1.5 The Evolution of Operations and Supply Chain Management

The concept of production is as old as humanity itself. If we look back in history and reflect on the great civilizations, such as those in China, Rome, and Egypt, we find example after example of the marvelous production accomplishments of the builders of these civilizations. Stonehenge, the pyramids of Egypt, the Great Wall of China, and the aqueducts and theaters of Rome are all examples of astounding production feats. Production during those early days was performed by skilled artisans who produced customized goods for individual customers. Nevertheless, organized and large-scale production of consumer goods began during the Industrial Revolution, generally around the late 18th to mid-19th century. Although the Industrial Revolution vastly changed how products were produced, it was during the 20th century that most operations innovations occurred.

Table 1.3 traces the evolution of production in today's state-of-the art operations and global supply chain management. Most dramatic and accelerated changes in the operations and supply chain management have taken place since the 1980s. We will discuss each of these topics in greater detail in subsequent chapters, but for now, the table offers a glimpse at how the operations management discipline has evolved.

During the late 1970s and early 1980s, intense global competition caused many companies to lose their competitive edge and market share. Until the early 1980s, people in the operations function were never involved in the formulation of a corporate strategy. Nevertheless, organizations began to realize that one way to survive was to define and execute a strategy through effective and efficient operations. That is, firms had to formulate operations strategies. Operations strategy uses an organization's resources efficiently to gain a competitive edge in the marketplace by achieving key operations objectives related to product quality, delivery, flexibility, cost, service, and innovation. That is, an operations strategy should outline the vision and road map for a firm's operational decision-making.

In the 1980s, facing the threat of global competition, companies adopted TQM programs to regain their competitive edge and achieve customer satisfaction. Total quality management (TQM) is a management philosophy that focuses on continuously improving the quality of a company's products and processes. According to the philosophy, every employee is responsible for improving the quality of a company's products and processes, and a quality culture should pervade the entire organization. Achieving total quality requires not only the commitment of the top managers of the company and its employees but also the involvement of the company's suppliers and even its customers. Furthermore, pursuing TQM is not the privilege of only large organizations. Even small companies can implement and reap the benefits of TQM. Pennril Datacomm Networks Inc. (Gaithersburg, MD), a designer and manufacturer of data communications and equipment, was experiencing defect rates that were so high that the company was reworking or scrapping about a third of everything it was producing. After embracing and implementing TQM, defects decreased by 81% and failures by 83% in the first three months, with a 73% reduction in warranty repairs in the first year.[17]

Motorola Solutions, Inc. (aka Motorola, Schaumburg, IL), in its efforts to reduce variations in its processes, started the Six Sigma quality initiative in 1986. The focus of Six Sigma is on improving quality through reducing the number of defects. Since the 1990s, several world-class corporations, such as General Electric (aka GE, Faifield, CT), have embraced the Six Sigma methodology and have witnessed dramatic improvements in product and process quality and profitability. The application of Six Sigma methodology has now expanded in scope and is used not only in the manufacturing sector but also in the service sector and in supply chains.

Lean manufacturing or lean production was championed as a management philosophy that originated in the 1990s based on the automaker Toyota Motor Corporation's (aka Toyota, Toyota City, Japan) production system. The basic idea behind lean production is that any activity or process that does not add value to the product or service is a waste and, therefore, should be eliminated. Several companies have benefitted from adopting lean manufacturing methods. For example, in 1997, Porsche AG (Stuttgart, Baden-Württemberg, Germany) was on the verge of bankruptcy before going lean and turning steady losses into profits. The success of the Porsche Boxter is the direct result of the company adopting lean manufacturing methods.

An extension of lean manufacturing is agile manufacturing, which is the ability of an organization to respond quickly to market changes with a set of processes, tools, and training available as needed. Whereas lean manufacturing can reduce, and perhaps eliminate, waste from production processes, it doesn't necessarily allow a company to respond quickly to sudden changes in customers' needs. Agile

1.5

Describe the evolution of operations and supply chain management from the Industrial Revolution to the present.

Operations strategies: strategies that use an organization's resources efficiently to gain a competitive edge in the marketplace by achieving key operations objectives related to product quality, delivery, flexibility, cost, service, and innovation. These strategies should outline the vision and road map for a firm's operational decision-making

Total quality management (TQM): a management philosophy that focuses on continuously improving the quality of a company's products and processes

Six Sigma: the methodology of improving quality through reducing the number of defects in a given process

Lean manufacturing: a management philosophy that originated in the 1990s based on Toyota's production system that states that any activity or process that does not add value to the product or service is a waste and, therefore, should be eliminated

Lean production: See **lean manufacturing**

Agile manufacturing: the ability of an organization to respond quickly to market changes with a set of processes, tools, and training available as needed

TABLE 1.3: Evolution of Operations and Supply Chain Management

TIME PERIOD	INNOVATIONS AND EVENTS	PRODUCTION EMPHASIS	NOMENCLATURE (COMMON TERMINOLOGY)
1700–1900	<ul><li>Steam engine</li><li>Interchangeable parts</li><li>Division of labor</li><li>Improvements in manufacturing technology</li><li>Formation of transportation networks</li></ul>	Internal production in factories	Factory management
1900–1920	<ul><li>Applications of scientific principles to manufacturing</li><li>Time and motion studies</li><li>Moving assembly lines</li></ul>	Internal and mass production	Scientific manufacturing and management
1920–1960	<ul><li>Production of war goods</li><li>Hawthorne studies</li><li>Motivational theories</li><li>Introduction of computers and quantitative tools</li></ul>	Internal mass production	Production management and operations research
1960–1980	<ul><li>Just-in-time (JIT) and material requirements planning (MRP) systems</li><li>Statistical process control</li><li>Increasing global competition</li></ul>	Internal production with some outsourcing, and the production of services	Production and operations management
1980–2000	<ul><li>Increased computerization</li><li>Business process reengineering</li><li>Total quality management (TQM)</li><li>Six Sigma quality</li><li>Lean manufacturing</li><li>Enterprise resource planning (ERP)</li><li>The Internet and electronic commerce (e-commerce)</li><li>Emerging global economies such as China and India as a result of reduced governmental trade barriers</li><li>Increased global sourcing and adoption of supply chain management practices for both goods and services</li></ul>	Emphasis on managing both internal operations and supply chains	Operations and supply chain management
2000–present	<ul><li>Global and sustainable supply chains</li><li>Advances in communication and transportation technologies, agile manufacturing</li></ul>	Emphasis on managing both global supply chains and operations across supply chains	Operations and global supply chain management

Business process reengineering (BPR): the radical redesign of a firm's existing workflows and resources to reduce operational costs and better meet the needs of customers and support a firm's overall mission

Business process management (BPM): a management approach that focuses on continuously improving the efficiency of business processes through innovation, flexibility, and the seamless integration of technology

manufacturing, by contrast, uses technology to bring together a firm's marketing, design, and the operations functions to do so. The Benetton Group (aka United Colors of Benetton, Treviso, Italy), a leading apparel manufacturer, was one of the pioneers in deploying and reaping the benefits of agile manufacturing. Zara, as the earlier Operations Profile demonstrated, is another clothing manufacturer that has successfully implemented agile manufacturing.

Fueled by a global recession and increasing foreign competition in the 1990s, companies were seeking innovative ways to improve their business processes and cut costs, to reestablish their competitive advantage, and increase customer satisfaction. A business process is a series of tasks or activities designed to produce a specific product, service, or output. For example, a company's accounting function is a business process that involves several individual activities such as accounts payable, accounts receivable, and billing, all of which are designed to move financial information within the company. Efforts to improve a company's business processes led to the approach of business process reengineering (BPR). BPR is the radical redesign of a firm's existing workflows and resources to reduce operational costs and better meet the needs of customers and support a firm's overall mission. The key focus of BPR is to achieve dramatic cost, quality, speed, and customer service improvements. By the mid-1990s, many Fortune 500 companies had initiated BPR efforts. More recently, business process management (BPM) has begun to replace BPR. BPM is a management approach that, like BPR, focuses on continuously improving the efficiency of business processes but also focuses on innovation, flexibility, and the seamless integration of technology.

Enterprise resource planning (ERP) systems were developed in the late 1990s. An ERP system is an information system that integrates information across all departments of an organization, such as finance, accounting, manufacturing, sales, and service. The purpose of ERP systems is to facilitate and manage the flow of information across all functions not only within an enterprise but also with its external stakeholders, including its suppliers and customers.

Of course, as we explained at the beginning of the chapter, the evolution of operations and supply chain management has continued to occur in the 21st century as a result of globalization and outsourcing. Many joint initiatives undertaken by countries around the world have provided an impetus for the globalization of businesses. For example, in 1947, to promote international trade, member countries of the United Nations negotiated and signed an international treaty called the General Agreement on Tariffs and Trade (GATT). The purpose of this agreement was to encourage free trade between member states by regulating and reducing tariffs on traded goods and by providing a forum for resolving trade disputes.

GATT lasted until 1993 and was replaced by the World Trade Organization (WTO) in 1995. In addition, in 1994, United States, Canada, and Mexico negotiated and implemented the North American Free Trade Agreement (NAFTA) to improve trade relations. NAFTA removed most barriers to trade and investment among these countries. Recently, the WTO expanded the scope of the rules of international trade to include services in addition to goods. Furthermore, the WTO also relaxed the restrictions and opened the markets for highly regulated industries such as agriculture, textiles, and telecommunications. Similarly, the formation of the European Union not only eliminated trade barriers among European countries but also led to strict quality and environmental standards that companies have to meet to do business with member countries. As a result of globalization, among global business partners, there has been a proliferation of strategic partnerships, joint ventures, licensing agreements, research consortia, direct marketing agreements—and above all—the formation of global supply chains.

Changes in Operations Management

1.6 Current and Emerging Issues in Operations and Supply Chain Management

1.6 Identify some of the current and emerging trends in operations and supply chain management.

Companies competing in today's global business environment are facing challenges and trade-offs that are making their operations and supply chains increasingly complex. Many companies are ill-equipped to do business in today's global markets and in the face of political upheaval. For most companies, the operations function and supply chains were designed to manage stable, high-volume production by capitalizing on low-cost labor opportunities available in China and other emerging economies. Nevertheless, with increasing global competition, the relative attractiveness of manufacturing locations (based on costs and availability of labor), as well as the ability to produce in high volumes at low costs, will change quickly in the future. That is, what makes us profitable today may not generate profits next year.

Fueled by the recent global economic downturn, some challenges, such as turbulent trade, are likely to become perennial problems for supply chain managers. The rising wealth of workers in many developing countries, especially those in central and eastern Europe, will make it harder to find reliable, low-cost suppliers. Many of these changes are beyond a company's control, and therefore, the senior executives responsible for formulating operations and supply chain strategies run a greater risk of making key decisions that could become unprofitable. To meet these challenges, companies worldwide will need to be aware of and capitalize on the operations and management trends we describe in this section.[18]

The Continuous Optimization of Resources

The trend toward optimizing the use of raw materials and labor by eliminating waste and maximizing productivity will continue. The application of lean and agile manufacturing techniques in conjunction with Six Sigma quality programs will gain popularity in both the manufacturing and service sectors. To demonstrate, the Korean steel manufacturer POSCO (Seoul, South Korea) combined lean manufacturing and Six Sigma methodologies to establish itself in the global marketplace as the leading provider of innovative steel products and services. In addition, firms will continue to optimize their inventory levels strategically throughout their supply chains along with their use of other resources, such as their transportation and production equipment. The responsibility to

Enterprise resource planning (ERP): an information system that integrates information across all departments of an organization, as well as facilitates and manages the flow of information across all functions within an enterprise and to its external stakeholders

balance the supply and demand of resources rests on the operations managers of every company within the supply chain.[19]

Greater Supply Chain Risks and Supply Chain Restructuring

Trends in Operations Management

Supply chain risk has been increasing sharply as a result of greater levels of outsourcing and offshoring, production of more complex products and services, fluctuating energy prices, and increasing financial volatility. As supply chains become more global, the greatest supply chain risks that companies are facing are the ability to obtain resources and labor and the integration of their IT systems with those of companies in their supply chains. Nevertheless, very few companies have meaningful strategies to respond to these risks.[20] To address these potential problems, companies need to invest in operations and supply chain management capabilities to respond more quickly to changes in the marketplace—much as Zara has done.[21]

Some organizations are responding to these challenges by restructuring their old supply chains. First, these organizations are splintering their traditional supply chains into smaller and more agile supply chains that can better respond to higher levels of business complexity, save money, and improve customer service. Second, these companies are reconfiguring their manufacturing facilities to respond to a range of potential market scenarios. Essentially, the firms are using their supply chains to hedge against uncertainty in the marketplace. Consider the example of a consumer durables manufacturer that manufactured most of its products in China. Because the delivery of the products from China took a long time, the company had to maintain high inventory levels. As a result, the firm was rapidly losing ground to competitors. To regain its market share, the company split its traditional one-size-fits-all supply chain into four smaller supply chains, or splinters. Products for which there was high, stable demand were assigned to the first splinter and continued to be manufactured in China. Products for which there was low, volatile demand were assigned to the second splinter and manufactured in the United States. The manufacturing of products with low but regular demand was split between the United States and Mexico and assigned to the third and fourth splinters. These changes helped the company reduce its cost of goods sold by 15%. Furthermore, the company was able to improve its quality levels across its full range of products, receive its products faster, and most important, improve its customer service levels by having the right goods available for them to purchase at the right times.[22]

Splintering: the practice of breaking traditional supply chains into smaller and more agile supply chains that can better respond to higher levels of business complexity, save money, and improve customer service

Sustainability: the use of methods, systems, and materials that won't deplete resources or harm natural cycles

Sustainability

Patagonia, the seller of outdoor clothing and equipment, is known for its sustainability initiatives and enjoys the reputation as an enlightened employer and champion of the environment.

AP Photo/Rick Bowmer

In recent years, customers have demanded that businesses operate in a socially responsible manner and produce products that do not harm the environment. Therefore, operations and supply chain strategies that focus solely on costs and time efficiency may not be enough. These strategies should also incorporate responsible labor practices and practices that minimize harm to the environment and use the world's resources wisely. Collectively these initiatives are referred to as sustainability. Sustainability is the use of *methods, systems, and materials that won't deplete resources or harm natural cycles*.[23] Companies need to integrate sustainability not only internally but also through all tiers of their supply chains, including their suppliers in developing countries. McDonald's, for example, forged closer relationships with its suppliers and provided them with a tool called the "environmental

scorecard." The suppliers were expected to improve over time their sustainability practices by measuring their use of water, their use of energy, their production of waste, and their air emissions. Such sustainable sourcing practices have not only improved McDonald's sales, but they have also helped reestablish the McDonald's brand. The company placed 12th on the 2016 Interbrand Best Global Brands list.[24]

Companies that take a creative and proactive approach to incorporating sustainability into their operations and supply chains can often drive down costs, mitigate risks, discover innovative approaches to developing products and services, and share the risks and rewards among their supply chain partners. Incorporating sustainability into a company's strategies, as cosmetics company Aveda (Aveda Corporation, Blaine, MN) does, also improves its reputation among consumers, which can allow a company to charge more for its products. Patagonia, Inc. (Ventura,

CA), the seller of outdoor clothing and equipment, is known for its sustainability initiatives and enjoys its reputation as an enlightened employer and champion of the environment. The company has a very simple but challenging goal: to produce the highest quality products with minimum possible harm to the environment. The company donates 1% of its total sales or 10% of its profit, whichever is greater, to environmental groups. From 1985 to 2005, Patagonia has donated US$25 million to more than 1,000 organizations. Although the company's products are priced higher than those of its competitors, the firm's operating margins typically are high for its industry—even with the donations figured in.[25]

 Corporate Social Responsibility

In recent years, many businesses worldwide have begun adopting practices that reflect a greater degree of **corporate social responsibility (CSR)**. CSR is the process of incorporating the interests of the public into a company's core business. One principle of CSR is that companies should make decisions with an eye toward what's good for the triple bottom line—which consists of people, the planet (environmental impact), and profits. Sony, for example, approaches CSR from two different perspectives. The first relates to the way it procures its materials. In March 2002, Sony established a set of "management regulations for environment-related substances to be controlled which are included in parts and materials"[26] These internal regulations require identification of environment-related substances that are banned or to be reduced along with applications where they are used. The second perspective

FIGURE 1.10: Linking Supply Chain and Operations Management

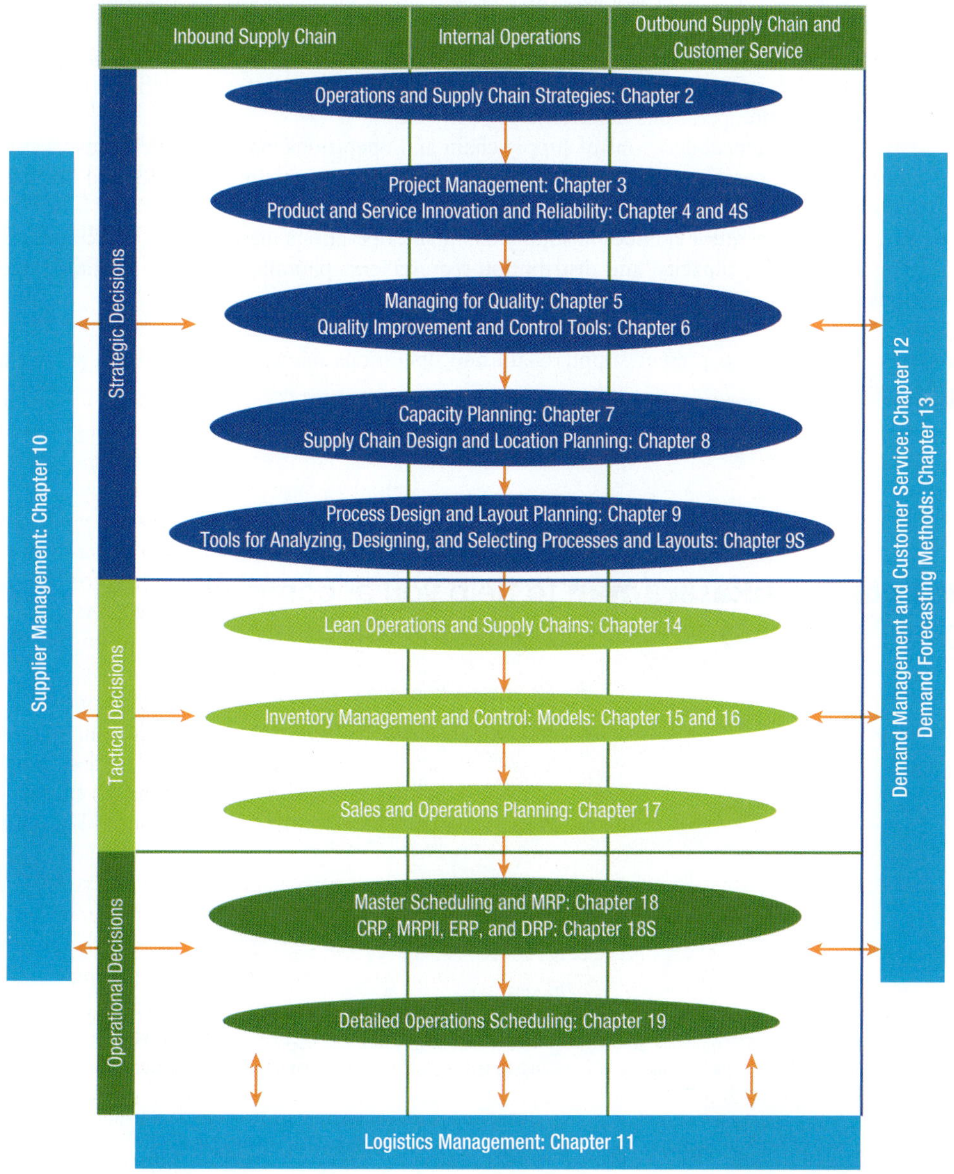

Inbound Supply Chain	Internal Operations	Outbound Supply Chain and Customer Service

Operations and Supply Chain Strategies: Chapter 2

Project Management: Chapter 3
Product and Service Innovation and Reliability: Chapter 4 and 4S

Managing for Quality: Chapter 5
Quality Improvement and Control Tools: Chapter 6

Capacity Planning: Chapter 7
Supply Chain Design and Location Planning: Chapter 8

Process Design and Layout Planning: Chapter 9
Tools for Analyzing, Designing, and Selecting Processes and Layouts: Chapter 9S

Lean Operations and Supply Chains: Chapter 14

Inventory Management and Control: Models: Chapter 15 and 16

Sales and Operations Planning: Chapter 17

Master Scheduling and MRP: Chapter 18
CRP, MRPII, ERP, and DRP: Chapter 18S

Detailed Operations Scheduling: Chapter 19

Logistics Management: Chapter 11

Supplier Management: Chapter 10

Strategic Decisions

Tactical Decisions

Operational Decisions

Demand Management and Customer Service: Chapter 12
Demand Forecasting Methods: Chapter 13

Corporate social responsibility (CSR): the process of incorporating the interests of the public into a company's core business

relates to the environment, human rights, and labor conditions. In supporting this initiative, Sony closely monitors and manages the chemicals used in its products at all stages of the manufacturing cycle, from the raw materials and components through the final shipment. To promote its social agenda, Sony procures parts and materials only from those suppliers who are designated as green partners.

1.7 Road Map: How This Text Is Organized

Figure 1.10 on the previous page shows the organization of this text. This figure outlines the flow of chapters against the backdrop of strategic, tactical, and operational decisions OM managers face. These decisions become progressively more relevant, not simply to internal operations but also impact inbound and outbound elements of the supply chain. Some chapters fit cleanly into this classification, and others, as we shall see, are not so easily categorized or operate on multiple levels. We will also consider them in turn.

- The remainder of Part 1 (chapters 2 through 9) corresponds to the strategic view of managing global supply chains and operations. The topics covered deal with such critical elements in supply chain and operations strategy as the design of products and services, project management, quality planning, location and capacity planning, and process selection and layout planning.
- Part 2, on the integrative decisions of supply chain and operations management, covers topics that are not easily categorized as strategic, tactical, or operational. The chapters on supplier management, logistics management, and demand management contain topics that are critical at each level and, thus, must be considered more comprehensively. Although not a separate part of the text, it is critical to understand these integrative concepts across all decision levels in the supply chain and operations hierarchy.
- Part 3, on the tactical decisions of supply chain and operations management, discusses critical issues in lean operations and supply chains, inventory management, and sales and operations planning.
- Part 4 covers operational issues in supply chain and operations management. It includes chapters on materials, capacity, and distribution requirements planning, as well as detailed operations scheduling.

The goal of this text is to present supply chain and operations management in global service and product industries.

Visit **edge.sagepub.com/venkataraman** to help you accomplish your coursework goals in an easy-to-use learning environment.

- Mobile-friendly eFlashcards
- Mobile-friendly practice quizzes
- A complete online action plan

- Chapter summaries with learning objectives
- Video and multimedia resources

CHAPTER SUMMARY

1.1 Explain how globalization has affected the management of supply chains and their operations. A company managing its global supply chain and operations faces numerous challenges, such as the costs of doing business abroad, the productivity and quality of the work of foreign workers, extended shipping times, and the difficulty of selecting suppliers that a firm isn't familiar with or familiar suppliers that don't always perform well. Firms that can handle these challenges well can create a competitive advantage for their organizations. This is particularly true for supply chain management. Supply chain management is the next great competitive frontier.

1.2 Describe the role of operations management within a company and in society. Operations management is a transformative function. It involves managing a set of processes required to design, produce, and deliver goods or services that add value throughout the supply chain and that benefit the final consumer. Operations management plays a pivotal role in our lives.

1.3 Trace the path of a raw material from the start of the supply chain to the final consumer. Supply chain management involves managing and integrating key business processes, relationships, and flows of materials, information, money, and people, with the ultimate goal of creating value for a firm's customers and stakeholders. An organization's supply chain is made up of numerous inbound and outbound partners. Each supply chain partner has to be managed for a firm to maximize its performance.

1.4 Explain why it is important to have an integrated view of operations from a larger supply chain framework. Critical decisions made in both operations and supply chain management at the strategic, tactical, and operational levels impact each other as the two are interrelated. First, upstream interfaces or relationships between operations and suppliers must be managed effectively to ensure the right quality materials are obtained at the right quantity and at the right time. Second, the downstream interfaces—the relationship that the firm's operations has with its customers—have to be managed effectively to improve the firm's product sales and growth. Finally, the vertical interfaces—the relationship the firm has with suppliers that provide the technology

and the skilled labor needed to design the firm's products, processes, and other services—have to be managed effectively to promote efficiency of operations, produce quality products, and minimize disruptions in production and the delivery of the final products to customers.

1.5 Describe the evolution of operations and supply chain management from the Industrial Revolution to the present. The Industrial Revolution vastly changed how products were produced. Most modern innovations took place in the 20th century. These innovations include TQM, Six Sigma, lean and agile manufacturing, BPM, and ERP. In the 21st century, increased globalization has led to a proliferation of strategic partnerships, joint ventures, licensing agreements, research consortia, direct marketing agreements—and above all—the formation of global supply chains.

1.6 Identify some of the current and emerging trends in operations and supply chain management. The trend toward optimizing the use of raw materials and labor by eliminating waste and maximizing productivity will continue. Methods such as such Six Sigma and lean and agile manufacturing will gain popularity not only in the manufacturing sector but in the service sector as well. Greater supply chain risks and the restructuring of supply chains are likely to continue, as are the trends toward sustainability and corporate social responsibility.

KEY TERMS

Agile manufacturing   17

Business process management (BPM)   18

Business process reengineering (BPR)   18

Corporate social responsibility (CSR)   21

Customer management   16

Demand management   15

Enterprise resource planning (ERP)   19

Inbound portion   11

Lean manufacturing   17

Lean production   17

Offshoring   2

Operations management (OM)   3

Operations strategies   17

Outbound portion   12

Outsourcing   2

Service support   16

Six Sigma   17

Splintering   20

Supplier management   16

Supply chain   3

Sustainability   20

Technology management   16

Total quality management (TQM)   17

Value chain   3

DISCUSSION AND REVIEW QUESTIONS

1. Compare and contrast outsourcing and offshoring. List some of the companies that have adopted these strategies in recent years and the reasons for them.

2. Wal-Mart (Wal-Mart Stores Inc., Bentonville, AR) has been one of the most successful companies in the retail industry because of its ability to sell products at "everyday low prices." What competitive strengths of Wal-Mart gave the company this advantage over its competition?

3. Define global supply chains. What are the inherent challenges that companies face in managing them?

4. Explain in some detail the critical role of the operations function in a company's success and its supply chain.

5. What are the key differences between goods and services?

6. Figure 1.5 presents the operations function as a system that transforms inputs into outputs. For the following scenarios, identify the inputs and outputs and the value created during the transformation process:
   a. A patient undergoing surgery in a hospital
   b. Airline travel
   c. Teaching students in a classroom
   d. Production of an automobile

7. One brand of The Campbell Soup Company (Camden, NJ) is condensed canned soup. Create a supply chain showing the movement of materials and information for this brand from the basic raw materials suppliers to you as the final consumer.

PROBLEMS

1. Give three examples of large firms that have international suppliers.

2. What are some key reasons why a firm should consider offshoring or outsourcing its work? Imagine you are the head of operations for Nike. What functions would it make sense to offshore or outsource, and which activities might you consider maintaining in-house? Why?

3. Why are companies setting up call centers and other service offices in India? If you were hiring Indian employees for such a call center, what characteristics would be critical for them to be hired?

4. After considering the various career options within supply chain and operations management, what underlying skills do you believe successful managers need to possess? Why?

5. Use the Internet to find examples of organizational transformation processes that are (a) physical, (b) locational, (c) transactional, (d) physiological, (e) psychological, or (f) informational? List a company's operations associated with each of these transformation processes [e.g., The Walt Disney Company (aka Disney, Burbank, CA) specializes in psychological transformations through guest experiences at its theme parks].

6. Consider the operation management interfaces with other business functions shown in Figure 1.4. Read the Zara Operations Profile. What interfaces in Figure 1.4 does Zara manage well? Why?

7. Give an example of a supply chain for a service.

8. Suppose you were considering hiring a supplier for a critical good your firm needs to make its products. Your final choices came down to three companies: one in Nigeria, one in Venezuela, and one in Bangladesh. Using the Corruption Index from Transparency.org, which company would seem the safest choice? Why?

9. Suppose you were considering hiring a supplier for a critical good your firm needs to make its products. Your final choices came down to three companies: one in Nigeria, one in Venezuela, and one in Bangladesh. Using the assessment of International Competitiveness from the World Economic Forum's website, which company would seem the best choice? Why?

10. Given the conflicting information in the two metrics (corruption and competitiveness) in questions 8 and 9, how would you resolve these discrepancies? That is, when dealing with supplier choices that involve multiple assessments, what should be the critical decision criteria for selecting suppliers? Why?

11. What are the advantages and disadvantages of having multiple layers of first- and second-tier suppliers?

12. What are some of the major costs in developing a supply chain? Hint: Identify the different upstream interfaces, and consider some of the likely costs associated with each of these interfaces.

13. What are some of the major downstream costs in developing a supply chain? Hint: Identify the different downstream interfaces, and consider some of the likely costs associated with each of these interfaces.

14. Why are the concepts of demand management and supplier management so critical to success operations and supply chain performance? Give examples of companies that specialize in excellent demand and supplier management practices?

15. Consider the evolution of operations and supply chain management (Table 1.3). Suppose you were tracing the likely development of Coca-Cola's operations from its founding in 1892 to the modern day. How might some of the innovations and production emphases over the past 125 years have affected Coca-Cola? Organize your answer in a table like the following:

Time Period	Innovations	Production Emphasis
1892–1910	Division of Labor	Factory Management
1910–1940	Assembly Lines and Automation	Mass Production

16. Why is sustainability so critical for successful operations and supply chain management in modern organizations?

17. Give an example of how ethics plays a role in supply chain management? (Hint: Think of the process of qualifying international, upstream suppliers. How would ethics factor into this decision?)

18. Consider the Lessons Learned about Apple. Why is it dangerous to use a single-source supplier when you are a company like Apple, which depends heavily on its ability to dazzle consumers with new products? How could employing multiple suppliers minimize Apple's risk in case one of its suppliers went out of business? What are the pros and cons of using cutting-edge materials or technologies in new products for a company like Apple?

CASE STUDY 1.1 MULTINATIONAL COMPANIES AND CHINA: INVESTING FOR THE LONG TERM

Multinational companies have had a long history of being careful in their investment decisions in China. When recalling his earlier days studying China's investment climate in 1981, Dr. Karl Harn, a magnate in the German auto industry, said, "For most multinational companies at that time, China was still a . . . [mystery]." In the decades since this observation, the pendulum has swung dramatically in the direction of working with Chinese firms as partners. In the Pudong district, Shanghai's central commercial hub, 98 international companies have invested in 181 projects worth US$8 billion.

The entry into China has been deliberate and carefully measured by many of these multinational firms. Until the mid-1990s, most multinational companies merely set up representative offices in China and mainly engaged in direct trade. Yet, since 1995, companies have penetrated the Chinese market for several reasons. First, the government has loosened its grip on economic policy, allowing for increasing interaction with corporate partners. Second, China's economy has grown and a significant percentage of the population is both well educated and has disposable income. China is more than a source for producing goods; it is now a hugely attractive market. Finally, China has continued to pursue economic and infrastructure projects to open and modernize its country even more, increasing its potential customers and business partners.

The multinational firms have responded to the obvious incentives in the Chinese market, and they now seek to establish production facilities in China and to enter into joint ventures and other partnership deals with Chinese firms. The list of multinational organizations that are firmly committed to the Chinese market reads like a *Who's Who* list: Omron Corporation (Kyoto, Japan); Hitachi, Ltd. (Tokyo, Japan); Panasonic Corporation (Osaka, Japan); Sanyo Electric Co., Ltd. (now part of Panasonic Corporation, Osaka, Japan); Fujitsu Ltd. (Tokyo, Japan); Toshiba Corporation (Tokyo, Japan); Isuzu Motors Ltd. (Tokyo, Japan); Siemens AG (Munich, Germany); Bayer AG (Leverkusen, Germany); Henkel Corporation (Düsseldorf, Germany); General Electric (aka GE, Faifield, CT); IBM (International Business Machines Corporation, Armonk, NY); Motorola Solutions, Inc. (aka Motorola, Schaumburg, IL); and Dell Inc. (Round Rock, TX).

Consider other multinational companies that have accelerated their large investment in China. McDonald's has built 52 factories in China. Sweden-Swiss ABB Group (Zürich, Switzerland) established 20 joint ventures. Volkswagen AG (Wolfsburg, Germany) set up four large joint ventures and one sole enterprise with a total investment of US$2 billion. In addition, The Boeing Company (Chicago, IL) has three large joint ventures with Chinese companies, and components used in more than 3,000 Boeing planes now flying worldwide were made in China. Moreover, multinational companies are investing in their localization strategy by hiring Chinese human resources instead of transferring their people overseas. For example, Microsoft (China) Co., Ltd. (Beijing, P.R. China) employs more than 500 Chinese workers, most of them possessing masters and doctorate degrees. In the ABB (China) Group (Shanghai, P.R. China), ten general managers are Chinese.

China is no longer just a source for low-wage labor. Multinational companies have begun locating their research and development departments there. By the end of 2010, Microsoft had invested US$80 million in a China Research Institute and declared recently that a US$50 million investment will be made in the Microsoft Asian Technology Center in Shanghai, the company's most advanced research institute in China. Siemens has also opened key technology centers in China. Motorola; Nortel Networks Corporation (formerly Northern Telecom Ltd., Mississauga, Ontario, Canada); IBM; Intel Corporation (Santa Clara, CA); DuPont China Holding Co., Ltd. (Shanghai, P.R. China); P&G (Procter & Gamble Co., Cincinnati, OH); Ericsson (Stockholm, Sweden); Panasonic; and Mitsubishi Motors Corporation (Tokyo, Japan) have all established research centers, technological development centers, and laboratories in the country. The Nokia Corporation (Espoo, Finland) has opened its first Chinese Bell Labs in Jinqiao, East of Shanghai, where it is ranked as a top 10 research center for the entire country.

A survey conducted by a Boston-based firm indicates that 90% of companies in Europe, the United States, and Japan have set a strategy to pursue opportunities in China ahead of other ventures: "Their race to invest and relocate their head offices in China clearly tells us that multinational companies have focused their key strategies on China, a stable and developing China cannot

be separated from the world, and the world cannot be independent of China, which is creating external business opportunities."[26]

Despite these advantages, multinational companies doing business in China face some risks and challenges. These risks include the need to conform to the Chinese government's mandate to form joint ventures with local Chinese companies instead of setting up independent business units as well as China's often lax handling of intellectual property rights. Consequently, companies face risk of loss of proprietary information and drain of key technological knowledge.

Questions:

1. How do you respond to the view that China's competitive advantage is based solely on a low-cost strategy that results from its workers' low wages?

2. Do you see dangers from over-reliance on China as a source for the inbound supply chain? That is, what risks do international firms run if they depend heavily on China for their inbound supply chain?

CASE STUDY 1.2 NINTENDO'S WII AND WII U: ABSENCE MAKES THE HEART GROW FONDER

Our story begins the week before Christmas in 2010, just about anywhere in the United States. A friend has tipped you off that a local toy retailer may be getting in a shipment of Nintendo Wii (Nintendo of America, Redmond, WA) consoles on a Friday night and that they will go on sale when the store opens Saturday morning. By 10 PM, you arrive at the store where you join a line of other customers for a long, overnight wait. You hope to be one of the dozen or so customers lucky enough to snag the game console in time to fulfill your children's holiday wishes. By morning, a member of the sales staff of the retailer distributes two dozen vouchers to the crowd. Your overnight vigil paid off as you will be one of the lucky few able to purchase a Wii in time for Christmas.

One of the most popular game console systems since its introduction, Nintendo's Wii was also one of the most difficult to find. This story of a lack of supply continued to repeat itself year after year, leading some to suspect that Wii shortages were simply created by Nintendo to maintain the public's fascination with the company's entertainment system. After all, they reasoned, was it likely that Nintendo's supply chain problems could continue to follow the same patterns since Wii's introduction in 2007?

Unfortunately, these problems have continued to plague Nintendo since the release of its newest Wii U gaming system. When it launched in 2013, the Wii U attracted so much consumer attention that within weeks, Nintendo once again cautioned that it would not be able to fill all orders for the upcoming holiday season. GameStop Corporation (Grapevine, TX), one of the largest U.S. game retailers, had already begun compiling a waiting list after pre-orders filled up. In no time at all, more than 250,000 names were on the list! Ironically, to generate initial enthusiasm for the product, Nintendo made the decision to sell the consoles at a marked-down price, meaning that for every console the company sold, it took a loss. This combination of a product in short supply and resulting losses means that Nintendo's supply chain has once again made it difficult for the company to realize the benefits from technological advances in gaming.

What has prompted the continued bottleneck, or delay, of Wii consoles? Some industry analysts believe that Nintendo bet that the shortages wouldn't cause customers to look for competing gaming consoles to buy instead. Although Nintendo has denied that this is its strategy and pointed instead to supply chain problems leading to delays, industry analysts suspect that a regular pattern of holiday shortages indicates otherwise. Whether intentional or not, there is no question that for several years this operating pattern paid

off: Customer demand for Wii consoles remained strong and, in fact, grew at a strong pace, even in the face of continued shortages.

The entertainment system industry is highly competitive, with rival systems from Sony [Play Station 4 (PS 4)] and Microsoft (Xbox One) pushing to capture some of Nintendo's market share. Not only has its system been highly popular with the public, but Nintendo has been consistently profitable in comparison with Sony and Microsoft, which have been losing money on every unit sold.

Can Nintendo's deliberate (or accidental) bottleneck strategy continue in the future? Industry analysts suspect that it cannot. As Bruce Richardson, chief research officer at AMR Research, Inc. (Boston, MA) noted, "In consumer electronics, you've got to pay close attention to the product lifecycle. . . . And if this stuff is all coordinated inside Nintendo, it doesn't appear that way in the U.S. market." This point was born out in recent industry sales numbers, as Wii U unit sales tumbled relative to its main competitor, Sony's PS 4. Several industry analysts traced declining sales to the chronic and continued supply chain problems in Nintendo's manufacturing and delivery systems.

Ultimately, it may simply be changes in the gaming market that prompt Nintendo to alter its supply chain and retailing strategy. The lack of availability of the Wii U could not have come at a worse time for Nintendo, which has seen its sales volume steadily declining since 2011 and in 2014 surrendered its industry leadership to Sony. The Wii U was Nintendo's strongest effort to reclaim the top spot in the gaming industry, but with a shaky and uncertain supply chain, it is anybody's guess how the latest round in this ongoing competition is likely to turn out. When Nintendo dominated console and game sales, it had the added luxury of slowing the speed of its supply chain if it wanted to. Now, however, the ability to profit from deliberate shortages is rapidly looking like a thing of the past.[27]

Questions:

1. Develop an argument either in favor of or against a deliberate shortage strategy, such as Nintendo has experienced in the past. What are the advantages and disadvantages of maintaining shortages?

2. With increased sales of competing devices, can Nintendo maintain a bottleneck strategy? What might be required for them to maintain such a strategy?

VIDEO CASE

Watch this video case to learn about how Rolls-Royce uses a global supply chain to their advantage in managing operations.

CRITICAL THINKING EXERCISES

Toyota, known for its quality automobiles, had its reputation tarnished by having to recall millions of its vehicles due to defective accelerators and brakes. The following article discusses the importance of accepting that quality problems can occur in any company and the need to have an effective crisis management mechanism in place.

Search for the article titled "Toyota Was in Denial. How About You" on Bloomberg.com and answer the questions that follow.

1. Why is the information in this article important to operations managers?

2. What are the basic reasons behind Toyota's recent product safety lapses?

3. How can hard questioning be good operations management? Can it be bad for operations management?

4. What can or should U.S. operators learn from Toyota's problems?

5. What is the future of the regulation of product safety in the United States?

CHAPTER 2

Operations and Supply Chain Strategies

LEARNING OBJECTIVES

After studying this chapter, you should be able to:

1. Compare the different levels of strategic planning, and identify the performance measures in each.

2. Define operations strategy, and describe how it is formulated and evaluated.

3. Contrast the formulation and evaluation of operating strategies for service organizations with those for manufacturing organizations.

4. Compare the different types of productivity measurements, and explain how firms use them strategically.

5. Describe how both manufacturers and service organizations formulate and evaluate their supply chain strategies.

6. Identify the key capabilities firms need to formulate and implement global operations and supply chain strategies and manage the risks related to them.

7. Describe what companies are doing to incorporate sustainability into their supply chain strategy and the problems they face in doing so.

OPERATIONS PROFILE: Pfizer's Revamped Supply Chain Strategy Saves the Company Millions

Pfizer, Inc. (New York, NY), a leading maker of pharmaceuticals, altered its supply chain strategy to improve its bottom-line profitability. Pfizer spends millions of dollars annually on consulting, legal, and financial services. The company uses consulting services for various technical and managerial tasks, ranging from laboratory processes to human resource training. It requires legal services for filing patents, defending against lawsuits, trademark protection, and so forth. As a first step in reducing these costs, the company set up a centralized procurement (buying) department and a new professional services team within it to examine the services the firm buys. Called the Knowledge Management Services (KMS) Group, it saved Pfizer a whopping US$370 million between 2007 and 2010. The KMS team concentrated on consulting services and legal services.

To develop a disciplined approach to using consulting services at Pfizer, the team created a process to review, classify, and approve outside consultants:

- **Procurement review and the approval of services.** The KMS team played a critical role in selecting and evaluating the company's consulting service providers as well as in deciding which projects required consulting in the first place. "One of the first things we worked on was selecting consulting firms that are very focused on the business units' needs," Joanne Lupatkin, a manager in Pfizer's procurement group, explained. "We now spend a lot of time on capability assessments and collecting feedback on work performed to ensure the money we're spending is on the right activities with the right firms."
- **The classification of designated firms.** Pfizer's key strategic suppliers, which provided the company with about 85% of all of its consulting needs, were classified as designated firms. These firms had been approved for their past performance and ability to deliver value for low cost. When Pfizer needs consulting services valued at more than US$100,000, these companies bid on the projects. Pfizer's senior executives then must sign off on the services and the bids before they can be provided.

On the legal side, the focus and goals differed, explained Elena Polansky, the director of Pfizer's procurement group. The team streamlined qualification processes and reduced from 85 to less than 20 the number of law firms with which the company works. Furthermore, they changed the billing structure for legal services. Legal firms now charge Pfizer an annual flat fee for all work performed during a calendar year, and each firm is responsible for managing its work within the flat fee. "The firms that are within the Pfizer Legal Alliance now understand that the focus is not on the billable hours, but on the value they are adding for Pfizer," said Polansky.

Robert S. Roseman, the senior director of Pfizer's procurement group, said he knew from the start that executive-level support, communication, and the skills of the KMS team were integral to the success of the initiative. The team members understand how legal and consulting services and the business units operate, according to Roseman. "The bottom line is these are not tactical purchasing people, but those who can think strategically. They are perceived, and act, as business partners."[1]

2.1 Levels of Strategic Planning

It's not enough for a company to produce a product, sell it, and hope to remain competitive forever. To continue to survive, companies have to develop and then frequently review and revamp their various strategies—including their operations and supply chain strategies.

A firm's strategy results from decisions made at the corporate, business-unit, and functional (departmental) levels. These levels are closely linked and form a

FIGURE 2.1: Strategic Planning Levels

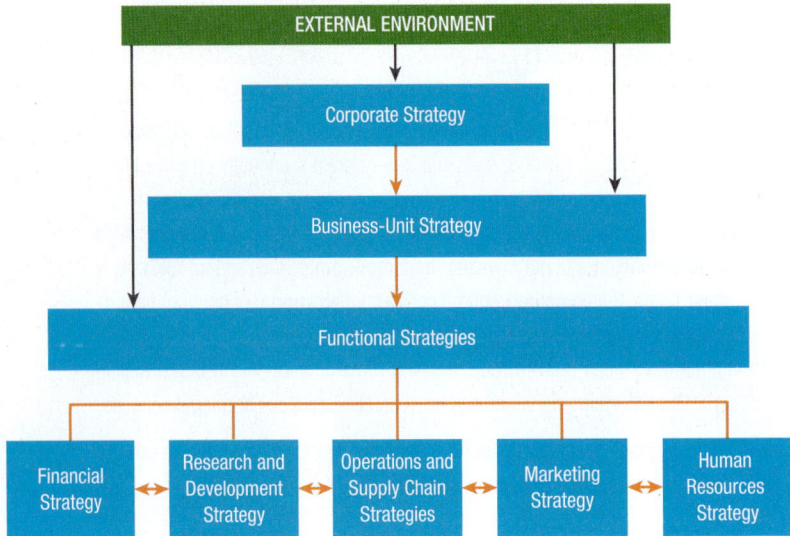

2.1

Compare the different levels of strategic planning, and identify the performance measures in each.

Corporate strategy: a strategy formulated by an organization's top managers and board of directors that attempts to address the fundamental question of what industries and markets the organization should enter and compete in

Triple bottom line: three performance targets that measure sustainability: the (a) economic value it provides its shareholders and the (b) environmental and (c) social value the company creates

Economic value: the traditional bottom line of economic performance

---

hierarchy, as shown in Figure 2.1. In this section, we look at each of these levels, the types of strategy decisions made at each level, and how the levels are linked.

Corporate Strategy

Large conglomerates own multiple businesses. Sony Corporation (Tokyo, Japan) operates eight strategic business units ranging from Sony Electronics to Sony Financial. General Electric (aka GE, Fairfield, CT) is organized around several diverse business units, ranging from oil and gas, to transportation, to aviation, to health care. A **corporate strategy**, which is formulated by an organization's top managers and board of directors, attempts to address the fundamental question of what industries and markets the organization should enter and compete in.

Corporate strategic planning is the broadest in scope (highest level in the hierarchy), has a long-term time horizon, and establishes the overall goals and directions for the corporation as a whole. Decisions made at this level typically include what businesses to acquire or divest, whether to acquire suppliers or distributors, and how to allocate resources between the different strategic business units of the corporation. These decisions, in turn, constrain the decisions made at lower levels in the hierarchy.

Traditionally, the primary objective of a corporate strategy was to improve the economic performance of the firm to create and sustain value to people who have invested in the company—its shareholders. More recently, however, several companies have expanded the scope of their corporate strategies to include stakeholders who affect the firm or are affected by it. These stakeholders can include communities, environmental resources, or future generations of trained workers. In other words, companies are increasingly considering sustainability when they formulate their corporate strategies.

Three performance targets measure sustainability. Together, they are called the **triple bottom line**. A firm's triple bottom line includes not only the economic value it provides its shareholders, but also the environmental and social value the company creates. Figure 2.2 illustrates the concept of triple bottom line with the three overlapping components of sustainability: economic, environmental, and social value.

Economic Value. One component in Figure 2.2 measures the traditional bottom line of the firm's economic performance. A business enterprise that is consistently losing money for its shareholders is not sustainable from an economic perspective even though it may be creating social and environmental value. The message of the triple bottom line, therefore, is not that a company should exclude the incentive to generate profits for itself and economic value to its shareholders. Instead, the triple bottom line strikes a balance between the profits a company generates with the external social and environmental costs associated with its production decisions.

Environmental Value. A company that creates economic value but exploits the environment and natural resources doesn't meet the standard of sustainability. First, the company risks running out of the natural resources it needs to operate. Fishing and logging companies, for example, must take care not to exhaust the fishing grounds and timberlands they harvest. Second, when firms do not include the environmental costs of their operations in their prices—for example, if a manufacturer fails to invest in equipment to lower the pollution emitted by its plants—customers will wrongly believe that the costs of the firms' products are lower than what they actually are. As a result, companies that do not include the environmental costs into the cost of production have an advantage over those companies that do report those environmental costs as part of their product costs. Nevertheless, although the polluters may benefit from this cost advantage in the short run, they may face serious problems in the long run. For example, the Peruvian government has declared an environmental state of emergency in the Pastaza River basin region because of the actions of Grupo Pluspetrol (Buenos Aires, Argentina), an Argentinan-based company developing its oil reserves, because of decades of pollution and mismanagement. The government has also fined Pluspetrol millions for its past actions.[2] One reason that companies do not report environmental costs is that these costs often are intangible and, hence, difficult to quantify. The problem of calculating environmental cost is further complicated because globally environmental regulations vary from one country to the next.

Operations managers can to help a corporation create environmental value. The Ford Motor Company's (aka Ford, Dearborn, MI) operation group has been working in conjunction with the company's car designers to build more sustainable cars. The cars' seat fabrics are made from 100% recycled materials, and renewable soy foam is used for the seat bases. Nevertheless, the operations function shouldn't restrict itself to figuring out just how to convert raw materials to finished products in a sustainable way. The department should also consider how products are packaged, how by-products and wastes are disposed of, and how energy and recycled materials are used. For example, to reduce waste and freight costs, several electronics firms in Korea are using rice husks converted into nontoxic packaging for stereo components and other electronics. The same material is subsequently reused to make bricks for Korea's construction industry.[3]

One approach that companies can use to evaluate environmental performance and to make improvements is life-cycle assessment (LCA). In this approach, the human and environmental impacts of a product's life from cradle to grave are quantified. At each stage of a product life cycle, the LCA considers alternative uses for the product, as well as associated waste streams, raw material extraction, material transport and processing, product manufacturing, distribution and use, repair and maintenance, and wastes or emissions associated with a product, process, or service as well as end-of-life disposal, reuse, or recycling.[4]

Social Value. Businesses depend heavily on the skills, education, and motivation of their employees. If a company mistreats or exploits its employees, it might create economic value in the short run, but it jeopardizes its sustainability because risks alienating its customers with its business practices and losing its employees to better firms. In 2001, Nike, Inc. (Beaverton, OR) admitted that it had contracted with factories in Pakistan and Cambodia that employed children to produce its expensive sportswear products. The children were being paid just pennies a day.

Nike didn't damage just itself though. Society suffered too. The inability of the children manufacturing its shoes to receive an education and develop more marketable skills and the inability of impoverished workers to purchase products and provide a robust consumer base for the enterprise and the economy are examples of these costs. A 2014 report by the risk analysis firm Verisk Maplecroft (Bath, U.K.), in its ranking of 197 countries, identified Eritrea, Somalia, Democratic Republic of Congo, Myanmar, and Sudan as the 5 places where child labor is most prevalent.[5] Multinational companies that contract with factories in these countries to produce their products should exercise great care in ensuring that children are not employed in producing their products.

As with environmental sustainability, if a firm fails to include social costs in its production and operating decisions, the prices of its products are likely to be artificially low, which in the short run gives these companies a cost advantage over companies that do attempt to capture these social costs.

FIGURE 2.2: Triple Bottom Line

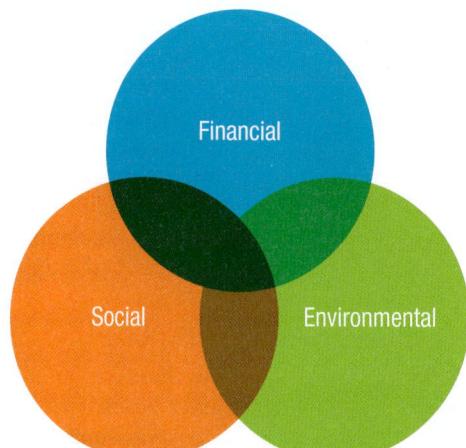

SOURCE: Reprinted from van den Berg, W. (n.d.). Does being wealthy mean being healthy? *Olive Leaf Foundation.* Retrieved from http://www.olf.org.za/article/does-wealth--health/

Why *Operations and Supply Chain Strategies* **Matter**

A company's operations and supply chain decisions are only as good as the strategy decisions made to implement them. Creating a strategy and using it to guide all subsequent operations decisions ensures that all internal operations and supply chain members are aligned with the company's goals.

Environmental value: the value created by sustainable practices

Social value: the value that results when the well-being of workers and other stakeholders is taken into account

Also, like environmental costs, it is hard to define social costs, and social sustainability practices of companies vary across the globe.

Patagonia, Inc. (Ventura, CA), a company that designs outdoor clothing and gear, is an example of a socially responsible company. Not only does Patagonia donate 1% of its total sales to environmental causes, the company also lets its employees take time off from their jobs and work for the environmental group of their choice, while continuing to pay these employees their salaries and benefits during their absence. Starbucks (Starbucks Corporation, Seattle, WA) is yet another company that promotes social values. The company treats its employees with respect and dignity, provides them with a friendly working environment, and pays them fair compensation and salary in accordance with laws and regulations. In cooperation with its employees, Starbucks ensures that safety regulations, practices, and training are followed so that accidents or injuries in the workplace can be prevented.

Business-Unit Strategies

Strategic Planning

For those companies that operate a single business, there is almost no distinction between a corporate and a business strategy. Nevertheless, for corporations that own a portfolio of businesses, each needs a business-unit strategy. Each of these businesses is typically referred to as a strategic business unit or SBU. A business-unit strategy establishes how each business unit should compete within its particular industry or market.

The focus of business strategies is on developing and leveraging the core competencies or competitive strengths within each SBU. The core competencies of the SBUs refer to the activities they excel at, or strive to excel at, such as the ability to produce high-quality or low-cost products. The aim of the process of identifying and developing core competencies is to arrive at a competitive plan that determines what products or services to offer in which market segments. Southwest Airlines Co.'s (Dallas, TX) core competency is offering low-cost, high-quality flights to price-conscious customers, who are their target market. Over time, this strategy has been successful as the company can operate inexpensively and maintain reasonable profit margins. For firms with multiple SBUs, the goal of the business strategy of each SBU is to achieve synergy by coordinating and integrating its activities to align with the overall corporate strategy of the firm.

Business-unit strategy: a strategy that establishes how each business unit should compete within its particular industry or market

Core competencies: the activities at which a firm excels or strives to excel

Competitive strengths: See **core competencies**

Functional strategies: Strategies that coordinate and integrate the activities and resources within each functional area of a company

Operations strategy: a strategy that uses the company's operational resources effectively to help it achieve a competitive advantage

Functional Strategies

The next level in the strategic planning process is the development of functional strategies for each area, such as marketing, operations, finance, and accounting. Functional strategies should coordinate and integrate the activities and resources within each functional area. As Figure 2.1 shows, the various functional strategies need to be designed to work in tandem with one another to support the higher level business strategies of the individual SBUs, as well as overall with the corporate strategy. Functional strategies are developed and implemented at a lower level in the corporate hierarchy, have shorter time horizons, and are more specific and detailed in terms of their action plans than are the higher-level business strategies.

Let's look at some examples of functional strategies. During difficult economic times or in markets in which there is intense competition, companies often adjust their marketing strategies to attract consumers and retain sales. McDonald's (Oak Brook, IL) decision to offer value meals is a marketing strategy. Similarly, BMW's (Bayerische Motoren Werke AG, Munich, Germany) engineering efforts to develop high-performance automobiles is a research and development strategy.

In this book, we concentrate on operations and supply chain strategies. Milliken & Co. (Spartanburg, SC), a textile manufacturer, is succeeding in an industry in which so many other American firms have failed. The firm's success results in part from its manufacturing innovations and a clever operations strategy that included diversifying out of traditional textiles and moving into niche products that built off its knowledge of textiles and specialty chemicals. For example, some Milliken innovations that have led to thousands of patents include the fabric that reinforces duct tape and the additives that make refrigerator food containers clear and children's art markers washable. Milliken also spread its 39 manufacturing centers to locations near their biggest markets in Europe and China.[6] Likewise, Wal-Mart's (Wal-Mart Stores Inc., Bentonville, AR) streamlining of its supply chain activities to achieve efficiencies and low costs is an example of a supply chain strategy. In the following sections, we will look more closely at the importance of operations and supply chain strategies and how they are formulated.

2.2 Formulating and Evaluating Operations Strategies

2.2

Define operations strategy, and describe how it is formulated and evaluated.

The purpose of a firm's operations strategy is to use the company's operational resources effectively to help it achieve a competitive advantage. An operations strategy, which provides the road map for all of the decisions managers of the firm's operations function make, is usually formulated in terms of the competitive priorities or core competencies of the firm, such as its ability to compete on prices and costs, quality, flexibility, time (speed), and innovation. These core competencies also typically constitute the objectives of the operations function.

In the past decades, companies were able to maintain their competitive advantage by emphasizing one or two of the competitive priorities, such as cost or quality. Nevertheless, advances in information technology, increasing globalization, and greater customer expectations have led to significant changes in the competitive priorities of firms. Today companies have to compete across multiple attributes of their core competencies.

Unfortunately, many organizations have found out the hard way that they cannot dramatically improve their operational capabilities in these multiple dimensions by using their existing resources. That is, these firms have discovered that to compete in the global arena, they have to rely on their supply chain partners and leverage *their* resources and operational capabilities. No longer is the competition between individual firms; instead, it is between supply chains, a topic we cover in Section 2.5.

Saab's inability to find its place in the car industry is an example of how a company's marketing and operational strategies must align for success.

©iStockphoto.com/Mikael Hjerpe

Until recently, managers in the operations function had little say in the formulation of a company's corporate objectives or business strategies and were viewed only as the function that improved production or service efficiency. Nor did a firm's operations strategy have much of an impact on its corporate strategy. A significant portion of the firm's resources and assets is tied to the operations function, however, and many structural decisions, such as plant locations and capacity investments, are directly related to the operations function. These structural decisions usually affect the firm in the long term, and once they are made, they are difficult to change. For example, if a company's decision to build a facility in a certain location is flawed, the facility can't be relocated easily. To avoid such a situation, the operations function should participate in the formulation of higher level strategies. In fact, in companies with a global reputation for operational excellence, the operations function not only participates in the formulation of the corporate and business-unit strategies but also, it is involved in major engineering and marketing decisions.

Nonetheless, all too often, firms have marketing-led strategies with the operations function serving only a supporting role. If the marketing strategies conflict with the operational capabilities of the firm, the firm might have to make costly structural changes, which can be time consuming and may come too late to have any meaningful competitive impact. Consider Saab (Saab Automobile AB, Trollhättan, Sweden), the Swedish auto manufacturer. For many years, it has hovered on the brink of bankruptcy. Historically, the company was known for its premium quality cars. Nevertheless, its sales have been declining steadily since the 1990s. A major reason for the company's difficulties is that its marketing strategy is misaligned with the operations strategy. Saab lacks the operational capabilities to compete based on economies of scale or costs. In addition, its products are not different enough to command top prices because the company hasn't invested enough in technology to improve its operational and design capabilities. In effect, Saab has not been able decide what it has to offer consumers.

Critical Elements of an Operations Strategy

An operations strategy has four critical elements—customers, operational capabilities or **critical success factors (CSFs)**, product factors, and core competencies—that can enable a company to achieve competitive advantage. Operations can come up with product-related features that customers most value or production technologies and processes that competition can't easily imitate. Figure 2.3 shows how a company's core competencies (value creation) can be enhanced as a result of addressing customer-related factors, operational CSFs, product factors, *or* some combination of all of these features. In the subsequent sections, we will discuss each of these elements in more detail.

PRODUCT FACTORS

Developing a manufacturing mission depends to a great extent on product factors: the nature of the product, its stage in the product life cycle, and the process used to produce that product. The nature of the product refers to the distinctive features or characteristics that identify the good or service. For example, as a result of their rapid obsolescence, computers and smartphones have very short product

Critical success factors (CSFs): strategic factors unique to a specific industry

FIGURE 2.3: Four Elements of an Operations Strategy

life cycles. Firms that manufacture and sell these products strive for superior innovation as their core competency.

Similarly, products that are in the mature stages of their life cycles require different core competencies. Mature products are typically not prone to rapid obsolescence, so an emphasis on innovation may not be necessary for firms producing such products. Nevertheless, a firm can still improve the profitability of these products. Such a firm might streamline its processes to make the delivery of the products more efficient. We will discuss the relationship between products and processes in much greater detail in Chapter 7.

CUSTOMERS

Customers are the people and groups that consume a firm's products or services. The ultimate aim of operations and supply chain strategies is to produce and deliver those products or services that not only satisfy but also delight customers, the people and groups who consume a firm's products or services. Although you are the end-consumer of the product or service delivered by a firm, each downstream partner of that firm in the supply chain is also a customer. For example, you may be the end-user of the Crest toothpaste produced by P&G (Procter & Gamble Co., Cincinnati, OH) but a retail store such as Wal-Mart is also an intermediate customer. Therefore, P&G has the responsibility of meeting not only your expectations but also those of Wal-Mart. Nevertheless, a firm must ultimately identify its critical customers—those that have the greatest impact on its success, perhaps even survival—and address the needs of those customers first.

CRITICAL SUCCESS FACTORS

Every industry has some unique strategic factors, such as resources or capabilities, which affect a company's ability to successfully compete. These elements are called critical success factors (CSFs). CSFs vary from company to company. Each firm should determine its CSFs based on what's important to the customers in the target market. The fundamental question the firm must answer is as follows: If your competitors are also offering the same or similar products or services, how will you distinguish yourself from the rest of the competition so that the potential customers will choose your product instead of your competitors? Then you have to decide what CSFs you need to achieve a sustainable competitive advantage. That is, how will you prevent your competitors from copying what's special about your product?

CSFs can originate from superior technology, operations and processes, logistics and distribution capabilities, marketing channels, information processing ability, or the skills of employees. A firm might derive a sustainable competitive advantage from its superior ability to design and introduce new products quickly, service a wide range of products, provide customized products or services on demand, or deliver products quickly.[7]

The CSFs that are the responsibility of the operations function become part of the company's *manufacturing mission*. The design, plan, and control of a firm's operations system should be geared toward accomplishing the manufacturing mission. Companies that are known globally for their manufacturing excellence have well-defined manufacturing missions.[8] Mitsubishi Motors North America, Inc. (Cypress, CA), a worldwide leader in manufacturing automobiles for the North American market, has the following manufacturing mission statement: "Mitsubishi Motors builds world class vehicles. We achieve the highest level of quality through effective teamwork and by practicing unwavering commitment to each other, our products, customers and the community."[9]

CORE COMPETENCIES

The manufacturing mission provides the basis for the operations function to identify and develop its core competencies (also known as competitive priorities, competitive strengths, or competitive weapons). Earlier we introduced the five core competencies: price, quality, time, innovation, and flexibility. In this section, we will take a closer look at each of these core competencies and discuss their importance. Note that although critical success factors are strategic factors that a company requires to compete in a given industry, core competencies are skills or key areas of expertise that a company has developed over time that distinguish the company from its competitors on the satisfaction of the costumer's needs. Also note that a company cannot excel in all five core competencies. Therefore, a company has to identify a subset of these core competencies that it can be good at, as well as develop and nurture it. Furthermore, in choosing the best strategy to compete in a given market, companies have to make inevitable trade-offs among these five core competencies. For example, a company relying exclusively on delivery speed as a competitive weapon runs the risk of producing a higher rate of defective items. Therefore, companies should find the right balance of core competencies (such as deliver speed and quality) that are critical to their business goals.

Price

Customers want products that are reliable and perform well over time but that can be bought at the lowest possible price. A firm has two ways to compete based on the price: One is to produce the product at a lower cost than the company's competitors. If the product is a commodity such as gasoline or sugar—a product that consumers mostly buy based on its price—then the firm can try to achieve economies of scale that drive the production cost per unit down. For example, the company might invest in extra equipment so it can process, ship, and sell more of the product at a lower price.

If the product offering is not a commodity, then the firm has to find alternative ways to reduce the cost of the product, such as lowering the cost of raw materials or labor. For example, Vizio Inc. (Irvine, CA), a company that designs flat panel LCD and plasma TVs, uses a low-price strategy. Nevertheless, the company's products are not only among the lowest priced but also of very high quality. Vizio is able to keep its product costs low because these products are manufactured in Thailand where labor costs are low.

The second way a firm can compete on price is to be willing to accept a smaller profit margin. Wal-Mart, for example, operates with lower profit margins by selling its products at low prices. Yet, the enormous sales volume the retailer generates more than compensates for the lower profit margin.

Quality

Quality describes a product's fitness for use depending upon the price the customer is willing to pay for it. Nevertheless, what constitutes quality to a particular consumer depends on the specific dimension of quality in the product that he or she is looking for. The eight most common characteristics of quality are *performance, conformance, features, durability, reliability, serviceability, aesthetics,* and *perceived quality*.[10] We discuss quality in detail in Chapter 5, but it is worth noting here that competing simultaneously on the basis of all eight quality dimensions would be expensive and difficult. In addition, the nature of the product might force the company to make trade-offs among them. Depending on the expectations of the target market, a firm might have to focus on only one characteristic. For example, the mileage a Honda Civic (Honda Motor Co., Tokyo,

Quality: a product's fitness for use depending on the price the customer is willing to pay for it

Vizio is able to produce high-quality products at low costs due to an operations strategy that has their products assembled in Thailand where labor costs are low.

Amanda Edward/Getty Images Entertainment/Getty Images

Japan) gets is very important to its target market. The mileage a Ferrari (Ferrari S.p.A., Maranello, Italy) gets? Not so much. The people who buy a Ferrari can usually afford to pay for a lot of gasoline.

Time

Time as a core competency has three attributes: product development cycle time, on-time delivery, and delivery speed.

1. *Product development cycle time.* **Product development cycle time** is the time it takes to conceptualize a new good or service, produce it, and make it available to customers. Firms that compete based on product development cycle time have the capability to introduce more quickly new products that customers want. The ability to reduce a product's development time can be a significant advantage. For example, apparel companies such as Zara (Coruña, Spain; see the Operations Profile in Chapter 1) and H&M (H & M Hennes & Mauritz AB, Stockholm, Sweden) can get their products from the concept stage to retail stores in just two weeks. In today's fast-paced and volatile economic environment in which customers have less discretionary income to spend, firms need to deliver the right products at the right time. Consequently, companies have to analyze the marketplace for current trends and then deliver that product before the trend has passed.

2. *On-time delivery.* On-time delivery is a firm's ability to deliver the products to its customers on or before the promised delivery date. Getting the products in the hands of the customer by the promised delivery date is the responsibility of not just the manufacturing firm but also of all of the firm's supply chain partners. For example, to get the finished product on time to the customer, the manufacturing firm's upstream supplier should deliver the raw materials, parts, and components on time. The manufacturing firm, in turn, has to ensure that finished products are produced on schedule. Finally, the logistics and transportation network of the supply chain needs to get the finished products to the firm's downstream supply chain partners when promised.

   The General Broach Company (Morenci, MI), a firm that designs and manufactures metalworking and machine tools for automotive customers, has a competitive advantage and is considered to be one of the top three suppliers in this niche market. Its customers include Chrysler (Fiat Chrysler Automobiles, Auburn Hills, MI), Ford (already introduced), and The General Motors Company (aka GM or General Motors, Detroit, MI). One of General Broach's advantages over the competition is its ability to maintain a rapid delivery schedule to customers. The company can meet its on-time commitments by using a special enterprise resource planning (ERP) system on its shop floor. The system optimizes the flow of products by identifying where backups can occur.[11] In the service industry, FedEx (FedEx Corporation, Memphis, TN) is a firm that has made its reputation for on-time and reliable delivery.

3. *Delivery speed.* In some markets, the ability to deliver the product or service faster than the rest of the competition can be a competitive advantage. An example of a company that has been successful by competing on its delivery speed is R&R Engineering Co. The firm is a manufacturer of low-cost, low-profit-margin machined components that manufacturers such as those in China use to produce inexpensive products. By investing heavily in machinery to speed up its output and by holding roughly 3.5 million pounds of steel in stock on a continuing basis, R&R Engineering Co. (Summitville, IN) is often able to ship orders on the same day as the order is placed. As a result, the company has rarely lost an order to a Chinese competitor.[12]

Innovation

Innovation is the process of implementing new ideas or changes that create value for customers. These changes, which can be radical or incremental, can be classified into two broad categories: product innovation and process innovation. *Product innovation* is the development and introduction of a brand new product or service or the improvement of an existing product or service through design changes or through the use of new components and materials. For example, the music industry has experienced some dramatic product innovation shifts. By the early 1990s, CDs had taken the place of long-play (LP) phonograph records, which in turn have been replaced in the past decade by music downloaded onto MP3 players. *Process innovation* refers to the changes in the way in which a product is produced or a service is delivered within the firm or across a supply chain. Many companies have achieved a competitive advantage in the marketplace through process innovation. Dell Inc. (Round Rock, TX), for example, differentiated itself by creating and implementing new business processes such as eliminating unnecessary steps in the supply chain, while offering customers the ability to create a personal computer (PC) with the features most important to them. Other examples of companies that have gained a significant competitive edge through process innovations are Amazon.com

Product development cycle time: the time it takes to conceptualize a new good or service, produce it, and make it available to customers

Innovation: the process of implementing new ideas or changes that create value for customers

(aka Amazon, Seattle, WA), which introduced the unique process of buying books online from the comfort of your home, and eBay Inc. (San Jose, CA), whose easy-to-use but revolutionary processes transformed e-commerce and the buying and selling of products in online auctions.

Other types of innovations that are initiated in an organization to gain a competitive edge are changes in the way work is organized and accomplished, and how work processes are managed in such areas as customer relationships, employee performance and retention, and knowledge management.

Flexibility

Flexibility as a core competency is a firm's ability to produce a range of different products or services or to respond efficiently to changes in demand. The first case is referred to as *product flexibility*; the second is referred to as *volume flexibility*. For example, when a firm's operations function can quickly incorporate engineering and design changes into its products or services, it has a significant strategic competitive advantage. Ford and Chrysler, for example, have the flexibility to produce different models of cars within the same plant or the same production line. Restaurants that can cope adeptly with both large and small numbers of customers that fluctuate widely before and after peak dining times demonstrate volume flexibility.

ORDER WINNERS VERSUS ORDER QUALIFIERS

The core competencies we just discussed, viewed from a customer's perspective, can be classified into order winners and order qualifiers.[13] An order winner is a competitive criterion (core competence) of a product that causes a customer to choose it instead of a competitor's product. An order qualifier is a competitive criterion that must be present in a product for it to be a viable competitor in the marketplace. For example, let's assume that a consumer in the market for a new dishwasher expects a certain level of quality in terms of performance. Let's also assume that the consumer has narrowed his or her choice down to five brands of dishwashers, which all meet this minimum performance quality requirement. All else being equal, the consumer will now most likely buy the brand of dishwasher that has the lowest price. For this consumer, quality is the order qualifier (necessary requirement), and the price is the order winner (the criterion that sealed the deal).

Both order winners and order qualifiers are equally important to a firm because it must meet both to survive. If a firm fails to provide the order-qualifying criterion, then the firm will lose sales. The qualifying criterion the firm failed to meet is called an order loser. Yugo (Zastava Corporation [now part of Fiat Chrysler Automobiles Serbia], Kragujevac, Serbia), for example, was a subcompact car produced in the former Yugoslavia and introduced in the United States in the mid-1980s. The base price of the car when it was introduced was US$3,990—thousands of dollars cheaper than other subcompacts in the market. Although there was an initial rush of customers to buy the cars because they were low priced, consumers soon lost interest in them because their quality was poor. That is, they failed to meet the order-qualifying criterion of the quality prevalent in the automobile industry at that time. Eventually the manufacturer of the cars went bankrupt.

Order-winning and order-qualifying criteria change over time and vary from market to market. In the automobile industry, during the late 1980 and early 1990s, quality was the order-winning criterion. In the current global economic environment, with minimal levels of quality expected, price has become an order winner and quality is an order qualifier. As customers' buying habits change over time and from market to market, firms also need to develop different strategies for different markets. These strategies also have to change to meet the different order-winning and order-qualifying criteria.

In addition, companies have to be careful when they make operational decisions in an attempt to meet new order-winning and order-qualifying criteria. For example, in the early 1970s, Steinway & Sons

The shift from LPs to cassettes to CDs to MP3s is an example of innovation in the music industry.

©iStockphoto.com/mattjeacock

Order winner: a competitive criterion (core competence) of a product that causes a customer to choose it instead of a competitor's product

Order qualifier: a competitive criterion (core competence) that must be present in a product for it to be a viable competitor in the marketplace

Order loser: a qualifying criterion a firm fails to meet

(aka Steinway, New York, NY) attempted to produce a high-quality vertical piano, with high quality as the order-winning criterion. Nevertheless, the production costs incurred were so high that the price of the piano, the order qualifier, exceeded what customers were willing to pay for it.

Maintaining the Fit Among Critical Elements

Part of developing and refining an operations strategy is the continual and never-ending process of maintaining the appropriate fit among the four critical elements: customers, product factors, operational CSFs or capabilities, and core competencies. Maintaining the fit is not always easy. Changing market trends, new technologies, different customer bases, evolving product life cycles, and competition can cause a mismatch among the four critical elements. When such a mismatch occurs, and depending on what critical element caused the mismatch, companies can pursue these courses of action:

- If the mismatch arose from changing market trends or from customers who no longer value the core competency provided by the firm's product, then the firm can try to sell its products to different customers in another country or market who do value the product. For decades, the Buick brand had a reputation for quality, great design, and solid technology. Yet, in the last 25 years, the sales of Buicks in the United States have plunged by more than 80%. GM has since shifted its marketing efforts for the brand to China, where Buicks have become a best seller.[14] In fact, one of the brand's fans was Henry P'u Yi, the last emperor of China.
- If the mismatch arose from a decline in the firm's operating capabilities because its technologies have become obsolete, then the firm should upgrade its operating capabilities by investing in state-of-the art technologies. For example, to improve its operating capabilities and reduce the emissions from its truck engines, Caterpillar Inc. (Peoria, IL) developed an innovative new technology called ACERT (advanced combustion emissions reduction technology). ACERT has reduced the emissions of the engines beyond the U.S. Environmental Protection Agency (EPA) requirements without sacrificing fuel efficiency and reliability.
- If the mismatch is the result of a change in the stage of a product's life cycle, then the firm has to emphasize the core competency that is appropriate for the stage. A new product progresses through several stages that are called a *product life cycle*. These stages are product introduction, growth, maturity, and decline. For a product that is at the introductory stage of its life cycle, the distinctive competencies that should be emphasized are quick response time and product innovation. Over time, as the product evolves into the maturity stage of its life cycle, the distinctive competencies to be emphasized are delivery dependability and flexibility in production. To respond to the new set of distinctive competencies, the firm has to change the operating capabilities of its production process.

To avoid any mismatches and ensure its long-term survival, a firm cannot ignore its strategic planning processes.

Strategic Structural and Infrastructural Decisions

Once the firm has decided which particular core competency it will emphasize in its competitive strategy, it can then make structural and infrastructural decisions. The decisions are wide ranging and address issues such as what operations resources are needed and how they should be configured to support the firm's business-unit strategy and overall corporate objectives. Structural decisions are long-term decisions about a firm's capacity, facilities, processes, and technology. Infrastructural decisions relate to sales and operations planning, materials management and control, quality systems, and workforce policies and practices. Tables 2.1 and 2.2 provide an overview of the decisions that need to be made in these two categories.

What makes one company superior to another is the extent to which that company's operations function *matches* its structural and infrastructural decisions to the firm's core competencies. Figure 2.4 presents a model that shows how a firm's operational, structural, and infrastructural decisions relate to its strategy formulation.

Figure 2.4 shows the interrelationship between structural and infrastructural decisions. As an example, structural decisions made about the type of capacity used will have an impact on infrastructural decisions about sales and operations planning. These decisions are also cross-functional. For

TABLE 2.1: Structural Decisions in Operations Management

DECISION AREA	QUESTIONS ASKED	FUNCTIONAL INTERFACES WITH OPERATIONS
Process and Capacity	What type of production process should be selected? What type of machine and labor capacity is needed? How much of that capacity is needed and when? When should it be expand or contracted and how?	Finance, Marketing
Facilities	Where should facilities be located? How many facilities are needed? What size should each be? What layout and design should each facility have? What work should be done in each facility?	Finance, Marketing
Technology	What kinds of technologies are needed? How often should these technologies be upgraded?	Information Technology, Finance, Engineering, Human Resources

TABLE 2.2: Infrastructural Decisions in Operations Management

DECISION AREA	QUESTIONS ASKED	FUNCTIONAL INTERFACES WITH OPERATIONS
Workforce	What type of workers and how many are needed? What skill levels and training do they need? What should be the workforce policies, incentives and reward systems, and level of employment security?	Human Resources
Sales and Operations Planning	How should demand be managed? What production planning procedures and decision rules should be in place? What quantities should be produced to meet demand effectively?	Finance, Marketing
Control Systems	What cost-control mechanisms should be in place? How should materials and inventory be managed and controlled? How should the company assess and control quality? How should performance be measured and monitored? How should workflow be controlled?	Finance, Human Resources
Product/ Process Innovation	What product and process improvement programs should be devised? How should knowledge be managed? How should change be managed? What is the timing and procedure for new product launches? How should intellectual property be managed?	Engineering, Human Resources
Organization	Should the organizational structure be centralized or decentralized? How many levels should there be in the organizational hierarchy? Who has the responsibility and authority for decision-making in each area?	Human Resources

example, an operations manager cannot make any capacity investment decision without the involvement of managers within the finance function, which is responsible for all capital budgeting decisions.

Evaluating the Performance of an Operations Strategy

The performance of an operations strategy is judged by how well it supports the firm's corporate and business strategies. A firm can use various performance measurement systems that combine financial and operational measures.

STRATEGIC PROFIT MODEL (SPM)

The **strategic profit model (SPM)**, also known as the *DuPont model*, provides a visual representation of an organization's financial performance in terms of its return on investment (ROI) and return on

Strategic profit model (SPM): a model that provides a visual representation of an organization's financial performance in terms of its return on investment and return on assets (also known as the DuPont model)

FIGURE 2.4: Operations Strategy Framework

[Diagram: Operations Strategy Framework showing hierarchy — Corporate Strategy → Business Strategy ↔ Distinctive Competencies ↔ Operations Strategy, which branches into Structural Decisions (Capacity, Technology, Facilities) and Infrastructural Decisions (Sales and Operations Planning, Control Systems, Innovation).]

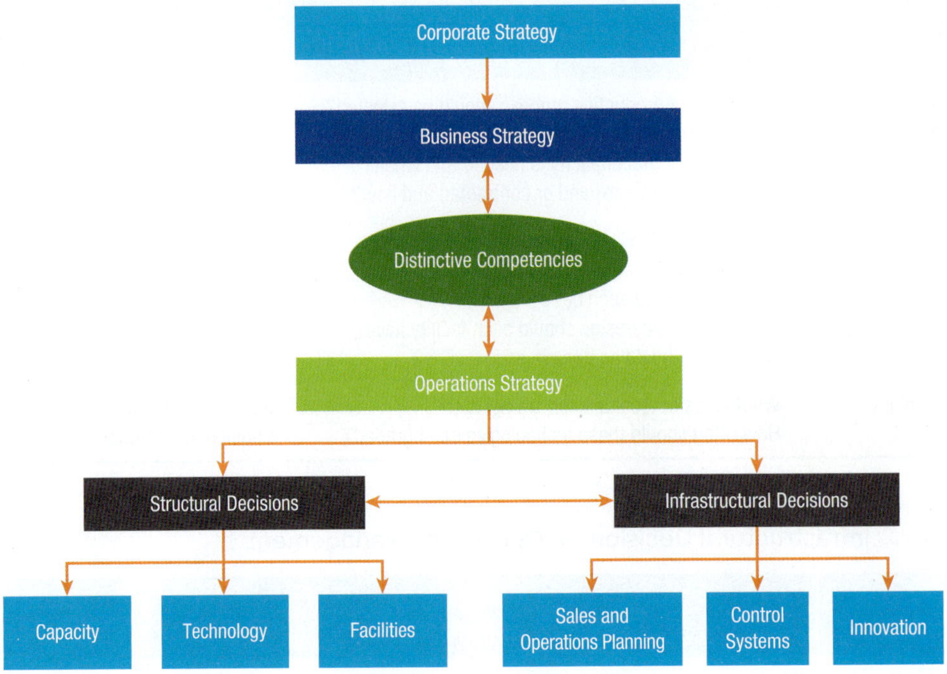

assets (ROA). According to this model, the tasks performed in every area of an organization have an impact on its ROI and the bottom line. For example, a firm can improve its ROI by reducing inventory or by improving its processes and productivity in its operations (as by speeding up production flows or minimizing delays). The model can be used to evaluate what-if scenarios. By asking questions such as, "What if productivity is improved by 2%, or we increase the number of units produced by 5%," managers can get answers to improve the firm's operations performance. Because these financial ratios and measures are linked, the organizations can manipulate one financial measure at a time to see its impact on other ratios and, ultimately, on the firm's bottom line. This process allows the company to determine from a variety of sources those variables that will improve its ROI the most. The SPM model is simple and relatively easy to use. Its only drawback is that all aspects of performance are translated into financial measures and other nonfinancial measures are not factored into the model.

BALANCED SCORECARD

The balanced scorecard, developed by Robert Kaplan and David Norton, is not only a performance measurement system but also a strategic planning and management system that is used extensively by profit, nonprofit, and governmental organizations worldwide. By using this system, managers are able to:

- Align a firm's activities with the vision and strategy of the organization.
- Improve the firm's internal and external communications.
- Track and monitor the firm's performance against its strategic goals.

Unlike the strategic planning model, the balanced scorecard includes strategic nonfinancial performance measures in addition to the traditional financial metrics. The inclusion of financial and nonfinancial measures offers managers a more balanced view of organizational performance.

The balanced scorecard transforms an organization's strategic plan by providing a framework that not only includes performance measurements but also helps planners identify what should be done in the future and what should be measured. It provides guidance for the organization on a day-to-day basis. Figure 2.5 shows how the approach works.[15]

Figure 2.5 shows that achieving an organization's vision and strategy requires balanced management of activities in the following four critical areas:[16]

The Balanced Scorecard

Balanced scorecard: a performance measurement system and a strategic planning and management system that allows managers to align a firm's activities with the vision and strategy of the organization, improve the firm's internal and external communications, and track and monitor the firm's performance against its strategic goals

FIGURE 2.5: Balanced Scorecard Approach

Financial

"To succeed financially, how should we appear to our shareholders?"

Objectives | Measures | Targets | Initiatives

Customer

"To achieve our vision, how should we appear to our customers?"

Objectives | Measures | Targets | Initiatives

Vision and Strategy

Internal Business Processes

"To satisfy our shareholders and customers, what business processes must we excel at?"

Objectives | Measures | Targets | Initiatives

Learning and Growth

"To achieve our vision, how will we sustain our ability to change and improve?"

Objectives | Measures | Targets | Initiatives

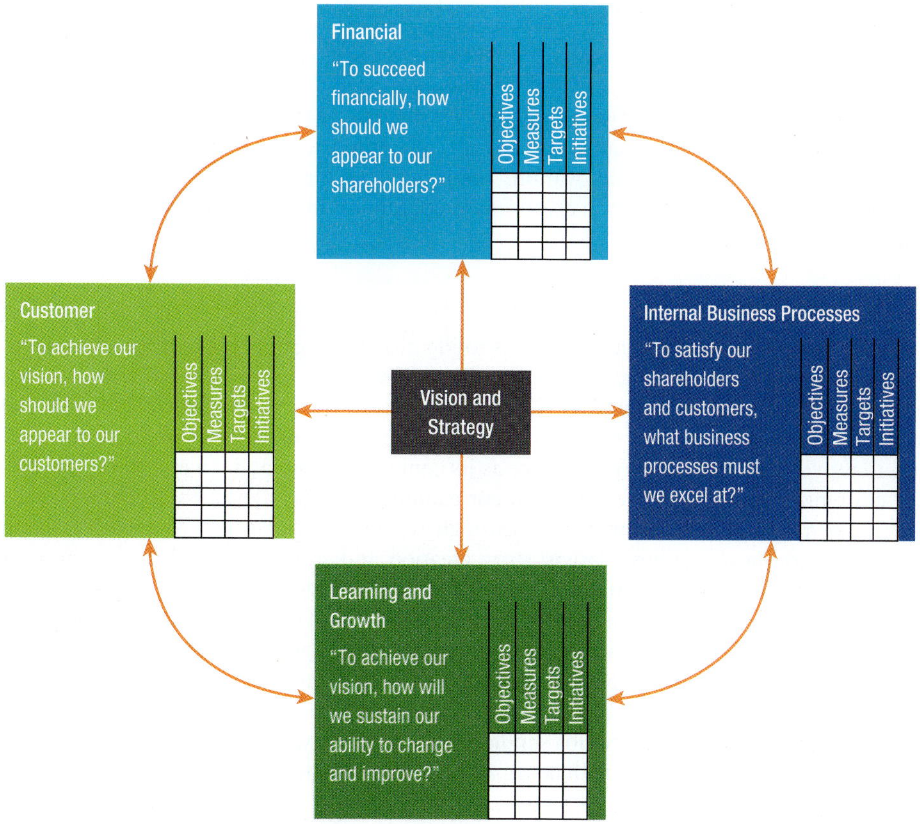

SOURCE: Adapted from Kaplan, R. S., & Norton, D. P. (1996, January–February). Using the Balanced scorecard as a strategic management system. *Harvard Business Review, 76.*

- **Learning and Growth.** Based on the premise that an organization's employees are its most critical resource, they should therefore be provided with adequate training, opportunities for learning and self-growth, and the free flow of information.
- **Business Processes.** Internal measurements of business processes should be implemented to monitor how well the firm is operating and to determine whether its clients are satisfied with its products.
- **Customer.** The firm should develop metrics to help it focus on customer satisfaction and to improve and monitor customer relations.
- **Financial:** Although financial data should not be the *only* indicator of strategic performance, for managing a business, timely and accurate financial data are still critical.

 More on the Balanced Scorecard

Figure 2.5 shows how each area requires a firm to address a pivotal question. For each question, the balanced scorecard approach requires that the firm develop objectives, metrics for each objective, target levels of performance for each metric, and an action plan for achieving each target. We can also see from Figure 2.5 that the balanced scorecard approach is a cyclical process of planning, doing, measuring, and providing feedback on performance. From an operations strategy perspective, the balanced scorecard helps to:

- Develop a road map for operational activities and to communicate specific goals and objectives.
- Develop metrics that indicate the extent to which each objective has been achieved.
- Prioritize areas for improvement in terms of their relative importance.
- Ensure that all efforts are aligned with the firm's corporate-level strategic objectives and goals.

Contrast the formulation and evaluation of operating strategies for service organizations with those for manufacturing organizations.

2.3 Formulating and Evaluating Strategies for Service Organizations

A strategic approach is required for managing service operations, just as it is for manufacturing companies. Figure 2.6 represents the hierarchical framework used in the strategic planning process for service operations. All of the core competencies that we discussed earlier for manufacturing companies also apply to service operations. That is, service firms also compete based on the core competencies of price, quality, time, flexibility, and innovation. The framework has three levels: strategic positioning, service operations strategy, and tactical execution. A continuous improvement cycle is used to provide feedback on the strategic plan.[17]

Strategic Positioning

The first step in developing the strategic plan is to identify the target market for its services—that is, its strategic positioning. The firm needs to define the customer base for its service offering. Second, the firm must determine its core competency. What is its unique ability or competitive strength that will add value and distinguish it from the competition? These core competencies could be the ability of the firm to provide the same quality of service as its competitors, but at a lower cost, or the ability to provide customized or differentiated services. For example, The Walt Disney Company (aka Disney, Burbank, CA) has three core competencies through which it has gained a competitive advantage. These are animatronics and show design, story creation and storytelling and themed atmospheric attractions, and the efficient operation of theme parks. The decision to emphasize these features has allowed Disney to create a unique niche that its customers recognize. After determining the core competencies, the firm must then define its mission and its high-level corporate goals and objectives. Firms at the strategic positioning level attempt to find answers to two questions:

- What services or service portfolios should we offer and to whom?
- What are our unique strengths that will add value to our customers?

Formulating the Service Operations Strategy

The service operations strategy level, which links the service firm's strategic position with its tactical execution, is next in the hierarchy. As in the case of manufacturing firms, the service operations strategy also describes how the firm's service operations interact with the other functions of the firm (e.g., marketing or finance) to support the service that will provide benefits and value to the customers. For example, if the service firm's order-winning criterion is flexibility, what actions will the firm take to ensure service flexibility and how will marketing promote this core competency to its customers? Decisions made at the service strategy level are geared toward ensuring that an organization can manage the costs and risks associated with its various services and that its services are designed not just for

FIGURE 2.6: Strategic Framework for Service Operations

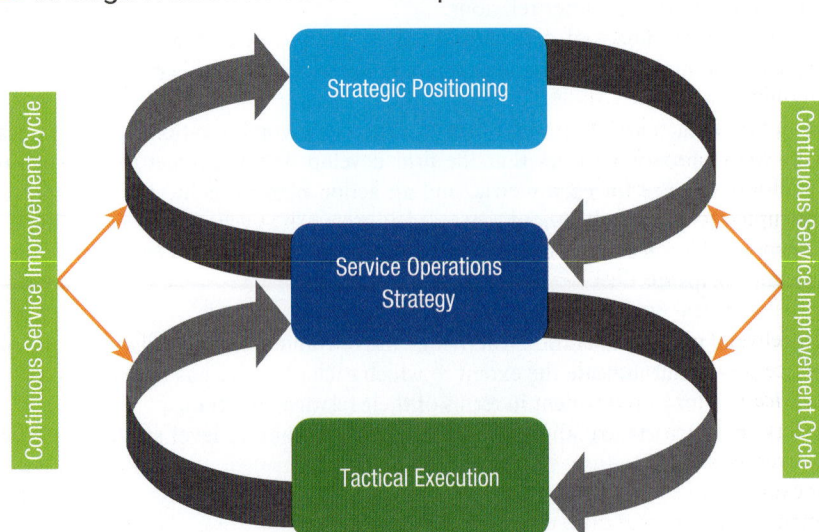

operational efficiency but also to give the company a distinctive performance edge. Decisions made at this level have far-reaching consequences, the impact of which will be felt only in the future. The service firm must define its service design concept and configure its operating and service delivery systems. Let us consider these steps in turn.

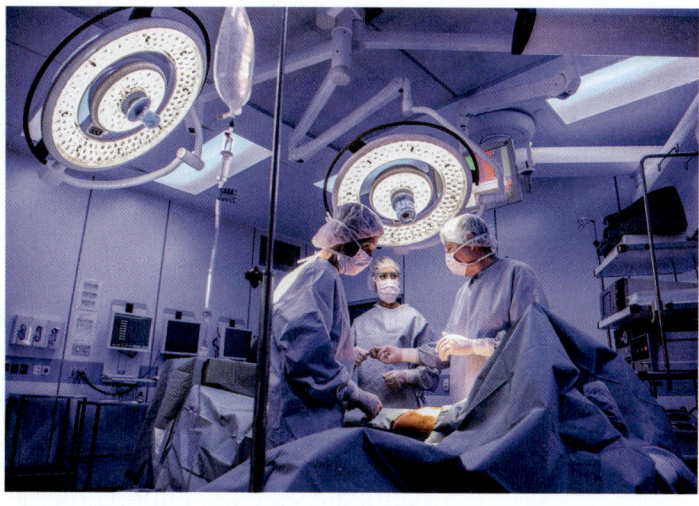

1. *The Service Design*

    The service design process begins with the firm first determining its core competencies (e.g., low cost, quality, service, or flexibility) and the order winners and order qualifiers in its target market. That is, the firm's core competencies must meet both the order-qualifying and order-winning criteria to compete successfully in the chosen target market. In this step, the firm attempts to answer the following question: How do we differentiate ourselves from competing alternatives offered in the target market?

    The service design phase focuses on the design and development of services and service management processes. The scope of the service design phase covers not only new services but also changes and improvements to existing services. In addition, the service design phase ensures that the firm has the capabilities it needs to manage the services it offers. Service design might involve making decisions about the location of the firm's facilities or how to manage their capacity.

    Designit (Aarhus, Denmark), Scandinavia's largest integrated strategic design consultancy, has created a new service design concept for Denmark's largest public hospital, Odense University Hospital (OUH). The service design concept, called the Patient House, is a state-of-the art facility that is expected to serve as a cost-effective blueprint for future public hospitals in Denmark and abroad. The focus of the design is on the services the hospital should offer as well as on finding a way to get patients to recover faster by involving them and their relatives in their treatment. The design concept also includes how the facility should be configured. For example, multifunction rooms with features such as ergonomic lighting give the hospital flexibility to treat different types of patients. Relatives will be able to stay overnight and dine at the hospital's restaurant, which offers a wide range of healthy food.[18]

2. *The Service Operations System*

    The service operations system encompasses all the activities and processes required for implementing the service. These activities and processes involve the interplay of people and equipment and may be visible (*front stage*) or invisible (*back stage*) to the customer. In the case of a hotel, the interior and exterior facilities, the equipment, and service personnel at the reservation desk are the visible components of the service operations system. The computerized reservation system and the people responsible for maintaining that system are examples of the invisible, or back stage, components of the service operations system.

    Determining capacity requirements, quality management systems, and management policies is also a part of a service operations strategy. Each feature should support the firm's core competencies so that the value customers receive is distinct and superior to that of competitors. The Patient House design concept for the Denmark hospital is an example. To be sure the system isn't disrupted, control mechanisms must be in place when changes are made to the design, scale, scope, and service levels. The control mechanisms might include implementing a patient safety-compliance checklist or having full-time doctors and nurses certified in critical care to ensure patients remain safe during the transition. The service operations system also guides the service delivery system, which is in the process of transferring the control of the service from the service provider to the customer.

3. *The Service Delivery System*

    The service delivery system is a unique feature of the service industry. The objective of the service delivery system is to provide a range of services as fast as possible when customers arrive as, for example, in a line at a supermarket or bank. The key performance criterion of the system is to manage and control the length of these queues.

Ergonomic Light is a new tool being used in a small number of leading hospitals. The ceiling system creates optimum lighting for each individual room in a hospital depending upon the purpose for which it's being used—preparing patients for operations, conducting operations, cleaning the rooms, and so forth.

©iStockphoto.com/Johnny Greig

 Strategies for Service Organizations

The purpose of the service operations strategy stage is to find answers to these questions:

- How do we truly create value desired by our customers and stakeholders?
- What is our rationale for making strategic investments in a particular service?
- How should service quality be defined, and given differing alternatives, which one should we emphasize to improve the quality of our service?
- If we offer multiple services, how do we efficiently allocate resources among them?

Tactical Execution

The final stage in the planning hierarchy is tactical execution. Tactical execution consists of the day-to-day activities required to support the service strategy. The activities in this phase include but are not limited to scheduling various tasks, staffing facilities, and improving the firm's output. For example, to get the Patient House up and running, the hospital will need to determine how many staff members it will need in various areas and how quickly patients can be treated and discharged.

Continuous Service Improvement

The continuous service improvement cycle in Figure 2.6 reflects the never-ending process of increasing the value customers receive by managing the quality of the service and making improvements to it. By continually looking at the firm's processes, organizations can achieve incremental and large-scale improvements in their service quality and operational efficiency. Both the balanced scorecard and the SPM are useful tools to evaluate and improve service performance. For example, many hospitals use the balanced scorecard approach to evaluate their performance and to implement improvements. In addition, linking improvement efforts and outcomes to the strategic planning process can also be done by using a feedback system called Plan, Do, Check, Act (PDCA):

Plan: Recognize an opportunity for improvement and plan for a change.

Do: Test the change by implementing a small-scale pilot study.

Check: Review and analyze the results of the test, and identify the lessons learned.

Act: Take action based on what was learned from the previous step.

Productivity: the ratio of outputs (goods and services) produced to the inputs used

Efficiency: how economically resources, particularly time and money, were used to complete an activity

Effectiveness: how well the task accomplished its intended purpose

If the change was successful, then incorporate lessons learned from the test into wider changes and use what was learned to plan for new improvements, beginning the cycle again. If the change did not work, then repeat the cycle again with a different plan. The Pearl River, New York, School District, a 2001 recipient of the Malcolm Baldrige National Quality Award, uses the PDCA cycle to define most of its work processes, including the district's overall strategic planning, needs, curriculum design and delivery, goal setting, and evaluation for its staff. Through the use of the PDCA cycle, the school district has been able to achieve a high student graduation rate and high student- and parent-satisfaction scores. The PDCA management method is also used for control and continuous improvement of goods production.

2.4 Measuring Productivity as Part of Strategic Planning

Compare the different types of productivity measurements, and explain how firms use them strategically.

A firm remains competitive by producing goods and services efficiently and effectively. In addition to the strategic profit model, the balanced scorecard, and the PDCA system, another important way to track how well a firm's operations functions is performing is by measuring its productivity.

In the context of operations, productivity is the ratio of outputs (goods and services) produced to the inputs used:

$$Productivity = \frac{Goods\ and\ services\ produced}{Inputs\ used}$$

This definition indicates that if a company wants to increase its productivity, it can do so by increasing its output of goods and services *or* by using fewer inputs to produce the same amount of output. Note that the concepts of efficiency, effectiveness, and productivity differ. Efficiency tells us how economically resources, particularly time and money, were used to complete an activity. Effectiveness, on the other hand, tells us how well the task accomplished its intended purpose. Productivity is a combination of both efficiency and effectiveness—not only the economical use of resources but also accomplishing the intended purpose or goal.

Types of Productivity Measures and Their Uses

A key step in measuring productivity is correctly identifying the relevant inputs and outputs and determining how they will be measured. There are two common types of productivity measures: single-factor productivity measures and multifactor productivity (total factor productivity) measures.

The single-factor productivity measure (which is also sometimes referred to as the *partial productivity measure*) is the simplest. This measure uses a single input, such as labor hours, for example, in the ratio. Suppose 2,000 units of a product were produced in a given time period using 400 hours of labor. Then:

$$\text{Single-factor productivity} = \frac{\#\,of\,units\,produced}{Labor\,hours\,used} = \frac{2000}{400} = 5 \text{ units per labor hour}$$

The firm produces an average of 5 units for each labor hour worked.

Single-factor productivity measures are easy to use and can reveal how well a single input is performing, which in this example was labor. Labor productivity is, in fact, a frequently used single-factor productivity measure. Nevertheless, this measure can be misleading because it does not include other inputs that may be contributing to the production process, such as mechanization and automation. Multifactor productivity is a productivity measure that uses all of the relevant inputs used to make the product or provide the service. These inputs include labor, materials, energy, capital, and miscellaneous factors such as purchased business services. Thus, multifactor productivity measure is a ratio of outputs to a set of combined inputs:

$$\text{Multifactor productivity} = \frac{Output}{Labor + Materials + Energy + Capital + Miscellaneous}$$

When calculating multifactor productivity, we need to use a homogenous unit of measurement, such as dollars, to value the inputs. For example, if 5,000 units of a product were produced in a given time period using labor hours, machine hours, capital, and energy at a cost of $2,000, $1,000, $1,500, and $500, respectively (all in U.S. dollars), then:

$$\text{Multifactor productivity} = \frac{5000}{\$2000 + \$1000 + \$1500 + \$500} = 1 \text{ unit per dollar}$$

In the multifactor productivity (total productivity) measure, all inputs used to make the product or provide the service are included. When multiple inputs such as capital, materials, energy, or labor are jointly included in the calculations, this measurement gets more complicated. A difficulty in using the multifactor productivity measure is identifying the inputs that contribute directly to the production of outputs and finding a common value for those inputs. For example, if the firm conducts team-building exercises to help its workers improve their performance, how should the cost of these exercises appear in the calculation? Other problems in measuring multifactor productivity are adjusting for different outputs that generate different revenues, adjusting output so that it is consistent with input measures, adjusting for differences in the quality of the different outputs, accounting for external factors that may cause changes in productivity, and so forth. Nonetheless, because the multifactor or total productivity ratio is an all-inclusive type of ratio, it is good for making overall productivity comparisons. It is too broad, however, to be used for improving specific areas because the ratio doesn't show the interaction between each input and output separately. Table 2.3 lists some examples of the various measures of productivity.

Productivity measures are used not only to assess the firm's performance but also to compare how well different departments within the firm are performing to determine whether their productivity has increased or decreased over time. Productivity measures can also be used to assess the answer to certain questions, such as whether new processes, equipment, or worker motivation techniques are improving the firm's performance. In addition, productivity measures can help a firm compare its productivity with that of its competitors. A firm that enjoys a higher level of productivity can lower its prices, increase its market share, and earn higher profits. Productivity measures can also be used to evaluate the performance of an entire industry. Likewise, by combining the productivity of various

TABLE 2.3: Examples of Various Types of Productivity Measures

Single-productivity measure	Output/labor Output/machines Output/energy Output/capital
Multifactor or total productivity measure	Goods and services produced/All inputs used

companies, industries, or segments of the economy, the productivity of an entire nation can even be evaluated.

Because productivity is relative, it can be meaningful or useful as a comparison tool only if it is adjusted. Therefore, organizations need to compute a **productivity index**. The productivity index is the ratio of productivity measured in a particular time period to the productivity measured in a base period. For example, if the base period's productivity measure were 1.83 and the next period's productivity were 1.98, the resulting productivity index would be 1.98 / 1.83 = 1.08. This result means that the firm's productivity increased by 8%. Now, let's assume that in the next period, productivity falls to 1.57. The productivity index is now 1.57 / 1.83 = 0.86. This result tells us that the organization's productivity is 86% of the base period. That is, productivity fell by 15%. Managers often use productivity indexes to track their firm's productivity over time. Doing so can help managers evaluate the success or failure of their decisions or of the projects undertaken by the firm.[19]

Factors Affecting Productivity

Numerous factors affect productivity in both positive and negative ways. These factors can be classified into the eight categories shown in Table 2.4. A firm can control some of these factors, but others are only marginally controllable or perhaps even uncontrollable.

There are many examples of how the factors listed in Table 2.4 have influenced the productivity of business operations. One example is the development of superconductivity systems, which increase the power of electrical products by lowering their resistance to electrical currents. This technological improvement radically increased the productivity of many businesses, especially those in the utility, health-care, electrical, and computer industries. Likewise, lean manufacturing and Six Sigma practices, which are discussed in Chapter 1 and in later chapters, are examples of process factors that improved productivity.

Steps to Improving Productivity

The two factors that can improve productivity rapidly are technology and the way in which the firm organizes and uses it resources, which we describe as processes. More often, though, productivity improvements are achieved incrementally, that is, a little at a time. Nonetheless, over a period of time, these improvements can add up. Yet, for these improvements to occur, a firm needs a measurement system that:

- Uses productivity measures that are relevant and appropriate for the business's operations. For example, an appropriate productivity measure for a retail store could be sales per square foot, whereas for a paper mill, it could be tons of paper produced per cord of wood.
- Is homogeneous in the sense that different types of inputs can be aggregated into a single measurement system and their productivity compared.
- Produces an index of productivity and combines productivity measurements into an overall rating of the firm's performance.
- Is flexible so that it can be used to accommodate changes in a firm's goals and policies over time.

Firms can take other steps to improve their productivity over time, such as:

- *Using benchmarking.* Benchmarking is a process that begins by identifying the best practices used by other firms within the industry and their achievements. The firm then adopts those methods to improve its productivity. For example, if the leading competitor's operations productivity index is 1.12, the firm would want to either match or exceed that index rating.

Productivity index: the ratio of productivity measured in a particular time period to the productivity measured in a base period

TABLE 2.4: Factors Affecting Productivity

FACTORS	EXAMPLES
Product	Poor product designs, lack of product standardization to achieve economies of scale, and poor quality standards will decrease productivity.
Process	The ability of a process to produce a large volume enhances productivity. A more subtle factor is the quality of the production process and methods used to produce the product.
Human Resources	A lack of education, skill levels, training, or challenging work can negatively affect the labor productivity of a firm's employees.
Management	Better planning, coordinating, scheduling, and controlling of activities will increase productivity. A participatory style of leadership can motivate workers to be more productive.
Technology	Use of state-of-the-art technology such as computer-aided design (CAD) and computer-aided manufacturing (CAM) can increase productivity by reducing wasted materials and time.
Capital	Good facilities, efficient plant layouts, and choosing the right machines and equipment can improve productivity.
Environment	Legislative and regulatory laws, climate and weather-related conditions, and the social environment can affect productivity. For example, strict product standards mandated by federal agencies such as the U.S. Food and Drug Administration (FDA) and EPA can lower productivity.
Geographic and Cultural	For companies operating abroad, language differences, the work culture, and additional holidays can decrease productivity.

- *Motivating employees.* Good pay, a comfortable workplace, and treating employees with respect and appreciation can help improve productivity, as will establishing meaningful performance metrics, mentoring and monitoring employees, and assessing and rewarding employees for a job well done.
- *Establishing open and clear channels of communication.* If employees trust their managers to communicate honestly with them, they will tend to be less afraid to take the initiative to improve the firm's productivity. This step reinforces the importance of early and consistent involvement by top management in any initiatives aimed at improving productivity.

Measuring Productivity in the Service Sector

Productivity is harder to measure in the service sector because the inputs used for measuring productivity can be more difficult to assess. Unlike the manufacturing sector, customers are active participants in the service production process. To measure service productivity, customers should be viewed as inputs. For example, if some customers in a drive-through line at a fast-food restaurant are slow to order, they will slow down the firm's productivity as measured by how many people it can serve per hour or per day. In addition, customers in a service organization often receive a variety of services as opposed to a goods-producing company where productivity measurements are based on a single output.[20] For example, interior designers usually provide many services to their clients, such as designing their clients' homes, hiring contractors to work on the homes, and shopping for furniture and décor. How should each activity be measured?

Typically, service productivity is measured by calculating the number of tasks performed or number of customers served in a given time period. Such a measure is relevant and meaningful as long as the tasks are routine and require minimal customization. For example, a fast-food restaurant can accurately measure the speed by which it serves customers.

Loading and unloading ultra-large container ships contributes to the congestion at U.S. ports.

©iStockphoto.com/Sami Sert

OPERATIONS PROFILE: LESSONS LEARNED
Bigger Ships, More Cargo, Bigger Headaches!

On any given day at the major ports in the United States, congestion and traffic have snarled an already slow loading and unloading process to one that is approaching a complete standstill. The Port of Virginia, for example, is one of the busiest ports in the country, and for thousands of truckers, their daily pick-up and delivery runs from the port to inland destinations have turned into a nightmare of snarled traffic, delays, and serious overcrowding. These truckers complain that the port's congestion has turned a routine, two-hour pickup process into an eight-hour ordeal of frayed nerves and poor performance.

This slowdown in the movement of imports and exports (totaling some US$900 billion worth of goods arriving and leaving U.S. ports annually) illustrates just how complicated the logistics of global trade has become. Ocean carriers, which continue to get larger as they are designed to carry massive numbers of containers (approximately 10,000, 20-foot container units), are clogging shipping ports on both the Atlantic and the Pacific seaboards. Some of these massive ships may seem to be a shipper's dream. They are more fuel efficient and can carry much more cargo than did their predecessors. Unfortunately, even though shipping lines have opted for bigger ships to improve their economies, no one has considered that the ports were designed to handle freight traffic that has been unchanged for more than 50 years. As a result, although the ships are getting bigger and more cargo can be delivered with each vessel's arrival, the ports where they must offload have become a huge bottleneck. What good is a larger cargo vessel if the ship must sit outside of port for weeks before it can be brought into the harbor for offloading?

The new era of big ships "has stressed the infrastructure to the breaking point," said Jock O'Connell, a senior trade advisor. He noted that "there needs to be a concerted effort to rethink and redesign the ports to accommodate these larger vessels and the additional cargo they're generating." When a ship arrives at its berthing station, cranes offload the containers and place them on the dock, where they are then collected and stacked, sometimes for days, in storage areas for redistribution. Containers destined for rail transportation are then hauled by trucks to the rail yard where they are put on rail cars for transportation. Most containers, however, sit in these collection areas until trucks assigned to collect and transport them can navigate their way through the crowded entrance to the port, identify their container, and leave the port area. Try to visualize a 13-lane wide, 10-truck-deep daily traffic jam at the port entrance! Even the most productive port in the United States, Los Angeles, can only move 80 containers per ship per hour. When hundreds of giant container vessels converge on the most popular ports, it is easy to imagine the potential for congestion on the docks. Greater levels of international trade, combined with bigger and bigger container ships, have stretched the ability of the nation's ports to maintain shipping flow.

Ports are working to resolve many of these problems. The Port of Miami has launched a multibillion dollar refurbishment project to expand the port and its loading and unloading facilities to handle these larger ships. Technology upgrades, including computerized systems for cargo-handling and global positioning system (GPS) container tracking, have helped speed the process of finding, identifying, and loading containers on to rail cars and transportation trucks. The Port Authority of New York and New Jersey has also addressed another implication of larger container ships by spending US$1.3 billion to the raise the Bayonne Bridge so that megaships can pass underneath. These and other remedial steps are being taken as U.S. port officials recognize that international trade and larger container ships bring a mixed blessing: Far more goods can pass between countries around the world, while causing congestion and supply chain challenges.[22]

Improving Productivity in Services

Nevertheless, if the tasks aren't routine or require varying levels of customization, then this measure of productivity is no longer meaningful. The amount of time a doctor spends will vary significantly from patient to patient depending on the patient's illness or symptoms. Therefore, the number of patients treated by a doctor on a given day is not an accurate measure of the doctor's productivity because, in this case, productivity is also closely related to the quality of the service—not just to its quantity.

Although it is more difficult to measure and monitor their productivity, service firms can reduce the variability in their processes and increase productivity by taking these steps:[21]

1. Identify the size and type of the customer base the firm serves, as well as the service agreements reached with the customers. Next, define and collect data uniformly across the service's processes.
2. Develop internal benchmarks. Benchmarking against other firms can be difficult if the service is complex. If the company's service is complex, it should use internal benchmarks. That is, it should compare itself against its own performance. If the firm's productivity falls, managers should try to determine why.
3. Develop broad but rigorous measurement systems to report and compare productivity across the different functions of the service company.

4. Monitor the productivity of employees by using business charting methods or a spreadsheet program.
5. Involve customers by conducting surveys and use their feedback to eliminate service elements that are unnecessary or inefficient.
6. Test and implement faster and more efficient ways to deliver the service. For example, an educational organization might find that delivering course materials online is fast, efficient, and more convenient for students.

2.5 Strategies for Supply Chains

So far we have discussed operations strategy in a single organization. Nevertheless, in this interconnected world, no firm can operate independently. Without the support of its trading partners, including its suppliers, wholesalers, retailers, and companies that provide transportation services, the firm cannot be expected to flourish. A complementary *supply chain* strategy is needed. Supply chain strategies provide clear directions that help the company maximize its supply chain efficiencies and drive down its operational costs.

As stated earlier, in today's highly competitive and global business environment, the competition is not between individual firms but between supply chains. As a result, supply chain partners have become more dependent on each other for their stability and success. Each is under pressure to perform and deliver as they exchange resources, currencies, and information, as well as share risks across national borders and multiple markets. A key reason that retailers such as Montgomery Ward (Chicago, IL) and Phar-Mor (Youngstown, OH) failed is that their supply chains were not efficient enough to compete with the supply chains of companies such as Wal-Mart.

Managing a supply chain requires making strategic, tactical, and operational decisions about the movement and storage of raw materials, work-in-process inventory, and finished goods from the point of their origin to the point of their consumption. Managing supply chains has become so important in the past decade that many companies have elevated the status of the supply chain management function in their organizations to that of other key functions such as marketing and finance. Although supply chain management usually refers to the coordination of activities across multiple firms, it can also refer to a single organization that owns multiple facilities and distribution centers. For example, large firms such as Sony and Toyota (Toyota Motor Corporation, Toyota City, Japan) own several manufacturing facilities and distribution centers throughout the world. Each of these firms needs a well-designed internal supply chain to coordinate and integrate the manufacturing, distribution, and logistics activities across these facilities.

Formulating Supply Chain Strategies

Formulating and implementing a supply chain strategy is a long-term process that requires a significant commitment of resources. It also requires structural and infrastructural decisions about the supply chain network to answer such questions as:

- What is the nature and number of operating facilities needed?
- What suppliers and how many are needed?
- What work should be outsourced or offshored?
- What type of relationships should the firm have with its suppliers?
- What should the distribution network be, and how should it be managed?

Other questions that must be addressed are:

- How should the firms in the network communicate critical information to one another, and what are ways to improve the network's efficiency?
- How should the life cycles of products be managed so that new and existing products can be easily integrated into the supply chain?
- How should customer relationships be managed?

2.5
Describe how both manufacturers and service organizations formulate and evaluate their supply chain strategies.

▶ Supply Chain Strategies

Wal-Mart and Procter & Gamble (P&G) have forged a powerful strategic alliance in the area of inventory purchasing and supplying.

Tim Boyle/Getty Images News/Getty Images

FIGURE 2.7: Decision Framework for Formulating a Supply Chain Strategy

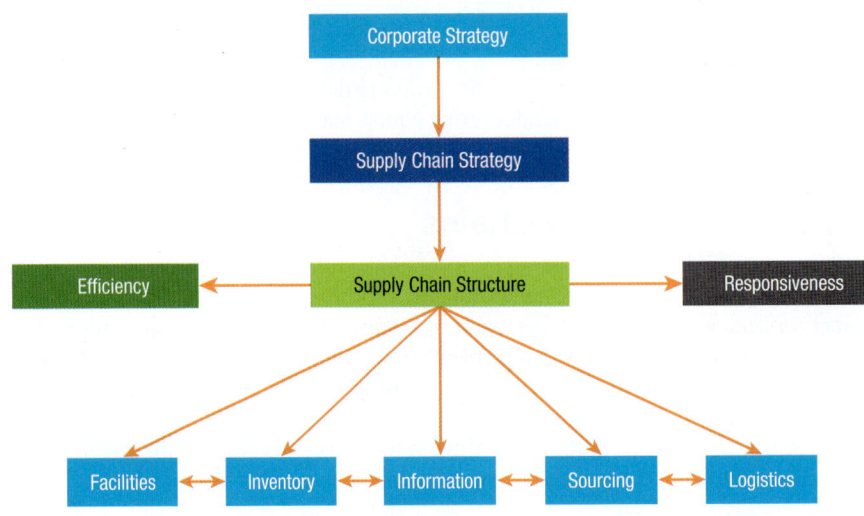

SOURCE: Adapted from p. 47 of Chopra, S., & Meindl, P. (2007). *Supply chain management* (3rd ed.). New York, NY: Pearson-Prentice-Hall.

Figure 2.7 presents a decision-making framework for formulating a supply chain strategy.[23]

A key decision that firms should make is how to structure their supply chains. For example, Dell's decision to sell its computers directly to consumers or Cisco's (Cisco Systems, Inc., San Jose, CA) decision to outsource its component manufacturing and assembly to outside contractors reflects how these two companies have broadly defined their supply chain structures. In addition, a firm's supply chain strategy also determines the types of transportation to be used, the type and number of operating facilities (including manufacturing plants, warehouse, and distribution centers), and inventory and information flows. Toyota's decision to build and operate production facilities in each of its major markets is an element of its supply chain strategy.[24]

Strategic fit, which we talked about earlier in the chapter when we discussed operations strategies, is equally applicable to supply chain strategies. Like its operations strategy, a firm's supply chain strategy should be aligned with and support the firm's overall corporate strategy. For example, suppose the competitive strategy of a firm is to provide a large variety of customized products quickly to its customers. Yet, to keep shipping costs low, the company uses inexpensive but slower modes of transportation, such as rail, or tries to achieve transportation economies by consolidating orders together for shipment. By using this approach, the corporate strategy of quick delivery to customers will not be achieved because delays are likely. The end result will be dissatisfied customers and the loss of those customers to competitors.

There are three successive steps that a company can follow to achieve a strategic fit:[25]

1. *Firms need to know their customers and the uncertainties associated with their supply chains.* A firm must make every effort to understand thoroughly the needs of its customers in its target markets. The firm should then assess the uncertainties in its supply chain in satisfying these needs. The uncertainties may arise from unpredictable demand, unexpected delays, and disruptions in the supply chain. The supply chain must be adequately prepared to respond to these uncertainties. That is, just as they need strategies for managing operational risks, firms also should be prepared to manage the risks related to their supply chains. See Case Study 2.1 at the end of the chapter for an example.

2. *Firms need to know the capabilities of their supply chains.* Different supply chains have different structures. Some supply chains are designed to be efficient (emphasizing low cost), whereas others are designed to be more responsive. Understanding your supply chain's capabilities can help the firm formulate viable alternatives to respond to supply chain uncertainties.

3. *Firms need to achieve a strategic fit.* If there is a mismatch between the supply chain's capabilities and the needs of customers, the firm has to either restructure the supply chain to support the competitive strategy or change its competitive strategy so there's a strategic fit between the two. Thus, a supply strategy should not only be in alignment with the firm's other strategies, but also it should be in alignment with the strategies of its supply chain partners. Moreover, supply chain

FIGURE 2.8: Supply Chain Operations Reference (SCOR) Model

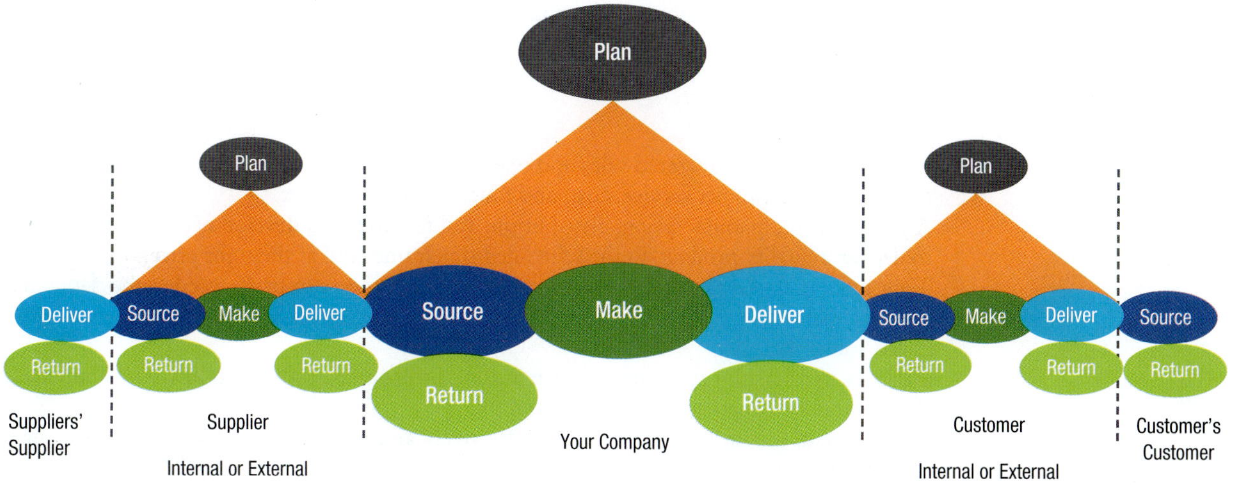

SOURCE: http://www.supply-chain.org.

partners should develop an overall strategy that supports the competitive strategies of the individual partner firms within the supply chain. Wal-Mart and P&G, for example, have forged a powerful strategic alliance in the area of inventory purchasing and supplying. The two firms use a **vendor managed inventory (VMI)** system that allows P&G to track and manage the inventory of all its products in all of Wal-Mart's stores. The advantage of such an alliance is that it frees Wal-Mart from having to use resources on mundane activities such as inventory management. In return, P&G gets premier shelf space for all its products in the giant's retailer's stores.

Evaluating the Performance of a Supply Chain Strategy

How do firms measure how well their supply chain strategies are working? Several key performance indicators such as inventory turns, cycle time, defects per million opportunities (DPMOs), and fill rate can be used to track supply chain performance. The supply chain operations reference (SCOR) model developed by the Supply Chain Council is a systematic way to measure supply chain performance. The SCOR model, which is shown in Figure 2.8, examines both high-level processes as well as individual processes that together define the scope of the supply chain. This model allows firms to identify the critical processes in a supply chain and, therefore, better understand exactly *what* to measure when assessing their performance. Furthermore, it allows organizations to compare the efficiency and effectiveness of their supply chains against those of their competitors.

The SCOR model divides supply chains into five distinct processes or building blocks:

1. *Plan*: Develop a plan for the supply chain that best meets the sourcing, production, and delivery processes needed to fulfill the expected demand for the firm's products.
2. *Source:* Procure the goods and services to meet the demand.
3. *Make:* Meet the demand by transforming the product into its finished state.
4. *Deliver*: Deliver the finished goods and services.
5. *Return*: Receive products, including defective or excess product, back from the customer for any reason.

The SCOR model has more than 150 key indicators. Like the model itself, the SCOR metrics are also organized in a hierarchical structure. Each higher level metric is developed from calculations from the lower level of the hierarchy. Typically, the lower level metrics relate to a narrower subset of processes within the supply chain. For example, the metric for a firm's delivery performance is calculated using the total number of products delivered correctly and on time. This information then is combined with other metrics to evaluate how well the firm's supply chain is performing overall and how it compares with the supply chains of competing firms.

Vendor managed inventory (VMI): a system that allows a firm to track and manage the inventory of all its products in all of its locations

2.6

Identify the key capabilities firms need to formulate and implement global operations and supply chain strategies and manage the risks related to them.

2.6 Global Strategies

Developing a coherent global supply chain and operations management strategy is clearly a complex process—one that requires managers to make a complicated and highly interwoven set of decisions. To develop and implement a viable global operations and supply chain strategy, every company needs six key capabilities. These are:[26]

- An effective global, integrated sales and operations planning process for key markets to ensure that the firm's customer service, cost, and time objectives are met.
- A procurement, manufacturing, distribution, and research and development network designed to deliver a quality product, in the scheduled timeframe, and at the right price.
- Tight links with their customers and suppliers so that they can better predict the demand for their products, gauge customer service levels, and reduce their working capital and cost-of-goods sold.
- Logistics partnerships to ensure the firm's efforts to source products to low-cost markets and to penetrate new markets are efficient and timely.
- The ability to recruit low-cost suppliers effectively and to ensure that their efforts are aligned with the firm's service objectives.
- A "go-to-market" strategy, which is a firm's plan to provide value to its customers by using the firm's internal and external resources. For emerging markets, this strategy involves decisions such as the number and type of products offered; wholesalers, distributors, and retailers to be used; and whether the products should be produced in-house or purchased from an outside vendor.

Integrating Operations and Supply Chain Strategies

Earlier in the chapter we examined the topics of formulating operations and supply chain strategies separately to present an overview of the similarities and differences in their development and implementation. Nevertheless, in reality, these two strategies must be tightly integrated with one another. This is especially the case for global operations and supply chains.

For example, because lower manufacturing costs (an operations issue) far outweigh higher transportation costs and longer shipping times (supply chain issues), more and more companies from more mature economies such as the United States, Europe, and Japan have drastically increased the outsourcing of the manufacturing of their products to firms in emerging markets such as China, India, Russia, Brazil, and Vietnam. Yet, a poorly executed global operations and supply chain strategy can all too often lead to dissatisfied customers and to a firm losing market share. Many companies don't anticipate the challenges associated with globalizing their operations and supply chains, including the ripple effect this globalization can have throughout the enterprise. Sony is an example. Sony invested heavily in manufacturing facilities in China as a precursor to expanding their markets into the country. Nonetheless, in 2002, the company was forced to move the production of some of its products from China back home to Japan. Sony believed China's manufacturers lacked the critical technological capabilities (an operations issue), supply chain flexibility, and the benefit of being close to the company's headquarters where strategic decisions were being made about the products.

Companies that have experienced greater success integrating their operations and supply chains globally have developed three capabilities:

- Supply chain adaptability, which is the ability of the supply chain to respond to changes in the marketplace to gain or maintain competitive advantage. For example, when new opportunities open up, can the firm quickly identify suppliers and new channels or resources for shipping and distribution?
- Financial-engineering capabilities, which is the ability to create new financial instruments to facilitate international exchanges and raise capital. Often, new international opportunities require unique methods for financial exchanges to occur. For example, when selling jet engines to national airlines in developing countries, General Electric sometimes needs to barter for partial payments made with commodities instead of cash. Imagine having to take a partial payment in oil or teak wood.
- Risk anticipation and mitigation capabilities, which refers to anticipating events that could disrupt global operations and developing mechanisms that reduce the impact of those risk should they occur.

Companies that attempt to penetrate new global markets may also need new strategies that involve redesigning their portfolio of products, the products themselves, and their distribution. Conversely, facing competition from lower cost competitors around the globe, domestic companies might need entirely new manufacturing, distribution, and sourcing strategies. Nevertheless, when formulating those strategies, both types of firms have to be careful that they don't compromise their other strategic objectives, such as fast delivery and good customer service. McDonald's, for example, serves 58 million customers daily in 119 countries. To satisfy its customers around the world, McDonald's offers a regionalized version of its menu with foods specific to that region and not offered elsewhere. Yet, whether the menu features Big Rosti (Germany) or the Chicken Maharaja Mac sandwich (India), there are some constants that have made McDonald's famous: fast delivery, consistently good customer service, and food that is affordable and portable.

Risk Management Strategies

Many unforeseen events can disrupt operational and supply chain activities, including environmental disasters such as earthquakes and hurricanes, labor strikes, technological glitches, and a key supplier going out of business. For example, in 2011, an earthquake and subsequent tsunami shut down the Fukushima Dai-ichi nuclear power plant in Fukushima, Japan, for months. The economic impact this disaster had on the Japanese economy, society, and the environment has been estimated to have been billions of dollars. It also left people and companies in the surrounding area without power for an extended period of time. Moreover, because so many firms have multinational operations and rely on international suppliers, a disruption in one area of the world will have resulting impacts elsewhere. Because of the tsunami, auto manufacturers around the globe—Toyota in particular—had to scale back their operations because their parts suppliers in Japan were shut down.

Risks in a Global Supply Chain

A firm's operations should have a risk management program that can anticipate uncontrollable events and implement contingency plans. In addition to having the backup generators and emergency batteries that were already in place, the Fukushima Dai-ichi plant could have maintained layer on layer of backup power to shut down its reactors safely should electricity from the grid fail. The plant should also have added more equipment to power the systems needed to cool the reactors.[27] Thus, a cutting-edge nuclear reactor is projected to become operational in 2019 along the icy shores of the Baltic Sea, in Olkiluoto, Finland. The 1,600-megawatt European Pressurized Reactor is the first of its kind to become operational after the Japanese disaster. It has new safety systems that can last for many decades, walls thick enough to withstand an airplane crash, and robustly designed components that can withstand the brutal Nordic winters. In addition, the nuclear reactor at Olkiluoto, has backup systems for power generation that include four large diesel generators, two smaller diesel generators, and a new reactor that can be connected to the joint backup systems of two older reactors.[28]

Corporations are working closely with their suppliers to safeguard their supply chains against future breakdowns. The tsunami convinced many organizations to begin dual sourcing—contracting with multiple sources for their materials and supplies—as a buffer against disruptions.

Businesses should also be concerned about disruptions to operations and supply chains from safety and security problems that arise accidently or are perpetrated intentionally, through acts of terrorism or corporate espionage. For example, organizations such as Motorola (Motorola Solutions, Inc., Schaumburg, IL) and Circle K Stores, Inc. (Tempe, AZ) have implemented formal crisis management teams to respond to crises and emergencies. Although it is impossible to prepare for every emergency or disaster that could affect a firm, crisis management teams learn from past incidents and formulate strategies for dealing with them should they occur in the future. After the September 11, 2001, attacks on the World Trade Center and Pentagon, many U.S. companies, including airlines, financial institutions, energy plants and dams, high-tech companies, sporting facilities, and public and commercial buildings, adopted security measures that included locking all facilities; providing only employees with electronic cards for entry and checking the IDs of visitors; installing video monitors, alarms, and blast-resistant glass in buildings; tightening the entry and security of their garage and parking facilities; and protecting their computer systems against unauthorized access and data theft.[29] Contingency planning is time-consuming and expensive but infinitely preferable to the alternative.[30]

2.7 Sustainability Issues

A research study conducted by Accenture PLC (Dublin, Ireland) on sustainability and supply chain strategy concluded that many leading-edge companies are incorporating sustainable practices into their supply chain practices, just as they do their operations practices. Not only are these firms designing

2.7

Describe what companies are doing to incorporate sustainability into their supply chain strategy and the problems they face in doing so.

Sustainability in
the Supply Chain

products with sustainability in mind, but also they are managing the carbon footprint of their supply chains—that is, managing the total amount of greenhouse gases they produce and using energy-efficient lighting, recycled materials, and so forth.

Nevertheless, the Accenture study also found that one third of supply chain executives had no awareness of the level of emissions in their supply chain network, and only one in ten companies actively managed the carbon footprint of their supply chains. The study further revealed that many European-based companies were well ahead of U.S. companies in the use of sustainable supply chains as a result of the environmental laws enacted in their countries. By contrast, firms in emerging economies such as India and China have typically lagged behind the West.

Developing an end-to-end sustainable supply chain is a huge undertaking. Not only does it involve a great deal of time and analysis, it often requires changes in the firm's structure and infrastructure. Yet, companies can no longer ignore this issue. At a minimum, companies should start evaluating the carbon footprint of their supply chains.[31]

$SAGE edge™ ....

Visit **edge.sagepub.com/venkataraman** to help you accomplish your coursework goals in an easy-to-use learning environment.

- Mobile-friendly eFlashcards
- Mobile-friendly practice quizzes
- A complete online action plan

- Chapter summaries with learning objectives
- Video and multimedia resources

CHAPTER SUMMARY ....

2.1 Compare the different levels of strategic planning, and identify the performance measures in each. Strategic planning sets the overall direction of the organization's future. Generally, firms have distinct but interrelated levels of strategies, including (a) a corporate-level strategy; (b) a business unit-level strategy, and (c) supply-chain- and operations-level strategies. Increasingly the corporate strategies firms formulate create three types of value: (a) economic value—the traditional bottom line of economic performance; (b) environmental value—the value created by sustainable practices; and (c) social value—the value that results when the well-being of workers and other stakeholders is taken into account.

2.2 Define operations strategy, and describe how it is formulated and evaluated. An operations strategy is a collection of decisions and action plans implemented within the operations function that creates value. An operations strategy focuses on four elements: (a) customers, (b) operational critical success factors, (c) product factors, and (d) a firm's core competencies. There are several ways to evaluate an operations strategy, ranging from financial modeling using the strategic profit model (SPM) to the balanced scorecard approach. The balanced scorecard approach aligns the firm's customer, financial, internal business process, and learning and growth goals.

2.3 Contrast the formulation and evaluation of operating strategies for service organizations with those for manufacturing organizations. The strategic planning process for service operations can be represented in a hierarchical planning framework that consists of three levels: strategic positioning, service operations strategy, and tactical execution, with a continuous improvement cycle as the fourth component.

2.4 Compare the different types of productivity measurements and explain how firms use them strategically. There are three common types of productivity measures: the single-factor productivity measure, the multifactor productivity measure, and the total

productivity measure. Productivity measures are used to assess the firm's performance and to compare how well different departments within the firm are performing to determine whether their productivity has increased or decreased over time. Productivity measures assess the impact of certain decisions, such as whether new processes, equipment, or worker motivation techniques are improving the firm's performance. In addition, productivity measures can help a firm compare its productivity with that of its competitors. The means for measuring productivity can be either relatively straightforward as in the case of manufacturing organizations or more complex as in the case of service organizations.

2.5 Describe how both manufacturers and service companies formulate and evaluate their supply chain strategies. To support their business strategies, firms need to create supply chain strategies. Supply chain strategies provide clear directions that maximize efficiencies within the supply chain and drive down operational costs. All elements of the firm's operations strategy must be fully integrated with the supply chain strategy. Strategic fit in a supply chain strategy requires a firm to know its customers and uncertainties related to its supply chain, know the capabilities of the supply chain, and match the capabilities to the needs and expectations of customers. The supply chain operations reference (SCOR) model can identify the critical processes in a supply chain and, therefore, better understand exactly *what* to measure when assessing their performance. Furthermore, it allows organizations to benchmark their supply chains against those of their competitors.

2.6 Identify the key capabilities firms need to formulate and implement global operations and supply chain strategies and manage the risks related to them. Companies that have experienced success integrating their operations and supply chains globally have developed three capabilities: supply chain adaptability to respond to changes in the marketplace, financial-engineering capabilities to create new ways to exchange and raise capital, and systematic ways to identify threats to their operations and supply chains and mitigate their effect.

2.7 **Describe what companies are doing to incorporate sustainability into their supply chain strategy and the problems they face in doing so.** Companies are incorporating

sustainability into their supply chain strategy by designing sustainable products, reducing carbon emissions, using energy-efficient lighting and recycled materials, and so forth. Yet, incorporating sustainability throughout a company's supply chain is difficult because it is time-consuming and may require changes in the firm's structure and infrastructure.

KEY TERMS

Balanced scorecard   40

Business-unit strategy   32

Competitive strengths   32

Core competencies   32

Corporate strategy   30

Critical success factors (CSFs)   33

Economic value   30

Effectiveness   44

Efficiency   44

Environmental value   31

Functional strategies   32

Innovation   36

Operations strategy   32

Order loser   37

Order qualifier   37

Order winner   37

Product development cycle time   36

Productivity   44

Productivity index   46

Quality   35

Social value   31

Strategic profit model (SPM)   39

Triple bottom line   30

Vendor managed inventory (VMI)   51

DISCUSSION AND REVIEW QUESTIONS

1. In what ways does the triple bottom line affect how the strategies for a firm's operations function are formulated and implemented?

2. FedEx's core competency is embedded in its slogan: *When it absolutely, positively has to be there overnight.* Identify that core competency.

3. Describe why an operations strategy is critical to a firm.

4. Why is it important to maintain a strategic fit among the four elements of an operations strategy? How can a company resolve any mismatches among them that result from changing markets trends or customers' order-winning criteria?

5. What do you think the order-winning and order-qualifying criteria for the furniture retailer IKEA (Delft, the Netherlands) is?

6. Suppose that you own a lawn mowing and snowplowing service and are planning to provide these services to homeowners in a wealthy neighborhood. How would you use the concepts of order winners and order qualifiers to formulate and implement your service operations strategy?

7. From an operations strategy perspective, how can the balanced scorecard be used as a performance measurement system?

8. Develop a balanced scorecard for a regional airlines company.

9. Compare the operations strategies for goods versus service firms.

10. A key supply chain strategy decision is to determine the structure of a firm's supply chain. How do you think the supply chains for Wal-Mart and IKEA are structured?

11. What are the distinguishing features of companies that lead the way with sustainable supply chain strategies?

12. What are the six capabilities needed for an integrated global operations and supply chain strategy?

13. Define productivity. What is the difference between productivity and efficiency?

14. Define single-factor, multifactor, and total productivity measures.

15. A multinational company has two manufacturing plants, one in Germany and the other in China. Both plants produce the same product, which is sold in their respective countries. By using a partial productivity measure for labor, an analyst for the company finds that the productivities of these two plants are significantly different.

    a. Explain some of the possible reasons for the difference.

    b. Why might a comparison of the two plants' productivity using a single factor be misleading?

    c. Can you think of another productivity measure that would be more meaningful?

16. What are some of the inherent problems in measuring productivity in the service sector?

17. Outline the factors that affect productivity.

18. What are the steps that you would take to improve productivity in a manufacturing organization? In a service organization?

SOLVED PROBLEMS

1. Jupiter Inc., a fictional company that processes fruits and vegetables, uses 6 workers to process 500 cases of canned cherries at the rate of 40 minutes per worker. What is the partial factor productivity of labor?

Solution

$$\text{Labor productivity} = \frac{\text{\# of cases of cherries produced}}{\text{Labor hours used}} = \frac{500}{6 \times \frac{2}{3}} =$$

125 cases/labor hour

2. Rollerblade, Inc. (Bordentown, NJ) produces 3,000 roller skates per day. The costs of producing these skates are: labor cost = $200;

material cost = $90; and overhead = $460 (all in U.S. dollars). Compute the multifactor productivity:

Solution

$$\text{Multifactor productivity} = \frac{\text{Number of roller skates produced}}{\text{Labor cost} + \text{material cost} + \text{overhead}} =$$

$$\frac{3000}{\$200 + \$900 + \$460}$$

Multifactor productivity = **4.0 skates per dollar input**

PROBLEMS

1. Develop an argument for the triple bottom line when selecting among strategic alternatives; that is, how do the concepts of environmental, economic, and social value influence strategy?

2. Suppose you were recently hired by the adidas Group (Herzogenaurach, Germany) to help the firm address its triple bottom line. Research adidas at http://www.adidas-group.com/en/group/profile/ to develop a picture of the company and its strategic goals. How does it currently address triple bottom-line issues? What suggestions would you offer for modifying its strategic vision? Why?

3. Suppose you were asked to determine and align the four elements of an operations strategy for The Boeing Company (Chicago, IL). Identify its customers, core competencies, operational critical success factors, and product factors. For each element, list no more than three examples.

4. Suppose you are a retail store owner trying to decide whether to extend your Black Friday hours to start on Thanksgiving afternoon. You know that you earn 40% of your annual sales revenue during the weeks between Thanksgiving and Christmas, with a big percentage occurring on Black Friday. How would the competing concerns for economic and social value complicate this decision?

5. Discuss how the following changes in a firm's external environment would affect its operations management (OM) strategy. What impact would these changes have on OM strategy:

   a. Threat of war between Pakistan and India
   b. Significant drop in oil prices as a result of new technologies
   c. Price deflation in the European Union
   d. New federal regulations limiting fossil fuel use
   e. Demographic changes leading to fewer young people entering the workforce
   f. New federal legislation mandating health-care coverage for firms employing 50 or more full-time workers

6. Identify five critical success factors for a firm competing in the software gaming industry.

7. Orion Tile & Marble Inc. (Anaheim, CA) supplies and installs ceramic tiles. The company tracks its workers' output over the past several weeks, and the data are as follows:

Week	Number of Workers	Tiles Installed
1	5	120
2	4	96
3	4	88
4	3	69
5	2	44
6	5	115
7	2	54

   a. In which week was labor productivity the highest?
   b. What are some possible reasons for the differences in productivity from week to week?

8. Udupi, a fictional catering service, prepares and serves meals at wedding receptions, anniversary celebrations, and birthday parties. The data in the following table provide the company's labor and material usage for the past four weeks for various events. The labor cost is US$10 per hour. Compute the multifactor productivity measure for each event, and explain the differences in productivity among the events:

Event	Labor Hours	Material Cost	Number of Meals Served	Price per Meal
Birthday party	50	$450	150	$10
Wedding reception	80	$2,400	200	$40
Graduation party	40	$720	120	$12
Anniversary celebration	50	$1,400	140	$15

9. A Swiss manufacturing company that operates two manufacturing plants—one in the United States and the other in India—shows the following results (all figures are in U.S. dollars):

	United States	India
Sales	2,500,000	1,800,000
Labor	300,000	350,000
Raw materials	170,000	120,000
Capital equipment	360,000	200,000

   a. Compute the partial productivity measure for labor, materials, and equipment. How would you account for productivity differences between these two locations?
   b. Compute the multifactor productivity measure using all inputs. Is this a better productivity measure? Why?

10. The fictional Taj Mahal Indian grocery store had sales of US$50,000 in August and US$62,000 in September. There are 10 full-time workers in the store, each of whom worked 40 hours a week. In August, the store also employed six part-time workers, each of whom worked 15 hours a week. In September, eight part-time workers were employed, each for 10 hours a week. Assuming there are four weeks in each month, and sales dollars are the output measure, what was the change in productivity from August to September?

11. You run a medium-sized farming equipment repair firm in North Dakota. Your busiest season is the late fall through winter months when area farmers need repairs done to their equipment. Because you have limited cash flow, keeping extra people on your payroll is expensive and undesirable. You have determined that each worker must work 120 hours per month and you can repair an average of 42 machines each month. If their labor productivity rate is 0.24, how many workers can you employ at your company?

12. GreenTile, Inc. is a fictional manufacturer of heat-absorbing ceramic tiles that can store and radiate heat for hours after sundown, saving homeowners heating costs during winter months. This year, GreenTile will produce 280,000 tiles at its plant in Phoenix, Arizona, to fill demand orders from its California retailers. To accomplish this, each worker at the plant must work 160 hours per month. If the labor productivity rate at the plant is 0.08 ceramic tiles per labor-hour, how many laborers should GreenTile have at its Phoenix plant?

13. The following data were collected by Orion Industries Inc. (Auburn, WA) to compile the monthly productivity report to be presented to its board of directors. By using these data, compute (a) the partial labor productivity, (b) partial machine productivity, and (c) the multifactor productivity (in units per U.S. dollar) of labor, machine, materials, and energy. The average cost of labor is $20 per hour, and the average cost of machine usage is $15 per hour.

Number of units produced	150,000
Labor hours used	12,000
Machine hours used	6,000
Materials cost	$50,000
Energy cost	$18,000

14. The fictional Enrobe Textile Inc. has garment production facilities in several locations around the globe. The average monthly cost of inputs (in U.S dollars) and output levels (in units) for each of these production facilities are given in the table.

	Chennai	Shanghai	Brussels	Sharjah
Finished goods in units	15,000	11,000	5,000	8,000
Work-in-process in units	1,500	2,000	700	1800
Labor costs	$10,000	$12,000	$7,000	$8,000
Material costs	$45,000	$50,000	$60,000	$64,000
Energy costs	$7,000	$9,000	$10,000	$5,000
Transportation costs	$5,000	$7,500	$11,000	$6,000
Overhead costs	$4,000	$5,500	$8,000	$6,500

Using the information in the table:

a. Compute the partial labor productivity for each facility.

b. Compute the multifactor productivity for each facility.

c. If Enrobe decides to close one of these facilities, which one would you recommend?

15. Adrian Thomas makes golf balls in his Erie, Pennsylvania, plant. Adrian wants to improve the overall productivity of his company given the increases in the cost of inputs in recent years. He has the following data on the inputs and outputs from two sample years:

	2014	2015
Number of units produced	10,000	11,000
Labor hours used	3000	2900
Machine hours used	1,000	1,200
Materials used (Pounds)	500	450
Energy (BTU)	40,000	29,000

Compute the percentage change in productivity for each category of input, and determine which category of input shows the most improvement.

16. Adrian Thomas (from Problem 15) has determined the costs of inputs for making golf balls as follows:

- Labor: $12 per hour
- Material: $6 per pound
- Machine: $8 per hour
- Energy: $0.60 per BTU

Compute the multifactor productivity (in units per U.S. dollar) for both last year and the current year, and determine the percentage change in productivity.

17. Rachel Dawson runs a small job shop that prints customized stationery. The job shop hires 10 workers, and each worker is paid US$15 per hour. During the third week of July, the 10 workers together produced 150 units of printed stationery. Each worker during this week of July worked 40 hours. Fifty out of the 150 units of stationery produced had minor defects and were sold at a reduced price of US$3 per unit at discount outlet stores. The remaining 100 pieces of stationery were sold at retail stores such as OfficeMax (now a subsidiary of Office Depot, Inc., Boca Raton, FL) and Staples Inc. (Framingham, MA) for a price of US$5 each. Compute the labor productivity in U.S. dollars per hour during the third week of July.

18. In May 2015, the Mercedes-Benz (Stuttgart, Baden-Württemberg, Germany) factory in Alabama produced 5,000 sport utility vehicles (SUVs). During this month, the labor productivity at this plant was estimated to be 0.08 SUVs per labor hour. The plant employed 250 workers during the month of May.

a. How many hours on the average did each worker work in the month of May?

b. If labor productivity can be increased to 0.10 SUVs per hour in the month of June 2015, how many hours on average would each worker work in the month of June?

CASE STUDY 2.1 SUPPLY CHAIN STRATEGIES AND DISASTER PLANNING

Volcanic eruptions, a global flu pandemic, the flooding of New Orleans and other locales, terrorist attacks, riots in the Middle East, and the Great Recession are all examples of events that have sent firms reeling. Likewise, the devastating earthquake and tsunami that struck Japan in 2011 left a trail of debris, death, and destruction in its wake. Despite the likelihood of disasters such as these, experts estimate that fewer than 10% of businesses have contingency plans in place to cope with disruptions in their major operations and supply chain.

"It is times like this that separate those companies that have their act together from those that don't," said Jim Lawton, the president and general manager of D&B Supply Management Solutions (Short Hills, NJ), a firm that provides business information, consulting, and management solutions worldwide. He went on to say at the time of the disaster, "What [firms do] in the first 24 hours [after the tsunami] is going to determine whether they land in a decent place or crash and burn."

Even companies that didn't have key suppliers in Japan were affected. Producers far up supply chains often still relied on basic components produced in the country. Japan supplies 25% of the world's silicon wafers, for example. What's more, many firms that had outsourced work to Japanese firms competed for a limited amount of manufacturing capacity in places such as Singapore, Vietnam, and Indonesia. Said Lawton at the time, "They really are all interconnected."

So, given these complexities, where does an organization start to develop a risk management plan for its supply chain? First, it is critical that the company get a detailed picture of its supply chain, not just first-tier suppliers but also the more distant suppliers of its suppliers. For example, although a firm may think that you are protected, what if one of its key suppliers relies too heavily on one source for its raw materials? Should the firm consider hiring additional suppliers to prevent a situation in which it would be without critical raw materials?

Second, firms must plan for disruptions and take the appropriate lessons to heart. Purchasing goods and services from a single supplier can hold down a company's procurement costs because the firm can often get volume discounts for its purchases. Nevertheless, the strategy can also be risky. Wherever possible, it's a good idea to funnel some work regularly to an alternative vendor. If Supplier A encounters a disruption, it's much easier for a company to go to Supplier B for emergency materials if it has a partnering history with that supplier.

Third, successful firms make risk management an ongoing part of supply chain strategy. It should not be a one-time-only undertaking; risk management strategies must be continually updated and reconsidered in light of changes in the global economy and the organization's operations.

Yet, because it so difficult to prepare for every type of emergency, most experts agree that successful risk management comes down to supply chain agility.

As Lawton noted, it helps to diversify the supplier base wherever possible. These organizations should think about shifting some production out of Asia or Latin America to be closer to home. They should seek to create an organization that can react quickly to whatever happens, including knowing precisely which individuals are responsible for executing an emergency-response plan and equipping them in advance with the tools necessary to do the job.[32]

Questions:

1. Take a position either for or against the following statement: "To prepare for disasters, you should stockpile inventory, other critical supplies, and raw materials."

2. Think of Heinz's (H. J. Heinz Company, Pittsburgh, PA) production of consumer goods and food products. How might you develop a risk management and disaster response for the company's supply chain?

3. Because it is impossible to plan for every disaster, how might you develop a method for identifying the most likely and serious risks your organization faces?

4. In your opinion, how much risk planning is sufficient? Why? Defend your answer.

VIDEO CASE ....

Watch this video case to learn about how Digital Benefit Advisors uses a customer-focused strategy to guide daily operations.

CRITICAL THINKING EXERCISES ....

The following article discusses how Nestlé S.A. (Vevey, Switzerland) coped with the volatility in food and raw material costs. The company crafted a strategy that didn't depend on commodity prices falling. This strategy relied on the efficiency of the operations function to reduce costs, while producing and launching premium, higher margin products in which raw material costs account for a smaller percentage of the retail price.

Search for the article titled "Nestlé's Recipe for Juggling Volatile Commodity Costs" on Bloomberg and answer the questions that follow.

1. Why is the information presented in this article important from an operations strategy perspective?

2. Based on this article, what in your opinion are Nestlé's distinctive competencies?

3. How can a low-cost strategy be good for operations management? Can it be bad? If so, how?

CHAPTER

3

Project Management

LEARNING OBJECTIVES

After studying this chapter, you should be able to:

1. Describe the importance of projects to a firm, identify the people and teams that work on projects, and list the qualities that make a project a success.

2. Identify the stages of the typical life cycle of a project.

3. Explain how scope management techniques, statement-of-work documents, work breakdown structures, and risk management principles enable firms to conceptualize, plan, and organize projects.

4. Use analytical tools to calculate project schedules.

5. Identify the main supply chain activities of a project and the qualities that should be considered when designing the project's supply chain.

6. Demonstrate how to execute, track, and terminate projects.

7. Identify the critical steps in planning for sustainability in projects.

8. Discuss issues related to global project management.

OPERATIONS PROFILE: Nissan Works to Eliminate Bugs That Could Eat Into the LEAF Project

©iStockphoto.com/joel-t

Nissan developed the LEAF, which is an acronym for *Leading, Environmentally friendly, Affordable, Family car*, to differ from the current generation of hybrids in one crucial way—it is not, strictly speaking, a hybrid at all because it lacks a gasoline engine. Standard hybrid cars use electricity at relatively low speeds over limited ranges, which make them ideal for commuters. Nevertheless, when traveling at higher speeds on highways or on longer trips, the batteries cannot power the cars, and their gasoline engines engage automatically. Hybrids typically average nearly 50 mpg for normal commuter driving and somewhat less than that for longer trips or highway travel.

By contrast, the LEAF uses no gasoline at all. The car was rated best-in-class for the environment because it emits no greenhouse gases and has no tailpipe emissions.

Nissan is working to minimize all potential risks as the company broadens its market for the vehicle in the United States. Nissan knows that dealerships and mechanics will initially experience some challenges working with the car, and Nissan wants them to have as few technical problems as possible. According to *Automotive News*, the Japanese manufacturer has assembled a rapid-reaction task force to resolve customer complaints immediately. The Los Angeles–based team is led by a group of 10 engineers that have been thoroughly trained on the vehicle's drivetrain, and each engineer has a squad of around 30 technicians to provide additional assistance as it's needed. Nissan is currently looking to install similar teams in both Europe and Japan.

The move is part of an effort to assuage any worries buyers may have about being among the first people to own the electric vehicles. In Japan, Nissan has even gone so far as to offer a program with free towing, unlimited free charging at dealerships, and a 24-hour hotline that owners can call with questions. In the near future, the company may do the same in the United States.

Hybrid automobile technology has been costly to develop. Toyota (Toyota Motor Corporation, Toyota City, Japan), which controls roughly two thirds of the global market for hybrid electric cars, is estimated to have spent upward of $10 billion on the technology over the course of 15 years. Environmental awareness and government incentives are pushing more American buyers to consider purchasing electric and hybrid vehicles, and their market share is expected to steadily increase.[1]

Describe the importance of projects to a firm, identify the people and teams that work on projects, and list the qualities that make a project a success.

Master the content.

edge.sagepub.com /venkataraman

3.1 Projects, Project Teams, and Measuring Success

A **project** is a unique venture with a beginning and an end, conducted by people to meet established goals within certain cost, schedule, and quality parameters.[2] Whether we are talking about building the latest generation of smartphone, designing a new composite material used to build airplanes, planning a major fund-raising event, or developing a high-speed rail network, the goal is to create something of value to address a business opportunity or prevent the loss of competitive advantage.[3]

Projects represent human accomplishments. Sometimes projects are grand in scale. The Hoover Dam and Space Station Freedom were grand projects. Sometimes their goals are to achieve small, incremental change; for example, when manufacturers come out with new and improved household products. Literally thousands of projects are undertaken daily by large and small companies alike, some with budgets of a few hundred dollars, and others with multibillion dollar budgets. Here are some examples of projects:

- Apple Inc.'s (Cupertino, CA) creation of the new iPad.
- Bechtel Corporation's (San Francisco, CA) construction of a large-scale chemical refining plant in South Africa.
- The West Coast High-Speed Route Modernization rail renovation project in the United Kingdom, designed to update the most heavily traveled passenger and freight rail network in Britain.
- Chile's rescue operation to free 33 miners trapped a half-mile below the surface after the catastrophic collapse of a mine.
- A World Bank project to reclaim nearly 3 million acres of poor soil for farming in the Uttar Pradesh state in India.
- The development of Chevrolet's Volt (The General Motors Company, Detroit, MI) electric car.
- The reconfiguration of Cummins Inc.'s (Columbus, IN) diesel engine assembly line to streamline the company's manufacturing processes.

Project management is the application of knowledge, skills, tools, and techniques to project activities to meet the project requirements.[4] Projects are different from organizational processes. A process is an ongoing, day-to-day activity in which an organization engages while producing goods or services. Processes use existing systems, properties, and capabilities in a fairly repetitive manner. An inventory reorder system, accounting operations to close out the books, or a manufacturing line are typical examples of processes. Projects are different. They are ways to address unique, one-time opportunities and business ventures.

All projects share the following characteristics:

1. **They are complex and unique.** Projects are complex because they require the coordinated effort of people across an organization (and often multiple organizations), such as employees from a firm's marketing, production, engineering, and design departments. Projects are unique in that they exist only as long as they are needed or until they have been completed. That is, they are not routine efforts.
2. **They have a clear goal or set of goals.** Project goals, also referred to as *deliverables*, are developed to address an opportunity or threat that a company perceives. They are designed to yield a tangible result—either a new product or service. For a project to be meaningful, it must have clear goals. "Improve operations flow" is *not* a meaningful project goal. On the other hand, "analyze and streamline the warehouse storage process to reduce processing costs by 10%" would be considered a clearly established goal for the project.
3. **They are limited by their budgets, schedules, and resources.** Projects are defined, to a degree, by their limits—limited financial and human resources for a specified time period. Unlike processes, projects do not go on indefinitely. Once a project is completed, the project team disbands and any leftover funds or other resources are transferred back to the organization. Likewise, projects are intended to be developed within a set budget and involve a select group of people.
4. **They are customer focused.** In the past, projects were considered successful if they met certain budget, schedule, and quality parameters. Nonetheless, this assessment left out a critical question: Does the project solve the concerns of the customer for whom it was developed? A project cannot be considered successful if it does not adequately address customer needs.

Project: a unique venture with a beginning and an end, conducted by people to meet established goals within certain cost, schedule, and quality parameters

Project management: the application of knowledge, skills, tools, and techniques to project activities to meet the project requirements

Projects allow companies to respond to the pressures of competing in today's markets, and there are several reasons that companies use projects to achieve their strategic goals.

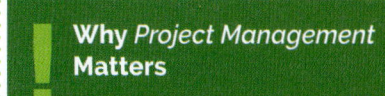

1. **Shortened product life cycles.** The life cycles of new products are increasingly being measured in months and, in some cases, even weeks. Consider the new smartphones manufactured by Samsung (Ridgefield Park, NJ), Nokia Corporation (Espoo, Finland), or Apple (already introduced in this chapter) and the huge number of applications for them that are being developed. These organizations are continually revising and updating their product lines to satisfy new customer demands.

2. **Narrow product-launch windows.** Opportunities in the marketplace are not open ended. Successful companies can get their goods and services into the marketplace quickly before the window of opportunity for them closes. Even while the Microsoft Corporation (Redmond, WA) was celebrating the release of its latest operating system, the company's employees were hard at work developing upgrades, extensions, and even considering the next version of the product.

3. **Increasingly complex and technical products and services.** Increasingly, products and services are complicated, technically sophisticated, and hard to produce efficiently. Today's cell phones have more processing power than the computers that controlled the Apollo 11, the first spacecraft to land on the moon. Firms are pressed to satisfy the public's insatiable demand for the next big thing—products that push the edges of the technological envelope

4. **The emergence and integration of global markets.** Former closed or socialist economies, such as those in Russia, India, and China have opened their doors to an influx of trade and millions of new customers. This new global environment, combined with technologies for quickly interacting with customers and suppliers, has made the business environment more fast-paced and open for development.

Project Teams

Because they are responsible for leading the teams of people who work on projects, project managers have a huge impact on a project's success or failure. In a sense, project leaders act as mini-CEOs for their projects, directing both the myriad of activities that need to be done and the people who need to do them. Part of the challenge project managers face is that the team members working on the project typically are loyal to their functional departments rather than to the project team. Sometimes the team members are employees of other organizations that a firm is partnering with. For example, the project team setting up the venue for the London Olympic Games, CLM, included the construction firms CH2M Hill, Inc. (Englewood, CO), Laing O'Rourke (Dartford, U.K.), and Mace (London, U.K.). Last, it is common for project managers to lead virtual teams. Rarely, if ever, do the members of these teams meet face to face. Instead, they communicate with one another over the Internet or by using other digital technologies. Virtual team members may live in different parts of the world. As a result, motivation and team building are critical skills for project managers to develop.

How Project Teams Are Structured

The highlighted portion of Figure 3.1, which is sometimes called a *matrix structure,* shows a common structure for a project team. Note that the project manager receives commitments for a number of resources, or employees, from each functional department contributing to the project team. The project manager negotiates for resources after deciding on the number of people needed to perform the project's various activities. As the figure shows, the project manager for Project Alpha receives a total of 7.5 resources (workers) from the marketing, production, finance, and research departments. In this example, a half resource is a way to indicate that a member of the project team is assigned on a part-time basis.

Figure 3.1 reveals a basic challenge for any project manager. Organizing a team involves negotiating and bargaining for resources as well as managing and motivating these temporary team members. Together the project manager and his or her team members are expected to meet the project's objectives within strict guidelines for performance, quality, time, and cost. Moreover, because each project is unique, there is usually no established road map for successfully developing projects. It is easy to see why project managers are so critical for the success of the projects they lead.

FIGURE 3.1: Example of a Matrix Project Structure

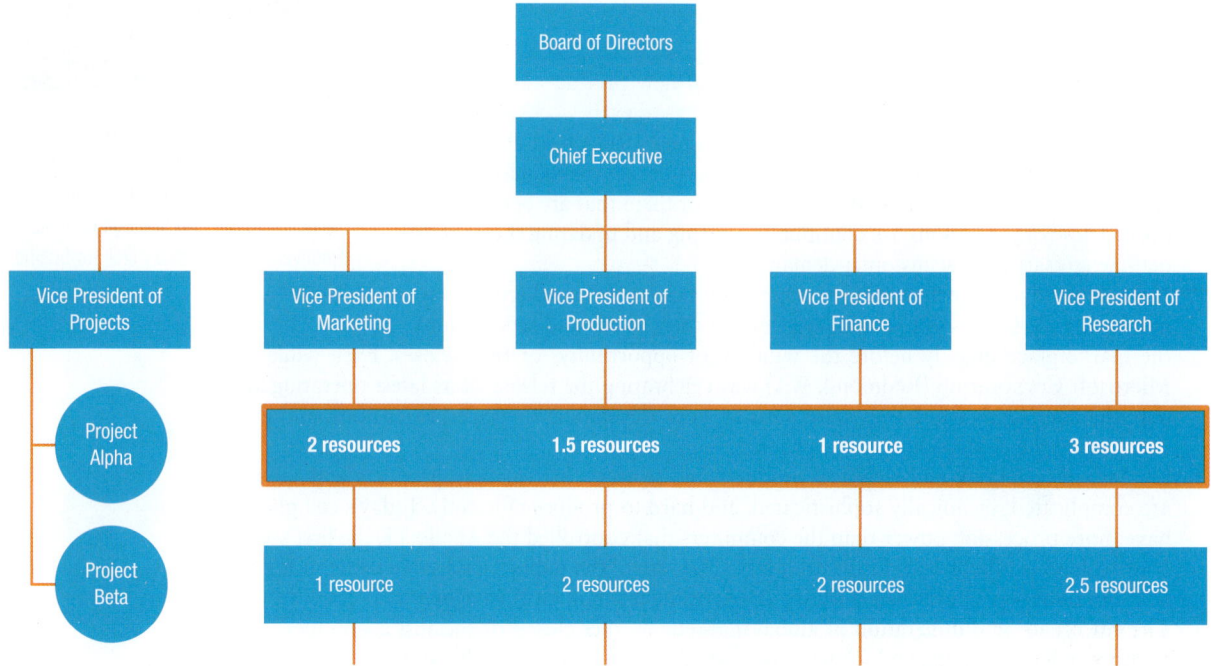

Projects can also be developed by people within a single functional group of an organization, such as the firm's marketing or production department, for example. This type of organizational structure is referred to as a *functional structure.* One advantage of a functional structure is that the members of the team generally share similar backgrounds and expertise. There are also no divided loyalties among the members because they all work in the same department. A functional structure makes sense when a project is designed primarily to benefit the department the team members work in. By contrast, when a project is designed to affect the entire organization or multiple groups within it, a matrix structure may make more sense.

Yet another structure is a *pure project structure,* which is often used by organizations that focus exclusively on projects. Construction firms, pharmaceutical developers, many software consulting, and research and development organizations are examples of project-focused organizations. Each project is a self-contained business unit with a dedicated project team. The firm assigns people from functional groups directly to the project for the time period they are needed, and the project manager has sole authority over them during that period. The functional department's chief role is to coordinate with project managers and ensure that there are sufficient resources available as they need them. Once the project is over, the personnel are reassigned to new projects. Figure 3.2 shows an example of a project organization.

What Makes a Project Successful?

A project's success must be evaluated by the elements that characterize the project. These elements are time (adherence to schedule), cost, and quality. This idea was originally referred to as the triple constraint of projects. In more modern times, customer satisfaction has been added as a criterion for projects. Because projects have the goal of satisfying a customer or client, it makes sense to use this new quadruple constraint as the basis for determining the success of a project.

- **Time.** Projects have a definite beginning and end. They are not supposed to continue indefinitely or routinely run past their expected delivery dates. Therefore, the first constraint for any project is that it should come in on or before the scheduled completion date.
- **Cost.** Projects are constrained by their budgets. The second criterion for a successful project is that the project must finish within its budget.
- **Quality.** All projects should be developed with a set of specifications that clearly states what the project is supposed to do or identifies the technical challenge it is supposed to address

Triple constraint: elements that characterize a project and are used to evaluate its success: time (adherence to schedule), cost, and quality

Quadruple constraint: a modern iteration of triple constraint that considers the goal of satisfying a customer or client. The elements of quadruple constraint are time, cost, quality, and customer satisfaction

FIGURE 3.2: Example of a Pure Project Structure

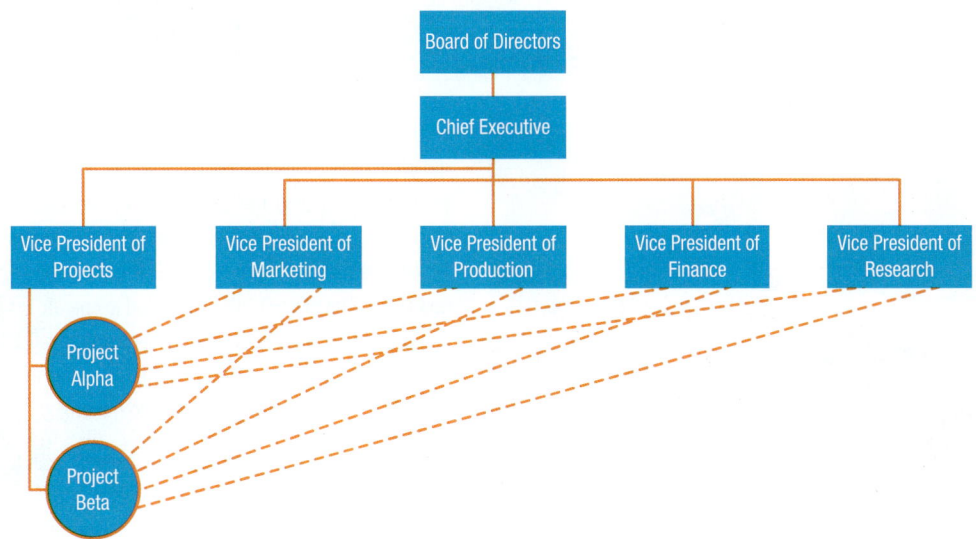

successfully. A project achieves quality if it meets its technical specifications. "On spec" is a term frequently applied to a project to assess its quality.

- **Client satisfaction.** The client for any project is the party (either internal or external to the organization) for whom the project is intended. Projects should be designed to satisfy the client's needs. Suppose an information technology (IT) department of a large organization creates a new order entry system for the logistics department without adequately understanding the logistics department's needs. If the logistics department rejects the system, it doesn't matter if the IT group managed the project well and brought it in under budget or on schedule. Because the clients were not satisfied with the project, it must be judged a failure. As a result, the final criterion for assessing the success of a project is the degree to which customers embrace and use it.

Triple Constraint

3.2 Project Life Cycles

A project's **life cycle** refers to the stages of its development. Figure 3.3 shows the four stages in a project life cycle. The stages are shown along the horizontal axis (the *x*-axis), and the measure of actual work being accomplished to complete the project is plotted on the vertical axis (*y*-axis) to the left.

3.2
Identify the stages of the typical life cycle of a project.

FIGURE 3.3: Project Life Cycle Stages

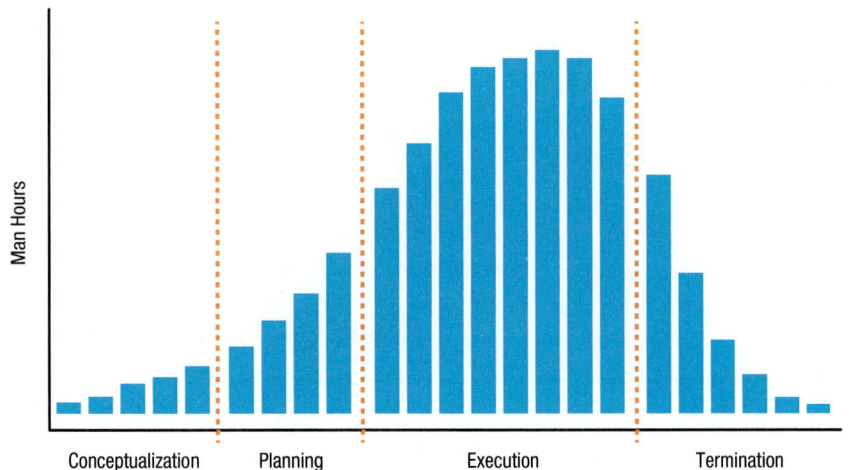

Life cycle: the stages of a project's development: conceptualization, planning, execution, and termination

SOURCE: Pinto, J. K., & Rouhiainen, P. (2001). *Building customer-based project organizations.* New York, NY: Wiley.

OPERATIONS PROFILE: The Expeditionary Fighting Vehicle

Scott J. Ferrell/CQ-Roll Call Group/Getty Images

One of the most difficult Congressional budget decisions in years was finally announced in early 2011: the cancellation of the Marine Corps' expeditionary fighting vehicle (EFV). The EFV is an armored amphibious vehicle designed nearly 20 years ago to replace a similar type of vehicle built in the 1970s. The EFV, which can carry up to 17 Marines, is designed to roll off a Navy assault ship, travel across the water's surface for distances of up to 25 miles, and then do battle onshore. Unfortunately, the project to build it has been a huge failure. As one reporter noted, "After 10 years and $1.7 billion, this is what the Marine Corps got for its investment in a new amphibious vehicle: A craft that breaks down about an average of once every 4½ hours, leaks, and sometimes veers off course." What went wrong?

Big defense projects are often of an incredibly long duration, and the EFV's record is no different. The EFV project was explored and launched in the 1980s by the U.S. Department of Defense (DoD). At one point, the project even won two DoD awards for successful cost and technology management. The original contract to engineer and design vehicle was awarded to General Dynamics Corporation (West Falls Church, VA) in 1996. In 2001, the company was awarded a subsequent contract for the system development and demonstration (SDD) phase of the program. During this critical stage, all the complex engineering, systems development, and functionality of the vehicle had to be successfully demonstrated.

Perhaps unwisely, General Dynamics only budgeted 27 months for total testing and system verification. This far-too-ambitious schedule soon became a problem after technical glitches surfaced. Two additional years were added to the SDD phase after more problems arose. When the prototypes of the vehicle were tested in 2004, their computer systems failed, causing the steering in the vehicles to seize up. In the same year, the hydraulic systems powering the vehicle's bow-flap, which was installed to make the EFV more seaworthy, began leaking and failing. The EFV was also supposed to operate for 70 hours on average prior to breaking down, but because of its reliability problems, the Marines reduced the figure to 43.5 hours. After these prototype tests, an additional two years were added to the project.

In 2006, the EFV was put through a series of tests to demonstrate that it could meet its performance requirements and was therefore ready to be produced. Its performance was terrible. The vehicles were only able to operate on average for 4.5 hours between breakdowns. and it took nearly 3.5 hours of corrective maintenance for every hour of operation. The EFV's reliability was so poor that it successfully completed only 3 of the 34 amphibious, gunnery, or mobility tests it had been assigned. In addition, the prototypes were nearly 1 ton overweight, suffered from limited visibility, and were so noisy that the driver was advised to wear earplugs while driving, making communicating with the EFV's commander nearly impossible.

Meanwhile, the project's costs just kept increasing. Originally, the Marine Corps planned to purchase 1,025 EFVs for a total of $8.5 billion. Because of the skyrocketing costs, however, the Marine Corps had to trim its order to 573 vehicles. In effect, the cost of the EFV had risen from about $8 million per vehicle to slightly more than $23 million per vehicle. In 2011, the DoD finally canceled the project. The only surprising thing about the cancellation was that it didn't happen sooner.

Has the Marine Corps learned its lesson with the EFV? It's hard to say. Quickly on the heels of the decision to cancel the EFV, the Marines announced the development of a new, improved EFV, called the amphibious combat vehicle (ACV), which it claims was designed to be a more realistic version of the EFV. The goal is to keep the ACV's costs to $10–$12 million per vehicle. Contractors have been given time to develop their prototypes, and the Marines are expected to choose the ACV around 2020. Critics argue that the Marines have still not learned the lessons of the disastrous EFV project, with the quick pivot to this alternative program. Furthermore, any more episodes of ballooning costs and poor performance may remove any chance of the Marines receiving a new combat vehicle for a generation. Even if it does work, and costs are within budget, a $10–$12 million per vehicle program would be a prime target for cuts in any new negotiations between Congress and the Pentagon.[5]

Note that as a project begins, the resources (man hours) needed for it are minimal but then increase sharply as the project moves further into development, before falling off again as the project moves to its conclusion. This pattern is typical for most projects. The four stages of the project life cycle are conceptualization, planning, execution, and termination.

- **Conceptualization.** In the conceptualization stage, the team members decide what they expect to achieve with the project. During this stage, the overall purpose of the project is determined and mutually agreed to by all affected parties, including the client. The scope of the project is determined, and all necessary resources needed to achieve it (people, budget, physical plant, and so on) are identified.
- **Planning.** In the planning stage, the team members determine how they are going to complete the project successfully. In this stage, they draw all the detailed schematics, set up schedules, identify performances specifications, and develop other plans for the project. The individual pieces of the project are identified (the actual steps), as well as the people needed to complete the complex and interrelated steps.
- **Execution.** The execution stage is the stage at which the actual work of the project is performed and the bulk of the resources allocated to it are consumed. The system is being developed, the structure built, or the product created and fabricated.
- **Termination.** In this stage, the finished project is transferred to its intended users, the project's resources get reassigned, and it is formally closed out. By this stage, the actual work done on the project is rapidly decreasing.

 Project Life Cycles

The advantage of the project life cycle is that it provides a useful graphic representation of how the project is ideally expected to perform, including the stages in its development. As such, we can use the life-cycle model to assess the status of the project at different points in its existence. In this chapter, we will use the product life cycle to divide the project management activities into the stages at which various tasks should be accomplished, starting with conceptualization and planning.

3.3 Conceptualizing and Planning Projects

In this section, we describe the tasks that must be completed to conceptualize and plan a project before it can be launched.

Conceptualization

During the conceptualization stage, the firm determines the purpose of the project, its objectives, and ways to meet those objectives. Some key pieces of information, such as those listed in the folllowing, must be either collected or developed early on for this purpose:

1. **The development of a problem, or need, statement:** A project begins with a statement of its goals—what the underlying problem or need is and how the project will either solve the problem or meet the need.
2. **An analysis of alternatives:** Usually there is more than one way to solve a problem or meet a need. Part of the conceptualization process is generating alternative solutions for the problem. For example, the Pittsburgh Penguins NHL hockey team had been playing in the oldest arena in the league when it built the Consol Arena, which opened in 2010. In deciding to build a brand new arena, the Penguins determined that modifying and updating a 50-year-old facility did not make sense in the long term.
3. **Information gathering:** The project manager and team need to know as much as possible about the project. For example, what are its specific target dates? Does the project have the support of the firm's top managers? Are there any restrictions that could affect the project's development, such as time or budget constraints, physical limitations, or client demands?
4. **Clearly stated objectives for the project:** Based on the need statement, the analysis of alternatives, and the information gathered about the project, the conceptualization phase concludes with the development of a clear statement of the final objectives for the project. The objectives should include its outputs (what it is supposed to accomplish), required resources, and timing.

A critical feature in conceptual development is project scope management. A project's scope identifies everything about the project—all activities expected to be performed, the resources consumed, and

 The Importance of Planning

the end products produced, including their quality standards.[6] **Scope management** is the process of determining the best way in which the project's goals can be accomplished given its constraints. The goal is to keep the project from getting out of control—either through cost escalation, schedule over-runs, or constantly changing project goals.

Many organizations have their project teams prepare a *statement of work (SOW)* as part of the scope management process. The statement of work is a detailed description of the work required for the project.[7] The document summarizes the work done during the conceptualization phase. Thus, it can help a project team stay on track in terms of what it is supposed to deliver. An effective SOW contains details about the project, a technical description of the project, and a timetable for completion.

1. The *introduction and background* discussion is a brief history of the organization or an introduction to the circumstances that identified the need to develop the project. Part of the introduction should contain the problem statement developed during the conceptualization phase.
2. The *technical description* of the project presents an analysis of the expected technical capabilities of the project or the technical challenges the project is intended to resolve.
3. The *timeline and milestones* break down the anticipated timeframe in which the key deliverables of the project will be completed along with the overall project.

Armed with an SOW, the project manager can begin identifying the specific steps necessary to execute it.

Keep in mind that the sooner the organization can articulate the project's specifications (its scope), the more confident it can be of developing a clear statement of work that will become the basis for all critical planning and scheduling. For many organizations, especially those with strong engineering and technical departments, a common problem with their project management is **scope creep**, the situation in which project specifications are continually modified or improved as new ideas emerge or new technical solutions become possible. Certainly, organizations want to produce the best possible projects with the most up-to-date technology, but the danger in scope creep is that constant meddling and modification of the project's goals can cause costs to rise and schedules to change. The modifications can prevent the project from getting started or completed.

Planning

Now we turn to the task that must be completed during the planning stage: creating work breakdown structures.

CREATING WORK BREAKDOWN STRUCTURES

A key task in planning a project is determining its **work breakdown structure (WBS)**. Any project is just a collection of steps, or activities, that collectively add up to the overall deliverable. The WBS is a process of breaking down a project's overall mission into step-by-step tasks. This process is critical because many people find that planning a project is daunting. Where do we start? How do we get from the beginning to the end? The WBS helps us break the project into its parts.

As a simple example, suppose you were asked to plan a wedding reception, which is at a local country club. You determine that among the general activities for a reception, you will need music, food and catering, decorations, invitations, and so forth. Under each of these deliverables are additional activities, usually referred to as **work packages**. For example, under the general heading of music are the work packages of (a) hiring a band, (b) approving the play list, (c) ensuring the sound system is compatible with the band's equipment, (d) scheduling their arrival and set-up times, (e) compensating the band, and (f) overseeing their cleanup and departure. Figure 3.4 illustrates a WBS for this project. Note that it is also relatively easy to create a WBS using Microsoft (MS) Project® (Microsoft Corporation, Redmond, WA), as Screenshot 3.1 demonstrates. Screenshot 3.1 shows a partial WBS for the wedding reception project created using the MS Project WBS option, which can distinguish among Project Level headings, Deliverable headings, and Work Package headings.

Employing Risk Management Techniques

Suppose your organization was contemplating spending more than a billion dollars to build a new international airport

---

Scope management: the process of determining the best way in which the project's goals can be accomplished given its constraints

Scope creep: a situation in which project specifications are continually modified or improved as new ideas emerge or new technical solutions become possible

Work breakdown structure (WBS): a process of breaking down a project's overall mission into step-by-step tasks

Work packages: activities that comprise the deliverables of a project

Due to a short production time line, the baggage conveyor system created by BAE Systems for the Denver airport ended up having so many flaws that they were forced to shut it down. This unexpected setback may have been avoided had they considered the project risk of a condensed timeline.

John Greim/LightRocket/Getty Images

Consider This 3.1:
Statements of Work: Then-and-Now

Modern weapon systems have traditionally contained many more specifications and greater detailed SOWs than did those of the past. Contrast the Army Signal Corps SOW for the Wright Brothers' heavier-than-air flying machine in 1908 to the Air Force's SOW for the Joint Strike Fighter, originally approved in 2001. The requirements in the 1908 SOW—for example, that the plane be easily taken apart for transport in Army wagons and be capable of being reassembled in an hour—and other contract conditions were specified on one page. The requirements section in the 2001 SOW for the Air Force Joint Strike Fighter is nearly 100 pages long with more than 300 paragraphs of requirements. Today's SOWs are much more complex requiring greater attention to detail perhaps because the products are so much more complex, the equipment and materials are technically challenging, and legal requirements need much greater specification.[8]

FIGURE 3.4: Partial Work Breakdown Structure

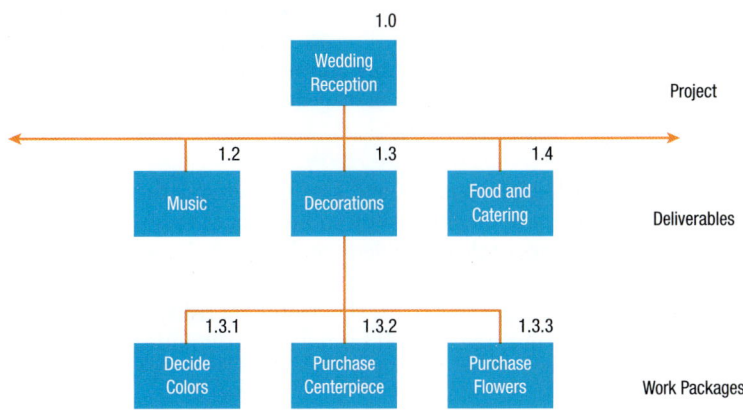

SCREENSHOT 3.1: Using MS Project to Develop a Work Breakdown Structure (WBS)

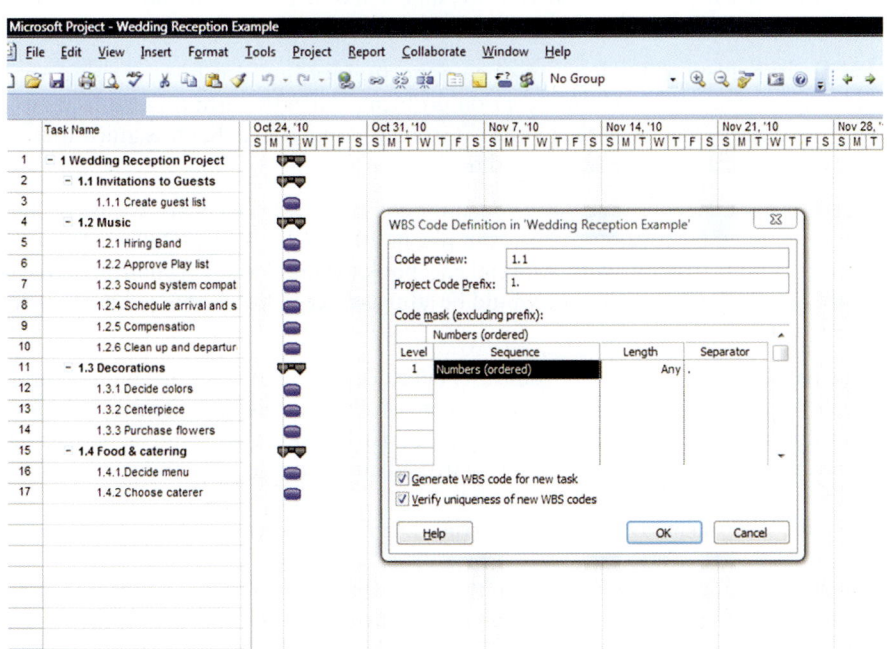

designed to upgrade the transportation facilities for your city and to attract new airlines to consider the site as a potential hub. As part of this huge project, the decision was made to develop a new and improved automated baggage handling system. This task is large because large, modern airports cover hundreds of acres of ground and the logistics of moving luggage quickly through these systems is complicated.

Such a situation actually occurred when a new international airport in Denver, Colorado, was built in 1994. Trying to automate the huge new airport fully within a tight timeframe proved to be beyond the capabilities of BAE Systems, Inc. (Arlington, VA), the company hired to create the conveyer system to route the luggage. During test runs, the bags were routinely misrouted, which delayed the opening of the airport. The conveyer system was so flawed that the airport had to go back to routing bags manually on carts. BAE worked frantically to isolate the problems with the system, all while millions of dollars in delay penalties were piling up.

BAE's project nightmare highlights a critical part of all projects: risk management plans. A **project risk** is any event that can negatively affect the viability of a project. Project risk is based on a simple formula:

$$\text{Project Risk} = (\text{Probability of Event}) \times (\text{Consequences of Event})$$

Thus, for a project risk to be significant, it must be highly likely, have very negative consequences, or both. For example, if the manager of the project fell ill, it would have terrible consequences for the project. Nevertheless, the probability of such an event occurring is likely to be relatively low. Critical personnel do change jobs, however, so the resignation of a key member of the project could seriously affect its success.

Risk management is the process of anticipating and figuring out how to respond to a project's risks prior to beginning the project. Project risk management requires the firm to ask the following questions:

- What adverse events are likely to happen, and how can we spot them?
- What can be done to minimize the probability and impact of these events occurring?
- What are the likely outcomes of these problems and our anticipated responses?

The risk management process involves three steps: (1) identifying risks, (2) analyzing the probability of risks occurring and their consequences, and (3) formulating risk mitigation strategies. Let us consider each of these steps in turn.

1. Identifying Risks

There are different types of risks.

Financial risks. The total monetary risk a firm exposes itself to when developing a project is the organization's financial risk. Denver invested well over a billion dollars in constructing its new international airport. The financial risk of the project was huge.

Technical risks. New technologies lead to opportunities but also to new risks. Apple's 4G iPhone was originally plagued by reception problems when the firm decided to wrap the antenna around the perimeter of the phone. Customers complained that this innovation resulted in poor reception, and Apple was forced to fix the problem.

Commercial risks. New products developed for commercial markets are always at the risk of not being accepted by customers. For example, in 2011, AT&T Inc. (Dallas, TX) introduced the HTC Status Smartphone with a special Facebook (Menlo Park, CA) button on the device's keyboard. AT&T figured the phone would be a huge success, but it bombed in the first month after its release.

Contractual (legal) risks. When a project is developed with strict terms and conditions that are legally enforceable, it contains contractual risk. Numerous terms and conditions can be embedded in contracts that make projects particularly risky. For example, a contract might contain serious penalties if the project is delivered late or exceeds its budgeted cost.

2. Analyzing the Probability of Risks Occurring and Their Consequences

The next step is to analyze the likelihood that the risks identified will occur and what their potential impact could be. For this purpose, project teams typically construct a risk impact matrix similar to

Project risk: any event that can negatively affect the viability of a project based on the formula: Project Risk = (Probability of Event) × (Consequences of Event)

Risk management: the process of anticipating and figuring out how to respond to a project's risks prior to beginning the project

the diagram shown in Figure 3.5. The risks identified in Step 1 are then assessed to determine the truly significant ones that must be addressed first. For the project shown in Figure 3.5, notice that the risk with the highest probability of occurring and the biggest impact is believed to be Risk D—that competitors will get their products into the marketplace before your firm can.

3. **Formulating Risk Mitigation Strategies**

After a project's risks that have been prioritized in terms of their potential impact, the team must decide what to do about them. There are many different ways to mitigate risks, but the five most basic approaches for doing so are as follows:

AT&T failed to identify the potential commercial risk associated with launching the HTC Status.

Bloomberg/Bloomberg/Getty Images

Accept the risk. Either the impact of the potential risk is minor or there is little that can be done about it. For example, annually the U.S. recording industry spends millions of dollars producing and promoting thousands of songs, knowing that fewer than 5% of them will be profitable. Yet, given that this is the nature of the industry, it is a risk recording companies accept.

Minimize the risk. Another strategy is to take reasonable steps to minimize the risk. For example, The Boeing Company (Chicago, IL) and Airbus SAS (Blagnac, France) both manufacture commercial planes. They depend on thousands of vendors for high-quality parts. One way both firms have sought to minimize potential quality risks across these multiple vendors is by creating quality teams that work with these vendors to ensure that all of the materials they produce for the planes pass rigorous quality standards.

Share the risk. When multiple organizations develop a project, they often share the risks proportionally. One type of contract that poorer, developing nations routinely sign with large industrial construction companies is a BOOT contract. BOOT is an acronym for Build, Own, Operate, Transfer. A BOOT contract requires the construction company to use its own money to develop the facility and ensure it is operating correctly *before* transferring ownership to

FIGURE 3.5: Risk Impact Matrix

Risk Factor	Consequence	Likelihood	Impact Potential
A. Loss of Lead Programmer	High	Low	Moderate
B. Technical Failure	High	Medium	Serious
C. Budget Cut	Medium	Low	Minor
D. Competitors First to Market	High	High	Serious

Consequences

	Low	Medium	High
High			D
Medium			B
Low		C	A

Likelihood

the government. This arrangement results in the construction company sharing some of the developmental risks of the project with the government.

Transfer the risk. In some circumstances, it may be possible to use a contract to transfer the risk effectively to another party. For example, if a customer is afraid of excessive cost overruns, it may insist on a fixed-cost contract, which specifies the project's price in advance. Likewise, a firm that is afraid of delays might insist on a contract that requires the project developer to pay a fine for every day the project is delayed.

Document the risk. Another way to deal with risks is to document them thoroughly as part of the project's development. One common practice in many firms is to create a lessons learned archive, so that future project teams have a better idea about how to mitigate the risks previous teams have experienced. This approach is useful, especially when a new project is similar to one that has been done in the past.

3.4 Scheduling Projects

3.4

Use analytical tools to calculate project schedules.

The most well-known project management activities relate to project scheduling. **Project scheduling** is the process of converting a project's goals into a logical method for completing them on time.

Estimating the Duration of a Project's Activities

Once we have identified all the activities necessary to complete a project, through the WBS, the next step is to come up with reasonable estimates for the time it will take to complete each activity, known as activity duration. This process can involve subjective as well as objective analysis. Typically, there are two ways to determine activity durations: **deterministic estimation** and **probabilistic estimation**. Deterministic estimation assumes that sufficient information from historical records or the opinion of experts is available to make this determination with a reasonable degree of accuracy. For example, it might possible to check the records or ask a senior engineer how long it took to finish a similar activity in the past. In the construction industry, sophisticated methods and well-understood building standards and procedures allow for deterministic estimation. Typically, deterministic estimates are associated with the *critical path method (CPM)* for planning and scheduling.

Nevertheless, suppose we are embarking on a new, cutting-edge project or attempting to harness a new technology. With no prior historical data or expert knowledge to guide us, we may not be able to accurately assign an expected duration to an activity. The **program evaluation and review technique (PERT)** was developed in the 1950s to solve problems like this. PERT uses probabilistic estimation—that is, it assigns probabilities to a range of time estimates for each activity. PERT recognizes that there are three time estimates related to any activity:

- The optimistic time (*a*)—the time an activity will take if everything happens as planned. When estimating the duration for *a*, you should allow only a 1% chance (1 / 100) that the activity time will be less than *a*—that is, that the activity will be completed even *faster* than planned if everything goes right.
- Most likely time (*m*)—the most realistic time to complete the activity.
- Pessimistic time (*b*)—the time an activity will take if nothing happens as planned, that is, if everything goes wrong or conditions are unfavorable. When estimating the duration for *b*, you should allow only a 1% chance (1 / 100) that the activity time will be greater than *b*—that is, that the activity will take *even longer* than planned if everything goes wrong.

Project scheduling: the process of converting a project's goals into a logical method for completing them on time

Deterministic estimation: a duration estimation that assumes that sufficient information from historical records or the opinion of experts is available to make this determination with a reasonable degree of accuracy

Probabilistic estimation: a duration estimation that assigns probabilities to a range of time estimates for each activity

Program evaluation and review technique (PERT): a duration estimation technique that uses probabilities by applying a weighted average of optimistic, pessimistic, and most likely estimates to derive an expected duration for an activity

Two assumptions are used to convert the values of *m*, *a*, and *b* into estimates of the expected time (TE) and variance (s^2) of the duration for the activity. One important assumption is that *s*, the standard deviation of the duration, equals one sixth of the range for reasonably possible times. The variance for an activity duration estimate is given by the formula:

$$s^2 = [1 / 6 \, (b - a)]^2$$

This equation, which expresses the first assumption, means that to achieve a probability distribution with a 99% confidence interval, observations should lie within 3 standard deviations of the mean in either direction. A spread of 6 standard deviations from tail to tail in the probability distribution, then, accounts for 99.7% of the possible activity duration alternatives.

Because the optimistic and pessimistic times are not symmetrical around the mean, the second assumption refers to the shape of the probability distribution. The beta, or asymmetrical, distribution better represents the distribution of the possible expected duration times (TE) for the activity (see Figure 3.6). The beta distribution suggests that the calculation for deriving TE is:

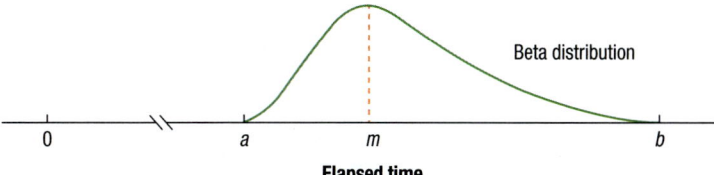

FIGURE 3.6: Using an Asymmetrical (Beta) Distribution to Estimate the Duration of an Activity

$$TE = (a + 4m + b) / 6$$

where

TE = estimated time for the activity

a = most optimistic time to complete the activity

m = most likely time to complete the activity, which is the mode of the distribution

b = most pessimistic time to complete the activity

In this calculation, the midpoint between the pessimistic and optimistic values is the weighted arithmetic mean of the mode and midrange, representing two thirds of the overall weighting for the calculated expected time (TE). The additional weighting is intended to highlight the clustering of expected values around the distribution mean, regardless of the length of both pessimistic and optimistic tails (total distribution standard deviation).

Let's take a look at an example. Suppose we wished to determine the expected times (TE) for a series of activities A through E, as listed in Table 3.1.

Including optimistic and pessimistic estimates can result in some important information regarding changes in the expected duration times for activities. For example, activity E has a most likely time of 5 days to complete. Nevertheless, because the pessimistic time is so much longer (12 days), the new expected duration for this activity is nearly one extra day longer or 5.83 days. In addition to the information on the TE for each activity, the variance in these expected durations varies dramatically. The variance for activity C is low (.11), whereas the variance for the TE of activity E is quite high (2.25). We will provide more in-depth examples of the method for calculating expected activity and project durations in the supplement for this chapter.

Creating Precedence Diagrams and Gantt Charts

Suppose we wished to hold an outdoor music festival to raise funds for the nonprofit group Habitat for Humanity. We know that we first need to identify the project's key activities using a WBS. The overall project includes a variety of deliverables such as finding sponsors, promoting the festival, and hiring the musical acts. Your particular job is to locate and prepare the site for the concert. After working with your project team, you prepare the WBS shown in Figure 3.7, which shows all of the activities related to your team's deliverables.

TABLE 3.1: Sample Project Duration Estimates

ACTIVITY	OPTIMISTIC TIME (a) (DAYS)	MOST LIKELY TIME (m) (DAYS)	PESSIMISTIC TIME (b) (DAYS)	EXPECTED TIME (TE): $(a + 4m + b) / 6$ (DAYS)	VARIANCE: $[1/6 \, (b - a)]^2$
a	2	5	8	5	36/36 = 1.0
b	1	3	7	3.33	36/36 = 1.0
c	2	3	4	3	4/36 = .11
d	5	7	10	7.17	25/36 = .69
e	3	5	12	5.83	81/36 = 2.25

FIGURE 3.7: Work Breakdown Structure for the Music Festival's Site Preparation

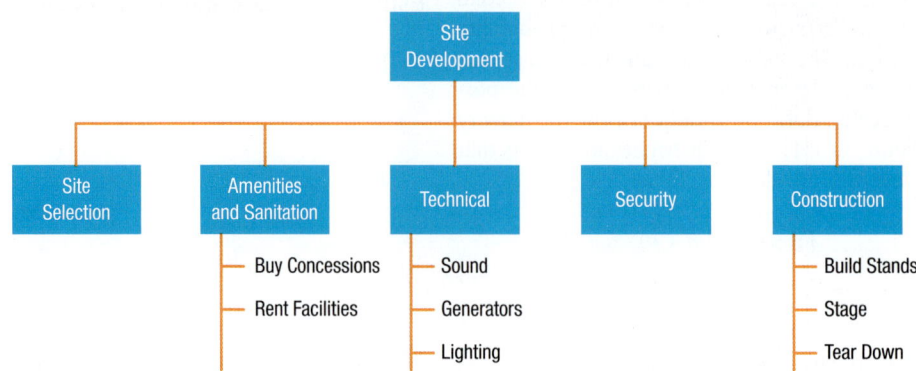

Once the team has identified the deliverables, you turn your attention to precedence diagramming and duration estimation. **Precedence diagramming,** which is also sometimes called *network diagramming,* is the process of creating a chart that shows a project's activities and indicates how they should logically be coordinated with one another. To construct such a diagram, you need to know which activities must precede, or be completed before, the others. Then you need to calculate duration estimates for the activities, which we will assume are being worked on during normal conditions and working hours. For example, you should use a standard eight-hour day to estimate the full-time work needed for each activity rather than building in overtime.

Although there are several ways to estimate durations, there is always some uncertainty about them. Here again, we can use past activities and the personnel who worked on them to guide our activities estimates or use PERT. Table 3.2 shows the project's activities, their predecessors, and the estimates for their duration.

There are two ways we can represent this information graphically in a network. The simplest and most powerful is the **Gantt chart,** which links project activities to a schedule, that is usually a calendar. Gantt charts look like bar charts, with activities stretched out horizontally in bars; the individual lengths of bars correspond to the duration of the activities. Figure 3.8 shows a Gantt chart for this project. Note that the overall estimated length of time to complete the project is determined by adding the lengths of the longest individual legs of each sequenced activity, which in this case are the activities A, B, F, and J. The estimated schedule for this project is 16 days.

We can also construct the Gantt chart using MS Project, as shown in Screenshot 3.2. The advantage of using a software package such as MS Project is that it automatically syncs the activities to a calendar and provides expected start and finish dates. The software assumes no work is done on

TABLE 3.2: Information for Site Preparation Example

ACTIVITY	DESCRIPTION	PREDECESSORS	DURATION (DAYS)
A	Site selection	None	4
B	Buy concessions	A	4
C	Rent facilities	A	2
D	Build stands	A	5
E	Generator and wiring installation	C	2
F	Security	B	4
G	Lighting installation	E	2
H	Sound system installation	E, F	2
I	Stage construction	D	3
J	Tear down	G, H, I	4

Precedence diagramming: sometimes called *network diagramming,* the process of creating a chart that shows a project's activities and indicates how they should logically be coordinated with one another

Gantt chart: a diagram that links project activities to a schedule, usually a calendar

FIGURE 3.8: Gantt Chart

ACTIVITY	DAY																
	1	2	3	4	5	6	7	8	9	10	11	12	13	14	15	16	17
A																	
B																	
C																	
D																	
E																	
F																	
G																	
H																	
I																	
J																	

SCREENSHOT 3.2: MS Project Gantt Chart for the Concert Site Preparation Project

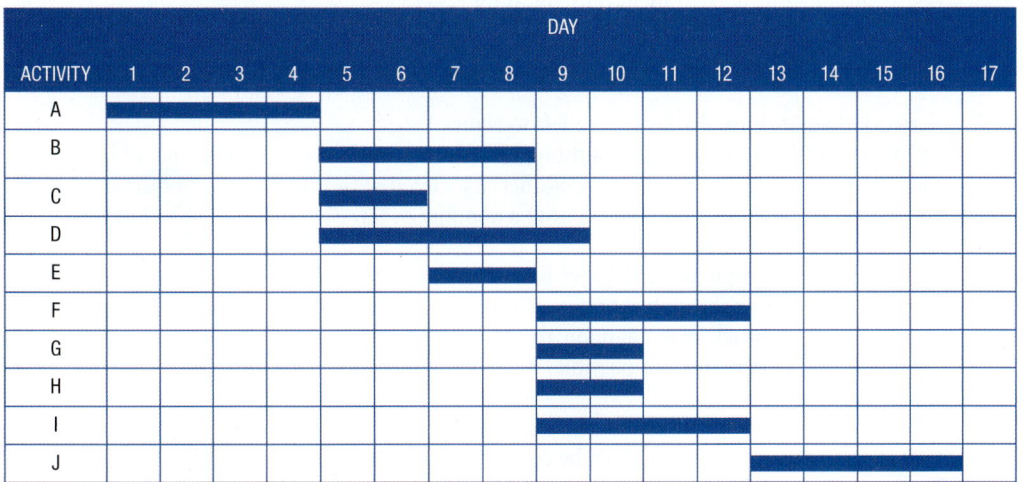

weekends. (Notice that Saturday and Sunday bars in Screenshot 3.2 are shaded.) If that is not the case, you must adjust the output the program calculates to allow for work on these days.

Determining a Project's Schedule: Creating Network Diagrams

Network diagramming is a logical, sequential process that requires the project manager to consider the order in which activities should occur to schedule projects as efficiently as possible. Gantt charts are useful because they clearly display the logical flow of activities needed to complete the project. Nevertheless, they don't necessarily show the exact sequencing of one activity to another. For example, in Figure 3.9, we can see that certain activities appear to precede others, but we can't be sure if this is the case. The Gantt chart also may not tell us which activities can be worked on simultaneously.

To get a better idea of how the activities should best be sequenced, it is useful to construct an **activity network**. There are two primary methods for creating activity networks. The most common type of activity network employs **activity on node (AON)** network representation. In the AON method, the node represents the individual project activity and the path arrows represent the sequencing of tasks from node to node through the network. The alternative method, **activity on arrow (AOA)**, uses arrows to represent the activities. The nodes separating the arrows are considered events that indicate the completion of one task prior to the beginning of the next. Figure 3.9 shows the two forms of network logic. Notice that in the AOA portion of the figure, the events are numbered because the arrows designate the activities. The numbers have no intrinsic meaning. They are simply labels used to keep track of the network's logic. The AON method is easier to visualize and more commonly used than the AOA method. In

Activity network: a diagram that illustrates how activities should best be sequenced

Activity on node (AON): a type of activity network that uses nodes to represent the individual project activity and the path arrows to represent the sequencing of tasks from node to node through the network

Activity on arrow (AOA): a type of activity network that uses arrows to represent the activities and nodes separating the arrows as events that indicate the completion of one task prior to the beginning of the next

FIGURE 3.9: Network Logic: AON Versus AOA

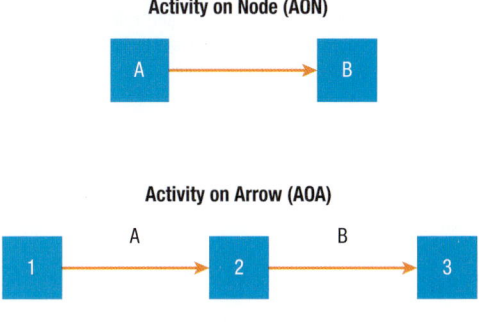

Network
Construction

fact, most popular project management software packages/programs, including MS Project, use AON exclusively. Consequently, we will focus only on AON.

When beginning to create the project activity network, it helps if we keep in mind some simple rules for their construction. The following rules will help us construct networks:[9]

1. Network diagrams usually flow from left to right.
2. Arrows can cross over each other, although for clarity, avoid doing so when possible.
3. Each activity should have a unique identifier associated with it (number, letter, code, etc.). For simplicity, these identifiers should occur in ascending order; each one should be larger than the identifiers of preceding activities.
4. An activity cannot begin until all preceding activities have been completed.
5. Looping, or recycling through activities, is not permitted.
6. Although not required, it is common to start a project from a single beginning node even when multiple start points are possible. A single node also is typically used as a project's end indicator.
7. Other than the starting and ending nodes, the network must not contain any dangling nodes. That is, every node, or activity, must be connected to a path that begins at the start activity and terminates at the end activity.

Figure 3.10 shows some common ways to represent the relationship of activities in a network diagram. These examples will help you construct your own networks diagrams.

LABELING NODES
The nodes for each activity should be clearly labeled with several different pieces of information. As you will see, if activity nodes have complete labels, it is easier to perform additional calculations such as, for example, calculating a project's total duration.

Figure 3.11 shows a close-up view of an activity node. We have marked the separate areas in which each piece of information should appear. (Figure 3.14 shows some nodes with actual information inserted in these areas.) Now let's look at what the labels mean:

FIGURE 3.10: Common Types of Activity Relationships (Using the AON Convention)

ACTIVITY RELATIONSHIPS	NETWORK LOGIC
Activity B can start when activity A is completed.	A → B
Activity C can start when both activity A and activity B are completed. Sometimes called a merge activity.	A, B → C
Activities B and C can start when activity A is completed. Sometimes called a burst activity.	A → B, C
Activity C can start when activity A is completed. Activity D can start when activities B and C are completed. Activity E can start when activity D is completed.	A → C, B → D, C → D, D → E
Activity C can only start when activities A and B are completed. Activities D and E can start when activity C is completed.	A → C, B → C, C → D, C → E

Early start time (ES): Earliest possible date on which an activity can start, based on the beginning and ending times for previous activities in the network.

Early finish time (EF): Earliest possible date on which an activity can be completed. Early finish is defined as ES + activity duration = EF.

Late start time (LS): Latest possible date that an activity may begin without delaying the project completion.

Late finish time (LF): Latest possible date an activity can be completed without delaying the project's completion. Late finish is defined as LS + activity duration = LF.

Activity slack: Amount of time an activity may be delayed from its ES without delaying the finish of the project. Slack (or float) is mathematically derived and can change as the project progresses and changes are made to the project plan. Activity slack = LS − ES (or LF − EF).

FIGURE 3.11: Labels for an Activity Node

Early Start	Identifier Number	Early Finish
Activity Slack	Activity Descriptor	
Late Start	Activity Duration	Late Finish

CONSTRUCTING THE CRITICAL PATH

Once we have identified the activities in a project and ordered them by their precedence, we can begin to construct the network diagram and find the critical path. Paths are simply sequences of activities in a network. Although it is common for networks to have multiple paths, the one that defines the overall length of the project (the longest individual path) is considered the critical path. All activities along this path are known as critical activities.

To illustrate the critical path, we use the site preparation example and the information in Table 3.2. Figure 3.12 shows the completed AON network diagram for our project and identifies four distinct paths:

Path 1: A – B – F – H – J

Path 2: A – C – E – H – J

Path 3: A – C – E – G – J

Path 4: A – D – I – J

We also know the estimated duration for each activity in the project network and can add them to determine the time necessary to complete each path. Thus:

Path 1: A – B – F – H – J = 4 + 4 + 4 + 2 + 4 = 18 days

Path 2: A – C – E – H – J = 4 + 2 + 2 + 2 + 4 = 14 days

Path 3: A – C – E – G – J = 4 + 2 + 2 + 2 + 4 = 14 days

Path 4: A – D – I – J = 4 + 5 + 3 + 4 = 16 days

Because path 1 is the longest, it is the critical path for our project, which is expected to take 18 days to complete. Activities A, B, F, H, and J are the critical activities.

Now, we will apply the rules for fully labeling the activity nodes in the network. We can accomplish this process using either the forward pass or the backward pass methods. The forward pass allows us to determine the earliest times each activity can begin and the earliest it can be completed. Follow these decision rules to apply the forward pass:

1. Add all activity times (ES + Dur = EF) along each path as we move through the network.
2. Carry the early finish (EF) time to the activity nodes immediately succeeding the recently completed node. That EF becomes the early start (ES) time of the next node unless the succeeding node is a *merge point* (a node with two or more immediate predecessors).
3. At a merge point, the largest preceding EF becomes the ES for that node.

Because activity A can start immediately, its early start time is 0. It appears in the upper left-hand part of the A node in Figure 3.13. The duration (Dur) of the activity is 4 days, and it appears at the bottom of the node. Adding the early start and the duration times gives us the early finish time of 4 (0 + 4 = 4), which appears in the upper right-hand corner of the node.

Early start time (ES): the earliest possible date on which an activity can start, based on the beginning and ending times for previous activities in the network

Early finish time (EF): the earliest possible date on which an activity can be completed. Early finish is defined as ES + activity duration = EF

Late start time (LS): the latest possible date that an activity may begin without delaying the project completion

Late finish time (LF): the latest possible date an activity can be completed without delaying the project's completion. Late finish is defined as LS + activity duration = LF

Activity slack: the amount of time an activity may be delayed from its early start (ES) without delaying the finish of the project. Activity slack is defined as Activity Slack = LS − ES (or LF − EF)

Critical path: the sequence of activities in a network that defines the overall length of the project (the longest individual path)

FIGURE 3.12: Network Diagram for the Site Preparation Project

FIGURE 3.13: Network Diagram With Completed Forward Pass Calculations

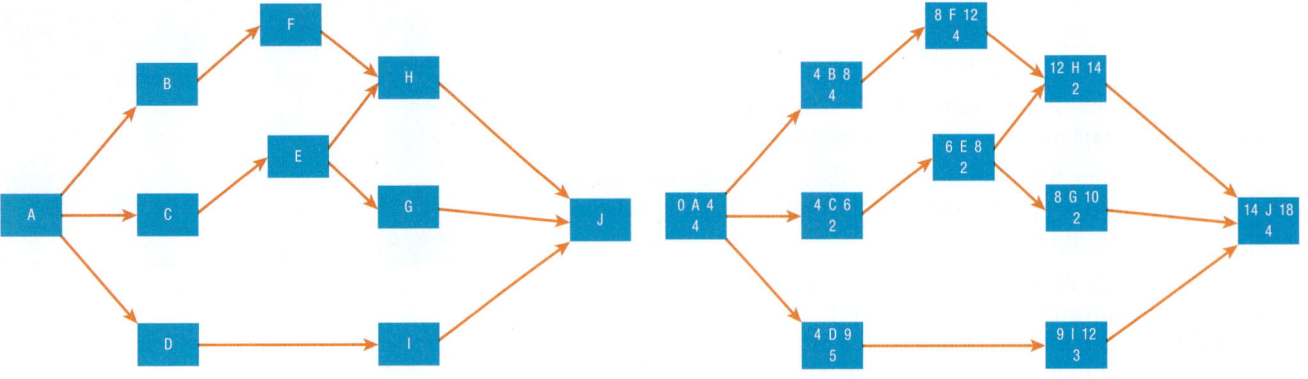

 The Critical Path

Activities B, C, and D are all successor activities to A, so the ES for each is 4 as the figure shows. We add their respective duration times to determine their early finish times and then make the early finish times from preceding tasks the early start times for succeeding tasks.

When we get to activity H, we find that this task is a merge point for activities E and F. We must apply the third decision rule in this case, and use the higher early finish time of the two activities, which in this case is 12 days. So, we use 12 as the early start time for activity H. Once the full forward pass calculations are completed through activity J, it becomes clear that the completion time for the total project is 18 days.

We next perform a backward pass on the network to ascertain the project's critical path and the total slack time for each activity. As Figure 3.14 shows, the backward pass starts at the end of the project (activity J) and works its way to the left toward the first node in the network. As with the forward pass, we follow three decision rules:

Forward pass: the process of fully labeling the activity nodes in a network to determine the earliest times each activity can begin and the earliest it can be completed

1. Subtract the activity times (LF – Dur = LS) along each path as we move through the network.
2. Carry back the LS time to the activity nodes immediately preceding the successor node. The LS becomes the LF of the next node unless the preceding node is a *burst point*, that is, a node with two or more immediate successors that have tasks flowing out of it.
3. In the case of a burst point, the smallest succeeding LS becomes the LF for that node.

Backward pass: the process of labeling the activity nodes in a network to determine the project's critical path and the total slack time for each activity

Backward passes start at the end node (activity J), as shown in Figure 3.14. Subtracting the duration from the late finish time, shown in the lower right-hand corner of each node, gives us the late start time, shown in the lower left-hand corner. This late start time is then transferred to the next nodes in the network. Notice that in this example, activity E would be considered a burst point because activities G and H emerge from it. By using decision rule 3, we would make the smallest late start time from these activities the late finish time for activity E. Because both activities G and H have 12 days as their late start times, we use 12 as the late finish time for activity E.

Once we have completed the backward pass, we can determine the slack time, or float, for each activity as well as for each path through the network. Recall that the slack tells us the amount of time an activity can be delayed without delaying the overall project. The slack time, which is shown in italics in the node, is found by using one of two equations: LF – EF = Slack or LS – ES = Slack.

To illustrate the implications of slack, suppose that activity C is delayed and cannot start until 3 days after the original schedule. What are the implications of this delay on the overall project? None. Because there are 4 days of slack for activity C, a delay of 3 days will not affect the overall length of the project or delay its completion.

One other important point to remember about activity slack is that it is determined as a result of performing

FIGURE 3.14: Project Network With Fully Labeled Nodes

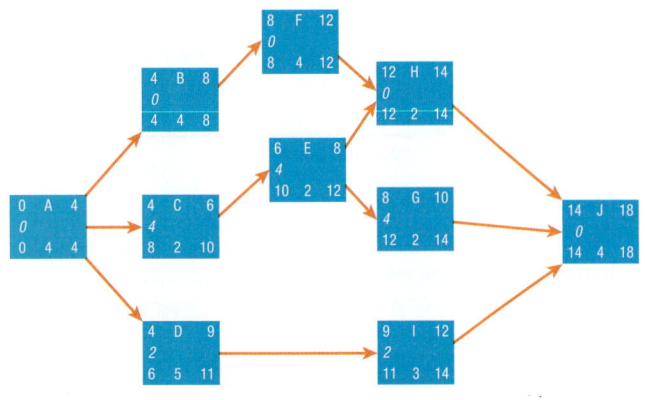

the forward and backward passes through the network. Until we have done the calculations for the ES, EF, LS, and LF, we can't be certain which activities have slack associated with them. Critical activities are those with zero slack. Using this information to determine the project's critical path suggests that the critical path is the longest path through the network and one with no slack associated with it. In our project example, we can determine the critical path by linking the nodes with no slack: A – B – F – H – J. We can also determine the slack for the noncritical paths. For example, the path A – D – I – J has 4 days of slack. Table 3.4 and Figure 3.14 show the information for the individual activities and the fully developed project network.

USING PROBABILISTIC ESTIMATES

Calculating the critical path showed us that the expected completion time for the site preparation project is 18 days; however, our original time estimates for each activity were deterministic. That is, they did not take into account the probability of different outcomes occurring. Suppose we wished to use probabilistic estimates, based on a beta distribution, to determine the likelihood of the project being completed on time. Applying probabilities to our estimates would help us know how much variance there is with regard to the project's duration. That is, what is the likelihood that the project will be delayed a little versus a lot? Variations in the completion times of the activities on the critical path can affect the project's overall completion time and possibly delay it significantly. Because this is a complex calculation, we have analyzed it more fully in the supplement for this chapter.

Calculating Activity Duration and Variance

Crashing the Project

Under some circumstances, it may be necessary to find ways to accelerate the completion of a project. There are several reasons to speed up the project:

1. The initial schedule was too optimistic.
2. The project is demanded earlier than anticipated because of changes in the marketplace. Perhaps we learn that a competitor is working on a similar product and will beat our product into the marketplace.
3. The project has slipped behind schedule, and we need to catch up.
4. Stiff financial penalties written into the contracts of the project make it important for it to be completed on time or early.

Crashing is the process of speeding up a project's remaining activities to move its completion date forward. Part of crashing a project includes calculating the dollar-per-day trade-off—that is, how much money must be spent to save one day in the project's schedule. Figure 3.15 shows that this trade-off is made by directly linking the costs for an activity (which are often labor costs) to the duration

Calculating Costs of Crashing Activities

TABLE 3.4: Project Activities With ES, EF, LS, LF, and Slack Labeled (in Days)

ACTIVITY	DURATION (DAYS)	EARLY START (ES)	EARLY FINISH (EF)	LATE START (LS)	LATE FINISH (LF)	SLACK
A	4	0	4	0	4	0
B	4	4	8	4	8	0
C	2	4	6	8	10	2
D	5	4	9	6	11	2
E	2	6	8	10	12	4
F	4	8	12	8	12	0
G	2	8	10	12	14	2
H	2	12	14	12	14	0
I	3	9	12	11	14	2
J	4	14	18	14	18	0

Crashing: the process of speeding up a project's remaining activities to move its completion date forward

FIGURE 3.15: Time–Cost Trade-off of Crashing an Activity

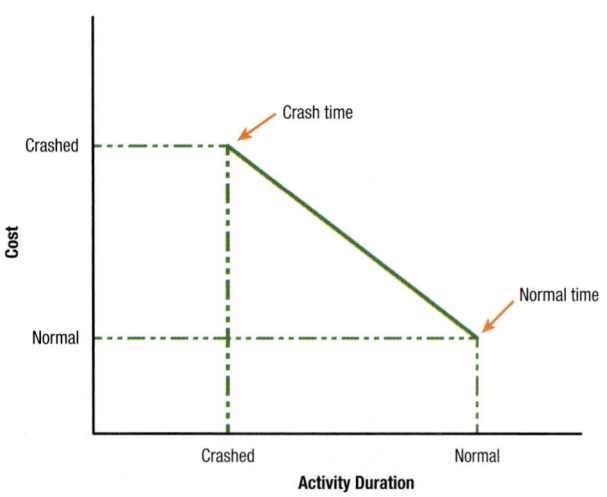

for that activity. For example, suppose we calculate that one person can complete an activity in 40 hours. The graph shows that adding two additional resources (people) to speed up the task will result in it being completed in a shorter amount of time. Nevertheless, the trade-off is potentially costly: We are now paying three people to do the work originally assigned to one person.

Prior to crashing a project, you need to scrutinize its schedule and prioritize the activities that should be crashed. For example, it makes no sense to crash noncritical activities because there is slack time for these activities. Therefore, we would be paying extra money to speed up activities that don't directly affect the final completion date for the project. Instead, we want to crash critical activities. We also we want to prioritize the critical activities that are less expensive to crash. Suppose that you need to hire an expensive programmer to crash one project activity. He will cost you an extra US$750 per day. On the other hand, suppose you can speed up different critical activities at a cost of only US$250 per day. From a cost perspective, you would first want to crash the cheaper activities before the more expensive one. An example of crashing is given in more detail in the supplement for this chapter.

3.5 Supply Chains for Projects

3.5 Identify the main supply chain activities of a project and the qualities that should be considered when designing the project's supply chain.

Increasingly, organizations are paying closer attention to the impact supply chains have on their projects. The goal is to create a coordinated planning network that allows for the optimal acquisition, scheduling, shipping, and distribution of goods and services used in a project.

As an example, suppose a member of a project team from company A has discovered that a competitor (company B) has started a project of its own to develop a very similar product. Unlike company A, however, company B's project team is in close touch with all of the company's external vendors, shippers, warehousing and facilities management personnel, and distributors. Company A concentrates solely on the project's development, trusting that its acquisitions and purchasing departments will be able to secure and deliver all materials when they're needed. In this scenario, company B stands the better chance of completing the project on time and getting the product to the market more quickly.

In the next section, we look at the role of the supply chain in a project and learn to design the supply chain for a project.

Supply Chain Activities for Projects

Supply Chains for Projects

There are three traditional activities of project supply chains: procurement, fabrication, and distribution.[10]

PROCUREMENT

The supply chain for developing a project begins with the inbound procurement of all services and parts needed for it. The inbound supply chain for many projects can be long and complex. It may have several tiers of suppliers. The Airbus A380, an enormous double-decker aircraft, requires the assembly of millions of individual parts from several thousand separate vendors and the coordination of facilities spread throughout several European Union countries. Airbus's project managers have to ensure that each vendor delivers the right number of products when needed and that they are of high quality.

When the delivery of goods or services used as inputs is uncertain, it makes it almost impossible to make accurate project plans. The key is to find trustworthy vendors. International quality assurance (QA) standards, such as International Organization for Standardization (ISO) 9001, are highly useful in providing a standard basis for supplier selection. The companies that have acquired ISO 9001 certification have demonstrated to a third-party auditor that their systems and operations fulfill certain standard criteria. Furthermore, these companies are audited regularly by independent auditors to ensure that they follow approved procedures and, in this way, maintain the requested level of quality in their operations.

Selecting good suppliers and working well with them sometimes isn't enough. Proactive firms try to predict future trends and problems and seek opportunities for procuring in different ways the materials needed to complete their projects. These organizations look beyond suppliers to the point where the actual raw materials for the project—either products or people—can be acquired. For example, as a result of tighter visa restrictions after the 9/11 terrorist attacks, Microsoft wasn't able to hire the talent it needed in the United States to work on its projects. The company addressed the problem in the short term by opening an office in Vancouver, Canada.[11]

FABRICATION

Fabrication is the manufacturing or assembling of materials to create the product or service. Fabrication has its own set of challenges and complexities. For example, when creating new software, programmers often have to write millions of lines of computer code, refining the process to streamline the subactivities for optimal speed. As another example, building an offshore oil-drilling vessel requires many individual steps be taken to fabricate, assemble, test, and commission the vessel. Whether the project is relatively routine or highly complex, at some point in its life cycle, it will require that the various steps be accomplished.

DISTRIBUTION

Distribution is the final link in the project development chain. It is the transfer of the product to its users. The distribution step signals that the project is complete. For many project-based firms, the distribution process has changed in recent years. For example, as we explained earlier in the section on risk management (Section 3.3), foreign governments anxious to defray some of the financial risks of developing plants in their countries are increasingly demanding BOOT contracts. As a result, construction companies such as Bechtel (already introduced); KBR, Inc. (Houston, TX); and Fluor Corporation (Irving, TX) are now required not only to build the plants but also to operate them jointly with their clients for a period of time before final transfer of ownership. In this way, clients stretch out the distribution process to reduce their risk of start-up problems.

If their project teams are highly skilled, distribution complexities such as this offer firms a way to gain a competitive advantage over their competitors. Price is an important factor when a client awards a contract, but so is finding a contractor that can minimize the client's project risk. For example, Technip Offshore (Pori, Finland) specializes in developing and building deep-water oil drilling platforms, each typically costing more than US$250 million. Technip works very closely with its clients to minimize their distribution risks. The firm is so good at minimizing risk by getting its clients' platforms up and running effectively and on time that it can charge a higher price for them than its competitors can.

Designing a Project's Supply Chain

Four fundamental steps are needed to create and manage a project supply chain. They are described in this section.

SETTING GOALS FOR THE SUPPLY CHAIN

What are the goals of our organization? Moreover, what do we want the supply chain to do, and how will it improve the firm's ability to develop the project? For many organizations, the goal is to design supply chains that can help them produce better projects more cost effectively and quickly than their competitors. For example, Apple has contracted with Chinese firms to manufacture many of its most popular products, such as the iPad, iPhone, and iPod. At just one plant in Shenzhen, more than 300,000 workers, including thousands of engineers, are housed on a self-enclosed campus and are able to respond rapidly to any requests or adjustments Apple needs to make to their products.[12]

DOING AN ENVIRONMENTAL ANALYSIS

Which suppliers are technically and financially capable of working with our firm, and what are the strengths and weaknesses of each? Also, what are the external threats and opportunities in developing the supply chain? For example, will the supply chain consist of suppliers located in other countries? If so, how will we deal with shifts in the business policies of the governments of these suppliers—shifts that could affect our firm's ability to depend on the suppliers? Would it be prudent to work with local suppliers as a backup plan? What are the risks in working with these suppliers? Will unscrupulous suppliers with access to your firm's copyrights or patents take advantage of your company? For example, The Ford Motor Company (aka Ford, Dearborn, MI) estimates that illegally counterfeiting of its auto parts in China costs the company more than US$2 billion each year.[13]

COORDINATING AND PLANNING

How should we structure our supply chain to ensure the flow of resources is efficient and cost effective? The key lies in two levels of coordinated planning. *Buyer–vendor coordination* is the first level. This type of coordination is the basic challenge of attaining a steady supply of the many resources needed to develop a project. *Production–distribution coordination* is the second level. It involves coordinating the transfer of the product to the customer. How will the transfer be accomplished? Is it a simple sign-off process once the performance of the project is checked? Is there a transition period to allow for ironing out bugs in the system? Or is there a more complex set of stages of transfer, similar to the BOOT processes? Regardless of the transfer method, careful planning needs to accompany the process and that planning must be incorporated into the beginning of the project's development.

CONTROLLING

Measuring the performance of the chain and adjusting the flow of resources or mixture of suppliers as needed is part of controlling a project. How can we be sure that we are getting maximum performance from our supply chain? How can we improve it? Controlling a project includes assessing the performance of a firm's suppliers, its quality, its prices, its reliability, and its future prospects. Will the firm remain financially viable? Will it go out of business, which would force us to scramble to find a new source of supply? Many corporations station quality assessment personnel at their suppliers' work sites to monitor the quality of the supplies they receive before they receive them.

Good project managers also constantly look for ways to streamline their supply chains, employ new and more efficient ways of working with their existing vendors, shift to new vendors when appropriate, experiment with new chains and delivery systems, and so forth. Once the supply chain is set up, it needs to be scrutinized continuously to ensure it is the most efficient, reliable, and highest quality chain attainable.

3.6

Demonstrate how to execute, track, and terminate projects.

3.6 Executing, Evaluating, and Terminating Projects

Once a project is under way, critical decisions still must be made and challenges still must be overcome. This section will discuss some of those challenges.

Evaluating a Project's Status: S-Curves and Earned Value Management

One of the recurring challenges with managing projects is assessing their status midstream. Is our project coming in on time? Is it likely to be late? The sooner we can detect negative trends, the sooner we can correct them and improve the chances of the project's success. The key lies in gathering accurate information in a timely way to ensure that it is actionable.[14] Put another way, it is critical to know what bits of information we should collect because they provide a clear picture of the status of the project and when they should be measured to let us take correction action.

Recall that projects are characterized as having a limited budget. The budget allows the project manager to keep track of costs. The projected cost of all of the project's activities are referred to as its *baseline budget*. The biggest cost for most projects is labor. Other typical costs are equipment charges, raw materials, and overhead. Once we have established the baseline budget, we have to evaluate it continually against the project's actual costs. The project team does this by monitoring the individual budgets of each activity and the cumulative (overall) budget for the project. The cumulative budget can be broken down by time over the project's projected duration.

THE S-CURVE: A BASIC PROJECT-STATUS TOOL

Let's consider the simple budget-control example shown in Table 3.5. The table gives a breakdown of the project's cumulative budget in terms of both deliverables and time. There are four deliverables (design, engineering, installation, and testing), a budget of US$80,000, and an anticipated duration of 45 weeks.

The project's status is evaluated as a function of the cumulative costs—both budgeted and actual—plotted against time as shown in Figure 3.16. The curves in the figure are derived by plotting the information in Table 3.5 on the graph. Notice the shape of the curves. The classic **S-curve** is typical of most projects. Initially expenditures are low and then increase rapidly during the project's execution stage. They then level off again as the project nears completion.

Let's now look at Table 3.5 and Figure 3.16 to see how to use the curves. Suppose that by week 20 the budgeted cumulative expenditures for the project were US$50,000. Nevertheless, our actual expenditures totaled only US$40,000. In effect, there is a US$10,000 difference, or negative variance, between the two as Figure 3.16 shows. The S-curve analysis is an easy visual way of showing a project's costs (both budgeted and actual) over the course of its schedule.

TABLE 3.5: Budgeted Costs for Project Tracy (in Thousands of U.S. Dollars)

	DURATION (IN WEEKS)									
	5	10	15	20	25	30	35	40	45	TOTAL
Design	6	2								
Engineering		4	8	8	8					
Installation				4	20	6				
Testing						2	6	4	2	
Total	6	6	8	12	28	8	6	4	2	
Cumul.	6	12	20	32	60	68	74	78	80	80

Monitoring the status of a project is also easy using S-curves. At the end of each period (week, month, or quarter), we simply total the project's expenditures to date and compare them with the budget. Any significant deviations between them reveal a potential problem. The S-curve also provides real-time tracking information because expenditures can be continually updated and the new values plotted on the graph.

EARNED VALUE MANAGEMENT

The problem with S-curves is that interpreting them isn't always obvious. For example, is the US$10,000 difference in our example the result of a delay in the project that put off spending on the project? Or is it the result of a more efficient process that has lowered the overall expenditures of the project to date? If you only compare actual versus budgeted costs, you ignore the fact that the client is spending that money to accomplish something—create a project.

What we need is a way to determine how the project is actually doing besides knowing just how much money has been spent.

The **earned value management (EVM)** method calculates the *value* generated by the project as well as the budgeted and actual costs at a certain point in time. Time is important because it becomes the basis for determining how much work should be accomplished at certain milestones. EVM also allows the project team to make future projections of a project's status based on its current state. At any point in the project's progress, we are able to calculate both schedule and budget efficiency. Schedule efficiency refers to how closely the project's progress is tracking relative to its original plan. Budget efficiency is the efficiency with which budget is being used relative to the value that is being created. Both the schedule and the budget efficiency allow the project manager to make future projections about the estimated cost and schedule to the project completion date. The calculation of earned value is discussed in the supplement for this chapter.

> **Earned value management (EVM):** a method to calculate the value generated by the project as well as the budgeted and actual costs at a certain point in time

Terminating the Project

The final stage in a project is its termination. A tremendous amount of paperwork must be archived during this stage, including schedule and planning documents, status reports, cost and resource-use documents, customer change-order requests, and specification change approvals. All legal documents must be stored, including the project's terms and conditions, and penalty, legal recourse, and incentive clauses. So too must the costs and other charges for all of the project's team members. Their time charged against the project's accounts and any company overhead in the form of the team's human resources benefits must be identified. Any nonemployees who worked on the project, such as contractors or consultants, must be contractually released, and these accounts must be paid off and closed.

FIGURE 3.16: Simple S-Curve

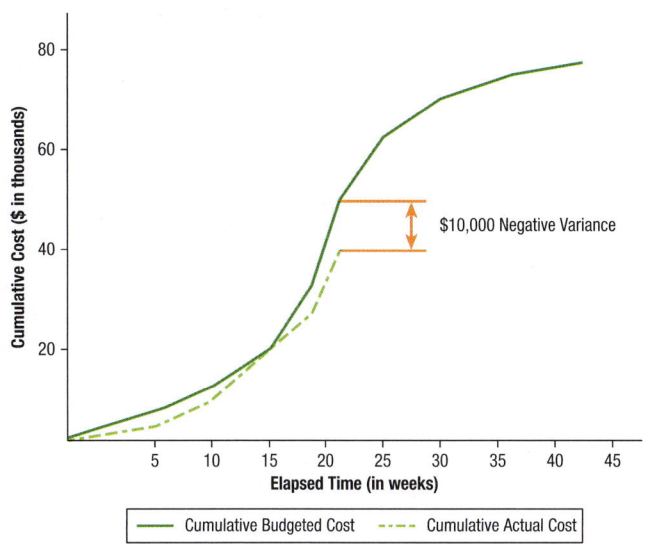

Closing Out
a Project

As we mentioned earlier, perhaps the most important part of closing out a project is conducting an in-depth "lessons learned" analysis documenting its highs and lows, unanticipated difficulties, and suggestions for future projects. The success of a lessons learned process is highly dependent on senior managers enforcing the archiving of critical historical information. The lessons learned serve as a valuable form of organizational learning whereby novice project managers can access and learn from information provided by other project managers reporting on past projects.

When they are pressed to document what went wrong with a project, project teams need to guard against making several mistakes For example, it's human nature to attribute your errors to external rather than to internal causes. Documenting that the client changed the specifications is much easier than admitting you and your team didn't do enough to determine the customer's needs for the project. It's also human nature to believe an error is just a one-time event. That way, you and your team don't have to look for underlying problems with your project management system and make adjustments to it. A team's members can also sometimes misinterpret the cause of a problem. In addition, the lessons from a terminated project are sometimes either ignored or subtly altered to support top management's views of how the project went.

Identify the critical steps in planning for sustainability in projects.

3.7 Sustainability Issues

Sustainability plays a key role in project management. The projects themselves may be undertaken to support sustainable activities. Renewable energy projects are common examples of projects that support green initiatives. Managers and organizations may employ sustainable practices. That is, projects may not only create sustainable outcomes but the way in which projects are run can support sustainable practices. In addition, the measurement of project success may take into consideration sustainable outcomes. For example, in addition to asserting a set of requirements for the project (budget, schedule, quality, and customer satisfaction), it may also be useful to identify, in advance, ways in which the project can achieve a firm's or a society's sustainability expectations.

Sustainability in Project Management

A useful way to integrate sustainability practices into project management is to set standards for ways in which a project can achieve green outcomes. Some critical steps in planning for sustainability in projects include:[15]

1. Set sustainability expectations. What are the requirements that project users and other critical stakeholders expect of the project?
2. Identify opportunities to reduce costs. Economizing on purchases and other project expenses will benefit the organization's bottom line and help maintain a focus on efficiency.
3. Use sustainability risk management. When project risk management is expanded to include green considerations for developing the project, the relevant project risks will expand to include a broader array of manageable concerns.
4. Emphasize value maximization. The goal of the project should be to produce value, not only economic returns. Different stakeholders view value differently, and among these critical value definitions is the concern of renewable and sustainable processes and outcomes.
5. Identify specific sustainability requirements that are to be pursued. Rather than treating sustainability as a vague or broad concern, use project scope management to focus specifically on how the project can target sustainable goals.
6. Engage suppliers and subcontractors in sustainable ways. Push the sustainability focus beyond the boundaries of your organization to consider ways you can require suppliers and other subcontractors to integrate sustainable operations in support of your project.
7. Motivate the project team. Sustainability is every project team members' concern, and when sustainable goals are communicated and rewarded, the organization's commitment is made explicit.

A real commitment to sustainability in business operations must be more than a simple greenwashing of current business practices. Project management offers several ways in which sustainable operations may be realized, through both the commitment of organizations to use their project activities in support of sustainable goals and initiatives as well as allowing sustainability to become part of a firm's project management practices. The more that organizations recognize the ways in which sustainable project management is both cost effective and a value creator, the more they will commit to it, for the greater good of both the firm and the larger economic and social environment.

OPERATIONS MANAGEMENT: LESSONS LEARNED
Unpopularity of Fossil Fuels Is Leading to Project Cancellations

A combination of social pressures, concern for the environment, and lower prices resulting from a recent glut of oil on the international market have led to the cancellation or postponement of several expensive projects in the United States. Overall, estimates suggest that more than a dozen projects, worth a combined US$33 billion, have been either rejected by regulatory agencies or withdrawn by their developers since 2012, with billions more tied up in reviews and legal actions. In 2016 alone, there have five recently cancelled projects, as shown in Table 3.4.

The current lowered price of oil has caused many of these energy projects to be judged as no longer profitable, and the cancellation decision was relatively easy. For example, many hydraulic fracturing ("fracking") wells have been shut down in the near term because of over-supplies of oil. Nevertheless, in many cases, the cancellations demonstrated that economic forces alone do not drive projects. Often social or environmental pressures can play a large role in reassessing the need for projects, particularly as they relate to sensitive topics such as energy policy. The decade-long battle, and final cancellation, of the Keystone Pipeline project by the Obama administration illustrates that project approval and final completion are often uncertain and prone to change. That is, it is a mistake to assume that projects of these types are routinely approved and, once having been approved, are never subject to reexamination later in their development cycle. It is also important to recognize the critical role that "intervenor groups," such as lobbyists, activists, and other environmental groups, can play in the decision to approve or cancel energy projects. For example, the same groups that are actively opposed to fossil fuels projects are in strong support of alternative energy options, including massive wind and solar farms.

TABLE 3.4: Fossil Fuel Projects Cancelled in 2016

PROJECT NAME	TYPE OF PROJECT	LOCATION	BUDGET (IN U.S. DOLLARS)
Gateway Pacific	Coal-export terminal	Washington	850 million
Constitution	Natural-gas pipeline	Northeast U.S.	875 million
Northeast Energy Direct	Natural-gas pipeline	Northeast U.S.	3 billion
Oregon LNG	Liquefied natural gas export facility	Oregon	6 billion
Jordan Cove & Pacific Connector	Liquefied natural gas terminal and connecting pipeline	Oregon	6.8 billion

The popularity of energy projects has been shown to be heavily dependent on broader federal and state energy policies. Economic conditions also affect the willingness to fund and support these projects; for example, during a recession, there is often a greater willingness to treat billion-dollar projects as public works undertakings to alleviate joblessness. Ultimately, one of the challenges with gaining wide acceptance of an energy project is winning the "hearts and minds" of the wider population who are affected by the results of the project. With fossil fuel projects, the debate often centers on "jobs vs. the environment" arguments that can lead to difficult trade-offs and passionate debate.[16]

3.8 Global Projects

Projects are occurring in settings around the planet. Whether sponsored by international economic agencies, the United Nations, the World Health Organization, or simply multinational organizations with offices worldwide, projects have increasingly become globalized with important implications for project management. For example, project management organizations have had to develop processes and methods for successfully managing these projects in other settings. The increasingly global nature of projects and project teams includes some important implications, including:

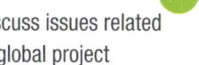

3.8

Discuss issues related to global project management.

Global Project
Management

1. The need to develop global project management standards. Standard practices enable project management professionals to undertake work in any setting because they are able to apply widely accepted methods for managing projects. International organizations like the Project Management Institute or the Association of Project Management publish standard bodies of knowledge that can serve as a basis for identifying the critical steps in project management. As a result, whether a project is being undertaken in Lima, Peru, or Novosibirsk, Russia, the steps necessary to complete it successfully are generally understood by all participants.

2. The increased use of geographically dispersed teams. Globalization allows project companies to create teams from parts of their organization that are separated by continents or multiple time zones. For example, a large project undertaken by Medtronic (Dublin, Ireland), a medical technology development company, may include team members located in Dublin, Ireland; Singapore; Seoul, South Korea; and Minneapolis, Minnesota. Scientists working in laboratories in Bangkok and Malaysia can work on the same team with technicians or medical professionals in Denver, Colorado, or Fort Worth, Texas. These geographically dispersed teams involve multiple nationalities and cultures, acceptable workplace behaviors, social taboos, and other challenges that make the ability to form a productive team difficult. Knowledge of multiple national cultural standards is just as important as having the technical means to bring team members together.

3. The use of virtual technologies. Communication methods for managing global projects are a challenge. Several virtual team communication devices have been developed to make these interactions as easy as possible. Platforms like Google Docs (Google, Inc., Mountain View, CA), Yammer (Yammer, Inc., San Francisco, CA), or Buzzword (Adobe Systems Incorporated, Palo Alto, CA) allow groups to work off similar documents. Basecamp (Chicago, IL), Skype (Microsoft Corporation, Redmond, WA), and Dropbox (San Francisco, CA) are effective online collaboration tools that link people either visually or through their shared project report documentation. Finally, there are numerous emerging virtual communication tools such as tele-immersion that create a virtual meeting space, providing all participants with visual images of their team members.

The globalization of projects represents a set of challenges and requires new operating methods for many organizations. As multinationals can make use of the expertise of their employees around the globe, the types of projects they will pursue will increasingly call for expertise in virtual settings, working with members of multiple cultures, and the joint challenges of building trust and establishing the best modes for communicating across national borders and multiple time zones.

 ....

Visit **edge.sagepub.com/venkataraman** to help you accomplish your coursework goals in an easy-to-use learning environment.

- Mobile-friendly eFlashcards
- Mobile-friendly practice quizzes
- A complete online action plan

- Chapter summaries with learning objectives
- Video and multimedia resources

CHAPTER SUMMARY ....

3.1 Describe the importance of projects to a firm, identify the people and teams that work on projects, and list the qualities that make a project a success. Shortened product life cycles, narrow product-launch windows, increasingly complex products, and global competition have made projects a principal way for modern organizations to gain a competitive advantage. Project managers function as mini-CEOs for their projects, directing the myriad of activities that need to be done on them and the people who need to do them. Typical structures for project teams are the matrix structure, functional structure, and pure project structure. A successful project is one that comes in on time and on budget and meets its quality and functionality specifications as well as the client's needs.

3.2 Identify the stages of the typical life cycle of a project. Projects have a definite beginning and end. As a result, they follow a life cycle that restricts the nature of the work as well as the resources committed to the project. The four phases of a project life cycle are the conceptualization, planning, execution, and termination stages. The conceptualization stage answers the question: "What are we hoping to achieve with the project?" The planning stage answers the question: "How are we going to complete the project successfully?" This stage includes all the detailed schematics, schedules, performances specifications, and other plans for the project. The execution stage is the stage where the actual work of the project is being performed, and the bulk of the resources allocated to it are consumed. The termination stage occurs when the finished project is transferred to its intended users, the project's resources get reassigned, and it is formally closed out.

3.3 **Explain how scope management techniques, statement-of-work documents, work breakdown structures, and risk management principles enable firms to conceptualize, plan, and organize projects.** During the conceptualization stage, the firm determines the nature of the project, its objectives, and ways to meet those objectives. Some key pieces of information that must be either collected or developed early on for this purpose include the development of a problem (or need) statement, an analysis of alternative solutions to the problem, information gathering to uncover the details of the project, and the generation of clearly stated objectives for the project. There are a variety of techniques and tools project managers can use for scope management—that is, to prevent projects from getting out of control. One tool is a statement of work (SOW), which is a detailed description of the work required for the project.[17] Another is a work breakdown structure (WBS). The WBS sets a project's scope by breaking down its overall mission into a cohesive set of synchronous, increasingly specific tasks. Risk management refers to a system for identifying, analyzing, and responding to a variety of risk factors that can seriously affect the project's success.

3.4 **Use analytical tools to calculate project schedules.** There are several methods and tools for scheduling projects, including the critical path method (CPM) and program evaluation and review technique (PERT). CPM works best when you can be reasonably certain of how long the project's activities are likely to take. PERT works best when you must use statistical probabilities to try to determine the duration of activities. Developing duration estimates and precedence diagrams allows us to determine the project's critical path (fastest time to completion) and all activities that are either critical (have zero slack) or have some slack time associated with them. Finally, it may be necessary to crash a project by accelerating its activities to speed up its completion.

3.5 **Identify the main supply chain activities of a project and the qualities that should be considered when designing the project's supply chain.** The major supply chain activities for developing a project begin with the inbound procurement of all the services and parts needed for it. Fabrication is the manufacturing or assembling of materials produced at another site to create the service or good. Distribution is the final link in the project development chain—that is, the actual transfer of the product to its users.

Four fundamental steps should be taken when creating and managing a supply chain for a project. (1) Setting the supply chain's goals: Determining what we want the supply chain to do, and how will it improve the firm's ability to develop the project. (2) Doing an environmental analysis: Determining which suppliers are technically and financially capable of working with our firm, and what the strengths and weaknesses of each are. (3) Coordinating and planning: Determining how to structure the supply chain to ensure the flow of resources is efficient and cost effective. (4) Controlling: Measuring the performance of the chain and adjusting the flow of resources or mixture of suppliers to improve the chain.

3.6 **Demonstrate how to execute, track, and terminate projects.** Two of the best known methods for tracking projects upon their execution are (1) S-curves, which relate the budgeted money spent on the project over its life cycle as a way to estimate the project's current status, and (2) earned value management (EVM), which links the percentage of activities completed, money spent, and schedule to give a more accurate estimate of the project's status. The EVM method also enables close estimates of the project's final budget and completion date. Terminating a project requires the completion of several administrative tasks, including archiving all legal and contractual documents, closing the project's cost accounts, and reassigning the project's team members. Creating a lessons learned document provides future project teams with information about what worked well and what did not so they can improve their performance.

3.7 **Identify the critical steps in planning for sustainability in projects.** A useful way to integrate sustainability practices into project management is to set standards for ways in which a project can achieve green outcomes. Seven critical steps in planning for sustainability in projects include (1) setting sustainability expectations, (2) identifying opportunities to reduce costs, (3) using sustainability risk management, (4) emphasizing value maximization, (5) identifying specific sustainability requirements that are to be pursued, (6) engaging suppliers and subcontractors in sustainable ways, and (7) motivating the project team.

3.8 **Discuss issues related to global project management.** Projects are occurring in settings around the planet. The rise of global business practices have necessitated a focus on processes and methods that allow for projects to be managed in international settings. The implications of global project management include (1) the need to develop global project management standards, (2) the increased use of geographically dispersed teams, and (3) the use of virtual technologies.

KEY TERMS

Activity network   75

Activity on arrow (AOA)   75

Activity on node (AON)   75

Activity slack   77

Backward pass   78

Crashing   79

Critical path   77

Deterministic estimation   72

Early finish time (EF)   77

Early start time (ES)   77

Earned value management (EVM)   83

Forward pass   78

Gantt chart   74

Late finish time (LF)   77

Late start time (LS)   77

Life cycle   65

Precedence diagramming   74

Probabilistic estimation   72

Program evaluation and review technique (PERT)   72

Project   62

Project management   62

Project risk   70

Project scheduling   72

Quadruple constraint   64

Risk management   70

Scope creep   68

Scope management   68

S-curve   82

Triple constraint   64

Work breakdown structure (WBS)   68

Work packages   68

DISCUSSION AND REVIEW QUESTIONS

1. Why are projects so important in modern society? What are their advantages and disadvantages for organizations?

2. What are some critical reasons why organizations are moving more of their operations to project-based work; in other words, what

are some societal and macroeconomic reasons why projects make sense?

3. Why is an understanding of project life cycles so useful for allocating resources (both people and money) to projects?

4. Consider the case of the Marine Corps' EFV. How did "scope creep" affect this project?

5. How do deterministic activity duration estimates differ from probabilistic duration estimates? Why would some projects use one method versus the other?

6. Consider a project discussed in this chapter, and conduct a risk management assessment on it. After identifying various types of risks, classify which of them can be transferred, shared, minimized, or accepted.

7. Think of a project you have been involved with. How did it go? What made it successful or not so successful? How could you

have improved its outcome given what you have learned from this chapter?

8. What are some reasons for crashing a project?

9. S-curves assume that a project's performance is directly related to the money spent to date. Explain the flaws with this reasoning.

10. Consider the Operations Profile on the recent number of cancellations of fossil fuel projects. What does this circumstance imply for the importance of comprehensive project risk analysis prior to the start of a new project? That is, when examining possible risks for new project opportunities, how broadly should the team assess its relevant environment for potential impacts?

SOLVED PROBLEMS

1. Assume that you have the following pessimistic, likely, and optimistic estimates for how long a project's activities are estimated to take. Using a beta distribution, estimate the activity durations for each task:

Duration Estimates

Activity	Pessimistic	Likely	Optimistic
A	7	5	2
B	5	3	2
C	14	8	6
D	20	10	6
E	8	3	3
F	10	5	3
G	12	6	4
H	16	6	5

Solution

Remember that the beta distribution calculates expected activity duration (TE) as:

$$TE = (a + 4m + b)/6$$

where

TE = estimated time for activity
a = most optimistic time to complete the activity
m = most likely time to complete the activity, the mode of the distribution
b = most pessimistic time to complete the activity

Therefore, in calculating expected activity duration (TE) for each task, we find:

Duration Estimates

Activity	Pessimistic	Likely	Optimistic	TE (Beta)
A	7	5	2	4.8
B	5	3	2	3.2
C	14	8	6	8.7
D	20	10	6	11
E	8	3	3	3.8
F	10	5	3	5.5
G	12	6	4	6.7
H	16	6	5	7.5

2. Assume that you have the following pessimistic, likely, and optimistic estimates for how long activities are estimated to take. Using the beta distribution, estimate the activity durations and variances for each task:

Duration Estimates

Activity	Pessimistic	Likely	Optimistic
A	7	5	2
B	5	3	2
C	14	8	6
D	20	10	6
E	8	3	3
F	10	5	3
G	12	6	4
H	16	6	5

Solution

Remember that the beta distribution calculates expected activity duration (TE) as:

$$TE = (a + 4m + b)/6$$

where

TE = estimated time for activity
a = most optimistic time to complete the activity
m = most likely time to complete the activity, the mode of the distribution
b = most pessimistic time to complete the activity

The formula for activity variance is:

$$s^2 = [(b - a)/6]^2$$

Therefore, in calculating expected activity duration (TE) and variance for each task, we find the value as shown:

Duration Estimates

Activity	Pessimistic	Likely	Optimistic	TE (Beta)	Variance
A	7	5	2	4.8	$[(7 - 2)/6]^2 = 25/36 = 0.69$
B	5	3	2	3.2	$[(5 - 2)/6]^2 = 9/36 = 0.25$
C	14	8	6	8.7	$[(14 - 6)/6]^2 = 64/36 = 1.78$
D	20	10	6	11.0	$[(20 - 6)/6]^2 = 196/36 = 5.44$
E	8	3	3	3.8	$[(8 - 3)/6]^2 = 25/36 = 0.69$
F	10	5	3	5.5	$[(10 - 3)/6]^2 = 49/36 = 1.36$
G	12	6	4	6.7	$[(12 - 4)/6]^2 = 64/36 = 1.78$
H	16	6	5	7.5	$[(16 - 5)/6]^2 = 121/36 = 3.36$

3. Assume you are given the following information about a project's activities and their predecessors. Construct the network diagram for this project:

Activity	Predecessors
A	—
B	A
C	A
D	B, C
E	B
F	D
G	C
H	E, F, G

Solution

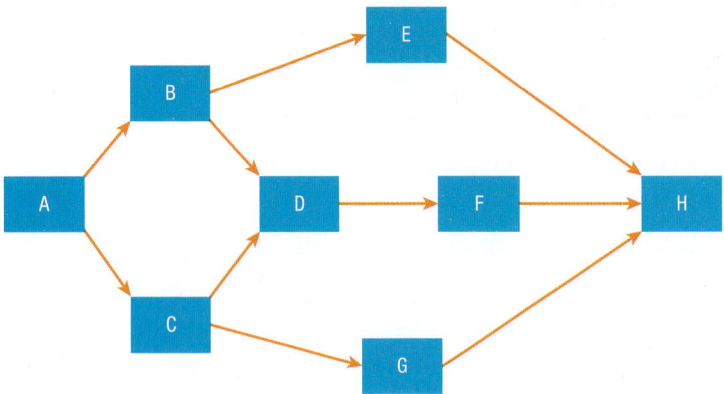

PROBLEMS

1. Suppose you were responsible for organizing one of the following events. Use a work breakdown structure (WBS) to organize and identify each task necessary to accomplish the project (for each WBS, employ a minimum of 3 deliverables and 10 total work packages):

   a. Graduation party

   b. Engagement reception

   c. Charity golf tournament

   d. Campus election campaign for student government

2. Suppose you are in charge of your group's final paper and presentation in an operations management class. You have identified your WBS and have labeled the various elements as 1.0 (project level), 1.1 (deliverables), and 1.1.1 (activities). Create a pyramid structure for your WBS with the following information:

   Project: Develop Transportation Control Plan

   Deliverables: 1. Final Paper, 2. Final Class Presentation

   Activities for the first deliverable (Paper): 1. Identify problem, 2. Literature review, 3. First draft of paper, 4. Editing and corrections, 5. Final draft of paper

   Activities for the second deliverable (Presentation): 1. Identify visuals for presentation, 2. Develop Microsoft PowerPoint slides, 3. Review slides, 4. Develop final slide deck for presentation, 5. Generate "hard copy" of slides

3. Consider a project, such as moving to a new neighborhood, completing a long-term school assignment, or even cleaning your bedroom. Develop a set of activities necessary to accomplish that project, and then order them in a precedence manner to create sequential logic. Explain and defend the number of steps you identified and the order in which you placed those steps for best completion of the project.

4. Imagine you are in charge of a project to change the format of your school's newspaper from the standard, print approach to a paperless, Web-based layout. You have a team of 8 students, with backgrounds in journalism, communications, and computer and software engineering to assist you in this assignment. Administrators at your school have given you a "hard" deadline of 12 weeks to complete the changeover. Identify five potential risks to this project that you should consider as part of your planning process. What are some risk mitigation strategies that you could employ to offset these risks?

5. Assume you are in charge of developing a new software product for your organization. Using the following information, develop a risk classification matrix. Then, develop mitigation strategies for each risk and offer arguments to support your strategy:

Risk Factor	Consequence	Likelihood	Impact Potential
A. Loss of lead programmer	High	Low	Moderate
B. Technical failure	High	Medium	Serious
C. Budget cut	Medium	Low	Minor
D. Competitor first to market	High	High	Serious

6. What is the time estimate of the following activity in which the optimistic estimate is 2 days, pessimistic is 12 days, and most likely is 4 days? Show your work.

7. What is the time estimate of the following activity in which the optimistic time is 5 days, the likely time is 8 days, and the pessimistic time is 14 days? Show your work.

8. You are developing duration estimates for activities for a construction project you are managing. In addition to "in-house" construction activities, you must contract with external vendors and suppliers who are responsible for delivering materials to the construction site in advance of their use. For one activity, you have identified an optimistic time of 4 days, a most likely time of 6 days, and a pessimistic time of 24 days. Your boss questions your last time estimate, asking why the pessimistic is so much higher than the other two estimates. Using risk analysis, what arguments might you offer your boss for such a large pessimistic estimate?

9. Using the following information, develop an activity network for Project Alpha:

Activity	Preceding Activities
A	–
B	A
C	A
D	B, C
E	B
F	D
G	C
H	E, F, G

10. Construct a network activity diagram based on the following information:

Activity	Proceeding Activities
A	–
B	A
C	A
D	A
E	B
F	C, D
G	E, F
H	F
I	G, H
J	I

11. Construct a network activity diagram based on the following information:

Activity	Preceding Activities
A	–
B	–
C	A
D	B, C
E	B
F	C, D
G	E
H	F
I	G, H

12. You have a partial network for your project, and you are about to conduct a forward pass through it. Explain why the early start (ES) for activity D is 12 days, not 8 days. Remember: Activity D is a merge activity.

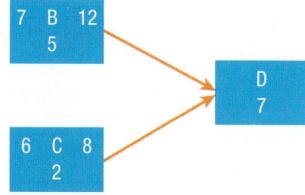

13. Referring to the figure for Problem 12, suppose that activity D was the last task in the network and you were about to start a backward pass.

    a. What is the project's duration? (Hint: Complete the forward pass.)

    b. What are the late finish (LF) and late start (LS) values for activities B, C, and D?

    c. Which activity has slack time? How many days?

14. Construct the following activity network, and identify the critical path. How long is the project expected to take to completion?

Task	Predecessors	Duration (weeks)
A	None	1
B	None	2
C	None	4

Task	Predecessors	Duration (weeks)
D	A, B	2
E	D	5
F	C, E	1
G	C	2
H	F, G	2

15. Consider the following network. What is the project's critical path? How many paths can you identify through the network? Name them.

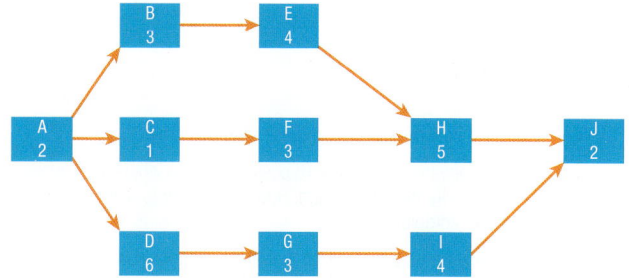

16. Use the following information to construct a project network with Gantt chart methodology. What is the total duration of this project?

Task	Predecessors	Duration (weeks)
A	None	12
B	None	8
C	None	5
D	A and B	10
E	C and D	10
F	A and B	5

17. Given the following information, answer the questions about this project:

Task	Predecessors	Duration
A	–	4
B	A	9
C	A	11
D	B	5
E	B	3
F	C	7
G	D, F	3
H	E, G	2
I	H	1

    a. Draw the network diagram representing this project.

    b. Fully label the network: identifying the critical path, all activity slack times, the early and late start times, and early and late finish times.

    c. What would happen if activities B and D each took 5 extra days to complete instead of the expected duration? How would the critical path change?

18. A construction manager is responsible for developing a new site for residential home construction. He has identified the following activities, their predecessor activities, and their expected duration:

Task	Predecessors	Duration (Days)
A. Final Purchase	–	2
B. Surveying	A	3
C. Permitting	A	5
D. Road Grading	B	4
E. Electrical Lines	C	3
F. Storm and Sewer	D	5
G. Paving	E, F	5
H. Tree Removal	E	3
I. Clearing Lots	H	7
J. City Inspection	G, I	1

a. Draw the network diagram representing this project.

b. Use the forward and backward pass method to label the network in full: Identify the critical path. How long is this project expected to take to complete?

c. How many paths are there through the network? How much slack time does each noncritical path have?

d. Which activities have slack, and which do not?

19. An advertising project manager has developed a program for a new advertising campaign. In addition, the manager has gathered the time information for each activity, as shown in the following table:

a. Calculate the expected activity times (round to nearest integer).

b. Calculate activity variances.

c. Calculate the activity slack times. What is the project's total length? Make sure you fully label all nodes in the network.

d. Identify the critical path. What are the alternative paths, and how much slack time is associated with each of them?

Time Estimates (weeks)

Activity	Optimistic	Most Likely	Pessimistic	Immediate Predecessor(s)
A	1	4	7	–
B	2	6	7	–
C	3	3	6	B
D	6	13	14	A
E	3	6	12	A, C
F	6	8	16	B
G	1	5	6	D, E, F

20. Consider the following project tasks and their identified best, likely, and worst case estimates of task duration. Assume the organization you work for computes TE based on the standard beta distribution formula. Calculate the TE for each of the following tasks (round to the nearest integer):

Activity	Best	Likely	Worst	TE
A	4	5	10	
B	4	6	9	
C	2	5	8	
D	5	8	10	
E	12	16	20	

Activity	Best	Likely	Worst	TE
F	6	10	12	
G	5	9	14	
H	14	16	22	
I	10	14	20	
J	1	2	5	

21. Using the information in the previous table, calculate the variances for each activity. Which activities have the highest variance?

22. Using the following information, create an AON network activity diagram. Calculate each activity TE (rounding to the nearest integer); the total duration of the project; its early start, early finish, late start, and late finish times; and the slack for each activity. Finally, show the project's critical path:

Activity	Preceding Activities	Best	Likely	Worst
A	–	12	15	25
B	A	4	6	11
C	–	12	12	30
D	B, C	8	15	20
E	A	7	12	15
F	E	9	9	42
G	D, E	13	17	19
H	F	5	10	15
I	G	11	13	20
J	G, H	2	3	6
K	J, I	8	12	22

Now, assume that activity E has taken 10 days past its anticipated duration to complete. What happens to the project's schedule? Has the duration changed? Is there a new critical path? Show your conclusions.

23. Using the following information, develop a simple S-curve representation of the expected cumulative budget expenditures for this project (figures are in thousands):

Duration (in days)

	10	20	30	40	50	60	70	80
Activities	4	8	12	20	10	8	6	2
Cumulative	4	12	24	44	54	62	68	70

24. Assume the following information (figures are in thousands):

Budgeted Costs for Sample Project
Duration (in weeks)

	5	10	15	20	25	30	35	40	45	Total
Design	6	2	1							
Engineer		5	10	12	6					
Install			7	15	30	8				
Test					1	5	8	5	2	
Total Monthly Cumul.										

a. Calculate the monthly budget and the monthly cumulative budgets for the project.

b. Draw a project S-curve identifying the relationship between the project's budget baseline and its schedule.

25. Assume the following information:

Budgeted Costs for Sample Project
Duration (in weeks)

	5	10	15	20	25	30	35	40	45	Total
Design	4	4	2							
Engineer		3	6	12	8					
Study			4	12	24	6				

Budgeted Costs for Sample Project
Duration (in weeks)

	5	10	15	20	25	30	35	40	45	Total
Test					2	6	6	4	2	
Total Monthly Cumul.										

a. Calculate the monthly budget and the monthly cumulative budgets for the project.

b. Draw a project's S-curve identifying the relationship between the project's budget baseline and its schedule.

26. Enter the information from problem #2 onto an MS Project template, and create a Gantt chart of the project's network.

CASE STUDY 3.1 PROJECT MANAGEMENT IN THE MOVIE BUSINESS

The global film industry is projected to generate gross revenues of US$35.3 billion by 2019. Thousands of films each year are produced by studios in many countries, most notably in Hollywood, California, but with strong participation by companies in India, China, Great Britain, France, and Germany. In fact, "Bollywood" in India is responsible for nearly 2,000 new films produced each year. Millions of people around the planet enjoy the wide variety of films produced by these companies every year, with more than 1.5 billion tickets sold in 2016.

Although it is common to apply project management ideas and concepts to a variety of ventures, including new product introductions, manufacturing, process improvement, and construction, in fact, one often-overlooked setting in which project management skills are highly valued is in the production of movies. Each movie includes a set of goals that defines the purposes of the film and the messages it intends to convey. Moreover, movie production is limited by several critical constraints (budgets and schedules) that executives must remain mindful of for the film to make money for investors.

The movie development cycle is related closely to the project life-cycle model of conceptualization, planning, execution, and termination. Like any good project, a successful film starts with a good idea: In this case, the idea is typically developed into a workable script. During the first stage of the movie-making process, development, the story is developed into a screenplay, which undergoes multiple rewrites and edits to keep the length within acceptable limits and address critical concerns. The project's goals and vision are conceptualized through these multiple treatments of the script to get it into final form. Financing is also organized during development, with producers signed on to secure a workable budget to complete the scripted film project. In movie "preproduction" stage, all the critical planning takes place before the camera rolls. Among the preproduction steps, movie companies employ the director and producer for the film, begin the casting of the various roles, and work out shooting locations, sets, and other backdrops necessary for the movie to be shot. Film "production" includes the actual work of shooting the scenes, setting up lighting, stage decoration, determining the sequence of the shots to be taken, rehearsals, shooting, and screening daily footage to determine whether the product of the day's work is usable or will have to be reshot on the following day. Finally, postproduction activities begin after all the footage has been captured and includes any activities or material that must be added to the film after the shots are completed, including editing, creating computer-generated imagery (CGI), generating a music score, color correction, and graphics and special effects.

Successful movie production requires strong project management. To create a profitable movie from what was only recently a series of ideas in an artist's imagination, it is necessary to be able to apply strong organizational skills, time and budget discipline, and good trouble-shooting abilities. Project management techniques have long been behind the creation of the most successful movies, generating millions in profits, and satisfying the demanding tastes of millions of customers at the box office.[18]

Questions:

1. Of the four measures of project success, which do you consider to be the most important for a movie project? Why?

2. Consider the following activities of a film. Using this information, construct a project activity network:

Activity	Description	Predecessors
A	"Green Light" the Project	—
B	Obtain Financing	A
C	Develop Screenplay	A
D	Casting	B, C
E	Identify Shooting Locations	C
F	Rehearsal	D, E
G	Shooting	B, F
H	Screening Daily Output	G
I	Editing	G
J	Sound Mixing	H, I
K	Music	J
L	Movie Release	K

VIDEO CASE ....

Watch this video case to learn about how Rolls-Royce manages products that can be highly technical and potentially hazardous.

CRITICAL THINKING EXERCISES ....

Conduct an Internet search for "project management disasters," and read a minimum of three of the publications you find. What common features or errors do these disasters have in common? In particular, do you believe that project management disasters are most often a failure of initial planning or subsequent execution? Defend your perspective with evidence or examples from the Internet.

SUPPLEMENT FOR CHAPTER

3

Project Management

LEARNING OBJECTIVES

After studying this chapter, you should be able to:

1 Calculate the probability of a project being completed on time.

2 Calculate the cost of "crashing" a project and the amount of time a project can be accelerated.

3 Calculate the earned value of an ongoing project to assess its current status throughout development.

OPERATIONS PROFILE: Fast Tracking Manchester's New Airport Development

David Goddard/Getty Images News/Getty Images

Manchester is the third-largest city in the United Kingdom with a population of nearly 7 million people in the metro and surrounding areas. Its international airport is one of the busiest in the country, servicing more than 70 airlines with 210 destinations to Europe, Asia, and the Americas. In 2015, its passenger numbers topped a record 22 million people. Manchester Airport brings more than US$2.5 billion to the regional economy every year, employing 20,000 people and supporting a further 25,000 jobs. As a result, Manchester International Airport is a regional asset that residents are motivated to continue developing.

The problem is that with the large volume of traffic through the airport over the years, its facilities have become increasingly run-down and the cost of simple upgrades and maintenance has become prohibitively expensive. The airport's main terminal (T1) was built in 1962 and is desperately in need of upgrading if the airport authority is to attract more passengers as well as local businesses to the Manchester area.

In 2015, the airport announced plans for a $1.5 billion renovation that would dramatically expand the size and capacity of the airport, while demolishing the outdated main terminal. The goal of the renovation is to remove as many disruptions and delays as possible to make travel to and from Manchester efficient and enjoyable. Among the renovations and service improvements are plans to:

- Add the latest technology to help passengers flow through the airport, speeding up peak-time security checks to less than 10 minutes, while making off-peak screening times five minutes or less.
- Create a U.S. customs preclearance facility for passengers returning to America to avoid lengthy customs lines at arrival.
- Create automated bag-drops for passengers so they are not required to hand-carry luggage throughout the terminal to counters and travel gates.
- Add 50 food and drink outlets, more gates for aircraft, and better links for passengers transferring from one plane to another.
- Attract more airlines to add more routes to Asia and America.

In 2016, preliminary documents were signed between the airport authority and the major contractors and work has begun on demolishing Terminal One. The airport hopes to complete the wholly revamped Terminal Two by 2023 and to complete all renovations by 2025. By 2050, it is hoped that 55 million passengers will use the hub every year, bolstering Manchester's revenues while taking some of the strain off London's two international airports: Heathrow and Gatwick, already operating at full capacity. The project is being funded by fast-tracking investment plans alongside borrowing, and it will ultimately include more than 60 changes to the current airport.

Charlie Cornish, chief executive of Manchester Airports Group, said: "Without doubt, with this level of investment Manchester will become one of the most modern and customer focused airports in Europe, demonstrating the importance of Manchester as a global gateway. It demonstrates that it's more than just being about Heathrow or Gatwick." He described the revamp as a "modern facility geared around a high level of customer service, stress-free, hassle-free with modern technology and communication." Mr. Cornish promised "minimal disruption" to passengers by working around terminal activity and only "knocking through" at the 11th hour. At the same time, he promised to work with the local community to mitigate disruption.

Building or renovating airports is a massive project undertaking, with numerous stakeholders and often, billions of dollars at risk. Having a clear sense of the project's goals, creating the means to minimize disruptions for current travelers, and making the process as risk-free as possible are the keys to a successful project that will benefit the citizens of Manchester and air travelers for decades to come.[1]

This supplement discusses three of the most common quantitative techniques used to manage projects: (1) calculations to determine the probability of a project being completed on time, (2) the costs associated with crashing it, and (3) the earned value method to track and control the project.

3S.1 Determining the Probability of a Project Being Completed on Time

3S.1

Calculate the probability of a project being completed on time.

 PERT Estimates

There are situations in which it is extremely difficult to estimate accurately the durations of a project's activities. In situations such as these, it's best to use the program evaluation and review technique (PERT) estimates we discussed in Chapter 3—that is, probabilistic estimates based on optimistic, most likely, and pessimistic times for each activity. Remember that the formula for the expected duration of an activity under these circumstances is:

$$TE = (a + 4m + b) / 6$$

where

TE = estimated time for activity

a = most optimistic time to complete the activity

m = most likely time to complete the activity, the mode of the distribution

b = most pessimistic time to complete the activity

To illustrate, let's look at the activities for Project Eagle, which are shown in Table 3S.1. Project Eagle is the name given to a market research project to be undertaken by a small firm in Columbus, Ohio. The firm's specific charge is to determine how receptive a suburban community would be to building a public swimming pool and changing station on the grounds of an older but underused park. After conducting a work breakdown structure (WBS) on the activities in the market research project, the project manager has determined that the following activities are needed. Furthermore, she has identified the order in which these activities must be performed. Table 3S.1 shows the listing.

If you use the information in Table 3S.1 to construct a network diagram, it will look the one in Figure 3S.1.

Recall that the formula for the variance of the duration of an activity is

$$s^2 = [1 / 6(b - a)]^2$$

where b is the most pessimistic time and a is the most optimistic.

TABLE 3S.1: Activities in Project Eagle

ACTIVITY	DESCRIPTION	PREDECESSORS
A	Contract signing	None
B	Questionnaire design	A
C	Target market ID	A
D	Survey sample	B, C
E	Develop presentation	B
F	Analyze results	D
G	Demographic analysis	C
H	Presentation to client	E, F, G

Determining the individual activity variances is straightforward. As an example, refer to Table 3S.2 to find the variance for activity A (Contract signing). Because we know the most optimistic and pessimistic times for this task (3 and 11 weeks, respectively), we calculate its variance as:

Activity A: $[(11 - 3) / 6]^2 = (8 / 6)^2 = 64 / 36$, or 1.78 weeks

This information is important because we want to know not just the likely times for activities but also how much confidence we have in these estimates. Thus, for activity A, we can see that although it's most likely to finish in 5 weeks, there is a considerable amount of variance in that estimate (nearly 2 weeks). As we did for activity A, we can calculate the expected variance and standard deviation for each of the project's other activities, as Table 3S.2 demonstrates.

Using the durations in Table 3S.2, we can complete the activity network for Project Eagle as Figure 3S.2 shows. We can also use the information in Table 3S.2 to calculate the variance for the overall project. The project's variance, which is found by summing the variances of all of its *critical* activities, can be found using the following equation:

σ_p^2 = project variance = Σ (variances of activities on the critical path)

Recall that the critical activities for this project are A – C – D – F – H. For the variance of the overall project, the calculation is:

project variance $(\sigma_p^2) = 1.78 + 1.00 + 4.00 + .69 + .25 = 7.72$

FIGURE 3S.1 Activity Network for Project Eagle

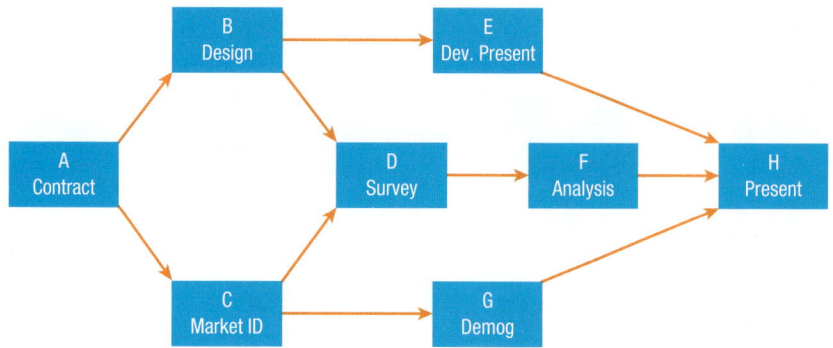

TABLE 3S.2: Expected Activity Durations and Variances for Project Eagle

ACTIVITY	OPTIMISTIC (a)	MOST LIKELY (m)	PESSIMISTIC (b)	EXPECTED TIME (TE)	VARIANCE $[(b-a)/6]^2$
A	3	4	11	5	$[(11-3)/6]^2 = 64/36 = 1.78$
B	2	5	8	5	$[(8-2)/6]^2 = 36/36 = 1.00$
C	3	6	9	6	$[(9-3)/6]^2 = 36/36 = 1.00$
D	8	12	20	12.7	$[(20-8)/6]^2 = 144/36 = 4.00$
E	3	5	12	5.8	$[(12-3)/6]^2 = 81/36 = 2.25$
F	2	4	7	4.2	$[(7-2)/6]^2 = 25/36 = .69$
G	6	9	14	9.3	$[(14-6)/6]^2 = 64/36 = 1.78$
H	1	2	4	2	$[(4-1)/6]^2 = 9/36 = .25$

The project standard's deviation (σ_p) is:

$$\sqrt{\text{Project variance}} = \sqrt{7.70} = 2.78 \text{ weeks}$$

The PERT estimates we just calculated also allow us to plot the normal probability distribution curve shown in Figure 3S.3. Under this assumption, the expected completion time of a project, the mean, is in the middle of the distribution. In our case, the mean is 30 weeks. The bell-shaped curve implies that there's a 50% chance that the project will be completed in 30 weeks or less and a 50 % chance that it will be completed in more than 30 weeks.

With this information, we can determine the probability that our project will be finished on or before a particular time. Suppose, for example, that Project Eagle must be completed on or before the 32-week mark. (Although the schedule calls for a 30-week completion, remember that our estimates are based on probabilities.) To determine the probability of the project finishing no later than 32 weeks, we need to pinpoint the area under the normal curve that corresponds to a completion date on or before week 32. We can use the following standard normal equation to determine this probability:

$$Z = (\text{due date} - \text{expected date of completion}) / \sigma_p = (32 - 30) / 2.78 \text{ or } 0.72$$

where Z is the number of standard deviations the target date (32 weeks) lies from the mean or expected date to completion (30 weeks). We can now use a normal distribution table (see Appendix A)

FIGURE 3S.2: Completed Activity Network for Project Eagle With the Critical Path Highlighted

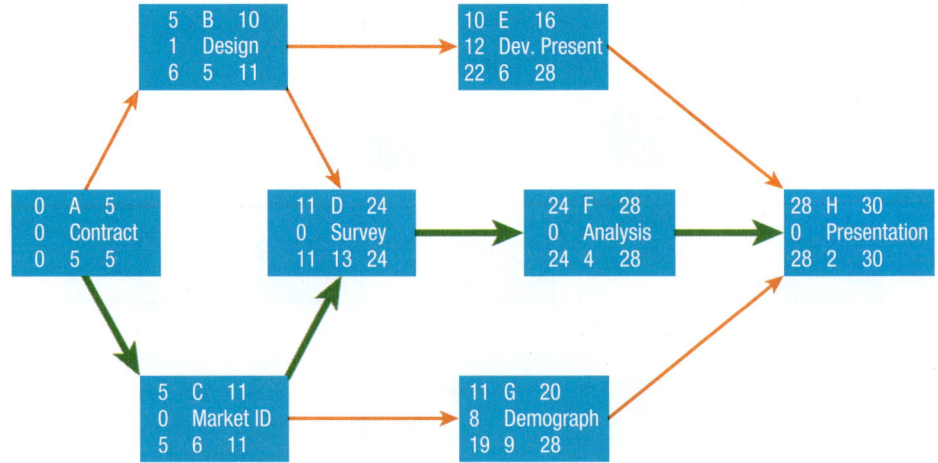

to determine that a Z value of 0.72 indicates a probability of 0.7642. Thus, there is a 76.42% chance that Project Eagle will finish on or before the critical date of 32 weeks. Visually, this calculation would resemble Figure 3S.4. The additional two weeks are represented by the shaded part of the normal curve showing the mean (30 weeks) plus two additional weeks.

Remember from this example that it is critical for the company to meet the 32-week deadline. How confident would we be working on this project if the likelihood of meeting that deadline were only 76.42%? Odds are the project team (and the organization) might find a 76% chance of success in meeting the deadline unacceptable. This concern leads to the question, how much time will the project team need to guarantee delivery with a high degree of confidence? More specifically, what is the minimal acceptable probability of completion that an organization needs when making this decision? For example, there is a big difference in requiring a 99% likelihood of completion versus a 90% likelihood.

Suppose that the organization managing Project Eagle requires a 95% likelihood of on-time delivery. Under this circumstance, how much additional time should be built into the project to ensure it's delivered on time? We can determine this value, again with the aid of Z score normal distribution tables. The tables indicate that for a 95% probability, a Z score of 1.65 most closely represents this likelihood. We can then rewrite the previous standard normal equation and solve for the due date as follows:

$$\text{Due Date} = \text{Expected date of completion} + (Z \times \sigma_p)$$
$$= 30 \text{ weeks} + (1.65 \times 2.78)$$
$$= 34.59 \text{ weeks}$$

If the project team can negotiate an additional 4.59 weeks, it has a very strong (95%) likelihood of ensuring that Project Eagle will be completed on time.

So far, we have only examined activities on the critical path because, logically, they define the overall length of a project. Nevertheless, there are some circumstances in which it may also be necessary to consider noncritical activities and their effect on a project's overall duration, especially if those activities have little slack time and a high variance. For example, for Project Eagle, activity B has only 1 day of slack time and a variance of 1.00. In fact, the pessimistic time for activity B is 8 weeks. Even though activity B is not on the critical path, if it were to take 8 weeks, the project would miss its deadline. Thus, it may be necessary to calculate the variances not only for critical activities but for all of the project's activities, especially those with higher variances. We can then calculate the likelihood of meeting our projected completion dates for all paths, both critical and noncritical.

FIGURE 3S.3: Probability Distribution for Project Eagle's Completion Times

30 Weeks

On-Time Completion

FIGURE 3S.4: Probability of Completing Project Eagle by Week 32

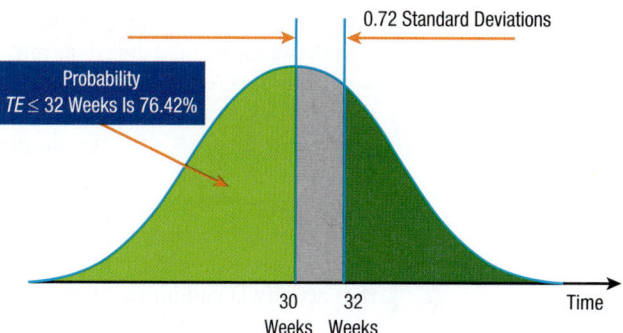

0.72 Standard Deviations

Probability $TE \leq 32$ Weeks Is 76.42%

30 Weeks 32 Weeks Time

3S.2 Calculating the Time–Cost Trade-Offs of Crashing a Project

Before crashing a project, you first need to assess the costs associated with each of its activities. You want to be sure the tasks you choose to accelerate will have the most impact on the schedule for the least cost. To determine how much could be gained by crashing a project's activities, we must first determine the actual fixed and variable costs associated with each. Assume that we have a reasonable method for estimating the total cost of project activities, in terms of both their normal duration times and crashed times. Recall from Chapter 3 that Figure 3.15 illustrates the relationship between an activity's costs and its duration. When we crash a project, the costs associated with the activity increase even more sharply. The crash point in the figure represents the fully expedited project activity—one in which no expense is spared to complete the task. Nevertheless, the slope of the line between the normal and crash points suggests that an activity can be speeded up to some degree less than the complete crash point. We want to find the point at which this time and cost trade-off is optimized.

3S.2

Calculate the cost of "crashing" a project and the amount of time a project can be accelerated.

We can calculate various time–cost trade-off combinations for a project's crash options by determining the slope for each activity using the following formula:

$$\text{Slope} = \frac{\text{crash cost} - \text{normal cost}}{\text{normal time} - \text{crash time}}$$

Cost of Crashing

To calculate the cost of crashing an activity, suppose that the normal activity duration of activity X is 5 weeks and it is budgeted to cost $12,000. The crash time for this activity is 3 weeks, and it is expected to cost $32,000. Using the previous formula, we can calculate the cost slope (in U.S. dollars) for activity X as:

$$\frac{32,000 - 12,000}{5 - 3} \quad \text{or} \quad \frac{\$20,000}{2} = \$10,000 \text{ per week}$$

That is, activity X will cost $10,000 for each week it's accelerated. Is this a reasonable price? To find out, you have to answer following questions:[2]

a. **What costs are associated with accelerating other project activities?** It may be that activity X's cost of $10,000 per week is a genuine bargain. Suppose, for example, that an alternative activity would cost $25,000 for each week's acceleration.

b. **What are the gains versus losses in accelerating the activity?** Do excessive late penalties make crashing a cheaper alternative? Alternatively, is there a huge potential payoff in being first to the market with the project?

EXAMPLE 3S.1: Suppose we have a project with the eight activities listed in Table 3S.3. The table also shows the normal durations and costs as well as crashed durations and costs of the activities. (Assume that the costs listed include both the fixed and variable costs for each activity.) Which activities should we crash and for how many days each?

We can then use the formula provided earlier to calculate the costs per unit of crashing each activity. (In this case, the units are days.) These costs are listed in Table 3S.4. The least expensive activities to crash are activity A ($250 per day), activity B ($300 per day), and activity G ($300 per day each). The most expensive activities to crash are activities H, E, and C, which cost $2,000 per day, $1,750 per day, and $1,500 per day, respectively. Remember that in this example, we are assuming that activity D cannot be shortened, so no crashing cost can be calculated for it.

TABLE 3S.3: Project's Activities and Costs (Normal vs. Crashed)

| ACTIVITY | NORMAL | | CRASHED | |
	DURATION	COST (IN U.S. DOLLARS)	DURATION	COST (IN U.S. DOLLARS)
A	5 days	1,000	3 days	1,500
B	7 days	700	6 days	1,000
C	3 days	2,500	2 days	4,000
D	5 days	1,500	5 days	1,500
E	9 days	3,750	6 days	9,000
F	4 days	1,600	3 days	2,500
G	6 days	2,400	4 days	3,000
H	8 days	9,000	5 days	15,000
Total costs =		$22,450		$37,500

TABLE 3S.4: Costs of Crashing Each Activity

ACTIVITY	CRASHING COSTS (PER DAY; IN U.S. DOLLARS)	ON CRITICAL PATH?
A	250	Yes
B	300	No
C	1,500	No
D	–	Yes
E	1,750	Yes
F	900	No
G	300	No
H	2,000	Yes

TABLE 3S.5: Cost of the Project Versus the Days Saved

PROJECT DURATION	CRASHED ACTIVITY	TOTAL PROJECT COST (IN U.S. DOLLARS)
27 days	A	22,450
26 days	A	22,700
25 days	A	22,950
24 days	E	24,700
23 days	E	26,450
22 days	E	28,200
21 days	H	30,200
20 days	H	32,200
19 days	H	34,200

Now let's transfer these crash costs to a network that shows the precedence of each activity. We can then make a trade-off between shortening the project and increasing its total costs by analyzing each alternative. Figure 3S.5 shows an activity-on-node (AON) network with only the activities and their crashed duration values included. We determined that the initial cost of the project using normal activity durations is $22,450. The network also shows that the project's critical path is A – D – E – H, or 19 days.

Crashing activity A is the least expensive. (Recall from our discussion in Chapter 3 that we first want to crash the activities that are the least costly to crash.) Crashing activity A by 1 day will increase the project's costs from $22,450 to $22,700. Fully crashing activity A will shorten the project's duration to 25 days, while increasing the project's costs to $22,950, as Table 3S.5 shows activities B and G are the next candidates for crashing at $300 per day each. Neither of these two activities is on the project's critical path, however, so the overall benefit of shortening them may be minimal. Activity D cannot be shortened. The cost per unit to crash E is $1,750, and the cost per unit to crash H is $2,000. Crashing activity E by 1 day will increase the project budget from $22,950 to $24,700. Fully crashing it by 3 days (shortening it from 9 days to 6) increases the budget to $28,200. As activity H costs $2,000 per day to crash fully, crashing it by 3 days (shortening it from 8 days to 5) will add another $6,000 to the budget. The total costs for each day the project is crashed are shown in Table 3S.5.

The fully crashed project network is shown in Figure 3S.5. Note that the critical path is unchanged. The trade-off between the costs and the project's duration is graphed in Figure 3S.6. As each project activity has been

Crashing a Project

FIGURE 3S.5 Fully Crashed Activity Network for the Project

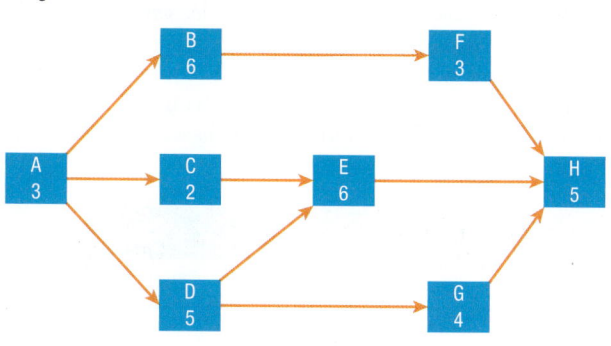

FIGURE 3S.6 Costs of the Project Versus the Days Saved: Graphic Representation

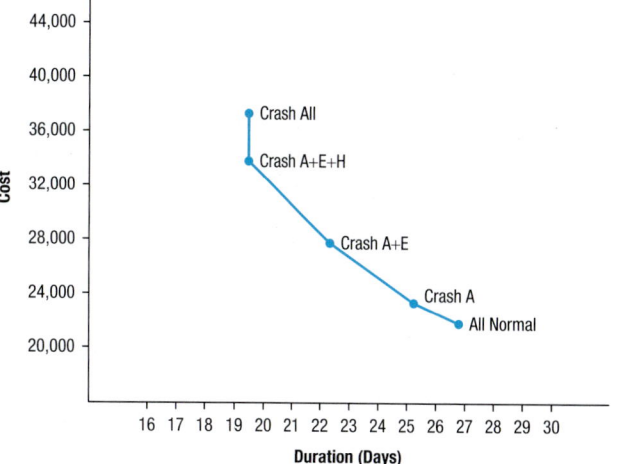

crashed in order, the overall project budget increases. Nevertheless, Figure 3S.6 also demonstrates that after crashing activities A, E, and H, there is little to be gained by crashing any of the other activities. The overall length of the project cannot shrink below 19 days, and the additional crashing merely adds costs to the budget. Therefore, the optimal crash strategy for this project is to crash only activities A, E, and H for a total cost of $11,750 and a revised project cost of $34,200.

Calculate the earned value of an ongoing project to assess its current status throughout development.

3S.3 Calculating a Project's Earned Value

As we explained in Chapter 3, the earned value management (EVM) method is valuable because it allows us to see how a project is truly performing. The method involves using a *time-phased* budget we regularly update—one that links the project's schedule and costs with the work actually completed on it.

Terminology for the EVM Method

The following are some key measures used to calculate a project's earned value and, more accurately, estimate its final budget and completion date.

Planned value (PV): a cost estimate of the budgeted resources scheduled across the project's life cycle (cumulative baseline)

Earned value (EV): the real budgeted cost, or "value," of the work actually performed to date

Actual cost of work performed (AC): the cumulative total cost of completing the project's work packages

Schedule performance index (SPI): the earned value to date divided by the planned value of work scheduled to be performed (EV/PV). This value allows us to calculate the project's schedule to completion

Cost performance index (CPI): the earned value divided by the actual, cumulative cost of the work performed to date (EV/AC). This value allows us to calculate the projected budget to completion

Budgeted cost at completion (BAC): the total budget for a project at its completion

PV	**Planned value.** A cost estimate of the budgeted resources scheduled across the project's life cycle (cumulative baseline).
EV	**Earned value.** The real budgeted cost, or "value," of the work actually performed to date.
AC	**Actual cost of the work performed.** The cumulative total cost of completing the project's work packages.
SPI	**Schedule performance index.** The earned value to date divided by the planned value of work scheduled to be performed (EV/PV). This value allows us to calculate the project's schedule to completion.
CPI	**Cost performance index.** The earned value divided by the actual, cumulative cost of the work performed to date (EV/AC). This value allows us to calculate the projected budget to completion.
BAC	**Budgeted cost at completion.** The total budget for a project at its completion.

Creating Project Baselines

The first step in developing an accurate control process is to create the baseline of the project, against which progress can be measured. We need baseline information regardless of the control process we use. Yet, baselines are critical to using the EVM method.

The first piece of information we need is the planned value (PV), or budgeted cost, of the project. The PV should include all costs relevant to the project, the most important of which are personnel costs, equipment and materials, and the project overhead, which is sometimes referred to as the *level of effort.* Overhead costs (level of effort) can include a variety of fixed costs that must be incorporated into the project's budget. The fixed costs may be for administrative or technical support, computer work, or the expertise of other staff (such as legal advice or marketing work). Establishing the project's baseline requires just two pieces of data: the work breakdown structure and a time-phased budget for the project.

1. The work breakdown structure identified the individual work packages and tasks necessary to accomplish the project. It also gave us some understanding of the hierarchy of tasks.
2. The **time-phased budget** takes the WBS one step further: It allows us to identify the correct sequencing of tasks, but more importantly, it enables the project team to determine the points in the project when budgeted money is likely to be spent as those tasks are completed. Say, for example, that our team determines that one activity, data entry, will require a budget of $20,000 to be completed and, furthermore, that the task is estimated to require 2 months to completion, with most of the work being done in the first month. A time-phased budget for this activity might resemble the following (in U.S. dollars):

ACTIVITY	JAN.	FEB.	. . .	DEC.	TOTAL
Data Entry	14,000	6,000		-0-	20,000

Once we have collected the WBS and applied a time-phased budget breakdown to it, we can create the project's baseline. The baseline is important because it's the standard against which we are going to compare all performance, cost, and schedule data as we attempt to assess the viability of the project as it is progresses. This baseline, then, represents our best understanding of how the project *should* progress. How the project is actually progressing, however, is, of course, another matter.

Why Use Earned Value?

Let us illustrate why the EVM method is valuable using the Project Tracy example. Return to the information presented in Table 3.5, which was plotted on the project's S-curve in Figure 3.16. Assume that it is now week 30 of the project and that we are attempting to assess the project's status. Also assume that there is no difference between the projected project costs and the actual expenditures; that is, the project's budget is being spent within the correct time frame. Nevertheless, suppose we were to discover that installation was only half-completed, and project testing had not yet begun. This example illustrates the problem with using S-curves and the strength of EVM. A project's status is relevant only when some measure of performance is considered in addition to the budget and elapsed schedule.

 Earned Value

Consider the revised data for Project Tracy listed in Table 3S.6. Note that as of week 30, the work packages related to design and engineering have been totally completed, whereas the installation is only 50% done, and testing has not yet begun. The percentages completed are based on the project team's assessment of the current status of the completion of the work packages. The question now becomes, what is the earned value of the work done to date? As of week 30, what is the status of this project in terms of budget, schedule, *and* performance?

TABLE 3S.6: Activity Completion Percentages for Project Tracy

	DURATION (IN WEEKS)									
	5	10	15	20	25	30	35	40	45	% COMP.
Design	6	2								100
Engineer		4	8	8	8					100
Install				4	20	6				50
Test						2	6	4	2	0
Total	6	6	8	12	28	8	6	4	2	
Cumul.	6	12	20	32	60	68	74	78	80	

Calculating the earned value of these work packages is fairly simple. As Table 3S.7 shows, we can modify the previous table to focus exclusively on the information we need to determine the earned value. We do so by multiplying the percentage of each work package completed by its planned value (budgeted cost) to determine the earned value to date for the package as well as the overall project. In this case, the project's earned value at the 30-week point is $51,000.

We can then compare the planned budget against the actual earned value using the project's original budgeted baseline, as shown in Table 3.5. This allows us to assess more realistically the status of the project because the earned value is plotted against the budget baseline. Compare this figure with the S-curve in Figure 3.16. Recall that by the end of week 30, our original budget projections suggested that $68,000 should have been spent. Instead, at week 30, only $51,000 had been spent. Unlike the standard S-curve evaluation, the EVM variance is meaningful because it is based not simply on the budget spent but also on value earned. In other words, we are not only showing a negative variance in terms of money spent on the project but also in terms of value created (performance) of the project to date. A negative variance of $10,000 in budget expenditures may or may not signal cause for concern; however, a $17,000 shortfall in value earned on the project to date represents a variance that has serious consequences.

Time-phased budget: a budget that identifies the correct sequencing of tasks and the points in the project when budgeted money is likely to be spent as those tasks are completed

TABLE 3S.7: Calculating the Earned Value (in thousands of U.S. dollars)

	PLANNED	% COMP.	EARNED VALUE
Design	8	100	8
Engineer	28	100	28
Install	30	50	15
Test	14	0	0
Cumulative Earned Value			51

Steps in the Earned Value Management Method

To assess a project using the EVM method, you need to follow these steps:[3]

Earned Value
Management

1. *Clearly define each activity that will be performed during the project, including its resource needs as well as a detailed budget.* As we demonstrated, the work breakdown structure identifies each of the project's activities and human or material resources assigned to it. This allows us to create the budget figure, or cost estimate, for each activity.
2. *Create the activity and resource usage schedules.* These schedules show the proportion of the total budget allocated to each task across a project's life cycle. That is, we determine how much of an activity's budget is to be spent each month (or other appropriate time period).
3. *Establish a time-phased budget that shows the project's expenditures across its life cycle.* The total (cumulative) amount of the budget becomes the project baseline and is referred to as the planned value (PV). The PV just means that we can identify the cumulative budget expenditures planned at any stage in the project. The PV, as a cumulative value, is found by adding the planned budget expenditures for each preceding time period.
4. *Total the actual costs of each activity to arrive at the actual cost of the work performed (AC).*
5. *Compute the value of the work done on each task by multiplying the percentage of it completed by its planned value (budgeted cost).* This calculation is referred to as the earned value (EV) and is the origin of the term for this control process. Then sum the earned value totals for the packages to arrive at the cumulative earned value—that is, the earned value for the overall project.
6. *Calculate both a project's budget variance and schedule variance while it is still in process.* Once we have collected the three key pieces of data (PV, EV, and AC), it is possible to make these calculations. The *schedule variance* is calculated by the simple equation: $SV = EV - PV$, or the difference between the earned value to date minus the planned value of the work scheduled to be performed to date. The budget, or cost, variance is calculated as $CV = EV - AC$, or the earned value minus the actual cost of work performed.

EXAMPLE 3S.2: Table 3S.8 lists the earned value results for Project Janus, which has a planned seven-month duration and an $118,000 budget (in U.S. dollars). The project began in January. We are interested in calculating its earned value as of the end of June. If we know the amount budgeted for each of the project's seven work packages and when that work is slated to be done, we can construct a budget table similar to that shown in Table 3S.8. Notice that each work package has a fixed budget across several time periods. For example, Staffing is budgeted to cost $15,000 and to be performed almost equally in January and February. The budget for Blueprinting is $10,000. That activity begins in March and concludes in April.

Each month, we can then plot the actual expenses for each activity. These sets of figures are added to the bottom four rows of the table. For example, note that by the end of March, we had planned to spend $21,000 on activities. Nevertheless, our actual cumulative costs were $27,000. The obvious question becomes, is this good news or bad news? On the surface, we might conclude that it was bad news because we overspent our budget. Yet, recall that the chief problem with the S-curve is that it only considers actual costs versus planned costs. This information alone won't help us truly determine the status of the project. To do that, we also need to how much of the project was completed by the end of March—not just the amounts budgeted and spent on the project.

TABLE 3S.8: Earned Value Table for Project Janus (in thousands of U.S. dollars)

ACTIVITY	JAN.	FEB.	MAR.	APR.	MAY	JUNE	JULY	PLAN	% C	VALUE
Staffing	8	7						15	100	15
Blueprinting			4	6				10	80	8
Prototype Development			2	8				10	60	6
Full Design				3	8	10		21	33	7
Construction					2	30		32	25	8
Transfer							10	10	0	0
Punch List						15	5	20	0	0
						$\Sigma =$		118		44
Monthly Plan	8	7	6	17	10	55	15			
Cumulative Planned	8	15	21	38	48	103	118			
Monthly Actual	8	11	8	11	10	30	0			
Cumulative Actual	8	19	27	38	48	78				

The key pieces of information that allow us to identify earned value are included in the right-hand columns. We are very interested in determining the current status of the project based on the number of tasks completed over the time budgeted to them. Therefore, the last columns show the planned expenditures for each task, the percentage of the tasks completed, and the calculated value. *Value* in this sense is simply the product of the planned expenditures and the percentage of these tasks completed. For example, under the activity Blueprinting, we see that this task was given a planned budget of $10,000 across two months total. To date, 80% of that activity was completed, resulting in $8,000 in value. If we total the columns for planned expenditures and actual value (EV), we come up with our project's planned budget ($118,000) and the value realized at the end of June ($44,000).

We now have enough information to make a reasonable determination of the project's status through using earned value management. The first value we require is the PV. This value can be found as the cumulative planned costs at the end of the month of June ($103,000). We have also calculated that the EV at the end of the month of June totals $44,000. The schedule variances that are of interest to us are the SPI and the estimated time to completion. The SPI is determined by dividing the EV by the PV. Table 3S.9 shows this calculation ($44,000 / $103,000 = .43). With the SPI, we can now project the length of time it should take to complete the project. Because the SPI is telling us that we are only operating at 43% efficiency in implementing the project, we take the reciprocal of the SPI times the original project schedule to determine the projected actual timeframe for the project's completion ($1/.43 \times 7 = 16.3$ months). This is bad news. Recall that the project was only supposed to last 7 months. At this pace, it will take a total of 16.3 months to complete.

How about the project's costs? Although we are running over 10 months late, can we make similar projections about how much the project will finally cost? The answer is yes. We can do so as long as we have two very important pieces of data—the AC of the work performed to date and the EV to date. The earned value has already been calculated ($44,000), and now we turn back to Table 3S.8 to locate AC. The cumulative actual cost at the end of June was $78,000. This amount is our AC and is entered into Table 3S.10.

We calculate cost variance by dividing the EV by AC, or $44,000 / $78,000 = .56. That is the CPI for this project. Determining the projected cost of the project involves taking the reciprocal of the CPI multiplied by the project's original budget ($118,000). The bad news is that this project is not only far behind schedule, but it is also projected to cost more than $210,000, which is a significant cost overrun.

TABLE 3S.9: Schedule Variances for Project Tracy (in U.S. dollars)

SCHEDULE VARIANCES	
PV	103,000
EV	44,000
SPI	EV / PV = 44,000 / 103,000 = .43
Estimated Time to Completion	(1/.43 × 7) = 16.3 months

TABLE 3S.10: Cost Variances for Project Tracy (in U.S. dollars)

COST VARIANCES	
Cumulative AC	78,000
EV	44,000
CPI	EV / AC = 44,000 / 78,000 = .56
Estimated Cumulative Cost to Completion	(1 / .56 × 118,000) = 210,714

Finally, as Figure 3S.7 illustrates, we can plot these variances on a graph that shows the difference between the EV and PV and AC. This example underscores how misleading simple S-curves can sometimes be. For example, in this case, we discovered that at the end of June, the difference between the AC ($78,000) and PV ($103,000) was $25,000. Although the analysis at that point showed that we had underspent our budget slightly, the status of the project in terms of its earned value shows that it is in trouble. This example demonstrates the advantages of using the earned value method to get a more accurate assessment of projects.

FIGURE 3S.7 Earned Value and Project-Status Slippage of Project Tracy

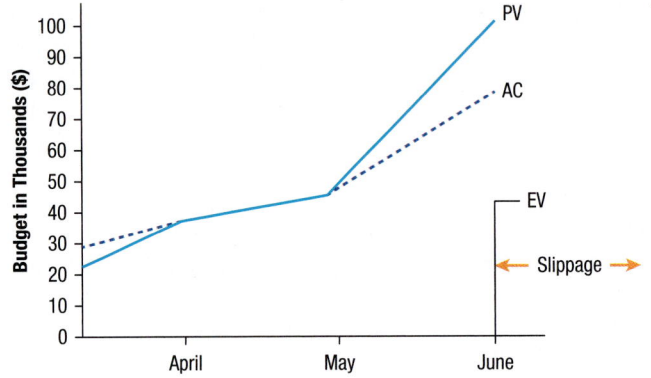

SUPPLEMENT SUMMARY

3S.1 Calculate the probability of a project being completed on time.
There are several situations in which it is extremely difficult to estimate the durations of a project's activities accurately. In situations such as these, it's best to use the PERT probabilistic estimates based on optimistic, most likely, and pessimistic times for each activity. Applying the relevant formulas for expected time and variance allows us to calculate the most likely time for each activity as well as the expected completion time for the project. Finally, apply the Z transformation to estimate the likely probability of the project being completed on time.

3S.2 Calculate the cost of "crashing" a project and the amount of time a project can be accelerated. Before crashing a project, first assess the costs associated with each of its activities. Be sure the tasks chosen to be accelerated will have the most impact on the schedule for the least cost. To determine how much could be gained by crashing a project's activities, first determine the actual fixed and variable costs associated with each. Calculate various time–cost combinations for a project's crash options by determining the slope for each activity using the formula:

$$\text{Slope} = \frac{\text{crash cost} - \text{normal cost}}{\text{normal time} - \text{crash time}}$$

3S.3 Calculate the earned value of an ongoing project to assess its current status throughout development. The earned value management (EVM) method is valuable because it indicates how a project is truly performing. The method involves using a *time-phased* budget that is regularly updated—one that links the project's schedule and costs with the work actually completed on it. The first piece of information needed is the planned value (PV), or budgeted cost, of the project. The PV should include all costs relevant to the project, the most important of which are personnel costs, equipment and materials, and the project overhead, which is sometimes referred to as the *level of effort.* Overhead costs (level of effort) can include various fixed costs that must be included in the project's budget, including the costs for administrative or technical support, computer work, and the expertise of other staff (such as legal advice or marketing work). Establishing the project's baseline requires just two pieces of data: the work breakdown structure and a time-phased budget for the project.

KEY TERMS

Actual cost of work performed (AC)   104

Budgeted cost at completion (BAC)   104

Cost performance index (CPI)   104

Earned value (EV)   104

Planned value (PV)   104

Schedule performance index (SPI)   104

Time-phased budget   105

DISCUSSION AND REVIEW QUESTIONS

1. Under what circumstances should you consider crashing a project's activities? What activities are the best candidates for crashing? When should you stop crashing the activities?

2. Why is it helpful to consider the variance of each activity in a project? Why do "large" variances create a problem for the project manager's estimation efforts?

3. What are the flaws of using S-curves to determine the "true" status of an ongoing project?

4. Why do you need to take "value" into consideration when determining the status of a project?

5. Why are SPI and CPI values important for the organization when determining a project's status?

6. The federal government requires the organizations it contracts with for projects to provide regular SPI and CPI updates for them. The government likes to see values close to 1.0 for these indexes. What does a 1.0 value suggest?

SOLVED PROBLEMS

1. Assume you are managing a project with the following information:

Activity	Predecessor	Optimistic Time (a)	Most Likely Time (m)	Pessimistic Time (b)
A	–	2	5	8
B	A	5	6	10
C	A	2	4	6
D	B,C	4	7	15
E	D	3	4	8
F	C	2	3	6
G	F	4	5	9
H	E,G	1	2	5

a. Construct the network diagram for this project.

b. What is the project's expected duration? What is the standard deviation of each activity?

c. Estimate the probability of finishing the project in 28 days or less.

d. You learn you can receive a significant bonus if the project finishes on day 25. What is the probability of this occurring?

e. To provide your top managers with a 95% assurance of finishing on time, how long should the project's duration be?

Solution

a. Construct the network diagram for this project.

FIGURE 3S.8 Network Diagram for Solved Problem #1

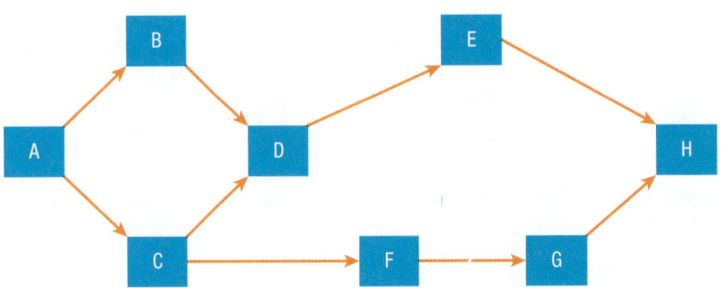

b. **What is the project's expected duration? What is the standard deviation of each activity?** Remember that the formula for determining a project's expected duration is:

$$TE = (a + 4m + b) / 6$$

where

TE = estimated time for activity
a = most optimistic time to complete the activity
m = most likely time to complete the activity, the mode of the distribution
b = most pessimistic time to complete the activity

We also know that the formula for determining the standard deviation of an activity is:

$$s = \text{square root } [1 / 6(b - a)]^2, \text{ where } b \text{ is the most pessimistic time and } a \text{ is the most optimistic}$$

Thus, the expected duration and standard deviation for each activity are:

Activity	Expected Duration	Standard Deviation
A	5	1.0
B	6.5	0.83
C	4.0	0.67
D	7.83	1.83
E	4.5	0.83
F	3.33	0.67
G	5.5	0.83
H	2.33	0.67

Next, we compute the expected duration and standard deviation for the longest path through the network. The network diagram shows three paths:

(1) A – B – D – E – H;
(2) A – C – D – E – H;
(3) A – C – F – G – H.

The critical path in Figure 3S.8 is A – B – D – E – H:

$$\text{Length} = 5.0 + 6.5 + 7.83 + 4.5 + 2.33 = 26.16 \text{ days}$$
$$\sigma_p = \text{square root } (\Sigma \text{ activity variances}_{path}) = \text{square root } (1.0^2 + 0.83^2 + 1.83^2 + 0.83^2 + 0.67^2) = 2.49 \text{ days}$$

c. **Estimate the probability of finishing the project in 28 days or less.**

We can now calculate the Z score for the critical path as:

$$Z = (\text{Target due date} - \text{Expected date of completion}) / \sigma_p = (28 - 26.16) / 2.49, \text{ or } 0.74$$

We can now use a normal distribution table (see Appendix A) to determine that a Z value of 0.74 indicates a probability of 0.7704. Thus, there is a 77% chance that our project will finish on or before the critical date of 28 weeks.

d. **You learn you can receive a significant bonus if the project finishes on day 25. What is the probability of this occurring?**

$$Z = \text{(Target due date} - \text{Expected date of completion)} / \sigma_p = (25 - 26.16) / 2.49, \text{ or } -0.47$$

The minus sign indicates that we have a less than 50% chance of finishing this critical path in 25 days or less. Using the normal distribution table (see Appendix A), a Z score for the positive value of 0.47 is approximately .68. For a negative value, we find the probability of finishing on or earlier than day 25 as $1 - 0.68 = 0.32$, or 32%.

e. **To provide your top managers with a 95% assurance of finishing on time, how long should the project's duration be?**

$$\begin{aligned}
\text{Due Date} &= \text{Expected date of completion} + (Z \times \sigma_p) \\
&= 26.16 \text{ days} + (1.65 \times 2.49) \\
&= 30.27 \text{ days}
\end{aligned}$$

2. Suppose you are considering crashing a project. The project's network diagram is as follows, along with a table identifying the critical activities, and the crash costs for all tasks.

    a. What is the cost of the project?

    b. Which activities are the best candidates for crashing?

    c. What is the expected duration of the project once it has been fully crashed?

    d. What will the cost of the fully crashed project be?

FIGURE 3S.9 Network Diagram for Solved Problem #2

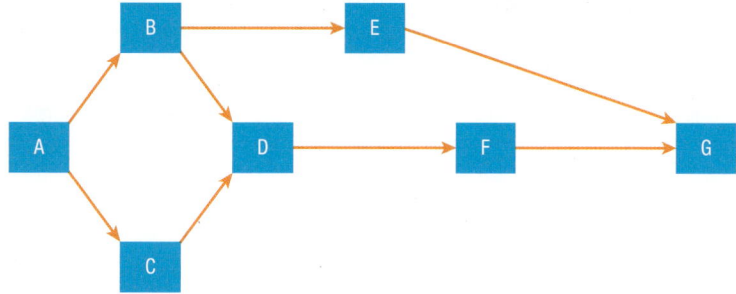

Solution

a. **What is the cost of the project?**

The critical path is A – B – D – F – G. As currently planned, the project will cost $16,300 and will take 26 days to complete.

Project Activities and Costs (Normal vs. Crashed)

Activity	Normal		Crashed	
	Duration	Cost (in U.S. dollars)	Duration	Cost (in U.S. dollars)
A	4 days	1,000	3 days	2,000
B	6 days	1,800	3 days	3,000
C	4 days	2,500	3 days	4,000
D	9 days	2,700	6 days	6,500
E	8 days	2,400	6 days	4,500
F	5 days	3,500	3 days	7,000
G	2 days	2,400	1 days	3,000
Total costs =		$16,300		$30,000

The Costs of Crashing Each Activity

Activity	Crashing Costs (per day in U.S. dollars)	On Critical Path?
A	1,000	Yes
B	400	Yes
C	1,500	No

Activity	Crashing Costs (per day in U.S. dollars)	On Critical Path?
D	1,267	Yes
E	1,050	No
F	1,750	Yes
G	600	Yes

b. **Which activities are the best candidates for crashing?**

The cheapest activities to crash are B ($400 per day) and G ($600 per day). Fully crashing each of these activities would bring the project's length to 22 day. Nevertheless, note that there are only 2 slack days associated with activity C. That means that after crashing activity B for 2 days, activity C is now also part of the critical path. To crash an additional day from activity B, it will also be necessary to crash activity C by one day. Activity C's crash cost per day is $1,500. Thus, crashing the project to save 4 days will require crashing activity B (3 days), activity C (1 day), and activity G (1 day). The total cost for crashing these activities is $3,300, increasing the project's budget to $19,600.

c. **What is the expected duration of the project once it has been fully crashed?**

Fully crashing each activity on the critical path will result in a project duration of 16 days and two joint critical paths: A – B – D – F – G and A – C – D – F – G.

d. **What will the cost of the fully crashed project be?**

The total cost of crashing these activities is $27,900. The only task that's not crashed is activity E. It's a noncritical activity, so crashing it would only add to the costs of the project.

3. Assume you are working on a one-year project with a budget of $125,000. Approximately four months into the project, you have been asked to assess its status and likely schedule and cost values upon completion. To date, you have generated the following information about the project (all cost data are in thousands of U.S. dollars):

Activity	Jan.	Feb.	Mar.	Apr.	Plan	% C	Value
Survey	3				3	100	
Clear	2	3			5	100	
Foundation		4	2		6	50	
Frame			6	4	10	20	
Finish				10	10		
Mo. Plan	5	7	8	14			
Cumul.	5	12	20	34			
Mo. Actual	6	10	10	16			
Cumul.	6	16	26	42			

a. Calculate the project's earned value (EV), planned value (PV), and actual cost (AC), and add the values to the table.

b. Given the data collected as of the end of April, calculate the schedule performance index (SPI) and the cost performance index (CPI). What does this information tell you about the final cost of the project and its likely completion date?

Solution

a. **Calculate the project's earned value (EV), planned value (PV), and actual cost (AC), and add the values to the table.**

The completed table shows that the EV as of the end of April was $13,000. The PV was $34,000, and the AC was $42,000.

Activity	Jan.	Feb.	Mar.	Apr.	Plan	% C	Value
Survey	3				3	100	3
Clear	2	3			5	100	5
Foundation		4	2		6	50	3
Frame			6	4	10	20	2
Finish				10	10		
					$\Sigma = 34$		$\Sigma = 13$
Mo. Plan	5	7	8	14			
Cumul.	5	12	20	34			
Mo. Actual	6	10	10	16			
Cumul.	6	16	26	42			

a. Given the data collected as of the end of April, calculate the schedule performance index (SPI) and the cost performance index (CPI). What does this information tell you about the final cost of the project and its likely completion date?

$$SPI = EV / PV = \$13{,}000 / \$34{,}000 = .38$$
$$CPI = EV / AC = \$13{,}000 / \$42{,}000 = .31$$

We use this information to calculate the estimated time to completion as:

$$(1 / .38 \times 12) = 31.58 \text{ months}$$

The estimated cost to completion is found by:

$$(1 / .31 \times \$125{,}000) = \$403{,}226$$

Unfortunately, based on the EV information you have acquired, this project is almost 20 months late and nearly $280,000 over budget.

PROBLEMS

1. You have a project with an expected completion time of 15 weeks and a project variance of 4 weeks.

    a. What is the probability the project will be completed in 12 weeks?

    b. What is the probability the project will be completed in 15 weeks?

    c. What is the probability the project will be completed in 18 weeks?

    d. If your investors need 95% probability assurance, what is the due date that yields this 95% likelihood of completion?

2. You and your father have taken on the project of remodeling your basement to turn it into a "mother-in-law" apartment for your relatives. You have calculated that you expect to complete the project in 68 days. Because your deliveries from suppliers are uncertain, you have had to assume a project variance of 21 days.

    a. What is the probability the project will be completed in 50 days?

    b. What is the probability the project will be completed in 70 days?

    c. What is the probability the project will be completed in 90 days?

    d. What is the due date that yields a 99% probability of completion?

3. Suppose for problem 2, you found a new supplier who could guarantee deliveries, allowing you to change project variance to 9 days.

    a. Recalculate the probabilities of finishing the project in 50, 70, and 90 days.

    b. What is the due date in this circumstance that will yield a 99% probability of completion?

4. You have a project with the following information:

Time Estimates (week)

Activity	Optimistic	Most Likely	Pessimistic	Immediate Predecessor(s)
A	1	4	7	—
B	2	6	7	—
C	3	3	6	B
D	6	13	14	A
E	3	6	12	A, C
F	6	8	16	B
G	1	5	6	D, E, F

a. Calculate each activity's expected duration (TE) and variance. Which activities have the greatest variance?

b. Create a network for this project. What is the expected duration?

c. What is the expected duration if we require a probability of 90% that the project will be completed on time?

5. The following table shows the time information for the activities needed to develop an ad campaign.

    a. Calculate the expected activity times (round to nearest integer).

    b. Calculate the slack for each activity. What is the project's total length? Make sure you fully label all nodes in the network.

    c. Identify the critical path. What are the alternative paths, and how much slack time is associated with each feeder path?

    d. Identify the burst activities and merge activities.

    e. Given the activity variances, what is the likelihood of finishing the project on week 24?

    f. Suppose you want to be 99% sure the project will finish on time. How many additional weeks would your project team need to ensure this likelihood?

Time Estimates (week)

Activity	Optimistic	Most Likely	Pessimistic	Immediate Predecessor(s)
A	1	4	7	—
B	2	6	10	—
C	3	3	9	B
D	6	13	14	A
E	4	6	14	A, C
F	6	8	16	B
G	2	5	8	D, E, F

6. Use the following information to determine the probability of the project finishing within 34 weeks of its scheduled completion date. Assume activities A – B – D – F – G are on the project's critical path:

Activity	Optimistic	Likely	Pessimistic	Expected Time	Variance
A	1	4	8		
B	3	5	9		
C	4	6	10		
D	3	7	15		
E	5	10	16		
F	3	6	15		
G	4	7	12		

a. Calculate the expected durations for each activity.

b. Calculate individual activity variances as well as the variance for the overall project.

c. What is the likelihood that the project will be finished by week 34?

d. If you wanted to be 99% confident of delivering the project on time, how much additional time would you need to add to the schedule?

7. An advertising project manager has developed a program for a new advertising campaign. In addition, the manager has gathered the time information for each activity, as shown in the following table:

Time Estimates (week)

Activity	Optimistic	Most Likely	Pessimistic	Immediate Predecessor(s)
A	1	4	7	—
B	2	6	10	—
C	3	3	9	B
D	6	13	14	A
E	4	6	14	A, C
F	6	8	16	B
G	2	5	8	D, E, F

a. Calculate the expected activity times (round to nearest integer).

b. Calculate the activity slacks. What is the total project length? Make sure you fully label all nodes in the network.

c. Identify the critical path. What are the alternative paths, and how much slack time is associated with each noncritical path?

d. Identify the burst activities and the merge activities.

e. Given the activity variances, what is the likelihood of the project finishing on week 24?

f. Suppose you wanted to have a 99% confidence in the project finishing on time. How many additional weeks would your project team need to negotiate for to gain this 99% likelihood?

8. You are deciding whether to crash your project. After asking your operations manager to conduct an analysis, you have determined the "precrash" and "postcrash" activity durations and costs, which are shown in the following table (assume *all* of the activities are on the critical path):

	Normal		Crashed	
Activity	Duration	Cost (in U.S. dollars)	Duration	Cost (in U.S. dollars)
A	4 days	1,000	3 days	2,000
B	5 days	2,500	3 days	5,000
C	3 days	750	2 days	1,200
D	7 days	3,500	5 days	5,000
E	2 days	500	1 day	2,000
F	5 days	2,000	4 days	3,000
G	9 days	4,500	7 days	6,300

a. Calculate the per day costs for crashing each activity.

b. Which activities are the best candidates for crashing? Why?

9. Suppose you are deciding on whether to crash a project's activities and you have the following information:

Activity	Predecessors	Duration
A	—	4
B	A	5
C	A	2
D	B	6
E	D	3
F	C	8
G	E,F	7

You also have the following cost information about the activities:

	Normal		Crashed	
Activity	Cost (in U.S. dollars)	Duration	Extra Cost (in U.S. dollars)	Duration
A	5,000	4 weeks	4,000	3 weeks
B	10,000	5 weeks	3,000	4 weeks
C	3,500	2 weeks	5,500	1 week
D*	4,500	6 weeks	4,000	4 weeks
E*	1,500	3 weeks	2,500	2 weeks
F	7,500	8 weeks	5,000	7 weeks
G*	3,000	7 weeks	2,500	6 weeks

a. Construct the project's network. What is the project's duration? What activities have slack time? What is the critical path?

b. Identify the sequencing of the activities to be crashed in the first four steps. Which critical activities should be crashed first? Why?

c. After four iterations involving crashing project activities, what has the critical path shrunk to?

d. Assume that a project penalty clause kicks in after 19 weeks. The penalty charged is $5,000 per week after 19 weeks. How would this information affect your decision to crash the project?

10. Using the following data, complete the table by calculating the planned and actual monthly budgets through the end of June. Complete the earned value column on the right. Assume the project is supposed to take 12 months and cost $250,000:

Activity	Jan.	Feb.	Mar.	Apr.	May	Jun	Plan	%C	Value
Staffing	8	7					15	100	_____
Blueprinting		4	6				10	100	_____
Prototype Development			2	8			10	70	_____
Full Design				3	8	10	21	67	_____
Construction					2	30	32	25	_____
Transfer						10	10	0	_____
Monthly Plan									
Cumulative									
Monthly Actual	10	15	6	14	9	40			
Cumul. Actual									

11. Using the data from Problem 10, calculate the following values:

Schedule Variances		Cost Variances	
Planned Value (PV)	_____	Actual Cost of Work Performed (AC)	_____
Earned Value (EV)	_____	Earned Value (EV)	_____
Schedule Performance Index	_____	Cost Performance Index	_____
Estimated Time to Completion	_____	Estimated Cost to Completion	_____

12. Use the following table to calculate project schedule variance based on the units listed (figures are in thousands of U.S. dollars):

Schedule Variance	A	B	C	D	E	F	Total
Planned Value	20	15	10	25	20	20	110
Earned Value	25	10	10	20	25	15	
Schedule Variance							

13. Using the following data, complete the table by calculating the planned and actual monthly budgets through the end of April. Complete the earned value column on the right and the rows for cumulative planned and actual expenditures. Assume the project is supposed to take 9 months and cost $100,000. All figures are in thousands ($).

Activity	Jan	Feb	Mar	Apr	Plan	% C	Value
Clearing	2	2			4	100	_____
Leveling	1	4			5	100	_____
Drainage		2	3		5	80	_____
Paving			1	5	6	50	_____
Construction				12	12	50	_____
Monthly Plan							
Cumulative							
Monthly Actual	3	9	5	20			
Cumul. Actual							

a. Using the data from Problem 13, calculate the following values:

Schedule Variances	
Planned Value (PV)	_____
Earned Value (EV)	_____
Schedule Performance Index	_____
Estimated Time to Completion	_____

b. Cost Variances

Cost Variances	
Actual Cost of Work Performed (AC)	_____
Earned Value (EV)	_____
Cost Performance Index	_____
Estimated Cost to Completion	_____

14. You are calculating the estimated time to completion for a project of 15 months' duration and a budgeted cost of $350,000. Assuming the following information, calculate the Schedule Performance Index and the estimated time to completion (figures are in thousands of U.S dollars):

Schedule Variances	
Planned Value (PV)	65
Earned Value (EV)	58
Schedule Performance Index	_____
Estimated Cost to Completion	_____

15. Suppose, for Problem 14, that your PV was 75 and your EV was 80. Recalculate the SPI and estimated time to completion for the project with this new data.

CHAPTER
4

Product and
Service Innovations

LEARNING OBJECTIVES

After studying this chapter, you should be able to:

1 Explain why new product development is vital for organizations.

2 Describe the approaches companies use to develop new products.

3 Demonstrate how new strategies have improved the way in which new products are designed and tested.

4 Discuss some new technologies that have allowed for faster new product development.

5 Explain the global product-development process, and describe how organizations are increasingly using it to gain a strategic advantage.

6 Describe how the collaboration of the members of a supply chain can improve product development.

7 Identify the unique challenges service organizations face when designing their products, including the tools and methods they use to do so.

8 Discuss some of the legal, ethical, and sustainability issues that affect firms developing new products and services.

OPERATIONS PROFILE: Developing New Products and Services in the Pet Industry

Americans love their pets. According to the latest estimates, 73 million homes have at least one pet, and these pet owners spend about US$50 billion annually on food and supplies, grooming services, veterinary care, and medicines for their animals. Moreover, the amount spent is growing.

Companies such as Nestlé S.A. (Vevey, Switzerland), Ralph Lauren Corporation (New York, NY), and P&G (Procter & Gamble Co., Cincinnati, OH), as well as thousands of smaller firms, are all eager to satisfy our desire to pamper our pets by producing new products and offering services for them. The products range from treats that resemble human snacks to Hermès (Hermès International SCA, Paris, France) collars encrusted with diamonds. The pet-products retailer PetSmart, Inc. (Phoenix, AZ) even offers doggy day care and pet hotels. Pet owners on their way to work can simply drop off their pets for day care services or for extended stays when going out of town. Dogs sleep on raised platform beds, and they can watch TV shows on the cable channel Animal Planet (Discovery Communications, Silver Spring, MD). Cats get live fish tanks to watch in their rooms, which have separate air-filtration systems, so the scents of dogs and cats do not mix and cause agitation. Meanwhile, other companies are offering day care and pet-sitting services for owners who feel guilty about the amount of time they spend at work or away from their pets.

Other new products and services offered for pet owners:

- **Natural foods and products to reduce a pet's carbon "paw" print.** From natural litters to toys, accessories, and organic food options, earth-friendly pet products are alternatives to more traditional pet foods and products.
- **Human products reformulated for pets.** Companies traditionally known for human products are going to the dogs, and cats, and reptiles. Big name companies such as Paul Mitchell (John Paul Mitchell Systems, Beverly Hills, CA); Omaha Steaks (Omaha Steaks International, Inc., Omaha, NE); Harley Davidson, Inc. (aka Harley, Milwaukee, WI); and Old Navy (subsidiary of Gap, Inc., San Francisco, CA) are now offering lines of pet products ranging from dog shampoo, to pet attire, to name-brand toys, to gourmet treats and food.
- **Pet accommodations.** Several hotel chains across the country have announced new pet-friendly policies and provide everything from oversized pet pillows, to plush doggie robes, to check-in gift packages that include a pet toy, dog treat, ID tag, bone, and turn-down treat. Some hotels even have a licensed dog masseuse on staff.
- **Pet products in stores for other goods and services.** Shopping for pet products is becoming easier than ever with an increasing variety of retail outlets now selling pet products. Shoppers can now find pet products such as doggie doors and yellow lawn spot removers at many lawn and garden stores, nurseries, and major home improvement stores such as The Home Depot, Inc. (Atlanta, GA).
- **Grooming and cleaning supplies.** Pet owners are taking grooming to new levels. Mouthwash and electric toothbrushes for canines have become routine steps in their beauty sessions. To keep the homes of pet owners cleaner, products such as self-flushing litter boxes, cleaning cloths for muddy paws that mimic traditional baby wipes, and scented gel air fresheners to keep rooms free of pet odors have made their way into the marketplace.
- **Computerized accessories.** High-tech products such as computerized identification tags, digital aquarium kits, automatic doors and feeders, enhanced reptile terrarium lighting systems, and touch-activated toys help pet owners take care of companion animals with ease and precision.
- **Convenience products.** Programmable feeding and drinking systems, automatic and battery-operated toys, and self-warming pet mats let pets practically care for themselves.
- **Wardrobe options.** Faux mink coats, hipster lumberjack vests, designer plaid jackets, matching jeweled and leather collar and leash sets, Halloween costumes, and holiday

outfits keep pets in fashion throughout the year. Upscale leather carriers complete with a cell phone and water bottle holder are the perfect accessories to keep the pet owner in style as well.

- **Travel accessories.** Whether it's a quick trip to the supermarket or a long ride to the beach, our household pets are now traveling animals too. Buckled up in a harness, seat-belt system, or a portable carrier, these pets stay safe and secure while on the road. Food and water along with safety supplies are on hand in all-in-one kits, waste disposal systems make for easy clean-up on quick stops, and motion sickness aids are available too.

- **Personalized gear.** From monogrammed sweaters and personalized food and water bowls to digitized collar tags and hand-made treats, owners embrace their pets as true members of the family, celebrating their fluffy, finned, and feathered companions with their very own belongings.

It seems that when it comes to spoiling "Rover," money is no object.[1]

4.1

Explain why new product development is vital for organizations.

 Product Innovation

4.1 Why Companies Develop New Products and Services

Innovative changes made to existing products can be incremental or substantial. To survive and compete, firms have to make changes to existing products and services in addition to introducing new and innovative products and services. These efforts are usually handled as projects and, therefore, require project management skills. This chapter, therefore, builds on the topic of product management discussed in Chapter 3. The skills needed to manage a product successfully are the same as those needed to develop a new product.

Broadly defined, a new product can be a tangible good, something that you can physically touch and feel, or an intangible offering, such as a service or an experience, that a company has not produced before. A new product can also be a variation of an existing product, such as a new flavor of Cherry Coke or Coke with orange (The Coca-Cola Company, Atlanta, GA) or an upgraded version of the product such as the many new versions of Apple's iPhones (Apple Inc., Cupertino, CA). In recent years, however, changes in technology have blurred the differences between products and services. Most products have a service component, and most services have a product component. For example, in most of its automobiles, General Motors (aka GM, The General Motors Company, Detroit, MI) offers the OnStar service package to aid in navigation, directions, and emergency calls. Companies therefore seek to create not simply the best products and services but also the best possible combination of products and services.

Responding to Market Challenges With New Products and Services

Companies introduce new products to improve their market share, stay ahead of the competition, and primarily, to survive in the marketplace. Businesses cannot survive if they offer the same products day in and day out. Their sales will eventually drop off, and their revenues and profits will erode.

The Virgin Group Ltd. (London, U.K.) is a company that has continued to reinvent itself as its market has evolved. Its first business was in the record (music) industry in the 1970s. To stay vital and enter new markets, the company has created a huge number of products and services and subsidiaries to produce them. These subsidiaries include Virgin Airlines, Virgin Cola, Virgin Wine, Virgin Radio, Virgin Megastores, Virgin Telecommunications, and Virgin Spa. Also, from the perspective of an individual company, when we say new products, these products may not necessarily be new to the market but are definitely new to the company. Within the fast-food industry, McDonald's (Oak Brook, IL), in addition to its existing burgers, frequently offers and markets new burgers.

Companies introduce new products and services to meet changing consumer needs and to adapt to changes in the product's life cycle. Leading companies, such as Motorola (Motorola Solutions, Inc. Schaumburg, IL),

The businesses the Virgin Group has expanded into over the past four decades are vast.

Bloomberg/Bloomberg/Getty Images

Toyota (Toyota Motor Corporation, Toyota City, Japan), Abbott Laboratories (Lake Bluff, IL), 3M (3M Company, Maplewood, MN), and American Express (American Express Company, New York, NY), view new product development as an ongoing, proactive process. They don't wait until their products become obsolete or their competitors introduce newer, better products. Instead, proactive firms always look to stay ahead of the competition, allocate resources to anticipate market changes, and seize on new product opportunities in response to these changes.

CHANGING CONSUMER TASTES

Consumer tastes change over time, and businesses need to respond proactively to these changing needs. Food packages display terms such as "natural," "organic," and "healthy" more prominently now than in the past. That's because consumers are becoming health conscious and are demanding healthy food products. These consumer preferences are forcing companies in the food industry to make significant changes, such as introducing products that are low in sugar and fat content. The Coca-Cola Company responded to these changes in consumer tastes by launching Coca-Cola Zero, which has a low-sugar content, as well as by promoting Dasani bottled water, one of the fastest growing consumer beverage segments in the marketplace. Changes in demographics such as consumers' ages, locations, or ethnicities can also encourage the introduction of new products or variations of existing products. For example, the development of fitness trackers like Fitbit (Fitbit, Inc., San Francisco, CA), Jawbone (San Francisco, CA), Misfit (Fossil Group, Inc., Richardson, TX), and Garmin (Garmin Ltd., Schaffhausen, Switzerland) are a result of the expanded interest in using technology to monitor health and activity levels among fitness enthusiasts.[2]

CHANGES IN THE STAGES OF THE LIFE CYCLES OF PRODUCTS

In Chapter 2, we described the stages in a product's life cycle: introduction, growth, maturity, and decline. Figure 4.1 shows the stages and examples of products in each stage. Although the time frame of a product's life cycle can vary, the pattern remains the same: Slow sales growth when the product is first introduced, then rapid sales growth as the product is more widely accepted and used, followed by mature or steady sales, and eventually decline. Table 4.1 lists the marketing and operational and supply chain implications for each stage.

 Product Life Cycles

As a result of technological and consumer taste changes, the life-cycle stages of products are becoming shorter. Wooden wagon wheels and buggy whips were great-selling products for centuries. By contrast, black-and-white televisions, turntables, and vinyl records all had relatively shorter life cycles (although vinyl records are now becoming more popular again). Some people argue that LCD and plasma flat-screen TVs are already entering the decline stage and will soon be replaced by multimedia online PC/TVs.

Because products are reaching the decline stage more quickly, companies are under pressure to introduce new products or updated and improved versions of the old ones to stimulate sales. For example, Microsoft (Microsoft Corporation, Redmond, WA) introduced the Xbox 360—an improved version of the original Xbox. Sony (Sony Corporation, Tokyo, Japan) revised its original PlayStation by producing a smaller version called PSOne and a slimmer, more powerful version called PlayStation 3.

CHANGES IN TECHNOLOGY

Advances in technology can enable companies to stay ahead of the competition and avoid product obsolescence by giving them strategic opportunities to introduce new products and services that are less expensive and of better quality. For example, miniaturization technology enabled Sony to produce and market a whole new class of portable consumer electronics such as radios, cassette tape recorders, the Sony Walkman, and CD players.

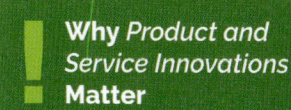

Why *Product and Service Innovations* **Matter**

To remain relevant and competitive in their markets, companies need to introduce innovative new products and services and to update existing products and services to meet their customers' needs. Successful operations managers possess the skills needed to develop, manage, and successfully launch a new product or service.

FIGURE 4.1: Four Products and Four Stages of the Product Life Cycle

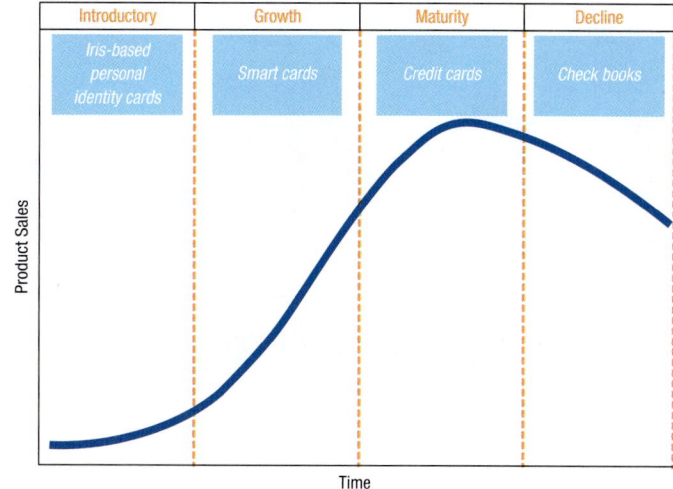

TABLE 4.1: Product Life Cycle Stages

STAGE	KEY FEATURES	EXAMPLES
Introductory	**Marketing aspects:** Demand is low and sporadic; emphasis is on generating awareness and developing a market for the product. **Operational and supply chain aspects:** Frequent changes in the product's design occur; the focus is on flexibility and quality; product's distribution is through a few select outlets.	3-D televisions, iris-based personal identity cards, and holographic projection devices
Growth	**Marketing aspects:** Demand growth is strong; competition intensifies; the focus is on increasing the product's market share. **Operational and supply chain aspects:** More product features are added; improving the product's quality and reducing its cost becomes more important; the product is distributed through a greater number and variety of outlets to make it more accessible.	Organic foods, smart cards, and tablet PCs
Maturity	**Marketing aspects:** Demand for the product levels off; the emphasis is on preserving market share and maximizing the profits from the product. **Operational and supply chain aspects:** The product is increasingly standardized; the emphasis is on the cost and availability of the product; a mass-market distribution strategy using all channels is typically used.	DVD players, credit cards, and laptops
Decline	**Marketing aspects:** Demand for the product declines; options include finding new uses or a new market for the product, lowering its costs, or discontinuing the product. **Operational and supply chain aspects:** An increasing emphasis is placed on cost reduction; supply chain relationships are critical to getting retail shelf space to continue to market the product.	Videocassette recorders, checkbooks, and hair curlers

AN EFFORT TO ACHIEVE BUSINESS GROWTH

One of the major reasons that companies introduce new products is the desire to grow their businesses. By successfully introducing new products into the market as the Virgin Group has done, companies can expand their customer bases, increase their sales and revenue, and earn higher profits. For example, after Novatel Wireless, Inc. (San Diego, CA) introduced a new PC card, called the Express Card, in 2006, the product quickly generated more than US$80 million for the company. In addition, by introducing new products, a company can penetrate previously untapped customer markets. Consider the Egg McMuffin. The sandwich was created in 1972 by the operator of a Santa Barbara McDonald's franchise who wanted to tap into the breakfast market. (McDonald's didn't have a breakfast menu at the time.) The huge success of the Egg McMuffin, which made the breakfast sandwich an integral part of the entire fast food industry, shows how new products launched on a small scale can quickly permeate a market.

The Sony Walkman was the first portable audio cassette player of its kind when it was introduced in 1979, and considered revolutionary. Only in 2010 did Sony finally discontinue the product.

Carl Court/Staff/Getty Images News/ Getty Images

CHANGES IN LEGAL AND REGULATORY REQUIREMENTS

Companies may also introduce new products or change the design of existing products to meet new legal and regulatory requirements imposed by government agencies such as the U.S. Food and Drug Administration (FDA) and the Environmental Protection Agency (EPA). For example, the U.S. Clean Air Act of 1963 (amended 1970, 1977, and 1990) has forced many automobile manufacturers to redesign cars to reduce the emission of harmful gases. Similarly, the ban on the use of materials such as asbestos, phosphates, and carcinogenic chemicals has forced companies to redesign existing products or come up with alternative designs for new products. In response to a new legal requirement in California, Coca-Cola and Pepsi (PepsiCo Inc., Purchase, NY) have asked their suppliers of the caramel coloring used in their colas to alter their manufacturing processes to reduce the amount of a carcinogenic chemical called 4-methylimidazole, or 4-MI.

Why Do New Products Fail?

Although to some extent the success of a new product may result from good luck and timing, invariably, a significant portion of the success is owed to:[3]

Product Failure

- Meticulous planning based on a thorough understanding of the market and the needs of customers.
- A solid price–value relationship; that is, the product is perceived by the buying public to offer good value for the price it has to pay for it.
- The skillful management of the product's development, sales, and marketing.

All too often, however, one or more of these factors is lacking. The project, therefore, isn't executed properly, and the product fails. Although there is no consensus on the percentage of new products that fail (the number probably varies from industry to industry), it is likely that more than 85% of them do. Stories about products introduced with considerable fanfare but that failed miserably are commonplace. Microsoft's Zune mp3 player was an example of such a product. It was developed to challenge Apple's iPod but never gained wide acceptance in the marketplace because it wasn't as easy to use and couldn't be linked with Apple's massive iTunes catalog. A classic example of a new product failure was McDonalds' McAfrika burger, which was launched in 2002. The McAfrika contained beef, cheese, tomatoes, and salad in a pita-like sandwich. Introduced in South Africa, critics suggested that the name alone demonstrated insensitivity. In addition, the product was brought to market at a time when South Africa was suffering through a string of famines, which made it even more of a public relations disaster. The burger was quickly withdrawn from the market.[4]

Yet another example of a new product that failed was the personal data assistant (PDA) device called Newton, which Apple introduced in 1993. Not only was this product expensive (at more than US$700), it was bulky, finicky, and had bugs. Even though the Apple Newton faded away, it did pave the way for the PalmPilot (Palm Inc., Sunnyvale, CA) in the late 1990s and eventually to the popular iPhones and other smartphones available now.

There are many reasons that new products can fail. The following list identifies some causes of failure:

- **Misunderstanding the target market.** A clear understanding of the product's **target market**, the potential set of consumers who might buy it, is vital to creating and launching a successful new product. Without knowing exactly who your potential consumers are, the chances are great you will develop, market, and sell the product in the wrong way. For example, the buying behavior of consumers who buy running shoes varies widely: There are consumers who buy running shoes instead of sneakers, there are consumers who refuse to pay a lot of money for running shoes, and there are those who will spend a lot on them. Consequently, when Nike (Nike, Inc., Beaverton, OR), New Balance (New Balance Athletic Shoe, Inc., Boston, MA), and other apparel companies develop a running shoe they have to define their target market clearly. If they don't, chances are great the products will fail just as McDonald's Arch Deluxe did.[5]
- **Incorrect product positioning.** Proper product positioning is the placement in the market of your product relative to competing products. Positioning requires a thorough understanding of the value offered by the product and the needs of the target market. If there is a mismatch between the two, the product will not succeed. For example, marketing an imported sports car such as a Ford Focus (The Ford Motor Company, Dearborn, MI) against an Alfa Romeo (Alfa Romeo Automobiles S.p.A, Turin, Italy) would be incorrectly positioning the product in terms of both its price and the needs of the target market.
- **Mismatch between the price of the product and its perceived benefits.** If the price of the product is too high compared with the benefits or value the product can provide, then the product is doomed to failure. For example, Blue-ray technology represented an improvement over basic DVD players, with enhanced clarity of picture and sound. However, the Blue-ray price tag (for both discs and players) was so high that sales never lived up to expectations because consumers couldn't perceive the actual benefits for the much higher cost. The Keurig Kold (Keurig Green Mountain, Waterbury, VT) soda maker was introduced at a price of more than US$350, when one of its top competitors in the home-chilled beverage market, SodaStream (SodaStream International Ltd., Airport City, Israel), was selling their top model for US$80, leading many

Target market: the potential set of consumers who might buy a product

OPERATIONS MANAGEMENT: LESSONS LEARNED
Poor Product Launches—What's in a Name?

When Nike launched a new tan-and-black–colored sneaker in 2012, the Nike SB Dunk Low, the company didn't expect it to turn into an embarrassing event. Nicknamed the *Black and Tan* after the popular alcoholic beverage of the same name, the shoe was introduced around the St. Patrick's Day holiday. One widely circulated ad noted, "'Tis the season for Irish beer and why not celebrate with Nike. The Black and Tan sneaker takes inspiration for the fine balancing act of a stout on top of a pale ale in a pint glass."

A firestorm soon developed. Unbeknownst to Nike, "Black and Tan" was the unofficial name for the English-backed paramilitary group the Royal Irish Constabulary Reserve Force. The group was known for its brutality toward Irish civilians in the 1920s during Ireland's Civil War. The name *Black and Tan* still evokes bitter memories for many people. One outraged Irish-American stated, "It's like calling a shoe the Al Qaeda!"

Although Nike apologized for the error in judgment, the company's ignorance about the shoe's name might not be much of an excuse. Just a few years earlier, Ben and Jerry's (Ben & Jerry's Homemade Holdings, Inc., South Burlington, VT) made a similar mistake when it launched a Black and Tan ice cream flavor. The product was quickly withdrawn after a similar media firestorm. This made Nike's decision to launch the shoe all the more bizarre. Ciaran Staunton, the president of the U.S.-based Irish Lobby for Immigration Reform, asked: "Is there no one at Nike able to Google 'Black and Tan'?"[6]

---

critics to argue that Keurig had priced itself out of the market, especially at a time when the U.S. public had moderated its demand for carbonated beverages.

- **Lack of understanding by consumers about the product's benefits.** New products often fail because customers aren't fully aware of or understand their benefits. This problem often results from the firm's failure to communicate in understandable terms the superior benefits provided by the product relative to competing products. Frequently, marketing personnel make a long laundry list of a product's features. Nevertheless, describing the product's benefits in relative terms, such as saying "this car is more fuel efficient and offers ten additional miles per gallon than other similar automobiles," are statements customers can appreciate and clearly understand. That is, it's not enough to create a great product. Companies also have to train their marketing and sales personnel to understand the product and its benefits so they can better educate and serve the potential buyers of it. For example, the Apple Watch is facing an uncertain future as consumers struggle to make sense of the small face, limited functions, and difficult-to-use display. Additionally, most people now wear watches as a fashion statement, rather than for their time-telling function. Thus, Apple is promoting a new product to consumers who are vague about its true purpose. After a gaudy introduction, sales have quickly leveled off and numerous industry analysts have suggested that the Apple Watch may end up an expensive failure.[7]

- **Poor product or service design.** Many companies spend thousands of dollars developing and marketing new products only to find out that consumers have completely rejected them because the products were poorly designed. One of the worst instances of a product failure was the Björk-Shiley synthetic heart valve (invented by American engineer Donald Shiley and Swedish heart surgeon Viking Björk), which tended to clog over time. Even after it was redesigned, the valve experienced problems. Unfortunately, the manufacturer ignored the early warning signs, which resulted in several hundred unnecessary deaths.[8]

- **Inadequate infrastructure and ancillary services.** To be successful, many products depend on infrastructures or ancillary services. For example, a company that designs a high-end, video-conferencing system should ensure that a dedicated, high-bandwidth network is in place when connecting the system in the customer's headquarters and remote offices. If this infrastructure does not exist, the video being broadcast will be interrupted frequently, and the product is not likely to be successful. The infrastructure provided by a supply chain can also be critical to the success of a new product. For example, the long-term success of vehicles that run on hydrogen fuel will likely depend on supply chain decisions about how and where hydrogen can be delivered to fuel the cars.[9] Likewise, the buyers of some products may need special training to use them to realize their full benefits. The firms that make these products either need to provide the infrastructure or services directly to customers or to contract with other firms to do so.

Types of Innovation

Broadly speaking, firms can choose between sustaining and disruptive innovations. A sustaining innovation is targeted toward an existing market and can be either radical or incremental. A *radical innovation* is a new product or solution associated with products in existing markets. Radical innovations do not, however, create new markets. Amazon.com (Seattle, WA) radically changed the way in which books are sold. Yet, there was a market for books long before Amazon began selling them. An *incremental innovation,* by contrast, is an improvement to an already existing product. Like radical innovations, incremental innovations do not create substantially new markets. For example, even though fuel-injectors have replaced carburetors in car engines, they did not create an entirely new automobile market.

A disruptive innovation is a product or service that takes root initially in simple applications, typically at the low end of a market. The innovation then gains momentum and moves up to the higher end of the market, eventually displacing established competitors. Unlike sustaining innovations, disrupting innovations create new and often unexpected markets because they offer a totally new set of value propositions. The digital file-sharing of music is an example of a disruptive innovation. Record companies abandoned single records in the 1990s, leaving customers with no way to purchase individual songs. This situation led to the development of peer-to-peer, song-sharing technologies that were initially free but were later taken over by digital content providers such as Apple's iTunes store and Amazon.com. This disruptive innovation has drastically undermined the sales of more expensive CDs. Other examples of disruptive innovations include cellular phones, community colleges, discount retailers, and medical clinics in retail stores. These products or services have gained popularity at the expense of landline telephones, four-year colleges, full-service department stores, and traditional doctors' offices.[10]

4.2 How New Products Are Developed

The Product Development Management Association defines new product development (NPD) as "the overall process of strategy, organization, concept generation, product and marketing plan creation and evaluation, and commercialization of a new product."[11] New product development is part of an overall strategic process known as product lifecycle management (PLM). PLM is a strategic, company-wide business approach that spans all aspects of a product's life cycle and its supply chain. It covers everything from the origination of the concept for the product, its design, sourcing of its components, testing, manufacturing, delivery, and service to improvements to the product based on how customers responded to it. PLM integrates people, processes, and information throughout the firm and along the supply chain. Figure 4.2 is a representation of the of PLM process.[12]

PLM has two uses, and they shouldn't be confused. The additional use is often referred to as product life-cycle management and abbreviated as PLCM. PLM focuses on managing the engineering aspects of a product throughout its useful life. In contrast, PLCM is a marketing concept that refers to managing the business side of the product during its life cycle, particularly its costs and sales performance. As an example of PLCM, companies may use various tactics to increase the sales of a product as they decline, which could include promotional campaigns, repackaging and redesigning the old product, reducing its price, and launching it in new markets. Consider the Toyota Qualis, which was originally launched in 1977. The Qualis was close to becoming obsolete in 1985 when it was redesigned for a third time. Nevertheless, when the automobile was launched in India, a new market, in 1986, it was a huge success until 2004.

There are several approaches to new product development. The two most common are (1) the traditional

Sustaining innovation: a product or service targeted toward an existing market that can be radical or incremental in nature

Disruptive innovation: a product or service that creates new and often unexpected markets through offering a totally new set of value propositions

New product development (NPD): the overall process of strategy, organization, concept generation, product and marketing plan creation and evaluation, and commercialization of a new product

4.2
Describe the approaches companies use to develop new products.

FIGURE 4.2: Product Lifecycle Management

SOURCE: Courtesy of MES Solutions Inc.

Product lifecycle management (PLM): a strategic, company-wide business approach that spans all aspects of a product's life cycle and supply chain, focusing on the engineering aspects of a product throughout its useful life

Product life-cycle management (PLCM): a marketing concept that refers to managing the business side of the product during its life cycle, particularly its costs and sales performance

approach, which begins by generating ideas for a new product and ends with its launch, or commercialization, and (2) the Stage-Gate® approach, which is a conceptual and operational road map that divides the process into distinct stages and uses cross-functional teams to move the product from one stage to the next. Let's now look at each of these approaches more closely.

The Traditional Approach to New Product Development

The traditional product development approach is shown in Figure 4.3. The actual number of steps in the process depends on the type of product and varies from company to company. The feedback loops, represented by the arrows in the figure, indicate the occasional need to return to a previous stage. For example, if no reasonable new product ideas survive the screening process, it would be necessary to return to Stage 1 to generate a new set of product ideas.

The Stage-Gate® Approach to New Product Development

Companies need to ensure that the new product development process is as rapid and efficient as possible—that is, it minimizes waste. As discussed in Chapter 3, the costs of a project can get quickly out of hand if they aren't closely managed. It has been estimated that companies waste about half of the resources allotted to the project on the conception, development, and launch of new products.

FIGURE 4.3: Traditional Approach to Developing New Products

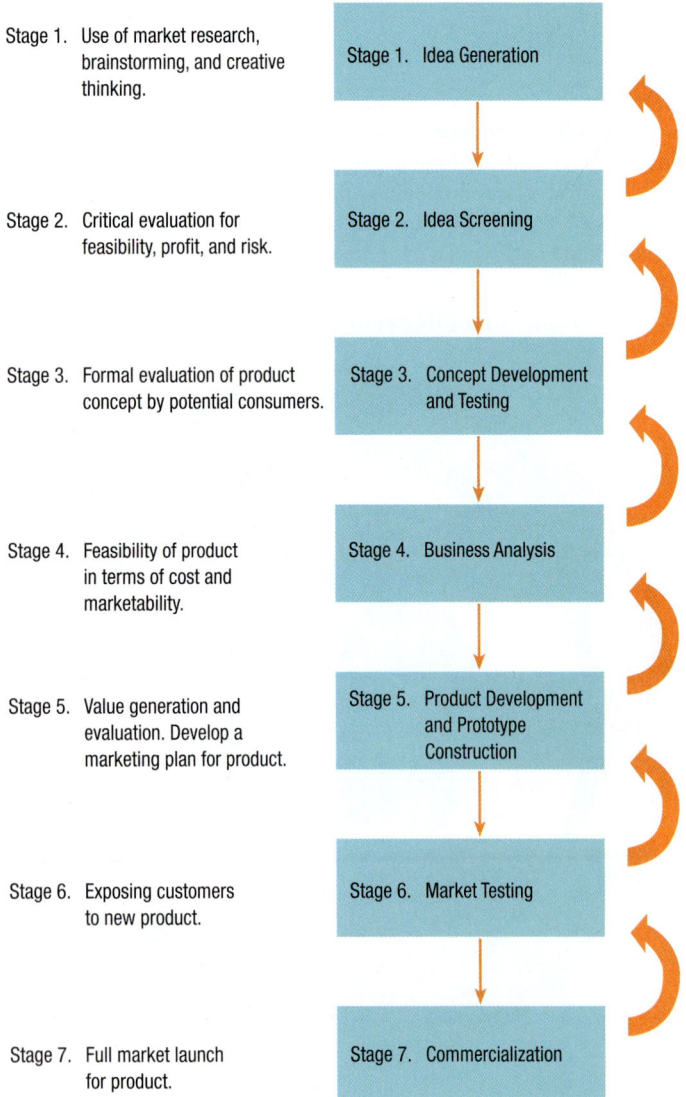

Stage 1. Use of market research, brainstorming, and creative thinking.

Stage 2. Critical evaluation for feasibility, profit, and risk.

Stage 3. Formal evaluation of product concept by potential consumers.

Stage 4. Feasibility of product in terms of cost and marketability.

Stage 5. Value generation and evaluation. Develop a marketing plan for product.

Stage 6. Exposing customers to new product.

Stage 7. Full market launch for product.

The **Stage-Gate® approach**, which is shown in Figure 4.4, is a method that helps prevent runaway, over-budget product development cycles. The stage-gate approach works like this: New projects are divided into *stages* (or *phases*), and *gates* separate consecutive stages. A *stage* refers to the critical activities that need to take place at a particular stage of the project. At each gate, a decision is made whether to continue with the project, typically by a senior manager or a steering committee. Is there still a need for the product? Are the technical challenges being overcome? Is the product's development still on time and within budget? If not, the project is kicked back to the previous stage for reconsideration and reworking. Additional resources are only allotted to the project once it has successfully completed all gate reviews after a development stage.

An estimated 70% to 85% of leading U.S. companies, including General Electric (aka GE, Fairfield, CT), now use the Stage-Gate® approach to launch their new products. A Stage-Gate® approach system designed and implemented by Nortel Networks Corporation (formerly Northern Telecom Ltd., Mississauga, Ontario, Canada), a global telecommunications equipment manufacturer, cost approximately US$1 million, but the benefits have been impressive. The company has been able to launch its new products faster, with fewer defects, and with less rework and recycling in the process.[13]

STAGE 0: DISCOVERY

The discovery stage is the first stage of any new product development project. During this stage, the new product development team collects and generates ideas for the new product. New product ideas can come from various sources, such as the firm's customers, market research and surveys, focus groups, customer service employees who listen to customers' complaints and suggestions, and the firm's suppliers and shippers, New product ideas can also be generated via **reverse engineering**, a process in which a firm dismantles a competitors' existing products to

FIGURE 4.4: Stage-Gate® Approach to Developing New Products

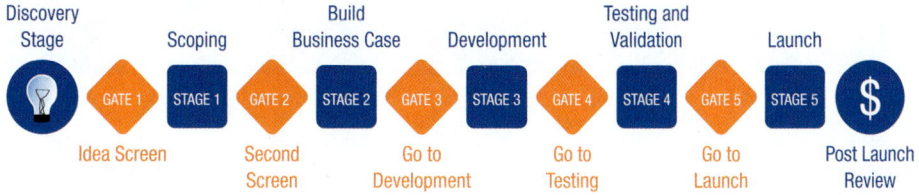

SOURCE: Adapted from Product Development Institute. (n.d.). Stage-Gate®—Your Roadmap for New Product Development. Retrieved from http://www.prod-dev.com/stage-gate.php. Stage-Gate® is a registered trademark of Stage-Gate Inc.

see how they work and whether they can be improved. The team members then decide which products their firm is capable of pursuing and choose the one that will deliver the greatest return. The product idea selected then moves to the first gate (Gate 1), where it is screened by the company's decision makers and a *Go/Kill/Hold/Recycle* decision about it is made. If the decision is to go ahead with the product idea, then an approved action plan along with a list of deliverables and date for the next gate is established.

Approaches to Product Development

STAGE 1: SCOPING

The focus of the scoping stage is to evaluate the technical merits of the product in relation to its potential target market. The team analyzes the strengths and weaknesses of the product and the value it can offer to the potential consumer. In addition, the team also identifies competing products and evaluates them. The purpose is to evaluate the threat these products pose to decide the nature of the product to be developed and how it should be positioned relative to them. As a result of these evaluations, the management team at the Gate 2 review can decide whether to proceed with the development of the new product and pass it on to the next stage.

STAGE 2: BUILD THE BUSINESS CASE FOR THE PRODUCT

Stage 2 is the most critical and, perhaps, the most difficult phase of the Stage-Gate® approach. It is the last stage of conceptualization before the actual development work on the product begins. Companies need to conduct a thorough analysis at this stage because a significant amount of resources will be expended after it. This stage includes four major processes: (1) Define and analyze the new product, (2) prepare the business-case document, (3) prepare the project plan, and (4) perform the feasibility analysis.

- **Define and analyze the new product.** In this step, the product development team will answer key questions about the proposed product: What benefits should the product provide? How does it compare with competitors' products? How will potential customers perceive its value? Through the use of surveys and market analysis, the firm identifies the potential markets for the product and can assess how consumers will react to it. Finally, a detailed analysis is done of the costs of producing, marketing, and launching the product.

- **Prepare the business-case document.** Based on the results of the previous step, the product development team prepares a business-case document, which includes a complete definition of the product and the rationale for developing it. As part of the business case, they must document the legal and regulatory (safety, health, and environmental) aspects of the project as well.

- **Prepare the project plan.** The team next prepares a project plan for the product's development. The plan should include the project's scope (see Chapter 3) as well as a detailed list of the project's activities, timeline for completion, and milestones. The plan also should specify the resources (personnel and financial) to be committed to the project.

- **Perform a feasibility analysis.** A feasibility analysis evaluates the difficulty of carrying out the project. Senior managers review all of the operational, financial, and market information collected during the previous processes to decide whether developing the product still makes sense or is feasible. For example, can the firm produce the product at a reasonable cost, so that the company can price it in a way that's affordable to consumers? If not, is it feasible to redesign or produce the product in another way?

**Stage-Gate®
approach:** a method that helps prevent runaway, over-budget product development cycles by dividing new projects into stages (or phases), with gates separate consecutive stages

**Reverse
engineering:** a process in which a firm dismantles a competitors' existing products to see how they work and whether they can be improved

OPERATIONS PROFILE: New Product Development at Coca-Cola: Illy Issimo

Even though it is more than 130 years old, The Coca-Cola Company is still committed to developing new products. The company has 500 different beverages in its portfolio. Coke, Diet Coke, Fanta, Sprite, Coca-Cola Zero, glacéau vitaminwater, Powerade, Minute Maid, Simply, and Georgia are just a few of them. The company is also the number one provider of sparkling beverages, juices and juice drinks, and ready-to-drink teas and coffees.

Coca-Cola uses the Stage-Gate® approach to develop its products. When analyzing the status of a new product, there are four options for the product after gate review:

- Return to the same stage for further improvements
- Terminate, if the management gate keepers fail to make a decision to move the product onward
- Suspend, if the product is lagging or failing to complete its necessary previous gate steps
- Proceed, if the project merits further development

Coca-Cola recently used the Stage-Gate® approach to create Illy Issimo, a new ready-to-drink coffee beverage. The stages for Illy Issimo's product development were as follows:

Stage 1: Idea Generation

People around the world continue to drink increasing amounts of coffee both at home and elsewhere. As a result, Coca-Cola decided to enter the coffee beverage market.

Stage 2: Building the Business Case

The company identified competing products in the past and present. It also researched the positioning of its product by mapping all similar products in local and regional markets, as well as throughout the world. At the global market level, the company discovered there was a niche, or opening, for its product in the premium-product segment. Next, the company partnered with the Italian coffee producer Illycaffè S.p.A. (Trieste, Italy) to create the product

Stage 3: Product Development

After the basic formula for the product was developed, two versions of it—one with milk and one without—underwent preliminary launches in the market. Coca-Cola predicted that the nonmilk version would account for 26% of the total sales of the product, whereas the milk-infused version would account for 74%. The percentages were based on people's coffee-drinking preferences—that is, the percentage of people who add milk to their coffee versus the percentage of those who do not.

Stage 4: Launch Preparations

In preparation for the product's full launch, Coca-Cola and Illy created the legal joint venture, ILKO Coffee International SRL (Milan, Italy). Illycaffè began setting up of the production facilities for the joint venture, identified suppliers for all of the product's ingredients, and developed standards for quality control and product testing. ILKO Coffee then developed the product's unique packaging, built a supply chain, and began the first commercial production runs.

©iStockphoto.com/memoriesarecaptured

Stage 5: Marketing Activities

ILKO Coffee made use of Coca-Cola's extensive marketing and advertising expertise to develop target markets, identify early adopters and other opinion leaders, and determine the appropriate distribution channels for the product, including which supermarkets to use and how best to promote it. For example, to promote a successful image, ILKO Coffee would not sell the Illy Issimo in low-cost grocery chains. Likewise, creating a new image for Illy Issimo has meant that Coca-Cola deliberately avoids trying to market and sell the beverage in all of its outlets and channels. A low-key, specialty approach for the drink is considered more appropriate.

First introduced to the marketplace in May 2009, Illy Issimo is now sold in 19 countries worldwide. Although it is still in its infancy stage of its life cycle, any beverage jointly produced by Coca-Cola and Illycaffè has to be considered a serious contender in the ready-to-drink coffee market.[14]

STAGE 3: DEVELOPMENT

During the development stage, the actual design and development of the new product occurs, along with some early and simple technical and market testing of the product. The product development team prepares a road map with a realistic timeline and well-defined milestones to track the product's progress. It is at this stage that the development of the product goes in to high gear and resources are expended on it. The final outcome of this stage is the construction of the product's prototype, which will have a Gate 4 review before being subjected to extensive testing and evaluation in the next stage of the Stage-Gate® approach. The company also develops operations and marketing plans for the new product during the development stage.

STAGE 4: TESTING AND VALIDATION

The purpose of this stage is to test and validate the entire project, including the product itself, the production process, and customers' acceptance of the product. Three types of tests are performed to validate the project: near testing, field testing, and market testing.

- *Near testing*: The purpose of near testing is to discover any defects or issues—safety or otherwise—with the product and eliminate or resolve them. The participants in this test are those who have an intimate knowledge of the products, including the company's customers, research and development personnel, and other interested stakeholders.
- *Field testing*: Also known as beta testing, field testing is done to obtain valuable feedback on the product. In addition to the company's customers and other stakeholders, the participants in this test can include anyone who is unfamiliar with the company producing the product. At this point, the product is identical in all aspects to the model that is to be launched. The objectives of this test are to determine whether the participants would still buy the product, the extent of their interest in the product, and the specific product features that they really like.
- *Market testing*: During this test phasing, consumers are exposed to the product along with its marketing campaign to find out whether they will, in fact, find the product attractive and respond to it as expected. This test phase is optional. If the company is confident that the product will sell and has solid marketing, operations, and launch plans in place, it may forego market testing and opt for a full product launch.

STAGE 5: LAUNCH

The final step of the Stage-Gate® approach is the product's launch. Prior to the launch, the company must determine how much of the product to produce based on what it believes consumers will initially demand. To ensure that the launch of the product goes smoothly, the company must also train its sales and support personnel about the product—how to sell it, install and use it, service it, and so forth. Recall from Chapter 3 that prior to the launch of the all-electric LEAF, Nissan (Nissan Motor Company Ltd, Yokohama, Japan) recognized that the car's brand-new technology would be difficult for dealerships and mechanics to support initially. To resolve any customer complaints before they got out of hand, Nissan developed a rapid-reaction taskforce of engineers and technicians specially trained in the technology. Two other aspects that a company should pay close attention to during the launch process are how the product will be priced and distributed. The company must devote sufficient time and effort to setting the correct price for the new product and develop appropriate distribution channels so that the product is available when there is a demand for it.

4.3 New Product Development Concepts and Strategies

Increasingly customers are demanding a greater variety of products with more and better features. Customers are also demanding customized products that are safer, longer lasting, easier to use, and less costly to maintain. In addition, increasing environmental and health concerns are forcing companies to adopt new strategies for designing, producing, delivering, and disposing of products. To cope with these myriad issues, companies are using different new practices. We describe those practices in this section.

Modular Design

Modular design is an approach in which independently created units called *modules* can be combined with others and easily rearranged, replaced, or interchanged to create different products. Dell Inc. (Round Rock, TX), for example, uses the modular design concept with its computers to respond to

Beta testing: field testing done to obtain valuable feedback on a product

Modular design: an approach in which independently created units called *modules* can be combined with others and easily rearranged, replaced, or interchanged to create different products

4.3

Demonstrate how new strategies have improved the way in which new products are designed and tested.

The A-10 Thunderbolt II, or Warthog, as it has been nicknamed, is an American fighter jet with a robust product design. The aircraft can operate under a wide variety of conditions and remain in the air even if it loses an engine, tail, or a half of a wing.

©iStockphoto.com/Hirkophoto

Robust product design: an approach to product or service design in which minor variations caused by various factors in a production process do not adversely affect how a product performs

Internal variation: product variations caused by the wear and tear of production equipment as it ages

External variation: product variations caused by environmental conditions, such as temperature, humidity, or dust

Unit-to-unit variation: product variations caused by variations in the materials, processes, or equipment used to produce a product

changing customer demands and to make its manufacturing process more flexible. Circuit boards and other components containing different levels of RAM and hard drive capacity can be interchanged easily to allow customers to customize every computer to suit their specific needs.

Rapid changes in technology can also quickly make electronics components and equipment obsolete. With modular product designs, businesses can replace components that become obsolete piece by piece rather than having to alter the entire product. Firms can also develop products faster by outsourcing the design or production of different components to different companies and then assembling them later. Modular design attempts to combine the advantages of standardization—high volumes of the components can be produced at a low cost—with the advantages of customization, so that a greater variety of products can be produced because the components can be assembled in different ways.

Robust Product Design

Genichi Taguchi, a Japanese quality expert, pioneered the concept of robust product design. With a robust product design, minor variations caused by various factors in the production process won't adversely affect how the product performs. Product variations can arise from three sources: internal variation, external variation, and unit-to-unit variation. Internal variations are caused by the wear and tear of production equipment as it ages. External variations are caused by environmental conditions, such as temperature, humidity, or dust. Products such as photoelectric cells, computer chips, and optical equipment must be engineered and produced in sterile settings. Even the slightest contamination can ruin the output. Finally, unit-to-unit variation is caused by variations in the materials, processes, or equipment used to produce a product. For example, if the grade of chocolate varied or was poorly mixed during the production process, there would be a significant variation in a candy maker's chocolate bars.

Anticipating the likely causes of variations and addressing them with a product's design is the idea behind robust product design. Some common examples of robust product design include umbrella fabric that will not deteriorate when exposed to varying environments (external variation), food products that have long shelf lives (internal variation), and replacement parts that will fit properly (unit-to-unit variation).

Value Analysis and Value Engineering

Intense worldwide competition in the global market place is forcing companies to provide high-value products and services to their customers. Before we discuss the tools and techniques used to create high-value products, we need a precise definition of value.

Value is defined by the following equation:

$$\text{Value} = \text{Function} \div \text{Cost}$$

This equation tells us that if we want to optimize the value of a product, we have to improve its functionality while holding its cost constant, or for a given level of functionality, we must reduce the cost of the product. Value analysis (VA) and value engineering (VE) provide firms with a set of tools they can use to improve the value of their products. Value analysis is used to improve, at a minimum cost, the functionality of a product without affecting its existing functions and standards. Value engineering, by contrast, is used to analyze and improve the value of *all* components used to develop a product from its design to its final delivery. Chevrolet's (manufactured by GM) redesign of the Malibu to increase its fuel efficiency is an example of value analysis (see Case Study 4.1).

Value engineering ensures that new products provide the value customers want, while simultaneously earning the producer of the product an excellent return on its investment. VE improves the value of a new product by significantly reducing its costs. A major portion of the cost of a manufactured product results from the cost of the materials that go into it, which is driven by the product's design. This circumstance is precisely where value engineering has produced impressive results. Companies in many different industries have used value engineering to reduce the costs not only of their products but also their processes and systems.[15]

Mass Customization

In response to consumer demand for customized products at low prices, some companies have adopted the strategy of **mass customization**. Mass customization is the mass production of individually customized products through the use of components assembled in several different configurations. It offers some benefits of customization at a relatively low cost. To use this strategy, companies should have the ability to design and produce the product quickly in response to customer requests. Dell has benefited from mass customization. It is possible to go to Dell's website and build a computer according to your specifications that has only the features that you want. You can, for example, create a computer with more RAM and a DVD player instead of a CD-ROM player and so forth. Automobiles manufacturers also rely on mass customization. Each car can be built on the assembly line to the buyer's specifications. Levi's (Levi Strauss & Co., San Francisco, CA) customized jeans and adidas's (addidas Group, Herzogenaurach, Germany) customized shoes are examples of mass customization in the apparel industry.

Mass Customization

Design for Manufacturing and Assembly

To build better quality products that consumers can buy at lower prices, some firms have begun using **design for manufacturing and assembly (DFMA)** principles, which are often implemented using software programs. Designs that reduce the number of parts in products are identified, making them easier to manufacture and assemble and less expensive to produce. Furthermore, because the manufacturing and assembly process is simpler, there is a chance of problems occurring, so the products are more reliable. Many companies have benefited from using this tool. For example, by using DFMA software, Texas Instruments Inc. (Dallas, TX) reduced from 129 minutes to just 20 minutes the assembly time for an infrared sighting device produced for the Pentagon. Similarly, through the use of DFMA, IBM (now Lenovo Group Ltd., Beijing, China) sliced the assembly time for its printers from 30 minutes to just 3 minutes.

A DFMA system has three major elements. The first element is the *raw material*. A good product design hinges on choosing the right material, such as standard materials that are readily available and possess all the correct mechanical and chemical properties to meet the design criteria for a product. In addition, to the extent possible, the type of the raw material chosen should be close to the finished parts to reduce additional processing. The second element is *choosing the right machines and processes*. Selecting the right machines and processes can drastically reduce the time needed to process the raw material and further increase the quality of the parts. The third element is the *assembly* of the finished product. The assembly provides the greatest opportunity to apply DFMA principles because fewer parts are needed to assemble the finished product.[16]

Design for Reliability (DFR)

A company, to be profitable, has to manufacture products that are reliable. That is, the product has to perform its intended function without failure. If the product fails, there are repercussions in the form of warranty costs, customer dissatisfaction, and even lawsuits. The recent reliability problems with Xbox 360 game systems cost Microsoft more than a billion dollars in addition to loss of business and market share. **Design for reliability (DFR)** is a process that encompasses the range of tools and practices that describe how, when, and in what order an organization needs to deploy them to design reliable products. A good DFR system ensures that:

1. The firm has designed reliability into its products and services.
2. The firm not only has the ability to determine the reliability of its products but also to achieve reliability.
3. The firm not only uses reliability practices early in the product design process but also has them integrated throughout the product development cycle.[17]

The supplement to this chapter discusses the concept of reliability in more detail and the approaches to evaluating reliability of products.

Value analysis (VA): analysis conducted to improve, at a minimum cost, the functionality of a product without affecting its existing functions and standards

Value engineering (VE): analysis conducted to improve the value of all components used to develop a product from its design to its final delivery

Mass customization: the mass production of individually customized products through the use of components assembled in several different configurations

Design for manufacturing and assembly (DFMA): a process that reduces the number of parts in a product, making it easier to manufacture and assemble and less expensive to produce

Design for reliability (DFR): a process that encompasses the range of tools and practices that describes how, when, and in what order an organization needs to deploy them to design reliable products

The MAKO Pro 16 Skiff boat (MAKO Boats, Springfield, MO) was designed using DFR principles. The inverted-V design of the hull creates a tunnel underneath the boat. The tunnel traps both air and water, which, along with the boat's engine, makes the boat more buoyant and provides a smoother ride.[18]

Design for Disposal, Remanufacturing, and Recycling (DFDRR)

Innovative product designs alone can greatly minimize how much of the product we use, waste, and discard. It is the job of product designers to determine the parts of a product to be designed for refurbishing and reuse, as well as the parts to be designed that are to be discarded, broken down, and recycled. This process is referred to as **design for disposal, remanufacturing, and recycling (DFDRR)**. For example, rechargeable nickel–cadmium batteries can be recycled to recover both cadmium and nickel for other uses. INMETCO Corporation (subsidiary of Horsehead Holding Corp., Pittsburgh, PA) and Accurec Recycling GmbH (Mülheim, Germany) are routinely recycling such batteries using a process called *pyrometallurgical distillation*.[19] The manufacturers of soaps and detergents use plastic containers that are easily recycled. Similarly, most paperboard used for cleaning product containers is made out of recycled paper, and the steel cans used for aerosols have 25% recycled steel content.[20]

Quality Function Deployment (QFD)

Quality function deployment (QFD) is a method companies use to translate customers' wants and needs into product or service features, to prioritize those features, and to set development targets for the product or service. Consider the Lockheed F-35, Joint Strike Fighter (Lockheed Martin, Bethesda, MD), which is a unique, hybrid aircraft with a blend of features and options designed to appeal to different branches of the military. The F-35 was designed with three main variants: The first is a conventional takeoff and landing variant for the Air Force; the second is a short take-off and vertical-landing variant for the Marines; and the third is a variant that allows the Navy to take off and land on more easily aircraft carriers (ships). After carefully considering the jet from the customers' point of view, Lockheed developed the F-35 deliberately for the widest possible use.

QFD helps planners to focus on the features of both new and existing products and services. The methodology originated in Japan in the mid-1960s, largely as a result of the work of Yoji Akao, a quality pioneer who is also recognized for developing *Hoshin Kanri*, the Japanese term for the strategic planning process. QFD has helped businesses to plan new products, figure out the processes to manufacture them and control those processes, document the specifications of existing products, and document competitive marketing strategies and tactics. Since the early 1970s, several leading companies such as Toyota, GM, IBM (International Business Machines Corporation, Armonk, NY), Kodak (Eastman Kodak Company, Rochester, NY), HP Inc. (formerly Hewlett-Packard, Palo Alto, CA), AT&T Inc. (Dallas, TX), P&G, and Motorola have used QFD with impressive results.

QFD makes use of cross-functional teams in four phases of product development. The process involves using a matrix in each of the four phases to translate the customer's requirements. The outputs of each phase then lead into the next phase.

Phase 1: This is the new product planning phase and is led by the marketing function. In this phase, the customer's requirements and the technical ability of the company to meet each of them are thoroughly documented. The success of the entire QFD process hinges on obtaining accurate and verifiable data from the customer in this phase. This phase is also called the **house of quality (HOQ)** phase and is represented by a planning diagram that resembles a house. Figure 4.5 shows a basic house-of-quality diagram. The six sections in the HOQ diagram are:

1. **Customer requirements.** This section of the HOQ lists the customers' requirements described in their own words (in the "voice of the customer"). The requirements are also ranked in terms of their importance to the customer.
2. **Engineering requirements.** These are the product's measurable technical characteristics that the QFD team believes will meet the requirements of customers. For example, the QFD team might determine that for a hairdryer, the appliance might require a certain number of fan speeds or heat settings.
3. **Interrelationships.** This is the main body of HOQ. It is where the QFD team considers each combination of customer and technical requirement to identify which are significant. For example, the QFD team may rate the level of the interrelationship between the customer's requirement of drying hair efficiently and the technical requirement of fan speed as high and denote that with a symbol in the HOQ matrix.

Design for disposal, remanufacturing, and recycling (DFDRR): a process that determines the parts of a product to be designed for refurbishing and reuse, and the parts to be designed that are to be discarded, broken down, and recycled

Quality function deployment (QFD): a method that translates customers' wants and needs into product or service features, to prioritize those features, and to set development targets for the product or service

House of quality (HOQ): the process of obtaining accurate and verifiable data from the customer in the first phase of the QFD process

4. **Competitive analysis.** The main purpose of this section is to compare how well the product identified by QFD meets the customer's requirements relative to the competition.

5. **Correlation matrix.** The triangular roof of the HOQ matrix is used to identify how the engineering requirements correlate with each other. That is, do the requirements support or impede one another? For example, a customer may want a new service that requires the work of a highly skilled worker but at a low cost. These two demands may be incompatible (have a low correlation).

6. **Targets.** This is the final section of the HOQ, and it summarizes the conclusions drawn from all the data in the matrix and the team's discussions. It consists of a set of engineering targets the new product design should meet.

FIGURE 4.5: House of Quality

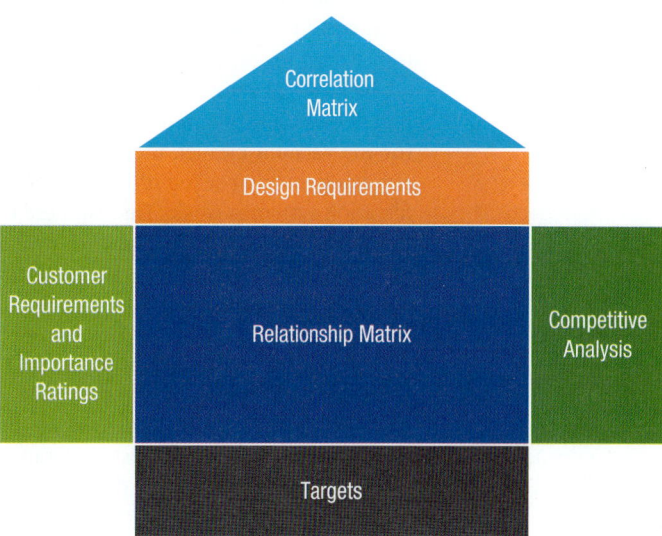

Figure 4.6, which shows a simple HOQ for a vacuum cleaner, may appear complicated because it has a considerable amount of information. But if we analyze this figure by examining its various elements (labeled in red), the benefits of the HOQ will become apparent. The most important part, customer requirements, is located on the left-hand side of Figure 4.6. This part provides information on what the customers want in a vacuum cleaner, along with an importance rating of each feature. The second important part, engineering requirements, is located vertically at the top of the house and denotes what your company can do to translate customer requirements into product and process design features. For example, to improve the cleaning ability of the vacuum cleaner (a customer requirement), your company can design the product with more suction power. The third part, located at the center of Figure 4.6, is the relationship matrix. This part shows the relationship and strength between each customer requirement and the product design attributes, including the relative strength of this

FIGURE 4.6: Simple House of Quality for a Vacuum Cleaner

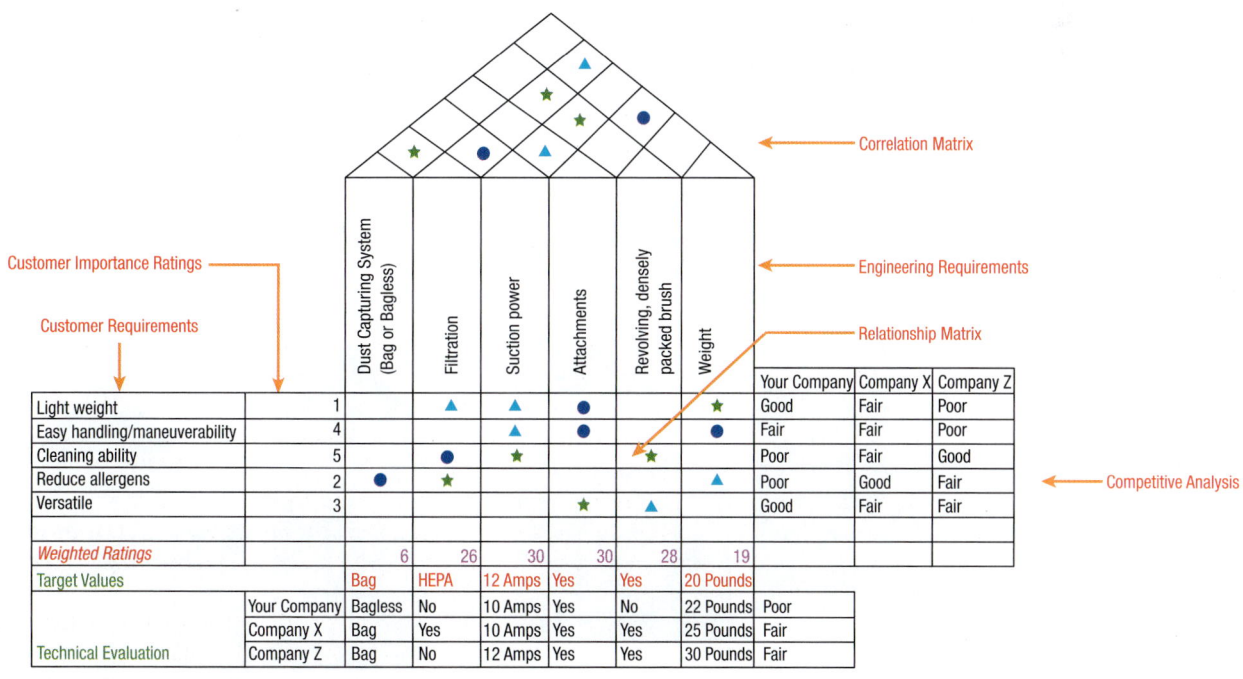

relationship. Thus, there is a strong relationship (denoted by a star symbol) between the customer requirement of reducing allergens and the design feature of a filtration system in the vacuum cleaner. That is, a filtration system in the vacuum cleaner is an important engineering feature to meet the customer need for reducing allergens.

Next, we examine the roof of the house in Figure 4.6, which is labeled the correlation matrix. This part shows the strength of the relationship among the various engineering requirements. For example, for the vacuum cleaner, there is a strong positive correlation between suction power and having a revolving thickly packed brush; however, the strength of the relationship between the weight and the filtration system is weak. That is, these two product features are not related to each other. The right-hand side of the figure includes an evaluation of your company's performance on customer requirements compared with two of your key competitors (designated as Companies X and Z). For example, although your company performs best in terms of the lightweight customer requirement, Company Z is the strongest for the customer requirement of cleaning ability.

The bottom portion of the figure has weighted ratings of engineering requirements, target values of technical specifications that your company wants to achieve, and technical evaluation, which is similar to the competitive evaluation. The weighted ratings for each engineering attribute are obtained by the sum of the product of the customer rating of each requirement by the numerical value of the strength of the relationship between that customer requirement and that engineering attribute. For example, for the engineering attribute of suction power, the value of 30 is obtained as follows: $(1 \times 1) + (4 \times 1) + (5 \times 5) = 30$. The weighted ratings and the target values will enable product designers to focus on the most important engineering attributes that will best meet customer needs. Thus, for the vacuum cleaner, the most important design features are more suction power and the inclusion of attachments, whereas a dust-capturing system is of relatively low importance.

Phase 2: The engineering department takes the lead in phase 2. During this phase, the product is developed and its part specifications are documented. Only those parts most critical to meeting the customer's needs are then deployed into the next phase of process planning.

Phase 3: During this phase, the manufacturing processes are organized into a flowchart and the parameters, or target values, of the process are determined and documented. For example, the parameters that would need to be determined for manufacturing a baked product include the product's wet weight and dry weights, temperature during mixing, baking temperature, baking time, and moisture content. The firm's manufacturing group leads this phase.

Phase 4: The final phase of QFD deployment is production planning with the operations and quality assurance departments taking the lead. Key performance indicators are established in this phase to monitor the production process, its schedules, and the skills training for operators. In addition, the processes that pose the greatest risks are identified in this phase, and controls are put in place to prevent failures.

The four phases of the QFD process are shown as cascading matrices in Figure 4.7.

FIGURE 4.7: Quality Function Deployment Process

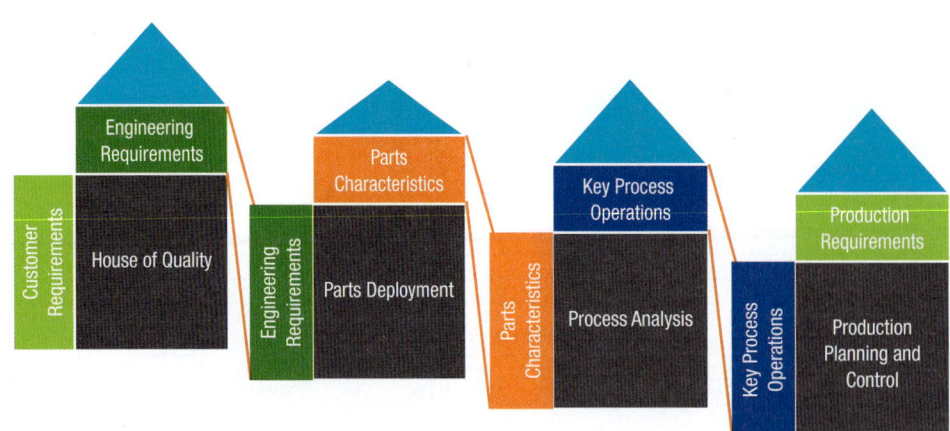

SOURCE: http://www.emeraldinsight.com/fig/1310010103001.png

Concurrent Engineering

Concurrent engineering, also sometimes referred to as *simultaneous engineering* or *integrated product development (IPD)*, is a new product development approach in which tasks are performed in parallel and every aspect of product development is considered early in the process. So, for example, instead of a company's engineering department designing a product and giving it to the firm's manufacturing department to produce, personnel from both groups work collaboratively to design the product and determine how it will be produced. There also is collaboration among members of the firm's other departments that have an impact on the product, such as marketing and customer service. Input from employees in all departments forces all the team to consider, from the very beginning, aspects such as quality, cost, schedule, and the requirements of users throughout the entire development of the product as well as all stages in its life cycle—from the concept stage to the disposal stage.

Robert Lutz, the former president of Chrysler (now part of Fiat Chrysler Automobiles, Auburn Hills, MI), recalled his early experiences with new car development at the troubled company. The culture of the company had created a separation and lack of communication between departments and functions at Chrysler that was so rigid, anyone not part of one's own department was treated as an outsider, separated by prejudices and cultural barriers. Making the problem with Chrysler's development process worse was the fact that it was linear and sequential, as represented in Figure 4.8. The design department sent its work to the engineering department, which either accepted or (more often) passed the design back with comments and corrections. After finally approving a car's design, the engineering group then sent it "over the fence" to the manufacturing department. The manufacturing group then requested changes and corrections. The result was that it took seven years for Chrysler to make an automobile. Meanwhile, other automakers were introducing new cars to the market in less than three years.[21]

Producing a product on a small scale during a pilot production phase using a serial approach as Chrysler did may pose no serious problems. Nevertheless, during large-scale production of the product, major difficulties often arise. The serial approach is slow, costly, and fraught with problems affecting product quality that require frequent engineering changes and cause production glitches and delays. Moreover, products produced this way are often uncompetitive in the marketplace.

Concurrent engineering attempts to overcome these problems by bringing together cross-functional teams—that is, members of different departments who collaborate from the outset of the project so the work is done correctly and as quickly as possible. Concurrent engineering might involve a firm's design and manufacturing engineers. Feedback is solicited from the representatives of the various functional groups before the product's specifications are finalized, and they agree on process, cost, quality, and other issues before manufacturing begins. Getting the design right during the early stages will save a lot of headaches for a firm later. General Electric's Aircraft Engines division used concurrent engineering to develop the engine for the F/A-18E/F fighter aircraft. By doing so, the company was able to reduce the time to design and fabricate some components from 22 weeks to just 3 weeks.

Concurrent engineering is a long-term business strategy for improving the development of products, not a quick fix. It requires an upfront and long-term commitment of a company's resources and

FIGURE 4.8: Sequential Product Development at Chrysler

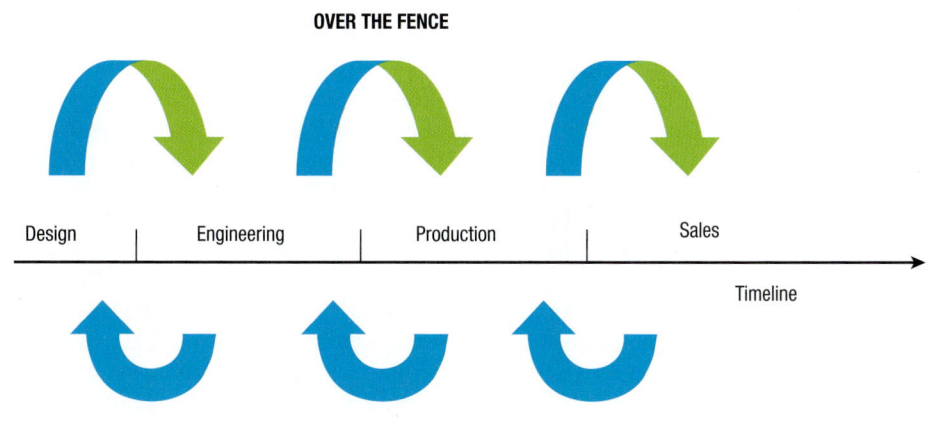

OVER THE FENCE

Design | Engineering | Production | Sales

Timeline

Rework Cycles

Concurrent engineering: a new product development approach in which tasks are performed in parallel and every aspect of product development is considered early in the process, also sometimes referred to as simultaneous engineering or integrated product development (IPD)

can take several years before the benefits of the approach are realized. Companies that are planning to implement concurrent engineering should be ready to make major organizational and cultural changes because the approach requires the integration of people, business processes, and technology. Getting different groups of people to work together closely when they haven't done so in the past isn't always easy. It requires the support of a firm's top managers and the commitment of personnel to work in cross-functional teams.

Time-Based Competition

Time-based competition is a strategy intended to reduce the time required to conceptualize, develop, manufacture, market, and deliver products so as to gain a competitive advantage. There are two types of time-based competition: *time-to-market speed* and *time-to-manufacture-and-deliver speed*. Firms that compete based on time-to-market speed aim to reduce the time it takes to develop new products or rapidly redesign them. Firms that compete based on time-to-manufacture-and-deliver speed aim to manufacture products quickly and deliver them quickly to customers.

Technology and Product Development

Competing on time can be a valuable strategy; research shows that companies that have developed new products that were 50% over budget but were launched into the market on time generated more profits than those products that were within budget but introduced into the market six months late.[22] In addition, firms with fast time-to-market speeds can introduce *more* new products or large numbers of improved or different products than can their competitors. Sun Microsystems, Inc. (acquired by Oracle America, Inc., Santa Clara, CA) became a market leader by reducing the time required to design and introduce engineering workstations by 50% compared with its competitors. Furthermore, firms that can reduce product development cycle time end up much farther along the learning curve than the competition, which creates barriers to entry for these competitors.

Other companies that have developed more products faster by using concurrent engineering include Black & Decker Corporation (Towson, MD), Ford, and AT&T. Still other companies have formed joint ventures and alliances or have acquired start-up firms to use the new technologies they have developed to bring out products faster. Yet another way companies are introducing new products quickly, while reducing costs, is to use a **product platform**. A product platform is a set of subsystems and components that form a common structure from which a family of products can be efficiently developed and produced. The auto industry, for example, uses product platforms to build vehicles quickly and reduce costs. As an example, General Motor's "Gamma" platform is used to manufacture the Chevrolet Spark, Buick Encore, and Opel Corsa. Although these vehicles look different than one another, they typically share a common chassis and internal parts. Similarly, manufacturers of hair dryers use similar materials or parts to produce different models with different features. The goal of using a product platform is to reduce costs by achieving economies of scale.[23]

4.4 Using Technology to Develop New Products

In recent years, advances in technology have reduced the time it takes to develop new products. These techniques also have improved their design quality and overall performance and have lowered their costs. We discuss some of these technologies in this section.

Rapid Prototyping and Virtual Reality

New product prototypes are usually an actual working model of the new product, a miniature version of the product, or a mock-up of the product. In the past, the developing prototypes used to take weeks or months. Today, new technology allows **rapid prototyping,** which is based on methods that are designed to create virtual reality games. Some companies have used the techniques to build three-dimensional (3-D) prototypes. Virtual reality is often used to describe a wide variety of applications commonly associated with immersive, highly visual, 3-D environments. Virtual reality is a visual communication tool in which images take the place of the real thing, but the user can still respond interactively. Virtual reality technology has its roots in computer-aided design. Once the product's design information is entered into a computer, that information can be used to create 3-D layouts of the product. With the help of virtual reality technology, changes to mechanical designs, restaurant layouts, or amusement park rides are all possible during the design stage, when it is much less expensive to make changes. Other companies use laser technology to develop product prototypes with complex shapes. In addition to reducing design time and costs, rapid prototyping and the use of virtual reality modeling can also improve the stability of a design and the product's performance, which in turn can lead to increased customer satisfaction.

4.4
Discuss some new technologies that have allowed for faster new product development.

Time-based competition: a strategy intended to reduce the time required to conceptualize, develop, manufacture, market, and deliver products so as to gain a competitive advantage

Product platform: a set of subsystems and components that form a common structure from which a family of products can be efficiently developed and produced

Rapid prototyping: quickly creating a miniature version of a product or a mock-up of a product using new technology based on methods that are designed to create virtual reality games

Computer-Aided Design

Computer-aided design (CAD) is part of a larger computer application known as *computer-aided engineering (CAE),* and it refers to the broad range of software that helps engineers design new products electronically rather than drawing by hand. The capability afforded by CAD eliminates routine mistakes, such as the scaling problems that can occur when a drawing is created manually, and reduces design times. Of course, this time savings in turn significantly increases the productivity of a firm's design staff and facilitates the faster launch of products.[24]

Furthermore, to ensure they function correctly, some newly designed products have to be tested under environmental conditions that vary throughout the year. For example, let's assume that an aircraft manufacturer has designed a new wing for an airplane. This new wing has to be tested to confirm that it can sustain extreme weather conditions and air turbulences. If the airplane manufacturer decided to test these wings physically in flight, it would take several trials on dozens of the new wings to make certain the wings operate successfully. Not only would these actual physical trials be very expensive, they could be dangerous.

Nevertheless, if these new wings were developed using CAD software, they can be tested virtually under conditions that simulate to real conditions.[25] PING (Phoenix, AZ) has successfully used CAD technology to design and test the stress points and aerodynamics of its golf clubs. This test design philosophy has allowed PING to save money by weeding out designs that do not meet its strict quality and performance expectations before ever producing prototypes of the clubs.[26]

4.5 Global Product Development

Intense global competition and political and economic pressures have had a dramatic impact on new product development for many industries. Today companies are using skilled engineering teams that are dispersed around the world to develop products collaboratively.[27] Likewise, major original equipment manufacturers (OEMs) and leading global product development companies seek to form strategic partnerships with their suppliers to develop better products faster and more cost effectively. For example, Ford has taken significant steps to combine its product development and purchasing organizations into an integrated global team to accelerate the creation of vehicles customers really want, reduce their costs, enhance their quality, and improve efficiency by eliminating duplicate engineering and purchasing efforts. These are examples of **global product development (GPD)**, which represents a major transformation for businesses. The overall objective of GPD is to introduce innovative new products that exceed customer expectations while maximizing the financial and operational productivity of the product development process. Global product development includes all activities, from generating new product ideas based on customers' needs to conceptualizing and designing the new product, to developing marketing and operation plans, to making ongoing refinements to products.

Companies that can achieve higher levels of productivity in product development compared with their competition gain a clear competitive advantage in the marketplace. Because productivity is defined as the amount of output per unit of input, the greater the level of output for a given level of input, the higher is the productivity level. Conversely, if for a given level of output, the level of input can be lowered, then again productivity is higher. If companies can then find ways to develop great products (output) while minimizing product development costs (input), they can enjoy a competitive advantage in terms of market share and profitability. It is estimated that by simply rearranging their product development activities and personnel in a global way—that is, so that certain functions are performed in some parts of the world and other functions are performed elsewhere—companies can quickly increase their product development productivity by 10% and realize significant cost savings.[28]

An example of a rapid prototype of a 3D model scooter.

©iStockphoto.com/Guru3Ds

4.5

Explain the global product-development process, and describe how organizations are increasingly using it to gain a strategic advantage.

Computer-aided design (CAD): part of a larger computer application known as computer-aided engineering (CAE), which refers to the broad range of software that helps engineers design new products electronically rather than drawing by hand

Global product development (GPD): the process of introducing innovative new products that exceed customer expectations while maximizing the financial and operational productivity of the product development process

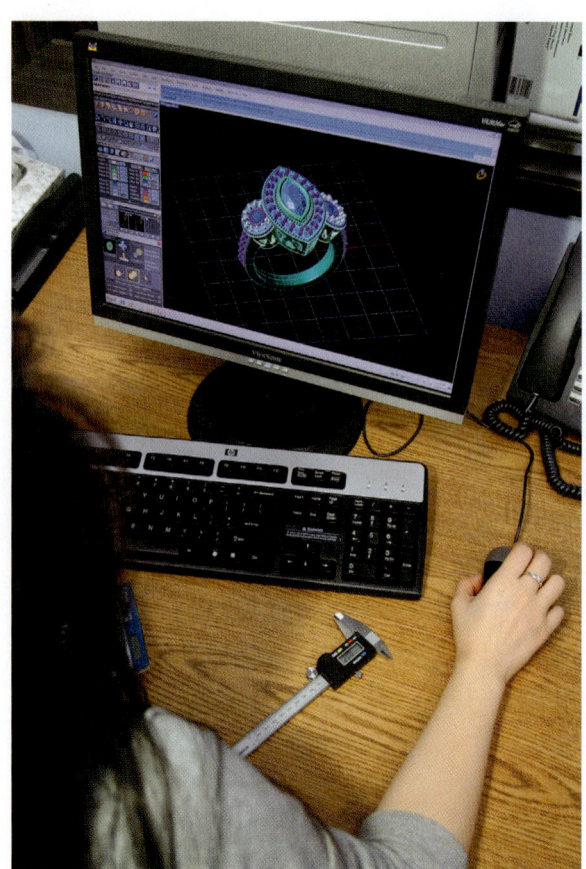

A technician developing a product using CAD.

Bloomberg/Bloomberg/Getty Images

The Evolution of Global Product Development

During the 1980s and 1990s, many manufacturing companies from high-cost industrialized countries such as the United States, the United Kingdom, Germany, France, Italy, and Japan steadily shifted their manufacturing activities to lower cost regions, such as India, China, Russia, Vietnam, and other Eastern European, South American, and Asian countries. In certain industries such as the textile and television industries, the practice of offshoring has shifted so much production to lower cost regions that there are now very few textile mills and television factories left in countries such as the United States. Even though offshoring is complex and involves issues such as quality control and longer lead times, the process is relatively straightforward and offers enormous cost advantages. For example, if an offshore manufacturing company in a low-cost region is given a complete set of design specifications for a product, including drawings and parts lists, it can typically fabricate and assemble the product and deliver finished goods directly to the customer or its distribution center at a fraction of the cost. An example of the result of the offshoring trend is the huge electronics manufacturing industry that now exists in Taiwan.

After successfully offshoring their manufacturing, some firms began to see the advantages of developing products in different parts of the world. Several leading manufacturing companies in the world, including General Electric (GE; already introduced), United Technologies Corporation (aka UTC, Farmington, CT), Siemens AG (Munich, Germany), and Cummins Inc. (Columbus, IN) adopted the principles of global product development. For example, GE plans and designs many of its products in India. GE's John F. Welch Technology Center, in Bangalore, India, where approximately 1,800 professionals are employed, is now the company's largest research and development center outside the United States. Many GE products are designed at the center, including some of GE's most complex jet engines.

In the mid-1990s, new software applications made it possible to work on products digitally, and with the help of the Internet, the work became instantaneously portable to nearly anywhere in the world. As a result, companies began to distribute select product-development functions to other countries, including the software-systems documentation process, quality assurance, and help-desk support. Information technology (IT) suppliers such as Infosys Limited (Bengaluru, India) and Tata Consultancy Services (TCS; Mumbai, India) sprang up to the meet the demand. Using the powerful new technologies such as state-of-the-art CAD, CAE, computer-aided manufacturing (CAM), and PLM, an increasing number of companies now have fully digital (or IT-enabled) product development processes that allow them to move at least some of the development process to regions of the globe that provide them with the best product-development capabilities at the lowest cost.

Challenges Related to Global Product Development

To develop products successfully in different parts of the world, companies must address several strategic and tactical issues.[29] Some of these issues are:

- **Protecting the firm's intellectual property (IP).** When developing a product offshore, firms often have to share valuable product information, designs, and technologies with companies in foreign nations. This sharing can make is harder to protect a firm's intellectual property (IP) rights. For example, many low-cost nations have no formal IP laws and have almost no respect for intellectual property rights. As a result, software piracy is rampant in these low-cost countries. Nevertheless, there are steps that companies can take to mitigate their IP risks. For example, if their products have a modular structure, firms can divide the various pieces of design or fabrication work and send it offshore, yet retain control of the finally assembly of the products. That way, no one supplier will have access to the complete product. That is, no single supplier will be familiar with all of its parts or know how the product is assembled. Second, by making a thoughtful and strategic assessment of the type of work to send abroad and the type of work to keep in-house, and by using information technology such as passwords and encryption to control the access to sensitive information, companies can reduce their IP risk.

- **Formulating a global process of development.** Manufacturing products in different places around the world requires companies to decide on a way to delegate tasks to the different global facilities. A process must be in place that breaks down the product's manufacture into clear steps, determines what steps are done by each facility, and then outlines how and where the necessary handoffs, reviews, and approvals take place.

- **Ensuring data and software systems are compatible.** When a company manufactures a product globally, the data related to it must be distributed among multiple, often geographically separated locations. Nevertheless, when each of these locations uses its own unique databases and systems, it is not always possible to access or review the data. For example, the development of the Airbus A380 (Airbus SAS, Blagnac, France) aircraft was significantly delayed because the engineering offices in Spain and France that worked on the plane didn't have a common software package. Because Spanish designers were using a different version of the software, when the planes were ready for assembly in Toulon, France, company engineers discovered that the electrical work on them had been done incorrectly and that the aircraft had to be rewired by hand. The total cost in time and money was enormous.[30] Global organizations must therefore establish best practices for both data and file management. In addition, a parent design or database system must be established so that all users will understand the impact of changes they make to the data.

- **Preparing staff members to work globally.** Developing products globally presents some challenges in terms of the roles staff members around the world must play and the skills they must acquire. To overcome these challenges, global organizations should carefully plan and properly train and educate all those who will work on the product. Firms need to find innovative ways for teams and individuals across times zones, languages, cultures, and companies to work together well. For example, doing business in India requires knowing the right people in the very tight network at the top of the Indian business establishment and cultivating relationships with them. Therefore, the key to foreign companies succeeding in India is to train their personnel on how they can tap into these business networks.

- **Understanding cultural differences.** Cultural differences pose yet another challenge in the global product development process. New product offerings require an intimate understanding of the cultural nuances of different countries. For example, in China, designing, manufacturing, and marketing black apparel is not a good idea because in China black is associated with evil, dirt, sin, disasters, and bad luck.[31] Likewise, the Kellogg Company's (aka Kellogg's, Battle Creek, MI) push to open the market in India for its breakfast cereals has hit a serious snag: Most Indians prefer a bowl of warm vegetables for breakfast, not corn flakes or other cold cereal. Although their new biscuit products are popular with children, Kellogg's is finding it tough to overcome cultural preferences for breakfast fare.[32]

 Global Product Design

4.6 New Product Development Issues for Supply Chains

4.6

Describe how the collaboration of the members of a supply chain can improve product development.

Typically, a company conceptualizes and designs a new product, and then a few weeks or months before the new product is launched, the company orders the necessary components required to produce it. What is missing in this "typical" scenario is the use of the full power of the supply chain as a product-development resource and cost-saving mechanism. Supply chain members can provide valuable input about how the product can best be designed or even design different aspects of the product. For example, firms such as Dell, HP, and Zara (Coruña, Spain) have shown that redesigning a firm's products to improve the performance of their supply chains, or, alternatively, redesigning the supply chain itself, can result in a sustainable competitive advantage. Zara, for example, by bringing in a new collection of apparel every 15 days and making it available to customers, was able to increase its market share. Zara aligned its offers to customer requirements, while building a customer-driven global supply chain.[33]

Many questions about the supply chain should be answered long before a firm starts producing a new product. That is, the organization of the supply chain should coincide with the product's creation phase. Specifically, as product engineers attempt to design and manufacture the new product and as

OPERATIONS MANAGEMENT: LESSONS LEARNED
The Impact of Supply Chain Delays

A motorcycle manufacturer in India had set the launch date for a brand new two-wheeler. It was a top-notch vehicle with power and capabilities not seen in the market before. The motorcycle was targeted toward the high end of the market, specifically for the growing number of young consumers in the middle class. The company had devised an excellent marketing plan and had prepared a full assembly line for production.

Just before the launch of the new motorcycle, however, an exclusive supplier of frames for the new motorcycle was unable meet the deadline to deliver them. The product launch date was pushed off again and again, and the delivery of the frames was eight months late. This fiasco had a ripple effect on the entire supply chain associated with the motorcycle. First, the assembly line that was dedicated to the production of the motorcycle remained idle when it could have been used to produce the one million other motorcycles the company produces every year. Second, the orders to suppliers producing other components for the new motorcycle were delayed. Third, the demand schedule for the motorcycle had to be completely revised because the peak period of demand for them had passed. Consequently, both the actual demand for the new motorcycle and the corresponding supplier requirements were much lower than originally planned. Fourth, the original lead times had to be revised, leading to additional costs and further delays. The net result was that the company lost a significant amount of revenue that it could have generated on the sales of this new motorcycle.

The company encountered these problems because it failed to estimate accurate lead times. Perhaps if the suppliers had been involved early during the development phase of the motorcycle, the frames would have been manufactured much earlier, and much could have been done to facilitate the introduction of this new motorcycle.[34]

marketing personnel attempt to estimate the demand for it, other important stakeholders, such as the firm's purchasing group, potential suppliers, and even the potential customers for the new product should be involved in the development process. The involvement of these stakeholders will help the product development team and the other participants get a better understanding of the product as well as the supply chain needed for it.

Suppose we are ready to develop a new product. The usual questions that we ask in preparing to produce this product and launch it into the market are as follows: What should be the cost of this new product? What will be the demand for this new product? When should we launch this product? In addition, we should also be asking the following questions about the supply chain:

- Who are the suppliers for the raw materials and components of this product?
- How long will it take the supplier to provide the inventory after it's ordered?
- Where will inventories be held in the supply chain, and at what cost?

Let us consider, for example, inventory levels. Two questions related to inventory levels are:

1. What are the optimum inventory levels for the new product that provide the lowest cost? Typically, for most new products, companies maintain high inventory levels to avoid stock-outs. Stock-outs result in poorer service and customer dissatisfaction, which are problematic for a new product. If the product is not available, customers may lose interest in it and the product could fail in the market.
2. Where should these inventories be located? A company has four options when making this decision. Inventories can be located at the manufacturer's facility, at a warehousing facility (perhaps near the largest market for the product), or at retail facilities. In addition, the company should consider in-transit inventory, which are items en route from one location to another. The correct choice, or combination of choices, requires a thorough analysis of the various costs associated with inventory. These include the costs of carrying the inventory, stock-out cost, transportation costs, and in-transit carrying costs. The best locations minimize a firm's total costs but allow a sufficient amount of inventory to be maintained to satisfy the customer demand.

Lead time: the total time it takes a supplier to both produce a product and deliver it after it's been ordered

Another supply chain issue relates to the **lead times** for suppliers. Lead time is the total time it takes a supplier to both produce a product and deliver it after it's been ordered. Lead times are rarely constant. A supplier might or might not have the inventory on hand and have to produce it, and delays can always occur during production and shipping. Therefore, suppliers should be involved during the development stage of the new product so that they have a clear understanding of the production lead times needed for the new product and are able to plan for delays. That way, they can then come up with better predictions on their stocking levels for the new product.

Collaboration Within Supply Chains

To achieve the benefits of information flows within a supply chain on product development, the company has to collaborate with its suppliers. We now look at an example to see how a company can accomplish the integration of its supply chain with the product development process.

The Supply Chain and Product Development

Assume a global company is working with a Brazilian manufacturer to produce a new product. The process begins with the global company providing the manufacturer the design specifications for the new product. Prior to full-scale manufacturing, the Brazilian company first produces samples of the product so that the global company can see how the product looks, how it operates, and whether it meets specifications. These interactions demonstrate the flow of supply chain information between the two companies. If the information is lacking, not accurate, or timely, the chances are the product won't make it into the market on time or be of the right quality.

There are four key ways that supply chain collaboration will have a direct impact on the success of the new product development process. They are the early involvement of the supply chain members, the creation of a clear supply chain design, multistage quality testing, and understanding the operating process of each supply chain member.

EARLY INVOLVEMENT OF THE SUPPLY CHAIN'S MEMBERS

In recent years, companies have embraced a more collaborative approach to new product development. By bringing all the key departments together—engineering, product design, marketing, purchasing, supply chain, and operations—communication among them occurs more frequently, and the information flow among the product development team, a firm's purchasing department, suppliers, and other interested stakeholders begins very early in the development cycle. Early involvement can help lower defect rates, improve lead times, and reduce a firm's operating costs.

The advantage of the collaborative process during new product development is best summed up by Sophie Bechu, vice president of Worldwide Engineering and Integrated Supply Chain for IBM. According to Bechu, "The designers often focus on performance and functionality, while the buyers focus on cost, supply and technology availability." Bechu believes that involving these different groups early in the design cycle is crucial to minimizing delays in getting the prototype of the product completed. [35] Involving the purchasing department, however, is only the first step. Getting suppliers involved as well is absolutely vital as their collaboration will reduce defects and operational costs and improve lead times.

CREATION OF A CLEAR SUPPLY CHAIN DESIGN

As you have learned, creating a supply chain requires a firm to make numerous decisions, such as which suppliers will handle which components and products, how they will be transported and assembled, and where they will be stored. Ideally, the chain designed for a new product should improve each phase of the product-development process. The best possible way to achieve this is to have a **process design** like that in Figure 4.9. Information flows are the key. As the figure shows, the order of events, both the flow of information and materials, is clearly mapped out based on the inputs from all of the firm's supply chain members.

After the design of the supply chain is agreed to, then the development of the prototypes for the product can begin. As the product's development progresses, the firm's suppliers, purchasing group, and the manufacturing function will need to forecast the demand for the product. The shipping logistics for the product will also have to be determined in conjunction with transportation companies. Designing a supply chain for a new product's development is not an easy task. If it's done correctly, however, and the supply chain costs are accurately calculated early during the product development phase, a company can save a great deal of time and money.

MULTISTAGE QUALITY TESTING

Defective products cost a company time, money, and customers. The best way to reduce the chances of producing defective products is to subject them to quality tests at key stages of the product development process. Ideal times for quality testing are:

- During the design phase to ensure there are no design flaws in the product
- At the supplier stage to ensure that standards for the product's raw materials meet its quality requirements

Process design: the supply chain for a new product in which the order of events is mapped out based on the inputs from all of the firm's supply chain members

FIGURE 4.9: Typical Manufacturing Supply Chain Process Flowchart

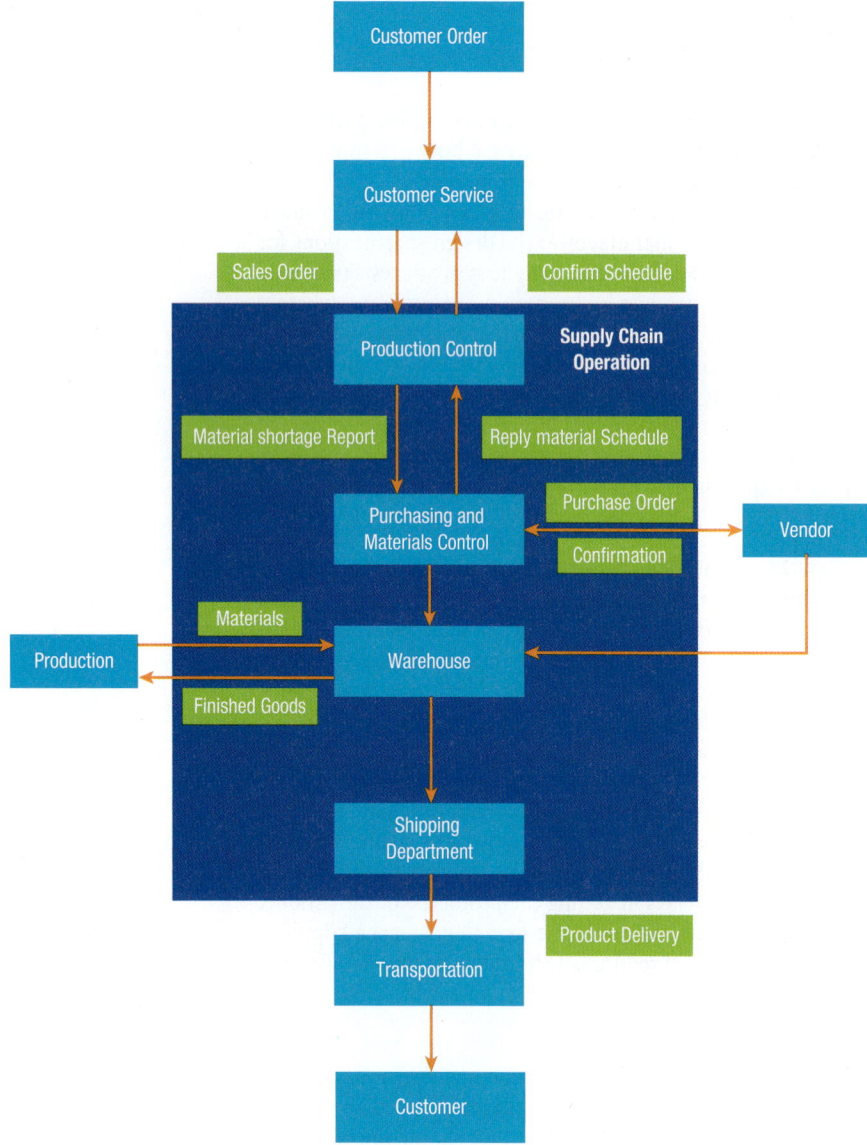

SOURCE: Retrieved October 10, 2014, from http://1.bp.blogspot.com/-IQRvhFlkBS0/TjUatxF7rwI/AAAAAAAABGc/OHpgKp8x83I/s400/Supply+Chain+Flow+Charts-1.jpg

- During manufacturing to eliminate defects during production
- Before the launch of the product to ensure it is free of defects before it reaches the market
- Prior to shipping the product to ensure it will be packaged properly and won't be damaged in transit

Consider the following example. During the late 1990s, Rane Brake Lining Limited (RBL, Chennai, India), a company in the automotive industry in India, was losing ground in the highly competitive global market because the company had a defect rate of 16,000 ppm (parts per million) and a process rejection rate of 2.1%. The process rejection rate is the percentage of processed parts that are rejected in a given period of time or in a processed lot of parts because they are of poor quality. To reduce the defect rate and improve quality, the company started using collaborative processes to design its new products, which dramatically improved the company's ability to get new and better products to the market as well as to the firm's supply chain. In one particular case, one of RBL's biggest customers reported a problem with the company's new brake pad, which was poorly designed and creating unnecessary friction on the cars' tires. To solve this problem, RBL suspended manufacturing and sent its own engineers to test the product both at the customer and at the supplier locations. The engineers found that the problem occurred in a minor, but critical step in the manufacturing process. The problem was corrected, and in less than a month, the rate of defect-free brake pads increased from 75% to 98%. Even though RBL quickly responded to the problem, had the company included the engineers during the manufacturing development phase of the new brake pad, it could have avoided the costs and time incurred from having to stop production to fix the problem, and the company would have reaped higher profits.[36] Collaborative, multistage quality testing does incur additional costs, but those costs are minimal, and the long-term benefits far outweigh the additional costs.

UNDERSTANDING THE OPERATING PROCESSES OF EACH SUPPLY CHAIN MEMBER

All too often companies receive goods from their suppliers that are not exactly what they ordered because the supplier either cannot deliver the goods in sufficient quantity or lacks a clear understanding of the new product. This problem tends to occur because the company developing the product hasn't properly evaluated the ability of the supplier to meet the requirements of the new product. Assessing a supply chain member's capabilities requires knowledge of the supply chain member's operating processes, the design of the supply chain, and the information flows in this design. To gain this understanding, the company should be willing to observe the operations of each of its supply chain members at the ground level and, if necessary, collaborate with them to improve their operations. The Boeing Company (Chicago, IL), for example, contracts with hundreds of suppliers located worldwide to manufacture the parts for its planes; however, the company retains total control over the production of those parts—even on their suppliers' assembly lines. All suppliers are carefully selected, and their manufacturing processes must meet or exceed Boeing's rigorous quality-control standards.

4.7 How Services Are Designed

There are unique challenges in the design of services. Unlike a product, services are intangible experiences offered to customers. It is difficult to standardize services precisely because they are unique experiences tailored for each consumer and delivered at varying points in time. The field of service design is still in its infancy. It is not exactly clear what service design means and how it helps businesses and their customers.[37] This statement from the Dutch service design agency 31 Volts (Utrecht, the Netherlands) conveys a sense of what service design is:

> When you have two coffee shops right next to each other, and each sells the exact same coffee at the exact same price, service design is what makes you walk into one and not the other.[38]

We can view service design as the process of not only planning, organizing, and improving an organization's existing services but also finding new and innovative ways to fulfill unmet customer needs. Service design is intended to enhance the customer's experience by examining the points of interaction between the service provider and the customer. Essentially, the aim of service design is to answer to these questions:

- What service should be provided?
- What is the nature of interaction between the customer and the service provider?
- Are the customers satisfied with it? If not, how can it be improved?

Customers and the service provider interact in several ways. These interaction touch points can occur face to face; via telephone, e-mail, and post mail; through websites and social media; through advertising and direct communication; after the delivery of the product; during the handling of complaints; and so forth. A company's service design should improve the different aspects of that interaction, which can range from written and verbal communication methods, to designing a customer-friendly, open office layout, to technologies supporting the company's service offerings, and so forth.

A firm should not only focus on the operations of its front office—that is, what customers see, such as the service staff—but should also evaluate its back office operations—the operations rarely seen by customers. A service design feature that focuses on the speedy processing of customers' written requests rarely involves the customer, but its impact is significant in terms of a customer's service experience with the company. In addition, a firm's service design can be used to improve the accessibility, usability, and content of a company's website, blogs, and social networking profile, which affect the customer's experience as well.

Many different service design tools and methods are available in providing a new service. Companies that provide services face important economic, social, cultural, environmental, and technological challenges where change is the only constant. Local and global customers are now better informed, more demanding, and better organized because of social networks. Service companies can meet these challenges and turn them into opportunities by using service design tools and methods to understand better their customers and their needs, goals, fears, and behaviors, so as to provide improved services to them.

The tools and methods used to design services are adapted from various disciplines including product design, interaction design and graphic design, the social sciences, and traditional business modeling and analytical methods. For example, designers often use *video-ethnography*. That is, the designers track their customers and record them as they use products and services so as to design better services for them. Another very useful tool for understanding the relationships among the different parts of a service system is the service system design matrix. The matrix establishes the relationship among three key factors of service: (1) the degree of contact between the consumer and the service provider, (2) the opportunity for sales, and (3) the service system's production efficiency. For example, the more contact a company has with a customer, the greater the chances are the firm will have an opportunity is to sell its service to the individual. This is the reason that checkout clerks

---

4.7

Identify the unique challenges service organizations face when designing their products, including the tools and methods they use to do so.

Service system design matrix: a tool that establishes the relationship among three key factors of service: (1) the degree of contact between the consumer and the service provider, (2) the opportunity for sales, and (3) the service system's production efficiency

FIGURE 4.10: Service System Design Matrix

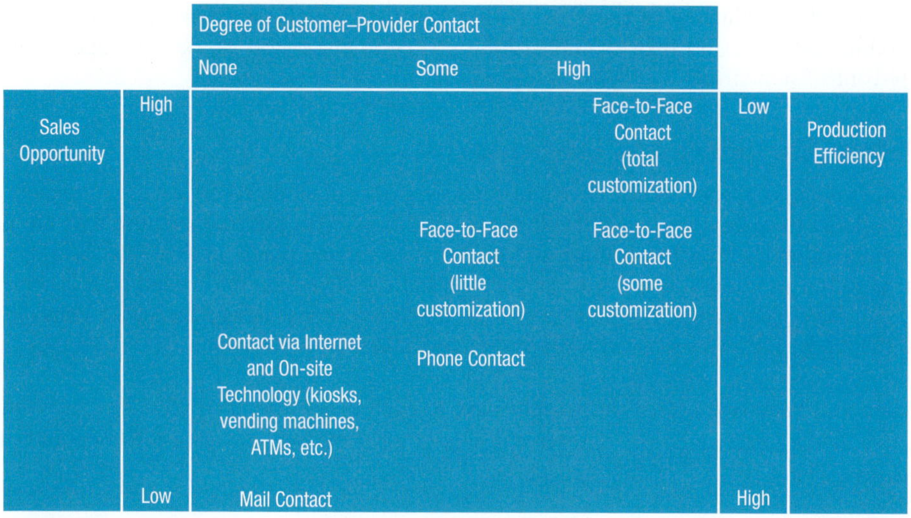

SOURCE: Studyblue. (n.d.). Service system management. Retrieved from https://www.studyblue.com/notes/note/n/-6-service-system-management/deck/6772308

at stores often ask you for your e-mail address, phone number, zip code, and other information. The matrix also establishes the relationship between the firm's production efficiency and degree of interaction it has with its customers. For example, services that require extensive customization and frequent customer input are less efficient.

The service system design matrix also categorizes the company's service delivery systems ranging from ordinary mail contact to face-to-face interaction involving the complete customization of products. The matrix is useful because it can identify whether a specific service operation needs attention or whether it can help assess the needs of the workers within the service system. For example, a customer of a bank may have very sophisticated and unique financial investment needs. In such a case, the employee of the bank assigned to this customer may need additional training, particularly on investments.

Figure 4.10 shows a service system design matrix. Let's now look at the six types of service delivery systems in the matrix.

1. **Face-to-face: Total customization.** This type of service delivery system has the highest degree of customer interaction. The customer and the service provider develop service specifications jointly. There is a high degree of latitude in this system as services can be tailored to the needs of the customer. Although the production efficiency of this service delivery system is low, the sales opportunities are very high. The financial investment services offered by a bank are an example this delivery system.

2. **Face-to-face: Some customization.** In this type of service delivery system, the overall service process is generally well understood. Nevertheless, there are some variations in the way in which the service can be delivered. In a bank, for example, the loan for a customer can be structured in many different ways or a client has different options for opening a checking account. Although not very efficient, this type of service also provides a high opportunity for sales. Customers are provided with the services that suit their needs, but unlike total customization, the services are chosen from standard products that the firm offers.

3. **Face-to-face: Little customization.** This type refers to a service delivery process in which there is very little variation because only a limited variety of services are available. A typical example of this type of service delivery process is the interaction between a customer and a teller in a bank. Although the production efficiency of this delivery system is greater than that of the other two systems just discussed, there are fewer sales opportunities.

4. **Phone contact.** Although most telephone inquiries these days are handled by automated menu systems, this type of service delivery may result in some customer interaction. For example, a bank customer may want to speak directly with a personal banker. In such cases, although some production efficiency is lost, the opportunity for a potential sale increases.

5. **Contact via Internet and on-site technology.** Kiosks, vending machines, and bank ATMs are examples of this type of service delivery. Fewer sales opportunities are associated with this type of service delivery system. Nevertheless, the system's production efficiency is high.

Internet banking is an exception because it allows for some customization and opportunities to generate sales.

6. **Mail contact.** Because direct customer contact is lacking in this type of service delivery system, the sales opportunities are low. An example of mail contact is the monthly statements sent by a bank.

The Ritz-Carlton (The Ritz-Carlton Hotel Company, L.L.C., Chevy Chase, MD), which is consistently rated among the top hotel chains in the world by customers, has adopted an effective service design. The Ritz-Carlton's mission is to satisfy its guests completely. The company's service philosophy is that the Ritz-Carlton is not offering its customers just a hotel room but also a great experience. Each employee at the Ritz-Carlton undergoes 120 hours of service training each year. For example, if a room attendant notices an empty soft drink container in a guest's room, per the company's service design guidelines, he or she has been trained to write down the type of beverage that the guest has been drinking. The next time the guests stay at a Ritz-Carlton hotel anywhere in the world, the same brand of beverage will be waiting in the person's room.

4.8 Legal, Ethical, and Sustainability Issues

4.8
Discuss some of the legal, ethical, and sustainability issues that affect firms developing new products and services.

Achieving quality products and services, focusing on customer needs, and finding the best methods to develop these new products and services are all critical functions of the operations and supply chain professional. Nevertheless, there are more issues involved in designing new products in addition to developing them efficiently. Consumers are increasingly concerned if the products do not perform as described or cause harm, and they also seek products that have a minimal impact on the environment. As a result, it is critical that we consider legal and ethical elements in product development, as well as the environmental and sustainability associated with new products and services.

Legal and Ethical Issues

When companies develop a new product, they are responsible for ensuring that the goods and services they produce do not harm consumers. From a legal point of view, organizations are clearly responsible for the design and safe use of their products. Many government regulatory acts such as the Federal Food, Drug, and Cosmetic Act of 1938 (amended in 2007) (United States), the Environmental Protection Act (U.K.), and the Hazardous Products Act (Canada) were intended to protect consumers. Both civil and criminal statutes provide consumers legal recourse when evidence shows that poorly designed goods or services have affected them adversely. Often, however, only the most serious and obvious offenses are settled this way. Many more difficult ethical issues related to product design crop up when the evidence is not very clear. For example, suppose a child accidently pressed the trigger of a power drill when the parent was not paying attention and was seriously injured. Who is responsible for this product's safety and its safe use? The parent? The power drill manufacturer? Should the power drill manufacturer have designed the drill with a simple and inexpensive lockout switch that would have to be pressed simultaneously when the trigger is pressed, thereby making it more difficult for the accident to happen?[39] Situations such as this demonstrate the complexity of designing safe products.

Most product designers are under immense pressure to accelerate the design process and to minimize costs. This pressure can encourage the designers to cut corners, leading to faulty product designs and workmanship that cause injuries and damages. Therefore, designers and the product development team should strictly adhere to legal and ethical standards. They should take the time needed to design products and services carefully to prevent expensive lawsuits and damage to the company's reputation.[40] For example, Volkswagen AG (Wolfsburg, Germany) came under considerable criticism for a decision it made to cheat on emissions testing in its diesel engines, which are used widely in both moderately priced and upscale brands, including Porsche (Porsche AG, Stuttgart, Baden-Württemberg, Germany) and Audi (Audi AG, Ingolstadt, Germany). Because of the discovery of Volkswagen's decision to install software designed to cheat emissions tests in 11 million cars worldwide, the company is now facing demands that it buy back nearly 500,000 of its vehicles. With fines and associated costs, it is estimated that Volkswagen stands to lose almost US$50 billion.[41] Wal-Mart (Wal-Mart Stores Inc., Bentonville, AR), on the other hand, is a company that makes customer safety a priority. Wal-Mart engages different independent third-party testing labs to ensure that the food, children's products, apparel, home, and pharmaceutical products that it sells comply with the highest safety standards set by state and federal government statutes.

Furthermore, ethically responsible companies introduce innovative products and services that go above and beyond meeting minimum legal requirements. The Buick Verano, introduced in 2012, has

TABLE 4.2: Sample Sustainability Checklist for New Product Development

SUSTAINABILITY-RELATED QUESTIONS	YES	NO
Will the product during the course of its full life cycle have a favorable impact on the planet?		
Will the product create sustainability-related risks in any form in which it will exist?		
During the new product development process, were various options or alternatives to determine environmental, social, and economic impacts evaluated?		
Can the product be manufactured using a method that involves lowest energy consumption?		
Can the product be manufactured using renewable energy sources?		
Can the product be manufactured by reusing existing materials, equipment, or both?		
Will the production process minimize the formation of by-products (chemical, radioactive, etc.) that can harm the environment or humans?		
By integrating or not integrating sustainability into the new product development process, what are risks the company faces in terms of its reputation, product differentiation strategy, and recruitment and retention of human resources?		
Does the company have or can it cost effectively acquire or develop production capabilities to integrate sustainability into the new product?		
What are the minimum legal environmental standards that the new product should meet?		

ergonomically designed seats that are not only comfortable but also alleviate back pain. General Motors, the maker of this car, was focusing on customer comfort and safety when it was designing the seats for this vehicle.[42]

Sustainability Issues

Globally, the number of consumers aware of and concerned about sustainability is growing. Regulatory requirements notwithstanding, companies across a wide range of industries are proactively responding to sustainability issues. Sustainability has an impact on two major areas of product development. The first is at the product–services level, and the other is at the operations level. At the product–services level, companies incorporate sustainability into the new product development process. For example, 3M, a globally diversified technology company and a leading proponent of the adoption and practice of sustainability, is incorporating sustainability by first considering the new product's purpose and then analyzing risks or factors that might inhibit its sales. The company then looks for ways to improve or modify the product to make it more sustainable. As part of this process, 3M assesses all environmental, health, and safety aspects of the product. Nevertheless, cost is rarely a deterrent for 3M when it comes improving the sustainability of a product perhaps because doing so helps give the product an edge over the competition.[43]

Although many leading companies are actively integrating sustainability into their new product development processes, the effort to do so is still in its infancy. Some of these companies are embedding sustainability into their Stage-Gate® approaches by using, whenever possible, quantitative measures of the triple bottom-line criteria. Although the specific criteria used to measure the sustainability of new products at the different stage gates can vary from company to company, they tend to combine some of the following:

- Economic sustainability criteria that include measures of technical feasibility and economic feasibility, such as production costs and the return on investment
- Environmental sustainability criteria that include measures of carbon emissions, recyclability, the use of renewable materials and natural resources, water and energy consumption, and waste
- Social sustainability criteria that include measures of health and safety, such as nutritional and hazardous material content, socially responsible sourcing, and the impact on employment in the firm and within the local community

Some criteria can be evaluated during the early stages of the product-development process after determining the technical and economic feasibility of the new product, whereas other criteria are best evaluated during middle stages of the process as more information becomes available about what the product will ultimately look like, how it will work, and so forth. Environmental and social criteria such as exhaust emissions and nutritional claims that are subject to regulatory legislation should be evaluated throughout the process. Tools, including questionnaires and checklists, can be used to evaluate sustainability during the Stage-Gate® new product development process.

A checklist of questions related to sustainability is listed in Table 4.2.[44]

One way to incorporate sustainability into products is the life-cycle assessment (LCA)—also known as life-cycle analysis—or the "cradle-to-grave" approach discussed in Chapter 2. The LCA approach over a product's entire life cycle, by analyzing and quantifying the environmental impacts caused by material inputs and outputs, such as energy use or air emissions, will enable both the companies producing the products and the consumers to make decisions that will benefit the environment.

Integrating sustainability into the new product development process is a challenge. Furthermore, the collaboration needed up and down supply chains to produce truly sustainable new products is rarely achieved. Much work remains to be done. Until sustainable new product development tools that are dynamic, cost effective, and easy to implement and use are developed, the process should be kept simple, along with educating employees and members of the supply chain about sustainable practices.[45]

Visit edge.sagepub.com/venkataraman to help you accomplish your coursework goals in an easy-to-use learning environment.

- Mobile-friendly eFlashcards
- Mobile-friendly practice quizzes
- A complete online action plan

- Chapter summaries with learning objectives
- Video and multimedia resources

CHAPTER SUMMARY

4.1 Explain why new product development is vital for organizations. Developing and introducing new products is vital to companies because they enable firms to expand their market share and stay ahead of the competition. They also allow the firm to survive in an intensely competitive global marketplace. Businesses will fail if they offer the same products day in and day out. Customers will stop buying the old products, sales will eventually drop off, and the firms' revenues and profits will decline. The product life cycle helps us understand the way in which most products are introduced, marketed, and eventually decline and fail.

4.2 Describe the approaches companies use to develop new products. Two common approaches to new product development approaches are (1) the traditional approach and (2) the Stage-Gate® approach. In the traditional approach, the process begins with generating ideas for a new product and ends with its final launch or commercialization. The Stage-Gate® approach is a conceptual and operational road map, in which the new product development process is divided into distinct stages and cross-functional teams are used to move the product from one stage to the next.

4.3 Demonstrate how new strategies have improved the way in which new products are designed and tested. In recent years, customers have demanded products with greater variety with more and better features, as well as products that are safer,

longer lasting, easier to use, and less costly to maintain. To respond to these customer expectations and to increasing environmental and health concerns, companies have devised new strategies for designing, producing, delivering, and disposing of products. Some of these strategies are modular design; robust product design; design for manufacturing and assembly; design for reliability; mass customization; design for disposal, remanufacturing, and recycling; and quality function deployment.

4.4 Discuss some new technologies that have allowed for faster new product development. The use of new technologies such as rapid prototyping, virtual reality, and computer-aided design have enabled companies to introduce quickly greater variety of products of higher quality and with better features, as well as products that are safe and environmentally friendly.

4.5 Explain the global product-development process and describe how organizations are increasingly using it to gain a strategic advantage. The global product development process involves working collaboratively with suppliers and skilled engineering teams dispersed around the world to develop new products. By forming such strategic partnerships with suppliers and other stakeholders, companies can create integrated global product teams to produce better products more quickly and more cost effectively. In addition to introducing innovative new products that exceed customer expectations, companies can also maximize the financial and operational productivity of the product development process.

4.6 **Describe how the collaboration of the members of a supply chain can improve product development.** Collaboration among supply chain members facilitates accurate and timely information flow among the members. Consequently, the right quality product is brought into the market on time. Elements of supply chain collaboration such as the early involvement of the supply chain members, creating a clear supply chain design, multistage quality testing, and understanding the operating process of each supply chain member greatly enhances the success of the new product development process.

4.7 **Identify the unique challenges service organizations face when designing their products, including the tools and methods they use to do so.** Design of services, unlike the design of a product, presents a unique challenge because services are intangible experiences offered to customers. Standardizing service is difficult because services are unique experiences that are customized for each consumer and must be delivered at varying points in time. The tools and methods used to design services are adapted from a variety of disciplines including product design, interaction design, and graphic design, the social sciences, and traditional business modeling and analytical methods. Some tools and methods used in service design include video-ethnography and service system design matrixes.

4.8 **Discuss some of the legal, ethical, and sustainability issues that affect firms developing new products and services.** From a legal perspective, companies involved in developing new products need to ensure that the goods and services they produce are safe and do not harm consumers. From an ethical perspective, companies must make every effort to ensure that the products they design are safe. Therefore, companies involved in developing new products should strictly adhere to legal and ethical standards, as well as develop strategies needed to design products and services with care that will prevent expensive lawsuits and damage to the company's reputation. In addition to legal and ethical requirements, sustainability issues also have an impact on the new product development process. To incorporate sustainability into new products, companies have to develop strategies that take into account all environmental, health, safety, and cost aspects of the product.

KEY TERMS

Beta testing   127

Computer-aided design (CAD)   135

Concurrent engineering   133

Design for disposal, remanufacturing, and recycling (DFDRR)   130

Design for manufacturing and assembly (DFMA)   129

Design for reliability (DFR)   129

Disruptive innovation   123

External variation   128

Global product development (GPD)   135

House of quality (HOQ)   130

Internal variation   128

Lead time   138

Mass customization   129

Modular design   127

New product development (NPD)   123

Process design   139

Product life-cycle management (PLCM)   124

Product lifecycle management (PLM)   124

Product platform   134

Quality function deployment (QFD)   130

Rapid prototyping   134

Reverse engineering   125

Robust product design   128

Service system design matrix   141

Stage-Gate® approach   125

Sustaining innovation   123

Target market   121

Time-based competition   134

Unit-to-unit variation   128

Value analysis (VA)   129

Value engineering (VE)   129

DISCUSSION AND REVIEW QUESTIONS

1. Why do new products fail? Pick an example of a product and a service that have failed, and discuss the reasons for their failure.

2. Discuss the reasons why businesses develop new products.

3. Compare and contrast sustaining and disruptive innovation using examples to describe each.

4. Compare and contrast product lifecycle management (PLM) and product life-cycle management (PLCM).

5. Provide examples of products in each of the following categories that are in different stages of their life cycles:

   a. Televisions

   b. Computers

   c. Pharmaceuticals

   d. Entertainment

6. Think of a new product and how the Stage-Gate® system could be used to develop it.

7. Name a product or company that you believe uses the following new product development concepts or tools:

   a. Robust design

   b. Mass customization

   c. Design for manufacturing and assembly (DFMA)

   d. Quality function deployment (QFD)

   e. Computer-aided design (CAD)

8. Pick a product or service, and using the house of quality, analyze how that company meets its customers' expectations.

9. Discuss the concept of time-based competition.

10. What are the fundamental aspects of globalized new product development?

11. Discuss the challenges of designing new products globally. What factors are critical to the success of such a strategy?

12. Discuss some supply chain issues that affect the development of new products.

13. Discuss the four key areas of supply chain collaboration that affect the success of the new product development process.

14. Outline the questions a service design should address.

15. Describe the service system design matrix, and explain how it helps companies develop better services for their customers.

16. Pick a new product, and discuss the three sustainability criteria you would look at when designing the product. Be specific.

17. What are some of the legal and ethical issues that companies need to consider while developing new products?

18. Pick a new product and use the Stage-Gate® system to outline how you would integrate sustainability into the product's development.

PROBLEMS

1. Construct a house of quality for a pair of expensive designer sunglasses. Make sure to identify some features that you think someone interested in buying such sunglasses would expect. Then complete the matrix to identify some attributes that you think an operations manager could measure in assessing how well his or her product meets customer expectations.

2. Construct a simple house of quality matrix for a table lamp. Begin by identifying (in your opinion) what attributes customers would want in a table lamp. Then complete the house of quality matrix to show how you as an operations manager would identify specific attributes that can be included in the table lamp to meet those customer needs.

3. Construct a house of quality matrix for Southwest Airlines.

4. You are planning to introduce a brand new refrigerator. You have also identified the following attributes that customers want in a new refrigerator: low price, low energy consumption, quiet operation, maintains food freshness, maintains temperature, dispenses purified water, storage flexibility, easy to clean, matches kitchen décor, and maximizes storage space. Your competition includes Maytag (manufactured by the Whirlpool Corporation, Benton Charter Township, MI), Whirlpool (manufactured by the Whirlpool Corporation), GE (manufactured by General Electric), and Frigidaire (Frigidaire Appliance Company, Charlotte, NC). Construct a house of quality matrix for the new refrigerator.

5. Identify three products that are, in your opinion, poorly named. Why do you find these products to be mid-named?

6. Conduct a simple value engineering exercise on a household appliance, such as a refrigerator, washing machine, or gas range.

7. Using the Chevrolet Malibu (Case Study 4.1) as an example, identify three or more ways that you might suggest applying value engineering principles to improving the product.

8. Identify five products that you recognize solely by their logos. What was it about these products that makes them instantly recognizable to you?

9. Conduct an Internet research for some examples of products that failed because of cultural differences. What are some common themes that you see emerging among these failures?

10. Using your research from problem 8, develop three lessons that all companies should pay attention to before attempting to launch products in other markets.

11. How will mobile and smartphone innovations continue to push common products further down the product life cycle toward obsolescence? How are the Venmo (subsidiary of PayPal Holdings, Inc., San Jose, CA) and PayPal (PayPal Holdings, Inc.) mobile payment apps likely to impact people's use of cash or debit card usage?

12. Identify a food product on the McDonald's menu that you would expect will fail within one year. Why do you believe this is the case?

13. You are a Marine procurement officer interviewing potential vendors for a new combat-zone communications device. How would you value features such as modular design, design for reliability, and robust product design? How might each of these features affect your decision on which communication system to recommend purchasing?

CASE STUDY 4.1 REDESIGNING FOR EFFICIENCY: THE CHEVROLET MALIBU

The future poses a serious challenge for automotive designers as they try to comply with federal fuel efficiency guidelines. After rising just 10 miles per gallon (mpg) in the past 30 years, U.S. fuel economy regulations are in the midst of a serious upward adjustment. By 2025, the average new vehicle is required to get 54.5 mpg—double the 2012 requirement of 27.3 mpg. In practical terms, that means that fuel economy is expected to increase by more than 2 mpg a year for the next decade. This dramatic increase makes it necessary for all automotive companies to improve fuel efficiency in their current fleet of cars, while looking for ways to get better mileage out of the new cars they design. Some choices the companies are making have been very creative:

- Honda's 2012 Civic (Honda Motor Co., Tokyo, Japan) uses specially coated engine pistons that reduce friction. This modification improved fuel efficiency by 2%.
- The 2012 Toyota Camry (Toyota Motor Corporation) weighs 150 pounds less than the previous year's model. The lower weight improved mileage.
- Chrysler (Fiat Chrysler Automobiles) is using a more efficient eight-speed automatic transmission in its 300 sedan model. This improved its highway mileage by 3 mpg.

General Motors is benefiting from a three-year project to find innovative ways to redesign its Chevrolet Malibu to enhance its fuel efficiency. The challenge was significant because GM did not want to redesign the Malibu completely. Among the ways that GM achieved fuel savings was by using lighter materials. For example, aluminum has replaced steel in the vehicle's hood and rear bumper beam. A new six-speed automatic transmission was installed in place of the car's five-speed shifter. GM also installed a smaller, fuel-injected engine that is more efficient but makes the car feel as if it has more power. To decrease its weight, the Malibu no longer has a spare tire. The tire has been replaced by a much lighter re-inflation kit (an air compressor and liquid sealant). Other changes are barely noticeable; for example, the front and rear and underbody have been redesigned to be more aerodynamic and improve fuel efficiency. The result of all these changes is that the Malibu will get at least seven more miles per gallon, and a tank of gas will take the vehicle an additional 92 miles.

One way or another, car manufacturers will find ways to wring additional mileage out of their automobiles. With the use of hybrid and electric power options, it is only a matter of time before all cars driven in the United States will be pushing the 50-mpg envelope.[46]

Questions:

1. Take a side in agreeing or disagreeing with the following statement: "The push to improve fuel efficiency is likely to cause engineers to pursue increasingly risky and untried technologies, ultimately to the detriment of the consumer."

2. How does a car company manage to follow efficiency guidelines and maintain an image of quality? That is, are these competing goals and, if so, how does the company balance them?

VIDEO CASE ···

Watch this video case to learn about what factors Rolls-Royce considers when developing new products.

CRITICAL THINKING EXERCISES ··

The purpose of this exercise is to promote entrepreneurial thinking among students by exposing them to some creative new products that were developed to meet the needs of everyday life.

Visit https://www.buzzfeed.com/peggy/genius-new-products-you-had-no-idea-existed?utm_term=.beppjxdBdP#.hjA7o4JxJv

This website lists some of the weirdest and some of the most ingenious new product ideas. Working as a team with some of your classmates, develop an idea for a simple new product or service that will satisfy an unmet need in your everyday life. You need to develop the product concept in full, delineating the features the product will have to satisfy your unmet need. Next, create on paper a visual representation of the product idea.

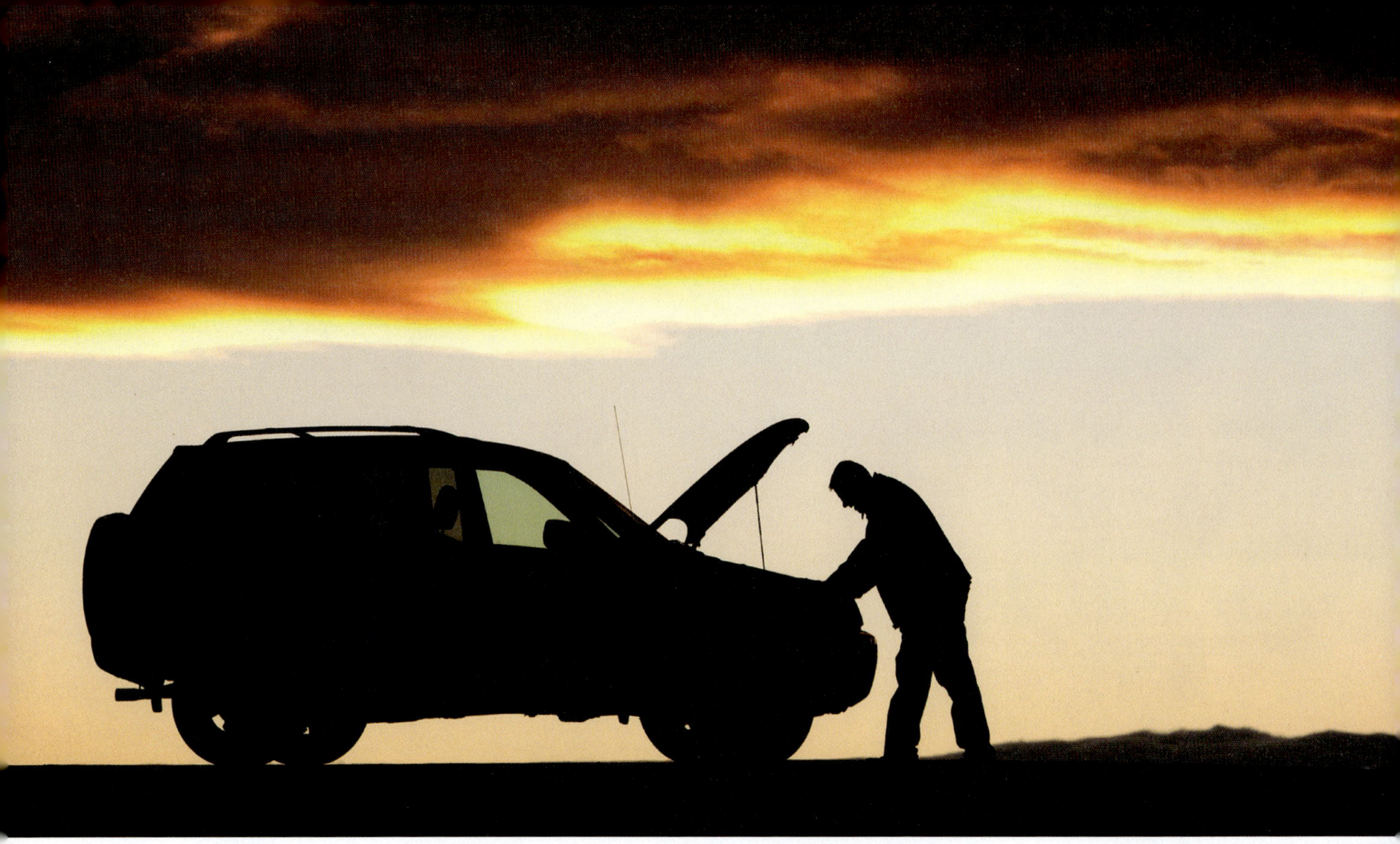

©iStockphoto.com/ImagineGolf

SUPPLEMENT FOR CHAPTER 4 Reliability

LEARNING OBJECTIVES

After studying this supplement, you should be able to:

1. Define reliability and compute the reliability of a product system.
2. Distinguish among the concepts of reliability, maintainability, and availability.

OPERATIONS PROFILE: Computer Glitch Grounds United Airlines

Under the best of circumstances, air travel can be aggravating and a constant test of our patience. Nevertheless, under conditions of computer failures, the impact on thousands of air travelers is decidedly vexing. On July 8, 2015, United Airlines (aka United, owned by United Continental Holdings, Inc., Chicago, IL) suffered a computer failure of a network router that disrupted its reservation system and degraded the network's ability to connect to perform a wide variety of applications. United was forced to cancel 59 flights and delay more than 800 flights as a result of the computer failure. This was not United's first brush with balky computer systems. A malfunction shut down the airline's computers in 2014, again delaying take-offs and leaving thousands of passengers fretting about connections. Computer troubles also were to blame for hundreds of delayed flights in August and November 2012.

Computer experts have suggested that the problems can be blamed on larger and more complicated computer systems with insufficient technical support, testing, and emergency backup systems. Anthony Roman, a former pilot and president of a large risk management firm, noted, "All major conglomerates should have redundant systems so that regardless of what fails you have a seamless operation." Yet, their computer systems are now connected to ticketing kiosks, automatic luggage drop-offs, mobile automated flight status notification systems, and other applications that are straining their capabilities.

Airline computer problems continue to persist, and are even increasing, according to experts, because the airline mergers forced carriers to find ways to combine their computer systems to support reservation booking and scheduling. Investing in new computers, including updating old legacy systems and providing sufficient backup and technical support, is becoming increasingly critical, not only for travel convenience but also for overall passenger safety. In a statement, United said that its network was reliable and includes several redundant systems, "but we continue to invest and improve on the reliability of those networks to deliver better service to our customers."[1]

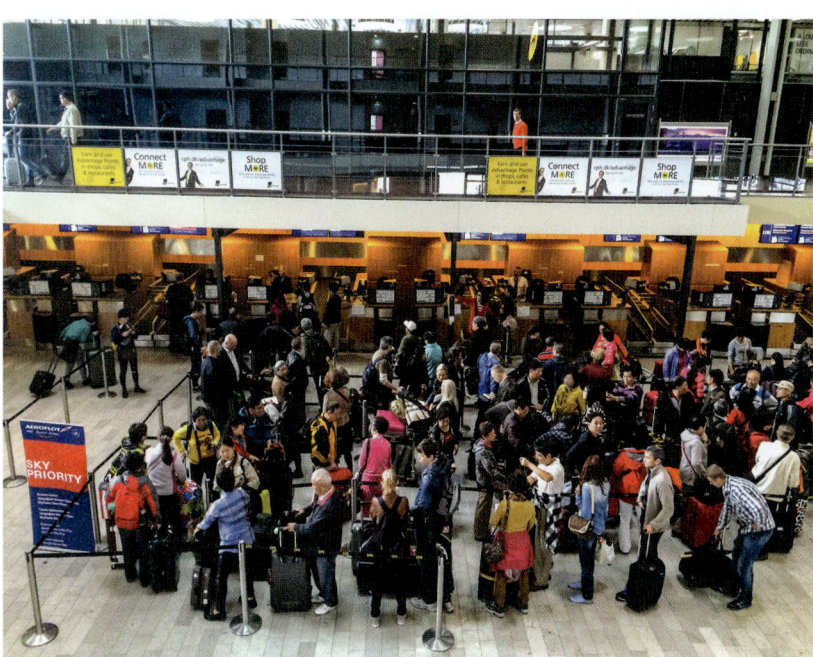

©iStockphoto.com/Anna Bryukhanova

Estimating
Reliability

Reliability: the
probability that a
component, product, or
system can perform its
intended function over
a period of time under
a given set of normal
operating conditions of
its use

Independent events:
components that, when
working or failing, in no
way affect the probability
that another will work
or fail

4S.1 Understanding Reliability

Define reliability and compute the reliability of a product system.

Product failure is familiar. At one time or another, everyone has faced the frustration of a computer crashing, a smartphone failing, or malfunctioning automobiles or household appliances. Airlines and electric utility companies experience mechanical problems or power outages as a result of system failures, bad weather, or accidents. Recently, a computer glitch caused the "big board" at the New York Stock Exchange to halt trading for nearly four hours, costing firms millions as jittery investors tried to dump stocks to get out of the market.[2] Because product failures can and do occur, companies introducing new products provide product warranties, maintenance guarantees, technical assistance, and part repair. With the propensity of a product or system to fail and the serious consequences that accompany such failures, a separate field of study known as *reliability* has evolved to analyze and estimate the likelihood of product and system failures over time.

Estimating Reliability

Reliability can be defined as the probability that a component, product, or system can perform its intended function over a period of time under a given set of normal operating conditions of its use. For example, a household vacuum cleaner having a 98% reliability means that 98% of the time it can perform its intended function of picking up dirt from a carpet without failure or malfunction for a specified duration (e.g., a year). The key phrase in the definition of reliability is *under a given set of normal operating conditions of its use*. In the case of a household vacuum cleaner, the given set of normal operating conditions is its use to clean carpets. If it is used to pick up gravel in your driveway or vacuum up spilled water, then it is not being used for the normal operating conditions for which the vacuum cleaner was intended. Similarly, when car manufacturers offer a three-year or 50,000-mile warranty on new cars, the given set of normal operating conditions of its use will require the car owner to observe the required maintenance procedures, including periodic inspections and oil and filter changes. The warranty on the car would be null and void if these maintenance procedures were never followed.

Because a product or system is made up of many components, the overall reliability of a product or system depends on the reliability of its individual components and the way in which they are arranged. By ascertaining the number of working or failing components, the reliability of the product or system can be established. For example, for a system to function properly, all of its individual components must also be working. In that case, the overall reliability of that system is a product of the reliabilities of its individual components. Thus, if there are n components in a system (S) with individual reliabilities of $R(C_1)$, $R(C_2)$, $R(C_3)$, etc., up to $R(C_n)$, then the overall reliability of the system $R(S)$ is given by:

$$R(S) = R(C_1) \times R(C_2) \times R(C_3) \ldots \times R(C_n)$$

Let us illustrate this formula with an example. Suppose a product has three components arranged in a series as shown in Figure 4S.1.

If each component has a reliability of 0.95, then the overall reliability of the system $R(S)$ is given by:

$$R(S) = R(C_1) \times R(C_2) \times R(C_3) = 0.95 \times 0.95 \times 0.95 = 0.857$$

We interpret this result to mean that at any given time, when using the product, there is an 85.7% likelihood that the product will function correctly for a specified duration. The reliability of the system in Figure 4S.1 is the product of the three component reliabilities. The computation of the reliability of the system assumes that the reliabilities of the three components are independent events. According to probability theory, the concept of independence in this context means that one component working or failing in no way affects the probability that another will work or fail.

Notice that the overall reliability of 0.857 for the system is significantly less than the reliability of 0.95 of the individual components. From the example, we can infer that for any product, as the number of components arranged in sequence increases, the overall reliability of the product decreases. Hence, in product design, simpler designs with fewer components are likely to improve reliability.

FIGURE 4S.1: Three Components Arranged in a Series

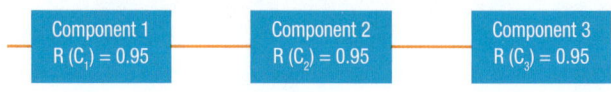

FIGURE 4S.2 Three Components with Redundancy in Component 2

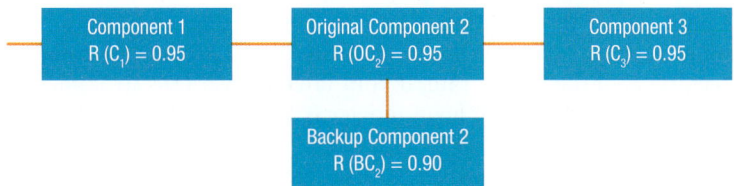

For many products or systems that perform "safety critical" functions, it is essential that they maintain high reliability because failure of these functions could result in loss of life, significant property damage, or damage to the environment. For example, the hydraulic systems that allow us to operate aircraft, brakes in a car, high-speed elevators, and early warning systems for missile defense must have the highest possible reliability. To maintain or increase the reliability of systems or products, the components or subsystems that perform the critical functions are often duplicated to serve as a backup if the original component or subsystem fails. This duplication of critical components is called redundancy, by which duplicate components operate in parallel to the original component, as shown for a system in Figure 4S.2.

In Figure 4S.2, the function performed by component 2 is critical and, hence, has a backup to the original component. If the original component fails [which can happen 5% (100% − 95%) of the time], then the backup component (which has a reliability of 90%) is automatically activated. To calculate the overall reliability of system depicted in Figure 4S.2, we first calculate the composite reliability of component 2 (original + backup) as follows:

$$R\ (C_2) = R\ (OC_2) + [1 - R\ (OC_2)] \times R\ (BC_2) = 0.95 + (1 - 0.95) \times 0.90 = 0.995$$

You can see that the backup component has increased the overall reliability of component 2 to 99.5%. As we still have a system of three components in series, the reliability of the overall system is calculated as shown:

$$R\ (S) = R\ (C_1) \times R\ (C_2) \times R\ (C_3) = 0.95 \times 0.995 \times 0.95 = 0.898$$

EXAMPLE 4S.1: An electrical power system has four major components with reliabilities of 0.99, 0.90, 0.95, and 0.96. All four components must function to prevent the failure of the electrical power system:

Reliability of an
Electrical Power
System

a. Compute the reliability of the overall power system.

b. If the designers of the electrical power system want to improve the reliability of the system by adding a backup component, which component should get the backup to achieve the highest reliability and compute the reliability of the system with the addition of the redundant component? Assume that the backup component has the same reliability as the original component.

SOLUTION

a. Compute the reliability of the overall power system:

$$P\ (S) = P\ (C_1) \times P\ (C_2) \times P\ (C_3) \times P\ (C_4) = 0.99 \times 0.90 \times 0.95 \times 0.96 = 0.8125$$

b. Since component 2 has the lowest reliability, it is the weakest link in the system and, hence, requires a redundant component as a backup. To calculate the overall reliability of the power system, we first calculate the composite reliability of component 2 (original + backup) as follows:

$$P\ (C_2) = P\ (OC_2) + [1 - P\ (OC_2)] \times P\ (BC_2) = 0.90 + (1 - 0.90) \times 0.90 = 0.99$$

As we have now a revised system of four components in series, the reliability of the overall system is calculated as:

$$P\ (S) = P\ (C_1) \times P\ (C_2) \times P\ (C_3) \times P\ (C_4) = 0.99 \times 0.99 \times 0.95 \times 0.96 = 0.8938$$

Redundancy: the duplication of critical components, by which duplicate systems operate in parallel with the original component

The reliability of a product or component can also be expressed as the average length of time elapsed before the product or component fails, known as the mean time between failures (MTBF). For example, a car transmission may have a mean time of 5,000 hours between failures. MTBF can also be calculated if the failure rate of the product or component is known by taking the reciprocal of the failure rate. If your lawn mower fails five times in 200 hours of operation, then the failure rate of the lawn mower is 5/200 = 0.025, and its MTBF = 1/0.025 = 40 hours.

When companies design a new product, a manufacturer can specify a desired MTBF as a quantifiable objective against which the actual reliability of the product or component achieved can be compared. Manufacturers of new products can develop MTBF measures through intensive product testing, based on actual past experience of similar products, or MTBF can be estimated by analyzing known factors that cause product failures. As reliability is an important dimension of product quality that determines the success of the product in the marketplace, companies should set reliability goals. With such goals in place, production efficiency can be achieved by reducing equipment failures and waste, as well as the ability of the production system to operate at an optimum level.

 4S.2

Distinguish among the concepts of reliability, maintainability, and availability.

4S.2 Availability and Maintainability

A concept that is different from, but closely related to, reliability, as well as one that is important to both costumers and designers, is availability of the system or equipment. Availability is the percentage of the time that the system or equipment is operating properly when it is needed for use. This definition of availability implies it is the fraction (or proportion) of the time that the equipment or system has not failed or is undergoing repairs. Note that when the system or equipment has availability, it does not necessarily mean that it also has high reliability. Reliability only considers the time it takes for a component, piece of equipment, or system to fail *while it is operating*, but it does not take into account any downtime associated with the repairs the system may need. That is, reliability does not take into consideration the time it would take to complete the repairs and bring the equipment or system back to working condition, and hence, make it *available for use*. If the equipment or system has been properly maintained, then it would take less time to repair and the availability of the equipment or system for use would be high. Therefore, availability is not only related to reliability, but it is also a function of maintainability. Maintainability is the ease with which the equipment or system can be repaired or serviced. For example, cars that use simple components that are easily replaced would be considered highly maintainable. On the other hand, a luxury automobile containing many complicated or highly interdependent systems would take a long time to service and have low maintainability. Table 4S.1 shows the relationship among the three concepts of reliability, maintainability, and availability.[3]

We can see from Table 4S.1 that to increase the availability of the equipment or system for use, either reliability and maintainability have to be constant or reliability has to increase with constant maintainability. We can also develop a quantitative measure for availability from MTBF, the metric for reliability, and mean time to repair (MTTR), which is a quantitative metric for maintainability, as follows:

$$\text{Availability} = \frac{MTBF}{MTBF + MTTR}$$

Mean time between failures (MTBF): the reliability of a product or component expressed as the average length of time elapsed before the product or component fails

Availability: the percentage of the time that the system or equipment is operating properly when it is needed for use

Maintainability: the ease with which an equipment or system can be repaired or serviced

Mean time to repair (MTTR): a quantitative metric for maintainability

TABLE 4S.1: Relationships Among Reliability, Maintainability, and Availability

RELIABILITY	MAINTAINABILITY	AVAILABILITY
Constant	Decreases	Decreases
Constant	Increases	Increases
Increases	Constant	Increases
Decreases	Constant	Decreases

Used with permission from ReliaSoft. Retrieved from http://www.reliasoft.com

EXAMPLE 4S.2: A laser printer can operate 300 hours between repairs (MTBF), and the MTTR of the printer is 3 hours. Compute the availability of the printer.

SOLUTION

$$\text{Given: MTBF} = 300 \text{ hours; MTTR} = 3 \text{ hours}$$

$$\text{Availability} = \frac{MTBF}{MTBF + MTTR} = \frac{300}{300 + 3} = \frac{300}{303} = 0.99\%$$

The implication of Table 4S.1 and the availability formula for designers is that as the MTBF increases (reliability increases) and MTTR decreases (maintainability increases), availability also increases. Thus, companies should design products that ensure a long time between failures. To reduce the MTTR, designers can incorporate design options in products that facilitate quick and easy repairs. For example, by incorporating a modular design in products such as computers and printers, MTTR can be decreased by replacing entire modules such as control panels, disk drives, and print cartridges when they malfunction.

Reliability refers to the probability that a component, product, or system can perform its intended function over a period of time under a given set of normal operating conditions. The reliability of a product or component can also be expressed as the average length of time elapsed before the product or component fails, known as MTBF. Because a product or system is usually made up of numerous components, the overall reliability of a product or system depends on the reliability of its individual components and the way in which they are arranged. As a result, by ascertaining the number of working or failed components, we can establish the reliability of the product or system.

Reliability, Availability, Maintainability

Two concepts that are closely related to reliability are the availability and maintainability of the system or equipment. Availability is the percentage of the time that the system or equipment is operating properly when it is needed for use. Maintainability is the ease with which a piece of equipment or system can be repaired or serviced.

$SAGE edge™

Visit **edge.sagepub.com/venkataraman** to help you accomplish your coursework goals in an easy-to-use learning environment.

- Mobile-friendly eFlashcards
- Mobile-friendly practice quizzes
- A complete online action plan
- Chapter summaries with learning objectives
- Video and multimedia resources

SUPPLEMENT SUMMARY

4S.1 Define reliability and compute the reliability of a product system. Reliability is the probability that a component, product, or system can perform its intended function over a period of time under a given set of normal operating conditions. The reliability of a product or component can also be expressed as the average length of time elapsed before the product or component fails, known as MTBF (mean time between failures). Because a product or system is made up of many components, the overall reliability of a product or system depends on the reliability of its individual components and the way in which they are arranged. By ascertaining the number of working or failed components, the reliability of the product or system can be established. For example, for a system to function properly, all of its individual components must also be working. The overall reliability of that system is a product of the reliabilities of its individual components. Thus, if there are n components in a system (S) with individual reliabilities of R (C_1), R (C_2), R (C_3), etc., up to R (C_n), then the overall reliability of the system R_S is given by:

$$R(S) = R(C_1) \times R(C_2) \times R(C_3) \ldots \times R(C_n)$$

4S.2 Distinguish among the concepts of reliability, maintainability, and availability. Reliability is the probability that a component, product, or system can perform its intended function over a period of time under a given set of normal operating conditions of its use. Availability is the percentage of the time that the system or equipment is operating properly when it is needed for use. The definition of availability implies it is that fraction of the time that the equipment or system has not failed or undergoing repairs. Maintainability is the ease with which the equipment or system can be repaired or serviced. Note that reliability does not take into consideration the time it would take to complete the repairs and bring the equipment or system back to working condition, making it, hence, available for use. If the equipment or system has been properly maintained, then it would take less time to repair and the availability of the equipment or system for use would be high.

KEY TERMS

Availability   154

Independent events   152

Maintainability   154

Mean time between failures (MTBF)   154

Mean time to repair (MTTR)   154

Redundancy   153

Reliability   152

DISCUSSION AND REVIEW QUESTIONS

1. What is the meaning of the term *reliability*?

2. Define the term *redundancy*, and discuss the role it can play in improving product design.

3. How are reliability and availability related? And how are they different?

4. Discuss how reliability, maintainability, and availability are related by using an example of a product or service that you are familiar with.

SOLVED PROBLEMS

1. Makework Industries (a fictional company) assembles industrial machines using four components in series that each have a reliability of 0.95. Customers who purchase these machines require a reliability of 0.94.

    a. Does the reliability of the machine meet customer expectations? If not, why?

    b. To achieve a reliability of 0.94 for the machine, what should be the reliability of the individual components?

    c. If the reliability of the individual components cannot be increased, but one redundant component with a reliability of 0.92 can be added as a backup to each original component, how many redundant components would be needed to achieve a reliability of 0.94 for the machine?

Solution:

a. The four components of the machine are arranged in series as shown:

Hence, the reliability of the machine R (M) is given by:

$$R (M) = R (S) = R (C_1) \times R (C_2) \times R (C_3) \times R (C_4) = 0.95 \times 0.95 \times 0.95 \times 0.95 = 0.814$$

The reliability of the machine does not meet customer expectations of 94% reliability. This is because the reliability of the individual components is not high enough to achieve an overall reliability of 94% for the machine.

b. The reliability of the components required to achieve a reliability of 94% for the machine is computed as shown:

$$\sqrt[4]{0.94} = 0.985$$

Thus, each of the four individual components needs to have a reliability of 0.985 to achieve a 94% reliability for the machine.

c. To determine the number of backup or redundant components needed to achieve a reliability of 0.94 for the machine, we proceed by calculating the overall reliability of the machine after adding one backup component at a time.

One redundant component

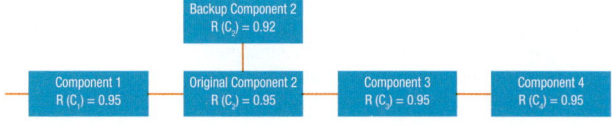

Thus, the combined reliability of component 2 is: $R (C_2) = R (OC_2) + (1 - R (OC_2)) \times R (BC_2) = 0.95 + (1 - 0.95) \times 0.92 = 0.996$

Therefore, the reliability of the machine is given by: $R (M) = R (S) = R (C_1) \times R (C_2) \times R (C_3) \times R (C_4) = 0.95 \times 0.996 \times 0.95 \times 0.95 = 0.854$

Since the reliability of the machine is still below the target value of 0.94, we add another backup component as shown:

Two redundant components

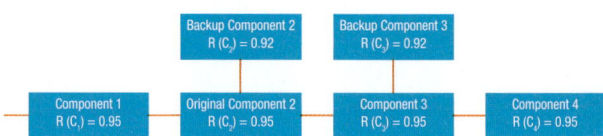

Thus, the combined reliability of component 3 is: $R (C_3) = R (OC_3) + (1 - R (OC_3)) \times R (BC_3) = 0.95 + (1 - 0.95) \times 0.92 = 0.996$

The reliability of the machine is given by: $R (M) = R (S) = R (C_1) \times R (C_2) \times R (C_3) \times R (C_4) = 0.95 \times 0.996 \times 0.996 \times 0.95 = 0.895$

Since the reliability of the machine is still below the target value of 0.94, we add a third backup component as shown:

Three redundant components

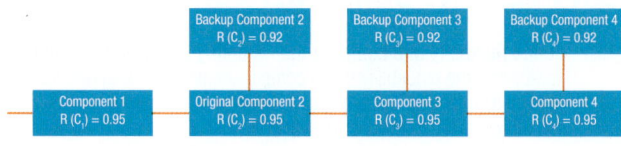

Thus, the combined reliability of component 4 is: $R (C_4) = R (OC_4) + (1 - R (OC_4)) \times R (BC_4) = 0.95 + (1 - 0.95) \times 0.92 = 0.996$

The reliability of the machine is now given by: $R (M) = R (S) = R (C_1) \times R (C_2) \times R (C_3) \times R (C_4) = 0.95 \times 0.996 \times 0.996 \times 0.996 = 0.939$

Since the reliability of the machine is very close to the target value of 0.94, we need three backup components.

2. Nicole Keller wants to choose a highly reliable satellite TV provider with minimum service disruptions. Nicole has collected the following data on mean time between failures (MTBF) and mean time to repair

(MTTR) for three fictitious satellite TV providers. Which TV provider should Nicole choose?

Satellite TV Provider	MTBF	MTTR
Crescent TV Network	300	5
Horizon TV Network	400	10
Perseus TV Network	600	15

Solution:

To help Nicole choose the right TV provider, we calculate the network availability for each TV provider by using the following formula:

$$\text{Availability} = \frac{MTBF}{MTBF + MTTR}$$

Satellite TV Provider	MTBF	MTTR	Availability
Crescent TV Network	300	7	$\frac{300}{300+7} = 0.977$
Horizon TV Network	400	10	$\frac{400}{400+10} = 0.975$
Perseus TV Network	600	12	$\frac{600}{600+12} = 0.98$

Nicole should choose Perseus TV network as it has the highest percentage of service availability.

PROBLEMS

1. Compute the reliability of the following system:

2. Compute the reliability of the following system:

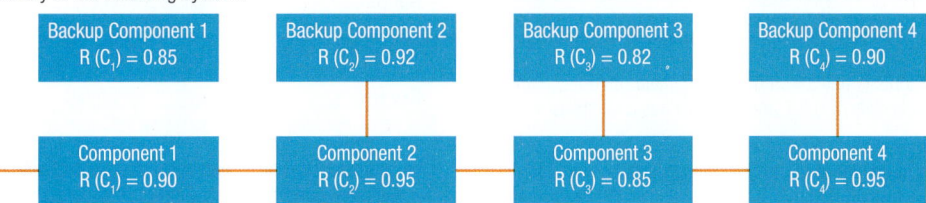

3. Which among the following systems is most reliable, A, B, C, or D? Why?

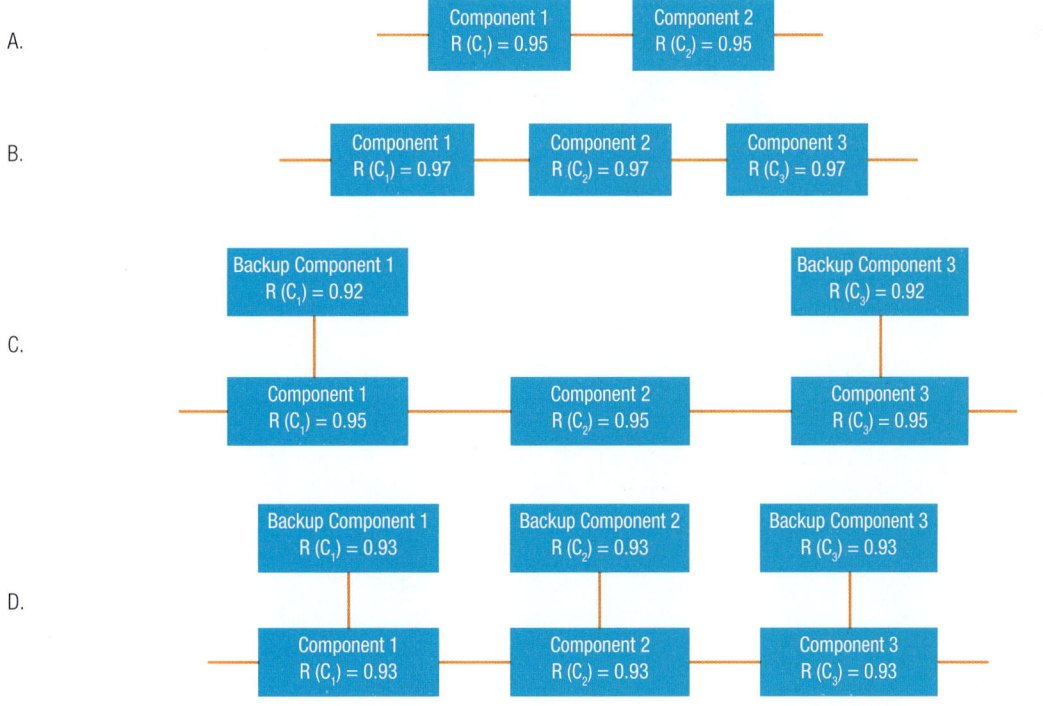

4. Image Tech, LLC (Oakland, CA) assembles cameras with the following structure from four major components:

Image Tech can purchase the four components from three different suppliers who have the following reliability data for each of the four components. If Image Tech wants to purchase all four components from one supplier, which one should it choose?

Component	Supplier A	Supplier B	Supplier C
1	0.95	0.88	0.90
2	0.90	0.92	0. 85
3	0.93	0.95	0.98
4	0.89	0.97	0. 93

5. Refer to problem 3. If the cost of the components varies according to their reliability levels as shown in the following table, and the cost to replace a failed system is $15,000, which of the four systems (A, B, C, or D) should be chosen?

Component Reliability	0.92	0.93	0.95	0.97
Cost (in U.S. dollars)	1,500	2,000	2,500	3,000

6. The hydraulic systems in an aircraft have three major modules. Two modules have a reliability of 0.98, and the third has a reliability of 0.99.

    a. What is the reliability of the hydraulic system?

    b. Given the safety-critical nature of an aircraft's hydraulic system, the manufacturer of the aircraft has decided to add redundant modules to each of the three major modules. If the reliabilities of the backup modules are identical to the original modules, what is the overall reliability of the hydraulic system with the backup modules?

7. Bobbie Peters, the office manager at the business school office at a university, is debating whether a new laser printer should be purchased for faculty use. The school currently has one laser printer that has an MTBF of 150 hours and an MTTR of 48 hours. Since the usage of the current laser printer has increased in recent years, Bobbie has decided that she would purchase another laser printer if the current laser printer's availability is less than 95%. What decision should Bobbie make?

8. Janet Grillo is unhappy with her current high-speed Internet service. She is considering switching to another Internet service provider. Janet has narrowed her choices to three fictitious Internet service providers and has collected the following data in hours on mean time between failures (MTBF) and mean time to repair (MTTR) for the three service providers. There is not much difference in the cost and speed service among the three Internet service providers. Given this information, which Internet service providers should Janet choose?

Internet Service Provider	MTBF	MTTR
Horizon	25	2
Star Cable	45	5
Sky Reach	70	7

9. An industrial robotic system can operate an average of 12 weeks for optimum performance and needs maintenance service to prevent system failure. The robotic system operates five days a week. If service maintenance takes an average of three days, what is the availability of this robotic system?

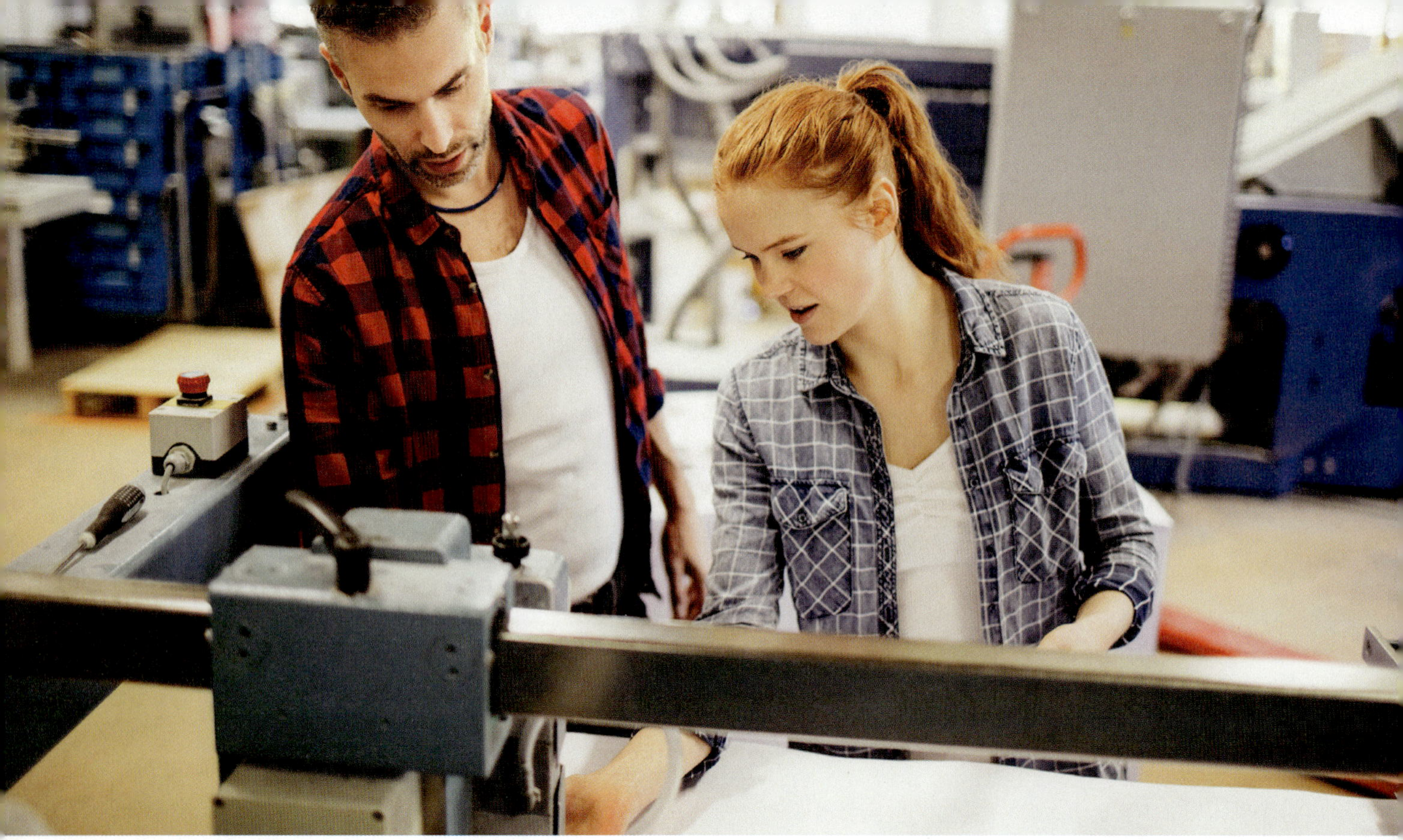

©iStockphoto.com/Geber86

CHAPTER 5 Managing for Quality

LEARNING OBJECTIVES

After studying this chapter, you should be able to:

1. Explain the importance of quality, the difficulties in measuring quality, and the differences in quality for different people or groups.
2. Outline the benefits and costs of creating quality products and services.
3. Describe the evolution of quality management and identify the pioneers who contributed to modern quality management methods.
4. Compare these major quality management initiatives: total quality management (TQM), the ISO 9000 family of quality standards, the Baldrige Award, Six Sigma, and DMADV methodologies.
5. Identify and describe some of the basic tools managers and employees use to manage quality in their firms.
6. Discuss the process of managing quality in supply chains.
7. Discuss the challenges of managing quality in global supply chains.
8. Describe the ethical and legal relationship among quality, sustainability, and corporate social responsibility.

OPERATIONS PROFILE: Louis Vuitton Spares No Expense to Gain the Quality "Seal of Approval" for Its Watches

tony french / Alamy Stock Photo

Although Louis Vuitton (Louis Vuitton Malletier, Paris, France) has long been known in the fashion world for its high-quality luggage, handbags, and accessories, it wasn't until six years ago, when Hamdi Chatti took over the brand's watch and jewelry division, that it set a new standard of quality for one of its product lines. The company recently announced that they have achieved the coveted Seal of Geneva standard for their watches and flew in guests and industry analysts worldwide to the Swiss city to celebrate their achievement. The Seal of Geneva is a rigorous set of quality and aesthetic standards that dates from 1886, when Geneva's reputation as a watchmaking center was under threat from counterfeiters, peddling fake Swiss watches. The canton of Geneva set up a system of optional inspection for watches made within its borders and, if standards were met, they would be engraved with the arms of the city of Geneva. Among the notable watchmakers with this quality seal are some of the most well-known luxury brands in the world, including: Cartier (Société Cartier, Paris, France), Chopard (Geneva, Switzerland), Roger Dubuis (Geneva, Switzerland), Vacheron Constantin (Geneva, Switzerland), and Ateliers deMonaco (Monte-Carlo, Monaco).

Gaining the Seal of Geneva quality recognition was so important to Vuitton that, in 2014, the company moved some of its manufacturing operations away from another district in Switzerland and built a factory on the outskirts of the city of Geneva, making them geographically eligible to be considered for the quality seal. At this new factory, Vuitton put together a quality team and a series of inspections and manufacturing processes that allowed them to master all the elements in watchmaking. Although it still uses components from Swiss sub-suppliers for some of its watches, for the highest quality pieces, all the design and components for prototypes and the first series are made in house. "If we need a bridge we can make it in a couple of days, if we need a dial we can make it in a week rather than waiting two months for it from an external supplier," said Mr. Chatti. He credited Vuitton's two master watchmakers with the emphasis on quality necessary to achieve the seal: "Together they have something like 70 years of experience. . . . Until you go into it, it is impossible to understand the detail, even the smallest screws have to be finished and polished in a particular way."

A watch bearing the Seal of Geneva is proof of this in-house craftsmanship. "It makes tangible something that we have done over the last 24 months during which we've centralized all the various trades that we have mastered over the last 12 years, from dial making to case making . . . to movement manufacture," said Michael Burke, President and Chief Executive of Louis Vuitton.[1]

5.1 Defining Quality

Quality means different things to different people. The producer of a product might define quality as the product's conformance to design specifications. By contrast, a consumer might define quality as the product's fitness for its intended use. A service provider, on the other hand, might see quality as the ongoing process of building and maintaining positive relationships with customers.

The following examples will demonstrate why it is so hard to define quality. Assume your firm's design engineers have specified that the diameter of a motor shaft should be between 2.95 inches and 3.05 inches. As long as the diameter of the motor shafts produced fall within this range, then they conform to specifications and meet quality standards. Although this definition of quality is directly measurable, it does not directly relate to the consumers' definition of quality, which is how well the product performs its intended function. That is, the firm might see its processes as creating a quality product, but the customer may never directly perceive that quality dimension.

In addition, the fitness for use aspect of quality is specific for each user and, therefore, it will vary from one consumer to another. Ferraris (Ferrari S.p.A., Maranello, Italy) and Toyota Land Cruisers (Toyota Motor Corporation, Toyota City, Japan) meet the basic requirement of transportation. Nevertheless, if a specific consumer is looking for a vehicle for driving on rough and mountainous terrain, then the Toyota Land Cruiser is clearly a better quality vehicle for this purpose. There are many dimensions of quality, including a product's appearance, durability, reliability, and others.

Given the multifaceted nature of quality, we need a more precise definition of it that captures the *value* it creates for both consumers and the providers of products and services. From the perspective of a consumer, quality is the value the consumer gains by buying a product or service at the lowest possible price. From the producer's perspective, quality refers to the value that is achieved by producing and selling a quality product or service and making the highest possible profit.[2]

The Quality Dimensions of Products

One of the issues companies have to contend with is that there are different dimensions of quality. There are eight basic dimensions.[3]

1. *Performance*. Performance is a product's primary attributes or operational features. For example, a consumer looking for the fastest automobile in the world (performance) can buy the super sport version of the Bugatti Veyron EB 16.4 (Bugatti Automobiles S.A.S., Molsheim, France) with a top speed of 268 mph, for an astounding US$2,600,000. Performance comes at a price.
2. *Conformance*. Conformance is the extent to which a product's design and operating features meet the specifications the producer of the product has established for it. For example, to be considered a high-quality product in terms of conformance, a Veyron EB 16.4 automobile must be able to reach a top speed of 268 mph and meet all of the other specifications Bugatti set for it in its engineering and design standards. Note that there is a significant difference between quality of conformance and quality of design. Quality of conformance is concerned with producing the product so that design specifications are met. Regardless of the quality of design, as long as the actual product produced completely meets design specifications, it would be considered an excellent quality product. An inexpensive automobile will have a high quality of conformance if the actual automobile produced completely meets design specifications.

   Quality of design, on the other hand, is concerned with building the level of quality into a product *based on what the customers want*. Thus, quality of design is determined before the actual product is produced. The product's completeness and correctness of specifications and its fitness for use as defined by the customer reflect the quality of design. As a result, if a firm does not separate quality of conformance from quality of design, it runs the risk of producing products that are of high quality (based on quality of conformance) while failing to satisfy user expectations (based on quality of design).
3. *Features*. Features are the bells and whistles added to a product's or service's basic functions. Siri voice-recognition software on an Apple iPhone (Apple Inc., Cupertino, CA), 3D television, and free meals or drinks on an airline flight are examples of quality features.
4. *Durability*. Durability is the average life of a product until it deteriorates and needs replacement. For expensive products, such as major appliances or automobiles, durability is often the most important dimension of quality.
5. *Reliability*. Reliability is the ability of a product to consistently perform its intended function without degrading or failing. Toyota automobiles have traditionally had a reputation for being

highly reliable. Nevertheless, in 2010, Toyota Motor Company's reputation suffered after some if its vehicles were found to have mysteriously accelerated, causing crashes. It took decades for the company to gain a reputation for reliability but just a short time to lose that reputation. For service industries, reliability refers to how trustworthy, prompt, and helpful a company is in providing customers with services when they need them. Four Seasons Hotels Ltd. (Toronto, Ontario, Canada), for example, are cited year after year as maintaining some of the highest reliability standards in their industry.

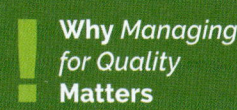

Quality means different things to different stakeholders: There are various dimensions of quality, costs of poor quality, and different quality programs that companies can implement to produce high-quality products and services. Building and monitoring the quality of products and services from design through delivery ensures that the needs of each stakeholder are met.

6. *Serviceability*. Serviceability, which is closely related to reliability, refers to the speed or ease of product repair. Consider a manufacturer that sells desktop computers assembled from modular units. Whenever there are problems with a computer, if a part can be quickly swapped out for a replacement, the computer meets the quality dimension of serviceability.

7. *Aesthetics*. This dimension of quality is subjective. Aesthetics refers to the product's look, feel, smell, sound, or taste. Because aesthetics are a matter of personal preference, it is difficult to please everyone on this dimension. Yet, aesthetics are often critical for creating an experience consumers value. For example, PING (Phoenix, AZ) manufactures high-end golf equipment. PING's market research revealed that golfers prefer clubs that make a pleasing sound when they strike a golf ball. Therefore, when it designs a new club, PING tests it to be sure that it sounds right acoustically. [4]

8. *Perceived Quality*. Perceived quality is the customer's view of the superior quality of a product or service relative to competing products or services. Often, it is an intangible feeling about a brand. For example, even though they might perform as well and be just as durable as one another, most handbag buyers perceive a Gucci (Gucci Group, Florence, Italy) handbag to be of higher quality than a handbag sold at Wal-Mart (Wal-Mart Stores Inc., Bentonville, AR) or Target (Target Corporation, Minneapolis, MN).

It may not be economically feasible or even possible for firms to compete on all eight dimensions of quality simultaneously. Not only would it be prohibitively expensive, but the type of the product would impose constraints that force trade-offs to be made among the dimensions. For example, instead of engineering a car that accelerates as fast as a Ferrari, the maker of an automobile targeted at middle-class customers might focus on achieving gas mileage that is equivalent or better than competing cars. The key is to determine which quality dimensions customers prize the most and then to deliver products that meet or exceed those dimensions.

The Quality Dimensions of Services

The goal of managing quality in the service sector is no different from that of the manufacturing sector. It also involves ensuring that the service organization meets or exceeds customer expectations. Nevertheless, because services are intangible and variable, measuring service quality can be much more difficult than it is for products. It is easy to tell if a product is or is not working. But what constitutes a good or bad haircut or good or bad service at a restaurant? It depends upon whom you ask.

Service Quality

Consumers evaluate the quality of a service based on what *they* expect it be. That is, service quality is determined by the size of the gap between what the customer expected to get and what she did get when the service was delivered. This gap, often referred to as a perception gap, is subject to each individual's interpretation. For example, the service delivered by your firm may, in actual fact, be better than your competitors. Yet, because perception is key, if your customer does not think she received service of as high quality as she could get elsewhere, your service will be judged to be of less quality. [5]

Research suggests that customers evaluate service quality based on five dimensions. [6]

1. *Service Reliability*: Service reliability is the ability of a service provider to deliver a service accurately and dependably. For example, for a restaurant, service reliability depends on the speed of service, its accuracy (did the restaurant staff get the order correct?), and the quality of the meals.

2. *Service Responsiveness*: Service responsiveness is the willingness of the service provider to promptly help a customer who needs special service. When a hotel arranges for a doctor to make a house call to treat a guest who gets sick while staying at the hotel, the hotel is displaying service responsiveness.

3. *Service Assurance:* Service assurance is the knowledge and courtesy of employees and their ability to convey trust and instill confidence in customers. For example, hospital personnel need to be able to assure patients that their care won't suffer during a shift change.

4. *Empathy:* Empathy is the service firm's ability to provide caring individualized service to its customers. For example, in the case of a sick guest, not only should the hotel respond quickly by calling the doctor, but it should do so in a manner that shows care and concern for that person.[7]

5. *Tangibles:* Tangibles are the physical features of the service facility, its ambience, equipment used, consumable goods, and personnel used in providing the service. Here again, service quality is judged by the impact these features have on customer satisfaction.

An organization that is well known for service quality excellence is The Ritz-Carlton Hotel Company, L.L.C. (Ritz-Carlton, Chevy Chase, MD). Among the "gold standards" of this two-time Malcolm Baldrige Award winner are its service values. You can see from this list how Ritz-Carlton has integrated into its service values several key service-quality dimensions.[8]

"Service Values – I am proud to be Ritz-Carlton"

1. I build strong relationships and create Ritz-Carlton guests for life.
2. I am always responsive to the expressed and unexpressed wishes and needs of our guests.
3. I am empowered to create unique, memorable and personal experiences for our guests.
4. I understand my role in achieving the Key Success Factors, embracing Community Footprints and creating The Ritz-Carlton Mystique.
5. I continuously seek opportunities to innovate and improve The Ritz-Carlton experience.
6. I own and immediately resolve guest problems.
7. I create a work environment of teamwork and lateral service so that the needs of our guests and each other are met.
8. I have the opportunity to continuously learn and grow.
9. I am involved in the planning of the work that affects me.
10. I am proud of my professional appearance, language, and behavior.
11. I protect the privacy and security of our guests, my fellow employees and the company's confidential information and assets.
12. I am responsible for uncompromising levels of cleanliness and creating a safe and accident-free environment.

Managing the quality of your customer service can lead to higher customer satisfaction. Satisfied customers become loyal to companies and brands and will refer others to them.

©iStockphoto.com/Steve Debenport

5.2 The Benefits and Costs of Managing Quality

Companies gain many benefits by managing quality. These benefits include the following:

- Higher customer satisfaction. Quality management programs establish quality standards for products and processes that are geared toward meeting or exceeding customers' expectations. When customers can get higher quality products and services at affordable prices, it increases their satisfaction with the companies that offer them.
- Revenue increases. Companies that have a viable quality management program in place not only have loyal customers who come back for repeat purchases of the company's products and services, but they also gain new customers. The net result is increased revenues and profitability.
- Reduced costs. By preventing defects and quality problems from occurring in the first place, the costs associated with reworking and scrapping products are significantly reduced. These cost savings, in turn, enable companies to offer their customers better prices on their products.
- Increases in productivity. When a company builds quality into their products, the amount of time it spends stopping production to fix problems and rework products is reduced. As a result, the productivity of the firm's workers and the company as a whole improves.

Quality programs are not without their costs; that is, we must recognize the underlying cost of quality that factors into a firm's decision about how to best manage for quality. Although different stakeholders value different dimensions of quality, the dimension most useful for understanding the cost of quality is conformance quality, or the adherence of a product to its specifications or standards. For example, many people view the aesthetic quality of the Lexus R350 (Toyota Motor Corporation, Toyota City, Japan) automobile as outstanding. Nevertheless, if a batch of the cars is defective, those cars would fail the conformance-quality test. This problem illustrates both the way in which quality issues can lead to cost decisions as well as the broad and varied nature of the cost of quality. There are four broad categories of quality costs: prevention costs, appraisal costs, internal failure costs, and external failure costs:

- **Prevention costs** are costs incurred to prevent defects and errors from occurring before manufacturing the product or delivering the service. The cost of training employees to properly use manufacturing equipment is an example of a prevention cost.
- **Appraisal costs** are the costs of measuring and inspecting products and services and the processes used to produce them. For example, companies routinely inspect or test the raw materials and parts they purchase to ensure that they meet quality standards. When Starbucks (Starbucks Corporation, Seattle, WA) sends inspectors into the coffee plantations of Central America to inspect crops, the company is incurring appraisal costs.
- **Internal failure costs** are costs that result from defects or quality problems *before* the product or service is delivered to the customer. For example, suppose a bank discovers a printing error in the standard mortgage application forms it uses. The costs associated with scrapping the forms and printing new ones before they are given to customers is an internal failure cost.
- **External failure costs** are costs that result from defects or quality problems *after* the product or service has been delivered to the customer. When Suzuki Motors (Suzuki Motor Corporation, Hamamatsu, Japan) recalled and fixed its XL-7 SUV because of a problem with its accelerator cables, this was an external failure cost. Likewise, because of a decade-long, mismanaged problem with its cars' ignition switches, in 2014, General Motors Company (Detroit, MI) announced the need to recall nearly 11 million cars worldwide and took losses of US$1.2 billion.[9]

Table 5.1 lists some examples of the types of costs that fall into each category.

5.2
Outline the benefits and costs of creating quality products and services.

Prevention costs: the costs incurred to prevent defects and errors from occurring before manufacturing the product or delivering the service

Appraisal costs: the costs of measuring and inspecting products and services and the processes used to produce them

Internal failure costs: the costs that result from defects or quality problems before the product or service is delivered to the customer

External failure costs: the costs that result from defects or quality problems after the product or service has been delivered to the customer

TABLE 5.1: Costs of Quality[10]

COST CATEGORY	COST COMPONENTS	
Prevention Costs	Quality systems development	Supervision of prevention activities
	Quality engineering	Quality data gathering, analysis, and reporting
	Quality training	Quality improvement projects
	Quality circles (volunteer groups of employees who meet regularly to solve work-related quality problems)	Technical support provided to suppliers
		Audits of the effectiveness of the quality system
	Statistical process control	
Appraisal Costs	Testing and inspection of incoming materials	Supervision of testing and inspection activities
	Testing and inspection of in-process goods	Depreciation of test equipment
	Final product testing and inspection	Maintenance of test equipment
	Supplies used in testing and inspection	Field testing and appraisal at customer's site
Internal Failure Costs	Net cost of scrap	Retesting of reworked products
	Net cost of spoilage	Downtime caused by quality problems
	Rework labor and overhead	Disposal of defective products
	Re-inspection of reworked products	Analysis of the cause of defects in production
External Failure Costs	Cost of servicing and handling customer complaints	Liability arising from defective products
	Warranty repairs and replacements	Returns and allowances arising from quality problems
	Repairs and replacements beyond the warranty period	Lost sales arising from a reputation for poor quality
	Product recalls	

OPERATIONS MANAGEMENT: LESSONS LEARNED
Yamada Electric and a Simple Solution to a Quality Problem

Yamada Electric Mfg. Co., Ltd. (Nagoya City, Japan) was experiencing a chronic quality problem in assembling a simple push-button switch. The switch had two buttons—on and off—each with a small spring underneath. The assembly of the switch was simple. Frequently, however, workers forgot to insert the springs. When customers complained about the defective switches, Yamada would send an inspector to the customer's plant to check every switch in the shipment and to fix those switches with the problem. Clearly this was a costly solution. Workers were then warned to be more careful, and the problem stopped occurring—for a while. Eventually, workers would again forget to insert the springs, and Yamada one again had to deal with disgruntled and dissatisfied customers. The defect occurred so regularly that it became an embarrassment to Yamada.

©iStockphoto.com/KM6064

To find a permanent solution to the problem, the company sought the help of Shigeo Shingo, an expert on quality control. Shingo suggested a very simple solution of placing a small dish next to the assembly station. At the beginning of each operation, two springs were taken from a parts box containing hundreds of springs and placed in the dish. The worker who assembled the switch would realize the mistake immediately if a spring remained in the dish after assembly and would reassemble the switch. This simple change in procedures eliminated the problem.[11]

Managing Quality

Companies that enjoy a reputation for quality invest in prevention methods because it is often less expensive to prevent quality problems from occurring in the first place than to fix them after defective products are in the hands of the customer. As the saying goes, an ounce of prevention is worth a pound of cure. Furthermore, as the following example illustrates, very simple and inexpensive procedures can often prevent defects.

5.3 Describe the evolution of quality management and identify the pioneers who contributed to modern quality management methods.

5.3 The Evolution of Quality Management and Its Pioneers

People have been trying to manage quality since the dawn of production. In this section, the evolution of quality management is traced, focusing specifically on the management practitioners who developed methods that were used from the 20th century to today.

Early Attempts at Quality Management

Prior to the 1700s, the primary way to control the quality of a product was to physically inspect it and the activities of the workers making it. Inspection is a quality-control technique used to determine whether products, processes, and services conform to quality by measuring, examining, and testing them against specified requirements. Initially, inspections weren't as systematic as the definition implies. Nevertheless, inspection worked well because the number of units being produced was often small.

More formal attempts to manage quality based on standardization began as early as the 1760s. Eli Whitney, the inventor of the cotton gin, encouraged musket makers to use interchangeable parts to produce identical components for the guns. During the early 20th century, Frederick W. Taylor advocated the standardization of manufacturing practices as well as parts. Taylor's suggestions to improve the manufacturing processes of firms through teamwork and cooperation laid some of the foundations for the modern quality management systems. Between 1915 and 1940, Henry Ford and Karl Friedrich Benz implemented process improvements and quality management practices in the operation of their automobile assembly lines.

Inspection: a quality control technique used to determine whether products, processes, and services conform to quality by measuring, examining, and testing them against specified requirements

Consider This 5.1:
Measuring Quality Costs

Measuring the costs of quality involves calculating all costs (1) to prevent poor quality, (2) to measure quality, and (3) to fix poor quality. Nevertheless, because many quality-related indicators, such as lost goodwill, can't be quantified easily, calculating costs of quality can be challenging. The following table presents an information-technology firm's cost-of-quality calculations using the PAF cost model; PAF stands for prevention, appraisal, and failure. Although the cost data presented are only for one year, much useful information can be gleaned that the company can use to reduce its quality-related costs. For example, the cost of bug fixes is a major portion of the company's overall quality costs. To reduce this internal failure cost, the company needs to improve the overall quality of its software development, perhaps by using better software-coding procedures. As the company gathers more data for subsequent years, the value of the cost of quality analysis will be much greater.[12]

CALCULATING THE QUALITY-RELATED COSTS OF AN IT ORGANIZATION USING THE PAF MODEL

PREVENTION COSTS		APPRAISAL COSTS	
Staff training	€134,750	Design review	€8,690
Requirements analysis	€154,572	Code inspection	€175,296
Early prototyping	€62,062	System FAT*	€330,484
Fault-tolerant design	€38,016	Training testers	€1,584
Quality planning	€6,160	UAT**	€183,656
Quality auditing	€1,804		
Quality improvement programs	€20,548	Total appraisal cost	€516,054
Clear specification	€18,392		
Accurate internal documentation	€145,992		
		*FAT: File allocation table	
Total prevention cost	€553,784	**UAT: User acceptance testing	

INTERNAL FAILURE COSTS		EXTERNAL FAILURE COSTS	
Bug fixes	€259,490	Technical support	€3,190
		Preparation of support answer books	€1,166
Total internal failure cost	€259,490	Investigation of customer complaints	€10,274
		Refunds and recalls	€0
		Coding/testing of interim bug-fix releases	€33,616
		Supporting multiple versions of the product	€8,316
		PR work to soften drafts of harsh reviews	€11,418
		Warranty costs	€0
		Total external failure cost	€67,980

WALTER A. SHEWHART

 A Pioneer of Quality

Major advances in modern quality management methods began in 1924, based on the work of Walter A. Shewhart. Shewhart, who worked as a statistician in Bell Laboratories during the 1920s, developed statistical quality-control charts, which subsequently became the foundation of statistical process control—a method of quality control using statistical methods. As Japan began rebuilding its economy after World War II, it sought the help Shewhart and others. At the time, products with "Made in Japan" labels were often considered shoddy. Yet, with the help of these quality gurus, Japan began to steadily improve the quality of its products.

W. EDWARD DEMING

W. Edward Deming, a disciple of Shewhart, taught statistical quality control methods to engineers and suppliers of the U.S. military during World War II. His methods led to improved quality of ammunition and other important military products. After World War II, Deming went to Japan and taught Japanese

TABLE 5.2: Deming's 14 Quality-Improvement Recommendations

1.	Create a constancy of purpose toward improvement of product and service, with the aim to become competitive and stay in business, and to provide jobs.
2.	Adopt the new philosophy. We are in a new economic age. Western management must awaken to the challenge, must learn their responsibilities, and take on leadership for change.
3.	Cease dependence on inspections to achieve quality. Eliminate the need for massive inspection by building quality into the product in the first place.
4.	End the practice of awarding business on the basis of a price tag. Instead, minimize total costs. Move towards a single supplier for any one item, on a long-term relationship of loyalty and trust.
5.	Improve constantly and forever the system of production and service, to improve quality and productivity, and thus constantly decrease costs.
6.	Institute training on the job.
7.	Institute leadership. The aim of supervision should be to help people and machines and gadgets to do a better job. Supervision of management is in need of overhaul, as well as supervision of production workers.
8.	Drive out fear, so that everyone may work effectively for the company.
9.	Break down barriers between departments. People in research, design, sales, and production must work as a team, to foresee problems of production and in use that may be encountered with the product or service.
10.	Eliminate slogans, exhortations, and targets for the work force by asking for zero defects and new levels of productivity. Such exhortations only create adversarial relationships, as the bulk of the causes of low quality and low productivity belong to the system and thus lie beyond the power of the work force. • Eliminate work standards (quotas) on the factory floor. Substitute leadership. • Eliminate management by objectives. Eliminate management by numbers, numerical goals. Substitute leadership.
11.	Remove barriers that rob the hourly worker of his right to pride of workmanship. The responsibility of supervisors must be changed from sheer numbers to quality.
12.	Remove barriers that rob people in management and in engineering of their right to pride of workmanship.
13.	Institute a vigorous program of education and self-improvement.
14.	Put everybody in the company to work to accomplish the transformation. The transformation is everybody's job.

scientists and engineers statistical process control methods and continuous improvement concepts, launching the quality revolution movement in Japan. He is best known for formulating a 14-point management philosophy for improving quality, productivity, and the competitive position of a company (Table 5.2).[13]

To honor Deming for his many contributions to the quality movement, in 1950, the Union of Japanese Scientists and Engineers instituted the Deming Prize. Although the prize was originally awarded to only Japanese companies that made major quality improvements, now non-Japanese companies are also eligible to receive the award. For decades, Deming and his work were relatively unknown in the United States, his home country. Only after Japan's high-quality vehicles began to compete successfully against U.S. vehicles in the 1980s did American carmakers seek his help.

JOSEPH M. JURAN

Joseph M. Juran went to Japan in 1954 to teach the Japanese how to use quality as part of strategic planning—that is, to set quality goals and design their processes to achieve them. He is also responsible for identifying the four costs associated with quality.

ARMAND V. FEIGENBAUM

Armand V. Feigenbaum was yet another quality expert. In 1951, Feigenbaum published a book on quality that emphasized the importance of the commitment to quality by all employees in an organization. In 1969, Japan, the United States, and European countries sponsored the first international conference on quality control in Tokyo. In the conference, Feigenbaum introduced the term *total quality control* for the first time. By the late 1970s, company-wide quality management was common in Japan, and many of the country's products had become recognized for their very high levels of quality. This is still the case. For the past four decades, Japanese automobiles have been regularly listed at the top of the J.D. Power and Associates (S&P Global Inc., New York City, NY) customer satisfaction rankings.

KAORU ISHIKAWA

Kaoru Ishikawa introduced the concept of the quality circle in 1962, which advocates volunteer groups of employees meeting regularly to identify and solve quality and production problems related to their work. In 1982, Ishikawa developed the cause-and-effect diagram (also known as the *fishbone diagram*)—a quality management tool that can be used to analyze and identify the root causes of problems in a process.

PHILIP CROSBY

In 1979, Philip Crosby, who published the book *Quality Is Free,* claimed that the savings a company realizes by establishing a quality program more than pays for the costs of such a program. In addition to the principle of doing it right the first time (DIRFT), Crosby proposed four other principles:

1. Quality means a product conforms to both its product specifications and the customer's requirements.
2. The goal of a system of quality is preventing defects, not evaluating the process after defects occur.
3. The performance standard for quality must be zero defects, not "acceptable levels" of quality.
4. The costs of measuring quality are found by assessing the process of producing a defective item.

SHIGEO SHINGO

Shigeo Shingo, a Japanese industrial engineer and leading expert on manufacturing practices, was one of the inventors of the Toyota Production System from 1948 to 1975. He coined the Japanese term poka yoke, which means "fail-safing" or "mistake-proofing." The term refers to any mechanism or device that can help an equipment operator avoid mistakes in a manufacturing process. The purpose of a poka yoke system is to eliminate product defects, particularly those that arise from human errors, to improve quality and reduce costs. For an example of poka yoke, see the "Operations Management: Lesson Learned—Yamada Electric and a Simple Solution to a Quality Problem" box discussed earlier in the chapter.

GENICHI TAGUCHI

In the 1980s, Genichi Taguchi created the Taguchi-loss function, which tracks the financial loss to society as a result of poor quality. Taguchi also developed the concept of robust design—designing products and processes so that they are insensitive (or robust) to factors outside the design engineer's control. (Recall that we discussed robust product design in Chapter 4.) He also is credited with the concept of design of experiments (DOE). DOE is the process of conducting design experiments and using their statistical results to identify a product's optimum configuration or design.

Table 5.3 summarizes the quality concepts and tools developed by these quality management pioneers.

TABLE 5.3: Pioneers of the Quality Management Movement

QUALITY MANAGEMENT PIONEER	QUALITY CONCEPTS AND TOOLS DEVELOPED
Walter A. Shewhart	Quality control and statistical theory
W. Edward Deming	Quality control and statistical theory, continuous improvement
Joseph M. Juran	Quality planning, quality improvement, quality control, and quality costs
Armand V. Feigenbaum	Total quality control (TQC)
Kaoru Ishikawa	Quality circle, cause-and-effect diagram (also known as the fishbone diagram)
Philip Crosby	Quality Is Free, doing it right the first time (DIRFT), zero defects
Shigeo Shingo	Poka yoke, which means "fail-safing" or "mistake-proofing"
Genichi Taguchi	Taguchi-loss function, robust product design, design of experiments (DOE)

Quality circle: a concept introduced by Kaoru Ishikawa in 1962, which advocates volunteer groups of employees meeting regularly to identify and solve quality and production problems related to their work

Cause-and-effect diagram: a quality management tool that can be used to analyze and identify the root causes of problems in a process, also known as the fishbone diagram

Poka yoke: a Japanese term that means "fail-safing" or "mistake-proofing," referring to any mechanism or device that can help an equipment operator avoid mistakes in a manufacturing process

Taguchi-loss function: a process created by Genichi Taguchi in the 1980s that tracks the financial loss to society as a result of poor quality designs

Design of experiments (DOE): the process of conducting design experiments and using their statistical results to identify a product's optimum configuration, or design

Compare these major quality management initiatives: total quality management (TQM), the ISO 9000 family of quality standards, the Baldrige Award, Six Sigma, and DMADV methodologies.

Kaizen: a Japanese term for continuous quality improvement

Plan, Do, Study, and Act (PDSA) cycle: a visual, circular representation of total quality management that illustrates the never-ending process of continuous improvement

Critical-to-quality (CTQ): the specific, measurable characteristics of a product or service that customers say are necessary for their satisfaction

5.4 Major Quality Management Initiatives

In this section, we will discuss some of the major quality initiatives used by businesses throughout the world. The initiatives include total quality management, the ISO 9000 and 14000 series of standards, the Malcolm Baldrige National Quality Program, and Six Sigma.

Total Quality Management (TQM)

As we discussed in Chapter 1, TQM focuses on the *continuous improvement* of the quality of a firm's products, services, and processes. It is a concept the Japanese call kaizen. Because continuous improvement is a never-ending process, it is represented as a circle in a model known as the Plan, Do, Study, and Act (PDSA) cycle. Although the PDSA cycle was originally developed by Walter Shewart, Edward Deming used it extensively in his work in Japan after World War II. Hence, the PDSA cycle, shown in Figure 5.1, is also often referred to as the Deming cycle.

The basic premise of TQM is that quality is the responsibility of everyone who is involved in the creation or consumption of a product or service. TQM implies that the management and workforce of the firm producing the product or service, its suppliers, and perhaps even the customers who buy it affect its quality. Figure 5.2 shows the various aspects of total quality management. Let's now look at each more closely.

Customer Involvement

- Because customers determine what acceptable quality means, firms need to get their feedback and ideas. Surveys, after-sales service programs, processes to deal with the complaints of customers, and websites that allow customers to provide feedback are some of the tools companies can use. From this information, a company derives critical-to-quality (CTQ) requirements, which are specific, measurable characteristics of a product or service that customers say are necessary for their satisfaction.

- **Employee Involvement.** Giving production workers more authority and responsibility, involving them in the decision-making process, and encouraging them to form quality circles are a few methods that firms can use to encourage their staff members to contribute to a TQM effort. The firm also can implement employee-suggestion systems and monetary and non-monetary incentive rewards to recognize employees who improve the quality of products and services.

- **Process Management.** A key TQM activity is continuously managing processes to make them safer, minimize waste, and reduce errors. Quality-control tools driven by statistics allow the firm to monitor a process before and after making changes to it.

- **Supplier Involvement.** Firms that treat their suppliers as partners can often enlist their help to develop quality planning and improvement programs. We will discuss supplier involvement in greater detail later in the chapter.

- **Committed Leadership.** If the firm's managers aren't committed to TQM, their employees won't be either. Top managers need to actively break up any organizational roadblocks hampering a continuous quality improvement effort so that steady quality improvements are made.

- **Fact-Based Decision Making.** A central feature of TQM is using statistical tools to collect and analyze data. Decisions are then based on those data rather than on the personal opinions of managers and employees.

- **Concurrent Engineering.** Because all of a firm's functional groups play a role in the success of a product, they each should have the opportunity to influence and shape the product during its design phase. For example, marketing can identify important product features based on customers' tastes, while production can identify product designs that are easier to produce.

FIGURE 5.1: PDSA Cycle

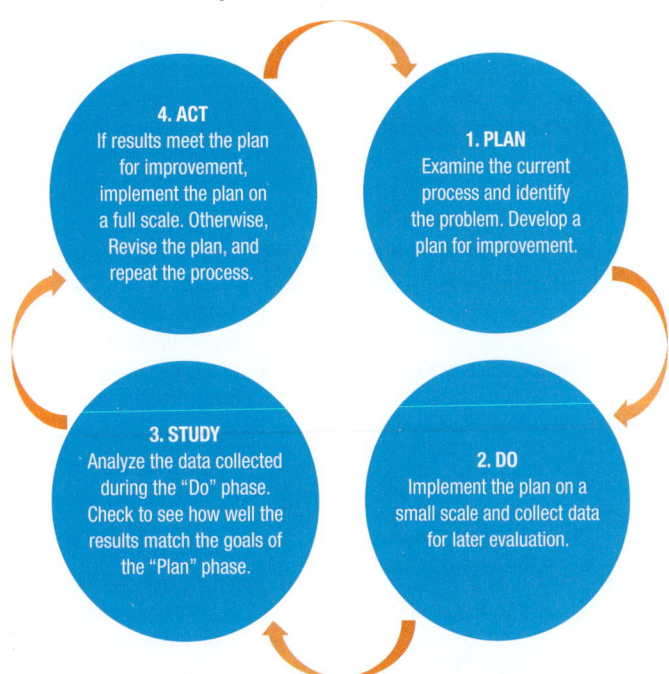

- **Strategic Quality Planning.** One of the essential elements of strategic quality planning is benchmarking. Benchmarking is the process of comparing the quality of your company's products or services and its processes with those companies considered to be world leaders in quality. Hyundai (Hyundai Motor Company, Seoul, South Korea) has successfully improved its image for quality among American car-buyers by routinely benchmarking its autos against the cars produced by Toyota and Nissan. Firms can even benchmark the best practices of companies in other industries to find out what they are doing well and adapt those practices to their own operations.

FIGURE 5.2: Key Aspects of Total Quality Management

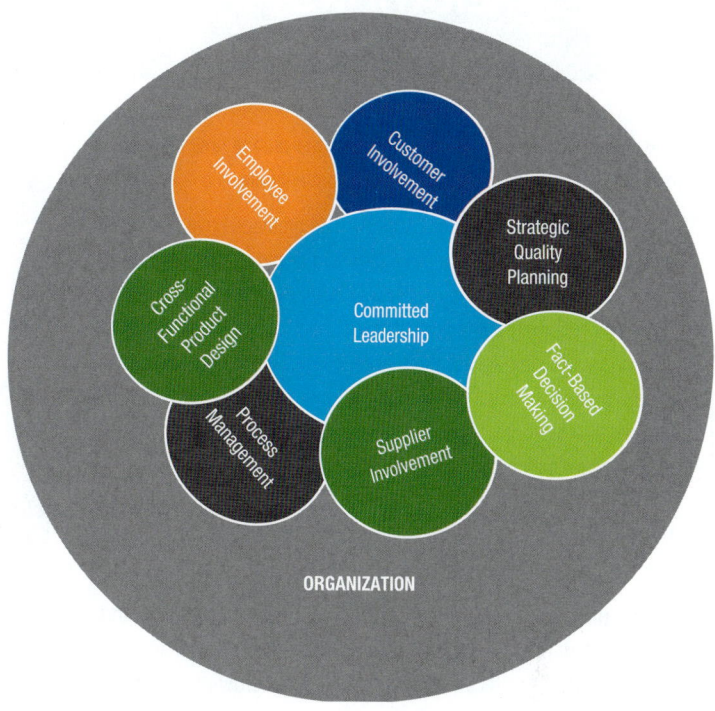

TQM isn't just for manufacturing firms. As the Operations Profile on page 172 illustrates, many service organizations such as hospitals have realized immense benefits by implementing TQM.

Despite its advantages, TQM is not a quick fix. Depending on the severity of an organization's problems, its full implementation may take several years. Nor is it costless. TQM can, in fact, increase a company's short-term costs as a firm revamps its practices. Organizations must be willing to invest time and money to implement TQM.

ISO Standards

The world's largest developer and publisher of international standards is the International Organization for Standardization (ISO), which was created in 1947 and is based in Geneva, Switzerland. The ISO has representatives from various national standards organizations that reach a consensus on the international standards prior to their publication.

Among the many standards published by International Organization for Standardization are the ISO 14000 standards, which help firms manage their processes to avoid damaging the environment, and the ISO 9000 family of standards for managing quality both in manufacturing companies and in service organizations. The standards outline criteria organizations should measure, including how products and services should be designed for quality, tested, manufactured, delivered, and continually improved. Organizations that meet the criteria can request to be certified by the ISO.

Among the advantages of an ISO 9000 certification is that it is a worldwide indicator of quality. Thus, it can increase a firm's credibility, the marketability of its products, and its attractiveness to investors. The certification can also help international organizations identify good, reliable supply chain partners with an equal commitment to quality.

To become ISO certified, companies must be audited by external governing groups that confirm they have met the requirements. A company begins the process by conducting its own internal audits to compare the ISO's standards to its own standards. The audits identify any deviations between the two, and the firm then tries to correct the deviations. Next, authorized bodies conduct external audits to ensure the company meets the standards of the ISO. If it does not, the firm can take steps to correct the problems and then be reassessed later. The process continues until the firm has met the standards. By going through multiple rounds of assessment, improvement, and reassessment, a firm can analyze its strengths and weaknesses and motivate the entire organization to strive for quality and other improvements.

Despite the many advantages of being ISO certified, some managers believe the certification process isn't useful for all organizations or is a not good use of resources. Certification is expensive and it sometimes can take years to complete. It also requires extensive recordkeeping, which takes time and effort. Consequently, companies should research the certification process before committing resources to it.

Benchmarking: the process of comparing the quality of your company's products or services and its processes with those companies considered to be world leaders in quality

International Organization for Standardization (ISO): The world's largest developer and publisher of international standards, created in 1947 and based in Geneva, Switzerland. The ISO has representatives from various national standards organizations that reach a consensus on the international standards prior to their publication.

OPERATIONS PROFILE: TQM Improves Hospital Operations

These are just a few of the health care organizations now using TQM methods to improve their operations and patient care.

Atlantic City Medical Center (ACMC). TQM methods have been used at this New Jersey facility for more than two decades. As George Lynn, the president of ACMC notes, "The idea is that the people who do the work are in control. Management gives them responsibility for quality, and doesn't simply hold them accountable." Under the old model, all departments operated independently, with patients moving among them as their treatment required. There was no sense of unity of purpose or coordination of patient care. "With the service philosophy, we start with the patient and work backward. The entire team plans and delivers care based on the need of the patient. Team members see total care, not just their own piece of it."

Florida Hospital Medical Center. This large hospital in the Orlando area adopted TQM to improve its operations. Before implementing TQM, patients often received food they had not ordered. "We had a 12% error rate," stated Randy Haffner, a former director at the hospital. Quality teams then analyzed all aspects of the food service and suggested ways to improve it. In only four months, the error rate fell to less than 2%. Quality teams also developed "care maps," which trace the treatment steps for each patient to reduce the rising costs associated with their respiratory care.

Alaska Native Medical Center. A recurring complaint heard at all hospitals is the long wait to be treated, particularly in emergency rooms (ER). At this Anchorage, Alaska, hospital the situation had become

©iStockphoto.com/SolStock

critical, leading to constant complaints, substandard treatment, and dissatisfaction on the part of the hospital's staff members. An analysis of patients' records indicated that 80% of them treated each day were not seriously ill. These people often were forced to wait as long as six hours before receiving treatment. Quality teams examined the problem and concluded the ER's processes needed to be completely redesigned. For example, 70% of patients who were not seriously ill came in between the hours of 9 a.m. and 6 p.m., yet resources were spread evenly throughout each 24-hour day. By separating the ER to treat serious and non-serious illnesses separately and by reassigning staff to correspond to the heaviest visitation times, the facility reduced waiting times from six hours to one hour, saved thousands of dollars, and improved the morale of its staff.[14]

Baldrige Standards

Quality Management Methods

The Baldrige National Quality Program and the associated Malcolm Baldrige National Quality Award were created by the Malcolm Baldrige National Quality Improvement Act of 1987. Both the program and award were named after Malcolm Baldrige, who was the U.S. Secretary of Commerce during the Reagan administration. The original award honored superior organizations that produced quality products and services provided. That focus has since shifted to a much broader, strategic focus on overall organizational quality, or performance excellence. To reflect that change in focus, the name of the program was changed in 2010 and is now known as the Baldrige Performance Excellence Program.

The Baldrige Award is not meant for individual products or services. It is given to organizations for their excellence. Up to 18 U.S. organizations that have demonstrated performance excellence in business, health care, and education, as well as in not-for-profit sectors, can win it annually. The award promotes awareness that the key feature of an organization's competitiveness is performance excellence and encourages successful organizations to share their performance strategies with other organizations.

Organizations applying for the Baldrige Award should have efficient operations, demonstrate continuous improvement delivering products or services, and have a mechanism in place for engaging and responding to customers and other stakeholders. An independent board of examiners and panel of judges composed of leading quality and continuous improvement experts from all sectors of the U.S. economy then evaluate the applications for the award. These experts look at a firm's achievements and improvements in the seven areas shown in Figure 5.3.

FIGURE 5.3: Criteria for the Baldrige Performance Excellence Program

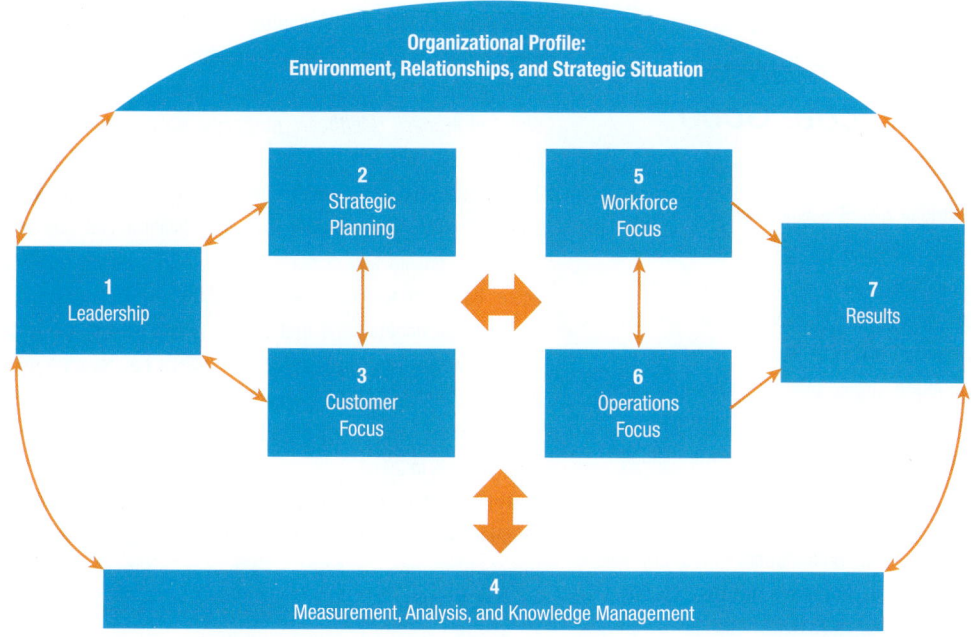

SOURCE: NIST. (2016). 2015–2016 Baldrige Excellence Framework. Retrieved from http://www.nist.gov/baldrige/publications/business_nonprofit_criteria.cfm

An organization applying for the award goes through an initial screening process. If the organization passes this hurdle, a team of examiners visits the company to verify information presented in the application. The organization then receives a written summary of strengths and areas of improvement for each area of the Baldrige criteria.

According to *Building on Baldrige: American Quality for the 21st Century* by the private Council on Competitiveness, "More than any other program, the Baldrige Quality Award is responsible for making quality a national priority and disseminating best practices across the United States." As of 2001, it was estimated that the program's net private benefits to the economy as a whole was US$24.65 billion, while the program's social costs were US$119 million. These figures translate the program's social benefit-to-cost ratio to be 207-to-1. A decade later, in 2011, another study of the 273 Malcolm Baldrige National Quality Award applicants since 2006 estimated that social benefit-to-costs had increased to 820 to 1.[15]

Six Sigma

Six Sigma, which we first mentioned in Chapter 1, was originally developed by Motorola (Schaumburg, IL) in 1986. It is a fact-based, data-driven quality management method that seeks to improve the quality of products and services by identifying and removing the causes of defects (errors) and minimizing process variations. "Process variations" refer to fluctuations that occur in process outputs. For example, assume that the target value of the diameter of a metal tube produced by a process is set at 3 millimeters. Nevertheless, not every metal tube produced by this process will have a diameter of exactly 3 millimeters. The actual diameters of the tube produced may vary as a result of tool wear, worker skill level, metal characteristics, and so forth. The world-class manufacturing and service organizations that have successfully implemented the Six Sigma methodology, include 3M Company (aka 3M, Maplewood, MN), Apple (Cupertino, CA), Beatrice Foods Company (Downers Grove, IL), The Boeing Company (Chicago, IL), Bryn Mawr Hospital (Bryn Mawr, PA), The Campbell Soup Company (Camden, NJ), Florida Department of Corrections (Tallahassee, FL), The Ford Motor Company (Dearborn, MI), General Electric (Fairfield, CT), HP Inc. (formerly Hewlett-Packard, Palo Alto, CA), Natural Gas Pipeline Company of America (Kinder Morgan, Houston, TX), Sony Corporation (Tokyo, Japan), Texas Commerce Bank N.A. (Houston, TX), United States Air Force (USAF, Washington, DC), United Parcel Service, Inc. (UPS, Sandy Springs, GA), and Xerox Corporation (Norwalk, CT).

Six Sigma derives its name from the Greek letter *sigma* (σ), which is the symbol for the standard deviation of values for the outcome of a process. The higher the process's standard deviation, the more inconsistent the process is. The "six" in Six Sigma refers to a value that is plus or minus six standard

Consider This 5.2:
Profile of a Malcolm Baldrige Award Winner: Advocate Good Samaritan Hospital

One of the 2014 Malcolm Baldridge Award winners was St. David's HealthCare (SDH) of Austin, Texas. St. David's, one of the largest hospital systems in Texas, operates six hospitals, six ambulatory surgery centers, four free-standing emergency departments, four urgent care clinics, rehabilitation facilities, and physician practices. With a workforce of more than 8,000, they are the fourth-largest private employer in the Austin, Texas, area. Net revenue for the system in 2013 was US$1.4 billion. Some of the reasons why the hospital won the award include the following:

- The hospital emphasizes superior standards that save lives. SDH's composite performance on critical measures reported by the Centers for Medicare and Medicaid Services (CMS, Woodlawn, MD) is at or better than the top 10% of health care systems nationally for each disease group.

- The hospital recognizes that people are the heart of success. SDH was the first health system in Texas to be named Texas Employer of the Year by the Texas Workforce Commission. It also has been recognized as one of the top 100 best places to work by *Modern Healthcare* magazine (Crain Communications Inc., Detroit, MI).

- The hospital uses a customer focus to improve customer satisfaction and loyalty. Through its Service Excellence Initiative and other efforts to address patient and customer needs, SDH's patient satisfaction scores have improved each year since 2009.

- The hospital understands that quality health care depends on a financially "healthy" medical system. SDH's net revenue growth between 2007 and 2013 increased more than 70%. Additionally, the return on assets has increased from approximately 17% in 2007 to 33% in 2013.

- The hospital fosters a love for community. St. David's Foundation (Austin, TX) has contributed more than US$200 million to community programs since 2007. Each year, grants are provided to more than 55 local agencies that provide primary care, mental health programs, community health programs, and dental health vans.[16]

deviations from the mean for any process, or a 99.9997% defect-free rate. This number translates into 3.4 defects per million opportunities.

A particular sigma quality level indicates how frequently defects are likely to occur. For example, in a process with a Six-Sigma quality level, defects are much less likely to occur than a process with a two-sigma quality level. Higher sigma levels of quality mean that product reliability and customer satisfaction are higher, the need for testing and inspection is lower, cycle time goes down, and costs decrease.

Why aim for a 99.9997% defect-free rate? Suppose we decided that a 99.9% defect-free rate was acceptable. This defect-free rate would result in the following outcomes:

- 5,000 incorrect surgical procedures per week
- Two landing errors at major airports every day
- 200,000 prescriptions incorrectly filled each year
- Seven hours per month of electrical brownouts or blackouts
- 20,000 pieces of mail lost every hour

By contrast, a 99.9997% defect-free rate would result in 1.7 surgical errors per week, one landing error at major airports every five years, 68 incorrectly filled prescriptions each year, 1 hour of electricity failure every 34 years, and seven articles of mail lost every hour. That's quite a difference. Table 5.4 shows the various defect rates associated with each sigma level.

Let us look at another example to put Table 5.4 into perspective. In a typical health care organization, the medical defects or error rates range from 67,000 to 309,000 (three sigma and two sigma) per million opportunities.[17] For health care organizations, such high numbers are unacceptable because lives may be at stake. Table 5.4 shows that if a hospital moves to a higher sigma quality level, medical error rates can be drastically reduced.

INTRODUCING SIX SIGMA INTO AN ORGANIZATION

Many of the practices that make TQM work in an organization are central to a Six Sigma effort as well. For example, there is an unwavering focus on understanding the needs of customers and their assessment of the quality of products and services. Six Sigma efforts undertaken depend on the process and are fact-driven, and they require the support of a firm's managers and the collaboration of employees across different functions. Moreover, like TQM, Six Sigma projects also have specific financial targets, such as decreasing costs and increasing profits by a certain amount.

Six Sigma projects are led by a team of employees who have received extensive Six Sigma training. Depending on the extent of their training, the employees have the titles of **Master Black Belts**, **Black Belts,** or **Green Belts**. Green Belts typically solve lower-level quality problems, such as reducing minor process variations. Black Belts and Master Black Belts tackle broader quality issues, such as improving entire operations and processes. Master Black Belts have the most statistical training. They serve as in-house coaches to Black Belts and Green Belts and check to see that Six Sigma efforts are applied consistently across an organization.

The Six Sigma process itself consists of a sequence of five steps: define, measure, analyze, improve, and control (DMAIC). These are described below and illustrated in Figure 5.4.

TABLE 5.4: Quality at Various Sigma Levels

SIGMA LEVEL	DEFECTS PER MILLION OPPORTUNITIES (DPMO)	OVERALL PERCENTAGE OF ACCURACY
One Sigma (1 σ)	690,000	31.0%
Two Sigma (2 σ)	308,000	69.0%
Three Sigma (3 σ)	66,800	93.3%
Four Sigma (4 σ)	6,200	99.4%
Five Sigma (5 σ)	233	99.97%
Six Sigma (6 σ)	3.4	99.99966%

1. **Define.** In this step, the project team determines the project's viability, creates a map of the process to be improved, and ensures that the people who are involved in it clearly understand what needs to be done. During this step, the project team creates a **project charter**, a document that identifies the project's objective, expected timeline, budget, scope, and the key personnel involved in the effort. The project charter also specifies how the project's progress and ultimate success will be evaluated. An important aspect of this step is identifying the critical-to-quality (CTQ) features expected to have the greatest impact on quality.
2. **Measure.** During the measure step, the project team gathers data to describe the current state of the process slated to be improved. The project team identifies existing defects and levels of quality. The purpose of this step is to determine the extent of the disparities between the process's current performance levels and goals the organization has set for it.
3. **Analyze.** During this step, the project team evaluates the disparities found in the previous step and analyzes their causes by identifying any problems that can lead to variation. Statistical tools are used to identify the causes and to determine the relationship between the suspected causes and their effects.
4. **Improve.** The project team makes improvements to existing processes during this step. Once the improvements are in place, a test run of the improved process is conducted. The same data obtained during the measure step are again gathered, and the two sets of data—those collected prior to the improvement and those after it—are compared. By using the appropriate statistical and data-analysis tools and charting techniques, the project team ensures that quality performance of the process has, in fact, improved sufficiently to meet the project's quality goal and also uncover any shortcomings that may still exist.
5. **Control.** In the control step, the project team takes actions to see that the variations in the process are permanently fixed and the quality improvements are sustained. Some of the tasks performed during this step include setting up the monitoring procedure for the process's data on an ongoing basis and taking corrective action if its performance begins to slip.

Master Black Belt: employees who have received the most statistical Six Sigma training and serve as in-house coaches to Black Belts and Green Belts, checking to see that Six Sigma efforts are applied consistently across an organization

Black Belt: employees who have received Six Sigma training and, along with Master Black Belts, tackle broader quality issues, such as improving entire operations and processes

FIGURE 5.4: Six Sigma Steps

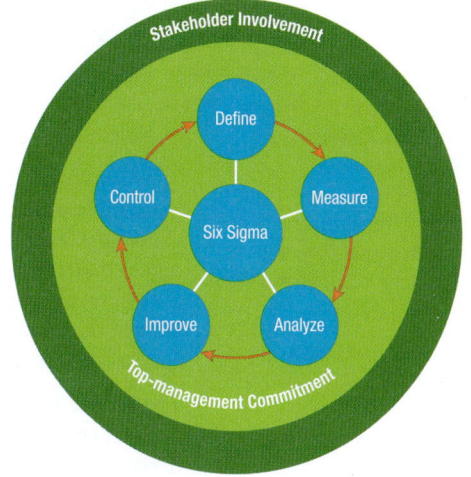

The Six Sigma DMAIC methodology should be used when there are quality problems with a company's existing product or process. Nevertheless, what if, after optimizing the process or product using the DMAIC methodology, product quality still has not improved? What happens if the product or process is new to a company and there is no existing system to try to optimize? In those circumstances, an alternative Six Sigma method may be employed, referred to as the DMADV (Define, Measure, Analyze, Design, Verify) methodology. The five steps of the DMADV methodology are:[18]

- **Define:** Define project goals and customer (both internal and external) deliverables.
- **Measure:** Measure and determine customer needs and specifications.
- **Analyze:** Analyze the various product and process design options that can meet customer requirements.
- **Design:** Design the product and the detailed process that will best meet the customer needs.
- **Verify:** Verify the design performance and ability to meet customer needs.

The benefit of the DMADV design and verify steps is that they reintroduce the team's solutions to the customer and verify them against customer needs; in other words, they are focused on the customer and ensure that any Six Sigma method undertaken by a company first and foremost recognize that improvement methodologies must address customer requirements.

5.5. Quality Management Tools and Techniques

5.5

Identify and describe some of the basic tools managers and employees use to manage quality in their firms.

Quality Management Tools

Several tools and statistical techniques help organizations analyze data to effectively manage and control quality. Table 5.5 describes them briefly, and Chapter 6 discusses them in more detail.

Service Quality Management Tools

Recall that measuring service quality often involves identifying the perception gap—the difference between what customers *expect* to receive from a service and their impression of what they *actually* received. Because both expectations and perceptions of performance are often based on intangibles, the perception gap is difficult to measure and manage. It also is likely to change over time. Firms can use a number of models to try to measure the gap. The RATER model and GAP model are among the better known models that firms can use to measure the perception gap.

THE RATER MODEL

The RATER model focuses on the five dimensions of customer expectations of service quality we discussed in section 5.1, which are ranked in terms of their importance to customers. Table 5.6 on page 179 shows the results of the ranking, which were determined by surveying many different service organizations, such as those in health care, finance, and education.[19]

Southwest Airlines Co. (Dallas, TX) is one of many companies that use the RATER model to improve their service quality. Southwest Airlines has been able to significantly improve its service quality using the RATER model because it is better aware of the critical service elements its customers expect.

THE GAP MODEL

The researchers who developed the GAP model identified five major gaps that organizations should measure, manage, and minimize.[20] Figure 5.5 on page 179 shows these gaps. The area above the horizontal dashed line in the middle of the exhibit corresponds to the customer. The area below it corresponds to the service provider. The black arrows show the flow of information and products.

The most critical gap is the one at the top of the figure, the customer gap. It is the difference between the customer's expectations about the service compared with the customer's perception of what was delivered. The other four gaps are provider gaps, which appear in the lower half of the figure. They are a direct result of the service provider's actions. Let's now look at each of the gaps in more detail.

The Knowledge Gap. The biggest gap in the figure, the knowledge gap is the provider's inadequate knowledge of the expectations of customers. It is the difference between what consumers actually expect from the service compared with what the provider thinks they expect. Cruise ship companies must understand what their guests expect, in both the tangible and intangible aspects of the cruise. Otherwise, the companies will waste resources providing services that customers never wanted or expected. The best approach the service provider can take to bridge this gap is through surveys of customers and potential customers.

The Service Design and Standards Gap. This gap is the difference between a provider's perception of what customers expect and what they actually experience. It exists when there is poor service design and a lack of customer-driven standards. For example, a service design gap may arise if a hotel room does not have free Internet access but the customer expects it.

Green Belt: employees who have received Six Sigma training and typically solve lower level quality problems, such as reducing minor process variations

Project charter: a document that identifies the project's objective, expected timeline, budget, scope, and the key personnel involved in the effort

TABLE 5.5: Tools and Techniques for Quality Control and Improvement

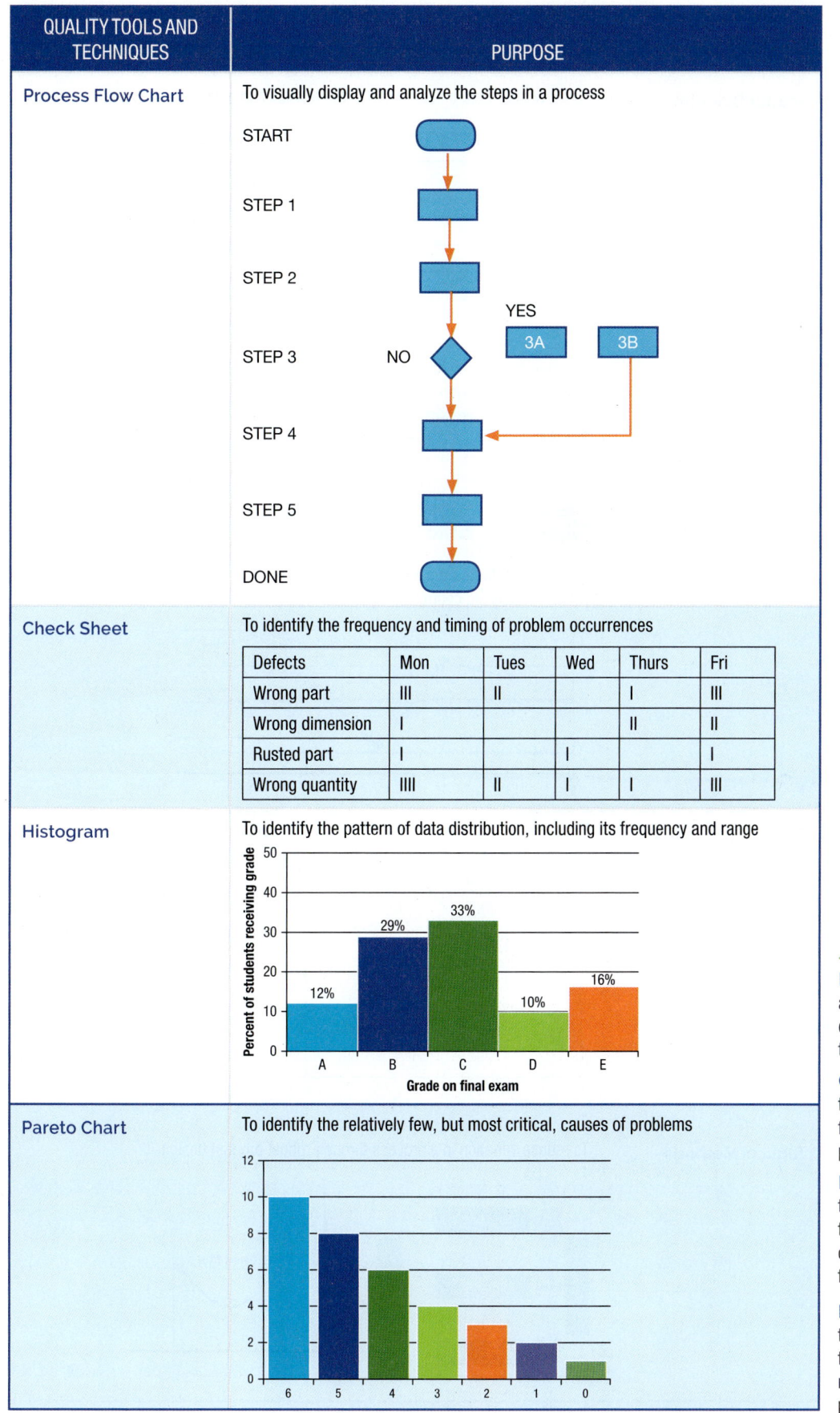

QUALITY TOOLS AND TECHNIQUES	PURPOSE
Process Flow Chart	To visually display and analyze the steps in a process
Check Sheet	To identify the frequency and timing of problem occurrences
Histogram	To identify the pattern of data distribution, including its frequency and range
Pareto Chart	To identify the relatively few, but most critical, causes of problems

Check Sheet table:

Defects	Mon	Tues	Wed	Thurs	Fri
Wrong part	III	II		I	III
Wrong dimension	I			II	II
Rusted part	I		I		I
Wrong quantity	IIII	II	I	I	III

Histogram: Percent of students receiving grade vs. Grade on final exam — A: 12%, B: 29%, C: 33%, D: 10%, E: 16%

Pareto Chart: values 6, 5, 4, 3, 2, 1, 0 — bars at 10, 8, 6, 4, 3, 2, 1

Process flow chart: a diagram that visually displays and analyzes the steps in a process

Check sheet: a chart that helps identify the frequency and timing of problem occurrences

Histogram: a graph that helps identify the pattern of data distribution, including its frequency and range

Pareto chart: a graph that helps identify the relatively few, but most critical, causes of problems

(Continued)

TABLE 5.5: (Continued)

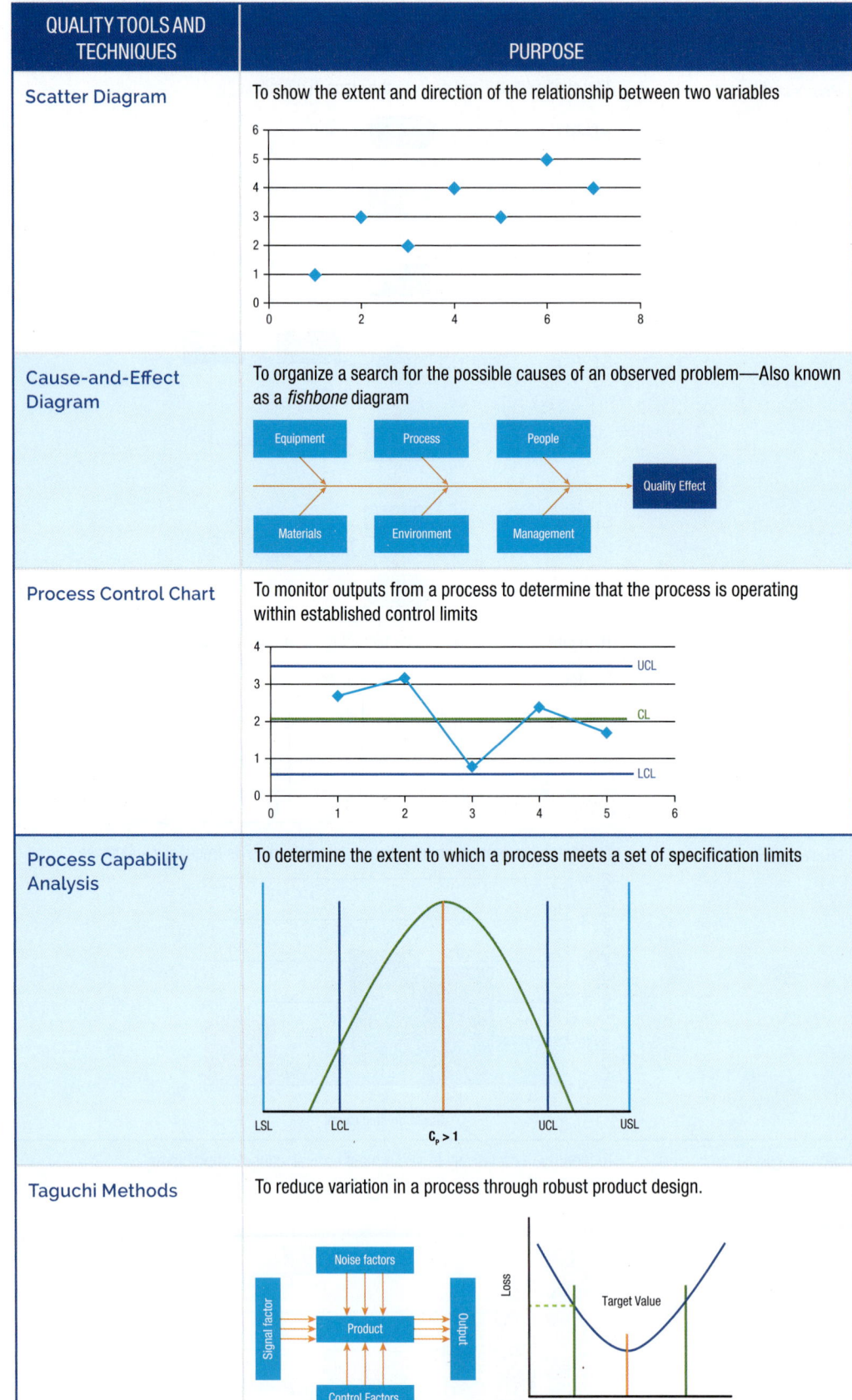

QUALITY TOOLS AND TECHNIQUES	PURPOSE
Scatter Diagram	To show the extent and direction of the relationship between two variables
Cause-and-Effect Diagram	To organize a search for the possible causes of an observed problem—Also known as a *fishbone* diagram
Process Control Chart	To monitor outputs from a process to determine that the process is operating within established control limits
Process Capability Analysis	To determine the extent to which a process meets a set of specification limits
Taguchi Methods	To reduce variation in a process through robust product design.

Scatter diagram: a graph that shows the extent and direction of the relationship between two variables

Process control chart: a graphic used to monitor outputs from a process to determine that the process is operating within established control limits

Process capability analysis: a graphic used to determine the extent to which a process meets a set of specification limits

Taguchi Methods: charts used to reduce variation in a process through robust product design

TABLE 5.6: Relative Importance of RATER Dimensions

DIMENSION	DESCRIPTION	RELATIVE IMPORTANCE
Reliability	Ability to perform the promised service dependably and accurately	32%
Responsiveness	Willingness to help customers and provide prompt service	22%
Assurance	Knowledge and courtesy of employees and their ability to convey trust and confidence	19%
Empathy	The individualized attention and caring that the firm provides to its customers	16%
Tangibles	Appearance of physical facilities, equipment, personnel, and communication materials	11%

The Service Delivery Performance Gap. This gap arises when the service delivered doesn't measure up to the firm's own standards or industry standards. When service at a drive-through window is chronically slow or orders are consistently wrong, that business is experiencing a service performance gap. Monitoring common customer experiences can help a business determine whether the service delivered matches its specifications.

FIGURE 5.5: GAP Model of Service Quality

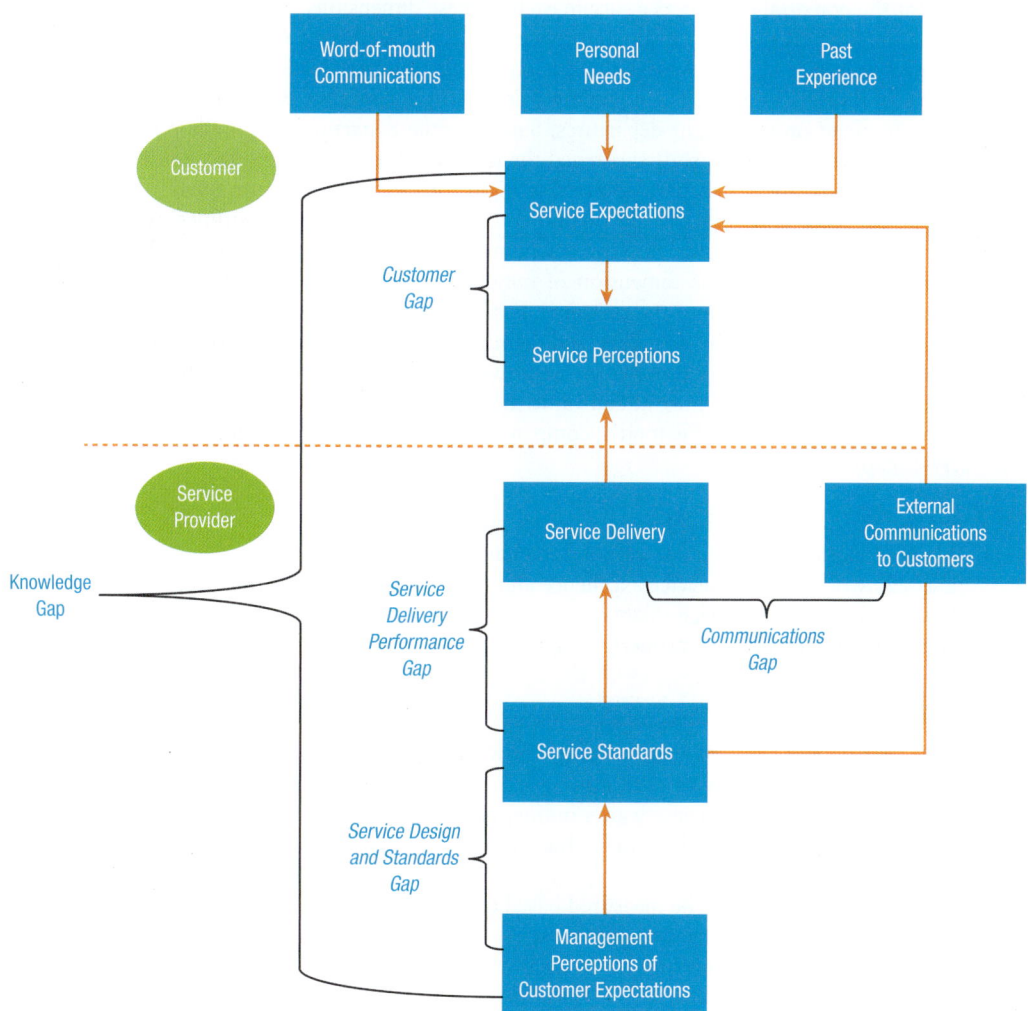

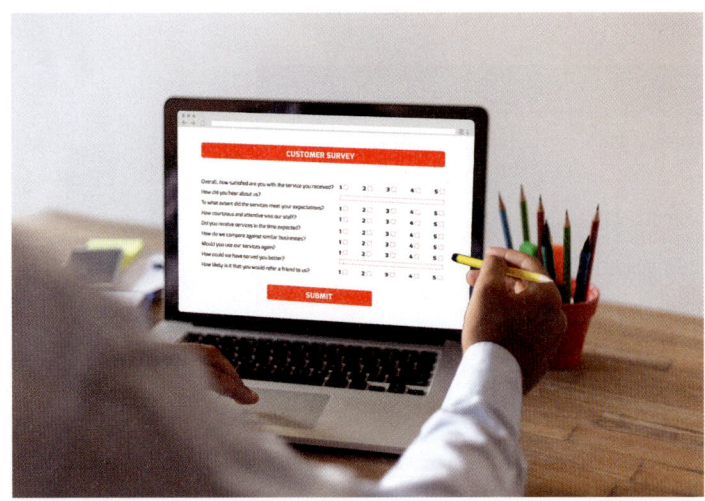

One tool companies use to close their knowledge gap is surveying customers and potential customers.

©iStockphoto.com/cigdemhizal

The Communications Gap. This is the gap between what was communicated to the customer about the service compared with the service provided. This gap can occur when service providers do not present customers with a realistic picture of the service and they end up disappointed. For example, to attract guests, a resort hotel in the Caribbean may use advertisements showing beautifully appointed hotel rooms, pristine beaches, luxurious lobby areas, and so forth. Nevertheless, when customers arrive and are greeted by noise, pollution, and an unsafe or poorly maintained environment, their satisfaction will plummet.

The Customer Gap. This gap results from the accumulation of the other gaps. That is, a combination of gaps in knowledge, service design and standards, service performance, and communications leads to an overall customer gap in service quality. Customers' expectations of service are formed on the basis of their personal needs and their own past experiences, and word-of-mouth information they gather ab*out the services provided by the company.*

The gap analysis model, often referred to as **SERVQUAL** analysis, uses surveys to determine the gaps that exist between the services that the customers expected to receive and what they actually received. Once these gaps are determined, the service provider will work to close or minimize these gaps, using the RATER model dimensions (reliability, responsiveness, assurance, empathy, and tangibles) to identify what the potential customers desire in each of these dimensions.

Let's use the RATER model to evaluate service quality at Southwest Airlines. In the area of reliability and responsiveness, Southwest Airlines is among the industry leaders with an on-time arrival rate in 2014 of more than 80%. The company was able to accomplish such a reliable performance by ensuring frequent on-time flight departures. Such on-time departures are made possible because the company's ticketing counter staff shortened the time for ticket purchases. In addition, the maintenance workers were able to prepare an arriving flight for the next departure quickly, often within 15 minutes. Assurance and empathy are pivotal components of Southwest Airlines' service quality. Southwest Airlines hires and trains employees who are fun loving, friendly, socially adept, and have the right attitude. Finally, on the dimension of tangibles, Southwest Airlines has made and implemented decisions that add value to the customer. For example, it uses 737 aircrafts because they are more reliable, require fewer crew members, and therefore have lower operating costs. In addition, the airline does not offer in-flight foodservice, as Southwest's market research found that it significantly increases ticket prices with very little added value to the customer.

In addition to using the RATER model, companies can also use the following broad guidelines to close service gaps:

- Involve their customers in the service-design process
- Make service improvements to respond to changes in the market
- Use teamwork to foster service excellence and continuously improve it
- Develop appropriate service-quality metrics
- Select the right employees, properly design their jobs, and train them

Electronic Service Quality (e-SQ)

Companies that deliver services electronically know that their success or failure is determined by their **electronic service quality (e-SQ)**. How good is the customer's electronic experience? Is the customer able to do what he or she wants online, via e-mail, or on the phone? How long does it take? Does the firm's technology help make the customer's transaction easier? That is, what constitutes good e-SQ?

Electronic service quality can be measured based on the quality of the information on the site and how well it is personalized for the shopper; the site's usability, reliability, and responsiveness; and the site's safety or security.[21] The importance of each can vary depending on the e-service offered. For

SERVQUAL: a gap analysis model that uses surveys to determine the gaps that exist between the services that the customers expected to receive and what they actually received

Electronic service quality (e-SQ): the level of success or failure of companies that deliver services electronically

example, online travel agencies have found that the functionality of their websites is a key factor in customer satisfaction with their services. Website functionality determines whether the customers will use them again. For companies that offer online financial services, security and safety to prevent the theft of account numbers are key factors.

Deficiencies in any of the aspects of electronic service quality can result in service gaps, such as these:

- *Marketing Information Gap.* This gap is created when the customer perceives that there is inadequate or incorrect information on the service provider's website or other electronic communication. For example, an online clothing website that neglects to list available sizes for skirts or coats will frustrate potential shoppers.
- *Design Gap.* This gap exists when a website, e-mail, or phone service is poorly designed. A slow, or non-intuitive, electronic connection can make it hard for shoppers to navigate around a website, through a phone tree, or get service by replying to an e-mail or text message sent by the provider.
- *Communication Versus Fulfillment Gap:* This gap occurs when, through its website or other electronic medium, a service provider makes a promise to a customer (such as guaranteeing overnight delivery or an instant refund), but then doesn't deliver on the promise.

With the large number of alternative electronic shopping options available today, it does not take much to disappoint potential customers and send them to competing service providers.

5.6 Managing Quality for Supply Chains

Discuss the process of managing quality in supply chains.

Managing Quality in the Supply Chain

Companies that manage the performance of their supply chains well can develop and market superior products and services. Conversely, if firms mismanage their supply chains and provide poor-quality products or services, they can damage their reputation, incur financial losses, and face lawsuits. In 2015, Chipotle Restaurants faced a series of *Escherichia coli* (*E. coli*) outbreaks at a number of its stores around the country. Among the causes was poor oversight of the variety of locally grown ingredients that Chipotle prides themselves on supporting. Unfortunately, this complicated supply chain proved impossible to reliably monitor as a result of the excessive costs of observing each producer and led to multiple, nationwide instances of tainted food. Likewise, another popular new consumer product, the hoverboard, has experienced a series of unexplained fires as the battery pack has a tendency to burst into flames with no warning. In late 2015, multiple airlines refused to allow customers to bring hoverboards on board or pack them in their luggage, fearing catastrophic mid-air fires.[22]

A quality problem can originate in any stage of the supply chain, from the acquisition of raw materials to the design of products and their production, transportation, and delivery to consumers. When such a problem occurs, it often affects all firms in the chain—even those not responsible for the problem.[23] These problems and the associated cost of solving them have led a number of companies to set more stringent quality standards for themselves and their vendors. By implementing a comprehensive supplier certification program, Alcoa Inc. (New York City, NY), a world leader in the production of aluminum products, was able to improve the quality of its products and reduce its costs as well of those of its suppliers.[24] Some firms require their suppliers to adopt Six Sigma practices, even going so far as to provide financial support for these efforts. When upstream suppliers become committed to Six Sigma, the improvement in the quality of the inputs they provide will naturally flow downstream to a firm's own operations as Figure 5.6 shows.

FIGURE 5.6: Supplier–Firm Six Sigma Quality-Improvement Chain

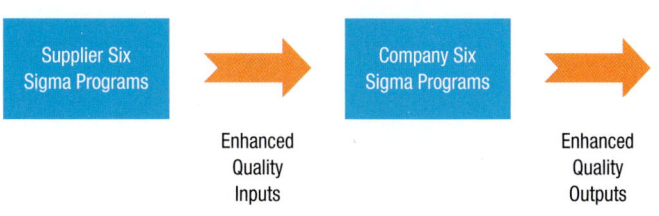

Consider This 5.3:
Service Quality at Amazon.com

As the largest online retailer in the world, Amazon sells everything from books, apparel, electronics, and digital downloads to gardening tools. The company has grown and maintained its competitive advantage by providing customers with superior service. Speed, accuracy, and courtesy are cornerstones of the company's operating philosophy.

Amazon keeps the quality of its service high in many different ways, including: understanding customer needs, adhering to customer-defined standards, and exceeding customer expectations.

Understanding Customers' Needs

Amazon attempts to understand the expectation of its customers as soon as they access its website. When a person makes a product selection, Amazon creates a customer profile of the person and attempts to offer alternative goods and services that may entice the customer. The more purchases the consumer makes while shopping on Amazon, the broader and more diverse the individual's profile becomes.

Adhering to Customer-Defined Standards

When consumers buy products from Amazon, they select the delivery method they want, and the company adheres to what they choose and the delivery timeframes specified. The company has also set strict standards for how quickly customers are informed when a product is unavailable (immediately), how quickly customers are notified whether an out-of-print book can be located (three weeks), how long customers can return items (30 days), and whether they pay return shipping costs.

Exceeding the Expectations of Customers

Apart from defining their service delivery standards, Amazon goes one step further. It exceeds its customers' expectations. Orders often arrive ahead of the promised dates, the orders are accurate, and usually in excellent condition because of careful shipping practices. Customers can also track packages and review previous orders at any time. Amazon's partners who sell used and new books and other related items must meet Amazon's high standards, and the company verifies the performance of each purchase by surveying the customer and posting the person's scores online for other customers to see. The company also has a "no questions asked" policy regarding returns and even includes return packaging materials with many of its deliveries to make the return shipping process as easy as possible.

Amazon has built a business model that not only avoids service gaps but is changing how retail shopping is conducted. The company has not simply become the best at what it does, it has proven that through an online, service-driven model, it can force traditional competitors to adapt to its new rules of the game, redefining the entire retail landscape.[25]

To attract customers, many vendors are voluntarily improving their quality management practices by adopting the quality standards of organizations such as the International Organization for Standardization (ISO), the American National Standards Institute (ANSI), and the American Society for Quality (ASQ). These vendors are finding that the benefits of doing so far outweigh the costs. Fewer defects and returned items, less scrap and rework, faster delivery and inventory replenishment times, and an enhanced reputation for the firm and its supply chain partners are among the benefits

In addition to adopting ISO, ANSI, and ASQ standards to enhance a product's quality, firms can implement other methods at different stages in its life cycle—from procurement and design to production and final delivery of the product to the consumer. [26]

Procurement Quality

A company's success or failure often hinges on the quality of the items its vendors supply. Supplier quality problems can quickly result in stock-outs or return charges. Moreover, it can be difficult to quickly replace the defective items because of the geographical distances that often separate producers and their suppliers. For this reason, many leading companies worldwide have invested significantly in systems and processes to improve the quality of their procurement activities. Table 5.7 shows some of the steps firms are taking instead of or in addition to requiring their suppliers to be certified or to adopt Six Sigma practices.

Design Quality

Design for supply chain: the process of designing a product so that it matches up well with the capabilities of a firm's supply chain members

As discussed in Chapter 4, tools such as concurrent engineering, design for manufacturing and assembly, and quality function deployment can be used not only to simplify the design and manufacturing of the product, but also to deliver a product that customers want. Likewise, product designs can be improved by involving a firm's supply chain partners. Design for supply chain is the process of

TABLE 5.7: Procurement Quality Steps

	STEPS	ACTIVITIES INVOLVED
1.	Measure, track, and recover the costs incurred from poor supplier quality	Typical examples of costs are scrap, line shutdowns, warranties, and product recalls. The firm should develop a cost-recovery system that holds suppliers accountable by charging quality costs back to them.
2.	Periodically audit suppliers	The purpose of an audit is to uncover quality problems in the supplier's processes. Following the audit, the supplier and manufacturer should work jointly to correct the problems within a mutually agreed upon timeframe.
3.	Create scorecards for suppliers and share their results with them	The scorecards can include the number of corrective actions required in the past, costs incurred from poor supplier quality, the number of customer complaints related to quality, and the relative ranking of the supplier in its industry.
4.	Develop a process to correct a supplier's quality problems	Investigate the cause of the quality problem, and then list the items that need to be fixed and implement appropriate changes. Examples of the changes are recalibration of manufacturing equipment and upgrading the skills of employees. The firms should document the changes for training purposes.
5.	Involve suppliers in quality management systems (QMS)	Create a system whereby suppliers (and other supply chain members) openly provide quality-related data to the company and vice versa.

designing a product so that it matches up well with the capabilities of a firm's supply chain members.[27] **Design for logistics** is the process of designing a product so that it can be transported easily through the supply chain.[28] This process includes designing the product's packaging or transportation routes. Similarly, firms can improve the quality of their products by working with their supply chain partners to implement value-engineering techniques (see Chapter 4) that focus on eliminating waste in products and manufacturing processes. For example, Schneider Electric SE (Rueil-Malmaison, France), a global electrical equipment manufacturer, worked with its suppliers to make significant changes to a component. The changes improved the quality of the product, sped up delivery times for the supply chain members, and lowered costs.[29]

Production and Delivery

Because of greater global competition, companies are increasingly focusing on logistics—the delivery of products and raw materials—as a key way to provide customers with quality and value so as to gain a competitive edge. Applying Six Sigma and TQM principles to logistics can improve the quality of products. In addition, when supply chain partners collaborate to develop logistics and inventory management systems, they increase the likelihood that quality is incorporated into the supply chain and that all of the partners benefit from it.

The transportation and packaging industries have also successfully used value analysis and engineering to improve the quality and safety of products and to speed up their delivery. Penske Logistics (Penske Corporation, Bloomfield Township, MI), a leading shipping and logistics services provider, is one such company. Penske also optimized the supply chain of one of its major customers by implementing uniform-ordering systems for its manufacturing plants.[30]

Design for logistics: the process of designing a product so that it can be transported easily through the supply chain

5.7 Global Quality Management

In the past decade, countries that offshored their production to emerging economies such as China and India sometimes faced serious quality problems in their consumer and industrial products. Not all quality management systems and standards can be readily transplanted from one country to another, and managing facilities around the globe can be challenging. Some countries may not have the technology or infrastructure needed to improve products, and not all cultures place a high priority on quality. Language and communication barriers sometimes make it difficult to share information and collect the data needed to improve quality. In addition, some team-based quality initiatives may require customization from country to country. For example, in some Asian

5.7

Discuss the challenges of managing quality in global supply chains.

Global Quality Management

OPERATIONS MANAGEMENT: LESSON LEARNED
Sleek Audio Tests Overseas Manufacturing

Sleek Audio (Bradenton, FL), a manufacturer of in-ear headphones for iPhones and other audio devices, thought they had made a good business decision by moving their manufacturing out of their original shop near St. Petersburg, Florida, to China to capitalize on the lower cost of labor and other incentives. They quickly learned that money isn't everything, as product quality plummeted, customer complaints soared, and whole shipments were either lost or defective. As part of the "reshoring" movement in the United States, Sleek Audio decided, to abandon their Chinese factories and move all operations back to the United States. Although their products are 15–20% more expensive as a result of the move, the company believes that the increase in quality more than makes up for the higher cost of manufacturing.[31]

Quality-control programs are critical for firms operating globally, however. If Boeing or Airbus (Blagnac, France), for example, were to contract for parts with a supplier in Vietnam, the company would work closely with the prospective supplier so that quality controls were in place. Some companies outsource some or all of their supplier-related activities, such as hiring suppliers and inspecting them, to independent **third-party quality assurance services** in the countries in which their suppliers are located. Using a third-party assurance service minimizes the language and cultural differences between a company and its suppliers. In addition, a third-party quality assurance service is better equipped to deal effectively with top managers and other employees in supplier organizations.[32] Finally, employing a third-party assurance service can eliminate the substantial travel expenses associated with sending a company representative abroad, as well as the time-consuming and lengthy paperwork needed to secure work visas or permits for the person. For more than a decade, General Motors has hired third-party quality providers to monitor its suppliers.

cultures, workers who are members of production teams feel it's inappropriate to suggest quality improvements to their superiors.

TQM and Global Quality

Applying TQM in global markets and operations presents some challenges, especially given the diverse expectations of customers in different countries. What customers value varies widely from country to country. Because resources are limited, it may be impossible for a firm to meet these various expectations. Nevertheless, it is still possible for companies to focus on the customer by thinking globally but acting locally. That is, they have to produce products and services that are locally acceptable, but are designed, developed, and manufactured according to global standards. For example, although The Coca-Cola Company (Atlanta, GA) uses the same formula and basic bottle shape for Coke worldwide, the labels on the bottles and their sizes vary depending upon the market.

All functions at all levels of the global corporation have to be involved in TQM for it to work, which can complicate its implementation. For example, the various operations functions such as fabrication and assembly are sometimes in different countries, and coordinating these activities from a TQM perspective is difficult. Measuring quality-related results across countries can also be impractical. To achieve continuous improvement, it can sometimes be more important to focus on the process of achieving the results than the results themselves.

In addition, the company may have to depend on foreign suppliers because the domestic suppliers do not meet quality standards, do not have competitive prices, or offer incompatible technologies. To meet this challenge, companies need to remain flexible. For example, production processes should be adaptable enough to simultaneously allow low volumes of production, high product variety, and low cost to meet the diverse global market requirements.

Other approaches some companies have used to improve global quality are risk assessment and prevention. Consider This 5.4 explains how Heinz (H. J. Heinz Company, Pittsburgh, PA) uses this approach to improve the quality of its food products.

Information Systems and Global Quality

Ideally, extending TQM throughout a global organization should provide benefits such as internal benchmarking and the transfer of knowledge from one part of the organization and its supply

Third-party quality assurance services: independent firms that manage supplier-related activities for other firms, located in the same country in which their suppliers are located

chain to others. The recent advances in information technology have made these benefits possible. Nevertheless, the information technology of various subunits of the organization must be integrated. Recall from Chapter 4 that the development of the Airbus A380 aircraft was significantly delayed because Airbus's engineering offices in Spain and France that worked on the plane didn't have a joint software package.

Most often it is not incompatibilities between hardware and software that cause problems, but outdated information infrastructure. Fully updated and integrated information networks among the various manufacturing units located in geographically dispersed countries are therefore critical to global TQM.

Information systems to monitor global quality are not cheap, but they can be an invaluable competitive advantage for their users. Defense contractor General Dynamics Corporation's (West Falls Church, VA) Bath Iron Works shipyard is responsible for building a number of the Navy's newest and most technologically advanced ships. To maintain the highest quality for the wide variety of systems to be installed on the multi-billion-dollar Zumwalt and Burke-class ships currently under construction, Bath Iron Works is heavily invested in computer-integrated manufacturing systems to control quality assurance, production scheduling, and systems integration.[34]

Technology Networks and Global Quality

Because economic and competitive factors can vary from country to country, not all of the supplier, production, distribution and marketing activities, and technological requirements across markets are likely to be contained within a single organization. That is, the sheer complexity of managing global quality makes it extremely difficult to maintain all critical elements within the firm. As a result, some emerging technologies or a scarce raw material may have to be acquired from outside the firm, from another country, or both. This coordination requires technology networks. A *technology network* is a resource pool made up of foreign firms and other domestic and foreign science and technology organizations that cooperate with one another. For example, India has launched a series of initiatives to improve Internet connectivity throughout the country, reasoning that digital networking is critical to overall economic progress. In 2014, less than 20% of the nation's 1.2 billion people used the Internet. In 2016, India launched "Digital India," partnering with Cisco Systems, Inc. (San Jose, CA) and companies within the country in a broad-based effort to digitally link the 250,000 local governments and promote more rapid use of the Internet and mobile communications.[35] Nevertheless, achieving an integrated and harmonious quality management and improvement system can still be difficult in these global alliances because the varying management styles and cultures can hinder organizational learning and transfer of knowledge. Therefore, in forming these strategic alliances, the global company should be aware of these obstacles.

Six Sigma and Global Quality

Six Sigma principles can be extended to manage global quality. There are several approaches a company can take to achieve continuous improvement globally through Six Sigma.[36]

- Establishing structures and quality improvement programs to support Six Sigma initiatives. For example, global corporations can hold periodic quality summit meetings in which regional vice presidents (general managers), sales managers, plant managers, and quality assurance managers from each region participate, and leaders from the firm's research and development groups and global operations groups attend.
- Establishing a Six Sigma steering committee under the leadership of a global Six Sigma manager. The members of the steering committee should include Six Sigma-trained representatives from each of the company's global manufacturing facilities.
- Overcoming the resistance of employees in different cultures to implement a Six Sigma project by making early and incremental changes. For example, implementing a Six Sigma initiative under the guidance of a Black Belt in one region initially can help employees in other divisions understand the process, recognize its advantages, and buy into the process. Establishing reporting structures can help with the progress. One reporting structure would be to have the Black Belts of the Six Sigma project report their progress to a local site leader, who in turn reports to a global Six Sigma manager. The Six Sigma manager would then disseminate the information to the company's other facilities.

Consider This 5.4:
Global Quality Management at Heinz

©iStockphoto.com/Christa Brunt

In addition to selling more than 650 million bottles annually of its iconic ketchup, Heinz also manufactures and sells various other food products in more than 50 countries around the world. Heinz has embraced ISO 9000 standards and has devoted time and money to develop a global quality strategy. Part of this strategy is the company's Global Quality

Risk Management Process, which is a food-safety risk assessment process designed to eliminate any biological, chemical, and physical hazards in the food it makes and sells. The goal is to continuously reduce food-safety risks, identify and share best practices among the company's facilities, and measure them all against a global common standard.

Using a combination of third-party assurance services and its own staff, the company has identified more than 40 categories of quality and safety critical to its products and assigned risk-control rating scores to each category at each plant. Each manufacturing or food-processing facility then establishes a plan to lessen its quality risks and achieve new target goals as part of the firm's continuous improvement efforts. For example, at plants in Massillon, Ohio, and Pocatello, Idaho, an electronic system identifies incorrect cartons that are traveling at very high speeds to prevent mislabeling any allergen risks—that is, to prevent applying labels that don't correctly identify products people could be allergic to, such as peanuts, eggs, or wheat. A Polish plant installed an X-ray machine to identify the presence of foreign materials in products.

In addition, Heinz routinely conducts risk assessment reviews through interviews and trouble-shooting sessions with its managers around the globe. As a result of their dedication to quality risk management practices, Heinz has had very few product recalls.[33]

Globally, Six Sigma has been a very successful and popular quality improvement methodology. In India, for example, several multinational companies, such as WIPRO Limited (Bangalore, India), Jet Airways (Mumbai, India), and Tesco PLC (Hertfordshire, England, U.K.) have implemented the Six Sigma method.

5.8

Describe the ethical and legal relationship among quality, sustainability, and corporate social responsibility.

Suppliers and Product Defects

5.8. Legal, Ethical, and Sustainability Issues

Many laws and regulations require products and services to meet certain quality standards—specifically, that they are safe and free of defects. If that level of quality is not met, a company must accept responsibility for the problem and correct it, even if it requires a worldwide recall of its products. Examples of companies that conducted recalls because their products were either defective or were contaminated include Toyota, Johnson & Johnson (New Brunswick, NJ), and Nestlé S.A. (Vevey, Switzerland; Perrier brand sparkling water), to name but a few. A company that knows it has produced a defective product and fails to inform buyers about it and take corrective action in a timely manner is engaging in unethical behavior that can seriously damage the firm's reputation and lead to lawsuits. We have previously noted the problems General Motors encountered with the faulty ignition switches they installed on millions of their cars. Some evidence exists to suggest that key executives at the company were aware of the faulty switches but opted to do nothing about it.[37]

In some cases, the source of the ethical and legal problems can originate with sub-contractors or other suppliers. Boeing's newest aircraft, the 787 Dreamliner, was plagued by a series of fires in the battery compartments of the aircraft, delaying delivery of the jets to their first customers and costing the company millions in lost revenue as they worked to identify and fix the problems with their batteries. After multiple inspections, Boeing discovered that the culprit was a lithium-ion battery manufactured by GS Yuasa Corporation (Kyoto, Japan), a Japanese sub-contractor. Boeing's quality control problems led the U.S. National Transportation Safety Board (NTSB) to temporarily ground the entire 787 fleet, while also citing GS Yuasa for their poor quality control and failure to test their batteries under more realistic conditions. Because the 787 program was already well behind delivery schedule, there has been some concern raised that Boeing was willing to too-quickly accept their sub-contractor's batteries without overseeing better testing controls.[38]

Although the costs of producing quality products and services can be substantial, the alternative is not acceptable: producing goods that lead to lost sales, dissatisfied customers, and in some cases, physical injury. In 2011, the Chinese government shut down a number of Wal-Mart stores in China, allegedly for selling expired, mislabeled, and substandard food. There are successful models that companies seeking to manage their supply chain operations for quality can use on which to base their initiatives. These range from global standards for quality (ISO 9000) to models and philosophies of superior quality (TQM and Six Sigma). The key is to identify the critical dimensions of quality that will drive sales and commit the time and money needed to support these dimensions.

Sustainability

Increasingly, consumers are demanding products that firms create with quality materials and that use manufacturing techniques that do not threaten the environment. Building quality into its products and services can help a company with its sustainability efforts in several ways. First, a high-quality product typically lasts longer. Second, higher product quality leads to higher productivity because a company doesn't have to stop to rework products. Avoiding rework can also help eliminate scrap and decrease a company's energy use. Third, efforts to achieve greater sustainability by designing products so they require fewer inputs lowers the chances of defective raw materials entering the production process. Minimizing defective materials, in turn, lowers production error rates and variability, improving a product's overall quality.

P&G's (Procter & Gamble Co., Cincinnati, OH) decision to create a concentrated version of its Tide detergent allowed the firm to reduce its packaging. The smaller package has helped the company lower its manufacturing and energy costs and achieve higher productivity.[39] When companies come up with sustainable ways such as this to improve a product's quality, the result is typically greater customer loyalty.

From a supply chain perspective, product quality has an impact on the environment. For example, if a product shipped from China is of poor quality, then the product must be returned or discarded. Either option is costly because returning the product increases transportation costs, which contributes to pollution, and discarding the product wastes scarce resources. ISO 14000 standards can help firms seeking to improve their sustainability.

Corporate Social Responsibility

Sustainability is a part of corporate social responsibility. Like sustainability, a company that practices corporate social responsibility is typically able to foster a better image for its products and even command higher prices for them. Nestlé endeavors to be socially responsible by working directly with the farmers and agricultural communities that supply about 40% of its milk and 10% of its coffee. Nestlé helped these suppliers by building infrastructure, training farmers, and paying fair market prices directly to them instead of using middlemen. In return, the suppliers provided Nestlé higher quality agricultural ingredients for its products. The strong relationships Nestlé formed as a result give it a reliable source of inputs, even when these raw materials are in short supply. For example, when the price of milk powder soared in 2007, Nestlé's supply chain and price risks were minimized, enabling the company to protect the interests of all its stakeholders—from its suppliers to the consumers of its products.[40] Nestlé releases its annual "Creating Shared Value" report, which demonstrates their steps to create social value through their products. So successful has Nestlé been with fostering social responsibility that, for 2013, they were named one of the top ten worldwide organizations for social responsibility. High-quality products that are sustainable don't happen by accident. They are the result of the deliberate actions socially responsible organizations take.

Visit **edge.sagepub.com/venkataraman** to help you accomplish your coursework goals in an easy-to-use learning environment.

- Mobile-friendly eFlashcards
- Mobile-friendly practice quizzes
- A complete online action plan

- Chapter summaries with learning objectives
- Video and multimedia resources

CHAPTER SUMMARY

5.1 Explain the importance of quality, the difficulties in measuring quality, and the differences in quality for different people or groups. Because there are different dimensions of quality, quality is often difficult to measure. Consequently, there is no single universal definition of quality that will suit all people for all circumstances. For example, the producer of a product might define quality as the product's conformance to design specifications. On the other hand, a consumer might define quality as the product's fitness for its intended use.

5.2 Outline the benefits and costs of creating quality products and services. Companies that systematically manage quality reap the benefits of higher customer satisfaction, increased revenues, reduced costs, and increases in productivity. In achieving and managing quality, companies have to contend with four broad categories of costs: prevention costs, appraisal costs, internal failure costs, and external failure costs.

5.3 Describe the evolution of quality management and identify the pioneers who contributed to modern quality management methods. Efforts to manage quality have evolved from inspection to statistical quality control, continuous improvement, quality planning, total quality control, quality circles, robust design, poka yoke methods, and total quality management. Some of the pioneers of the quality movement include Walter Shewhart, Edward Deming, Joseph Juran, Armand Feigenbaum, Kaoru Ishikawa, Philip Crosby, Shigeo Shingo, and Genichi Taguchi.

5.4 Compare these major quality management initiatives: total quality management (TQM), the ISO 9000 family of quality standards, the Baldrige Award, Six Sigma, and DMADV methodologies. Among the major quality initiatives undertaken by businesses throughout the world, TQM focuses on the *continuous improvement* of the quality of processes, services, and processes. To achieve that goal, everyone who is involved in the creation or consumption of a product or service, including management and the workforce of the firm, its suppliers, and perhaps even the customers, should be responsible for its quality. The International Organization for Standardization (ISO) is the world's largest developer and publisher of international standards for quality. Among the many standards published by ISO, the ISO 9000 family of standards focuses on managing quality in both manufacturing and service organizations. Organizations that meet the criteria can request to be certified by the ISO. The initial focus of the Baldrige Award was on the quality of products and services provided by superior organizations. This focus, however, has since changed and the award is now given annually to organizations in business, health care, education, and not-for-profit sectors that demonstrate "performance excellence." Six Sigma, which was originally developed in 1986 by Motorola, is a fact-based, data-driven quality management method. It seeks to improve the quality of products and services by identifying and removing the causes of defects (errors) and minimizing process variations. The Six Sigma method consists of a sequence of five steps: define, measure, analyze, improve, and control (DMAIC). In certain situations, the DMADV (define, measure, analyze, design, and verify) methodology will offer

better results. To be successful, Six Sigma efforts require the support of a firm's managers and the collaboration of employees across different functions.

5.5 Identify and describe some of the basic tools managers and employees use to manage quality in their firms. A number of analytical tools and statistical techniques are available to analyze data to effectively manage and control quality. Some of these tools include process flowcharts, check sheets, histograms, Pareto charts, scatter diagrams, cause-and-effect diagrams, process control charts, process capability analysis, and Taguchi methods. For managing service quality, two of the commonly used tools are the RATER model and GAP model.

5.6 Discuss the process of managing quality in supply chains. Supply chain partners can improve their quality management practices by adopting the quality standards of organizations such as the International Organization for Standardization (ISO), the American National Standards Institute (ANSI), and the American Society for Quality (ASQ). In addition to adopting ISO, ANSI, and ASQ standards, firms involved in a supply chain can use other methods at different stages in the product life cycle—from procurement and design to production and final delivery of the product to the consumer.

5.7 Discuss the challenges of managing quality in global supply chains. Managing quality in the global setting can be a very serious challenge for organizations. Not all quality management standards can be transplanted from one country to another, and managing facilities around the globe can be difficult when some countries may not have the technology or infrastructure needed to improve products and not all cultures place a high priority on quality. Language and communication barriers can also make it difficult to share information and collect the data needed to improve quality. Firms often employ technology networks and information systems to link together their geographically dispersed plants and offices. Furthermore, they must find the means to maintain sufficient levels of quality control among supply chain partners to ensure that no defective or substandard materials become part of the production process, leading to inferior products.

5.8 Describe the ethical and legal relationship among quality, sustainability, and corporate social responsibility. Many laws and regulations require that products and services meet certain quality standards so that they are safe and free of defects. If those quality standards are not met, then the company has the responsibility to fix the quality problem even if it requires a worldwide recall of its products. In addition, if a company knows it has produced a defective product, it is ethically responsible to inform its customers about it and to take corrective action in a timely manner. Otherwise, the company can seriously damage its reputation and it may face lawsuits. Customers are increasingly demanding products that are created with quality materials, and they expect companies to use manufacturing techniques that do not threaten the environment. Therefore, building quality into its products and services can help a company with its sustainability efforts because a high-quality product typically lasts longer. Also, higher quality products lead to higher productivity and efficient use of energy because wasteful actions such as product rework and scrap are eliminated. Efforts to achieve greater

sustainability by designing products that require fewer input materials improves product quality because it lowers the chances of defective raw materials entering the production process.

KEY TERMS

Appraisal costs   165

Benchmarking   171

Black Belt   175

Cause-and-effect diagram   169

Check sheet   177

Critical-to-quality (CTQ)   170

Design for logistics   183

Design for supply chain   182

Design of experiments (DOE)   169

Electronic service quality (e-SQ)   180

External failure costs   165

Green Belt   176

Histogram   177

Inspection   166

Internal failure costs   165

International Organization for Standardization (ISO)   171

Kaizen   170

Master Black Belt   175

Pareto chart   177

Plan, Do, Study, and Act (PDSA) cycle   170

Poka yoke   169

Prevention costs   165

Process capability analysis   178

Process control chart   178

Process flow chart   177

Project charter   176

Quality circle   169

Scatter diagram   178

SERVQUAL   180

Taguchi Methods   178

Taguchi-loss function   169

Third-party quality assurance services   184

DISCUSSION AND REVIEW QUESTIONS

1. List the eight dimensions of product quality. Pick the product offerings of any two competing firms. What are the similarities and differences between the products when it comes to each dimension? Given these similarities and differences, what strategic implications do they hold for the companies in relation to their target markets?

2. List and briefly explain the costs of quality.

3. What are the consequences of poor quality products?

4. Why is being ISO 9000 certified important to global firms?

5. What practices characterize TQM?

6. Explain how improving the quality of products and services can increase a firm's productivity and lower its production costs.

7. What are the criteria for the Baldrige Performance Excellence Program?

8. What is the Six Sigma approach to quality management? Briefly explain the DMAIC process.

9. What are the dimensions of service quality?

10. Discuss the five gaps in the GAP model of service quality.

11. What is electronic service quality (e-SQ)? What four gaps can form between a consumer and an electronic-service provider?

12. Choose an electronic service provider you have done business with, and evaluate its service quality using the four gaps we discussed.

13. List the approaches that can be used to improve a product or service's quality during the different stages of its life cycle, including the procurement phase.

14. What can global companies do to improve the quality of their goods and services?

15. Explain why product quality and sustainability are closely linked.

16. Describe the relationship between product quality and a company's ethical behavior.

PROBLEMS

1. Compare and contrast two hotel chains on the five service value dimensions: reliability, responsiveness, assurance, empathy, and tangibles. Give examples of how a premium hotel chain, such as the Four Seasons or Ritz Carlton would differ from a low-price motel option.

2. How have you seen examples of successful companies in your hometown profit by superior emphasis on product or service quality?

3. How have the "costs of quality" (prevention, appraisal, internal failure, and external failure costs) played a role in the success of Mercedes-Benz (Stuttgart, Baden-Württemberg, Germany), BMW (Bayerische Motoren Werke AG, Munich, Germany), or Audi AG (Ingolstadt, Germany)? Use the Internet to investigate examples of luxury car companies addressing these costs.

4. What are the advantages and disadvantages of using the PAF model to calculate the costs of quality? What advice would you give to a CEO who is considering using the PAF model for his or her product quality assessments?

5. What are the advantages and disadvantages of the Six Sigma approach to quality? Would you advise an air traffic controller organization to commit to Six Sigma? Why or why not? What about a neighborhood bakery?

6. Construct a GAP model to analyze patient/customer service quality for a health care facility.

7. Construct a RATER assessment of a local restaurant? On which dimensions were they superior, and on which were they poor? Based on your perspective, how would you rate the relative importance of the five dimensions in a restaurant service encounter? Why?

8. Think of an outstanding electronic service encounter you have had in the past year and contrast it with a poor example. What characterized the excellent service encounter, and how did it differ from the poor quality example?

9. Assume you are a consultant working with a software company that is interested in developing on-line and e-service options for their customers. What advice would you offer for a company on how to improve its electronic service quality?

CASE STUDY 5.1 PFIZER FIXES PROBLEMS WITH ITS CLEANING PROCESSES

Prior to the start of Pfizer, Inc.'s (New York, NY) "Right First Time" Six Sigma quality initiative, manufacturing teams throughout the company often faced what it called black hole issues—chronic problems that seemed to suck up resources and ideas and yet never get resolved. One black hole was the cleaning of some of the company's tri-blender machines.

Tri-Blenders are machines specially designed to thoroughly and efficiently blend dry ingredients and liquids, while minimizing the air introduced into the process. Their performance is critical to producing high-quality pharmaceuticals, whether as pills or liquids. The tri-blenders for one key product at Pfizer's Kalamazoo, Michigan, plant are cleaned about 400 times per year. The tri-blender cleaning could not be done safely with solvents. Instead, the equipment had to be taken down and parts cleaned by hand, put into an automated washer, then manually unloaded and dried. Every cleaning required a 100% inspection by the plant's cleaning validation lab. This task alone consumed about a quarter of the lab's time and resources. Part cleaning also had a high failure rate, necessitating extensive re-cleaning.

Tabitha Bratt, the cleaning validation lab manager with a Six Sigma Black Belt, was chosen to head up an eight-person cross-functional team to solve the tri-blender troubles. The team members met frequently and conducted several walkthroughs and mapped every step in the cleaning process. Each team member was responsible for a different step in the cleaning process, and they compared notes during the meetings. The group then began to develop a list of causes, starting with listening to the team members who worked on the floor. For example, one operator had been frustrated with

the consistently poor cleaning of one particular small part. "Why don't we just throw the thing away?" he wondered. That's what they did, and Pfizer started to use disposable parts.

Eventually, the team drafted new operating procedures and videotaped the cleaning process for computer-based training for all operators. A few months later, the process was finally validated by demonstrating its reliability and effectiveness. The key was getting the operators involved from the start, said Jill June, the director of the "Right First Time" initiative at the plant. "You have to put people in positions of responsibility who understand what the problem is," she explained. The operators were "living it, breathing it, and seeing it every day." A key to the success of this Six Sigma project was getting the operators to become more accepting of change and willing to drive it. As a result, Pfizer's Kalamazoo plant has established a new standard for cleaning and employing its tri-blenders, all supported by equipment operators.[41]

Questions:

1. Pfizer's experience demonstrates that correcting quality problems is often complex, time-consuming, and expensive. Why, in your opinion, does it make sense for companies to invest time and money to make these corrections?

2. Search for "Six Sigma projects" on the Internet. What similarities do you see among the projects you found? What conclusions can you draw about organizations that undertake these projects?

CASE STUDY 5.2 PARTNERING TO IMPROVE QUALITY

AmeriCal Manufacturing, Inc* (AMI), an American manufacturing firm located in the Midwest, recently partnered with a supplier in China. The supplier provides power transmissions, bearings, and specialty components to a variety of industries, including the aerospace industry. After receiving some of these parts, AMI realized they did not meet all of AMI's specifications. The company then contracted with a third-party quality assurance firm to inspect the Chinese supplier.

To verify that the products shipped to AMI conformed to specifications, the firm sent an experienced quality engineer to the supplier's manufacturing plant to assess the plant's processes. Using AMI's specifications and work instructions, the engineer reviewed the documents that accompanied the manufacturing work orders. He followed a standardized checklist for inspecting each part and determining how it was manufactured, noted any deficiencies, and communicated them to AMI. He then worked with the supplier to correct the problems.

The engineer discovered that there were differences in how the supplier and AMI gauged the product's specifications. To resolve this problem, the supplier changed its methods of gauging specifications to match AMI's methods. It was then able to conduct statistical studies on the production

runs and make the adjustments needed so the product conformed to AMI's specifications.

Ultimately, the engineer was able to finish the project within a reasonable amount of time, educate the supplier about the customer's expectations, and provide it with some quality management tools. This type of scrutiny and interaction would have been almost impossible or too costly without a third-party quality assurance service.[42]

Questions:

1. This case illustrates how complex it is to implement quality standards across a global supply chain. To minimize quality problems, what steps can a supplier and its customer take prior to signing a contract?

2. Develop three morals of this story. Consider the perspectives of the manufacturer and the supplier and explain how they might conflict with each other.

3. Why do you think this conflict might be the case?

4. What are the advantages and disadvantages of using third-party quality assurance services?

* Not its real name.

CASE STUDY 5.3 3M: FINDING THE DELICATE BALANCE BETWEEN SIX SIGMA AND INNOVATION

3M, an American corporation, is known for innovative products such as masking tape, Thinsulate, and Post-It Notes. In 2000, 3M hired as its CEO James McNerney, an advocate of Six Sigma. Over the next 4.5 years, McNerney introduced Black Belt training companywide, identified and supported numerous Six Sigma projects throughout 3M's operating divisions, eliminated many sources of waste, and cut costs.

Initially, investors were ecstatic because the company's stock price rose and its profit margins increased. Unfortunately, at the same time, people were noticing that a company founded on the idea of radical innovation and disruptive technologies was losing its way; new product ideas were declining. For a company that prided itself on drawing one-third of its revenues from products that had been introduced within the past five years, the number of new products was steadily slipping. What was happening?

Programs like Six Sigma are process improvement–focused and can lead to reductions in cost and increases in quality. Nevertheless, there is a danger that, along the way, the focus on improving the bottom line can stifle the attitudes a company needs to foster creativity. "Invention is by its very nature a disorderly process," said George Buckley, who in 2004 succeeded McNerney and reversed many of his initiatives. "You can't put a Six Sigma process into that area and say, 'well, I'm getting behind on invention, so I'm going to schedule myself for three good ideas on Wednesday and two on Friday.' That's not how creativity works."

Managing the twin goals of efficiency and innovation was difficult. "The more you hardwire a company on total quality management, [the more] it is going to hurt breakthrough innovation," notes Vijay Govindarajan, a management professor at Dartmouth's Tuck School of Business. "The mindset that is needed, the capabilities that are needed, the metrics that are needed, the whole culture that is needed for discontinuous innovation, are fundamentally different."

To reinvigorate new product development at 3M, Buckley increased the company's R&D budgets and channeled money toward 3M's core business areas. Six Sigma continues to play an important role in managing the bottom line, but not at the expense of the creativity. Buckley (who has since retired) "brought back a spark around creativity," explained Timm Hammond, the company's director of strategic business development. Added Bob Anderson, a business director in 3M's radio frequency identification division: "We feel like we can dream again."[43]

Questions:

1. In your opinion, does this case illustrate significant problems with the Six Sigma philosophy? Why or why not?

2. Do you agree with the assessment that a company can either focus on quality or innovation? Why do you think 3M had such a difficult time balancing these two goals?

CASE STUDY 5.4 VAN HALEN, BROWN M&M'S, AND QUALITY CONTROL

Few rock bands have had the longevity and impact Van Halen has enjoyed over its career. As one of the premier bands in the world, the group has the luxury of commanding high fees and generous perks. The band's requests were described in the detailed riders in its performance contracts. A rider is a list of expectations, requirements, and outright demands that artists attach to the contracts they sign with concert promoters, who arrange for them to perform. Chauffeured transportation, luxurious accommodations, and lavish backstage buffets are often listed in the riders.

At the height of its popularity, Van Halen took the terms in its riders to extremes. For example, the band demanded that a bowl of M&M candies be provided but that all the brown M&Ms be removed. The presence of a single brown M&M was grounds for Van Halen to cancel a scheduled appearance.

Was this simply an example of artistic arrogance taken to the extreme? In fact, the "no brown M&Ms" contract clause served a practical purpose: to provide an easy way to determine if the technical specifications of the contract had been thoroughly read and complied with. As David Lee Roth, the band's former lead singer, relates in his autobiography:

> Van Halen was the first band to take huge productions into tertiary, third-level markets. We'd pull up with nine 18-wheeler trucks, full of gear, where the standard was three trucks, max. And there were many, many technical errors. . . . The contract rider read like a version of the Chinese yellow pages because there was so much equipment, and so many human beings to make it function. So just as a little test, in the technical aspects of the rider, it would say "Article 148: There will be fifteen amperage voltage sockets at twenty-foot spaces, evenly, providing nineteen amperes. . . ." This kind of thing. And Article 126, in the middle of nowhere, was: "There will be no brown M&Ms in the backstage area, upon pain of forfeiture of the show, with full compensation."
>
> So, when I would walk backstage, if I saw a brown M&M in that bowl . . . well, line-check the entire production. Guaranteed you'd run into a problem. Sometimes it would threaten to just destroy the whole show. Something like, literally, life-threatening.

The band believed that if arena personnel were careful enough to remove brown M&Ms from the bowl, they had probably done everything else to ensure that the production would be fully supported and safe for all concerned. The presence of brown M&Ms was a visible signal to the band that the quality control was lacking.

Skeptics may view the brown M&Ms test as an unreasonable way to determine whether quality controls were being maintained. Nevertheless, David Lee Roth offered some evidence to suggest that it actually was a pretty good quality check:

> The folks in Pueblo, Colorado, at the university, took the contract rather kinda casual. They had one of these new rubberized bouncy basketball flooring in their arena. They hadn't read the contract, and weren't sure, really, about the weight of this production; this thing weighed like the business end of a 747.
>
> I came backstage. I found some brown M&Ms, I went into full Shakespearean, "What is this before me?" . . . and promptly trashed the dressing room. Dumped the buffet, kicked a hole in the door, twelve thousand dollars' worth of fun.
>
> The staging sank through their floor. They didn't bother to look at the weight requirements or anything, and this sank through their new flooring and did eighty thousand dollars' worth of damage to the arena floor. The whole thing had to be replaced.[44]

Questions:

1. Comment on the decision to use brown M&Ms as a safety check for the band's performances. Does this seem a good way to verify quality to you? Why or why not?

2. Suppose you were just promoted to assistant manager at a local restaurant and, as part of your duties, you are asked to improve basic food preparation and service delivery quality. Based on this case, how might you develop a quality test at the restaurant to verify that all necessary food preparation and safety procedures were being followed?

VIDEO CASE ....

Watch this video case to learn about how Beefsteak, a restaurant in Washington, D. C., consistently offers fresh, high-quality dishes.

CRITICAL THINKING EXERCISES ....

The purpose of this exercise is for the students to become aware that a company to deliver a quality product to its customers has to ensure that the quality of its product is maintained throughout the supply chain – from supplier to the final customer.

Do a search on the web for the following key phrase: "Toyota accelerator recall." Then read some of the news articles you found about the recall.

1. Why is the information in the articles important to operations managers?
2. How did Toyota identify and fix the defect?
3. How can Toyota prevent their recurrence in the future?

CHAPTER
6

Quality Improvement and Control Tools

LEARNING OBJECTIVES

After studying this chapter, you should be able to:

1. Explain the difference between quality control and quality assurance.

2. Apply the various tools for appraising the quality of products and processes.

3. Apply the various tools for preventing defects in products and processes, including control charts, a process capability analysis, and how to calculate Six Sigma levels of quality.

4. Use quality design tools to improve product or process design.

OPERATIONS PROFILE: Using Technology to Improve the Quality of Helicopter Rescue

©istockphoto.com/john Kirk

Helicopter rescue, especially using air ambulances for emergency transportation, has long been a dangerous job. The accident rate for civil helicopters was 3.6 events per 100,000 flight hours in 2014, roughly the same as in 2010 and 2011, according to the government–industry team leading the safety campaign. That rate was about one-third higher in 2012 and 2013. To address the challenges of air rescue and improve the quality of its services, Air Methods Corporation (Dove Valley CDP, CO), the country's largest operator of emergency medical helicopters, has become the first to create an all-weather fleet able to use satellite data and simulators routinely to upgrade the training and capabilities of its flight crews. Operating in 48 states with more than 400 total rotorcraft and fixed-wing medical transport aircraft, Air Methods is comparable in size to Southwest Airlines Co. (Dallas, TX).

In the past, access to satellite imagery was limited by the Federal Aviation Administration (FAA), who instead mandated that air emergency vehicles use expensive radar systems and on-board sensors to ensure flight safety in stormy weather or low visibility. The regulations were prompted by very high accident rates for helicopters in general, and air ambulances in particular. The National Transportation Safety Board (NTSB) also urged steps to tighten safety requirements. As a result, a large proportion of Air Methods' fleet was barred from operating in bad weather, often the time when air rescue services are most needed. The management of Air Methods decided to adopt stricter quality standards for training its pilots and flight crews in an effort to get relief from these restrictions and continue flying. The company used two methods for improved training: reliance on up-to-date satellite imagery and extensive simulator training.

Until recently, helicopter simulator training was not widely available for helicopter pilots, requiring them to do most of their training in real-life situations. Although this training was fine in good weather, it could not prepare pilots for the challenges they were likely to face in severe situations. Additionally, improved weather satellites and better communications made it easier for Air Methods to argue that, rather than investing in expensive radar systems, satellite displays would be just as effective in allowing crews to avoid severe weather or areas of dangerously low visibility. Satellite weather data typically are updated every few minutes. From a financial standpoint, it also is favored by operators because it reduces the weight and maintenance costs associated with helicopter radars. Earlier this year, the FAA authorized the Colorado-based company to identify hazards from storms by relying on weather information streamed from satellites instead of using traditional on-board radar systems.

Quality Assurance
and Quality Control

Air Methods was able to persuade the FAA to relax the standards in its case by proving that Air Methods's quality control standards were significantly higher than current federal law requires. As a result of its investment in advanced technology and wide use of simulators, the FAA granted the company an exemption to resume operations, partly arguing that meteorological conditions and forecasts transmitted by satellites are comparable to information gleaned from radars, and that the company's enhanced pilot training and advanced operational control center offer additional safeguards for pilots, patients, and medical personnel.[1]

6.1 Quality Control Versus Quality Assurance

Although the term **quality control (QC)** is used synonymously with another similar concept called quality assurance, there is a subtle difference between the two. Quality control is concerned with the quality of a product or service after it is produced or delivered. By contrast, **quality assurance (QA)** is a set of procedures to improve a product's or a service's quality *before* it is delivered. In this chapter, we will examine several quality improvement tools and techniques that managers use to manage quality (Figure 6.1). The tools fall into two broad categories: appraisal tools and defect prevention tools.

FIGURE 6.1: Overview of Quality Improvement Tools

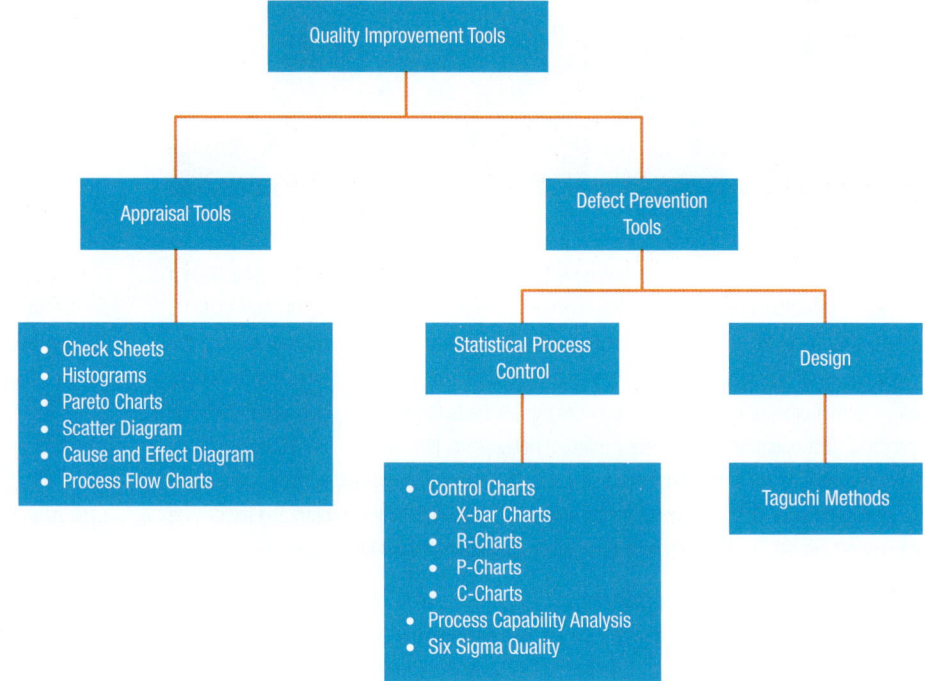

6.2 Quality Appraisal Tools

The appraisal tools that managers and employees use include check sheets, histograms, Pareto charts, scatter diagrams, cause-and-effect diagrams, and process flowcharts.

Check Sheets

Check sheets, which are useful for manufacturing processes and operations that are repeated, are forms used to collect and record quality-related data. The sheets are one of the simplest quality control tools because they are easy to understand, require very little effort to design, and are based on events that have actually occurred. Figures 6.2 and 6.3 are examples of check sheets for product and service operations. Note that the two kinds of organizations collect data in different categories. The categories chosen help a quality control manager review and analyze quality trends and isolate problems. For example, by using a check sheet a manager could identify day of the week in which defects occur most frequently in a manufacturing process and then determine whether a specific worker or work station was responsible for them. By looking at Figure 6.2, you can conclude that the defects that occur in the process of making printed circuit boards are most frequent on Monday and Friday. You can also tell that the most common type of defect is misaligned components followed by misaligned mounting

6.1
Explain the difference between quality control and quality assurance.

6.2
Apply the various tools for appraising the quality of products and processes.

Quality control (QC): the quality of a product or service after it is produced or delivered

Quality assurance (QA): a set of procedures to improve a product's quality or a service's quality before it is delivered

FIGURE 6.2: Check Sheet for a Manufacturing Process

Printed-Circuit-Board Check Sheet
Name of data recorder: JKP
Location: Rome, Italy
Data collection dates: 04/23 to 04/27

DEFECT TYPE	M	Tu	W	Th	F	TOTAL
Misaligned components	IIII	II	II	I	II	11
Adhesive failure	II	I			I	4
Incorrect board dimension	III				II	5
Circuitry failure	IIII	I			II	7
Misaligned mounting holes	II	I	II	I	II	8

FIGURE 6.3: Check Sheet for a Service Process

Hotel Operation Check Sheet
Name of data recorder: RVR
Location: Chennai, India
Data collection dates: 05/23 to 04/27

DEFECT/ COMPLAINT TYPE	M	Tu	W	Th	F	TOTAL
Inefficient housekeeping	IIII	II	I	I	III	11
Room service delay	II	I			III	6
Discourteous hotel staff	III	II	II	III	IIII	14
No internet service	II	I			II	6
Noisy hotel guests	I			I	IIIII	7

holes. Similarly, Figure 6.3 tells you that the complaints related to a hotel's operations occur most frequently on Friday and Monday. The most frequent complaints are discourteous hotel staff and inefficient housekeeping.

Histograms

A histogram can be used to show the distribution of a set of quality-related data. A histogram is a vertical bar chart that shows the frequency of occurrences of values. The shape and size of the histogram can provide meaningful information on the values that occur most frequently and the ranges they occupy. In the histogram shown in Figure 6.4 on page 198, you can see that if the manufacturing specifications require the thickness of the metal sheets to be between 4.0 mm and 5.0 mm, then this process meets specifications only about 73% (16/22) of the time.

Pareto Charts

A Pareto chart is also a vertical bar chart. Nevertheless, unlike in a histogram, the bars are arranged in decreasing height from left to right. The height of an individual bar represents how often a particular problem has occurred. The taller the bar is, the more significant is the problem. The chart is based on the Pareto principle, which states that 80% of quality problems stem from 20% of causes. Pareto charts help quality control managers focus their efforts on the activities that are responsible for most of the quality problems. A Pareto chart is a good tool to use when the data from a manufacturing or a service process can be broken down into categories and the frequency of occurrences in each category can be counted. Figure 6.5 on page 198 shows how a Pareto chart pinpoints the dissatisfaction of patients in a hospital. This Pareto chart shows that roughly 84% (155 / 185) of the dissatisfaction occurs from inept doctors and nurses, patient disrespect, and poor physical facilities.

Scatter Diagrams

A scatter diagram is a tool that can be used to determine visually whether two variables are related or correlated. It can show whether changes in one quality variable have an influence on another quality variable. Plotting the data related to these two variables can show whether they are positively or negatively related or have no relationship.

The terms *independent* and *dependent* are commonly used to describe these variables. An independent variable is the variable whose value changes for one reason or another. A dependent variable is a variable directly affected as a result of a change in an independent variable. For example, the more number of hours of training employees receive, the fewer defective products they are likely to produce. In this case, employee training is the independent variable, and the number of defects is the dependent

Why *Quality Improvement and Control* **Matters**

There are several approaches to monitoring and controlling the quality of products and services through the various stages of the supply chain. Using the correct tools and techniques to monitor and control quality can help businesses achieve their quality standard goals across their supply chains.

 Appraising Quality

FIGURE 6.4: Histogram for a Manufacturing Process

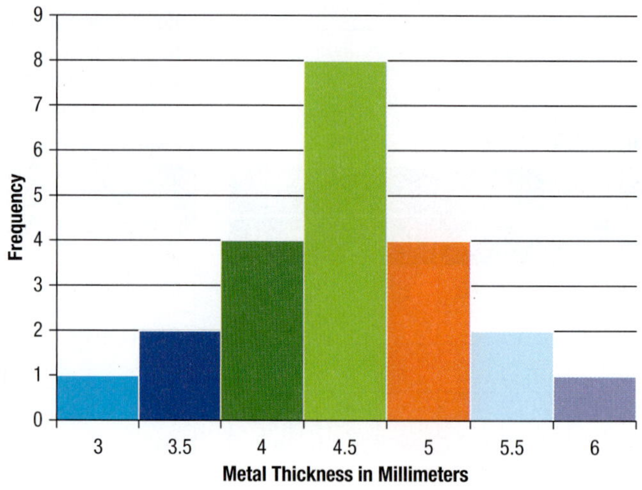

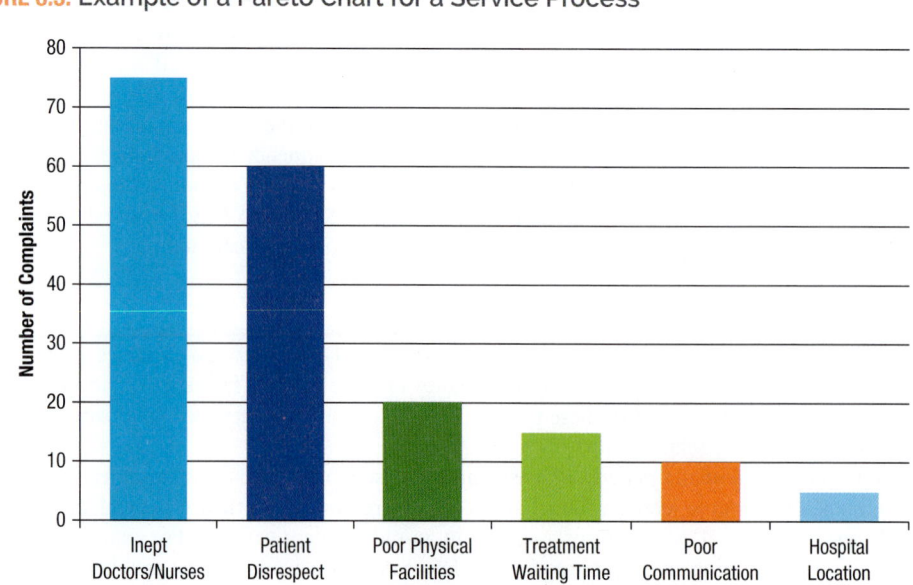

variable. Figure 6.6 shows this relationship. In the scatter diagram, the variables for employee training and product defects are negatively correlated: As the number of training hours employees are provided with *increases,* the number of product defects *decreases.* Scatter diagrams are used to determine whether two variables are correlated. Note, however, just because two variables are correlated does not necessarily imply causality (one effect *causing* the other to occur). If you measure the heights and weights of a group of individuals, you will find high correlation between the two variables height and weight. This high correlation does not, however, imply that height causes weight or vice versa.

Cause-and-Effect Diagrams (Fishbone Diagrams)

A cause-and-effect diagram (also known as a *fishbone diagram* because of the way it looks) is a quality control tool that identifies, sorts, and graphically displays the potential causes of a quality problem. The diagram also helps managers identify the interrelationships among factors that have an impact on a manufacturing process. The first step in constructing a cause-and-effect diagram is to begin with the observed quality problem (the effect). Next, the main categories contributing to the problem should be identified. In operations and supply chain management, the categories usually pertain to a firm's machines, methods, materials, people, and environment such as location, time, temperature, humidity, or culture in which it manufactures its product or provides its services. A hypothetical example of a cause-and-effect diagram for an airline quality problem is shown in Figure 6.7.

FIGURE 6.5: Example of a Pareto Chart for a Service Process

FIGURE 6.6: Training Hours Versus Product Defects

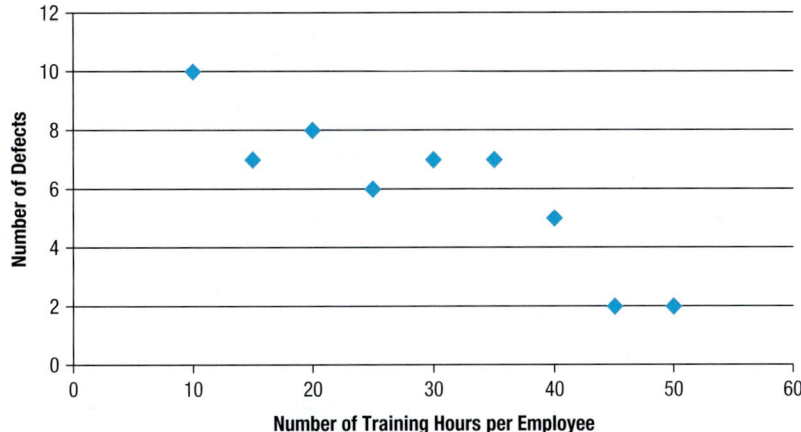

Constructing a cause-and-effect diagram enables decision makers to zero in on the causes of the quality problems. In the airline example in Figure 6.7, the reason the customer may have been unhappy was a delayed departure as a result of overbooking (methods). If that is the case, then the airlines' reservation and system should be improved to reduce overbooking in the future.

Process Flowcharts

A process flowchart graphically displays the steps in a manufacturing process and its flow. Before beginning any process quality improvement effort, it is a good idea to represent the process in its current state using a flowchart. Doing so helps a firm's quality improvement team understand how the process currently works and identify quality-related issues and redundant steps that could be eliminated. Figure 6.8 on page 200 shows an example of a supply chain process flowchart.

6.3 Quality Defect Prevention Tools

Some of the important tools used to prevent defects are statistical process control (SPC), (including control charts), process capability analysis, and Six Sigma. Let's now look at each.

Statistical Process Control (SPC)

Statistical process control (SPC) uses statistical methods to monitor a process to determine whether it is stable and producing a product that conforms to specifications. Although SPC is most frequently used to monitor manufacturing processes, it is equally applicable to services. For example, hospitals, restaurants, and banks use SPC to track patient and customer waiting times, and airlines use SPC to monitor flight delays and lost bags.

6.3

Apply the various tools for preventing defects in products and processes, including control charts, a process capability analysis, and how to calculate Six Sigma levels of quality.

FIGURE 6.7: Cause-and-Effect Diagram for a Service Process

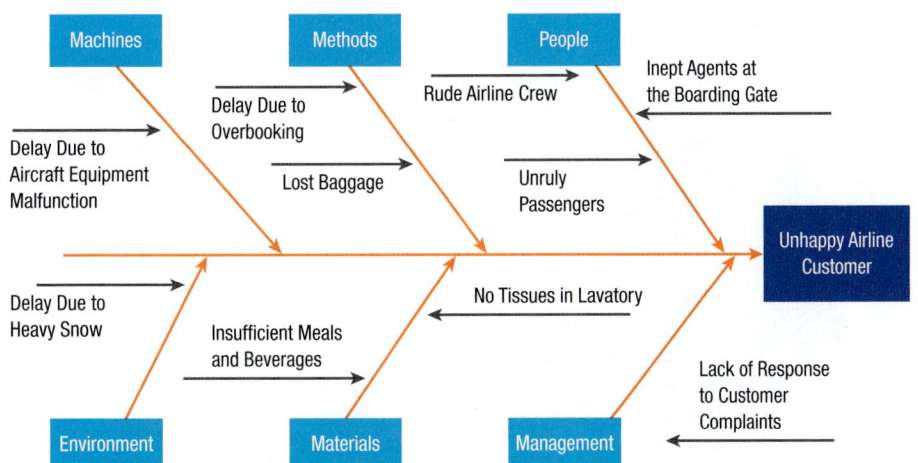

FIGURE 6.8: Process Flowchart for a Supply Chain

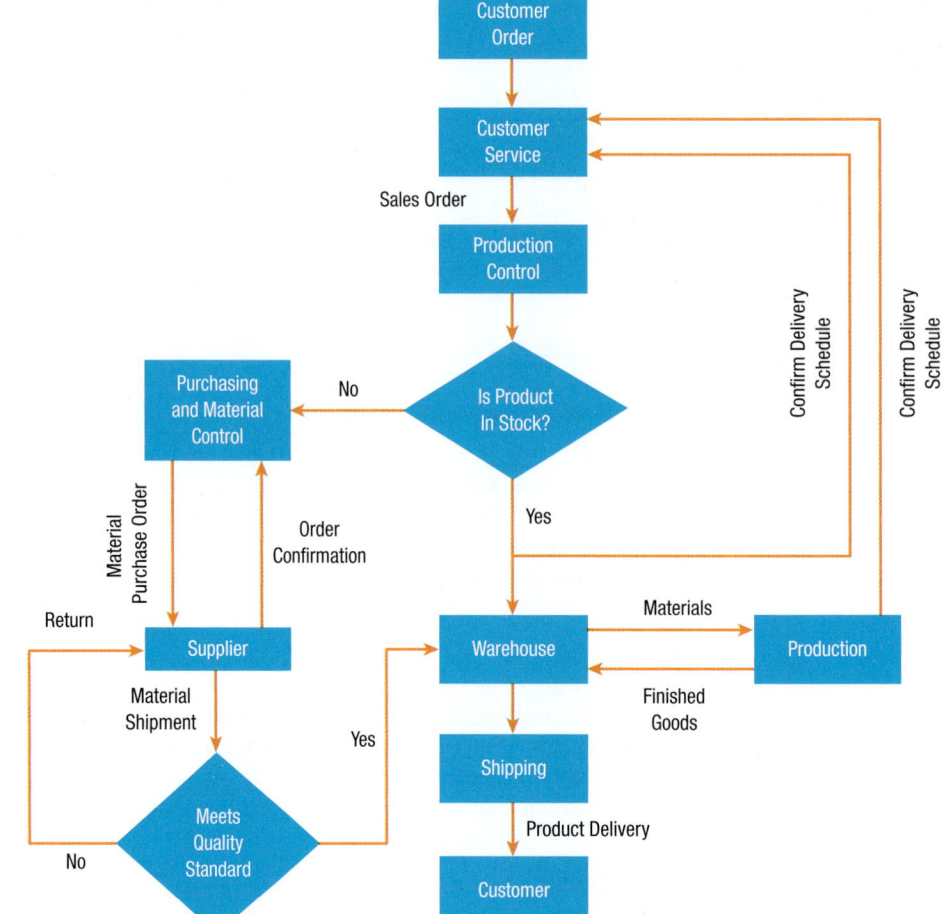

Attribute: a quality characteristic that is counted using whole numbers and often categorized using either/or measures

Variable: a quality characteristic that is measured on a continuous, or incremental, scale

Common cause variations: variations in quality that arise from random natural differences

Special cause variations: variations in quality that are not normally present in the process and can be attributed to unique or assignable causes

Service industries use statistical process control to track waiting times.

©iStockphoto.com/Alina Vincent Photography, LLC

MEASURES OF QUALITY

Testing raw materials, subassemblies, finished products, and services for quality is part of SPC. But what exactly are we evaluating? What we look for is either a quality characteristic called an **attribute** or a quality characteristic called a **variable**. Attributes are characteristics that are counted using whole numbers and often categorized using either/or measures such as good or bad, whole or broken, defective or nondefective, and so forth. The number of defects a product has is an example of an attribute. By contrast, variables are quality characteristics that are measured on a continuous, or incremental, scale. The length of time customers are made to wait (2.5 minutes), the diameter of a pipe (3.75 feet), and the weight of a box of cereal (16.4 ounces) are examples of variable quality characteristics.

VARIATIONS IN A PROCESS

Every process, regardless of its nature, displays variation. Some of the variations arise from random natural differences. They result from small differences in the raw materials used in a process, slight differences in the types of equipment used, and so on. These variations are called **common cause variations**.

Variations that are not normally present in the process and can be attributed to unique or assignable causes are known as **special cause variations**. These variations, which can be identified and corrected, typically occur because of equipment wear and tear, defective raw materials and components, or poorly trained workers. Out-of-shape or low-compression (flat) tennis balls produced by a process using faulty equipment is an example of a special cause variation. By contrast, minor differences in the color of the balls are a common cause variation. Perhaps the dye supplied to the manufacturer to produce the tennis balls was a slightly different shade than previous batches. The goal of SPC is to eliminate special cause variations—those that can have a measurable impact on a product's quality.

Control Charts

The tool used in SPC to monitor and control the consistency, or stability, of a process is called a **control chart**. A control chart is a graph that shows whether a process has remained stable or has undergone some change over time. It is a statistical tool used to distinguish between common cause variations and special cause variations. Figure 6.9 is an example of a control chart.

A statistical process control chart has three features:

- A *center line (CL)*, which represents the target value of the quality characteristic the firm is trying to achieve.
- An *upper control limit (UCL)*, which represents the upper-limit value of variation in the process.
- A *lower control limit (LCL)*, which represents the lower-limit value of variation in the process.

In general, if all of the values on the control chart plotted over time are randomly distributed around the center line and between the upper and lower control limits, then the variation is normal, and the process is presumed to be stable and in control. If, however, several of the points plotted fall outside of these limits or if the points follow a pattern instead of being randomly distributed, then the process is considered to be out of control and attributed to assignable or special causes. In an out-of-control process, there is no way to predict whether the process will meet its target value. It is like driving a car in which the brakes may or may not fail and you have no way of knowing when that will occur.

Using a well-designed control chart, a quality control manager can tell with a quick visual inspection of the chart whether a process is in control or out of control and quickly stop it if it is going awry. Nevertheless, a control chart will only tell the manager whether the average value lies around the target value and the approximate direction of the shift of the average value over time. That is, the control chart will only indicate if a process is in control or not—not what is causing it to go out of control. If the process is not in control, the manager has to investigate the particular time period when the trouble began to establish its causes.

WHEN AND WHERE TO USE CONTROL CHARTS

Because the frequent use of control charts can be time consuming and costly, as it involves repeated data collection and testing using samples of product outputs, they are best used at critical stages of a

FIGURE 6.9: Design of Control Limits Based on the Normal Distribution

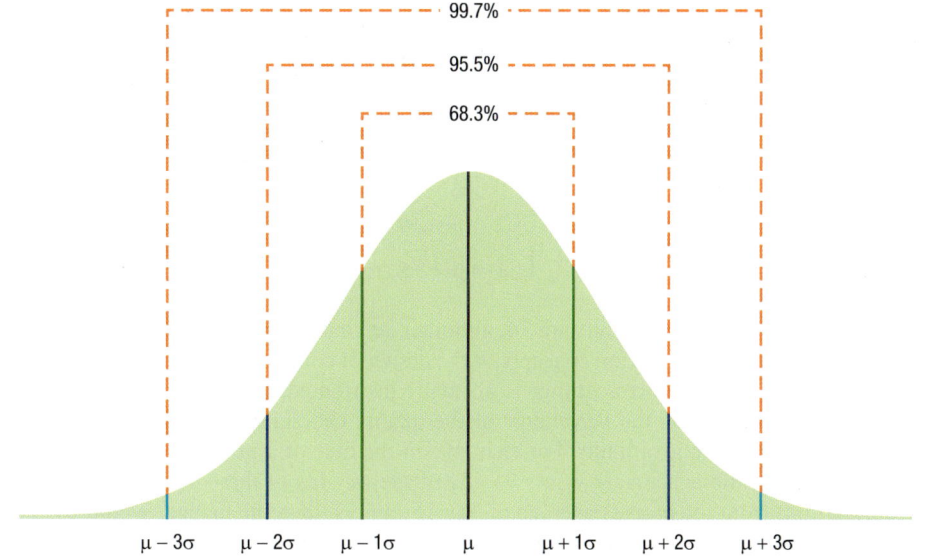

process where the process is most likely to go out of control and defects are likely to occur. Control charts are best used at these critical stages:

- At the beginning of a manufacturing process to check that the raw materials and components used in the process are defect-free.
- Before an operation, such as painting or packaging, that might mask defects.
- Before costly or irreversible operations are performed.
- Before delivery in the case of a service.

TYPES OF CONTROL CHARTS

There are two categories of control charts: one for monitoring attributes and the other for monitoring variables. All control charts, regardless of their type, require us to determine the values for the features we discussed earlier: the center line (CL), upper control limit (UCL), and lower control limit (LCL). Yet, the CL, the UCL, and the LCL depend on the specific control chart we design.

DESIGNING CONTROL CHARTS

When designing a control chart, a quality control manager should first determine whether the chart is going to measure every product or only a sample of the total produced. Typically, samples are used because measuring every product or service produced is time consuming and costly. For example, The Hershey Company (Hershey, PA) produces more than 1.4 million chocolate bars daily (1,000 every minute). It would be impossible to measure each chocolate bar. If the decision, then, is to use samples, the quality control manager should ensure that the sample data collected truly represents the *population*, or total amount produced. In addition, the samples should be taken over time and come from the same or similar processes so that special causes of variation can be distinguished from common cause variations.

The typical procedure is to take samples at periodic intervals and then calculate the statistics on the samples, such as the mean for each sample or the percentages or number of defective units. These statistics are then plotted on control charts so the randomness of the variations in the process can be observed. How the values in a sample are distributed on the chart is called a sampling distribution. A sampling distribution describes the randomness of the variation in a sample's values.

The most frequently made assumption is that the sample values are normally distributed. This assumption is based on the central limit theorem, which states that as the size of a sample gets larger and larger, its distribution also approaches the normal distribution, even if the underlying population from which the samples were collected is not normally distributed. Thus, when the plotted sample observations are assumed to be normally distributed, we can expect the following percentages of observations to be included within the following standard deviation limits:

$$\mu \pm 1\sigma - 68.3\%$$
$$\mu \pm 2\sigma - 95.5\%$$
$$\mu \pm 3\sigma - 99.7\%$$

Note that the numbers 1, 2, and 3 are the Z-values found in the Standard Normal Distribution table. In designing control charts, the center line that represents the process average corresponds to the mean of the normal distribution. The upper and lower control limits are computed based on the percentage of the process output that we want to be within certain limits. Thus, if we want 99.7% of the process outcomes to be within certain control limits, then the upper and lower control limits are given by:

$$UCL = \mu + 3\sigma$$
$$LCL = \mu - 3\sigma$$

The most commonly used control limits are 3σ, although 2σ control limits are occasionally used. The application of the normal distribution concepts to the design of control charts is illustrated in Figures 6.9 and 6.10. Assuming the process output is normally distributed, a quality control manager can design control charts based on the percentage of the quality characteristic of sample outputs from the process to fall within control limits. For example, in the case of a process that packs cornflakes into boxes, if the operations manager wants 95.5% of the weights of these boxes to fall within ± 2 standard deviations from the process average of, say 15 ounces, then the manger would use 2σ control limits to design the control chart. Thus, by plotting on a control chart the sample observations

Sampling distribution: how the values in a sample are distributed on the chart

Central limit theorem: a theorem that states that as the size of a sample gets larger and larger, its distribution also approaches the normal distribution, even if the underlying population from which the samples were collected is not normally distributed

collected from a process, the quality control manager can determine whether the process is operating within the pre-established control limits.

The usual approach for companies is to use 3σ control limits because narrower control limits may lead a manager to erroneously conclude that the process is out of control when, in fact, the variation that led to the points falling out of the control limits was purely random. In general, if the manager is confident that the process is relatively stable, then using the wider 3σ control limits is appropriate. On the other hand, if the manager suspects that special cause variations may exist in the process, then using a narrower control limit such as 2σ to detect these nonrandom variations would be the right approach. The approach shown in Figure 6.10 is to divide the area on either side of the center line into three zones. Each zone is 1, 2, or 3 standard deviations from the center line. Then, by using the rules given in the next section, we can determine whether a process is in control.

WHEN IS A PROCESS OUT OF CONTROL?

From a quality control perspective, an out-of-control manufacturing or service process means that it is probably not meeting customer requirements or achieving a firm's quality goals. The following rules can be used to detect if a process is in control:

FIGURE 6.10: Control Chart Zones

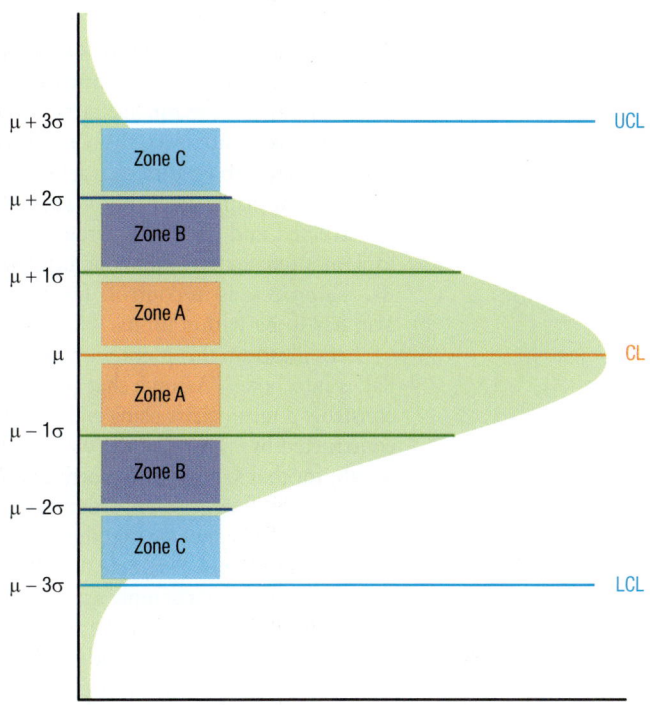

- Given 3σ control limits, all sample data plotted fall within the control limits.
- The plotted points are clustered around the center line and are randomly distributed and have no discernible pattern.
- An approximately equal number of plotted points fall above and below the centerline.
- There are no runs of eight successive points on either side of the center line.
- Two out of three successive points do not fall within zone C.
- Four out of five consecutive points do not fall within zone C, zone B, or both.
- Fifteen consecutive points are not within zone A.

Figure 6.11 shows a control chart of an out-of-control process. Note that after the seventh hour, something went wrong with this process in that the thickness measure began to steadily increase, as the run of eight points above the center line shows. The process eventually went out of control after

FIGURE 6.11: Out-of-Control Process

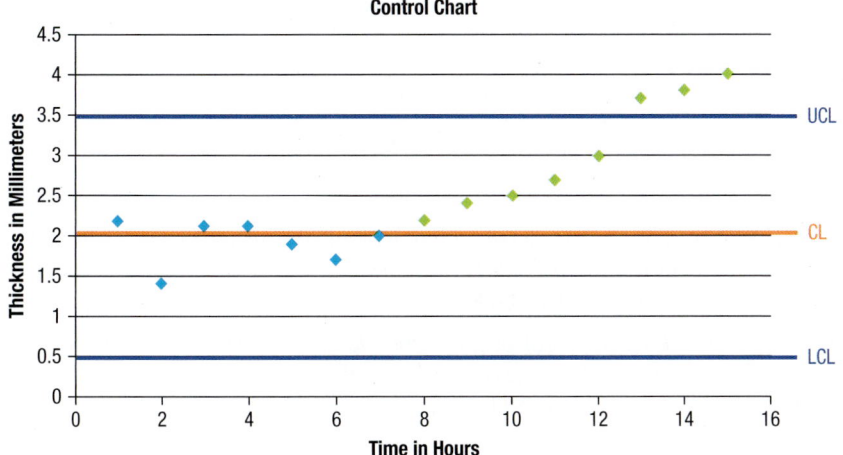

the twelfth hour. The quality control manager should have stopped the process between the seventh and eight hour to investigate what went wrong.

CONTROL CHARTS FOR VARIABLES: MEAN CHARTS AND RANGE CHARTS

The most frequently used control charts for monitoring the variable quality characteristics are mean charts and the range charts. A **mean chart** monitors the variation *between* samples, whereas a **range chart** monitors the variability *within* samples. Recall from our earlier discussion that variables refer to quality characteristics that can be measured on a continuous scale (for example, weight or waiting time). For a variable analysis, both a mean chart and a range chart have to be constructed and used concurrently to conclude that the process is in control. It is not enough to look at a mean chart and conclude that, because the average values of the samples are within limits, the process is in control. The variability *within* the samples as determined by the range chart also has to be within limits.

Let's illustrate this point with an example. Suppose we were monitoring a process that packs corn flakes into boxes. Assume that the target value of this process is an average of 10 ounces. We then construct a mean chart using eight samples of 10 boxes each during an 8-hour day. The mean chart is constructed by measuring the weight of each of the ten boxes in each sample, calculating an average weight for that sample, and plotting those values on the control chart. Now, let's assume that all of the eight sample averages were around the target value of 10 ounces. If we use a mean chart only for this process, we will conclude that the process is in control. Nevertheless, suppose that although the average weight of the boxes in sample no. 5 is exactly 10 ounces (exactly on target), the individual weights of the ten boxes in that sample are as follows: 9.9, 10, 10.1, 10.2, 9.8, 10, 9.9, 10.1, 20, and 0 ounces. You can see from this example that even though the mean for this sample is on target, the variability of the sample is not: The ninth box was overfilled, and the last one came up empty. If we had also constructed a range chart for this process, which tracks the difference between the maximum value and the minimum value in each sample, our conclusion would have been that the process is out of control.

Constructing a Mean Chart. Take the following steps to construct a mean chart:

Step 1. Calculate the mean of each sample $(\bar{x}_i)$.

- Add all of the measurements together and divide by the sample's size, n.

Step 2. If the mean (μ) and standard deviation (σ) of the population are not known, then calculate the grand mean, $\bar{\bar{X}}$, which is the average of all the sample means from the previous step.

- This will give you the overall average of all the sample's data points.

- The grand mean will be the centerline (CL) on the control chart.

Step 3. Calculate the standard error of the mean ($\sigma_{\bar{X}}$) if the standard deviation (σ) *of the population* is known or can be estimated. Otherwise, go to step 6. The standard error of the population mean ($\sigma_{\bar{X}}$) is given by:

$$\sigma_{\bar{X}} = \sigma / \sqrt{n}, \text{ where n is the sample size.}$$

Step 4. Calculate the center line (CL), upper and lower control limits ($UCL_{\bar{X}}$, $LCL_{\bar{X}}$) for the mean chart using the following formulas:

$$CL = \mu \text{ or } \bar{\bar{X}}$$
$$UCL_{\bar{X}} = \mu \text{ or } \bar{\bar{X}} + z \times \sigma_{\bar{X}}$$
$$LCL_{\bar{X}} = \mu \text{ or } \bar{\bar{X}} - z \times \sigma_{\bar{X}}$$

If we want 99.7% of the sample data to fall within 3σ control limits, then z = 3. Alternatively, if you specify the percentage of observations you want within control limits, the value of z can be determined from any Standard Normal Distribution table.

Step 5. If the standard deviation (σ) of the population is not known or is too difficult to compute, then we can use the range value (the difference between the maximum and minimum values) in each sample to compute the control limits for the mean and range charts. The procedure is as follows:

Mean chart: a control chart that monitors the variation between samples

Range chart: a control chart that monitors the variability within samples

a. Calculate the mean (or average) of the ranges $(\overline{R})$.

$\overline{R} = (R_1 + R_2 + R_3 + \ldots + R_k) / k$, where k is the number of samples.

b. Calculate the upper and lower control limits for the mean chart using A_2 values for the given sample size, which are shown in Table 6.1:

$$UCL_{\overline{X}} = \overline{\overline{X}} + A_2 \times \overline{R}$$

$$LCL_{\overline{X}} = \overline{\overline{X}} - A_2 \times \overline{R}$$

Tables such as 6.1 are published in many statistical quality control manuals and handbooks. They provide factors that approximate 3σ and can be used to compute control limits for both the mean chart and the range chart for varying sample sizes. The term $A_2 \times \overline{R}$ is an approximation of $3 \times \sigma_{\overline{X}}$. Note, in practice, as σ is typically unknown, in constructing variable control charts, we typically

TABLE 6.1: Table of Values for Computing 3σ and Control Limits for Mean and Range Charts

SAMPLE SIZE	A_2	D_2	D_3	D_4
2	1.880	1.128	—---	3.268
3	1.023	1.693	—---	2.574
4	0.729	2.059	—---	2.282
5	0.577	2.326	—---	2.114
6	0.483	2.534	—---	2.004
7	0.419	2.704	0.076	1.924
8	0.373	2.847	0.136	1.864
9	0.337	2.970	0.184	1.816
10	0.308	3.078	0.223	1.777
11	0.285	3.173	0.256	1.744
12	0.266	3.258	0.283	1.717
13	0.249	3.336	0.307	1.693
14	0.235	3.407	0.328	1.672
15	0.223	3.472	0.347	1.653
16	0.212	3.532	0.363	1.637
17	0.203	3.588	0.378	1.622
18	0.194	3.640	0.391	1.608
19	0.187	3.689	0.403	1.597
20	0.180	3.735	0.415	1.585
21	0.173	3.778	0.425	1.575
22	0.167	3.819	0.434	1.566
23	0.162	3.858	0.443	1.557
24	0.157	3.895	0.451	1.548
25	0.153	3.931	0.459	1.541

SOURCE: Adapted from Institute for Quality and Reliability. http://world-class-quality.com/images/download/20081104091341_Control%20Chart%20Constants%20 and%20Formulae.pdf

prefer the use of range as a measure of dispersion rather than standard deviation.

Step 6. Graph the mean chart by plotting the sample means (along the y-axis) over the time periods in which the items were sampled (along the x-axis).

Step 7. Determine whether the process is in control using the criteria we discussed earlier. If not, take the necessary corrective action to bring the process back in control.

Let's use these steps to construct a mean control chart for the following example and determine whether the process is in control.

Review Example 6.1 to learn how a bottling plant can determine whether their process is out of control.

©iStockphoto.com/ARSELA

 Example 6.1

EXAMPLE 6.1: A filling machine in a soft drink bottling plant is used to fill 16-ounce bottles of cola. The output of this process is normally distributed with a mean (μ) of 16 ounces and a standard deviation (σ) of 1 ounce. Quality control personnel monitor the filling process by checking independent samples of 25 bottles every hour.

a. Construct a mean chart for this process.

b. During an 8-hour day, the following sample means were obtained (in ounces): 16.05, 16.1, 15.94, 16.2, 15.95, 15.9, 16.05, and 15.93. Is there any evidence that the process is out of control?

SOLUTION

Step 1: Calculate the mean of each sample ($\bar{x}_i$).

The sample means were given to us in the example. They are: 16.05, 16.1, 15.94, 16.2, 15.95, 15.9, 16.05, and 15.93.

Step 2: If the mean (μ) of the output and its standard deviation (σ) are not known, then calculate the grand mean, $\bar{\bar{X}}$, which is the average of all the sample means from the previous step).

Because the mean (16 ounces) and the standard deviation (1) is already given to us, we can skip this step and use μ instead of $\bar{\bar{X}}$ to define the center line.

Step 3: Calculate the standard error of the mean if the standard deviation (σ) is known or can be estimated. Otherwise, go to step 6.

Because we know the standard deviation (σ =1 ounce) and the size of the sample (n = 25), we can compute the standard error of the mean using the following formula:

$$\sigma_{\bar{X}} = \sigma / \sqrt{n} = 1/\sqrt{25} = 0.2$$

Step 4: Calculate the center line (CL) and the upper and lower control limits (UCL, LCL) for the mean chart using the following formula:

$$CL = \mu = 16.0 \text{ ounces}$$
$$UCL_{\bar{X}} = \mu + 3 \times \sigma_{\bar{X}} = 16.0 + 3 \times 0.2 = 16.6 \text{ ounces}$$
$$LCL_{\bar{X}} = \mu - 3 \times \sigma_{\bar{X}} = 16.0 - 3 \times 0.2 = 15.4 \text{ ounces}$$

Because we know the mean (μ) of the output and its standard deviation (σ), we will skip step 5 and go to step 6.

Step 6: Graph the mean chart by plotting the sample means (along the y-axis) over the time periods in which the items were sampled (along the x-axis).

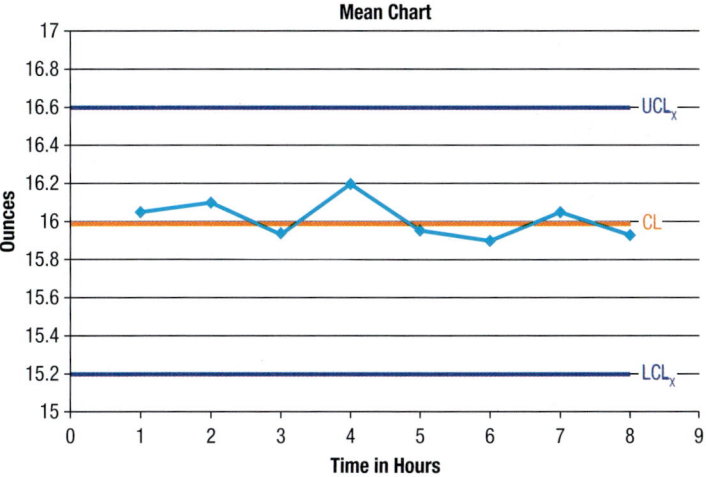

Step 7: Determine whether the process is in control. If not, take the necessary corrective action to bring the process back in control.

Because none of the criteria rules we listed earlier have been violated, the process is assumed to be in control. No intervention is necessary at this time.

EXAMPLE 6.2: Crescent (Apex Tool Group, LLC, Sparks MD) is a manufacturer of socket tools and the extension or handle fittings for those tools. For the socket to fit the handle, the inside diameter of the socket fitting must be greater than the outside diameter of the handle fitting. The company wants to construct a mean chart to monitor the manufacturing process used to produce the socket tools. Although the inside diameters of the tools produced by this process are normally distributed and the mean historically has been 13mm, the company is not sure if the process is meeting this target value. The process's standard deviation is also not known. The company collected independent sample data on the inside diameter of these socket tools over a 10-hour period using a sample size of four (listed in the table as "Item 1" through "Item 4"), and the values in millimeters are given in the following table. Construct a mean chart for this process:

Example 6.2

SAMPLE NUMBER	ITEM 1	ITEM 2	ITEM 3	ITEM 4
1	13.1	13.9	12.8	13.2
2	13.8	13.0	12.5	12.7
3	14.0	12.9	13.1	13.5
4	12.3	13.3	12.8	13.6
5	13.1	12.6	13.3	12.9
6	12.5	13.4	12.8	13.3
7	13.6	12.7	13.3	13.8
8	12.5	13.5	13.1	12.9
9	13.0	13.6	12.7	13.2
10	12.8	12.9	12.7	13.3

SOLUTION

Step 1: Calculate the mean of each sample ($\bar{x}_i$).

Because the size of each sample is four, the ten sample means are calculated by using the

formula: $\left(\sum_{i=1}^{n} x_i\right) / n = (x_1 + x_2 + x_3 + x_4) / 4$

The ten sample means are: 13.25, 13.00, 13.38, 13.00, 12.98, 13.00, 13.35, 13.00, 13.13, and 12.93.

Step 2: If the mean (μ) of the output and standard deviation (σ) are not known, then calculate the grand mean, $\overline{\overline{X}}$, which is the average of all the sample means from the previous step.

In this example, the mean (μ) and standard deviation (σ) are not known. The grand mean $\overline{\overline{X}}$ is calculated using the following formula:

$$\overline{\overline{X}} = \sum_{i=1}^{n} \overline{x}_i \,/\, k, \text{ where } k \text{ is the number of samples}$$

$$\overline{\overline{X}} = (\overline{x}_1 + \overline{x}_2 + \ldots + \overline{x}_{10}) \,/\, k$$

$$\overline{\overline{X}} = (13.25 + 13.00 + 13.38 + 13.00 + 12.98 + 13.00 + 13.35 + 13.00 + 13.13 + 12.93) \,/\, 10$$

$$\overline{\overline{X}} = \textbf{13.10 } mm$$

Since the standard deviation (σ) is not known or cannot be estimated, we go to step 5.

Step 5a: If the standard deviation *(σ) of the output* is not known, determine the range value, which is the difference between the maximum value and minimum value in each sample. Then calculate the mean (or average) of the ranges $(\overline{R})$.

$$\overline{R} = (R_1 + R_2 + R_3 + \ldots + R_k) \,/\, k, \text{ where } k \text{ is the number of samples.}$$

In this example, the range values (the difference between the maximum and minimum values in each sample) are: 1.10, 1.30, 1.10, 1.30, 0.70, 0.90, 1.10, 1.00, 0.90, and 0.60. Hence, the mean of the ranges $\overline{R}$ is:

$$\overline{R} = (1.10 + 1.30 + 1.10 + 1.30 + 0.70 + 0.90 + 1.10 + 1.00 + 0.90 + 0.60) \,/\, 10 = \textbf{1.0 } mm$$

Step 5b: Calculate the center line (CL) and the upper and lower control limits (UCL, LCL) for the mean chart. Use Table 6.1 to find the A_2 value for the given sample size.

The sample size n = 4. The value of A_2 from Table 6.1 is 0.729.

$$CL = \overline{\overline{X}} = 13.10$$

$$UCL_{\overline{x}} = \overline{\overline{X}} + A_2 \times \overline{R} = 13.10 + 0.729 \times 1 = 13.829$$

$$LCL_{\overline{x}} = \overline{\overline{X}} - A_2 \times \overline{R} = 13.10 - 0.729 \times 1 = 12.371$$

Step 6: Graph the mean chart by plotting the sample means (along the y-axis) over the time periods in which items were sampled (along the x-axis).

The control chart for this example is as follows:

Mean Chart for the Inside Diameter of Socket Tools

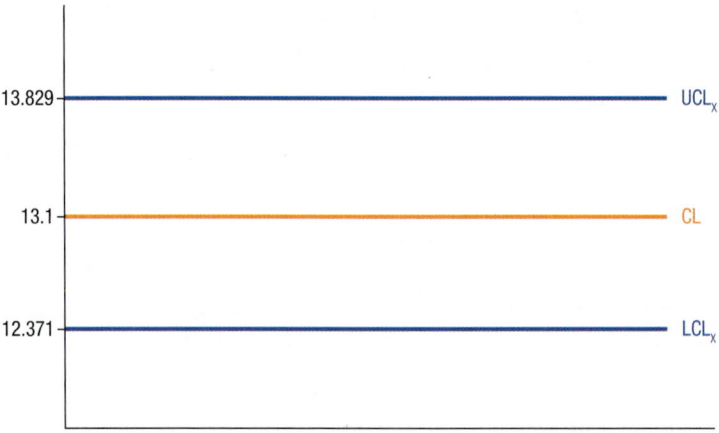

Crescent computed the following sample means of the inside diameter of socket tools for the next 8 hours of operation. The means were 13.2, 12.8, 12.9, 13.3, 12.7, 13.4, 12.5, and 13.6. We've plotted them on the following mean chart:

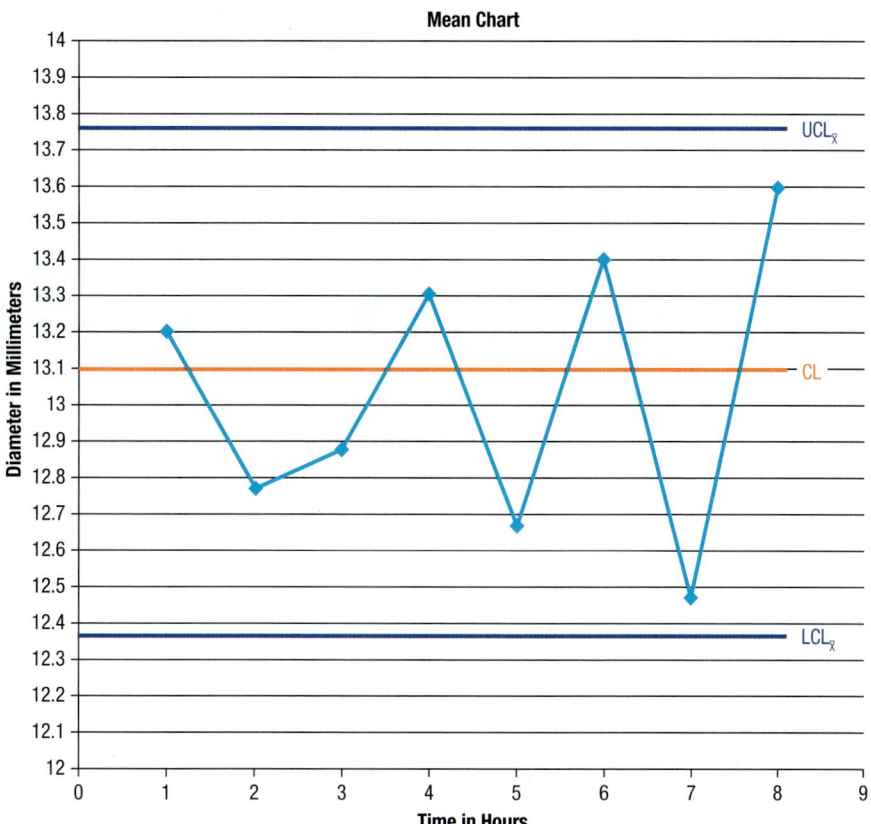

Step 7: Determine whether the process is in control. Based on the chart, the process appears to be in control. Nevertheless, the funnel-shaped distribution of plotted points may indicate a potential problem. The quality control manager must reconstruct another mean chart with a much larger sample size to see if there is a shift in the mean. In addition, a range chart should also be constructed.

Constructing a Range Chart. Recall that range charts are constructed to monitor the variability within samples. For a variable quality characteristic, the mean chart may indicate that the average value over a period is close to the target value. Yet, the process may exhibit variations on a day-to-day or hour-to-hour basis that may make it unstable. For example, variations in the quality of raw materials and/or variations in the skill levels of individual workers can cause significant deviations from the target value. Hence, in addition to a mean chart, a range chart is also needed to monitor the variability of a process to see if it is in control. To construct a range chart, take the following steps:

Step 1: Calculate the range for each sample (R_i), which is the difference between the maximum and the minimum data values in each sample.

Step 2: Calculate the average, or mean, of the ranges ($\bar{R}$).

$$\bar{R} = (R_1 + R_2 + R_3 + \dots + R_k) / k, \text{ where k is the number of samples.}$$

Step 3: Calculate the center line (CL) and the upper and lower control limits (UCL, LCL) for the range chart using $\bar{R}$ and the values of D4 and D3 for the given sample size, which are found in Table 6.1.

$$CL = \bar{R}$$
$$UCL_R = D_4 \times \bar{R}$$
$$LCL_R = D_3 \times \bar{R}$$

Step 4: Graph the range chart by plotting the sample ranges (along the y-axis) relative to the time periods in which items were sampled (along the x-axis).

Step 5: Determine whether the process is in control using the criteria outline earlier. If not, take the necessary corrective action to bring the process back in control.

EXAMPLE 6.3: Refer to Example 6.2. Using the sample data given in the table, construct a range chart.

SOLUTION

Step 1: Calculate the range for each sample (R_i), which is the difference between the maximum value and the minimum value in each sample.

The data from Example 6.2 are as follows, and the sample ranges have been calculated:

SAMPLE NUMBER	ITEM 1	ITEM 2	ITEM 3	ITEM 4	SAMPLE RANGE (MAX-MIN)
1	13.1	13.9	12.8	13.2	1.10
2	13.8	13.0	12.5	12.7	1.30
3	14.0	12.9	13.1	13.5	1.10
4	12.3	13.3	12.8	13.6	1.30
5	13.1	12.6	13.3	12.9	0.70
6	12.5	13.4	12.8	13.3	0.90
7	13.6	12.7	13.3	13.8	1.10
8	12.5	13.5	13.1	12.9	1.00
9	13.0	13.6	12.7	13.2	0.90
10	12.8	12.9	12.7	13.3	0.60

Step 2: Calculate the average, or mean, of the ranges ($\overline{R}$).

$$\overline{R} = (R_1 + R_2 + R_3 + \ldots + R_k) / k, \text{ where k is the number of samples.}$$

$$\overline{R} = (1.10 + 1.30 + 1.10 + 1.30 + 0.70 + 0.90 + 1.10 + 1.00 + 0.90 + 0.60) / 10 = \mathbf{1.0} \text{ mm}$$

Step 3: Calculate the center line (CL) and the upper and lower control limits (UCL_R, LCL_R) for the range chart using $\overline{R}$ and the values of D_4 and D_3 for the given sample size, which are shown in Table 6.1.

For a sample size of 4, the D_4 and D_3 values from Table 6.1 are: 2.282 and 0, respectively.

$$CL = \overline{R} = 1.0$$
$$UCL_R = D_4 \times \overline{R} = 2.282 \times 1 = 2.282$$
$$LCL_R = D_3 \times \overline{R} = 0 \times 1 = 0$$

The range chart for the inside diameter of the socket tools is shown as follows:

Range Chart for the Inside Diameter of Socket Tools

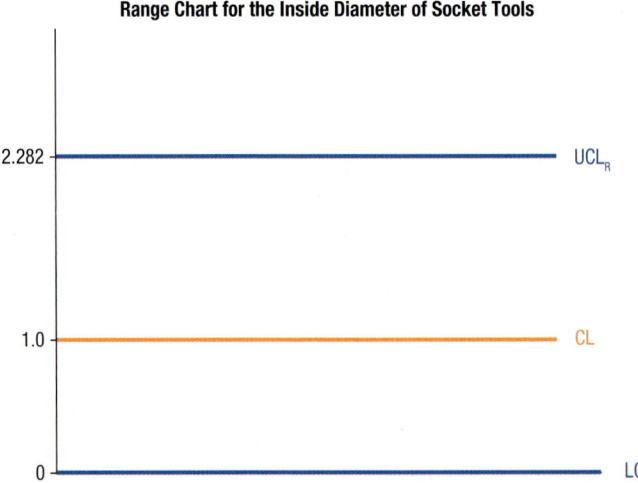

Crescent computed the following inside diameter sample ranges for the next 8 hours of operation. They are 1.2, 0.8, 1.9, 1.3, 1.7, 2.0, 2.2, and 2.3. Is the process in control?

The sample ranges are plotted in the following chart:

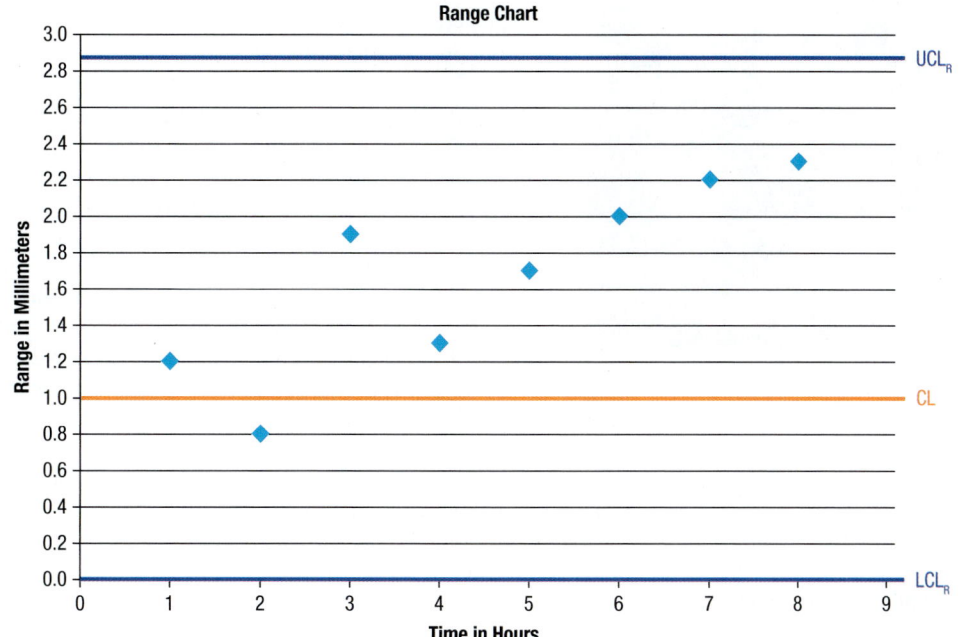

The process is *not* in control because seven of eight plotted points fall above the center line. In addition, the variation in data seems to be a result of special causes because there is a pattern visible in the point: Notice that beginning in hour four, the points have increasing values.

CONTROL CHARTS FOR ATTRIBUTES: C-CHARTS AND P-CHARTS

Recall that attributes refer to quality characteristics that cannot be measured. Instead, they must be counted and categorized. For example, when we monitor quality features such as the number of incorrect mail deliveries per day, or sort items into "nondefective" and "defective" categories, we are tracking attribute quality characteristics. The two most common types of attribute control charts are c-charts and p-charts. C-charts are used to monitor countable occurrences, such as the number of non-conformities or defects per unit. The unit can be a unit of a product, a unit of time, a unit of area, a unit of volume, and so forth. P-charts are used to monitor the fraction, or proportion, of defects or errors in a product or service. In general, control charts for attributes, unlike variables, require larger sample sizes to develop meaningful quality measures. In addition, although the zone rules that we discussed for variable control charts do not apply for attributes, the rules for trending patterns in data or shifts in the average value do. The important difference between a p-chart and a c-chart is that although p-charts can only classify an item as defective or non-defective, a c-chart goes further and identifies the number of defects in each unit. For example, in an inspection of 20 automobiles, the p-chart can only sort which of the cars are defective or non-defective. Nonetheless, in an automobile that is declared non-defective by a p-chart, there may be a number of minor defects such as scratches or poorly fitted components that may not be readily apparent. Using a c-chart can help identify the number of such non-conformities or defects in each car.

CONSTRUCTING A C-CHART

The theoretical basis for constructing a c-chart is the Poisson distribution, a type of probability distribution typically covered in a basic statistics course. The Poisson distribution is based on the following assumptions:

- The probability of occurrence of an event (defect) over a narrow interval of time, area, or space is small and directly proportional to the size of that interval.
- The probability of two such events (defects) occurring in that same narrow interval is so small that it is negligible.

C-chart: an attribute control chart that is used to monitor countable occurrences

P-chart: an attribute control chart that is used to monitor the fraction, or proportion, of defects or errors in a product or service

P-charts would help a mechanic understand how many of their cars have defects, but the c-charts would better classify the level of defectiveness.

©iStockphoto.com/Minerva Studio

- The probability of an event (defect) occurring is constant from one interval to the next and does not change.
- The probability of occurrence of an event (defect) in any given interval is independent of that event occurring in any other interval.

Let's consider an example to understand these assumptions. Suppose you are hired as a consultant to monitor the number of accidents occurring on the intersection of a major highway and provide suggestions for improving the intersection's safety. If you examine the number of vehicles passing through that intersection on any given day, it is extremely large. Nevertheless, if you slice the day into narrow (say, 2-minute) intervals, then the probability of an accident occurring during any given 2-minute interval (for example, 11:00 am to 11:02 am) is small and does not change from one interval to the next. Also, the probability of two accidents occurring in the same 2-minute interval of 11:00 to 11:02 is so small that for all practical purposes it is equal to zero. In addition, the fact that an accident occurred in a particular time interval has no influence on another accident occurring in yet another narrow time interval.

You can see from this example that whether or not to use a c-chart depends on how the data were generated and whether they meet the assumptions of a Poisson distribution. In general, c-charts are used if all of the following conditions are met:

- When the product, service, or process is important or complex; that is, a simple classification of "defective" or "non-defective" is not good enough.
- When there is a need to monitor the number of defects or nonconformities in each unit or sample.
- When the samples examined for occurrences of defects are drawn from a very large population.
- When the potential errors or nonconformities that could occur are known prior to data collection.
- When the sample size is fixed.

For c-charts, even though the underlying probability distribution is a Poisson distribution, for practical reasons the normal approximation to the Poisson distribution is used. In constructing c-charts, at least 20 to 25 samples or subgroups should be used to have a reliable representation of the variability in the system.

The steps for constructing a c-chart are as follows:

Step 1. Ensure that the data to be collected meets the assumptions of a Poisson distribution and the sample size is large enough to assume it's normally distributed.

Step 2.

- Decide on the data collection frequency and ensure that the order of the data collected is maintained from sample to sample. In other words, if the data are collected daily on an hourly basis, say on Monday 9 am, 10 am, etc., then the same order should be followed on Tuesday, Wednesday, and so on.
- Choose the number of samples (k) to be collected, which should be greater than 20.
- Record the number of defects or nonconformities (c_i) in each sample.

Step 3. Compute the process average or mean ($\bar{c}$) using the following formula:

$$\bar{c} = (c_1 + c_2 + c_3 + \ldots + c_k) / k, \text{ where k is the number of samples.}$$

This will be the center line for the c-chart.

Step 4. Compute the upper and lower control limits (UCL$_c$, LCL$_c$) using the following formulas:

$$UCL_c = \bar{c} + z \times \sqrt{\bar{c}}; \; LCL_c = \bar{c} - z \times \sqrt{\bar{c}}, \text{ where z can be 1, 2, or 3.}$$

Step 5. Draw the c-chart by graphing the center line (CL) and the upper and lower control limits (UCL$_c$, LCL$_c$). Plot the number of defects or nonconformities for each sample.

Step 6. Interpret the chart to see if the process is in control by checking for special cause variations such as points beyond the control limits and run of consecutive points above or below the center line.

EXAMPLE 6.4: A hotel, in its ongoing efforts to improve its service to its guests, is planning to develop a c-chart to monitor the number of customer complaints it receives each day. The data collected are assumed to have come from a population that has an underlying Poisson distribution. Additionally, the sample data collected are large enough to assume it is normally distributed. Data on customer complaints for 20 days were collected and are given in the following table:

Example 6.4

Days	1	2	3	4	5	6	7	8	9	10	11	12	13	14	15	16	17	18	19	20
Number of Complaints	4	3	4	5	2	1	7	2	1	5	3	5	6	3	2	1	5	2	3	1

Construct a c-chart for this hotel example using 3σ upper and lower limits. Is this process in control?

SOLUTION

Step 1. Ensure that the data to be collected meets the assumptions of a Poisson distribution and that sample size is large enough to assume it is normally distributed.

Based on the information given in the problem, these assumptions are met.

Step 2.

- Decide on the data collection frequency and ensure that the order of the data collected is maintained from sample to sample.
- Choose the number of samples (k) to be collected, which should be greater than 20.
- Record the number of defects/errors/nonconformities (c_i) in each sample.

  All of these requirements have been met in the hotel example.

Step 3. Compute the process average, or mean ($\bar{c}$), using the following formula:

$$\bar{c} = (c_1 + c_2 + c_3 + \ldots + c_k) / k.$$
$$\bar{c} = (4+3+4+5+2+1+7+2+1+5+3+5+6+3+2+1+5+2+3+1) / 20 = 3.2$$

This is the central line for the c-chart.

Step 4. Compute the upper and lower control limits (UCL$_c$, LCL$_c$) using the following formulas:

$$UCL_c = \bar{c} + z \times \sqrt{\bar{c}}; \; LCL_c = \bar{c} - z \times \sqrt{\bar{c}}, \text{ where z can be 1, 2, or 3.}$$

As we are required to use 3σ control limits $z = 3$. Therefore,

$$UCL_c = \bar{c} + z \times \sqrt{\bar{c}} = 3.2 + 3 \times \sqrt{3.2} = 8.66$$

A negative number of customer complaints does not make sense, so we set the LCL equal to 0.

$$LCL_c = \bar{c} - z \times \sqrt{\bar{c}} = 3.2 - 3 \times \sqrt{3.2} = -2.16 = 0$$

Step 5. Draw the control chart by graphing the center line (CL) and the upper and lower control limits (UCL_c, LCL_c). Plot the number of defects or nonconformities for each sample collected earlier.

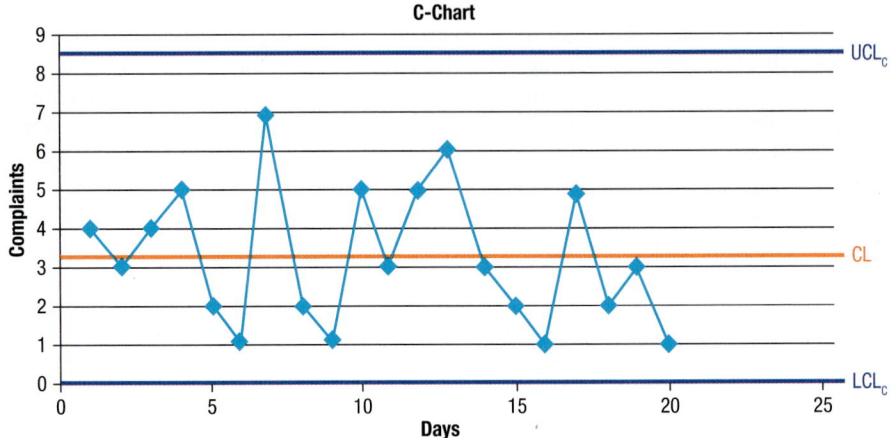

The process appears to be in control because none of the plotted points fall outside of the control limits. In addition, there does not appear to be any pattern to the variation.

CONSTRUCTING A P-CHART

As we explained earlier, a p-chart is another attributes chart. It is used to monitor the proportion of nonconforming or defective items rather than the actual number of defects as a c-chart does. Also, unlike a c-chart, the size of the samples can vary. Consequently, p-charts track the percentage of defective units rather than the actual count. Since p-charts describe attributes as "defective" or "non-defective" or "good" or "bad," the population (total output) from which items are sampled is assumed to have a binomial distribution. A binomial distribution is a discrete probability distribution with two discrete outcomes: success or failure, defective or non-defective, and so forth. Yet, if the sample sizes are large enough, then, based on the central limit theorem, we can assume that the distribution of the data collected is normally distributed.

Like all other control charts, p-charts are also used to monitor process changes over time. For example, the manager of an accounting department can use a p-chart to plot the proportion of weekly accounts-payable billing errors by counting bills that were accurate and those that were not. Likewise, the manufacturer of printed circuit boards can use a p-chart to monitor the proportion of defective boards produced on a daily basis. When you construct a p-chart, the sample size should be large enough so that the chances of finding nonconforming units in the sample are reasonably high. One rule of thumb to determine the sample size for a p-chart is $n \times p \geq 5$, where n is the sample size and p is the proportion of defective units relative to the total output produced. The requirement of $n \times p \geq 5$ is vital because the p-chart relies on the normal approximation to the binomial distribution, which is typically valid only if $n \times p \geq 5$ and $n \times (1 - p) > 5$. For example, if we know the proportion of defective units historically generated by a process is 5%, then the sample size, n, should at least be equal to 100 ($n \times p \geq 5 = 100 \times 0.05 = 5$).

The steps for constructing a p-chart are as follows:

Step 1. Ensure that the data to be collected are from a binomially distributed population and the sample size is large enough to assume it is normally distributed.

Step 2.

- Decide on how frequently the data will be collected.
- Choose a large sample size (n) and the number of samples (k) to be collected.
- Record the number of defective, or nonconforming, units, and calculate the proportion of them (p_i) for each sample.

Step 3. Compute the average, or mean, proportion of defective units ($\bar{p}$) in the samples using the following formula:

$$\bar{p} = (p_1 + p_2 + p_3 + \ldots + p_k) / k, \text{ where k is the number of samples.}$$

If the sample size, n, is constant from sample to sample, then

$$\bar{p} = \frac{\text{Total number of defective units from all samples}}{\text{Number of samples} \times \text{Sample size}}$$

This will be the center line for the p-chart.

Step 4. Compute the upper and lower control limits (UCL_p, LCL_p) using the following formulas:

$$UCL_p = \bar{p} + z \times \sigma_p$$

$$LCL_p = \bar{p} - z \times \sigma_p, \text{ where z can be 1, 2, or 3, and}$$

$$\sigma_p = \sqrt{\frac{\bar{p}(1 - \bar{p})}{n}}, \text{ where n is the sample size.}$$

Step 5. Draw the control chart by graphing the center line (CL) and the upper and lower control limits (UCL_p, LCL_p). Plot the percentage of defective units for each sample collected earlier on the control chart.

Step 6. Interpret the chart to see if the process is in control by checking for special cause variations such as points beyond the control limits and runs of consecutive points above or below the center line.

EXAMPLE 6.5: A tire company in Jodhpur, India, wants to construct a p-chart to monitor the quality of tires it manufactures. To collect data for the chart, the quality control manager of the company uses a sample size of 100 and records the number of defective tires and non-defective tires on a daily basis. The number of defective tires recorded for 20 samples is shown in the following table. Assume that the distribution of the total output is binomial and n x p ≥ 5:

Example 6.5

Days	1	2	3	4	5	6	7	8	9	10	11	12	13	14	15	16	17	18	19	20
Number of Defects	5	3	8	7	6	10	7	4	6	8	4	3	6	3	2	5	5	4	6	3

a. Construct a p-chart for this example using 3σ control limits.

b. Is this process in control?

SOLUTION

Step 1. Ensure that the data to be collected are from a binomially distributed population and the sample size is large enough to assume it is normally distributed.

Based on the information given in the problem, these assumptions are met.

Step 2.

- Decide on how frequently the data will be collected.
- Choose a large sample size (n) and the number of samples (k) to be collected.
- Record the number of defective units and calculate the proportion of them (pi) for each sample.

All of this information has been provided for this company example.

Step 3. Compute the average, or mean, proportion of defective units ($\bar{p}$) in the samples using the following formula:

$$\bar{p} = (p_1 + p_2 + p_3 + \ldots + p_k) / k, \text{ where k is the number of samples.}$$

If the sample size n is constant from sample to sample, then

$$\bar{p} = \frac{\text{Total number of defective units from all samples}}{\text{Number of samples} \times \text{Sample size}}$$

This will be the center line for the p-chart.

Because the sample size is a constant (n =100), we have

$$\bar{p} = \frac{\text{Total number of defective units from all samples}}{\text{Number of samples} \times \text{Sample size}} = 105/ (20 \times 100) = 0.0525$$

This is our centerline for the p-chart.

Step 4. Compute the upper and lower control limits (UCL_p, LCL_p) using the following formula:

$$UCLp = \bar{p} + z \times \sigma_p; LCLp = \bar{p} - z \times \sigma_p, \text{ where z can be 1, 2, or 3, and}$$

$$\sigma_p = \sqrt{\frac{\bar{p}(1-\bar{p})}{n}}, \text{ where n is the sample size.}$$

We first need to calculate σ_p, which is given by

$$\sigma_p = \sqrt{\frac{\bar{p}(1-\bar{p})}{n}} = \sqrt{(0.0525) \times (1 - 0.0525) / 100} = 0.0223$$

Hence, for 3σ limits:

$$UCLp = 0.0525 + 3 \times 0.0223 = 0.1194, \text{ and } LCLp = 0.0525 - 3 \times 0.0223 = -0.0144 = 0$$

Step 5. Draw the control chart by graphing the center line (CL), the upper and lower control limits (UCL_p, LCL_p). Plot the percentage of defective units for each sample collected earlier.

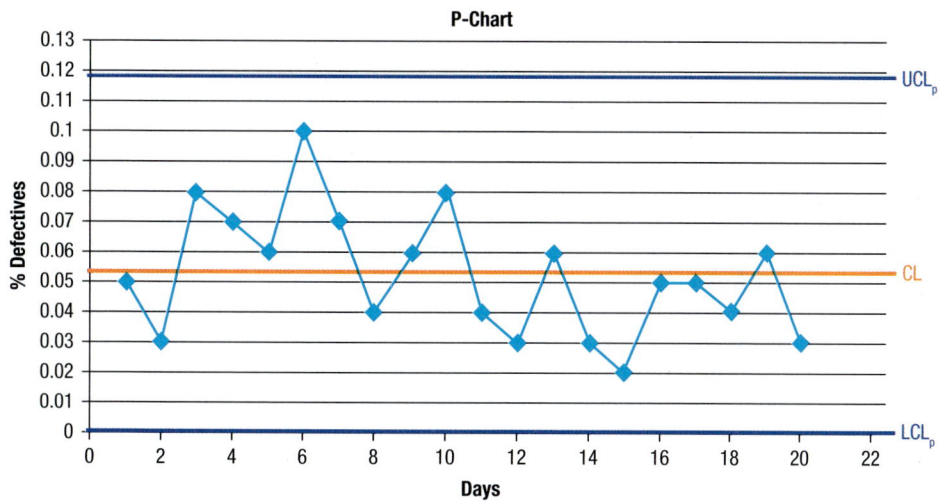

Step 6. Interpret the chart to see if the process is in control by checking for special cause variations such as points beyond the control limits and runs of consecutive points above or below the center line.

The chart shows that the process appears to be in control. Nevertheless, after day 10, more of the plotted points are clustered near or below the center line. The quality control manager should investigate to see if the process average has shifted downwards and address the reasons for that shift.

Process Capability Analysis

Process capability analysis is a technique used to determine whether a process is able to meet a set of **design specification limits,** or normal level of variations, that reflect the customer's requirements for a product or service. These limits are different than control chart limits. (We will discuss the differences in more detail in a moment.) Design specification limits, also known as **tolerances,** are numerical maximum and minimum values within which the outputs produced by a process are expected to fall to be considered as having acceptable quality *to the customer*. These limits are calculated ± the designed target value for that process. For example, consider a packaging process that packs oatmeal serial into boxes. Let us also assume that the mean (μ) for this process is 16 ounces with a tolerance of ± 0.5 ounces. Thus the *upper specification limit* (USL) of the process is 16.5 ounces, and the *lower specification limit* (LSL) is 15.5 ounces. In other words, the process is expected to produce boxes of oatmeal each with a net weight that falls between 15.5 ounces and 16.5 ounces. If there are boxes that have a net weight outside of this range, the normal variations that occur during the process exceed the design specification limits set for it, and it is not capable of meeting the customer's requirements.

DESIGN SPECIFICATION LIMITS VERSUS CONTROL CHART LIMITS

The upper and lower control limits of a control chart are sometimes mistakenly interpreted as design specification limits. Yet, they are completely different concepts. The control limits in a control chart are parameters established based on the observed dispersion of the sample outputs of a process. They represent the "voice of the process" because they are calculated based on the actual past performance of the process. They should *not* be confused with the design specification limits, which are determined based on the customer's requirements and hence represent the "voice of the customer." For example, suppose a firm learns that the customers who purchase the screws it produces want the diameter of the screw heads to have a target value of 12mm with a tolerance of plus or minus 0.5mm. In other words, the customer wants the finished screw-head diameter to fall somewhere between a lower specification limit (LSL) of 11.5mm and an upper specification limit (USL) of 12.5 mm. These values are the design specification limits for the process producing the screws.

Now suppose that, based on actual past performance of the screw-producing process, the firm finds the screws heads to be an average of 12.1mm in diameter with a standard error of the mean of 0.3mm, then the 3σ control limits for this process is 12.1 plus or minus 3 × 0.3. This translates into

Design specification limits: numerical maximum and minimum values within which the outputs produced by a process are expected to fall to be considered as having acceptable quality to the customer, also known as tolerance limits

Tolerances: *See* Design specification limits

a lower control limit of 11.2mm and an upper control limit of 13mm. You can see from this example that there is a difference between the control limits for the process and the specification limits desired by customers. Consequently, the current manufacturing process cannot consistently meet customer requirements. The relationship between control charts limits and design specifications limits is illustrated in Figure 6.12.

In Figure 6.12a, the natural process variation captured by the limits of a control chart is greater than the design specification limits or tolerances for variations allowed for the product. This means that the process is not capable of producing the product to design specifications. Consequently, the process will lead to a situation in which a large proportion of the products produced will be classified as defective or non-conforming.

Figure 6.12b depicts a situation in which the control limits and design specification limits are identical. This means that the process is just barely capable of operating to design specifications. In this scenario, if the control limits are based on ± 3σ, then 99.73% of the items will be classified as conforming to specifications and only a small proportion (about 0.27%) of items will be classified as defective or non-conforming. Figure 6.12c shows a situation in which the process is off center—that is, it consistently deviates in one direction away from the target value. In this case, the process at the current level at which it is operating is not capable because a certain percentage of the process output is falling outside the upper specification limits. If the process is adjusted to bring the process average to the target value (re-centered value), then the process can become capable of meeting design specifications.

Figure 6.12d depicts a situation in which the process is not only centered but also the design specification limits are greater than the limits of the control chart. This situation means that the natural random variations in the process as captured by the control chart are within the limits of the design tolerances. This process is always capable of producing products that meet the customer's requirements.

FIGURE 6.12: Determining Process Capability

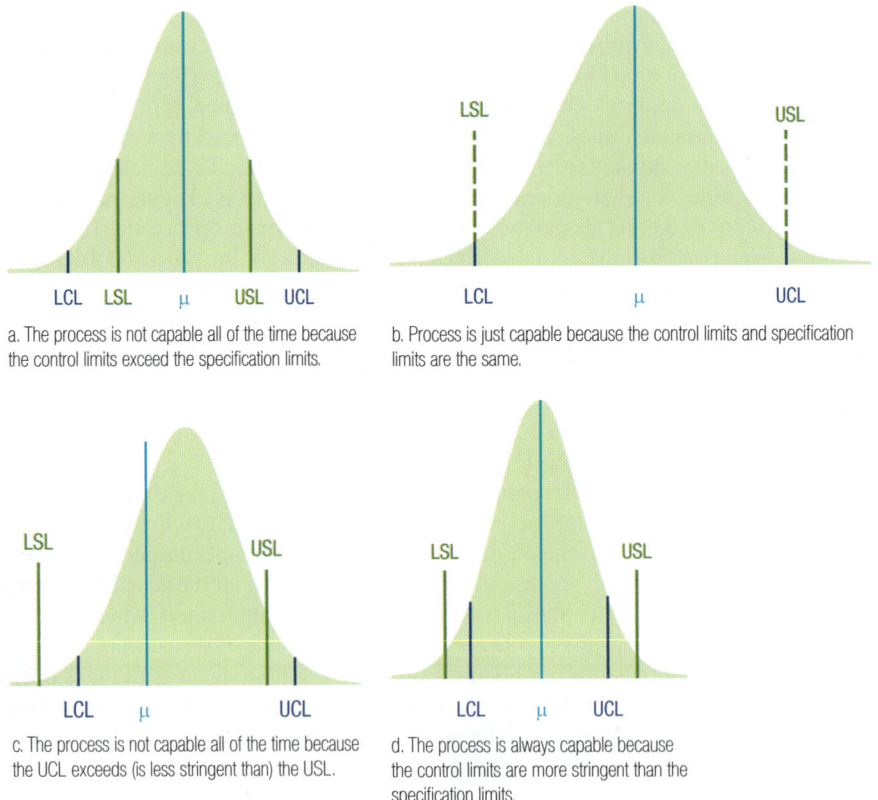

a. The process is not capable all of the time because the control limits exceed the specification limits.

b. Process is just capable because the control limits and specification limits are the same.

c. The process is not capable all of the time because the UCL exceeds (is less stringent than) the USL.

d. The process is always capable because the control limits are more stringent than the specification limits.

SOURCE: Kapadia, M., (n.d.), http://www.symphonytech.com/articles/pdfs/processcapability.pdf

MEASURES OF PROCESS CAPABILITY

You should now understand why measuring the capability of a process is important. Companies need to not only get a sense of the variability of their processes but also determine whether they are capable of meeting their design specifications. Two commonly used measures to calculate the capability of a process versus graphing them like we did in Figure 6.12 are the process capability index (C_p) and the process centering capability index (C_{pk}).

THE PROCESS CAPABILITY INDEX (C_p)

The **process capability index (C_p)** is a measure of how well a procees meets its specification limits. The measure is defined as the ratio of the range of design tolerances (specification limits) to the range of the variability of the process.

$$C_p = \frac{\text{Tolerance Range or Specification Width}}{\text{Range of Process Variation}}$$

The higher the value of C_p, the better is the process capability. Process variability is typically set at 6σ. Therefore,

$$C_p = \frac{(\text{Upper specification limit} - \text{Lower specification limit})}{6\sigma}$$

If C_p is less than 1, the specification width—that is, the difference between the upper and lower specification limits—is less than than the variation, or range, of the process. Therefore, it is not capable of consistently meeting its design specifications as shown in Figure 6.12a. If C_p is equal to 1, then the tolerance range matches the variation, or range, of the process, and it is just barely capable of meeting its design specifications as shown in Figure 6.12b. If C_p is greater than 1, then the specification width is greater than variation, or range, of the process, and it is always capable of meeting its design specifications as shown in Figure 6.12d. It is common for companies to aim for a process capability index value of 1.33 or greater because this number provides some margin for error. With values of C_p significantly greater than 1, the company is in a much better position to deal with many unexpected, but short-term variations in the process.

EXAMPLE 6.6: A company manufactures piston rings for automotive companies. Design specifications require the diameter of the piston rings to have a target value of 75mm with a tolerance of ± 0.5mm. The current manufacturing process produces piston rings with an average diameter of 74.8mm and a standard deviation (σ) of 0.15mm. Is the company's manufacturing process capable of meeting design specifications?

 Example 6.6

SOLUTION

With a target value of 75mm and a tolerance of ± 0.5mm, the design specification limits are 75.5mm and 74.5mm. Therefore:

$$C_p = \frac{(\text{Upper specification limit} - \text{Lower specification limit})}{6\sigma}$$

$$C_p = \frac{(75.5 - 74.5)}{(6 \times 0.15)}$$

$$C_p = 1.11$$

The process capability index of 1.11 indicates that the company's manufacturing process is capable of meeting the design specifications.

Process capability index (C_p): a measure of how well a procees meets its specification limits

THE PROCESS CENTERING CAPABILITY INDEX (C_{PK})

The process capability index (C_p) is the primary measure used to track process capability. It works well as long as the mean of the process is centered between the upper and lower specificiation limits and hitting its target value—the value the firm is shooting for. But consider a process like the one shown in Figure 6.12c. In this case, the process capability index (C_p) will not indicate that the process is not capable. To deal with a distribution in which the mean of a process is not centered, we need another measure of process capability—the **process centering capability index (C_{pk})**. This index measures how well the process is centered between the design specification limits. The higher the value of C_{pk}, the more centered is the process. The formula for the C_{pk} is:

$$C_{pk} = \text{Minimum} \left(\frac{\text{Process Mean} - \text{LSL}}{3\sigma}, \frac{\text{USL} - \text{Process Mean}}{3\sigma} \right)$$

From this formula we can infer that if the values for the numerators are equal to each other—that is, if $C_p = C_{pk}$—then the mean is centered between the two limits. By contrast, if the numerators don't equal one another, then the mean is off center and has drifted away from the firm's target value, which, of course, lies directly between the upper and lower specification limits. In cases where the process is off center, we can apply a correction factor (K) to the C_p. The off-centering correction factor K is computed as follows:

$$K = | D - \text{Mean} | / (1/2 \times (\text{USL} - \text{LSL})), \text{where}$$

$$D = (\text{USL}+\text{LSL})/2, \text{the specification target value.}$$

The correction factor (K) expresses the deviation of the mean away from the center relative to the specification width.

Once we compute K, we can now adjust the process capability index, C_p, for the effect of the non-centering as follows:

$$C_{pk} = (1 - K) \times C_p$$

If K = 0, then the process is perfectly centered, and $C_{pk} = C_p$. Nonetheless, as the mean drifts away from its target value, K increases, and the C_{pk} values become smaller than C_p.

 Example 6.7

EXAMPLE 6.7: Refer to Example 6.6. Compute C_{pk} and the off-center correction factor K.

SOLUTION

From Example 6.6, USL = 75.5mm; LSL = 74.5mm; mean = 74.8mm and D = (75.5+74.5)/2 = 75. Using the formula for C_{pk} and K, we have:

$$C_{pk} = \text{Min} [((74.8 - 74.5)/3 \times 0.15), ((75.5 - 74.8)/ 3 \times 0.15)] = \text{Min} [0.67, 1.55] = 0.67$$

ALTERNATE SOLUTION

$$K = | 75 - 74.8| / ((75.5 - 74.5)/2) = (0.2/0.5) = 0.4$$

Given $C_p = 1.11$ from the solution to problem 6.6, we have:

$$C_{pk} = (1-K) \times C_p = (1-0.4) \times 1.11 = 0.67$$

Even though the solution to Example 6.6 ($C_p = 1.11$) indicates that the process is capable, the 0.67 value for the C_{pk} indicates that the process is off center and lies toward the lower specification limit. In other words, there is an increased likelihood of producing piston rings with diameters that fall below the lower specification limits. The correction factor K = 0.4 indicates the extent to which the mean, or average value, is deviating from the target value the firm has set for the product and thus the extent of improvement that need to be made to re-center the process.

As a rule-of-thumb, to do a process capability analysis, you should collect a minimum of 20 samples each with a sample size of at least five items. In addition, when the nonconformity of a product could have serious negative consequences, the C_{pk} should be calculated at the start of the production run to ensure the process is working as well as it should be and then calculated again frequently to ensure that the mean has not shifted.[2]

Process centering capability index (C_{pk}): a measure of how well the process is centered between the design specification limits

FIGURE 6.13: Determining Process Quality on the Six Sigma Scale

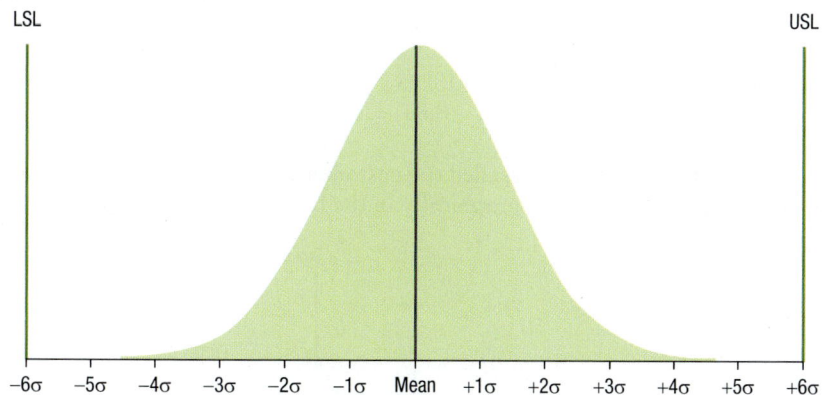

Revisiting Six Sigma: Calculating Six Sigma Quality of a Process

For some organizations, such as those in the health-care industry, operating at the 3σ quality level can be too risky. For example, at the 3σ quality level, there will be at least 20,000 prescriptions incorrectly filled, and 15,000 babies accidentally dropped by doctors and nurses each year. It is precisely for this reason that Motorola (Schaumburg, IL) invented the Six Sigma quality program. Recall that the goal of a Six Sigma effort is to produce no more than 3.4 defects in a million opportunities. In a Six Sigma process, a defect is defined as anything that falls outside of customer specifications limits (USL and LSL). This means 99.9997% of the time the value of a quality characteristic should be between six standard deviations of the mean and the lower or upper specification limit. Thus, once the specification limits are established, the quality level of a process on the Six Sigma scale can be calculated by determining the distance between the mean and the specification limits in terms of the actual standard deviation of the process. This concept is illustrated in Figure 6.13.

To calculate the Six Sigma level of any process, we can use the following equation:

$$\text{Sigma quality level} = \frac{(\text{USL} - \text{Mean})}{\sigma} \quad \text{or} \quad \frac{(\text{Mean} - \text{LSL})}{\sigma}$$

The percentage of defects from the process can be calculated using the Standard Normal Distribution Tables in Appendix A at the end of this book or by using Microsoft Excel (Microsoft Corporation, Redmond, WA) and the following formula:

$$\text{Percentage of Defectives} = (1 - \text{NORMSDIST} (\text{Process } \sigma))$$

EXAMPLE 6.8: The customers of a pizza delivery shop expect their pizzas to be delivered within 20 to 30 minutes. To improve its customer service levels, the shop collected past data on delivery times and found that the average delivery time was 27 minutes with a standard deviation of 3 minutes. What is the Six Sigma quality level of this pizza delivery process and the percentage of late deliveries?

SOLUTION

$$\text{Upper Sigma quality level} = \frac{USL - Mean}{\sigma} = \frac{30 - 27}{3} = 1$$

$$\text{Lower Sigma quality level} = \frac{Mean - LSL}{\sigma} = \frac{27 - 20}{3} = 2.33$$

The low values of 1 and 2.33 indicate that the distance between the mean of the process and the upper and lower specification limits are 1 and 2.33 standard deviations, respectively. Therefore, the current pizza delivery process is not operating at the Six Sigma quality level. Both the average delivery times and the variation in delivery time need to be reduced. Because we are interested only in late deliveries, we are looking for the percentage of times pizza deliveries exceeded 30 minutes—the customer's upper specification limit. By using Microsoft Excel with the following formula, we have:

$$\text{Percentage of defectives} = (1 - \text{NORMSDIST (Process } \sigma)) = (1 - \text{NORMSDIST (1)})$$
$$= (1 - 0.84) = 16\%$$

This means that pizza deliveries exceeded the customer's upper tolerance level of 30 minutes 16% of the time. This result is shown graphically in the following figure:

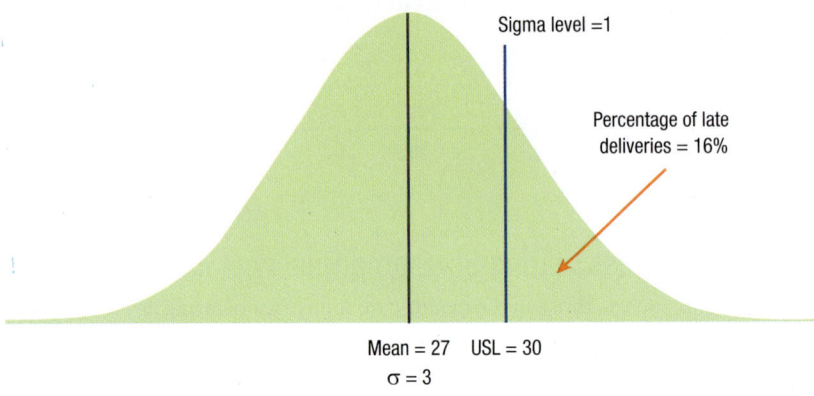

Sigma level = 1

Percentage of late deliveries = 16%

Mean = 27   USL = 30
σ = 3

6.4 Quality Design Tools

Use quality design tools to improve product or process design.

Quality control charts, statistical process control, and Six Sigma efforts have helped many companies minimize the variability in their manufacturing or service operations and improve the quality of their products. Nevertheless, it has been found that a product's design has the greatest impact on its quality. Therefore, many companies focus closely on this aspect of quality and how to improve it. Next, let's look at some of the methods they use.

The Taguchi Method (Robust Design)

Web: Quality and Product Design

Recall that in Chapter 4 we discussed robust design, which is also called the Taguchi method. The concept of robust design involves designing a product or process so that it is insensitive to factors such as different environmental conditions, machine wear and tear, variation resulting from differences in raw materials, and so forth. Three of the most important robust design tools are the Taguchi-loss function, parameter design process, and design of experiments (DOE).

THE TAGUCHI-LOSS FUNCTION

The traditional view of quality is that as long as a product or service simply meets or conforms to its design specifications, it is of appropriate quality. Yet, the Japanese quality pioneer, Genichi Taguchi, had a different view of quality. The following are three of his premises:

- When every quality characteristic of a product meets its target value, the loss in terms of quality is at a minimum.
- Any deviation from the product's quality characteristic target value results in losses, including loss to the society. In other words, not only does the manufacturer incurs losses, such as the time needed to fix the problem and the loss of revenues and its reputation, consumers also incur losses. For example, they may incur time and money costs to return the item and even suffer physical injuries or ailments caused by it. The greater the deviation, the greater the loss.
- The losses associated with poor quality should be expressed in monetary units.

The Taguchi-loss function, which is known as the *quadratic function* or *quality-loss* function, is a simple equation used to quantify the monetary losses incurred by the manufacturer and the consumer as a result of a product's deviation from the its target values. The blue curves in Figure 6.14a and Figure 6.14b represent the function in two different scenarios. Figure 6.14a shows that a small

FIGURE 6.14a: Taguchi-Loss Function for Smaller Deviations From the Target Value

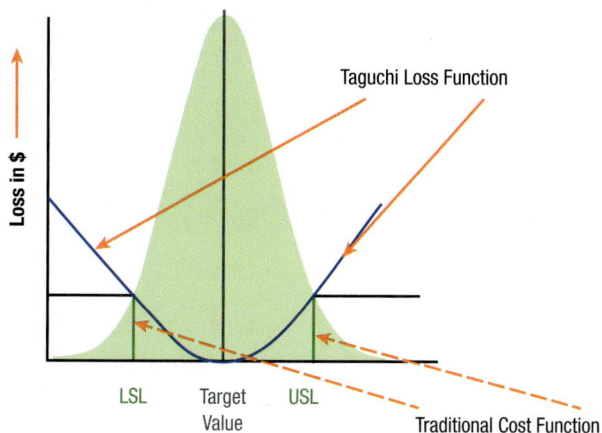

FIGURE 6.14b: Taguchi-Loss Function for Larger Deviations From Target Value

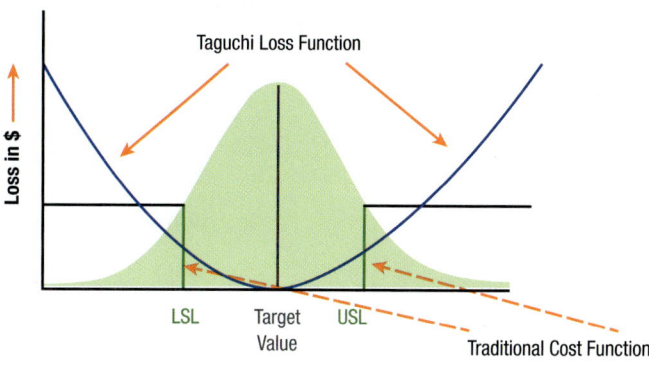

deviation from the target value for a product results in a small Taguchi loss. By contrast, Figure 6.14b shows that a large deviation from the target value results in a large loss. Furthermore, as the deviation increases, the loss increases in a nonlinear fashion. Also, both figures show that the losses as defined by Taguchi are higher than the traditionally understood losses.

The equation for the Taguchi-loss function, which is as follows, compares the measured value, X, of the quality characteristic of a unit to the target value, T:

$$L(X) = k \times (X - T)^2$$

where

k = the loss coefficient

X = the measured value of the quality characteristic

T = the target value

$L(X)$ = the expected loss associated with the specific value of X

The equation simply states that the loss is directly proportional to the square of the deviation of the measured value, X, from the target value, T. This means that any deviation from the target value will diminish the customer's satisfaction. Taguchi's definition of quality differs from the traditional definition of quality in the following way. In this equation, the value of k, the loss coefficient, is a constant. It can be easily determined if the values of X and the associated expected loss $L(X)$ are both known. Once the value of k is known, we can determine the average loss for a sample set of data and the total loss for all samples using the following equations:

Average loss per sample set: $L = k \times (s^2 + (\overline{X} - T)^2)$, where

s = the standard deviation of the sample data

$\overline{X}$ = the mean of the sample data

The total loss = the average loss per sample set × the number of samples

EXAMPLE 6.9: Crescent produces socket tools that have inside diameters with a target value of 0.5 inches, and a tolerance of ± 0.050 inches. As a result of wear and tear, the equipment used to make the tools needs to be replaced, but the firm's managers are delaying the replacement because they feel like the company still makes good tools. The tools have been meeting the target value, although several of them were rejected at the assembly stage. Recently, a tool produced by the process did not meet its target value because it had an inside diameter of 0.550 inches. The failure costs associated with a defective socket tool is US$50.00. Using the following sample data collected from a recent production lot and the Taguchi-loss function formula, justify why replacing the equipment may benefit the company and the customer:

SAMPLE #	SAMPLE SIZE					
	ITEM 1	ITEM 2	ITEM 3	ITEM 4	ITEM 5	ITEM 6
1	0.460	0.476	0.492	0.501	0.512	0.526
2	0.459	0.495	0.495	0.503	0.515	0.525
3	0.462	0.483	0.498	0.505	0.513	0.527
4	0.474	0.495	0.500	0.509	0.521	0.534
5	0.462	0.489	0.502	0.510	0.521	0.532
6	0.478	0.491	0.502	0.511	0.524	0.534

SOLUTION

The mean and the standard deviation for the six sets of samples are: $\overline{X} = 0.501$ and s = 0.0215.

The target value of the inside diameter of the socket tool $T = 0.5$.

The measured inside diameter of a particular socket tool $X = 0.550$.

The expected loss for a defective socket tool L(X) = \$50.00.

$L(X) = k \times (X - T)^2$

$50 = k \times (0.550 - 0.500)^2$

Therefore, $k = 50/ (0.550 - 0.500)^2 = 20,000$. So, the average loss per socket tool in this sample is

$L = k \times (s^2 + (\overline{X} - T)^2) = 20,000 \times [(0.0215)^2 + (0.501 - 0.500)^2] = 9.28$, or \$9.28.

The total loss for all of the sample sets is given by:

L = the average loss per sample set × the number of samples

Using this example, and projecting the total loss for 50 such sample sets, we have

Total loss = \$9.28 × 50 = \$464.

The total loss computed indicates that the company should replace the equipment because the losses are bound to increase with its continued wear and tear. This example also shows that the Taguchi-loss function is expressed in monetary terms, which makes it easily understood by all of the departments within a company.

PARAMETER DESIGN

Parameter design focuses on determining the optimal design of a product and the processes used to produce it so as to minimize variations. According to Taguchi, factors that affect the design of any product or system can be divided into two categories: *control factors* and uncontrollable, or *noise factors*. Control factors are variables affecting a process that a designer can easily control. *Signal* factors are input factors that are also controlled by the designer or operator of the product so that the product can perform its intended functions (setting the temperature of the thermostat to cool a room or turning the ignition key to start a car). By contrast, noise factors are factors affecting a process that are difficult for a designer to control.

As an example, let's assume that in a chemical process, two factors, reaction time and ambient temperature, affect the yield (how much is produced by the process). The reaction time is a control factor because it can be easily manipulated and controlled by the designer. Therefore, the designer will choose the setting for the reaction time that will maximize the yield. Ambient temperature is the room temperature surrounding the process. It also affects the yield. If the designer cannot control the temperature, it is a noise factor. Because the designer has no control over the ambient temperature, she needs to find a setting for the reaction time that minimizes the variation in the yield when there is a change in the ambient temperature. This is the essence of parameter design.

Parameter design: an approach to design that focuses on determining the optimal design of a product and the processes used to produce it so as to minimize variations

The first step in the parameter design process is to create a **P-diagram** that identifies the various factors that have an effect on the design and performance of a product or process. The P-diagram is illustrated in Figure 6.15.

The P-diagram in Figure 6.15 shows that the firm's output is influenced by *signal*, *control*, and *noise* factors. The second step in the parameter design is to identify the signal (input) factors and the output associated with the design concept. For example, in the design of a cooling system for a room, the temperature setting of the thermostat is the signal factor, and the resulting room temperature is the output. The size of the air conditioning unit, the number of registers to be used, where they should be located, and the type of insulation used are determined by the designer and, hence, are classified as control factors. Nonetheless, the frequency of opening and closing windows, the number of occupants in a room, and the outside temperature are factors that are beyond the control of the designer and, hence, are classified as noise factors.[3] The designer's job is to use the control factors and their related settings so that design is not greatly influenced by the noise factors. For example, the designer might use sealed window units in the room and/or limit the number occupants in the room and so forth. Ignoring noise factors during the early design stages of a product's development is a frequent cause of quality losses and product failures.[4]

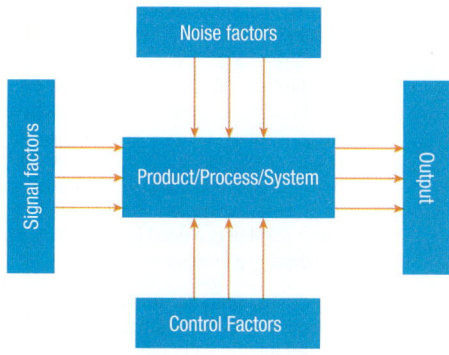

FIGURE 6.15: P-Diagram

DESIGN OF EXPERIMENTS (DOE)

Recall that we first discussed design of experiments in Chapter 5. Design of experiments is a set of statistical techniques used to determine which controllable factors and which noise factors are the significant variables that will have an impact on product/process or system performance. The purpose of using DOE is to come up with settings for the controllable factors at those levels that will make the product or process insensitive to the noise factors. By using DOE techniques the designer can establish parameter settings such as temperature settings or drill speeds at those levels that will make the process resilient or robust to variations in the operating environment.

In summary, the use of parameter design and DOE enables product designers to establish product parameter settings that are robust to variations caused by uncontrollable factors. Once the parameter design is in place, the designers can then test the impact of deviations of the parameter values from the target by using the Taguchi-loss function. The purpose of this exercise is to come up with an optimum design that is not only robust, but also balances the added cost of tighter tolerances against the benefits to the customer. The net result is a successful product produced at a low cost.

P-diagram: a diagram that identifies the various factors that have an effect on the design and performance of a product or process

Visit **edge.sagepub.com/venkataraman** to help you accomplish your coursework goals in an easy-to-use learning environment.

- Mobile-friendly eFlashcards
- Mobile-friendly practice quizzes
- A complete online action plan

- Chapter summaries with learning objectives
- Video and multimedia resources

CHAPTER SUMMARY

6.1 Explain the difference between quality control and quality assurance. Quality control is concerned with the quality of a product or service after it is produced or delivered. By contrast, quality assurance (QA) is a set of procedures to ensure a product or service's quality *before* it is delivered. Various quality appraisal and quality control tools are covered in the chapter.

6.2 Apply the various tools for appraising the quality of products and processes. The appraisal tools that managers and employees use include check sheets, histograms, Pareto charts, scatter diagrams, cause-and-effect diagrams, and process flowcharts. Check sheets are forms used to collect and record quality-related data. The sheets are one of the simplest quality control tools because they are easy to understand, require very little effort to design, and are fact-based. A histogram is a vertical bar chart that shows the frequency of occurrences of values. A Pareto chart is also a vertical bar chart with the bars arranged in decreasing height from left to right. The height of an individual bar represents how often a particular problem has occurred. A scatter diagram is a tool that can be used to visually determine whether two variables are related or correlated. A cause-and-effect diagram is a quality control tool used to identify, sort, and graphically display the potential causes of a quality problem. A process flowchart graphically displays the steps in a process and its flow. Before beginning any process quality improvement effort, it is a good idea to depict the process in its current state using a flowchart.

6.3   **Apply the various tools for preventing defects in products and processes, including control charts, a process capability analysis, and how to calculate Six Sigma levels of quality.**
The three basic statistical process control methods are: control charts, process capability analysis, and assessing Six Sigma–level quality. The chapter describes the difference between variable and attribute quality and the underlying theory behind control charts. Two control charts for monitoring variable quality and two control charts for attribute quality are discussed. Process capability analysis is used to determine whether the process is stable, centered, and the process output falls within specification limits.

In a Six Sigma process, a defect is defined as anything that falls outside of customer specifications limits (USL and LSL). This means 99.9997% of the time the value of a quality characteristic should be between six standard deviations of the mean and the lower or upper specification limit. Thus, once the specification limits are established, the quality level of a process on the Six Sigma scale can be calculated by determining the distance between the mean and the specification limits in terms of the actual standard deviation of the process.

6.4   **Use quality design tools to improve product or process design.**
The concept of robust design involves designing a product or process so that it is insensitive to factors such as different environmental conditions, machine wear and tear, variation resulting from differences in raw materials, and so forth. Three of the most important robust design tools are the Taguchi-loss function, parameter design process, and design of experiments (DOE). The costs associated with poor quality can be evaluated using the Taguchi-loss function. These costs of poor quality provide valuable information to quality managers to reduce variation using robust design methods. By using parameter design and design of experiment tools, product and process designers can establish product parameter settings that are robust to variations caused by uncontrollable factors. As a result, the designers can determine the optimal design of a product and the processes used to produce it so as to minimize variations.

KEY TERMS

Attribute   200

C-chart   211

Central limit theorem   202

Common cause variations   200

Control chart   201

Design specification limits   217

Mean chart   204

Parameter design   224

P-chart   211

P-diagram   225

Process capability index (C_p)   219

Process centering capability index (C_{pk})   220

Quality assurance (QA)   196

Quality control (QC)   196

Range chart   204

Sampling distribution   202

Special cause variations   200

Tolerances   217

Variable   200

DISCUSSION AND REVIEW QUESTIONS

1. What is a control chart?

2. What is the difference between an attribute and a variable?

3. Why should a mean chart and a range chart be used together to determine whether a process is in control?

4. What is the difference between a c-chart and a p-chart?

5. What is the difference between specification limits and control limits?

6. What conditions should be met to conclude that a process is in control using control charts?

7. What is the Taguchi-loss function, and how is it used to improve the quality of designs?

8. Select a fast-food restaurant, a bank, and a hotel and identify some of the processes in each of these businesses for which control charts could be useful.

9. What information on a process's capability do the C_p and C_{pk} indices provide individually and jointly?

10. If you conclude using a control chart that a process is in control, can you assume that the process is also capable?

11. State the difference between tolerance and control limits.

12. Visit a hospital, a bank, and a grocery store and identify the different processes that can be monitored using a control chart.

SOLVED PROBLEMS

1. A mythical Sirius Airlines flight from Chicago to New York was delayed by 2 hours. Draw a cause-and-effect diagram to identify the possible causes and their categories for the delayed flight departure.

Solution:

The major categories for flight delays can be machines, people, methods, materials, environment, and management. Some of the possible causes can be bad weather, overbooked flights, poorly trained staff, aircraft equipment problems, fuel or food shortage, and so forth. The following is a cause-and-effect (fishbone) diagram for delayed flight departure:

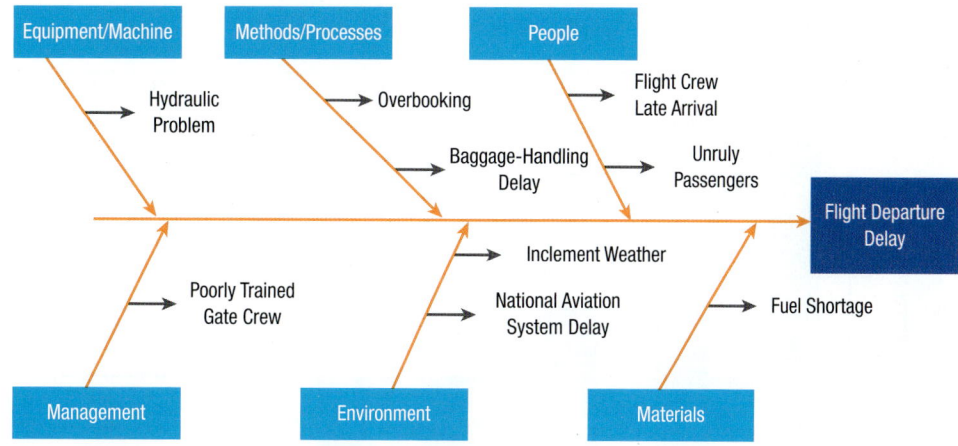

2.   A local Ford Service Center had the following car repair shop data:

Ticket No.	Repair Work	Ticket No.	Repair Work
1	Alternator	21	Brakes
2	Batteries	22	Brakes
3	Tires	23	Oil & Filter
4	Oil & Filter	24	Oil & Filter
5	Tires	25	Alternator
6	Tires	26	Batteries
7	Tires	27	Oil & Filter
8	Oil & Filter	28	Bearings
9	Oil & Filter	29	Alternator
10	Brakes	30	Oil & Filter
11	Transmission	31	Oil & Filter
12	Oil & Filter	32	Brakes
13	Brakes	33	Tires
14	Batteries	34	Transmission
15	Batteries	35	Oil & Filter
16	Alternator	36	Brakes
17	Tires	37	Oil & Filter
18	Oil & Filter	38	Tires
19	Brakes	39	Oil & Filter
20	Oil & Filter	40	Oil & Filter

Prepare a check sheet and then construct a Pareto diagram for the previous data.

Solution:

Check Sheet for the Ford Service Center Repair Work

Repair Work	Tally	Frequency of Occurrences
Tires	##	7
Oil & Filter	## ## ##	15
Batteries	##	4
Brakes	##	7
Alternator	##	4
Transmission		2
Bearings		1

Pareto Chart for the Ford Service Center Repair Work

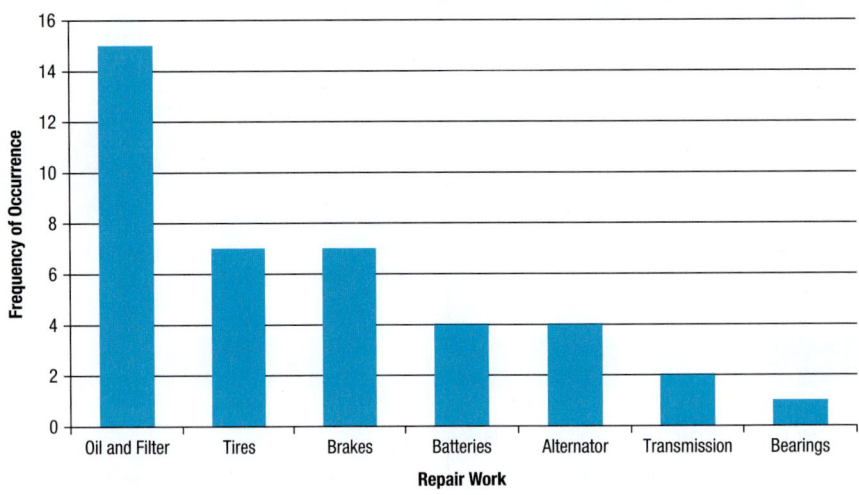

3. The fictional Super-Charge Company manufactures batteries. It collects data using a random sample of six batteries from the output of batteries it produces each hour. The voltage of each battery is tested and recorded to ensure that the process is in control. The following table shows the data:

Sample	Mean	Range	Sample	Mean	Range
1	4.98	0.42	9	5.05	0.48
2	4.88	0.58	10	5.14	0.57
3	4.87	0.54	11	5.41	0.41
4	5.24	0.78	12	5.15	0.61
5	5.10	0.75	13	5.02	0.37
6	5.04	0.22	14	4.88	0.42
7	5.11	0.54	15	4.97	0.55
8	5.08	0.89	16	5.08	0.36

a. Use this data from the table to design and construct a mean chart and a range chart.

b. Plot the data on the control charts.

c. Is this process in control? If not, what action should the firm's quality control manager take?

Solution:

Mean ($\bar{X}$) Chart

$$\bar{\bar{X}} = (4.98+4.88+4.87+5.24+5.10+5.04+5.11+5.08+5.05+5.14+5.41+5.15+5.02+4.88+4.97+5.08)/16$$

$$\bar{\bar{X}} = \textbf{5.06}$$

$$\bar{R} = (0.42+0.58+0.54+0.78+0.75+0.22+0.54+0.89+0.48+0.57+0.41+0.61+0.37+0.42+0.55+0.36)/16$$

$$\bar{R} = \textbf{0.53}$$

From Table 6.1, for a sample size of n = 6, the factors A_2, D_3, and D_4 are: 0.483, 0, and 2.004.

$$\text{Center line} = \bar{\bar{X}} = \textbf{5.06}$$

$$\text{Upper control limit (UCL}_{\bar{X}}) = \bar{\bar{X}} + A_2 \times \bar{R} = 5.06 + 0.483 \times 0.53 = \textbf{5.32}$$

$$\text{Lower control limit (UCL}_{\bar{X}}) = \bar{\bar{X}} - A_2 \times \bar{R} = 5.06 - 0.483 \times 0.53 = \textbf{4.81}$$

Range Chart

$$\text{Center Line} = \bar{R} = \textbf{0.53}$$

$$\text{Upper control limit (UCL}_R) = D_4 \times \bar{R} = 2.004 \times 0.53 = \textbf{1.06}$$

$$\text{Lower control limit (LCL}_R) = D_3 \times \bar{R} = 0 \times 0.53 = \textbf{0}$$

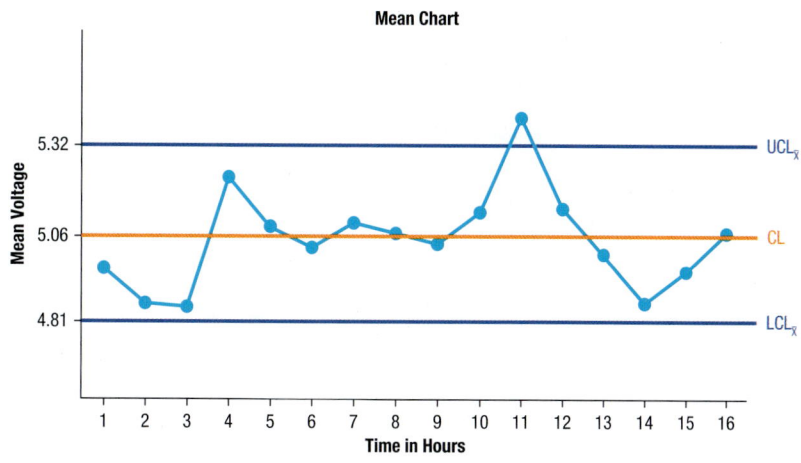

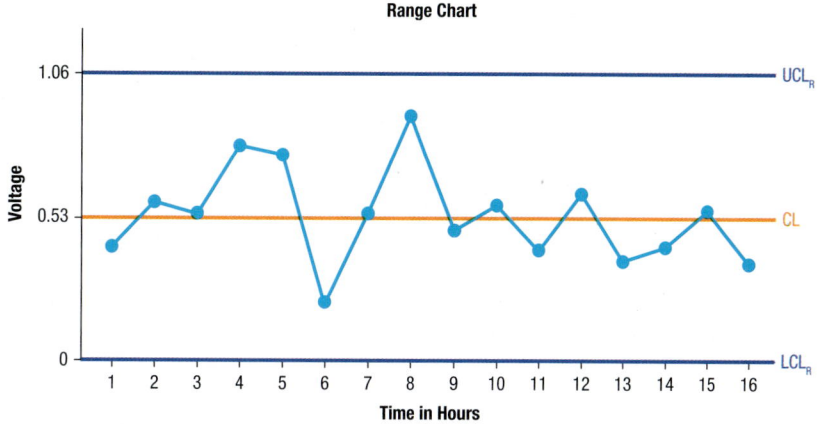

Solution:

The range chart shows the process is in control, but the mean chart does not. In the mean chart, the data point for sample 11 falls above the upper control limit. So this process is not in control. The data for sample 11 should be investigated for special cause variations. The solution to this problem is shown in the following screenshot from an Excel spreadsheet:

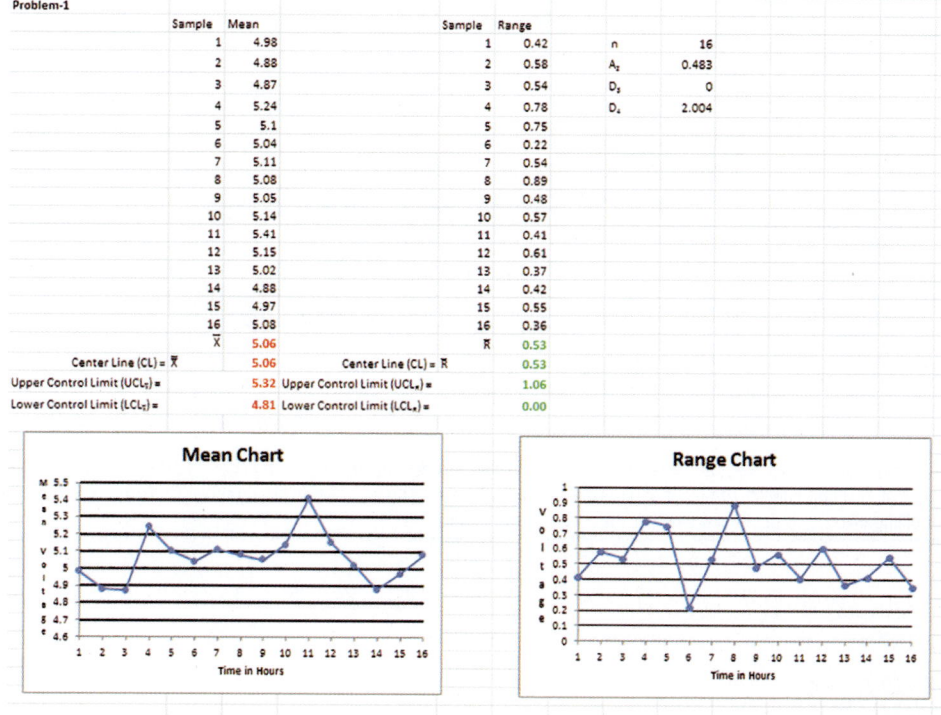

4. A pipe manufacturer produces 12-foot sections of brass pipes with an average inside diameter of 4 inches and a standard deviation of 0.2 inch. The distribution of the output is approximately normal. The process is monitored using sample means with a sample size of 25 pipes.

    a. Determine the center line and the upper and lower control limits that will include 96% of the sample means within control limits.

    b. During a 10-day period of production, the following sample means were recorded: 4.001, 4.005, 4.003, 3.999, 4.002, 3.998, 3.997, 4.000, 3.995, and 4.001. Is the process in control?

Solution:

Given: $\mu = 4.0$ inches; $\sigma = 0.2$ inch; sample size n = 25.

Because μ and σ are known, the center line, the upper and lower control limits are given by the following formulas:

$$CL = \mu$$

$$UCL_{\overline{X}} = \mu + z \times \sigma_{\overline{X}}$$

$$LCL_{\overline{X}} = \mu - z \times \sigma_{\overline{X}}$$

$$\sigma_{\overline{X}} = \sigma/\sqrt{n} = 0.2/\sqrt{25} = 0.04$$

Because 96% of the sample means should fall within the control limits for the process to be in control, the Z-value for the previous formula can be determined from the Standard Normal Distribution Table included in Appendix A. The Z-value is approximately 2.054. Therefore,

$$CL = \mu = 4.0$$

$$UCL_{\overline{X}} = \mu + z \times \sigma_{\overline{X}} = 4.0 + 2.054 \times 0.04 = 4.082$$

$$LCL_{\overline{X}} = \mu - z \times \sigma_{\overline{X}} = 4.0 - 2.054 \times 0.04 = 3.918$$

The solution to this problem is shown in the following screenshot from an Excel spreadsheet. The Excel graph shows that all sample means are within control limits with no assignable causes of variation. Hence, the process is in control:

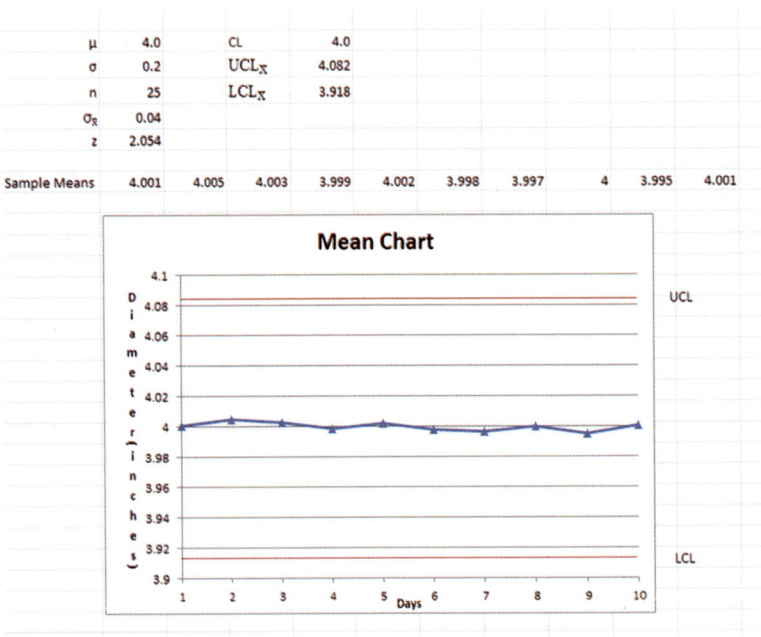

5. After receiving a number of complaints about errors in its billing statements, a hospital decided to monitor its billing statements over a 20-day period using a sample size of 100 statements. The number of billing errors each day is shown in the following table. Construct a 2σ control chart to monitor the proportion of billing errors and determine whether the process is in control:

Sample	1	2	3	4	5	6	7	8	9	10	11	12	13	14	15	16	17	18	19	20
# of Billing Errors	7	5	5	3	6	4	7	6	8	5	9	2	5	4	8	6	6	7	5	4

Solution:

Given: sample size (n) = 100; number of samples =20. Therefore,

$$\overline{P} = \frac{(7+5+5+3+6+4+7+6+8+5+9+2+5+4+8+6+6+7+5+4)}{20\times100} = 0.056$$

$$\sigma_p = \sqrt{0.056*(1-0.056/100} = 0.023$$

$$\text{Center line} = \overline{P} = 0.056$$

$$UCL_p = 0.056 + 2 \times 0.023 = 0.102$$

$$LCL_p = 0.056 - 2 \times 0.023 = 0.010$$

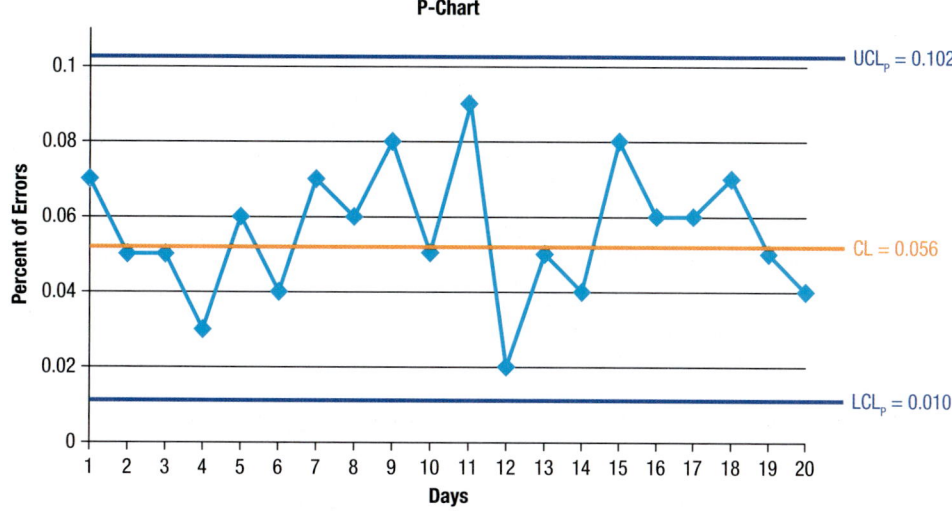

The plot of the data in the p-chart shows that the process is stable and in control. The solution to this problem is shown in the following screenshot from an Excel spreadsheet:

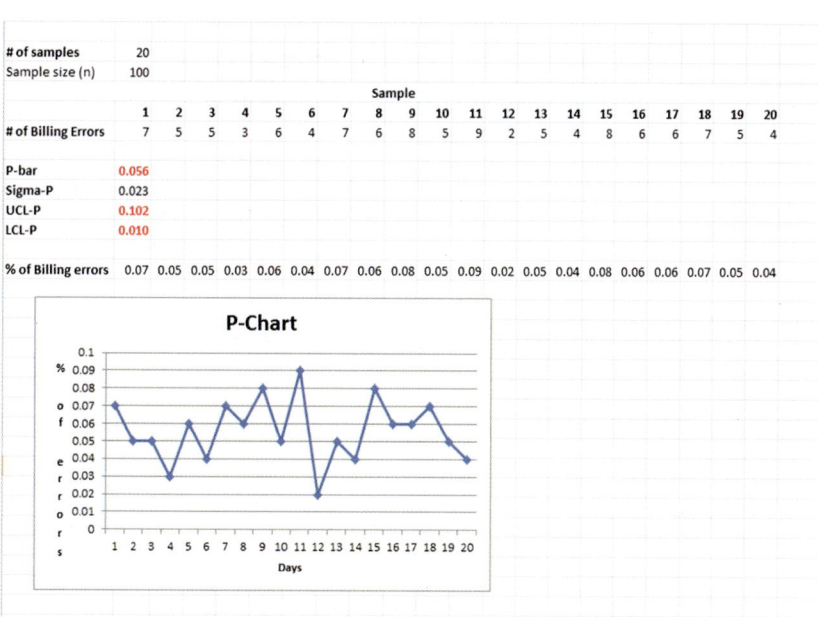

6. The manager of a manufacturing plant wants to use a c-chart to monitor the number of injuries that occur each month in the plant. The number of injuries she recorded in one particular month are shown in the following table:

Month																							
1	2	3	4	5	6	7	8	9	10	11	12	13	14	15	16	17	18	19	20	21	22	23	24

No. of Injuries																							
2	5	3	3	5	4	7	6	3	5	6	9	7	4	8	5	1	7	8	4	2	5	6	4

a.   Why is a c-chart used to monitor this process?

b.   Using 3σ control limits, construct a c-chart for this process and determine whether it is in control.

Solution:

a.   In this problem, the variation in the number of injuries in the manufacturing plant is being monitored. The sample size in this case is the plant. The operational definition for an injury is any injury that occurs in the plant in any given month. The opportunity for injuries (defects) to occur is very large because there are many opportunities for injuries to occur. Nevertheless, the number of injuries (defects) that actually occur (relative to the number of opportunities for injuries to occur) is small. Hence, a c-chart is appropriate under these conditions.

b.   For 3σ control limits, the center line and the upper and lower control limits for the c-chart are:

$$CL = \overline{c}, UCL_c = \overline{c} + 3\sqrt{\overline{c}}, \text{ and } LCL_c = \overline{c} - 3\sqrt{\overline{c}}$$

$$\overline{c} = (2+5+3+3+5+4+7+6+3+5+6+9+7+4+8+5+1+7+8+4+2+5+6+4)/24 = 4.96$$

$$UCL_c = \overline{c} + 3\sqrt{\overline{c}} = 4.96 + 3\sqrt{4.96} = 2.227 = 11.64$$

$$LCL_c = \overline{c} - 3\sqrt{\overline{c}} = 4.96 - 3\sqrt{4.96} = -1.72 = 0$$

The control chart and the plotted data are as follows. The process is in control:

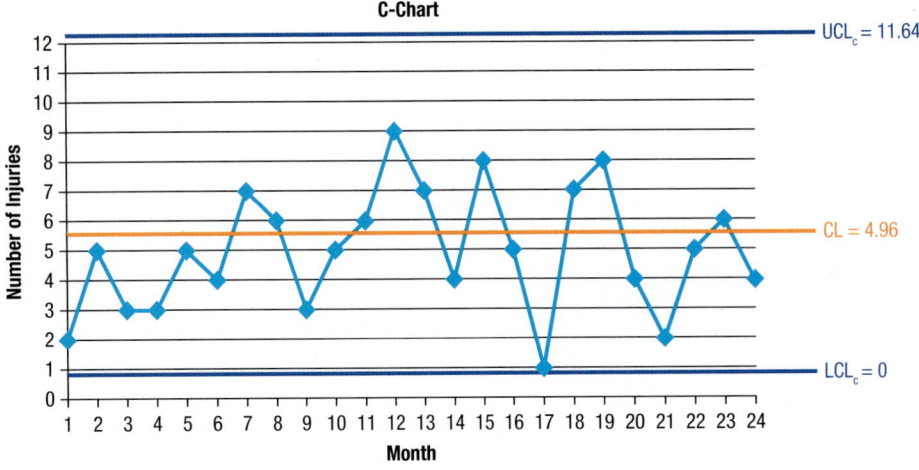

The solution to this problem is shown in the following screenshot from an Excel spreadsheet:

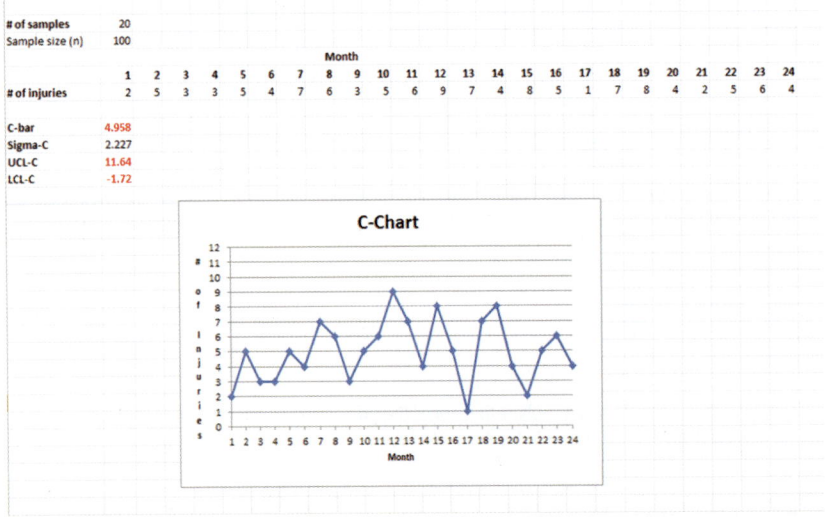

7.   A manufacturing process has a process sample mean ($\bar{x}$) of 16mm and a sample standard deviation (s) of 2mm. The upper specification limit is 21 and the lower specification limit is 9. Compute the C_p and the C_{pk} and determine whether the process is capable and centered. What is the value of the implicit off-centering correction factor, K?

Solution:

Because the mean (μ) and standard deviation (σ) are not known, we will use $\bar{x}$ and s instead in our calculations.

$$Cp = \frac{(USL - LSL)}{6s} = \frac{(21-9)}{6(2)} = 1.0$$

The value of C_p = 1.0 means that the process is just capable as long as it is centered. Yet, it is desirable to have a value of C_p > 1.33 to conclude that the process is capable. To determine whether the process is centered, we need to calculate C_{pk}.

$$C_{pk} = \text{Min}\left[\frac{USL - \bar{x}}{3s}, \frac{\bar{x} - LSL}{3s}\right] = \text{Min}\left[\frac{21-16}{3(2)}, \frac{16-9}{3(2)}\right] = \text{Min}(0.833, 1.167) = 0.833$$

The process is not centered because the C_{pk} is less than 1. To make the process capable, either the variability should be reduced or the process needs to be centered. The implicit off-centering correction factor, K, is calculated as follows:

$$C_{pk} = (1 - K) \times C_p$$

Therefore:

K = 1 − (C_{pk} / C_p) = 1 − (0.833/1.0) = 0.167

The solution to this problem is shown in the following screenshot from an Excel spreadsheet:

Sample mean ($\bar{x}$)	16.0
Sample standard deviation (s)	2.0
USL	21.0
LSL	9.0
Process Capability Index (C_p)	1.00
Process Centering Capability Index (C_{pk})	0.833
Off-centering correction factor (K)	0.167

8.   For its repair work, an automobile repair shop has set a target value of eight customer complaints with 10 complaints being the upper limit. The shop received 14 complaints in May. It directly costs the company US$100 per complaint to correct the repair work problems. In addition, the cost associated with lost sales later as a result of each complaint is estimated to be $200. Using the Taguchi-loss function, show how reducing the number of customer complaints per month will benefit the company.

Solution:

The total loss to the shop per customer complaint: $100 + $200 = $300.

The acceptable deviation from the target value = (X − T) = 10 − 8 = 2.

Therefore,

$$L(X) = k \times (X - T)^2$$

$$k = L(X) / (X - T)^2 = 300 / 4 = \$75$$

Because we have determined the value of the loss coefficient k, we can now calculate the total loss the shop incurred for the 14 complaints in May as follows:

$$L(X) = k \times (X - T)^2 = 75 \times (14 - 8)^2 = \$2700$$

Clearly, the shop will benefit from improving the quality of its repair work by reducing the number of customer complaints. The solution to this problem is shown in the following screenshot from an Excel spreadsheet:

Cost of correcting repair work per complaint	100.0
Intangible cost of lost sales	200.0
Total Loss per complaint	300.0
Target value for complaints (T)	8.0
Acceptable deviation from target (X -T)	2.0
Actual number of complints received in May-12	14.00
Loss Coefficient (k)	75.000
Total Loss for complaints in May-12	**2700.000**

9. The fictional Martian Wear Inc., which sells outdoor clothing and gear online, guarantees it will ship its customers' orders within 34 to 82 hours of order receipt. The company's shipment data for the past 6 months indicate that the average shipment time was 62 hours with a standard deviation of 8 hours.

    a. Is the company achieving a Six Sigma level of quality?

    b. If not, how can the company do so?

Solution:

Given: μ = 62 hours; σ = 8 hours.

$$USL = 82 \text{ hours}; LSL = 34 \text{ hours.}$$

a. If the company is achieving a Six Sigma level of quality, then the distance between the mean and the USL and LSL should be greater than or equal to six standard deviations. Given the firm's data, the actual upper and lower limits that can be achieved by the company at the Six-Sigma level are:

$$\text{Actual upper limit} = 62 + (6 \times 8) = 110 \text{ hours}$$

$$\text{Actual lower limit} = 62 - (6 \times 8) = 14 \text{ hours}$$

Both the upper and lower specification limits (82 hours and 34 hours) are closer to the target (62 hours) than the actual upper and lower values (110 hours and 14 hours). Clearly, this clothing designer is not achieving a Six Sigma level of quality for its shipping process.

b. To achieve a Six Sigma level of quality, the distance from the mean to both the USL and the LSL should be equal to or greater than six standard deviations.

$$USL - \mu = 82 - 62 = 20, \text{ and}$$

$$\mu - LSL = 62 - 34 = 28$$

To achieve Six Sigma level of quality, the smaller of the two deviation values should be equal to 6σ. Therefore,

$$6\sigma = 20 \text{ or, } \sigma = 20 / 6 = 3.33 \text{ hours.}$$

The company needs to reduce its process standard deviation from 8 hours to 3.33 hours to achieve a Six Sigma level of quality.

The solution to this problem is shown in the following screenshot from an Excel spreadsheet:

Process mean (μ)	62.0
Process standard deviation (σ)	8.0
USL	82.0
LSL	34.0
Actual upper limit	110.00
Actual lower limit	14.00

To achieve six-sigma level quality, the distance from the mean to both the USL and LSL should be greater than or equal to six standard deviations.

USL - μ	20.0
μ-LSL	28.0

To achieve six-sigma level quality, the smaller of the two deviation values should be equal to 6σ.

$\sigma = (USL - \mu)/6$	3.333333

The company needs to reduce its process standard deviation from 8 to 3,33 hours to achieve six-sigma level quality in its delivery process.

PROBLEMS ....

1. You live in Buffalo, New York. As you were getting ready to leave for work on a Monday morning, your car won't start (effect). Identify the possible causes for your car's failure using a cause-and-effect (Fishbone) diagram.

2. You are waiting in the Buffalo International Airport to take a JetBlue Flight (JetBlue Airways Corporation, Long Island City, NY) to New York City. Your JetBlue aircraft that was expected to arrive at 8 am has been delayed (effect) by 2 hours. Identify the possible causes for the aircraft delay using a cause-and-effect (Fishbone) diagram.

3. Apple was planning to launch its new iPhone version (iPhone7) on January 31, 2017. Nonetheless, as a result of concerns over defective components in the product and cost overruns (80% over budget), the new product launch has been delayed (effect) by 6 months. Identify the possible causes for the iPhone7 product failure using a cause-and-effect (Fishbone) diagram.

4. The Pennsylvania State Police issued tickets for the following infractions during the month of November, 2015. Construct a check sheet and a Pareto chart for these infractions. What are your conclusions?

Day	Violations
Sunday	DUI, Over-speeding, Stop sign violation
Monday	Parking violation, Expired registration, Illegal right-turn
Tuesday	Over-speeding, Stop sign violation, Parking violation
Wednesday	DUI, Over-speeding, Expired registration, Illegal right-turn
Thursday	Over-speeding, Stop sign violation, Parking violation, DUI
Friday	Over-speeding, Expired registration
Saturday	Over-speeding, Stop sign violation, Illegal right-turn
Sunday	Parking violation, Expired registration, DUI
Monday	Over-speeding, Stop sign violation, Parking violation
Tuesday	Parking violation, Expired registration, Illegal right-turn
Wednesday	DUI, Over-speeding
Thursday	Over-speeding, Stop sign violation, Parking violation
Friday	Stop sign violation, Parking violation
Saturday	Over-speeding, Expired registration
Sunday	Illegal right-turn, Stop sign violation
Monday	DUI, Over-speeding, Stop sign violation
Tuesday	Over-speeding, Stop sign violation
Wednesday	Over-speeding, Parking violation
Thursday	Parking violation, Expired registration
Friday	Over-speeding, Expired registration
Saturday	Over-speeding, DUI
Sunday	Parking violation, Stop sign violation
Monday	Stop sign violation, Over-speeding, Expired registration
Tuesday	Illegal right-turn, Stop sign violation
Wednesday	Over-speeding, Expired registration, DUI
Thursday	Over-speeding, Stop sign violation, Parking violation
Friday	Parking violation, Expired registration
Saturday	Over-speeding, Stop sign violation

5.   An airline company received the following complaints from customers who flew in its flights last year.

Type of Complaints	Number of Complaints
Lost / Damaged Luggage	51
Flight Cancellations	69
Poor Customer Service at the Gate	60
Rude Flight Attendants	45
Overbooked Flights	133
Cost	197
Arrival/Departure Delays	245
Security Checks	156
In-Flight Meal Service	44
Total	1000

a.   Construct a Pareto chart summarizing these complaints.

b.   If you are responsible for managing the customer complaints for this airline, what are the two predominant issues that you would address to improve customer service?

6.   A national pizza chain guarantees delivery of pizza orders within 20 minutes from the time of accepting an order; otherwise, the customer gets the pizza free of charge. Assume that actual delivery times in minutes for a random sample of seven customer orders were: 18, 17, 19, 20, 15, 25, and 30. Given this information,

a.   How would you define variation in the pizza delivery process?

b.   In the random sample of seven customers, how many customers got a free pizza?

c.   What is the accuracy rate of this current delivery process?

d.   If this pizza chain wants to be called a Six Sigma operation, what percentage of deliveries should it complete within 20 minutes from the time of accepting an order?

7.   The specifications for the diameter of a motor shaft are between 2.3 inches and 2.5 inches. Any motor shaft that falls outside of these limits is considered to be defective. The average diameters of motor shafts produced by a production process over a 24-hour period are given in the following table. Prepare a run chart, and state your conclusions:

Time	Diameter (in inches)	Time	Diameter (in inches)
8:00 AM	2.36	8:00 PM	2.42
9:00 AM	2.34	9:00 PM	2.38
10.00 AM	2.37	10:00 PM	2.41
11:00 AM	2.37	11:00 PM	2.40
12 PM	2.35	12 AM	2.39
1:00 PM	2.32	1:00 AM	2.36
2:00 PM	2.34	2:00 AM	2.35
3:00 PM	2.35	3:00 AM	2.35
4:00 PM	2.45	4:00 AM	2.37
5:00 PM	2.46	5:00 AM	2.37
6:00 PM	2.48	6:00 AM	2.38
7:00 PM	2.40	7:00 AM	2.39

8.   The Illinois Department of Transportation has the following set of data on age of drivers and accident rates. Draw a scatter diagram for this data to determine the apparent relationship (if any) between the two variables and explain in your own words the nature of the relationship. To draw the scatter diagram, put one variable on the horizontal axis and the other variable on the vertical axis:

Age	25	31	23	24	30	33	27	36	57	38	46	54	28	19
Accident rate	6	3	9	8	4	3	5	2	1	2	2	1	5	11

9.   Prepare a process flowchart for actions to be taken in an academic dishonest process. Your process flowchart should include the following items: cheating/plagiarism is suspected; the professor communicates that no action is required; the professor decides whether a violation has occurred;

the professor meets with the student suspected of a violation; the professor checks the college records for prior violations by the student; if the student has a prior record, the professor communicates with the academic integrity board; if no prior record exists, the professor gets approval from the department chair for a penalty; a hearing is held before the academic integrity board; the professor communicates the penalty imposed with the student; the student accepts or appeals the penalty decision; the student accepts the decision of the academic integrity board; the case is closed.

10. The mythical Prime Meridian Hotel has been receiving an unusually large number of complaints from customers staying overnight in the hotel in the past month. Prepare a cause-and-effect diagram for this problem.

11. The fictional Zantec Tool Company manufactures metal washers used as locking devices. One of the parameters that determine the quality of a washer is its diameter. The company's manufacturing process used to produce the washers has a mean of 50 millimeters with a standard deviation of 1 millimeter. The company monitors the production process every hour by measuring the average diameter of the washers using a sample size of 25.

    a. Construct a mean chart for this process using 3σ control limits.

    b. During a 10-hour operation of this process, the washers had the following average diameters (in mms): 50.3, 49.9, 50.2, 49.7, 51.0, 49.5, 49.8, 50.3, 50.6, and 49.8. Is the process in control?

12. Orion Inc., a fictional company, produces automotive parts, accessories, batteries, and maintenance items for a variety of vehicles, including cars and vans. Orders for the company's products are shipped from distribution centers located in various regions using trucks. One of the measures that the company uses to monitor the performance of its supply chain is its ability to get the orders to its customer on time. The order-fulfillment time is the time it takes for the company to deliver an order after it receives it. To ensure this quality measure is being met, the distribution centers are required to collect sample data every month. The following table presents one such sample set of data of order-fulfillment lead times in days for 20 samples of six orders each:

Sample	Fulfillment Time (in days)	Sample	Fulfillment Time (in days)
1	1.0, 2.0, 1.5, 1.8, 2.1, 0.5	11	2.7, 2.4, 1.8, 1.2, 2.4, 1.6
2	1.7, 2.3, 1.9, 1.1, 2.3, 1.5	12	2.5, 1.9, 2.9, 3.1, 1.4, 2.1
3	1.2, 2.0, 1.9, 2.1, 2.5, 1.8	13	1.0, 2.2, 1.2, 0.5, 2.7, 3.1
4	2.5, 1.3, 2.9, 3.1, 2.4, 3.5	14	1.4, 2.3, 2.5, 0.8, 2.1, 1.6
5	2.0, 1.1, 2.2, 0.7, 2.0, 3.0	15	3.5, 1.0, 1.8, 1.8, 2.7, 1.6
6	1.5, 2.0, 1.5, 1.8, 2.7, 0.6	16	2.0, 1.7, 1.9, 2.1, 2.4, 1.5
7	2.1, 1.8, 2.4, 3.0, 1.4, 2.5	17	2.0, 1.0, 2.4, 1.1, 2.7, 2.5
8	0.5, 1.0, 2.0, 3.0, 2.7, 0.9	18	1.1, 2.3, 2.4, 1.7, 2.4, 0.5
9	3.5, 1.7, 1.9, 2.6,1.4, 2.5	19	1.4, 2.3, 1.9, 2.1, 3.4, 2.5
10	1.5, 0.3, 1.9, 2.7, 2.0, 1.1	20	1.9, 2.7, 0.9, 1.1, 2.5, 0.8

    Construct a mean and a range chart for this process using 3σ control limits and determine whether it is in control.

13. Madan Lal & Sons is a fictional Indian manufacturer of high-quality cricket balls. The balls are 100% handmade and consist of high-quality leather and other materials. To maintain its reputation as a high-quality producer, the company has strict quality control standards. The weight of a cricket ball has a huge impact on its quality. Typically, a ball weighs between 156 grams and 163 grams. Every day the company weighs a sample of five balls produced that day and records their weights. The following table shows the weights of the balls sampled during a 20-day period:

Sample	Weight (in grams)	Sample	Weight (in grams)
1	155.3, 156.0, 160.1, 154.9, 158.7	11	154.9, 155.8, 160.7, 155.9, 158.1
2	155.0, 156.9, 162.1, 159.9, 157.7	12	156.3, 157.0, 158.1, 159.9, 162.7
3	161.3, 159.0, 158.6, 164.2, 160.5	13	164.3, 162.8, 158.1, 156.4, 157.7
4	165.3, 164.0, 160.9, 161.9, 159.7	14	158.3, 157.4, 162.4, 163.1, 156.4
5	160.0, 158.0, 164.1, 158.9, 157.7	15	165.3, 159.4, 159.1, 162.5, 163.5
6	155.8, 157.5, 159.1, 157.9, 160.3	16	161.3, 159.1, 161.1, 153.9, 154.9
7	158.4, 153.0, 157.1, 158.2, 156.5	17	156.7, 162.0, 154.1, 157.9, 166.7
8	160.0, 155.5, 162.7, 161.5, 156.2	18	159.3, 164.5, 162.8, 156.3, 158.0
9	157.8, 159.0, 163.3, 158.9, 156.7	19	165.3, 159.5, 162.8, 157.9, 163.7
10	165.7, 162.9, 156.1, 159.9, 163.7	20	158.0, 156.7, 160.8, 157.9, 160.3

    a. Design a mean and a range chart for the cricket-ball production process using 3σ control limits.

    b. For the month of May, the company recorded the following 10 sample means and sample ranges.
       Sample means: 158.3, 164.0, 158.3, 159.0, 161.5, 157.8, 160.3, 155.9, 163.1, and 158.6.
       Sample ranges: 4.1, 6.3, 5.4, 5.9, 6.1, 6.4, 6.6, 6.7, 6.9, and 7.0.
       Was the process in control during the month of May?

    c. How would increasing the sample size from five to 20 affect the control chart? Would it change your conclusion in part b?

14. Spencer's Food Mart (Spencer, OK) monitors its customers' checkout times using mean and range charts. Eight samples of $n = 20$ checkout time observations (in minutes) were collected, and the following sample means and corresponding sample ranges were calculated:

    Sample means: 4.06, 5.1, 3.75, 6.3, 5.8, 4.7, 3.9, and 5.0.

    Sample ranges: 0.7, 1.0, 0.5, 1.3, 0.9, 0.6, 0.4, and 0.9.

    a. Construct a mean chart and a range chart for the checkout time process using 3σ control limits.
    b. The following sample means and sample ranges were observed on a particular day:
       Sample means: 4.1, 6.0, 4.25, 5.7, 4.9, 5.2, 4.5, and 5.8.
       Sample ranges: 0.8, 1.2, 0.5, 0.3, 0.4, 0.9, 0.7, and 1.9.

    Is this process in control?

15. Quasar Exports Ltd, a fictional Turkish manufacturer of glass, wants to use a c-chart to monitor the number of defects in the sheets of glass it produces. The company wants to use the chart to address the production problems it is experiencing and use it on an ongoing basis as a monitoring tool. To construct the chart, the company collected data over 5 days by inspecting 30 sheets of glass and recording the number defects per sheet. The data are as follows:

Sample	Defects per Sheet	Sample	Defects per Sheet	Sample	Defects per Sheet
1	7	11	5	21	8
2	11	12	8	22	12
3	5	13	1	23	7
4	12	14	11	24	4
5	3	15	14	25	9
6	14	16	8	26	3
7	6	17	9	27	13
8	8	18	5	28	5
9	10	19	3	29	9
10	9	20	4	30	4

    a. Why did the company choose a c-chart to monitor this process?
    b. Using the data in the table, construct a c-chart using 3σ control limits.
    c. After making quality improvements to the process and concluding that it is in control in the current week, the quality control manager of Quasar collected data on the number of defects per sheet for the following week using 20 glass sheets. The defects per sheet were as follows: 2, 7, 4, 5, 6, 4, 8, 1, 5, 3, 4, 4, 7, 2, 8, 3, 5, 6, 4, and 3.
       Plot the data on the c-chart, and determine whether the process is in control.

16. Trinity Hospital in the Philippines has been experiencing an increase in the errors related to the medication administered to patients. Over the course of 30 days, the hospital collected the following data on the number of medication errors per day:

Sample	Errors per Day	Sample	Errors per Day	Sample	Errors per Day
1	5	11	2	21	2
2	1	12	4	22	1
3	7	13	7	23	6
4	10	14	10	24	5
5	9	15	4	25	4
6	5	16	6	26	3
7	3	17	5	27	5
8	2	18	9	28	8
9	1	19	7	29	9
10	9	20	6	30	2

    a. What control chart would you use to monitor this process? Why?
    b. Construct the appropriate control chart for this process using 3σ control limits.
    c. Plot the data and determine whether the process is in control.

17. A logistics company supplies electronic parts to various retail stores daily. The company uses late deliveries as a metric to track its supply chain performance. Any order that is not delivered on the same day is considered late. The numbers of late deliveries for each of the past 20 days are as follows:

Sample	Late Deliveries per Day	Sample	Late Deliveries per Day
1	7	11	3
2	12	12	5
3	5	13	3
4	11	14	13
5	6	15	8
6	8	16	7
7	5	17	4
8	3	18	10
9	4	19	6
10	7	20	9

Construct a c-chart for this process using 3σ control limits and determine whether the process was ever out of control.

18. Omega Electronics (Jaipur, India) mass produces monitors that are used for medical imaging technology. To monitor the quality of the production process, the company draws samples of 100 tubes each, inspects them, and then classifies them into good or bad units. The inspection data for 15 days of production is shown in the following table. Construct a p-chart with 3σ control limits, and determine whether the process is in control:

Sample	1	2	3	4	5	6	7	8	9	10	11	12	13	14	15
Number of Defective Units	11	12	10	9	5	7	3	8	4	8	5	7	6	8	4

19. The Trinity Hospital Quality Improvement (QI) team wants to monitor the C-section deliveries of pregnant mothers admitted to the hospital's obstetrics unit. The team decided to construct a p-chart using 2σ control limits and collected the following data for the past 24 weeks:

Week	Pregnant Mothers Admitted	No. of C-Section Deliveries	Week	Pregnant Mothers Admitted	No. of C-Section Deliveries
1	64	14	13	44	8
2	85	16	14	25	2
3	72	12	15	64	7
4	50	12	16	52	8
5	77	8	17	48	9
6	42	7	18	38	10
7	51	12	19	54	6
8	92	16	20	25	5
9	37	5	21	65	7
10	87	10	22	54	11
11	46	6	23	77	13
12	54	16	24	62	6

a. Why did the QI team decide to use a p-chart?
b. Construct a p-chart using the data given in the table.
c. Determine whether the process is in control, as the hospital is worried that too many C-sections are being performed to the detriment of patients?

20. Erie Furniture Store, a fictional company, buys chests of drawers made out of teakwood. One of the features that determines whether a chest of drawers is of good quality is the presence or absence of dust panels (thin sheets of wood) between the drawers in the body of a chest or desk. These panels make the products structurally stronger and also keep dust away from the contents inside of the drawers. To monitor the quality of the Brazilian firm that supplies the chests, Erie Furniture collected the following data on the number of chests with missing dust panels. The data were gathered over the course of 15 months, and each sample collected contained 100 chests:

Sample	1	2	3	4	5	6	7	8	9	10	11	12	13	14	15
Number of defective units	10	8	7	8	5	6	9	11	6	8	4	9	3	5	8

Construct a p-chart with 3 sigma limits, and determine whether the process is in control.

21. A courier company guarantees its customers that the average time to pick up their packages is 20 minutes with a tolerance of ± 6 minutes. The company collected data on 30 actual arrival times and determined that the standard deviation of this sample was 5 minutes. Compute the C_p and C_{pk} and determine whether this process is capable.

22. The diameter of a motor shaft has the following specifications in millimeters: 120 ± 10. The manufacturing process used to produce these shafts is normally distributed, and control charts show it to be in control. To determine whether this process is capable, a quality control manager collected a random sample of 30 shafts and determined that the process diameter had a sample standard deviation of 2.5 millimeters. Compute the C_p and C_{pk} values, and determine whether this process is capable.

23. The fictional Patient Transport Co.'s target time to get customers to hospitals is 16 minutes. To evaluate whether it is reaching that target, for 20 consecutive days, the firm tracked patients' actual times to the hospital using sample sizes of n = 5 each day. Using the sample data, the company estimated the mean of the process to be $\bar{X}$ = 19.8 minutes and the standard deviation to be s = 8.5 minutes. Assume that the process is normally distributed and that the mean and range charts for it indicate it is in control. Using the Taguchi-loss function, comment on the efficiency of the process and make specific recommendations for its improvement.

24. Refer to problem 23. In addition to the information provided in the problem, Patient Transport Co. has also specified an upper tolerance limit of 20 minutes for its transportation time.

    a. Is the company achieving Six Sigma–level quality?
    b. If not, how should it do so?

25. Elite Auto Service Station services different makes and models of cars and SUVs. The auto station, to determine the quality of service it provides, conducts a weekly survey of five of its customers. The survey is a 100-point customer satisfaction rating instrument where a perfect score of 100 denotes that the customer is completely satisfied. The following table provides the results of the survey that the auto service station conducted over the past 12 weeks:

Week	Customer Rating Score				
1	90	96	88	80	92
2	100	94	82	87	94
3	97	99	78	85	90
4	60	88	91	93	94
5	89	95	90	84	78
6	98	90	100	92	84
7	80	98	86	88	96
8	92	74	89	93	82
9	88	97	85	90	86
10	93	87	95	97	90
11	74	82	83	79	92
12	81	89	99	83	94

    a. Construct a mean and a range chart to monitor customer satisfaction at the auto service station using 3σ control limits.
    b. Determine whether the manager of this service station is capable of achieving a customer rating score between 90 and 96.

26. Crescent Manufacturing, a fictional firm, produces camshafts used in automobiles. A lathing machine is used in the cutting process of producing the camshafts. The production manager of the company uses X-bar and R control charts to monitor the variation in the cutting process. When a shift towards a control limit is detected, he finds that the cutting tool is wearing and so replaces it, bringing the process back into control. The cutting tool wears at the rate of 0.003 centimeters per piece. The cutting process is normally distributed and has a process standard deviation (σ). Specifications for the camshaft diameter are between 10 centimeters and 10.2 centimeters. Both the lower and upper specifications include a 3σ cushion to minimize the risk of production output falling outside of specifications. Determine the number of camshafts that this process can turnout before replacement of the cutting tool becomes necessary.

27. A hospital administrator wants to monitor the quality of service that the patients receive at his hospital. To facilitate this process, 50 patients are asked to complete weekly patient feedback forms. The completed forms typically contain one or more critical complaints about the hospital's service. The following table shows the number of critical patient complaints each week for a 15-week duration:

Week	1	2	3	4	5	6	7	8	9	10	11	12	13	14	15
Critical Complaints	5	3	2	7	10	8	4	9	1	12	6	3	8	11	7

Construct a control chart to monitor patient satisfaction at the hospital using 3σ control limits. Is the process in control?

28. A glass manufacturer wants to measure flaws in sheets of float glass produced using control charts. The company would like to address problems that the chart highlights until the process becomes stable, then use the chart as an ongoing quality monitoring tool. The company has given you the following data on the number of flaws per sheet of float glass for the past 19 days of production:

Day	1	2	3	4	5	6	7	8	9	10	11	12	13	14	15	16	17	18	19
Flaws	3	11	8	5	10	2	1	0	8	5	4	13	9	7	2	3	14	2	1

a. What control chart would you use to monitor this process and why?
b. Using 3σ limits, construct the appropriate control chart for this process.
c. Plot the data given, and determine whether the float glass production is in control.

29. The following table provides results of DNA samples taken over the past 15 days using a sample size of 100:

Day	1	2	3	4	5	6	7	8	9	11	12	13	14
Defects	8	7	7	10	6	7	0	9	8	2	1	0	3

a. Using this information, construct a 3-sigma *p*-control chart.
b. The following defects were observed on the next 5 days: 11, 4, 12, 6, and 13. Is the process in control?

30. A company that manufactures hydraulic pumps buys valves from a supplier in China. The Chinese supplier has submitted the company with a new valve and claims that it will improve the efficiency of the company's manufacturing process. The Chinese supplier claims that the process producing the valve has a mean of 10 mm and standard deviation of 0.05 mm. The company desires a μ = 10mm and a σ = 0.055. What is the C_{pk} of this valve?

CASE STUDY 6.1 J.D. POWER AUTOMOBILE SURVEYS: WHAT DOES "QUALITY" MEAN, ANYWAY?

Americans, it was once said, have a love affair with the automobile. In fact, it isn't just Americans who are automobile enthusiasts anymore; car ownership around the planet has grown dramatically since the turn of the millennium, as more families find themselves with sufficient income to afford a car. One long-standing question that concerns us as consumers is the quality of the car we are considering to purchase. A host of consumer organizations and industry groups, like Consumers Union (Yonkers, NY) or J.D. Power and Associates (S&P Global Inc., New York City, NY) surveys, serve as a means by which we can seek third-party information on the quality of cars, track trends in cars, and identify potential trouble before spending thousands of dollars on a new purchase.

One of the problems with assessing automobile quality is finding a reasonable definition of what "quality" is intended to mean, especially for rating organizations. For example, J.D. Power and Associates publishes an annual quality assessment guide, the Initial Quality Study (IQS), based on the response to its surveys by new car owners. One interesting feature of these surveys has been the sometimes dramatic upward or downward movement of automobile manufacturers in these surveys, sometimes from one year to the next. For example, from 2014 to 2015, industry data on Lexus's quality dropped them six places, from third to ninth overall. Audi dropped from 11th to 16th, whereas Kia rose from seventh to second. Does quality really change that quickly or, to put it another way, have Lexus and Audi cars' quality demonstrated that level of quality drop-off in just one year?

One potential problem is that most people conflate high quality with a lack of defects. On the other hand, if we adopt Webster's definition of quality as "the degree of excellence which a thing possesses," we may start to understand part of the problem with measuring new car quality. J.D. Power's surveys take this broader approach to quality. The IQS was designed to capture a vehicle's defects, which could be either a fault in the assembly of the vehicle or a design issue. A fault might include a loose electrical cable or a

non-working light switch. A design issue is usually something the car's owner doesn't like based on his or her personal preference—for example, an overly complicated radio or hard-to-read display system.

When quality surveys measure both faults and design problems, consumers run the risk of misunderstanding how quality should be measured. Is a leaking sunroof of the same poor quality as a confusing navigation system? It may be the case that, to recall the old adage, one should never buy the first year introduction of a new car until all the bugs have been ironed out. Certainly, evidence suggests that the more new car models a manufacturer introduces in one year, the lower its rating on quality surveys like the IQS administered by J.D. Power. Nevertheless, it is important for people who are considering the purchase of a new car to carefully distinguish what "quality" means to them: Is the absence of defects more important than the concern for design issues? Are design issues more critical? In an age when the search for quality drives consumers' attitudes and behaviors, for auto companies to be competitive, it never hurts to recognize what "quality" means to prospective buyers.[5]

Questions

1. Think of a car that you would automatically rank of high quality. What are the features the car possesses or the image it conveys that would suggest it was of high quality?

2. Contrast your rating of a high-quality car with one you would rank "low quality." What are the reasons you rank one high and the other low quality?

3. What role does car price have in our quality assessment? Can you think of a low or moderately priced car that you would consider high quality? Why?

VIDEO CASE

Watch this video case to learn more about how Beefsteak, a restaurant in Washington, D. C., measures and evaluates the effectiveness of their products to ensure consistent, high-quality dishes.

CRITICAL THINKING EXERCISES ....

The purpose of the following exercises is three-fold. First, they are intended to make the students learn in-depth about process capability analysis. Second, they are intended to make the students become aware that quality control is a key area where ethical violations can occur, and to force them to think about approaches that can be used to prevent such unethical behavior. Third, students are forced to think about applying Taguchi methods to systems other than manufacturing.

1. When analyzing the capability of a process, you find that the value of C_p is greater than 1, but the value of C_{pk} is less than 1. Is this process capable? If not, what steps should you take to correct the problem?

2. Use some examples to discuss some of the areas in quality control that have the potential for unethical behavior. What steps would you take to prevent such behavior?

3. Apply the Taguchi-loss function to an Information System.

4. Please read the following mini-case studies and answer the questions that follow:

The Taguchi-loss function argues that a system should have a minimum loss to society over its entire lifecycle. Suppose you were asked to lead a team designing a new patient registration system for your hospital and you wanted to ensure quality standards for the system. How might Taguchi's methods help you with your planning and decision making? In other words, where would you focus your efforts to minimize costs of the new system?

For example, suppose you had identified a variety of costs of the new system, including costs related to:

1. Planning and designing the system. There are a number of potential costs to consider related to designing a system.

    a. Non-conformance costs: under-designing a system so it doesn't perform all the activities necessary or over-designing the system to include features that your staff don't need or will not use.

    b. Cost of lost opportunities: loss of benefits as a result of a system that does not provide its users or customers with needed information.

2. Warranties: Warranties are security protection to ensure that sensitive patient information is kept confidential. Consider the costs of creating a patient registration system that could accidentally leak critical insurance or medical history information.

3. Maintenance and support costs: What will the costs to the hospital be in the case where the system is prone to breakdowns or needs to be constantly monitored (personnel costs for continuous monitoring)?

4. Disposal, upgrade, and replacement costs: Your team needs to consider whether there will be disposal costs associated with replacing old equipment (what about environmental costs of this disposal?) or upgrade costs, including downtime, while all the hospital's systems are linked to the new patient registration system?[6]

Questions

1. Referring back to the principles behind the Taguchi-loss function, what are some strategies your team can adopt to minimize costs associated with each of these four elements in the new information system implementation?

    a. Strategies for minimizing planning and design costs.
    b. Strategies for minimizing warranty costs.
    c. Strategies for minimizing maintenance and support costs.
    d. Strategies for minimizing disposal, upgrade, and replacement costs.

2. Suppose you were to apply a similar approach to improving food service at a local restaurant. Using the principles behind the Taguchi-loss function, what are some strategies your team can adopt to identify and minimize costs associated with some of the critical cost centers you identified in the restaurants operations?

CHAPTER
7

Capacity Planning

LEARNING OBJECTIVES

After studying this chapter, you should be able to:

1. Explain why capacity planning is important and how capacity decisions are made.

2. Evaluate the difficulties associated with capacity planning for services, and explain how they can be overcome.

3. Describe the challenges of planning for capacity in supply chains, and explain what supply chain partners can do to improve their joint capacity planning.

4. Predict the effect of sustainability and ethics on the future capacity decisions of firms and supply chains.

5. Identify the challenges in developing a global capacity planning strategy, including the opportunities and threats in the global arena.

OPERATIONS PROFILE: Missoni for Target: Too Popular, Too Soon

Reuters / Alamy Stock Photo

"Woof! We are suddenly extremely popular. You may not be able to access our site momentarily due to unusually high traffic. Please stay here and we'll try to get you in as soon as we can!"

With this message posted to its website in 2011, Target (Target Corporation, Minneapolis, MN) acknowledged what crowds of shoppers had discovered the previous day: Target completely underestimated how popular one of its hottest promotions, a new partnership with Italian fashion house Missoni (Varese, Italy), would be. Missoni's clothing usually costs in the hundreds or thousands of dollars, but it had designed several cheaper items for Target, such as a US$40 skirt and a US$600 patio set. Although the collection, consisting of some 400 pieces including apparel, accessories, and housewares, was supposed to be available in stores and online for six weeks, the demand was so great that Target's website was swamped, and the company quickly ran out of stock. The rush was not confined to their online shopping site either. In New York City, Target's East Harlem store was stripped of merchandise in 15 minutes, and the collection sold out at the retailer's Atlantic Avenue location in Brooklyn in about 10 minutes. Those early-bird shoppers lucky enough to make their Missoni purchases immediately began listing their finds online at above-retail prices. By the next afternoon, eBay Inc. (San Jose, CA) had 27,870 Missoni for Target items listed, up from 1,473 just 24 hours before. A navy maxi dress went for US$202.50 with 13 bids. Its retail price: US$64.99.

Limited partnerships such as this one, in which high-end designers create cheaper versions of their fashions for lower end stores, have become popular because they appeal to cost-conscious customers who want to be stylish but can't afford designer prices. Target, in particular, has become known for creating buzz around its limited partnerships with designers and fashion brands, including partnerships with Liberty Ltd. (London, U.K.) and Neiman Marcus (Dallas, TX). In 2010, Target offered 300 items with Liberty, which is known for its floral prints, and sold out of most merchandise in a couple of days. Although the company began replenishing some merchandise over the next few days, it only trickled in at a rate that did not meet the demand.

Master the content.

edge.sagepub.com
/venkataraman

 SAGE edge™

During the promotion with Missoni, the real beneficiaries may have been the lucky shoppers able to get through on the website. Many buyers who purchased the products listed them on eBay for more than double the price. "It's a little bit embarrassing for one of the nation's largest retailers to have a Web site that can't support a rush—it's not like they're any strangers to rushes," said Ian Schafer, chief executive of the digital marketing firm Deep Focus, Inc. (New York, NY). "It's saying, 'We're so popular we had to turn people away at the door.' Then get a bigger place."[1]

7.1 Capacity Planning

7.1 Explain why capacity planning is important and how capacity decisions are made.

Suppose your firm, which produces the jerseys of players for the National Basketball Association (NBA), experienced a banner year in 2016. Because of the fan enthusiasm that followed the strong and unexpected performance of the Golden State Warriors' player Stephen Curry, you anticipate a major spike in the demand for his jerseys in 2017. Does your company have the capacity to meet this sizable increase in demand, or are you about to lose a significant portion of Stephen Curry fans to the competition? The answer to these questions depends on capacity planning—how well your company planned to meet the future demand for your products and services.

Capacity planning is a key strategy for operations and their supply chains. In the context of operations, capacity is the maximum amount of output an operation is capable of producing in a given time period. Capacity planning is the process of determining the capacity that an operations system will need to meet this demand effectively. All operations and supply chain managers face uncertainty in projecting the demand for their products and services. Moreover, there is always a gap between the capacity available in the system and the capacity that is required to meet demand. Such a gap can lead to inefficiency, either in the form of idle or underused resources or unhappy customers whose demands were not met. The goal of capacity planning is to minimize this gap.

As Table 7.1 shows, capacity planning can be done over different time horizons. Long-term capacity planning or strategic capacity planning requires managers to forecast demand over several years and look at demand and growth trends as well as at cyclical demand patterns. Deciding to expand, contract, or change facilities in the long term is an example of strategic capacity planning, and it is closely related to decisions about facilities location. These decisions generally involve huge capital expenditures. Once they are made, they cannot be easily undone, so careful planning is necessary. Medium- and short-term capacity planning requires managers to forecast variations such as seasonal changes in demand.

Rough-cut capacity planning and capacity requirements planning (CRP) are part of medium-term capacity planning. Rough-cut capacity planning (RCCP) is a rough check of production plans and schedules to determine whether the required capacity and available capacity are in balance. The check takes into account the amount of labor, machinery, storage space, and the capacity of your suppliers. Capacity requirements planning (CRP), which follows RCCP, is the process of doing a more detailed comparison of the available capacity and required capacity by projecting your resource requirements for labor, equipment, and so forth.

If available capacity is insufficient in the medium term, a firm might hire more workers, ask them to work overtime, or use a subcontractor. Capacity planning in the short term, often referred to as

Capacity: the maximum amount of output an operation is capable of producing in a given time period

Capacity planning: the process of determining the capacity that an operations system will need to meet this demand effectively

Strategic capacity planning: the process of forecasting demand over several years and looking at demand and growth trends as well as at cyclical demand patterns

Rough-cut capacity planning (RCCP): the process of doing a rough check of production plans and schedules to determine whether the required capacity and the available capacity are in balance

Capacity requirements planning (CRP): the process of doing a more detailed comparison of the available capacity and the required capacity by projecting your resource requirements for labor, equipment, and so forth

TABLE 7.1: Capacity Planning Levels

CAPACITY PLANNING HORIZON	CRITICAL ISSUES
Long term	Strategic ventures Building new facilities Purchasing new equipment
Medium term	Rough-cut Analyzing capacity versus monthly production plans Hiring workers, operating multiple shifts Working overtime Contracting
Short term	Capacity control Analyzing weekly schedules and bottlenecks Balancing the workload

FIGURE 7.1: A Bottleneck

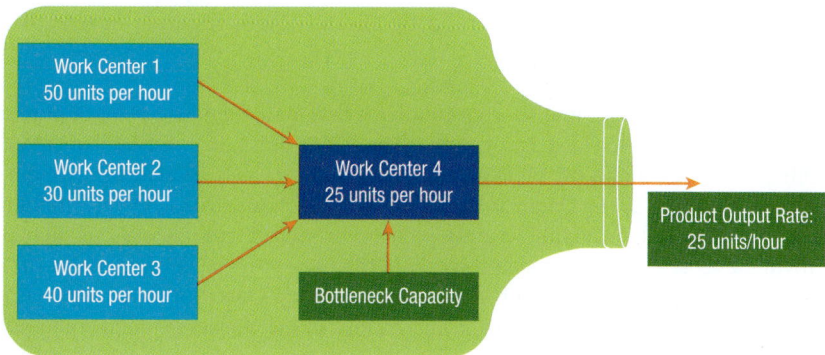

Work Center 1
50 units per hour

Work Center 2
30 units per hour

Work Center 4
25 units per hour

Work Center 3
40 units per hour

Bottleneck Capacity

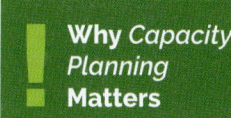

Product Output Rate:
25 units/hour

capacity control, involves analyzing a facility's existing capacity relative to its weekly production schedules. The purpose of capacity control is to achieve as balanced a workload as possible among the various work centers. A **work center** is part of a production facility where all activities related to a particular phase of the production process (such as assembly, milling, grinding, etc.) are performed. Managers need to be aware of where in the production process the bottleneck capacities are, as well as to manage bottlenecks such that the throughput, or output rate, of the operations system is close to but does not exceed these bottleneck capacities.

A **bottleneck** is a limit or constraint on the workflow in an operation. Consider Figure 7.1. In a production system with four work centers arranged in sequence, the work center with the lowest capacity, at 25 units per hour, is the bottleneck. It does no good to run work centers 1, 2, and 3 at full capacity because work center 4 cannot keep up with the volume produced by the preceding work centers. It is badly overloaded. It can only process 25 units per hour, but it is receiving 120 units from the other workstations. If the capacity of work center 4 can't be increased, the workload on the other three work centers should be balanced such that they also produce only a total of 25 units per hour. If the output of the work centers 1 to 3 isn't synchronized with work center 4, work-in-process inventory in the form of partially completed units will accumulate at the bottleneck.

Managing bottlenecks is typically a short-term capacity planning issue. We will address capacity planning decisions in the medium and short term in Chapters 18S and 19. We will also discuss the topic of constraint management later. In this chapter, our discussion will focus on long-term or strategic capacity planning.

The Strategic Importance of Capacity Decisions

Capacity decisions are strategic for several reasons:

- *Capacity decisions affect an organization's ability to meet future demand.*
  The inability to meet demand can cause great harm to a company and even to the general public. The pharmaceutical industry has been facing drug shortages as a result of the increasing demand for many specialty drugs, such as those used in chemotherapy. Nevertheless, there has been a general failure to increase the manufacturing capacity for these drugs because they are less profitable than other drugs. As a result, there is a real danger that cancer patients will lack effective treatment.[2]
- *Capacity decisions have an impact on operating costs.*
  If available capacity is insufficient to meet future demand, companies may have to use supplemental resources such as overtime, contract workers, and additional shifts. These alternatives increase operating costs substantially because they are more costly than typical production inputs.
- *Capacity decisions can require a major capital investment.*
  Long-term capacity planning decisions such as the purchase of a new machine or construction of a new facility typically require significant outlays of capital. This initial cost for investing in capacity influences top management decisions. For example, before a nuclear power plant can generate electricity, the utility will require a long-term commitment of resources to build it,

Capacity control: analyzing a facility's existing capacity relative to its weekly production schedules, also called capacity planning in the short term

Work center: a part of a production facility where all activities related to a particular phase of the production process are performed

Bottleneck: a limit or constraint on the workflow in an operation

The Importance of
Capacity Planning

without earning revenue to offset these expenditures. Furthermore, any delays in construction are serious. According to estimates, of the 67 nuclear power plants currently under construction worldwide, at least 49 have experienced significant delays, resulting in tens of billions in additional costs.[3]

- *Capacity decisions can be inflexible.*

  Long-term capacity decisions such as building a new manufacturing plant or purchasing new equipment are inflexible. That is, once these decisions are made and implemented, mistakes are difficult to correct and the plant or equipment cannot easily be changed without incurring substantial costs. In 2016, Qatar Solar Technologies (QSTec, Doha, Qatar) announced completion of a US$1 billion manufacturing plant to produce materials used in solar panels and photovoltaic cells. The plant, which took more than five years to develop and staff, represents a commitment to solar power in a highly volatile industry. Once the investment was made, any changes to the cost of solar products or fluctuations in the market demand could not be easily absorbed.[4]

- *Capacity decisions can be a source of competitive advantage.*

  The firm's ability to respond quickly by altering existing capacity to meet changes in demand can give that company a competitive edge. A company achieves this ability by building a production system with flexible capacity.

- *Globalization adds to the complexity of capacity decisions.*

  With increasing globalization, individual companies have to be concerned not only with their own capacity but also with the capacity of their supply chains. For example, changes in demand for a company that sells its products to several foreign countries forces the company to alter not only its own capacity but also the capacity of its suppliers, distribution centers, and warehouses.

Types of Capacity and Capacity Measurements

Capacity can be measured by using either inputs or outputs. A recycling company, for example, can measure its plant capacity based on inputs, such as the truckloads of material it receives. Similarly, a hospital can measure its capacity based on the number of available beds in a given time period (an input measure). On the other hand, many manufacturing facilities use output to measure capacity. A textile company can measure its capacity based the amount of yarn produced. Similarly, a hospital can measure capacity on the number of patients treated in a given time period (an output measure).

We have so far used anecdotal or theoretical examples of capacity. Companies, however, often find it useful to measure capacity quantitatively to assess its effectiveness and efficiency. **Design capacity** is the maximum rate of output achieved by an operation, a process, or a manufacturing or service facility that is producing under ideal conditions. **Effective capacity** is the capacity that can be achieved given the actual changes in product mixture, machines, and equipment that require periodic maintenance, scheduling changes, and workers who take time off for lunch, absences, and other needs. Effective capacity is typically less than design capacity. The **actual output**, or the actual capacity, rarely exceeds effective capacity. The actual output reflects all production factors, not just regular changes in the production process. These factors include machine breakdowns, unusual material shortages that stall production, and labor shortages and strikes.

Two other measures of capacity performance can be defined using actual output, effective capacity, and design capacity. These measures are capacity efficiency and capacity utilization. **Capacity efficiency** tells us how well the available effective capacity is being used to produce the actual output. It is the percentage of effective capacity used to produce the actual output:

$$\text{Capacity efficiency} = \frac{\text{Actual Output}}{\text{Effective Capacity}} \times 100\%$$

Capacity utilization, by contrast, tells us the extent to which the capacity designed and installed is actually used. It is the percentage of design capacity used to produce the actual output.

$$\text{Capacity utilization} = \frac{\text{Actual Output}}{\text{Design Capacity}} \times 100\%$$

Both measures are expressed as percentages, and both have to be used jointly to track capacity. Using one measure only and ignoring the other can lead to misleading conclusions about capacity performance. The following example demonstrates why.

Design capacity: the maximum rate of output achieved by an operation, a process, or a manufacturing or service facility that is producing under ideal conditions

Effective capacity: the capacity that can be achieved given the actual changes in product mixture, machines, and equipment that require periodic maintenance, scheduling changes, and workers who take time off for lunch, absences, and other needs

Actual output: also called *actual capacity*, the capacity that can be achieved given all production factors, not just regular changes in the production process

Capacity efficiency: a measure of how well the available effective capacity is being used to produce the actual output

Capacity utilization: a measure of the extent to which the capacity designed and installed is actually used

EXAMPLE 7.1: A Kia Service Center has the design capacity to perform an average of 60 repairs per day. Yet, given the complexities of the repairs, shift changes, and worker skill levels, the effective capacity of this repair shop is an average of 40 repairs day. The actual number of repairs that are completed on average is 36 repairs per day. What is the utilization capacity and efficiency capacity of this repair shop?

Example 7.1

$$\text{Capacity efficiency} = \frac{\text{Actual Output}}{\text{Effective Capacity}} \times 100\% = \frac{36}{40} \times 100\% = 90\%$$

$$\text{Capacity utilization} = \frac{\text{Actual Output}}{\text{Design Capacity}} \times 100\% = \frac{36}{60} \times 100\% = 60\%$$

This example demonstrates that whereas the capacity efficiency is high (90%), the extent to which the capacity is being used is only 60%. The remaining 40% of the time there is idle capacity in the system. Similarly, focusing exclusively on the utilization measure of capacity is misleading because there is potential for unnecessary bottlenecks in the system and waste in the form of inventory buildup. Capacity utilization does not take into account capacity that we can realistically achieve from varying worker skill levels, equipment breakdown, and so forth that can cause bottlenecks in the system. Therefore, to improve actual capacity performance, both measures have to increase. The way to improve actual output is by increasing effective capacity because it acts as a constraint on the actual capacity that can be achieved.

Several factors influence effective capacity. Some of these factors include the size and location of facilities, the nature of the product or service, process factors such as quality, complexity of tasks performed by workers, supply chain factors, and so forth. For example, if a company's facilities are located in an area where there is little room for expansion, the firm's effective capacity will be limited. Effective capacity is also limited for firms that manufacture multiple products because they have to retool their assembly lines or substitute different parts when switching from one product to another. In contrast, firms that produce a single highly standardized product, as is the case in sugar and oil refining companies, have a high effective capacity because there is no need to spend time on the retooling equipment and substitution of parts.

Capacity gap: the difference between the capacity required and capacity available

Leading strategy: the process of increasing capacity in anticipation of future increases in demand for products or services

Strategies for Capacity Planning

In capacity planning, three fundamental questions must be addressed by the operations and supply chain staff:

- *When is capacity needed?* This depends on whether the company is planning for capacity for the long term, intermediate, or short term and on the life-cycle stages of products.
- *What kind of capacity is needed?* The kind of capacity needed may be new facilities, new equipment, or operating a second shift or using overtime. Long-term capacity planning decisions typically involve acquiring new facilities, whereas short-term capacity decisions often involve use of overtime or a second shift. The type of capacity needed also depends on the kinds of products the company produces and their life-cycle stages. When a product is in the introductory stages of its life cycle, acquiring new production capacity for it is typical. During the decline stage, the firm lowers its capacity so it doesn't end up with a lot of useless equipment when the product is discontinued.
- *How much capacity is needed?* This question addresses the issue of the capacity gap—the difference between the capacity required and the capacity available.

Example 7.1 illustrates how a service center can calculate their utilization capacity and efficiency capacity.

©iStockphoto.com/SusanChiang

Companies can choose from three strategies for capacity planning. A leading strategy is the most aggressive of the three. Companies that pursue this strategy increase their capacity in anticipation of future increases in demand for their products or services. Extra capacity such as this is called a **capacity cushion**. For example, Suntech Power Holdings of China (now Wuxi Suntech Power Co., Ltd., Wuxi Jiangsu Province, P.R. China) was the world's largest producer of photovoltaic cells for converting light energy into electricity. In anticipation of America and Europe's continued drive for alternative energy sources, Suntech aggressively expanded plant construction and capacity development worldwide to take advantage of the expected steady growth in the solar power industry.[5] Companies that pursue a leading strategy can lure customers away from competitors that do not have the resources to increase their capacity when demand skyrockets. The big disadvantage of a leading strategy is that if the anticipated demand increases do not occur, then the company is stuck with idle capacity, excess inventory, or both. As an example of this risk, Suntech was forced to declare bankruptcy in 2015 because its anticipated higher demand for photovoltaic cells never materialized. Because of cheaper oil prices and the U.S. government's decision to protect home-grown companies by putting tariffs on Suntech's exports, the company found that it's too-rapid expansion had made it impossible to remain profitable.

When a firm uses a **matching strategy**, it increases its capacity in small increments to keep pace with increases in demand. This strategy can be cumbersome because it requires frequent tinkering and the adding and shifting of capacity. Nonetheless, it incurs less risk than a leading strategy.

The least aggressive strategy is a **lagging strategy**. When a company pursues a lagging strategy, it increases its capacity only when there is a *sizeable* increase in demand. That way the firm doesn't end up with idle capacity or excess inventories if the demand is significantly lower. Yet, if demand increases quickly, the company may lose customers to competitors that pursue leading and matching strategies.

Generally, companies want a greater capacity cushion when the demand for a product is variable but the reward for having the capacity is substantial. For example, the largest oil storage area in the country is in Cushing, Oklahoma. The various storage units there can hold 46.3 million barrels of oil. In the event of an oil crisis and a spike in the price of oil, a firm with a great deal of capacity there can absorb a significant portion of the demand. For products that have stable demand patterns, companies have smaller capacity cushions. Airline companies know that approximately 10% of booked passengers will be no-shows. So to maximize their per-seat profits, the companies routinely overbook their flights (exceed their capacity), knowing that the revenue on extra tickets sold will offset the costs of inconveniencing and rebooking passengers when the firms' capacity forecasts fail.[6]

The Capacity Planning Process

Capacity planning is complicated, and the five-step procedure shown in Figure 7.2 can help managers make capacity planning decisions. Note that the capacity planning process is ongoing and continuous.

Step 1: Determine future capacity requirements.

Because capacity planning requires decisions be made over different time horizons, we need to forecast the demand for our products and services each time period and then convert the forecasts into capacity requirements. Chapter 13 discusses the various methods for forecasting demand.

Step 2: Analyze the available capacity and identify any capacity gaps.

After forecasting the capacity requirements, the next step is to compute accurately the capacity that is currently available. The purpose is to identify the capacity gaps that need to be bridged.

Step 3: Develop capacity alternatives to meet capacity requirements.

When developing capacity alternatives, planners should:

- *Design flexible capacity systems.* Capacity systems should be designed so that they are flexible enough to accommodate future capacity expansions. It is much less costly to expand an existing facility that has extra capacity than it is to close it and relocate it elsewhere. Furthermore, several subsequent operations system design and control decisions such as layout of facilities and equipment selection are impacted by the flexibility of capacity systems.

- *Consider product life-cycle stages.* Capacity requirements are difficult to predict during the introductory stages of a product's life cycle. Hence, the capacity at this stage should be

Capacity cushion: the extra capacity added in anticipation of future increases in demand for products and services

Matching strategy: the process of increasing capacity in small increments to keep pace with increases in demand

Lagging strategy: the process of increasing capacity only when there is a sizeable increase in demand

FIGURE 7.2: Steps in the Capacity Planning Process

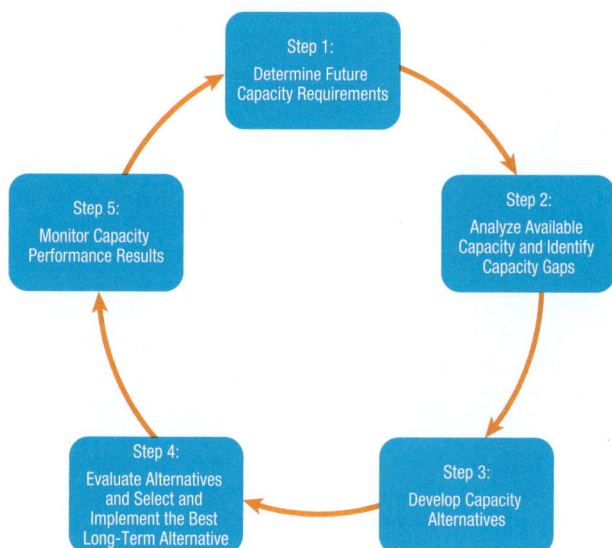

EXAMPLE 7.2: A manufacturing firm is planning to purchase new machines for processing three products that the company manufactures. Demand information and processing time data for the three products are shown in the table. Each machine will be operated 8 hours per day for 300 days per year. How many new machines should the company purchase to meet the capacity requirements?

PRODUCT	ANNUAL DEMAND (IN UNITS)	STANDARD PROCESSING TIME (IN HOURS PER UNIT)	PROCESSING TIME NEEDED (IN HOURS)
A	500	6.0	500 × 6 = 3,000
B	400	8.0	400 × 8 = 3,200
C	800	3.0	800 × 3 = 2,400
Total			8,600

SOLUTION: Because the company operates 8 hours per day for 300 days a year, the total available capacity per machine per year is 300 × 8 = 2,400 hours. Because the total time per year needed to process the three products is 8,600 hours, the number of machines the company should purchase is:

$$\frac{8,600}{2,400} = 3.58 \text{ or } 4 \text{ machines}$$

flexible enough to accommodate changes not only in demand but also in product designs. During the growth stage, increases in demand will require companies to keep pace by increasing their capacity. During the mature stage of a product life cycle, demand tends to be stable and organizations can make full use of their capacity to reduce their costs. Finally, during the decline stage of a product's life cycle, declining demand for the product results in underuse of capacity. At this stage, the company can either dispose of the excess capacity by selling it or introduce new products or services using the existing capacity system.

• *Consider the interrelationships among the components of the capacity system.* A capacity system is a collection of subsystems that are closely interrelated. For example, when building a hospital, managers need to consider the interrelationships among the various units of the facility such as the number of operating rooms, the size of the intensive care unit, and so forth, to determine the number of patient beds. For hospital capacity planning, health-care professionals recognize the need for avoiding bottlenecks, ensuring that patients can move from the

Capacity planning is critical for manufacturers such as Nestlé due to the seasonal variation in demand for its products like chocolate, many of which are perishable.

Bloomberg/Bloomberg/Getty Images

emergency room or the operating room directly to a bed in a recovery unit with no waiting time.[7]

• *Deal with problems resulting from step-by-step increases in capacity.* Companies that attempt to increase their capacity to meet their demand requirements rarely find a perfect match. This is because capacity increases typically do not occur in smooth, step-by-step increments but in large chunks, which can result in idle or underused capacity. Consider this situation to see how a company can adjust its existing capacity to handle an increase in demand. In late December, a Southwest Airlines (Dallas, TX) flight from Chicago to Los Angeles with a capacity of 250 seats is fully booked. There are 100 passengers on the waiting list to board this flight. Southwest Airlines can resolve this capacity problem by adding another flight. Nevertheless, if the company does so, the second flight will have 150 empty seats. One way to fill up the empty seats is for Southwest to schedule the second flight so that it stops in another city, say, Nashville, to pick up Los Angeles–bound passengers.

• *Deal with fluctuations in capacity requirements.* Factors such as the random nature of demand and seasonality, or random events such as inclement weather, can cause fluctuations in capacity requirements. The demand for snow-removal trucks increases in snowy weather. Similarly, companies that manufacture products such as bathing suits, ice cream, and ski equipment experience seasonal demand for them. The problem that these companies face is that their production capacity alternates between underuse and overuse. Adding more snow trucks, for example, will certainly alleviate the problems associated with snowy days, but during warmer weather days, this will result in excess capacity.

Many of Nestlé's (Vevey, Switzerland) food products have seasonal demand. The company experiences high demand for its chocolates mainly during the winter season (during Christmas and Easter holiday seasons), and then demand tapers off during the summer months. Depending on the time of year, Nestlé uses a combination of different capacity plans to adjust to the changes in demand. One plan the company uses is a **level capacity plan**. In this case, the company doesn't ramp up production during the peak season. Instead, it produces the products at a steady rate and then stores them until they are demanded. The advantage of a level capacity plan is that it leads to stable employment, low per-unit costs, and a high rate of capacity utilization. The disadvantage is that inventory builds up during periods of slack demand. Furthermore, a company such as Nestlé that produces perishable goods runs the risk of their spoiling if they remain in inventory for too long.[8]

Level capacity plan: the process of producing products at a steady rate and then storing them until they are demanded

Economies of scale: a decrease in the cost per unit of output as the volume of output increases

Diseconomies of scale: an increase in the volume of output beyond a point at which the cost per unit increases

• *Determine the optimum operating level for each capacity alternative.* Every capacity alternative, whether it is a large, medium, or small plant or equipment, has an optimum production or operating volume level. At the optimum level, the cost per unit of output is the lowest for that capacity alternative. If the output rate of the alternative is less than the optimum level, then increasing it contributes to **economies of scale**. Economies of scale occur when the cost per unit of output decreases as the volume of output increases. Essentially what is happening is that the firm's fixed costs are being spread over a larger number of units produced, thereby reducing the cost of each unit produced. Producing beyond the optimum level causes **diseconomies of scale**. Diseconomies of scale occur when the volume of output increases beyond a point at which the cost per unit increases. This happens because producing more and more output becomes harder and more costly given the firm's limited resources. For example, if employees have to work overtime to produce the extra output, the cost per unit increases. Figure 7.3 illustrates these concepts. The optimal operating level is a function of the amount of capacity a facility's capacity has. For example, as shown in Figure 7.4, larger facilities can achieve higher optimal output rates at a lower minimum cost than can smaller facilities, which have lower optimal output rates but at a higher minimum cost. The optimum operating level and, therefore, the type of capacity to be acquired to a great extent depends on the future demand for a company's products. Yet, it also depends on the company's ability to acquire capital and its choice of the particular capacity planning strategy.

Step 4: Evaluate the alternatives and select and implement the best long-term capacity alternative.

After developing several capacity alternatives, the company has to evaluate them from numerous perspectives. Although cost considerations are used most often, the company should also consider the capacity alternative's useful life, its compatibility with current operations, worker skill levels, and so forth. In addition, a company's management also needs to assess qualitative factors such as sustainability and ethics, the community's attitude toward the location of the alternative, and the impact of adding new capacity. The evaluation could include a breakeven analysis or using linear or integer programming, waiting-line models, simulations, and decision theory techniques. We will discuss some of these techniques in the section on quantitative modules later in the book. Decision trees are a popular tool for evaluating capacity alternatives and are discussed in Module F: Decision Making Tools. The outcome of this step is that the company can select and implement the best capacity alternative.

Step 5: Monitor the capacity's performance results.

The final step is to monitor how well the capacity alternative meets the firm's needs. Figure 7.2 is arranged in a circle to indicate that if demand requirements or market conditions change, then the capacity planning process should start all over again.

FIGURE 7.3: Optimal Capacity and Economies and Diseconomies of Scale

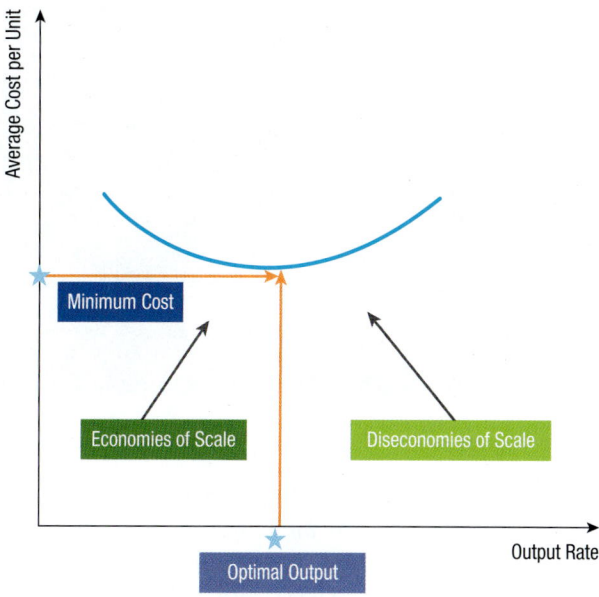

7.2 Service Capacity Planning

Service organizations such as consulting firms, banks, information technology (IT) outsourcing firms, and restaurants face some unique problems when planning their capacity. Services are generally consumed at the time they are produced, and as a result, using inventory to serve as a buffer is not an option when more capacity is needed. Consequently, the capacity of service firms at all times has to be equal to or greater than what is needed to meet demand. Otherwise, the service company runs the risk of alienating or losing the customer. For example, an airline may have 40% of its seats unused for its 7:00 am flight, but its 7:00 pm flight on the same day may be fully sold out. The unused capacity from the earlier flight is lost and cannot be used to cover the passengers on the waiting list for the later flight. Restaurants usually operate at full capacity during breakfast, lunch, and dinner times, but there is idle capacity during the other slack periods of the day. Thus, periodic capacity underuse is inevitable for service firms.

7.2

Evaluate the difficulties associated with capacity planning for services, and explain how they can be overcome.

 Service Planning Capacity

FIGURE 7.4: Optimal Output Levels for Facilities of Different Sizes[9]

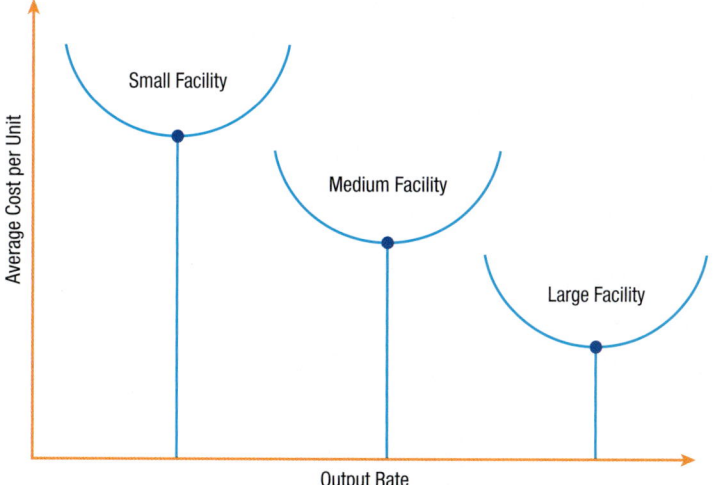

SOURCE: Reid, R. D., & Sanders, N. R. (2015). *Operations management* (5th ed.). New York, NY: Wiley.

It may be difficult for a hotel to determine the demand for their concierge services on a given day. In order to meet this demand, the hotel may opt to staff additional concierges to expand their capacity.

©iStockphoto.com/mmac72

Factors Influencing Service Capacity

There are three critical factors that influence service capacity. These three factors are customer proximity, services capacity, and demand volatility and capacity. We will discuss each of these factors next.

CUSTOMER PROXIMITY

One of the most important order-winning criteria for service firms is customer convenience. Therefore, service firms want to be near, or in close proximity to, their customers. For example, a hotel located in the downtown area of a large city will have good customer proximity. Nonetheless, the service location decision can have a significant impact on the firm's overall capacity. For instance, the hotel may not be able to add capacity by building additional rooms because it might not be possible to expand in a downtown area already crowded with buildings.

SERVICES CAPACITY

As for all businesses, inadequate capacity will inevitably lead to delays in the delivery of a service, resulting in customer dissatisfaction and lost customers. Yet, maintaining a capacity cushion can lead to higher costs. For example, increasing the number of tellers to maintain high service levels in a bank might be necessary for a bank to retain its customers. The capacity will come at a cost in the form of wages paid to those workers during slow periods when they are idle.

DEMAND VOLATILITY AND CAPACITY

The degree of the volatility of the demand for a service can have an impact on capacity planning as well; that is, the number of customers in the service delivery system and the nature of the services they require will influence capacity. For example, on any given day, hospitals experiencing higher demand volumes may have to pay nurses to be on call should they be needed. Likewise, a hotel may experience unexpected demand for its concierge services and need to maintain extra capacity in the form of on-call concierge staff. In short, service delivery firms have to plan for capacity based on *peak* demand levels so that they don't have to turn away customers and have enough capacity to provide critical services.

Capacity Planning for Services

Although there are exceptions, such as airline companies, service firms generally require lower capital investments to satisfy the increased demand of their customers. Many service firms can meet increases in demand (at least initially) by adding more staff. The key capacity planning decisions for service companies are the size of workloads or length of processing times needed to deliver the service.

Regardless of the type of service provided, whether it's installing brakes on a car or preparing a mortgage application in a bank, the key capacity constraint is the amount of time it takes to complete the specific task. All too often, the constraint or bottleneck in service firms is the department that has limited capacity in the form of personnel or resources. For example, consider a software developer trying to schedule capacity across multiple consulting projects. If several of the projects require advanced programming skills and the firm only has one programmer sufficiently trained to perform them, that individual effectively becomes the critical constraint in the system, and all job scheduling has to be done around her availability.[9]

Each service organization is unique. Therefore, there is no one-size-fits-all capacity planning procedure for service firms. Nevertheless, some basic steps, shown in Figure 7.5, should be followed by all service organizations when developing their capacity plans.

Step 1: Determine the service level requirements.

Determining the service level requirements involves determining the processing requirements or workloads, determining a unit for work measurement, and determining the service levels for each workload.

- Determine the processing requirements.

    The first step in the service capacity planning process is to categorize the processing requirements or workloads of each department of the service organization and to quantify customer expectations for that job. This requires determining which employee or department will do the work, the type of work that needs to be done (e.g., processing a loan application or a bank teller processing of cash withdrawal), and how that work will be completed (online or face-to-face). Analyzing workloads by each department of the service firm allows planners to determine performance expectations and service level requirements for each of those departments.

- Determine a unit for work measurement.

  For the purposes of capacity planning, it is useful to define an output as a unit of measurement of work performed. For example, in measuring the work done at a fast food restaurant, the number of customers served or the number of hamburgers prepared can be a more useful measure than using the resources (inputs) needed to accomplish the work, such as the amount of French fries, raw ground beef, or pickle slices used to prepare the food served to customers.

- Determine the service levels for each workload.

  Once the workloads and units to be measured are determined, planners can establish the service levels. A service level is an implicit or explicit agreement between the service provider and the consumer that defines acceptable levels of service. Service levels are often defined from the customer's perspective, typically in terms of response times or waiting times or the number of customers served. Using workloads to establish service levels makes sense because they measure service performance in a way that customers understand. For example, at a Dunkin' Donuts (Canton, MA) drive-through, as soon as an order is received over the intercom, a timer starts by the service window. Dunkin' Donuts employees are expected to process and complete the order within two minutes, the time determined through customer surveys to satisfy their expectations.

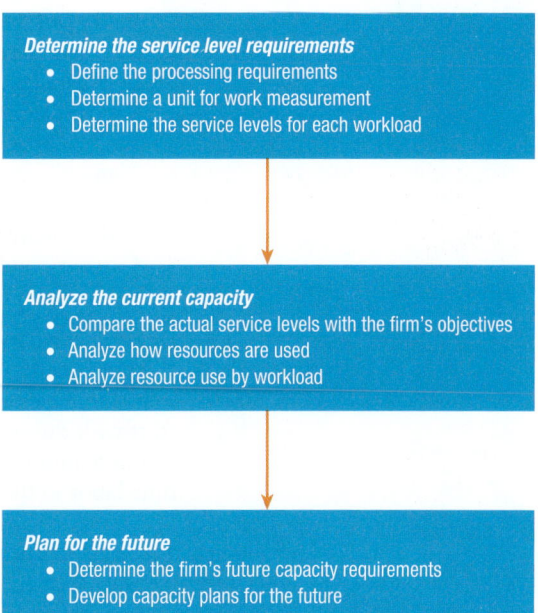

FIGURE 7.5: Capacity Planning Process for Services

Determine the service level requirements
- Define the processing requirements
- Determine a unit for work measurement
- Determine the service levels for each workload

Analyze the current capacity
- Compare the actual service levels with the firm's objectives
- Analyze how resources are used
- Analyze resource use by workload

Plan for the future
- Determine the firm's future capacity requirements
- Develop capacity plans for the future

Step 2: Analyze the current capacity.

- First, compare the actual service levels with the objectives that were established. In the case of the Dunkin' Donuts drive-through, we measure the actual times customers had to wait to receive service. Gathering this data over several days for both the peak and slack periods of demand, we can compute the average waiting time separately for both peak and slack periods. We can then compare these measurements with the service level objectives. This comparison will indicate whether the system has adequate capacity to meet the preestablished service level objectives.

- Second, analyze how the various resources (labor, computer systems, and so forth) of the service system are used. This analysis will help identify highly used resources or shortages of bottleneck resources that may cause bottlenecks now or in the future. An analysis of resources in a hospital would pinpoint the departments (cardiology, radiology, psychiatry, emergency, and so forth) that are the major users of critical resources (doctors and nurses). This analysis will enable us to focus our attention on those workloads or departments that are making the greatest demands on the system's resources.

- Within each department, determine where the most time is being spent. In a hospital, a neurosurgeon may be spending the greatest amount of time during surgery, whereas the registered nurses assigned to that unit may be spending most of their time during pre- and postoperative care.

Step 3: Plan for the future.

- Determine the firm's future capacity requirements. Although the existing capacity may be providing satisfactory service levels now, is this capacity enough to meet the future needs of the service organization? To answer this question, we need to determine future capacity requirements:

- The expected growth in the business of the service firm will affect future capacity requirements. For example, a bank planning to open a new branch will experience additional demand for its services, which will increase the organization's workloads and the need for additional resources.
- The firm needs to predict and plan for the requirements needed to implement the new services. Banks introducing new programs such as mobile banking, remote deposit services, or serving as "identity brokers" to insurance or credit agencies need to provide adequate support for these initiatives.
- Planned acquisitions or divestitures. For example, the acquisition of smaller, community banks by larger, regional banks would likely create additional workloads and capacity requirements for the larger financial institutions.
- Capacity budget limitations. Budget shrinkages may lead to the consolidation or reallocation of resources, which can affect the firm's future capacity requirements.

- Develop capacity plans for the future.

    After identifying the future capacity requirements for the service system, the final step is to develop a capacity plan to meet those requirements. The best approach is to start with the existing capacity plan and determine whether it can be modified to meet future requirements. The capacity alternatives may range from using overtime or part-time labor in the short run to adding a new service facility in the long run.

Following these steps can help service firms be prepared for the future and acquire only those resources they need to ensure their service levels are adequate

7.3 Capacity Planning for Supply Chains

Describe the challenges of planning for capacity in supply chains, and explain what supply chain partners can do to improve their joint capacity planning.

Many companies find that their existing processes, technologies, and associated capacities are not flexible enough for them to do business efficiently on a global scale.[10] For example, historically, many companies have used the Panama Canal as a major shipping route between the Pacific and the Atlantic and between west coast and east coast ports. As the Canal was built more than 100 years ago, capacity has become more and more strained. It is estimated that nearly 40% of the newest and biggest container ships are too wide to fit through the canal locks. Because of these capacity challenges, Panama embarked on a large project to widen the canals and add additional locks and shipping channels. As a result of this increase in capacity, ports in Boston, Miami, and Charleston have spent millions on expanding their facilities as they recognize that more traffic through the Panama Canal will result in greater cargo loads entering these shipping ports. This example highlights the cascading effect that capacity planning can have, as changes to one element in a supply chain naturally affect other components.[11]

Capacity Planning for the Supply Chain

When companies plan their capacity in the context of their supply chain, they need to answer questions such as these:[12]

- How much capacity should the individual supply chain members have to meet the long-term capacity requirements of the chain?
- How much of the total supply chain capacity requirements can each supplier provide during peak periods? Which supply chain members could become potential bottlenecks?
- Given the capacity of each supply chain member, how much of the raw materials and products should be allocated to various suppliers, plants, and warehouses to meet the demand of customers in various market regions? How much of the demand should be met from inventory, production, or a combination of the two?

Capacity planning is more challenging and dynamic for a supply chain than it is for an individual company because there are so many more organizations and functions involved, especially when the supply chain is global. Uncertainties for any individual firm ripple through the entire supply chain. To best illustrate this uncertainty phenomenon, let us consider the impact of demand uncertainty, technological uncertainty, and supply uncertainty on capacity planning in the aerospace industry.

Demand Uncertainty

In the volatile aerospace industry, demand uncertainty has caused significant capacity planning problems for supply chains. For example, after the September 11, 2001, terror attacks, many airlines canceled or postponed orders for aircraft. As a consequence, The Boeing Company (Chicago, IL)

OPERATIONS MANAGEMENT: LESSONS LEARNED
Pratt and Whitney Battles Capacity and Supply Chain Problems for a New Jet Engine

Pratt & Whitney (East Hartford, CT) is an American aerospace manufacturer and one of the three largest commercial and military jet engine makers in the world, competing directly with Rolls-Royce Holdings plc (London, U.K.) and General Electric (aka GE, Fairfield, CT) for market share. The two main airplane manufacturers, Boeing (introduced earlier) and Airbus SAS (Blagnac, France), have dominated the market for commercial aircraft, with a current backlog (airplanes ordered for delivery) of more than 10,000 airplanes of various types. With newer regional jet manufacturers like Canada's Canadair Ltd. (Montreal, Quebec, Canada) and Bombardier Inc. (Montreal, Quebec, Canada), Brazil's Embraer S.A. (São José dos Campos, São Paulo, Brazil), and China's Comac (Commercial Aircraft Corporation of China, Ltd., Shanghai, P.R. China) also competing for orders from the airlines and engines accounting for up to one third of the value of a new jet, it is estimated by some experts that jet engine makers' revenues could total US$1 trillion over the next 20 years.

Pratt & Whitney, a division of United Technologies Corporation (aka UTC, Farmington, CT), used to dominate the market for jet engines, but these days it is in third place behind GE and Rolls-Royce. Pratt is hoping to find its way back to the top with a next-generation technology designed to appeal to aircraft makers and their commercial airline customers: the "geared turbofan." Recent developments in the market, including a need by commercial airlines for more fuel-efficient and powerful engines, have increased the highly competitive nature of the jet engine manufacturing and services business. Pratt's geared turbofan engines have a gearbox that lets the fan at the front of the engine turn at a different speed to the compressors inside it. By allowing each to run at optimal speeds, it makes the engine more efficient while lowering noise levels. Pratt's commitment to this technology includes investing US$10 billion and more than two decades worth of research and development in the project.

The initial reception to the new engines has been overwhelmingly positive, with Pratt officials noting that shortly after its introduction, it had more than 7,000 orders for the geared turbofan. Pratt's priority is to manage its supply chain in a manner that allows the company to exploit this surge in demand. Its goal is to ramp up production of the engine from 15 in 2015 to 1,200 a year by 2020. The supply chain challenge is significant; for the first time, 80% of parts of the geared turbofan are made by companies other than Pratt and then shipped to its manufacturing centers in the United States, Canada, and Germany. Pratt has also invested US$1.3 billion in expanding its facilities as a capacity buffer. Also, as an additional guard against capacity and supply problems, the company is requiring suppliers to provide buffers of extra parts as insurance against any halts to the production process. In a final step toward improving capacity in the supply chain, Pratt has tried to double the number of suppliers, including signing contracts with duplicate makers for many of the engine parts to make sure supplies are on hand.

Unfortunately, the supply chain has not cooperated in ways that Pratt & Whitney hoped. United Technologies Chief Executive Gregory Hayes estimated that nearly 50% of the company's 1,600 suppliers—including the 500 to 600 who supply parts and materials for the engines themselves—weren't meeting the company's on-time delivery and quality control targets. The combined effects of these supply chain disruptions has led to delays in supplying jets for pending orders and has resulted in some airlines canceling their orders for aircraft powered by the new engine. "We have all the capacity we need—the challenge is to get all the parts in on time," insisted Danny DiPerna, Pratt's senior vice president for operations and the chief official overseeing the company's supply chain. "It's a dogfight every day."

Pratt & Whitney have now taken steps to address these concerns. If a supplier is not meeting its quality or production goals, Pratt sends engineers to help fix the problem at the source. The company also has taken a long-term view to ensure that capacity and suppliers are coordinated for future deliveries. They have shifted their focus to monitoring suppliers 100 weeks ahead of when parts are due to arrive at the manufacturing centers, up from just 20 weeks lead time in 2015. Pratt hopes that these supply chain adjustments will allow it to control capacity and plan for a smoother and faster supply chain, from parts delivery to assembly to shipping to its customers.[15]

slashed its production by half and laid off 35,000 people.[13] Such an unanticipated uncertainty in demand was painful not only for Boeing but also for its whole supply chain because the attack not only disrupted Boeing's production plans and schedules but also that of its supply chain partners after Boeing's customers canceled orders for parts and components. Decisions affecting demand management in capacity planning are complex, and the topic is covered in detail in Chapter 12.

Technological Uncertainty

To benefit from technological changes, aerospace firms must invest heavily in research and development to improve their products. These technological advances, however, can be risky because they create uncertainty that can resonate through a supply chain.[14] Technological uncertainty often goes

The Panama Canal is one of the most frequently used shipping routes in the world. As demand continues to increase over the years, the canal has needed to undergo major renovations to alleviate the strain on its capacity.

©iStockphoto.com/stellalevi

hand in hand with the need for continuous technology upgrades.[16] For example, Boeing's decision to make major components of its newest aircraft, the 787, out of composite materials led to the need for much more intensive testing of every component to resolve these new uncertainties. The company also spent years ensuring it got the manufacturing and assembly processes error free. Depending on the degree to which organizations adopt new technologies and the uncertainties associated with them, it is possible to experience disruptions in the manufacturing processes that make it hard to deliver orders reliably.[17] Gaps between demand and capacity such as these can lead to undesirable and long-lasting business consequences for the members of a supply chain—consequences that are difficult to resolve. For example, Apple Inc.'s (Cupertino, CA) plan to release the newest versions of its iPhone with a super scratch-resistant sapphire screen resulted in its decision to cancel the product after having invested more than US$1 billion in its development. Apple discovered that its industry supplier, GT Advanced Technologies (Merrimack, NH), did not have the capability to grow effectively the sapphire crystals needed for the iPhone screens. After repeated delays in the newest iPhone's introduction, Apple scrapped the sapphire screen innovation and went back to its old technology.[18]

Supply Uncertainty

There are two types of supply uncertainty, both of which can adversely affect the capacity and sales of a firm's downstream supply chain partners. The first type is a shortage of inbound raw materials and components. For example, the high demand for new aircraft can create a shortage of scarce raw materials such as the titanium used in the planes. The second type of supply uncertainty is the inability of an individual supplier to fulfill its obligations. Those obligations may involve quality expectations, promised delivery dates, or even the manner in which the goods are themselves manufactured. For example, with more and more citizens and national governments concerned about climate change, Indian companies supplying to multinational chains like L'Oreal S.A. (Clichy, France), Dell Inc. (Round Rock, TX), Unilever N.V. (Rotterdam, the Netherlands), the Colgate-Palmolive Company (New York, NY), and Jaguar Land Rover Limited (Whitley, Coventry, U.K.) are under threat of losing their contracts unless they show clear steps to address the amount of carbon they produce. A United Kingdom–based international organization released a study that pointed to several Indian supplier organizations that, to date, had made little attempt to alter their production processes in light of climate and water risks.[19] In addition, strategic supply chain capacity planning requires a company to focus not only on its own capacity investment decisions but also on the investments of the other partners in the supply chain. Because the capacity investment of a single firm in the supply chain can affect the entire the chain, it can have a big impact on all of the firm's upstream and downstream supply chain partners.[20]

Supply Chain Uncertainty

A Framework for Strategic Supply Chain Capacity Planning

In firms with global operations, no individual company can afford to make capacity planning decisions without regard for their effect on the members of the supply chain. Strategic capacity planning is not just an acquisition or expansion issue, but it also involves coordinating and integrating the supply chain. Because of the inherent uncertainty in demand, technology, and supply factors, supply chain partners must forge close relationships—relationships that help the chain plan and control the manufacturer's capacity with its upstream suppliers and its downstream customers to maximize the value of the entire supply chain. A framework that identifies these coordinating and integrating relationships is shown in Figure 7.6.

SHARING INFORMATION AND INTEGRATING BUSINESS PROCESSES

Effective strategic capacity planning requires disseminating accurate information to all members in the supply chain. To accomplish this, the supply chain members should be able to share accurate and timely information. Integrating and automating the information systems of the partners enables them to collaborate and synchronize their capacity planning. In addition, the supply chain members should also integrate and simplify their business processes to avoid technology uncertainty. For example, if an

FIGURE 7.6: Capacity Planning Framework for a Simple Supply Chain

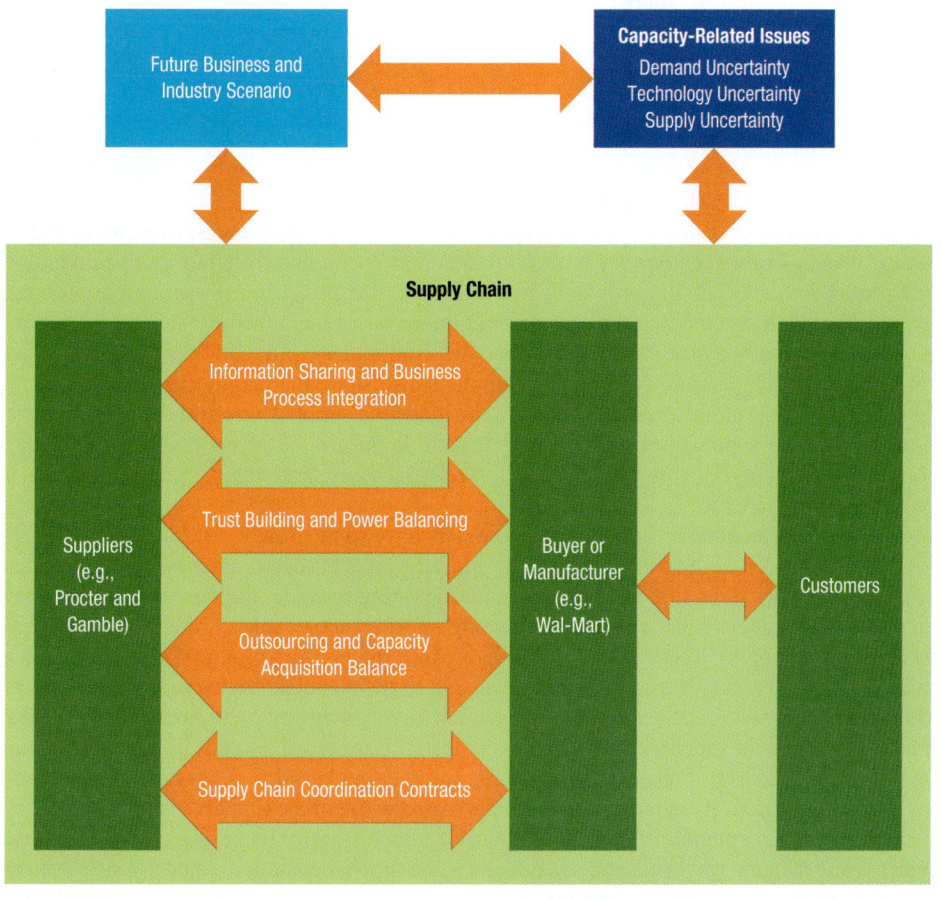

SOURCE: Wang, Buxton, Farr, & MacCarthy, *op. cit.*, Figure 2-1, p. 15.

organization is using enterprise resource planning (ERP) software by SAP (SAP SE, Walldorf, Germany) or Oracle (Oracle Corporation, Redwood City, CA), then a high degree of coordination can be achieved with its other supply chain partners if they also have similar compatible ERP systems in place.

BUILDING TRUST AND BALANCING POWER

Building trust and balancing power among supply chain members can offset many supply chain uncertainties and help nurture one-to-one relationships between firms. For this to occur, the partners must first clearly recognize the mutual benefits provided by the relationship as well their mutual dependence on one another. The ideal situation is to have the supply chain tasks divided among the partners in such a way that no one supply chain member has the upper hand. Yet, such a balance of power is rarely achieved; some members of the supply chain enjoy more clout either because of their market leadership or because they have more resources.

BALANCING OUTSOURCING AND CAPACITY ACQUISITION

In supply chains, there are typically two options for meeting capacity requirements: capacity acquisition or outsourcing. This choice is often considered a "make or buy" decision: whether to acquire capacity for in-house production or outsource production to a third party. Each option has its advantages and disadvantages. The advantage of outsourcing is that by outsourcing those activities that do not directly contribute to the company's bottom line, manufacturers can reduce capital investment and production costs. The disadvantage, however, is the possible loss of control over the production of the work that has been outsourced. By keeping the production in-house, a firm has more control over it, but it could end up with excess or unused capacity if demand falls short of expectations.

Furthermore, demand and supply uncertainties influence capacity and outsourcing decisions. For example, during an economic downturn, suppliers may be forced to cut back on capacity so they don't end up with excess inventory should demand weaken further. As a result of the suppliers' reluctance to expand, the downstream buyers in their supply chain might not have enough raw materials to fill their orders. In this instance, a buyer might want to reserve capacity with the supplier by offering to buy a certain portion of the supplier's future capacity. In exchange, the supplier commits to increase its capacity so that the buyer can meet its demand.[21] High-tech manufacturers, for example, such as telecommunications and semiconductor firms, have long manufacturing lead times and short product life cycles, and they have very large budgets for R&D. If these firms have their supplies disrupted, they will be unable to launch new products. Consequently, they reserve capacity with their suppliers to avoid such disruptions.[22]

ESTABLISHING SUPPLY CHAIN CONTRACTS

During periods of high demand volatility, suppliers often face the risk of excess capacity in their manufacturing plants. Consequently, they issue contracts that encourage their buyers to purchase more of their products to alleviate the problem. One such type of contract is a **revenue-sharing contract**. Under a revenue-sharing contract, the supplier and the buyer or manufacturer share the revenue generated from the sale of the products. The suppliers sell components and materials to the manufacturer at a price below their marginal cost, but the suppliers also share the manufacturer's revenue, which offsets this loss. The manufacturer benefits from the increased supply levels and the reduced purchase price of the supplies it purchases. Thus, when demand is uncertain, buyers and suppliers can enter into revenue-sharing agreements (which are often referred to as share-the-pain agreements) to share the burden of overcapacity.[23]

Despite these advantages, revenue-sharing contracts have some drawbacks. In general, the supplier carries a greater burden of the risk, including the administrative burden of monitoring the manufacturer's sales and revenues to be sure the firm isn't underreporting them. In addition, the supplier may not be motivated to expand its capacity for fear of ending up with excess capacity if demand remains weak. If this occurs, the supplier loses revenue not only because the product produced by the manufacturer did not sell but also because the goods the supplier sold to the manufacturer were sold for a low price.

With a **capacity-reservation contract**, the manufacturer has the option of reserving additional production capacity with the supplier to be exercised in the future as needed. The advantage of such contracts is that they offer benefits to both the manufacturer and the supplier; that is, they have the potential to reduce the manufacturer's procurement costs and increase the use of the supplier's capacity. For instance, the manufacturer may commit to a certain amount of future capacity by paying upfront a reservation fee, which is less than the wholesale price. In exchange, the supplier commits to increase its capacity sufficiently to satisfy the manufacturer's demands. Capacity-reservation contracts are an increasingly popular method for allocating risks across suppliers and buyers in high-tech supply chains.[24]

7.4. Ethical and Sustainability Issues

7.4 Predict the effect of sustainability and ethics on the future capacity decisions of firms and supply chains.

Capacity planning decisions and sustainability are closely related. Capacity decisions focus on the company's acquisition of critical human, technological, financial, and organizational resources, as well as on their organization, deployment, and use to reduce operating costs and waste. Reducing waste improves the environment and reduces operating costs. Sustainability practices that focus on reducing resource usage and waste lead to more efficient use of existing capacity. For example, by using new methods to produce a car, The Ford Motor Company (aka Ford, Dearborn, MI) has been able to reduce its water use in the United States by 71% and by 62% globally—saving 10.6 billion gallons between 2000 and 2012. This is equivalent to the annual water consumption of about 100,000 U.S. homes, according to the U.S. Environmental Protection Agency (EPA).[25]

Ethics, likewise, play a critical role in implementing capacity planning decisions. For companies that have global supply chains in which their overseas suppliers and subcontractors use labor as their primary capacity resource, there are many opportunities for trimming costs. Such cost cutting comes at the expense of an uneducated, poor labor force because in many of these suppliers' countries, labor standards are lower and there are fewer environmental regulations. Consequently, such ethical violations as the abuse of labor occur frequently in these countries. Nike, Inc. (Beaverton, OR), for example, was forced to adjust its labor policies when it became publicly known that the Asian factories in which it outsourced its shoemaking routinely employed underage workers and subjected them to unreasonable working conditions and long hours for minimal pay. An egregious example occurred in 1984 when a Union Carbide Corporation (now a subsidiary of Dow Chemical Company, Houston, TX) pesticide plant located in Bhopal, India, leaked poisons into the surrounding community, killing thousands and injuring hundreds of thousands of other people living nearby in shanty-towns. The company had allowed the plant to deteriorate as a result of poor maintenance and safety management.[26] Alternatively, after the terrible fires and loss of 1,100 lives in Bangladeshi garment factories in April 2013, Wal-Mart (Wal-Mart Stores Inc., Bentonville, AR) issued a zero-tolerance policy for unauthorized subcontracting.

Revenue-sharing contract: an agreement where the supplier and the buyer or manufacturer share the revenue generated from the sale of the products

Capacity-reservation contract: an agreement where the manufacturer has the option of reserving additional production capacity with the supplier to be exercised in the future as needed

Each of these examples demonstrates that the goals of sustainability and ethical management of operations and supply chains should not be treated as a luxury or as a concern to be addressed outside of the firm's normal activities. That is, too many times firms assume that adding ethics or sustainability to their capacity calculations will simply result in added costs or inefficient operations. In fact, the opposite is usually the case: Managing ethically and with sustainable standards can not only help a firm's bottom line but it will also improve the environment and lives of people around the globe.

Ethics of Careful Capacity Planning

7.5. Global Capacity Management

Globalization of the supply chains, scarcity of supply, and uncertain demand dictate that global manufacturers align capacity with projected demand on a global basis. Increasingly, global manufacturers, including automotive and industrial equipment manufacturers, use a common global platform across multiple regions. A **global platform** is a set of standards and practices that allows companies geographically dispersed around the globe to share information, developments, products and components, payment methods, and other relevant information. As a result, it is increasingly common for global companies to use components sourced in one region for assembly in another region. Therefore, to compete effectively in the current highly competitive global business environment, companies need to manage capacity globally, which requires a consolidated view of global demand and supply. Unfortunately, the processes and systems used by most global manufacturers are unable to respond to this capacity challenge. This inability is often because the supply chains of these manufacturers are planned and managed by disparate regional systems, even though the supply chains are getting increasingly more complex. That is, these firms continue to manage locally, even though they are thinking globally. As a result, they are unable to manage their capacity dynamically in response to revised demand forecasts and changes in capacity constraints.[27]

To develop systematic and accurate global capacity plans and to manage capacity effectively, companies need to consider supply risks, exchange rate risks, risks from foreign government policies, laws and regulations, labor availability and stability in foreign countries, demand and transportation risk, and so forth. Specifically, to generate accurate global capacity plans, firms need to estimate in advance the timing and impact of these risks. In addition, as several of these risks may be interrelated, the global capacity planning process should also take such interrelationships into consideration. For example, production delays caused by risky supplies of key raw materials can, in turn, lead to transportation problems, which will eventually lead to delivery delays to a subsequent destination in the supply chain. In fact, the primary impact of poorly developed global capacity plans is the failure to deliver the product or service on time. To mitigate and respond to these risks, companies need to develop capacity plans that have flexibility in resource use in both their domestic and overseas operations. For example, Ford plans to increase its global factories by nearly one third over the next several years. By 2017, Ford will have around 80 factories worldwide and it expects 90% of them to be running three shifts (full production capacity) to increase production by 30%. Ford began building 14 new factories as part of a global expansion in 2011 in countries such as China and India. The automaker is betting that this advance capacity planning will allow it to respond more quickly to changing consumer tastes. Ford expects to launch 114 new or modified vehicles worldwide by 2017.[28]

Ford's efforts illustrate some of the challenges of global capacity planning. The purpose of developing a global capacity plan is to determine the total capacity needed to meet the projected global demand for a company's products. Managing global capacity first requires a regular capacity planning cycle that ranges from the intermediate to long-term time horizon (1 to 4+ years), and the capacity plans developed need to be flexible and responsive enough so that plans can be updated as needed. Developing such capacity plans is an iterative and collaborative process. Once developed, a capacity plan serves as a key input into supply network design, into decisions regarding new plant construction (such as Ford's decision), and into planning for other capital investments. The second step in effective global capacity management is monitoring and response. The time horizon for this phase is from the short to the intermediate term (0 to 1 year). The focus of this step in global capacity management is to ensure that there are no capacity misalignments from changes in supply, changes in demand, or both, and to determine the best

7.5

Identify the challenges in developing a global capacity planning strategy, including the opportunities and threats in the global arena.

Global platform: a set of standards and practices that allows companies geographically dispersed around the globe to share information, developments, products and components, payment methods, and other relevant information

Survivors of the Bhopal Gas Disaster of 1984 gathered in 2015 on the 31st anniversary of the incident.

Anadolu Agency/Anadolu Agency/ Getty Images

Consider This 7.1:
Working to End Child Labor

One of the most contentious and important issues in recent years concerns the use of child labor. Child labor is often used in developing and impoverished nations, particularly when unscrupulous subcontractors and local supply chain partners exploit their workers. As a result of the increased exposure of these practices over the past decade, most organizations have begun actively campaigning to end child labor and have fashioned corporate policies and practices deliberately designed to promote safe and fair labor policies in the organizations (and, in some cases, in the countries) where their goods are produced.

These are some examples of child labor abuses:

- Barry Callebaut (Zürich, Switzerland), a large international cocoa producing company, has extensive contracts with farms in West Africa, where child labor was used. The firm worked with local governments and cocoa producers to find a way to protect children and safeguard the environment. In fact, the firm has spent more than US$75 million to support some 40 programs throughout West Africa that benefit cocoa farming families and their communities.

- In 2011, Apple terminated its contracts with a Chinese factory in which it had found 42 underage workers. Apple decided to cut ties with the factory because it had "determined that management had chosen to overlook the issue and was not committed to addressing the problem." At other factories, Apple mandates the maximum hours per week employees can be required to work and specifies the minimum safety and health standards all of its contractors must follow.

- Wal-Mart has embarked on a corporate-wide initiative to promote sustainability and eliminate the use of child labor by its numerous subcontractors. The retailer has developed an ethical sourcing manual that governs the practices of its global supply chain. Clear guidelines about child labor are specified in the manual, and Wal-Mart has terminated all contracts with companies that have violated the guidelines.[29]

 Capacity and the Unexpected

response should unexpected events occur that can potentially affect both short-term and long-term capacity plans. The third step in managing global capacity, which has the same time horizon focus as capacity monitoring, is constraint management. Constraint management focuses on effectively managing available capacity by modifying supply allocations and production and supplier schedules, expediting in-bound or out-bound shipments, using alternative suppliers or components, modifying existing capacity through shifts and overtime, and so forth.[30]

$SAGE edge™

Visit **edge.sagepub.com/venkataraman** to help you accomplish your coursework goals in an easy-to-use learning environment.

- Mobile-friendly eFlashcards
- Mobile-friendly practice quizzes
- A complete online action plan
- Chapter summaries with learning objectives
- Video and multimedia resources

CHAPTER SUMMARY

7.1 Explain why capacity planning is important and how capacity decisions are made. The dilemma that all operations and supply chain managers face is that the demand for products and services is uncertain. There is always a gap between the capacity available in the system and the capacity that is required to meet demand. Managers have to plan for capacity in the short, medium, and long terms. Not only do they have to decide when capacity is needed but also the kind of capacity needed and how much of it. Appropriate capacity planning strategies and accurate capacity measurements such as capacity efficiency and capacity utilization are used to help make these decisions,

7.2 Evaluate the difficulties associated with capacity planning for services, and explain how they can be overcome. Services are generally consumed at the time they are produced. As a result, it is not possible to inventory extra quantities of them to serve as a buffer when demand increases. The key capacity planning decisions for service organizations deal with workloads or the processing times needed to deliver the various types of services. Many service firms require less capital investment to satisfy the increased demand of their customers. These firms can often meet increases in demand by adding more staff, at least in the short run.

7.3 Describe the challenges of planning for capacity in supply chains, and explain what supply chain partners can do to improve their joint capacity planning. Capacity planning is more challenging for a supply chain than it is for an individual company because there are more organizations and functions involved. Uncertainties for any individual firm have an effect that ripples throughout the entire supply chain. For firms that operate in global markets, the task is challenging. Among the steps firms can take to effectively plan for capacity within their chains are to (a) share information and integrate their business processes, (b) build trust and share power with one another, (c) balance outsourcing and capacity acquisitions, and (d) establish supply chain contracts that allow for risk sharing.

7.4 **Predict the effect of sustainability and ethics on the future capacity decisions of firms and supply chains.** Capacity planning decisions and sustainability are closely related. Capacity decisions focus on the company's acquisition of critical human, technological, financial, and organizational resources, as well as on their organization, deployment, and use to reduce operating costs and waste. Reducing waste improves the environment and reduces operating costs. Sustainability practices that focus on reducing resource usage and waste lead to more efficient use of existing capacity. Ethics, likewise, plays a critical role in implementing capacity planning decisions. Too many times firms assume that adding ethics or sustainability to their capacity calculations will increase costs or result in inefficient operations. In fact, the opposite is usually true. Firms increasingly are factoring sustainability and ethical business choices into their decisions

regarding capacity planning and use of overseas suppliers and other contractors, as well as for developing their supply chains.

7.5 **Identify the challenges in developing a global capacity planning strategy, including the opportunities and threats in the global arena.** Globalization of the supply chains, scarcity of supply, and uncertain demand dictate that global manufacturers align capacity with projected demand on a global basis. To compete globally, companies need to manage their capacity, which requires a consolidated global view of demand and supply. Unfortunately, the approaches used by most global manufacturers are unable to address this capacity challenge. This inability is often because the supply chains of these manufacturers are planned and managed by disparate regional systems, even though the supply chains are getting increasingly more complex. To combine these disparate plans into a coherent, broad strategy requires that companies also consider the broad variety of risks including supply risks, exchange rate risks, risks from foreign government policies, laws and regulations, labor availability and stability in foreign countries, as well as demand and transportation risk.

KEY TERMS

Actual output   248

Bottleneck   247

Capacity   246

Capacity control   247

Capacity cushion   250

Capacity efficiency   248

Capacity gap   249

Capacity planning   246

Capacity requirements planning (CRP)   246

Capacity utilization   248

Capacity-reservation contract   260

Design capacity   248

Diseconomies of scale   252

Economies of scale   252

Effective capacity   248

Global platform   261

Lagging strategy   250

Leading strategy   249

Level capacity plan   252

Matching strategy   250

Revenue-sharing contract   260

Rough-cut capacity planning (RCCP)   246

Strategic capacity planning   246

Work center   247

DISCUSSION AND REVIEW QUESTIONS

1. What is the difference between effective capacity and design capacity?

2. Why is it important to consider both capacity utilization and capacity efficiency measures when evaluating a firm's capacity performance?

3. What are capacity cushions, and why do companies need them?

4. Briefly discuss the caveats that companies should be aware of when developing capacity alternatives.

5. Discuss the factors that make capacity planning in supply chains difficult.

6. What are some unique capacity planning challenges that service companies face?

7. Discuss briefly the steps involved in capacity planning for services.

8. Discuss briefly the various aspects of capacity planning for a service facility such as a hospital.

9. What are supply chain contracts, and how are they used to address capacity-related issues?

10. Explain how capacity can be managed to implement sustainability principles.

11. What are some challenges of global capacity management?

12. Discuss briefly the three key elements of the global capacity management process.

SOLVED PROBLEMS

1. The manager of a chemical plant is trying to decide which type of machinery to buy: Type 1 or Type 2. Either type can be used to process two chemical products: polyvinyl chloride and polypropylene. Demand information and processing time data for the two products are shown in the following table. Each machine would be operated 8 hours per day, 300 days a year. The cost to purchase the Type 1 machinery is US$25,000. The cost to purchase Type 2 machinery is US$20,000.

   a. Which type of machines should the plant purchase? How many of them are needed to meet the capacity requirements?

Product	Annual Demand (in tons)	Standard Processing Time (in hours per ton)		Processing Time Needed (in hours)	
		Type 1	Type 2	Type 1	Type 2
Polyvinyl Chloride	600	3.0	5.0	$600 \times 3 = 1{,}800$	$600 \times 5 = 3{,}000$
Polypropylene	500	6.0	5.0	$500 \times 6 = 3{,}000$	$500 \times 5 = 2{,}500$
Total				4,800	5,500

Solution:

Since the plant operates 8 hours per day for 300 days a year, the total available capacity is $300 \times 8 = 2,400$ hours per machine. Given that the total processing time needed for the Type 1 machinery is 4,800 hours, the number of Type 1 machines needed is:

$$\frac{4,800}{2,400} = 2$$

Given that the total processing time needed for Type 2 machinery is 5,500 hours, the number of Type 2 machines needed is:

$$\frac{5,400}{2,400} = 2.29 \text{ or } 3$$

The total cost for two Type 1 machines is US$25,000 $\times$ 2 = US$50,000, and the total cost for three Type 2 machines is US$20,000 $\times$ 3 = US$60,000.

Hence, the chemical plant should buy two Type 1 machines.

2.   The design capacity of a Niagara Car Wash (Erie, PA) line is 15 cars per hour. If a line's effective capacity and efficiency are estimated to be 12 cars per hour and 0.8, respectively, how many wash lines at the minimum does Niagara Car Wash need to service an estimated 300 cars in an 8-hour day?

Solution:

Since:

$$\text{Capacity Efficiency} = \frac{\text{Actual Output}}{\text{Effective Capacity}} \times 100\%$$

$$\text{Actual Output} = \text{Capacity Efficiency} \times \text{Effective Capacity} = 0.8 \times 12 = 9.6 \text{ cars}$$

Thus, each wash line can actually service 9.6 cars per hour. Therefore, during an 8-hour day, each wash line can service $9.6 \times 8 = 76.8$ cars. To service 300 cars during an 8-hour day, the number of wash lines needed is $300 / 76.8 = 3.90$, or 4 wash lines.

PROBLEMS

1.   A company that manufactures soft drinks wants to assess the capacity performance of its production line. The system has a design capacity of 100,000 bottles per 8-hour shift. Due to maintenance requirements and the changeover of equipment needed to produce different flavors of the soft drinks, the effective capacity of the system is 80,000 bottles per 8-hour shift. Nonetheless, during the past month, the production line's average actual output was only 72,000 bottles per 8-hour shift. Compute the production line's capacity utilization and capacity efficiency measures for this time period. If the plant manager wants further improvement in these measures, what are some actions that he should take?

2.   XYZ International is planning to increase its capacity to overcome the bottlenecks in its production line. The firm plans to do this by the addition of a new machine. The company received proposals for this new equipment from two vendors. The cost revenue data for the two machines proposed by the vendors is as follows:

Vendor	Fixed Costs (in U.S. dollars)	Variable Costs (in U.S. dollars)
A	80,000	10 per unit
B	100,000	8 per unit

The revenue that will be generated from the sale of each product produced by the machines is $25 per unit.

a.   What is the breakeven volume for each machine?

b.   For what volume range is each machine superior?

3.   The Sam & Irene Black School of Business at Penn State Erie, The Behrend College, has the facilities and faculty to accommodate an enrollment of 1,500 new students per academic year. Yet, to maintain small class sizes (less than 45), the school's chancellor, Ralph Ford, placed a ceiling of 1,300 on the enrollment of new students. Despite a healthy demand for business courses in the previous academic year, only 1,000 students took business courses because of their conflicting schedules. What are the capacity utilization and efficiency measures for this system?

4.   The design capacity at the fictitious Quick Lube service bay is 8 cars per hour. If the effective capacity and efficiency of a Quick Lube service bay are 6 cars per hour and 0.78, respectively, how many service bays at the minimum does a Quick Lube need to service an estimated 250 cars in an 8-hour day?

5.   The effective capacity of the loan processing department of the fictional Union City Bank is only 60% of design capacity, and the actual output is 85% of effective capacity. If the bank desires an actual output of 10 loan processing jobs per week, what should be the design capacity?

6.   The following diagram illustrates a production system with four work stations arranged in sequence along with their number units each can produce per hour:

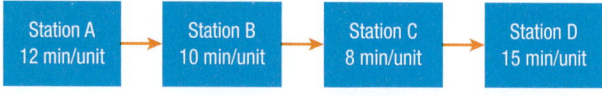

| Station A 12 min/unit | Station B 10 min/unit | Station C 8 min/unit | Station D 15 min/unit |

a.   Which work station is the bottleneck?

b.   If you could increase the capacity of any two of these work stations, which two would you focus on? By how much would you increase the capacity of these two work stations? What would be the effective capacity of the total system after these improvement were made?

7.   A local manufacturing plant has three work stations (as shown in the following figure) with two machines operating in parallel in workstation 1. In other words, before proceeding to station 2, the product can be processed in either one of the two machines in workstation 1:

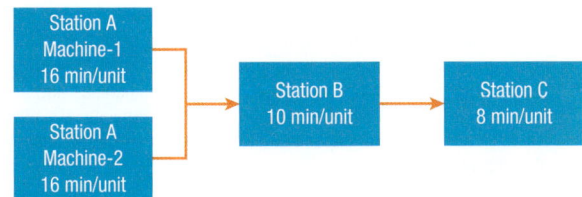

a. Which workstation among the three is the bottleneck workstation?

b. If the company operates 8 hours per day, 7 days per week, what is the weekly capacity of this work cell?

c. If you could increase the capacity of any one of three work stations, which one would you focus on? By how much would you increase the capacity of this work station?

d. What would be the effective capacity of the total system after these improvements are made?

8. A manufacturing firm is planning to purchase new machines for processing four products it manufactures. Demand information and processing time data for the four products are shown in the following table. Each machine the firm purchases will operate 8 hours per day, for 250 days a year. How many new machines should the company purchase to meet its capacity requirements?

Product	Annual Demand	Standard Processing Time (in hours per unit)
A	300	5.0
B	500	4.0
C	750	8.0
D	675	2.0

9. An operations manager, to increase the capacity of his manufacturing plant, decides to buy an additional machine. He has three alternatives: Machine I at a cost of $60,000; Machine II at a cost of $40,000; or Machine III at a cost of $100,000 (all in U.S. dollars). Annual demand forecasts for the four products that will use this machine and the processing times for the three types of machines are given in the following table:

Product	Demand Forecast (in units)	Processing Time (in minutes per unit)		
		Machine I	Machine II	Machine III
A	20,000	4	5	3
B	14,000	5	4	4
C	8,000	6	6	5
D	36,000	3	2	1

a. Considering only the purchase cost of these machines, which machine, and how many of that machine type should the operations manager buy? Assume the plant operates 8 hours a day and 300 days a year.

b. In addition to the purchase cost of the machines, the operations manager needs to consider the hourly operating cost of these machine, which are given as follows:

Machine I: $12 an hour; Machine II: $14 an hour; and Machine III: $15 an hour.

To satisfy capacity processing requirements and to minimize total purchasing and operating costs, which type of machine, and how many should the operations manager buy?

10. The business school of Loyola College, Chennai, India, has the capacity to enroll 1,500 business students in its class offerings every semester. Nevertheless, the dean of the college, Fr. Francis Bertram, to facilitate student learning and interaction, has limited the enrollment to 1,200 students. Despite a high demand for business courses, schedule conflicts and financial needs allowed only 1,100 students to enroll in business courses. Compute the capacity utilization and efficiency of this educational system.

11. XYZ Manufacturing has computed for the current month the following effective capacities and efficiencies for three of its departments.

Department	Effective Capacity	Capacity Efficiency
Milling	45,200	0.92
Sawing	34,500	0.88
Assembly	97,600	.97

What is the expected production next month for each of the three departments?

12. RanBaxy Pharmaceuticals Inc. (subsidiary of SUN PHARMA Company, Princeton, NJ) is currently manufacturing a drug that has a variable cost and selling price of $1.20 per unit $2.00 respectively (in U.S. dollars). The current fixed costs are $25,000, and the sales volume is 25,000 units. The company is considering adding new equipment to the production that can improve the production efficiency of this drug. The new equipment will add an additional $9,000 to the fixed cost, and variable cost per unit would decrease to $1.00. At what sales volume would adding this new equipment be profitable?

13. Laurel Nelson owns a beauty salon. Laurel's fixed costs are $15,000 per month. The average variable cost for the beauty supplies she sells is $10 per unit. The average selling price of a product that the salon sells is $15 per unit (all in U.S. dollars). What is the breakeven sales volume?

14. Refer to problem 13. Suppose Laurel plans to expand her business. The new fixed cost would be $20,000. The average variable cost reduces to $9 per unit and sales price remains at $15 per unit.

a. What is the new breakeven sales volume?

b. At what sales volume would Laurel be indifferent to the capacity scenarios outlined in problems 13 and 14?

15. The production process at ABC Manufacturing is as shown in the following figure:

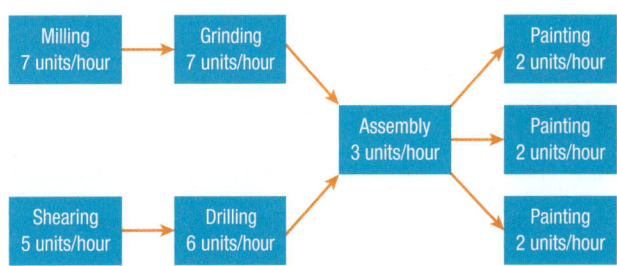

A product in this production process needs to go through only one of the painting operations:

a. Which one of the operations in the previous figure is a bottleneck operation?

b. If Orion Manufacturing operated 8 hours/day, 25 days/month, what is the monthly capacity of the company's production process?

16. A manufacturer of a small appliance produces motors for the appliance using two identical processes. Each process has a design capacity of 300 units per day and an effective capacity of 250 units per day. The actual output currently is an average of

220 units per day. The current annual demand for the motors is 60,000 units. The company's production manager has undertaken process reengineering efforts that will increase actual output to 240 units per day. The company expects that the annual demand for the appliance, and hence, for the motors, will double in the next year. How many processes will the company require to satisfy the expected demand next year? Assume 250 working days a year.

17. Refer to problem 15. Which action would result in the greatest increase in process capacity: (a) increase milling operation capacity by 10%; (b) increase grinding operation capacity by 20%; (c) increase shearing operation capacity by 15%; (d) increase assembly operation capacity by 10%; and (e) increase painting operation capacity by 20%.

18. What is the capacity of the production system shown in the following figure?

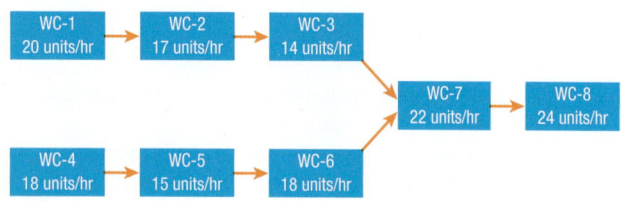

19. A process has been designed to produce 3,000 units per day. The effective capacity of the process, however, is impacted by an inherent scrap rate of 10%. In addition, the actual output of the process is affected by variations in worker efficiencies and fatigue by a factor of 8%. Determine the design capacity, effective capacity, actual output, capacity utilization, and capacity efficiency of this process.

20. Determine the capacity of the production system shown in the following figure. To increase the output of the system, which work center capacity should be increased, and by how much?

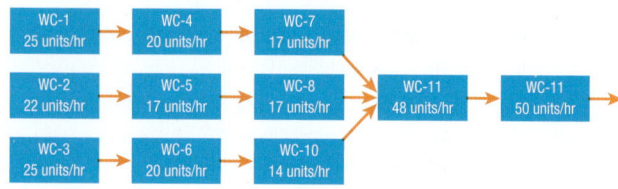

CASE STUDY 7.1 KIRWAIN'S CAPACITY PLANNING CHALLENGE

Kirwain Sound Systems, a fictional company, specializes in manufacturing stereo loudspeakers for outdoor locations, usually around patio and pool areas. Because the company's speakers are expected to hold up to extreme weather conditions, they must be rugged and well made. One critical component in the speaker is the rubberized gasket that protects the delicate speaker assembly in each unit. These gaskets create an airtight seal around the speaker box that protects the electronics from dust and moisture.

The assembly process used to attach the gaskets to the speaker boxes is manual. The gaskets are made from a special rubber that is resistant to extreme temperatures and weather conditions. The gasket is cut to the required length and pasted to the speaker box with a special adhesive and held in place by clamps. The operation requires 3.5 minutes per assembly with the help of three factory workers. Kirwain has contracted with a vendor in India that produces the sealed speaker boxes for US$18 per unit. Using standard freight shipping, Kirwain typically receives regular monthly supplies of completed speaker boxes.

Kirwain is about to sign a contract with Assumption Audio (Abbotsford, Victoria, Australia), the largest vendor of stereo equipment in the world. The orders Kirwain receives from Assumption are expected to increase its

business substantially within six months. Although the current factory is expected to handle this higher workload, Kirwain is concerned that the gasketing operation that is currently outsourced could become a serious bottleneck. Assumption demands high quality, and products must be available when they are ordered.

As a result, Kirwain is considering alternatives for dealing with this potentially serious capacity problem. Assume you are part of a consulting team that has been asked to assess Kirwain's systems. How would you advise Kirwain to adjust its capacity planning? As part of your answer, consider the following issues:

Questions

1. How does seasonal demand affect the firm's capacity planning and constraint management?

2. Identify the most critical issues in the case, and develop a strategic capacity plan for Kirwain.

3. What long-term issues should be considered? Medium term? Short term? Make sure that your analysis considers the implications for each of these planning horizons.

VIDEO CASE

Watch this video case to learn about how MPK Foods, a family-owned company that produces seasoning mixes sold to grocery stores, plans and manages the capacity of their suppliers and manufacturing operations to meet varying levels of demand.

CRITICAL THINKING EXERCISES ···

The following article highlights some capacity planning challenges that companies face in meeting demand for their products in a growth market. Specifically, the article discusses the success of Fiat Chrysler Automobile's (Auburn Hills, MI) operation in Brazil and the capacity planning challenges the company had to deal with to support its growth in South America.

Read the article Perry, J. (2014, October 10). Fiat Brazil: Quest for growth. *Automotive Manufacturing Solutions.* Retrieved from http://www.auto motivemanufacturingsolutions.com/people/fiat-brazil-getting-bigger-and -better

1. Highlight some capacity planning challenges that Fiat faces with its Betim factory and desire to grow its markets in South America. How do the efforts to increase capacity lead to the identification of production bottlenecks? Give examples.

2. What are some challenges with increasing production capacity at older plants?

3. How can local government initiatives help a company like Fiat with its capacity planning challenges?

Demonstrate your understanding of **capacity planning and management** at Littlefield Labs.

Littlefield Laboratories is a highly automated, state-of-the-art blood testing facility for clinics and hospitals. The lab will operate 24 hours a day for a total of 210 days. You're asked to step in as the operations manager on Day 30, and are tasked wit managing the capacity of the lab for the duration of its operation. Because Littlefield Labs guarantees results within a specific time frame, delays in testing and processing times can cost you money. Based on historic data and predicted demand patterns, you must buy or sell machines in order to optimize capacity and maximize the lab's profits.

Compete against your classmates to prove your understanding of the chapter concepts:

• LO 7-1: Explain why capacity planning is important and how capacity decisions are made.

• LO 7-2: Evaluate the difficulties associated with capacity planning for services, and explain how they can be overcome.

The team with the most cash in hand at the end of the 210-day time frame wins!

©iStockphoto.com/PonyWang

CHAPTER
8

Supply Chain Design and Location Planning

LEARNING OBJECTIVES

After studying this chapter, you should be able to:

1. Discuss the factors that affect supply chain design and facility location decisions.

2. List and describe the phases in the supply chain design and location decision-making process.

3. Describe and compare the analytical methods managers use to evaluate locations.

4. Identify the effect of sustainability and ethics on the location decisions of firms and supply chains.

5. Identify the factors that can influence the choice of global locations.

OPERATIONS PROFILE: Mexico, the Next Great Automaker

Most people do not think of Mexico as a region known for auto manufacturing. Yet, since the early 2000s, the country on America's southern border has steadily become one of the world's most attractive places for automakers to locate their factories. Because of Mexico's pursuit of free trade agreements, it is an ideal export base for automakers from Europe, China, Japan, and the United States. More than 80% of the cars built in Mexico are exported to other countries, about two thirds of them to the United States. "I can export duty free to North America, South America, Europe and Japan," says Volkswagen of Mexico's (subsidiary of Volkswagen AG, Wolfsburg, Germany) Vice President of Corporate Affairs Thomas Karig. "There's not another country in the world where you can do that."

Nissan (Nissan Motor Company Ltd, Yokohama, Japan), Mercedes-Benz (Stuttgart, Baden-Württemberg, Germany), and BMW (Bayerische Motoren Werke AG, Munich, Germany) have plans to manufacture cars in Mexico, as has Hyundai-Kia (Hyundai Motor Company, Seoul, South Korea). Audi (Audi AG, Ingolstadt, Germany) has recently constructed a US$1.3 billion factory that builds luxury SUVs in Mexico. In 2016, Mexico was the world's eighth-largest auto producer, on pace to surpass Brazil. By 2020, Mexico should be sixth behind China, the United States, Japan, India, and Germany, with an annual production of 4.7 million vehicles. Mexico's gain further benefits the United States because Mexican factories use four times as many American-made components as Chinese factories do.

Locating a plant in Mexico offers four key advantages. First, China's manufacturing wages have increased significantly since 2000 and are now up to 30% higher than in Mexico. This makes China less competitive and Mexico's wages more attractive to auto companies. Second, the North American Free Trade Agreement (NAFTA) benefited Mexican businesses by allowing them to implement free trade agreements with more than 40 countries, which is greater than the United States and China combined. Third, Mexican manufacturing businesses pay far less for natural gas than do Chinese manufacturers because natural gas prices in Mexico are tied to U.S. prices. Finally, Mexican businesses can take advantage of industry clusters of auto parts manufacturers that have flocked to the country over the past several years, allowing them to take advantage of reduced transportation costs.

In Aguascalientes, a city located some 500 kilometers northwest of Mexico City, in North Central Mexico, a progressive governor and local mayor courted foreign auto manufacturers. They

Bloomberg/Bloomberg/Getty Images

attracted Nissan, which built a massive 21-million-square-foot factory. In 2012, the governor helped set up an arrangement in which the government sold the land, just 4 miles from another Nissan factory, to the Japanese carmaker at an attractive price. Nineteen months later, the US$2 billion plant, one of the largest industrial investments ever made in Mexico, was up and almost running, which was a record for Nissan. Production began in late 2013 and quickly ramped up to full capacity of 175,000 vehicles a year, operating 23 hours a day, 6 days a week. Approximately 3,000 jobs were created, and another 9,000 at supplier companies. Across the street, connected by a newly built bridge, is a logistics center where railcars are standing by to transport vehicles to the United States and Brazil. In addition to these primary markets, Nissan ships to 50 countries from Mexico. Between the two plants in Aguascalientes, Nissan produces one vehicle every 38 seconds, which is on par with its flagship plant in Kyushu, Japan.[1]

Aguascalientes is a success story in supply chain management and plant location planning, which are the topics of this chapter. We discuss these ideas by first addressing the nature of supply chain design and facility location decisions. We then examine the design and location process—that is, the steps by which organizations intentionally develop with supply chain partner networks and make critical facility location decisions. Finally, we consider the wide variety of methods that organizations use to locate plants and evaluate various location options. Our goal is to offer a chapter that clearly demonstrates why location planning is critical and takes us on a journey through the ways in which firms identify facility location.

8.1

Discuss the factors that affect supply chain design and facility location decisions.

Supply Chain Design

8.1 Supply Chain Design and Facility Location Decisions

Managing supply chains is more than the efficient movement of goods. Decisions have to be made about (a) what and how much of a product to produce at each stage of the supply chain process; (b) the amount of inventory to be held at each stage; (c) how and what type of information should be shared among supply chain partners; and (d) where plants and distribution centers should be located, what manufacturing processes should be performed at each facility, what the capacity of the facilities should be, what markets should each facility serve, and which supply sources should provide raw materials to each facility.[2]

All of these supply chain design decisions are interrelated, and each has an impact on the overall performance of the supply chain in terms of its cost and on responsiveness in terms of its ability to meet customer demand on time and react purposefully to changes in the marketplace. For example, Amazon.com (aka Amazon, Seattle, WA) found that it could not operate efficiently by using a single Seattle-area warehouse to supply books and other products throughout the United States. To improve its shipping times, the company had to add additional warehouses in other parts of the country. Similarly, in 1988, Toyota (Toyota Motor Corporation, Toyota City, Japan) opened its first U.S. assembly plant in Lexington, Kentucky. The location has been a good one. The plant has been more cost-efficient than many older, union-staffed American car manufacturing facilities.

The decisions about transportation, inventory, and information sharing can be changed fairly easily depending on changes in the supply chain, customer demand, and the marketplace. For example, it is easy for a firm to change how it transports products. Instead of trucking them, it might opt to send them by rail. Nevertheless, the decisions made about where to locate facilities cannot be changed easily. These choices have a long-term effect. Relocating a multibillion-dollar automotive assembly plant in Mexico as a result of fluctuations in demand, transportation costs, raw material prices, or an unstable political environment is much harder to do.

Decisions about distribution centers and warehouses in the supply chain, many of which are equipped with costly and sophisticated state-of-the art materials handling equipment, can be difficult to undo as well. Once these facilities are established, they can't be easily relocated. Yet, if the locations of the facilities are suboptimal, the result will be higher costs throughout the lifetime of these facilities.[3]

Factors That Affect Supply Chain and Location Decisions

Many factors that influence supply chain design and location decisions are environmental; that is, they are conditions over which a firm has no control. In addition, technological factors, such as the nature and availability of production technologies, are also critical. In fact, flexibility, economies of scale, and fixed costs associated with production technologies along with product requirements in different markets influence the choice of whether a company needs to locate a few large facilities or several small local facilities. In the soft drinks industry, for example, companies such as Pepsi (PepsiCo Inc., Purchase, NY) and Coca Cola (The Coca-Cola Company, Atlanta, GA) have many bottling plants all over the world. The availability of natural resources, skilled labor, capital, and information resources also have an effect on location decisions. Wine-makers locate in regions such as Napa Valley in California, New South Wales in Australia, and Bordeaux in France because of their ideal soil conditions and climates.

Commerce restrictions and conditions such as taxes, tariffs, and quotas are also factors. For example, Boeing's (The Boeing Company, Chicago, IL) decision to locate a new factory in North Charleston, South Carolina, to assemble the 787 air-craft was influenced by the tax incentives offered and right-to-work laws (allowing nonunion labor) in that state. Similarly, trade agreements such as NAFTA, General Agreement on Tariffs and Trade (GATT), and the establishment of the European Union have reduced or eliminated tariffs and quotas, making it attractive to com-panies to locate abroad.

Political factors include the political stability of a country, the existence of well-established legal systems, rules of commerce, corporate ownership, and the transfer of earnings, which are critical to global supply chain decisions. The lack of a legal system that enforces copyrights and patents has prevented many inter-national firms from entering the Chinese market. Critics have charged that the Chinese government has been slow to uphold international copyright agreements.[4] Likewise, Venezuela's 2010 decision to nationalize the facilities of U.S.-based Owens-Illinois Inc. (Perrysburg, OH), which describes itself as the world's largest glass container maker, was just one in a long string of government seizures of private commercial property, ranging from gold mines, to banks, to power companies.[5]

The infrastructure of different countries, the competition, target market customer preferences, and logistics and facility costs are also important in supply chain design decisions. To provide easy access to customers in the target market, many service businesses such as banks and logistics companies oper-ate and maintain several sites. In addition to its super hub and headquarters in Memphis, Tennessee, the FedEx Corporation has a national hub in Indianapolis and several regional hubs throughout the United States. The company's hub in Indianapolis's airport alone helps FedEx connect with customers in more than 220 countries and territories on six continents. The number of locations a firm needs and their sizes depend on the target markets.

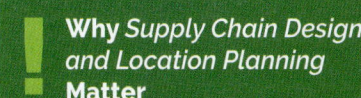

> **Why** *Supply Chain Design and Location Planning* **Matter**
>
> Deciding where a company's facilities are located and how its supply chain is designed has a huge impact on revenues, costs, and operations. These decisions also determine the ability of a company to meet sustainability goals such as protecting natural resources and reducing carbon emissions.

Competitive Strategies That Affect Supply Chain and Location Decisions

How a company designs its supply chain and where it locates its facilities will depend on the factors we just described as well as a firm's particular competitive strategy. Let's look at some of these strat-egies next.

STRATEGY: LOWER THE FIRM'S COSTS

Businesses across the globe were hit hard by the financial and economic turmoil that began in 2008. In the years that followed, companies and their suppliers were under intense cost pressures to reeval-uate low-cost sourcing and manufacturing strategies. One key part of these strategies is facilities man-agement—that is, selecting the best locations and planning for the optimal manufacturing or service capacity for the facilities. For example, lower labor costs are the main reason that companies like General Motors (General Motors Company, Detroit, MI), General Electric (aka GE, Fairfield, CT), and Motorola (Motorola Solutions, Inc., Schaumburg, IL) have facilities in China and India. Credit card companies routinely operate call centers from sites in India or the Philippines. Similarly, more than 3,000 companies, including large multinational firms such as Toyota (already introduced), Panasonic (Panasonic Corporation, Osaka, Japan), Hitachi (Hitachi, Ltd., Tokyo, Japan), and Zenith Electronics (division of LG Electronics, Seoul, South Korea) operate manufacturing plants along the U.S.–Mexican border to take advantage of the low Mexican wages there. More than a million workers are employed in these plants.

STRATEGY: GROW THE FIRM'S BUSINESS

Firms that focus on market growth often locate their facilities in reasonable proximity to the new market that they are planning to enter. Mexico, for example, is a key location for spring boarding Nissan's market growth in the Americas. Consequently, as mentioned earlier, in addition to its new plant in Brazil, Nissan has built a US$2 billion manufacturing complex in Mexico.[6] Likewise, because the United States is the world's largest luxury car market, BMW, Mercedes-Benz, Lexus (division of Toyota Motor Corporation, Nagoya, Japan), and Acura (division of Honda Motor Co., Tokyo, Japan) have all built plants in North America to enhance their local market opportunities. Service industries, including banks, fast food chains such as Taco Bell (subsidiary of Yum! Brands, Inc., Irvine,

In 1990, McDonald's opened its first restaurant in Russia in Moscow's Pushkin Square. The store serves more than 30,000 customers a day, and is as busy as it was on opening day. With the exception of cabbage pie among other traditional Russian food items, the menu is essentially the same as in the United States.

Alexander Nemenov/AFP/Getty Images

CA) and McDonald's (Oak Brook, IL), retail stores, and supermarkets are locating abroad for the same reason. McDonald's, by establishing its first restaurant in Russia in January 1990 and subsequently expanding to more than 60 Russian cities, was able to set up its restaurants in many of the top locations in that country. Starbucks (Starbucks Corporation, Seattle, WA), on the other hand, only entered the country in 2007, which has made the company's search for prime locations more complicated. In addition, many companies have been able to extend the life cycles of their mature products by offering them in foreign countries. For example, the Suzuki Cultus (Suzuki Motor Corporation, Hamamatsu, Japan), originally manufactured and sold in Western countries in 1983, is still being manufactured in Pakistan and enjoys strong sales throughout the Far East.

STRATEGY: ACCESS NEW SOURCES OF MATERIALS AND RESOURCES

Depleted raw materials or natural resources sometimes force organizations to relocate. Mining, petroleum, fishing, and logging businesses are often forced to relocate to tap into new supplies of resources. Shortages of iron ore and coking coal in China and elsewhere have forced many steel companies to prospect for new locations worldwide that have rich iron-ore deposits. For example, the world's largest steel producer ArcelorMittal, S.A. (Luxembourg City, Luxembourg) and South Korea's POSCO (Seoul, South Korea) are spending US$32 billion to build steel mills in eastern India. The Australian mining company Fortescue Metals Group Ltd (East Perth, Western Australia) is also exploiting China's depleted resources and need for steel by exploring for iron ore in western Australia.[7]

STRATEGY: ACCESS TALENT IN ORDER TO DEVELOP INNOVATIVE PRODUCTS

Location is critical for companies whose operations strategies depend on innovation. There are innovation hubs all around the world for various industries. These innovation hubs are social communities or research centers that provide subject-matter expertise on technology trends, knowledge management, and industry-specific insights. Israel, Sweden, and Finland attract firms engaged in wireless communications. The United States is an innovation hub for firms in the pharmaceutical industry. Research Triangle Park, an area in North Carolina, serves as a secondary location for dozens of the world's top computer and technology firms, including BASF SE (Ludwigshafen, Germany), DuPont (E. I. du Pont de Nemours and Company, Wilmington, DE), IBM (International Business Machines Corporation, Armonk, NY), United Therapeutics (Silver Spring, MD), and Cisco (Cisco Systems, Inc., San Jose, CA). Similarly, there are concentrations of software developers in places such as California's Silicon Valley, Boston, and the Indian city of Bangalore. This phenomenon is called clustering, and it often occurs when there is a concentration of critical resources in a particular region. All of these firms are located where there is a large talent pool of scientists and engineers and strong links between universities and industry.[8] These organizations reason that it is often easier to bring facilities to the talent rather than trying to lure talent to remote facility locations.

TAKE ADVANTAGE OF FAVORABLE FINANCIAL, LEGAL, AND REGULATORY ENVIRONMENTS

Clustering: a phenomenon where several companies in the same industry are located in the same area because of a concentration of critical resources in a particular region

Firms often relocate to take advantage of the financial incentives offered by governments. Indiana and Louisiana have attracted companies from neighboring states with more restrictive labor laws. Many American companies have moved their headquarters abroad to escape property and corporate income taxes and to take advantage of tax rebates and lower tax rates offered to these companies by foreign governments. For example, several American companies, including pharmaceutical firms Pfizer, Inc. (New York, NY), and Actavis Generics (Dublin, Ireland, and Parsippany-Troy Hills, NJ), have set up locations in Ireland to take advantage of more favorable tax rates. U.S. stem cell companies are establishing their operations in Asia because of the willingness of the governments in Asian countries to invest in stem cell research and the fewer regulatory requirements there.[9]

Why Supply Chain and Location Decisions Sometimes Backfire

Some companies such as McDonald's and Wal-Mart (Wal-Mart Stores Inc., Bentonville, AR) have enjoyed remarkable long-term success operating across the United States and around the world. Other companies have been less successful. Let's look at some drawbacks associated with supply chain design and location decisions, particularly when they involve operations in foreign countries.

CULTURAL ISSUES

Companies with locations in other countries must learn to do business in an environment with a different culture and with different laws. To be successful, a firm's managers need to be fluent in the country's language to supervise the workers and relate to customers and other businesspeople in

In an increasingly global marketplace, it is important for organizations to understand the cultures of their business partners and international divisions to effectively communicate goals, priorities, and challenges.

©iStockphoto.com/Dean Mitchell

the country. It is also critical to understand the religious and cultural practices in overseas locations. In 2004, McDonald's offended Muslims and tarnished its reputation when it printed the Saudi Arabian flag on several takeout containers. The flag contains a verse from the Koran, which according to Islamic religion, should never be placed on objects meant to be thrown away.

Companies have to deal with gender differences in labor practices and in promoting products that can be sold to consumers. For example, in many African nations, women are limited in the types of work they can perform. Thus, hiring women for some factory jobs is inappropriate. Finally, it is critical to recognize that not every product will appeal to consumers in other cultures. For example, P&G (Procter & Gamble Co., Cincinnati, OH) would be unable to sell disposable razors to women in a culture in which women do not normally shave their legs.[10]

PRODUCT QUALITY AND SAFETY PROBLEMS

Quality and safety problems can occur when companies outsource their manufacturing operations to firms abroad. A 2015 exposé by CBS's *60 Minutes* (New York, NY) on regulatory standards violations prompted the decision by Lumber Liquidators, Inc. (Toano, VA), to stop selling laminate flooring made in China. Unfortunately, many quality and safety issues are not uncovered until the products reach the hands of consumers.

Often workers in low-cost manufacturing countries lack adequate supervision and the training they need to produce safe, high-quality products. Moreover, these production workers are often under pressure to meet stringent output and time deadlines, which can lead to lower quality products. In addition, in several developing countries, different cultural attitudes regarding the importance of hard work can result in lower productivity and quality.[11]

TRANSPORTATION ISSUES

Companies that have operations in overseas locations have experienced logistical and transportation problems such as congestion in ports, dock strikes, theft, risk of piracy, and security risks from terrorism. If goods produced in an overseas location are to be transported to other countries, then the extended distances and potential transportation disruptions can lead to higher costs that can negate any savings in labor and material costs.

CURRENCY AND EXCHANGE RATE RISKS

The global economic and financial turmoil that we have witnessed in recent years has exposed the currencies of many struggling countries to the risk of devaluation—a reduction in the value of their currencies. China, for example, has taken significant steps to prop up the value of its currency, the yuan, to prevent capital from leaving the country for other currencies like the U.S. dollar or euro. For global corporations with facilities in a foreign country, the devaluation of that country's currency frequently results in lower revenues and profits in there. This is because in competitive markets, these companies usually cannot increase their prices beyond a point to cover the losses from the lower exchange rate that resulted from the devaluation. Furthermore, a country whose currency has been devalued typically experiences other economic problems such as inflation, unstable financial markets, and possibly a recession. The inability to plan for such financial problems can have a negative impact on the firm's

Devaluation: a reduction in the value of currencies

bottom line. For example, after the latest in a series of devaluations of the Venezuelan bolívar, Pepsi announced a loss of US$126 million for 2014 and took even larger losses the next year. Coca-Cola lost more than US$660 million during that same period from its operations in Venezuela, and a group of airlines said last year that the government owes them a combined US$4 billion.[12]

IMPORT/EXPORT RESTRICTIONS

Companies operating in foreign locations often face import and export restrictions, many of which can be stringent. For example, the United States has restricted the amount of steel and lumber that can be imported. The restrictions are intended to prevent foreign producers from dumping low-cost lumber and steel in the United States to drive domestic producers out of the market. Similarly, manufacturers in Brazil continue working to protect their markets by lobbying the government to impose tariffs on numerous imported products, including shoes, chemicals, textiles, and cars. In addition, some countries place restrictions on the transfer of earnings that companies can export out of the country or the amount they can deposit in foreign banks. Also, many countries such as China, Mexico, the Philippines, and Thailand severely restrict the foreign ownership of firms within their countries. For example, foreign companies that wish to locate their operations in China have to partner with a local Chinese firm.

THE POTENTIAL LOSS OF PROPRIETARY TECHNOLOGY

When a company considers locating in a foreign market, the firm must evaluate the country's legal climate—especially to determine whether proprietary patents and technologies are legally protected there. According to the 2015 International Property Rights Index (IPRI), Venezuela, Haiti, Angola, Bangladesh, and Myanmar are the five worst countries in the protection of private and intellectual property rights.[13] Although laws in China protecting intellectual property rights have been in place since 1979, violations of these rights are still prevalent, particularly in the automotive and electronic industries.[14] For example, Volkswagen assembles its autos in China under a joint-venture contract with its Chinese partner, the FAW Group Corporation (aka FAW, Changchun, Jilin, P.R. China). In 2012, Volkswagen's executives accused FAW of stealing the designs for an automatic transmission. Previously FAW had stolen Volkswagen's blueprints for a new engine and had built a new factory to produce it. Unfortunately, Volkswagen could do little besides formally protest these thefts. Because China is one of the company's biggest foreign markets, the German automaker is in the awkward position of trying to protect its patents while avoiding offending its Chinese hosts and maintaining its sales in the country.[15]

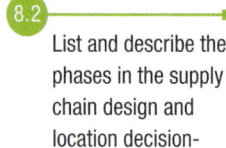

List and describe the phases in the supply chain design and location decision-making process.

The Location Decision Process

8.2 Phases in the Supply Chain Design and Location Decision-Making Process

Several design models, including sophisticated mathematical optimization models, are often used to determine the best possible network of facilities. The transportation model is one such technique, which will be discussed in Section 8.3. First, however, let's look at the four decision-making phases related to designing a supply chain and locating facilities. Notice how many of the factors that we have discussed feed into the decisions that need to be made in each phase.

Phase I: Design the Supply Chain

In this phase, the firm outlines the basic design of the supply chain. The design chosen will reflect the number of stages in the supply chain, the activities that will be performed at each stage, and whether these activities will be performed in-house or outsourced. The first input to supply chain design is the firm's competitive strategy because the supply chain should be arranged to satisfy the needs of customers. The second input is the forecast of the potential global competition that is likely to exist in each of the firm's markets and whether this competition will be from local or global companies. Third, the company should identify any internal constraints on its available capital and determine whether the firm's future growth can be accomplished with its existing facilities, by building new facilities, or through partnering with a member of the supply chain. With the help of these inputs, the company can determine the design of the supply chain.

Phase II: Determine the Configuration of Regional Facilities

In this phase, expected demand by country, the volume of the demand, and customer requirements are analyzed. If the customer requirements are fairly homogeneous in that they do not change from region to region, then locating a few large consolidated facilities would be satisfactory. On the other hand, if customer requirements vary, the firm would need several smaller localized facilities. Another factor that influences the location and size of facilities is whether existing production technologies can reduce costs through economies of scale. Firms in the semiconductor industry, for example, require just a few high-capacity locations to achieve cost reduction through economies of scale. As we have explained, tax incentives, tariffs, exchange rates, and import and export restrictions also influence the choice of regional locations for the firm's supply chain. In general, regions that are politically stable and have favorable taxes and exchange rates are better locations than those that may include political instability or other factors that can negatively affect operations. In addition, factors such as the competitiveness of markets, the potential total logistics costs, and expected time to respond to the requirements of each market should be considered in deciding the location of regional facilities. The overall objective of this phase is to determine the number of facilities needed for the supply chain, the regions where they will be located, and the role each facility will play in meeting the market requirements.

Phase III: Select Potential Sites for Locating Facilities

Once the firm decides on the regions where facilities would be located, it must then identify potential sites within each region for setting up these facilities. The main factors to be considered at this stage are the availability of the necessary infrastructure, including suppliers, transportation services, utilities, availability of skilled workers, and community attitude toward the location of the industry facility.

Phase IV: Choose Locations

In this phase of the decision process, the firm selects the exact sites for locating the various facilities in the supply chain. The objective in Phase IV is to come up with a final supply chain design that will maximize the profits for the company, given its labor and logistics costs, taxes and tariffs, and other site specific costs for each location in the supply chain.

Many factors, which vary from industry to industry, affect location decisions. For example, when deciding where to locate a manufacturing facility, its proximity to raw materials and the availability of labor and low labor costs are clearly important. Health-care and emergency facilities such as fire stations and paramedic units must be located near population centers. By contrast, issues such as pollution and public safety generally force companies to locate chemical plants and nuclear power stations far away from residential areas. Locations decisions are sequential and made in three stages, which we describe next. Various factors in each stage need to be considered. These critical success factors are listed in Table 8.1.

STAGE 1: SELECT THE COUNTRY

The choice of a country generally depends on economic and market conditions and the legal system. For example, after nearly 20 years of negotiations with the Chinese central government and at a final cost of US$5.5 billion, The Walt Disney Company (aka Disney, Burbank, CA) has opened a Disneyland-style theme park in Shanghai. Despite significant governmental restrictions, Disney's choice of China as its next global location was motivated by that nation's huge market—1.3 billion potential customers.[16]

STAGE 2: SELECT THE REGION

After selecting the country, the firm must decide which specific geographic region is most conducive for locating the manufacturing or service facilities. The decision is based on the availability of skilled labor, transportation networks, tax incentives, and demographics. For example, Disney's Shanghai theme park encompasses more than 1,700 acres—as large as the company's park in Florida. Disney picked Shanghai largely because of its transportation network and the relatively higher discretionary income of its residents. In the absence of a strong transportation network, the logistical challenges of accommodating and catering to visitors at a huge resort can be enormous.

Hospitals need to be located in populous areas, like Johns Hopkins Hospital in Baltimore, MD, to be accessible to most people.

©iStockphoto.com/Delmas Lehman

TABLE 8.1: Critical Success Factors at the Location Decision Stages

LOCATION DECISION	CRITICAL SUCCESS FACTORS
Country	• Labor climate • Transportation costs • Markets and customer proximity • Proximity to suppliers and resources • Competitors' locations • Sustainability factors (environmental quality and labor laws and regulations.) • Political environment and the stability of the government • Tax laws and structure • Cultural and social factors such as language differences, norms and customs, religious holidays, customer attitudes and characteristics, and the standard of living • Economic factors such as the stability of a nation's currency, its exchange rates, interest rates, inflation rate, and employment level • Other factors such as utility costs, water and power supplies, infrastructure, and telecommunications
Region	• Proximity to markets • Proximity to raw materials • Availability and cost of utilities • Labor availability, costs, and degree of unionization • Taxes and incentives • Environmental laws and regulations • Attractiveness of the community such as the quality of life, availability of housing and recreational facilities, schools • Transportation networks available such as rail, truck, water, pipeline • Other factors: climate, company preferences and desires, and regional and local governmental policies and attitudes
Site	• Size of site • Space to expand • Construction and land costs • Zoning and environmental restrictions • Transportation infrastructure, such as airports, ports, and highways • Proximity to customers and other supporting industries • Visibility and traffic patterns • Customer safety

Another reason that the company chose Shanghai is that about 330 million potential customers live within three hours of the site, which is located between the city's airport and downtown.[17]

STAGE 3: SELECT THE SITE

Next the company must choose the specific site to locate the facilities. Factors that can affect this decision include construction and land costs, zoning and environmental restrictions, space to expand the facility (if desired), and proximity to supporting industries. The location decisions for service and retail firms are influenced by factors that are somewhat different from manufacturing firms. Minimizing costs is a major objective for manufacturing firms. Instead, service companies generally look for locations that will have a big impact on their volumes sold, or revenues.

In general, for the service sector, the critical success factors in locating facilities are the proximity of competitors, convenient access for customers, traffic volumes and patterns, parking availability, and, demographics such as the age and income levels of customers, as well as the size of the population. One reason that doctor's offices and hospitals are often located near one another is for the convenience of patients who have been referred from one to the other. For service firms such as banks, customer safety, and security are also important on the decisions about branch location. On the other hand, for many retail businesses such as department stores, fast-food restaurants, automobile dealers, and gas stations, traffic volumes are the predominant success factors. In addition, decisions about location vary depending on the type of service firm. For example, although it's important for hospitals and supermarkets to be near their customers, this criterion is not important for service firms such as call centers, catalog companies, e-tailors, and other online businesses.

Figure 8.1 shows the three-stage, decision-making process for locating an Alcon, Inc. (Fort Worth, TX, and Hünenberg, Switzerland) facility. Alcon sells a wide range of surgical, pharmaceutical, and vision-care products in more than 180 countries. One of Alcon's manufacturing facilities is located in Brazil. Alcon

FIGURE 8.1: Stages in the Location Decision for an Alcon Facility

| Country Decision (Brazil) | Region Decision (Sao Paulo) | Site Decision (City of Sao Paulo) |

chose the Brazilian location because it foresaw the country's potential as an emerging economy. Alcon's decision to locate the manufacturing facilities in the state and city of Sao Paulo was further motivated by the availability of skilled labor, market size, regional governmental support, and tax incentives. The company chose the particular site because the firm needed to build a facility large enough to include sales and marketing offices, a state-of-the-art manufacturing plant, and a distribution center. Approximately 400 Alcon employees work in the 6,000-square-foot facility. Note that companies seldom find an ideal location. Typically, they find several satisfactory or acceptable locations to choose from.

8.3 Analytical Methods for Evaluating Locations

8.3 Describe and compare the analytical methods managers use to evaluate locations.

Decision-making tools can be used to select the best possible location. The most popular and commonly used ones are:

- Factor rating method
- Breakeven analysis
- Center-of-gravity method
- Geographic information system (GIS) method

In this section, we look at each of these methods. Another method, the transportation method, which is a more advanced quantitative technique, is presented in Module B.

The Factor Rating Method

In this method, the various location alternatives are evaluated by rating the relevant factors. To use this method, you would take the following steps:

1. Identify and list the most relevant factors in the location decision.
2. Rate the importance of each factor on a scale of 1 to 5 (with 1 being low and 5 being high).
3. For each factor, rate each location on a scale of 1 to 10 (with 1 for very low and 10 for very high).
4. For each factor and each location, compute a score by multiplying the factor rating and the location rating.
5. Compute a total score for each location by summing up the scores calculated in the previous step.
6. Select the site that has the maximum total score.

 Example 8.1

EXAMPLE 8.1: For its first overseas expansion, Harry Potter Magic Kingdom, a fictional British chain of family-oriented theme parks, is evaluating two alternative locations: Chennai, India, and Shanghai, China. Table 8.2 shows the relevant factors and their importance, a rating for each factor for each potential location. Using the factor rating method, we can determine the most suitable location for the theme park.

The total factor rating score for the Shanghai location is higher than that of Chennai. Hence, the Shanghai location is the preferred choice. Nevertheless, this decision should also take into account other relevant information, particularly a cost–volume analysis, often referred to as breakeven analysis, discussed next.

Factor rating method: the process of evaluating the various location alternatives by rating relevant factors

TABLE 8.2: Analyzing Locations: An Example of the Factor Rating Method

FACTORS	FACTOR RATINGS (IMPORTANCE) (1–5)	RATING FOR CHENNAI (1–10)	RATING FOR SHANGHAI (1–10)	SCORE FOR CHENNAI LOCATION	SCORE FOR SHANGHAI LOCATION
Tax Incentives	4	7	5	4 × 7 = 28	4 × 5 = 20
Availability of Labor	5	3	3	5 × 3 = 15	5 × 3 = 15
Proximity to Customers	3	6	5	3 × 6 = 18	3 × 5 = 15
Per Capita Income	5	3	4	5 × 3 = 15	5 × 4 = 20
Transportation Network Availability	3	4	3	3 × 4 = 12	3 × 3 = 9
Community Attitude	5	4	5	5 × 4 = 20	5 × 5 = 25
Quality of Educational System	4	1	6	4 × 1 = 4	4 × 6 = 24
Provision for Site Expansion	2	10	6	2 × 10 = 20	2 × 6 = 12
Proximity to Supporting Industries	2	7	9	2 × 7 = 14	2 × 9 = 18
Utilities Availability	3	5	8	3 × 5 = 15	3 × 8 = 24
TOTAL SCORE				161	182

Breakeven Analysis

When comparing several potential locations, if we assume that the revenue per unit is the same regardless of where the goods are produced, then the total revenues can be eliminated from consideration and the potential locations can be compared on the basis of their total costs. By performing a **breakeven analysis**, we can find the location that has lowest total cost for a given volume range.[18]

To conduct a breakeven analysis by location, take the following steps:

1. For each location, determine its fixed costs and variable cost per unit. Fixed costs are the portion of total costs that remain constant regardless of the volume produced or output level. Variable costs are the portion of total costs that varies directly with the output level.
2. On a graph, plot the total costs (fixed costs + variable costs) for each location against a range of annual production volumes. Plot the total costs on the vertical axis and the annual production volume on the horizontal axis.
3. Choose the location that has the lowest total costs for the expected production volume.

EXAMPLE 8.2: Tipton Metals, a mythical manufacturer of metal castings, needs an additional plant to expand its capacity. The company's managers have identified three potential locations: Sandusky, Ohio; Erie, Pennsylvania; and Pittsburgh, Pennsylvania. All three locations will generate the same revenue per unit of the product produced but have different cost structures as Table 8.3 shows. Given this cost information:

1. Determine the most economical location for an expected annual volume of production of 3,000 units.
2. Determine the breakeven volumes for the locations and the range of annual volumes of production at which each of three locations would become most economical.

TABLE 8.3: Cost Structures for Three Locations

LOCATION	FIXED COSTS (IN U.S. DOLLARS)	VARIABLE COSTS PER UNIT (IN U.S. DOLLARS)
Sandusky, Ohio	30,000	40
Erie, Pennsylvania	55,000	30
Pittsburgh, Pennsylvania	100,000	20

Breakeven analysis: a technique that is used to determine the production quantity at which total revenues are equal to total costs and net profits are equal to zero

3. Total Cost = Fixed Cost + (Production Volume) × (Variable Cost per Unit) = FC + QVC

Example 8.2

$$\text{Total cost for Sandusky} = 30,000 + 3,000 \times 40 = \$150,000$$
$$\text{Total cost for Erie} = 55,000 + 3,000 \times 30 = \$145,000$$
$$\text{Total cost for Pittsburgh} = 100,000 + 3,000 \times 20 = \$160,000$$

Erie has the lowest total cost for a production volume for 3,000 units and therefore seems to be most economical location. Nevertheless, suppose we are not entirely sure how much output we expect to produce at the plant? That is, if we vary the total expected annual output, will that affect our location decision?

To determine the range of production volume at which each location is most economical, we let Q be the breakeven volume—that is, the production volume where the total costs for the locations are the same.

For the Sandusky and Erie locations:

$$30,000 + Q \times 40 = 55,000 + Q \times 30$$
$$Q \times (40 - 30) = 55,000 - 30,000$$
$$10 \times Q = 25,000$$
$$Q = 2,500$$

To determine the production volume where the total costs for the Erie and Pittsburgh locations are the same:

$$55,000 + Q \times 30 = 95,000 + Q \times 20$$
$$Q \times (30 - 20) = 100,000 - 55,000$$
$$10 \times Q = 45,000$$
$$Q = 4,500$$

Hence, Q, the breakeven volume for both the Sandusky and Erie locations, is 2,500 units. The breakeven volume for the Erie and Pittsburgh locations is 4,500 units. This means that for these volumes, you are indifferent to choosing either location—either Sandusky or Erie for 2,500 units and either Erie or Pittsburgh for 4,500 units. Nonetheless, if the production volume is below 2,500 units, then Sandusky is the economical location. Between 2,500 and 4,500 units, Erie is the preferred choice. Beyond an expected production volume of 4,500 units, Pittsburgh should be selected.

Note that we did not compute a breakeven volume for Sandusky and Pittsburgh because for a range of production volume between 2,500 and 4,500 units, the Erie location has the lowest total costs and is clearly the best choice (see Screenshot 8.1).

SCREENSHOT 8.1: Analyzing Locations: An Example of a Breakeven Analysis Using Excel

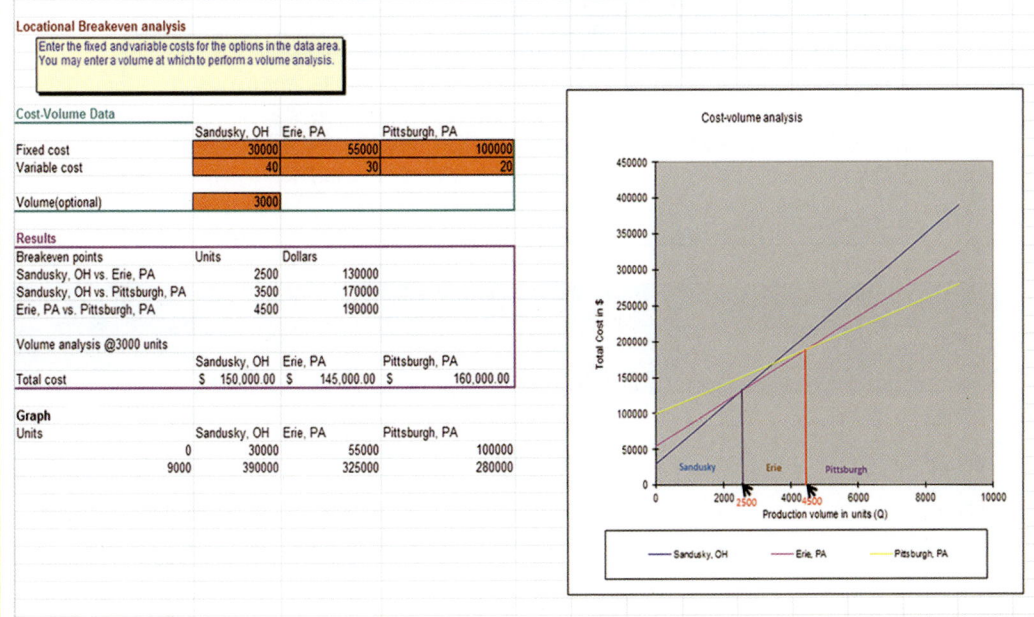

The Center-of-Gravity Method

The center-of-gravity method is a quantitative technique used to determine the location of a single warehouse or distribution center to minimize its distribution costs. Distribution costs typically depend on several factors, such as the weight of a product, the quantity of it shipped, and the distance and speed at which it must travel. Nevertheless, the center-of-gravity method assumes that distribution costs are a linear function of only the distance and the quantity shipped. That is, the method attempts to locate a facility at the center of movement within a geographic area based on these two factors. The method makes use of a map and a coordinate system to identify the coordinates of a central location relative to all other locations.

The first step in the center-of-gravity method is to place the existing locations on either a grid or a map using x (longitude) and y (latitude) coordinates. The scale used and the origin of the coordinate system can be arbitrary as long as the relative distances of the existing locations are accurately represented. To determine the center of gravity or the coordinates for the central location of the new facility, the following formulas are used:

$$x\text{-coordinate of the new facility at the center of gravity} = \frac{\sum_{i=1}^{n} x_i Q_i}{\sum_{i=1}^{n} Q_i}$$

$$y\text{-coordinate of the new facility at the center of gravity} = \frac{\sum_{i=1}^{n} y_i Q_i}{\sum_{i=1}^{n} Q_i}$$

where,

$x_i = x$-coordinate of the existing facility i
$y_i = y$-coordinate of the existing facility i
$Q_i =$ annual quantity/weight shipped to and from existing facility i

 Example 8.3

EXAMPLE 8.3: The fictional Royal Lobster restaurant chain currently has one restaurant in each of the following locations: Buffalo, New York; Chicago; Atlanta; and Jersey City, New Jersey. The company wants to construct a new central distribution center to process and package ingredients before shipping them to the various restaurants. The annual demand for these ingredients in trailer loads is shown in the following table. The ingredients are transported in 40-foot truck trailers, each with a capacity of 35,000 pounds. Using the center-of-gravity method, determine a possible location for the distribution center.

RESTAURANT LOCATION	NUMBER OF CONTAINERS SHIPPED ANNUALLY
Atlanta	135
Buffalo	75
Chicago	145
Jersey City	125

Center-of-gravity method: a quantitative technique used to determine the location of a single warehouse or distribution center at the center of movement within a geographic area to minimize its distribution costs

RESTAURANT LOCATION	X- COORDINATE VALUES (X_i)	Y- COORDINATE VALUES (Y_i)	NUMBER OF CONTAINERS SHIPPED ANNUALLY (Q_i)	$X_i \times Q_i$	$Y_i \times Q_i$
Atlanta	550	100	135	74,250	13,500
Buffalo	700	950	75	52,500	71,250
Chicago	200	700	145	29,000	101,500
Jersey City	1,000	650	125	125,000	81,250
TOTALS			480	280,750	267,500

$$x\text{-coordinate of the new facility} = \frac{\sum\limits_{i=1}^{n} x_i Q_i}{\sum\limits_{i=1}^{n} Q_i}$$

$$= 280{,}750 \div 480 = 585$$

$$y\text{-coordinate of the new facility} = \frac{\sum\limits_{i=1}^{n} y_i Q_i}{\sum\limits_{i=1}^{n} Q_i}$$

$$= 267{,}500 \div 480 = 558$$

The new location for the distribution facility with coordinates (585, 558) is near Cleveland, Ohio. You could plot the data we calculate manually, or use Excel, as Screenshot 8.2 shows.

SCREENSHOT 8.2: Analyzing Locations: An Example of the Center-of-Gravity Method Using Excel

The GIS (Geographic Information System) Method

An important location tool that can be used for both manufacturing and service location analysis is a geographic information system (GIS). A GIS is a computerized system that can store, relate, and display data collected from a physical environment or a geographical location. For example, the geographic databases of many GISs include detailed census and demographic data, maps, utilities, physical features such as rivers and mountains, major airports, colleges, and hospitals in every city, county, zip code, and block in the country. Because a GIS has the ability to overlay existing data with new information and display it in color on a computer screen, it can be used to analyze and make business decisions, urban development decisions, and decisions related to disaster planning. Like service businesses, many retailers use geographical information systems to identify good locations.

GIS was used to identify Starbucks locations based on median household incomes in the Chicago area. Although there are Starbucks locations throughout the Chicago metro area, the highest concentration of them are in the "Loop" or downtown business district. This high concentration of Starbucks locations is because even though downtown Chicago is not a predominantly residential area, there is a high volume of traffic in that area on a daily basis. In fact, within one particular half-square mile area in the middle of downtown Chicago, there are 11 Starbuck's stores. In addition, the highest median

Geographic information system (GIS): a computerized system that can store, relate, and display data collected from a physical environment or a geographical location

Consider This 8.1:
GIS and Location Decisions

Adam Rousselle needed to move his expanding firm, Utility Risk Management Corp, which was based in Doylestown, Pennsylvania, 25 miles outside Philadelphia. Utility Risk Management uses sophisticated technology to identify trees that threaten to take down power lines. Rouselle expected to increase his company's eight-person staff with dozens of new engineers, programmers, and mathematicians. But Doylestown was too small to attract that much talent quickly.

Rouselle didn't opt to move the company to a large city though. Surprisingly, he relocated the firm to the ski town of Stowe, Vermont. His decision attracted the attention of then-Vermont Governor Jim Douglas and other leaders in government, industry, and academia, all eager to bring technology jobs to the state, which heavily relies on tourism. It was attention his small firm didn't get in Pennsylvania. "The governor came to welcome 18 people who came to my job fair," he said.

Rousselle considered three states besides Vermont: Michigan, Florida, and elsewhere in Pennsylvania. In the end, he said, the labor force, support from state officials, and an estimated US$380,000 in cash incentives, made Vermont the best fit. Rousselle said he could get up to US$5,000 per employee each year to train them in specific skills that his customers want. And, he said, he could offer lower salaries than he needed to in Pennsylvania and still be competitive in the labor market.

So was Vermont the perfect location? "There is no such thing," said Anatalio Ubalde, the co-founder of GIS Planning, Inc., a San Francisco company that analyzes geographic data for economic developers. "Is there a better location than another one? The answer is yes."

GIS Planning launched a site called ZoomProspector.com designed to evaluate potential sites based on the attributes entrepreneurs believe matter most to their businesses. Other websites such as City-data.com provide local information, but Ubalde said that ZoomProspector's proprietary data, much of it collected from the company's economic development clients, offers small business owners access to the same information large companies use when they decide where to site new locations.

"Most small companies aren't simply looking for the cheapest place to do business," Ubalde said. Instead entrepreneurs tend to ask where they can find the best workers, as Rousselle did. "That's why cities like New York and San Francisco remain attractive despite their high costs," according to Ubalde. Aside from the labor pool, tax rates differ significantly from state to state, which may be more important for small businesses with few employees. "Areas with low taxes often also have lower costs, and the combination can entice entrepreneurs who are priced out of places that are more in-demand," stated economist Josh Barro.

Small business owners have long taken a haphazard approach to choosing a location, according to ZoomProspector's Ubalde, which puts them at a disadvantage. That might be a minor inconvenience in a healthy, growing economy but during tougher economic times, location choices can mean the difference between surviving and going out of business. "For some businesses it's the difference of literally millions of dollars each way in affecting the bottom line," Ubalde said.[19]

household incomes are clustered to the North and West of downtown Chicago. Consequently, the highest concentrations of Starbucks locations are in the northern and western suburbs.[20]

8.4 Ethical and Sustainability Issues

8.4

Identify the effect of sustainability and ethics on the location decisions of firms and supply chains.

The increased focus on sustainability has led companies to reevaluate some of their supply chain decisions, including where they locate their facilities and how they design their supply chains. The region and site selection for a facility is particularly important when it comes to sustainability. In terms of sustainability, the firm must answer these questions:

- Is the facility in the right location for protecting natural resources?
- Does the facility have an efficient transportation infrastructure that can help minimize transportation activities to reduce carbon emissions?
- Does the facility have access to renewable energy sources, such as wind and solar energy?
- Does the facility have access to recycling opportunities for the company's waste?
- Does the facility meet all applicable environmental laws and regulations?
- Is the facility cost effective given that the location is sustainable?

As an example of the role sustainability plays in facilities location decisions, consider the decision to find the best location for a health-care facility. If the facility is to be in a rural area, with the open land typically

Ethics and Challenges of Location Decisions

available in such areas, the facility may need storm-water retention ponds and geothermal energy fields to achieve sustainability. If the facility is in an urban area, sustainability would be determined by public transportation networks or recycling centers. Yet another way in which the location of a health-care facility can affect sustainability is through its ability to enhance the physical, social, and economic health of its surrounding community. Companies should understand which strategies align well for a given facility site.

The ethical dilemmas that companies face when locating their facilities result from choices that companies have to make between doing what is right and doing what is good for business.[21] When companies relocate manufacturing facilities, they often lay off employees in the process. Hundreds of thousands of Americans jobs were lost when U.S. manufacturers relocated their plants to Mexico after the passage of NAFTA. The aftermath of terminating operations in an existing location is higher unemployment that, in turn, leads to lower standards of living, economic turmoil, and higher crime rates in the community, state, or country that lost the jobs. During its boom years in the 1950s, Detroit boasted a population of 2 million people and one of the healthiest economies in the United States. As a result of foreign competition and outsourcing, Detroit faced some of the severest challenges in the country, including a serious budget deficit, declining services, alarming levels of unemployment, and a dwindling population. In 2014, several thousand high-paying jobs in Wichita, Kansas, and Winston-Salem, North Carolina, were lost when Boeing and Dell Inc. (Round Rock, TX) closed plants in each of these respective locales. Companies that relocate facilities and domestic jobs can face bad publicity and a loss of goodwill from consumers. On the other hand, the Maine-based small business company, Atayne, LLC (Brunswick, ME), which makes high-performing outdoor and athletic apparel from recycled plastic bottles and recycled fabric, is committed to sourcing and manufacturing its product domestically. The company makes its products in Tennessee, North Carolina, Vermont, and Massachusetts, and the company's sales have doubled each year.[22]

8.5 Global Location Planning

8.5

Identify the factors that can influence the choice of global locations.

Increased globalization and advances in technology that have occurred in recent decades have induced companies to explore global locations to gain a competitive advantage for their businesses. Specifically, advanced communication technology, such as geographical information system (GIS) technology, has simplified the global site location process. Global location planning, however, is still a complex task because companies have to evaluate many factors that can influence the choice of a global location. Some of these foreign location factors include:[23]

Global Location Planning

- *Host country market size*: Companies must be sure that potential locations have a large enough number of potential customers to make the investment in global location profitable.
- *Total cost*: Companies must determine the maximum cost (both tangible and intangible costs) it may incur for each potential location alternative. Tangible costs include distribution, land, labor, taxes, utilities, and construction costs. Intangible costs can include lack of customer responsiveness to the company's business.
- *Infrastructure*: Potential global locations should have the necessary infrastructure such as proximity to highways to facilitate transportation, communications technology services, water, and electricity.
- *Labor availability*: Companies must determine whether each potential global location has the sufficiently skilled labor pool they will need. For example, China's fifth-largest auto maker, BAIC Group (Beijing Automotive Industry Holding Co., Ltd., Beijing, P.R. China), opened a technical center in Fremont, California, in Silicon Valley. BAIC's choice of location was no accident. Fremont is the same city where Tesla makes its Model S and Model X electric vehicles. Because BAIC intends to enhance its electric car capabilities, particularly in the Chinese market, it has developed local partnerships with suppliers, while working to lure engineers from auto makers with greater experience in the industry to gain from their knowledge.[24]
- *Free trade zones*: In choosing potential foreign locations, companies must consider countries that are free-trade zones, as goods can be brought into that country without customs duties and other requirements. As described in the Operations Profile in this chapter, Mexico is poised to become the largest auto manufacturing location in the world, thanks to its liberal free trade policies.
- *Political risk*: In choosing potential foreign locations, companies must evaluate the inherent political risk associated with those locations. For example, some countries in the Middle East and South Asia have unstable political environments, and risk of political upheaval and turmoil can have a negative impact on the company's long-term operations.
- *Governmental regulations*: Governments of many countries, to protect local businesses, have barriers and heavy restrictions and regulations for foreign companies operating within their borders.

There are a number of factors to consider when planning locations overseas, including the size of the host country's market, the total cost, infastructure, availability of labor, free trade zones, political risk, and government regulations in the host country.

©iStockphoto.com/franckreporter

Therefore, companies must evaluate these governmental barriers, environmental regulations, as well as cultural nuances, language barriers, and other obstacles in these host countries when developing location strategies. IKEA (Delft, the Netherlands), the Swedish-founded furniture retailer, announced its intention to open its first store in India by 2017. This was IKEA's second attempt to enter the Indian market, and it only opted to do so after the Indian government announced its willingness to relax laws that required international retailers to get their materials exclusively from small and medium Indian enterprises. With India's government willing to modify the law for companies like IKEA, the company has announced its intention to develop 25 stores nationwide by 2025.[25]

In addition to these factors, companies must also consider the host country's economy, the quality and availability of transportation in that country, protection of intellectual property, and so forth.

Given these many factors and the risks involved in locating in a foreign country, companies typically choose locations in collaboration with economic development groups to keep the operating and start-up costs low. Furthermore, to respond to the intense competition in the global marketplace, companies need to move into the new global location quickly to begin operations. Therefore, most companies, instead of building new facilities, tend to lease existing facilities. In addition, while developing global location strategies, companies must consider adapting their product or service offerings that will meet the unique needs of consumers in the foreign market. Otherwise, the company's venture in the new global location is bound to fail. As an example, the Vodafone Group, the London, U.K.–based telecommunications company, attempted to enter the Japanese market by selling handsets used in Europe. The venture failed, and Vodafone had to abandon the Japanese market because the consumers in that country were using completely different technology from the one used in Europe.[26]

$SAGE edge™

Visit **edge.sagepub.com/venkataraman** to help you accomplish your coursework goals in an easy-to-use learning environment.

- Mobile-friendly eFlashcards
- Mobile-friendly practice quizzes
- A complete online action plan
- Chapter summaries with learning objectives
- Video and multimedia resources

CHAPTER SUMMARY

8.1 **Discuss the factors that affect supply chain design and facility location decisions.** Many factors that influence supply chain design and location decisions are environmental factors—that is, they are conditions over which a firm has no control. How a company designs its supply chain and where it locates its facilities will ultimately depend on environmental factors as well as on a firm's particular competitive strategy, such as its desire to grow its business, decrease it costs, or relocate near key resources.

8.2 **List and describe the phases in the supply chain design and location decision-making process.** Four decision-making phases

are related to designing supply chains and locating facilities. In the first phase, the firm establishes the basic design of its supply chain, including the number of stages in the supply chain, the activities that will be performed at each stage, and whether these activities will be performed in-house or outsourced. During the second phase, the configuration of the chain's regional facilities is determined. This phase begins with an analysis of expected demand by country, the volume of the demand, and the nature of customer requirements. During the third phase, managers determine potential sites within each region for setting up these facilities. Then, at this stage, the firm assesses the availability of the necessary infrastructure, including suppliers, transportation services, utilities, availability of skilled workers, and the community attitude toward the location of the industry facility. During the fourth phase, location choices are made.

8.3 Describe and compare the analytical methods managers use to evaluate locations. Using the factor rating method, managers list the most important factors for the location decision and then rate each location based on each of those factors to arrive at a total score for it. The location with the highest score is then chosen. A breakeven analysis can be used to determine the location that has the lowest total cost for a given volume range of production. The center-of-gravity method is a quantitative technique used to determine the location of a single warehouse or distribution center to minimize distribution costs. A geographic information system (GIS) is a computerized system that can store, correlate, and display data collected from a physical environment or a geographical location. GISs include detailed census and demographic data, maps, utilities, physical features such as rivers and mountains, major airports, colleges, and hospitals in every city, county, zip code and block in the country.

8.4 Identify the effect of sustainability and ethics on the location decisions of firms and supply chains. The increased focus on sustainability has led companies to reevaluate such supply chain decisions as where they locate their facilities and how they design their supply chains. The region and site selection for a facility is particularly important when it comes to sustainability. For example, is it in the right location to protect natural resources? Is it located in a way that helps minimize transportation activities to reduce carbon emissions? Does it meet all applicable environmental laws and regulations? Closely related to sustainability issues are ethical dilemmas that companies face when locating their facilities. Companies that relocate facilities and domestic jobs can face bad publicity and a loss of goodwill from consumers. Relocating facilities in countries with poor environmental and labor regulations are also becoming issues for consumers.

8.5 Identify the factors that can influence the choice of global locations. Global location planning, however, is a complex task because companies have to evaluate many factors that can influence the choice of a global location. Some of these foreign location factors include (a) host country market size, (b) total costs, (c) infrastructure, (d) labor availability, (e) free trade zones, (f) political risk, and (g) governmental regulations. In addition to these factors, companies must also consider the host country's economy, the quality and availability of transportation in that country, and protection of intellectual property. Given these many factors and the risks involved in locating in a foreign country, companies typically choose locations in collaboration with economic development groups to keep the operating and start-up costs low.

KEY TERMS

Breakeven analysis 278

Center-of-gravity method 280

Clustering 272

Devaluation 273

Factor rating method 277

Geographic information system (GIS) 281

DISCUSSION AND REVIEW QUESTIONS

1. Discuss briefly each of the four phases of designing a supply chain network.
2. Discuss the strategic importance of facility location decisions.
3. What are some reasons why companies find new locations or relocate their existing facilities?
4. What are some disadvantages of relocating facilities to a foreign country?
5. The global facility location decision process occurs in a sequence of three stages:

   (1) country decision, (2) regional/community decision, and (3) site decision.

   List and briefly explain each critical success factor for the first decision stage of choosing the country.

6. How do the location strategies for service facilities differ from the location strategies for manufacturing facilities?
7. Why would the location decision for a hospital be different than the location decision for a supermarket? In terms of critical success factors, what are the similarities and differences?
8. What minimum set of criteria should service firms establish when selecting new locations?
9. What is a GIS? How can a restaurant use this tool to select a new facility for its operation?
10. What sustainability and ethical issues do companies need to consider when making location choices?
11. ArcelorMittal is planning to build a steel plant in India. Discuss some critical country-, region-, and site-related factors the company needs to evaluate to build the plant?

SOLVED PROBLEMS

1. The fictional Omega Steel Works is planning to build a new steel plant in India. The firm's managers have identified three Indian states, Orissa, Jharkand, and Karnataka, as the potential regions for the steel plant. In addition, the managers have identified the critical success factors for a steel mill location, developed scores (0 to 100) to rate them on this basis, and set factor weights (0 to 1) to reflect their relative importance. The factors, their weights, and the scores for the three states are given in the following table. Where should the company build the plant?

Factor	Weight	Orissa	Jharkand	Karnataka
Labor Availability and Costs	0.1	60	70	65
Transportation Availability and Costs	0.1	55	50	60
Proximity to Iron Ore Reserves	0.5	65	60	70
Infrastructure Availability (Power, Water, and Waste Disposal)	0.3	50	60	70
Total	1.0			

Solution:

- For each factor and each location, compute a score by multiplying the factor rating score and the weight assigned to the factor.
- Compute a total score for each location by summing up the scores calculated in the previous step
- Select the location that has the maximum total score.

The necessary calculations required for the steps listed are shown in the following table:

Factor	Weight	Score Orissa	Score Jharkand	Score Karnataka	Weighted Score Orissa	Weighted Score Jharkand	Weighted Score Karnataka
Labor Availability and Costs	0.1	60	70	65	$60 \times 0.1 = 6.0$	$70 \times 0.1 = 7.0$	$65 \times 0.1 = 6.5$
Transportation Availability and Costs	0.1	55	50	60	$55 \times 0.1 = 5.5$	$50 \times 0.1 = 5.0$	$60 \times 0.1 = 6.0$
Proximity to Iron Ore Reserves	0.5	65	60	70	$65 \times 0.5 = 32.5$	$60 \times 0.5 = 30.0$	$70 \times 0.5 = 35.0$
Infrastructure Availability (Power, Water, and Waste Disposal)	0.3	50	60	70	$50 \times 0.3 = 15.0$	$60 \times 0.3 = 18.0$	$70 \times 0.3 = 21.0$
Total	1.0				59.0	60.0	68.5

Karnataka has the highest total score, so it is the preferred location. (See Screenshot 8.3 for a solution to this problem in Microsoft Excel.)

SCREENSHOT 8.3: Solved Problem 8.1

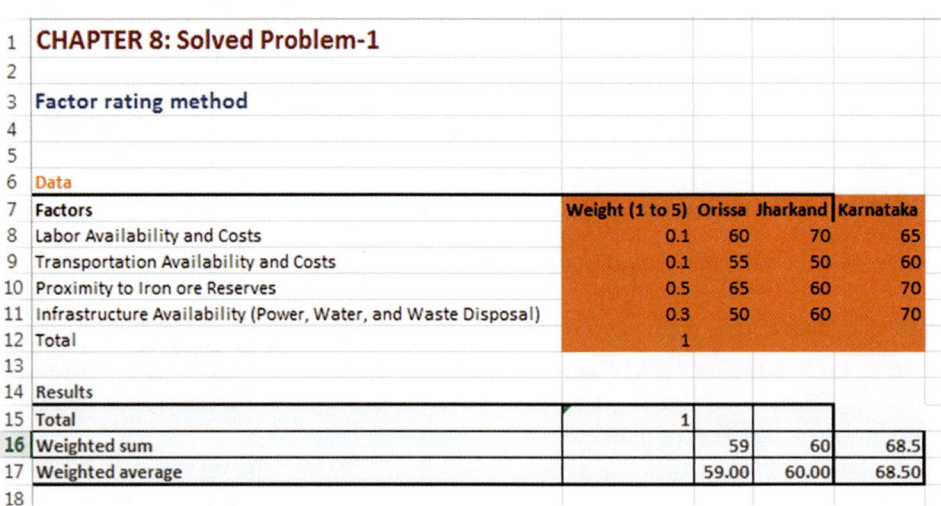

2. Omega Steel Works conducted a cost analysis for the potential plant locations in the three Indian states. The analysis indicates that the fixed costs per year for plants in Orissa, Jharkand, and Karnataka are $1.5 million, $750,000, and $3.0 million, respectively, and the variable costs are $300, $400, and $200 per ton, respectively (all in U.S. dollars). The expected selling price of a ton of steel is $800, and the company expects to produce and sell a volume of 2,500 tons per year:

   a. Determine the most economical location for an expected annual production volume of 2,500 tons.

   b. Determine the breakeven volumes for the locations and the volume ranges over which each of the three locations would operate most economically.

Solution:

a. Total Cost = Fixed Cost + (Production Volume) × Variable Cost per Unit) = FC + Q × VC

   For Orissa: Total Cost = $1,500,000 + 2,500 \times 300 = \$2,250,000$

   For Jharkand: Total Cost = $750,000 + 2500 \times 400 = $ **$ 1,750,000**

   For Karnataka: Total Cost = $3,000,000 + 2500 \times 200 = \$3,500,000$

Jharkand is the most economical location for a production and sales volume of 2,500 tons.

b. To determine the range of production volume at which each location is economical, we let Q be the breakeven volume, that is, the production volume where the total costs for the locations are the same.

For Orissa and Jharkand locations:

   $1,500,000 + Q \times 300 = 750,000 + Q \times 400$

$Q \times (400 - 300) = 1,500,000 - 750,000$

$100 \times Q = 750,000$

$Q = 7,500$

To determine the volume where the total costs for the Orissa and Karnataka locations are the same:

$1,500,000 + Q \times 300 = 3,000,000 + Q \times 200$

$Q \times (300 - 200) = 3,000,000 - 1,500,000$

$100 \times Q = 1,500,000$

$Q = 15,000$

Based on the calculations earlier, if the annual sales volume is less than 7,500 tons, then Jharkand is the preferred location for the steel plant. If the annual sales volume is greater than 7,500 tons but less than 15,000 tons, then the steel plant should be located in Orissa. For an annual sales volume greater than 15,000 tons, Karnataka is the best location. These results are shown graphically in the following figure. Note that we did not calculate the volume where the total costs for Jharkand and Karnataka are the same because it is clear from the figure that if the volume falls between 7,500 and 15,000 tons, then Orissa is the preferred choice. (See Screenshot 8.4 for a solution to this problem in Microsoft Excel.)

SCREENSHOT 8.4: Solved Problem 8.2

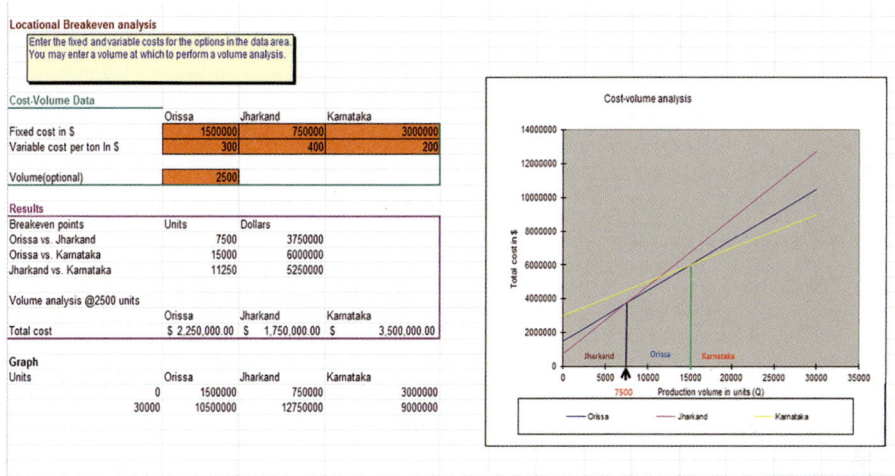

3. The mythical Sirius Textile Factory has garment retail outlets stores in the European cities of Brussels, Milan, Paris, and Berlin. The company is looking to construct a new central distribution center to stitch labels on its garments before shipping them to its various outlet stores. The annual demand for these garments in metric tons is given in the following table. The garments are transported in 13.5-meter truck trailers, each with a capacity of 35 metric tons. Using the center-of-gravity method, determine a possible location for the distribution center.

Retail Store Location	Number of Metric Tons Shipped Annually
Brussels, Belgium	90
Milan, Italy	75
Lyon, France	60
Berlin, Germany	150

The calculations required are shown in the following table.

Retail Store Locations	x- Coordinate Values (x)	y- Coordinate Values (y)	Number of Metric Tons Shipped Annually (Q)	$x_i \times Q_i$	$y_i \times Q_i$
Brussels	100	850	90	9,000	76,500
Milan	600	100	75	45,000	7,500
Lyon	120	140	60	7,200	8,400
Berlin	700	1,300	150	105,000	195,000
Totals			375	166,200	287,400

$$x\text{-coordinate of the new facility} = \frac{\sum_{i=1}^{n} x_i Q_i}{\sum_{i=1}^{n} Q_i} = 166{,}200\,/\,375 = 443$$

$$y\text{-coordinate of the new facility} = \frac{\sum_{i=1}^{n} y_i Q_i}{\sum_{i=1}^{n} Q_i} = 287{,}400\,/\,375 = 766$$

SCREENSHOT 8.5: Solved Problem 8.3

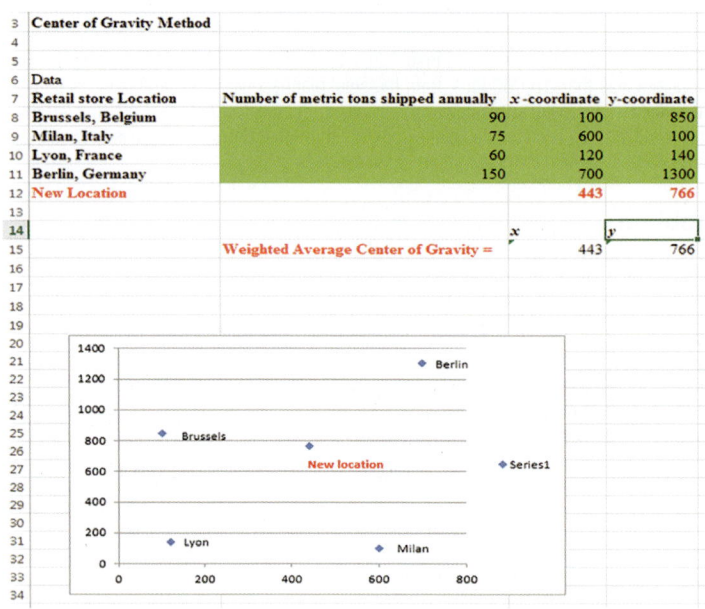

The coordinates of this new facility are graphically depicted in the screen capture from an Excel file. The new location for the distribution facility with coordinates (443, 766) is near Frankfort, Germany.

PROBLEMS

1. The fictional Reliance Retailers are planning to locate a new retail facility in the Chicago area. The firm has narrowed its location choices to three Chicago suburbs: Oakbrook, Evanston, and Arlington Heights. The company has selected four factors as the basis for evaluation. The factor scores and the factor weights are shown in the following table. Which location should Reliance Retailers choose?

Factor	Weight	Score (on a 100-point scale)		
		Oakbrook	Evanston	Arlington Heights
Community's Disposable Income	0.4	80	50	70
Public Transportation Availability	0.2	40	80	60
Community Growth Potential	0.1	50	60	70
Labor Availability and Costs	0.2	50	70	60
Total	1.0			

2. Solar Flare Inc., a mythical manufacturer of solar panels, is planning to build a new facility in a South American country. Bill Johnson, the manager responsible for this decision, has identified Argentina, Brazil, and Chile as the potential alternatives for the new location. The critical success factors, their relative importance, and the scores for these countries based on the factors are shown in the following table.

Factor	Weight	Score (on a 10-point scale)		
		Argentina	Brazil	Chile
Social and Cultural Factors	0.1	6	7	6
Availability of Technology	0.3	7	8	6
Political and Legal Issues	0.2	5	6	7
Skilled Labor Availability and Costs	0.4	7	6	5
Total	1.0			

a. In which country should Johnson choose to locate the facility?

b. After making the decision, Johnson learned that civil unrest and a political coup could occur in Chile. Consequently, the score for Chile's political–legal factor was changed to 3. Will the change affect Johnson's decision?

3. A U.S. hospital chain is planning to enter the Indian market by building its first medical facility in southern India. The director, Dr. Uma Raman, is a native of that region and is familiar with the economic, social, and cultural aspects of that region. After a preliminary analysis, she chooses three cities as potential locations. The pertinent factors, their weights, and rating scores are given in the following table. Both the factor weights and scores are based on a 10-point scale.

Location Factor	Weight	Scores		
		Bangalore	Chennai	Hyderabad
Facility Utilization	9	9	7	6
Average Time Per Emergency Trip	8	6	6	8
Employee Preferences	5	5	6	3
Accessibility to Major Roadways	5	5	4	5
Land Costs	4	5	4	6

a. Which city should Dr. Raman select?

b. If a minimum score of 5 is required for all factors, which city should be chosen? A

4. A manufacturer of high-technology medical equipment is planning to expand and build a new plant in one of the following countries in Southeast Asia: Philippines, Singapore, and Malaysia. John Beaumont, the VP of Strategic Operations, has identified five critical success factors for evaluating the locations in these three countries. John used a 5-point scale (1—least favorable country; 5—most favorable country) to evaluate each factor. The weights used to reflect the importance of each factor are between 0% and 100%. The results for each country using the factor rating method are given in the following table:

Factor	Weight	Score (on a 5-point scale)		
		Philippines	Singapore	Malaysia
Social and Cultural factors	0.1	3	5	2
Availability of Technology	0.3	3	4	4
Political and Legal Issues	0.1	5	3	3
Skilled Labor Availability	0.3	1	5	2
Economic Factors	0.2	5	1	4
Total	1.0			

a. Which country should John select?

b. What would be John's conclusion if the weights for political and legal issues and skilled labor availability are reversed?

5. The Great Lakes Institute of Technology (Erie, PA) is planning to open a new campus in one of the following five countries: India, Singapore, Bangladesh, Thailand, and China. The dean of the university, Vipin Gupta, is considering seven factors in his choice of location. The factor scores (based on a 10-point scale) and factor weights (in percentages) are given in the following table.

Factor	Weight	Score (on a 10-point scale)				
		India	Singapore	Bangladesh	Thailand	China
Social and Cultural Factors	0.1	6	7	6	4	5
Ability to Converse in English	0.1	7	8	6	5	4
Political and Legal Issues	0.1	6	7	5	6	5
Faculty Availability and Costs	0.3	9	8	4	5	7
Communication Infrastructure	0.2	6	9	3	4	7
Population Demographics	0.1	9	7	6	6	9
Housing Availability	0.1	5	4	5	8	3
Total	1.00					

a. Which country should Vipin Gupta select?

b. How would Dean Gupta's decision change if "communication infrastructure" is not an issue?

6. Reliance Home Inc., a fictional manufacturer of dishwashers, washers, and dryers, is planning to construct a new warehouse and distribution center in Asia to serve the markets in that continent. The company has narrowed its choice of locations to the following port cities: Singapore, Pontianak, Chennai, Osaka, and Shanghai. The critical location factors and their weights, and the score corresponding to each location for each factor, are given in the following table.

Factor	Weight	Score (0 to100)				
		Singapore	Pontianak	Chennai	Osaka	Shanghai
Site Cost	0.05	60	90	70	50	50
Labor Availability	0.20	70	60	80	70	90
Labor Cost	0.20	50	90	70	60	60
Political Stability	0.05	90	60	70	80	90
Transportation Infrastructure	0.10	85	65	60	80	95
Duties and Tariffs	0.10	55	85	70	40	75
Port Congestion	0.15	75	90	70	60	80
Governmental Regulations	0.15	80	70	90	70	65

a. Which location should the company choose?

b. What location should the company choose if the factor weights are all equal?

7. Varun Excelo, a fictional construction company in Chennai, India, is planning to construct a new beachfront resort along the eastern coast of India. The company has narrowed its choice to the following five locations: Mahabalipuram, Pondicherry, Bheemunipatnam, Covelong, and Puri. The critical location factors and their weights, and the score corresponding to each location for each factor, are given in the table below.

Factor	Score (0 to100)				
	Mahabalipuram	Pondicherry	Bheemunipatnam	Covelong	Puri
Site Cost	50	60	90	70	80
Beach Quality	75	70	80	70	90
Infrastructure	90	80	60	75	70
Highway Proximity to Beach	90	80	75	80	70
Shopping Malls and Restaurants	85	75	60	70	65

As the weights indicating the relative importance of each factor are not given, use your judgement to allocate weights to each factor and recommend to Varun Excelo the best location for the beach resort.

8. Peter Boyle is planning to build a new recycling plant. The fixed and variable costs for three potential sites are as follows (in U.S. dollars):

Cost	Chicago	Erie	Dallas
Fixed Cost	$1,200,000	$700,000	$900,000
Variable Cost per Unit	$75	$110	$90

a. Over what range of recycling volume is each city optimal?

b. For a recycling volume of 5,000 units, which site is the best?

9. A ski equipment manufacturer is planning to build a manufacturing plant in Europe. The fixed and variable costs (in U.S dollars) for four potential plant sites are shown as follows:

Potential Site	Fixed Cost per Year	Variable Cost per Unit
Bern, Switzerland	$150,000	$ 5
Vienna, Austria	85,000	8
Brussels, Belgium	100,000	4
Zagreb, Croatia	50,000	12

a. Graph the total-cost lines for the four potential sites.

b. Over what range of annual production volume is each location optimal?

c. If the expected production volume of the ski equipment is 8,000 units, which location would you recommend?

10. Dolphin Motors is evaluating three sites—A, B, and C—to locate a plant to build its new Sedan Dolphin XL600. The total annual cost is the sum of the annual fixed costs and variable costs of production. Dolphin Motors has gathered the following cost data for each site (in U.S. dollars):

Cost	A	B	C
Annual Fixed Cost	$12,000,000	$20,000,000	$23,000,000
Variable Cost Per Sedan Produced	$3000	$2200	$1200

a. Over what range of annual production volume is each location optimal?

b. If the expected production volume is 20,000 sedans, which location would you recommend?

11. A local electronics company has several production facilities scattered throughout the midwestern United States. The company is looking to establish a distribution center to ship its products to Best Buy (Richfield, MN), Wal-Mart, and other retailers that sell electronic products in the cities listed in the following table. The location coordinates of these cities and the shipping loads to these cities are also shown. Compute the center-of-gravity location for the proposed new distribution center:

City	Map Coordinates (x, y)	Shipping Loads
A	(2, 2)	25
B	(3, 12)	12
C	(4, 14)	7
D	(8, 8)	22
E	(9, 18)	16
F	(13, 16)	11
G	(15, 4)	18
H	(17, 17)	21

12. A publisher is planning to add another distribution center to its operations in India. The coordinates of the cities where its books are to be shipped and the shipping loads for each are shown in the following table. What is the center-of-gravity location for the proposed new distribution center?

Cities	Map Coordinates (x, y)	Shipping Loads per Day
Chennai	(10, 3)	3
Bangalore	(5, 5)	3
Bombay	(2, 7)	2
Delhi	(5, 15)	6
Hyderabad	(5, 6)	5
Kolkata	(12, 7)	3
Ahmedabad	(1, 8)	10

13. A grocery chain is planning to construct a state-of-the art distribution facility to serve its seven store locations in the greater Chicago land area. As fresh meat and produce are transported to these store locations several times a day, the site location for the new distribution center is critical for efficient distribution. Given the following map coordinates for the seven store locations, and the number of round trips made by trucks to each of these store locations, use the center-of-gravity method to determine the map coordinates for the new distribution facility:

Store Locations	Map Coordinates (x, y)	# of Truck Round Trips per Day
1	(9, 4)	4
2	(4, 7)	4
3	(12, 13)	3
4	(8, 8)	7
5	(14, 4)	6
6	(2, 11)	2
7	(7, 7)	12

14. An army division in eastern Afghanistan has six troop encampments in the Hindu Kush Mountain ranges. The army division commander wants to use the center-of-gravity method to determine the best location for a supply depot to serve these camps. The map coordinates (in miles) of the six camps and the daily shipment in tons required at each camp are given in the following table:

Camp Location	Map Coordinates (x, y)	Daily Shipment (in tons)
1	(90, 110)	75
2	(50, 280)	150
3	(420, 300)	95
4	(200, 520)	50
5	(580, 380)	120
6	(150, 270)	200

What is the best location for the supply depot using the center-of-gravity method?

15. An Italian restaurant chain is planning to open a distribution center to prepare and ship the food ingredients required by five of its restaurants in Germany. The map coordinates and the annual truck-load shipments to each of these restaurants are given in the following table.

Restaurant Location	Map Coordinates (x, y)	Annual Truckload Shipment (in tons)
Frankfurt	(10, 70)	150
Munich	(20, 20)	100
Rosenheim	(25, 15)	85
Berlin	(30, 140)	70
Dresden	(35, 100)	45

a. Determine the best location for the distribution center using the center-of-gravity method.

b. Based on your answer to part a), identify the closest town to the map coordinates to locate the distribution center.

c. Is there a better location than the one identified in part b)? If yes, explain.

16. The fictional Crown Shoes Inc. imports dress shoes and sneakers from several manufacturers in India. Container shipments of these items arrive from India at the following three ports in the United States: Houston, Charleston, and New York City. The company plans to open a distribution center to examine these container loads of imported items for defects and to repackage them before shipping in truckloads to five retail customer warehouse locations. The map coordinates of the ports and warehouses and the annual truckloads of shipments are shown in the following table:

Ports and Warehouse Locations	Map Coordinates (x, y)	Daily Shipment (in tons)
Houston	(1000, 700)	55
Charleston	(2800, 1600)	30
New York	(2900, 2400)	65
A	(300, 1100)	20
B	(1600, 1600)	45
C	(900, 2300)	35
D	(1100, 2500)	32
E	(2000, 2400)	18

Determine the best location for Crown's distribution center using the center-of-gravity method.

17. A textile factory produces men's clothes at the following five locations in Southern India: Tirunelveli, Palakad, Tiruppur, Tumkur, and Vijayawada. The company now needs to determine the best location to distribute bolts of cloth to the five manufacturing locations. The map coordinates of the five manufacturing locations and the weekly quantity to be shipped to each of the five locations are given in the following table:

Manufacturing Location	Map Coordinates (x, y)	Weekly Shipment Quantity (in bolts)
Tirunelveli	(15, 5)	20
Palakad	(5, 20)	25
Tiruppur	(10, 25)	45
Tumkur	(8, 35)	30
Vijayawada	(35, 70)	35

a. Determine the best location for the distribution center using the center-of-gravity method.

b. Based on your answer to part a), identify the closest town to the map coordinates to locate the distribution center.

c. Is there a better location than the one identified in part b)? If yes, explain.

18. Mary Beth Olsen, owner of a pizza shop, is planning to expand her operation by adding one additional pizza shop. She has narrowed her choices to three locations. Labor and materials costs per pizza for all three locations is $3.70. The selling price per pizza is $5.80 each for all three locations. The fixed costs in the form of rent and equipment are $6,000 per month for location A, $6,550 per month for location B, and $7,200 per month for location C (all in U.S. dollars):

a. What should be the sales volume at each location to realize a monthly profit of $8,500?

b. If forecasted pizza sales per month at locations A, B, and C are $19,500, $21,200, and $24,200, respectively, determine the profit for each of the three locations.

c. At what range of sales volume would each location be profitable?

19. Blue Moon Airways (BMA), a fictional airline company with headquarters in India, is planning to open a second service hub in response to surge in demand for air travel to and from India to cities in North America and Europe. Several cities in North America have shown great interest in securing BMA's business because of the surge in employment levels an airline service hub can generate. Consequently, choice of location is critical for BMA both from cost and revenue perspectives. Jonty Rhodes, BMA's V.P. of Strategic Operations, has narrowed the choices to four cities in each of the North American and European continents. The critical location factors and their weights, as well as the score corresponding to each location for each factor, are given in the following table:

Factor	Weight (0 to 100)	Score (on a 100-point scale)							
		London	Paris	Brussels	Rome	Houston	Cleveland	Raleigh	Chicago
Demographics	70	80	70	70	60	80	75	90	95
Site Cost	60	40	40	60	70	85	90	70	40
Expansion Potential	70	50	60	70	75	65	85	70	50
Skilled Labor Availability	90	90	80	75	60	85	75	85	95
Wage Rates	80	35	40	60	80	70	85	80	30
Financial Incentives	80	40	35	60	80	65	90	70	30
Economy	80	70	70	75	60	80	65	90	60
Political Issues	60	70	50	70	70	80	70	90	65
Competition	85	40	45	50	80	85	90	90	35
Total	1.0								

a. Which location should BMA choose for its hub?

b. What location should BMA choose if the factor weights are all equal?

c. If the weight financial incentive factor is lowered to 50, would your decision be different from your answer in part a)?

20. Refer to the following grid map that shows seven stores (labeled as demand locations D_1 to D_7) for a retail chain. The company is planning to locate a distribution center to distribute efficiently merchandise on a weekly basis. Weekly truckloads of shipment to these seven demand locations are given in the following table. Use the center-of-gravity method to find the best location for the distribution center:

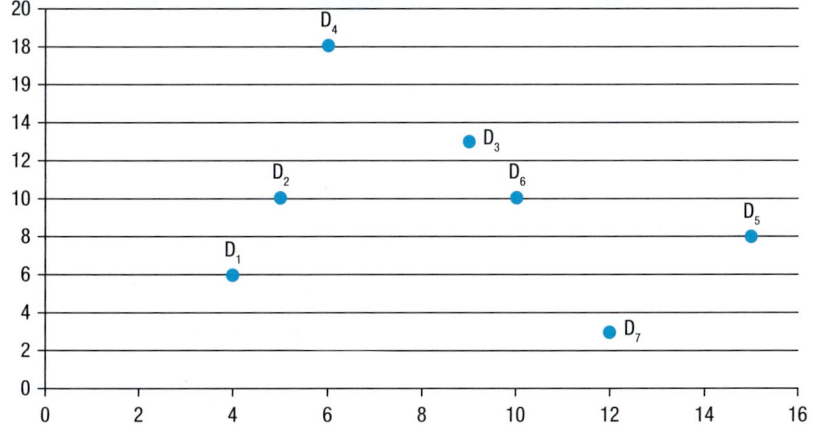

Stores	Weekly Truckload Shipments
D_1	15
D_2	10
D_3	25
D_4	8
D_5	13
D_6	17
D_7	7

CASE STUDY 8.1 COUNTERING THE COUNTERFEITERS

When we think of the wide variety of issues that companies must consider when deciding where to locate partners as part of their supply chain, one unique, but increasingly important, factor to consider is the impact that local counterfeiting may have on their operations. The Agreement on Trade-Related Aspects of Intellectual Property Rights (TRIPs) defines pirated copyright goods as "any goods which are copies made without the consent of the right holder or person duly authorized by the right holder in the country of production and which are made directly or indirectly from an article where the making of that copy would have constituted an infringement of a copyright or a related right under the law of the country of importation." Although it is well understood what constitutes product piracy in many industries, how do firms address the potential for counterfeiting within their industries, particularly when they manufacture critical or high-risk products?

In the pharmaceutical industry, buying or using counterfeit medicine has the potential for creating safety and health risks. The problem is that in the pharmaceutical supply chain, from the initial raw materials to manufacturing to distribution, there are many opportunities for shady suppliers to provide fake or mislabeled materials and ingredients, leading to possibilities to create a counterfeit product. An example of what occurs when the pharmaceutical chain is not properly controlled and verified against alteration took place in Panama in 2006. Cough medicine that was manufactured and sold there used

unauthorized ingredients originating from China. The tainted medication led to more than 78 deaths. Panamanian authorities found that diethylene glycol, which is often used in antifreeze, was used in the cough medicine instead of glycerin, an inactive ingredient used in medicines to make syrup. The barrels had been mislabeled to indicate they contained glycerin when they actually contained diethylene glycol.

Another example of problems with the pharmaceutical supply chain occurred in the United States in 2012, in which Genentech Inc.'s (South San Francisco, CA) cancer treatment drug, Avastin, was impacted by fraud. A Canadian supplier sold counterfeit Avastin that did not contain any of the active ingredients required for the medicine.

The impact from counterfeit products is felt by the brand owner, the consumer, and the companies that unknowingly use or sell counterfeit products. They are all harmed by the distribution of counterfeit products. Substandard drugs that are made from poor quality raw materials, using an improper dosage of the active ingredients, inadequate storage or transportation, or products made from a process that does not follow good manufacturing practices, all create dangerous risks for the consumer. Counterfeiting in the health-care industry is so bad in places that health organizations have found instances of fake drugs that contained harmful ingredients such as boric acid, brick dust, chalk dust, cement powder, talcum powder, floor polish, shoe polish, and antifreeze!

Manufacturers seeking to develop their overseas supply chains must be aware of the potential dangers to be found in their location decisions. In addition to considering the more common factors of ease of operations, political conditions, and so forth, it is critical that they calculate a related, but perhaps often not considered, cost: the potential for local supplier counterfeiting and the equal potential for devastating impact of such counterfeiting on an organization's reputation and ongoing profitability.[27]

Questions

1. What are some of the most common reasons for the counterfeiting of materials at a company's overseas supply source?

2. What are some steps a company can take to lessen the impact of counterfeiting its raw materials or finished goods through supply chain partners?

VIDEO CASE

Watch this video case to learn about how MPK Foods, a family-owned company that produces seasoning mixes sold to grocery stores, works with suppliers to get their products on the shelves.

CRITICAL THINKING EXERCISES

The following article highlights the importance of making global location decisions based on the total cost of ownership. In other words, companies need to make global location choices by evaluating all the factors that impact the total cost of doing business in a foreign location. Global location decisions should not be based on just availability of cheap labor or raw materials, but they should include factors such as labor productivity, distance, and protection of intellectual property rights.

Search for the article titled "Time to Head Home for Some Manufacturers" in Businessweek and answer the discussion questions.

1. Why is the information in this article important to operations managers?

2. What are the business reasons for relocating factories back in the United States?

3. How will relocating manufacturing facilities in the United States affect how operations and supply chains are managed?

4. What is the U.S. government's role in fostering or creating manufacturing work in the United States? Who will finance this role?

5. What is the near-term future of manufacturing employment in the United States?

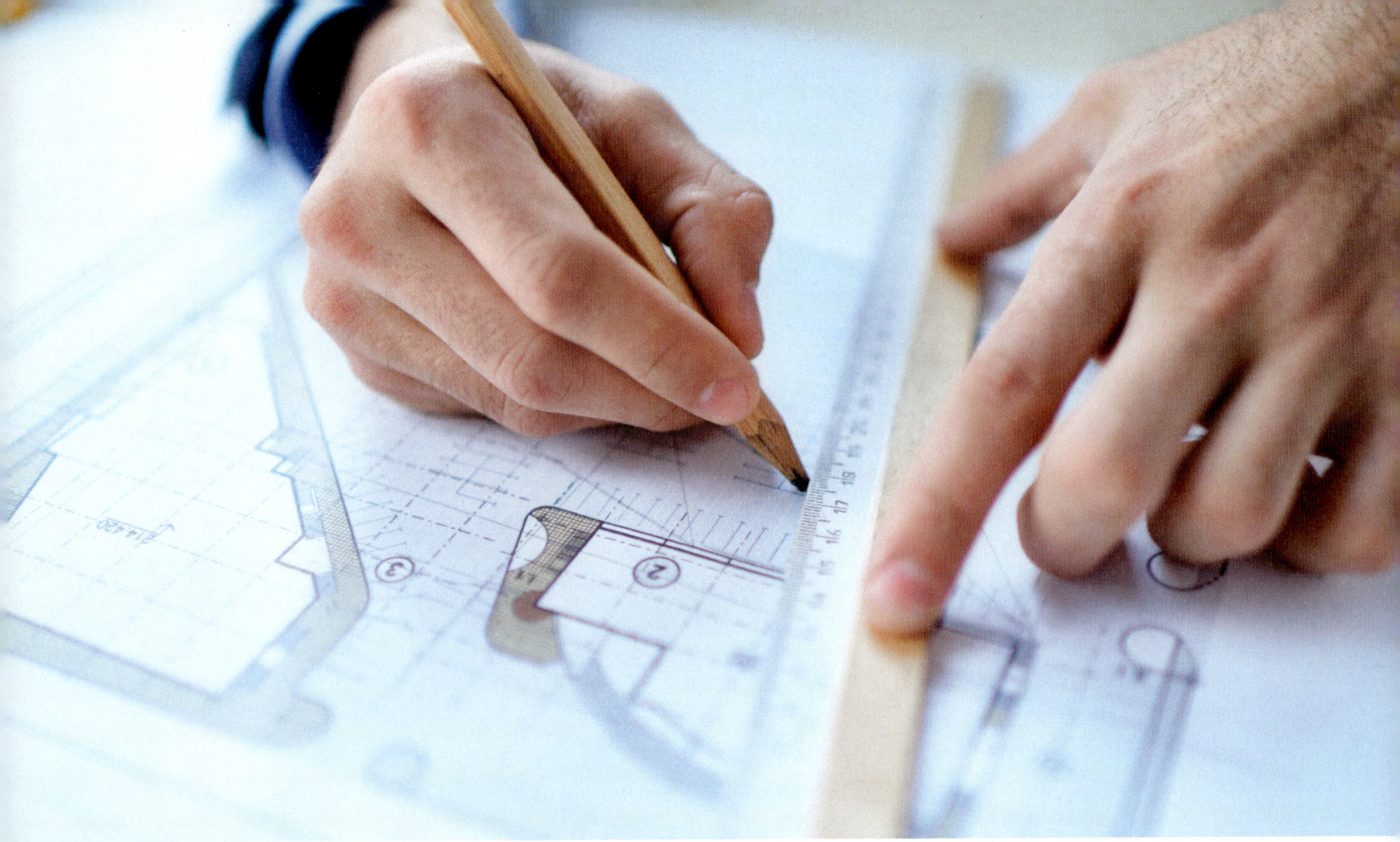

©iStockphoto.com/mediphotos

CHAPTER 9 Process Design and Layout Planning

LEARNING OBJECTIVES

After studying this chapter, you should be able to:

1. Argue for the strategic importance of process selection to an organization, and identify factors that affect process choice.
2. List the unique features in the design of service processes.
3. Defend the reasons that it is important for companies to synchronize their internal processes with the external processes of their supply chain partners.
4. Describe the unique challenges involved in designing global processes.
5. Construct the different layout types, and identify their features.
6. List strategies that companies can take to address the legal, ethical, and sustainability issues in process design and layout planning.

OPERATIONS PROFILE: Process Redesign at Mars: Moving Toward Sustainability and Social Responsibility

Patrick Hertzog/Afp/Getty Images

Mars, Incorporated (McLean, VA), one of the largest privately held organizations in the world, employs more than 70,000 people in more than 400 offices and factories in 73 countries. The firm's products range from candy to teas and coffee to pet food—all manufactured with the goal of social responsibility and sustainability. The company sponsors many sustainability initiatives:

- Sustainability workshops are held at Mars sites worldwide, and employees are encouraged to dedicate a week to generating ideas for new processes to save energy and water and to reduce waste. Since 2007, these efforts have helped the company cut its energy usage by 6%, water usage by 18%, and landfill waste by 51%.

- Mars has invested millions of dollars to improve the efficiency of equipment used to produce its Wrigley's gum and confectionary products. These improvements have helped streamline production and have significantly reduced the energy required to produce the products.

- Mars's goal is to acquire 100% of its cocoa, fish and seafood products, black tea, coffee beans, and palm oil from sustainable sources worldwide. The company works to acquire 100% of its materials from certified sources—that is, suppliers that have the highest ethical standards in growing food and supporting their workers.

- All of the company's product packaging has been redesigned to reduce its weight, ensure it's 100% recyclable, or make use of recycled materials.

Although many companies affirm their support of social responsibility and sustainable operations, Mars offers a model for other organizations to emulate.[1]

Because of the long-term impact on the organization, designing quality products and services, capacity planning, along with process design and layout planning are among the most important and strategic decisions that operations managers have to make. These decisions also have implications for a wide range of subsequent tactical and operational activities, as well as the organization's supply chain. In the current competitive global economy, businesses are under intense pressure to reduce the time to market, lower the cost of their products and services, and meet the goals of sustainability. From the point of originating a new product or service idea to its introduction in the global marketplace, companies face myriad options for achieving this transition. One of the critical decisions that operations managers have to make is to evaluate these various options in a systematic and robust manner and choose the best way to achieve this transition using existing resources. This chapter on process design and layout planning addresses this issue of transition—converting inputs into outputs in the most efficient manner.

Argue for the strategic importance of process selection to an organization, and identify factors that affect process choice.

Master the content.

edge.sagepub.com /venkataraman

9.1 Designing, Selecting, and Redesigning Manufacturing Processes

Companies face many options in the way they produce their goods and services and in their choice of production methods. A process is a collection of interrelated tasks that convert specific inputs into specific outputs. A process design is the most cost-effective way to achieve this transformation to produce goods or services that satisfy customers' needs and achieve the firm's sustainability goals while accommodating the firm's technological and managerial constraints. Operations managers are responsible for evaluating processes in a systematic way as well as selecting among them (process selection), choosing the right technologies and then analyzing the processes and redesigning them, if necessary.

The particular process a company selects is influenced by its process strategy, which is the strategy a firm opts to take in producing goods and services determined by the availability and mixture of labor, equipment, and automation. The extent and the ease with which the firm can adjust its processes to changes in demand, technologies, product and service design requirements, and the availability of resources also affect a process strategy. In addition, a process strategy is influenced by the degree to which customers can affect a product's design specifications. First, however, let's look at some of the basic types of processes that companies use.

Basic Process Types

Depending on the product or service, companies have the option of choosing from five basic types of processes: project, job-shop, batch, repetitive, or continuous flow processes. Table 9.1 compares the five process types.

- A project process is used when the product is unique and typically produced one at a time to the customer's specifications. Examples include construction projects, new product development projects, or the production of a movie. This type of process works best when there is low demand for a product, nonroutine work, a large investment of resources, and stringent time and budget constraints for completion.
- A job-shop process is used when the processing requirements are intermittent and different for each product because it is unique and produced in low volumes or sporadically. For example, Orange County Choppers (Newburgh, NY), a manufacturer of custom-designed motorcycles, uses a job-shop process. In the service sector, a job-shop process is used in a doctor's office where various patients with different ailments are treated. Each treatment is unique based on the patient's specific needs.
- A batch process is used to produce a moderate variety of products in moderate volumes in groups or batches. In the case of paint manufacturing, a moderate variety of paints such as flat, semi-gloss, and storm-coat is produced in batches in different colors and in modest volumes. A service firm such as a credit card company uses a batch process to process bills. Instead of receiving a separate bill for each credit card transaction, the customer receives a bill each month for all of that month's credit card transactions.
- When a high volume of standardized products needs to be produced, a repetitive process should be used. Low unit costs, high efficiency, and high volume of productions are the goal. Repetitive manufacturing processing systems include automobile assembly lines and the production of television sets and computers. In the service sector, automatic carwashes and fast food restaurants use repetitive processes.
- When very large volumes of a highly standardized product are to be produced, a continuous flow process is appropriate. Continuous flow processes are used to produce sugar, chemicals, oil, beer, and steel and to generate power—output that typically can't be counted individually. This type of processing system is highly automated, often operating 24 hours a day, and the entire plant is devoted to the production of a single highly standardized product.

Figure 9.1 on page 300 is a matrix of the five types of processes; it ranks each process according to its product and service variety and the volumes produced. Note that when there is the need for a high product and service variety with low volumes of demand, a project or job-shop process is best. Conversely, when little or no product variety is required but high volumes are needed, the choice should be a continuous flow process. Process choice also depends on the product's stage in its life

---

Process: a collection of interrelated tasks that convert specific inputs into specific outputs

Process selection: the decisions of selecting the kind of process that can give a firm a competitive advantage in terms of speed to market, responsiveness to customers, and cost savings

Process strategy: the strategy a firm opts to take in producing goods and services determined by the availability and mixture of labor, equipment, and automation

Project process: a process that is selected when the product is unique and typically produced one at a time to the customer's specifications

TABLE 9.1: Five Process Types

PROCESS TYPE	DESCRIPTION	ADVANTAGES	DISADVANTAGES
Project	Process for producing a single product, often unique, and the process is of limited duration.	Unique product tailored to the customer's specifications.	High risk of cost and schedule overruns and subsequent customer dissatisfaction.
Job-shop	Process for producing a low volume of customized products and services.	High product variety, low capital investment, and high process flexibility.	High variable cost per unit, low-capacity utilization, low production volumes, the need for highly skilled labor, careful production planning, and complex control.
Batch	Process for producing semi-standardized products and services.	Moderate product variety and process flexibility, and moderate production volumes.	Production planning and control moderately complex.
Repetitive	Process for producing standardized products and services.	Low variable cost per unit, high-capacity utilization, high production volume, need for skilled labor low, production planning and control less difficult.	Limited product variety, high capital investment, and low process flexibility.
Continuous Flow	Process for producing highly standardized products and services.	Very high volumes of production, and very high-capacity utilization and efficiency.	Highly rigid process with no flexibility. The process is costly to redesign and is associated with high costs when the process is interrupted or down.

cycle. During the introductory stage of a product life cycle, demand is low and sporadic, and the product design may change several times. Hence, the appropriate process for it at this stage is a job-shop process. As the product or service enters the growth stage, the demand for it increases and it requires fewer design changes. Thus, a batch process may be appropriate for this stage.

Shifting from one production process to another is often difficult and expensive. A company may have to scrap its existing processes and start anew. For example, suppose fast food restaurant KFC (subsidiary of Yum! Brands, Louisville, KY) wants to add the Indian delicacy tandoori chicken to its menu. This new offering would require many operational changes. The operations manager would need to decide whether to purchase additional ingredients such as lemon juice, yogurt, and a variety of spices; process the chicken by marinating it in these ingredients for at least 8 hours to get the right flavor; buy new equipment to bake the chicken in a tandoor, a bell-shaped clay oven; redesign the layout for the process and space in the kitchen for the new equipment; train employees to produce the new product; and so forth. This seemingly small product addition can lead to large process challenges.

Mass Customization Processes

If a company's production process does not lie on the diagonal of options in Figure 9.1—that is, the process does not align with the volume and variety demanded of the product—then, generally speaking, the company made a bad process choice. Nevertheless, if the firm has designed an innovative process that combines the advantages of any two of the basic processes, then the company can gain a competitive advantage even though the newly designed process does not fall along the diagonal of options shown in the figure. Mass customization, which we introduced in Chapter 4, combines the advantages of job-shop and repetitive or continuous flow processes. A mass customization process allows a firm to produce customized products at the speed, volume, cost, and quality of a repetitive or continuous flow processes. Dell Inc. (Round Rock, TX) uses a mass customization strategy to produce its computers to customer specifications but at mass production prices. There are several characteristics of mass customization. Let's look at them next.

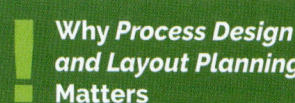

Why *Process Design and Layout Planning* Matters

Process design and layout planning are issues of strategic importance, enabling a company to produce and deliver goods or services in the most cost-effective way that satisfies customers' needs. They can also help the firm achieve its sustainability goals while accommodating technological and managerial constraints.

Job-shop process: a process that is selected when the processing requirements are intermittent and different for each product because it is unique and produced in low volumes or sporadically

Batch process: a process that is selected to produce a moderate variety of products in moderate volumes in groups or batches

FIGURE 9.1: Product–Process Matrix: Process Choice as a Function of Product Variety and Volume

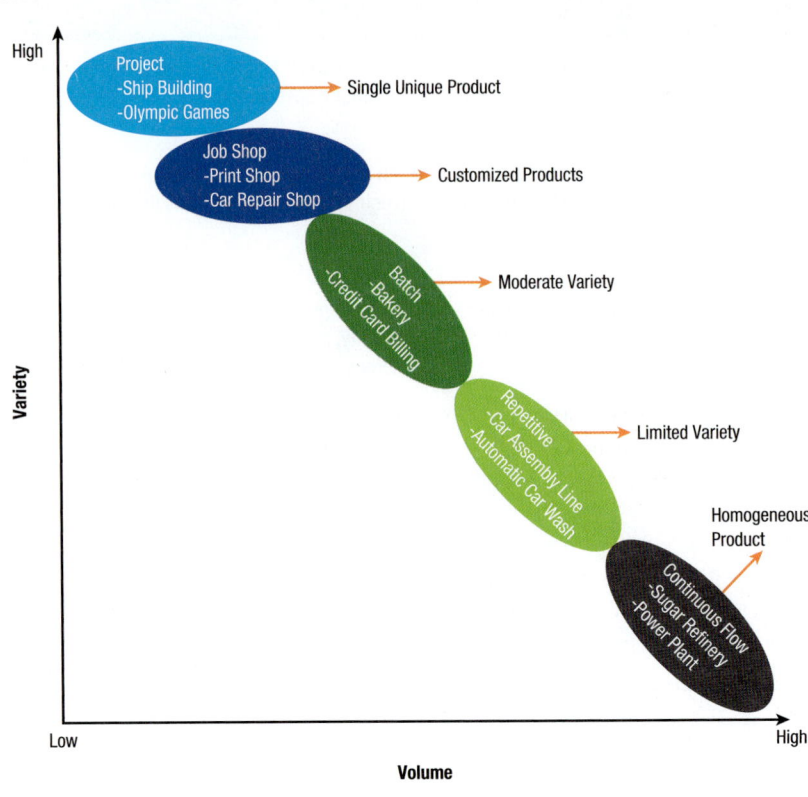

RAPID AND INNOVATIVE PRODUCT DESIGNING SYSTEMS

Achieving successful make-to-order product designs requires that companies use technologies such as computer-aided design (CAD) and rapid prototyping, which are design techniques we discussed in Chapter 5. CAD and rapid prototyping enable a company to come up with several versions of a product, sometimes in a matter of minutes. Using its website, customers of the Swiss-based shoe producer Bally (subsidiary of JAB Holding Company, Luxembourg) can specify design options, colors, and other details and then see the design of the shoes prior to ordering them.

FLEXIBILITY

Flexible processes are required for mass customization. To achieve this process flexibility, mass customization combines three production strategies: lean manufacturing, synchronous manufacturing, and agile manufacturing. Lean manufacturing, which we have already discussed, allows a company to achieve efficient levels of high-volume, low-cost production. Synchronous manufacturing adds process flexibility by synchronizing customers' orders with the tasks performed at the various workstations. If the work done by the first workstation is on the first customer order, then the work done by the second workstation will also be on that first customer order, and so forth. This system allows the firm to produce a wide variety of products by using the job-shop process. Many products, including automobiles and lawn mowers, are produced this way. A mass customization strategy also uses agile manufacturing, which as you may recall from Chapter 1 is the ability of an organization to respond quickly to market changes with a set of processes to produce high-quality products at a reasonable cost. For example, the Italian apparel manufacturer the Benetton Group (aka United Colors of Benetton, Treviso, Italy) delays the dyeing of its knitted garments until very late in the production process when it receives the most recent demand estimates for its garments. The strategy prevents Benetton from producing too many garments in colors customers do not want or too few garments in colors customers want.

RESPONSIVE SUPPLY CHAINS AND TIGHT INVENTORY CONTROL

Another key requirement for mass customization is to have an agile and responsive supply chain. The firm's supply chain partners have to realize that survival of the network depends on satisfying customers. Parts, materials, information, and decisions should flow through the company's supply chain network quickly and accurately. To keep tight control over inventory, the firm must know how much and what type of inventory exists in the pipeline so that there are no unwanted or obsolete items in the supply chain. Many organizations have adopted enterprise resource planning (ERP) software,

Repetitive process: a process that is selected when a high volume of standardized products needs to be produced

Continuous flow process: a process that is selected when very large volumes of a highly standardized product are to be produced

Mass customization process: a process that allows a firm to produce customized products at the speed, volume, cost, and quality of repetitive or continuous flow process configurations

Synchronous manufacturing: a manufacturing strategy that adds process flexibility by synchronizing customers' orders with the tasks performed at the various workstations

TABLE 9.2: Features, Advantages, and Disadvantages of Mass Customization

FEATURES	ADVANTAGES	DISADVANTAGES
• Make or build-to-order • High- or low-volume production • Use of lean, agile, and synchronized manufacturing methods • Continuous flow work cells • Multiskilled and empowered employees	• Customized products • Volume flexibility • Low cost • High quality • Highly flexible and responsive processes and equipment • Quick equipment changeover • Low inventories • Short lead and cycle times	• High capital investment • Excess capacity • Requires unique operational capabilities • Can only be adopted by certain industries

SOURCE: Adapted from Rockford Consulting Group, Ltd. (2006). Mass customization. *RCG University*. Retrieved from http://rockfordconsulting.com/mass-customization.htm

such as SAP (SAP SE, Walldorf, Germany) or Oracle (Oracle Corporation, Redwood City, CA), so that they can receive constant updates on the status of their inventory in their supply chains.

Not every company can, or even should, produce products using a mass customization system. Yet, when implemented properly, it can give companies a competitive edge because they can meet customers' needs by offering them highly customized products in large volumes quickly and at reasonable prices. Table 9.2 lists some of the features, advantages, and disadvantages of mass customization.[2]

Process Selection Decisions

Selecting the right processes, or process selection, can give a firm a competitive advantage in terms of speed to market, responsiveness to customers, and cost savings. Nevertheless, process selection decisions can be expensive. Implementing them generally requires a substantial capital investment and significantly affects other downstream decisions such as the layout of facilities. In this section, we examine some of the strategic decisions operations managers have to make when selecting a production process.

 Making Process Selection Decisions

ALIGNING PROCESS SELECTION DECISIONS WITH THE MARKET'S REQUIREMENTS

To avoid mismatches, operations managers need to understand how their firms' processes align with the needs of their markets. Consider, for example, the U.S. banking industry. After the financial-market meltdown of 2008, the federal government imposed new restrictions on bank operations. This changing set of market requirements increased regulatory pressure on banks (such as maintaining more liquidity and restricting loans to more credit-worthy borrowers), and it altered the way they competed and were able to satisfy their customers. Banks had to modify their lending practices and change the processes used to gather information to *align* these processes better with new market requirements.

Product profiling is a way to evaluate the alignment of the needs of a company's markets with its processes. Product profiling identifies the key product and service dimensions of a market to uncover misalignments that can occur over time.[3] These dimensions include the product variety that customers want, the expected demand for the product, competitors' pricing and cost strategies, and the market's order-winning criteria. To see the benefit of product profiling, suppose that a company uses a job-shop process to produce a range of products to satisfy the order-winning criteria of quality and customization customers are demanding and that these products account for 35% of the company's sales revenue. Also assume that the company is considering investing US$40 million in its processes to target the market segment in which the order-winning criterion is price. Managers believe the firm could generate 20% of its total business sales to price-conscious consumers by doing so. To achieve this increase, the company would have to change the scheduling of its processes. This change in process scheduling could threaten its ability to meet the needs of its existing market segment—that is, customers who want quality, customized products, and who are willing to pay a premium for them. In a very short period of time, this investment, if made without careful analysis, could result in a manufacturing conflict. Had the company created a product profile prior to this process investment, it would have uncovered the mismatches between the existing and the new processes and the demands of the marketplace.

DETERMINING WHETHER TO USE IN-HOUSE PRODUCTION OR OUTSOURCING

Many parts and components go into manufacturing a product. Most companies do not have the capability to produce all of these parts and components. Therefore, a key decision companies have to make before selecting a process is to determine which parts and components will be produced in-house and which will be procured from an outside vendor. The decision of whether to manufacture a part or component in-house or to outsource it depends on the answers to the following questions.

Product profiling: a way to evaluate the alignment of the needs of a company's markets with its processes through identifying the key product and service dimensions of a market to uncover misalignments that can occur over time

1. *Do we have enough capacity to produce the component?*

   A company may choose to manufacture a part or component or perform a service in-house rather than buy it from an outside vendor if it has enough idle or unused capacity. On the other hand, if the capacity available in-house is not sufficient to produce all of the components or to perform the service, then the company has to decide which parts or services should be outsourced and which should be done in-house. In general, if the demand for the product is highly variable or if it is a highly customized product or service, then the production of all parts or the service performed should be done in-house so that the demand can be better managed. Producing the product or service in-house enables the company to have workers with the necessary skills levels available to produce products that meet customers' quality expectations. In contrast, outsourcing is a good alternative for highly standardized products that have a high and steady volume of demand.

2. *Do we have the core competencies to produce the component?*

   If the company has the core competencies to produce quality products or services that give it a competitive advantage, then it should do so. The company can enhance the effectiveness of the product or service by focusing on what it does best. This decision is particularly true if the technology or competency is valuable and proprietary—that is, if the technology is only available to the company rather than widely available. Often, however, the components of a product are so highly specialized that they require special equipment or a specific knowledge or skill. In this case, an outside vendor or contractor can deliver a better product or service. For example, a company producing liquid natural gas (LNG) must transport it to other sites at extremely low temperatures (–260° Fahrenheit) in extremely cold tanks. Many LNG producers contract with companies that specialize in manufacturing these tanks rather than make them themselves.

3. *Are our suppliers reliable?*

   The decision to outsource depends to a large extent on the availability of suppliers that are reliable in the quality of the goods and services they provide and in their delivery. Delivery delays and poor quality shipments from suppliers can jeopardize a company's production process, and it is for this reason that some companies require their suppliers to meet quality and delivery standards, such as those specified by the International Organization for Standardization (ISO) 9000 standards (see Chapter 5).

4. *Does outsourcing entail significant risks?*

   Buying goods and services from an outside vendor can be risky, particularly if the supplier is located in a foreign country. These risks include the loss of direct control over operations, the loss of proprietary information as a result of knowledge sharing, and the violation of intellectual property rights. Firms doing business in China have had problems with theft of intellectual property. Typically the Chinese government requires Western firms to establish joint ventures with Chinese firms in the country. These joint ventures have led to numerous cases in which the Chinese partner appropriated the technologies and patents provided by the Western firm and then established its own company in China to compete with the Western partner, often with governmental support.[4] In addition, the outsourcing company may lose goodwill and suffer damage to its reputation if the foreign supplier engages in unethical practices, such as the use of child labor. The human rights organization Amnesty International charged Apple Inc. (Cupertino, CA), Sony Corporation (Tokyo, Japan), and Samsung (Ridgefield Park, NJ) with child labor violations for purchasing cobalt ore from mines in the Democratic Republic of the Congo. Cobalt is a vital ingredient in lithium ion batteries, used to power many of these companies' devices. According to the reports, Congolese mines employ workers as young as nine years old to fill the cobalt orders from these firms. Apple, Sony, and Samsung are charged with failing to conduct basic checks to ensure that minerals used in their products are not mined by children.[5]

5. *What are the costs of outsourcing?*

   Although the cost of purchasing the item from an outside vendor includes the purchase price, transportation costs, taxes, tariffs, and so forth, the cost of in-house production includes labor, material, overhead, and inventory costs. In general, all other things being equal, outsourcing is a viable alternative if and only if the cost advantages of purchasing from an outside vendor are significant.

Figure 9.2 presents a decision framework that can be used to compare in-house production with outsourcing.

DETERMINING THE TECHNOLOGY AND EXTENT OF AUTOMATION NEEDED

Technological innovations can have a significant impact on how products and services are produced and delivered, their quality and costs, the firm's productivity, and whether the firm can achieve competitive advantage by adopting these innovations. Some examples of technological innovations include three-dimensional (3-D) printing, laser technology being used in surgical processes, digitized processes to collect and maintain patients' medical information, and the use of mobile data terminals (MDTs) in moving cabs, trains, and buses to improve communication among personnel and better manage transportation systems. The decision to integrate new technology in a production process should be made only after a thorough study of its advantages and disadvantages. Operations managers need to assess what the technology can and cannot do, the cost and time needed to implement the new technology, and its potential impact on the firm's existing human resources needs. For example, the firm may need to hire additional employees with different skills or train its current employees to use the technology.

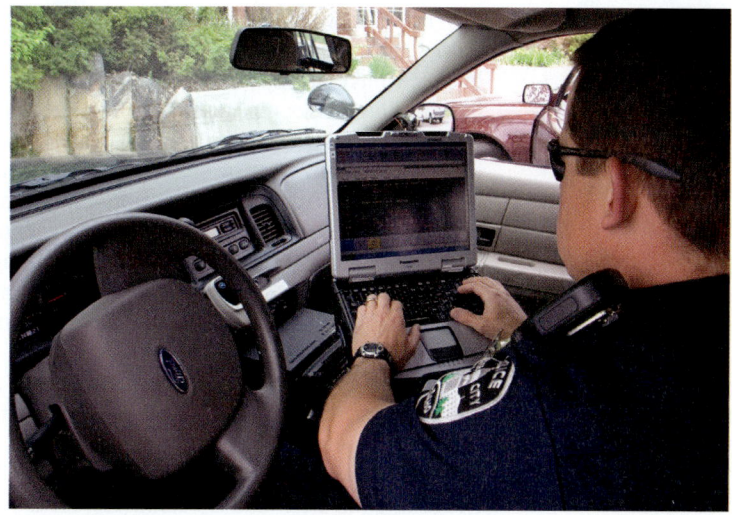

A mobile data terminal such as the one shown in this police car is a computerized device that includes a screen and a keyboard. It is used in public transit vehicles, taxi cabs, police cars and so forth as a means to communicate with the central dispatch office.

ddpphotos340872/NEWSCOM

FIGURE 9.2: Decision Framework for In-house Production or Outsourcing

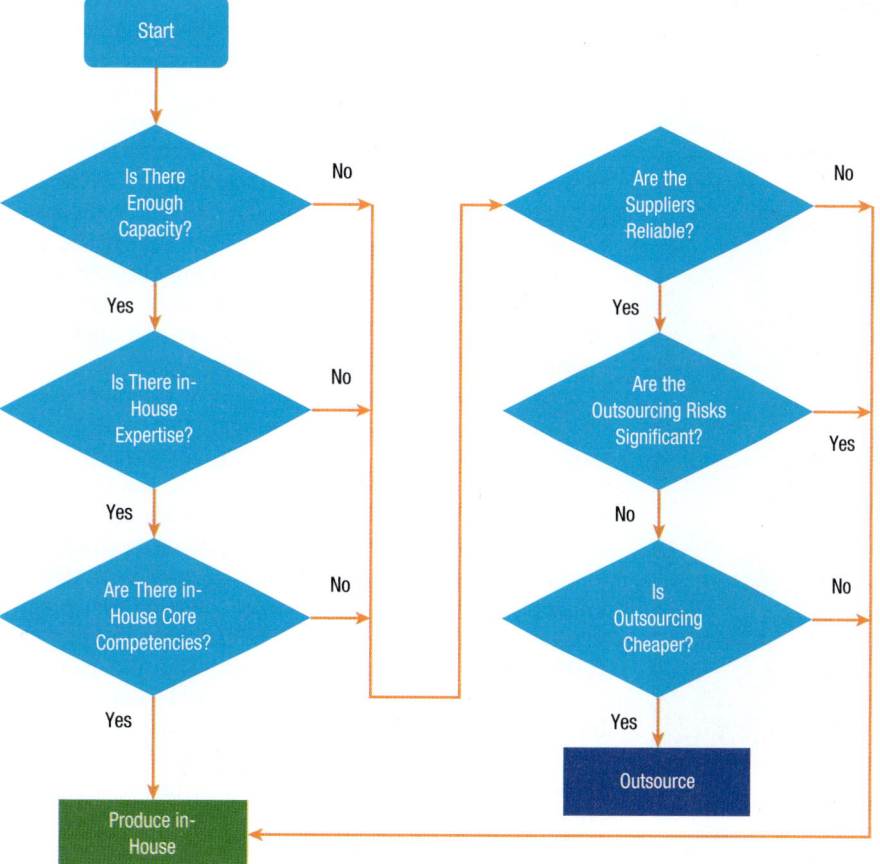

Fixed automation: the process of producing a product or component in a fixed sequence of operations

Flexible automation: the process of using high-cost, general-purpose machines to produce a variety of products in low volumes or in small batches

Numerically controlled (NC) machines: machines that are programmed with a specific set of instructions that tell the machines the details of the operations to be performed

The extent to which a firm's processes should be automated is closely related to technology. The most significant advantage of automation over human labor is the consistency of performance and quality. Unlike human labor, where there is high variability in performing the same tasks, machines perform these tasks repeatedly in the same amount of time and at the same general level of quality. Furthermore, unlike human resources used for labor, automated equipment does not suffer from fatigue, boredom, or go on strikes. Yet another advantage of automation is that it can reduce a firm's labor costs. Nonetheless, automation requires a firm's processes to be standardized, which makes it harder to produce a wide variety of products or customized products. Other disadvantages are the high initial cost of investing in automatic equipment, the high volumes of production needed to justify the investment, and the potential for decreased morale and productivity among workers who fear that they may lose their jobs as a result of automation. Thus, the decision of whether to automate and by how much requires careful analysis.

Automation in manufacturing processes can be broadly classified into two types: fixed automation and flexible automation. **Fixed automation** is the process of a producing a product or component in a fixed sequence of operations. This type of automation is appropriate for processes designed to produce large volumes of standardized products that have relatively long life cycles. For example, chemical companies and oil refineries use a fixed automated process. Fixed automation is highly efficient and produces products at a low variable cost. Yet, any major redesign of the product or the existing process will be very expensive. It could require purchasing new equipment or having to reconfigure the firm's factory.

Flexible automation evolved from *programmable automation.* High-cost, general-purpose machines are used to produce a variety of products in low volumes or in small batches. These machines are controlled by computer programs that provide instructions for the sequence of operations to be performed on each product. The ability to reprogram these machines to handle varying degrees of product customization is the major advantage of this type of automation. Numerically controlled machines and industrial robots are examples of programmable automation. **Numerically controlled (NC) machines** are programmed with a specific set of instructions that tell the machines the details of the operations to be performed. The most common NC machines are milling machines, lathes, and grinders. NC machines are used to produce products such as industrial components. An **industrial robot** is a versatile machine that can perform routine tasks such as cutting and boring, welding, assembly, and materials handling without any human intervention. Most of the millions of industrial robots around the world are used to produce automobiles and metal and machinery products, electrical and electronic products, and rubber and plastic items.[6] The advantage of using robots in manufacturing processes is that they can perform many of the difficult tasks such as heavy lifting, and dirty, repetitive, and dangerous jobs. Yet another application of programmable automation in manufacturing processes is **computer-aided manufacturing (CAM)**, which uses computer software and hardware to control machine tools and other related machinery. In modern computer NC systems, CAM, along with CAD (computer-aided design), is used to automate end-to-end component design and manufacture. CAM is used in various major industries such as silicone manufacturing, tanning, dairy, and the beverage manufacturing. **Computer-aided process planning (CAPP)** is another technological application; it involves the use of computer technology to assist in planning the processes required to manufacture a part or product. CAPP provides a link between product design and manufacturing.

A more advanced application of flexible automation is a flexible manufacturing system. A **flexible manufacturing system (FMS)** is a processing method that can produce parts, allow changes to be made to products being manufactured, and handle varying levels of production.[7] Many of The Ford Motor Company's (aka Ford's, Dearborn, MI) plants use FMS not only to improve efficiency but also to introduce new models of cars quickly. In a dynamic manufacturing environment, an FMS can increase a firm's

Automated storage and retrieval systems are useful in situations that require controlled access to high-value and sensitive materials that need be stored and retrieved in harsh environments that may be hazardous to workers.

manufacturing efficiency and reduce the downtime of its equipment. The biggest drawback of an FMS is the high initial cost of developing it because it requires firms to acquire sophisticated equipment and machinery.

The complete automation of the manufacturing plant can be accomplished using computer-integrated manufacturing (CIM) technology, in which a manufacturing plant uses computers to control all processes. CIM can be used with computer-aided design and manufacturing (CAD and CAM), computer-aided process planning (CAPP), NC machines, robots, FMS, and in different combinations of these processes, all of which are fully integrated. CAD and CAM are particularly important because they greatly facilitate the automation of product designs and manufacturing processes through the use of computer software. Dassault Systèmes SE (Vélizy-Villacoublay, France), for example, provides CIM software technology for aerospace customers like The Boeing Company (Chicago, IL) and Airbus SAS (Blagnac, France) to allow them to evaluate different design alternatives for their aircraft prior to full production. Although CIM can allow a firm to produce and deliver high-quality, customized products quickly and efficiently, it has some drawbacks. For example, the complexity of CIM manufacturing operations requires fully integrating all equipment, some of which may not be compatible with others.

Table 9.3 lists some other advances in technology that have improved productivity and efficiency for processes in both the manufacturing and service sectors. These technologies have been applied in a wide variety of areas, such as process control, materials handling, transportation, and patient care in hospitals.

ANALYZING AND REDESIGNING PROCESSES

Markets change over time, and a process that once worked well may no longer achieve the firm's goals, particularly if the firm participates in global markets. It often is necessary to reexamine a process to determine whether it can be improved to make it more cost efficient or more responsive to customers. In some cases, the process may need to be entirely redesigned. Changes in the process may also be necessary to accommodate new product mixes or to integrate new technologies. To determine when it is time to redesign a process, the operations manager must answer questions like these:

- Does the existing process give the company a competitive edge in terms of the order-winning criteria of cost, quality, flexibility, and delivery time?
- Are there redundant steps or steps that do not add value in the process that can be eliminated?
- How can the process be improved or redesigned to enhance value provided to the customer?

Industrial Robot: a versatile machine that can perform routine tasks such as cutting and boring, welding, assembly, and materials handling without any human intervention

Computer-aided manufacturing (CAM): an application of programmable automation in manufacturing processes that uses computer software and hardware to control machine tools and other related machinery

Computer-aided process planning (CAPP): a technological application that involves the use of computer technology to assist in planning the processes required to manufacture a part or product

TABLE 9.3: Examples of Advances in Process and Manufacturing Technologies

TECHNOLOGY	DESCRIPTION	APPLICATIONS
Standard for exchange of product, model data (STEP)	An ISO standard for representing and exchanging the design and manufacturing-related information of a product in computer-interpretable format.	A Eurofighter designed by four industry partners using STEP technology to exchange product design and manufacturing data.[8]
Computer-aided process planning (CAPP)	The use of computer technology to assist in planning the processes required to manufacture a part or product. Provides a link between product design and manufacturing.	CAPP can be used to link a product's design with the machines and tools used in the production process.[9]
Automated storage and retrieval system (ASRS)	A computer-controlled system that uses various methods for the automatic placement and retrieval of loads to and from specific storage locations within a warehouse.	Automated storage and retrieval systems are useful in situations that require controlled access to high-value and sensitive materials that need be stored and retrieve loads in harsh environments that may be hazardous to workers.[10]
Automated guided vehicles (AGVs)	Electronically guided mobile vehicles are directed by wires or markers embedded on the floor or by radio frequencies, vision, or lasers to move materials in manufacturing, warehousing, and service facilities.	AGVs are used in many industries in the manufacturing sector for efficient, cost-effective movement of materials and for improving operations in many manufacturing facilities and warehouses.

TABLE 9.4: Tools for Process Analysis and Redesign

TOOLS	DESCRIPTION	USES
Assembly drawing	An enlarged view of the product that has detailed listing of all parts and subassemblies.	Enables the user to understand how various parts of a product can be put together quickly and easily.
Assembly chart	A step-by-step pictorial representation of the assembly process.	Facilitates the assembly of a product through a well-defined sequence of steps.
Process route sheet	A document that describes the sequence of different operations, places, or people involved in a process.	Enables anyone to see all of the details of a work or customer order.
Process mapping	A graphical technique that shows all process-related activities, including inputs and outputs, decision points such as approvals and exceptions, and any cross-functional relationships.	Provides an integrated and unifying view of business processes, so that all stakeholders have a clear understanding of the individual roles they play in the overall system.
Value stream mapping (VSM)	A process mapping technique used to analyze and design the flow of materials and information across multiple processes required to bring a product or service to a consumer.	Enables a process analyst to identify activities that do not add value so that that they can be eliminated to reduce waste and improve efficiency.
Process simulation	A technique that uses computer software to provide a dynamic view of the actual process.	Enables a process analyst to estimate the variability of task times and explore several what-if scenarios without changing or disrupting the actual process.
Service blueprinting	A technique used to analyze service processes, particularly those that have high service content and require customer interaction, such as hospitality services, teaching, and counseling.	Enables a service provider to focus on customer interaction as an integral part of the design process so that overall service quality can be improved.

Several tools can help an operations manager answer these questions and analyze a firm's processes. Many of these tools, such as process charts and assembly charts, are discussed in more detail in the supplement to this chapter. Table 9.4 contains a brief overview of them. A more comprehensive discussion of value-stream mapping, yet another useful process analysis tool, is presented in Chapter 9S.

List the unique features in the design of service processes.

Flexible manufacturing system (FMS): a processing method that can produce parts, allow changes to be made to products being manufactured, and handle varying levels of production

Computer-integrated manufacturing (CIM): a technological application in which a manufacturing plant uses computers to control all processes

9.2 Designing Service Processes

To design processes for services, the operations manager must understand the degree of customer interaction when performing the service and customization needed to satisfy the customer. Although service operations managers prefer to offer standardized services to reduce their firms' costs, customers prefer customized services that address their unique needs. Nonetheless, firms are also aware that customers value services they perceive as being tailored especially for them. High-end retail stores such as Saks Fifth Avenue (subsidiary of the Hudson's Bay Company, New York, NY), Neiman Marcus (Dallas, TX), and Nordstrom, Inc. (Seattle, WA) adopt this customized approach by employing personal shoppers to work directly with customers to find the most flattering colors and styles of clothing for them. The approach these firms use differs from the standard displays of clothing on racks that many retailers use. This trade-off between customers' expectations and service providers' desire for efficiency is what makes the design of service processes challenging. The better a company is at bridging this gap, the more competitive it will be.

Classifying Processes Within the Service Process Design Matrix

The service process design matrix shown in Figure 9.3 classifies from high to low various service processes in terms of their degree of customer interaction and customization and in their degree of labor intensity. The degree of customer interaction is the extent to which to which the customer can participate in the service process. For example, a high degree of interaction means the customer can tailor the service provided by demanding more or less of some aspects of the service. Customization is the need and ability to alter the service so the individual customer's needs and expectations can be met. The degree of labor intensity is the labor time and effort required in comparison with the use of equipment or automation. A service process that uses a high level of automation, such as an ATM machine, with very little labor time and effort has a low degree of labor intensity.

Figure 9.3 includes examples of service processes that fall into each quadrant. The lower left quadrant, labeled *service factories*, contains service processes that have a low degree of labor intensity, customer interaction, and customization. This quadrant is similar to the repetitive assembly and continuous flow processes of goods-producing firms shown in Figure 9.1. Service firms in this quadrant operate like factory assembly lines, employing cheaper, unskilled labor and taking advantage of economies of scale. Service processes that have a low degree of labor intensity but a high degree of customer interaction and customization are shown in the lower right quadrant, labeled *service shops*. Livery cabs, hospitals, auto repair shops, and high-end restaurants fall into this quadrant. The upper left quadrant, labeled *mass services*, contains service processes that have little variety but high volumes. Not only is customization of the service to meet the individual needs of customers negligible, but also there is often limited contact between the customer and the service provider. Yet, the high volume of service requires high labor intensity. Examples of these processes include rail services, the services offered by retailers and wholesalers, and

FIGURE 9.3: Service Process Design Matrix

SOURCE: Schmenner, R. W. (1986, Spring). How can service businesses survive and prosper? *Sloan Management Review*, 212.

online schools. Finally, those service processes that have a high degree of labor intensity and a high degree of customer interaction and customization fall in the upper-right quadrant labeled *professional services*. This quadrant is similar to the specialized job-shop and batch processes in the goods-producing industries shown in Figure 9.1. Doctors' offices, law and accounting firms, graphic designers, and tutors are examples of professional services.

Designing Service Processes

We can use Figure 9.3 to determine how an organization can best design its service operations by finding the best combination of labor intensity (customer interaction) and customization for its needs. By drawing a diagonal arrow from the upper-right corner to the lower-left corner as Figure 9.3 shows, we can infer that processes that require high levels of customer interaction and customization, such as professional services, or processes that involve a high degree of labor intensity experience high variability and, therefore, are less productive than standardized operations.

Positioning and Repositioning Processes Within the Service Process Design Matrix

Organizations can use the service process matrix to position their services relative to their competitors. Consider Nordstrom. Even though Nordstrom's service process falls into the mass services category, the company has made a conscious effort to position itself more toward the right of that cell (toward the professional services cell) by having highly trained Nordstrom employees personally interact with each customer to meet his or her unique needs and expectations.

Similarly, most hotels belong in the service shop category. Nevertheless, because the labor intensity and customer interaction is very high at luxury hotels such as the Red Carnation Hotels UK Ltd. (London, U.K.), its service process lies on the border between the service shop and professional services categories. The process was not created by accident. The values of Red Carnation include giving "personalized, warm and consistently exceptional service" and creating "positive, memorable experiences for every guest." If guests have a problem or need something special, the hotel's highly trained employees are empowered to do whatever it takes to resolve the situation immediately, even if they have to break away from their regular duties. Clearly, given its mission and value set, Red Carnation did not want to belong to the service factory category and made a strategic decision to position itself toward the service shop and professional services category.[11]

Managers can also use the service process matrix to understand the effect of a strategic change intended to reposition the firm's operations. For example, assume that for competitive reasons a firm in the service factory category wants to move into the service shop category. To implement this strategic change, the firm will need to provide a higher degree of customer interaction and customization as well as manage higher costs that arise from the loss of economies of scale, which was an advantage that the company had by being in the service factory category. Furthermore, moving to a service shop requires higher labor skill levels that add to the cost of providing service. Also, the span of supervision in a service shop tends to be wider. Hence, the firm's managerial hierarchy needs to be flatter and less rigid.[12]

By contrast, to reduce the variability of its output and improve its productivity, a service firm might want to move the other way—down the diagonal in Figure 9.3 toward the service factory category. That is, the firm might want to decrease the degree of customer interaction and customization it provides along with the labor intensity of its processes. Over the past decade, many law firms have increased their television advertising to seek clients interested in will preparation, bankruptcy, and uncontested divorces. The law firms have chosen these tasks because these are standard cases that require minimum customization, and a law firm can handle many of them in a single trip to the courthouse. It is a way for the law firm to replace customized services with standardized services. Banks that rely on ATMs for routine transactions and warehouse stores such as Costco (Costco Wholesale Corporation, Issaquah, WA) and Sam's Club (Sam's West, Inc., subsidiary of Wal-Mart Stores, Inc., Bentonville, AR) are examples of other service firms that have shifted their service processes toward the service factory category through significant reductions in labor intensity.

Even hospitals whose service processes traditionally belong to the service shop category have moved toward the service factory category. Consider, for example, the Hospital for Special Surgery in New York City, which specializes only in the diagnosis and surgical and nonsurgical treatment of musculoskeletal conditions. The hospital offers standardized services, which allow it to be run more like a service factory. Managers of service firms moving in this direction face several challenges. They must make capital decisions such as choice of plant and equipment, manage costs, keep track of technological advances, carefully manage demand, and schedule the delivery of services because services can't easily be inventoried.[13]

Many other service businesses have also attempted to reposition their processes in relation to the service process matrix. For example, to achieve efficiency, some restaurants, which have traditionally fallen in the service shop quadrant because of their high degree of customization and customer interaction, have moved to the service factory quadrant typified by the fast food industry. In contrast, some fast food restaurants have moved away from the service factory model to one that allows for a limited amount of product customization and more variety of products to choose from. For example, the McItaly menu introduced in Italy by McDonald's (Oak Brook, IL) consists of hamburgers made with all Italian meat and features Italian products such as extra virgin olive oil, parmesan cheese, bresaola (low-fat dry beef, sliced thinly and eaten cold), ham, artichokes, onions, and pancetta. The McItaly Marchigiana, for example, was introduced for the Marche region in Italy, and it includes locally sourced, fresh mozzarella cheese.[14]

Using Technology to Improve Service Processes

Advances in technology have improved service processes. Using the right technology can help firms improve the quality of their services, provide them more quickly and efficiently, and offer them at a lower cost. Voice recognition and call-routing technologies have improved service processes by directing the potential service consumer to the right department or employee who can address the customer's needs. In addition, "live chat," which is available on many websites, enables you to "talk" to a customer service representative instead of waiting endlessly on hold or waiting for an email reply. A tangible benefit of such technologies is that there is less delay in service delivery, thus, saving the service firm time and money.

One of the most important benefits of recent advances in technology is that service processes have become more flexible. Customers now have the option of choosing how the services they want should be delivered. For example, self-checkout lines in retail outlets or ticketing kiosks at airports enable customers to get the services they want without interacting with the employees of the service organization, thus saving the customer

Self-checkout lanes are a win-win proposition: they give shoppers the flexibility to choose how they want to checkout and provide merchants with efficiencies and cost savings.

Bloomberg/Bloomberg/Getty Images

time and allowing the service firm to reduce the number of employees it must employ at the service site. Customers uncomfortable with these innovations or who want the human touch can use regular checkout lines. Colleges and universities have embraced technology in their process of educating their students. By offering online classes, they provide students the flexibility and convenience of how and where they want to learn. Thus, the schools can educate students with smaller investment in physical plant (classrooms) and staff.

Technology has also enabled service firms to provide critical and timely information to their customers. Internet ticketing sites such as Orbitz, Travelocity, and Expedia (all three of which are owned by Expedia, Inc., Chicago, IL) have enabled airline companies to sell tickets directly to customers and scale back their ticketing phone lines. Mobile or smartphone apps remind fliers of departure, check-in, and arrival times, as well as notify them of flight delays. Through the use of the Internet, telephone, and social media, customers now have more efficient ways of requesting or ordering the products or services they want. In the final analysis, regardless of the technology used, the key objective is to use technology to simplify service processes so that they are easy to use and improve the service experience.

9.3 Designing Processes for Supply Chains

To provide the customers with high-quality products and services at the lowest possible cost, and at the locations most convenient for customers, companies need to design their individual internal processes in ways that maximize the performance of their supply chains. In effect, companies need to synchronize not only their individual internal processes but also link up with the external processes of their supply chain partners. For example, a well-synchronized supply chain process for canned soup will produce and deliver defect-free cans of soup in the right quantities and at the right time to all grocery stores and supermarkets. In the section, we focus on designing a manufacturing process that is synchronized across the supply chain.

Classifying Manufacturing Processes by the Degree of Product Customization

Companies need fast and flexible manufacturing processes that can adapt quickly to change. To achieve this objective, the different manufacturing processes should be integrated across a customer-focused supply chain. In a manufacturing supply chain, depending on the type of product, different processes link multiple supply chain partners. Consider the processes in the supply chain for making shirts. First, yarn, which is a standardized product, is manufactured using a continuous flow process. The yarn manufacturer at this stage in the supply chain sells its products to a downstream weaving firm. The second step in the supply chain consists of another continuous flow process: weaving the finished yarn into fabric using looms. A manufacturer further down the chain then finishes the fabric by cutting it into patterns and sewing it into sweaters. Note that the cutting and sewing portion of the supply chain is more labor intensive and that a batch-type process is used to make different types and quantities of sweaters. Before being packed and shipped, the manufacturer may use more batch processes to customize the sweaters even more, such as dyeing them and stitching different labels on them. Figure 9.4 on page 310 illustrates the use of different manufacturing processes in a supply chain.[15] The product customization begins after the fabric weaving process.

The basic types of customization occurring within manufacturing supply chains can be classified into four categories:

- **Make-to-stock (MTS):** This type of manufacturing method is used for products that typically require little or no customization, are produced in large volumes, and are stored as inventory for future use. They include crude oil, chemicals, and many consumer products such as sugar, flour, and salt that are sold in retail stores.
- **Make-to-order (MTO):** In this method, products are manufactured only after receiving a customer's order. A combination of standard and custom-made components is used to make the product, but its final configuration is specific for the customer. High-end automobiles, such as a Ferrari (Ferrari S.p.A., Maranello, Italy) or Porsche (Porsche AG, Stuttgart, Baden-Württemberg, Germany), engagement rings, wedding invitations, custom-built homes, and custom-tailored clothing are examples of products manufactured using this method.
- **Assemble-to-order (ATO):** In this process, the basic parts and components of a product are standardized and have already been manufactured and are kept in stock. After receiving an order, these parts are quickly assembled based on the customer's requirements. This

---

9.3

Defend the reasons that it is important for companies to synchronize their internal processes with the external processes of their supply chain partners.

Make-to-stock (MTS): a manufacturing method used for products that typically require little or no customization, are produced in large volumes, and are stored as inventory for future use

Make-to-order (MTO): a manufacturing method in which products are manufactured only after receiving a customer's order

Assemble-to-order (ATO): a hybrid of the MTS and MTO methods in which the basic parts and components of a product are standardized, have already been manufactured, and are kept in stock until an order is received, when they are quickly assembled based on the customer's requirements

FIGURE 9.4: Manufacturing Processes in the Supply Chain for Shirts

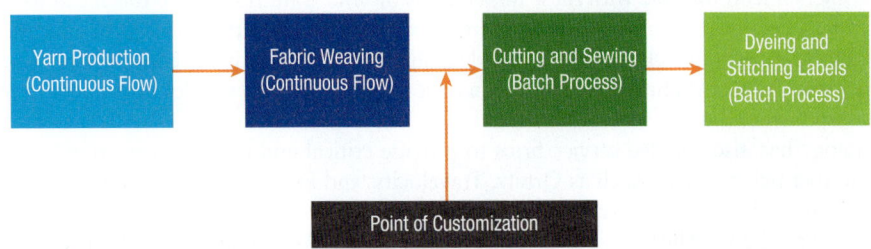

SOURCE: Adapted from Bozarth, C. C., & Handfield, R. B. (2013). *Introduction to operations and supply chain management* (3rd ed., p. 44). Englewood Cliffs, NJ: Pearson Prentice-Hall.

method is a hybrid of the MTS and MTO methods because it combines the advantages of both. Customization occurs at the last stage of the manufacturing process, and even then the degree of customization is still limited. By focusing on enhancing their information processing, General Electric (aka GE, Fairfield, CT) is creating more than 400 "brilliant factories," which allow customization and assembly-to-order manufacturing in a wide range of products, from locomotives to oil extraction machinery. Other examples of products produced using the ATO method include many automobiles, specialty chemicals, and sports t-shirts with team or organizational logos.

- **Engineer-to-order (ETO):** This process offers the highest degree of product customization. In the ETO method, products are designed, manufactured, and assembled to the customer's specifications from start to finish. ETO products include industrial equipment, tools, molds and dies, power generation equipment, custom signs, boats, and specific types of medical equipment.

Engineer-to-order (ETO): a method in which products are designed, manufactured, and assembled to the customer's specifications from start to finish

As the matrix in Figure 9.5 shows, the four manufacturing methods can be categorized along the dimensions of demand variability and production complexity. Demand variability means that there are likely to be modifications or multiple variations in the output produced by the manufacturing process. Production complexity refers to the complexity and time involved in producing the product.

Mapping Manufacturing Methods Across Supply Chains

FIGURE 9.5: Mapping Process Types to Manufacturing Methods

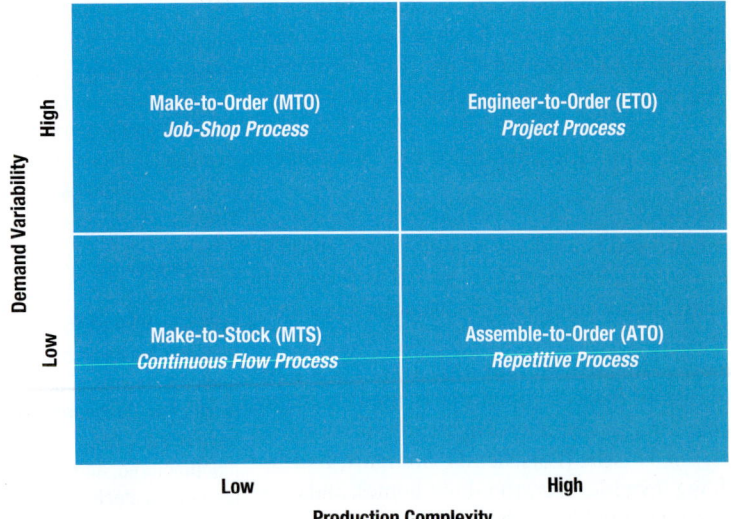

The manufacturing methods—MTS, MTO, ATO, and ETO—that a company within a supply chain should choose depend on factors such as the competitive business environment; the proliferation of products, customers, and distribution channels; and demand variability. To respond to all these factors, companies often use a mixture of these manufacturing processes; that is, they find the best blend of manufacturing processes. For example, Dell's mass customization strategy is a hybrid of job-shop and repetitive processes. This combination allows Dell to offer unique products to its customers as quickly as possible.

Before we apply the various manufacturing methods to a supply chain, let us look at two manufacturing systems companies usually rely on—systems we will discuss in more detail in Chapter 14. A *push manufacturing* system is one in which production is based on forecasted demand or projected sales. Demand is often forecast using historical data or past trends; for example, manufacturers in many industries accelerate production to coincide with periods of high demand. Air conditioner manufacturers gear up for peak sales in the spring and summer.

SOURCE: Adapted from Flores, H. (n.d.). *Manufacturing Strategy: An Adaptive Perspective.* White paper. Montreal, Quebec, Canada: Technology Evaluation Centers. Retrieved from https://www.technologyevaluation.com/research/white-paper/Manufacturing-Strategy-An-Adaptive-Perspective.html

Companies that produce highly standardized products with relatively low demand variability and production complexity use push manufacturing systems with the goal of maximizing their capacity. MTS manufacturing processes are often a part of push systems.

Processes and the Supply Chain

In contrast, when the demand for a product is highly variable or its production is complex, companies often use a *pull manufacturing* system, which is based on actual customer orders rather than on demand forecasts. Ford Australia, for example, produces cars only after it receives an order from the customer. An MTO manufacturing process is often a part of a pull system. Supply chains that use pull manufacturing systems have the capacity and flexibility needed to produce a variety of products in an environment with variable demand.

Most companies use a mixture of push-and-pull manufacturing. As firms grow and expand their product lines, the variability in the demand for their products increases as does their production complexity. As a result, it becomes more difficult for companies to rely exclusively on either push or pull manufacturing systems. The hybrid manufacturing practices are also reflected in their supply chains. That is, certain portions of a supply chain rely on push manufacturing, whereas other portions rely on pull manufacturing methods.

The firm must determine which combination of push-and-pull systems best enables it to combine efficiency and customer responsiveness in their supply chains. As more companies embrace mass customization, they have to determine which portion of the supply chain can be managed using a push approach and which portion works best as a pull system. The interface between the two is called the push–pull boundary or decoupling point.[16] This is the point where customization occurs, splitting the supply chain into the distinct pull-and-push parts. Figure 9.6 shows how manufacturing processes use the decoupling point to divide the supply chain.[17]

The decoupling point is also often referred to as the point of postponement (POP).[18] The POP is the point that divides the supply chain into the supplier side and the customer side. Push systems are aimed at gaining maximum efficiency by managing and streamlining the supply chain, whereas pull systems are intended to satisfy the demands of customers. The exact point where decoupling or the POP occurs depends on the type of the manufacturing process (MTS, ATO, MTO, and ETO). The POP point is:

- The point at which the variability in the demand for the product increases significantly
- The point that denotes the longest lead time the customer will tolerate
- The point of trade-off between inventory flexibility and capacity flexibility

The supply chain process for companies that operate in an MTS manufacturing environment is completely forecast based, and it begins with the acquisition of raw materials and ends with the

FIGURE 9.6: Determining Manufacturing Processes Based on the Decoupling Point in a Supply Chain

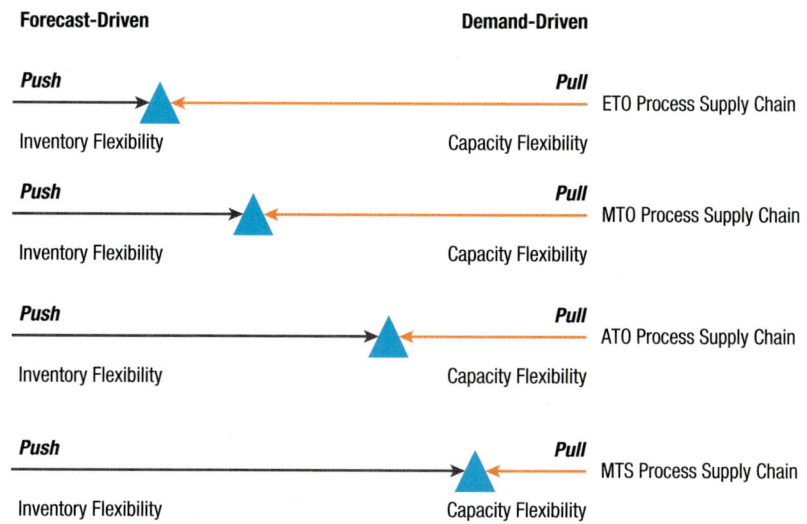

Push–pull boundary: the interface between the parts of a supply chain that can be managed using a push approach and the parts that can be managed as a pull system

Decoupling point: See push–pull boundary

Point of postponement (POP): the point that divides the supply chain into the supplier side and the customer side

SOURCE: Adapted from Flores, H. (n.d.). *Manufacturing Strategy: An Adaptive Perspective.* White paper. Montreal, Quebec, Canada: Technology Evaluation Centers. Retrieved from https://www.technologyevaluation.com/research/white-paper/Manufacturing-Strategy-An-Adaptive-Perspective.html

creation of finished goods. The firm takes customer orders and delivers products to them from the inventory in stock. The key supply chain challenge in this process is to maintain inventory flexibility because demand has to be met from inventory in stock. When the push influence on the MTS supply chain increases, there is a greater need for inventory flexibility, and the POP occurs further down the supply chain, as Figure 9.6 shows.

Figure 9.6 also shows that when there is greater demand variability for a product and more customization is needed, the firm should use ATO and MTO processes. Therefore, the pull influence on the supply chain is also stronger and greater capacity flexibility is needed. That is, the supply chain must be prepared to handle fluctuations. Work-in-process (WIP) inventory is often used as a buffer to increase the chain's flexibility to respond to demand changes. Items in WIP inventory are partially finished and waiting for work to be completed on them or they are finished goods that have not yet been packaged and inspected. WIP inventory may also contain raw materials that have been moved to the production area. In a computer manufacturing company, many of the components such as the processor or printed circuit boards may be initially stored as work-in-process inventory. Subsequently, when a customer order for a computer is received, these WIP items are assembled in specific configurations to meet customer requirements. Whenever there is a high degree of product variety, as in MTO and ATO processes, the breadth and volume of WIP are also high.

The amount of WIP inventory determines where the POP occurs in the supply chains that use MTO and ATO processes. In an ATO process supply chain, the volume of WIP inventory is higher and occurs farther down the supply chain (closer to the finished product) than in an MTO process supply chain. In an ATO process supply chain, because the degree of customization is high and the volume of WIP inventory held as buffer is low, the POP occurs further upstream than in a MTO process supply chain.[19]

Finally, with the ETO manufacturing process, supply chain activities, such as ordering raw materials, production, etc., are triggered only after a firm customer order is received because the degree of customization is very high and occurs very early in the supply chain. Consequently, the POP occurs much farther upstream in the supply chain. Industries that have ETO process supply chains include aerospace and defense, capital equipment, and specialized machinery industries.

The careful design or redesign of production processes can enhance the performance of a supply chain. Strategies such as combining different processes and resequencing production operations to shift the POP can provide important benefits. First, shifting the POP enables companies in the supply chain to make production decisions after first getting more accurate estimates of the demand for a product, which then reduces the need to carry unnecessary inventory. Second, it enables the supply chain to be more responsive while keeping costs low. For example, the hybrid strategy that characterizes mass customization helps supply chains produce and deliver unique products, often with minimal increases in lead times. Benetton, the Italian clothing manufacturer, benefited from shifting its POP. By delaying the dyeing of its knitted garments until late in the production process, Benetton was able to respond rapidly to changes in customer demand for different colors of clothing. This postponement strategy not only made Benetton's supply chain highly adaptable and responsive, but it also created superior customer value.

9.4 Global Process Design

9.4
Describe the unique challenges involved in designing global processes.

Companies with global operations have to answer the following three questions when designing their production processes:[20]

1. If the company is producing similar products in several plants located in different countries, should the company be using similar processes in all locations to produce these products?
2. If the company decides to use similar processes, how should they be designed?
3. If the company decides to produce new products that satisfy the unique needs of the consumers in a given country, then what should be the design of these new processes?

Adaptive manufacturing: a process that combines lean and agile manufacturing with flexible manufacturing systems to adapt production in response to changing market conditions

Companies that operate production facilities in a foreign country have to redesign their products to varying degrees to suit the needs of the local market. This high degree of variability makes mass customization necessary. The most important factor influencing sales is fulfillment speed; cost, quality, and availability are secondary. To increase how fast they can respond to customers, companies use concurrent engineering to integrate their product and process designs and collaborating more closely with their supply chain partners. Firms also use adaptive manufacturing, which combines lean and agile manufacturing with flexible manufacturing systems to adapt production in response to changing market conditions. Adaptive manufacturing relies on technology to create hybrid manufacturing processes, which may include MTS processes. In an adaptive process, the POP is flexible and can be adjusted to employ techniques of all manufacturing processes, such as MTS, ATO, MTO, and ETO.

With annual sales of US$150 billion and projected steady increases for the next decade, the jewelry industry remains strong and highly profitable. Adaptive manufacturing allows jewelry makers to shift their focus constantly from customized, individual pieces of expensive jewelry that are created on an MTO basis to more generic rings or broaches that can be made with a wider, MTS approach. The result is to allow jewelry manufacturers the broadest flexibility for responding to the newest trends in the industry, including unbranded jewelry and online, special order shopping.[21] This example illustrates the advantages of using an adaptive manufacturing strategy and a hybrid approach to capitalize on flexible processes and supply chains.

9.5 Layout Planning

A layout describes the physical arrangement of work and storage areas, departments, or equipment within the confines of some physical structure such as a plant, office, warehouse, or a service facility. A typical manufacturing facility has some or all of the following components: front area, production area, warehouse, shipping and receiving, maintenance and production support, and employee services and amenities. Warehouses may have their own shipping and receiving, maintenance, and employee services areas. All of these have people, equipment, and materials traveling and interacting with each other. Layout planning decisions involve arranging these components for new facilities and rearranging them in existing facilities. The goal is to arrange people, equipment, materials, and processes so that the work flows smoothly and rapidly at all times. Other goals of layout planning are:

- Achieving the appropriate product or service quality
- Eliminating waste through the efficient use of workers and space
- Eliminating bottlenecks in product or service flows
- Minimizing material and manufacturing costs
- Eliminating the movement of materials, workers, and customers that do not add value to the product or service
- Improving productivity
- Maximizing the utilization of production capacity
- Reducing accidents and health hazards to ensure employee safety
- Reducing customer waiting times
- Making supervision and control easier

The Strategic Nature of Layout Decisions

Layout decisions are strategic decisions because they affect the cost and efficiency of manufacturing and warehouse operations or, in the case of a service facility, the efficiency and quality of the customer service. In addition, firms often decide to change their layouts to respond more rapidly to market opportunities or to correct or improve operating efficiencies. Another reason the decisions are strategic is that an organization has to make a significant commitment of money, time, and effort when building a facility or when making changes to it—requiring planning, analysis, testing, and verification as well as the purchase of new machinery. Sometimes operations have to be suspended until the new layout is completed, equipment installed, and workers trained to operate within the new layout. Moreover, mistakes made in the layout planning and implementation process cannot be easily rectified and any problems will take time to emerge and correct.

Basic Types of Layouts

There are many different types of layouts. We will first discuss the three basic layout types: process, product, and fixed-position layouts, and then we will describe alternatives.

PROCESS LAYOUTS

A process layout, often referred to as a functional layout, is used when a firm produces low volumes of products using job-shop or batch production processes. A process layout enables the firm to meet the different needs of a variety of customers. Similar activities or machines in work centers or departments are grouped together based on the type of the work or function they perform. Machines performing lathing operations are located in the lathing department; machines performing drilling

Process Design for Global Operations

9.5

Construct the different layout types, and identify their features.

Layout: the physical arrangement of work and storage areas, departments, or equipment within the confines of some physical structure such as a plant, office, warehouse, or a service facility

Process layout: a layout type that is used when a firm produces low volumes of products using job-shop or batch production processes, often referred to as a functional layout

FIGURE 9.7: Process Layout for a Manufacturing Facility

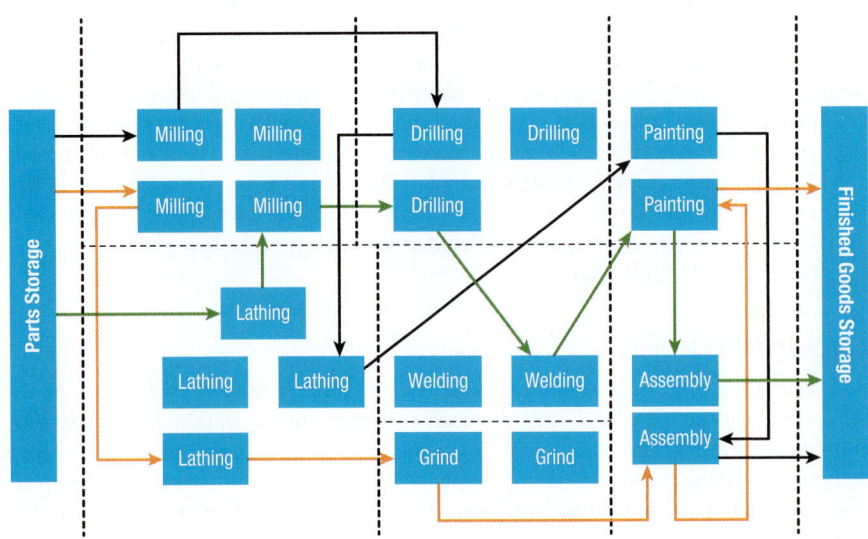

operations are grouped in the drilling department; casting operations are in another location, and so on. The physical arrangement of departments in a process layout has no set sequence because the sequence of operations required to complete an order varies from customer to customer. Figure 9.7 shows a process layout for a manufacturing facility. Although the machines are grouped into departments, the principal focus is on making special orders for each customer. One order may go directly to the milling department and then proceed to drilling, welding, painting, and so forth. Another order may first be sent to the lathing department and then directly to painting for final finishing before being assembled. Although equipment is organized into departments, the actual process flow is not uniform but varies from product to product.

Many service facilities also use process layouts. Figure 9.8 shows a process layout for a hospital. Notice how similar it is to the job-shop process for manufacturers. The arrangement is like that for a manufacturing process in the sense that it is based on the work done in each department. In a hospital, each patient receives customized treatment in a sequence that is unique to the patient's problem. So, for example, a patient enters the hospital and, after registering, is directed to the different departments that will administer treatment.

The biggest advantage of a process layout is that it allows a firm to treat each order as a special case, enabling the firm to process a variety of customer orders. The biggest disadvantage is its relative inefficiency. It is common for jobs to queue up on the department floor at various points because processing or service times will vary from job to job or from customer to customer. These variances make it difficult to schedule workflows because companies must work on one order at a time, each of which has its unique characteristics and production or service requirements.

FIGURE 9.8: Process Layout for a Hospital

Psychiatry			Kitchen	Laundry	
Waiting Rooms			Cafeteria	Pediatrics	Neonatal Unit
Surgery	Anesthesiology			OB/GYN	Labor Rooms
Post-Operative Care	Cardiology	Waiting Rooms	Reception and Lobby	Waiting Rooms	Pulmonology
					Ear/Nose/Throat
Clinical Pathology Labs	Microbiology Labs			Radiology	Orthopedics
				Administration Offices	Physiotherapy

FIGURE 9.9: Product Layout for a Sugar Factory

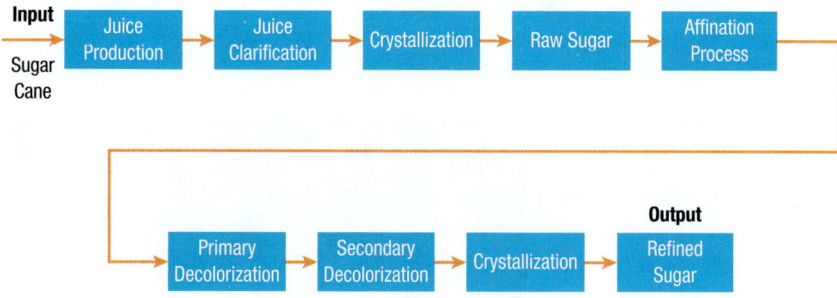

PRODUCT LAYOUTS

A product layout, also referred to as a *straight-line layout*, works well for repetitive or continuous flow processes used to produce a highly standardized product with high and constant demand. The machines or work centers are arranged according to a predetermined sequence of operations needed to produce the product. Materials enter the system at the first work center at one end of the line, and finished products come out from the last work center at the end of the line. In between, partly finished goods travel automatically from one work center to another, and the output of one work center becomes the input for the next. For example, if you visited a sugar factory, you would see that raw sugar cane fed in at one end of the mill comes out as refined sugar at the other end. Figure 9.9 shows a product layout for a sugar factory. A similar layout can be observed in a paper mill. The wood pulp is fed into the first work center and eventually comes out as paper at the other end.

The biggest advantage of a product layout is that high levels of efficiency and capacity utilization can be achieved. Product layouts can also provide a sort of closed system that works well if the production is highly automated and the product being produced cannot be contaminated, such as when pharmaceuticals are being manufactured. The greatest disadvantage of the layout is its inflexibility because it is built for a single purpose. Any change in the design of the product or significant increases or decreases in demand will require a complete redesign of the layout.

When increased communication and teamwork among workers on the shop floor is needed, then a U-shaped layout like that shown in Figure 9.10 is better than a product layout. Many household appliances such as blenders, coffeemakers, and toaster ovens can be produced using a U-shaped layout. A U-shaped layout is an improvement over the straight-line layout because it is more compact, which minimizes the handling of materials. It is also more flexible because workers can handle jobs in multiple workstations. In addition, U-shaped layouts allow workers, material handlers, and supervisors to have an unobstructed view of the entire line and to travel efficiently between workstations because there are typically fewer walls and partitions in a U-shaped layout. Research has also shown that under certain conditions, U-shaped layouts can significantly improve the labor productivity of assembly line processes.[22]

FIGURE 9.10: U-shaped Layout

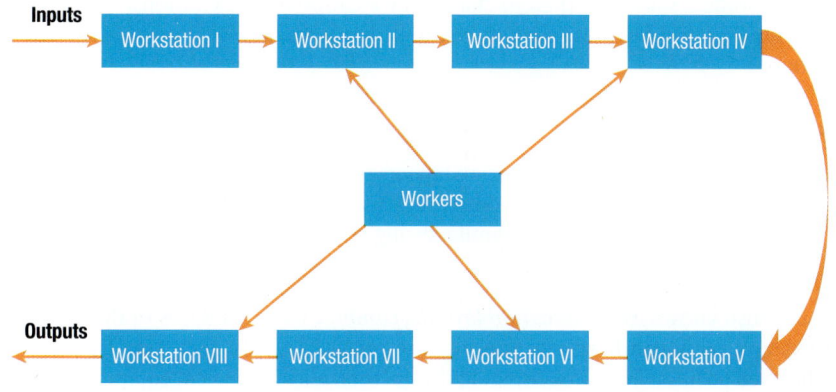

Product layout:
a layout type that is used for repetitive or continuous flow processes used to produce a highly standardized product with high and constant demand, also referred to as a straight-line layout

U-shaped layout:
a compact layout in the shape of a U that allows workers to handle jobs in multiple workstations, gives workers an unobstructed view of the entire line, and allows workers to travel efficiently between workstations

OPERATIONS MANAGEMENT: LESSONS LEARNED
Boeing and "The Move to the Lake"

Not all earthquakes are a disaster. Boeing's move to the lake after an earthquake in 2000 had a positive effect on the firm's manufacturing productivity. The Renton, Washington, area was hit by a powerful earthquake that rattled Boeing's corporate headquarters and left several buildings of the complex unsafe. One of the spaces hardest hit was a building in which 1,400 Boeing engineers worked on the 737 aircraft. The 737 was Boeing's most successful product and the backbone of its fleet.

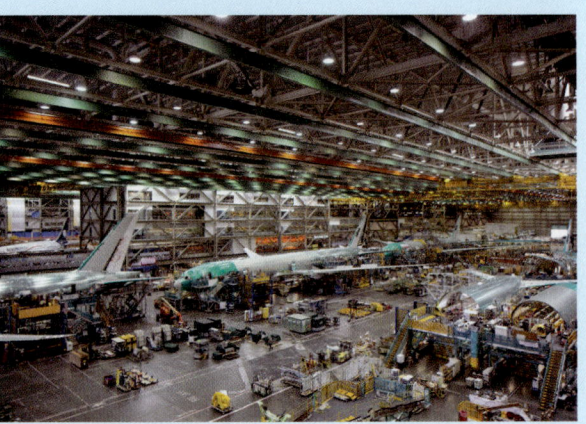

After the earthquake, Carolyn Corvi, then the vice president and general manager of Boeing's airplane production, saw an opportunity to make many changes in the organization, its manufacturing processes, and its culture. Corvi's idea was to relocate the engineering staff to the factory floor. Until that time, Boeing engineers worked in a large building that was separated from the manufacturing operations, slowing communication and making it more difficult for engineers to receive real-time information or address critical manufacturing needs quickly. The changes made after the earthquake brought the engineers closer to the assembly workers. "There was always a huge gap between the people who design the product and those who build it on the factory floor," stated Corvi. "Everyone's got to be focused on the airplane and you can't be focused on the airplane if you're in an office a quarter of a mile away."

Working with consultants, Corvi and her team redesigned some vacant warehouse space at the company's 737 plant on the shores of Lake Washington to house 2,500 engineers. The decision was later dubbed *the move to the lake*. The engineers were located in and around the production area, so they could observe the airplanes' progression through various manufacturing stages. Open areas and workspaces promoted communication and the exchange of ideas.

By 2005, Boeing engineers were working closely with 737 shop-floor mechanics and technicians and interacted with the production crews. Moreover, Boeing's manufacturing speed improved to the point where it took 11 days, not 22, to make a 737. The move to the lake not only changed old corporate culture of separation and disengagement, but it also brought critical engineering skills to the place where they are most needed. In addition, it changed not only how a factory should operate but also even how it should look. Corvi summed up the results this way: "It started out as an idea about a facilities change. It quickly turned into an opportunity for all of our people to work together to continuously improve and trust one another to get the work done. We have places to concentrate and public spaces for people to come together and collaborate."[23]

FIXED-POSITION LAYOUTS

In a fixed-position layout, the product remains stationary in the plant. The resources such as workers, materials, machines, and tools needed to produce the product are brought to the product's location. This type of layout works well for project-type processes such as shipbuilding and house construction in which the product produced is bulky or fragile. It requires less time and money to move the resources to the product's location than to change the location of workstations.

Table 9.5 presents the features, advantages, and disadvantages of process, product, and fixed-position layouts.

Other Types of Layouts

In addition to the more popular manufacturing layouts discussed to this point, some additional layout types either combine characteristics of the ones previously covered, offer a degree of flexibility in that they can be modified to address specific manufacturing requirements, or relate to service operations.

HYBRID LAYOUTS

Hybrid layouts, also known as *combination layouts*, combine the advantages of the three basic layout types. For example, although hospitals typically use process layouts, they may frequently use some aspects of the fixed position layout by bringing the doctors, nurses, medical equipment, and medicines

Fixed-position layout: a layout type in which the product remains stationary in the plant

Hybrid layout: a layout type that combine the advantages of the three basic layout types, also known as a combination layout

TABLE 9.5: Features, Advantages, and Disadvantages of the Three Basic Types of Layouts

LAYOUT	FEATURES	ADVANTAGES	DISADVANTAGES
Process Layout	• High product variety with low volumes of production can be handled. • General-purpose equipment and skilled workers can be used. • No predetermined sequence of operations because each job has its unique sequence.	• Flexibility. • Low fixed costs because general-purpose equipment is used. • Job variety motivates workers. • The availability of multiple machines reduces the impact of equipment failure.	• Managing queues of WIP inventory is challenging because jobs to be completed have to wait for the workstation to be available. • Relatively inefficient because idle workers and equipment cause low-capacity utilization. • The variety and volume of WIP inventory require large amounts of storage space. • High levels of WIP inventory generate high-variable costs. • Frequent setups cause high setup costs. • Job complexity results in large supervisory costs. • Accounting, purchasing, and inventory control are complex.
Product Layout	• Sequential production because of the highly standardized nature of the product. • Adaptable to high and constant product demand.	• High efficiency and capacity utilization. • Straightforward and routine accounting, purchasing, and inventory control. Low supervisory costs because of the low complexity of jobs. • High volumes of production lead to economies of scale and low variable costs. • Job specialization and reduced training result in low labor costs.	• The inflexible layout makes product and process redesign difficult. • High capital investment is needed for the highly specialized equipment. • Low employee morale because the jobs are boring and routine. • Risk of idle labor and equipment time if the equipment breaks down.
Fixed-Position Layout	• Product is large, bulky, heavy, or fragile and cannot be easily moved. • Production is based on a project type of process. • Resources such as labor and equipment are brought to the project site. • Project completion time and product quality are critical.	• Most useful when the product is unique and requires a specialized project type of process.	• Limited space can cause the worksite to be crowded and clogged. • High variable costs because of the need for specialized workers. • Low equipment utilization, idle time, and cost overruns can occur if there are unexpected project delays. • The narrow span of supervision and higher administrative burdens results in high supervisory costs.

to the patient. Similarly, supermarkets and grocery stores predominantly employ a process layout. Nevertheless, by using fixed-path equipment such as conveyors in stockrooms and at the cash registers, the stores combine some aspects of a product layout. Many manufacturers use hybrid processes with layouts that combine the advantages of both process and product layouts. Manufacturers that use flexible manufacturing systems, as discussed earlier in the chapter, typically rely on hybrid layouts.

CELLULAR MANUFACTURING LAYOUTS

A popular hybrid layout is a cellular manufacturing layout. Cellular manufacturing layouts are based on the principles of group technology (GT), a parts coding and classification system in which parts or products with similar characteristics are grouped into families. The families of parts are distinguished by shape, size, or similar manufacturing or routing requirements. A typical cell in this type of manufacturing process is a self-contained production unit (within the larger plant) that is completely responsible for producing a product or process. Figure 9.11 on page 318 shows a cellular layout. Notice how unlike a process layout, the milling isn't all done in one area, the lathing in another, and

Cellular manufacturing layout: a popular hybrid layout in which a self-contained production unit (within the larger plant) is completely responsible for producing a product or process

Group technology (GT): a parts coding and classification system in which parts or products with similar characteristics are grouped into families

FIGURE 9.11: Cellular Layout

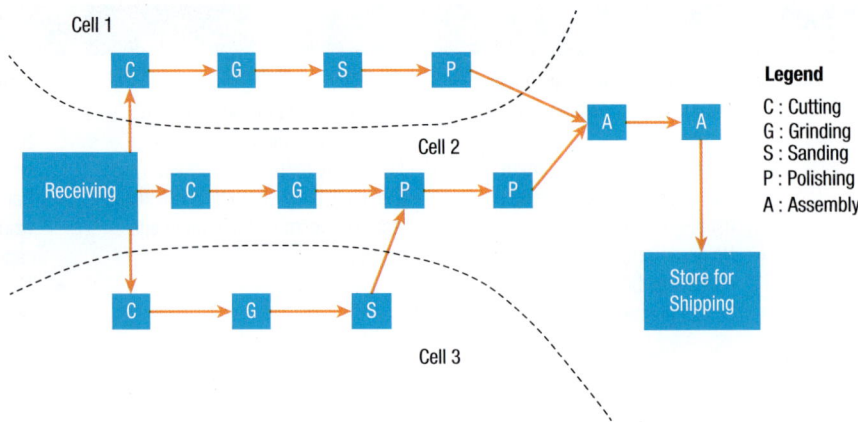

so on. Instead, these functions are done in different cells, which are each responsible for producing different parts or products.

Cellular layouts can improve materials flows significantly because the operations needed to produce a family of parts are done entirely in a small cell, thereby eliminating the need to transport in-process parts to other areas of the factory. In addition, grouping products with similar processing requirements into a cell minimizes machine setups and changeovers. Cellular manufacturing also allows a company to modify the cells more easily to create new parts or products.

Finally, each cell has a significant amount of operational autonomy because the work done within it is contained. The cell's workers are able to perform multiple processes, and they are responsible for making quality improvements, reducing waste, and maintaining the equipment in the cell, which reduces boredom and increases motivation. Because employees are empowered in this way, lead times and inventory can often be reduced and the number of workers required to complete the tasks is kept to a minimum. The net result is that cellular manufacturing layouts give a company flexibility and the ability to produce small batches of high-quality products at a low cost.[24]

Cellular manufacturing has some disadvantages:

- For products that are highly customized, require high precision work, or are produced in low volumes, cellular layouts won't result in smooth and efficient workflows.
- For processes that require expensive equipment with low utilization, cellular layouts are not cost effective.
- Given different sequences of operation in a cellular layout, it is more difficult to balance the flow of work than it is with a single-product assembly line.
- Job rotation is a key element of cellular manufacturing, but workers might not be motivated to acquire the different skills needed. Furthermore, as cellular layouts require teamwork, there is a potential for personality conflicts among team members.
- It doesn't work well if a product has many components that can be assembled quickly or requires only one operation, or if the entire product cannot be assembled or completed within the manufacturing facility. For example, many consumer goods and automobile manufacturers prefer an assembly line rather than cellular manufacturing.

SERVICE LAYOUTS

To meet the different needs of their customers, hospitals, supermarkets, restaurants, banks, and law offices often uses process layouts. Yet, service companies can use the other basic layout types. For example, landscaping and home-repair businesses used fixed-position layouts by bringing resources needed for the jobs to the customer's site. Similarly, services such as automated carwashes, dinner buffets, and school cafeteria lines use a product layout.

Despite their similarities to manufacturing layouts, different factors have to be taken into consideration when planning service layouts. One is the physical surroundings, known as the servicescape, in which a service is assembled and delivered and the seller and customer interact.[25] When laying out facilities, the right ambience and décor should be used to increase the satisfaction of customers. For example, Starbucks (Starbucks Corporation, Seattle, WA) has deliberately created a servicescape that

Servicescape: the physical surroundings in which a service is assembled and delivered and the seller and customer interact

mimics a homey, comfortable atmosphere, with Wi-Fi, couches, and comfortable décor. Patrons can sit and get work done or leisurely enjoy their coffee.

WAREHOUSE LAYOUTS

Warehouse layouts need to be designed with clearly defined objectives that align with a firm's overall corporate strategy. The objectives can be as broad as minimizing warehouse costs or maximizing customer service. They can also be as specific as maximizing the use of space and increasing flexibility or increasing warehousing efficiency without adding more resources. Operations managers need to analyze information that affects the warehouse's operations as compared with the firm's objectives. If the analysis shows that the objectives can be met, then the next step is to create a detailed plan for the warehouse.

The detailed plan should map out all of the warehouse's functions, such as receiving and shipping, case picking, pallet storage, broken case picking, and packing, and correctly linking them together. In the process, questions such as the following need to be asked:

- Is the warehouse large enough, or should more square footage be added?
- How much of the process can be (or should be) automated?
- Does the warehouse provide efficient paths for the movement of personnel and material handling equipment, such as forklifts?
- How many loading bays are needed?
- How many racks and storage structures must be installed?
- Where should products be stored?

Generally, items ordered more frequently are placed in the most convenient storage area, typically in the front of the warehouse. For example, a tire warehouse will store its most popular brands and sizes of tires where they are more easily accessible. Infrequently ordered items are typically stored in the rear of the warehouse or away from the busiest flow areas. Many modern warehouses use a procedure called **cross docking** to save warehouse space and minimize materials handling. With cross docking, materials from incoming transportation carriers are unloaded, and instead of storing them in the warehouse, they are directly loaded on outbound carriers intended for different destinations.

In addition, warehouses use different methods of storage and materials handling for different products, which can include liquid, minerals, and agricultural products. For products such as these, the layout should be designed to accommodate bulk material handling equipment such as conveyor belts, elevators, or silos. The layout should also be flexible to accommodate current and future business needs, such as anticipated growth, the adding of new functions including office support personnel, the adding of future loading docks, and providing for sufficient truck parking space.[26]

The resources allocated to implementing the layout and the estimated start and finish time for completing it need to be determined as well. For example, if the firm decides to use robots in the warehouse, it is first necessary to lay out tracks for the robots before pouring concrete for the floor. The next step is to ensure that all changes made in the warehouse are reflected in the warehouse management system. Modern warehouse management systems use automated storage and retrieval systems (ASRS). Wal-Mart, for example, uses sophisticated ASRS technology that transmits point-of-purchase information directly from stores to the firm's warehouses, where shipments are then arranged for transport to replenish the stock at the stores. Suppliers get the same information so that they can begin manufacturing new products, which are then shipped to the warehouse. In this way, the ASRS links every stage of the supply chain: Retail purchases trigger warehouse shipments, which in turn signal suppliers to manufacture and ship more products to the warehouse. A well-designed ASRS adds value and decreases costs by saving space and increasing the efficiency of warehouse operations.

The last step is post-implementation review. The new layout should be reviewed to determine that the design is working and that there are no operational problems that have occurred as a result of the new layout.[27]

OFFICE LAYOUTS

There are two common types of office layouts: *traditional* and *cubicle*. A traditional office layout has offices with walls and doors to reflect the status of employees in the organization's hierarchy, reduce noise, and maintain privacy. In a cubical layout, rows of cubicles are separated by aisles to facilitate communication among the cubicles' occupants. Many office layouts now have low-rise partitions instead of walls to separate offices. Office layout considerations are safety, facilitating teamwork, and maximizing working conditions, all of which are applicable to both factory and service layouts.

 Office Layouts

Cross docking: a process in which materials from incoming transportation carriers are unloaded and directly loaded on outbound carriers intended for different destinations

Many modern offices have adopted an open office layout design to leverage the power of modern technologies such as laptops, Wi-Fi, and the Internet. An open layout opens up the traditional workplace by lowering or eliminating cubicle walls to facilitate more interaction and collaboration among colleagues and relocating private offices to provide everyone in the workplace access to a window view. The open layout also takes advantage of mobile technology by creating alternative workspaces in alcoves, bistro areas, lounges, cafeterias, and outdoor plazas. The benefits of an open office layout include more efficiency, higher productivity, increased flexibility, and collaboration. In addition, many modern offices now have cubicles that don't have permanent occupants. Instead, employees work at home and come in and work in unassigned cubicles when they need to.

Retail store layouts should emphasize aisle space, traffic flows, and the visibility of best-selling and high profit-margin products.

©iStockphoto.com/fiphoto

RETAIL LAYOUTS

Most retailers use process layouts. The primary objective of the layout is to increase sales and profitability by increasing the customer's exposure to as many products as possible. To increase potential sales, a good retail layout employs aisle spaces that allow customers to move around easily and browse the entire store. This maximizes the amount of time the customer spends in the store and the opportunity for potential sales. In addition, retailers typically locate high-selling and high-profit items in the periphery of the store or in prominent locations to attract customers who initially may not want to venture into the store or off of the aisles. Lighted display cases can be used for expensive items to discourage theft and draw customers' attention to the displays. Other strategies to increase exposure include placing products with high profit margins on shelves at eye level or at the end of the aisles where they will be easily seen.

Retail Layout Design

Open office layout: a layout type that opens up the traditional workplace by lowering or eliminating cubicle walls, relocating private offices, and taking advantage of mobile technology by creating alternative workspaces in alcoves, bistro areas, lounges, cafeterias, and outdoor plazas

9.6 List strategies that companies can take to address the legal, ethical, and sustainability issues in process design and layout planning.

RESTAURANT LAYOUTS

A restaurant layout should be designed to help customers enjoy their dining experience and facilitate the movement of customers and restaurant staff. Service quality is a primary determinant of satisfaction. Other important layout considerations are:[28]

- *Entrance.* The entryway is made as attractive as possible because this is the part of the restaurant that customers see first. Open floor plans and room to meet guests and mingle help promote a positive first impression.
- *Waiting and Dining Areas.* The waiting and dining areas should have comfortable seats along with menus that customers can browse. The goal is to minimize wait times or provide a setting where waiting customers can enjoy themselves while waiting. Many sports bars, for example, put television screens in waiting areas to distract customers. The atmosphere of the dining area typically emphasizes the restaurant's image; for example, fine dining uses soft lighting, music, and elegant features to reinforce customers' impressions.
- *Bar.* The bar area provides for the efficient flow of guests and workers because this is also the area where servers order and pick up drinks for their tables.
- *Kitchen.* The layout of the kitchen area is determined by the type of food served and the type of equipment needed to prepare food. An Italian restaurant might include a large pizza oven in the kitchen area. The size, layout, and location of the kitchen will have a significant effect on the efficiency of restaurant operation and the customers' dining experience.
- *Restrooms.* The same effort that was expended in creating the design and ambience for other areas of the restaurant should carry through to restroom layout.

9.6 Legal, Ethical, and Sustainability Issues

In addition to producing products and services that are cost effective, companies have added sustainability goals to their requirements for process selection. These goals are protecting people, guarding the environment, and making profits. The methods for designing and operating sustainable processes vary from industry to industry. Yet, they generally include the following:

- Using materials in production processes that are nontoxic, are recyclable, and require a minimum amount of energy.
- Designing or redesigning processes that prevent wasting resources or reduce the production of harmful by-products.
- Designing or redesigning processes so that by-products or scrap materials can be recycled or reused.
- Designing or redesigning processes and work areas to maintain the physical well-being of workers and the general public.

Designing lean processes, a practice that has been embraced by both manufacturing and service industries, can also help a company achieve sustainability. (Lean processes are discussed more extensively in Chapter 14.) Companies that design lean processes can also reduce their inventories and the sizes of their plants as well as lower defects, shorten the lead times for products, and reduce rework and scrap. In addition, lean processes tend to reduce the variations in a company's workloads, resulting in smoother production flows.

Ethical companies design their processes so that the safety of workers and consumers is not compromised. Consider what happened to British Petroleum (BP plc, London, U.K.) in 2010 when one of its drilling rigs in the Gulf of Mexico exploded as a result of a buildup of flammable gas. A review of BP's processes found a consistent pattern of using minimal or substandard safety and maintenance procedures. As part of the settlement, BP had to pay nearly US$8 billion in legal penalties and fines to the U.S. government and to more than 100,000 plaintiffs.

It's not always easy to determine what constitutes an ethical course of action when it comes to designing a process. Sometimes it can be difficult to determine what impact a process will have on the safety of workers and consumers or on the environment. Moreover, being too cautious in introducing new processing technologies could prevent the companies from passing on to consumers the benefits that new technologies offer, such as lower costs and better quality products. For example, the use of fracking technology to extract natural gas and oil (from depths that were unreachable by conventional technologies) can employ a lot of people and make countries more energy independent. Nonetheless, concerns over the potential impact of this technology on the environment may prevent some U.S. states and other countries from authorizing it within their borders.

TABLE 9.6: Sustainability of Retailers: 10 Biggest Users of Solar Power in the United States*

COMPANY	ENERGY GENERATED (IN MEGAWATTS)
1. Wal-Mart (Bentonville, AR)	105.1
2. Kohl's (Menomonee Falls, WI)	50.2
3. Costco (Issaquah, WA)	48.1
4. Apple (Cupertino, CA)	40.7
5. IKEA (Delft, the Netherlands)	39.1
6. Macy's (New York, NY)	20.8
7. Johnson & Johnson (New Brunswick, NJ)	17.8
8. Target (Minneapolis, MN)	14.9
9. McGraw-Hill (New York, NY)	14.1
10. Staples (Framingham, MA)	13.7

* 2014 data.
SOURCE: Adapted from Winter, C. (2014, October 20). Big box retail's latest bright idea: Solar power. *Bloomberg Businessweek*. Retrieved from http://www.businessweek .com/articles/2014-10-20/big-box-retails-latest-bright-idea-solar-power

Processes and
Sustainability

Sustainable layouts promote energy efficiency, safety, and worker comfort, and they minimize environmental degradation. Starbucks excels at using minimal workspace as efficiently as possible; there is a lot going on behind the counter in a relatively small area. The Nike shoe factory in Ho Chi Minh City in Vietnam has achieved a comfortable work environment using sustainable building practices. A natural ventilation system cools the factory, and warm air is expelled through roof-mounted ventilation towers. In addition, the factory achieves natural ambient day lighting by installing high, open mesh windows that reach above surrounding rooftops to admit daylight to the factory interior.[29]

Historically, factories were large, multifloored buildings because of the space limitations in cities. By the 1960s, however, more and more production facilities were built in suburban and even rural settings, where the cheap land allowed for many buildings and large campuses. The sheer sprawl of these complexes made them expensive to heat and cool, led to increased property taxes, and resulted in higher infrastructure and maintenance costs. In recent decades, factories have returned to a vertical structure, and the buildings have been built using green technology.

Organizations are also turning to sustainable energy sources for their facilities, often by using solar panels or wind power. For example, retailers use solar power as a way to save money by generating most of the energy they need for their stores. In fact, not only are companies saving money with wind and solar power, but also they are generating excess power that can be sold to other people and firms.[30] Table 9.6 shows that the top 10 U.S. companies with on-site solar energy capacity cumulatively have installed 1.2 million solar panels capable of producing US$47.3 million worth of electricity a year. In fact, Wal-Mart and Costco alone have more photovoltaic (PV) capacity than the entire state of Florida.[31]

Visit **edge.sagepub.com/venkataraman** to help you accomplish your coursework goals in an easy-to-use learning environment.

- Mobile-friendly eFlashcards
- Mobile-friendly practice quizzes
- A complete online action plan

- Chapter summaries with learning objectives
- Video and multimedia resources

CHAPTER SUMMARY

9.1 Argue for the strategic importance of process selection to an organization, and identify factors that affect process choice.
Companies use the information they receive from the external environment, including customer demand for goods and services, technological changes, and the type of product or service to help them make choices about capacity planning and process selection. All processes have to be implemented in the situations in which they will bring the highest benefit to the organization. Some factors that affect the choice of process are the type of product or service, varieties of products or services offered, risk of customer dissatisfaction, capital investment, and process flexibility. Understanding and correctly interpreting the effects that these different factors have on the choice of process can be critical. Other factors that should be included in process selection are market requirements, technological considerations, degree of automation available and desired, and sustainability.

9.2 List the unique features in the design of service processes.
Service process design focuses on how the most efficient

combinations of customization and customer interaction should interact with labor intensity for service operations. Most service organizations seek to optimize these elements and find an efficient means to produce their services. The service process design matrix allows firms to categorize their services as compared with others in their industry and strike a balance between customization and labor intensity. Thus, in industries that gravitate toward efficient operations, which are organized as a service factory, it may be possible to market high-end services by employing more labor or customization of the product line to offer customers more choices.

9.3 Defend the reasons that it is important for companies to synchronize their internal processes with the external processes of their supply chain partners. To provide customers with high-quality products and services at the lowest possible cost, and at the locations most convenient for them, companies need to design their individual internal processes in ways that maximize the performance of their supply chains. That is, companies need not only to synchronize their individual internal processes but also to link them with the external processes of their supply chain partners. To succeed in a global competitive environment, companies need fast and flexible manufacturing processes that can adapt quickly to change. To achieve this objective, the different manufacturing processes should be integrated across a customer-focused supply chain. In a manufacturing supply chain, depending on the nature of the product, different types of processes link multiple supply chain partners.

9.4 Describe the unique challenges involved in designing global processes. Companies with global operations often have several plants located in different countries, and they must decide what processes to use and how should they be designed. These companies have to redesign their products and processes to varying degrees to suit the needs of the local market. Because of the variability in global markets, companies must respond quickly to meet the requirements of their customers. In most cases, they rely on mass customization and adaptive manufacturing.

9.5 Construct the different layout types, and identify their features. After firms decide on the appropriate processes (usually intended to provide the best efficiency while allowing the firm to maximize its responsiveness), these decisions shape the design of layout. For both service and manufacturing operations, layout analysis and design contribute to the firm's competitive advantage. Layout planning decisions encompass designing layout for new facilities as well as redesigning layouts for existing facilities. Several different layout options are available for an organization to choose from, depending on

such features as the demand for their products, the type of products, and flexibility in producing the products. Among the more common layouts are process, product, and fixed position. An innovative layout is cellular manufacturing methods, which can offer workers a wider range of activities and job responsibilities, even though it requires extra training and may not motivate all employees. Service layout should consider the servicescape or the ambiance in the physical features and environment surrounding the service and how they affect service delivery satisfaction. There are various service layouts, each with its own features that must be considered in enhancing the servicescape. Among the types of service layouts are warehousing, office, retail, and restaurants.

9.6 List strategies that companies can take to address the legal, ethical, and sustainability issues in process design and layout planning. A challenge for organizations in both the manufacturing and service industries is to design processes and layouts that are sustainable. Some strategies companies can use to design and operate sustainable processes include using nontoxic and recyclable materials, designing lean processes to prevent waste, and designing processes that ensure the safety of workers and the general public. Sustainable layouts employ a variety of strategies to ensure energy efficiency, safety, and the comfort of workers and prevent environmental degradation. Finding better means to ventilate, provide electricity and light, improve working conditions to minimize worker fatigue, or economize on power sources are all necessary steps in making our layouts both more efficient and more sustainable.

KEY TERMS

Adaptive manufacturing 312

Assemble-to-order (ATO) 309

Batch process 299

Cellular manufacturing layout 317

Computer-aided manufacturing (CAM) 305

Computer-aided process planning (CAPP) 305

Computer-integrated manufacturing (CIM) 306

Continuous flow process 300

Cross docking 319

Decoupling point 311

Engineer-to-order (ETO) 310

Fixed automation 304

Fixed-position layout 316

Flexible automation 304

Flexible manufacturing system (FMS) 306

Group technology (GT) 317

Hybrid layout 316

Industrial Robot 305

Job-shop process 299

Layout 313

Make-to-order (MTO) 309

Make-to-stock (MTS) 309

Mass customization process 300

Numerically controlled (NC) machines 304

Open office layout 320

Point of postponement (POP) 311

Process 298

Process layout 313

Process selection 298

Process strategy 298

Product layout 315

Product profiling 301

Project process 298

Push–pull boundary 311

Repetitive process 300

Servicescape 318

Synchronous manufacturing 300

U-shaped layout 315

DISCUSSION AND REVIEW QUESTIONS

1. This chapter suggests that capacity planning and process selection serve as a link between external, market-driven demands and internal operational processes. Why is this the case?

2. Under what circumstances would an organization consider producing a component in-house versus outsourcing it?

3. Give examples of products that can be produced using the following process types:
   a. project
   b. job-shop
   c. batch
   d. repetitive
   e. continuous flow

4. Why might an organization consider using agile manufacturing? What pressures could the firm be facing? What advantages and disadvantages would it receive from using it?

5. How has the rise in automation dramatically altered the ways in which an organization develops its flow of processes? Give examples of automation and the subsequent changes that have occurred in a process.

6. Explain the service process design matrix. How can organizations use it when examining their service processes?

7. Explain the following manufacturing methods, and give an example of each one:

   a. make-to-stock

   b. assemble-to-order

   c. make-to-order

   d. engineer-to-order

8. The point of postponement (POP) is a useful idea for developing manufacturing strategies. Explain why an organization needs to be aware of the decoupling point as it develops its supply chain strategy.

9. Explain the three types of layouts, and give examples of products manufactured with these layouts:

   a. process

   b. product

   c. fixed-position

10. What are the advantages of cellular manufacturing layouts? What are their disadvantages?

11. List three principles that should affect the design and operations of a warehouse.

12. Visit a local restaurant, and analyze its layout. What do you see as some limitations or drawbacks with how the facility is laid out? What suggestions might you make for redesigning it?

PROBLEMS

1. You have just been hired to redesign the layout of a moderately priced restaurant in midtown New York City. You serve two meals daily—lunch and dinner. In analyzing some of the critical elements in restaurant design (entrance, waiting and dining areas, bar, kitchen, and restrooms), what recommendations would you have for prioritizing your limited budget? In other words, which elements are the most critical to you and why?

2. Suppose that you were now considering the redesign of a low-priced, family-style restaurant in South Florida. How might your budget priorities for the various design elements change? Why?

3. The goal of a retail layout is to maximize profit per square foot of floor space. How does this principle affect your decision on how many products to stock in a retail clothing outlet?

4. Referring to problem 3, is there a critical mass for stocking products on retail floors? In other words, how would you evaluate a retail clothing store that crowded the aisles with clothing displays? How would you expect stock display congestion patterns to differ at a Wal-Mart versus a high-end retailer like Nordstrom?

5. Suppose you worked in a mass production environment for a company producing LED video screens and you were asked to help redesign their operations flow. What layout planning concerns would be a priority? Why?

6. What do you see as advantages and disadvantages of do-it-yourself process flows, such as self-checkout at grocery stores?

7. How would you characterize the primary goals of a product process design, and how would you differentiate these goals from those for a service process design, such as a hospital?

8. Examine the service process design matrix in Figure 9.3. Identify at least two other businesses that would be classified in each of the four quadrants. What are the implications of these different process design configurations; in other words, what are some keys to success for firms operating in each of these quadrants?

CASE STUDY 9.1 SUSTAINABLE FOOD DEVELOPMENT: THE FUTURE IS LOOKING UP

When we think of cities, few of us picture crops growing as far as the eye can see. Nevertheless, someday that might be exactly what we see if a new agricultural revolution called *vertical farming* takes root. Vertical farming is based on a simple idea: Instead of growing food far away and trucking it into urban centers, which costs money and creates pollution, grow it as close to the consumers as possible in vertical greenhouses in urban areas.

A 12-story vertical farm is going up in Linköping, Sweden. The layout for this agriculture factory has been carefully developed. After being planted, an outdoor elevator will take boxed plants to the top floor. The plants will then travel from the top floor to the bottom to take advantage of natural sunlight and to make their harvesting easier. The company building the vertical factory plans to produce 300 to 500 metric tons of leafy greens a year.

Another example of new process design for sustainability is taking place in a former meatpacking plant in Chicago: Vegetables are being grown on floating rafts and fertilized by waste from nearby fish tanks. There are even farms around the United States that hang their crops in the air and spray the roots with nutrients. Neither soil nor water is used. Farming is an example of human ingenuity. Today it is coupled with the desire for sustainable operations and a willingness to experiment with process designs. Although no one is ready to declare that farming will become completely vertical and urbanized, creativity combined with technology are offering some truly unique opportunities for one of the world's oldest industries.[32]

Questions

1. Think of other examples of sustainability that are motivating corporations worldwide to redesign their processes. What are some critical factors that have led to this movement, as well as some process designs and layouts that have changed as a result?

2. What are some of the advantages and disadvantages of sustainable processes and plant layouts?

VIDEO CASE ....

Watch this video case to learn about what factors the Rockefeller Gastropub took into account when planning the layout design of the restaurant.

CRITICAL THINKING EXERCISES ....

Visit or research online a manufacturing facility and a service organization in the area where you live:

1. In terms of the product-process matrix in Figure 9.1, to which category does the manufacturing facility belong and how would you classify the layout of the manufacturing facility?

2. In your opinion, what are the drawbacks of process design and layout of the manufacturing facility? What suggestions do you have for improvement?

3. In which quadrant of the service process design matrix in Figure 9.3 would you classify the service organization you visited? What suggestions do you have, if any, for a redesign of this service process?

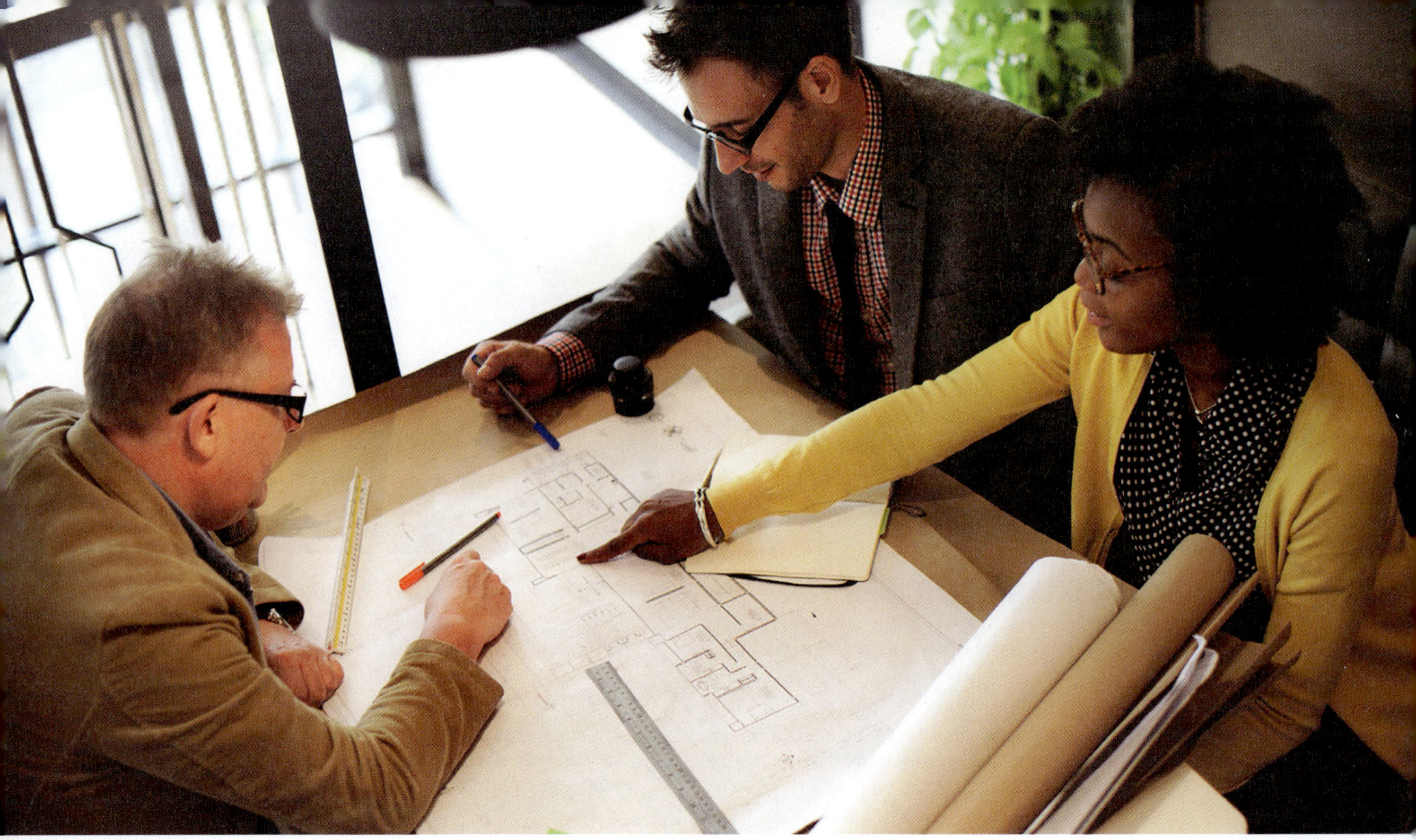

©iStockphoto.com/Rawpixel

SUPPLEMENT FOR CHAPTER 9

Tools for Analyzing, Designing, and Selecting Processes and Layouts

LEARNING OBJECTIVES

After studying this supplement, you should be able to:

1. Employ tools for process selection, analysis, and design.
2. Describe and use the techniques for designing process and product layouts.

OPERATIONS PROFILE: Relieving Congestion at St. Francis Hospital

St. Francis Hospital, located in Indianapolis, Indiana, had been working to improve the service delivery time for patients entering the emergency department (ED). Because of overcrowding and inefficient ED work flow layout, the average time for a patient's length of stay was nearly 4 hours. When a patient arrives, hospital staff needs to get both registration information and clinical information about the patient's condition. At most hospitals, these processes are usually handled by separate staff and at separate locations in hospitals, requiring patients to move from one wait to the next and often experiencing significant delays in care and treatment. These problems and delays prompted low patient satisfaction evaluations, as well as poor door-to-bed times. Looking for ways to improve this situation, the ED team at St. Francis Hospital set out to integrate their registration and clinical information processes, as well as to standardize how long it took a nurse to triage a patient.

For example, the team reorganized the registration and triage nursing functions by combining the two physical areas, putting the ED triage nurse and lead registrar in the same workstation. This was an easy option because it only involved moving their work areas closer together. Then the team took the integration further, identifying four questions that overlapped between what the triage nurse and registrar needed, and had them change practices to work together to answer the questions. In another effort to minimize unnecessary patient flow, St. Francis acquired a workstation on wheels (WOW), which allowed the registrar to complete the registration process in patient rooms, further cutting down on the time the patient had to spend in the waiting room.

Within one year of the implementation of this practice, St. Francis decreased their patients' length of stay from 253 minutes to 173 minutes. Also, the rate of patients who left without being seen decreased from 3.86% to 2.62%, all during a period of increased ED volume.[1]

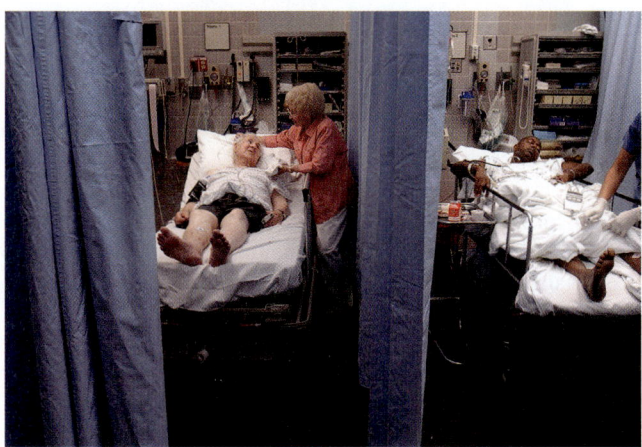

Cyrus McCrimmon/Denver Post/Getty Images

9S.1 Process Selection, Design, and Analysis Tools

9S.1

Employ tools for process selection, analysis, and design.

Numerous tools are available to use in making process choices and for analyzing processes and layouts. Let's first look at some tools that can be used for process selection and analysis and then those that can be applied for layout analysis.

Tools for Process Selection

One of the simplest tools used to compare and select processes is a cost–volume, or breakeven, analysis. We used breakeven analysis in location decisions in Chapter 8. To use this tool to make process selection decisions, we calculate the total costs of the processes we're considering for various

Example 9S.1

production volumes. We then plot on a two-dimensional graph the total cost lines for each process and choose the one that has the lowest cost for the number of units we expect to produce. If the lines intersect, it indicates that the total costs of the processes are identical at a certain production volume. So, if the operations manager plans to produce that amount, he or she will be indifferent about which process is chosen. For this reason, the points of intersection are sometimes referred to as points of indifference.

EXAMPLE 9S.1: Dantzig Corporation, a fictional company, would like to evaluate three production processes (A, B, and C) to accommodate the changes in demand for its products. The fixed and variable costs per unit for each of these processes are shown in Table 9S.1.

TABLE 9S.1: Fixed and Variable Costs

PROCESS	FIXED COST (IN U.S. DOLLARS)	VARIABLE COST PER UNIT (IN U.S. DOLLARS)
A	25,000	42
B	50,000	32
C	90,000	22

a. Determine the most cost-effective process for an expected annual production volume of 3,000 units.
b. Determine the production volumes at the points of indifference between these processes and the range of annual volumes of production at which each of three processes would become most economical.

SOLUTION

a. Total cost = Fixed cost + (Production volume × Variable post per unit) = FC + (Q × VC)

$$\text{Total cost for Process A} = 25{,}000 + (3{,}000 \times 42) = \$151{,}000$$
$$\text{Total cost for Process B} = 50{,}000 + (3{,}000 \times 32) = \$146{,}000$$
$$\text{Total cost for Process C} = 90{,}000 + (3{,}000 \times 22) = \$156{,}000$$

Process B has the lowest total cost for a production volume of 3,000 units and, therefore, seems to be the most economical process. Nevertheless, suppose we are not entirely sure how much output we expect to produce as a result of changes in demand? In other words, if we vary the total expected output, then our process choice decision may also change.

b. To determine the range of production volume at which each process is most economical, we let Q be the production volume at the indifference points (points of intersection of the total cost lines).

To determine the volume where the costs of Process A and Process B are equal:

$$25{,}000 + (Q \times 42) = 50{,}000 + (Q \times 32)$$
$$Q \times (42 - 32) = 50{,}000 - 25{,}000$$
$$10 \times Q = 25{,}000$$
$$Q = 2{,}500$$

To determine the volume where the costs of Process B and Process C are equal:

$$50{,}000 + (Q \times 32) = 90{,}000 + (Q \times 22)$$
$$Q \times (32 - 22) = 90{,}000 - 50{,}000$$
$$10 \times Q = 40{,}000$$
$$Q = 4{,}000$$

Points of indifference: the intersection of two lines on a breakeven analysis graph that show the point at which total costs of two processes are identical

Hence Q, the production volume at the point of indifference between processes A and B, is 2,500 units. Between processes B and C, it is 4,000 units. This means that for these volumes, Dantzig Corporation will be indifferent to choosing either of these processes because the total cost is the same for both. Yet, if the production volume is below 2,500 units, then process A is most economical. Between 2,500 and 4,000 units, process B is the preferred choice. Beyond an expected production volume of 4,000 units, process C should be selected. These decision choices are illustrated graphically in Figure 9S.1.

FIGURE 9S.1: Choosing a Process Based on a Cost–Volume Analysis

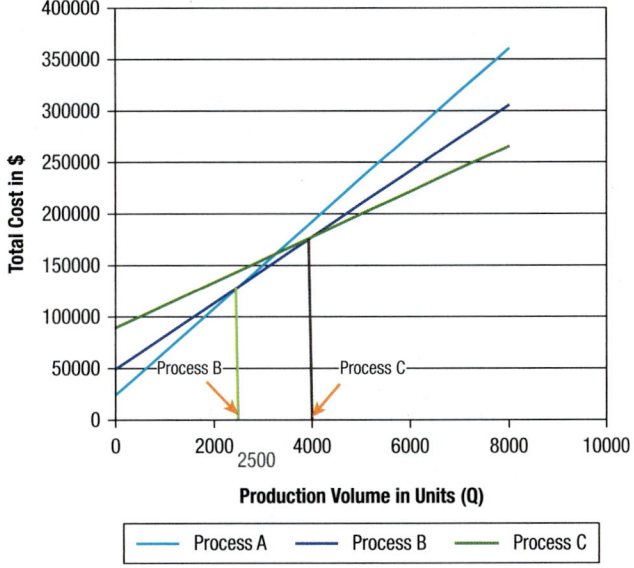

Tools for Process Analysis and Design

Other tools can be used to analyze and understand a process's complexities so as to design or redesign it. The tools include assembly drawings, assembly charts, route sheets, process mapping, value stream mapping (VSM), process simulation, and service blueprinting for analyzing service processes.

Assembly Drawings and Charts and Route Sheets

An assembly drawing is an enlarged view of a product that shows all of its parts and subassemblies. Assembly drawings, which are also referred to as working drawings, provide complete information for the manufacture or assembly of a product or structure.

An assembly chart, which is sometimes called a *gozinto* chart, maps how a product's parts go together and the order in which they are assembled. Detailed instructions for all major parts of the product and all assembly and subassembly operations and inspections are included on the chart. An example of an assembly chart is shown in Figure 9S.2 on page 330.

A route sheet is a document that describes the sequence of different operations, places, or people involved in a process. The sheet helps organize work orders by tracking the parts for products and the status of jobs during their scheduling, production, and quality control phases. Setup and processing times and any additional details such as the equipment or special tools needed to produce the product also are included on the sheet. It is an excellent communication tool because it enables anyone to see when a work order was generated, who worked on it and where, the order's status, the customer's key requirements or concerns, and any past or future communication with the customer. Route sheets store this information all on one document so that order status can be compared with all other open work orders. An example of a route sheet for a bracket part is shown in Figure 9S.3 on page 331.

PROCESS CHARTS AND VALUE STREAM MAPS AND SIMULATIONS

A process chart uses graphics to show all activities related to a process, including its inputs and outputs, decision points such as approvals and exceptions, and any cross-functional relationships. All steps in the process are identified. For a restaurant, for example, this would include the customer's arrival and seating, ordering of food, the beverage service, preparing the food, its delivery and consumption, and payment for it followed by table cleaning. Process charts can help pinpoint problems such as likely bottlenecks and delay points, wasteful activities such as rework, and locations where redundant

Assembly drawing: an enlarged view of a product that shows all of its parts and subassemblies

Assembly chart: a chart that maps how a product's parts go together and the order in which they are assembled, sometimes called a *gozinto* chart

Route sheet: a document that describes the sequence of different operations, places, or people involved in a process

Process chart: a diagram that uses graphics to show all activities related to a process, including its inputs and outputs, decision points such as approvals and exceptions, and any cross-functional relationships

FIGURE 9S.2: Assembly Chart for a Bicycle

STEPS:

Handlebar Assembly Operation-1 (A-1)
Loosen the bolt and slide the handlebars onto the frame. Adjust the height of the handlebars and tighten the bolt.

Seat Assembly Operation-2 (A-2)
Slide the seat post into the bike frame. Adjust the height.

Inspection: Check that it's straight, and then tighten the bolt all the way.

Wheel Assembly Operation-3 (A-3)
For both wheels, install skewers by unscrewing the bolt on one side of the skewer, sliding it through the axle of the wheel, and screwing the end back on. Then place the front wheel into the front fork of the bike frame and the back wheel into the rear chainstays and tighten the skewers down.

Inspection: Make sure that the wheel is centered and spins freely.

Pedal Assembly Operation-4 (A-4)
Slide the right and left pedals on the respective crank arms and tighten the bolts.

Final Inspection: Check that the wheel spins freely and that both the wheels and handlebars are centered.

SOURCE: eHow Contributor. (n.d.). How to assemble a bicycle. eHow.com. Retrieved from http://www.ehow.com/how_4781732_assemble-road-bicycle.html#ixzz-2BGejiV8U

A Process Chart

Value stream mapping (VSM): a process-mapping technique used to analyze and design the flow of materials and information across multiple processes

or unnecessary activities occur. Symbols such as arrows, circles, diamonds, triangles, and boxes are used to identify various decision points, activities, or events. An example of a process chart is shown in Figure 9S.4 on page 332. The chart shows all of the steps needed to treat a patient in an emergency room. All operations and activity flows are identified as well as downtime or delay points. As the figure shows, the emergency-room visit took 126 minutes and included only 81 minutes of value-added time (examination and treatment). The rest could be viewed as not adding value, time lost from delays, or time spent transporting the patient. Process charts are an extremely useful tool for first mapping and then analyzing an organization's primary processes to find ways to improve it.

Value Stream Maps and Process Simulations

Value stream mapping (VSM) is a process-mapping technique used to analyze and design the flow of materials and information across multiple processes. Beginning with the customer, VSM examines all

FIGURE 9S.3: Route Sheet for a Bracket

MATERIAL SPECS:___	PART NAME: BRACKET	PART #: BR 1320
STOCK SIZE: ___	USAGE: BRACKET ASSEMBLY	DATE ISSUED: 11/5/12
# OF PIECES/STOCK __	ASSEMBLY #: BR 1324	DATE SUPPLIED: 11/6/12
WEIGHT: ___	SUBASSEMBLY #:	ISSUED BY: RRV

Operation Sequence	Operation Description	Department and Machines	Setup Time	Processing Time/Unit
1	Shear to length	Shear: Machine # 2	10 minutes	.025
2	Shear 45° corners	Shear: Machine # 2	6 minutes	.020
3	Drill holes	Drill: Drill press	20 minutes	3.5
4	Bend 90°	Brake: Brake press	9 minutes	.025

processes, including the organization's supply chain, to determine where value is added or is not added across the system. Although value stream mapping is often used in lean manufacturing environments, it can be used in any value chain process including logistics, supply chain, software, and product development, and even in service-related industries such as health care. Because of its common tie-ins to lean manufacturing, we will discuss value stream mapping in greater detail in Chapter 14.

The charting and graphical techniques we've discussed so far in this supplement can only provide a static view of a process. That is, they offer a snapshot of how a process is performing. A process simulation, by contrast, can provide a dynamic view. Using computers, multiple inputs, work centers, and processing techniques can help an operations manager look at the variability of a process under different conditions. So, for example, she can explore several what-if scenarios to analyze several process alternatives without changing or disrupting the actual process. Process simulations can be considerably more complex to set up and run. Many commercial simulation software programs now perform this task. These programs can be used to model and analyze not only manufacturing processes but also service processes.

Tools for Analyzing Service Processes

SERVICE BLUEPRINTS

Many of the process analysis tools we have discussed can also be used to analyze service processes. Another tool for analyzing services is a service blueprint. Service blueprints are especially useful for analyzing service processes that have high service content such as the intensive customer interaction observed in hotels like Ritz Carlton (The Ritz-Carlton Hotel Company, L.L.C., Chevy Chase, MD). To create a blueprint, we use the following steps:[2]

1. Identify the service process to be blueprinted and the customers who will experience the service.
2. Envision the service from the perspective of customers. Try to perceive how they view and are likely to respond to a service, *not* how the organization wishes them to respond.
3. Envision the actions of the service delivery personnel—including employees who have face-to-face contact with customers (onstage personnel) and employees who have no direct contact with the customers (backstage personnel) but who contribute to the service process.
4. Ensure all likely service scenarios and how they should play out ideally, and then make sure that support functions like clean-up or technical support are available in case of problems. For example, if a table is not readily available for a restaurant customer, make sure that the customer is escorted to the waiting area to be seated. In this way, at every step in the service pipeline, the elements of effective service are available when needed.

A service blueprint has several levels, as Figure 9S.5 on page 335 shows. Level 1 in the figure represents the physical environment or surroundings of the restaurant, such as its ambience and décor. Level 2 maps the activities under the control of the restaurant's customers. Level 3 identifies the

Process simulation: a technique that provides a dynamic view of a process using computers, multiple inputs, work centers, and processing techniques to help operations managers look at the variability of a process under different conditions

Service blueprint: a tool for analyzing processes that have high service content by specifying how the service will be provided

FIGURE 9S.4: Process Chart for an Emergency-Room Visit

				PROCESS CHART	

Current Process: ☒   Proposed Process: ☐

Subject Charted: ***Patient with shoulder injury***   Date: 11/06/15

Department: Emergency Room (ER)   Chart prepared by: RRV   Sheet: 1 of 1

Steps	Distance (in feet)	Time (in minutes)	Chart Symbols	Process Description
1	15	1.0	○ ⇨ □ D ▽	Patient enters emergency room and reaches the admission window.
2	——	12.0	○ ⇨ □ D ▽	Patient fills out his or her medical history.
3	35	1.0	○ ⇨ □ D ▽	Patient is taken to the ER triage room by a nurse.
4	——	5.0	○ ⇨ □ D ▽	Nurse inspects patient's shoulder and checks his temperature and blood pressure.
5	35	1.0	○ ⇨ □ D ▽	Patient escorted to the waiting room.
6	——	6.0	○ ⇨ □ D ▽	Patient waits for an ER bed to become available.
7	50	1.5	○ ⇨ □ D ▽	Patient is escorted to an ER bed.
8	——	5.0	○ ⇨ □ D ▽	Patient waits for the doctor.
9	——	10.0	○ ⇨ □ D ▽	Doctor examines the injured shoulder, talks to the patient, and advises patient to take X-rays.
10	300	4.5	○ ⇨ □ D ▽	Nurse takes patient to the radiology department.
11	——	10.0	○ ⇨ □ D ▽	Technician takes X-rays of patient's shoulder.
12	300	4.5	○ ⇨ □ D ▽	Patient escorted back to ER bed.
13	——	5.0	○ ⇨ □ D ▽	Patient waits for doctor.
14	——	15.0	○ ⇨ □ D ▽	Doctor examines X-rays, provides injury diagnosis, and advises patient to have a shoulder cast.
15	——	20.0	○ ⇨ □ D ▽	Patient has a cast put on his shoulder.
16	——	5.0	○ ⇨ □ D ▽	Doctor calls hospital pharmacy for prescription pain and sleep medication and advises patient on shoulder care and for a follow-up appointment.
17	50	1.5	○ ⇨ □ D ▽	Patient is escorted back to the checkout window.
18	——	2.0	○ ⇨ □ D ▽	Patient checks out.
19	400	5.0	○ ⇨ □ D ▽	Patient goes to hospital pharmacy.
20	——	5.0	○ ⇨ □ D ▽	Patient waits for prescription medication.
21	——	2.0	○ ⇨ □ D ▽	Patient pays and collects the medication.
22	250	4.0	○ ⇨ □ D ▽	Patient leaves hospital.

PROCESS CHART					
Summary Report					
Activity	**Symbol**	**Number of Steps**	**Distance (in feet)**	**Time (in minutes)**	**Value-Added Time (in minutes)**
Operation	○	7	——	66	66
Transport	⇨	9	1,435	24	15
Inspection	□	2	——	15	
Delay	D	4	——	21	
Storage	▽	0	——	0	
Total		**22**	**1435**	**126**	**81**

onstage activities of employees who directly interact with customers. Level 4 identifies the backstage activities, which are typically invisible to the customer. The blueprint also shows potential service failure points, which are marked by the letter F, along with the remedial measures that can be taken to reduce the customer's dissatisfaction.

The various levels of the service blueprint create different challenges for managers. For example, they have to be concerned about issues such as employee selection and training to ensure that the onstage activities provide the necessary levels of customer satisfaction. Managers also have to examine the backstage activities to try to achieve process innovations and ensure they augment the activities performed onstage.

9S.2 Layout Analysis Tools and Techniques

In this section, we will discuss some tools used to design and analyze the three basic layout types discussed in Chapter 9.

9S.2

Describe and use the techniques for designing process and product layouts.

Techniques for Designing Process Layouts

In process layouts, the process facilities are shared by many different products. Consequently, the relative positioning of the various departments is a compromise. A good process layout minimizes the materials handling or transportation costs or employee and customer traveling or waiting time.

 Layout Analysis

PROCESS LAYOUT ANALYSES USING
QUANTITATIVE DATA: THE COST MINIMIZATION METHOD
The most common way to design a process layout (as well as a fixed layout) for a manufacturing facility is to arrange departments or work centers so that the total cost of materials handling is minimized. This can be accomplished by reducing the number of nonadjacent moves between the most frequently interacting departments. That is, the departments that have the most frequent and largest flow of parts and materials should be placed next to each other horizontally, vertically, or diagonally. The total cost of materials handling in manufacturing process layouts depends on three factors:

1. The cost of moving a load between departments.
2. The number of loads to be moved between departments.
3. The distance between departments.

Given this information, the total cost of handling materials in a process layout can be computed using the following formula:

$$\text{Minimize total cost} = \sum_{i=1}^{n} \sum_{j=1}^{n} C_{ij} X_{ij} D_{ij}$$

where

n = the total number of departments or work centers
i, j = the individual departments

FIGURE 9S.5: Service Blueprint for a Restaurant

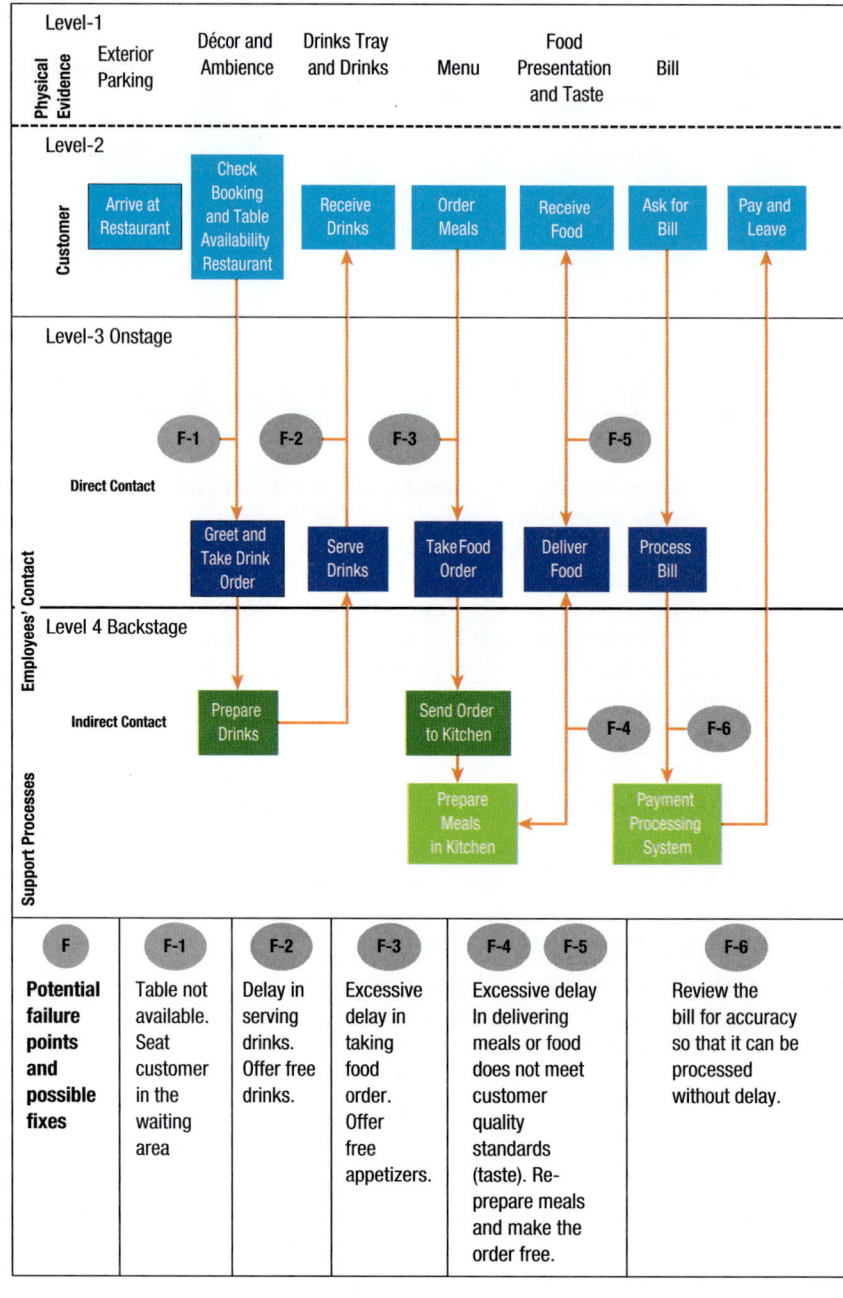

SOURCE: Adapted from http://www.hotelmule.com/attachments/2010/01/26_2010010704581522KeF.jpg; accessed November 2012.

C_{ij} = the cost to move a load between departments i and j
X_{ij} = the number of loads moved between departments i and j
D_{ij} = the distance between departments i and j

The equation to minimize the total cost of handling materials is a function of the distance (D_{ij}) between departments and the number of loads (X_{ij}) to be moved between departments. To design a process layout to minimize the cost, do the following:

1. Construct a table that shows the number of loads moved between each pair of departments.
2. Determine the total space requirements for each department.
3. Develop an initial layout.

4. Determine the total cost of the layout using the equation to minimize total cost.
5. By trial-and-error or other methods, revise the layout by placing departments that have the highest interaction in terms of loads adjacent to each other. Then compute the total cost that will result from the new layout.
6. Repeat step 5 until you determine which configuration will result in the lowest cost.

EXAMPLE 9S.2: Design a process layout for a factory with six departments with the objective of minimizing the total cost of handling materials. The dimension of each department is 20 × 20 feet, and the building is 80 feet long and 60 feet wide. The cost of moving a load between each pair of departments is US$1. The initial layout of this factory along with information on the number of loads in a week and the distance between each pair of departments are shown in the following tables. Develop a revised layout by eliminating nonadjacent moves between work centers with high interactions, and compute the total cost. Note: Departments diagonal to one another are considered to be adjacent.

INITIAL LAYOUT

Assembly (1)	Painting (2)	Machining Center (3)
Materials Storage (4)	Shipping (5)	Inspection (6)

Interdepartmental Workflows Matrix: Number of Loads Moved per Week

DEPARTMENT	ASSEMBLY (1)	PAINTING (2)	MACHINING CENTER (3)	MATERIALS STORAGE (4)	SHIPPING (5)	INSPECTION (6)
Assembly (1)		60	100	0	0	30
Painting (2)			40	60	20	0
Machining Center (3)				30	0	1000
Materials Storage (4)					60	0
Shipping (5)						0
Inspection (6)						

Distance between Departments (in feet)

DEPARTMENT	ASSEMBLY (1)	PAINTING (2)	MACHINING CENTER (3)	MATERIALS STORAGE (4)	SHIPPING (5)	INSPECTION (6)
Assembly (1)		10	35	10	15	40
Painting (2)			10	15	10	15
Machining Center (3)				40	15	10
Materials Storage (4)					10	30
Shipping (5)						10
Inspection (6)						

SOLUTION

The layout of the departments and the workflows between them are shown in the following figure:

INTERDEPARTMENTAL WORKFLOWS

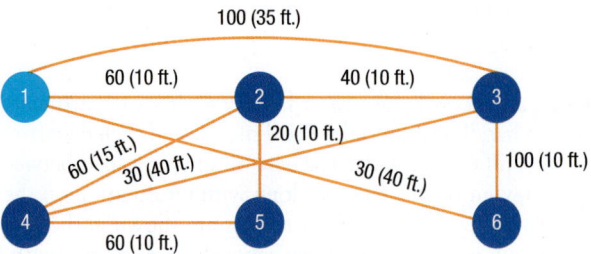

The total cost of materials handling for the layout is (in U.S. dollars):

$$\text{Total cost} = \sum_{i=1}^{n}\sum_{j=1}^{n} C_{ij} X_{ij} D_{ij}$$

$= 1 \times 60 \times 10 + 1 \times 100 \times 35 + 1 \times 30 \times 40 \text{ (1 and 2) (1 and 3) (1 and 6)} + 1 \times 40 \times 10 + 1 \times 60 \times 15 + 1 \times 20 \times 10 \text{ (2 and 3) (2 and 4) (2 and 5)} + 1 \times 30 \times 40 + 1 \times 100 \times 10 + 1 \times 60 \times 10 \text{ (3 and 4) (3 and 6) (4 and 5)}$

$= \$600 + \$3,500 + \$1,200 + \$400 + \$900 + \$200 + \$1,200 + \$1,000 + \$600$

$= \mathbf{\$9,600}$

In the initial layout, the nonadjacent moves occur between the assembly work center (1) and machining work center (3). These two work centers also have one of the highest interactions with a movement of 100 loads between the two. Hence, we place these two work centers adjacent to each other. This revision also changes the distance between some other pairs of departments. The revised distances and interdepartmental flows are shown in green in the following figure:

REVISED INTERDEPARTMENTAL WORKFLOWS

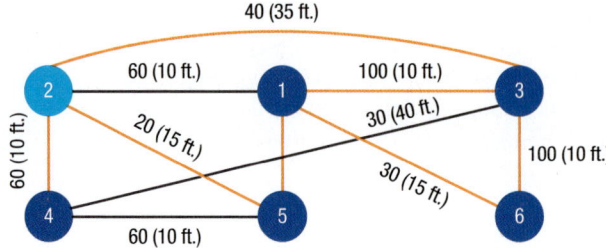

The total cost of materials handling for this revised layout is (in U.S. dollars):

$$\text{Total cost} = \sum_{i=1}^{n}\sum_{j=1}^{n} C_{ij} X_{ij} D_{ij}$$

$= 1 \times 60 \times 10 + 1 \times 100 \times 10 + 1 \times 30 \times 15 \text{ (1 and 2) (1 and 3) (1 and 6)} + 1 \times 40 \times 35 + 1 \times 60 \times 10 + 1 \times 20 \times 15 \text{ (2 and 3) (2 and 4) (2 and 5)} + 1 \times 30 \times 40 + 1 \times 100 \times 10 + 1 \times 60 \times 10 \text{ (3 and 4) (3 and 6) (4 and 5)}$

$= \$600 + \$1,000 + \$450 + \$1,400 + \$600 + \$300 + \$1200 + \$1000 + \$600$

$= \mathbf{\$7,150}$

Thus, the revised layout reduces the total cost of materials handling by $9,600 − $7,150 = $2,450.

Revised Layout

Painting (2)	Assembly (1)	Machining Center (3)
Materials Storage (4)	Shipping (5)	Inspection (6)

In an ideal scenario, there would no nonadjacent moves in the layout. Yet, in practice, eliminating all nonadjacent moves is rarely possible. So, different layout configurations should be tried until one is found that reduces the total cost as much as possible.

With some modifications, the method described here can be applied to several process layout decisions. For example, for service facilities, if the objective of the layout is to minimize the time employees or customers spend moving about as the product or service is produced, then those times could be used in Equation 1 instead of costs.

PROCESS LAYOUT ANALYSES USING QUALITATIVE DATA: THE RELATIONSHIP RATING METHOD

When quantitative data are not readily available, qualitative criteria, such as the best judgment of a firm's managers, can be used to design a process layout. The relationship rating technique developed by Richard Muther is a method used to design new layouts or change old ones based on qualitative criteria. Managers rate the best locations for departments relative to one another, and the information is displayed in a grid known as Muther's grid.[3] Symbols or letters represent the relationships between departments. Figure 9S.6 shows an example of a Muther's grid decided on by a grocery store's managers.

The grid in Figure 9S.6 should be read like a mileage table on a road map. The difference is that the letters displayed on a Muther's grid indicate the desirability of the location of pairs of departments instead of the distances between cities. The letter "A" in the figure indicates that closeness between two departments is absolutely necessary, whereas the latter "X" indicates closeness is undesirable. Thus, the "A" at the intersection of convenience and impulse products and checkout stands means it's absolutely necessary to locate these two departments close to each other. By contrast, the "X" rating between the checkout stands and the fresh-meat department indicates that it is undesirable to locate these two departments close together. For example, the store's managers might have agreed that having the fresh-meat department near the checkout stands would adversely affect the front on the store's appearance and ambience. Using a numbering system, the managers' reasons for the ratings could also be included in the grid. For the sake of simplicity, the numbers have been omitted from this figure.

Technique for Designing Product Layouts: Line Balancing

In a product layout, machines or work centers are arranged based on a predetermined sequence of operations for the product. The goals are to achieve high levels of efficiency and capacity utilization while ensuring that the product flows smoothly through the line with no bottlenecks. The technique of line balancing is used to achieve these goals. Line balancing involves assigning productions tasks so that the time required to complete them is approximately equal across workstations. This prevents some workstations from having to wait on others to finish their work on products traveling down the

FIGURE 9S.6: Muther's Grid for a Grocery Store

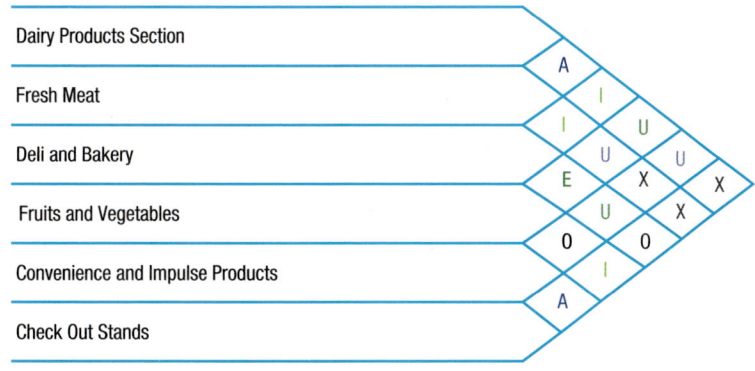

Letter Code	Closeness Rating
A	*Absolutely Necessary*
E	*Especially Important*
I	*Important*
O	*Ordinary Closeness*
U	*Unimportant*
X	*Undesirable*

Relationship rating: a technique developed by Richard Muther used to design new layouts or change old ones based on qualitative criteria

Muther's grid: a visual representation of a relationship rating in which symbols or letters represent the relationships between departments

Line balancing: assigning production tasks in such a way that the time required to complete them is approximately equal across workstations

FIGURE 9S.7: Some Tasks in an Automobile Assembly Line

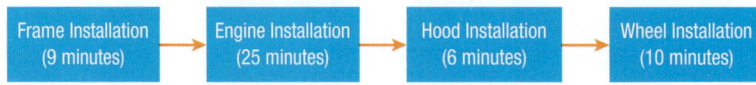

line. Whenever there is **idle time**, or the difference between the total time available and the total time used to complete a process, between workstations, a line is said to be unbalanced, and bottlenecks occur. Line balancing also helps minimize the number of workstations a firm needs.

Achieving a perfectly balanced line is easier said than done, though. In part this is due to precedence relationships, which require some tasks to be done before others. Space restrictions on a plant's floor can create precedence relationships that have the potential to constrain a system. More often, however, they are a result of the sequential nature of a line process. For example, prior to being painted, cars on an assembly line have to be inspected to ensure any dents and scratches on them are detected and fixed. Similarly, for safety-related reasons or to prevent contamination, some operations done have to be performed sequentially. For example, the painting operation can't be combined with any other operation that involves silicone-based materials because silicon contamination can cause craters, or defects, in the paint on cars.

Cycle time is another constraint that can make it difficult to balance a line. Cycle time is the time required for the line to produce one unit to achieve an output rate that allows a firm to meet its demand requirements.

To understand precedence-relationship and cycle-time constraints better, look at Figure 9S.7, which shows some tasks involved in assembling an automobile. The precedence constraint means the order in which the four operations in the figure can be done cannot be violated. For example, the hood can only be installed after the engine has been installed. Now let's look at the cycle time. Assume that the cycle time for this assembly line is 30 minutes. This means that the firm's goal is to have one car coming off the assembly line every 30 minutes. If we assume that we use a separate workstation to perform each of the four operations, it takes 50 (9 + 25 + 6 + 10) minutes for each car to be processed. This time is referred to as flow time, which is the time required to produce an item completely if only one unit is being produced at a time. Obviously, 50 minutes exceeds the desired cycle time.

Nevertheless, in an assembly line, it is usually common for work on several items to take place simultaneously, not one at a time. In our example, by having four different workstations, four different cars can be produced at the same time, each one at a different assembly stage. Thus, in the assembly line in Figure 9S.7, after completing the work of frame installation on the first car in the first workstation, workers in that station can begin the frame installation on the second car. In the meantime, the crew in the second workstation will be working on engine installation on the first car. After completing engine installation, the first car can be moved to the third workstation for hood fitting and then to the final station to be fitted with wheels. Accordingly, once the frame has been installed on the second car, it now moves to a second workstation for engine installation, and so on. Assuming no time is lost in moving a car from one workstation to another, the throughput or flow time of the assembly line is determined by the operation that takes the longest time in the assembly line. In this example, it is 25 minutes—the time spent on engine installation. Therefore, after assembling the first car in 50 minutes, each subsequent car can be assembled every 25 minutes. Note that the flow time may or may not be equal to the cycle time desired by managers. Note too that the cycle time also dictates the *maximum* time available for a workstation to complete its tasks. So, in this example, for the line to be balanced, no workstation can take longer than 30 minutes or bottlenecks will occur. Example 9S.3 will explain in more detail how the cycle-time constraint works.

STEPS IN LINE BALANCING

The process of line balancing involves the following steps:

1. *Compute the desired cycle time (C), which is given by:*

$$C = \frac{Daily\ production\ time\ available}{Units\ to\ be\ produced\ daily}$$

2. *Draw a precedence graph based on the precedence relationships among operations.*

Precedence relationships: the relationship between two or more tasks that requires certain tasks to be done before others

Cycle time: the time required for the line to produce one unit to achieve an output rate that allows a firm to meet its demand requirements

Flow time: the time required to produce an item completely if only one unit is being produced at a time

TABLE 9S.2: Options for Balancing an Assembly Line

RULE OF THUMB	DESCRIPTION
Most-following-tasks rule	Assign tasks in the order of most number of following tasks. In Figure 9S.7, the frame installation has the most number of following tasks (3). Hence, it will be assigned first to the first workstation and so on. In the case of a tie, assign the task with the longest operating time first.
Ranked-positional-weight rule	Assign tasks in the order of highest positional weight. The positional weight of a task is computed as the sum of each task's time and the sum of all tasks following it. Thus, in Figure 9S.7, the positional weight of frame installation is equal to $9 + 25 + 6 + 10 = 50$. Similarly, the positional weights of engine installation, hood installation, and wheel installation are 41, 16, and 10, respectively. Since frame installation has the highest positional weight, it will be assigned first to the first workstation and so on. In the case of a tie, assign the task with the longest operating time first.
Longest-operating-time rule	Assign in the order of the task with the longest operating time.
Least-number-of-following-tasks rule	Assign tasks in the order of the least number of following tasks.
Shortest-operating-time rule	Assign in the order of the task with the shortest operating time.

3. *Compute the theoretical minimum number of workstations (N) required.*

$$N = \frac{\text{Sum of all task times}}{\text{Cycle time}} = \frac{\sum_{i=1}^{n} t_i}{C}$$

4. *Compute the theoretical minimum amount of idle time (I)*

$$I = \text{Total time available} - \text{Total time used} = N \times C - \sum_{i=1}^{n} t_i$$

5. *Balance the assembly line.*
   This step involves assigning tasks to the workstations (determined in step 3) without violating the precedence and cycle time requirements. Because line balancing is basically a trial-and-error process, it may be necessary to try several options shown in Table 9S.2 to determine the best possible solution—that is, the one that has the minimum number of workstations and the least amount of idle time.

6. *Compute the* balance efficiency *(E)*

$$E = \frac{\text{Total time used}}{\text{Total time available}} = \frac{\sum_{i=1}^{n} t_i}{N x C}$$

EXAMPLE 9S.3: An assembly line to be balanced has 11 tasks with precedence relationships. The task times are shown in Table 9S.3. Based on demand forecasts for the product to be assembled in the line, management has decided on an output rate of 120 units per day. The line operates eight hours a day. Given this information, balance the assembly line using both the most-following-tasks rule and the ranked-positional-weight rule (see Table 9S.2).

 Example 9S.3

SOLUTION

1. *Compute the desired cycle time (C)*
   Because the line operates eight hours a day, the total production time available is 60 minutes per hour × 8 hours = 480 minutes. Since the daily production needs to be 120 units, the cycle time is given by:

$$C = \frac{\text{Daily production time available}}{\text{Units to be produced daily}} = \frac{480\, minutes}{120\, units} = 4 \text{ minutes per unit}$$

2. *Draw a precedence graph based on the precedence relationships among the operations.*

Balance efficiency: the measure of how well a process uses the time available to complete it

TABLE 9S.3: Assembly Task Times

TASKS	IMMEDIATE PREDECESSOR	TASK TIME (IN MINUTES)
A	NONE	4
B	A	2
C	A	2
D	B, C	3
E	C	1
F	D, E	4
G	F	3
H	F	1
I	G	3
J	H	1
K	I, J	3

FIGURE 9S.8: Precedence Graphs for Various Relationships

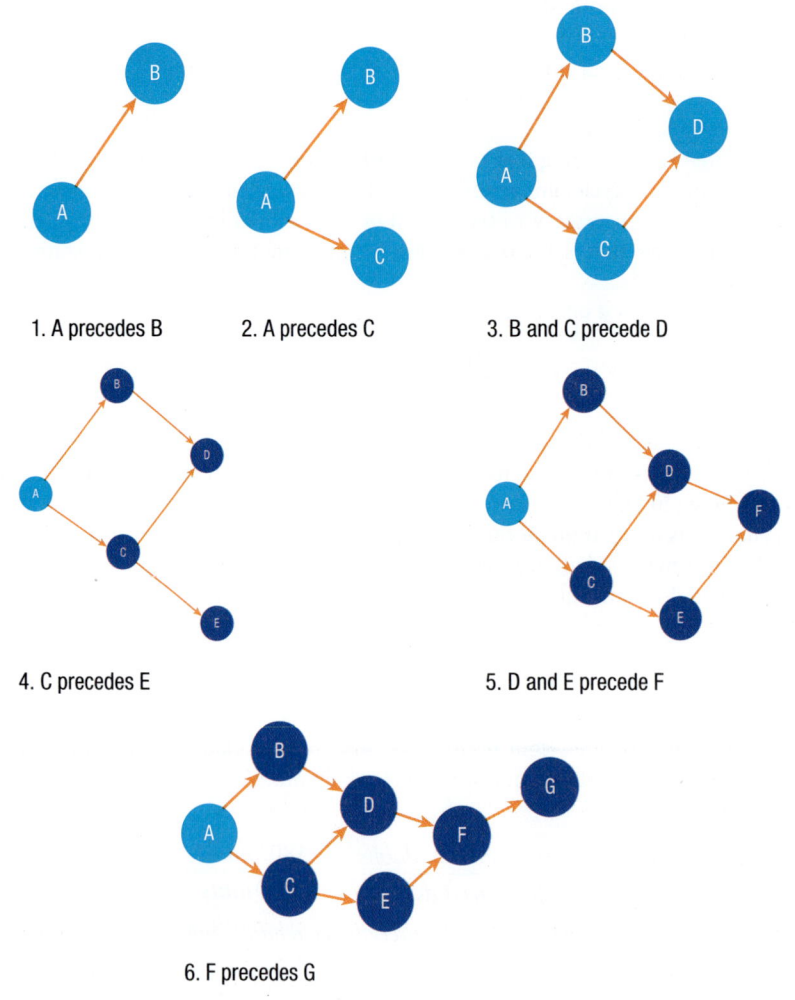

1. A precedes B

2. A precedes C

3. B and C precede D

4. C precedes E

5. D and E precede F

6. F precedes G

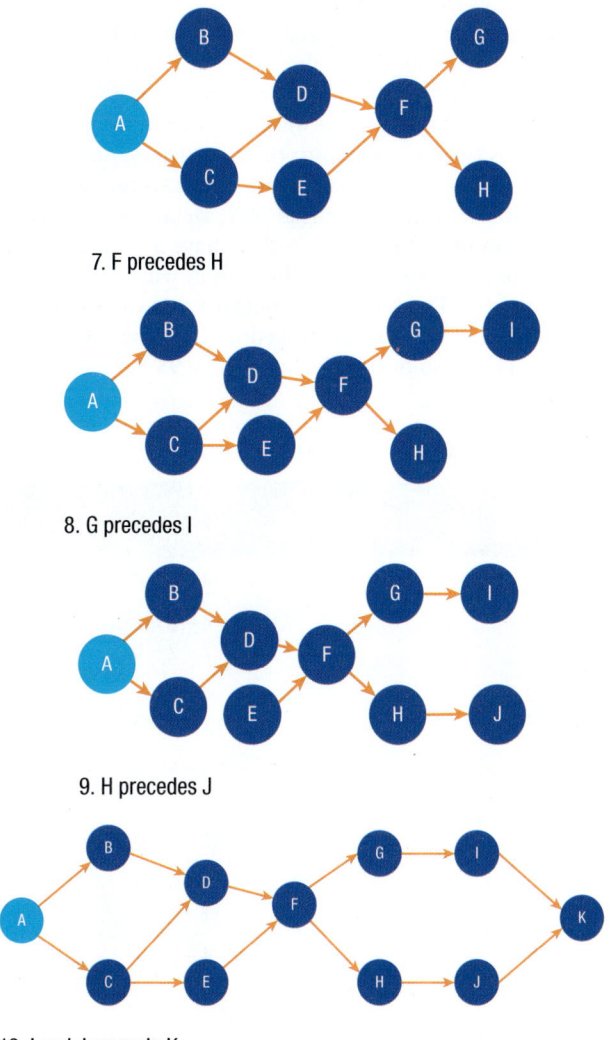

7. F precedes H

8. G precedes I

9. H precedes J

10. I and J precede K

The diagram obtained after step 10 is the final precedence diagram for this example.

3. *Compute the theoretical minimum number of workstations (N) required.*

The sum of all task times is the total of all 11 task times listed in column 3 of the previous table:

$$N = \frac{\text{Sum of all task times}}{\text{Cycle time}} = \frac{\sum_{i=1}^{n} t_i}{C} = \frac{(4+2+2+\dots+3)}{4} = 6.75$$

Since we cannot have fractional workstations, we round up the number to 7.

4. *Compute the theoretical minimum amount of idle time (I)*

$$I = \text{Total time available} - \text{Total time used} = N \times C - \sum_{i=1}^{n} t_i = 7 \times 4 - 27 = 1$$

Thus, the minimum desired idle time in the system we would like to have is 1 minute.

5. *Balance the assembly line.*

Assign the 11 tasks to the 7 workstations with just 1 minute of idle time in the system using the most-following-tasks and the ranked-positional-weight rules. The tasks should be assigned so that the precedence-relationships and the cycle-time constraints are not violated.

i. *Most-following-tasks rule:*

Using the precedence graph we created, we list for each task the number of tasks following it. Thus, task A = 10, C = 8, B = 7, D = 6, E = 6, F = 5, G = 2, H =2, I = 1, J = 1, and K =0. Hence, the task that should be assigned to the first workstation is A followed by C, then B, and so on. Because the maximum amount of time available in any workstation is 4 minutes (which is equal to the cycle time), only task A can be assigned to the first workstation. Next, we assign tasks to the second workstation. Since C has the next highest number of following tasks of 8, we assign C to the second workstation. Because C consumes only 2 minutes, and we have a total of 4 minutes available in the second workstation, we can assign to the second workstation task B, which also has a task time of 2 minutes. Thus, B and C are tasks that can be performed concurrently in workstation 2. We follow the same procedure for assigning the remaining tasks to the workstations, and the results are shown in Table 9S.4.

TABLE 9S.4: Task Assignments to Work Stations

WORKSTATION	TASK ASSIGNMENT	TIME REMAINING (IN MINUTES)	IDLE TIME (IN MINUTES)
I	A	4 − 4 = 0	0
II	C B	4 − 2 = 2 2 − 2 = 0	0
III	D E	4 − 3 = 1 1 − 1 = 0	0
IV	F	4 − 4 = 0	0
V	G H	4 − 3 = 1 1 − 1 = 0	0
VI	I J	4 − 3 = 1 1 − 1 = 0	0
VII	K	4 − 3 = 1	1

Because the 11 tasks have been assigned to the 7 workstations with 1 minute of idle time in the system, we have met our objectives, and the line is balanced. Its layout is shown in Figure 9S.9.

FIGURE 9S.9: Balanced Layout

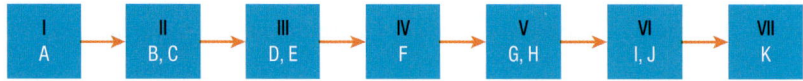

ii. *Ranked-Positional-Weight Rule*

Because this rule requires that we assign the task with the highest positional weight first, we calculate the positional weights of all 11 tasks first. Using the precedence graph and the tasks times provided in the previous table, we calculate the task positional weights as follows:

$$A: 4 + 2 + 2 + 3 + 1 + 4 + 3 + 1 + 3 + 1 + 3 = 27$$
$$C: 2 + 3 + 1 + 4 + 3 + 1 + 3 + 1 + 3 = 21$$
$$B: 2 + 3 + 4 + 3 + 1 + 3 + 1 + 3 = 20$$
$$D: 3 + 4 + 3 + 1 + 3 + 1 + 3 = 18$$
$$E: 1 + 4 + 3 + 1 + 3 + 1 + 3 = 16$$
$$F: 4 + 3 + 1 + 3 + 1 + 3 = 15$$
$$G: 3 + 3 + 3 = 9$$

H: 1 + 1 + 3 = 5
I: 3 + 3 = 6
J: 1 + 3 = 4
K: 3

The task that should be assigned to the first workstation is A because it takes 4 minutes to complete, which is also the maximum time (cycle time) available in the first workstation. No additional tasks can be assigned to this workstation. The task with the second highest positional weight is C, which is assigned to the second workstation. Because task C takes only 2 minutes, we can assign additional tasks to the second workstation. Because task B has the next highest positional weight, we assign it to the second workstation because it too takes only 2 minutes. If you continue this process, you will find that the ranked-positional-weight rule results in the same layout as the most-following task rule.

6. *Compute the balance efficiency (E)*
   We balanced the line using 7 workstations and a cycle time of 4 minutes. The total time consumed by all of the 11 tasks is 27 minutes. Therefore:

$$E = \frac{Total\ time\ used}{Total\ time\ available} = \frac{\sum_{i=1}^{n} t_i}{N x C} = \frac{27}{7 x 4} = \frac{27\ minutes}{28\ minutes} = 96.3\%$$

Thus, we have achieved a balance efficiency of 96.3%. The 3.4% balance inefficiency (100% – 96.3%) is caused by the 1 minute of idle time in the system.

Computer Software for Designing Process Layouts

Layout problems that are relatively small can be solved manually or by using graphical approaches. Yet, typically real-life layout problems are large, complex, and require the use of software. Fortunately, many such software programs are commercially available to solve both process and product layout problems. For example, for large process layout problems that involve quantitative criteria such as cost minimization, a computer program called CRAFT, which is an acronym for Computerized Relative Allocation of Facilities Technique, can be used. CRAFT computes the total cost of materials handling for a process layout. Then it systematically examines pairs of departments at a time to see whether bringing them closer together will reduce the cost. The iterations of layouts continue until no further cost reduction is possible, with the last iteration being the best possible layout.

FIGURE 9S.10: Example of a Hospital Layout Problem Solved Using CRAFT

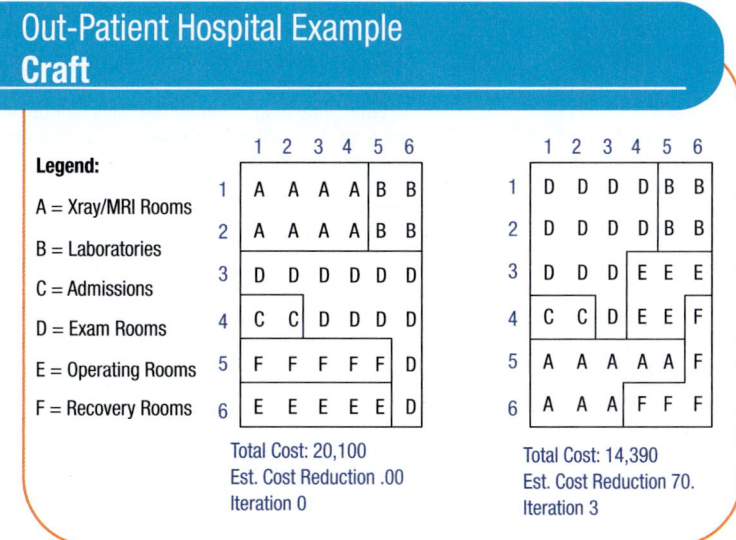

NOTE: The software program went through three iterations to achieve the best possible layout for a total cost reduction of ($20,100 – $14,390 = $5,710.

SOURCE: Reprinted from http://image.slidesharecdn.com/layout-1223621497671389-9/95/layout-21-728.jpg?cb=1223616922

For large process layout problems whereby the relationships between departments are expressed in qualitative terms, a computer software programs called ALDEP (which stands for Automated Layout Design Program) or CORELAP (which stands for Computerized Relationship Layout Planning) can be used. All of these programs provide good, if not necessarily perfect, layout solutions. The programs also offer more capabilities such as the ability to generate charts, make cost comparisons, and so forth. Large line balancing problems for product layouts can be solved quickly using IBM's COMSOAL (Computer Methods for Sequencing Operations for Assembly Lines; International Business Machines Corporation, Armonk, NY) or GE's ASYBL (Assembly Line Configuration Program; General Electric, Fairfield, CT). Like the ones used for process layout problems, the programs do not guarantee optimal solutions. Nonetheless, they can provide good layouts for balancing a line using one of the five rules of thumb in Table 9S.2.

Visit **edge.sagepub.com/venkataraman** to help you accomplish your coursework goals in an easy-to-use learning environment.

- Mobile-friendly eFlashcards
- Mobile-friendly practice quizzes
- A complete online action plan

- Chapter summaries with learning objectives
- Video and multimedia resources

SUPPLEMENT SUMMARY

9S.1 Employ tools for process selection, analysis, and design.
One of the simplest tools used to compare and select processes is a cost–volume, or breakeven, analysis. To use this tool to make process selection decisions, we calculate the total costs of the processes we're considering for various production volumes. We then plot on a two-dimensional graph the total cost lines for each process and choose the one that has the lowest cost for the number of units we expect to produce.

Several tools can be used to analyze and understand a process's complexities so as to design or redesign it. The tools include assembly drawings, assembly charts, route sheets, process mapping, value stream mapping (VSM), and process simulation. Although an assembly drawing is an enlarged view of a product that shows all of its parts and subassemblies, an assembly chart maps how a product's parts go together and the order in which they are assembled. A route sheet is a document that describes the sequence of different operations, places, or people involved in a process. The sheet helps organize work orders by tracking the parts for products and the status of jobs during their scheduling, production, and quality control phases. A process chart graphically shows all activities related to a process, including its inputs and outputs, decision points such as approvals and exceptions, and any cross-functional relationships. All steps in the process are identified. Value stream mapping (VSM) is a process-mapping technique used to analyze and design the flow of materials and information across multiple processes. Beginning with the customer, VSM examines all processes, including the organization's supply chain, to determine where value is added or not added across the system. Process simulation provides a dynamic view of the process. Using computers, multiple inputs, work centers, and processing techniques can help operations manager look at the variability of a process under different conditions.

Although many of the process analysis tools we have discussed can also be used to analyze service processes, a very useful tool for analyzing services is a service blueprint. Service blueprints are especially useful for analyzing service processes that have high service content such as the intensive customer interaction observed in luxury hotels.

9S.2 Describe and use the techniques for designing process and product layouts. In process layouts, the process facilities are shared by a wide variety of different products. Consequently, the relative positioning of the various departments is a compromise. A good process layout minimizes the materials handling or transportation costs or employee and customer traveling or waiting time. The most common way to design a process layout for a manufacturing facility is to arrange departments or work centers so that the total cost of materials handling is minimized. This can be accomplished by reducing the number of nonadjacent moves between the most frequently interacting departments.

When quantitative data are not readily available, qualitative criteria, such as the best judgment of a firm's managers, can be used to design a process layout. The relationship rating technique developed by Richard Muther is a method used to design new layouts or change old ones based on qualitative criteria. Managers rate the best locations for departments relative to one another, and the information is displayed in a grid known as Muther's grid.

In a product layout, machines or work centers are arranged based on a predetermined sequence of operations for the product. The goals are to achieve high levels of efficiency and capacity utilization while ensuring that the product flows smoothly through the line with no bottlenecks. The technique of line balancing is used to achieve these goals. Line balancing involves assigning production tasks so that the time required to complete them is approximately equal across workstations. This prevents some workstations from having to wait on others to finish their work on products traveling down the line.

Whenever there is idle time between workstations, a line is said to be unbalanced, and bottlenecks occur. Line balancing also helps minimize the number of workstations a firm needs.

As real-life layout problems are typically large, arriving at an optimal solution to such problems is nearly impossible. Hence, heuristic approaches are used to generate solutions that are not necessarily optimal but are satisfactory. Many commercially available computer packages such as CRAFT, CORELAP, and ALDEP can be used to reduce the effort required to solve large-scale process layout problems. Nevertheless, these programs also rely to a great extent on heuristic approaches. Large line balancing problems for product layouts can be solved quickly using IBM's COMSOAL or GE's ASYBL. These computer programs, however, do not guarantee optimal solutions.

KEY TERMS

Assembly chart 329	Line balancing 337	Process simulation 331
Assembly drawing 329	Muther's grid 337	Relationship rating 337
Balance efficiency 339	Points of indifference 328	Route sheet 329
Cycle time 338	Precedence relationships 338	Service blueprint 331
Flow time 338	Process chart 329	Value stream mapping (VSM) 330

DISCUSSION AND REVIEW QUESTIONS

1. How can you use the following process analysis tools to improve or redesign existing processes?
   a. An assembly chart
   b. A process routing sheet
   c. A process chart

2. What advantages does a process simulation have over the charting techniques used to analyze a process?

3. Discuss service blueprinting and how it's useful for analyzing service processes.

4. What is a Muther's grid, and how is it used in process layout decisions?

5. What is line balancing?

6. What is the difference between flow time and cycle time?

7. How does the variability in task times affect balancing a line?

8. Why are rule-of-thumb approaches used to analyze layouts?

9. What are some constraints that layout analysts have to address in balancing a line?

10. How would you calculate the percentage of idle time in an assembly line that is balanced?

SOLVED PROBLEMS

1. Anita Patel Enterprises is a fictional process-oriented machine shop that has been experiencing rapid growth. The owner, Anita Patel, is planning to move her factory to a new, larger facility. The new facility has eight departments, and Anita has designed a process layout for it. Material movements in terms of loads for any given month between each pair of departments and the distances between them are shown in the following tables. The cost of moving one unit of materials one foot is US$2. How would you help Anita improve the layout to minimize the total materials handling cost of the new facility?

Initial Layout

Materials Storage (1)	Welding (2)	Drilling (3)	Lathing (4)
Grinding (5)	Assembly (6)	Inspection (7)	Testing (8)

Interdepartmental Workflow Matrix: Number of Loads Moved per Week

Department	Materials Storage (1)	Welding (2)	Drilling (3)	Lathing (4)	Grinding (5)	Assembly (6)	Inspection (7)	Testing (8)
Materials Storage (1)		120	120	0	0	0	0	0
Welding (2)			0	60	30	0	0	0
Drilling (3)				40	40	0	0	0
Lathing (4)					30	0	0	30

(Continued)

(Continued)

Department	Materials Storage (1)	Welding (2)	Drilling (3)	Lathing (4)	Grinding (5)	Assembly (6)	Inspection (7)	Testing (8)
Grinding (5)						30	0	10
Assembly (6)							40	0
Inspection (7)								0
Testing (8)								

Distance Between Departments (in feet)

Department	Materials Storage (1)	Welding (2)	Drilling (3)	Lathing (4)	Grinding (5)	Assembly (6)	Inspection (7)	Testing (8)
Materials Storage (1)		10	20	0	0	0	0	0
Welding (2)			0	20	10	0	0	0
Drilling (3)				10	20	0	0	0
Lathing (4)					30	0	0	10
Grinding (5)						10	0	30
Assembly (6)							10	0
Inspection (7)								0
Testing (8)								

Solution:

To visualize the movement of loads between departments, we construct an interdepartmental workflow graph for Anita's initial layout. It's shown in the following figure:

Interdepartmental Workflows

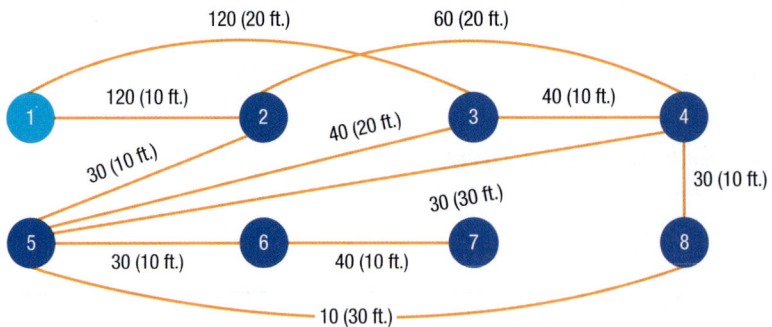

Using Equation 1, Let's now calculate the total cost of materials handling for the layout:

$$\text{Total Cost} = \sum_{i=1}^{n}\sum_{j=1}^{n} C_{ij} X_{ij} D_{ij}$$

= 2×120×10 + 2×120×20 + 2×60×20 + 2×30×10 + 2×40×10 + 2×40×20 (1 and 2) (1 and 3) (2 and 4) (2 and 5) (3 and 4) (3 and 5)
+ 2×30×30 + 2×30×10 + 2×30×10 + 2×10×30 + 2×40×10 (4 and 5) (4 and 8) (5 and 6) (5 and 8) (6 and 7)

= \$2,400 + \$4,800 + \$2,400 + \$600 + \$800 + \$1,600 + \$1800 + \$600 + \$600 + \$600 + \$800

= **\$17,000**

Thus, the total cost of materials handling for the initial layout is $17,000.

In this layout, two significant nonadjacent moves occur: One between the materials storage work center (1) and the drilling work center (3), and a second between the welding work center (2) and the lathing work center (4). These two pairs of work centers also have the highest interactions, with a movement of 120 and 60 loads, respectively. Hence, we should place these two pairs of work centers adjacent to each other. In other words, we place work centers 1 and 3 adjacent to each other, and 2 and 4 adjacent each other. Doing so also changes the distances between some other pairs of departments. The revised distances and the interdepartmental flows, which are highlighted in green, are shown in the following figure.

Revised Interdepartmental Workflows

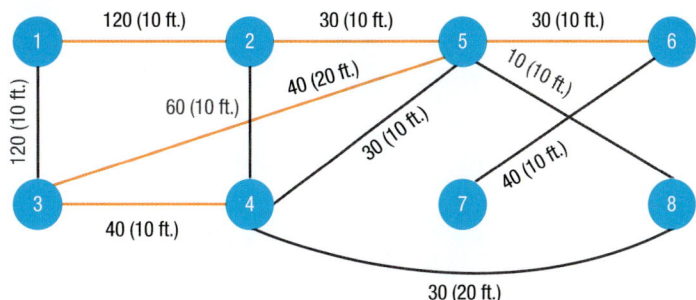

Using Equation 1, let's now calculate the total cost of materials handling for the revised layout.

$$Total = \sum_{i=1}^{n}\sum_{j=1}^{n} C_{ij} X_{ij} D_{ij}$$

$= 2 \times 120 \times 10 + 2 \times 120 \times 10 + 2 \times 60 \times 10 + 2 \times 30 \times 10 + 2 \times 40 \times 10 + 2 \times 40 \times 20$ (1 and 2) (1 and 3) (2 and 4) (2 and 5)

(3 and 4) (3 and 5) $+ 2 \times 30 \times 10 + 2 \times 30 \times 20 + 2 \times 30 \times 10 + 2 \times 10 \times 10 + 2 \times 40 \times 10$ (4 and 5) (4 and 8) (5 and 6) (5 and 8) (6 and 7)

$= \$2,400 + \$2,400 + \$1,200 + \$600 + \$800 + \$1,600 + \$600 + \$1,200 + \$200 + \$600 + \$800$

$= \mathbf{\$12,400}$

Thus, the revised layout reduces the total cost of materials handling by $17,000 − $12,400 = $4,600.

2. The closeness ratings of nine departments on the first floor of a retail store are presented in the following Muther's grid:

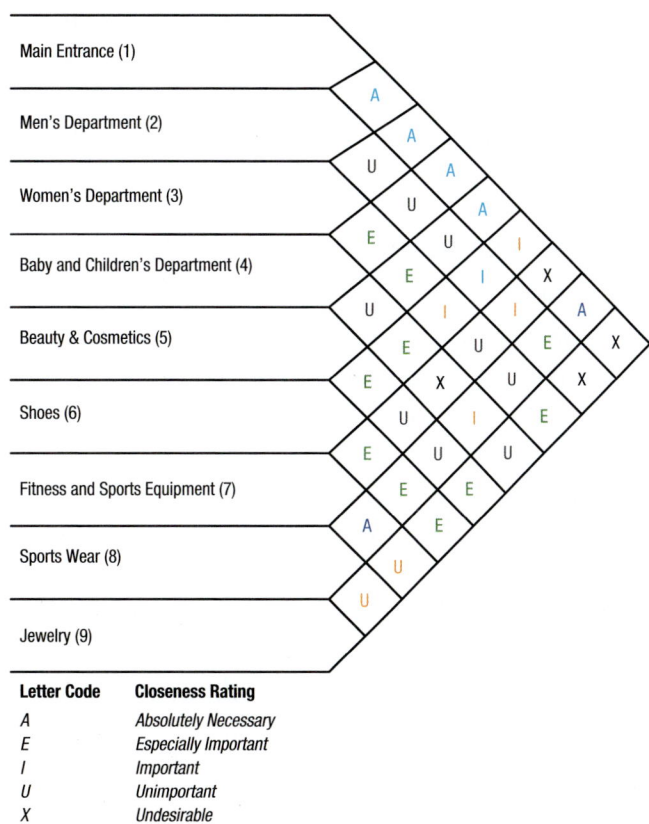

Letter Code	Closeness Rating
A	Absolutely Necessary
E	Especially Important
I	Important
U	Unimportant
X	Undesirable

Lay out the nine departments so that the closeness ratings reflected in the grid are satisfied.

Solution:

We begin by placing in the layout plan the department that has highest number of "A" ratings. This is the main entrance area (1) with 5 "A" ratings. Next we place the departments that have an "A" rating next to the main-entrance area. Then we place departments that have an "E" rating as close to each other as possible, and so on. Departments that have an "X" rating are placed as far away from each other as possible. A possible layout for this example is as follows:

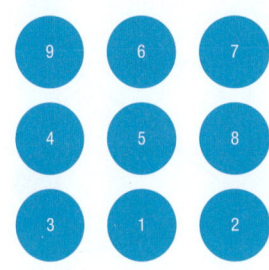

Jewelry	Shoes	Fitness and Sports Equipment
Baby and Children's Department	Cosmetics	Sportswear
Women's Department	Main Entrance	Men's Department

3. Airbus SAS (Blagnac, France) has determined the tasks, their precedence relationships, and the task times needed to assemble a wing component on one of the airplanes it produces. This information is shown in the following table:

Tasks	Immediate Predecessor	Task Time (in minutes)
A	NONE	12
B	A	10
C	B	4
D	B	5
E	A	11
F	C, D	4
G	F	6
H	E	11
I	G, H	3

In addition, Airbus has determined that its productive daily operating time is 7 hours and that 35 units of this component need to be assembled per day:

a. Determine the cycle time for the component.

b. Draw a diagram that shows the precedence relationships among the tasks needed to assemble the component.

c. What is the minimum number of workstations required to balance this assembly line?

d. Assign tasks to workstations using the most-following-tasks rule.

e. Compute the layout's balance efficiency.

Solution:

1. *Compute the desired cycle time (C).*

   Because the line operates seven hours a day, the total production time per day is 60 minutes per hour × 7 hours = 420 minutes. Since the daily production needs to be 35 units, the cycle time is:

$$C = \frac{Daily\ production\ time\ available}{Units\ to\ be\ produced\ daily} = \frac{420\ minutes}{35\ units} = 12\ minutes\ per\ unit$$

2. *Draw a precedence graph based on the precedence relationships among the operations.*

   The precedence diagram is as follows.

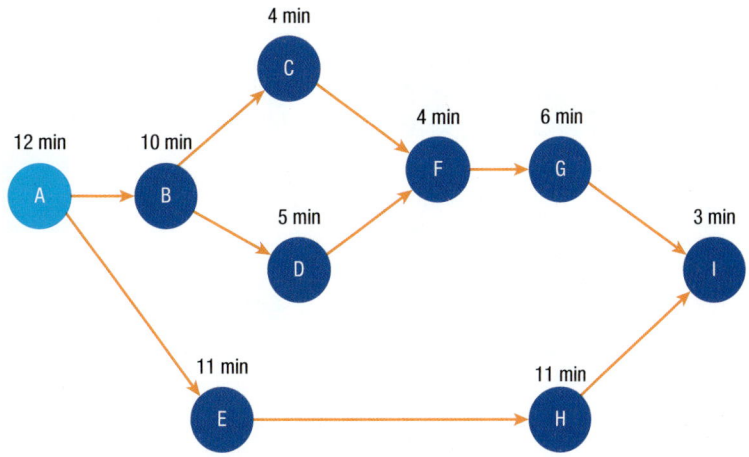

3. *Compute the theoretical minimum number of workstations (N) required.*

The sum of the task times is the total of all the 9 task times listed in column 3 of the table or (12 + 10 + 4 + 5 + 11 + 4 + 6 + 11 + 3) = 66 minutes:

$$N = \frac{\text{Sum of all task times}}{\text{Cycle time}} = \frac{\sum_{i=1}^{n} t_i}{C} = \frac{66}{12} = 5.5$$

Since we cannot have fractional workstations, we round up the number to 6. Thus, the minimum number of workstations we will need to balance the line is 6.

4. *Compute the theoretical minimum amount of idle time (I).*

$$I = \text{Total time available} - \text{Total time used} = N \times C - \sum_{i=1}^{n} t_i = 6 \times 12 - 66 = 6$$

Thus, the minimum desired idle time in the system we would like to have is 6 minutes.

5. *Balance the assembly line using the most-following-tasks rule.*

We want to assign the 9 tasks to the 6 workstations with 6 minutes of idle time. Using the precedence graph we created, we list for each task the number of tasks following it: Task A = 8, B = 5, C = 3, D = 3, E = 2, F = 2, G = 1, H =1, and I = 0. Hence, the task that should be assigned to the first workstation is A followed by B, then C and D, and so on. Because the maximum time available in any workstation is 12 minutes (which is equal to the cycle time), only task A can be assigned to the first workstation. Since task B has the next most number of following tasks (5 tasks), we assign it first to the second workstation. No additional tasks can be assigned to the second workstation as a result of the cycle time constraint of 12 minutes. Because both tasks C and D have the same number of following tasks (3 tasks), they can be performed concurrently. In addition, the sum of their task times is only 9 minutes (4 + 5). Consequently, C and D both can be assigned to workstation 3. No additional tasks can be assigned to the third workstation. The next candidates for assignment are tasks E and F. They are tied in terms of the most number of following tasks (2 tasks). Yet, because E has the longest task time, it should be assigned to the fourth workstation. Note that E also has task A as its predecessor.

Ideally, B and E should have been assigned to the second workstation. But because the sum of their task times will exceed the cycle time of 12 minutes, that assignment is not feasible. Therefore, a secondary path has to be created with workstation 4 following the first. Task F is now assigned to the fifth workstation and takes 4 minutes. That leaves 8 (12 − 4) more minutes available in this workstation, so additional tasks can be assigned to it. Tasks G and H are the next candidates for assignment because they are tied for the most number of following tasks (1 task). Although H has the longer operating time, it cannot be assigned to the fifth workstation as a result of the cycle-time and precedence-relationship constraints. Hence, G should be assigned to the fifth workstation. H is assigned to the sixth workstation, which follows workstation 4 in the secondary path. Finally, task I is assigned to workstation 7. The assignment of the 9 tasks to the seven workstations is as follows.

Workstation	Task Assignment	Time Remaining	Idle Time (in minutes)
I	A	12 − 12 = 0	0
II	B	12 − 10 = 2	2
III	C	12 − 4 = 8	
	D	8 − 5 = 3	3
IV	E	12 − 11 = 1	1
V	F	12 − 4 = 8	
	G	8 − 6 = 2	2
VI	H	12 − 11 = 1	1
VII	I	12 − 3 = 9	9

The following figure shows the layout of the line:

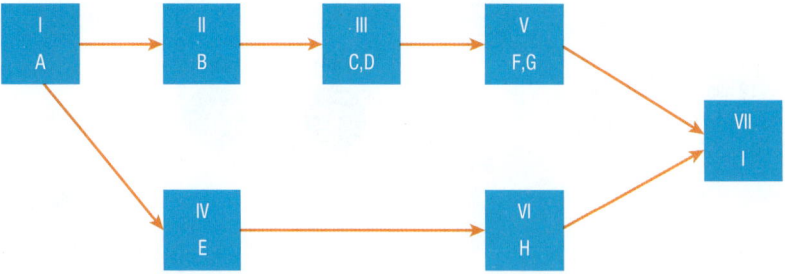

Because the 9 tasks require 7 workstations, and there's a total of 18 minutes of idle time in the system, we have not met our objectives—that is, we were unable to balance the line with 6 workstations and 6 minutes of idle time.

6. *Compute the balance efficiency (E)*

The line required 7 workstations and has a cycle time of 12 minutes. The total time consumed by all the 9 tasks is 66 minutes. Therefore:

$$E = \frac{Total\ time\ used}{Total\ time\ available} = \frac{\sum_{i=1}^{n} t_i}{N \times C} = \frac{66}{7 \times 12} = \frac{66\ minutes}{84\ minutes} = 78.6\%$$

Thus, the balance efficiency achieved is only 78.6%. The 21.4% (100% − 78.6%) balance inefficiency is caused by the 18 minutes of idle time in the system.

The precedence-relationship and cycle-time constraints forced us to use a seventh workstation. The only way to balance the line with 6 workstations is by reducing the task times. For example, if we can reduce the time it takes to complete task I from 3 to 2 minutes by adding more resources to perform that task, then we could use workstation 5 to accommodate task I, thereby eliminating the need for workstation 7. Furthermore, we will also reduce the total idle time in the system to 6 minutes, the line will be balanced, and our objectives will be met.

4. XYZ Pet Products is setting up an assembly line to produce ultra-slim radio dog collars. The line will operate 12 hours a day and produce 480 collars daily. The tasks needed to produce a collar along with their task times and precedence relationships are shown in the following table. Balance the line using the ranked-positional-weight rule:

Task	Immediate Predecessor	Task Time (in seconds)
A	NONE	80
B	NONE	30
C	B	60
D	A	20
E	B, C	40
F	D	80
G	D, E	10
H	F, G	30
I	H	10
J	H	40
K	I, J	10
Total		410 seconds

Solution:

1. *Compute the desired cycle time (C).*

Because the line operates 12 hours a day, the total production time available is 60 seconds per minute × 60 minutes per hour × 12 hours per day = 43,200 seconds. Since the daily production needs to be 480 collars, the cycle time is given by:

$$C = \frac{Daily\ production\ time\ available}{Units\ to\ be\ produced\ daily} = \frac{43200\ seconds}{480\ collars} = 90\ seconds\ per\ collar$$

2. *Draw a precedence graph based on the precedence relationships among the operations.*

The precedence graph based on the information given in the table is as follows:

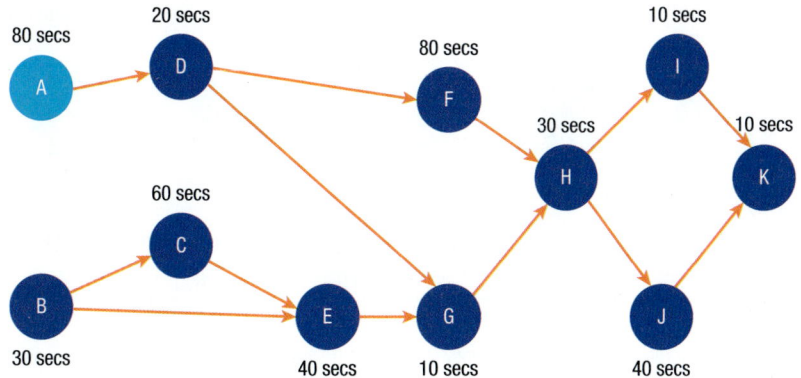

3. *Compute the theoretical minimum number of workstations (N) required.*

The sum of all task times is the total of all 11 task times listed in column 3 of the table: $(80 + 30 + 60 + 20 + 40 + 80 + 10 + 30 + 10 + 40 + 10) =$ 410 seconds.

$$N = \frac{\text{Sum of all task times}}{\text{Cycle time}} = \frac{\sum_{i=1}^{n} t_i}{C} = \frac{410}{90} = 4.6$$

Since we cannot have fractional workstations, we round up the number to 5. Thus, the minimum number of workstations we will need to balance the line is 5.

4. *Compute the theoretical minimum amount of idle time (I)*

$$I = \text{Total time available} - \text{Total time used} = N \times C - \sum_{i=1}^{n} t_i = 5 \times 90 - 410 = 40 \text{ seconds}$$

Thus, the minimum idle time in the system we would like to have is 40 seconds.

5. *Balance the assembly line using the ranked-positional-weight rule:*

To balance the line, we need to assign the 11 tasks to the 5 workstations and have 40 seconds of idle time in the system. Using the precedence graph we created, we can calculate each task's ranked positional weight:

A: 80 + 20 + 10 + 80 + 30 + 10 + 40 + 10 = 280
B: 30 + 60 +40 + 10 + 30 + 10 + 40 + 10 = 230
C: 60 + 40 + 10 + 30 + 10 + 40 + 10 = 200
D: 20 + 10 + 80 + 30 + 10 + 40 + 10 = 200
F: 80 + 30 + 10 + 40 + 10 = 170
E: 40 + 10 + 30 + 10 + 40 + 10 = 140
G: 10 + 30 + 10 + 40 + 10 = 100
H: 30 + 10 + 40 + 10 = 90
J: 40 + 10 = 50
I: 10 + 10 = 20
K: 10

Based on the positional weights and their rank, we assign task A to the first workstation. Given the precedence-relationship and cycle-time constraints, no additional tasks can be assigned to this workstation. Task B, which has the next highest positional weight, is assigned to the second workstation. Because B takes only 30 seconds, there are 60 more seconds (90 − 30) available in the second workstation. Therefore, we can assign task C, which has the next highest positional weight, to the second workstation without violating the constraints. Even though tasks C and D are tied in terms of their ranking (both have a score of 200; we chose to assign C to the workstation because as it has the longer task time). We continue the procedure for assigning the remaining tasks to the other workstations. The results are shown in the following table:

Workstation	Task Assignment	Time Remaining (in minutes)	Idle Time (in minutes)
I	A	90 − 80 = 10	10
II	B	90 − 30 = 60	
	C	60 − 60 = 0	0
III	D	90 − 20 = 70	
	E×	70 − 40 = 30	20
	G	30 − 10 = 20	
IV	F×	90 − 80 = 10	10
V	H	90 − 30 = 60	
	J	60 − 40 = 20	0
	I	20 − 10 = 10	
	K	10 − 10 = 0	

NOTE: We assigned task E instead of F to the third workstation even though task F has a higher positional weight. This is because assigning task F to the third workstation would violate the cycle-time constraint of 90 seconds.

Because the 11 tasks have been assigned to the 5 workstations with 40 seconds of idle time in the system, we have met our objectives, and the line is balanced. The layout of the line is as follows:

6. *Compute the balance efficiency (E)*

The line required 5 workstations and has a cycle time of 90 seconds. The total time consumed by all the 11 tasks is 410 seconds. Therefore:

$$E = \frac{\text{Total time used}}{\text{Total time available}} = \frac{\sum_{i=1}^{n} t_i}{N \times C} = \frac{410}{5 \times 90} = \frac{410 \, seconds}{450 \, seconds} = 91.1\%$$

Thus, the balance efficiency achieved is 91.1%. The 8.9% balance inefficiency (100% − 91.1%) is caused by the 40 seconds of idle time in the system.

PROBLEMS

1. Create an assembly chart for putting together a McDonald's Big Mac.

2. Create a process chart for orange-juice processing.

3. Create a process chart for course registration at your university.

4. Prepare a service blueprint for a local hair salon.

5. Murali Aromatics Inc. is a fictional manufacturer of aromatic oils and perfumes. Demand for the company's products has been increasing steadily for the past five years, and capacity of the existing process cannot support any future demand growth, Therefore, the owner of the company, Capt. Muralidharan, is planning to invest in a new process that will have the production capacity handle any demand increases in the future for the company's products. He has two alternatives processes to choose from: Process A will require an initial investment of US$50,000 for plant and equipment, and the variable cost per unit of output (labor and material) will be US$10. Process B will require an initial investment of US$30,000 for plant and equipment, and the variable cost per unit will be US$15.

   a. Which process should Capt. Muralidharan choose if the annual expected production volume is 7,000 units?

   b. At what production volume would Capt. Muralidharan be indifferent between choosing either process A or process B?

6. MegaTech is a fictional manufacturer of electronic products. Recent growth in the demand for the company's products requires it to invest in new production methods. The company has three alternatives: (a) invest in a small production facility that uses mature technology; (b) invent in a larger more automated facility with state-of-the art equipment; or (c) outsource production to an electronic manufacturer in China. The cost scenarios for each production alternative are given in the following table. At what production volumes should each alternative be chosen?

Process Alternative	Fixed Cost (in U.S. dollars)	Variable Cost per Unit (in U.S. dollars)
Process A	250,000	50
Process B	750,000	20
Process C	0	60

7. Fly High Inc. is a fictional manufacturer of snowboards. The company has designed a new ski board and needs to choose a new production method. The process types the company can choose from and their associated cost data are provided in the following table:

Process Type	Fixed Cost of Plant and Equipment (in U.S. dollars)	Labor	Materials	Energy
		Variable Cost Per Unit (in U.S. dollars)		
Intermittent	900,000	25	30	22
Continuous	2,000,000	20	18	12
Repetitive	1,600,000	22	20	14
Mass customization	1,200,000	30	25	14

The expected annual demand for the new snowboard is 30,000 units.

a. Which process type is the best for a production volume of 30,000 units?

b. Which process type is the best for a production volume between 50,000 and 70,000 units?

c. At what production volume will the company be indifferent to choosing between the mass customization process and the repetitive process?

8. Alistair Cook's fictional machine shop has four work centers: I, II, III, and IV. The distances in feet between each pair of work centers are as follows.

	I	II	III	1V
I	———	5	10	8
II	———	———	7	9
III	———	———	———	11
IV	———	———	———	———

The loads moved between each pair of work centers are as follows:

	I	II	III	1V
I	———	900	800	500
II	———	———	400	300
III	———	———	———	700
IV	———	———	———	———

If the materials handling cost is US$2 per load per foot, what is the total materials handling cost for this layout?

9. A Chicago job-shop operates with four departments—machining, drilling, assembly, and painting. The shop's production manager, Karen Grillo, has data on the distances between pairs of departments and the number of loads between them. This information is shown in the following tables. The cost of moving one unit of the material one foot is US$1.

The distance between departments in feet are as follows:

	M	D	A	P
M	———	22	14	10
D	———	———	7	11
A	———	———	———	5
P	———	———	———	———

The loads moved between each pair of work centers per week are as follows:

	M	D	A	P
M	———	800	2000	400
D	———	———	600	400
A	———	———	———	2000
P	———	———	———	———

a. What is the total materials handling cost for this layout?

b. Assembly and painting and assembly and machining are two pairs of departments with high loads moved between them. An improved layout can be obtained by switching the assembly and painting departments, which will alter the distance between certain pairs of department. What is the total materials handling cost for this revised layout?

10. Trinity Hospital is planning to open a new clinic in Mylapore, Chennai, India. Based on historical data from similar facilities, the hospital's design committee collected the following data on the movement of patient in terms of the number of trips they make between departments:

From	Patient Trips To					
	1	2	3	4	5	6
1. Intake	–	60	20	30	20	120
2. Exam room		–	40	50	30	30
3. Radiology		50	–	30	70	50
4. Laboratory		20	20	–	20	50
5. Gynecology		40	30	20	–	40
6. Waiting area	50	70	60	30	60	–

The committee has also determined an initial layout for the facility. The distances in feet between departments for the layout are shown in the following table:

From	To					
	1	2	3	4	5	6
1. Intake	–	80	120	100	120	80
2. Exam room		–	120	300	150	200
3. Radiology			–	220	80	270
4. Laboratory				–	80	120
5. Gynecology					–	120
6. Waiting area						–

Initial layout

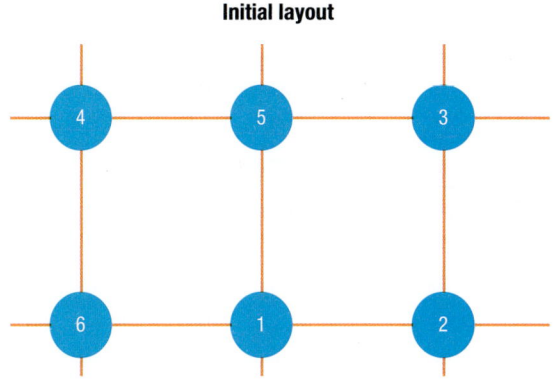

Given the previous information,

a. Calculate the number of trips × distance score for the initial layout.

b. Design an improved layout that will minimize the number of nonadjacent trips and compute the number of trips × distance score for the revised layout.

11. A law firm has six departments and you are asked to prepare a layout for this law firm office. The distance between adjacent departments is 30 feet, and the number of trips between the departments is given in the following table. Prepare a layout that will minimize the number of nonadjacent trips between departments

	Number of Trips					
From\To	1	2	3	4	5	6
1	–	20	30	70	15	58
2		–	100	27	33	47
3			–	46	24	18
4				–	20	55
5					–	40
6						–

12. Given the following Muther's grid, design a revised layout:

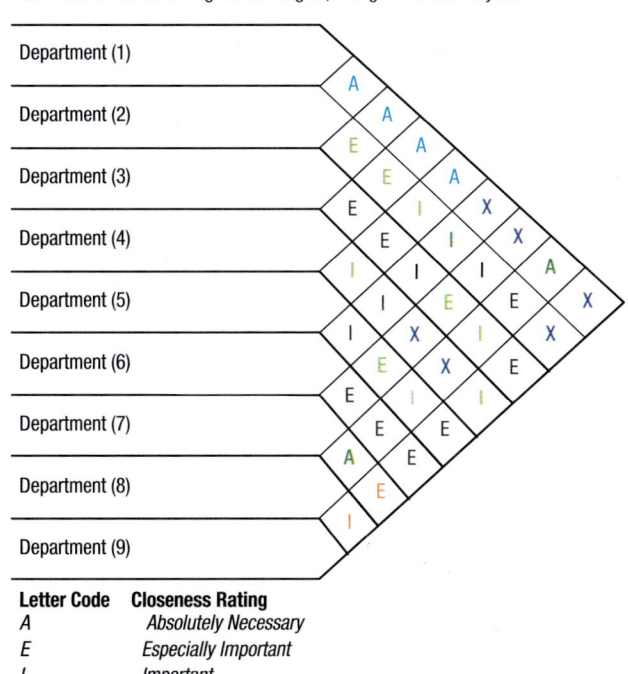

Letter Code	Closeness Rating
A	Absolutely Necessary
E	Especially Important
I	Important
U	Unimportant
X	Undesirable

13. The fictional Reliance Department Store is opening a new store in City Center Mall. Data from existing stores on customer movements between the departments are given in the following table. Design a layout for the company's new store that will minimize nonadjacent customer movement:

From/To	Customer Movements					
	Men's	Women's	Girls	Boys	Infants	Electronics
Men's	–		20	30		70
Women's	40	–	60	50	50	10
Girls		50	–	30		20
Boys	30		40	–		50
Infants		40			–	
Electronics	50					–

14. An assembly line with 16 tasks needs to be balanced. The line operates 7 hours a day, and the desired daily output rate is 70 units. The total time for all the 16 tasks is 38 minutes:

    a. What is the cycle time?

    b. What is the theoretical minimum number of workstations required?

    c. What cycle time will provide a daily output rate of 105 units?

15. An operations manager wants to balance a line as efficiently as possible. The desired daily output rate is 60 units, and the line operates 9 hours a day. Given the precedence diagram, assign the tasks to workstations according to the following heuristics:

    a. Most following tasks rule.

    b. Ranked positional weight rule.

    c. Compute the balance efficiency for both rules. Which assignment is better?

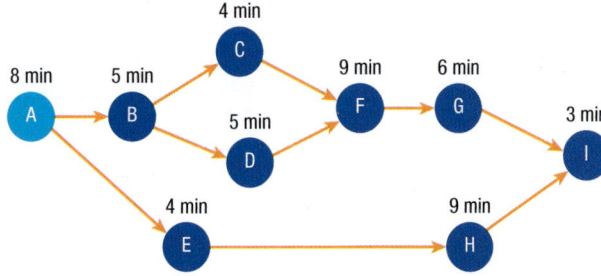

16. Assembling the subassembly of the landing gear of the Airbus A320 aircraft requires 13 tasks. The tasks, their precedence relationships, and task times as given in the following table. In addition, Airbus has determined that its productive daily operating time is 8 hours and requires 48 units of the subassembly to be assembled per day:

Tasks	Immediate Predecessor	Task Time (in minutes)
A	NONE	8
B	A	3
C	A	3
D	A	3
F	D	7
G	C, E, F	5

Tasks	Immediate Predecessor	Task Time (in minutes)
H	G	3
I	G	2
J	G	5
K	H	8
L	J	5
M	I, K, L	10
Total		68

Given this information:

a. Determine the cycle time.

b. Draw a precedence diagram that shows the precedence relationships among tasks for this assembly operation.

c. What is minimum number of workstations required to balance this assembly line?

d. Assign tasks to workstations using the most following tasks rule.

e. Assign tasks to workstations using the ranked positional weight rule.

f. Compute the balance efficiency for both rules.

g. Which rule achieves a better balance?

17. Excelsior Technologies (not a real company) designs layouts for a variety of companies. Damien Motors, a fictional German automobile company, is planning to open an assembly line plant in Hamburg for its new car Sting Ray-II. The tasks, their precedence relationships, and the task times are given in the following table. In addition, Damien Motors has determined that its productive daily operating time is 8 hours and requires 40 units of the new model to be assembled per day:

Tasks	Immediate Predecessor	Task Time (in minutes)
A	NONE	7
B	A	3
C	A	3
D	A	2
E	B	6
F	D	7
G	C, E	5
H	G	3
I	G, F	5
J	G	5
K	H	8
Total		54

Given this information:

a. Determine the cycle time.

b. Draw a precedence diagram that shows the precedence relationships among tasks for this assembly operation.

c. What is minimum number of workstations required to balance this assembly line?

d. Assign tasks to workstations using the most following tasks rule.

e. Assign tasks to workstations using the ranked positional weight rule.

f. Compute the balance efficiency for both rules.

g. Which rule achieves a better balance?

18. Refer to Solved Problem 9S.3. Suppose production requirements dictate that the cycle time be reduced from 12 to 11 minutes. Using the data given in the table in Solved Problem 9S.2, rebalance the line using the new cycle time.

19. James Stuart & Associates, a fictional reputed law firm, is moving into a new facility. Historical data on employee movements per month among the six departments in the old office facility are given in the following table. Design a layout for the new office facility on a 2 × 3 grid that will minimize the distance that the employees in the lawyers' office must travel:

Trips From	Trips To					
	1	2	3	4	5	6
1	–	120				90
2		–			220	
3		80	–			
4			70	–		
5	80				–	50
6		70			140	–

20. Given the following Muther's grid, design a revised layout on a 2 × 3 grid:

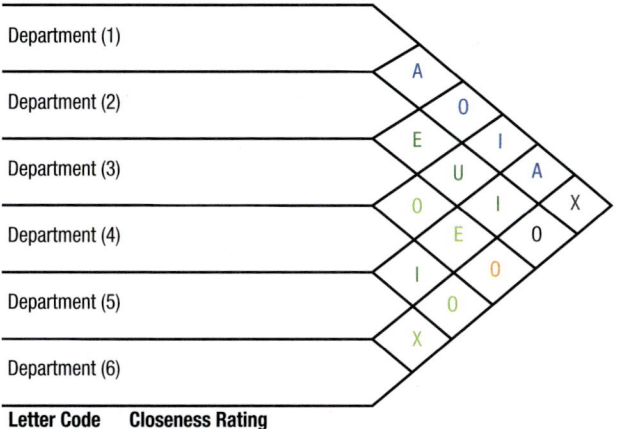

Letter Code	Closeness Rating
A	Absolutely Necessary
E	Especially Important
I	mportant
U	Unimportant
X	Undesirable

21. Voyage Enterprises is a fictional manufacturer of handcrafted leather suitcases and travel bags. Assembly of suitcases is a labor-intensive process and requires completion of seven task elements shown in the following table:

Tasks	Immediate Predecessor	Task Time (in minutes)
A	NONE	40
B	A	20
C	B	15
D	A	5
E	None	10
F	D and E	15
G	F	10

Given this information:

a. Draw a precedence diagram that shows the precedence relationships among tasks for this assembly operation.

b. Compute the total time required to assemble one suitcase and the cycle time required for assembling 60 suitcases in a 40-hour week.

c. Balance the line using the most following tasks rule, and compute the balance efficiency.

d. What changes should be made to the line to produce 90 suitcases in a 40-hour week?

22. The following is a precedence diagram of tasks and their time in minutes to assemble a dresser:

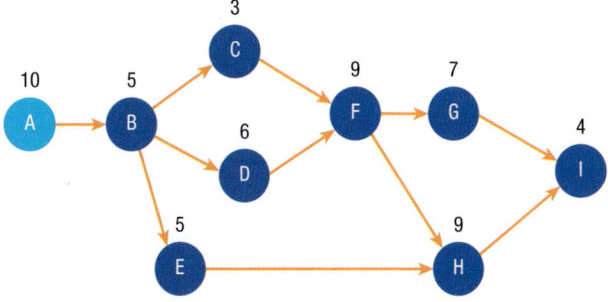

a. If 200 dressers are to be assembled in a 40-hour work week, what is the cycle time?

b. Balance the line using the positional weight rule, and compute the efficiency of balance.

c. Balance the line using the most following tasks rule, and compute the efficiency of balance.

d. Which rule is more efficient and why?

23. Hackers Golf Club Inc. (not a real company) is contemplating a new finish for the golf clubs it manufactures. Bernd Hacker, the company CEO, has come up with three choices: (a) Refurbish the old machine at a cost of $1200, (b) purchase a new machine at a cost of $2500, or (c) make major design modifications to the old machine at a cost of $1600. If the refurbishing alternative is chosen, variable costs would amount to $2.50 per club. Variable costs for the alternative of major design modifications would be $1.20, and for the new machine it would be $ 0.80 (all in U.S. dollars):

a. Construct a total cost graph for the three alternatives.

b. What alternative would Bernd Hacker choose if the sales volume for the golf clubs is expected to be 5,000 units?

c. What would be the best alternative of the sales volume for the golf clubs if they will be between 2,000 and 3,000?

24. Ergonomics Kitchen Cabinetry has designed a new Lazy Susan wooden cabinet and needs to choose a new production method. The process types the fictional company can choose from and their associated cost data are provided in the following table:

Process Type	Annualized Fixed Cost of Plant and Equipment (in U.S. dollars)	Variable Cost per Unit (in U.S. dollars)		
		Labor	Materials	Energy
Intermittent	1,000,000	40	32	20
Continuous	2,200,000	25	24	11
Repetitive	1,700,000	30	19	14
Mass customization	1,300,000	27	20	15

The expected annual demand for the new Lazy Susan cabinet is 25,000 units, and each unit of Lazy Susan will sell for $200.

a. Which process type will maximize profit for producing this cabinet, and what is the value of this annual profit?

b. Which process type is the best if the annual demand is between 15,000 and 20,000 units?

CRITICAL THINKING EXERCISES

1. Suppose you have been hired to improve a hospital layout. Choose any nine departments of the hospital, and develop a Muther's grid for them. Explain your preferences for rating the relationships between departments. For example, if you chose an "A" rating (Absolutely Necessary) for the relationship between the emergency room and the hospital's front entrance area, explain why.

2. Develop a service blueprint for an automobile service shop. Make sure you identify potential service failure points in your service blueprint.

CHAPTER
10

Supplier Management

LEARNING OBJECTIVES

After studying this chapter, you should be able to:

1. Identify the goals of supplier management.

2. Describe the various tasks of the supplier management process and demonstrate how metrics are used to rate supplier performance.

3. Evaluate the issues involved in managing service providers.

4. Describe the unique challenges involved in managing global suppliers.

5. Identify some reasons why firms actively promote ethically and socially responsible behavior in supplier management.

OPERATIONS PROFILE: Factory Fires: Fixing the Garment Supplier Pipeline

STR/AFP/Getty Images

The year 2012 was a bad one for suppliers of clothing for the fashion industry. On November 24, a fire broke out at the Tazreen Fashions plant (Tazreen Fashions Ltd., Dhaka, Bangladesh), a Bangladesh garment factory located outside the capital of Dhaka. The fire killed 112 people and injured several hundred others. The factory made clothing for Wal-Mart Stores Inc. (Bentonville, AR) and Sears (Sears, Roebuck & Co., Hoffman Estates, IL), as well as designer labels Sean John (New York City, NY), ENYCE (Sean John, New York City, NY), C&A (Cofra Holding AG, Vilvoorde, Belgium), and other brands. The death toll was surprisingly high because the factory did not have fire escapes, sprinklers, or other safety equipment. Even worse, managers padlocked doors and directed workers to remain at their stations while the fire raged. In September, a fire at a garment factory in Karachi, Pakistan, killed 264 people. Again, the factory had no emergency doors, no extra stairways, and no easy exits from the building. The youngest casualty of this disaster was just 10 years old. Seventeen more fires wreaked havoc on Bangladeshi textile and garment factories in the four weeks following the Tazreen fire.

At the time, Bangladesh had grown to become the world's third-largest exporter of apparel after China and Vietnam; the textile and apparel manufacturing industries have estimated export sales of US$21 billion annually. Bangladesh has some of the lowest wages for garment workers in the world: just US$43 per month. In the immediate aftermath of the Dhaka fire, then-Wal-Mart CEO and president Mark Duke stated, "We're still stepping back again and saying, 'What else can we do?'" But the *New York Times* reported that, in 2011, Wal-Mart officials had resisted improving the safety standards at its suppliers' factories in Bangladesh. Why? Because, said a Wal-Mart official at the time, raising safety standards would be a "very extensive and costly modification."

Clearly, Wal-Mart's policy of keeping its thousands of suppliers at arm's length was becoming a liability. In 2013, the company and other major corporations announced a series of steps to improve the working conditions at their suppliers' factories and those of their subcontractors. Wal-Mart dramatically increased its supervision of overseas suppliers and severed ties with suppliers that had subcontracted work to less-safe factories without the retailer's knowledge.

Wal-Mart's tougher policies replaced its former "three strikes" approach with its suppliers, but this is only a first step. To curtail the use of non-approved suppliers, the company is publishing on its website the names of factories not authorized to do business with its suppliers. The goal is to be sure that Wal-Mart's suppliers can't claim they did not know the banned firms weren't allowed to work on products being sold to the retailer. Wal-Mart also announced it would audit its suppliers before doing business with them and that it will require factories, such as those in Bangladesh, to implement additional safety measures. Suppliers must also station their own employees at subcontractors' factories rather than relying on third-party agents to monitor them. "We want the right accountability and ownership to be in the hands of the suppliers," said Rajan Kamalanathan, Wal-Mart's vice president of ethical sourcing. "We are placing our orders in good faith."

Other major retailers have also taken steps to better manage their garment suppliers. After Tommy Hilfiger (Phillips-Van Heusen Corporation, New York City, NY) learned that 29 workers had died in a fire at one of its suppliers' factories in Bangladesh, the retailer worked with Bangladeshi labor-rights groups to develop more stringent safety standards for its suppliers and provided nearly US$2 million in funding to enforce the standards. Tommy Hilfiger also convinced The Gap, Inc. (San Francisco, CA), another retailer that had contracted with factories that put workers' lives at risk, to sign on to the same standards.[1]

As this profile suggests, supplier management is both a critical component of an organization's operations function as well as a very complicated piece in the supply chain puzzle. This chapter explores the important elements of supplier management.

10.1

Identify the goals of supplier management.

▶ Goals of Supplier Management

10.1 Supplier Management and Its Goals

Supplier management is a business process that enables a company to identify and select the best possible suppliers and negotiate the best possible prices for the resources it purchases from them. Many companies refer to supplier management as purchasing, procurement, or vendor management. The resources a company acquires from a vendor can be tangible (physical goods) or intangible, such as services and information. For example, for a plastics company, the suppliers could be those who supply raw materials such as poly vinyl chloride (PVC), resins, and color pigments. Nevertheless, the company will also need nontangible supplies such as transportation for its products, banking, and internet services. Managing suppliers is equally important for service organizations as it is for manufacturers. Like manufacturers, service firms purchase both tangible products and intangible products. Done properly, supplier management will not only ensure that a company is working with the best possible network of suppliers but that all companies in the network remain profitable.

The main goals of supplier management are to ensure that the supplies a firm acquires: (a) meet their quality standards, (b) are available when needed, and (c) minimize their cost, and that the supply chain (d) fosters sustainability, (e) promotes ethical behavior, and (f) develops innovative products and processes. Let's examine these goals in more detail.

Meeting Quality Standards

A product's final quality is determined to a great extent by the quality of the materials and components that go into it. For many companies, such as automobile manufacturers, medical device makers, and food manufacturers, the quality of the materials they buy from their suppliers is the key to their reputation and profitability. Any problems with the quality can lead to factory shutdowns and quickly result in stock-outs and lost sales. Consider, for example, the problem Toyota (Toyota Motor Corporation, Toyota City, Japan) had with accelerator pedals and brakes in several of its automobile models that were manufactured between 2009 and 2011. The problem was caused by substandard parts and components provided by Toyota's suppliers. For a period of time, the reputation that Toyota worked so hard to build over the decades took a serious hit.

The lesson learned from the Toyota fiasco is that every manufacturer must have a systematic process of verifying that the materials and components purchased from its suppliers meet its quality standards.[2] Furthermore, the **cost of poor quality (COPQ)**, such as the extra materials and production costs associated with scrap and rework, can make up a significant portion of an organization's expenses. Given the adverse effect that poor quality supplies can have, many companies worldwide now require their suppliers be prequalified by having ISO 9001 (International Organization for Standardization) or some other type of quality certification (see Chapter 5).

Making Deliveries on Time

Cost of poor quality (COPQ): additional production and material expenses incurred as a result of scrap and rework

It is critical that materials and other resources are delivered on time if a firm is to meet its manufacturing production schedules and, hence, the demand for the finished products it sells. Any production stoppage as a result of shortages of raw materials or components will lead to delays and lost revenue. In addition, if a manufacturer's equipment and labor remain idle because resources are unavailable, the company incurs losses from the idle time. The massive earthquake and tsunami that struck Japan's east coast in 2011 seriously disrupted supply chains and production schedules for several firms, including Toyota, Sony Corporation (Tokyo, Japan), Honda Motor Co. (Tokyo, Japan), Toshiba Corporation

(Tokyo, Japan), and even Citroen Peugeot of France (Groupe PSA, Paris, France). The disruption was so severe it actually contributed to the decline in the GDP (gross domestic product) for countries in Asia and North America.[3] Similarly, the last global recession left some suppliers insolvent and led to supply-chain disruptions. (We will talk about supply risks in more detail later in the chapter.)

To offset risks such as these, many large manufacturing firms buy raw materials in bulk and maintain inventories of some of their critical resources. Nonetheless, stockpiling supplies is costly and not always a viable option, especially for smaller firms. For this reason, many companies collaborate with established suppliers to guarantee that their manufacturing operations are not disrupted. If a manufacturer is confident

that its suppliers will deliver the supplies it needs when they are needed, then the firm can eliminate bulk buying and reduce the costs associated with carrying unnecessary inventory. For example, collaboration with component suppliers enables Sony Corporation, makers of Xperia smartphones and PlayStation consoles, to successfully operate its just-in-time (JIT) inventory system. In Japan, Sony insists that their component suppliers' warehouses be located in close proximity to Sony factories so they are able to quickly supply Sony with components as and when they are needed. This JIT inventory system decreases Sony's inventory costs, and the costs saved on these components are improving the company's profitability. Sony is using supplier management to cut costs to spur a revival in an industry hit hard by declining demand for televisions, cameras, and personal computers. Sony is working to find new products to capture a consumer shift to mobile devices from Apple Inc. (Cupertino, CA) and Samsung Electronics Co., Ltd. (Suwon, South Korea). As part of their supplier management program, Sony is trimming their current supplier base of more than 1,000 firms to a more responsive and cost-efficient 250 "strategic partners."[4]

Minimizing Costs

The purchases from suppliers often constitute more than 50% of a firm's expenses. The amount spent to acquire its supplies can, to a great extent, determine the firm's financial viability and success. The supplies used to make products are expenses that fall under the category of cost of goods sold (COGS). Any savings achieved in this area will directly affect a firm's bottom line. For example, suppose a company reduces its purchasing costs, and therefore its COGS, by $2 million. If the firm has an 8% margin on sales, then it must sell $25 million in goods to achieve the same $2 million in cost savings ($25 million × .08 = $2 million; all in U.S. dollars).

Reducing the COGS is critical in industries with low profit margins and industries in which it is difficult to increase revenues. The food and grocery industry and the building materials industry are examples. Internet technology and improved global logistics networks have enabled firms in these industries to save millions of dollars in shipping and materials costs. These advancements demonstrate how important supplier management has become.

When determining its supply-related costs, a firm needs to look at the total cost of ownership (TCO) of the supplies—not just their purchase price. The total cost of ownership includes the overall costs (both direct and indirect) associated with purchasing, transporting, handling, inspecting, storing, and insuring the products, and then disposing of them.[5] Also included are the pre-transaction costs of finding suppliers, evaluating and prequalifying them, and then integrating them into the firm's production, IT, and other systems. Post-transaction costs typically are costs of poor quality resulting from poor supplier quality and late deliveries. These costs include the idle time from production shutdowns, scrap and rework, the cost of returns and product recalls, liability and warranty costs, lost sales, and damage to a company's reputation as a result.[6] For example, Toyota's suppliers are able to improve their designs, enhance the quality of the parts and systems they develop for Toyota, and thus minimize waste because Toyota apprises its suppliers of its long-term plans.[7]

The massive earthquake and resulting tsunami in Japan in 2011 caused serious disruptions to supply chains and production schedules for Japanese companies as well as their trading and business partners.

©iStockphoto.com/winhorse

 Why *Supplier Management* **Matters**

Suppliers are a vital link in a company's supply chain; it is important to select the right suppliers and manage them effectively to ensure that they provide quality resources at the lowest possible cost. They also help the company achieve its sustainability goals by providing materials that do not harm the environment, as well as assist the company in developing innovative products and processes.

Cost of goods sold (COGS): expenses incurred from purchasing the supplies used to make products

Total cost of ownership (TCO): the overall costs (both direct and indirect) associated with purchasing, transporting, handling, inspecting, storing and insuring the products, and then disposing of them

OPERATIONS MANAGEMENT: LESSONS LEARNED
"Do You Want Fries With That?" Supplier Management Problems Lead to Horse Meat in Hamburgers

In 2013, the Irish government announced that DNA testing revealed that Polish meat labeled as beef and sold to several frozen-meat suppliers contained up to 80% horse meat. Authorities quickly traced the source of the tainted products to two companies. One was Silvercrest Foods (ABP Food Group, Ardee, Ireland), a frozen meat supplier in Ireland. Tesco PLC (Hertfordshire, England, U.K.), Aldi (Essen, Germany), and The Co-operative Group (Manchester, U.K.), three large supermarket chains that sell a variety of "value range" beef patties, all buy large quantities of their frozen beef products from Silvercrest. After the finding by the Irish government's food inspectors, the companies quickly dropped Silvercrest as a supplier. Burger King (Restaurant Brands International, Oakville, Ontario, Canada), which has stores in England and Ireland and sometimes used Silvercrest meat, also stopped using Silvercrest as a supplier after finding traces of horse DNA in its hamburger meat.

SEBASTIEN BOZON/AFP/Getty Images

The second source of the tainted products, Rangeland Foods Ltd. (Castleblayney, Ireland), conducted its own tests on the burgers it sells to the catering and wholesale industries and found they contained between 5% and 30% horse meat. The company contacted its customers about the discovery after the test results and began pulling meat off shelves.

Silvercrest and Rangeland Foods bought the meat from Irish and British importers, who in turn, contracted with meat packers in Poland. Polish authorities vehemently denied that the contamination occurred in their country, suggesting instead that other parties further up the supply chain may have been guilty of tampering with the food. "Somebody, someplace, is drip-feeding horse meat into the burger-manufacturing industry," notes Alan Reilly, the chief executive of Ireland's food safety authority, "We don't know yet exactly where this is happening."[8] The investigation subsequently led to the discovery across Europe of similar issues in France, Germany, and the Netherlands.

Determining the true, or total, cost of ownership is particularly important but often difficult when a firm contracts with global suppliers. Consider, for example, a U.S. company buying goods from a supplier in Bangladesh. Although the purchase price of the goods may be low because labor costs in Bangladesh are low, there may be other hidden costs. Some of the hidden costs are those related to long lead times and transportation, poor quality, the need to carry inventory because of uncertain delivery times, and the complexity associated with international shipping, such as customs clearance, liquidated damages for delayed unloading of cargo, and security concerns. These costs, along with increasing wages abroad and fluctuating fuel and transportation costs, have led many firms to revert back to using domestic suppliers. Wal-Mart, for example, over the next decade is planning to buy US$50 billion worth of goods from U.S. suppliers for its Wal-Mart and Sam's Club stores.[9]

Developing Better Products and Processes

Economic forces in global markets push firms to improve their products and processes through innovation to remain competitive. Yet, most companies cannot keep pace with the rapid rate of technological advances. In fact, many companies that did their own research and development work in the past are now outsourcing parts of this process to their suppliers.[10] Automakers increasingly rely on their suppliers for innovations to keep them one step ahead of the competition. For example, Faurecia Automotive Seating (The Faurecia Group, Nanterre, France), a supplier of car seats, has developed a smartphone app that enables a vehicle's owners and occupants to use their phones to adjust their seats.[11]

10.2 The Supplier Management Process

10.2 Describe the various tasks of the supplier management process and demonstrate how metrics are used to rate supplier performance.

Figure 10.1 shows the supplier management process. It consists of seven tasks: strategic sourcing, purchasing, supplier performance management, supplier information management, supplier relationship management, supplier risk management, and supplier phase-out.

FIGURE 10.1: The Supplier Management Process

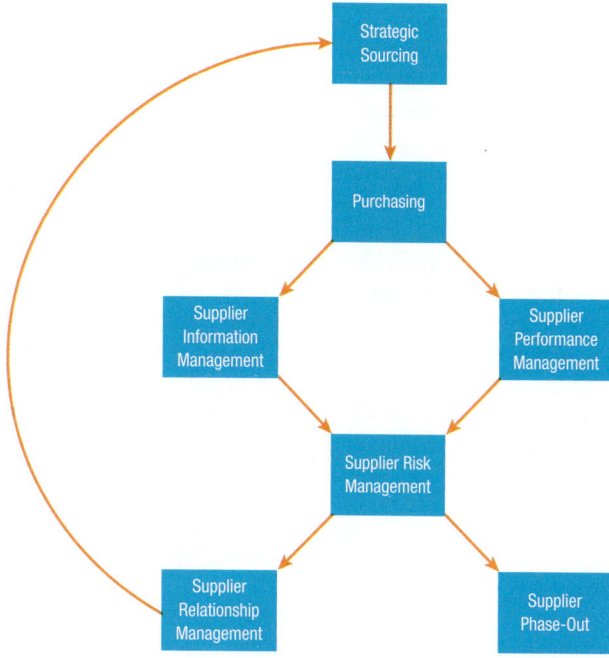

Strategic Sourcing

Strategic sourcing is a systematic process that seeks to align a firm's purchasing strategies with its overall strategy in a cost-effective manner. In contrast to the day-to-day procurement of goods and services, strategic sourcing takes a long-term approach and focuses on working with suppliers to optimize what they can contribute to the organization. Through strategic sourcing, The Walt Disney Company (Burbank, CA) has been able to save hundreds of millions of dollars annually. It has also used its voice to point toward more ethical approaches to sourcing; for example, Disney announced that it will no longer do business with several large paper suppliers in Asia that engage in questionable environmental policies. These firms were charged with endangering the Indonesian rainforest and contributing to the destruction of the habitat. [12]

Strategic Sourcing

The strategic sourcing process consists of the six steps shown in Figure 10.2. [13]

ANALYZING SPENDING PATTERNS

A systematic strategic sourcing process begins with the company collecting, classifying, and analyzing expenditure data as part of a **spend analysis**. [14] The purpose of a spend analysis is to determine:

- What products is the company really spending the most money on?
- Who are the suppliers on whom the company is spending the most money?
- Is the company getting what has been promised for the money spent?

Unfortunately, very few companies systematically organize and analyze their spend data and therefore have no concrete means to answer these three questions. As a result, global firms are losing hundreds of billions annually. These losses reflect the inability of some companies to identify suppliers that provide the best value for the money or result from the failure of suppliers to deliver the required items of appropriate quality on time. On the other hand, for those firms who actively

Spend analysis: an examination of what products and suppliers a company spends the most money on, and if the company is getting what has been promised for the money spent

FIGURE 10.2: The Strategic Sourcing Process

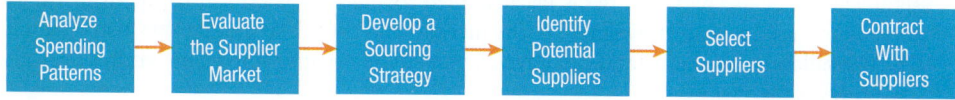

monitor and control their spending, it is estimated that the average company saves 0.25% to 1% on total spend dollars. For a company with $1 billion in spending, this equates to $2.5 million to $10 million in new cost savings every year (all in U.S. dollars).[15] The availability of accurate, timely, complete, and detailed expenditure data and the analysis of those data can provide critical information about procurement spending patterns, supplier compliance and performance ratings, and the status of inventory and parts that can uncover both money-saving opportunities and sourcing strategies.

Businesses that have company-wide spending visibility, which means a clear and comprehensive view of all spending activities including access to all spending data; that use enterprise-wide data classification schemes; that are capable of auditing, detecting, and correcting inaccurate or corrupt records from the data set; and that classify data efficiently have had the most success analyzing their spending.[16] Some large companies that have used aggressive enterprise-wide spend analysis practices have reported savings of more than US$40 million per year.[17] For example, Owens Corning (Toledo, OH), the world's largest manufacturer of fiberglass and related products, developed an enterprise-wide spending analysis capability that allowed the company to access and analyze data on spending and vendor commitments. Owens Corning's analysis led to cost reductions and improved supplier management that saved the company US$2 million annually.[18]

EVALUATING THE SUPPLIER MARKET

The main purpose of evaluating the supplier market is to help a company choose its purchases with greater cost effectiveness as well as minimizing its supply-related risks. In this step, the company gathers the following information:

- The current and the likely future capacity available in the supplier market, such as the number and size of suppliers and where they are concentrated.
- The number, size, demand requirements, and purchasing capacity of the procuring company's competitors.
- The ranking of the procuring company in the supplier market relative to its competitors in terms of current and future purchase volumes, quality requirements, and so forth.

The information gathered can help the company understand the extent of the competition in the market for supplies, whether there are single or multiple sources of supply, and the risks and opportunities involved in entering supplier-buyer relationships. Evaluating the supplier market also involves identifying alternate suppliers in addition to those in the existing pool.

DEVELOPING A SOURCING STRATEGY

The combination of the first two steps—analyzing spending patterns and evaluating the supplier market—provides a company with the information it needs to develop a sourcing strategy. Sourcing strategies can vary significantly by the type of items purchased. Consequently, the firm needs to develop a framework to classify its sourcing strategies based on the different items it purchases. Figure 10.3 is an example of such a framework. The various sourcing strategies are categorized based on the supply risk associated with them—that is, how likely the supplies are to be unavailable—and the impact supplies have on a firm's value or profitability if they aren't available.

- *Noncritical Purchases.* The supply risk for these items is low as is their impact on the firm's profitability. Items such as office supplies fall under this category. The focus of a sourcing strategy for these items is to reduce the costs of purchasing them—that is, to make the purchases routine so employees don't waste a lot of time buying the items. The departments that need the items typically buy them directly from local suppliers using purchasing cards (company-issued credit cards), which simplifies the process.
- *Leveraged Purchases.* These items have a high impact on a firm's value or profitability. Nevertheless, they are nonetheless items a firm can try to save money on because multiple suppliers sell them. The sourcing strategy is to use the firm's purchasing power to consolidate purchases from a few suppliers to achieve volume discounts. Examples of leveraged purchases include bulk chemicals, heating oil, and standardized semi-finished goods such as electric motors.
- *Bottleneck Purchases.* Although the amount of money spent on these items is generally not significant, they are high-risk items because their availability is critical to the firm. Typically, these items are not readily available in the market, and there may not be very many suppliers. The unavailability of these items can have an immediate negative impact on a firm's operations.

FIGURE 10.3: Sourcing Strategies for Different Types of Purchases

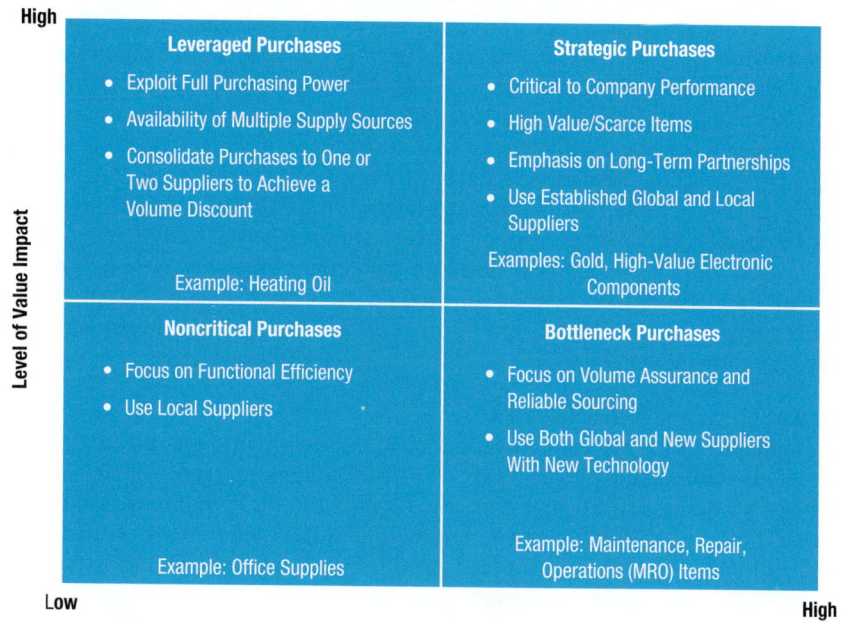

SOURCE: Adapted from Kraljic, P. (1983). Purchasing must become supply management. *Harvard Business Review, 61*(5), 112.

For example, suppose a firm produces hydraulic pumps, which have many components. The non-availability of a specialized check valve can delay production. To get these items, the firm may have to use both existing local and global suppliers and locate new suppliers who have the technology to produce these items.

- *Strategic Purchases.* These items, like the bottleneck items, are critical to the firm because they contribute directly to the company's profitability. Yet, the supply risks associated with them are high because they are unique, may not be readily available in the market, or may have very few suppliers. Alternative fuel engines for the automobile industry are an example. The sourcing strategy for such items typically involves building long-term partnerships with suppliers with a focus on collaboration and innovation.

By using the framework in Figure 10.3, a company can decide in which category its purchases fall. Armed with this information, developing a sourcing strategy involves (a) optimizing the supply base, (b) choosing the location of the suppliers, and (c) determining the nature and length of the contractual relationship

Optimizing the Supply Base

A supply-base optimization means determining the best number of suppliers from which to purchase. On the one hand, too many suppliers may result in a lack of control and make communication more complex. On the other hand, too few suppliers increase a firm's risk of shortages and leave it vulnerable to unexpected price increases. As a result, supply-base optimization does not necessarily mean reducing the number of suppliers. Instead, it is a repeatable process for determining the best number of suppliers for the various types of purchases.[19]

A company opts for a single-sourcing strategy by contracting with a single supplier when purchasing a particular item. Using a single-sourcing strategy enhances the cooperation between

Supply-base optimization: the process of determining the best number of suppliers to purchase from

Single-sourcing strategy: a plan to contract with a single supplier when purchasing a particular item, enhancing the cooperation between the buyer and the supplier

Companies may contract with multiple sources or businesses in the same field to force competition within their supply chain.

©iStockphoto.com/400tmax

the buyer and supplier. Perhaps the supplier has made significant investments in plant and equipment to produce a customized item sold only to the buyer and is also guaranteed a sufficient amount business from the buyer for an extended period of time. Single-sourcing strategies are often used by automakers when they purchase specialty parts such as the types of seats they install in the vehicles they manufacture. When a single-sourcing strategy is used, the supplier must be well-established because the impact on the purchasing firm will be great if the supplier goes out of business.

For bottleneck purchases, a company may want to rely on a multiple-sourcing strategy (use of multiple suppliers) so backup supplies are available. For leveraged purchases, the company could use a single-sourcing strategy or a *dual-sourcing strategy* (buying from just two suppliers) to achieve volume discounts. For example, many retailers dual-source their shipping between UPS (United Parcel Service, Sandy Springs, GA) and Federal Express (FedEx Corporation, Memphis, TN) to force these firms to compete with each other by discounting shipping prices. It has the added benefit of safeguarding against supply chain disruptions should one source experience difficulties; for example, threat of a labor strike or a natural disaster.[20]

Choosing Between Local and Global Suppliers

Despite the expanding global economy and competition, many organizations, particularly small- to-medium-sized companies, still rely on local suppliers located close to them. The close proximity helps a buying firm to invest in and support the local economy and to resolve any problems with the supplier quickly by visiting their facilities. A number of supermarket chains have begun routinely using locally sourced produce as a way of helping local farmers and investing in the communities they service.[21]

Sometimes firms rely on local suppliers simply because they are unfamiliar with the global supplier market. Nonetheless, advances in communication technology and e-commerce have made it easy for companies to gather information on any supplier, local or global, and their prices, delivery times, and customer service. Being able to take advantage of lower labor costs around the globe, and the manufacturing specialization that exists in some regions, such as electronics production in the Far East, can provide firms with a competitive advantage.

Global sourcing has some disadvantages, though. In some markets, it may be cheaper to buy from local suppliers. It is often difficult to achieve on-time or speedy delivery if your firm is buying supplies abroad. Exchange-rate fluctuations, import duties, customs clearance, the protection of intellectual property rights, and problems with quality can also be drawbacks. We will talk more about global sourcing later in the chapter.

Determining the Nature and Length of the Buyer-Supplier Relationship

The nature and duration of the buyer-supplier relationship depends on the item being purchased. In general, buyer-supplier relationships can be broadly classified into one of the three categories shown in Figure 10.4.

Transactional relationships are simple buy-and-sell exchanges of goods or services. They are typical for noncritical or one-time purchases, as is the case for commodities that can be purchased from hundreds of suppliers. To purchase these items, companies only need to have a purely transactional relationship with their suppliers that is based on price. Very little effort goes into these purchases, and there are rarely any cost savings in these transactions.[22]

Buyers and suppliers enter into *collaborative relationships* if there is a significant degree of mutual benefit to both parties. Perhaps the savings from doing so is significant or major product innovations can be achieved if the two companies collaborate. Early supplier involvement is typical in most collaborative relationships, particularly when the parties are seeking product innovations.[23]

Strategic alliances are the highest level of collaborative relationships between the buyer and the supplier. In strategic alliances, the firms share knowledge and expertise, expenses and risks. An example of a strategic alliance is a joint venture. In a joint venture, the two firms create an independent company by sharing their resources and capabilities. A joint venture is typically used when both firms are seeking a competitive advantage or are hoping to reduce the risk when venturing into new markets. Microsoft Corporation (Redmond, WA) and Oculus VR, LLC (Menlo Park, CA), the maker of virtual reality goggles, announced a partnership in which Microsoft provides an Xbox controller with

Multiple-sourcing strategy: a plan to contract with several suppliers to ensure that backup supplies are available

Joint venture: a strategic alliance in which two firms create an independent company by sharing their resources and capabilities

FIGURE 10.4: The Buyer-Supplier Relationship Continuum

Transactional Relationship — Collaborative Relationship — Strategic Alliance

every purchase of the Oculus Rift headset. They are also allowing purchasers the ability to stream Xbox One games to the virtual reality device. The benefits to both companies are huge: Microsoft gets a head start on its game device competitors into the virtual reality marketplace and Oculus Rift, a small start-up firm, gets the brand recognition that comes from Microsoft.[24]

A strategic alliance common among Japanese businesses is the Keiretsu network. In a Keiretsu network, manufacturers and their suppliers of raw materials and components form a coalition. Many Japanese automobile companies such as Toyota, Honda, and Nissan (Nissan Motor Company Ltd (Yokohama, Japan) belong to Keiretsu networks. The companies in these networks maintain long-term relationships and collaborate as partners by providing mutual financial support and technical expertise to one another.

IDENTIFYING POTENTIAL SUPPLIERS

After developing a sourcing strategy (see Figure 10.2), the buyer needs to identify a set of potential suppliers. The process of identifying potential suppliers will depend on the extent of value added and the supply risk of the items to be purchased (see Figure 10.3). For noncritical and lower-cost items, suppliers can be identified by searching locally, on the internet, or in trade magazines and directories. For high-value or high-risk purchases, the buying company should develop a set of criteria used to identify, prequalify, and select suppliers. Table 10.1 lists examples of supplier selection criteria.

SELECTING SUPPLIERS

The process of selecting suppliers begins with the buying company preparing a request for proposal (RFP), which is sometimes called a request for quotation (RFQ), and sending it to potential suppliers. An RFP includes details such as the specifications for the product being purchased, its quality requirements, delivery and service requirements, evaluation criteria, pricing, and shipping and payment terms. To generate interest among suppliers and to be sure that all of them compete on a level playing field, the buying firm should have a plan indicating how it will communicate with suppliers during the RFP process.[25] The plan, which is an internal document, should identify the buying company's goals and objectives, the steps in the communication process, and the policy for sending key messages to and from the suppliers.

Depending on the type of items being purchased and the amount of money being spent on them, the buying organization can use one of the following approaches to select its suppliers: competitive bidding, online reverse auctions, and negotiation.

Competitive Bidding. With competitive bidding, the buying firm publishes its RFP or RFQ electronically, and each interested supplier submits a bid, usually also electronically. Competitive bidding is used when:

- A large enough pool of qualified suppliers is available to make the bidding competitive, and the buyer-supplier relationship is transactional.
- The items are standardized, are in the mature stage of their product life cycle, and have well-defined specifications.
- The price is the predominant selection criterion, and the amount spent on the purchase will be high enough to generate competition among potential suppliers.

If the spending level on the item is high enough, the buying organization might want to create a cross-functional team to carefully evaluate each bid against the requirements specified in the RFP. The cross-functional team might also visit the suppliers' facilities to evaluate the quality of their operations and processes, financial viability, credibility and reputation in the market, delivery and technical capabilities, managerial style, sustainability practices, labor climate and attitudes, culture, and their strategic direction.

 Selecting a Supplier

Keiretsu network: a strategic alliance common among Japanese businesses in which manufacturers and their suppliers of raw materials and components form a coalition

Request for proposal (RFP): a document prepared by a buying company and sent to potential suppliers detailing the specifications for the product being purchased, its quality requirements, delivery and service requirements, evaluation criteria, pricing, and shipping and payment terms

Request for quotation (RFQ): See request for proposal

Competitive bidding: the process of allowing interested suppliers to review a company's RFP or RFQ electronically and submitting a bid for the job

TABLE 10.1: Selection Criteria for Potential Suppliers

• Price or products	• Commitment to sustainability
• Product and service quality	• Financial stability
• Product safety	• Flexibility and agility
• Delivery reliability	• Prior experience and past performance
• Service support	• Technical capabilities

When multiple suppliers provide bids, choosing the right supplier is not always easy. In situations such as this, the buyer can use tools such as the Analytic Hierarchy Process (AHP), optimization models, and factor rating method to help in the selection process. AHP is a decision methodology that uses a hierarchy of criteria against which each decision alternative (such as different suppliers) is evaluated. Optimization models are mathematical models that enable the buyer to choose the best alternative under a given set of constraints (such as scarce resources). In the context of supplier selection, in the factor rating method relative weights are assigned to factors relevant in selecting a supplier. Next, each supplier for each factor is then rated by assigning a score (say between 0 and 100). For each factor and each supplier, a score is computed by multiplying the factor rating and the supplier rating. A total score is computed for each supplier by summing up the scores calculated in the previous step. The supplier that has the maximum total score is the preferred supplier. We discussed the factor rating method in Chapter 7 for making location decisions. The following example will show you how to use the factor rating method to select a supplier.

EXAMPLE 10.1: Tri-Star Technologies' (El Segundo, CA) cross-functional team is planning to outsource the production of an electronic component needed for its products. The company has identified three potential suppliers and the critical supplier criteria (factors). Tri-Star has also assigned factor weights ranging from 0 to 1 to reflect the relative importance of each factor. The team has also developed scores (1 to 100) to rate the three suppliers on the various criteria. The factors, their weights, and the scores for each supplier are listed in the table. Which supplier should the company select?

FACTOR	WEIGHT	SCORE		
		SUPPLIER A	SUPPLIER B	SUPPLIER C
Delivery Reliability	0.1	80	70	60
Purchase Price	0.1	50	70	60
Quality Performance	0.5	60	60	70
Technological Capabilities	0.3	50	60	70
Total	1.0			

SOLUTION

- For each factor and each supplier, compute a score by multiplying the factor rating score and the weight assigned to the factor.
- Compute a total score for each supplier by summing up the scores calculated in the previous step.
- Select the supplier that has the highest total score.

The calculations are shown below:

Factor	Weight	SCORE			WEIGHTED SCORE		
		Supplier A	Supplier B	Supplier C	Supplier A	Supplier B	Supplier C
Delivery Reliability	0.1	80	70	60	80×0.1=8.0	70×0.1=7.0	60×0.1=6.0
Purchase Price	0.1	50	70	60	50×0.1=5.0	70×0.1=7.0	60×0.1=6.0
Quality Performance	0.5	60	60	70	60×0.5=30.0	60×0.5=30.0	70×0.5=35.0
Technological Capabilities	0.3	50	60	70	50×0.3=15.0	60×0.3=18.0	70×0.3=21.0
Total	1.0				58.0	62.0	**68.0**

Supplier C has the highest total score and therefore should be selected.

Online Reverse Auctions. An **online reverse auction** is an e-procurement solution for selecting suppliers. It was first introduced by General Electric (GE, Fairfield, CT) in the 1990s and has been used extensively for sourcing since then. In online reverse auctions, the roles of buyers and suppliers are reversed. Instead of buyers competing with each other and bidding up the price of a product as in a regular auction, suppliers compete for the buyer's business by offering their products or services at lower and lower prices. The buyer allows qualified suppliers to submit online competitive bids for supplying products or services whose various attributes have been specified by the buyer.

There are four types of online reverse auctions:

- *Sealed-bid, first-price auction.* Within a specified time period, each potential supplier submits a sealed secret bid online in response to the buyer's RFQ. The buyer opens the sealed bids at the expiration of the auction time period and awards the contract to the supplier with the lowest price.
- *English auction.* The bidding starts with the buyer listing an initial price for the item it wants to buy. Suppliers then submit their bids and the auction continues as long as each successive bid is lower than the previous bid. The contract is awarded to the supplier with the last lowest bid. In an English auction, all of the suppliers are able to see the current lowest bid as the auction progresses.
- *Dutch auctions.* The buyer starts with an initial low price and then gradually raises the price of the item until one of the suppliers agrees to provide it at that price.
- *Second-price (Vickrey) auction.* Each potential supplier submits a sealed bid in response to the buyer's RFQ. The contract is awarded to the supplier that bids the lowest price, but the contract price is set at the level quoted by the *second-lowest* bid. It is a win–win situation for both the buyer and the supplier because the buyer is able to select the supplier willing to bid the lowest, but the supplier is able to increase its profit margin by being awarded the contract for a price higher than the price it quoted.

Online reverse auctions offer buyers several advantages: The intense competition among suppliers allows the buyer to realize large savings. The auction can also be completed in a very short period of time once suppliers agree to participate. In addition, many online-reverse-auction websites already have suppliers registered to place bids. This registered listing helps buyers to expand their supplier bases and contact multiple suppliers simultaneously. Buyers can also scan the suppliers on a site and decide which of them should be invited to participate in the auctions.

Online reverse auctions have disadvantages, though. First, because price is the primary focus of competitive bidding, there is potential for distrust and deterioration of the buyer–supplier relationship. In addition, the pressure to provide increasingly lower bids can result in quality problems throughout the supply chain. For example, when a supplier wins a competitive bid to supply cotton gloves, it may have to cut its costs to maintain its profit margin. Its cotton suppliers are then stressed to maintain *their* margins, leading to cheaper quality materials or lowered standards for growing the cotton. At every stage in the supply chain, there are ripple effects tied to the lower cost of the winning bid. Despite these disadvantages, online reverse auctions do offer an alternative approach to sourcing goods and services, and the potential cost savings can have a significant impact on a company's operations.[26] General Electric and Quaker Oats Company (Chicago, IL) are among just a few of the companies that have been able to save millions of dollars on their procurement costs by using them.

Negotiation. During a **negotiation**, the buyer and the supplier bargain on the contractual terms of a purchase, such as its price, payment terms, and delivery. Negotiated contracts are generally used for strategic purchases or if there is only a single supplier of an item or a supplier that is particularly qualified to provide it. Negotiation is also desirable if there is a high degree of supply risk or if early supplier involvement is required, as in the case of new product development.

Negotiation can lead to favorable outcomes only if both the buyer and the supplier perceive that there is value to be gained by entering into a contractual relationship. Any difference in value to be gained between the buyer and the supplier is called the **bargaining surplus**. The purpose of negotiation is for each party to gain as much of this bargaining surplus as possible. Both the buyer and the supplier should have a clear idea of the value each party brings to the relationship to estimate the bargaining surplus. Once both parties have set a value on the bargaining surplus, the next step is to arrive at a fair and equitable distribution of this surplus based on the extent of contribution made or the extent of supply risk each party assumes. Ideally, the buyer and supplier should negotiate on multiple elements of the contract, not just the price, because doing so provides opportunities for compromise. For example, if the buyer is more concerned about the quality and delivery time of the purchases than

Online reverse auctions: an e-procurement solution for selecting suppliers in which suppliers compete for the buyer's business by offering their products or services at lower and lower prices

Negotiation: a process in which a buyer and supplier bargain on the contractual terms of a purchase, such as its price, payment terms, and delivery

Bargaining surplus: any difference in value to be gained between the buyer and the supplier

Negotiations between buyers and suppliers can be used strategically if both parties agree on the value of entering into the agreement.

©iStockphoto.com/Christopher Futcher

the price, and the supplier cannot lower the price but can improve its delivery times, negotiating on all the three factors—the price, quality, and delivery time—can benefit both parties.[27]

CONTRACTING WITH SUPPLIERS

When implementing sourcing decisions, the winning supplier or suppliers are notified and invited to participate in developing the supply contract that put into writing the decisions upon which both parties have agreed. A supply or purchase contract formally specifies the terms of the buyer–supplier relationship and the contract's performance requirements. There are two basic types of supply or purchase contracts: *fixed-price* and *cost-plus contracts*.

A fixed-price contract sets a price that is not subject to any change regardless of changes in the external environment, such as economic fluctuations, competition, or variations in market prices or supply levels. A fixed-price contract also includes a fair and reasonable incentive and a ceiling that requires the contractor to assume an appropriate share of the risk. Buyers and suppliers usually enter into fixed-price contracts when definite specifications of the items being purchased are available and the supplier can estimate the cost of producing these items with reasonable accuracy. The administrative burden of signing a fixed-price contract is small. Yet, the contract subjects the supplier to a maximum amount of financial risk in the event of cost escalations and the buyer to a financial loss if the market price of the products drop. To demonstrate, suppose that a buyer enters into a three-year, fixed-price contract for liquid natural gas (LNG). After 12 months, new sources of LNG have significantly lowered the market price for the commodity. Under a fixed-price contract, the buyer is locked in at the higher price.

A cost-plus contract allows a supplier to be paid in full for all reasonable expenses incurred up to a preset limit as well as an additional sum so that the supplier realizes a profit on the transaction. These types of contracts also include an incentive for the contractor to manage the contract effectively. Cost-plus contracts are typically used when the purchases are complex or expensive and there is uncertainty about what material and labor required to produce the product will cost. Although cost-plus contracts typically favor suppliers because they have low financial risk, cost-plus contracts can also benefit the buyer by lowering overall costs if the contract is managed carefully. For example, because of the technical challenges involved, the United States Air Force and Lockheed Martin (Bethesda, MD) signed a cost-plus contract with Rolls-Royce Holdings plc (London, U.K.) to produce an engine used in the F-35 Lightning II fighter jet.[28]

In addition to cost-plus contracts, three other types of contracts are commonly used to help buyers and sellers share the risks of entering into an agreement:[29]

- **Buyback contracts.** Also referred to as *returns contracts*, buyback contracts include a buyback or returns clause that allows the supplier to buy back some of the buyer's unsold inventory up to a specified amount at an agreed-upon price. Buyback contracts are usually appropriate for products with little variable costs, such as software, music, or books. For example, a college bookstore can enter into a buyback contract with a book publisher and return the unsold books back to the publisher. The publisher, in turn, can take back the books and sell them in the future once the demand goes up. Buyback contracts encourage a buyer to purchase more from the supplier and sell the goods, thereby increasing the profit potential of both parties.

- **Revenue-sharing contracts.** Under a revenue-sharing contract, the supplier charges a lower price for the items being purchased but also shares in a percentage of the buyer's revenue. As with buyback contracts, the lower price encourages buyers to purchase more, thus increasing the product's availability, which can lead to higher profits for both the supplier and the buyer. In addition, the lower initial purchase price also reduces the buyer's cost of overstocking. For example, Redbox (Redbox Automated Retail, LLC, Oakbrook Terrace, IL), the automated DVD and Blu-ray disc rental company with greater than 35,000 kiosks located around the United States, entered into revenue-sharing agreements with a number of the major movie studios, such as NBCUniversal, Inc. (New York City, NY). Redbox agreed to pay a portion of

Fixed-price contract: an agreement in which set prices are not subject to any change regardless of changes in the external environment

Cost-plus contracts: an agreement that allows a supplier to be paid in full for all reasonable expenses incurred up to a preset limit as well as an additional sum so that the supplier realizes a profit on the transaction

Buyback contract: an agreement that includes a buyback or returns clause that allows the supplier to buy back some of the buyer's unsold inventory up to a specified amount at an agreed-upon price (also known as a returns contract)

its rental income in exchange for a reduction in the initial purchase price of the DVDs from NBCUniversal. NBCUniversal also agreed to make their movies available to Redbox within 28 days following their home entertainment release.[30]

- **Quantity-flexibility contracts**. Under these contracts, the buyer has the flexibility to change the quantity purchased based on the buyer's updated demand forecasts for the product. Automakers such as Ford (Ford Motor Company, Dearborn, MI) and Maruti (Maruti Suzuki India Limited, New Delhi, India) and companies in the high-tech industries typically enter into these types of contracts with their suppliers.

The type of contract will vary depending on whether the supplier is a current or new supplier to the buyer. The contracts for current suppliers should reflect any changes in specifications, expectations for improvements in the delivery or service requirements, or pricing. For new suppliers, in addition to preparing a new contract, the buyer should use a communication plan to manage the transition from the old supplier to the new supplier. The communications plan should include every department of the buyer's organization that is affected by the spend category. It is particularly important to monitor the new supplier's performance closely during the first several weeks to see that it is equal to or better than the previous supplier.

The six-step strategic sourcing process shown in Figure 10.2 offers both buyers and suppliers opportunities to improve supply chains. Nonetheless, this process should be implemented carefully. First, the strategic sourcing process should be well documented. Otherwise, without clear procedural guidelines, performance expectations, and obligations spelled out, the process can stagnate and the desired goals may not be achieved. Second, the process should have deliverables that can be measured and reported to demonstrate the contribution of strategic sourcing to achieving business objectives and improving the bottom line. Third, throughout the sourcing process, all new information should be documented. Information in this instance can refer to any changes in supplier marketplace dynamics such as new entrants, supplier contracts, and any learning that has occurred during the process. Fourth, the sourcing process should have a well-established timeline so that tasks can be easily scheduled. Finally, it is important to verify that the suppliers and the buyer's purchasing department comply with the performance terms that were agreed upon during the sourcing process. For example, the suppliers' performance should be measured against clearly defined metrics. In addition, the purchasing department must maintain contact with the suppliers on an ongoing basis to solidify the relationship.[31]

Purchasing

The second task of the supplier management process shown in Figure 10.1 is purchasing. The purchasing process begins when the buyer creates a **purchase order** (PO) and sends it to the supplier. Purchase orders normally include the terms and conditions specified in the contract between the buyer and supplier. The purchase order authorizes the supplier to produce and ship the item and send the invoice to the buying company afterward.

There are several types of POs:[32]

- **Standard purchase orders** are used for one-time purchases.
- **Planned purchase orders** are used for purchases to be made on approximate dates at specified quantities when inventories run low.
- **Blanket purchase orders** are used for long-term purchases made on multiple delivery dates scheduled over a period of time.

The purchasing process typically uses online and automated tools such as e-mail, fax, an enterprise resource planning (ERP) system, electronic data interchange (EDI), or e-procurement. Fewer companies are sending purchase orders via the mail and fax because doing so is relatively more labor intensive and slower than e-procurement. In the past, companies have used e-procurement for purchasing relatively inexpensive items and the non-automated approach for purchasing expensive products. Nevertheless, companies as diverse as insurance, heavy manufacturing, banking, and real estate firms have realized the benefits of e-procurement even for high-value purchases. When the goods are received, the buyer cross-checks the invoice against the purchase order to be sure the items are in the right condition, in the proper quantity, and that their price on the invoice is accurate. If everything is accurate, the supplier is then paid.

Material purchases fall into two major categories: **direct materials purchases** and **indirect materials purchases**. Direct materials are materials that are *directly* incorporated to the production of

Quantity-flexibility contract: an agreement in which the buyer has the flexibility to change the quantity purchased based on the buyer's updated demand forecasts for the product

Purchase order: a form that includes the terms and conditions specified in the contract between the buyer and supplier and authorizes the supplier to produce and ship the item and send the invoice to the buying company afterward

Standard purchase order: a purchase order used for one-time purchases

Planned purchase order: a purchase order for purchases to be made on approximate dates at specified quantities when inventories run low.

Blanket purchase order: a purchase order used for long-term purchases made on multiple delivery dates scheduled over a period of time

Direct materials purchase: the purchase of materials that are directly incorporated to the production of finished goods and include most raw materials and components

Indirect materials purchase: the purchase of materials not directly used in the finished product but that support their production

finished goods and include most raw materials and components. They are part of the finished product, and the amount of their usage can be tracked on a per-product basis. Examples of direct materials are microchips for high-technology manufacturers; bricks, lumber, shingles, and siding for house construction; and a fiberglass or metal reflector for a satellite dish. Because of the high impact direct material purchases have on a firm's profit margins, developing close relationships with the suppliers of these materials is essential.

Indirect materials, by contrast, are materials not directly used in the finished product but that support their production. Replacement parts, maintenance items such as oil for machinery, and office products used for administrative purposes are examples of indirect materials. Although the percentage of money spent on indirect materials is typically not as high as the percentage spent on direct materials, it can still be significant. For example, in 2011, GM (General Motors Company, Detroit, MI) spent US$77 billion on direct material purchases and US$9 billion on indirect material purchases.

Supplier Performance Management

The third task of supplier management is managing the performance of a company's suppliers. Historically, companies in the manufacturing sector have used **supplier scorecards**, like the one in Figure 10.5, to rank their suppliers and track their performance improvement over time. A supplier scorecard contains measures used to evaluate the performance of suppliers. For the measures to be meaningful, they should be derived from the buyer's corporate goals. For example, if a corporate goal is to deliver quality products to its customer, one of the supplier performance measures must gauge the delivery of high quality and defect-free materials or components. On the other hand, if the corporate goal is to provide goods and services to customers quickly and respond quickly to changes in demand, the metrics must be used to evaluate delivery speed, on-time delivery, and a supplier's ability to respond to last-minute order changes.

Each measure is assigned a percentage weight that reflects its importance, and the weighted category scores are then combined into an overall score for each supplier that appears on the scorecard. The information on the scorecard can also be used when the company negotiates with its suppliers.

Rather than just using scorecards, some companies are taking a more comprehensive approach called *supplier performance management (SPM)* to improve their supply chains. SPM is a continuous process of assessing suppliers and their capabilities, monitoring and evaluating their performance, and identifying areas for improvement. The SPM process requires uninterrupted information exchanges that synchronize the buyer's requirements with the supplier's capabilities. The focus of SPM is to resolve problems between buyers and suppliers before they become conflicts that need to be resolved. For example, to be sure that suppliers are complying with environmental, health, and safety (EHS) regulations, Hewlett-Packard (HP Inc., Palo Alto, CA) uses an integrated corrective action management approach as part of their SPM process to quickly resolve any EHS deficiencies. HP allows a supplier 30, 180, or 360 days to resolve the problem based on the severity of the deficiency. To foster open communication, HP encourages its suppliers to identify deficiencies and collaborates with them to resolve problems.[33] Designing and implementing more meaningful performance metrics, identifying unusual supply situations, and minimizing supply disruptions are all aspects of supplier management.

To implement an SPM process, a buyer should take the following steps:[34]

1. Develop an SPM strategy that aligns with the firm's corporate objectives.
2. Develop the performance criteria suppliers should meet.
3. Choose appropriate performance evaluation tools and identify the steps for collecting, monitoring, and measuring the performance of suppliers.
4. Collect qualitative and quantitative data and determine the timeframes (monthly, quarterly, so on) for collecting them.
5. Analyze the performance data against the criteria and communicate the results to suppliers and other stakeholders.
6. Collaborate with suppliers to identify areas of improvement and set improvement goals with them.
7. Periodically review and recalibrate the goals, strategy, and metrics to respond to changing business needs.

Supplier scorecard: a form that contains measures used to evaluate the performance of suppliers

The buying company should maintain an SPM database to not only analyze the performance trends of individual suppliers over time but to also compare the performance of many suppliers over time.

FIGURE 10.5: Example of a Supplier Scorecard

SUPPLIER RATING SCORE CARD

Company Name/Logo

Supplier: _____ Assessment Period: _____

RATING ELEMENT / PERSPECTIVE	RATING*	WEIGHT	SCORE	COMMENTS
Quality Performance				
• Material Acceptance (Conformance to requirements specified on Purchase Orders, Drawings, and associated Standards/Specifications)		X 7.0		
• Responsiveness to Issues (Timeliness & Effectiveness of Corrective Actions)		X 4.0		
(55 points max) Subtotal				
Cost and Service Performance				
• Price Competitiveness & Value Added		X 1.0		
• On-Time Delivery		X 3.0		
• Lead Time & Cycle Time		X 1.0		
• Ease of Doing Business (i.e. Requesting Quotes, Placing Orders, Tracking Status, Flexibility, Response to Changes & other Requests)		X 1.0		
• Accuracy & Timeliness of Paperwork/Data (i.e. Quotes, Packing Slips, Invoices)		X 1.0		
(35 points max) Subtotal				
Supplier Capability				
• Production Capability		X 1.0		
• Infrastructure (i.e. Quality, Manuf, Admin, Systems, Culture)		X 1.0		
(10 points max) Subtotal				

(100 points max) Total Earned Score ☐ Overall Rating ☐

QA Concurrence | Purchasing Concurrence | Production Control Concurrence

*Ratings (as a % of max points)	1= Unacceptable 0-39%	2=Needs Improvement 40-59%	3=Average 60-79%	4=Above Average 80-89%	5=Excellent 90-100%	Rev. TBD MMDDYY

Note: Colors were removed to comply with QMD Conference Paper Submittal Guidelines. Add colors (Red, Tan, Yellow, Green, and Blue) to the Scale and Scores.

SUPPLIER PERFORMANCE RATINGS – RANKING

Company Name/Logo

Supplier Type: _____ Assessment Period: _____

RATING ELEMENT / PERSPECTIVE	Maximum Points	Supplier A	Supplier B	Supplier C	Supplier D	Supplier E
Quality Performance • Material Acceptance • Responsiveness to Issues.	55					
Cost and Service Performance • Price Competitiveness & Value Added • On-Time Delivery • Lead Time • Ease of Doing Business • Accuracy & Timeliness of Paperwork	35					
Supplier Capability • Production Capability • Infrastructure	10					
Totals	100					
% Business						
$ Volume						
# Parts						
# Deliveries						
# Different Parts						

QA Concurrence | Purchasing Concurrence | Production Control Concurrence

Ratings Scale (as a % of max points)	1= Unacceptable 0-39%	2=Needs Improvement 40-59%	3=Average 60-79%	4=Above Average 80-89%	5=Excellent 90-100%	Rev TBD MMDDYY

Note: Colors were removed to comply with QMD Conference Paper Submittal Guidelines. Add colors (Red, Tan, Yellow, Green, and Blue) to the Scale and Scores.

SOURCE: Lindsey, M. (2012). Supplier performance ratings – scorecards, rankings, and awarding business. *American Society for Quality.* Retrieved from www.asq-qm .org/resourcesmodule/download.../@random4baa558b6db9c/

OPERATIONS PROFILE:
Coca-Cola: Managing an Orange's Journey to the Customer

Simply Orange Juice may be misnamed because there is nothing simple about it, either in its production or its supply chain. As the maker of Minute Maid and Simply Orange Juice, The Coca-Cola Company (Coke, Atlanta, GA) implemented some sophisticated supplier management processes to increase its market share in the not-from-concentrate orange juice market, for which consumers are willing to pay a 25% premium over frozen concentrated orange juice.

At the world's largest juice bottling plant, situated an hour south of Disney World in Central Florida, Coca-Cola employs an algorithm, known as Black Book, to coordinate its supply chain for orange juice. Black Book is much more than a supply chain coordinating process, however. For example, to analyze customers' preferences, Black Book's algorithm includes detailed data about the more than 600 flavors that all go into the orange. The data are matched to customer preferences for acidity, sweetness, and other attributes of every batch of juice. Using this formula, Coke is able to custom blend its orange juice to maintain its consistency, regardless of where it gets its supplies, when they are picked, or how they are shipped. Black Book also can incorporate weather patterns, cost data, and expected crop yields, enabling Coke to plan for its supplies up to 15 months in advance.

Coke's biggest international partner, Brazil-based Cutrale Group (Rio de Janeiro, Brazil), is its orange juice supplier. Cutrale uses satellites to monitor crops in Brazil and direct the company's growers to pick crops at just the right time and ship them to Florida, where they join oranges that Coke and Cutrale buy from Florida growers every year. Cutrale also constructed a 1.2-mile underground pipeline from its Orlando-based processing plant to Coke's packaging and storage facility. The pipeline replaced 70 tanker trucks required daily to deliver the juice to the Coke processing site.

In peak season, from April to June, oranges can go from grove to glass in less than 24 hours. Using fiber-optic cables, operators at both Coke and Cutrale closely monitor the flow of juice to make sure the pipeline is steady and keeps up with processing and packaging flows; that is, the speed at which orange juice can be processed and put into packages. Black Book verifies that the weekly recipe is constantly adjusted to account for variations in the growing season and quality of the oranges. Cutrale has also constructed enormous silos at the site that store thousands of gallons of orange juice. As a result, whether its summer or winter, Coke always has steady supplies of consistent orange juice for its customers.

From a sustainability perspective, nothing in the orange juice processing cycle is wasted. Cutrale constructed a US$10 million facility to ship orange pulp to China, where it is processed into Minute Maid Pulpy, a citrus drink that is Coke's first billion-dollar brand in China. Oils from the skins of the oranges are bottled and sold as scent, flavoring, and for use in household cleaning supplies. Finally, the peel is pressed into pellets and sold as cattle feed. From start to finish, Coke and its supply chain partners and suppliers have demonstrated through their orange juice processes exactly how to organize and manage a complicated brand management and distribution system through a combination of Black Book and attention to detail.[37]

The main purpose of maintaining an SPM database is to select, reward, and, if necessary, eliminate suppliers with poor-performance records from the company's supply base.[35]

Supplier Information Management

A buying organization should adopt a disciplined approach to collecting and managing basic information about its current and potential future suppliers. Too often, each department or region in large firms handles its own supplier pool; for example, operations has a large set of suppliers they deal with, research and development has their own suppliers, and so on. As a result, the same supplier may exist at several different places and even with different company names. The buying teams across functions or regions may each purchase products from the same supplier—each with different payment terms or prices—without even being aware that other parts of the organization had supplier contracts with them. This problem happens when no one across the departments is coordinating or managing overall supplier information and coordinating shipments or negotiating discounts that can affect multiple groups. When Target (Target Corporation, Minneapolis, MN) left the Canadian market in 2015, one reason cited was its poor supplier management system that frequently left store shelves bare because of their inability to coordinate shipments across their Canadian locations.[36]

To best manage their global supply chain, sourcing, and procurement activities, organizations must be able to quickly answer questions about their suppliers' or vendors' companies, contracts, raw materials, past performance, and safety and environmental compliance records. A formal supplier information program can serve as a central repository of all relevant supplier information used by both the buying organization and the supplier organization to access and maintain information in a collaborative way. Although the nature and type of supplier information required may vary depending on the size and culture of the buying organization, there are some desirable information features that can serve as a standard for a basic supplier information management platform. These features include:

- The supplier's ability to produce quality products at competitive prices.
- The supplier's stability and financial standing.
- The supplier's responsiveness to buying organization needs.
- The supplier's commitment to continuous improvement.
- The supplier's ability to deliver goods and services on time and as promised.
- The supplier's commitment to sustainability improvements and corporate social responsibility.

Tracking and managing supplier information that presents a holistic picture of a firm's suppliers is a complicated undertaking. Often, the information is dispersed across multiple, disconnected systems. The records are also often incomplete and out-of-date, and it can be difficult to segment and prioritize suppliers when the buying organization uses large numbers of them. As a result, the first step in creating a valuable supplier management information system is collecting and updating all supplier information, making it internally consistent (using the same record systems), and ensuring that all vendor and supplier purchases and contacts are centrally controlled.[38]

Supplier Risk Management

Whether in the manufacturing sector or the service sector, if key suppliers become operationally or financially unable to do business, it can be detrimental to the firm's performance. Consequently, a key part of supplier management is having a supply-risk management process in place. Table 10.2 presents five major types of supply risks and the strategies that companies can use to mitigate and manage those risks.

Supply-risk management should include an evaluation of the past performance of a firm's suppliers, its reputation in the market relative to its competitors, its modes of communication with its customers, its ordering and delivery policies, and its procedures. Suppliers should also be assessed for their ability to overcome events such as natural disasters, economic downturns, and threats from

TABLE 10.2: Types of Supply Risks and Mitigation Approaches[39]

TYPE OF SUPPLY RISK	DESCRIPTION	MANAGEMENT AND MITIGATION APPROACH
Strategy Risk	Stems from the choice of a company's sourcing strategy. For example, a small family-run business may not have the resources to support a global sourcing strategy.	Choose the right sourcing strategy up front to identify and qualify the right suppliers using reliable market intelligence.
Market Risk	Stems from volatility in market prices caused by fluctuations in stock prices, exchange rates, interest rates, and commodity prices.	Use approaches such as price hedging, forward contracts, quantity discounts, multiple suppliers, and supplier incentives, or postpone decisions to counter volatility in market prices.
Implementation Risk	Stems from suppliers' inability or unwillingness to meet delivery lead times or increase production because of capacity problems or because the buyer is not a key customer.	Identify and select new suppliers quickly to minimize disruptions in production, lead times, etc.
Performance Risk	Stems from ongoing quality and financial issues with the supplier.	Continuously monitor all suppliers using technology to detect early-warning signals to avoid disruptions caused by bankruptcies, performance problems, ownership changes, labor strikes, geopolitical changes, or the inability to meet compliance regulations. Use prequalified suppliers and clearly establish tolerances for product quality standards and consequences of quality failures.
Demand Risk	Stems from fluctuations in demand and inventory levels.	Use multiple suppliers and suppliers that have the capacity flexibility to respond to demand changes.

piracy or acts of terrorism that could delay deliveries. External sources of information about suppliers include news and financial articles regarding changes in a supplier's financial condition, management team, demand for its products and the prices being paid for them. The buyer should also keep track of employee strikes, security breaches, sustainability indices, and violations of safety and health regulations. Internal sources of information include the firm's own experience with the quality of the supplier's products and any delivery delays, noticeable lags in the suppliers' response times, and supplier-generated information that isn't accurate or transparent.[40]Armed with this knowledge, the buying firm can assess the risk of each supplier and put risk plans in place to mitigate problems.[41]

Supplier Relationship Management (SRM)

Most successful companies have strong relationships with their suppliers. For example, BNSF Railway Company (Fort Worth, TX) has forums for its suppliers and an annual awards ceremony for the top performers. In companies like BSNF, there is greater awareness of the need to build bridges between their organizations and their suppliers by establishing strong buyer–seller relationships. The process of doing so is known as *supplier relationship management (SRM)*. Supplier performance management (SPM) is a subset of supplier relationship management. The main focus of SPM is to determine whether suppliers are meeting their contractual obligations. SRM is a much broader concept in the sense that it focuses on enhancing the value of the relationship to both the buyer and the supplier through collaboration.[42]

Companies such as Toyota and Honda show dedication and diligence in managing supplier relationships by exchanging best practices, sharing information, honing innovation, and learning how suppliers work. For example, to develop new technology, Toyota works with its suppliers by hosting engineers from the supplier companies to work in collaboration with its own engineers for two or three years.[43]

Supplier Phase Out

The final task of the supplier management process presented in Figure 10.1 is supplier phase out. A buying organization phases out its suppliers for reasons such as these:

- The supplier has consistently failed to provide the goods and services that meet the organization's requirements, including sustainability requirements.
- Cheaper and more reliable suppliers are available.
- Suppliers with better offerings, technology, or processes are available.
- The risks associated with doing business with the supplier cannot be mitigated.
- The supplier is bankrupt or goes out of business.

Apple regularly audits its suppliers to determine whether it wants to continue to do business with them. The company will work with a firm the first time it encounters a problem to see that the problem does not happen again. Yet, if there are major repeat violations, the supplier's contract is terminated.[44] Similarly, Wal-Mart has switched from a "three strikes" rule to a zero-tolerance policy regarding its suppliers.

Phasing out existing suppliers and switching to new suppliers is costly and can disrupt the operations of both buying firms and selling firms. For example, after the crash of an Air France (Société Air France, S.A., Tremblay-en-France, France) flight in 2009, the European Aviation Safety Agency ordered all airlines with Airbus A330 and A340 planes in their fleets to voluntarily remove their speed sensors, which were manufactured by Thales Group (Thales S.A., La Défense, France), and replace them with sensors manufactured by Goodrich Corporation (Charlotte, NC). Airbus, as result of this forced change in supplier, not only had to pay for the new sensors but also the costs of installing and testing them. In addition, because Goodrich became the sole supplier of the sensors, the company experienced its own production and supply issues as it ramped up production to meet demand.[45] As you can see, the decision to switch to a new supplier should not be taken lightly but made only after carefully considering all factors, not just the price of the item being supplied. Also, the buying organization should establish guidelines early during the contracting phase, negotiating exit clauses into the contract to ensure that penalties exist for early contract termination and to avoid alienating the supplier whose services you may need at a later date.

10.3 Managing Service Providers

10.3
Evaluate the issues involved in managing service providers.

Service providers vary from those that provide information technology, telecommunications, and internet services to those that provide storage, legal, marketing, call center, financial, accounting, and educational services. Just like suppliers that provide tangible products, services providers must be managed as well. The procedure in Figure 10.1 is equally relevant for managing the providers of services. The only difference is that, rather than referring to the acquisition of goods as procurement or purchasing, the acquisition of services in many organizations is called service contracting. We now discuss how the supplier management process can be applied to services.

Sourcing Service Providers

In this stage, the company analyzes, evaluates, and selects its service providers based on certain specifications and requirements. The process begins with first defining the overall business needs of the company and then identifying the specific service requirements that support them. An important aspect of defining the service requirements is to determine which services are strategic and which are not. Strategic services are those that have a direct impact on the company's business operations, are used by the company's customers, or require unique or highly skilled workers. If the company has the in-house expertise to perform these services, then strategic sourcing might not be needed. Nonstrategic services are standard services that are easily available from several service providers. Examples of nonstrategic services are the services provided by call centers and by automated billing and administrative services firms.

Companies should also a conduct a spending analysis to identify the extent of money spent on the various services. Such an analysis will help the company categorize the service providers and to arrive at a short list of potential providers. The next step in the sourcing process is defining the criteria for selecting the service provider, sending RFQs, evaluating the responses, and selecting the preferred service providers using a weighted factor rating model.

Cost savings is the basis for standard services that can be purchased from multiple service providers. For strategic services, the price alone is not often the main criterion. Other terms and conditions will often matter more. For example, L.L. Bean, Inc. (Freeport, ME) prides itself on its service and sees it as a competitive advantage. Firms such as this will be more likely to select a call center service provider that provides high-quality customer service rather than the call center with the lowest cost. Strategic service acquisition can be handled by a negotiation team. The negotiation team should include members from the business units with the best insight into what services are and are not required as well as members from the firm's procurement, legal, and IT departments.

Service Provider Risk Management

Buying firms face several risks when they hire service providers. Some of these risks and approaches to mitigate them are as follows:

- *Security risks*. Security risks include the theft of data, intellectual property rights, and patents, as well as privacy concerns. Some firms that have outsourced work to Chinese service providers have found that these service providers used their proprietary information to go into direct competition with them. Companies should carefully evaluate whether contracting with a service provider will compromise its ability to compete. If the risk is too great, then the company should perform these services in-house. There are additional risks related to offshoring work to service providers. We will discuss them later in the chapter.

Working with Service Providers

- *Failure to deliver the needed services on time*. Penalty clauses should be included in the contract to encourage the service provider to meet its delivery deadlines and to minimize the adverse effect of delivery delays on the buying firm's operations. For example, many firms use liquidated damages clauses in delivery contracts to increase the likelihood that their suppliers deliver services on time. A liquidated damages clause specifies a fixed, per-day amount that the service provider must pay for failure to deliver the contracted service.
- *Failure to realize the expected cost savings:* This type of risk can occur as a result of cost escalations because the actual services required by the client company varied from the original estimates or costs weren't accurately calculated in the first place. Firms cannot assume that the low labor costs of a service provider will directly translate into cost savings. DepoExpress, Inc. (San Francisco, CA), a company that provides deposition summaries for litigators, stopped outsourcing work to Indian contractors after experiencing problems with quality control and differences in language, even though the Indian contractors were paid only 60% of what their U.S. counterparts would cost.[46]

Service Provider Performance and Relationship Management

Managing a service provider is more complicated than simply agreeing to contract terms and then trusting that the services will be delivered as promised. To monitor and manage the service provider's performance, a firm will typically establish a vendor management team with expertise in both relationship management skills and project management skills. This team is responsible for establishing cost, delivery, and other performance metrics, and reviewing them periodically to not only evaluate the performance of its service providers but also to evaluate the vendor management team's ability to manage the service provider effectively. In addition, the firm providing the service will often also use an internal customer liaison who has the responsibility of working closely with the buying firm's business units to understand its service needs and verify that the services that have been negotiated are delivered as required.

Managing Suppliers

Many of the approaches we discussed to manage supplier information apply to managing the information related to a firm's service providers. Information on a supplier's capabilities, financial standing, service quality, delivery performance, compliance record on sustainability, focus on continuous improvement, and security measures should be collected and evaluated. Likewise, as with supplier relationship management, the purpose of *service provider relationship management* is to ensure that the interaction between the supplier and buying organization is streamlined and efficient and to enhance the value of both companies through collaboration. Service provider relationship management also involves implementing technologies, processes, policies, and procedures to improve the firm's communication with the service provider and its operational efficiency. Nonetheless, there are some additional considerations that the buying organization should include when managing relationships with service providers:[47]

- *Management strategy.* Outsourcing services requires the buying company to develop specialized skills in-house, develop multi-sourcing strategies to better leverage the outsourcing operations and find more specialized service providers, determine the appropriate service level agreements during the contracting phase, and use appropriate relationship management techniques.
- *Organizational structure.* As outsourcing services shifts work performed in-house to third-party service providers, changes in the organizational structure are inevitable. For example, by agreeing to contract their customer support services to an agency in the Philippines, Citibank National Association (New York City, NY), Safeway, Inc. (Pleasanton, CA), and Aetna, Inc. (Hartford, CT) all eliminated their own in-house helpdesks and call centers. Often, there is a transition of employees between the client company and the service provider. Hence, an essential feature of outsourcing relationship management (ORM) is to build the appropriate in-house management and oversight structure and mechanisms.
- *IT infrastructure.* One of the inevitable consequences of outsourcing services is that the client company's existing IT infrastructure must be reconfigured to accommodate, monitor, and manage the network of third-party service providers.

10.4 Global Supplier Management

Describe the unique challenges involved in managing global suppliers.

Global Supplier Management

Evaluating and selecting suppliers domestically can be difficult, but the job becomes even more challenging and complex when a company begins choosing from an array of geographically dispersed global suppliers. Gathering critical information from geographically dispersed supplier organizations is time-consuming and expensive. Political instability in other countries, natural disasters, dock or port strikes, communications failures, power failures, currency risks, cyber-attacks, and terrorism and piracy are other challenges a buying firm may encounter. For example, in 2010, severed undersea cables led to a communication blackout that disrupted the supply of goods from India to buyers in other countries.[48]

Moreover, although labor costs are significantly lower in countries such as Vietnam and India, they cannot be the only factor considered. Companies buying goods and services abroad also need to account for the hidden costs of offshoring—those related to costs of poor quality, exchange rate fluctuations, and so forth. Extended shipping times, weather disruptions and their effects, customs-clearance times, and other governmental red tape all need to be considered in the decision to work with global suppliers. Clearly, there are supply risks that have the potential to disrupt the operations of a firm's global supply chain partners. Buyers can use several strategies to mitigate these risks. Let's look at them.

Have a Backup Pool of Suppliers

It is easier to manage a few suppliers, but it is also riskier if one of them experiences problems and cannot meet its obligations. As we mentioned earlier in the chapter, as a backup strategy, a buyer can contract with alternative suppliers and, in the case of global sourcing, suppliers in other countries. For example, the alternative suppliers may be located in countries that are more politically stable or have stable currencies, have more reliable power supplies, and have more efficient transportation infrastructure. If the primary supplier fails to deliver, this backup strategy minimizes the negative effects on the buyer.

Choose Suppliers From Countries That Have Better Laws and Regulations and Infrastructures

Another strategy is to source suppliers only from countries that have well-defined laws and regulations for adhering to sustainability requirements, intellectual property rights, and well-developed infrastructures. Assuming the price is comparable across countries, it is safer to work with suppliers located in more stable countries.

Establish Collaborative Relationships With Global Suppliers

Another strategy is for the buying organization to spend the time, effort, and money to build collaborative relationships with its suppliers. Collaborative relationships may require the buying organization to provide financial assistance and support to its primary and secondary global suppliers to safeguard their financial health and competitiveness. A reason for the long-term success of Toyota, for example, has been its commitment to building and maintaining collaborative relationships with its suppliers worldwide.

Use Technology for Greater Supplier Visibility

Technology, such as an ERP system, can contribute to supply reliability. For example, Lubrizol Corporation (Wickliffe, OH), a Berkshire Hathaway company that produces specialty chemicals, uses SAP's global ERP system to manage its suppliers. The global ERP system expedites decision making by allowing the company to implement risk-mitigation strategies in real time in the event of any supply disruptions. In the event of shortage of key raw materials, the system immediately identifies what product that raw material goes into, the manufacturing locations where that raw material is used, and the number of approved alternative global suppliers for that raw material. This information allows Lubrizol to immediately contact its backup sources of supply, minimizing disruptions in the manufacturing processes.[49]

Select Suppliers From a Country Whose Language and Culture You Can Understand

An additional tactic is to select suppliers from countries with minimal language barriers; for example, English is widely spoken in India but may not be in parts of South America, Russia, and East and Southeast Asia. In addition, it is important to understand that cultural differences from one country to another as they relate to religious holidays, social norms, and a region's work ethic can have an impact on suppliers and their productivity and relationships.

Despite its many challenges, global sourcing offers many benefits, including lower costs, faster time-to-market, and a broader pool of suppliers and service providers. The purpose of global sourcing is to acquire a product or service by exploiting global efficiencies that exist across geopolitical boundaries. As global sourcing aims at finding better sources of supply around the world that offer better product and services at lower prices, it is vital that these vital sources of supply are effectively managed.

10.5 Legal, Ethical, and Sustainability Issues

Supply chain sustainability is important because approximately 50% of all energy and carbon emissions for a company are related to its supply chain.[50] Many countries now require companies to report their sustainability practices, including their efforts to limits carbon emissions. As a result, firms are demanding that suppliers reduce their carbon emissions and disclose the impact their products and processes have on the environment. To have a toxic-free supply chain by 2020, the clothing and accessories retailer Zara (Coruña, Spain) requires its suppliers to publicly disclose data about the chemicals they use and to comply with bans on dangerous chemicals used in textiles.[51] Companies that have greater market power often make sustainability requirements part of their supplier-selection criteria. McDonald's (Oak Brook, IL), to assure its customers that its ingredients are fresh, locally sourced, and of decent quality, have developed an app for smart phones called "Track My Maccas" that allows customers to read lists of ingredients for McDonald's menu items.

10.5
Identify some reasons why firms actively promote ethically and socially responsible behavior in supplier management.

McDonald's smart phone app called "Track My Maccas" allows McDonald's customers to use their smart phones to see where the various ingredients of their food came from in a very fun and engaging format.

Tomohiro Ohsumi/Getty Images News/Getty Images

 An Ethical Supply Chain

The food giant Dannon (Danone S.A., Paris, France), whose products include Dannon, Oikos, and Danimals, sells one-third of the yogurt purchased in the United States. In recent years, they have sought to respond to the public's growing concern about the source of its food by creating a direct supplier relationship with a set of dairy farms that supply the company with milk. Under a new supply system, farmers in the program must adhere to Dannon-dictated animal welfare standards and work to improve and conserve soil on their farms. Furthermore, they are expected to feed their livestock with non-GMO (genetically modified organism) ingredients. In exchange, the seven large dairy farms that Dannon has contracted with will receive price guarantees for their milk, which ensures a steady level of profit for the farms. In this way, Dannon, its customers, and their suppliers all benefit from a sustainable and healthier supplier relationship. "Engaging in this direct way with our milk suppliers allows us to join them in a journey to improve agricultural practices and reduce their footprint on the environment, which in turn reduces Dannon's footprint on the environment," said Mariano Lozano, chief executive of the Dannon Company.[52]

Companies are realizing that supply chain sustainability improvements can result in sizable financial returns. For example, Patagonia, Inc. (Ventura, CA), an outdoor clothing store based in California, by urging its fans and customers to join the brand's sustainability cause of "buy less" and by instituting sustainability measures increased its sales from $362 million in 2012 to $543 million in 2013 (in U.S. dollars).[53] Given the impact sustainability initiatives can have on a firm's financial measures, some firms have created return-on-investment (ROI) measures and profit and loss (P&L) statements that focus on the benefits of these improvements.[54]

In addition to concern for sustainability in supplier management operations, it is important to recognize ways in which they can promote ethically and socially responsible behaviors. Companies face immense pressure from consumers, investors, business partners, regulators, and media organizations to behave ethically. These stakeholders expect not only individual companies but their entire supply chains to be ethical. To incorporate ethical behavior into its business practices, Coca-Cola invested millions of dollars to provide training and support for almost 40,000 fruit farmers within its supply chain in Uganda and Kenya, including 17,000 women. Through its 5by20 program, Coca-Cola has the goal of economically empowering five million women entrepreneurs as supply chain partners by the year 2020. As of 2015, their goal was on track, with more than 600,000 women positively affected by this policy.[55] Yet, with so many firms in a supply chain, it is inevitable that eventually one of them will make an ethical breach. Sometimes it is the leader, or dominant firm, in the supply chain. At other times, it is the firm's suppliers. Nevertheless, when a breach does happen, the leader often ends up bearing the brunt of the blame, regardless of who is at fault. For example, in 2015, PETCO (Petco Animal Supplies, Inc., San Diego, CA) and PetSmart, Inc. (Phoenix, AZ), national pet food chains, both pulled China-made jerky dog treats off their shelves after receiving reports during the previous year that greater than 1,000 dogs had died from the contaminated products. Their concern was that customers would focus their anger and blame on the retailer who sold the products, rather than the Chinese company who made them.[56] Because ethical violations such as these can seriously harm a firm's reputation and profitability, companies need to try to prevent them.

SAGE edge ....

Visit **edge.sagepub.com/venkataraman** to help you accomplish your coursework goals in an easy-to-use learning environment.

- Mobile-friendly eFlashcards
- Mobile-friendly practice quizzes
- A complete online action plan

- Chapter summaries with learning objectives
- Video and multimedia resources

CHAPTER SUMMARY

10.1 Identify the goals of supplier management. The goals of a well-managed supplier management program are to improve an organization and its supply chain performance by enhancing the quality of goods and services, ensuring their timely delivery and reducing their cost, fostering sustainability, improving product and process innovations, and promoting ethically and socially responsible behavior.

10.2 Describe the various tasks of the supplier management process and demonstrate how metrics are used to rate supplier performance. The key elements of the supplier management process are:

a. Strategic sourcing
b. Purchasing
c. Supplier performance management
d. Supplier information management
e. Supplier risk management
f. Supplier relationship management
g. Supplier phase out

There are numerous measures that can be used for rating supplier performance, including quality performance, cost and service performance, and supplier capability assessment.

10.3 Evaluate the issues involved in managing service providers. The process of managing service providers is similar to the one used for managing suppliers in the manufacturing sector. Yet, given the intangible nature of services, there are also some unique challenges that organizations have to address. Service risk management and

relationship management are two key components in managing service providers.

10.4 Describe the unique challenges involved in managing global suppliers. Unique challenges have to be addressed when managing global suppliers. They include differences in languages and cultures, long lead times, and security threats. Additionally, political instability in other countries, natural disasters, dock or port strikes, communications failures, power failures, currency risks, cyberattacks, terrorism, and piracy are all unique characteristics that can affect a firm's ability to proactively manage its global suppliers.

10.5 Identify some reasons why firms actively promote ethically and socially responsible behavior in supplier management. Supply chain sustainability is important because approximately 50% of all energy and carbon emissions for a company are related to its supply chain. Because many countries now require companies to report their sustainability practices, these firms are demanding that suppliers reduce their carbon emissions and disclose the impact their products and processes have on the environment. In addition to concern for sustainability in supplier management operations, it is important to recognize ways in which they can promote ethically and socially responsible behaviors. Companies face immense pressure from consumers, investors, business partners, regulators, and media organizations to behave ethically. These stakeholders expect not only individual companies but their entire supply chains to be ethical. Companies can face fines or public shaming (with resulting loss of sales) when they are found to operate without regard to ethical business practices.

KEY TERMS

Bargaining surplus   369

Blanket purchase order   371

Buyback contract   370

Competitive bidding   367

Cost of goods sold (COGS)   361

Cost of poor quality (COPQ)   360

Cost-plus contracts   370

Direct materials purchase   371

Fixed-price contract   370

Indirect materials purchase   371

Joint venture   366

Keiretsu network   367

Multiple-sourcing strategy   366

Negotiation   369

Online reverse auctions   369

Planned purchase order   371

Purchase order   371

Quantity-flexibility contract   371

Request for proposal (RFP)   367

Request for quotation (RFQ)   367

Single-sourcing strategy   365

Spend analysis   363

Standard purchase order   371

Supplier scorecard   372

Supply-base optimization   365

Total cost of ownership (TCO)   361

DISCUSSION AND REVIEW QUESTIONS

1. Discuss why supplier management is important for both manufacturing organizations and service organizations.

2. What are the goals of supplier management? Discuss how achieving those goals can improve a company's supply chain performance?

3. How can suppliers' failure to meet sustainability requirements hurt a buying organization? Name some companies that have suffered from this problem.

4. How would a service company like Marriott Hotels (Marriott International, Inc., Bethesda, MD) use a spend analysis to manage its suppliers?

5. What is supply-base optimization and why is it important in supplier management?

6. Give an example for each of the four categories of purchases presented in Figure 10.3 for a company like Apple. What sourcing strategy would you use for each of these purchases?

7. What are the three approaches for selecting suppliers and how do they relate to the purchase categories?

8. What are the two basic types of supply contracts, and what is the difference between them?

9. Briefly discuss the three basic types of purchase orders.

10. How do direct and indirect material purchases differ?

11. List the benefits of e-procurement.

12. Why is it necessary to manage, at the strategic level, the performance of your suppliers?

13. What types of supply risks do companies face when they contract with suppliers from countries like China and India? Why do these risks have to be managed? Discuss your answers by using some company examples.

14. What are the three different types of supplier relationships discussed in the chapter?

15. What are the features of a well-designed supplier relationship management program?

16. What are some of the unique challenges companies face when managing their service providers?

17. What factors make managing global suppliers more complex?

SOLVED PROBLEM

Omega Steel Works is planning to purchase from global suppliers the iron ore it needs to make its products. The company has identified suppliers in Bangladesh, China, and India. It has also identified the critical factors for selecting suppliers and developed scores (0 to 100) for rating the suppliers on the factors. Weights ranging from 0 to 1 have been chosen to reflect the relative importance of the factors. The factors, their weights, and the scores for the suppliers are shown in the table below. Which country's supplier should the company select?

Factor	Weight	Score		
		Bangladesh	China	India
Delivery Reliability	0.15	60	70	60
Purchase Price	0.10	50	60	70
Quality Performance	0.25	40	60	70
Technological Capabilities	0.15	50	60	70
Sustainability Compliance	0.25	40	50	60
Financial Viability	0.10	60	80	70
Total	1.0			

a. For each factor and each supplier, compute a score by multiplying the factor rating score and the weight assigned to the factor.

b. Compute a total score for each supplier by summing up the scores calculated in the previous step.

c. Select the supplier that has the highest total score.

Solution:

Factor	Weight	Score			Weighted Score		
		Supplier From Bangladesh	Supplier From China	Supplier From India	Supplier From Bangladesh	Supplier From China	Supplier From India
Delivery Reliability	0.15	60	70	60	60×0.15 = 9.0	70×0.15 = 10.5	60×0.15 = 9.0
Purchase Price	0.10	50	60	70	50×0.1 = 5.0	60×0.1 = 6.0	70×0.1 = 7.0
Quality Performance	0.25	40	60	70	40×0.25 = 10.0	60×0.25 = 15.0	70×0.25 = 17.5
Technological Capabilities	0.15	50	60	70	50×0.15 = 7.5	60×0.15 = 9.0	70×0.15 = 10.5
Sustainability Compliance	0.25	40	50	60	40×0.25 = 10.0	50×0.25 = 12.5	60×0.25 = 15.0
Financial Viability	0.10	60	80	70	60×0.10 = 6.0	80×0.10 = 8.0	70×0.10 = 7.0
Total	1.0				47.5	61.0	**66.0**

Omega Steel Works should make the supplier from India its preferred supplier and the Chinese supplier, which has a slightly lower score of 61.0, its backup supplier.

PROBLEMS

1. A manager of a restaurant must choose between two suppliers for his primary food and cleaning supplies.

   a. What do you consider would be some of the critical factors on which to base the choice of supplier?

   b. Develop a supplier scorecard that will help her rate the critical issues and allow for a more accurate selection of supplier.

2. Suppose, in Problem 1 above, the restaurant had a strong incentive to operate in sustainable ways and promote sustainable

operations. How might you adjust the supplier scorecard to take into consideration a minimum of three (3) sustainable features?

3. Look up "fair trade" on the internet and examine the principles that govern the movement. How can "fair trade" be applied to supplier management to create a more ethical supplier management system?

4. XYZ Corporation is looking to switch suppliers for its commercial building operations. Its last supplier was notorious for promising on-time delivery to construction sites and was frequently late or delivered the wrong components. You have been hired to develop a supplier risk management system. Identify a minimum of five types of supplier/delivery risks and develop some mitigation strategies to resolve them as part of your new supplier selection.

5. Suppose another division of XYZ Corporation develops state-of-the-art computer processing equipment and is considering moving to a low-bid process with its suppliers, which is likely to result in new contracts with Asian and Indian firms. What are some of the supplier risk and mitigation strategies to consider with these overseas suppliers?

6. A U.S. bank is planning to outsource its IT services to a service provider in India. After a thorough spend analysis and market evaluation, the bank has identified three possible providers. The critical factors, their weights, and the scores for each service provider are shown in the following table. Both the factor weights and scores are based on a 10-point scale.

Critical Factors	Weight	Scores		
		Supplier 1	Supplier 2	Supplier 3
Service Reliability	9	9	7	6
Data Security	8	6	6	8
Cost Savings	5	5	6	3
Labor Stability	5	6	5	5
Employee Skills	4	6	5	6

a. Which supplier should the bank select?

b. If a minimum score of 5 is required for all factors, which supplier should be chosen?

7. An electronics company is planning to outsource the production of the semiconductor chips needed for its products. The company has decided to adopt a multi-sourcing strategy to ensure it has alternative supply sources should the primary supplier fail to meet its contractual obligations. Accordingly, the company wants to classify its suppliers as potential, approved, and preferred suppliers by using a weighted-factor rating model. The company is planning to use the following schema to classify the suppliers based on their total weighted scores:

Potential suppliers: 55 to 65; Approved suppliers: 66 to 79; Preferred suppliers: >80.

The company has already identified three firms from China, Vietnam, and Singapore as possible suppliers. In addition, the team has identified the critical supplier criteria/factors and factor weights (0 to 1) to reflect their relative importance. The team has also developed scores (1 to 100) to rate the three suppliers on these criteria. The factors, their weights, and the scores for the three suppliers are shown in the following table. Categorize each supplier as potential, approved, or preferred.

Critical Factors	Weight	Score		
		China	Vietnam	Singapore
Delivery Reliability	0.2	60	50	85
Purchase Price	0.1	70	80	50
Quality Performance	0.3	60	60	80
Technological Capabilities	0.3	70	60	90
Sustainability Compliance and Ethical Behavior	0.1	60	50	80
Total	1.0			

CASE STUDY 10.1 THE BOEING 787, BATTERIES, AND SUPPLIER MANAGEMENT[57]

Ntsb/ZUMA Press/Newscom

The launch of Boeing's newest aircraft, the 787 Dreamliner, was supposed to be a triumphant moment in the history of Boeing. The Dreamliner set a record for booking the most advance orders ever recorded for a new airplane.

Unfortunately, the path to glory has been marred by a problem with the planes' battery systems. In 2013, smoke filled the cabin of a 787 in flight and another 787 made an emergency landing in Japan. Yet another 787 caught fire while on the ground in Boston. The Federal Aviation Administration (FAA) grounded all 787s shortly thereafter. Not only were American planes being grounded. All Nippon Airways Co., Ltd. (Tokyo, Japan) and Japan Airlines Co. Ltd. (Tokyo, Japan) grounded their fleets of Dreamliners, and other carriers, such as Air India Ltd. (New Delhi, India) and LATAM Airlines Group S.A (Santiago, Chile), also temporarily grounded theirs.

Boeing worked frantically to isolate the cause of the battery problems. The 787 was the first commercial aircraft to use lithium-ion batteries. GS Yuasa Corporation (Kyoto, Japan), a Japanese manufacturer, was the supplier. The company also supplied batteries for the International Space Station and electric railcars. Lithium-ion batteries are known for their high-energy storage capacity, low weight, and no memory degradation, but they have also been linked to heat-related problems in the past in various electronic devices. GS Yuasa said it could take months to determine whether the issue is limited to the battery or involves the jet's entire electrical system.

Boeing's supplier management system is complex, with multiple interdependencies among international organizations, all which need to be carefully managed. For example, GS Yuasa's batteries must link with the Dreamliner's electrical power conversion system, which is manufactured by France's Thales SA. United Technologies Corporation's (Farmington, CT) UTC Aerospace Systems (Charlotte, NC) unit supplies the overall power system for each aircraft, which uses 1.45 megawatts of electricity, enough to power 400 homes. Thus, although Boeing oversees its entire supply chain, Thales SA originally selected GS Yuasa to supply the batteries.

The problems that Boeing faced turned the Dreamliner into something of a nightmare. The company's stock price fell, and Boeing's backlog of some 850 orders for its aircraft was in jeopardy amid concern about the plane's safety. Moreover, buyers demanded deep discounts because delivery schedules for the planes were delayed.

Questions

1. Take a position on the following statement: "Boeing dug its own grave by outsourcing so much of the 787 to its supply chain. The firm could not possibly do an effective job managing so many suppliers." Do you agree or disagree? Why?

2. What are the advantages and disadvantages of Boeing allowing its suppliers to award contracts for their own supplies of the plane's components?

3. In your opinion, what is the moral of this story from a supplier management point of view?

VIDEO CASE

Watch this video case to learn about how effectively managing suppliers helps the Rockefeller Gastropub ensure that they can deliver the best products to satisfy customers.

CRITICAL THINKING EXERCISES

Royal Enfield (Chennai, India) is a manufacturer of five models of motorcycles in the United States. All of the five models use the same engine but the engines will require special tooling during the manufacturing process. The company has identified two reliable suppliers of these engines: one in India and the other in China.

1. If Royal Enfield wants to perform a total cost of ownership analysis, what data should collected from each of these suppliers?

2. If the company wants to establish a collaborative supplier relationship with the supplier selected, identify the nature and areas of collaboration.

3. Assume that Royal Enfield selected the supplier in China. Develop a supplier scorecard to evaluate this Chinese supplier.

CHAPTER
11

Logistics Management

LEARNING OBJECTIVES

After studying this chapter, you should be able to:

1. Identify the components of an integrated logistics management system.

2. List the steps in the order fulfillment process.

3. Identify the decisions involved in transportation management.

4. Describe the role of packaging in the transport, distribution, storage, sale, and use of goods.

5. Define materials handling, and discuss its critical role in a logistics system.

6. Describe the functions of a warehouse and the different types of warehouses.

7. Explain why good inventory management is important to logistics management.

8. Discuss the importance of facilities network design in a logistics system.

9. Discuss the unique challenges of managing global logistics.

10. Define logistics outsourcing, and explain why companies outsource their logistics function.

11. Describe the unique logistical needs and challenges in the service sector.

12. Explain how sustainability issues are affecting the decisions made in logistics.

OPERATIONS PROFILE: Piracy on the High Seas—Another Global Logistics Problem

The sea lanes along the northeast coast of Africa are among the most critical and heavily trafficked in the world, with tankers transporting oil and chemical products from fields in the Middle East, and many cargo ships carrying everything from raw materials to finished products and goods. Ships traveling from the Far East and India routinely pass along the Horn of Africa that projects out into the Indian Ocean and marks the tip of the African continent into the eastern ocean. Since the early 1980s, the small African country of Somalia has been embroiled in civil and religious wars, resulting in a crippled economy with few opportunities for its people to earn a living beyond subsistence fishing and farming. Around 2008, a huge increase in the piracy of tanker and container ships occurred in this historically troubled region of the world.

Small, fast boatloads of Somalian pirates arrive swiftly through stealth and surprise, and they board and commandeer large ships along the coast. Pirates seized 52 ships from 2009 to 2010. By negotiating with private shipping firms and the governments of the kidnapped sailors, the pirates earned US$146 million in 2011, which works out roughly to US$5 million per captured ship. Although the numbers have since dropped, the attacks had a significant impact on international trade by impeding the delivery of shipments and increasing shipping expenses.

Combating piracy has been challenging for several reasons. First, pirates may attack anywhere along the 2,400-mile-long coastline, making it nearly impossible to patrol the region fully. Second, whose responsibility is it to rid the coast of pirates? Should it be the nations under which these vessels are flagged or an international patrolling force? Third, what should be done with Somalian nationals caught in the act of piracy? Where should the captured pirates be held? Is this crime under the jurisdiction of the United Nations, or should pirates be prosecuted in Somalia?

It's easy to blame the Somalian pirates for violating international law, flouting kidnapping and hijacking rules, and openly engaging in criminal activity. The number of Somalis who engage in this criminal activity is quite small, however; most Somalis are subsistence farmers. Furthermore, Somalis place some blame on the shipping companies for dumping toxic chemicals and waste from bilges, poisoning the fishing grounds that Somalis depend on for their survival. The decreased catches force many to turn to piracy. The pirates also have the support of local coastal communities, who see them as a sort of ad hoc coast guard, defending their territorial waterways from exploitation by larger, wealthier countries. As one expert put it, "It's almost like a resource swap: Somalis collect up to $100 million a year from pirate ransoms. . . . and the Europeans and Asians poach around $300 million a year in fish from Somali waters."

STRINGER/AFP/Getty Images

By 2013, the frequency of pirate attacks on shipping in the Indian Ocean was negligible. With increased international patrolling by air and sea and heightened vigilance on the part of ships' crews, Somali pirates were finding the pickings increasingly slim. Although it seems that the worst is over, the surge in piracy off the Somali coast in the Indian Ocean is just one example of the many logistics challenges that organizations can face when transporting goods around the globe.[1]

In this chapter, we will discuss the logistics function, which includes the activities needed to transport, warehouse, and distribute products. Increasing globalization and liberalization of trade has triggered intense competition, forcing both private and public firms to be more innovative and efficient in designing their logistics activities. Consequently, it is one of the most important functions in today's business world. Companies such as Wal-Mart (Wal-Mart Stores Inc., Bentonville, AR) and FedEx (FedEx Corporation, Memphis, TN) excel in their logistics and reap the benefits of improved profitability and enhanced reputations as a result. As an example of their proficiency, when Hurricane Katrina devastated New Orleans, Wal-Mart beat the Federal Emergency Management Agency and the American Red Cross to the hardest hit areas, delivering relief supplies. Wal-Mart was able to respond so rapidly because the company performs these activities every day and has mastered the art of logistics.[2]

11.1 Identify the components of an integrated logistics management system.

Integrated Logistics Management

11.1 Integrated Logistics Management

Most businesses devote between 10% and 35% of their gross sales, depending on the nature of business, its geographic location, and the weight and value of its products, to logistics costs.[3] **Integrated logistics management (ILM)** refers to the practices used to control the movement of these products (and the associated costs) so that there is a continuous and uninterrupted flow of materials and products from suppliers to manufacturers to the final consumers. Integrated logistics management systems can help keep logistics costs down, improve the satisfaction of customers, and help a firm become more competitive to grow its revenues.

Figure 11.1 shows the various activities of an integrated logistics management system. In the following sections of this chapter, we examine what each part of this system accomplishes.

11.2 List the steps in the order fulfillment process.

11.2 Order Fulfillment

Order fulfillment is the process by which a company responds to customer orders. It includes all the activities from the initial contact with the customer to the delivery of that order. Order fulfillment is a critical logistics activity because it influences customer satisfaction and often determines whether customers will do business with the firm again. A company can receive an order from a customer by mail, fax, or telephone, through its sales staff, using an electronic data interchange (EDI, which is the

Logistics: the activities needed to transport, warehouse, and distribute products

Integrated logistics management (ILM): the practices used to control the movement of products (and the associated costs) so there is a continuous and uninterrupted flow of materials and products from suppliers to manufacturers to the final consumers

Order fulfillment: the process by which a company responds to customer orders

FIGURE 11.1: Integrated Logistics Management System

computer-to-computer exchange of business data), or online via the Internet. Once an order is received, it must be processed quickly. Most companies use computerized order-processing systems to reduce order shipping and billing cycle times. For example, when General Electric (aka GE, Fairfield, CT) gets an order, its computer-based order processing system checks whether the item is in stock, where it is located, and the customer's credit standing. Next, the computer generates a shipment order, bills the customer, updates the inventory records, sends a production order for stock replenishment, and relays the message back to the sales representative that the customer's order is on its way—all in less than 15 seconds.[4]

The order fulfillment process seems simple enough. Nevertheless, it varies in complexity from company to company because each order can be different. For example, some orders can be filled from a firm's inventory of made-to-stock items. For items made-to-order, the fulfillment process is more complicated. It may begin with acquiring the necessary materials and components, manufacturing the product to the customer's specifications, and then packaging and shipping it to the customer. Any failure in the process can lose customers and damage the reputation of the company. On the other hand, if the correct order is delivered on time, personalized, and meets the expectations of the customer, then it is highly likely customers will come back to the company for repeat buys. L.L. Bean, Inc. (Freeport, ME), which sells outdoor apparel and equipment, has become highly successful by emphasizing the order fulfillment component of its logistics management.

Most small companies and new businesses handle the order fulfillment process in-house. Many large companies, however, have outsourced their order fulfillment process to **fulfillment centers** to save time and to focus on their core businesses. Most of these fulfillment centers will offer the basic order fulfillment services of warehousing, order processing, and returns and exchanges. Given the fierce competition in the e-commerce market, using fulfillment centers can help firms to differentiate from the competition. Because many fulfillment centers are highly automated and operate efficiently, they can deliver most orders the same day they are received. In addition, many of these fulfillment centers can also offer specialized services such as product assembly and call center services.[5]

11.3 Transportation Management

Transportation management involves overseeing the movement of goods and raw materials and is a vital component of nearly every business and industry. In the grocery retail businesses, for example, any disruption in transportation can result in goods spoiling. Bananas waiting to be shipped to Europe from Costa Rica can't sit in intermodal containers on loading docks for an extended period. Likewise, fresh fish from Alaska must be shipped via jumbo jets to markets in Japan. Envision a transportation network as a collection of highways, pipelines, shipping sea lanes, or any other structure that facilitates vehicular movement or flow of goods. Transportation includes the inbound movement of raw materials and components from the suppliers to the manufacturer and the subsequent outbound movement of finished goods from the manufacturer to the customer.

Transportation costs are a significant portion of a firm's total supply chain expenses. In fact, more than 50% of total logistics costs result from transportation costs. Furthermore, with increasing globalization and uncertain oil prices, transporting products and materials to and from countries overseas is a complex undertaking. Efficiently managing transportation in the supply chain is further complicated by changing governmental regulations in overseas markets, global security concerns, and green initiatives to reduce carbon emissions.

Strategy and Transportation Performance Metrics

The role transportation plays in an individual firm depends on the firm's competitive strategy. If the company's target market consists of price-conscious customers, then a company is more likely to use slower modes of transportation to maintain low product prices. Yet, such a strategy may also require the company to carry higher levels of inventory to avoid the risk of lost sales. Conversely, if the target market demands high levels of responsiveness or if the company wants to reduce unnecessary inventory levels, then the firm might choose to use faster transportation modes. Benetton (aka United Colors of Benetton, Treviso, Italy), the Italian-based fashion apparel designer and manufacturer, uses airfreight for all of its exports to get the fashions consumers want to them quickly. Similarly, unlike other furniture retailers that transport assembled furniture, IKEA (Delft, the Netherlands), by transporting its furniture parts in flat packs, optimizes carrier space and thus reduces its costs compared with other furniture retailers. IKEA's price-conscious customers often have to assemble the products when they get them, but they are able to purchase them at a low cost.

IKEA packs its furnuture in flat packages for more efficient and cheaper shipping.

©iStockphoto.com/tunart

A firm's strategy will in turn affect the transportation performance metrics most important to it. The key transportation metrics are:

- *Cost*: The price charged for shipment.
- *Speed*: The elapsed transit time from the initial pickup point to the final delivery point.
- *Reliability*: Consistent delivery in terms of time and quantity.
- *Capability*: The ability to transport a variety of different products.
- *Capacity*: The volume of freight that can be transported at one time.
- *Flexibility*: The ability to adapt to shipping changes and contingencies.

There are four different participants in managing transportation:

- The **consignor** is typically the seller of goods. The consignor may offer to move its freight to designated places for transportation.
- The **consignee** is typically the buyer of the goods and receives the freight shipment.
- The **carrier** is typically a transportation company responsible for transporting goods or people via land, sea, or air. A **common carrier** is a transportation firm such as UPS (United Parcel Service, Inc., Sandy Springs, GA) or Fed Ex hired by the general public for interstate transportation. A common carrier has published rates and schedules. A **contract carrier**, on the other hand, is a for-hire transportation company that provides transportation for one or a limited number of shippers under a specific contract, but it does not serve the general public. Fremont Contract Carriers, Inc. (Fremont, NE), is an example.
- **Transportation infrastructure owners** can be either publicly or privately owned entities. Highways, airports, and ports are typically owned and operated by state or local governments. Nonetheless, other types of transportation owners are owners of infrastructure, railroads, and the pipelines that are operated by companies in the private sector.

The participants have different goals and objectives. The transportation carriers and infrastructure owners, for example, invest in airplanes, trucks, ships, rail lines, and pipelines and, hence, make decisions that focus on maximizing the return on their investments. The shipper, on the other hand, makes transportation decisions that minimize the **total landed cost**, which is the total cost of making and delivering the product so that it generates revenue. Finally, the buyer invariably expects high levels of responsiveness at a minimum cost. The optimal management of a supply chain requires striking a balance between the goals of these key participants.

Transportation Modes: Basic and Intermodal

There are two modes of transportation: basic and intermodal. The five basic modes are air, motor carriers (trucks), rail, water, and pipeline. Figure 11.2 shows a breakdown by the various basic transportation modes of the total transportation costs in the United States in a recent year, which topped $800 billion. A sixth mode is intermodal transportation. It is a combination of any of the five basic modes.

The mode of transportation used by a company influences the cost, speed, flexibility, and capacity with which it can ship its products. But the mode also has an impact on the many other aspects of the product, such as its packaging, the type of materials handling equipment used to load and unload the product, and the design of the shipping and receiving docks. For example, if a company uses water as its primary mode of transportation, then goods to be shipped must be packaged so that they are not damaged by humidity, temperature, or other environmental conditions.

AIR

The air mode of transportation is ideal when delivery speed or reliability is critical and the goods to be transported have a low weight-to-value ratio. It is the fastest mode of transportation for shipments that have to be transported across distances of 600 miles or more. Yet, it is also the most expensive

Consignor: the seller of goods

Consignee: the buyer of goods and receiver of freight shipments

Carrier: a transportation company responsible for transporting goods or people via land, sea, or air

Common carrier: a transportation firm hired by the general public for interstate transportation

Contract carrier: a for-hire transportation company that provides transportation for one or a limited number of shippers under a specific contract but does not serve the general public

Transportation infrastructure owners: publicly or privately owned transportation entities or owners of infrastructure, railroads, and the pipelines that are operated by companies in the private sector

FIGURE 11.2: Breakdown by Mode of the Share of Total Transportation Costs (in billions of U.S. dollars) in the United States

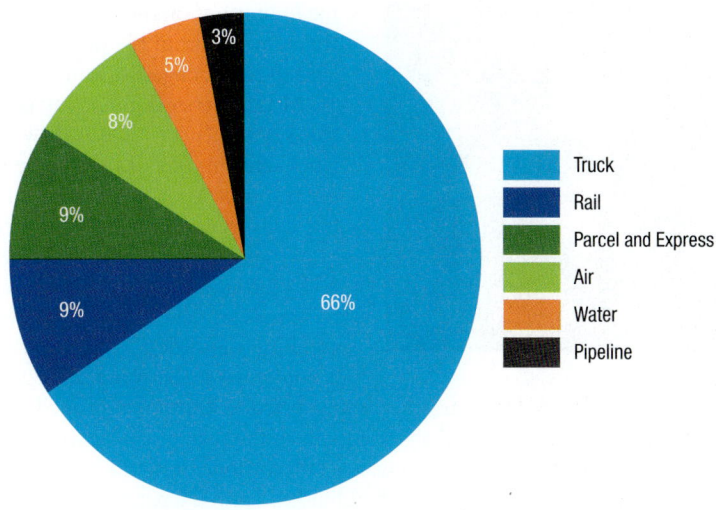

Percentage Share of U.S. Transportation Cost in 2015 by Mode

- Truck — 66%
- Rail — 9%
- Parcel and Express — 9%
- Air — 8%
- Water — 5%
- Pipeline — 3%

SOURCE: Reprinted from Council of Supply Chain Management Professionals (CSCMP). (2015, June 23). *26th Annual State of Logistics Report.* Lombard, IL: Author. Retrieved from https://cscmp.org/member-benefits/state-of-logistics

mode of transportation, as the line-haul cost, which is the cost of moving the goods from the point of origin to the final destination point, is the highest compared with all other modes of transportation. Consequently, many companies cannot afford to use air transportation, and as Figure 11.2 shows, it is one of the least-used modes of transportation. In addition, most shippers and consignees aren't near airports, which means secondary forms of transportation are required to get the goods from the shipper's location to the origin airport and from the destination airport to the buyer's location. The need for secondary transportation increases transportation costs, transit times, and shipping and handling costs, and it increases the potential for lost and damaged goods. Despite these disadvantages, many products of small size but high value, emergency shipments, or perishable goods, use air transportation. Air transportation is used for cut flowers, fruits and vegetables, diamonds, jewelry, blood supplies, and medical products. Most air freight is transported in passenger planes. Increasing airport congestion and inclement weather such as fog, thunderstorms, and snow as well as increased security measures in airports in response to threats of terrorism have had a negative impact on the reliability of air transportation.

 Transporting Goods

MOTOR CARRIERS (TRUCKS)

As Figure 11.2 shows, 66% of the total transportation costs in the United States in 2015 were motor-carrier costs. The percentage is nearly the same in the European Union. The development and access to the 47,000 miles of Interstate Highway System has supported the extensive use of trucks in the United States. In fact, the success of many companies such as Wal-Mart and its supply chain efficiency can be attributed to the logistical opportunities and advantages provided by the Interstate Highway System. Factory location decisions made by many automobile manufacturers, such as BMW (Bayerische Motoren Werke AG, Munich, Germany), Nissan (Nissan Motor Company Ltd, Yokohama, Japan), Honda (Honda Motor Co., Tokyo, Japan), and Toyota (Toyota Motor Corporation, Toyota City, Japan), have been influenced by proximity to the Interstate Highway System.

An advantage of motor carriers is that they provide a greater reach and more flexibility than any of the other modes of transportation. Unlike air and water transportation, trucks can access remote inland areas that do not have ports. Consequently, trucks are used in conjunction with most air and ocean shipments to transport goods to the remote areas of a country. Trucks provide quicker delivery times for short and medium distances compared with rail and water transportation and are able to transport large and heavy loads at reasonable costs compared with air. In addition, using trucks can sometimes eliminate the need to warehouse goods. Some manufacturers ship products straight to retail facilities. In essence, the trucks serve as mobile warehouses.

Total landed cost: the total cost of making and delivering the product so that it generates revenue

Line-haul cost: the cost of moving goods from the point of origin to the final destination point

Less-than-truckload shipments from various shippers are often combined in a single container to increase efficiency.

©iStockphoto.com/tunart

The disadvantages of the motor carriers are high fuel costs (compared with pipeline and rail shipments, for example), disruptions during inclement weather, legal restrictions on the type and nature of goods that can be transported, and the limitations on the volume of goods that can be transported. From the public's standpoint, trucks lead to road congestion and greater pollution.

Motor carrier shipping can be either **less-than-truckload (LTL)** or **full truckload (FTL)**. Less-than-truckload shipping, as the name implies, refers to the transportation of freight that does not fill the full delivery-load capacity of a truck. The weight of partial shipments in LTL trucks can range from 151 to 20,000 pounds. When shippers are asked to transport less-than-full loads, they typically combine the orders from several shippers to fill a container to be more efficient in transporting goods. Trucks with full delivery loads are then transported to **terminals** (a facility where freight is moved between trucks), where the partial shipments from the several consignors are sorted and then reloaded onto smaller trucks for further shipment to the various destinations of the consignees. The number of terminals used and the frequency of handling and moving partial shipments are determined primarily by the transportation distances of the shipments. Most small companies use transportation or logistics-related software to coordinate their shipping procedures and LTL shipping arrangements. The primary advantage of LTL shipping is that it is cheaper than **package or parcel carriers**, such as Fed Ex and UPS, which specialize in shipments weighing less than 150 pounds. These carriers use a combination of air, truck, and rail transportation for rapid and reliable delivery of emergency or time-sensitive shipments. The primary disadvantage of LTL shipping is that transit and delivery times are considerably longer than they are with FTL shipping because of the time spent transferring the small shipments to and from trucks at the various terminals. In addition, shippers also run a higher risk of product damage or loss because of the frequent freight handling at the terminals.

FTL involves transporting quantities of homogeneous goods that are large enough to fill the entire truck or a semi-trailer. Some of the major full-truckload carrier companies in the United States are J.B. Hunt Transport Services, Inc. (Lowell, AR); Swift Transportation (Phoenix, AZ); Schneider National (Green Bay, WI); and Werner Enterprises, Inc. (Omaha, NE). Some of the major full truckload carrier companies in other countries are Norbert Dentressangle SA (Lyon, France); Seino Transportation Co., Ltd. (Gifu Japan); and TransForce Inc. (Saint-Laurent, Montreal, Canada). An FTL carrier will typically transport a full truckload of goods to a single shipper at a single destination.

Full truckload carriers are often contracted for transporting specific types of cargo. For example, some full truckload carriers will exclusively transport only food and perishable items, whereas others may specialize in transporting poisonous and hazardous materials. Federal laws control the types of goods that can be transported together in a single truck, and special equipment may be needed for different types of freight, such as refrigeration trucks for perishable food items.

The transit times of FTL carriers are shorter because they make fewer stops to transfer goods. The risk of damage to products and their loss is lower because, unlike LTL carriers, freight is never handled or repackaged en route. In addition, because FTL carriers typically have only one shipment origin and destination and carry large amounts of freight, the economies of scale achieved results in lower transportation costs for shippers. The main disadvantage of using FTL carriers is the **backhaul**, or return journey, of the trucks to their origins after the freight is delivered if the trucks are empty. If the trucks go back empty, the shipper pays a higher rate for the transportation of the product.

RAIL

Of the five basic transportation modes, railroads generate the most revenue in terms of ton-miles shipped. As of 2014, the top seven railroads operating in North America generated total freight revenue of approximately US$75.1 billion.[6] The U.S. railroad industry is dominated by only four freight carriers: the BNSF Railway Company (Fort Worth, TX), CSX Transportation (subsidiary of CSX Corporation, Jacksonville, FL), Norfolk Southern Railway (Norfolk, VA), and Union Pacific Railroad (Omaha, NE). Consequently, potential customers who rely on transporting freight via rail are faced with limited service options and pricing inflexibility.

Less-than-truckload (LTL): the transportation of freight that does not fill the full delivery-load capacity of a truck

Full truckload (FTL): the transportation of freight that fills the full delivery-load capacity of a truck

Terminal: a facility where freight is moved between trucks

Package or parcel carriers: common carriers that specialize in shipments weighing less than 150 pounds

Backhaul: the return journey of the trucks to their origins after the freight is delivered if the trucks are empty, resulting in the shipper paying a higher rate for the transportation of the product

A wide variety of products can be shipped via rail, but it is generally used to transport low-value, high-volume freight over long distances. Examples include bulk commodities such as coal, chemicals, farm products, and nonmetallic minerals. Next to water transportation, rail is superior to air, trucks, and pipelines in terms of its capability of transporting a wide variety of different products. Furthermore, the growth of intermodal transportation has given railroads the ability to transport higher value products, including manufactured and packaged goods. For some railroads, such as BNSF, intermodal shipments are now the biggest part of their business. Rail transportation is also one of the safest modes of transport, having fewer disruptions from accidents and breakdowns; nevertheless, the use of rail transportation includes some important disadvantages as well. Unlike motor transportation, the rail mode is inflexible as the routes and timings are predetermined. It is also slower than shipping by air or truck. In addition to higher cost, loading and unloading of rail road freight at terminals can lead to significant delays and potential for product damage. For small volumes of freight and for movements that involve short distances, rail transportation is uneconomical.

Lanai, Hawaii, produces very little of its own food. The island's residents rely on regular barges from Maui to replenish its food and fuel supplies, as well as serve as a source for autos, appliances, and other large items.

AP Photo/Ronen Zilberman

WATER

The water mode of transportation is used for both the domestic and the international movement of freight. It is the most dominant transportation mode for international freight. Domestic water transportation in the United States takes place on inland waterways (the Great Lakes and rivers) or over the ocean to Hawaii, Alaska, and Puerto Rico. There are approximately 24,000 miles of navigable inland waterways used by domestic shipping lines in the United States.[7] The freight transported by inland waterway carriers is mostly done on barges and consists of low-value bulk commodities such as petroleum, grain, coal, and chemicals. About 40% of the inland waterways' cargo is petroleum, which is carried in tank barges.

Water transportation via ocean carriers has grown in popularity since the turn of the century because of the efficiency and per-mile cost effectiveness of water transportation. With the availability of ports in every country with a seacoast, it is easy to transport freight overseas via ocean carriers. Some of the major ocean carriers are Maersk Line (division of A.P. Moller – Maersk Group, Copenhagen, Denmark), American President Lines Ltd. (now APL, France), and Evergreen Group (Taipei, Taiwan).

The primary advantage of water transportation is its ability to carry a heavy volume of cargo at relatively low cost compared with other modes of transportation. It is also safer compared with trucks and rail, which are not infrequently involved in vehicular crashes or derailments, as well as more energy efficient. For example, one gallon of fuel can move one ton of cargo 202 miles by train and only 59 miles by truck, whereas one gallon of fuel will allow a barge to transport the same one ton of cargo 514 miles.[8] Consequently, the water mode of transportation is more than twice as energy efficient as rail and more than eight times as efficient as trucks. Third, switching to water transportation reduces roadway congestion. The major disadvantages of water transportation are long transit and delivery times. Other problems are delays resulting from customs and excise restrictions, port congestion, the safe management of containers to avoid serious accidents, and security risks caused by hurricanes, terrorism, and high seas piracy.

PIPELINES

There are about 409,000 miles of pipelines in the United States, and they transport about 17% of total ton-miles of freight. Although the two primary categories of products moved via pipelines are oil and gas, occasionally dry bulk commodities, such as coal in the form of slurry, are also transported using pipelines. Most pipelines are buried underground or travel along sea floors.

Compared with other modes of transportation, pipelines offer some distinct advantages. First, pipelines are one of the most cost-efficient modes of transportation. The cost of transporting a barrel of petroleum by pipeline from Houston to the New York harbor is only about US$1.[9] Second, pipelines are reliable—they can transport large volumes of a product without interruption or intermediate handling.

Intermodal forms of transportation are used for transporting items long distances and are known as intermodals because they can switch transportation modes with ease.

©iStockphoto.com/John Kirk

For example, the 800-mile-long Trans-Alaska Pipeline System has a maximum capacity of two million barrels per day. There are fewer disruptions from inclement weather and fewer worker strikes and absenteeism than in other modes because the movement through pipelines is electronically monitored and controlled. Third, products transported through pipelines are generally very safe and secure. The risks such as shrinkage or loss by theft, fire, damage, spillage, and evaporation are insignificant.[10] Unlike other inland modes of transportation, pipelines offer important environmental benefits as they do not crowd the highways and cause air pollution. In addition, compared with trucks and barges, pipelines have a lower spill rate per barrel of oil transported.

Pipelines are only capable of carrying products that are liquids, liquefiable, or gaseous. Pipelines are also the slowest modes of transportation. Even though pipelines have a lower spill rate than other modes of transportation have, when they do leak, the damage can be catastrophic.

INTERMODAL TRANSPORTATION

Intermodal transportation is a newer mode of transportation in which freight stored in containers is carried by two or more other modes of transportation. The containers are constructed in sizes ranging from the standard 20-foot containers to large 53-foot units. There are also different types of intermodal containers, depending on the type of freight to be moved. Common container types include tank (for liquids and gases), flat-rack (for heavy machinery), and refrigerated (for perishable or temperature-sensitive goods) containers. For companies that are engaged in international trade, intermodal transportation is often the only option as manufacturing facilities and markets are not always located close to the ports and therefore require that firms combine multiple modes of transportation.

The major advantage of intermodal freight transportation is the flexibility it provides in moving goods. Shippers can choose the combination of modes that is the most cost- and time-efficient way for them to move freight. For example, the truck–rail intermodal combination exploits the cost advantages of the rail mode with the flexibility and delivery speed advantages of the truck mode of transportation. A disadvantage of intermodal transportation is the high cost that results from the type and the number of transportation modes used. For example, intermodal transportation that involves air is invariably expensive. Other disadvantages are delays caused by lack of communication between the different transportation modes and the high cost associated with idle time of the transportation mode used, particularly when that mode (such as trucks) moves from one location to another without carrying a load (empty).

In summary, each of the five basic modes of transportation has relative advantages and disadvantages in terms of the key supply chain performance criteria of capability, flexibility, cost, reliability, traceability, and transit time. Table 11.1 ranks the five basic modes of transportation across the six

Intermodal transportation: a newer mode of transportation in which freight stored in containers is carried by two or more other modes of transportation

TABLE 11.1: Ranking the Five Basic Modes of Transportation in Terms of Key Supply Chain Performance Metrics

MODE	KEY SUPPLY CHAIN PERFORMANCE METRICS					
	COST	SPEED	RELIABILITY	CAPABILITY	FLEXIBILITY	CAPACITY
Air	1	5	2	2	3	1
Truck	2	4	4	3	5	2
Rail	3	2	3	4	4	4
Water	5	1	1	5	2	3
Pipeline	4	3	5	1	1	5

Legend: 5 = Best; 1 = Worst.

dimensions of key supply chain performance criteria. The table shows that the rail mode of transportation falls somewhere in the middle. It is less expensive and has more capability and capacity than the air and truck modes of transportation do, but it takes longer. Nevertheless, compared with pipeline and water modes of transportation, the rail mode of transportation is more expensive but is faster. The relative advantages and disadvantages of the intermodal transportation, of course, depend on the different types of basic modes used.

Transportation Network Design Options

Well-designed transportation networks have a positive impact on a firm and the performance of its supply chain. Next we will look at some transportation network design options from the point of view of a firm that has multiple locations and gets its raw material and finished goods from many suppliers. The design options are not mutually exclusive. A company can—and should—choose to use some suitable combination of them depending on the product and its demand in different locations.

DIRECT SHIPMENTS

As Figure 11.3a shows, when the firm uses a direct-shipment design, each supplier sends shipments directly to each of the buying firm's locations. The only decisions the buying company's purchasing manager has to make are the quantity to be shipped of the good and the transportation mode to be used. This design option works well when the shipments are large (FTL). The key advantages of this option are delivery speed and elimination of the need for intermediate warehouses. Home Depot (The Home Depot, Inc., Atlanta, GA) has, at times, used the direct-shipment option because the order quantities of its stores are large.

DIRECT SHIPMENTS WITH MILK RUNS

A milk run is a delivery system in which a single truck picks up shipments from several suppliers and the goods are delivered to a single location. Sometimes shipments are picked up from a single supplier and delivered to multiple locations. Figure 11.3b shows how a direct shipment with milk runs works. In this figure, a truck picks up deliveries intended for buyer 2 from suppliers C, B, and A; after delivery to buyer 2, the truck returns to the location of supplier C. The advantages of this option are lower transportation costs because shipments can be consolidated in a single truck and intermediate warehouses are not required. The key to this transportation option lies in determining the appropriate route that each milk run should take to achieve transportation efficiency. By using frequent milk runs from multiple suppliers, Toyota has been able to operate more efficiently by reducing its shipment sizes, thereby reaping the benefits of steady and level material flows and just-in-time (JIT) deliveries.[11]

SHIPMENTS USING A CENTRAL DISTRIBUTION CENTER

As Figure 11.3c shows, with this option, suppliers deliver shipments to distribution centers (DCs) designated to serve the buyer's locations. The DCs are useful as intermediate storage locations and as cross-docking points, where goods to the various buyer locations can be sorted and shipped. Recall from Chapter 9 that cross-docking is a logistics practice in which inbound shipments from a carrier are unloaded, sorted, and loaded onto outbound carriers with little or no intermediate storage in between. Cross-docking is widely used in the retail industry. Wal-Mart uses distribution centers and cross-docking systems to deliver 85% of its merchandise to its stores. Inbound transportation costs are lower with DCs because suppliers achieve economies of scale by sending large shipments to them.

SHIPMENTS USING DCS AND MILK RUNS

Under this option (Figure 11.3d), milk runs are used to deliver shipments from the distribution center in sequence (Buyer 1, Buyer 2, and Buyer 3) to the buyer's different locations. This option works well when shipments to one location are not large enough to fill a truck. In Japan, 7-Eleven, Inc. (Irving, TX) uses this option by cross-docking deliveries from its fresh-food suppliers and then sending out milk runs to deliver the small shipments to the individual retail stores. Milk runs from a DC can also help several buyers minimize their costs by consolidating runs into a single shipment.

As we noted, a company can choose a combination of the design options depending on the product and its demand in different locations. For example, direct shipments can be used for products that experience high demand in certain high-demand locations, whereas low-demand products for low-demand locations can be shipped by using some combination of DCs, milk runs, and LTL and FTL carriers. Dell Inc.'s (Round Rock, TX) competitive strategy of direct sales to customers eliminates

Direct-shipment design: a transportation network design in which each supplier sends shipments directly to each of the buying firm's locations

Milk run: a delivery system in which a single truck picks up shipments from several suppliers and the goods are delivered to a single location

FIGURE 11.3: Transportation Network Design Options

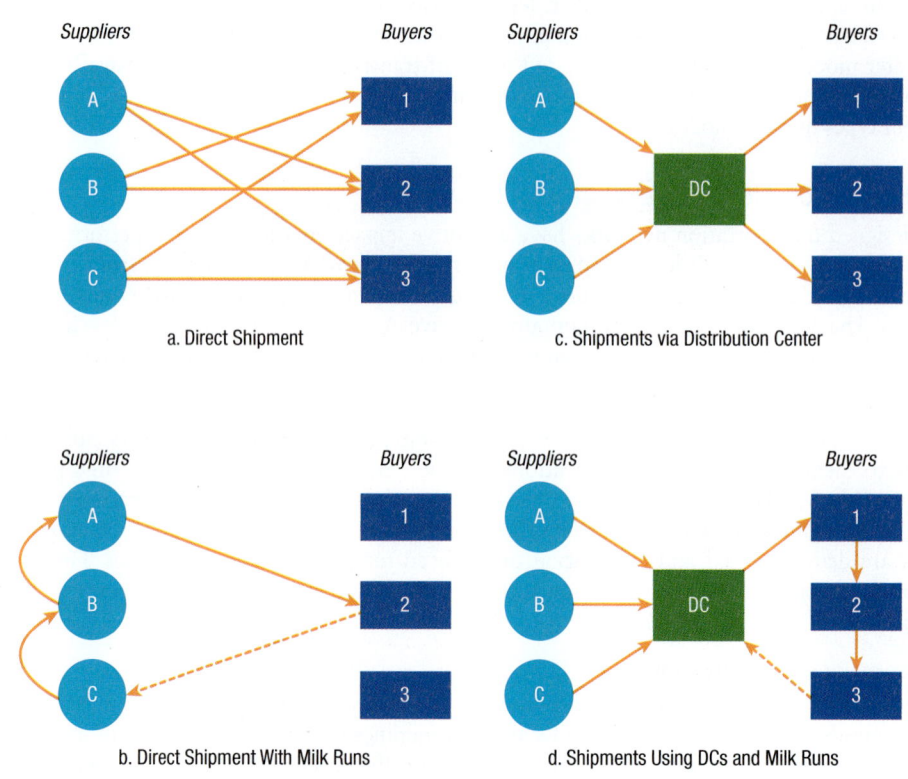

a. Direct Shipment

b. Direct Shipment With Milk Runs

c. Shipments via Distribution Center

d. Shipments Using DCs and Milk Runs

SOURCE: Chopra, S., & Meindl, P. (2010). *Supply chain management: Strategy, planning, and operation* (4th ed., ch. 13, pp. 371–375). Upper Saddle River, NJ: Prentice-Hall.

the need for intermediate warehouses and distribution centers to store inventory. In addition, to keep inventory costs low and to meet its customer responsiveness goal (a 72-hour order fulfillment time), Dell uses air transportation for many components, such as the printed circuit board (PCB) assemblies for its computers, which are manufactured by Asian suppliers.

The trade-off between transportation costs and a firm's responsiveness to its customers also has an impact on transportation modes and network design options. To improve its responsiveness, a firm might need to maintain higher inventory levels, have more distribution centers, and select expensive and multiple transportation modes that inevitably increase transportation costs and compromise efficiency. For example, if a company's goal is high customer responsiveness, then to deliver customer orders quickly, it has to either use faster modes for LTL shipments or have more distribution centers located closer to customer demand locations. The first alternative will increase transportation costs, whereas the second alternative will increase inventory costs for products stored in multiple distribution centers. Conversely, if the company wants to reduce its transportation costs, then it can accumulate customer orders over a period of time so that FTL shipments can be made to achieve economies of scale. This process of combining customer orders over a period of time is known as temporal aggregation. It will reduce transportation costs but will decrease the firm's responsiveness to customers if shipments are delayed.

Given these trade-offs, companies need to design innovative new processes that strike the best possible balance between transportation and inventory costs and customer responsiveness. For example, Ambuja Cements Limited (Mumbai, India), India's largest exporter of cement, was able to reduce transportation costs while improving its customer responsiveness by implementing process innovations. Transportation costs account for a significant proportion of the company's operating expenses. Its plants are usually located close to limestone and crushed-rock mines, which produce the raw materials needed for the cement, but they are often located far away from the company's customers. Ambuja developed a "split plants" design to reduce these costs. For the initial stages of cement processing, all operations are completed at plants located close to the mines, which significantly trims the weight of the material that has to be transported to construction sites and buyers. The intermediate lightweight cement material is then transported for final processing to grinding and packaging plants that are located closer to the company's target markets.[12]

Temporal aggregation: the process of combining customer orders over a period of time

11.4 Packaging

Packaging is the process of enclosing or protecting goods for transportation and for distribution, storage, sale, and use. In addition to protecting products, packaging also serves the functions of promoting, identifying, and providing relevant information about the product to the consumer. Let's look at these various functions:[13]

- *Protection.* Packaging physically protects goods and products from compression, outside vibrations, and shock during transit, and from environmental elements, such as temperature, dust, oxygen, and water vapor. For example, corrugated fiberboard partitions are used in boxes for shipping glassware to prevent breakage.
- *Efficiency.* Accumulating several small identical objects and grouping them into a single packaging unit can improve the efficiency of physically handling them. For example, to be able to ship more units per box of coffee, many manufacturers have replaced their traditional cylindrical metal cans with rectangular, vacuum-sealed packs.
- *Information Dissemination.* Packages and labels communicate how to use, transport, recycle, or dispose of the package or product. Packages for food and for pharmaceutical, medical, and chemical products often must convey information about the products as mandated by governmental agencies. In the United States, state and federal laws such as the Fair Packaging and Labeling Act (FPLA of 1966, P.L. 89-755) govern the labeling of consumer products.
- *Promotion.* Marketers use packaging and labeling to attract potential customers. Innovative techniques in the design and materials used in packaging can promote a company's brand and convey positive messages about product quality and specific features. For example, a company may use recycled or "green" materials in their packaging to target environmentally conscious consumers.
- *Security.* Packaging plays an important role in reducing theft, deterring tampering, and ensuring the security of goods during shipment. For example, in Chicago in 1982, several people died after taking Tylenol (McNeil Consumer Healthcare McNeil-PPC, Inc., subsidiary of Johnson & Johnson, Fort Washington, PA), possibly as a result of deliberate tampering when the bottles were on store shelves. After that event, tamper-resistant packaging became mandatory for pharmaceutical products. In addition, packages can be designed to detect tampering and be made more resistant to discourage tampering and pilferage; they can also include anti-theft devices, such as dye-packs and radio-frequency identification (RFID) tags. Dye packs are radio-controlled incendiary devices used to prevent theft. RFID tags use radio waves to communicate with readers and can be used in the area of logistics to track goods in stock or in transit. The traceability of goods is very important to shippers because they want to know where their goods are at all times. For high-dollar loads, it is not uncommon for shippers to put RFID tags and GPS devices on their freight and containers.

Describe the role of packaging in the transport, distribution, storage, sale, and use of goods.

Security and Packaging

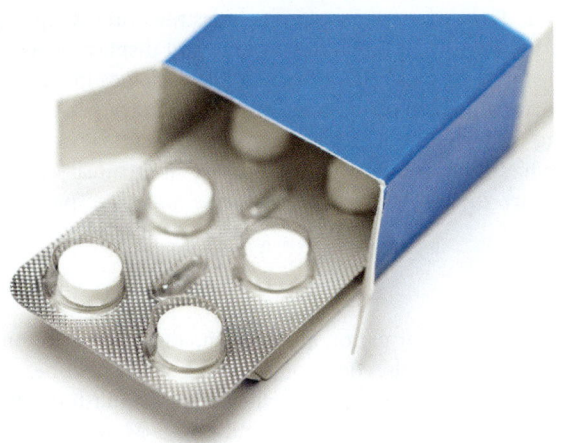

The tablets shown here are enclosed in a blister package, which was then packaged in a secondary folding carton made of paperboard.
©iStockphoto.com/fcafotodigital

Coffee packaging has evolved over time to make shipping more efficient.
©iStockphoto.com/NoDerog

- *Convenience.* Packages can be designed with features that make them more convenient to transport, display, open, dispense, reclose, reuse, recycle, and dispose of. For example, juice boxes have been replacing bottles and have become very popular because of their convenience and ease of shipping. In some instances, boxes are used for wine and single-serving margaritas instead of bottles. These boxes in turn can be assembled into pallets for ease of handling. Similarly, fresh fruits and vegetables are packaged in bags, crates, hampers, baskets, cartons, bulk bins, and placed on pallets.
- *Controlled Usage.* Packages can be designed to accommodate controlled usage of some products for health reasons. For example, bulk commodities such as sugar and salt can be packaged for single servings or dosages to dispense a precise amount of their contents for controlled consumption.

Packaging Factors

The various physical, chemical, and microbiological characteristics of the product and the severity (such as heat or humidity) of the distribution environment affect packaging choices. For example, the specific packaging requirements for a product will vary depending on whether it is a solid, liquid, or gas. Many gaseous products such as nitrogen, oxygen, and hydrogen are compressed and packaged in aluminum, steel, or composite material cylinders for transportation and storage. By contrast, liquids can be packaged in bottles, cans, or fluid pouches. Some perishable products such as fresh produce, fish, or meats, whose characteristics change the longer they stay in the logistics channel, require special packaging to retain their freshness from their source of origin to destination. Other physical characteristics of products that affect their packaging include their density (weight-to-volume ratio), fragility, and hazardous nature, as well as their ability to withstand the elements such as rain and hot or cold weather conditions.

The size and shape of products and how they are packaged for shipment has a direct impact on the number of goods that can be transported in a single load. Poor packaging leads to inefficiencies because of excessive air spaces in boxes, stacked pallets, and containers. Packaging inefficiencies are also caused by excessive use of packaging materials that are not recycled or reused, leading to waste. Apple Inc.'s (Cupertino, CA) packaging designs lead the industry in terms of their material-usage efficiency. For example, the company has been able to reduce the packages for its iPhones allowing it to transport significantly more units in a single shipping container.[14] Poor packaging can also require workers to engage in the cumbersome, or time-consuming, activities of unpacking of materials and disposing of packaging waste.

Packaging Types

To make packaging as effective as possible, a three-level hierarchy of primary, secondary, and tertiary packaging is used. Primary packaging is the material that covers and holds the product and is in direct contact with its contents. Examples of primary packages include the tube used to hold the toothpaste or the can used to hold a soft drink. Secondary packaging includes the outer wrappings that envelop and protect primary packages. In addition, it facilitates storage and display, transportation, and the dissemination of product information. Examples of secondary packages include the box that holds tubes of toothpaste or the cartons used to group and hold the primary packages of cans of soft drink. Finally, tertiary packaging typically involves the grouping of secondary packaging for the purposes of protecting and bulk handling products during storage and transportation. The most commonly seen tertiary packages are the corrugated brown boxes and large pallets of shrink-wrapped boxes.

Package Labeling

Package labels are used to promote products, provide information about them, and track them once they have been shipped. The labels can have writing, symbols, codes, or drawings on them. For example, standard symbols are put on labels to show product or industry certifications, establish proof of purchase, and provide information to consumers about a product's use and safety. Many European countries use a Green Dot (♻) symbol to indicate that a package is recyclable. The retail and logistics industries use bar codes, universal product codes (UPCs), and RFID labels for automatic identification and information management of products. Package carriers have developed their own coding schemes for tracking packages. UPS, for example, uses a coding scheme known as MaxiCode 2-D for package tracking.

Primary packaging: the material that covers and holds the product and is in direct contact with its contents

Secondary packaging: outer wrappings that envelop and protect primary packages

Tertiary packaging: the grouping of secondary packaging for the purposes of protecting bulk handling products during storage and transportation

11.5 Materials Handling

Materials handling refers to the short-distance movement, storage, control, and protection of materials and of people within a plant or a warehousing facility. Materials handling plays a critical role in integrated logistics management for several reasons. First, materials handling costs are a significant portion of overall logistics costs. Several studies conducted across various industries have found that the cost of handling alone accounts for about 20% to 25% of total manufacturing costs.[15] Thus, well-designed material handling systems can greatly improve both labor and equipment productivity and reduce materials-handling costs. Second, poor materials handling is the main cause of product damage. Each part as it passes through the chain of a manufacturing process can be handled 50 to 60 times.[16] Each handling increases the risk of damage to parts and materials. State-of-the-art materials-handling systems and methods cannot only reduce the frequency of the handling but also, along with proper packaging, can reduce the potential for damage to parts, materials, and products. Third, poor materials handling is a major cause of injuries to workers, accounting for about 21% of permanent disabilities and more than 25% of temporary disabilities.[17] Proper materials-handling equipment and methods can reduce the risks of these injuries.

> **11.5**
> Define materials handling, and discuss its critical role in a logistics system.

A range of equipment and tools is used as part of materials-handling systems. The equipment can broadly be classified into the following four categories:

- *Storage and Handling Equipment.* This type of equipment is used for the temporary storage and handling of materials prior to their long-term storage for shipment or in a warehouse. Examples of such equipment are pallet racks, stacking frames, shelves, and elevated platforms referred to as mezzanines.
- *Engineered Systems.* Engineered systems use computer-aided materials-handling equipment. They have automatic settings that can be adjusted depending on changes in the system and the process. Some examples of such systems are automated storage and retrieval systems (AS/RS), automatic guided vehicles (AGVs), conveyor systems, and robotic delivery systems.
- *Bulk Materials-Handling Equipment.* Bulk materials-handling equipment is used for storing, handling, and transporting large quantities of loose or packaged bulk materials such as chemicals, grains, powdered minerals, and liquids. Examples of bulk materials-handling equipment are conveyor belts, stackers, reclaimers (used to recover materials from a large stockpile), bucket and grain elevators, hoppers, and silos.
- *Industrial Trucks.* Motorized vehicles such as pallet trucks, forklifts, platform trucks, hand trucks, and cranes can be used to move and transport goods and materials. These trucks may be manual or powered by electricity.

Supply warehouses: part of a manufacturing plant used for the long-term storage of goods

Cross-docking warehouse: a warehouse where incoming shipments from various suppliers are sorted and batched and then delivered to buyers, spending little or no time in storage

11.6 Warehousing Management

Warehouses are storage facilities used to store incoming goods temporarily (such as raw materials, finished goods, partially finished goods, and component parts) for eventual distribution to consumers or other businesses. Warehousing management, the fifth component of integrated logistics management, ensures these goods are properly stored, tracked, and distributed so they get to the right destinations. Warehouses can be categorized as supply warehouses, cross-docking warehouses, or distribution centers. Supply warehouses are typically part of a manufacturing plant and are used for the long-term storage of goods, including raw materials, parts, and partially finished goods. In cross-docking warehouses, incoming shipments from various suppliers are sorted and batched and then delivered to buyers and spend little or no time in storage. Distribution centers, which we have already discussed, are typically used for storing finished goods for a short period of time before they are sorted and shipped to their destinations.

Warehousing adds another significant, but often necessary, layer of cost to the logistics function. In 2012, for example, warehousing accounted for $126 billion, which is about 15% of the overall

> **11.6**
> Describe the functions of a warehouse and the different types of warehouses.

🖥 Materials Handling

In the Warehouse

transportation costs in the United States. There are a several reasons that warehouses are used as intermediate storage facilities. First, an imbalance always exists between the quantity of goods produced and the demand for these goods. Using a warehouse enables companies to regulate the rate of flow of goods between production and consumption points. For example, most toymakers use constant production rates throughout the year to use their existing production capacity in full and prepare for the high demand for toys in November and December. Warehouses are used throughout the rest of the year to store the toys until demand increases. Likewise, for certain commodities produced only in particular seasons, such as wheat, warehousing is needed to make them available in the offseason. Second, warehouses are needed because businesses frequently purchase and store large quantities of goods from their suppliers because they anticipate a scarcity of the goods or increase in their prices, or because the buyers get volume discounts from producers. For example, candy manufacturers such as The Hershey Company (Hershey, PA) often buy large quantities of sugar and use warehouses to store it as a hedge against price increases.

Since the turn of the century, many companies have consolidated warehouses in the design of their supply chain network. Instead of having several decentralized warehouses, companies consolidate their distribution activities by having fewer, more centralized warehouses. Thus, for a global company with operations in China, instead of having 10 decentralized warehouses to cater to the customer base across China, they may choose to have only three or four centralized warehouses. The benefits of warehouse consolidation include reduction in overall cost, decreased inventory levels, and improved customer service by meeting higher customer demand through the ability to store a large variety of products. A drawback in consolidation is the potential lack of agility in responding quickly to customer needs. When warehousing operations are centralized, there may be additional steps involved in collecting customer orders, submitting them, and fulfilling orders.

Warehouse Functions

Warehouses perform a variety of functions. Nonetheless, given the many activities that need to be coordinated, most companies now use technologies such as **warehouse management system (WMS)** software to track products, control inventory, and improve order picking and loading as well as unloading-dock logistics. Companies such as P&G (Procter & Gamble Co., Cincinnati, OH), Pfizer, Inc. (New York, NY), and Wal-Mart (introduced earlier in the chapter), to speed up warehouse operations, use WMS programs that have state-of-the art technologies such as voice-activated receiving and packaging, RFID, and pick-to-light technology. The following are major warehouse functions:

- *Order Picking.* This is the process of selecting products stored in the warehouse to fulfill orders. Modern warehouses use technologies such as automatic storage and retrieval systems, voice picking equipment, and pick-to-light systems to facilitate order picking. For example, pick-to-light technology improves order picking along warehouse conveyor belts by monitoring and identifying products for specific shipments. An order picker scans a barcode representing a specific order to be filled. Based on the barcode, a light will indicate the specific bin from which an operator is expected to pick an item. A light above the bin will also illuminate with the quantity to be picked. The picker then selects the item or items for the order, and to confirm the pick, the picker presses the lighted indicator button. If the light switches off, the order has been successfully filled.
- *Inventory Management.* Good inventory management gives a firm the ability to locate and pick items quickly that are stored within a warehouse for subsequent loading and outbound shipment. The firm must strike a balance between the costs of paying for inventory and storing it versus maintaining a sufficient amount of stock to meet the demands of customers. One of the most useful technologies that is used in this area is RFID, which can significantly improve the ability to manage inventory effectively and track the location of specific goods within the warehouse.
- *Consolidation.* Consolidation (also referred to as accumulating) is the receipt of goods from various sources of supply and combining smaller orders into a large shipment to a specific destination. The purpose of consolidation is to achieve lower outbound transportation charges through FTL shipments.
- *Bulk Breaking.* **Bulk breaking** refers to the process in which a warehouse (typically a distribution center) receives a large bulk shipment of goods from a single supplier and then splits (or breaks) it

Warehouse management system (WMS): technologies used to track products, control inventory, and improve order picking and loading as well as unloading-dock logistics

Bulk breaking: the process in which a warehouse (typically a distribution center) receives a large bulk shipment of goods from a single supplier and then splits (or breaks) it into individual orders for shipment and local delivery to multiple buyer destinations

into individual orders for shipment and local delivery to multiple buyer destinations. The purpose of this function is to achieve lower inbound transportation charges through larger consolidated FTL shipments.

- *Cross-Docking*. Warehouses perform cross-docking. Items that are cross-docked spend very little time in storage.
- *Assembly*. To support the manufacturing operations of their firms, many warehouses preassemble products and components received from a variety of second-tier suppliers.
- *Packaging and Labeling*. Warehouses may pack and label products to protect them against damage and to make it easy to identify them accurately.
- *Reverse Logistics*. Reverse logistics are activities such as managing product returns, repairing and remanufacturing products, and disposing or recycling of packaging material.

Warehouse Types

In addition to deciding whether to use supply or cross-docking warehouses, distribution centers, or some combination of the three, companies must also decide whether to rent a public warehouse, use a contract warehouse, own a private warehouse, or choose a mixture of them.

Public warehouses charge clients a certain fee to store their goods, depending on the volume of warehouse space used and any additional warehouse services that the clients desire. Among the services public warehouses may offer are order picking, packaging and labeling, inventory management, and shipping. Companies use public warehousing to avoid the costs of having to build and operate their own facilities. Some companies, such as those producing seasonal chemical products like herbicides and pesticides, don't need warehouse space throughout the year and use public warehouses instead. The disadvantages of using a public warehouse can include a lack of control, a lack of space availability if other shippers are using the warehouse, and possibly poor customer service.

Contract warehouses, like public warehouses, charge their clients a fee for leasing their facilities. Yet, the contractual agreement is for a longer term and the clients have to pay despite whether the space is used. In addition, the risk of storing the goods is shared between the owner of the goods and the warehouse company. Consequently, public warehousing usually costs less than contract warehousing does. Like public warehouses, contract warehouses also offer services such as packaging and labeling, cross-docking, inventory control, and assemble products. The advantage of contract warehousing is its superior customer service because the warehouse owner has expertise in warehouse operations and the benefits of a long-term contract. A drawback of contract warehouses is that the firm might be locked into disadvantageous long-term contracts if market conditions or the firm's warehousing needs change.

Private warehouses are typically owned and operated by firms producing or owning the goods. The most significant advantages of a private warehouse are the control the company has over its goods and the flexibility it offers in terms of managing the warehouse. In addition, the company owning the private warehouse has the ability to integrate the warehouse's operations with other activities in the logistics system. The most obvious disadvantage of a private warehouse is the cost required to build and maintain it. Furthermore, the services and flexibility offered by public warehouses and contract warehouses, along with the ability of these warehouses to achieve economies of scale, has contributed to a decline in the use of private warehouses.

11.7 Inventory Management

Many logistics decisions such as the location and number of warehouses, modes of transportation, and materials-handling requirements depend on how a company manages its inventory. Inventories account for a significant portion of a company's operational and supply chain costs. For example, out of the total logistics costs of $1.449 trillion in 2014 for the United States, inventory carrying costs alone accounted for $475.3 billion (32.8%).[18] As we have explained, higher levels of inventory in the logistics pipeline will enable a company to provide its customers with superior service through the timely delivery of orders but will escalate the company's inventory costs. Low levels of inventory will lower a company's costs, but the firm may not be able to meet the demand by customers or their delivery expectations because of inventory shortages. The company's supply chain offers another level of complexity. Because it is composed of many organizations, each with its own inventory management practices, managing and coordinating inventory decisions across the chain can be extremely difficult. Furthermore, tools such as RFID and GPS can be very useful in inventory management as tracking and tracing items. For example, Challande & Fils SA (Nyon, Switzerland), a Swiss waste-management

Reverse logistics: activities such as managing product returns, repairing and remanufacturing products, and disposing or recycling of packaging material

Public warehouse: a warehouse that charges clients a certain fee to store their goods, depending on the volume of warehouse space used and any additional warehouse services that the clients desire

Contract warehouse: a warehouse that charges clients a fee for leasing their facilities for a longer term where clients have to pay despite whether the space is used

Private warehouse: a warehouse owned and operated by firms producing or owning the goods

11.7
Explain why good inventory management is important to logistics management.

Managing Inventory

and material-transportation company, uses RFID tags on bins and GPS to track the locations of its containers and waste bins as they are deposited at construction sites and other locations.[19]

The use of RFID and other technological tools is particularly important in the case of product recalls and for tracking inventory in-transit in global supply chains. Also, inventory management involves ensuring that the oldest products go out first, expiration dates are tracked, products pulled that are expired, and returns from retailers with excess inventory are accounted for. Given the importance of inventory on a company's bottom line, on its supply chain costs, and on customer satisfaction, we will devote all of Chapter 15 to the management of inventory.

Discuss the importance of facilities network design in a logistics system.

Facilities Networks

11.8 Facilities Network Design

We have discussed facilities network design in Section 7.1 on supply chain design and facilities location decisions. In the context of an integrated logistics system, a facilities network design is the strategic placement of warehouses, distribution centers, service centers, and manufacturing plants throughout the supply chain. The optimum numbers and types of facilities, their locations, and the nature of their operations are decisions that have to be made as part of the facilities network design process.

The seven primary logistics activities discussed in Sections 11.2 to 11.8 are interwoven to create an integrated logistics system. Each activity is vital, and collectively, these seven logistical activities have a significant impact on the overall logistical and supply chain performance.

Discuss the unique challenges of managing global logistics.

Global Logistics

11.9 Global Logistics

Global logistics is the design and management of a system that plans, implements, and controls the efficient and effective flows of materials into, through, and out of a company facility and that cuts across national boundaries to achieve its specific corporate objectives. Figure 11.4 shows the framework of a global logistics system.

The rapid expansion of the global marketplace has made it necessary for firms to manage their logistics on a global scale. The elimination of trade barriers through formal trade agreements such as the North American Free Trade Agreement (NAFTA) and the economic integration among European countries with the formation of the European Union has promoted free movement of goods, services, and factors of production among participating countries. In 2014, for example, the combined trade among the three NAFTA partners amounted to US$1.2 trillion, making it the second largest trading bloc next to the 27-member European Union.[20]

This growth of free trade among countries has had a tremendous impact on global logistics. Logistics and supply chain managers must manage all of the logistics activities we have discussed not only domestically but also globally, which includes multiple countries, languages, cultures, governments, and regulations. In addition, these managers have to contend with other logistical factors. Let's look at them next.

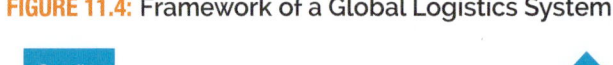

FIGURE 11.4: Framework of a Global Logistics System

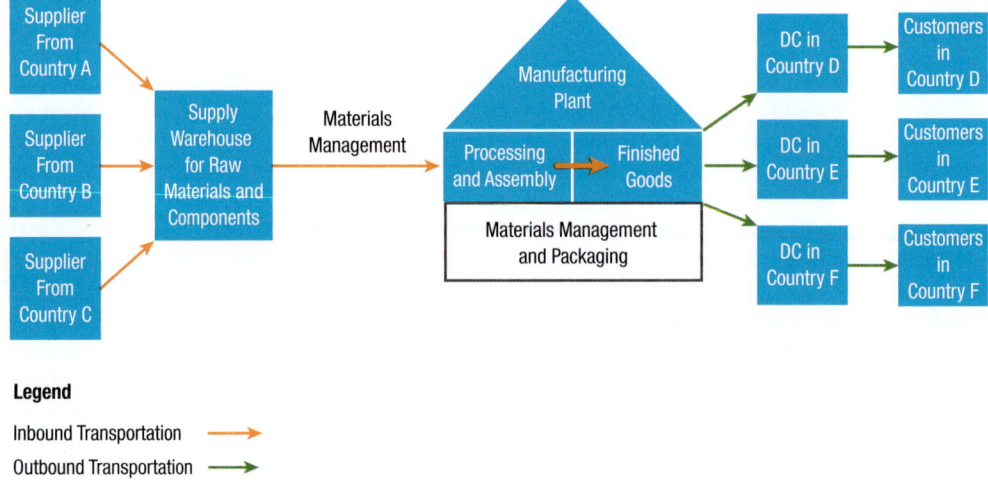

Political Factors

Political restrictions placed on international trade by different countries make global logistics challenging. Some of these restrictions are trade barriers, such as governmental laws and regulations in the form of tariffs, which are taxes levied on specific items exported from or imported to a country. Import quotas are another type of trade barrier. They limit the quantity of certain goods that can be imported to a country in a given period of time. Many countries do not allow agricultural or plant products to be imported without thoroughly inspecting them.

Other trade restrictions may take the form of greater scrutiny by central governments of countries of companies engaged in global logistics. This is because global logistics has a significant impact (favorable or unfavorable) on a country's balance of trade, which is the net difference between the monetary value of exports and imports of that country during a specific period. For example, a country may be more favorably disposed toward the logistics activities conducted by exporting companies because they have a more favorable impact on its balance of payments than importing companies do.

Economic Factors

Global trade and, by implication, global logistics activities are affected by economic factors such as currency fluctuations, market sizes, infrastructure (roads, bridges, and rail systems), and income levels of the populations of trading countries. In an extremely poor country, such as Bangladesh, most people cannot afford to buy products in large quantities or to buy expensive products. Consequently, companies that export goods to countries like these face logistical decisions such as the kinds of products to offer for sale and the type of packaging that should be used. Thus, exporting computerized washing machines to a developing country like Bangladesh might replace workers and therefore could conflict with that country's employment goals. Furthermore, the level of servicing needed for such a product may be unavailable in such countries. Consequently, products like these washing machines may have to be modified before exporting to developing countries.

A country's infrastructure is yet another economic factor that has a huge impact on global logistics. Many foreign ports may not have adequate or appropriate materials-handling equipment or modern warehouses to handle or store shipments. In India, for example, warehouses are typically small, with a maximum size of only 25,000 square feet, and they often have dirt instead of cement floors. In addition, these warehouses rarely use any materials-handling equipment and operate with a low level of technology. Consequently, managing Indian warehouses is complex, and warehouse spaces are used inefficiently.[21]

Cultural Factors

Global logistics must be designed and managed to deal with work practices and environments that vary from country to country. Logistics managers need to understand the unique cultural differences in the way consumers in other countries perceive and demand products and services, and they must accommodate these cultural preferences if global logistics operations are to be successful. Saudi Arabia, for example, does not allow alcoholic beverages or Christmas trees to be imported into the country under any circumstances. These goods will be destroyed at the Saudi border. In addition, language differences, national holidays, and time zone differences have an impact on day-to-day logistics activities. In India, for example, there are more than 40 national, public, and religious holidays. Workers take time off for these holidays, which can have an impact on logistics schedules.

Distance

Order-to-delivery lead times are significantly longer and uncertain over the greater distances that generally separate buyers and suppliers operating in different countries. For example, ocean carrier shipments from China to the West Coast of the United States can be delayed up to a week in bad weather. The undesirable consequence of such a delay will be that the trucks gathered at port terminals on the West Coast will have to remain empty and idle until the shipments arrive, which can cause financial difficulties for shippers. Unpredictable losses from problems such as these are typical in global logistics.

International Documentation

The documents needed to comply with the prevailing laws and regulations of different governments are extensive and complex. We will describe a few of the more commonly used documents: certificates

---

Tariffs: taxes levied on specific items exported from or imported to a country

Import quota: another type of trade barrier that limits the quantity of certain goods that can be imported to a country in a given period of time

Balance of trade: the net difference between the monetary value of exports and imports of that country during a specific period

of origin, bills of lading, commercial invoices, shipper's export declarations, and shipper's letter of instructions. A **certificate of origin** is a document that specifies the country in which the goods in a particular shipment were manufactured or processed. A **bill of lading** is a document that delineates the terms of the contract between the shipper and the transportation company. It indicates who has the title to the goods—that is, who owns them—and who has the contractual agreement with the carrier. It also serves as a receipt for the goods. A sample bill of lading document is shown in Figure 11.5. A **commercial invoice** is a customs declaration document provided by an exporter of goods that crosses international borders. It includes key information about the parties involved in the shipment, a description and quantity of the goods being transported, the terms of sale, and the method of payment. The **shipper's export declaration** is a document completed by the shipper of goods and shows the value, weight, destination, and other features of export shipments. The **shipper's letter of instructions** is a document required by the carrier or certain logistics service providers to obtain the authorization to issue and sign the air waybill on behalf of the shipper.[22] An air waybill is a receipt and a non-negotiable instrument issued by an international airline for goods and serves as a contractual agreement with the airlines, but it does not serve as a document of title to the goods.

Security

Security is a growing problem for logistics managers. In the past two decades, shipping and logistics firms have beefed up their security in response to the threats of theft, piracy, and terrorism. To avoid pilferage, firms use packaging materials that include straps, seals, and shrink wrapping, and they avoid writing brand names on packages for international shipments (as well as for domestic shipments). To help cope with piracy, firms have begun to use private armed guards on ships operating in the high-risk area. In addition, the World Maritime Council has advised shipping vessels that intend to transit through areas at risk for piracy to communicate with naval forces in the region. A few firms have started using alternative routes to avoid the risk of piracy.

To combat terrorism, many national governments such as the United States have several mandatory and voluntary security programs such as the Customs-Trade Partnership Against Terrorism (CTPAT) and Operation Safe Commerce. CTPAT requires its members to take steps to protect the supply chain, identify security gaps, and implement specific security measures and best practices. Operations Safe Commerce is a program that works with businesses to identify supply chain vulnerabilities and develop improved methods and technologies to ensure the security of cargo entering and leaving the United States.

Global Channel Intermediaries

Companies rarely rely only on in-house personnel to conduct the all of the complex activities associated with global logistics. Instead, the firms often use the services of intermediaries that have the expertise to handle many or all of the activities. These service providers include:

- *Global Freight Forwarders.* **Global freight forwarders** perform such international shipment functions as obtaining rate quotes, chartering and booking space on carriers, preparing all the necessary documentation, arranging for cargo insurance, arranging and tracing inland surface transportation, and providing translation services.
- *Export Management Companies.* **Export management companies** help companies that lack the resources or expertise to ship their products abroad themselves. They provide value-added services such as conducting market research in prospective countries, developing appropriate distribution channels, and ensuring foreign labeling requirements are met.
- *Export Trading Companies.* **Export trading companies** help domestic companies locate potential importers of their products and provide services such as preparing export documents that meet the foreign government's import requirements and arranging for transportation.
- *Custom-House Brokers.* **Customs-house brokers** oversee the movement of goods through customs and verify that accompanying documents are complete and accurate.
- *Export packers.* **Export packers** provide the necessary packaging services for export shipments.

International Transportation Modes

As a result of increased demand for international transportation, many Asian countries such as China, Vietnam, and the Philippines have been importing growing quantities of raw materials

---

Certificate of origin: a document that specifies the country in which the goods in a particular shipment were manufactured or processed

Bill of lading: a document that delineates the terms of the contract between the shipper and the transportation company, indicating who has the title to the goods and who has the contractual agreement with the carrier, and serves as a receipt for the goods

Commercial invoice: a customs declaration document provided by an exporter of goods that crosses international borders

Shipper's export declaration: a document completed by the shipper of goods and shows the value, weight, destination, and other features of export shipments

Shipper's letter of instructions: a document required by the carrier or certain logistics service providers to obtain the authorization to issue and sign the air waybill on behalf of the shipper

Global freight forwarder: a service provider that performs international shipment functions

Export management company: a service provider that helps companies that lack the resources or expertise to ship their products abroad themselves

FIGURE 11.5: Example of a Bill of Lading

Non-Negotiable

BILL OF LADING

No.

_____ OF _____

Port/Place of Loading	Voyage Number	Vessel Name	Port/Place of Discharge	On-Carriage Final Destination

SHIPPER		CONSIGNEE		CHARGES
Name		Name		
Street Address		Street Address		
City, State		City, State		
Notify/Contact	Phone	Notify/Contact	Phone	

DESCRIPTION OF GOODS PROVIDED BY SHIPPER

UNITS	HMO		WEIGHT

SHIPPER'S CERTIFICATION REGARDING HAZARDOUS GOODS

Placards, stickers, markings, etc.:	Emergency Contact:	ERG No.:

Shipper hereby certifies that the packing of each container has been carried out in accordance with the provisions of 49 C.F.R. §176.27(c), and that the above-named materials are properly classified, described, packaged, marked and labeled, and are in proper condition for transportation according to the applicable regulations of the Department of Transportation [49 C.F.R. §172.204].

Authorized Signature: _____   Date: _____

CARRIER'S LIABILITY FOR LOSS/DAMAGE TO GOODS

Shipper's attention is directed to Section 9 on the reverse side of this Bill of Lading. All goods shall have an agreed release value of $500 per package unless Shipper declares, and Carrier accepts, a higher release value directly below.

Shipper's Initials: _____   Release Value: $ _____ per pound   Carrier's Acceptance: _____

ORIGIN		DESTINATION		
date/time in:		date/time in:		Received in good order, count and condition unless noted otherwise above.
date/time out:		date/time out:		

SHIPPER	ORGANIZATION	CONSIGNEE
_____	_____	_____
Authorized Signature Date	Authorized Signature Date	Authorized Signature Date

---

SOURCE: Photo of a bill of lading document. Retrieved from http://www.docstoc.com

and increasing their exports of manufactured goods. Because of the great distances involved in global trade, the modes of transport used most often are water and air. There are, however, notable exceptions in the use of surface transportation in global trade. For example, the member nations of NAFTA and the European Union often rely on trucking. Despite the relatively insignificant role of surface transportation in global logistics, it is vital that companies engaged in international trade thoroughly understand a country's logistics infrastructure and its modal operating characteristics. In a country such as India, which has only 2,000 kilometers of highways, gridlock and shipping delays are a major problem.

The Indian economy loses $12.54 billion each year due to logistics and supply chaos from traffic congestion.

©iStockphoto.com/shigemitsu

Other Features of Global Logistics

Payment and possession risks are greater with global logistics than they are with domestic logistics. For example, who owns the goods if they are pirated or damaged in transit across countries? Which party must bear the loss? In this discussion we describe some of the documents used to minimize the risks.

TERMS OF SALE

The terms of sale refers to the rights and obligations of each party in the transport of goods. When and where the transfer of physical goods and the legal title to goods occur, payment for goods, freight charges, and insurance for goods in-transit, required documentation, and who has the responsibility for control and caring for the goods in-transit are spelled out in the terms of sale.

PAYMENT METHODS

With global shipments, there is much greater uncertainty about how and when the buyer will pay the seller for the goods purchased. As for domestic logistics, the seller of the goods wants payment for them as soon as possible. Uncertainty about the timing of payments as a result of transportation delays, unexpected economic and political turmoil in countries, and incorrect international documents can complicate matters. There are four types of payment methods in global logistics transactions: cash-in-advance, letters of credit, documentary collections, and open-account.

The least attractive payment method for importers is the cash-in-advance payment method. This method enables the seller, or exporter, to avoid all risk and receive payment before the ownership of the goods is transferred to the foreign buyer. The buyer runs the risk of not receiving the goods if the payment is made in advance. Exporters that insist on this payment method will often lose business to competitors that offer more attractive payment terms. A letter of credit (LC) is the most secure payment method available to international traders. It is a document issued by a bank according to the instructions of the importer (buyer) of goods. The letter authorizes the exporter (seller) to draw a specified sum of money, usually after the receipt by the bank of certain documents such as bill of lading, invoice, packing list, or certificate of origin as proof of delivery within a specified time. An LC is a commitment by the buyer's bank to make the payment as long as the terms and conditions stated in the LC have been met. It is a useful payment method when the exporter lacks sufficient credit information about the foreign buyer but is satisfied with the creditworthiness of the buyer's foreign bank. With the documentary collections mode of payment, a bank used by the seller sends the required shipment documents to the buyer's bank, along with instructions for payment. The buyer's bank, acting as an intermediary, collects payment from the buyer and remits it to the exporter's bank in exchange for the shipping documents that confirm the transfer of title to the goods to the buyer. The only drawback with this method of payment is that the seller has limited recourse in the event of nonpayment as the banks act only as a facilitator for its clients.

With the open account payment method, goods are shipped and delivered before payment is made. The buyer is typically offered payment credit terms of 30 to 90 days. Clearly, this payment method is the most risky option to the exporter and, therefore, is the most beneficial option to the

Export trading company: a service provider that helps domestic companies locate potential importers of their products and provides services such as preparing export documents that meet the foreign government's import requirements and arranging for transportation

Customs-house broker: a service provider that oversees the movement of goods through customs and verifies that accompanying documents are complete and accurate

Export packers: a service provider that provides the necessary packaging services for export shipments

Terms of sale: the rights and obligations of each party in the transport of goods

foreign buyer. The exporter can substantially mitigate the risk of nonpayment by using trade finance techniques, such as export credit insurance, which gives the exporter conditional assurance that payment will be made if the foreign buyer is unable to pay. [23]

PACKAGING ISSUES

As with domestic shipments, when goods are bound for international destinations, they must be packed, secured, and crated correctly. Nevertheless, there are additional factors to consider such as shipping methods, the corrosive effects from environmental conditions, and the impact of vibration and static shock during transit. In addition, the packaging needs and requirements may vary from country to country. Hence, packaging should not only provide protection and space efficiency, but it should be tailored to the consumer purchasing patterns of the country the product is being shipped to, the language differences, and the environmental and legal requirements related to packaging.

INVENTORY ISSUES

The combination of potential delays and long lead times make carrying larger inventory levels a necessity for companies engaged in global logistics. A larger inventory, of course, is more costly than a small inventory is. In addition, depending on the country where the goods are produced, stored, or consumed, the value of inventory changes when the value of currencies and exchange rates fluctuate. In a country in which the currency becomes unstable as a result of economic turmoil, firms tend to maintain greater amounts of inventory because it is considered less risky than holding cash, which could depreciate quickly. Finally, companies involved in global trade must carefully think through their inventory policies as products held as inventory in one country may not be useful in another country. Consider, for example, electrical products produced in the United States that have voltage requirements of 120 volts. These products cannot be sold in India or Europe without a voltage converter and an adaptor because many countries use 220 volts in their electrical lines. Warehousing is another issue. As we discussed earlier in Section 11.6, many developing countries such as China and India have poor and inefficient warehousing facilities and practices. Consequently, inventory costs in these countries tend to be higher because the risk associated with insufficient storage space, product obsolescence, theft, and product damage are higher. [24]

11.10 Logistics Outsourcing

Logistics outsourcing, or contract logistics, is a practice in which third-party logistics providers (3PL) perform some or all of the logistics functions—such as warehousing, outbound transportation, export packing, carrier negotiation, and freight consolidation—for a company. Many companies outsource some or all of their logistics functions to the 3PL providers, such as A&R Global Logistics, Inc. (Midland, MI) and Penske Logistics (subsidiary of Penske Corporation, Bloomfield Township, MI), so as to reduce their logistics costs and focus on their core businesses. Yet another factor that has spurred logistics outsourcing is the accelerated growth in global trade. Global 3PL providers are often better equipped to handle in-country activities and serve as freight forwarders, export trading companies, and customs house brokers, among other logistics duties.

Although it can improve the effectiveness of a company's supply chain, logistics outsourcing is complex and risky. The shipper needs to build long-term partnerships with the 3PL providers, which can be beneficial for both companies if they treat problems as mutual issues for resolution. For example, when the customers of Overhead Door Corporation (Lewisville, TX), a garage door manufacturer, complained about damage to the company's products and poor customer service and delivery, the firm partnered with one of its 3PL providers, Ryder (Ryder System, Inc., Miami, FL), to implement a solution. The solution included a mixture of inbound and outbound supply chain management activities, such as a progressive fuel-management and backhaul program. These solutions enabled the Overhead Door Corporation to reduce the in-transit damage to its products, improve customer satisfaction levels, reduce fuel costs, and generate US$1.5 million in third-party backhaul revenues. [25]

Logistics outsourcing is prevalent in both domestic and global operations and is continuously evolving. Two new types of organizations have evolved in recent years: fourth-party logistics providers (4PLs) and fifth-party logistics providers (5PLs). There is no consensus yet on the definitions of 4PL and 5PL. For our purposes, however, a 4PL provider can be defined as a company that integrates and assembles the resources, capabilities, and technology not only for its own organization but also for other 3PL providers to design, build, and implement comprehensive supply chain solutions. The focus of fifth-party logistics (5PL) firms is e-business solutions, including developing information systems for managing and tracking shipments through the supply chain. [26]

TABLE 11.2: Comparing Logistics Providers

Third-party logistics provider (3PL)	A provider of outsourced logistics services to companies for some or all of their supply chain management processes.
Fourth-party logistics provider (4PL)	An independent supply chain integrator that assembles the resources and technology needed for the activities of the shipper and other logistics providers (2PL and 3PL) to build supply solutions for the shipper.
Fifth-party logistics provider (5PL)	An independent logistics service provider that mainly specializes in e-business solutions, including developing information systems for managing or tracking shipments through the supply chain.

Describe the unique logistical needs and challenges in the service sector.

Logistics for Services

Fourth-party logistics providers (4PL): a company that integrates and assembles the resources, capabilities, and technology not only for its own organization but also for other 3PL providers to design, build, and implement comprehensive supply chain solutions

Fifth-party logistics providers (5PL): e-business solutions, including developing information systems for managing and tracking shipments through the supply chain

11.11 Logistics in the Service Sector

Although service industries do not move and store the large volumes of goods that manufacturing industries do, they have their own unique logistical needs and challenges. Because services are time-critical, the transportation needs of service firms must be met quickly. Hospitals must have medicines, the needed instruments, and a wide range of materials and supplies readily available before a surgeon can perform an operation or procedure. The transportation needs to deliver such items are often met by carriers that can make overnight deliveries. Likewise, banks must process checks and deliver the cashed checks quickly to the issuing bank. Many paper processing and movement tasks in service firms are accomplished via linked computers. The traditional logistical activities of transportation, distribution, and warehousing of physical goods also occur in services. Hotels require many supplies and logistical services, including the delivery of food and beverages, furnishings, and bedding, as do host of other companies such as pest-control and lawn-care companies, and entertainment, housekeeping, and tax preparation firms.

Managing logistics in the service sector is relatively new and, therefore, a fertile area for achieving business improvements and innovations. The health-care industry, in particular, has reaped huge benefits from innovative logistics solutions. Innovative transportation, warehousing, packaging, and labeling systems combined with tracking technology, such as RFID, have enabled products to be traced using serial numbers and have ensured they are delivered on time, accurately, and safely. Logistical solutions have also been developed to monitor and handle medications and devices that may be time or temperature sensitive. For example, Abbott Laboratories (Lake Bluff, IL) frequently examines ways to optimize the use of transportation modes, distribution channels, and routes to maximize the efficiency of its health-care logistics as well as to save fuel.[27]

The food services industry is increasingly using 3PLs. Many commercial food service companies (restaurant chains) and noncommercial food service establishments such as school and hospital cafeterias rely on 3PLs for their food service logistics and distribution needs. For example, the Papa John's Pizza (Papa John's International, Inc., Jeffersontown, KY) chain contracts with 3PL providers, to coordinate its inbound logistics needs of delivering cheese, dough, pepperoni, and tomato sauce to its more than 3,000 stores in a timely and streamlined fashion.

Logistics also play a key role in the hospitality industry, which relies heavily on customer satisfaction for its success. For companies such as Royal Caribbean Cruises Ltd. (Miami, FL), logistics disruptions (missed deliveries and products held up in customs) can mean a ship has to sail without the food and beverage choices or other supplies critical to its guests' comfort. The logistics activities for cruise lines also must be coordinated so that essential freight arrives in ports of call to meet their loading windows. Because of logistical complexities such as these, many companies in the hospitality industry turn to 3PLs providers to manage the movement of food, beverages, raw ingredients, and supplies.

Explain how sustainability issues are affecting the decisions made in logistics.

11.12 Ethical and Sustainability Issues

Ethical behavior and sustainability initiatives go hand in hand. Deceptive packaging, misleading information on package labels, covering up damaged products going out for shipment, and manipulating inventory figures are examples of unethical behaviors that occur in the world of logistics. Bribing customs officials, using child labor, and ignoring the safety of workers and mistreatment in countries with weak regulations are other examples. Fortunately, most companies realize that ethical violations are counterproductive and can damage their reputation. Consequently, there has been a concerted effort by many companies in the logistics industry to develop and adhere to codes of ethical conduct as well as to focus on sustainability.

Historically, logistical costs have been defined in purely monetary terms. In recent years, however, the increasing concerns for environmental protection, coupled with demands from consumers and other stakeholders to be more socially responsible, has led companies to redefine the cost associated with logistics activities. In addition to internal costs, companies must now account for the external costs of logistics activities that may deplete of natural resources, contribute to climate change, cause air and water pollution, cause noise or vibration, or result in accidents. Hence, companies are now faced with the challenge of achieving a more sustainable balance among economic, environmental, and social objectives as shown in Figure 11.6.

Although the logistics industry is an increasingly significant contributor to the growth of national firms and the global economy, it is also a high consumer of fossil fuels and a significant producer of carbon dioxide emissions because of its transportation activities. A report by the scientific group Intergovernmental Panel on Climate Change found that transportation accounts for nearly 15% of greenhouse gas emissions. Similarly, high-volume, large-scale warehouses and distribution centers consume a considerable amount of energy and materials as does the use of excess packaging that cannot be recycled or reused.

FIGURE 11.6: Goals of Sustainable Logistics

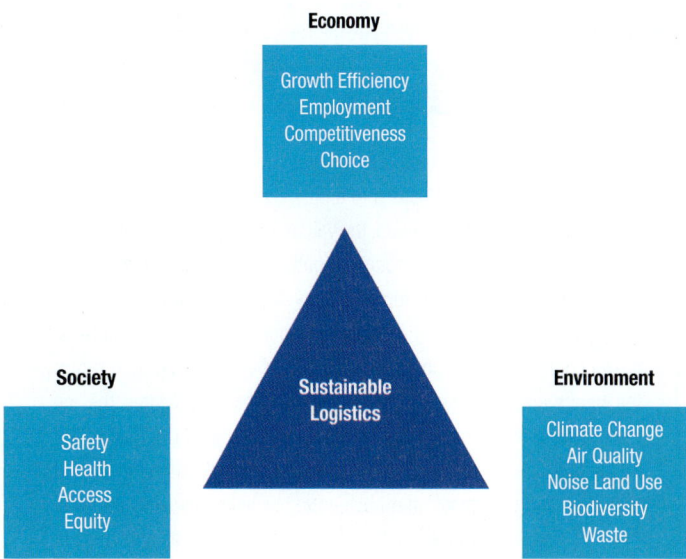

SOURCE: Green Logistics. (n.d.). What is green logistics? Retrieved from http://www.greenlogistics.org/

Because of these negative consequences, consumers and public officials are not only demanding more transparency and accountability from the logistics sector but also expecting companies to come up with logistics strategies to conserve resources, minimize the impact on the environment, and ensure the safety and health of people. Consequently, sustainability has become a critical goal for companies in the logistics industry. Maersk Line won Supply Chain Asia's "Shipping Line of the Year Award" in 2012 for achieving outstanding service reliability in a sustainable manner. Over the course of 5 years, the company had reduced its carbon dioxide emissions per container moved by 16% through various sustainability initiatives.[28] Furthermore, companies in the logistics sector that have embraced sustainability and have developed strategies to meet the sustainability challenges head on have attracted new customers.

Companies can implement many operational strategies to improve sustainability in logistics activities. Let's look at some of them.

Packaging

The global consumer industry uses annually a total of 253 metric tons of packaging materials in the form of paper and plastic. Just the production of paper packaging materials results in the loss of approximately 7 million trees each year. Using efficient and smarter packaging methods can help companies reduce the amount of packaging material they use, improve the space required on pallets and in containers, and reduce emissions. The following are strategies for achieving sustainable packaging:[29]

 Sustainable Packaging

- *Measure and monitor packaging.* To develop metrics for evaluating the impact of packaging in the retail industry, companies such as Staples, Inc. (Framingham, MA); Nike, Inc. (Beaverton, OR); and Target (Target Corporation, Minneapolis, MN) have joined to form a group known as the Sustainable Packaging Coalition. Similarly, a coalition of manufacturers and retailers has launched the Global Packaging Project to develop industry-wide standards for sustainable packaging by testing more sustainable packaging materials and techniques for future use.
- *Use Safe, Light, Recyclable, and Reusable Packaging Materials.* In 2012, Best Buy (Richfield, MN) eliminated 803 tons of PVC plastic and 713 tons of other environmentally harmful plastic materials from its Exclusive Brands packaging. In addition, Best Buy is also using recycled packaging materials, nonsolvent coatings, and organic inks wherever possible. Switching from 60-gauge to 75-gauge shrinkwrap alone can save tens of thousands of pounds of it annually.[30]

OPERATIONS MANAGEMENT: LESSONS LEARNED
Making Trucking More Cost Effective and Sustainable Through Collaboration

It makes good sense to cooperate with your competitors in the trucking industry at least when it comes to empty containers and semitrailers. In the United States and Canada, the Voluntary Interindustry Commerce Solutions Association has brought together major carriers, retailers, and manufacturers to develop an Empty Miles program to minimize waste through sharing transporting arrangements. With FTL carriers, it was common to ship containers to point of delivery and then return the trucks empty to their point of origin. It's been estimated that as many as one third of all trucks on the road are empty. The goal of the Empty Miles program is to match retailers and manufacturers that need transportation with those that have empty or below-capacity carriers. The J. C. Penney Company (aka JCPenney, Plano, TX) was able to save US$5.6 million in transport costs in 2009 by taking advantage of the empty space in containers for its shipments.

A similar program launched in the United Kingdom has been adopted by more than 40 of Britain's biggest retailers and manufacturers that agreed to share transportation. In the first three years of the program, more than 2,000 trucks were eliminated from the roadways, and 120 million miles weren't driven, saving nearly 16 million gallons of gas in the process. Not only are the programs decreasing supply chain costs for participating organizations, but they are also decreasing the carbon footprint of road transportation carriers.[34]

Similarly, a firm can improve its sustainability by finding ways to use its warehouses and office capacity more effectively. Kardex Remstar, headquartered in Zurich, Switzerland, has designed a dynamic storage system called the Lektriever Electric Lateral Filing (ELF) system, which the company claims can reduce floor space by 70%, improve worker ergonomics, and increase productivity by up to 160%. By reducing the physical space required to store items and deliver stored items to the operators at ergonomic heights, the ELF storage system achieves the goal of improving the triple bottom line of sustainability—that is, the planet, people, and profits.[35]

- *Use Innovative Package Designs.* Puma SE (Herzogenaurach, Germany) is using bags instead of boxes for its shoes. The bags look and feel like regular plastic shopping bags but are made of 100% corn starch and are completely biodegradable and compostable; they even dissolve in water.[31]
- *Converting Waste into Energy.* Some companies are devising strategies to enhance their sustainability by converting waste products into renewable energy sources. The health-care logistics unit of the 3PL provider GENCO (owned by Fed Ex, Pittsburgh, PA), for example, processes and ships seven million pounds of outdated pharmaceuticals for incineration. GENCO, in partnership with Covanta Energy in Indianapolis, has started converting this waste material into steam energy that is used to heat and cool 220 homes a year in city neighborhoods.[32]

Consolidating Facilities

Although there are many ways in which individual companies can reduce waste, energy consumption, and carbon emissions, there is even greater potential to achieve logistics sustainability within the entire supply chain. In many supply chains, functions such as packaging and distribution, returns processing, and disposal are managed independently in different locations. Combining these functions into one location can reduce carbon emissions and save money. For example, companies within the supply chain can collaborate to create consolidation centers and multiuser warehouses, which can improve the use of transportation carrier space through FTL shipments, while keeping warehousing costs to a minimum. DHL Express (division of Deutsche Post DHL, Bonn, Germany), which was contracted to manage London's Heathrow airport distribution center, was able to achieve environmental and operational benefits by consolidating 700 inbound deliveries a week into 300 outbound runs. In 2008, the consolidated deliveries of the DHL fleet saved a total of 218,000 km of transport that resulted in 158,000 kg fewer carbon emissions and a significant reduction in congestion. DHL was so successful in its role managing the consolidation center at Heathrow that London's other major airport, Gatwick, contracted with DHL to manage its logistics consolidation center.[33]

Using a Mixture of Transportation Modes and Optimizing Transportation Routes

The carbon emissions of different modes of transportation vary substantially. On average, an airplane emits 1.2 kg of carbon dioxide (CO_2) per ton-km. A ship is significantly more efficient. It emits less than 0.02 kg of CO_2 per ton-km.[36] Given the constraints of delivery speed and cost, a firm's sustainable transportation strategies may include finding opportunities to switch transportation modes from air to road or from road to rail or the use of intermodal transportation options. For example, between 2005 and 2010, Baxter International Inc. (Deerfield, IL), an American medical supply company, by using a mixture of transportation modes (rail for long distances and trucks for short distances to deliver goods to the final destination), reduced carbon emissions by 14,000 metric tons.[37]

Optimizing the transportation routes and scheduling of trucks will not only save money but also cause less damage to the environment. Many logistics companies attempt to reduce their carbon footprint by using dynamic vehicle planning and routing software systems. These systems integrate up-to-date traffic data to calculate the most efficient delivery routes, help trucks bypass traffic jams and detours, and enable them to exchange shipments during trips to speed up their delivery. In addition to achieving higher productivity per trip, planning and routing software systems reduce the distances traveled by vehicles and CO_2 emissions.

Managing Capacity

One of the biggest problems in the logistics industry today is the underuse of asset capacity warehouses, trucks, trains, and containers. For example, in the European Union, approximately 25% of the total kilometers traversed by trucks are made by empty trucks on backhauls. Empty trucks are not only wasteful economically but also have a harmful impact on the environment. Capacity underutilization from empty trips and the accompanying CO_2 emissions can be minimized by increasing the number of loaded or full backhauls, training dispatchers to optimize capacity utilization, and installing a real-time information tool such as GPS tracking technology to monitor the availability of vehicles. In addition, to use truck capacity effectively, companies should coordinate their purchasing, sales, and logistics functions; manage demand fluctuations; match product shipments to vehicle sizes and their weight restrictions; and implement just-in-time delivery methods.

Visit **edge.sagepub.com/venkataraman** to help you accomplish your coursework goals in an easy-to-use learning environment.

- Mobile-friendly eFlashcards
- Mobile-friendly practice quizzes
- A complete online action plan
- Chapter summaries with learning objectives
- Video and multimedia resources

CHAPTER SUMMARY

11.1 Identify the components of an integrated logistics management system. Integrated logistics management refers to the activities used to control the movement of products and associated costs so that there is a continuous and uninterrupted flow of products. The key components of an integrated logistics management system are order fulfillment, transportation management, packaging, materials handling, warehouse management, inventory management, and the design of a network of facilities.

11.2 List the steps in the order fulfillment process. Order fulfillment is the process by which a company responds to customer orders. It includes all the activities from the point of initial contact with the customer to the point of delivering that order. The order fulfillment process is a critical logistics activity because it is a key determinant of customer satisfaction and of whether customers will do business with you again.

11.3 Identify the decisions involved in transportation management. Transportation management involves overseeing the movement of goods and raw materials and is a vital component of nearly every business and industry. Decisions in transportation management include selecting a transportation mode and a network design strategy. The most common transportation modes are air, truck, rail, water, and pipeline. Each mode has its benefits and drawbacks. Intermodal transportation is the movement of freight stored in containers using two or more modes of transportation. Transportation network design strategies involve establishing an infrastructure that facilitates scheduling and routing decisions. The goal is to optimize the satisfaction of customers at the least possible cost. Among the critical trade-offs when designing a transportation system are transportation versus inventory costs and transportation costs versus customer responsiveness.

11.4 **Describe the role of packaging in the transport, distribution, storage, sale, and use of goods.** Product packaging affects a firm's transportation and logistics strategies and requires an organization to focus on a variety of issues such as product protection, convenience, and efficiency that affect packaging. Packaging protects the product, and it can be designed to make it easier to transport and sell a product. The various physical, chemical, and microbiological characteristics, and the shape and size of the product and the severity of the distribution environment, affect packaging choices. Firms use different types of packaging to handle and ship products as safely and efficiently as possible.

11.5 **Define materials handling, and discuss its critical role in a logistics system.** Materials handling is the short-distance movement, storage, control, and protection of materials within the confines of a plant or a warehousing facility. Materials handling plays a critical role in logistics because it has an impact on overall logistics costs, product protection, and physical safety of workers.

11.6 **Describe the functions of a warehouse and the different types of warehouses.** Major warehouse functions include order picking, inventory management, consolidation, assembly, bulk breaking, cross-docking, packaging and labeling, and reverse logistics. Public warehouses, private warehouses, and contract warehouses are the three major types of warehouses. In addition, supply warehouses, cross-docking warehouses, and distribution centers are storage facilities used to store incoming goods temporarily both at the point of origin and between the origin and consumption points.

11.7 **Explain why good inventory management is important to logistics management.** Good inventory management gives a firm the ability to locate and pick items quickly that are stored within a warehouse for subsequent loading and outbound shipment. Part of inventory management is striking the optimum balance between the costs of carrying inventory in storage against maintaining a sufficient amount of stock to meet the demands of customers.

11.8 **Discuss the importance of facilities network design in a logistics system.** In the context of an integrated logistics system, a facilities network design refers to the strategic placement of warehouses, distribution centers, service centers, and manufacturing plants throughout the supply chain. The optimum numbers and types of facilities, their locations, and the nature of their operations are decisions that have to be made as part of the facilities network design process.

11.9 **Discuss the unique challenges of managing global logistics.** When designing a global logistics framework, managers need to take into account standard logistical challenges, as well as political, economic, cultural, and distance factors. They also must complete international documentation for each shipment.

11.10 **Define logistics outsourcing, and explain why companies outsource their logistics function.** Logistics outsourcing consists of employing third-party (3PL) logistics experts who perform some or all of the necessary logistics functions of warehousing, outbound logistics, export packing, carrier negotiation, and freight consolidation. In recent years, other layers of contract logistics have become widely used, including 4PL and 5PL providers. Many companies outsource some or all of their logistics functions so as to reduce their logistics costs and focus on their core businesses. In addition, accelerated growth in global trade has spurred logistics outsourcing as the global 3PL providers are often better equipped to handle in-country activities and serve as freight forwarders, export trading companies, and customs house brokers, among other logistics duties.

11.11 **Describe the unique logistical needs and challenges in the service sector.** The traditional logistical activities of transportation, distribution, and warehousing of physical goods also occur in services. Yet, as a result of the time-critical nature of service businesses, their logistical needs must be met quickly. Innovative transportation, warehousing, packaging, and labeling systems combined with tracking technology, such as RFID, are used by many service businesses to ensure products and services are delivered on time. Because of the unique logistical complexities, many service companies turn to 3PL providers to manage their logistics functions.

11.12 **Explain how sustainability issues are affecting the decisions made in logistics.** Sustainability has shaped the decisions managers make about the logistics functions of their firms with regard to the packaging, transportation, storage, and waste generated by their operations. Companies can implement many operational strategies to improve sustainability in logistics activities, including focusing on smarter and greener packaging, consolidating facilities, employing better mixtures of transportation modes, and managing capacity.

KEY TERMS

DISCUSSION AND REVIEW QUESTIONS

1. Discuss the importance of logistics management for effective supply chain management. What factors have contributed to the evolution and growth of logistics management?

2. What are the key benefits of an integrated logistics management system?

3. What is transportation management, and why is it a critical part of an integrated logistics management system?

4. Identify the key modes of transportation, and discuss the benefits and drawbacks of each mode.

5. "If a company's target market consists of price-conscious consumers, then the firm is more likely to use slower modes of transportation." Discuss why this is so.

6. What are backhauls, and why are they often an unnecessary drain on a company's transportation resources?

7. What are some common examples of intermodal transportation? Briefly describe how each works.

8. Describe a milk-run delivery system. When would a firm use such a system?

9. How does cross-docking work?

10. Discuss the critical trade-offs related to transportation management: (a) transportation vs. inventory costs and (b) transportation costs vs. customer responsiveness. Why do these trade-offs typically occur?

11. What are the critical functions served by packaging?

12. What four strategies can improve packaging efficiency?

13. Identify the four broad categories of materials handling.

14. Explain the differences among supply warehouses, cross-docking warehouses, and distribution centers.

15. What are the functions of a warehouse?

16. What are the various critical factors to consider in global logistics?

17. Discuss and distinguish the functional differences among 3PL, 4PL, and 5PL providers.

18. What are some critical functions played by logistics in the service sector?

19. How are ethical and sustainability considerations addressed through logistics management?

PROBLEMS

1. You have just taken a job with a diversified manufacturing firm, and as your first assignment, you must make some transportation decisions on behalf of your organization for shipping its various products. Given the following set of products, argue for using air, truck, rail, or water assets to ship the product. Why would one be more appropriate than another method?

   a. Petroleum distillates from Fresno, California, to Chicago, Illinois

   b. Critical, time-sensitive medical supplies from Tampa, Florida, to Bogota, Columbia

   c. Automobile parts for secondary markets from Long Beach, California, to Shanghai, China

   d. Refurbished office equipment from Atlanta, Georgia, to Charlotte, North Carolina

2. Suppose you were designing packaging for organically grown tea. What are some of the features you would emphasize? Why? How would the various functions of packaging affect how you would package your product?

3. Assume you are the logistics manager for fictional StayFresh Grocery Stores, in Cleveland, Ohio. You are responsible for 7 stores in the metropolitan area. How might you employ cross-docking at your biggest regional warehouse to improve the distribution of goods to each of the stores? Identify how cross-docking works, and how it could aid in on-time (and fresh) produce deliveries.

4. Consider the challenges of global logistics management for selling supply chain textbooks to universities in South Africa. Identify how packaging, labeling, and inventory issues can all play critical roles in successfully managing the logistics, shipping, and distribution of the textbooks.

5. Use the Internet to search for examples of sustainable product packaging. What are some key features that many of these packages have in common?

6. Identify the three main goals of sustainable logistics. Using a product such as bottled water, explain how an organization can be creative in packaging and delivering bottled water to its markets worldwide.

CASE STUDY 11.1 HOW SUSTAINABLE LOGISTICS SOLUTIONS AND TECHNOLOGIES HAVE HELPED WAL-MART BECOME MORE EFFICIENT

Wal-Mart is the world's largest retailer in sales. The company was voted No. 1 for Retail and among the top 50 in all industries on *Fortune* magazine's "World's Most Admired Companies 2015" list. Wal-Mart earned this award in part because of its commitment to sustainability, corporate philanthropy, and employment opportunity. The importance Wal-Mart attaches to these goals can be observed in the ambitious environmental targets the company pursues. As part of its sustainability efforts, the retailer set three main goals: to be supplied 100% by renewable energy; to create zero waste; and to sell products that sustain people and the environment. To realize these targets, Wal-Mart established initiatives such as sustainable sourcing practices, energy efficiency, renewable energy, waste reduction, and life-cycle management.

Because Wal-Mart operates one of the largest private trucking fleets in the United States and the United Kingdom, many of its sustainability initiatives address the efficiency of its fleet and distribution networks. Back in 2005, the company defined measurable fleet efficiency goals for the United States to be achieved by 2008 (a 25% efficiency increase) and 2015 (a 100% efficiency increase), respectively. To achieve these goals, Wal-Mart focuses on sustainable logistics solutions and innovative technologies.

Sustainable Solutions

Wal-Mart identified routing and loads as two of the major areas of sustainability improvement. By increasing the load per truck, the total number of vehicles needed was reduced and the number of empty truck miles decreased. From 2008 to 2009, Wal-Mart decreased the number of miles per driver by more than 7%, while delivering almost 1.5% more cases of goods. This decrease in miles driven combined with improved truck technologies helped Wal-Mart avoid emitting greater than 180,000 metric tons of CO_2 emissions in 2009 and saved the company US$170 million. Furthermore, the company's affiliate in the United Kingdom, ASDA (Asda Stores Limited, Leeds, West Yorkshire, U.K.), made further achievements by increasing the flexibility of its distribution systems, thus, saving 8 million trucking miles in 2008. Backhauls were increased, so trucks that usually traveled back empty from stores to distribution centers could be used by suppliers for direct deliveries to their distribution centers. In addition, more suppliers could make use of front hauls by filling their residual capacity with ASDA goods if they were heading in the same direction. Moreover, the existing infrastructure was upgraded: distribution centers were provided with retrofitting equipment, including more efficient light bulbs and energy-demand monitoring systems that turn off lights and equipment when not in use. In addition, some distribution centers are already partially run on renewable energy. Since 2007, Wal-Mart has opened several high-efficiency stores that use 20% to 45% less energy than a typical Wal-Mart Supercenter.

Continued Efforts

Technological innovations mainly focused on the actual vehicles circulating between suppliers and distribution centers. Wal-Mart added several new technologies to its fleet to reduce emissions. The company has also tested many new technologies to see whether they are viable for business and provide a return on investment. The different measures range from installing fuel-saving technologies on trucks, to running routes with aerodynamic trucks, to using vehicles that run on alternative fuel sources, as well as to using different types of hybrid vehicles. In addition, the initiatives were expanded to the passenger cars the company makes available to its associates. By the end of 2009, Wal-Mart had managed to increase the efficiency of its U.S. fleet by 60%.

How have their sustainability targets been met to date? In 2015, the company announced that it had exceeded the goal, set in 2010, to eliminate 20 million metric tons of greenhouse gas emissions from its global supply chain. In fact, it has eliminated 28.2 million metric tons to date, the equivalent of the emissions of nearly 6 million cars over a year. Wal-Mart also has doubled the fuel efficiency of its fleet since 2005, through its innovations in loading, routing, and driving techniques, as well as through new tractor and trailer technologies, saving US$1 billion along the way. Other goals are proving more elusive. For example, the target that it "be supplied 100% by renewable energy" by 2015 has not been met; in fact, Wal-Mart reported that 26% of its energy usage is currently from renewable sources. On the other hand, the company's goal of being "waste free" is nearly complete as it reported an 83% diversion of waste from its facilities in the United States.

Wal-Mart continues to make further efforts and, thus, has extended its sustainability program to its logistics suppliers. Wal-Mart announced plans to develop a worldwide sustainable product index. The effort includes supplier assessments, the creation of a life-cycle analysis database, and a simple tool to help consumers make more sustainable choices through product labeling. Said Mike Duke, former president and CEO of Wal-Mart, "The sustainability product index will bring about a more transparent supply chain, drive product innovation, and ultimately provide consumers with the information they need to assess the sustainability of products. If retailers work together with suppliers and logistics suppliers, we can create a new retail standard for the 21st century."[38]

Questions

1. Why are the logistics decisions of a retailer like Wal-Mart so important for other firms to be aware of and emulate?

2. Why has Wal-Mart taken a more environmentally conscious approach to logistics?

3. How does sustainable logistics equal ethical logistics?

VIDEO CASE

Watch this video case to learn about how MPK Foods, a family-owned company that produces seasoning mixes sold to grocery stores, makes decisions about logistics for their business.

CRITICAL THINKING EXERCISES

A company involved in global distribution of its products faces many challenges. Discuss some strategies that you would implement for distribution of a company's products in Japan.

1. Suppose, in the first instance, that the products were high-technology electronics that were very fragile and required careful room-temperature monitoring.

2. Now, in the second instance, suppose you were looking to distribute timber products for residential construction.

How might your distribution strategy change in these two circumstances? Identify the critical issues you need to address for each scenario.

CHAPTER
12

Demand Management and Customer Service

LEARNING OBJECTIVES

After studying this chapter, you should be able to:

1 Explain the importance of demand management for organizations, and identify the factors that affect it.

2 Describe the challenges of global demand management and the strategies that can be used to address them.

3 Identify the unique nature of services demand management, and discuss the risks from excess and insufficient capacity.

4 Propose and apply the four supply chain dimensions of customer service.

5 Discuss the sustainability and ethical issues in customer service.

OPERATIONS PROFILE: Demand Management Is Fueling Sales Success at Levi-Strauss

©iStockphoto.com/@laurent

During the economic downturn of 2008–2010, retailers around the world were stuck with high inventories when consumers stopped shopping. This drop in demand forced the retailers to take steep markdowns and resulted in low profit margins. Since that time, many of these firms have paid more attention to forecasting and demand management. By researching what products sell best in various markets, they have made better ordering decisions and have stocked the right brands and product lines in individual stores and geographic locations. The retailers have also cut down on over-buying and on having to mark down merchandise to sell it.

An annual survey of apparel spending patterns conducted in 2010 by AMR Research, Inc. (Boston, MA) suggested that the main way clothing firms planned to fuel growth was to increase their sales of existing products. "There are a number of macro-challenges facing retailers today that all tie back to why they're asking about demand forecasting and replenishment," said Mike Griswold, VP of retail research at AMR. Among these challenges are the growth of their own brand-name products, increases in multiple selling channels, and more fickle shoppers. These events make it harder for retailers to predict and satisfy customers' demands. Shoppers are knowledgeable about products and styles even before setting foot inside a retail store. "Eighty-five percent of shoppers do some kind of online research prior to entering your store," Griswold explained, noting that they care about quality, but price remains a critical issue. "Price is also one of the top decision-makers for consumers in terms of where they shop and what they buy, and being able to understand movement relative to price is incredibly important for retailers," Griswold stated.

Figuring out how to deal with demand changes is a critical part of Levi Strauss & Co.'s (San Francisco, CA) operating strategy—one that benefits the company's bottom line. The clothing maker sells its products at the wholesale level and through its own network of retail stores, the numbers of which have been growing rapidly. The firm uses a software system to forecast the demand for its goods both within geographic regions and at specific stores. The system allows Levi-Strauss to conduct volume and location-level forecasting, as well as to replenish stocking by store grading: Higher graded (more profitable) stores get replenished first. The clothing firm also adjusts store inventory levels based on seasonal shifts and, on average, can replenish stores twice a week.

How has all of this helped Levi-Strauss? Since the implementation of the system, the value of the company's stock on-hand have been reduced by 20%, excess stock is down by 30%, and lost sales because of stock-outs have been reduced by 5%. Executives at the company also note that they have improved their ability to react to stores selling certain items more quickly and are far better at anticipating inventory needs arising from seasonal shifts and changing fashion trends. Levi-Strauss has also used the software system to manage its logistics and store-shipment transit times to maximize its sellable space through more frequent replenishment runs if need be.[1]

12.1

Explain the importance of demand management for organizations, and identify the factors that affect it.

Master the content.

edge.sagepub.com
/venkataraman

Effective Demand Management

Bullwhip effect: the result of a change in consumer demand that causes a company in a supply chain in close proximity to the consumer (such as a retailer) to order more goods from the immediate upstream supplier (such as a wholesaler or distributor) to meet the demand

Demand forecasting: the process of estimating the demand for a firm's products in the near future

Demand planning: the process of accurately forecasting the demand for a company's products and services well into the future to give the company and its supply chain partners a basis for all the planning needed to acquire the supplies to meet that demand

12.1 Demand Management

Demand management is the process of first determining accurately what the customer wants, and then coordinating the processes and procedures both within the firm and across its supply chain to meet that demand quickly and efficiently. If a huge snowstorm is forecast for the Midwest region of United States, companies such as Home Depot (The Home Depot, Inc., Atlanta, GA) and Lowe's (Lowe's Companies, Inc., Mooresville, NC), among others, rely on demand management to stock their midwestern stores with snow shovels and snowblowers so that the total demand—actual customer orders as well as forecasted demand—is matched against capacity. Mismatches between the two will result in lost sales or inventory that sits on store shelves.

In addition, companies in almost every industry face challenges that come from high customer expectations, governmental regulations, changing market dynamics, and the ongoing impact of technologies such as smartphone apps. To respond to these challenges, like Levi-Strauss, firms seek new approaches to forecast and manage demand by using best-in-class techniques and state-of-the-art technologies that exploit every link in their supply chains.[2]

Effective demand management is important not only for a company's operational function but also for a company's other functional areas. These are some of the functional areas in which demand management activities have an impact:

- **Supply chain.** Demand influences the supply chain design decisions, such as when the firm must find new sources of supply.
- **Finance.** Demand influences capital investment decisions, such as investments in technology and changes in capacity.
- **Marketing.** Demand influences new product introductions and product portfolio planning.
- **Human resources.** Demand determines how many employees are hired or let go, as well as overtime for current workers.

Accurate demand planning and effective demand management have numerous benefits, including the mitigation of the **bullwhip effect** that causes unwanted inventories in the supply chain. The bullwhip effect suggests that in response to changes in customer demand, inventory fluctuations increase as you move further up in the supply chain from the retailer to the raw material supplier. By generating accurate forecasts of product quantities that will be demanded at specific times and places, demand planning and management activities can facilitate implementation of just-in-time production systems. Inaccurate demand planning and poor demand management, on the other hand, can lead to excess inventories in the supply chain, unwanted or idle capacity, lost wages, and so forth.

Factors That Affect Demand Management

Managers have to consider how economic, technological, and internal company factors could influence customer demand and production processes and schedules. For example, economic factors such as average household incomes, employment levels, inflation, and interest rates will affect customers' purchasing power and, hence, the demand for a company's products. Similarly, other economic factors, such as general price levels, will determine the cost of raw materials or transportation costs, which in turn will affect the company's production levels that are needed to meet demand. New technologies that create new products and new processes affect a company's demand management process as well. For example, technological advances have created demand for new product possibilities such as drones, self-driving automobiles, and three-dimensional (3-D) televisions. Similarly, process improvements resulting from technological advances, such as bar coding and radio-frequency identification (RFID), have all led to improved product and service quality, increases in productivity, and reductions in the costs of production. Internal company factors also influence the ability of an organization to manage demand effectively. These internal factors include the human, technological, financial, and physical resources available to the company and its ability to acquire these resources and make effective use of them to manage demand. Figure 12.1 shows the various stages of the demand-management process, which we will discuss in detail in the rest of this chapter.

Demand Planning

Demand management begins with **demand forecasting**, in which the firm estimates the demand for a firm's products in the near future. **Demand planning** goes further. It requires accurately forecasting the demand for a company's products and services well into the future and gives the company and its

FIGURE 12.1: Demand-Management Process

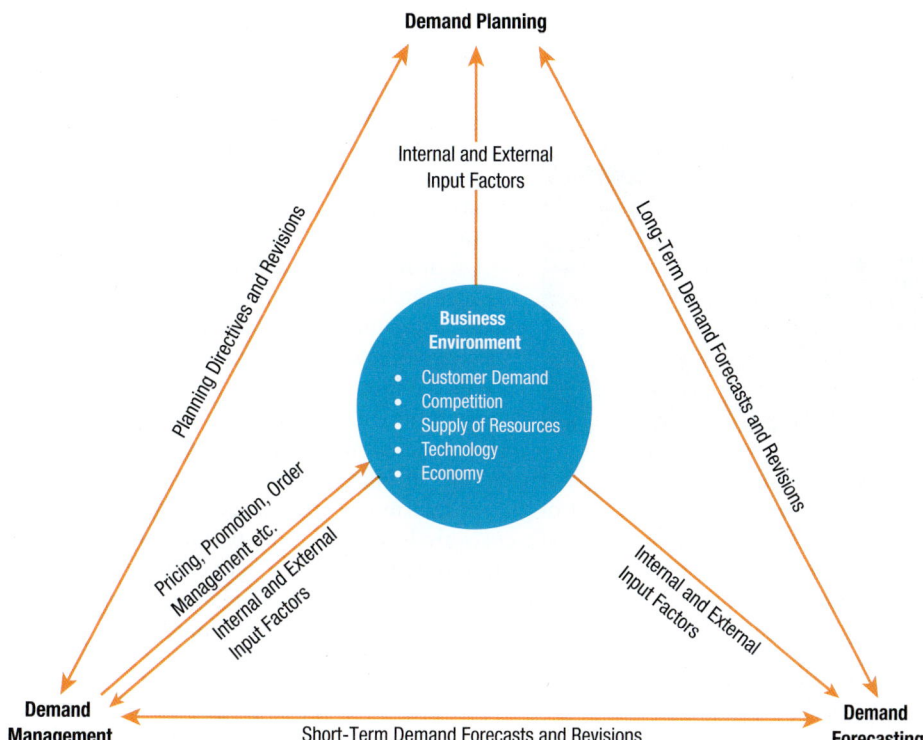

supply chain partners a basis for all the planning needed to acquire the supplies to meet that demand. Demand planning is important for the following reasons:[3]

- **It provides a way to track a firm's progress toward achieving its revenue and profit targets.** Every company has an annual operating plan for achieving its revenue and profit targets. By developing a monthly demand plan, the company can track its progress toward achieving these annual targets. If the demand plan indicates that the firm's performance will fall short, corrective actions, such as reducing operating costs, can be taken to achieve the desired profit targets.
- **It provides a clear picture of the market dynamics that affect demand.** The process of demand planning goes beyond short-term demand forecasting and includes an analysis of product and market trends, seasonal demand, price, promotions, and customer activities that determine sales volume. The information generated by this analysis provides the company's sales and marketing departments with a clear picture of the dynamics affecting the demand for products so they can engage in activities to increase sales and maximize the firm's revenues.
- **It helps a firm provide superior customer service.** By identifying what products are being demanded by which customers and when, demand planning also tracks the variability in demand. The company can then stock extra inventory or expedite production to be sure that products are available when the customers need them.
- **It reduces operational costs.** Companies that engage in demand planning are constantly tracking demand, which enables them to achieve optimal supply chain efficiency by ensuring that materials arrive on time, reducing waste in the form of excess and obsolete inventories, reducing the use of overtime and idle time during production, and reducing or eliminating the need for expedited deliveries. As a result of such operational efficiencies, material, production, and logistics costs are reduced.
- **It promotes innovation.** Because part of demand planning includes evaluating customers' needs and desires on an ongoing basis, the process helps companies identify opportunities for introducing new products and services. By looking at a variety of demand scenarios and ranges, a company can evaluate the benefits and risks of new product introductions. For example, retailing organizations are better able to coordinate their Internet and social media communications to link directly with their customers, passing along coupons and other

Investments in transportation such as rail networks are based on long-term demand management decisions.

©iStockphoto.com/mizoula

special offers. They are also better able to analyze the purchase data they receive to fine-tune their product offerings, product orders from suppliers, and inventory levels.

LONG-TERM DEMAND PLANNING DECISIONS

Long-term demand planning decisions involve issues that will concern the organization for several years and will require the firm to project its aggregate demand from the present to the future. In terms of a firm's supply chain, for example, long-term issues include designing a supply chain and planning for supply chain capacity. What will the projected volume flows through the supply chain be? Will the flow be through existing routes or require new routes? Does the existing supply chain network have enough warehouse and transportation capacity to handle the volumes and so forth? For example, in North America, railroads are expected to generate huge new revenues as a result of greater intermodal transportation, trade with countries abroad, and the fact that fuel and shipping costs are lower per ton mile for rail than they are for truck or air. The U.S. Department of Transportation estimates that freight demand is likely to grow to $27.5 billion by 2040, and North America's Railroad companies are anticipating this demand by investing $14 billion in additional track, rail yards, and refueling stations.[4]

INTERMEDIATE-TERM PLANNING DECISIONS

Making demand projections and product portfolio and financial planning decisions are the focus of intermediate demand planning, which typically ranges from three months to three years. The objective of these decisions is to establish profit and revenue targets, the optimum mixture of products needed to meet the demand, and the procurement of the resources needed to meet production targets. For example, rare earth minerals are critical to companies in the high-tech and green industries such as those that manufacture smartphones, tablets, or solar panels. Nevertheless, these materials are scarce. Therefore, procurement decisions for these materials have to be made well in advance of production.

SHORT-TERM DEMAND PLANNING DECISIONS

The time horizon for short-term demand planning decisions is three months or less. Operational decisions, including inventory planning and control, purchasing, and transportation for inbound and outbound materials, are the focus. The demand projections related to these activities are more detailed in the sense that the forecasts are at the individual product and facility levels, often in daily or weekly time intervals. These decisions aim to guarantee that the firm can fulfill customer orders and has adequate stocks of inventory.

Demand Forecasting

 Forecasting Demand

As we explained, demand forecasting is the process of estimating the demand for a firm's products. Consider, for example, a retailer such as Nordstrom, Inc. (Seattle, WA), with stores in cities across North America, including New York, Chicago, Los Angeles, Dallas, and San Francisco. The logistics manager for Nordstrom needs to know the expected sales in a given period for a specific store, such as the one in San Francisco or Dallas. With this information, the manager can coordinate shipments of specific quantities of goods at specific times to these individual stores. Hence, logistics systems need accurate demand forecasts by product, by individual stocking location, and by time periods to function effectively and efficiently.

Note that demand forecasts are rarely accurate in predicting the exact, actual demand that will occur in every future period. According to AMR Research, forecasting errors—the deviations of actual demand from the forecast—for most products are in the range of 11% to 28%. Forecasts are typically inaccurate because many factors influence demand, and it is almost impossible for a forecaster to identify all of them and their effects. Hence, the best forecasting approaches are those that minimize forecasting errors. By improving its forecast, for a given level of inventory, the firm can provide superior customer service or, for given desired level of customer service, hold less inventory.[6]

Forecasters view actual demand as a combination of predictable and random variations. Predictable variations are those that follow a pattern, such as the increase in ice cream consumption during the

Forecasting errors: the deviations of actual demand from the forecast

Consider This 12.1:
Strong Demand Spells Shortages for Subaru of America

High U.S. demand for its automobiles in 2013 put Subaru of America (subsidiary of Subaru, Cherry Hill, NJ) in the difficult position of trying to increase a production process that was already operating at full capacity. Because of strong ratings in consumer outlets, such as *Consumer Reports*, the demand and sales forecasts for Subaru cars, particularly its Forester SUV model, rapidly outstripped the company's ability to keep up, leading to shortages and a production backlog. At one point, the company had only a 16-day supply of Foresters in the United States.

Subaru's growth strategy for the future in the United States involves investing heavily in its Lafayette, Indiana, plant and increasing its production volume by 50%. The Lafayette plant is the only Subaru manufacturing facility in the world outside of Japan, and the company was concerned that healthy demand in America made it impossible for production facilities on the other side of the Pacific to keep up. Subaru announced the investment of US$140 million to expand its facilities and hire 1,200 new employees. As a longer term solution, it was a step in the right direction, although in the short term, it was too late to prevent some lost sales. Yasuyuki Yoshinaga, the company's CEO, noted that unexpected demand was bound to lead to supply shortages in the short term. Even if dealers want more, there is little the company can do soon, he said.[5]

summer months. Random variations are minor changes in demand that are caused by unknown factors and cannot be foreseen. Various mathematical and statistical approaches can be used to generate forecasts. To reduce the magnitude of forecasting errors, forecasters try to choose a forecasting method that will include all relevant factors and account for the randomness in the actual demand.

Historical data are used to predict the average or trend of actual demand, based on the assumption that the past behavior of demand is a reliable predictor of its future. Yet, expansion of product lines and globalization has further increased the randomness and volatility of the demand for products. Hence, past demand is just one possible indicator of future demand. Consequently, in today's volatile business environment, forecasts prepared using mathematical and statistical approaches should be viewed as one of many inputs in the demand planning process. Chapter 13 contains a complete discussion of the most frequently used forecasting methods.

Two additional approaches that can reduce the inaccuracy of forecasts are (1) collaborative forecasting between the company, its customers, and its suppliers and (2) acceleration of the forecasting process to reduce forecasting errors.[7]

COLLABORATIVE FORECASTING

Collaborative forecasting is the process-gathering information from within and outside of the organization to forecast the demand for a product. Among the factors considered are (a) historical demand, including patterns, similar products, seasonality, and macro- and microeconomic trends; (b) demand changes resulting from promotions and advertising campaigns; (c) new product introductions and competitors' activity; and (d) the unique insight and judgment of the company's supply chain partners. The inputs to the forecasting process typically include updated forecasts of the demand for a firm's products or product families from the company's sales force, distributors, and wholesalers; historical demand data; recent demand information from actual point-of-sale data; and information from the company's marketing department about market changes, trends, and transitions from one product to another.

Collaborative forecasting is part of **collaborative planning, forecasting, and replenishment (CPFR)**, a highly popular and successful business process in supply chain management. Wal-Mart (Wal-Mart Stores Inc., Bentonville, AR), in 1995, was the first to use the CPFR process. Since then hundreds of companies from a wide variety of industries have adopted it. CPFR seeks to enhance the integration and efficiency of supply chains by encouraging supply chain partners to collaborate on activities such as demand planning and forecasting, inventory management, and information sharing. Supply chains partners that have successfully implemented CPFR have reduced merchandising, inventory, logistics, and transportation costs significantly.[8]

Figure 12.2 illustrates the four major collaborative activities that buyers and sellers in a supply chain need to undertake to satisfy the demands of the end consumer. The key features of the CPFR process through all these four phases of activities are cooperation and information sharing among supply chain partners.[9] During the strategy and planning phase, the buyers and sellers in the chain establish common business goals and delineate the scope of collaboration and the response to events that cause supply chain disruptions. The next step in this phase is for

Collaborative forecasting: the process of gathering information from within and outside of the organization to forecast the demand for a product

Collaborative planning, forecasting, and replenishment (CPFR): a process that enhances the integration and efficiency of supply chains through collaboration between supply chain partners on activities such as demand planning and forecasting, inventory management, and information sharing

FIGURE 12.2: Collaborative Planning, Forecasting, and Replenishment (CPFR) Process

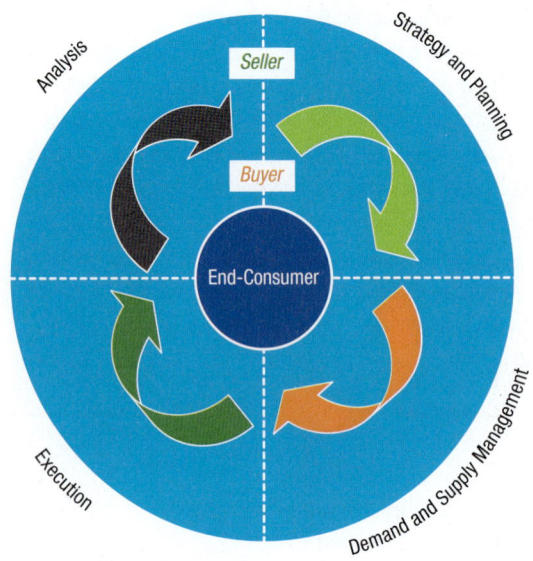

Exception management: the continuous monitoring of shortages or sudden changes in the quality of materials

Godiva Chocolatier uses a program called SmartForecasts to track inventory and demand in real time and make more accurate forecasts.

©iStockphoto.com/Bosca78

the buyers and sellers to develop a joint business plan that identifies some of the significant events, such as marketing promotions, inventory policy changes, or new-product introductions that could affect supply and demand.

There are two tasks in the demand and supply management phase. The first is sales forecasting, and the second is order planning. Based on the sales forecasts, the firm will plan its orders. Order planning involves determining future product ordering and delivery requirements, inventory levels, transit lead times, logistical constraints, and other factors that affect the supply required to meet end-consumer demand. During the execution phase, goods are produced, stocked, shipped, and delivered to meet demand. The tasks during the analysis phase include exception management and performance assessment. Exception management is the continuous monitoring of shortages or sudden changes in the quality of materials. These unexpected events are referred to as exceptions. Performance assessment involves the development and calculation of key metrics to evaluate how well the organization has achieved business goals. Performance assessment also is used to monitor trends in the industry so that alternative strategies can be developed quickly if deemed necessary. Problems implementing CPFR arise if supply chain partners cannot determine common goals, collaborate, and share sensitive (proprietary) information with one another.[10]

ACCELERATING THE FORECASTING PROCESS

Accelerating the forecasting process is another way to improve the accuracy of forecasts.[11] Forecasts can be accelerated when processes used to collect demand data are automated, enabling the forecaster to consolidate and review the information quickly. The faster the forecaster can access current changes in demand, the more accurate the forecast will be. When companies receive the most current and updated demand forecasts from all of their supply chain partners, they can determine in which distribution centers and warehouses inventories should be stocked. This will ensure that demand from end-consumers for the top-selling products will always be met.

Developing a unified database that gives all the participants in the forecasting process immediate information about demand is another way to reduce forecasting errors. As a result of advances in information technology, information flows in real time within and across businesses result in better forecasts. Godiva Chocolatier (subsidiary of Yıldız Holding, New York, NY), a manufacturer of high-quality confections, is one of the many companies in the consumer industry that uses technology to manage demand. The program adopted by Godiva is called SmartForecasts. It uses three years of demand history to generate its monthly forecasts, and it projects these forecasts 18 months into the future. The technology has been very successful at reducing stock-outs and at maintaining the highest possible service level.[12] Developing ways to aggregate and disaggregate demand data across product families and time periods to generate demand forecasts for individual products and time periods can improve the timeliness and accuracy of forecasts as well.

Proactively Managing Demand

The third phase of the demand management process is to manage consumer demand proactively to meet the company's revenue and profit targets. Whereas demand planning has a long-term time horizon, managing consumer demand focuses on the short term. The goal is to monitor current consumer demand so that the company does not reduce its profits as result of temporary fluctuations in the demand for its products.[13] Demand can be managed proactively through promotions, sales incentives, and price changes to increase demand. Firms can also shift demand to different time periods by staggering customer order fulfillment or delivery due dates. Companies often adopt this tactic to avoid lost revenue if their existing production capacity is insufficient to meet all of the customers' demand in the current period. In the event of a stock-out, the firm can attempt to market a product with comparable features or a lower price. The Shaw Industries Group, Inc. (subsidiary of Berkshire Hathaway, Inc., Dalton, GA), a leading carpet manufacturer in the world, implemented a life-cycle planning solutions technology to respond rapidly to demand changes for its products. The use of this technology enabled the company to improve forecast accuracy by 19%, reduce its obsolete inventory by 30%, and improve its gross margins by more than US$1 million a year.[14]

A company's internal demand management activities need to be well coordinated too if a firm is to manage its demand proactively. For example, the company's sales and marketing personnel, who are responsible for creating and driving demand, should be aware of any production constraints, such as the firm's available capacity to produce a product. Otherwise, the marketing group will devote resources to promoting a product that operations cannot deliver. Conversely, operations personnel should be aware of and do everything they can to meet the product delivery dates sales representatives have promised customers and to understand the priorities associated with various customer orders.

12.2 Global Demand Management

The primary challenge of global demand management is ensuring that inventories are readily available when demand arises in many, geographically dispersed locations. If supply chains are more localized, companies have greater flexibility in responding to demand fluctuations. For example, if demand for a company's products softens, it is typically easier for the firm to cancel orders with local suppliers on a short notice than with more distant suppliers. On the other hand, if demand increases above anticipated levels, the firm can place new orders with local suppliers with reasonable assurance that the suppliers will deliver on time. The reason that localized supply chains are more responsive to order changes is that they often have shorter lead times (usually days or weeks). Global suppliers have more difficulty responding because, in a long, multitiered global supply chain, lead times (as much as a year) between actual demand and the point at which the needed supplies to meet that demand enter the supply pipelines can be lengthy. By the time an organization can determine that a change in demand has occurred, inventories are already in the supply pipeline. If there is a downturn in demand, companies have few options other than selling the products at a deep discount to reduce the excess inventory. For example, by the time companies could understand the severity of the global economic crisis starting in 2009, they had already committed to their inventory orders, even though the larger quantities weren't needed. Nevertheless, a business that reduces inventory substantially when demand wanes can eventually be harmed if consumers are left with too few products and product choices. For example, when customers expect clothing to be available in many sizes and colors, a fashion retailer must stock this range of items or lose sales to competitors.[15]

Global demand volatility also affects a company's upstream suppliers. Because of the long end-to-end replenishment lead times, a company's suppliers also hold additional inventories of raw materials or intermediary products in anticipation of the company placing definite orders. If the company cancels its orders as a result of a demand downturn, the suppliers are stuck with inventories for which demand no longer exists. Conversely, during periods of demand upswings, the long lead times of global supply chains also affect a company's ability to meet demand because it will take significantly longer time to get goods flowing again through the supply chain.

To mitigate these costs and risks, companies need to improve their global demand planning, synchronize all of their supply chain operations, and adopt the demand planning and management strategies discussed earlier in this chapter. That is, they need to (a) use point-of-sale (POS) data, (b) increase the frequency of forecasting so forecasts can be evaluated more often against actual demand to determine forecasting errors, (c) collaborate and share timely information with their supply chain partners, and (d) coordinate their internal demand management activities.

Technology is important in implementing these strategies. For example, one of the world's largest pharmaceutical companies implemented demand-planning solutions—a software program to get an accurate and undistorted view of the company's global demand for its products and to improve forecasting accuracy. By implementing demand planning solutions, the company was able to aggregate forecasts across markets in multiple units of measure. In other words, the company was able to aggregate its forecasts in terms of individual items, cases, or any other appropriate units of measure. As a result, the company was able to gain an accurate and undistorted view of global demand forecasts

12.2

Describe the challenges of global demand management and the strategies that can be used to address them.

 Global Demand Management

for its pharmaceutical products, which allowed the company to synchronize its manufacturing and production processes. The pharmaceutical manufacturer now has a comprehensive demand-planning system that is managed centrally, flexibly supporting both local market analysis and enabling global best practices.[16]

Another global demand management strategy that has been very effective is postponement. Recall from Chapter 9 that with this strategy, the manufacturing or the distribution of the final product is delayed until the customer's order is received. This option requires manufacturing firms to purchase components or retailers to order products that can be instantly configured as close to the point-of-sale as possible. The final product configuration is postponed until the last possible moment to allow for maximum customization while maintaining the minimum inventory necessary to manufacture or assemble the product. For example, for a product such as a smartphone, a customer can theoretically select from more than 2,500 options as part of the phone and service. Yet, through proper cell phone design, a manufacturer can offer these various options by assembling and configuring the cell phones from just 200 different components and software choices. The mobile phone manufacturer now has to forecast demand and produce only the right amounts of these 200 different components. Then, by using the postponement strategy, the firm can build the 2,500 various options as and when customers demand them.[17]

In general, most companies that have implemented postponement strategies have been able to match supply with demand and reduce their inventory, while responding promptly to changing customer demands. The companies have been able to offer a wider range of customized products and reduce the number of outdated products in their inventory.[18] There are, however, drawbacks of a postponement strategy. First, it is not a strategy that will work in all situations. For example, a supplier of medical equipment and critically needed medical supplies cannot use postponement as its supply chain strategy. The second drawback is the higher cost associated with customizing products and the need to have universal parts in inventory.

12.3 Services Demand Management

12.3

Identify the unique nature of services demand management, and discuss the risks from excess and insufficient capacity.

Like manufacturers of goods, businesses in service sectors, such as hospitals, movie theaters, motels, restaurants, information processing, and airlines, also experience fluctuating demand. The demand fluctuations can be short term, such as hourly or weekly (for example, happy hour at a local pub), or long term, such as the seasonal increase in demand experienced by accountants and tax preparation services prior to April 15 every year. Unlike manufactured goods, however, services cannot be inventoried to satisfy demand at a future date. Therefore, their fluctuating demand is a challenge for service providers. This problem is particularly critical for companies in service industries, such as transportation, hospitality, entertainment, and health care that have capacity limits. The capacity constraints in these industries can take the form of a shortage of needed equipment or skilled workers.

Service providers face two types of risks if they do not accurately predict and manage their demand:

- Excess capacity in the form of idle resources, which add to costs without providing value. Think of a restaurant that overscheduled its wait staff on a slow night. These workers must be paid even though they are underused.
- Insufficient capacity, which leads to poor service quality and prevents the business from growing. Consider a health-care clinic opening in a part of town without adequate medical care. Initially, the clinic may be so flooded with patients that the medical staff cannot keep up, leading to inadequate care and a loss of patients to other facilities.

Managing the demand for a service business hinges on calculating the service capacity it will need well in advance of the demand and being flexible enough to use its available capacity effectively. The process should begin by determining the productive capacity (resources) that the service provider requires. For example, a restaurant needs cooks, wait staff, cleaning staff to clear and reset tables, bartenders, and greeters. The next step is to determine the reasons that demand fluctuates. In the case of the restaurant, the highest demand often occurs on weekends and at lunch and dinner times. Armed with this information, service providers can develop demand management strategies, such as making sure the restaurant is appropriately staffed to handle these peak service flows.

In the short term, if demand and available capacity are well matched, then the demand for services can be managed by redistributing capacity so that critical services such as emergency services in hospitals are not affected. Many service providers redistribute capacity by using appointment and reservation systems. For example, doctors' and lawyers' offices meet the demand fluctuations for their services by scheduling appointments for their patients and clients. Hotels, restaurants, and car rental agencies also try to use reservations systems to manage the demand for their services and to minimize customer-waiting times. Similarly, information technology (IT) service providers handle the demand for limited broadband capacity by rescheduling the processing of some of the less important tasks away from peak times. For example, a bank may use its IT service provider to reconcile accounts late at night or on weekends, when the need for their services is minimal. This is a cost-effective way of maintaining service delivery quality without paying the added expense from increasing the broadband width.

Regardless of the methods used (appointments, reservations, or the rescheduling of tasks), to achieve efficiency, service providers will generate short-term (daily or weekly) forecasts of demand for their services. For example, banks need to determine how much cash to maintain in their ATMs and reasonable replenishment schedules so they don't run out of it, while ensuring too much cash isn't sitting idle in the machines and not earning interest for the bank. Therefore, bank cash management services use forecasting algorithms to determine the optimum amount of cash needed at specific points in time.

Over the medium to long term, the organization uses demand forecasts primarily for financial, capacity, and workforce planning and for the acquisition or creation of the assets needed to deliver services. Although service providers can increase their capacity during peak periods by expanding their capacity and hiring additional employees, these changes always increase costs. If the demand wanes, the firm will then be stuck with the extra capacity. Therefore, service providers should first gauge their existing capacity to identify and eliminate bottlenecks and to assess whether it is possible to redistribute the workload over the long term to offer a high-quality service without increasing capacity. For example, in the banking industry, common bottlenecks in a mortgage application approval process are home inspection and appraisal. Similarly, in a hospital, a lack of adequate resources such as specialized equipment and skilled labor needed to conduct sequences of activities such as physical exams, CT scans, or surgery can create bottlenecks.

Accurately forecasting the demand for their services involves taking into consideration historical data and current trends, involving real-time developments that can better align a company's resources to match demand in both the short and the long term. The most successful service providers have adopted stringent demand planning and forecasting processes by involving and integrating all functions within the company into these processes and by using relevant demand planning and forecasting software technologies. As a result, these service providers have achieved the dual and often conflicting objectives of reducing costs and delivering quality services.

12.4 Customer Service and Demand Management

Demand management and customer service are closely linked. Recall that order fulfillment is a key determinant of how satisfied our customers are and whether a firm can retain them for future sales. Customers want the right product, at the right price, in the right condition, delivered to the right place, and at the right time. Therefore, from a supply chain perspective, customer service can be defined as the ability to satisfy customers in terms of time, reliability, communication, and convenience.[19] Let us consider these four supply chain dimensions of customer service.

The Role of Customer Service in Supply Chains

TIME
The time dimension is the ability of the supply chain to reduce the cycle time involved in fulfilling a customer order from the point an order was received. Customers in a supply chain, whether it is a retailer or end-consumer, prefer companies that fulfill their orders quickly. The success of online grocery stores such as AmazonFresh (Amazon.com, Seattle, WA) or Peapod (Peapod, LLC, Skokie, IL) rests on their ability to receive orders, process them, and deliver products to customers' homes within a day of ordering.

RELIABILITY
Reliable customer service consists of **order cycle time consistency**, delivery safety, and order delivery completeness.[20] Downstream customers in a supply chain, such as retailers, value consistent order cycle times because they are predictable. In Chapter 14, we will show that with consistent order cycle times, these customers can better plan the inventory levels they need to satisfy their customers. **Delivery safety** is the ability of companies to deliver products to customers without loss or damage. **Order delivery completeness** is the ability of a company to deliver the orders placed by customers

---

Managing Demand for Services

12.4 Propose and apply the four supply chain dimensions of customer service.

Order cycle time consistency: a factor of reliable customer service

Delivery safety: the ability of companies to deliver products to customers without loss or damage

Order delivery completeness: the ability of a company to deliver the orders placed by customers fully and completely

fully and completely. Like lost or damaged products, incomplete order deliveries can cause customer dissatisfaction and lead to out-of-stock situations for retailer customers. One measure companies often use to track order delivery completeness is the **order fill rate**, which is the percentage of customer orders that can be fully and completely filled from items in stock. Of course, reliability, in terms of order cycle time consistency, safe deliveries, and order delivery completeness may not be completely achievable as a result of factors beyond a company's control. Nonetheless, companies that do perform at high levels across these three elements are often cited for their outstanding customer service. For example, L.L. Bean, Inc. (Freeport, ME), the apparel maker and retailer, is often rated highly in consumer surveys for its outstanding customer service, particularly for its consistent and speedy order deliveries and order fill rate.

COMMUNICATION

Effective communication between the seller and the customer is a key part of customer service because it is the channel for obtaining critical customer feedback on the company and its supply chain performance. In addition to a company's customer service, representatives need full and complete information to resolve any issues customers might have in addition to having the communication skills of listening, empathizing, and speaking clearly. Live chat, social media sites, and e-mail have facilitated communications. Yet, personal and face-to-face communication remain essential to good customer service. Companies that operate in the global environment should be aware that telephone and face-to-face communication with customers is still the norm in many countries.

CONVENIENCE

"Convenience" in customer service refers to making the product or service available when and where the customer wants it. Increasingly, customers today are basing their purchasing decisions on the dimension of convenience. In many countries, businesses now operate longer hours and are open even on weekends. For example, some banks in the United States and Canada have late-evening hours of operation and are open even on Saturdays and Sundays to provide superior service and convenience to their customers. Likewise, many medical offices now schedule early morning walk-in hours and Saturday morning appointments to accommodate working families who do not have the flexibility to come during regular office hours. Online banking, booking car pickups through Uber (Uber Technologies, Inc., San Francisco, CA), online travel booking apps, and online shopping also fulfill customers' demands for convenience.

To provide greater convenience to their customers, companies have responded by developing **multichannel marketing systems**—that is, systems that allow customers to purchase products and have them delivered in different ways. For example, brick-and-mortar stores such as Best Buy (Richfield, MN), Sears (Sears, Roebuck & Co., Hoffman Estates, IL), Home Depot (already introduced in this chapter), Target (Target Corporation, Minneapolis, MN), and Wal-Mart (already introduced) allow customers to purchase products on the company's website and pick them up at the stores or have them delivered to their homes. Future Shop (former subsidiary of Best Buy, Burnaby, BC, Canada), a Canadian-based electronics retailer, guaranteed customers could pick up items they ordered online in just minutes at convenient pick-up booths outside of the stores (Best Buy discontinued Future Shop in 2015 and consolidated it into the Best Buy chain).

A distinguishing feature of companies that are known for delivering world-class customer service is the commitment of their employees. The retailer Nordstrom is a company that excels at customer service because its employees are famous for going out of their way to please customers. Nordstrom devotes a lot of resources on training and developing its employees to deliver top-notch customer service. In addition to training and development, these companies treat their employees well and motivate and reward employees who deliver outstanding customer service with bonuses and raises. Furthermore, these companies also empower their employees by providing them complete autonomy to serve their customers in any way they deem appropriate. The Ritz-Carlton Hotel Company, L.L.C. (aka Ritz-Carlton, Chevy Chase, MD), a past winner of the Malcolm Baldrige National Quality award, gives every employee, including the hotel housekeepers, the authority to spend up to US$2,000 to solve a customer problem.[21]

Order fill rate: the percentage of customer orders that can be fully and completely filled from items in stock

Multichannel marketing systems: systems that allow customers to purchase products and have them delivered in different ways

Customer Service Management

One approach to managing customer service is to look at four key features: customer profitability analysis, establishing customer service objectives, customer service measurement, and service failure and recovery.[22] We will briefly discuss each of these four features of managing customer service.

Consider This 12.2:
Transforming Customer Service Management

Shoppers are aware of their purchasing alternatives and are very demanding of retail organizations and what they can offer. In addition to being able to buy products online and pick them up in stores, customers want the following:

Goddard Automotive / Alamy Stock Photo

"My Account"

Customers don't think in terms of sales channels; that is, the producers' methods for bringing products or services to market for consumer purchase. Instead, a retailer's success is tied to its ability to link channels together in ways that encourage shoppers. This means providing customers with a single account that allows them to navigate from one channel to another without using different login information. Delta Air Lines, Inc. (Atlanta, GA) offers its customers a single account that allows them to access their flight information and updates, bonus miles, and other important data.

Store Inventory Visibility

Shoppers hate to have their desired purchases back-ordered, whether through an online catalog or when visiting a store. When consumers aren't sure of inventory availability, it is likely that they will simply buy from a competitor that guarantees their order fulfillment and delivery preferences. Wayfair.com (Wayfair, LLC, Boston, MA), for example, is a retail website for décor and home improvement. Not only is its website easy to navigate, it also shows how many items are in inventory and has alerts indicating when stock is low. If an item is out of stock, the system will electronically notify shoppers when it is back in stock.

Sales Associate Ordering

Customers use their smartphones and tablets to find information about the products they discover in bricks-and-mortar stores. Do retailers' employees have the same tools and ability to access product information? Sixty-five percent of shoppers expect employees to be able to check the prices of products when asked about them. Fifty-five percent expect employees to be able to look up inventory when it's out of stock and find out when it will be back in stock—or if it's in stock at one of the retailer's other stores.

Kiosks

Touchscreen displays have led to a much wider use of the in-store kiosk. Although kiosks used to be somewhat clunky for shoppers, these in-store displays have gotten much more sophisticated. Audi AG (Ingolstadt, Germany), for example, has a digital showroom in London that only houses one actual car. A large interactive display then allows car buyers to customize the car's features and choose its colors.[23]

SOURCE: Reprinted from http://www.audi.co.uk/audi-innovation/audi-city.html

CUSTOMER PROFITABILITY ANALYSIS

A customer profitability analysis (CPA) is the process of allocating revenue and costs to specific customer segments or individual customers to determine the profitability of those segments or individual customers. Not all customers are equally important to an organization. Because some are more valuable than others (that is, they generate more revenue for the organization), the resources a firm expends on customer service should be based on each customer's value to the company. Although it's a straightforward idea, CPA can be complicated in practice. For example, it is easy to determine the revenues each customer or customer segment generates for the firm. Apportioning the costs incurred for each segment is more difficult because most firms treat the costs associated with customer service as a general overhead expense.[24]

Customer profitability analysis (CPA): the process of allocating revenue and costs to specific customer segments or individual customers to determine the profitability of those segments or individual customers

ESTABLISHING CUSTOMER SERVICE OBJECTIVES

The purpose of establishing customer service objectives is to ensure that a company's employees know exactly what they need to do to provide the high quality of customer service a firm wants. A firm's customer service objectives should be aligned with the company's top-level goals and be

Customer Service Objectives

realistic and achievable. They should also be measurable so employees can compare their performance against them.

Establishing customer service goals and objectives begins with the customer and his or her point of view. Thus, it is the customers who determine what aspects of service are important, how well the company currently provides those services, and what additional services they would like. In addition to getting the input of their customers on these aspects, companies will often compare their service-level performance against the performance of their toughest competitors. Thus, if a start-up airline sought to develop customer service objectives, it might consider benchmarking its performance against Virgin Atlantic Airlines (Crawley, U.K.), a company known for its attention to enhancing customer service.[26]

CUSTOMER SERVICE MEASUREMENT

After a company has established its customer service objectives, what measures should it use to assess service quality? Some of the measures a restaurant might consider would be the number of customer complaints received or, alternatively, compliments from comment cards. It might also solicit direct feedback on cleanliness, service promptness, courtesy of all staff, and waiting time.

Data collected using the wrong measures or measures that are simply easy to collect will be misleading and may not indicate what is truly important to customers. For example, a call center may choose the number of calls processed in any given time period as a measure of customer service quality. Nevertheless, "number of calls handled" may not necessarily reflect customer service quality if no assessment of customer satisfaction is considered. In fact, this measure could perversely encourage call personnel to do what is necessary to get off the line quickly, including providing abrupt or unhelpful service to callers. That is, the measures used to assess quality should indicate to employees what their focus should be. Therefore, the measures of customer service should be sufficient in both scope and number, reflect customer perceptions of service quality, and send the right message to employees about what, in the company's view, is and is not good-quality customer service.[30] Some of the commonly used measures, listed in Table 12.1, are based on the dimensions of customer service that we discussed earlier in this section.

SERVICE FAILURES AND RECOVERIES

A **service failure** occurs when an organization's service performance fails to meet the customer's expectations. Despite the best efforts of an organization, service failures will occur. Examples of service failures include late deliveries, delivering incomplete or incorrect orders, and damaged or lost products. A **service recovery** is an effort by the organization to appease dissatisfied customers such as offering them refunds, credits, discounts, apologies, or free items or services. The success of a service recovery hinges on the strength of the relationship between the customer and the organization and the severity of the service failure. If the customer has had a long-standing relationship with the organization and has been satisfied with the past service performance by the firm, his or her satisfaction can often be quickly restored with prompt service recovery efforts. Yet, a customer who tends to focus more on the transaction and has no prior relationship with the organization may require more immediate or expensive service recovery efforts. Consider a situation in which an airline overbooks a flight or cancels it outright, causing customers to spend the night in a local hotel or even on the floor of the terminal. A service recovery in this instance may be impossible.[32]

Service failure: the result of an organization's failure to meet customers' expectations for service performance

Service recovery: an effort by the organization to appease dissatisfied customers such as offering them refunds, credits, discounts, apologies, or free items or services

TABLE 12.1: Commonly Used Customer Service Measures[31]

CUSTOMER SERVICE DIMENSION	MEASURE
Time	• Order fulfillment or order cycle times • Inquiry response times
Reliability	• Perfect and complete orders • On-time deliveries
Communication	• Customer complaints • Order status information communicated
Convenience	• Ease of the returns process • Response times to emergency situations

OPERATIONS MANAGEMENT: LESSONS LEARNED
Trapped on an Airplane

Anyone who has flown has probably experienced delays of one form or another. Nonetheless, a recent spate of airline delays has taken service failures to a whole a new level: Passengers have found themselves trapped on aircraft for extended periods of time—sometimes up to 19 hours. Passengers have been forced to cope with minimal food and water, overflowing toilets, and stifling heat on planes while waiting for their flights to depart. Consider some recent examples:[25]

©iStockphoto.com/eriktham

- Bad weather delayed a Sunwing Airlines Inc. (Toronto, ON, Canada) flight from for more than 13 hours. While the plane remained on the tarmac, all passengers received were granola bars and bottled water. The airplane, which should have taken off at 6:30 am, finally returned to the terminal at 8:00 pm, and passengers were allowed to deplane to eat dinner and were given vouchers for food and future travel. The airplane was reboarded at 10:00 pm, and the flight departed Toronto at midnight.

- Sixty-mile-an-hour winds forced a Virgin America (Burlingame, CA) flight from Los Angeles to New York City to divert to Newburgh, New York, where passengers were stranded on the aircraft for 7 hours. At one point, food supplies aboard the plane were so low that Pringles (Kellogg Company, Battle Creek, MI) chips had to be rationed: Each passenger received four chips. One woman suffered a panic attack and had to be escorted off the aircraft. The passengers finally deplaned at midnight and were forced to ride a bus for another 2.5 hours before finally arriving at their destination at 3 am.

- A JetBlue (JetBlue Airways Corporation, Long Island City, NY) flight from Fort Lauderdale, Florida, to Newark, New Jersey, left more than 100 travelers stranded on the tarmac at the wrong airport for more than 7 hours. The JetBlue pilot ultimately had to call airport officials and plead with them to send police, telling them he "can't seem to get any help from our own company." Passengers on the JetBlue flight were left onboard the plane without food, water, or functioning bathrooms. "It was a nightmare," one passenger told news reporters afterward. "The bathrooms were getting nasty."

Whether enduring canceled flights, seemingly endless security lines and delays, overbooking, overworked and cranky airline personnel, or excessive delays on the tarmac, airline travel is often burdensome and unpleasant. Airline companies argue that the situations that create these events are often beyond their control; for example, conditions such as unanticipated weather problems are a major source of delay. Passengers, however, point to the common practice of double-booking seats and funneling more and more aircraft into air traffic hubs that are becoming too congested to handle the volume of traffic assigned to them. In effect, they argue that poor demand forecasting, coupled with the desire to fill the maximum number of seats possible on each flight, is leading to delays and poor customer service. The U.S. Department of Transportation has introduced a "Three Hour" rule, whereby aircraft are prohibited from delaying on the tarmac longer than three hours before having to return to a gate and disembarking passengers. If the government determines that any airline is violating the tarmac delay rule, that carrier could be fined as much as US$27,500 per passenger.

The number of complaints from passengers reflects a growing dissatisfaction with air travel. "As the industry continues to consolidate, capacity is rationalized and reduced, seats are packed closer and closer together, and load factors get higher and higher. The travel experience becomes punishing," said Robert Mann of R.W. Mann & Company, Inc. (Port Washington, NY), an airline industry analysis and consulting company. "Add fees for services previously considered part of the bargain and you have the recipe for discontent."[27]

In the event of a service failure, the extent to which it affects the customer's relationship and commitment to the organization depends on its severity. If the original service failure was a major problem for consumers, the organization runs the risk the losing the trust and commitment of the customer. Furthermore, the resulting customer dissatisfaction is likely to lead to negative publicity for the company. Evidence used to suggest, for example, that those experiencing a dissatisfying service encounter tell, on average, 10 or more others of their experiences. Nevertheless, in the age of social media platforms like Twitter (Twitter, Inc., San Francisco, CA), Pinterest (San Francisco, CA), and Facebook (Menlo Park, CA), these numbers have multiplied dramatically.[28] When the service failure is severe, to mend the relationship with the customer, the recovery effort needs to be immediate and strong.

(Continued)

OPERATIONS MANAGEMENT: LESSONS LEARNED
Trapped on an Airplane

(Continued)

As part of their customer service management process, organizations need to track and identify occurrences of service failures as well as their severity. This process is complicated because the view of a service failure varies from customer to customer. To manage service efforts effectively, managers need to take two steps. First, they need to gather information at the time of service failure from the complaint provided by the customer so that the necessary action can be taken for immediate service recovery and improvement of future performance. Second, managers should conduct a postrecovery assessment to evaluate recovery performance against the customer.[29]

CUSTOMER-FOCUSED SUPPLY CHAIN MANAGEMENT

In the global business environment, an individual company cannot manage and provide quality customer service without the help of its supply chain. Customer-focused supply chain management (CFSCM) is based on the idea that the long-run profitability and efficiency of an enterprise depends on the customers' overall satisfaction with the company's and its supply chain partners' products or services.[33] In CFSCM, every supply chain member is linked to the customer. Therefore, quality customer service requires collaborative relationships throughout the supply chain, from upstream raw material suppliers to downstream final users of the product or service. Implementing an effective CFSCM program requires the following steps:

- Establish free and open two-way communications with customers and suppliers.
- Understand customers' strategic service needs: speedy delivery, flexibility, etc.
- Establish functional interfaces between your company and your supply chain partners to collaborate with them on customer service.

In a customer-focused approach to supply chain management, all supply chain activities are synchronized as the actual demand information captured at the point-of-sale is communicated through the supply chain using information technology. With the availability of such up-to-date and accurate information on customer service needs, each supply chain partner can take the necessary steps to support the supply chain's overall customer service goals. By collaborating with supply chain partners, key customer service performance factors such as reliability, responsiveness, flexibility, lower costs, and better resource management can be achieved faster and more effectively than by the individual efforts of any one member of the supply chain.

Discuss the sustainability and ethical issues in customer service.

12.5 Ethical and Sustainability Issues

Sustainability, the balancing of economic, social, and environmental factors, is an important feature of quality customer service. Customers demand that businesses act in an ethically and socially responsible manner. Furthermore, as customers are becoming more knowledgeable about environmental issues such as global warming and carbon emissions, they do not want to purchase products and services that they perceive are damaging to the planet. Consequently, more and more customers want to purchase only from those companies that produce or deliver products and services that are environmentally friendly. In addition, the ethical credentials and the socially responsible behavior of businesses have an influence on the consumers' purchasing decisions. With the increasing transparency resulting from the widespread use of social media platforms such as Facebook and Twitter, companies can no longer hide their unsustainable, unethical, and harmful business practices. For example, according to a study conducted in the United Kingdom, 64% of consumers avoided a company's product because of its unethical behavior and 60% of consumers purchased a product or service from a company because of its ethical behavior. Furthermore, according to this study, 59% of consumers had recommended a product or service to a friend because of a company's ethical practices. In 2009, a Canadian musician witnessed his guitar case being tossed around carelessly by airline baggage handlers, resulting in significant damage. When United Airlines (United Continental Holdings, Inc., Chicago, IL) refused to recognize his claims for compensation, he uploaded music videos to YouTube (YouTube, LLC, San Bruno, CA) with songs that complained about United's behavior. The videos were ultimately viewed

Customer-focused supply chain management (CFSCM): a management method in which every supply chain member is linked to the customer, requiring collaborative relationships throughout the supply chain

more than 16 million times, and the resulting bad public relations was one reason that United ultimately settled the musician's claims.[34]

Clearly, as sustainability has a direct impact on how a customer feels about a product or service, it has become an integral element of customer service. Hence, if, as part of their customer service program, companies can convince customers that their products and services will have no detrimental impact on the environment and that they are ethically and socially responsible, they will reap the benefits of improved profits and customer loyalty. On the other hand, if an organization cannot convince its customers that it is on a path of sustainable development, then it will lose its customers. Several companies have received bad publicity because of their unsustainable behavior. For example, Nestlé's (Vevey, Switzerland) reputation was damaged when it came to light that the company was using palm oil in its products. The use of palm oil implies that Nestlé was directly or indirectly responsible for destruction of rain forests and, thus, contributed to damage to the environment. Another concern is the use of antibiotics in animal feed for products that eventually make their way to consumers' tables. The use of antibiotics in animal feed has come under fire by consumers and medical groups because its overuse on animals is causing these drugs to be less effective when administered to humans, who are developing resistance to them. As a result, Perdue Farms (Salisbury, MD) has announced that it will no longer use antibiotics in chicken feed at its facilities.[35]

Perdue Farms has stopped using antibiotics in their chickens due to concerns from their customers.

John Greim/LightRocket/Getty Images

In the final analysis, as an integral part of customer service, an organization should not only exhibit sustainable behavior but also create a perception in the minds of consumers that the company acts in an ethically, socially, and environmentally responsible manner. These behaviors are critical because more and more potential customers expect organizations to operate in ethical ways. Successful firms work hard to understand the expectations of their customer base. Sustainable business practices not only serve the greater good, but also they demonstrate a commitment to customer service that is increasingly valued in modern organizations.

 Sustainability and Customer Service

$SAGE edge™

Visit **edge.sagepub.com/venkataraman** to help you accomplish your coursework goals in an easy-to-use learning environment.

- Mobile-friendly eFlashcards
- Mobile-friendly practice quizzes
- A complete online action plan

- Chapter summaries with learning objectives
- Video and multimedia resources

CHAPTER SUMMARY

12.1 Explain the importance of demand management for organizations, and identify the factors that affect it. Demand management is the process of determining accurately what the customer wants and then coordinating the processes and procedures both within the firm and across its supply chain to meet demand in an efficient and timely manner. Effective demand management has numerous benefits including the mitigation of the bullwhip effect that causes unwanted inventories in the supply chain. The demand management process consists of demand forecasting, demand planning, and demand management. A wide range of economic, technological, and internal company factors can have an impact on customer demand.

12.2 Describe the challenges of global demand management and the strategies that can be used to address them. The key challenges of global demand management include inventory availability in geographically dispersed regions and demand volatility. Some strategies that can be adopted to meet these challenges include using point-of-sale (POS) data, increasing the frequency of forecasting, collaborating and sharing timely information with supply chain partners, and coordinating their internal demand management activities.

12.3 Identify the unique nature of services demand management, and discuss the risks from excess and insufficient capacity.

The focus of services demand management lies in calculating the required service capacity well in advance of the demand for services and being flexible enough to use this available capacity effectively to meet the demand. Service providers face the risk of excess capacity in the form of idle resources, which add to costs without providing value, and insufficient capacity, which leads to poor service quality and prevents the business from growing if demand is not predicted accurately and managed well.

12.4 **Propose and apply the four supply chain dimensions of customer service.** Customer service is the series of activities designed to enhance the level of customer satisfaction. There are four supply chain dimensions of customer service: (a) time—the ability to reduce cycle time in fulfilling customer orders;

(b) dependability—consists of consistency, delivery safety, and order completeness; (c) communication—dialogue between the seller and the customer; and (d) convenience—making the product or service available when and where the customer wants it.

12.5 **Discuss the sustainability and ethical issues in customer service.** As customers are becoming more knowledgeable about environmental issues such as global warming and carbon emissions, they do not want to purchase products and services that could harm our planet. In addition, customers demand that businesses act in an ethically and socially responsible manner. Consequently, companies that produce or deliver products and services that are environmentally friendly, and conduct business in an ethically and socially responsible manner, will have a positive influence on the consumers' purchasing decisions.

KEY TERMS

Bullwhip effect   418

Collaborative forecasting   421

Collaborative planning, forecasting, and replenishment (CPFR)   421

Customer profitability analysis (CPA)   427

Customer-focused supply chain management (CFSCM)   430

Delivery safety   425

Demand forecasting   418

Demand planning   418

Exception management   422

Forecasting errors   420

Multichannel marketing systems   426

Order cycle time consistency   425

Order delivery completeness   425

Order fill rate   426

Service failure   428

Service recovery   428

DISCUSSION AND REVIEW QUESTIONS

1. Discuss the importance of demand management from the perspectives of both a manufacturing firm and a service organization. What are the five key reasons why demand management is so critical for an organization's success?

2. "If we don't take care of our customers, someone else will." Explain the nature of this statement. Why does customer service management matter in the modern, global environment?

3. Give examples of long-term, intermediate-term, and short-term decisions made as part of demand planning. Use one manufacturing and one service organization for each example.

4. How is demand forecasting similar to demand planning, and how is it different?

5. What are the strengths and weaknesses of a demand forecasting system? What limitations to the systems must we be aware of?

6. What is collaborative forecasting, and why is it so important in demand management?

7. What are the four steps to managing demand effectively?

8. How does global demand volatility affect an organization's upstream and downstream suppliers? Use a grocery store as an example.

9. Why can postponement be an effective demand management strategy? How does it work for a service firm? A manufacturer?

10. How does services demand management operate? Why is it so critical for service organizations (Hint: use the concept of "capacity-constrained" in your response)?

11. What does "customer service" mean to you?

12. What are the four supply chain dimensions of customer service?

13. Service recovery success hinges on two elements. What are they?

PROBLEMS

1. Imagine that you were considering the potential of opening an upscale restaurant in a remote area of the Oregon coast. What demand management (economic and technological) factors should you consider as part of the decision of whether such a restaurant would be feasible?

2. Suppose you were a senior manager at an oil refinery in Texas and you were considering partnering with a major railroad and investing money to help them upgrade their rail lines used for shipping oil from Canada south to your refinery. Prior to making this investment decision, what other long-term and intermediate-term issues should be considered as part of this important decision?

3. How has Amazon Prime demonstrated the truth of the statement that demand management and customer service are closely linked? (Hint: Remember that order fulfillment is a key determinant of how satisfied customers are and whether you can retain them for future sales.)

4. Think of an example of a service failure that you experienced. It could be any of a variety of examples from retail, food and dining, health care, etc. Analyze and evaluate the situation. What were the causes of the service failure? How could the firm have done a better job?

5. Referring to problem 4, did the firm engage in a service recovery act? If so, what did they do? How did its service recovery change your opinion of the firm's overall performance, and what is the implication of service recovery for improving your perceptions of the business?

6. Imagine you are shopping for a new car. What are some customer service metrics that the auto dealer should be using to evaluate its performance? Based on your experience with buying a car, did you see evidence that these metrics were being used? How or how not?

7. Imagine you were shopping for a new smartphone at a large wireless service provider. How do the metrics of customer service (time, dependability, communication, and convenience) determine how satisfied you were with this retail encounter?

CASE STUDY 12.1 MCDONALD'S REINVENTS ITSELF, AGAIN

McDonald's (Oak Brook, IL) has never been content to sit back and wait for consumer tastes to change. Rather, the company continually tries to shape the face of fast food and influence the marketplace with new offerings and other image changes. In the face of stiff competition from healthier alternatives, such as Subway (Subway Corporation, Milford, CT) and a general feeling by the public that major fast-food companies are not much different from one another in terms of their prices, quality, service levels, and product offerings, McDonald's has had to reinvent itself.

When fast food seemed synonymous with "greasy," "over-cooked," and "fried," McDonald's met the challenge by adding healthy menu options, such as wraps, grilled chicken, fresh fruit, and yogurt-based smoothies. These menu changes were doubly effective: They allowed McDonald's to compete directly with other stores that promoted healthy alternatives, and they diffused the arguments of their harshest critics, including the San Francisco Board of Supervisors, who, in 2011, banned McDonald's inclusion of a toy in their Happy Meals, claiming that the "pester power" of children could induce parents to buy these unhealthy lunch choices. McDonald's responded by offering healthy options such as milk and apple slices in Happy Meals, and instead of eliminating the toys, McDonald's charged ten cents for the addition of a toy, with the proceeds benefitting the charity the Ronald McDonald House.

McDonald's efforts in staying current in a changing industry are based on managing demand, forecasting trends, determining what the customer wants, and where possible, influencing their perceptions. Thus, McDonald's must address both sides of the supply chain. It does so by forecasting demand for its products based on reappraising taste and current trends, and working with suppliers to provide menu items that are of consistently high quality and available.

McDonald's continues to be the leader in the fast-food industry. When competitors offer their own healthy menus, they are often seen as simply copying and therefore acknowledging McDonalds' prescience in staying ahead of the consumer trend curve. Critics have charged that the fast-food industry offers poor choices to patrons who don't know any better. Unlike some competitors who seem content to keep their menus unchanged and their products unhealthy, McDonald's has been doing what is necessary to change who it is, reinvent itself, and keep its fingers firmly on the pulse of its international customer base.[36]

Questions

1. In your opinion, what is the future of fast food around the world? Are consumer taste changes and concerns about healthy eating likely to diminish the demand for fast food?

2. How would you evaluate McDonald's reinvention strategy? Do the changes represent a fundamental shift in the company's competitive model, or are they cosmetic?

3. If McDonald's hired you to advise it with regard to future trends and the changes it should consider, what would you suggest? Defend your suggestions.

4. Research the current state of McDonald's, particularly in light of the retirement in March 2015 of CEO Don Thompson. How has reinvention been difficult for the company? How might a reinvention strategy sometimes seem to the general public?

CASE STUDY 12.2 PREDICTING THE FUTURE DEMAND FOR RURAL HEALTH CARE

The United States faces many challenges when it comes to predicting the demand for health-care services. Nowhere is this truer than in rural settings. Many senior citizens are concentrated in rural areas in the temperate climates of the South and the West. As the U.S. population ages, its health-care needs increase dramatically. For example, citizens who are 75+ years of age are four times more likely to require in-patient health care than are people 55 to 64 years of age, according to the National Center for Health Statistics. The problem is exacerbated because the overall health of Americans is declining as a result greater inactivity combined with poor diet. A larger percentage of the rural population displays these at-risk behaviors, which include alcohol and tobacco use, inactivity, and obesity, when compared with the urban and suburban populations. These risk factors are, in turn, linked to chronic illnesses, such as diabetes, heart disease, and cancer, which account for nearly 75% of all health-care spending.

Another factor that plays a role in trying to predict future demand for rural health care is the decline in the support of a cohesive family unit. With senior citizens living longer and family members increasingly mobile, they are unable to provide care. This lack of support network will shift the duty of providing care from the family unit to health-care organizations. Finally, the demand for in-home and community-based services, such as assisted living and adult day-care services, is expected to rise.

In this setting, government and health-care providers are trying to anticipate future demand for services to support older people. Rural hospitals, for example, will have to create a coherent long-term strategy to stay profitable. Among the issues they will need to focus on are:

• **Health provider recruitment and retention.** How will health-care organizations acquire and retain family practice physicians, surgeons, nurses, and other health-care professionals, especially in rural settings, which may not be as attractive to health-care professionals as larger cities or population centers?

• **Cost-effective treatment for the uninsured and under-insured.** Rural populations include a large number of people without medical insurance or ready access to health care. Although health-care organizations are morally obligated to treat these underserved groups, they represent a financial drain on hospital resources.

• **Community economic development.** Health-care organizations have a vested interest in supporting local economic development because the influx of new businesses (and jobs) tends to decrease poverty rates and the number of uninsured in a geographic area.

• **Expanding senior services.** Seniors will need more than traditional ambulatory and hospital care. How will health-care organizations address the demand for in-home and community-based options in a cost-effective manner?[37]

Questions

1. Imagine you are a member of the demand planning staff for a hospital in a rural part of Florida. How would you begin developing a plan for the future demand for health care at your hospital? What demographic and other factors would you consider critical to developing such a plan?

2. Research some of the provisions in the Affordable Health Care Act (officially Patient Protection and Affordable Care Act of 2010, P.L. 111-148). Give one example of how the act's new regulations will affect demand forecasting and planning.

VIDEO CASE ··

Watch this video case to learn about how Bart's Books puts customers first and provides a positive experience for their patrons.

CRITICAL THINKING EXERCISES ···

1. Why is demand planning difficult in high-tech companies? What are the consequences of the lack of an effective demand-planning process in such companies?

2. Visit a local bank in your neighborhood. Interview the manager of that bank, and write a report on the demand-planning process used by the bank.

Demonstrate your understanding of **demand management** at Littlefield Labs.

Littlefield Laboratories is a highly automated, state-of-the-art blood testing facility for clinics and hospitals. The lab will operate 24 hours a day for a total of 210 days. You're asked to step in as the operations manager on Day 30, and are tasked with managing the lab's demand by setting prices and by limiting the number of jobs allowed in the lab at one time. You are also tasked with managing the lab's capacity to meet demand. Based on historic data you must manage demand and capacity to maximize the lab's profits.

Compete against your classmates to prove your understanding of the chapter concepts:

• LO 12-1: Explain the importance of demand management for organizations, and identify factors that affect it.

• LO 12-2: Describe the challenges of global demand management and the strategies that can be used to address them.

• LO 12-3: Identify the unique nature of service demand management, and discuss the risks from excess and insufficient capacity.

The team with the most cash in hand at the end of the 210-day time frame wins!

Londres

New York

Bogotá

©iStockphoto.com/stevecoleimages

CHAPTER

13

Demand Forecasting Methods

LEARNING OBJECTIVES

After studying this chapter, you should be able to:

1 Demonstrate the importance of forecasting for business operations.

2 Recognize the characteristics of good forecasts.

3 Illustrate and distinguish between qualitative and quantitative types of forecasting methods, including their strengths and weaknesses.

4 Use the four forecast error measures to track forecast accuracy.

5 Employ the methods used to monitor and control forecasts.

6 Identify the steps involved in forecasting for supply chains.

7 Illustrate the role ethics and ethical decision-making can play in selecting and using forecasting models.

OPERATIONS PROFILE: Challenges in Forecasting Demand for L.L. Bean's Famous "Duck Boots"

Sunpix Travel / Alamy Stock Photo

L.L. Bean, Inc. (Freeport, ME) is an iconic American brand, known for its outdoor clothing and equipment, high customer satisfaction, and product reliability. One of its most popular brands is the "Bean Boot," more commonly known by its popular name, the Duck Boot. The hand-sewn tan leather and black-webbed rubber boot has found a resurgence as a winter fashion essential for two reasons: first, because the wearer can splash through the worst winter ice and melting snow with warm, dry feet and second, because they have developed something of a cult following as a fashion statement. In other words, although they originally debuted in 1912 and have been in the catalog for over 100 years, they have become cool again.

L.L. Bean has had a hard time keeping up with demand for the boots since 2015. If you were to order a pair today, you might find that they have been backordered for 6 months. In fact, the retailer projected a shortfall of nearly 50,000 pairs of boots for 2016 despite manufacturing half a million pairs, more than three times the number made in 2005. They have become so popular that competitors like Sperry (Lexington, MA) and North Face (The North Face, Inc., Alameda, CA) have begun producing their own brand of Duck Boot. Made in America and with a solid reputation for quality (and a no-questions-asked replacement policy), L.L. Bean's boots have shed their utilitarian image in favor of appearing more fashionable in the marketplace. This rapid increase in popularity caught the company by surprise and has left it scrambling to adjust its sales forecasts for future demand for the boots. In fact, Duck Boots have been selling out every year since 2011.

Why can't L.L. Bean keep up with demand? There are several answers to this question, one of which is the company's decision to keep all manufacturing local, at its Brunswick, Maine, facility. Rather than contract with Chinese manufacturers, L.L. Bean has made the decision to use locally sourced materials and American labor to hand-produce each pair of boots. Another reason for their constant backordering lies in developing forecasts for demand year-to-year. The challenge for L.L. Bean in forecasting demand for its boots has to do with taking a reasonable look at the reasons for the current popularity of the boots and balancing these data with longer term knowledge of the brand. For example, when the company considers its products' life cycles, it is critical that it understand the difference between short-term fads and steady demand for popular goods. For fashion items, the demand is relatively constant and allows for reasonably accurate forecasts for the future. Fad items are different; with a short life-cycle, high initial demand, and equally strong drop-off, fad items are hard to predict and, as a result, make demand forecasting very inaccurate. "I think that one of the things that's so interesting is that it's really the opposite of fast fashion, because these [boots] are really made to last," said Eric Smith, a public relations representative for L.L. Bean. "They're made to last not just years, but literally, generations." UGG (Goleta, CA) brand boots, for example, have been a fashion item for a long time, allowing their manufacturer to forecast future demand with some accuracy. For L.L. Bean, the rapid increase in popularity of the Duck Boot caught the company by surprise, as consumers gravitated toward a classic, modestly priced and American-made product.

"The demand for Bean Boots has cycled up and down during the hundred years we've [been] making it. We don't go out of our way to find those trends," said Smith. "The trends keep coming back to us. Then people will go away for a while and they keep coming back. We're just happy to be in one of those cycles, when it's the largest of those cycles we've seen."[1]

13.1
Demonstrate the importance of forecasting for business operations.

13.1 Introduction to Forecasting and Its Applications

This chapter begins where Chapter 12 left off in our quest to understand demand forecasts. You'll recall that we discussed the time frame for demand-planning decisions in Section 12.1. The forecasts used as a basis for these decisions are reviewed in Table 13.1, which also identifies the types of activities that qualify as short-run, medium-range, and long-term. We can also think of these decisions as operational, tactical, or strategic. The distinctions shown in this table will help us in studying the specific forecasting techniques that are the focus of this chapter.

To get started, let's define forecasting precisely: Forecasting is the estimation of the future value of some variable. Our specific interest is on forecasting demand, but forecasts can be used to predict price, capacity, or other variables such as the availability of supply, the time required to complete an activity, or tracking the progress of a project. The forecast may describe a scenario of a future event.

Different companies at different stages of a supply chain will require different types of forecasts for their planning activities. Consider, for example, the demand for facial care products. A retailer such as Macy's (Macy's, Inc., Cincinnati, OH) may need to know the projected number of potential customers for facial care products within various market segments. Macy's will use this information to plan overall orders for different products from the various tiers of manufacturers in its supply chain and for allocating inventories to the individual stores in the different market segments.

At the next stage of the supply chain, a supplier of facial care products such as L'Oreal S.A. (Clichy, France) may not only require regional market forecasts, but also global forecasts of demand in the facial care industry. For example, the demand forecast for facial care products for 2017 was US$67.1 billion with an estimated sale of 9.6 billion units. As the world leader in this market with close to 14% market share, L'Oreal used this forecasted information to target its products to the Asia-Pacific market, which was the fastest-growing market for facial care products.[2] At the third stage of the supply chain, suppliers of individual products or raw materials to L'Oreal may require forecasts of inputs to skincare products to plan for acquiring necessary raw materials and ingredients.

13.2
Recognize the characteristics of good forecasts.

13.2 The Characteristics of Good Forecasts

To be useful, demand forecasts should be:

- Accurate: Any deviations (forecast errors) from actual demand should be small.
- Consistent: Forecasts should be consistent in their ability to track actual demand. That is, a forecasting technique that sometimes overestimates and at other times underestimates the actual demand does not provide consistent forecasts, and it is therefore not reliable.
- Timely: Forecasts should be available within a reasonable timeframe so there is adequate time to make decisions and make necessary changes.
- Simple: Forecasts should be easy to interpret so that users of the information have confidence in the forecast.
- Efficient: The costs of preparing the forecast should not outweigh its benefits.

As Chapter 12 explained, forecasts cannot precisely estimate actual demand levels because many different factors influence actual demand. Some types of forecasts tend to be more accurate than others, however.

Good Forecasts

TABLE 13.1: Demand-Forecast Time Horizons of Business Activities

	OPERATIONAL	TACTICAL	STRATEGIC
Forecast Time Horizon	Short-term: Typically less than 3 months but can be as long as 1 year	Medium-term: Can range between 3 months and 3 years	Long-term: Greater than 3 years
Examples of Forecasted Activities	Production scheduling, worker assignments	Sales and production planning, budgeting	New product development, facilities planning

- *Short-Term Forecasts Tend to Be More Accurate Than Long-Term Forecasts.* Short-term demand forecasts for products tend to be more accurate than long-term forecasts because the factors that affect them are more likely to remain fairly consistent in the short term. In the long run (say, 3 to 5 years from now), factors such as new technology and changing consumer preferences can dramatically affect demand, and it is difficult to gauge their impact. Therefore, forecasts far into the future tend to be less accurate. Nevertheless, this is usually not a serious problem because long-term forecasts are typically used for strategic planning, where absolute accuracy is not required.
- *Aggregate Forecasts for Groups of Products or Services Tend to Be More Accurate Than Forecasts for Individual Products.* A company can prepare more accurate forecasts for aggregated products such as a product line rather than for individual products. For example, Toyota (Toyota Motor Corporation, Toyota City, Japan) can more accurately forecast the total number of cars needed for next year rather than the total number of maroon Sienna minivans with an option package of all leather seats and sunroofs. With aggregate forecasts, the forecast errors (overestimation or underestimation of actual demand) for individual product items tend to cancel out each other. As a result, the total demand for cars will be far more accurate.
- *The Forecasts for Dependent-Demand Items Are More Accurate Than Forecasts for Independent-Demand Items.* A dependent demand item is a part or component of an end product. Its demand depends on the demand for the end product. The end product, on the other hand, is an independent demand item whose demand is unrelated to the demand of any other product or item. For example, cars are independent demand items, whereas tires are dependent demand items. Treating tires as an independent demand item is meaningless in this case and will result in excess inventory or shortages. Their demand is predictable and can be easily calculated once the estimates of demand for cars become available. Thus, if a production plan calls for 400 cars of a particular model, then the derived demand of 1600 (400 × 4) tires should be used.

13.3 Qualitative Versus Quantitative Forecasting Methods

Table 13.2 lists the two broad categories of forecasting methods, qualitative and quantitative methods, and the most commonly used techniques for each method. Next, we will look at each of these methods.

Qualitative Methods

Qualitative methods are used if no measurable, reliable, historical, or statistical data are available. These methods are primarily based on intuition, judgment, or informed opinions of experts in the

TABLE 13.2: Demand Forecasting Methods

QUALITATIVE METHODS	QUANTITATIVE METHODS

a. Expert opinion
b. Delphi method
c. Sales force opinions
d. Market research
e. Historical life-cycle analogy
	• *Time Series Analysis*
	  a. Naïve approach
	  b. Moving average
	  c. Weighted moving average
	  d. Exponential smoothing
	  e. Trend-adjusted exponential smoothing
	  f. Linear trend analysis/simple linear regression analysis
	  g. Techniques for seasonality
	  h. Linear trend multiplicative model
	  i. Techniques for evaluating cyclical variations
	
	• *Causal Methods*
	  a. Simple linear regression analysis
	  b. Multiple linear regression analysis

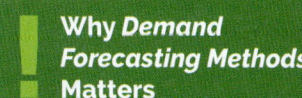

Why *Demand Forecasting Methods* Matters

Demand forecasting is a fundamental prerequisite for all strategic, tactical, and operational planning decisions. An effective demand planning system can generate accurate forecasts at the individual product, product group, customer group, and regional levels, as well as for different planning horizons.

13.3

Illustrate and distinguish between qualitative and quantitative types of forecasting methods, including their strengths and weaknesses.

Dependent demand: a part or component of an end product

Independent demand: an item whose demand is unrelated to the demand of any other product or item

Qualitative method: a forecasting method based on intuition, judgment, or informed opinions of experts in the industry, used if no measurable, reliable, historical, or statistical data are available

industry. For example, in its attempt to forecast demand for a new product, a company may rely on a qualitative technique such as the opinion of its sales force. Some of the frequently deployed qualitative forecasting methods are expert opinion, Delphi method, sales force opinions, market research, and historical life-cycle analogy.

EXPERT OPINION

Demand forecasts can be obtained by relying on expert opinion—that is, the intuition or the experienced judgment of experts such as senior executives in the industry, marketing consultants, trade associations, or academics. The accuracy of these forecasts depends on the degree of insight the expert has into the overall market in that industry. Relying on the judgment of experts alone, without the backup of more rigorous methods, can be risky because there is a potential for bias and because the competitive environment is uncertain.

THE DELPHI METHOD

The Delphi method attempts to eliminate or minimize the problem of bias in the opinion of a single expert by using a panel of experts to generate forecasts. Each expert is first asked independently to provide a demand forecast. After the initial forecasts are made, they are shared among all members of the panel. Because an expert may refine his or her opinion after reading the opinions of others in the panel, each expert is then asked to make a subsequent forecast. The process continues until the forecast is refined in each successive round and the experts reach a consensus.

SALES FORCE OPINIONS

Because a company's sales representatives are in close contact with customers, they are often a good source of demand estimates that can be assembled into a composite forecast for a company. This forecasting approach, however, has several drawbacks. First, a salesperson may not be able to distinguish between what customers say they intend to buy and what they actually buy. Second, the most recent demand levels (high or low demand) could introduce bias into the estimates of future demand. Third, the salespeople have an incentive to provide lower estimates if their sales quotas will be based on these demand forecasts.

MARKET RESEARCH

Since end consumers determine the actual demand for a company's products, asking the customers directly what they will buy makes sense. Surveys, such as questionnaires, that solicit personal, demographic, economic, and marketing information are used for this purpose. Yet, surveys are expensive, time-consuming, and often have low response rates.

HISTORICAL LIFE-CYCLE ANALOGY

The historical life-cycle analogy method is used to forecast demand for a new product or service that is similar to existing products. The basic premise of the historical life-cycle analogy method is that by determining the demand for former or similar products experienced during the various stages (introduction, growth, maturity, and decline) of their life cycles, it is possible to provide fairly accurate demand estimates for a new product in each of its life-cycle stages. For example, by analyzing the demand pattern of LED TVs, it is possible to estimate the demand a newer 3D TV would experience during its life-cycle stages.

Expert opinion: the intuition or the experienced judgment of experts

Delphi method: a qualitative method that attempts to eliminate or minimize the problem of bias in the opinion of a single expert by using a panel of experts to generate forecasts

Historical life-cycle analogy: a method used to forecast demand for a new product or service that is similar to existing products

Quantitative method: a forecasting method based on measurable, historical data and evidence that shows past demand is indicative of its future demand

Because of their close contact with customers, salespeople can often contribute to qualitative data tracking demand.

©iStockphoto.com/Jimmy Fam Photography

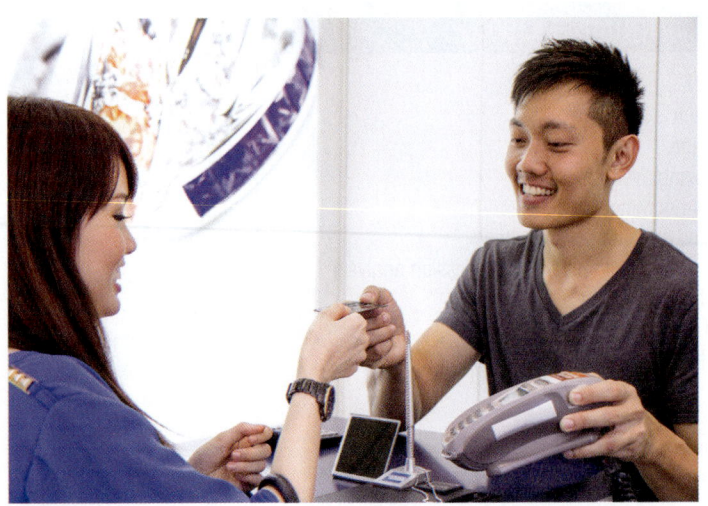

Quantitative Methods

Quantitative methods can be used if measurable, historical data are available and if there is evidence that past demand is indicative of its future demand. For example, Nike, Inc. (Beaverton, OR) may rely on a quantitative technique that uses demand data from past months to estimate the total sales of its golf apparel. Quantitative methods are also appropriate for demand forecasting if there are causal relationships between explanatory variables (such as disposable household income or advertising dollars spent) and demand. These methods are usually used for short or medium-to-intermediate timeframes. These techniques can be further classified into two subcategories: time series analysis and causal methods.

Types of Quantitative Methods: Time Series Forecasting

A **time series** is a time-ordered sequence of observations taken at regular intervals over a period of time. For example, 24 months of sales data for the Ford Taurus (from January 2015 to December 2016) would constitute a time series. The underlying premise of time series analysis is that past behavior of demand is indicative of its future behavior; therefore, past demand data can be used to construct forecasts of demand. Because actual demand is a mixture of several components, the first step in time series forecasting is to identify and evaluate the major components that make up a time series. These components include trend, seasonal, cyclical, irregular, and random variations in demand. Figure 13.1 shows each of these components.

The **trend** is the long-term movement (increasing or decreasing) of data over time. This definition implies that time is the explanatory or independent variable and the actual set of demand observations is the dependent variable. There are several possible patterns that can occur when demand is tracked solely as a function of time. First, the demand level may remain more or less constant over time. The second possible pattern is that data as a function of time may have a linear relationship. This **linear trend** can be either positive or negative, in which demand either increases or decreases in successive periods. Figure 13.1a shows a positive linear trend line. The third possible scenario is that demand, when plotted as a function of time, may exhibit a **nonlinear trend** pattern, such as **exponential growth** or **decline**. In the case of exponential growth, each succeeding observation increases by some constant factor; in exponential decline, each succeeding observation decreases by some constant factor. In these cases, in addition to time, other factors such as population shifts and changes in income levels influence demand. A fourth possible pattern is a **damped trend**. With a damped trend, the level of demand increases initially, but over the long run it levels off (see Figure 13.2 on page 442). A damped trend often occurs when new products are introduced. Initially they experience growth, but then the growth stabilizes.

Seasonal variations are periodic, fairly short-term fluctuations in demand often caused by human activities or weather. They usually relate to the time of year, month, or even a particular day of the week. Examples of seasonal variations are increased retail sales in December, peak demand for snow shovels during the winter, or the spikes in banking activity on Fridays and the first of the month (pay-day for many people). **Cyclical variations** are wave-like oscillations in demand about the trend line caused by changes in economic or business cycles, such as boom or recession or as a result of changes in political conditions (see Figure 13.1b). These variations typically last for more than a year. **Irregular variations** are unusual variations in demand caused by factors such as union strikes or extreme weather conditions such as tropical storms or heavy blizzards. The unusual demand for basic necessities, such as food, clothing, and water, in the aftermath of a natural disaster is an example of such irregular variations. These variations in demand are not expected to recur with any predictable regularity; they therefore are treated as outliers and are eliminated from consideration for forecasting purposes.

All other variations in demand, not accounted for by any of the previous four classifications, are considered to be **random variations**. These variations can be identified only after the fact. In other words, they can't be predicted.

Time series: a quantitative method in which time-ordered sequence of observations are taken at regular intervals over a period of time

Trend: the long-term movement (increasing or decreasing) of data over time

Linear trend: a pattern in which demand either increases or decreases in successive periods

Nonlinear trend: a pattern in which demand either increased or decreases irregularly

Exponential growth/decline: examples of nonlinear trends

Damped trend: a pattern in which the level of demand increases initially and levels off in the long term

Seasonal variations: periodic, fairly short-term fluctuations in demand often caused by human activities or weather

FIGURE 13.1: Components of a Time Series

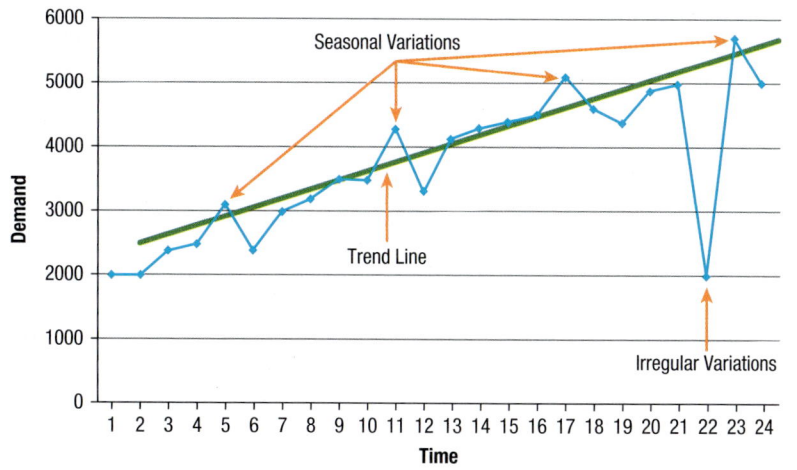

a.

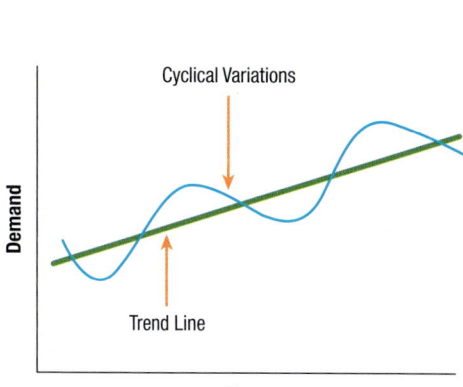

b.

FIGURE 13.2: Different Possible Trend Patterns

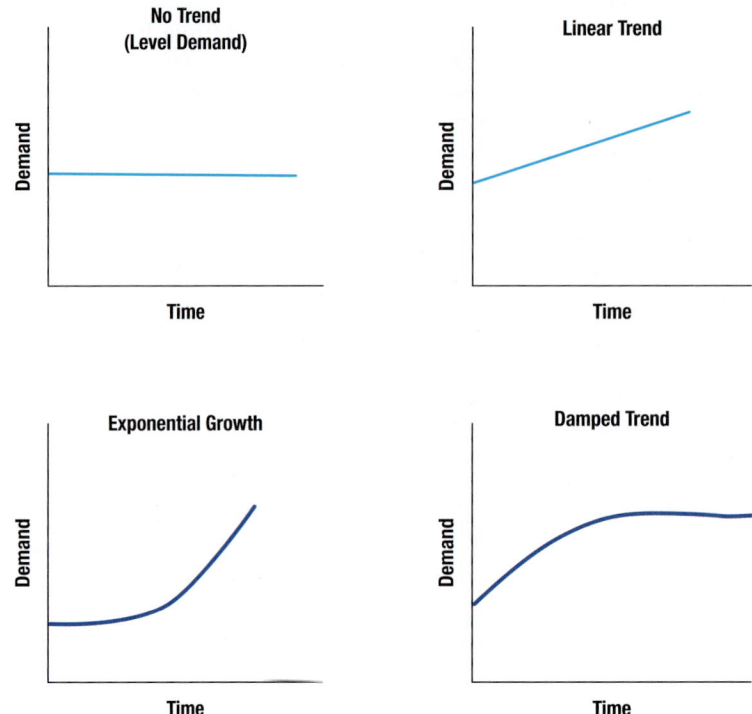

Short-Term Time Series Forecasting Methods

In many situations, a forecast of what will happen in the immediate future is often required without much regard for what will happen in the longer term. This is a common situation in many production processes. Orders that are going to be received in the next period have to be forecasted so that production schedules can be set. For the most part, short-term forecasts do not require sophisticated analysis techniques. If historical data in the form of a time series exist, the forecaster can use any of the following techniques for short-term forecasting: the naïve approach, simple averages, moving averages, and exponential smoothing. We will use the data from Table 13.3 to illustrate these forecasting techniques.

Table 13.3 shows the number of patients who arrived at a health-care facility during a 15-week period.

1. NAÏVE APPROACH

When forecasters use the **naïve approach,** they assume that the demand in the next period will be the same as it is in the current period. This approach to forecasting is simple and can be used as a base to compare the performance of other more advanced or complex forecasting techniques. Also, in the absence of any other information, the approach could be used to determine the forecast for the next reporting period. A naïve forecast for the data in Table 13.3 would provide an estimate of demand for period t+1 as:

$$F_{t+1} = A_t$$

where F_{t+1}, is the forecast value for period t + 1 and A_t, is the actual value at time t.

Thus, for the health-care facility data given in Table 13.3, the forecast of patients arriving at the facility in week 16 is given by:

$$F_{16} = A_{15} = 110$$

2. MOVING AVERAGE AND WEIGHTED MOVING AVERAGE

With a **moving average**, rather than using all past demand values, the forecaster averages the most recent demand periods to predict demand in the future period. The assumption is that the most recent events are the best indicators of the future. The choice of the number of periods to be included in the moving average is arbitrary and is left to the judgment of the forecaster. In general, however, if the demand in the past periods exhibits significant random fluctuations, then the forecaster would include more past periods' demand to calculate a moving average forecast. By including such past periods of data, we can smooth random fluctuations by canceling out the highs and lows in the time series. The formula for the moving average (MA) is:

$$MA_n = F_{t+1} = (\Sigma \text{ actual data values for } n \text{ recent previous periods} / n) = (\sum_{i=1}^{n} A_{t+1-i}) / n$$

That is,

$$MA_n = F_{t+1} = (A_t + A_{t-1} + A_{t-2} + \ldots + A_{t-(n-1)}) / n$$

EXAMPLE 13.1: Using the moving average technique, compute the forecast for period 16 for the health-care facility for three different values of n (3, 4, and 5) using the data in Table 13.3.

SOLUTION

$$MA_3 = F_{16} = (A_{15} + A_{14} + A_{13}) / 3 = (110 + 100 + 88) / 3 = 99.3 \text{ or } 100 \text{ patients}$$

$$MA_4 = F_{16} = (A_{15} + A_{14} + A_{13} + A_{12}) / 4 = (110 + 100 + 88 + 94) / 4 = 98 \text{ patients}$$

$$MA_5 = F_{16} = (A_{15} + A_{14} + A_{13} + A_{12} + A_{11}) / 5 = (110 + 100 + 88 + 94 + 94) / 5 = 97.2 \text{ or } 98 \text{ patients}$$

TABLE 13.3: Patient Demand at a Health-Care Facility

WEEK	NUMBER OF PATIENTS
1	77
2	83
3	89
4	92
5	99
6	108
7	122
8	115
9	122
10	107
11	94
12	94
13	88
14	100
15	110

The three-, four-, and five-week moving average forecasts for all weeks of demand data from the health-care facility example are shown in the Microsoft Excel spreadsheet (see Screenshot 13.1; Microsoft Corporation, Redmond, WA). Although the director of the health-care facility would use only the forecast for week 16, the forecasts for the prior weeks would show how well the forecasts track actual demand. That is, they would be used to indicate the accuracy of the forecasting method.

SCREENSHOT 13.1: Example of Moving Average

	A	B	C	D	E
1					
2					
3	Week	Number of Patients	Three-Period Average	Four-Period Average	Five-Period Average
4	1	77			
5	2	83			
6	3	89			
7	4	92	83.0		
8	5	99	88.0	85.3	
9	6	108	93.3	90.8	88
10	7	122	99.7	97.0	94.2
11	8	115	109.7	105.3	102
12	9	122	115.0	111.0	107.2
13	10	107	119.7	116.8	113.2
14	11	94	114.7	116.5	114.8
15	12	94	107.7	109.5	112
16	13	88	98.3	104.3	106.4
17	14	100	92.0	95.8	101
18	15	110	94.0	94.0	96.6
19	16		99.3	98.0	97.2
20					
21					
22			=AVERAGE(B19:B21)		

FIGURE 13.3: Smoothing Effects of Three-, Four-, and Five-Week Moving Average Forecasts

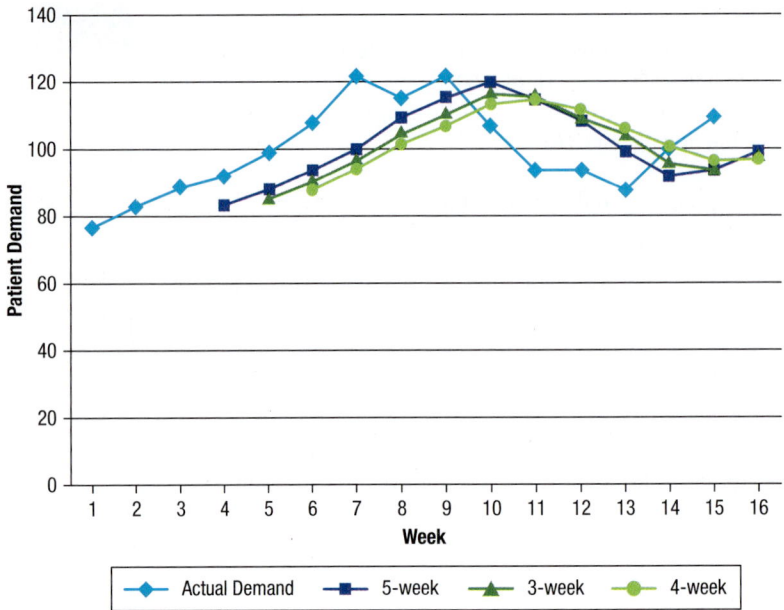

All three moving average forecasts tend to smooth out the fluctuations in actual demand. It appears, however, that the three-week moving average forecasts track actual demand better than the other two moving average forecasts. The smoothing effect can be observed in Figure 13.3, where all three moving average forecasts have been superimposed on the graph of the original patient demand values.

Although the moving average method uses the data from most recent periods, it still assigns equal importance to all periods of data included in the base of the moving average. Consequently, even with this method there is bound to be some forecast lag. That is, the forecast will underestimate demand if the actual demand in recent periods has been increasing. This problem can be resolved to a certain extent by using an extension of the moving average called the **weighted moving average**. In this method, forecasters assign more weight to most recent values in the time series if they feel that these values reflect how the actual demand will behave in the near future. For example, the most immediate observation might be assigned a value of 0.5, the next most recent value a weight of 0.3, and so on. The value of the weights assigned to the demands in the different time periods can vary and is left to the judgment of the forecaster. The sum of the weights, however, should be equal to 1. Using this method, the forecast for the next period is given by:

$$F_{t+1} = \sum_{i=1}^{n} W_{t+1-i} A_{t+1-i}$$

where

$$\sum_{i=1}^{n} W_{t+1-i} = 1$$

For example, using a weighted moving average with four recent periods (n = 4) and using weights of $W_1 = 0.5$, $W_2 = 0.3$, $W_3 = 0.2$, $W_4 = 0.1$, the forecast is:

$$F_{t+1} = F_5 = \sum_{i=1}^{4} W_{t+1-i} A_{t+1-i} = W_1 A_4 + W_2 A_3 + W_3 A_2 + W_4 A_1 = 0.5A_4 + 0.3A_3 + 0.2A_2 + 0.1A_1$$

3. EXPONENTIAL SMOOTHING

Exponential smoothing is a popular forecasting method that is simple to compute and can be made as sensitive as required. With this method, the next period's forecast is a weighted average of all previous observations that gives progressively less weight to older observations. This approach is called exponential smoothing because the forecast is made up of an exponentially weighted average of all the

Weighted moving average: a short-term time series forecasting method in which forecasters assign more weight to most recent values in the time series if they feel that these values reflect how the actual demand will behave in the near future

Exponential smoothing: a forecasting method in which the next period's forecast is a weighted average of all previous observations that gives progressively less weight to older observations

EXAMPLE 13.2: For the health-care facility data in Table 13.3, compute the forecast of patient demand for week 16.

SOLUTION

$$F_{t+1} = F_{16} = \sum_{i=1}^{4} W_{t+1-i} A_{t+1-i} = W_1 A_{15} + W_2 A_{14} + W_3 A_{13} + W_4 A_{12}$$

$$F_{16} = 0.5 \times 110 + 0.3 \times 100 + 0.2 \times 88 + 0.1 \times 94 = 112 \text{ patients}$$

An Excel spreadsheet calculating the weighted moving average technique is shown in Screenshot 13.2.

SCREENSHOT 13.2: Weighted Moving Average

	A	B	C	D	E	F	G	H
1								
2								
3	Weights	W_1		W_2	W_3	W_4		
4			0.5	0.3	0.2	0.1		
5								
6								
7	Week	Number of Patients						
8	1	77						
9	2	83						
10	3	89						
11	4	92						
12	5	99						
13	6	108						
14	7	122						
15	8	115						
16	9	122						
17	10	107						
18	11	94						
19	12	94						
20	13	88						
21	14	100						
22	15	110						
23								
24	Forecast (F_{16})	112 ────→	=($B$4*b22+$C$4*b21+$D$4*b20+$E$4*b19)					

previous observations. The averaging techniques discussed earlier are known as smoothing processes because they remove the random fluctuations from the time series so that the underlying trend can be seen more clearly and be used for making a forecast that is not subject to random swings. Exponential smoothing techniques are used to make short-term forecasts, primarily for the time period following the latest observation. The basic exponential smoothing formula is:

$$F_{t+1} = \alpha A_t + (1 - \alpha) F_t$$

where α is a smoothing constant and is a fraction between 0 and 1.

The formula for basic exponential smoothing can be rewritten as:

$$F_{t+1} = \alpha A_t + F_t - \alpha F_t = F_t + \alpha (A_t - F_t)$$

This formula can be interpreted as:

New forecast = old forecast + α × (latest observation – old forecast)

The greatest weight is assigned to the most recent observation. The weight assigned to each of the preceding demand observation decreases exponentially by a fixed fraction $(1 - \alpha)$.

The sensitivity of the forecast to changes in the most recently observed data are controlled by the value assigned to α. If α is set to 1, the new forecast (smoothed value) will be equal to the latest observation and no smoothing will occur. The implication in this case is that the new forecast should respond immediately to changes in the actual observation seen in the most recent period. Thus, when α is set to 1, the exponentially smoothed forecast is equivalent to the naïve forecast. On the other hand, if α is set to 0, then all variations in the actual values from the old forecast are essentially ignored, and the new forecast remains the same as the previous forecast rather than the latest observation. This decision implies that the actual value in the most recent period is purely a random occurrence and hence should be ignored. In practice, however, the forecaster chooses high values for α if the underlying average is likely to change, and low values for α are chosen if the underlying average is relatively stable.

To begin exponential smoothing, a forecaster needs two pieces of information: an initial forecast and a value for α. The value of α is left to the judgment of the forecaster. An initial forecast can be obtained using the naïve approach by assuming that it is equal to the actual demand value of any of the previous period.

Example 13.3

EXAMPLE 13.3: Use the health-care facility data from Table 13.3 to generate forecasts using exponential smoothing. Assume that the forecast of patient demand for week 2 is the actual demand in week 1 (the naïve forecast). That is, $F_2 = A_1 = 77$. Assume a value for α = 0.3.

SOLUTION

Using the exponential smoothing formula, the solution is:

New forecast = old forecast + α × (latest observation − old forecast)

The forecast for week 3 is:

$$F_3 = F_2 + \alpha \times (A_2 - F_2) = 77 + 0.3(83 - 77) = 78.8$$

Similarly the forecast for week 4 is:

$$F_4 = F_3 + \alpha \times (A_3 - F_3) = 78.8 + 0.3(89 - 78.8) = 81.86$$

For week 5 it is:

$$F_5 = F_4 + \alpha \times (A_4 - F_4) = 81.86 + 0.3(92 - 81.86) = 84.90$$

This process can be repeated for the remaining weeks to get the following smoothed series:

$F_6 = 89.1$ $F_{12} = 105.2$
$F_7 = 94.8$ $F_{13} = 101.8$
$F_8 = 103.0$ $F_{14} = 97.7$
$F_9 = 106.6$ $F_{15} = 98.4$
$F_{10} = 111.2$ $F_{16} = 101.9$
$F_{11} = 109.9$

Thus, the forecast for period 16 is given by $F_{16} = 101.9$, or 102 patients.

SCREENSHOT 13.3: Exponential Smoothing

	A	B	C	D	E	F
1						
2						
3	Assume	$F_2 = A_1$				
4		α	0.1	0.3	0.5	
5	Week	Number of Patients	Forecast-1	Forecast-2	Forecast-3	
6	1	77				
7	2	83	77.0	77.00	77.0	
8	3	89	77.6	78.80	80.0	
9	4	92	78.7	81.86	84.5	
10	5	99	80.1	84.90	88.3	
11	6	108	82.0	89.13	93.6	
12	7	122	84.6	94.79	100.8	
13	8	115	88.3	102.95	111.4	
14	9	122	91.0	106.57	113.2	
15	10	107	94.1	111.20	117.6	
16	11	94	95.4	109.94	112.3	
17	12	94	95.2	105.16	103.2	
18	13	88	95.1	101.81	98.6	
19	14	100	94.4	97.67	93.3	
20	15	110	95.0	98.37	96.6	
21	16		96.5	101.86	103.3	
22						
23						
24			=(C20 +$C$4*(B20-C20))			

We see that this series does produce a smooth trend, but it also shows a marked lag. That is, forecasts underestimate demand when the actual demand is increasing. The sensitivity of the forecasts can be improved by substituting a higher value of α. In addition to the forecasts for $\alpha = 0.3$, exponentially smoothed forecasts using α values of 0.1 and 0.5 for the health-care facility data are shown in the Excel screenshot 13.3.

It appears that, for the most part, the forecasts for $\alpha = 0.5$ track actual demand better than the other two forecasts. The smoothing effect can be observed in Figure 13.4. All three exponentially smoothed forecasts have been superimposed on the graph of the original patient demand values. Notice the highly damped smoothing and the considerable lag associated with the forecasts generated using $\alpha = 0.1$ when compared with those forecasts generated by using α values of 0.3 and 0.5.

FIGURE 13.4: Exponentially Smoothed Forecasts for α Values of 0.1, 0.3, and 0.5

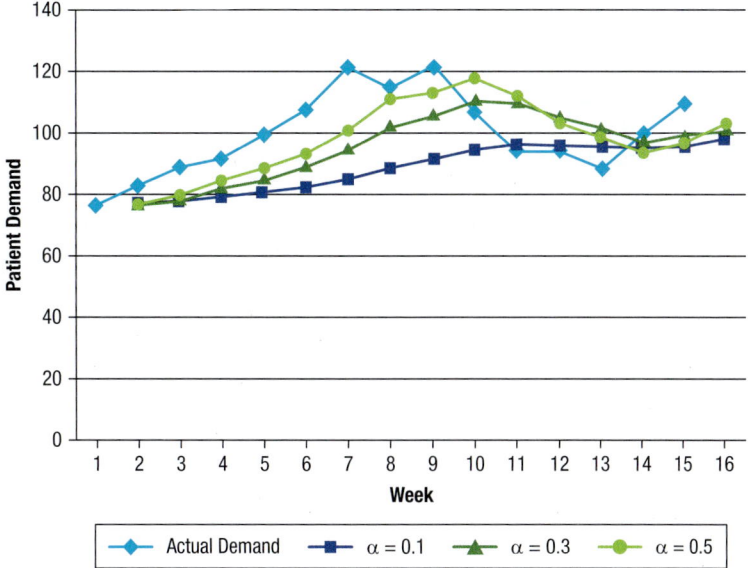

4. TREND-ADJUSTED EXPONENTIAL SMOOTHING

The exponential smoothing approach discussed earlier is an appropriate forecasting technique if the time series exhibits a horizontal pattern (no trend) with random fluctuations. Nevertheless, if the time series does exhibit a trend, forecasts based on simple exponential smoothing will lag the trend. For example, global demand for crude oil showed a declining trend from 2004 to 2010. Use of exponential smoothing for forecasting demand during any period in this duration would have overestimated the actual demand for crude oil. In such cases, a variation of simple exponential smoothing called **trend-adjusted exponential smoothing** can be used as a forecasting technique. The trend-adjusted forecast (TAF) has two components:

1. A forecast based on simple exponential smoothing.
2. A trend factor.

$$TAF_{t+1} = F_{t+1} + T_{t+1}$$

where

F_{t+1} = An exponentially smoothed forecast
T_{t+1} = Trend estimate
TAF_{t+1} = Next period's trend-adjusted forecast
$F_{t+1} = \alpha A_t + (1 - \alpha) F_t$
$T_{t+1} = \beta (F_{t+1} - F_t) + (1 - \beta) T_t$, where T_t = Previous period's trend factor

The factors α and β are smoothing constants with values between 0 and 1.

Note that the formula used for estimating the trend is similar to the formula used for simple exponential smoothing. The trend factor computed is a weighted measure of the change between the current

Trend-adjusted exponential smoothing: a variation of simple exponential smoothing that includes a trend factor, a weighted measure of the change between the current forecast and the next period's forecast

forecast (F_t) and the next period's forecast (F_{t+1}). To use this method, the forecaster must choose an initial estimate of the trend and a value for β in addition to choosing an initial forecast and a value for α. These initial values are usually selected based on the judgment of the forecaster or through trial and error. The value of β selected reflects the forecaster's judgment on the changes in trend.

EXAMPLE 13.4: Use the data from the health-care facility in Table 13.3 to illustrate this forecasting method. Use values of $\alpha = 0.3$ and $\beta = 0.4$ to generate the forecasts. In addition, assume that the initial forecast for week 2 is equal to the actual demand in week 1 and an initial trend factor for week 1, $T_2 = 0$.

SOLUTION

Because we have a long sequence of data of 15 periods, we should have a fairly good estimate of the trend by the time we forecast for week 16.

We begin by generating an unadjusted forecast for week 3 by using a simple exponential smoothing model:

$$F_3 = \alpha A_2 + (1 - \alpha) F_2 = 0.3 \times 83 + 0.7 \times 77 = 78.8$$

Using this unadjusted forecast, we now compute the trend factor for week 3:

$$T_3 = \beta (F_3 - F_2) + (1 - \beta) T_2 = 0.4 \times (78.8 - 77) + 0.7 \times 0 = 0.72$$

The trend-adjusted forecast for week 3 is:

$$TAF_3 = F_3 + T_3 = 78.8 + 0.72 = 79.52$$

Similarly for week 4:

$$F_4 = \alpha A_3 + (1 - \alpha) F_3 = 0.3 \times 89 + 0.7 \times 78.8 = 81.86$$

Using the unadjusted forecast, we compute the trend factor for week 4:

$$T_4 = \beta (F_4 - F_3) + (1 - \beta) T_3 = 0.4 \times (81.86 - 78.8) + 0.6 \times 0.72 = 1.66$$

The trend-adjusted forecast for week 4 is:

$$TAF_4 = F_4 + T_4 = 81.86 + 1.66 = 83.52$$

This process can be repeated for the remaining weeks to get the trend-adjusted forecasts as shown in the Excel screenshot 13.4. The trend-adjusted forecast for week 16 is calculated as follows:

$$F_{16} = \alpha A_{15} + (1 - \alpha) F_{15} = 0.3 \times 110 + 0.7 \times 98.37 = 101.86$$

Using this unadjusted forecast, we will now compute the trend factor for week 16:

$$T_{16} = \beta (F_{16} - F_{15}) + (1 - \beta) T_{15} = 0.4 \times (101.86 - 98.37) + 0.6 \times (-1.30) = 0.62$$

The trend-adjusted forecast for week 16 is:

$$TAF_{16} = F_{16} + T_{16} = 101.86 + 0.62 = 102.48 \text{ or } 103 \text{ patients}$$

The Excel spreadsheet calculation is shown in Screenshot 13.4.

Figure 13.5 compares the trend-adjusted and simple exponential smoothing forecasts with the original patient demand values. Notice that the trend-adjusted forecast captures the trend factor (the rise and fall) of the actual time series data a little better than the unadjusted forecasts constructed using simple exponential smoothing.

Excel solutions using the four forecasting techniques of moving averages, weighted moving averages, simple exponential smoothing, and trend-adjusted exponential smoothing for Examples 13.1 to 13.4 can be found in an Excel spreadsheet provided with the study materials for this text.

SCREENSHOT 13.4: Trend-Adjusted Exponential Smoothing

	A	B	C	D	E
1					
2					
3	**Assume**	F$_2$ = A$_1$ AND T$_1$ = 0	α	β	
4			0.3	0.4	
5	**Week**	**Number of Patients**	**Unadjusted Forecast (α = 0.3)**	**Trend Factor (β =0.4)**	**Trend-adjusted Forecast**
6	1	77		0	
7	2	83	77.0	0	77.0
8	3	89	78.8	0.72	79.5
9	4	92	81.9	1.66	83.5
10	5	99	84.9	2.21	87.1
11	6	108	89.1	3.02	92.1
12	7	122	94.8	4.08	98.9
13	8	115	103.0	5.71	108.7
14	9	122	106.6	4.87	111.4
15	10	107	111.2	4.77	116.0
16	11	94	109.9	2.36	112.3
17	12	94	105.2	-0.50	104.7
18	13	88	101.8	-1.64	100.2
19	14	100	97.7	-2.64	95.0
20	15	110	98.4	-1.30	97.1
21	16		101.9	0.61	102.5
22					
23			=(C20 +$C$4*(B20-C20))		=(C21+D21)
24					
25				=(D$4*(C21-C20)+(1-D$4)*D20)	

FIGURE 13.5: Comparison of the Trend-Adjusted Forecasts and the Simple Exponential Smoothing Forecasts

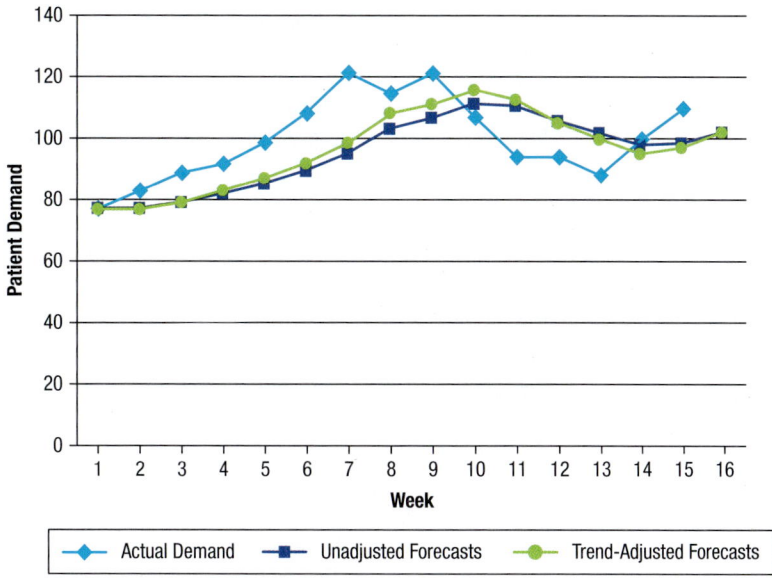

Exponential smoothing is a forecasting method widely used in many industries. Exponential smoothing models are more adaptive, create accurate forecasts, can be easily applied and automated, and lend themselves to large-scale forecasting. Because each forecasting method assumes that future patterns and trends will approximate current patterns and trends, the techniques are most useful for shorter-term forecasting of 24 months or less. Nevertheless, the assumption behind exponential models—that is, that greater emphasis should be given to more recent demand data—becomes less plausible in the longer term. The further out into the future you forecast, the less likely this is to hold true.

Also, exponential smoothing consists of a family of models that can be used to estimate and forecast future demand if the time series has up to three underlying data components—level, trend, and seasonality. For example, the simple exponential smoothing model (also called *first-order smoothing*) can be used when demand is constant, or level, with random variations. In contrast, the trend-adjusted

---

OPERATIONS PROFILE: Using Forecasting to Solve Hospital Staffing Challenges

Staffing in many hospitals accounts for over 50% of their costs. If the staff is too small, there are declines in the quality of care; if the staff is too large, the cost will be a financial burden on the hospital. More than half of all administrators still use manual methods to schedule their staff, and they base those schedules on information that is not useful, such as total number of beds available or on historical averages. This process is time-consuming, outdated, and often inaccurate. New advances in forecasting based on analytics are being introduced to the hospital staffing problem to help predict patient demand, reduce staffing shortages and overages, and improve the scheduling process for hospital staff and their managers.

Hospitals increasingly rely on methods for anticipating and adjusting their staffing through the use of forecasting models. Sophisticated analytics models generate patient forecasts that are as much as 20% more accurate than predictions made on historical averages alone. Some of these new solutions can flexibly handle certification time, paid time off requests, shift swaps, and more to generate patient-optimized schedules. Finally, the sophisticated forecasting methods are able to provide comprehensive measures of staffing requirements that allow administrators to monitor patient wait times, nurse-to-patient ratios, paid hours per visit, and other hospital-specific, predetermined metrics.

Among the critical elements in effective hospital staffing are forecasting methods that:

1. Recognize that staffing can be specific, so they work to predict staffing needs hour-by-hour, or by day of the week.

2. Adjust for changes in projected needs. For example, if a competitor opens a specialty outpatient clinic nearby, the staffing approach must adjust for changes in demand for its services.

3. Make adjustments for each facility's (or unit's) special circumstances. For example, rural outpatient services must adjust staffing for unique events, such as the start of hunting season.

4. Recognize changes to the hospital's staffing demographics. For example, the forecasting method must be able to make modifications for extended family leave for staff having children.

When hospitals commit to careful patient forecasts, they are able to make better staffing decisions that minimize patient wait times, avoid over-stressing their human resources and equipment, and ensure higher quality patient care as well as hospital profitability.[3]

smoothing (also known as second-order or double smoothing) model is useful when demand exhibits different types of changing trend patterns. Third-order or triple exponential smoothing demand forecasting models that exhibit both trend and seasonal patterns are also available, but explaining the calculations used in these models is beyond the scope of this textbook.

Medium- to Long-Term Time Series Forecasting Methods

We have thus far discussed techniques that can be used to forecast demand for the short term. We will now discuss some of the techniques commonly used to forecast demand for the medium- to long-term time horizons.

1. LINEAR TREND ANALYSIS

In the medium to long term, a time series graph of increasing demand will invariably exhibit a trend pattern—linear, damped, or exponential growth. We will not explain how to calculate damped and exponential growth trends because those techniques are the topic of more advanced statistics classes, but if we consider demand to be linear, we can use linear regression analysis to forecast demand in the medium to long term. Linear regression is a predictive technique that models the relationship between a dependent variable and one or more independent variables. The formula for a simple linear regression analysis is:

$$\hat{y}_t = a + bt$$

Linear regression analysis: a predictive technique that models the relationship between a dependent variable and one or more independent variables

where

    b is the slope of the straight line.

    a is the intercept of the line with the *y* axis at *t* = 0.

    $\hat{y}_t$ is the forecasted demand (the dependent variable) at time period *t* (the independent variable).

The goal of a linear regression analysis is to determine the values for *a* and *b* for a given set of time series data. To graph a linear regression, you draw a straight line that best fits the scatterplot of past values of actual demand (*Y*, the dependent variable) that have been plotted over time (*t*, the independent variable). Best fit means drawing a straight line that keeps the differences between the actual *Y*-values and the predicted ŷ-values (represented by the straight line) to a minimum. These differences are nothing but forecasting errors.

The method used to draw this line of best fit is the **least-squares method.** This method results in a straight line that minimizes the sum of the squares of the differences between the line and each of the actual observations. That is, the line of best fit is the line that minimizes the sum of the squares of forecasting errors. We square the differences so that positive differences do not offset negative differences. In essence, the least-squares method enables us to draw a line where the scatter of the observed demand data around the line is at its smallest. This line of best fit is called the *regression line* or the *trend line* for the observed set of data. Figure 13.6 illustrates the least-squares approach.

The formula for minimizing the sum of the squares of the deviations of all of the data points from the line is:

$$\text{Minimize} \sum_{t=1}^{n}\left(Y_t - \hat{y}_t\right)^2$$

The formula for the expression can be minimized using the partial differentiation, a technique discussed in calculus courses. By using partial differentiation, we can get formulas for *a* (the intercept) and *b* (the slope) of the regression line, which you recall is:

$$\hat{y}_t = a + bt$$

For a time series of *n* demand observations, the slope *b* of the line is given by:

$$b = \frac{n\Sigma ty - \Sigma t\,\Sigma y}{n\Sigma t^2 - \left(\Sigma t\right)^2}$$

FIGURE 13.6: Least-Squares Method for the Line of Best Fit

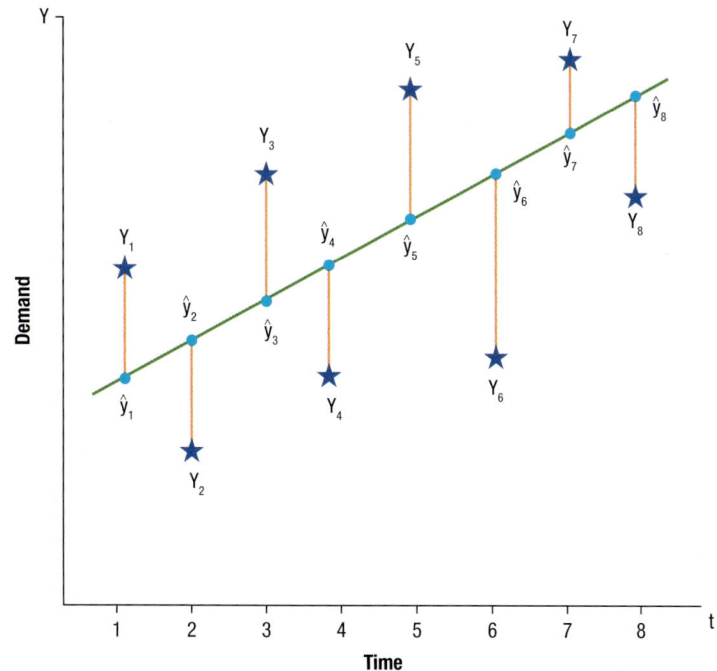

Least-squares method: a method used to draw the line of best fit

The intercept a of the line is given by:

$$a = \frac{\Sigma y - b\Sigma t}{n}$$

where

t = the number of time periods in the series.

Y = the observed demand value in a given time period.

a (y-intercept) = the average value of $\hat{y}_t$ when $t = 0$.

B = the slope, which denotes by how much the estimated $\hat{y}_t$ changes for each one unit increase in t.

Let's look at a simple example for developing a linear trend equation using a linear regression analysis.

Example 13.5

EXAMPLE 13.5: The cell phone sales for a Pennsylvania firm for the past 20 months are shown in Table 13.4.

TABLE 13.4

MONTHS	SALES (IN UNITS)	MONTHS	SALES (IN UNITS)
1	6,120	11	9,420
2	6,920	12	9,330
3	6,840	13	10,230
4	6,730	14	9,430
5	7,240	15	9,450
6	7,640	16	10,080
7	7,410	17	11,200
8	7,630	18	9,460
9	8,950	19	11,050
10	9,210	20	11,770

a. Plot the data to visually check if a linear trend model would provide an accurate forecast.

b. If so, determine the linear trend line using regression analysis.

c. Using the linear trend equation, forecast cell phone sales for months 21 and 22.

SOLUTION

a. The plot in Figure 13.7 shows that a linear trend model is appropriate.

FIGURE 13.7: Plot of Cell Phone Sales Over Time

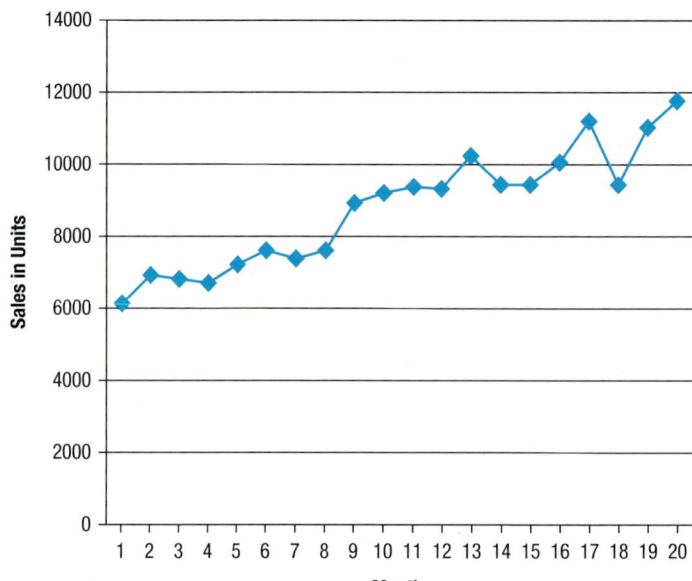

b. The calculations for determining the slope and intercept of the regression line are shown in the Excel Screenshot 13.5.

SCREENSHOT 13.5: Linear Trend Analysis

	A	B	C	D	E	F	G	H	I
1									
2	n	20							
3	Month (t)	Sales in Units (Y)	t*Y	t²	Y²				
4	1	6120	6120	1	37454400				
5	2	6920	13840	4	47886400				
6	3	6840	20520	9	46785600				
7	4	6730	26920	16	45292900				
8	5	7240	36200	25	52417600				
9	6	7640	45840	36	58369600				
10	7	7410	51870	49	54908100				
11	8	7630	61040	64	58216900				
12	9	8950	80550	81	80102500				
13	10	9210	92100	100	84824100				
14	11	9420	103620	121	88736400				
15	12	9330	111960	144	87048900				
16	13	10230	132990	169	104652900				
17	14	9430	132020	196	88924900				
18	15	9450	141750	225	89302500				
19	16	10080	161280	256	101606400				
20	17	11200	190400	289	125440000				
21	18	9460	170280	324	89491600				
22	19	11050	209950	361	122102500				
23	20	11770	235400	400	138532900				
24	210	176110	2024650	2870	1.6E+09				
25									
26	Slope	b		263.9023	→=(($B$2*$C$24)-($A$24*$B$24))/(($B$2*$D$24)-($A$24*$A$24))				
27	Intercept	a		6034.526	→=(($B$24)-($C$26*$A$24))/$B$2				
28	Forecast for Month 21	Y₂₁		11576.47	→=($C$27+$C$26*21)				
29	Forecast for Month 22	Y₂₂		11840.38					

The slope of the line is given by:

$$b = \frac{n\Sigma ty - \Sigma t\,\Sigma y}{n\Sigma t^2 - (\Sigma t)^2} = \frac{20\times 2024650 - 210\times 176110}{20\times 2870 - 210^2} = 263.9$$

The intercept of the line is given by:

$$a = \frac{\Sigma y - b\Sigma t}{n} = \frac{176110 - 263.9\times 210}{20} = 6034.5$$

The resulting linear trend equation is:

$$\hat{y}_t = a + bt = 6034.5 + 263.9 \times t$$

c. The forecast for period 21 is:

$$\hat{y}_{21} = 6034.5 + 263.9 \times 21 = 11{,}576.4 \text{ or } 11{,}577$$

The forecast for t = 22 is:

$$\hat{y}_{22} = 6034.5 + 263.9 \times 22 = = 11{,}840.3 \text{ or } 11{,}841$$

Based on the linear trend equation that we developed using regression analysis, we can now estimate that the expected cell phone sales will be 11,577 units for period 21 and 11,841 units for period 22.

Both linear trend analysis and trend-adjusted exponential smoothing can be used to evaluate the trend component of a time series. The advantage of linear trend analysis over trend-adjusted exponential smoothing is that it is easier to project the trend line to generate forecasts for future periods.

Nevertheless, trend-adjusted exponential smoothing adjusts the trend period-by-period based on the behavior of demand in the most recent periods. The choice of the particular technique depends on the data and the preference of the forecaster.

2. TECHNIQUES FOR FORECASTING SEASONALITY

No matter how smooth the trend line, most time series have seasonal variations in demand. The best way to evaluate seasonal variations is to first generate a set of seasonal indices or factors that capture the seasonal contribution to demand in each period during the year. For example, if the times series is comprised of monthly data, then 12 indices are generated to indicate the seasonal contribution of each month. On the other hand, if the time series consists of quarterly data, then four indices are generated to capture the seasonal contribution of each quarter. The seasonal indices are then combined with the trend forecasts to generate composite estimates of demand.

There are two models of combining the trend and the seasonal components. One is an additive model in which the seasonal indices are added to the projected trend data to create a combined forecast. In this model, both the trend and the seasonal components are expressed in units expected to be sold. The other method is the multiplicative model in which the seasonal indices are expressed as percentages and the combined forecast is expressed as percentage adjustments of the underlying trend. Thus, if we assume that a time series has only the trend and seasonal components, then the combined forecast generated using the two models are as follows:

$$\text{Additive model: } \hat{Y}_t = \hat{y}_t + \hat{s}_t$$

where $\hat{Y}_t$, $\hat{y}_t$, and $\hat{s}_t$ are in units.

$$\text{Multiplicative model: } \hat{Y}_t = \hat{y}_t \times \hat{s}_t$$

where $\hat{Y}_t$, and $\hat{y}_t$, are in units, and $\hat{s}_t$ is expressed as a percentage.

In the models,

$$\hat{y}_t = \text{the trend forecast for period } t,$$

$$\hat{s}_t = \text{the projected seasonal index for period } t, \text{ and}$$

$$\hat{Y}_t = \text{the combined or composite forecast for period } t.$$

The decision to use an additive or a multiplicative model depends on the pattern of seasonal variations. If the variations remain constant over time, then the additive model should be used. On the other hand, if the variations become more or less pronounced as the trend component increases or decreases, then a multiplicative model is appropriate. Figure 13.8 shows the seasonal variations around the trend.

Let us examine two methods for calculating seasonal indices: the simple average method and the centered moving average method.

3. THE SIMPLE AVERAGE METHOD

The simple average method has three steps:

Step 1: Compute the average demand for each season from past time series data.

Step 2: Compute the average total demand for the entire time series data.

Step 3: Divide the average demand for each season (computed in Step 1) by the average total demand (computed in Step 2) to arrive at the seasonal indices for each month.

Example 13.6 illustrates this method.

Seasonal indices: factors that capture the seasonal contribution to demand in each period during the year

Additive model: a model of combining trends and seasonal components in which the seasonal indices are added to the projected trend data to create a combined forecast

Multiplicative model: a model of combining trends and seasonal components in which the seasonal indices are expressed as percentages and the combined forecast is expressed as percentage adjustments of the underlying trend

Simple average: a method for calculating seasonal indices by dividing the average demand for each season by the average total demand to arrive at the seasonal indices for each month

Generating a set of seasonal indices for seasonal products can help companies determine the demand for their products during each period of a year.

©iStockphoto.com/ktaylorg

FIGURE 13.8: Additive and Multiplicative Seasonal Patterns

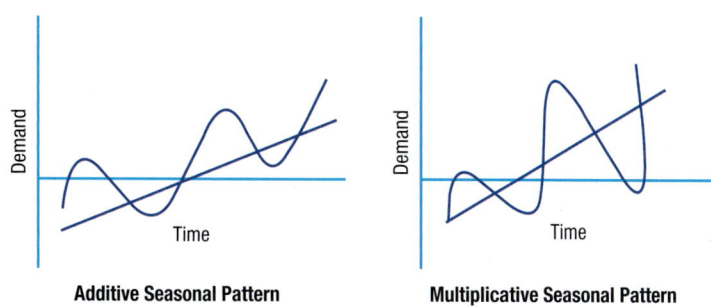

Additive Seasonal Pattern   Multiplicative Seasonal Pattern

EXAMPLE 13.6: A Pennsylvania-based cell phone dealer wants to develop monthly seasonal indices for the company's cell phone demand. Monthly demand data for the past 3 years (2015 to 2017) are shown in Table 13.5. Compute the seasonal indices for each month using the simple average method.

TABLE 13.5

MONTH	DEMAND		
	2015	2016	2017
January	90	96	116
February	80	96	96
March	90	104	91
April	100	108	118
May	122	138	145
June	120	128	132
July	110	115	124
August	99	115	120
September	93	100	105
October	85	88	95
November	80	83	87
December	88	78	83

Step 1: Calculate the average demand for each month. For example, the average demand for January is: (90+96+116)/3 = 100.67.

Step 2: Calculate the average total demand from January 2015 to December 2017.

$$(90+80+...+87+83)/36 = 103.28.$$

Step 3: Divide the average demand for each month by the average total demand to get the seasonal indices. For example the seasonal index for January is:

$$100.67/103.28 = 0.97.$$

The seasonal index calculations for all the remaining months are shown in the Excel spreadsheet in Screenshot 13.6.

Centered moving average method: a method for calculating seasonal indices in which moving averages for each season are centered

SCREENSHOT 13.6: Computing Seasonal Indices Using Simple Average Method

	A	B	C	D	E	F	G
1							
2					=AVERAGE(B5:D5)		
3							
4	Month	2015	2016	2017	Average Monthly Demand	Average Total demand	Seasonal Indices
5	January	90	96	116	100.67	103.28	0.97
6	February	80	96	96	90.67	103.28	0.88
7	March	90	104	91	95.00	103.28	0.92
8	April	100	108	118	108.67	103.28	1.05
9	May	122	138	145	135.00	103.28	1.31
10	June	120	128	132	126.67	103.28	1.23
11	July	110	115	124	116.33	103.28	1.13
12	August	99	115	120	111.33	103.28	1.08
13	September	93	100	105	99.33	103.28	0.96
14	October	85	88	95	89.33	103.28	0.86
15	November	80	83	87	83.33	103.28	0.81
16	December	88	78	83	83.00	103.28	0.80
17							
18						=AVERAGE($B$5:$D$16)	=(E16/F16)

The pattern of monthly seasonal variation is shown in Figure 13.9.

FIGURE 13.9: Plot of the Seasonal Indices Calculated Using the Simple Average Method

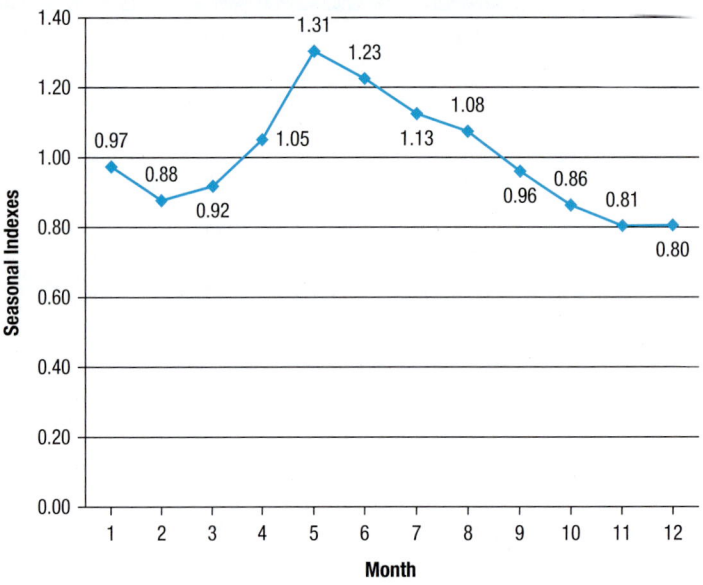

4. THE CENTERED MOVING AVERAGE METHOD

The centered moving average method has five steps.

Step 1: For the demand data in the time series, calculate a moving average equal to the length of the season. For example, if the seasonal variation data are collected quarterly, then a four-period moving average is used because there are four seasons in a year. On the other hand, if the data are collected daily, then a seven-period moving average is used because there are seven days in a week.

Step 2: Center the moving averages. If the number of seasons is an odd number, then the moving average is centered in the middle period. For example, for a seven-day moving average used for capturing daily seasonal variation data, the moving average will be centered on day 4. For an even number of seasons, an additional step is necessary to center the moving average. In this case, an average of two successive moving averages should be calculated. For example, in the case of quarterly data, the four-period moving average values of quarter 1 to quarter 4 and quarter 2 to quarter 5 are averaged to center the data. That is, data for quarter 5 is also incorporated in the second moving average so a center for it can be found.

Step 3: Calculate the ratio of actual demand to the centered moving average value for each seasonal period.

Step 4: For each seasonal period, calculate an unadjusted seasonal index by averaging the ratio of values calculated for that period in Step 3.

Step 5: Adjust the total of the seasonal indices to equal the number of seasons in a year. For example, for quarterly seasonal indices the total should sum to 4. The resulting numbers are the adjusted seasonal indices for each period.

EXAMPLE 13.7: An electronics store has recorded the following quarterly sales of computers for the last 4 years (see Table 13.6). Compute the quarterly seasonal indices using the centered moving average method.

TABLE 13.6

Quarter	1	2	3	4	5	6	7	8	9	10	11	12	13	14	15	16
Sales	730	1120	1170	1730	780	1130	1350	1960	790	1180	1290	2020	820	1350	1430	2150

SOLUTION

Step 1: For the demand data in the time series, calculate a moving average equal to the length of the season. Because the seasonal variations data are collected quarterly in this example, we will compute a four-period moving average. For example, the first moving average for the first four periods is calculated as follows:

$$(730+1120+1170+1730)/4 = 1187.5.$$

This value is the entry in cell D-8 in the column titled MA-4 in Screenshot 13.7. Similarly, the average of sales from periods 2 to 5 is calculated and is 1,200. This value is the next entry in cell D-9 in that column. These are the four-period moving averages.

Step 2: Center the moving averages. The four-period moving average values of period 1 to period 4 and period 2 to period 5 are averaged to center the data. For example, the first two four-period moving average values are averaged to get the following centered moving average:

$$(1187.5+1200)/2 = 1193.75.$$

This value is entered in cell E-6 under the column Centered MA-2 in period 3. Similarly the second and third four-period moving average values are averaged to get the second centered moving average value of 1,201.25. The rest of the centered moving average values are calculated in a similar manner and are shown in column 5.

Step 3: Calculate the ratio of actual demand to the centered moving average value for each seasonal period. For example, for period 3, the ratio is given by:

Sales in period 3/Centered MA-2 for period 3 = 1170/1193.75 = 0.98.

The ratios for the remaining periods are calculated similarly and are shown in the column labeled Ratio in the Excel screenshot.

Step 4: For each seasonal period, calculate an unadjusted seasonal index by averaging the ratio of values calculated for that period in Step 3. For the example problem, the unadjusted seasonal indices for each quarter are calculated by computing the average of the values for those quarters in the column labeled Ratio. For example, the unadjusted seasonal index for quarter 1 is the average of the ratio values in period 5 (0.64), period 9 (0.60), and period 13 (0.59), which is:

$$(0.64+0.60+0.59)/3 = 0.61.$$

This value of 0.61 is entered in the column labeled Unadj. SI for periods 1, 5, 9, and 13, representing quarter 1. The unadjusted seasonal indices for the remaining quarters are calculated the same way.

Step 5: Adjust the total of the seasonal indices to equal the number of seasons in a year. For example, *the total* of quarterly seasonal indices in this example should sum to 4. The resulting numbers are the adjusted seasonal indices for each period. The adjustment is done as follows:

The sum of the unadjusted quarterly seasonal indices = 0.61 + 0.91 + 0.99 + 1.47 = 3.98.

The adjusted seasonal indices are:

Quarter 1: (4 × 0.61)/3.98 = 0.61

Quarter 2: (4 × 0.91)/3.98 = 0.91

Quarter 3: (4 × 0.99)/3.98 = 1.00

Quarter 4: (4 × 1.47)/3.98 = 1.48

The total of the four indices is: 0.61 + 0.91 + 1.00 + 1.48 = 4.0.

The adjusted seasonal indices are shown in the column labeled Adj. SI in Screenshot 13.7.

SCREENSHOT 13.7: Moving Average Calculations for Seasonality Indices

	A	B	C	D	E	F	G	H	I	J
1										
2						=(C6/F6)				
3	Period	Quarter	Sales	MA-4	Centered MA-2	Ratio	Unadj.SI	Adj. SI		
4	1	1	730				0.61	0.61		
5	2	2	1120				0.91	0.91		
6	3	3	1170		1193.75	0.98	1.00	1.00		
7	4	4	1730		1201.25	1.44	1.48	1.48		
8	5	1	780	1187.5	1225	0.64	0.61	0.61		
9	6	2	1130	1200	1276.25	0.89	0.91	0.91		
10	7	3	1350	1202.5	1306.25	1.03	1.00	1.00		
11	8	4	1960	1247.5	1313.75	1.49	1.48	1.48		
12	9	1	790	1305	1312.5	0.60	0.61	0.61		
13	10	2	1180	1307.5	1312.5	0.90	0.91	0.91		
14	11	3	1290	1320	1323.75	0.97	1.00	1.00		
15	12	4	2020	1305	1348.75	1.50	1.48	1.48		
16	13	1	820	1320	1387.5	0.59	0.61	0.61		
17	14	2	1350	1327.5	1421.25	0.95	0.91	0.91		
18	15	3	1430	1370			1.00	1.00		
19	16	4	2150	1405			1.48	1.48		
20				1437.5						
21							Unadj.SI	Adj. SI		
22					Quarter-1		0.609877	0.610802	=(4*F22)/$F$26	
23					Quarter-2		0.911441	0.912824		
24					Quarter-3		0.996034	0.997546		
25					Quarter-4		1.476587	1.478828		
26					SUM		3.993939	4		
27										
28					=(F8+F12+F16)/3					

Both the simple average method and the centered moving average method can be used to compute the seasonal indices for time series data. Nevertheless, the simple average method is better to use when the time series data exhibit seasonal variations around a constant or level demand pattern. The centered moving average method is more widely used and is considered to be a more accurate method of calculating seasonal indices if the time series data exhibit any type of linear or nonlinear trend pattern. The obvious disadvantage of the centered moving average is that it is computationally more cumbersome than the simple average method. Moreover, the simple average method is a good technique for computing seasonal indices even if a trend is present in the data as long as the variations in demand about the trend line are relatively large. For example, demand for air travel or for primary care physicians show an increasing trend but experience significant seasonal fluctuations.

5. THE LINEAR TREND MULTIPLICATIVE METHOD

Linear trend multiplicative method: a method in which the seasonal indices are expressed as percentages and the combined forecast is expressed as percentage adjustments of the underlying linear trend

In the linear trend multiplicative method the seasonal indices are expressed as percentages and the combined forecast is expressed as percentage adjustments of the underlying linear trend. The linear trend multiplicative method can be used if the time series demand data exhibit a linear trend with seasonal variations and seasonal index values are available. For example, the method can be used to forecast automobile sales, which have exhibited an increasing trend in recent years, but with seasonal variations. The linear trend multiplicative method has four steps:

Step 1: Deseasonalize the actual demand in each period by dividing by the seasonal index for that period. Deseasonalizing means eliminating the seasonal variations in demand data so that the resulting time series data reflect only the trend values.

Step 2: Construct a linear trend equation with the deseasonalized data.

Step 3: Using the linear trend equation, generate the trend forecast for the desired future period.

Step 4: Multiply the trend forecast by the seasonal index for that period to arrive at a seasonalized forecast.

We will illustrate these steps using the data from Example 13.7.

EXAMPLE 13.8: An electronics store has recorded the following quarterly sales of computers along with the quarterly seasonal indices for the last 4 years (see Table 13.7). Compute seasonalized forecasts for the four quarters for year 5.

TABLE 13.7

PERIOD	1	2	3	4	5	6	7	8	9	10	11	12	13	14	15	16
Sales	730	1120	1170	1730	780	1130	1350	1960	790	1180	1290	2020	820	1350	1430	2150
Seasonal Indices	0.61	0.91	1.00	1.48	0.61	0.91	1.00	1.48	0.61	0.91	1.00	1.48	0.61	0.91	1.00	1.48

SOLUTION

Step 1: Deseasonalize the actual demand in each period by dividing by the seasonal index for that period. For example, the deseasonalized demand for period 1 is: 730/0.61 = 1196.7.

Similarly, for period 2, the deseasonalized demand is 1120/0.91 = 1230.8, and so on.

The deseasonalized demand values obtained from the computations are shown in Screenshot 13.8.

Step 2: Develop a linear trend equation using the deseasonalized data. The calculations required to develop the linear trend equation are shown in Screenshot 13.8.

SCREENSHOT 13.8: Linear Trend Multiplicative Model

	A	B	C	D	E	F	G	H
1								
2	n	16			=(C4/D4)			
3	Period (t)	Quarter	Sales	Seasonal Indices	Deseasonalized Sales (y)	t*y	t²	
4	1	1	730	0.61	1195.1	1195.1	1	
5	2	2	1120	0.91	1227.0	2453.9	4	
6	3	3	1170	1.00	1172.9	3518.6	9	
7	4	4	1730	1.48	1169.8	4679.4	16	
8	5	1	780	0.61	1277.0	6385.0	25	
9	6	2	1130	0.91	1237.9	7427.5	36	
10	7	3	1350	1.00	1353.3	9473.2	49	
11	8	4	1960	1.48	1325.4	10603.0	64	
12	9	1	790	0.61	1293.4	11640.4	81	
13	10	2	1180	0.91	1292.7	12926.9	100	
14	11	3	1290	1.00	1293.2	14224.9	121	
15	12	4	2020	1.48	1365.9	16391.4	144	
16	13	1	820	0.61	1342.5	17452.5	169	
17	14	2	1350	0.91	1478.9	20705.0	196	
18	15	3	1430	1.00	1433.5	21502.8	225	
19	16	4	2150	1.48	1453.9	23261.7	256	
20	136				20912.4	183841.4	1496.0	
21	Slope	b	17.9					
22	Intercept	a	1154.9		=($C$22+$C$21*20)			
23	The Linear Trend equation is : 1154.9 + 17.9*t							=(C28*E28)
24		Period	Deseasonalized forecast		Seasonal Indices	Seasonalized forecast		
25		y₂₁	1459.2		0.61	890.1		
26		y₂₂	1477.1		0.91	1344.1		
27		y₂₃	1495.0		1	1495.0		
28		y₂₄	1512.9		1.48	2239.0		

The formulas are as follows.
The slope b of the trend line is:

$$b = \frac{n\Sigma ty - \Sigma t\,\Sigma y}{n\Sigma t^2 - (\Sigma t)^2} = \frac{16 \times 183841.4 - 136 \times 20912.4}{16 \times 1496 - 136^2} = 17.9$$

The intercept a of the line is:

$$a = \frac{\Sigma y - b\Sigma t}{n} = \frac{20912.4 - 17.9 \times 136}{16} = 1154.9$$

The resulting linear trend equation is:

$$\hat{y}_t = a + bt = 1154.9 + 17.9 \times t$$

Step 3: Using the linear trend equation, forecast the trend future periods. Thus, the deseasonalized trend forecasts for Periods 17, 18, 19, and 20 (as shown in Screenshot 13.8) are:

$$\hat{y}_{17} = 1154.9 + 17.9 \times 17 = 1459.2$$

$$\hat{y}_{18} = 1154.9 + 17.9 \times 18 = 1477.1$$

$$\hat{y}_{19} = 1154.9 + 17.9 \times 19 = 1495.0$$

$$\hat{y}_{20} = 1154.9 + 17.9 \times 20 = 1512.9$$

Step 4: Multiply the trend forecast by the seasonal index for that period to arrive at a seasonalized forecast. Given the seasonal indexes of $S_1 = 0.61$, $S_2 = 0.91$, $S_3 = 1.00$, and $S_4 = 1.48$ for the four quarters, respectively, the seasonalized forecasts for periods 17, 18, 19, and 20 (as shown in the spreadsheet) are:

Seasonalized forecast for period 17: $\hat{y}_{17} \times S_1 = 1459.2 \times 0.61 = 890.1$

Seasonalized forecast for period 18: $\hat{y}_{18} \times S_2 = 1459.2 \times 0.91 = 1344.1$

Seasonalized forecast for period 19: $\hat{y}_{19} \times S_3 = 1459.2 \times 1.00 = 1495.0$

Seasonalized forecast for period 20: $\hat{y}_{20} \times S_4 = 1459.2 \times 1.48 = 2239.0$

Techniques for Evaluating Cyclical Variations

Cyclical variations caused by economic or business conditions (such as a recession or boom, for example) form wave-like oscillations about the trend line; they usually last for more than a year. Cyclical variations are similar to seasonal variations but are more difficult to forecast because they are more irregular. Isolating, analyzing, and forecasting the cyclical variations in a time series requires advanced filtering and mathematical and statistical techniques, and their discussion is beyond the scope of this textbook. Although the naïve and moving average approaches can be used to track cyclical variations, forecasts using these approaches lag behind actual cyclical variations by several periods.

Leading indicators are frequently used to track cyclical fluctuations. These are variables such as the number of housing starts in the economy, number of unemployment insurance claims, inventory changes, and stock prices. Changes in the values of leading indicators typically precede changes in the economy or the business cycle. For example, information about the number of housing starts can be used to predict the demand for durable goods such as refrigerators, washers, and dryers. Therefore, if there is a consistent correlation between the demand for a product and one of the indicators, then a mathematical relationship between them can be established and a forecast made.

Leading indicators: variables such as the number of housing starts in the economy, number of unemployment insurance claims, inventory changes, and stock prices used to track cyclical fluctuations

Types of Quantitative Methods: Causal or Associative Methods

Associative methods are a form of quantitative analysis that uses causal techniques to identify related variables for making forecasts. So, for example, we can use bank lending interest rates to predict sales of homes. Interest rates and home sales would be considered related variables; changes to interest rates can often be used to forecast changes to home sales. There are several associative methods for forecasting, including linear regression analysis and multiple regression analysis.

1. LINEAR REGRESSION ANALYSIS

In our earlier discussion of linear trend analysis, we used linear regression analysis to evaluate the trends in a time series. In that regression equation, we assumed that the dependent variable demand

(Y) is a function of the independent variable t (the time period). The linear regression technique can be used in a similar way to determine the association or relationship between two variables.

For example, suppose the demand for houses is a function of price. If that's the case, the price is the independent or predictor variable, and demand is the dependent or predicted variable. We can then use regression for forecasting purposes. The only difference between the trend equation we used in the linear trend analysis and the linear regression equation we will use as an associative method is that the independent variable will be denoted by x instead of t. Other than this difference, the procedure for using the linear regression equation is exactly the same—the least-squares method. When there is an associative relationship between two variables, the linear regression equation takes the following form:

Using linear regression analysis in the real estate market can show the relationship between the price of a house (the independent variable) and the demand for it (the dependent variable).

©iStockphoto.com/LOU OATES

$$y_c = a + bx_i$$

where y_c is the computed or forecasted value of demand, and the slope (b) of the regression line is:

$$b = \frac{n\Sigma x_i y_i - \Sigma x_i \Sigma y_i}{n\Sigma x_i^2 - (\Sigma x_i)^2}$$

The intercept of the line is given by:

$$a = \frac{\Sigma y_i - b\Sigma x_i}{n}$$

EXAMPLE 13.9: Milton Tile and Carpet Store (Odessa, TX) wants to forecast demand for its ceramic tiles. The store manager, Jessica Milton, believes that the store's tile sales are directly related to the number of new housing starts in Ector County. She collected the data in Table 13.8 from the county on the number of monthly house construction permits issued and Milton's corresponding ceramic tile sales.

TABLE 13.8

MONTH	1	2	3	4	5	6	7	8	9	10	11	12
Monthly Tile Sales	6000	13000	7000	8000	6000	15000	7700	6800	14200	8000	4000	5700
Monthly Construction Permits	18	32	14	20	12	40	22	19	33	25	10	13

a. Construct a linear regression equation for the previous data.

b. Interpret the values for the slope (b) and the intercept (a).

c. Forecast tile sales if 27 housing permits were issued in a given month.

SOLUTION

Even though a linear trend line can be used to analyze the data, an associative method is more appropriate because the sales of tile are more directly related to housing permits issued than time periods. The calculations for the slope and intercept of the regression equation are shown in Screenshot 13.9.

a. The linear regression equation is of the form:

$$y_c = a + bx_i$$

Independent or predictor variable: a variable that, when changed, causes an effect on a dependent or predicted variable.

Dependent or predicted variable: a variable that is affected by an independent or predictor variable

SCREENSHOT 13.9: Linear Regression Analysis: Associative Method

	A	B	C	D	E	F	G	H	I	J
1										
2	n		12							
3	Monthly Construction Permits (x)	Tile Sales in Units (Y)	x*Y	x^2	y^2	y_c	$(y-y_c)^2$			
4	18	6000	108000	324	36000000	7167.028	1361954			
5	32	13000	416000	1024	1.69E+08	12298.92	491518.2			
6	14	7000	98000	196	49000000	5700.774	1687988			
7	20	8000	160000	400	64000000	7900.155	9969.064			
8	12	6000	72000	144	36000000	4967.647	1065753			
9	40	15000	600000	1600	2.25E+08	15231.42	53557.14			
10	22	7700	169400	484	59290000	8633.282	871014.8			
11	19	6800	129200	361	46240000	7533.591	538156.2			
12	33	14200	468600	1089	2.02E+08	12665.48	2354752			
13	25	8000	200000	625	64000000	9732.972	3003192			
14	10	4000	40000	100	16000000	4234.52	54999.69			
15	13	5700	74100	169	32490000	5334.211	133801.9			
16	258	101400	2535300	6516	9.99E+08		11626656			
17										
18		x-bar	21.5							
19		Y-bar	8450							
20	Slope	b	366.5634675		=(($B$2*$C$16)-($A$16*$B$16))/(($B$2*$D$16)-($A$16*$A$16))					
21	Intercept	a	568.8854489		=(($B$16)-($C$20*$A$16))/$B$2					
22	The Linear Regression Equation is: 568.89 + 366.56 * x									
23	Forecast for x =27	Y_{27}	10466.09907		=($C$21+$C$20*27)					
24	Forecast for x =22	Y_{22}	8633.281734							

where y_c is the computed, or forecasted, value of demand, and the slope of the regression line is given by:

$$b = \frac{n\Sigma x_i y_i - \Sigma x_i \Sigma y_i}{n\Sigma x_i^2 - (\Sigma x_i)^2} = \frac{12 \times 2535300 - 258 \times 101400}{12 \times 6516 - (258)^2} = 366.56$$

The intercept of the line is given by:

$$a = \frac{\Sigma y_i - b\Sigma x_i}{n} = \frac{101400 - 366.5635 \times 258}{12} = 568.89$$

Therefore, the linear regression equation is:

$$y_c = 568.89 + 366.56 \times x_i$$

b. The value of the slope (b = 367) means that for each new housing permit issued sales of ceramic tiles increase by 367 units. The value of the intercept (a = 569) means that even if no new housing construction permits were issued there will still be a demand for 569 units of tiles.

c. The forecast for ceramic tile sales if 27 construction permits were issued (x =27) is:

$$y_c = 568.89 + 366.56 \times x_i = 568.89 + 366.56 \times 27 = 10,466 \text{ tiles.}$$

2. EVALUATING THE GOODNESS OF FIT OF THE REGRESSION LINE

The purpose of using a regression equation is to establish if there is a relationship between the predictor (x) and the predicted variable (y). Nevertheless, after writing the regression equation, we also need to evaluate how well it describes the extent of the relationship between the two variables. That is, we need to assess how well the line of best fit is in relation to the observed data. We can use three measures to evaluate this, and therefore, the validity of the regression equation for forecasting. These measures are the coefficient of determination (R^2), the correlation coefficient (r), and the standard error of the estimate (s_{yx}).

Coefficient of determination: the proportion of variation explained by regression

Total sum of squares: a measure of the variation of the actual Y-values around the mean Y

Regression sum of squares: a measure of the difference between the mean Y and the predicted or computed value of Y using regression

The **coefficient of determination** (R^2) is the proportion of variation explained by regression—that is, by the relationship between X and Y. There are three measures of variation that must be calculated prior to finding R^2: the **total sum of squares** (SST), which measures the variation of the actual Y-values around the mean Y ($\overline{Y}$).

$$SST = \Sigma (Y_i - \overline{Y})^2$$

• The explained variation, or the **regression sum of squares** *(SSR),* which measures the variation resulting from the relationship between x and Y—that is, the difference between the mean Y and the predicted or computed value of Y ($\hat{y}_i$ or y_c) using regression.

$$SSR = \Sigma (\hat{y}_i - \overline{Y})^2$$

- The unexplained variation, or **error sum of squares** *(SSE)*, which measures the variation not explained by the regression but resulting from other factors or variables.

$$SSE = \Sigma\,(Y_i - \hat{y}_i)^2$$

The R^2 can then be computed using the following formula:

$$R^2 = \frac{SSR}{SST} = \frac{\Sigma\left(\hat{y}_i - \overline{Y}\right)^2}{\Sigma\left(y_i - \overline{Y}\right)^2} = \frac{a\Sigma y_i + b\Sigma x_i y_i - n\left(\overline{Y}\right)^2}{\Sigma y_i^2 - n\left(\overline{Y}\right)^2}$$

R^2 has a value between 0 and 1. The higher the value of R^2, the better is the line of fit. That is, the higher the R^2 value, the more confidence we have that the estimate is accurate.

The **correlation coefficient** *(r)* statistic measures the strength of the relationship between x and Y, and takes on a value between -1 and +1. The closer the correlation coefficient is to +1 or -1, the stronger is the relationship between the variables. The formula for r is given by:

$$r = \frac{\Sigma x_i y_i - n\overline{x}\,\overline{Y}}{\sqrt{\Sigma x_i^2 - n(\overline{x})^2}\,\sqrt{\Sigma y_i^2 - n(\overline{Y})^2}}$$

Note: For simple linear regression only with just two variables, r can also be calculated by taking the square root of R^2.

The standard error of the estimate (s_{yx}) measures the random variation, which is the variation of the actual (observed) y values from the predicted y values $(\hat{y}_i)$, by the standard error of the estimate. The smaller the value of s_{yx}, the smaller is the variation of the actual (observed) y values from the predicted y values $(\hat{y}_i)$. The interpretation of the standard error of the estimate is similar to that of standard deviation, which measures the variability or dispersion around the mean. That is, the standard error of the estimate measures the variability of the actual Y values around the fitted regression line.

$$s_{yx} = \frac{\sqrt{SSE}}{\sqrt{n-2}} = \frac{\sqrt{\Sigma(Y_i - \hat{y}_i)^2}}{\sqrt{n-2}} = \frac{\sqrt{\Sigma y_i^2 - a\Sigma y_i - b\Sigma x_i y_i}}{\sqrt{n-2}}$$

EXAMPLE 13.10: Using the data from the solution to Example 13.9 of the Milton Tile and Carpet Store (see Screenshot 13.9), evaluate the goodness of fit of the regression equation developed for that example. Specifically, compute the values of R^2, r, and s_{yx} and interpret the results.

SOLUTION

From the solution to Example 13.10, we have the following data:

$$n = 12,\ \Sigma x = 258,\ \overline{x} = (\Sigma x/n) = 258/12 = 21.5,\ \Sigma Y = 101{,}400,\ \overline{Y} = (\Sigma Y/n) = 8450,$$

$$\Sigma xY = 2{,}535{,}300,\ \Sigma x^2 = 6516,\ \Sigma Y^2 = 998660000,\ a = 568.89,\ b = 366.56,$$

$$R^2 = \frac{a\Sigma y_i + b\Sigma x_i y_i - n\left(\overline{Y}\right)^2}{\Sigma y_i^2 - n\left(\overline{Y}\right)^2} = \frac{(568.89 \times 101400) + (366.56 \times 2535300) - 12 \times 8450^2}{998660000 - 12 \times 8450^2} = 0.918$$

$$r = \frac{\Sigma x_i y_i - n\overline{x}\,\overline{Y}}{\sqrt{\Sigma x_i^2 - n(\overline{x})^2}\,\sqrt{\Sigma y_i^2 - n(\overline{Y})^2}} = \frac{2535300 - 12 \times (21.5) \times (8450)}{\sqrt{6516 - 12 \times (21.5)^2}\,\sqrt{998660000 - 12 \times (8450)^2}} = 0.958$$

$$s_{yx} = \frac{\sqrt{\Sigma y_i^2 - a\Sigma y_i - b\Sigma x_i y_i}}{\sqrt{n-2}} = \frac{\sqrt{998660000 - 568.89 \times 101400 - 366.56 \times 2535300}}{\sqrt{(12-2)}} = 1079$$

All of the statistics indicate that the regression line obtained in Example 13.10 is a very good fit. The regression equation gives Jessica Milton the ability to predict ceramic tile sales for her store with a high degree of confidence. Specifically, the value of R^2 of 0.918 means that 91.8% of the variation in ceramic tile sales (Y-values) is accounted for by changes in the housing construction permits (x-values). Similarly, the r value of 0.958 indicates that the variables of housing construction permits (x) and ceramic tile sales (Y) are almost perfectly positively correlated (close to the value of 1). Finally, the s_{yx} value indicates that actual ceramic tile sales (Y) deviate from the predicted $(\hat{y}_i)$ values by about 1,079 units.

Error sum of squares: a measure of the variation not explained by the regression but resulting from other factors or variables

Correlation coefficient: a statistic that measures the strength of the relationship between x and Y, and takes on a value between -1 and +1

Standard error of the estimate: a measure of the variation of the actual (observed) y values from the predicted y values $(\hat{Y}_i)$

An Excel spreadsheet of the solution to Example 13.10 is given in Screenshot 13.10.

SCREENSHOT 13.10: Goodness of Fit of Regression Line

	A	B	C	D	E	F	G	H
3	Data From Example 13-6							
4	n		12					
5	Monthly Construction Permits (x)	Tile Sales in Units (Y)	x*Y	x^2	Y^2	Y_c	$(Y-Y_c)^2$	
6	18	6000	108000	324	36000000	7167.028	1361954	
7	32	13000	416000	1024	1.69E+08	12298.92	491518.2	
8	14	7000	98000	196	49000000	5700.774	1687988	
9	20	8000	160000	400	64000000	7900.155	9969.064	
10	12	6000	72000	144	36000000	4967.647	1065753	
11	40	15000	600000	1600	2.25E+08	15231.42	53557.14	
12	22	7700	169400	484	59290000	8633.282	871014.8	
13	19	6800	129200	361	46240000	7533.591	538156.2	
14	33	14200	468600	1089	2.02E+08	12665.48	2354752	
15	25	8000	200000	625	64000000	9732.972	3003192	
16	10	4000	40000	100	16000000	4234.52	54999.69	
17	13	5700	74100	169	32490000	5334.211	133801.9	
18	258	101400	2535300	6516	9.99E+08		11626656	
20		x-bar	21.5					
21		Y-bar	8450					
22	Slope	b	366.5634675					
23	Intercept	a	568.8854489					
24	Coeeficient of Determination	R^2	0.918023998		=((C21*B16)+(C20*C16)-(B2*C19*C19))/((E16)-(B2*C19*C19))			
25	Correlation Coeeficient	r	0.958135689		=(C16-(B2*C18*C19))/((SQRT(D16-(B2*C18*C18))*(SQRT(E16-(B2*C19*C19)))))			
26	Standard Error of the Estimate	S_{yx}	1078.269741		=SQRT(E16-(C21*B16)-(C20*C16))/SQRT(B2-2)			

A linear regression analysis can be a powerful forecasting tool. Nevertheless, the validity of a linear regression model depends on four assumptions:

- The independent and dependent variables have a *linear relationship*.
- The deviations between the actual values and the predicted values using the regression equation (the error terms) are *independent*. That is, the error terms have no correlation.
- The error terms have a constant variance.
- The error terms are normally distributed.

If the observed data do not fulfill any of these assumptions, then linear regression analysis should not be used. To use the linear regression model, the assumptions of the model must be validated. Validation of the model can be achieved by analyzing the forecast error values. In addition, any forecast made using the linear regression equation should be only within the range of observed values.

3. MULTIPLE LINEAR REGRESSION ANALYSIS

In our discussions and examples using simple linear regression analysis for evaluating the trend shown in a time series and for evaluating causal relationships, we assumed that the model consists of only two variables—a dependent variable and an independent variable. Yet, often several independent variables may influence a dependent variable such as demand. For example, the demand for a product may be a function of both the price of the product and the promotional dollars spent by the company that produced it. A multiple linear regression can be used when several independent variables affect a dependent variable, a. The formula for a multiple linear regression equation is:

$$y_c = b_0 + b_1 x_1 + b_2 x_2 + b_3 x_3 + \ldots + b_i x_i$$

where y_c is the computed value of the dependent variable; x_1, x_2, x_3, and x_i are the independent variables; b_0, b_1, b_2, b_3, and b_i, and so on, are the regression coefficients and represent the amount by which y changes for a unit change in x_i, assuming all other independent variables are held constant.

Multiple linear regression: a predictive technique that models the relationship between a dependent variable and several independent variables

A complete discussion of the multiple linear regression equation is beyond the scope of this textbook. In addition, even for a problem with only two independent variables, the calculations needed in the formulas for the regression coefficients are cumbersome and require the use of software. Nonetheless, we will illustrate in the Solved Problems how a multiple regression problem can be solved using Excel. Students interested in learning more about multiple regression procedure should consult a statistics text.

13.4 Measuring and Monitoring the Accuracy of Forecasting Methods

To choose the best forecasting method, the forecaster should examine the performance of a range of forecasting methods over time and choose the one that results in the fewest forecasting errors. We discuss several ways to measure forecasting errors.

Mean Absolute Deviation (MAD)

The **mean absolute deviation (MAD)** is one of the easiest forecasting error measures to compute. The MAD is the average of the sum of the absolute differences between the actual and the forecasted demand values and is given by:

$$MAD = \frac{\sum_{t=1}^{n}|A_t - F_t|}{n}$$

Forecasting Accuracy

where

A$_t$ = the actual demand in time period t
F$_t$ = the forecasted demand in time period t
n = the number of time periods
$|A_t - F_t|$ is the absolute value of the forecast errors

Cumulative Sum Error (CSE) and Bias

The **cumulative sum error (CSE)** is the sum of the differences between the actual and the forecasted demand values:

$$CSE = \Sigma(A_t - F_t)$$

Although positive and negative differences tend to offset each other, a large positive CSE value indicates that the forecast is consistently understating the actual demand. In contrast, a large negative CSE value indicates that the forecast is consistently overstating the actual demand. Thus, by calculating the *average value* of the CSE, we can measure if there is *bias* in the forecasting method—that is, a tendency to consistently produce a particular type of forecast (say, high or low) that isn't accurate. The bias is the average value of the CSE, its formula is:

$$Bias = \Sigma(A_t - F_t)/n$$

Mean Squared Error (MSE)

The **mean squared error (MSE)** is the average of the sum of the squared differences between the actual and the forecasted demand values, and its formula is:

$$MSE = \frac{\sum_{t=1}^{n}(A_t - F_t)^2}{n-1}$$

The forecasting errors (A$_t$ - F$_t$) are squared to minimize the distortion effect of positive and negative differences offsetting each other.

Mean Absolute Percentage Error (MAPE)

The **mean absolute percentage error (MAPE)** measures the absolute error as a percentage of the actual demand, and its formula is:

$$MAPE = \frac{\sum_{t=1}^{n}\frac{|A_t - F_t|}{A_t} * 100}{n}$$

The MAPE is the average of the absolute percent error.

Each of the four measures of forecast accuracy has advantages and disadvantages. The MAD is simple and easy to compute. Although it provides information on whether the forecast is around the target on average, it provides no information about the forecasting bias. The CSE tracks the forecasting bias, but the cancellation of positive and negative forecast errors can distort the information. The MSE tracks both the accuracy of the forecast and the forecasting bias, but large errors tend to be magnified because they are squared. The MAPE, unlike the MAD and the MSE, can be used to compare different data sets because it provides a common measure—the percent of the error.

We will demonstrate the use of these error measures using the data from the health-care facility example. Specifically, we will compute the four forecasting error measures for weeks four to fifteen.

EXAMPLE 13.11: For the health-care facility data in Table 13.3, compute the forecasting error measures for the forecast generated using a 3-week moving average. Then do the same for the forecast generated with simple exponential smoothing when $\alpha = 0.3$. Compare the accuracy of the two forecasting methods.

SOLUTION

The Excel spreadsheet shows the calculations of the error measures for the three-period moving average (Screenshot 13.11) and the exponential smoothing forecasts (Screenshot 13.12).

SCREENSHOT 13.11: Forecast Error Measures for Three-Period Moving Average

	A	B	C	D	E	F	G
1							
2							
3	Week	Number of Patients (A_t)	3-Period MA-Forecasts (F_t)	(A_t - F_t)	|A_t - F_t|	(A_t - F_t)^2	(|A_t - F_t|/A_t) *100
4	4	92	83	9	9	81	9.78
5	5	99	88	11	11	121	11.11
6	6	108	93.3	14.7	14.7	216.09	13.61
7	7	122	99.7	22.3	22.3	497.29	18.28
8	8	115	109.7	5.3	5.3	28.09	4.61
9	9	122	115	7	7	49	5.74
10	10	107	119.7	-12.7	12.7	161.29	11.87
11	11	94	114.7	-20.7	20.7	428.49	22.02
12	12	94	107.7	-13.7	13.7	187.69	14.57
13	13	88	98.3	-10.3	10.3	106.09	11.70
14	14	100	92	8	8	64	8.00
15	15	110	94	16	16	256	14.55
16	Total			35.9	150.7	2196.03	145.84
17							
18		MAD		12.6 ——→ =(E16/12)			
19		Bias		3.0 ——→ =(D16/12)			
20		MSE		183.0 ——→ =(F16/12)			
21		MAPE		12.2 ——→ =G16/12			

$$MAD = \frac{\sum_{t=1}^{n}\left|A_t - F_t\right|}{n} = 150.7/12 = 12.6$$

$$Bias = \Sigma(A_t - F_t)/n = 35.9/12 = 3.0$$

$$MSE = = \frac{\sum_{t=1}^{n}\left(A_t - F_t\right)^2}{n} = 2196.03/12 = 183.0$$

$$MAPE = \frac{\sum_{t=1}^{n}\frac{\left|A_t - F_t\right|}{A_t} *100}{n} = 145.84/12 = 12.2$$

$$MAD = \frac{\sum_{t=1}^{n}\left|A_t - F_t\right|}{n} = 156.86/12 = 13.1$$

$$Bias = \Sigma(A_t - F_t)/n = 66.6/12 = 5.6$$

$$MSE = = \frac{\sum_{t=1}^{n}\left(A_t - F_t\right)^2}{n} = 2508.73/12 = 209.1$$

$$MAPE = \frac{\sum_{t=1}^{n}\frac{\left|A_t - F_t\right|}{A_t} *100}{n} = 149.51/12 = 12.5$$

The forecasting error measures indicate that the 3-week moving average produces more accurate forecasts because it has lower values for all four error measures compared with the simple exponential method. It appears that the 3-week moving average does a better job smoothing out the random variations in the data.

SCREENSHOT 13.12: Forecast Error Measures for Exponential Smoothing

	Week	Number of Patients (A_t)	EXP.Smoothing-Forecasts (F_t) ($\alpha = 0.3$)	($A_t - F_t$)	$|A_t - F_t|$	$(A_t - F_t)^2$	$(|A_t - F_t|/A_t)*100$
4	4	92	81.9	10.14	10.14	102.82	11.02
5	5	99	84.9	14.10	14.10	198.75	14.24
6	6	108	89.1	18.87	18.87	356.02	17.47
7	7	122	94.8	27.21	27.21	740.28	22.30
8	8	115	103.0	12.05	12.05	145.10	10.47
9	9	122	106.6	15.43	15.43	238.14	12.65
10	10	107	111.2	-4.20	4.20	17.62	3.92
11	11	94	109.9	-15.94	15.94	254.03	16.96
12	12	94	105.2	-11.16	11.16	124.48	11.87
13	13	88	101.8	-13.81	13.81	190.71	15.69
14	14	100	97.7	2.33	2.33	5.44	2.33
15	15	110	98.4	11.63	11.63	135.33	10.58
16	Total			66.66	156.86	2508.73	149.51
17							
18		MAD	13.1 ——▶ =(E16/12)				
19		Bias	5.6 ——▶ =(D16/12)				
20		MSE	209.1 ——▶ =(F16/12)				
21		MAPE	12.5 ——▶ =G16/12				

13.5 Monitoring and Controlling Forecasts

The ability of a given forecasting method to accurately track demand can diminish over time because of changes in consumer tastes, market turmoil, or fluctuations in the business cycle. Therefore, companies need to monitor the performance of their preferred forecasting techniques over time to be sure the forecasts are accurate. If the current technique is not consistent in its ability to accurately track demand, the company should change the forecasting method it uses. Companies typically use two methods for monitoring and controlling forecasts: tracking signals and control charts.

The use of tracking signals involves establishing an upper and a lower control limit to determine whether the forecasting errors related to a method are within these limits. A tracking signal value that goes outside of these control limits is an indicator that the forecasting method being used should be modified or changed. Because most time series forecasting methods rely on historic demand patterns to predict demand, tracking signals are useful for determining whether the pattern of demand has changed.

Employ the methods used to monitor and control forecasts.

Tracking signals are set using both the MAD and CSE and therefore monitor not only whether the forecasts lie around the target but also whether they are consistently too high or too low. The only two numbers required for calculating tracking signals are the actual demand values and forecasts. Consequently, tracking signals can be used with a variety of forecasting methods. The only drawback is that the tracking signal may falsely flag a forecasting method as out of control when small deviations occur in one direction that may not really reflect a real change in demand pattern. The formula for calculating a tracking signal is:

$$\text{Tracking Signal} = \frac{\sum_{t=1}^{n}(A_t - F_t)}{MAD}$$

To create tracking signals using this formula, the calculations for the CSE (in the numerator) and the MAD must be done on a period-by-period basis. To establish the control limits for tracking signals, companies assume that forecasting errors are normally distributed, and the relationship between the MAD and the standard deviation of the forecast errors (σ_e) is:

$$\sigma_e = 1.25MAD$$

where

$$\sigma_e = \sqrt{\frac{\sum_{t=1}^{n}(e_t - \bar{e})^2}{n-1}}$$

e_t = the forecasting error in period t = ($A_t - F_t$)

$$\bar{e} = \text{the average forecasting error} = \frac{\sum_{t=1}^{n}e_t}{n}$$

Because forecasting errors are assumed to be distributed normally, companies often use 3σ (or 3.75 MAD) control limits for the use of tracking signals. With forecasting errors being measured in

Tracking signals: upper and lower control limits used to determine whether the forecasting errors related to a method are within these limits

MAD units, the 3σ (or 3.75 MAD) control limits imply that the probability that the forecasting errors are attributable to random variation is 99.7%. Typically, a tracking signal that stays between 3σ or 3.75 MAD is considered acceptable, which means the errors are attributable to random variations in demand. Nevertheless, if the tracking signal falls outside of these limits, then the probability that the errors result from random variation is low; in other words, the likelihood that there are other factors that are causing changes in the demand pattern and the existing forecasting method requires modification. Most companies use control limits that range from ± 2 to ± 5 MAD. We will demonstrate the use of tracking signals for the linear regression method and the data in Example 13.6. Recall that the linear regression equation in this example is:

$$y_c = 568.89 + 366.56 \times x_i$$

EXAMPLE 13.12: For the Milton Tile and Carpet Store in Example 13.9, compute the linear regression forecasts and the tracking signals for each of the 12 periods. Plot the tracking signals using ± 4 MAD control limits and determine whether the forecasts are within control.

SOLUTION

Using the previous linear regression equation, we will first calculate the forecasts and then the CSE, MAD, and tracking signals.

For Period 1:

The linear regression forecast is: $y_1 = 568.89 + 366.56 \times 18 = 7166.97$.

$$(A_1 - F_1) = (6000 - 7166.97) = -1166.97$$

$$CSE = -1166.97$$

$$MAD_1 = |A_1 - F_1| = |-1166.97| = 1166.97$$

$$\text{Tracking signal} = \frac{\sum_{t=1}^{n}(A_t - F_t)}{MAD_1} = -1166.97/1196.97 = -1$$

The remaining calculations for the other periods are shown in the Excel spreadsheet in Screenshot 13.13.

The plot of these tracking signals over time is shown in Figure 13.10. The plot shows that 10 of the 12 tracking signals are within ± 4 MAD control limits. The tracking signals for periods 4 and 6, however, fall outside of the upper control limit of $+4$. The cause for these unusual values should be investigated for irregular variations in demand.

SCREENSHOT 13.13: Tracking Signals for Milton Tile and Carpet Store

⊿	A	B	C	D	E	F	G	H
1								
2								
3	y_c	568.89 + 366.56*xi				=(F7+E8)		
4	a	568.89					=(F8/G8)	
5	b	366.56						
6	Time Period	x		Actual Demand (At)	Linear Regression Forecast (Ft)	(At - Ft)	CSE	|At - Ft|	Tracking Signal
7	1	18		6000	7166.97	-1166.97	-1166.97	1166.97	-1
8	2	32		13000	12298.81	701.19	-465.78	701.19	-0.66
9	3	14		7000	5700.73	1299.27	833.49	1299.27	0.64
10	4	20		8000	7900.09	99.91	933.4	99.91	9.34
11	5	12		6000	4967.61	1032.39	1965.79	1032.39	1.90
12	6	40		15000	15231.29	-231.29	1734.5	231.29	7.50
13	7	22		7700	8633.21	-933.21	801.29	933.21	0.86
14	8	19		6800	7533.53	-733.53	67.76	733.53	0.09
15	9	33		14200	12665.37	1534.63	1602.39	1534.63	1.04
16	10	25		8000	9732.89	-1732.89	-130.5	1732.89	-0.08
17	11	10		4000	4234.49	-234.49	-364.99	234.49	-1.56
18	12	13		5700	5334.17	365.83	0.84	365.83	0.00

FIGURE 13.10: Plot of the Tracking Signals for the Linear Regression Forecasts of Milton Tile and Carpet Store

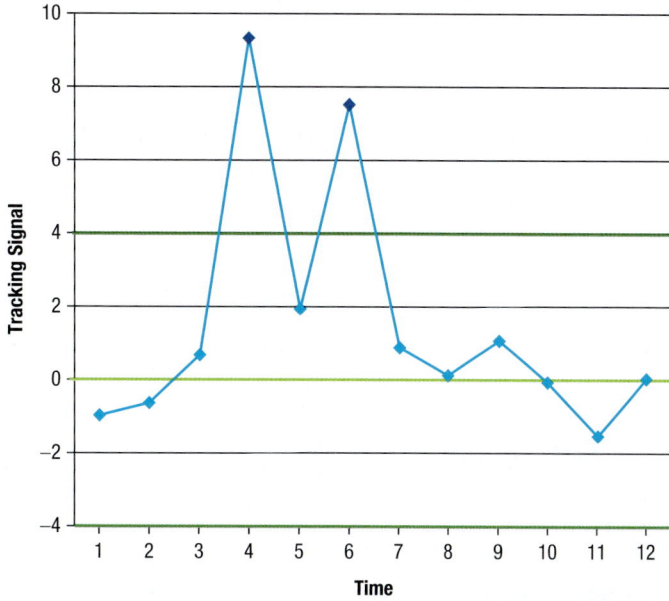

The second tool that can be used in monitoring and controlling forecasts is a *control chart*, which we discussed in Chapter 6. Constructing a control chart is similar to calculating a tracking signal except that we use the standard deviation of forecast errors to construct the control limits and plot the computed forecasting errors on the control chart. A control chart for this example could be designed using $3\sigma_e$ control limits, which would require 99.7% of the forecasting errors to be within this range.

13.6 Forecasting for Supply Chains

The effectiveness of a demand planning system depends on its ability to generate forecasts, not only at the individual product level but also at product group, customer group, and regional levels, as well as for different planning horizons. Each partner in the supply chain will engage in similar forecasting processes for its own company. The coordination of the individual company forecasts allows an organization to synchronize its own forecasts to its supply chain. In this section, we describe the steps in the forecasting process that a company in the consumer products industry can use when forecasting for its supply chain.[4]

13.6

Identify the steps involved in forecasting for supply chains.

1. *Determine the purpose of the forecast.*

   The first step is to decide on the business activity to forecast. This decision will determine whether the forecast is for the short term, medium term, or long term. If demand for a product is immediate and is expected to occur within the next few weeks, then operations managers will need short-term forecasts to assist them in making decisions about production scheduling issues that span only those next few weeks. For example, electricity suppliers require short-term load forecasts for the control and scheduling of power systems. These forecasts help determine which devices to operate in a given time period and how to meet demand even when local failures occur in the system. If, on the other hand, the business activity is strategic (for example, developing a new product or facility planning), forecasts for longer-term planning horizons are needed. Once we know the purpose for which the forecast will be used, the forecaster can also determine the level of detail (for example, individual items, product families, or regional market forecasts) that will be needed. Typically, for short-term activities such as production scheduling, demand forecasts of individual items are needed. On the other hand, medium time-frame decisions, such as sales and operations planning, require aggregate demand forecasts of product groups or families.

2. *Collect and clean historical data.*

   One important step in the data collection is to ensure the quality and integrity of the data by cleaning up or filtering the original data. For example, collected demand data should reflect the

Coordinating Forecasts

Consider This 13.1:
Forecasting Using Excel

The solutions using the various forecasting techniques discussed in this chapter can also be obtained using Microsoft Excel. We can solve these problems in Excel either directly using the available commands or by creating customized worksheets. To generate forecasts directly from Excel, you need to do the following:

1. From the tools menu at the top of the Excel worksheet, select the "Data" option and then the "Data Analysis" option. The following data analysis tools window will be displayed, as shown in Screenshot 13.14.

SCREENSHOT 13.14: Data Analysis Window

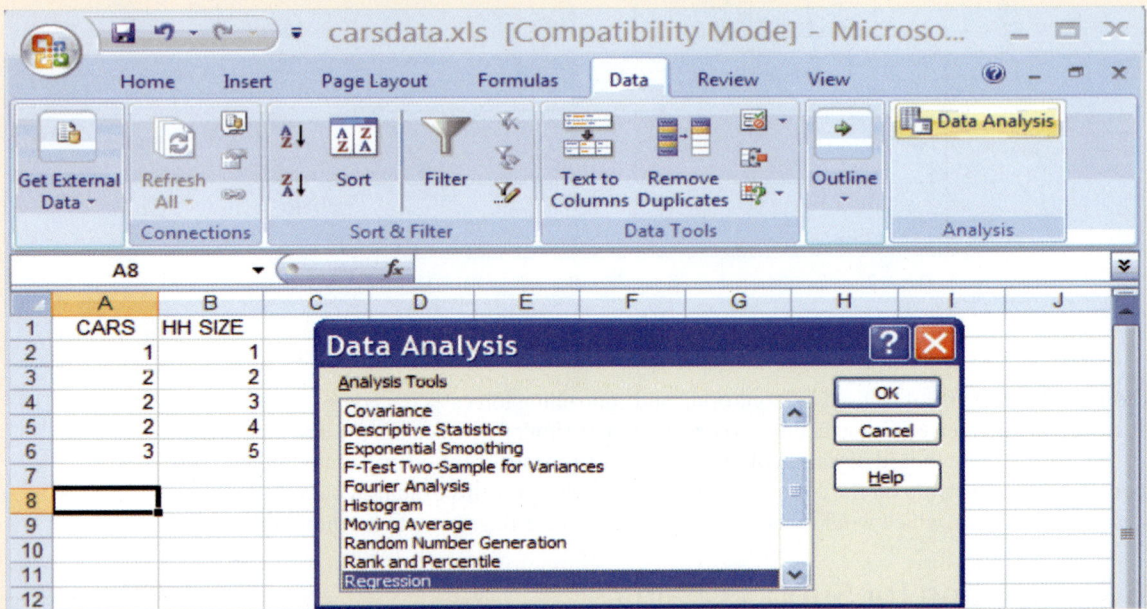

2. Next click on the forecasting technique you want to use. For example, if you choose exponential smoothing, then the resulting exponential smoothing window will be displayed (Screenshot 13.15).

SCREENSHOT 13.15: Exponential Smoothing Window

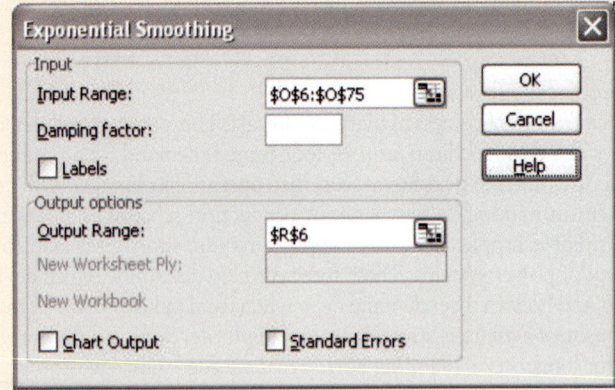

3. In the "Input Range" box, enter the range of the actual demand data. Enter the value of α in the box labeled "Damping Factor." In the box labeled "Output Range," specify the range in the worksheet where you want the forecasted values to be displayed. After clicking "OK" the forecast values will be displayed in that range.

Similar procedures in Excel can be used for the other forecasting techniques.

SOURCE: Reprinted from http://www.audi.co.uk/audi-innovation/audi-city.html

true demand that occurred in the market and not simply what the company sold. For example, the data from company sales will not include the impact of stockouts or other negative events that occurred because the company was unable to meet actual demand. Similarly, the original data may include outliers such as unusually low or high demand caused by random events (such as unusual weather patterns) and need to be eliminated. Other factors that need to be considered to enrich the original historical data include promotions that were used during a given period or the various structural changes such as acquisition of new production capacity within the company or the entry or departure of a competitor that may have occurred within the industry.[5]

3. *Select an appropriate forecasting technique and generate the demand forecasts.*

    In general, quantitative forecasting techniques are used for generating short-term and medium-term forecasts, whereas qualitative methods are used for long-term forecasting. The Hard Rock Cafe International, Inc. (Orlando, FL), for example, uses the technique of weighted moving averages and regression analysis to determine the food items most likely to be demanded on its menu. One possible approach for choosing an appropriate forecasting technique is to use past knowledge of demand and then plot the available demand data you have to assist in determining correct functional specification. As the data are plotted, the forecaster can determine whether to use a linear model or whether something else, such as seasonal variation, might need to be included in the forecast. Most companies rely on one of the many available forecasting software packages to generate their demand forecasts. These software packages can select from several statistical methods to identify the best forecast approach for each individual product item or product group.

4. *Adjust the forecast with judgmental inputs.*

    Using forecasting software does not guarantee that you will generate good and accurate forecasts. In the grocery industry, retailers historically used manual ordering and intuition to replenish stock, which frequently led to problems of over-ordering, stock-outs, and a failure to anticipate surges in demand. In current practice, big grocery chains, like California-based Unified Grocers (Commerce, CA), have combined demand forecasting software with human judgment. They find that software forecasts alone do not accurately allow for variations among stores in the chain, but a combination of forecasts coupled with human assessments gives them a very accurate means for stock ordering and shelf-life estimates.[6] Insights from sources such as sales representatives, suppliers, and recent changes in market conditions might be used to adjust the statistical forecasts generated from the previous step. The net result of these adjustments is a baseline forecast.

5. *Adjust the baseline forecast for marketing promotions.*

    Marketing promotions are used to increase sales volume for specific periods during the calendar year. If a company is planning to use promotions during the forecast planning horizon, then the baseline forecasts need to be adjusted as these events influence sales volume.

6. *Share the forecast information with suppliers and downstream customers.*

    If the company has any collaborative arrangements with its suppliers and customers, such as the Collaborative Planning, Forecasting and Replenishment (CPFR) program discussed in Chapter 11, the forecast information from Step 4 should be communicated to all stakeholders, including suppliers and customers and the internal managers responsible for these programs. Sharing this information may lead to additional adjustments to the forecast.

7. *Generate a "single number" forecast.*

    The culmination of efforts from the previous six steps is to arrive at a single forecast number that will be used in the next important process of sales and operations planning. During the sales and operations planning process, this single forecast number will enable the senior management from key areas of the company to agree on an execution plan that will drive both the demand side and the supply side of the enterprise.

8. *Monitor the forecast.*

    The forecast generated should be monitored to assess its ability to track actual demand in a consistent manner. If the forecast performance is unsatisfactory, the forecast needs to be revised by using a different technique, reexamining the assumptions, accuracy, and validity of data.

13.7 Ethical Issues

Forecasts can contribute to ethical decision-making in two ways: We use ethics to make our forecasts, and ethics affect the results of our forecasting efforts. Let us consider these in turn, after first considering the circumstances in which ethics determine how an organization makes its forecasts.

13.7

Illustrate the role ethics and ethical decision-making can play in selecting and using forecasting models.

In the 1970s, Ford used forecasts to determined that replacing deadly fuel tanks in the Ford Pinto would be more costly than settling cases for traffic deaths caused by the faulty parts. The goal of these forecasts was to determine profitability, but obscured a moral and ethical decision that could have saved lives.

Bettmann/Bettmann/Getty Images

Forecasting and Ethics

The ethical challenge that lies at the heart of building such a tool is deciding *which* predictors, or fact variables, are acceptable to use. Do we select just those variables that present our projections in the best possible light? That is, do we choose to suppress certain data while "cherry picking" other information that will allow our forecasts to arrive at predetermined results? Another ethical problem relates to decisions about using questionable or potentially inappropriate variables as part of the forecasting model. Suppose, for purposes of predicting supply chain losses from theft, our company was considering whether to employ a predictive model based on racial or ethnic background of the factory workers. Would such criteria be considered ethical? If not, what about using predictors such as residential location, which could indirectly communicate workers' racial identity? In short, are variables such as the possession of a past criminal record or the neighborhood a person resides in (factors that *could* be used as prediction variables) fair factors to consider? More important, *should* they be considered in a model to forecast supply chain losses? We can see these questions deal with ethical issues in forecasting and further see that our models are frequently shaped by prior assumptions.

Ethics influence decisions companies make after they have made the forecasts. Their challenge lies in determining what to do with the data they have generated, particularly when the information may contain bad news or place the firm in a morally ambiguous situation. Perhaps the most notorious example was Ford Motor Company's (Dearborn, MI) decision in the 1970s to deliberately suppress its forecasts for the traffic deaths that resulted from the location of the Pinto's fuel tank. In running its projections, it reasoned that the cost of retrofitting millions of Pinto fuel tanks was more expensive than the cost of settling lawsuits in the case of traffic fatalities. Specifically, it determined that modifying the car would cost an additional $11 per vehicle. Ford compared this with the likely injury claims forecast for the death, severe burns, and repair costs of Pinto accidents. The bill for reengineering the cars, the cost of production delays, and the extra parts for hundreds of thousands of cars came to $113 million, but the cost of compensation payouts, reckoned Ford, would be $49 million (all in U.S. dollars). As a result, Ford made a fateful decision to increase its profits instead of acting ethically.[7]

Ethics can play a prominent role in forecasting, and it is critical that we understand the ways in which our decision-making can affect both the quality of the forecasts we make as well as the decisions we adopt as a result of forecasts. The notion that numbers don't lie is a dangerous assumption if we consider the huge number of choices, decisions, and options we employ in developing forecasting models. At the same time, accurate forecasts are only a first step; the choices we make *as a result* of these forecasts are influenced by our ethical standards, as well as those of the organizations we work for.

$SAGE edge™ ....

Visit **edge.sagepub.com/venkataraman** to help you accomplish your coursework goals in an easy-to-use learning environment.

- Mobile-friendly eFlashcards
- Mobile-friendly practice quizzes
- A complete online action plan

- Chapter summaries with learning objectives
- Video and multimedia resources

CHAPTER SUMMARY

13.1 Demonstrate the importance of forecasting for business operations. Forecasting involves generating estimates of future values for some variable or a scenario that corresponds to some future event. Demand forecasting is a critical and fundamental process for any business and is essential to the strategic, tactical, and operational planning for a company and its supply chain. Effective forecasts need to be accurate, consistent, timely, simple, and efficient.

13.2 Illustrate and distinguish between qualitative and quantitative forecasting methods, including their strengths and weaknesses. Forecasting methods can broadly be classified into two categories: qualitative and quantitative methods. Qualitative methods are typically used for forecasting for the long term or if no measurable, reliable, historical, or statistical data are available. Some common qualitative forecasting methods are expert opinion, Delphi method, sales force opinions, market research, and historical life-cycle analogy. Quantitative forecasting methods are typically used for the short-term to medium-term time frame and if measurable, historical data are available and if evidence that past behavior of demand is indicative of its future behavior. Techniques such as moving averages, exponential smoothing, and regression methods are some of the more commonly used quantitative forecasting methods.

13.3 Recognize the characteristics of good forecasts. Good forecasts have several characteristics that demonstrate their quality. For a forecast to be useful to its organization, it must be (a) accurate—any forecast errors should be small; (b) consistent—they should demonstrate reliability in tracking actual demand; (c) timely—to be useful, forecasts should be available within some minimal time period to give decision makers opportunities to adjust their options; (d) simple—forecasts should be easy to interpret; and (e) efficient—the costs of preparing the forecast should not outweigh its benefits.

13.4 Use the four forecast error measures to track forecast accuracy. The best forecasting method is the one that consistently minimizes forecasting errors. Several forecast error measures are used to track the performance of forecasting methods. The *mean absolute deviation (MAD)* is one of the easiest forecasting error measures to compute. The MAD is the average of the sum of the absolute differences between the actual and the forecasted demand values. The *cumulative sum error (CSE)* is the sum of the differences between the actual and the forecasted demand values. The *mean squared error (MSE)* is the average of the sum of the squared differences between

the actual and the forecasted demand values. The *mean absolute percentage error (MAPE)* measures the absolute error as a percentage of the actual demand.

13.5 Employ the methods used to monitor and control forecasts. Companies typically use two methods for monitoring and controlling forecasts: tracking signals and control charts. The use of *tracking signals* involves establishing an upper and a lower control limit to determine whether the forecasting errors related to a method are within these limits. A tracking signal value that goes outside of these control limits is an indicator that the forecasting method being used should be modified or changed. The second tool that can be used in monitoring and controlling forecasts is a *control chart*. Constructing a control chart is similar to calculating a tracking signal except we use the standard deviation of forecast errors to construct the control limits and plot the computed forecasting errors on the control chart.

13.6 Identify the steps involved in forecasting for supply chains. Forecasting important information within the broader context of the organizational supply chain is a challenging and complicated undertaking. The effectiveness of a demand planning system depends on its ability to generate forecasts, not only at the individual product level but also at product group, customer group, and regional levels, as well as for different planning horizons. The relevant steps for forecasting for supply chains include (a) determining the purpose of the forecast, (b) collecting and cleaning historical data, (c) selecting an appropriate forecasting technique and generating the demand forecasts, (d) adjusting the forecast with judgmental inputs, (e) adjusting the baseline forecast for marketing promotions, (f) sharing the forecast with suppliers and downstream customers, (g) generating a single number forecast, and (h) monitoring the forecast.

13.7 Illustrate the role ethics and ethical decision-making can play in selecting and using forecasting models. Forecasts can contribute to ethical decision-making in two ways: We use ethics to make our forecasts, and ethics affect the results of our forecasting efforts. The ethical challenge that lies at the heart of building such a tool is deciding *which* predictors, or fact variables, are acceptable to use. Ethics influence decisions companies make after they developed and used these prediction models. Their challenge lies in determining what to do with the data they have generated, particularly when the information may contain bad news or place the firm in a morally ambiguous situation.

KEY TERMS

DISCUSSION AND REVIEW QUESTIONS

1. Give some examples of a company's operational planning activities that require demand forecasts.

2. When is it appropriate to use qualitative forecasting methods?

3. Discuss the qualitative forecasting technique of a historical life-cycle analysis.

4. What is a time series and the rationale for forecasting based on a time series analysis?

5. Discuss briefly the various components of a time series.

6. What are the advantages of the simple exponential smoothing method of forecasting over the moving average technique?

7. In exponential smoothing, what is the rationale for choosing a low versus a high value of α?

8. Under what circumstances is the trend-adjusted exponential smoothing method of forecasting superior to a linear trend analysis?

9. What is the difference between the linear trend equation and the linear regression equation for a causal model?

10. In a multiple linear regression model with two independent variables, how would you interpret the regression coefficients b_1 and b_2?

11. In what ways is the MAPE superior to the other forecasting error measures discussed in this supplement?

12. Which forecasting technique would be best for each of the following scenarios:

    a. The demand for Valentine's Day greeting cards?

    b. The demand for ice cream during a year?

    c. The demand for a new solar-powered car?

    d. The demand for services in a beauty salon during a week?

SOLVED PROBLEMS

1. The weekly demand for 50-pound bags of fertilizer at Evergreen Garden and Floral Center for the last 12 weeks is shown in Table 13.9.

    a. Develop a 3-year moving average forecast from week 4 to week 13.

    b. Develop a three-period weighted moving average forecast from week 4 to week 13 with weights of $W_1 = 0.5$, $W_2 = 0.3$, and $W_3 = 0.2$.

Note: The most-recent period's demand is assigned the higher weight, and progressively lower weights are assigned to past periods.

    c. Compute the MAD to determine the better of the two forecasting methods.

    d. What is the naïve forecast for week 13?

Solution

a. The three-period moving average forecast for weeks 4 and 5 are shown as follows:

$$MA_4 = F_4 = (A_3 + A_2 + A_1) / 3 = (410 + 610 + 400) / 3 = 473.3 \text{ or } 474 \text{ bags}$$

$$MA_5 = F_5 = (A_4 + A_3 + A_2) / 3 = (520 + 410 + 610) / 3 = 513.3 \text{ or } 514 \text{ bags}$$

Forecasts for the remaining weeks are calculated in a similar manner and are shown in the Excel screenshot.

TABLE 13.9

Week	Demand (50-Pound bags)
1	400
2	610
3	410
4	520
5	990
6	800
7	740
8	870

Week	Demand (50-Pound bags)
9	1150
10	1380
11	1450
12	1560

b. The three-period weighted moving average forecasts for weeks 4 and 5 with weights of $W_1 = 0.5$, $W_2 = 0.3$, and $W_3 = 0.2$ are calculated using the following formula:

$$F_{t+1} = \sum_{i=1}^{3} W_{t+1-i} A_{t+1-i} = W_1 A_t + W_2 A_{t-1} + W_3 A_{t-2}$$

$$WMA_4 = F_4 = (0.5 \times A_3 + 0.3 \times A_2 + 0.2 \times A_1) = (0.5 \times 410 + 0.3 \times 610 + 0.2 \times 400) = 468 \text{ bags}$$

$$WMA_5 = F_5 = (0.5 \times A_4 + 0.3 \times A_3 + 0.2 \times A_2) = (0.5 \times 520 + 0.3 \times 410 + 0.2 \times 610) = 505 \text{ bags}$$

Forecasts for the remaining weeks are calculated in a similar manner and are shown in the Excel screenshot.

c. Compute the MAD to determine the better of the two forecasting methods.

To compute the MAD, we first compute the absolute value of the forecast errors and then compute the average of these absolute values as follows.

$$MAD = \frac{\sum_{t=1}^{n} |A_t - F_t|}{n}$$

These calculations are shown in the Excel screenshot 13.16.

SCREENSHOT 13.16: Solved Problem 13.1

	A	B	C	D	E	F	G	H	I	J	K	L	M	N	O	P
1	Chapter 13-Solved Problem-1															
2										Problem 1a						
3	Week	Demand (50-Pound bags)	MA₃ Forecast	WMA3 Forecast		MA₃ Error	WMA₃ Error	MA₃ - MAD	WMA₃ - MAD		The three-period moving average forecast for week 13 is 1463.3					
4	1	400														
5	2	610								Problem-1b						
6	3	410								W₁	0.5					
7	4	520	473.3			468	46.7	52.0	46.7	52.0	W₂	0.3				
8	5	990	513.3			505	476.7	485.0	476.7	485.0	W₃	0.2				
9	6	800	640.0			733	160.0	67.0	160.0	67.0	F₁₃	1491	=($K$6*B15+$K$7*B14+$K$8*B13)			
10	7	740	770.0			801	-30.0	-61.0	30.0	61.0						
11	8	870	843.3			808	26.7	62.0	26.7	62.0	The three-period weighted moving average forecast for week 13 is 1491					
12	9	1150	803.3			817	346.7	333.0	346.7	333.0						
13	10	1380	920.0			984	460.0	396.0	460.0	396.0	Problem-1c					
14	11	1450	1133.3			1209	316.7	241.0	316.7	241.0						
15	12	1560	1326.7			1369	233.3	191.0	233.3	191.0		MA₃	WMA₃			
16	13		1463.3			1491			233.0	209.8	MAD	233.0	209.8			
17																
18			=AVERAGE (B13:B15)					=AVERAGE (G7:G15)		Problem-1d						
19																
20										F₁₃	1560	=B15				
21																
22										The Naive forecast for week 13 is 1560						

Based on these calculations, the weighted moving average is a better forecasting method because it has a lower value of MAD (209.8) compared with the simple three-period moving average.

d. The naïve forecast for week 13 is: $F_{t+1} = A_t$

$$F_{13} = A_{12} = 1560$$

2. The fictional Cookies & Cream is a popular homemade ice cream shop in Chennai, India. The owners of the shop would like to forecast the demand for their ice cream to plan their production during the coming summer season. They have gathered the sales data (in gallons) for their ice cream for the past 12 months (see Table 13.10).

TABLE 13.10

Month	1	2	3	4	5	6	7	8	9	10	11	12
Sales	320	490	700	820	920	960	880	720	540	460	550	480

a. Compute an exponentially smoothed forecast for month 13. Assume an initial forecast of $F_2 = 320$ gallons and $\alpha = 0.2$.

b. Compute an exponentially smoothed forecast for month 13. Assume an initial forecast of $F_2 = 320$ gallons and $\alpha = 0.4$.

c. Compare the two forecasts in (a) and (b) using the MSE and determine which method is more accurate.

Solution

a. Compute an exponentially smoothed forecast for month 13. Assume an initial forecast of $F_2 = 320$ and $\alpha = 0.2$.

Using the exponential smoothing formula:

New forecast = old forecast + (latest observation - old forecast), the forecast for week 3 is given by:

$$F_3 = F_2 + \alpha \times (A_2 - F_2) = 320 + 0.2 \times (490 -- 320) = 354 \text{ gallons}$$

Similarly, the forecast for week 4 is:

$$F_4 = F_3 + \alpha \times (A_3 - F_3) = 354 + 0.2 \times (700 - 354) = 423.2 \text{ gallons}$$

For week 5:

$$F_5 = F_4 + \alpha \times (A_4 - F_4) = 423.2 + 0.2 \times (820 - 423.2) = 502.6 \text{ gallons}$$

This process can be repeated for the remaining weeks to get the following smoothed series (Table 13.11).

TABLE 13.11

Month	1	2	3	4	5	6	7	8	9	10	11	12
Sales	320	490	700	820	920	960	880	720	540	460	550	480
Forecast		320	354	423.2	502.6	586	660.8	704.7	707.8	674.2	631.4	615.1

Thus, the forecast for period 13 is given by:

$$F_{13} = F_{12} + \alpha \times (A_{12} - F_{12}) = 615.1 + 0.2 \times (480 - 615.1) = 588.1 \text{ gallons}$$

b. Compute an exponentially smoothed forecast for month 13. Assume an initial forecast of $F_2 = 320$ and $\alpha = 0.4$.

Using the exponential smoothing formula:

$$F_3 = F_2 + \alpha \times (A_2 - F_2) = 320 + 0.4 \times (490 - 320) = 388 \text{ gallons}$$

Similarly the forecast for week 4 will be:

$$F_4 = F_3 + \alpha \times (A_3 - F_3) = 388 + 0.4 \times (700 - 388) = 512.8 \text{ gallons}$$

For week 5:

$$F_5 = F_4 + \alpha \times (A_4 - F_4) = 512.8 + 0.4 \times (820 - 512.8) = 635.7 \text{ gallons}$$

This process can be repeated for the remaining weeks (see Table 13.12) to get the following smoothed series.

TABLE 13.12

Month	1	2	3	4	5	6	7	8	9	10	11	12
Sales	320	490	700	820	920	960	880	720	540	460	550	480
Forecast		320	388	512.8	635.7	749.4	833.6	852.2	799.3	695.6	601.4	580.8

Thus, the forecast for period 13 is given by:

$$F_{13} = F_{12} + \alpha \times (A_{12} - F_{12}) = 580.8 + 0.4 \times (480 - 580.8) = 540.5 \text{ gallons}$$

c. Compare the two forecasts in (a) and (b) using the MSE and determine which method is more accurate.

The mean squared error (MSE) is:

$$MSE = \frac{\sum_{t=1}^{n}(A_t - F_t)^2}{n}$$

To compute the MSE for the two forecasting methods, we will use the previous formula.

For $\alpha = 0.2$, beginning with period 2:

$$(A_2 - F_2)^2 = (490 - 320)^2 = 28900$$

Similarly, for period 3:

$$(A_2 - F_2)^2 = (700 - 354)^2 = 119{,}716$$

We compute the square of the arithmetic errors for the remaining periods the same way.

For $\alpha = 0.4$, beginning with period 2:

$$(A_2 - F_2)^2 = (490 - 320)^2 = 28{,}900$$

SCREENSHOT 13.17: Solved Problem 13.2

	A	B	C	D	E	F	G
1							
2					Squared Error (α = 0.2)	Squared Error (α = 0.4)	
3	Month	Sales	Forecast-1 (α = 0.2)	Forecast-2 (α = 0.4)	(At - Ft)^2	(At - Ft)^2	
4	1	320					
5	2	490	320.0	320.0	28900.0	28900.0	
6	3	700	354.0	388.0	119716.0	97344.0	
7	4	820	423.2	512.8	157450.2	94371.8	
8	5	920	502.6	635.7	174256.2	80837.9	
9	6	960	586.0	749.4	139840.1	44349.0	
10	7	880	660.8	833.6	48031.8	2148.8	
11	8	720	704.7	852.2	235.0	17473.4	
12	9	540	707.7	799.3	28135.6	67242.8	
13	10	460	674.2	695.6	45877.0	55501.4	
14	11	550	631.4	601.4	6618.1	2637.1	
15	12	480	615.1	580.8	18246.9	10162.9	
16	13		588.1	540.5	767306.8	500969.0	
17				MSE	69755.2	45542.6	
18			=0.2*B15+0.8*C15				
19	Problem 2a			=E16/11			
20	The forecast for period 13 for α = 0.2 is: 588.1						
21							
22	Problem 2b						
23	The forecast for period 13 for α = 0.4 is: 540.5						
24							
25	Probem 2c						
26	The exponential smoothing method with α = 0.4 has a lower MSE value, and hence it is a more accurate forecasting method.						
27							

Similarly, for period 3:

$$(A_2 - F_2)^2 = (700 - 388)^2 = 97{,}344$$

The calculated results for remaining periods are shown in the Excel screenshot.

Given these calculations:

$$MSE\ (\alpha = 0.2) = \frac{\sum_{t=1}^{n}(A_t - F_t)^2}{n} = \frac{\sum_{t=2}^{12}(A_t - F_t)^2}{n} = 767306.8\ /\ 11 = 69755.2$$

$$MSE\ (\alpha = 0.4) = \frac{\sum_{t=1}^{n}(A_t - F_t)^2}{n} = \frac{\sum_{t=2}^{12}(A_t - F_t)^2}{n} = 500969\ /\ 11 = 45542.6$$

Because the exponential smoothing method with $\alpha = 0.4$ has a lower MSE value, it is a more accurate forecasting method.

3. Rahul Dravid is the manager of Kohinoor Service Station, a fictional company that sells CNG (compressed natural gas), a fossil fuel substitute for gasoline. Dravid wants to develop forecasts of demand for CNG so that he can order a sufficient number of liters of CNG to meet demand. He has gathered data on sales of CNG for the past 15 months (see Table 13.13).

TABLE 13.13

Month	CNG Sales (in gasoline gallon equivalent)
1	820
2	740
3	650
4	530
5	670
6	700
7	770
8	840
9	1100
10	1220
11	1000
12	940
13	880
14	810
15	720

a. Compute a forecast for month 16 using the trend-adjusted exponential smoothing model. Assume $F_2 = 820$, $T_2 = 0$, and $\alpha = 0.3$, $\beta = 0.5$.

b. Compare the trend-adjusted forecast with the unadjusted forecast using the forecast error measure the MAPE.

Solution

a. We will begin by first generating an unadjusted forecast for week 3 by using the simple exponential smoothing model.

$$F_3 = \alpha A_2 + (1 - \alpha) F_2 = 0.3 \times 740 + 0.7 \times 820 = 796$$

Using the unadjusted forecast, we will now compute the trend factor for week 3.

$$T_3 = \beta (F_3 - F_2) + (1 - \beta) T_2 = 0.5 \times (796 - 820) + 0.5 \times 0 = -12$$

The trend-adjusted forecast for week 3 is:

$$TAF_3 = F_3 + T_3 = 796 + (-12) = 784.0$$

Similarly for week 4:

$$F_4 = \alpha A_3 + (1 - \alpha) F_3 = 0.3 \times 650 + 0.7 \times 796 = 752.2$$

Using the unadjusted forecast, we will now compute the trend factor for week 4.

$$T_4 = \beta (F_4 - F_3) + (1 - \beta) T_3 = 0.5 \times (752.2 - 796) + 0.5 \times (-12) = -27.90$$

The trend-adjusted forecast for week 4 is:

$$TAF_4 = F_4 + T_4 = 752.2 + (-27.90) = 724.3$$

This process can be repeated for the remaining weeks to get the trend-adjusted forecasts shown in the Excel screenshot. The trend-adjusted forecast for week 16 is:

$$F_{16} = \alpha A_{15} + (1 - \alpha) F_{15} = 0.3 \times 720 + 0.7 \times 900.5 = 846.3$$

Using the unadjusted forecast, we will now compute the trend factor for week 16:

$$T_{16} = \beta (F_{16} - F_{15}) + (1 - \beta) T_{15} = 0.5 \times (846.3 - 900.5) + 0.5 \times (-20.97) = -37.56$$

The trend-adjusted forecast for week 16 is:

$$TAF_{16} = F_{16} + T_{16} = 846.3 + (-37.56) = 808.8 \text{ (GGE)}$$

SCREENSHOT 13.18: Solved Problem 13.3

	A	B	C	D	E	F	G	H	I
1									
2									
3	Assume	F2 = A1 AND T1 = 0	α		β				
4			0.3		0.5		Unadjusted	Adjusted	Unadjusted	Adjusted
5	Month	CNG Sales	Unadjusted Forecast (α = 0.3)	Trend Factor (β =0.4)		Trend-adjusted Forecast	$|A_t - F_t|$	$|A_t - F_t|$	$(|A_t - F_t|/A_t)$ *100	$(|A_t - F_t|/A_t)$ *100
6	1	820		0	0.0					
7	2	740	820.0	0		820.0	80.00	80.00	10.81	10.81
8	3	650	796.0	-12.00		784.0	146.00	134.00	22.46	20.62
9	4	530	752.2	-27.90		724.3	222.20	194.30	41.92	36.66
10	5	670	685.5	-47.28		638.3	15.54	31.74	2.32	4.74
11	6	700	680.9	-25.97		654.9	19.12	45.09	2.73	6.44
12	7	770	686.6	-10.12		676.5	83.39	93.50	10.83	12.14
13	8	840	711.6	7.45		719.1	128.37	120.92	15.28	14.40
14	9	1100	750.1	22.98		773.1	349.86	326.68	31.81	29.72
15	10	1220	855.1	63.97		919.1	364.90	300.93	29.91	24.67
16	11	1000	964.6	86.72		1051.3	35.43	51.29	3.54	5.13
17	12	940	975.2	48.67		1023.9	35.20	83.87	3.74	8.92
18	13	880	964.6	19.06		983.7	84.64	103.70	9.62	11.78
19	14	810	939.2	-3.17		936.1	129.25	126.08	15.96	15.57
20	15	720	900.5	-20.97		879.5	180.47	159.50	25.07	22.15
21			846.3	-37.56		808.8			226.00	223.74
22								MAPE	16.14	15.98
23			=(C20+$C$4*(B20-C20))	=($D$4*(C21-C20)+(1-$D$4)*D20)	=(C21+D21)					
24	Problem 3a								=(H21/14)	
25	The trend-adjusted forecast for week 16 is: 808.8									
26										
27	Problem 3b									
28	The trend-adjusted forecast has a lower MAPE and hence is a better forecasting method									

b. The computations necessary for computing the MAPE are shown in the following Excel screenshot. Given this information, the MAPE for the unadjusted forecast is:

$$MAPE = \frac{\sum_{t=1}^{n} \frac{|A_t - F_t|}{A_t} * 100}{n} = 226/14 = 16.14\%, \text{ and}$$

The MAPE for the trend-adjusted forecast is:

$$MAPE = \frac{\sum_{t=1}^{n} \frac{|A_t - F_t|}{A_t} * 100}{n} = 223.74/14 = 15.98\%$$

4. Omega Solar Systems is a fictional Belgian manufacturer of solar panels. The company must base its quarterly production schedule on the demand forecasts for its solar panels. The company has quarterly data for the past 3 years on its sales of solar panels (see Table 13.14).

TABLE 13.14

Quarter	Demand for Solar Panels
1	650
2	720
3	515
4	700
5	835
6	770
7	920
8	955
9	890
10	1030
11	1155
12	1100

a. Develop a linear trend line equation for the data.

b. Using the linear trend line equation, generate forecasts for the next four quarters.

Solution

a. The calculations required to develop the linear trend line equation appear in the Excel screenshot. Given these calculations:

The slope of the trend line is:

$$b = \frac{n\Sigma ty - \Sigma t\,\Sigma y}{n\Sigma t^2 - (\Sigma t)^2} = \frac{12 \times 73525 - 78 \times 10240}{12 \times 650 - (78)^2} = 48.7$$

The intercept of the line is:

$$a = \frac{\Sigma y - b\Sigma t}{n} = \frac{10240 - 48.7 \times 78}{12} = 536.7$$

The resulting linear trend equation is:

$$\hat{y}_t = a + bt = 536.7 + 48.7 \times t$$

b. The forecasts for periods 13, 14, 15, and 16 are given by:

$$\hat{y}_{13} = 536.7 + 48.7 \times 13 = 1169.9$$

$$\hat{y}_{14} = 536.7 + 48.7 \times 14 = 1218.6$$

$$\hat{y}_{15} = 536.7 + 48.7 \times 15 = 1267.3$$

$$\hat{y}_{16} = 536.7 + 48.7 \times 16 = 1316.0$$

SCREENSHOT 13.19: Solved Problem 13.4

5. The manager of the fictitious Italian Cuisine wants to come up with more accurate estimates of the number of customers arriving at the restaurant for an evening meal. The manager knows that demand for an evening meal is seasonal and depends on the day of the week. He has gathered data in Table 13.15 on the number of customers who came to the restaurant for an evening meal for the past 4 weeks.

TABLE 13.15

Week 1	Number of Customers	Week 2	Number of Customers	Week 3	Number of Customers	Week 4	Number of Customers
Monday	85	Monday	80	Monday	78	Monday	85
Tuesday	78	Tuesday	75	Tuesday	74	Tuesday	77
Wednesday	80	Wednesday	82	Wednesday	84	Wednesday	86
Thursday	90	Thursday	92	Thursday	96	Thursday	90

Week 1	Number of Customers	Week 2	Number of Customers	Week 3	Number of Customers	Week 4	Number of Customers
Friday	120	Friday	124	Friday	130	Friday	138
Saturday	140	Saturday	144	Saturday	142	Saturday	146
Sunday	60	Sunday	62	Sunday	58	Sunday	56

a. Compute the seasonal index for each day of the week using the simple average method.

b. Compute the seasonal index for each day of the week using the centered moving average method.

Solution

a. Compute the seasonal index for each day of the week using the simple average method.

Step 1: Calculate the average demand for each day (Monday, Tuesday, and so on). For example, the average demand for Monday is: $(85 + 80 + 78 + 85) / 4 = 82$.

Step 2: Calculate the average total demand from week 1 to week 4. For example:

$$(85 + 80 +……+ 146 + 56)/28 = 94.7.$$

Step 3: Divide the average daily demand by the average total demand to get the seasonal indices. For example, the seasonal index for Monday is:

$$82/94.7 = 0.87.$$

The seasonal indices' calculations for all the remaining days are done similarly and are shown in the Excel screenshot.

b. Compute the seasonal index for each day of the week using the centered moving average method.

Step 1: For the demand data in the time series, calculate a moving average equal to the length of the seasons in a year. In this example, as the seasonal variations are captured daily, we will compute a 7-period moving average. For example, the first moving average for the first four periods is calculated as follows:

$$(85 + 78 + 80 + 90+120+140+60)/7 = 93.3.$$

This value is entered in row 2 of the column titled MA-7 in the following table. Similarly, the average number of customers from periods 2 to 8 is entered in row 3 of the column titled MA-7.These 7-period moving average computations are also shown in the Excel screenshot.

Step 2: Center the moving averages. Because there is an odd number of weekly data, the 7-period moving average values will be centered on day 4. For example, the first 7-period moving average value will be centered on Thursday, the next on Friday, and so on. These values are entered under the column titled "Centered MA" in the Excel screenshot.

Step 3: Calculate the ratio of actual demand to the centered moving average value for each seasonal period. For example, for Thursday (period 4), the ratio is given by:

$$\text{Number of customers in period-4/Centered MA for period-4} = 90/93.3 = 0.96.$$

The ratios for the remaining periods are calculated similarly and are shown in the screenshot under the column labeled "Ratio."

Step 4: For each seasonal period, calculate an unadjusted seasonal index by averaging the ratio of values calculated for that period in Step 3. For this problem, the unadjusted seasonal indices for each day of the week are calculated by computing the average of the values for that day in the column labeled "Ratio." For example, the unadjusted seasonal index for Thursday is the average of the "ratio" values in period 4 (0.96), period 11 (0.98), and period 18 (1.02), which is:

$$(0.96 + 0.98 + 1.02)/3 = 0.986.$$

The value of 0.986 is entered in the column labeled "Unadj. SI" in the table for periods 4, 11, 18, and 25, which are Thursdays. The unadjusted seasonal indices for the remaining days of the week are calculated the same way and are shown in the Excel screenshot.

Step 5: Adjust the total of the seasonal indices to equal the number of seasons in a week. For example, the total of the daily seasonal indices for the example should sum to seven. The resulting numbers are the adjusted seasonal indices for each period. The adjustment is done as follows:

The sum of the unadjusted quarterly seasonal indexes is:

$$0.859 + 0.792 + 0.880 + 0.986 + 1.325 + 1.511 + 0.637 = 6.99.$$

The adjusted seasonal indexes are:

Monday: $(7 \times 0.859)/6.99 = 0.86$

Tuesday: $(7 \times 0.792)/6.99 = 0.79$

Wednesday: $(7 \times 0.880)/6.99 = 0.88$

Thursday: $(7 \times 0.986)/6.99 = 0.99$

Friday: $(7 \times 1.325)/6.99 = 1.33$

Saturday: $(7 \times 1.511)/6.99 = 1.51$

Sunday: $(7 \times 0.637)/6.99 = 0.64$

The total of the seven indexes is $0.86 + 0.79 + 0.88 + 0.99 + 1.33 + 1.51 + 0.64 = 7.0$.

The adjusted seven seasonal indices are shown in the Excel screenshot under the column labeled "Adj. SI."

SCREENSHOT 13.20: Solved Problem 13.5a and 13.5b

	A	B	C	D	E	F	G	H
4	Day	Week-1 customers	Week-2 customers	Week-3 customers	Week-4 customers	Average Daily demand	Average Total demand	Seasonal Index
5	Monday	85	80	78	85	82	94.7	0.87
6	Tuesday	78	75	74	77	76	94.7	0.80
7	Wednesd	80	82	84	86	83	94.7	0.88
8	Thursday	90	92	96	90	92	94.7	0.97
9	Friday	120	124	130	138	128	94.7	1.35
10	Saturday	140	144	142	146	143	94.7	1.51
11	Sunday	60	62	58	56	59	94.7	0.62
12						94.7		
14						=AVERAGE(F7:F13)	=(F14/G14)	

	A	B	C	D	E	F	G	H	I	J	K	L	M
1											=(F10+F17+F24)/3		=(7*K3)/$K$10
2	Period	Day	Customers	MA-7	Centered MA	Ratio	Unadj.SI	Adj. SI			Unadj.SI	Adj. SI	
3	1	Monday	85				0.86	0.86		Monday	0.859453	0.860353	
4	2	Tuesday	78				0.79	0.79		Tuesday	0.792256	0.793086	
5	3	Wednesday	80				0.88	0.88		Wednesd	0.880615	0.881538	
6	4	Thursday	90		93.3	0.96	0.99	0.99		Thursday	0.985707	0.98674	
7	5	Friday	120		92.6	1.30	1.33	1.33		Friday	1.325897	1.327287	
8	6	Saturday	140		92.1	1.52	1.51	1.51		Saturday	1.511711	1.513295	
9	7	Sunday	60		92.4	0.65	0.64	0.64		Sunday	0.637033	0.6377	
10	8	Monday	80	93.3	92.7	0.86	0.86			SUM	6.992672	7	
11	9	Tuesday	75	92.6	93.3	0.80	0.79						
12	10	Wednesday	82	92.1	93.9	0.87	0.88	=(C6/E6)					
13	11	Thursday	92	92.4	94.1	0.98	0.99						
14	12	Friday	124	92.7	93.9	1.32	1.33						
15	13	Saturday	144	93.3	93.7	1.54	1.51						
16	14	Sunday	62	93.9	94.0	0.66	0.64						
17	15	Monday	78	94.1	94.6	0.82	0.86						
18	16	Tuesday	74	93.9	95.4	0.78	0.79						
19	17	Wednesday	84	93.7	95.1	0.88	0.88						
20	18	Thursday	96	94.0	94.6	1.02	0.99						
21	19	Friday	130	94.6	95.6	1.36	1.33						
22	20	Saturday	142	95.4	96.0	1.48	1.51						
23	21	Sunday	58	95.1	96.3	0.60	0.64						
24	22	Monday	85	94.6	95.4	0.89	0.86						
25	23	Tuesday	77	95.6	96.6	0.80	0.79						
26	24	Wednesday	86	96.0	97.1	0.89	0.88						
27	25	Thursday	90	96.3			0.99						
28	26	Friday	138	95.4			1.33						
29	27	Saturday	146	96.6			1.51						
30	28	Sunday	56	97.1			0.64						

6.   Management of the fictional Mayo Department Store want to use time series data to forecast the retail sales of its Cool-Breeze air conditioners for the four quarters of 2015. Demand for these air conditioners has grown steadily during the past 3 years. The quarterly sales for the past 3 years are in Table 13.16. Seasonal indices for the four quarters have been found to be 0.70, 1.10, 1.30, and 0.90, respectively. Compute a seasonally adjusted sales forecast for the sales of Cool-Breeze air conditioners for the four quarters of 2015.

TABLE 13.16

Year	Quarter	Sales (in U.S. dollars)
2012	1	70
	2	120
	3	150
	4	100
2013	1	85
	2	135
	3	165
	4	95
2014	1	90
	2	140
	3	200
	4	90

Solution

Step 1: Deseasonalize the actual demand in each period by dividing by the seasonal index for that period. For example, for the first quarter of 2012:

$$\text{Deseasonalized demand} = \text{Actual demand/quarter-1 Seasonal index} = 70/0.7 = 100.$$

The deseasonalized demand for the remaining quarters are calculated similarly and are shown in the following Excel screenshot.

Step 2: Develop a linear trend equation using the deseasonalized data and a linear regression.

The calculations to determine the slope (b) and the Y-intercept (a) are shown as follows:

The slope **"b"** of the trend line is given by:

$$b = \frac{n\Sigma ty - \Sigma t \Sigma y}{n\Sigma t^2 - (\Sigma t)^2} = \frac{12 \times 9507.3 - 78 \times 1421.9}{12 \times 650 - (78)^2} = 1.85$$

The intercept **"a"** of the line is given by:

$$a = \frac{\Sigma y - b\Sigma t}{n} = \frac{1421.9 - 1.85 \times 78}{12} = 106.4$$

The resulting linear trend equation is:

$$\hat{y}_t = a + bt = 106.4 + 1.85 \times t$$

Step 3: Using the linear trend equation, generate the forecast for the desired future period.

The trend forecast for quarters 1, 2, 3, and 4 of 2015 is as follows:

$$\hat{y}_{13} = 106.4 + 1.85 \times 13 = 130.45$$

$$\hat{y}_{14} = 106.4 + 1.85 \times 14 = 132.3$$

$$\hat{y}_{15} = 106.4 + 1.85 \times 15 = 134.15$$

$$\hat{y}_{16} = 106.4 + 1.85 \times 16 = 136.0$$

Step 4: Multiply the trend forecast by the seasonal index for that period to arrive at a seasonalized forecast.

Given the seasonal indices of $S_1 = 0.70$, $S_2 = 1.10$, $S_3 = 1.30$, and $S_4 = 0.90$ for the four quarters respectively, the seasonalized forecasts for periods 13, 14, 15, and 16 are:

Seasonalized forecast for Period 13: $\hat{y}_{13} \times S_1 = 130.45 \times 0.70 = 91.3$, or 92 air conditioners.

Seasonalized forecast for Period 14: $\hat{y}_{14} \times S_2 = 132.30 \times 1.10 = 145.5$, or 146 air conditioners.

Seasonalized forecast for Period 15: $\hat{y}_{15} \times S_3 = 134.15 \times 1.30 = 174.4$, or 175 air conditioners.

Seasonalized forecast for Period 16: $\hat{y}_{16} \times S_4 = 136.0 \times 0.90 = 122.4$, or 123 air conditioners.

SCREENSHOT 13.21: Solved Problem 13.6

	A	B	C	D	E	F	G	H
1								
2						=(D5/E5)		
3			n		12			
4	Year	Quarter	Period (t)	Actual Sales	Seasonal Indices	Deseasonalized Sales (y)	t*y	t^2
5	2010	1	1	70	0.7	100.0	100	1
6		2	2	120	1.1	109.1	218.1818	4
7		3	3	150	1.3	115.4	346.1538	9
8		4	4	100	0.9	111.1	444.4444	16
9	2011	1	5	85	0.7	121.4	607.1429	25
10		2	6	135	1.1	122.7	736.3636	36
11		3	7	165	1.3	126.9	888.4615	49
12		4	8	95	0.9	105.6	844.4444	64
13	2012	1	9	90	0.7	128.6	1157.143	81
14		2	10	140	1.1	127.3	1272.727	100
15		3	11	200	1.3	153.8	1692.308	121
16		4	12	90	0.9	100.0	1200	144
17				78	1440		1421.9	9507.4	650
18								
19	Slope	b		1.85				
20	Intercept	a		106.45				
21	The Linear Trend equation is : 106.45 + 1.85 * t							
22		Period	Deseasonalized forecast	Seasonal Index	Seasonalized forecast	=(C23*D23)		
23		Y_{13}	130.5	0.7	91.4			
24		Y_{14}	132.4	1.1	145.6			
25		Y_{15}	134.2	1.3	174.5			
26		Y_{16}	136.1	0.9	122.5			

7.   Champion Auto Group, a fictional Fiat car dealership in Shanghai, China, is planning to boost sales of the new Fiat model—the Viaggio—in Shanghai. The company's managers believe car sales are closely related to the amount of money spent on advertising. The firm gathered the data in Table 13.17 that show the number of cars sold and the advertising money (in U.S. dollars) spent for each month of 2014.

   a.   Develop a linear regression equation for forecasting car sales as a function of advertising money spent.

   b.   Forecast car sales if the advertising money spent is $35,000 in a given month.

   c.   Evaluate the goodness of fit of the regression equation by computing the values of R^2, r, and s_{yx} and interpret the results.

TABLE 13.17

Month	Number of Cars Sold	Advertising (in U.S. dollars)
January	20	25
February	14	17
March	30	42
April	35	60
May	48	100
June	52	105
July	28	53
August	22	48
September	19	30
October	26	33
November	10	22
December	13	30

Solution

The calculations required to compute the linear regression equation are shown in the following Excel screenshot:

   a.   The linear regression equation for car sales as a function of advertising dollars spent is:

$$y_c = a + bx_1, \text{ where}$$

y_c is the computed or forecasted value of car sales, and the slope "b" of the regression line is given by:

$$b = \frac{n\Sigma x_i y_i - \Sigma x_i \Sigma y_i}{n\Sigma x_i^2 - (\Sigma x_i)^2} = \frac{12 \times 18936 - 565 \times 317}{12 \times 35789 - (565)^2} = 0.437.$$

The intercept "a" of the regression line is given by:

$$a = \frac{\Sigma y_i - b\Sigma x_i}{n} = \frac{317 - 0.437 \times 565}{12} = 5.86.$$

Therefore, the linear regression equation for the relationship is:

$$y_c = 5.86 + 0.437 \times x_i.$$

b.   The forecast of car sales if $35,000 (x = 35) were to be spent on advertising is:

$$y_c = 5.86 + 0.437 \times x_i = 5.86 + 0.437 \times 35 = 21.2 \text{ or } 22 \text{ cars.}$$

c.   From the solution to problem 7a, we have the following data:

$$n = 12, \Sigma x = 565, \overline{x} = (\Sigma x/n) = 565/12 = 47.08, \Sigma y = 317, \overline{y} = (\Sigma y/n) = 26.42,$$

$$\Sigma xy = 18{,}936, \Sigma x^2 = 35{,}789, \Sigma y^2 = 10{,}303, a = 5.86, b = 0.437,$$

$$R^2 = \frac{a\Sigma y_i + b\Sigma x_i y_i - n(\overline{Y})^2}{\Sigma y_i^2 - n(\overline{Y})^2} = \frac{(5.86 \times 317) + (0.437 \times 18936) - 12 \times 26.42^2}{10303 - 12 \times 26.42^2} = 0.91$$

$$r = \frac{\Sigma x_i y_i - n\overline{x}\,\overline{Y}}{\sqrt{\Sigma x_i^2 - n(\overline{x})^2}\sqrt{\Sigma y_i^2 - n(\overline{Y})^2}}$$

$$r = \frac{18936 - 12 \times (47.08) \times (26.42)}{\sqrt{35789 - 12x(47.08)^2}\sqrt{10303 - 12x(26.42)^2}} = 0.95$$

$$S_{yx} = \frac{\sqrt{\Sigma y_i^2 - a\Sigma y_i - b\Sigma x_i y_i}}{\sqrt{n-2}} = \frac{\sqrt{10303 - 5.86 \times 317 - 0.436 \times 18936}}{\sqrt{(12-2)}} = 4.2$$

SCREENSHOT 13.22: Solved Problem 13.7

	A	B	C	D	E	F	G	H	I
1									
2	n		12				Explained	Unexplained	Total
3	x-Advertising in (000 $)	Y-Car Sales in units	x*Y	x^2	y^2	y_c	$(y_c - \overline{y})^2$	$(Y-y_c)^2$	$(Y-\overline{y})^2$
4		25	20	500	625	400	16.8	92.9	10.39350736	41.17361
5		17	14	238	289	196	13.3	172.5	0.513123884	154.1736
6		42	30	1260	1764	900	24.2	4.9	33.66879493	12.84028
7		60	35	2100	3600	1225	32.1	31.8	8.670159657	73.67361
8		100	48	4800	10000	2304	49.5	533.7	2.303226034	465.8403
9		105	52	5460	11025	2704	51.7	639.3	0.089755797	654.5069
10		53	28	1484	2809	784	29.0	6.7	0.999220057	2.506944
11		48	22	1056	2304	484	26.8	0.2	23.20195701	19.50694
12		30	19	570	900	361	19.0	55.6	0.001691457	55.00694
13		33	26	858	1089	676	20.3	37.8	32.84970186	0.173611
14		22	10	220	484	100	15.5	119.9	29.88199157	269.5069
15		30	13	390	900	169	19.0	55.6	35.50816352	180.0069
16		565	317	18936	35789	10303		1750.8354	178.0812931	1928.917
17									
18		X-bar		47.08333					
19		Y-Bar		26.41667					
20	Slope	b		0.437					
21	Intercept	a		5.862					
22	The Linear Regression Equation is: 5.862 + 0.437 * x								
23	Forecast for x = 35	y_c		21.1					
24	Coeeficient of Determination R^2			0.907678				=(G16/I16)	
25	Correlation Coeeficient	r		0.95272				=SQRT(C24)	
26	Standard Error of the Estimate s_{yx}			4.2				=(SQRT(H16))/(SQRT(B2-2))	
27									

All of the statistics indicate that the regression line obtained for problem 7 is a very good fit. In other words, our regression equation gives Champion Auto Group the ability to predict car sales with a high degree of confidence based on advertising money spent. Specifically, the value of R^2 of 0.91 means that 91% of the variation in car sales (y-values) is accounted for by changes in the money spent on advertising (x-values). Similarly, the **r** value of 0.95 indicates that the variables advertising dollars (x) and car sales (y) are almost perfectly positively correlated (close to the value of 1). Finally, the S_{yx} value of 4.2 indicates that, on average, the actual car sales (y) deviate from the predicted values (y_c), by about 4.2 units.

8. Green Line Trucking Company, a fictitious transportation firm, believes that the maintenance expenses on its trucks are a function of the number of miles driven and the age of the trucks. The company wants to develop a forecasting model to estimate the annual maintenance expenses using the two variables. Past year's data on miles driven, age, and maintenance expenses on the company's fleet of 10 trucks are shown in Table 13.18.

TABLE 13.18

Truck Number	Age	Miles Driven	Annual Maintenance Expenses (in U.S. dollars)
1	7	15,200	1,280
2	8	15,820	1,690
3	4	8,370	930
4	4	10,220	1,080
5	9	17,440	1,900
6	5	11,380	1,125
7	1	5,770	435
8	2	6,350	510
9	8	17,720	1,815
10	9	18,540	2,350

Based on this data, use Excel to develop a multiple regression equation.

a. Interpret the coefficients b_0, b_1, and b_2.

b. Forecast the annual maintenance expenses for a truck that is 6 years old and will be driven 12,000 miles next year.

Solution

a. The Excel solution to this problem is as follows:

SCREENSHOT 13.23: Solved Problem 13.8

	A	B	C	D	E	F	G	H	I
1	Chapter 13-Solved Problem 8-Multiple Regression Model								
2									
3	SUMMARY OUTPUT								
4									
5	*Regression Statistics*								
6	Multiple R	0.96490507							
7	R Square	0.931041794							
8	Adjusted R Square	0.911339449							
9	Standard Error	184.812112							
10	Observations	10							
11									
12	ANOVA								
13		*df*	*SS*	*MS*	*F*	*Significance F*			
14	Regression	2	3228063.883	1614032	47.25538	8.61095E-05			
15	Residual	7	239088.6173	34155.52					
16	Total	9	3467152.5						
17									
18		*Coefficients*	*Standard Error*	*t Stat*	*P-value*	*Lower 95%*	*Upper 95%*	*Lower 95.0%*	*Upper 95.0%*
19	Intercept	-67.9324064	283.0596664	-0.23999	0.817212	-737.2621582	601.3973	-737.2621582	601.3973454
20	Age	99.83732554	126.8861362	0.786826	0.457191	-200.2007092	399.8754	-200.2007092	399.8753603
21	Miles driven	0.06390345	0.075888918	0.842066	0.42758	-0.115545326	0.243352	-0.115545326	0.243352226
22									
23	Solution								
24	Probem 8a	The multiple regression equation is: $y_c = b_0 + b_1X_1 + b_2X_2 = -67.93 + 99.8 \times X_1 + 0.064 \times X_2$							
25	Probem 8c	$y_c = -67.93 + 99.8 \times X_1 + 0.064 \times X_2 = -67.93 + 99.8 \times 6 + 0.064 \times 12,000 = \$1,298.87$							
26									

The multiple regression equation is:

$$y_c = b_0 + b_1 X_1 + b_2 X_2 = -67.93 + 99.8 \times X_1 + 0.064 \times X_2.$$

b. The Y-intercept (b_0) is -67.93. The theoretical interpretation is that the annual maintenance expenses decrease by $67.93 when the age of the truck and the number of miles driven are zero. Nevertheless, from a practical standpoint, these values are nonsensical, as the values of age and number of miles driven are outside the range of observed values and have no significance. The increase in the annual maintenance expenses for each year the truck gets older, holding the number of miles driven constant (b_1), is $99.8. The increase in the annual maintenance expenses for each extra mile driven by the truck, holding the age of the truck constant (b_2), is $0.064.

c. Using the multiple regression equation developed, we can forecast the annual maintenance expenses for a truck that is 6 years old and will be driven 12,000 miles next year to be as follows:

$$y_c = -67.93 + 99.8 \times X_1 + 0.064 \times X_2 = -67.93 + 99.8 \times 6 + 0.064 \times 12,000 = \$1,298.87.$$

The table shows that the high values of the correlation coefficient (multiple R) and the coefficient of determination (R^2) of 0.96 and 93% indicate that the two variables, age of the truck and number of miles driven, have a high positive correlation. The annual maintenance costs and 93% of the variation in annual maintenance expenses can be explained by the variation in the age of the truck and number of miles driven. The standard error value of 184.8 means that, on the average, the actual maintenance expense deviates from each predicted value by $184.8.

9. For the Champion Auto Group data in Solved Problem 7, compute the linear regression forecasts and the tracking signals for each of the 12 periods. Plot the tracking signals using ±4 MAD control limits and determine whether the forecasts are within control.

Solution

Using the linear regression equation from Solved Problem 7, we will first calculate the forecasts, and then the CSE, MAD, and tracking signals. For example,

For Period 1:

The linear regression forecast is: $y_1 = 5.86 + 0.437 \times 25 = 16.785$.

$$(A_1 - F_1) = (20 - 16.785) = 3.215$$

$$CSE = 3.215$$

$$MAD_1 = |A_1 - F_1| = |3.215| = 3.215$$

$$\text{Tracking signal} = \frac{\sum_{t=1}^{n}(A_t - F_t)}{MAD_1} = 3.215/3.215 = 1$$

The remaining calculations for the other periods are shown in Excel screenshot 13.24.

The table shows that six of the 12 tracking signals are within control limits. The tracking signals for periods 2, 4, 5, 6, 7, and 9, however, fall outside of the control limits. The forecasts for this data appear to be out of control and the causes for these unusual values should be investigated.

SCREENSHOT 13.24: Solved Problem 13.9

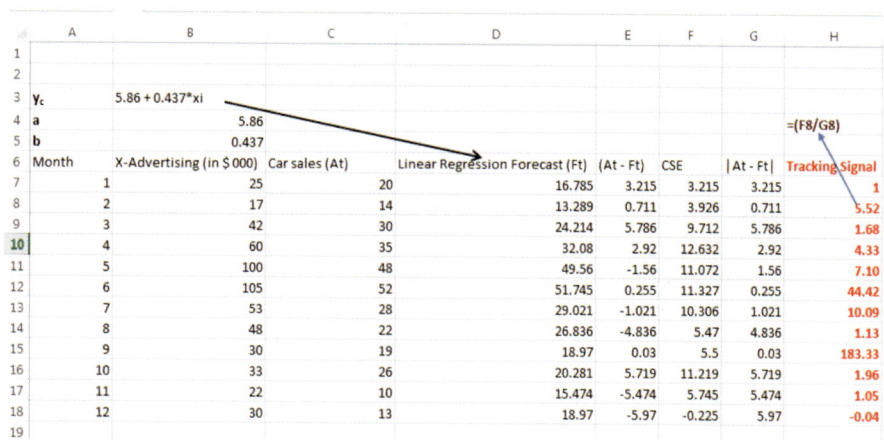

PROBLEMS

1. The demand for automobiles at Crescent Auto Dealers for the last 8 weeks is as follows:

Week	1	2	3	4	5	6	7	8
Auto Demand	9	11	8	12	10	13	7	12

   a. Develop a 3-week moving average forecast for weeks 4 through 9.

   b. Develop a 3-week weighted average forecast for weeks 4 through 9 with weights of $W_1 = 0.6$, $W_2 = 0.3$, and $W_3 = 0.1$. (The most recent week is assigned the highest weight, and weights assigned to past weeks decline progressively).

   c. Use the MAD to determine which of the two forecasting methods is more accurate.

   d. What is the naïve forecast for week 9?

2. Vidhya Balan is planning to liquidate her investments in mutual funds and invest in real estate. Before making the change in her investment strategy, Vidhya wants to forecast the price of mutual funds for the next 2 months. She has collected the following data on the average fund prices for the past 10 months:

Month	1	2	3	4	5	6	7	8	9	10
Average Fund Price (in U.S. dollars)	55.10	53.80	53.40	52.95	52.15	52.75	52.65	51.50	52.25	51. 70

   a. Using a five-period moving average, forecast the average fund price for period 11.

   b. Using exponential smoothing with $\alpha = 0.3$, forecast the average fund price for period 11. Assume an initial forecast for month 6 (F_6) as $52.15.

   c. Compute the MAD to determine the more accurate of the two forecasting methods.

3. James Triton, owner of the fictitious Triton Auto Parts, wants to use simple exponential smoothing to forecast the demand for automobile batteries for his store. He has collected the following data from his store for the past 6 months:

Month	January	February	March	April	May	June
Battery Sales (in U.S. dollars)	18	23	17	28	32	26

   a. Forecast the sales for July using simple exponential smoothing with $\alpha = 0.2$. Assume that the forecast for February (F_2) is the naïve forecast.

   b. Forecast the sales for July using simple exponential smoothing with $\alpha = 0.4$. Assume that the forecast for February (F_2) is the naïve forecast.

   c. Which of the two forecasting methods should James Triton use? Compute the MAD to help James decide.

4. Trinity General Hospital had the following number of patient admissions during the past 8 weeks:

Week	1	2	3	4	5	6	7	8
Patient Admissions	120	145	95	112	130	110	100	140

   a. Develop a 3-week weighted average forecast for week 4 through 9 with weights of $W_1 = 0.5$, $W_2 = 0.3$, and $W_3 = 0.2$.

   b. Forecast patient admissions for week 9 using simple exponential smoothing with $\alpha = 0.2$. Assume that the forecast for week 4 (F_4) is the naïve forecast.

   c. Use the MSE to determine which of the two forecasting methods is more accurate.

5. Calangute Beach Resort, a fictional sea-side luxury hotel in Goa, India, had the following occupancy rates for 12 months of 2014:

Month	1	2	3	4	5	6	7	8	9	10	11	12
Occupancy rate in %	65	68	72	75	78	83	92	88	76	65	64	69

   a. Forecast the occupancy rate for January 2015 using simple exponential smoothing with $\alpha = 0.4$. Assume that the forecast for month 2 (F_2) is 65%.

   b. Forecast the January 2015 occupancy rate using trend-adjusted simple exponential smoothing with $\alpha = 0.4$ and $\beta = 0.2$. Assume that the forecast for month 2 (F_2) is 68% and the trend factor for month 2 is $T_2 = 0$.

   c. Which of the two forecasting methods is more accurate? Compute the MSE/Bias forecasting error measure to answer the question.

6. Bear Creek Ski Resort in Vail, Colorado, had the following guest occupancy for the 8 weeks of November and December of 2014. Forecast the number of guests for January 2015 using trend-adjusted simple exponential smoothing with $\alpha = 0.5$ and $\beta = 0.3$. Assume that the forecast for week 2 (F_2) is 220 and the trend factor for month 2 is $T_2 = 0$:

Week	1	2	3	4	5	6	7	8
Number of Guests	194	220	232	248	256	270	274	290

7. The marketing manager of a shoe store has developed the following linear trend equation to predict monthly sales for the store's popular brand of ladies shoes.

$$F_t = 220 + 27 \times t, \text{ where}$$

F_t is monthly sales (in 00s), and t is in months.

    a.   By how much do monthly sales increase or decrease?

    b.   Using the regression equation, forecast shoe sales for month 9.

8. St. Xavier College, a fictional educational institution, wants to forecast the enrollment in its business department for the next academic year. The combined enrollment for full-time and part-time students expressed in full-time equivalents (FTE) for the past 10 semesters are:

Semester	Enrollment
1	884
2	921
3	1007
4	1030
5	1048
6	1074
7	1103
8	1128
9	1165
10	1220

    a.   Plot the data. Does the data appear to have a linear trend?

    b.   Forecast the enrollment for the next four semesters using the linear trend equation.

9. Martin Guenther, the manager of Lloyd's Savings Bank (fictitious) in Hamburg, Germany, wants to forecast the number of new checking accounts that will be opened in the next 2 months. He has data for the past 12 months on new checking accounts opened, which is shown in the following table:

Month	1	2	3	4	5	6	7	8	9	10	11	12
New Checking Accounts	120	144	178	228	245	252	255	262	277	282	290	295

    a.   Forecast the number of new checking accounts that will be opened in month 13 using trend-adjusted exponential smoothing with $\alpha = 0.4$ and $\beta = 0.5$. Assume that the forecast for month 2 (F_2) is the naïve forecast and the trend factor for month 2 is $T_2 = 0$.

    b.   Forecast the number of new checking accounts that will be opened in month 13 using a linear trend equation.

    c.   Which of the two forecasting methods is more accurate? Use the MAPE to answer the question.

10. In the busy port of Chennai, India, the number of containers loaded onto ships during a 15-week period is as follows:

Month	1	2	3	4	5	6	7	8	9	10	11	12
Number of Containers Loaded	180	225	260	240	285	320	380	410	490	530	545	550

    a.   Develop a linear trend equation to forecast container loadings.

    b.   Using the equation, forecast the number of containers that will be loaded in weeks 15 and 16.

    c.   The current loading equipment in the port can handle a loading volume of up to 600 containers. If the loading volume exceeds 600 containers, then the port has to purchase new loading equipment. If the current trend continues, when should the port purchase the new equipment?

11. The director of an emergency room, Simran Kaur, has observed that patient traffic at the emergency room follows a seasonal pattern with a higher patient traffic during weekends than weekdays. She has gathered the following data on daily patient admissions during the last 4 weeks:

	Week			
Day	1	2	3	4
Monday	110	105	109	112
Tuesday	95	100	92	88
Wednesday	89	85	80	84
Thursday	93	96	78	90

| | Week | | | |
Day	1	2	3	4
Friday	150	155	152	148
Saturday	255	260	268	275
Sunday	160	166	170	175

Given this information:

a.   Compute the daily seasonal indices of patient admissions using the simple average method.

b.   Compute the daily seasonal indices of patient admissions using the centered moving average method.

12.   The fictitious Haskin & Collins Ice Cream Store needs an accurate estimate of demand. The owner of the store believes that the demand for ice cream has a quarterly seasonal pattern. To analyze the pattern, the owner gathered the following quarterly ice cream sales data in gallons for the last 4 years:

| | Year | | | |
Quarter	1	2	3	4
January–March	370	380	470	530
April–June	550	500	620	700
July–September	770	820	980	990
October–December	420	440	510	530

Given this information:

a.   Compute the quarterly seasonal indices for ice cream sales using the simple average method.

b.   Compute the quarterly seasonal indices for ice cream sales using the centered moving average method.

13.   A BMW car dealer in Sicilia, Italy, has the following monthly new car sales data for January through December 2014. The dealer believes that new car sales follow a monthly seasonal pattern and computed the seasonal indices for each of the 12 months, which are also given in the following table:

Month	1	2	3	4	5	6	7	8	9	10	11	12
New Car Sales	720	742	695	798	740	830	785	900	990	920	890	840
Seasonal Indexes	0.85	0.85	0.65	0.9	0.85	1.00	0.96	1.20	1.30	1.30	1.35	1.35

a.   Plot the car sales data. Does there appear to be a trend?

b.   Deseasonalize the actual car sales to isolate the trend component.

c.   Develop a linear trend equation using the deseasonalized data.

d.   Develop a trend forecast for January and February 2015.

e.   Develop a seasonalized forecast for January and February 2015.

14.   For the data in problem 11, using the seasonal indices developed for that problem and using the simple average method, do the following:

a.   Deseasonalize the admissions data.

b.   Develop a linear trend equation using the deseasonalized data.

c.   Develop a trend forecast for Monday and Tuesday of week 5.

d.   Develop a seasonalized forecast for Monday and Tuesday of week 5.

15.   Use the seasonal indices developed for problem 12 and the centered moving average method to:

a.   Deseasonalize the ice cream sales data.

b.   Develop a linear trend equation using the deseasonalized data.

c.   Develop a trend forecast for the first quarter of year 5.

d.   Develop a seasonalized forecast for the first quarter of year 5.

16.   A home improvement store has the following actual quarterly sales for its lawn mowers for the past 2 years. Quarterly seasonal indices for quarters 1, 2, 3, and 4 are $S_1 = 1.0$, $S_2 = 1.2$, $S_3 = 0.96$, and $S_4 = 0.85$:

Year	Quarter 1	Quarter 2	Quarter 3	Quarter 4
2014	98	140	112	80
2015	92	152	104	88

Predict the sales for the second quarter of 2016.

17. The chancellor of a small regional college is concerned about the declining freshmen enrollment at his college. A number of factors have contributed to the decline, but the chancellor believes it is directly related to annual tuition increases. He has collected the following data for the past 8 years:

Year	1	2	3	4	5	6	7	8
Freshman enrollment	6550	6230	5980	5540	4960	4630	4520	4220
Annual tuition (in U.S. Dollars)	32000	37000	45200	45700	46200	46700	52200	57700

  a. Develop a linear regression equation for forecasting freshman enrollment as a function of the annual tuition.

  b. Forecast freshman enrollment if the annual tuition increases to US$9,000 in year 9.

  c. Evaluate the "goodness of fit" of the regression equation by computing the values of R^2, r, and s_{yx} and interpret the results.

18. The managers of Mayo Department Store want to evaluate the relationship between the sales of air conditioners and the average weekly temperature. The following weekly sales data along with the average daytime temperatures for 10 one-week periods are shown in the following table:

Week	1	2	3	4	5	6	7	8	9	10
Air-Conditioner Sales (in units)	100	85	103	110	70	115	150	120	97	85
Average Temperature (in degrees Fahrenheit)	78	70	85	90	75	94	101	98	86	80

  a. Develop a linear regression equation for air conditioner sales as a function of the average weekly temperature.

  b. Forecast air conditioner sales if the average weekly temperature is 88 degrees Fahrenheit.

  c. Evaluate the "goodness of fit" of the regression equation by computing the values of R^2, r, and s_{yx} and interpret the results.

19. Champion Auto Group believes that car sales are closely related to the amount of money the firm spends on advertising and the personal income levels of consumers in various target markets. The company gathered the data on the number of cars of a new model sold in Shanghai given the advertising money (in U.S. dollars) spent and the average personal income of the consumers. The information is shown in the following table:

Number of Cars Sold	Personal Income (in U.S. dollars)	Advertising (in U.S. dollars)
20	52	25
14	40	17
30	73	42
35	83	60
48	110	100
52	125	105
28	66	53
22	60	48
19	47	30
26	58	33
10	35	22
13	39	30

  a. Based on this data, use Excel to develop a multiple regression equation.

  b. Interpret the coefficients b_0, b_1, and b_2.

  c. Interpret the statistics "multiple R" and the coefficient of determination (R^2) in the regression output.

  d. Forecast the car's sales if the average personal income of the target market is US$81,000 and the amount spent on advertising is US$52,000.

20. A major shoe manufacturer is considering launching a brand new pair of running shoes. Before introducing the shoes to the market, the company wants to determine the impact the price and in-store promotions will have on the sales of the new shoes. A sample of 24 shoe retail stores was selected for test marketing. The data obtained from the study are as follows:

Store	Price (in U.S. dollars)	In-store Promotion (in U.S. dollars)	Shoe Sales (in U.S. dollars)	Store	Price (in U.S. dollars)	In-store Promotion (in U.S. dollars)	Shoe Sales (in U.S. dollars)
1	55	2,500	410	13	75	5,000	270
2	55	2,500	380	14	75	5,000	310
3	55	2,500	320	15	75	5,000	380
4	55	5,000	350	16	75	7,500	300

Store	Price (in U.S. dollars)	In-store Promotion (in U.S. dollars)	Shoe Sales (in U.S. dollars)	Store	Price (in U.S. dollars)	In-store Promotion (in U.S. dollars)	Shoe Sales (in U.S. dollars)
5	55	5,000	450	17	75	7,500	330
6	55	5,000	470	18	75	7,500	420
7	55	7,500	490	19	95	2,500	180
8	55	7,500	510	20	95	2,500	200
9	55	7,500	540	21	95	5,000	190
10	75	2,500	250	22	95	5,000	220
11	75	2,500	300	23	95	7,500	240
12	75	2,500	290	24	95	7,500	270

a. Based on this data, use Excel to develop a multiple regression equation.

b. Interpret the coefficients b_0, b_1, and b_2.

c. Interpret the statistics "multiple R" and the coefficient of determination (R^2) in the regression output.

d. Forecast shoe sales if the price is US$65 and the amount spent on advertising is US$4,400.

21. Based on 12 months of demand data, an apparel store generated the following forecasts using judgmental methods. Compute the tracking signals for the forecasts using ±4 MAD limits and comment on the performance of the forecasting method used:

Month	Demand	Forecast
1	1,772	1,774
2	1,790	1,780
3	1,796	1,792
4	1,783	1,794
5	1,775	1,772
6	1,770	1,764
7	1,765	1,758
8	1,777	1,779
9	1,782	1,765
10	1,794	1,782
11	1,755	1,768
12	1,779	1,795

22. Multiple regression analysis in Excel produced the following tables:

	Coefficients	Standard Error	t Statistic	p value
Intercept	720.9429	154.5534	3.990108	0.000947
X_1	−3.2897	2.333548	−1.43058	0.170675
X_2	1.17015	0.335605	5.30407	5.83E-05

	df	SS	MS	F	p value
Regression	2	121,783	60,891.48	14.76117	0.000286
Residual	15	61,876.68	4,125.112		
Total	17	183,659.6			

a. State the multiple regression equation.

b. Interpret the meaning of the coefficients X_1 and X_2 in the table.

c. Forecast the value of the dependent variable if $X_1 = 20$ and $X_2 = 9$.

23. A market research analyst used multiple regression analysis to determine the impact of price and promotion on the sale of a new brand of cereal. The analyst collected data from three variables from 30 different stores, formulated a multiple regression model, and solved the model in Excel. The partial Excel regression output is reproduced in the following tables:

	Coefficients	Standard Error	t Statistic	P-value
Intercept	4857.845	503.627	2.892	9.27689E-07
Price	−47.326	5.4287	−6.61249	9.735284E-09
Promotion	5.3581	0.77463	4.55487	9.54095E-05

	Df	SS	MS	F	P-value
Regression	2	121783	60891.48	14.76117	0.000286
Residual	15	61876.68	4125.112		
Total	17	183659.6			

a. State the multiple regression equation for this problem.

b. Interpret the meaning of the coefficients of price and promotion in the Excel output.

c. Forecast the value of the sales during a month if the price of a box of the new cereal is US$3.29 and the monthly promotional expenditure is US$600.

24. Euro Rail ridership during the summer months is believed to be closely related to the number of tourists visiting Europe. The following table shows the data on number of tourists and Euro Rail ridership for the past 15 years:

Year	Number of Tourists (in millions)	Euro Rail Ridership (in millions)
2000	9	2.3
2001	4	1.9
2002	7	1.7
2003	5	1.8
2004	12	2.8
2005	13	2.9
2006	14	2.4
2007	20	4.8
2008	7	1.3
2009	5	1.1
2010	9	1.9
2011	11	2.1
2012	16	3.3
2013	14	2.8
2014	18	3.6
2015	17	3.2

a. Develop a linear regression equation for Euro Rail ridership as a function of the average number of tourists visiting Europe.

b. Forecast Euro Rail ridership if the average number of tourists visiting Europe is 19.2 million.

c. Evaluate the "goodness of fit" of the regression equation by computing the values of R^2, r, and s_{yx} and interpret the results.

25. A math instructor who teaches calculus at a university in Western Pennsylvania believes that there is a relationship between the number of optional homework problems that the students complete during the semester and their final score for the course. To examine this relationship the instructor gathers data (given in the following table) on the homework problems completed and the final score for the course for a randomly selected sample of 16 students:

Student	Number of Completed Homework Problems	Final Score for the Course
1	20	60
2	45	72
3	56	78
4	61	70
5	64	71
6	67	71
7	70	85

Student	Number of Completed Homework Problems	Final Score for the Course
8	74	90
9	77	88
10	79	88
11	39	66
12	52	81
13	28	55
14	47	71
15	35	63
16	80	92

a. Develop a linear regression equation for the final course score as a function of the average number optional homework problems completed.

b. Forecast a final course score if the average number of homework problems completed is 59.

c. Evaluate the "goodness of fit" of the regression equation by computing the values of R^2, r, and s_{yx} and interpret the results.

26. James Trott, the manager the fictitious Blue Line Trucking Company, wants to develop a forecasting model to predict the maintenance expenditures on the company's trucks. The manager believes that a truck's maintenance expenditures are closely related to the age of the trucks and the number of miles driven. He collected the data on these three variables for 10 different trucks, and they are given in the following table:

Age of the Truck (in years)	Number of Miles Driven	Maintenance Cost (in U.S. dollars)
5	15,200	1230
8	22.520	2480
7	18,945	2320
4	12,405	1080
4	13,897	1042
6	17,235	2260
3	11,648	970
10	35,985	4570
9	37,790	5780
1	6,400	350

a. Develop a multiple regression equation for this problem using Excel.

b. Interpret the meaning of the coefficients of age of the truck and miles driven in the Excel output.

c. Forecast the maintenance cost if the age of the truck is 7 years and the number of miles driven is 32,300.

27. Refer to problem 26.

a. Using Excel, develop a linear regression model for predicting maintenance cost as a function of age of the trucks. Forecast maintenance cost if the age of the truck is 7 years.

b. Using Excel, develop a linear regression model for predicting maintenance cost as a function of the number of miles driven. Forecast maintenance cost if the number of miles driven is 32,300.

c. Evaluate the "goodness of fit" of the regression equations developed in both part a and part b by computing the values of R^2, r, and s_{yx}. Which model is a better fit and why?

d. How do the forecasts developed in parts a and b compare with the one developed in problem 24?

28. Orion Electronics, a fictitious chain of electronics stores, operates a website to encourage potential customer to buy its products online. Because the website is expensive to maintain, the VP of Marketing is unsure if the online sales of the company's products is directly related to the number of hits on the website. To evaluate this relationship, the marketing manager of the company is directed to gather monthly data on the number of hits and the corresponding sales for the past 24 months. The data are presented in the following table:

Number Hits (in 000s)	Customer Orders (in 000s)	Number Hits (in 000s)	Customer Orders (in 000s)
42.3	9.4	48.8	11.3
29.6	6.1	44.3	9.9
38.4	9.7	57.1	12.5
45.7	8.3	54.3	11.9
24.3	5.1	65.9	14.8

Number Hits (in 000s)	Customer Orders (in 000s)	Number Hits (in 000s)	Customer Orders (in 000s)
55.4	11.7	36.8	6.9
*3.9	0.5	27.4	5.4
30.7	7.3	24.1	4.9
29.2	6.7	40.1	10.8
33.9	7.4	47.8	10.9
28.5	5.5	45.5	11.1
21.6	4.9	32.3	7.7

* Data highlighted in red reflects data in the month when the company's website was shut down for the majority of the month as a result of a security breach.

a. What should you do with the data highlighted in red for forecasting purposes? Include it in the model or omit it?

b. Develop a linear regression model using Excel by including all 24 pieces of data.

c. Develop a linear regression model using Excel after excluding the highlighted data in red.

d. Compare the Excel outputs from both "b and c," and determine which linear regression model is a better fit.

29. A company that produces protein bars used different forecasting techniques to predict demand for its protein bars. The actual demand and the forecasted demand for cases of protein bars using the two different forecasting methods are presented in the following table:

Month	1	2	3	4	5	6	7	8	9
F_1	97	80	82	54	81	88	89	86	80
F_2	95	77	89	62	84	93	89	84	74
Actual Demand	99	86	90	68	79	82	96	88	76

a. Compute MAD for the results of each forecasting method. Which one is more accurate?

b. Compute MSE for the results of each forecasting method. Which one is more accurate?

c. Compute MAPE for the results of each forecasting method. Which one is more accurate?

d. As a forecaster, what factors would lead you to choose one forecasting error measure over the other two?

30. Aarthi Medicals, a fictitious company, has been monitoring the sales of a health drink for diabetics. As the demand for the health drink has been steadily increasing, the owner of the store, Nicole Carter, wants to develop good forecasts for this product to determine how many cases of this drink to order every week from the manufacturer. Nicole has compiled the demand data shown in the accompanying table for the past 12 weeks. Nicole wants to evaluate forecasts using the exponential smoothing method using smoothing constants values of $\alpha_1 = 0.20$ and $\alpha_2 = 0.40$.

Week	Demand in Cases	Week	Demand in Cases
1	48	7	48
2	52	8	46
3	49	9	55
4	35	10	54
5	47	11	58
6	53	12	57

a. Assuming a forecast for week 2 of 48 cases ($F_2 = 48$), generate forecasts for weeks 13 to 15 using exponential smoothing for both values of the smoothing constant ($\alpha_1 = 0.20$ and $\alpha_2 = 0.40$).

b. Compute the forecast error measures of MAD and MSE and determine which value of the smoothing constant provides more accurate forecasts.

31. Great Lakes Blood Bank (fictional) is the primary supplier of blood to various hospitals in Erie County, Pennsylvania. The number of pints of the rare blood type AB- supplied by the blood bank to the hospitals in Erie County during the past 8 weeks are given in the following table:

Week	1	2	3	4	5	6	7	8
Pints Supplied	270	350	370	352	325	344	295	367

a. Forecast the demand for the AB- blood type for week 9 using a four-period moving average.

b. Forecast the demand for the AB- blood type for week 9 using a four-period weighted moving average, with weights of $W_1 = 0.4$, $W_2 = 0.3$, $W_3 = 0.2$, and $W_4 = 0.1$. Note the higher weights are assigned to the most recent weeks.

c. Compute the forecast for week 9 using simple exponential smoothing. Assume $F_1 = 270$ and $\alpha = 0.3$.

32. A company has observed the following demand during the past 10 months for one of its popular products:

Month	1	2	3	4	5	6	7	8	9	10
Demand	60	80	40	80	120	70	110	120	80	100

   a. Plot these data on a graph. Do you observe any pattern such as trend, seasonal, cyclical, or random variations in the data?

   b. Compute 3-month moving average forecasts from month 4 to month 11. Plot the forecast in the same graph that you generated in a.

   c. Compute forecasts from month 4 to 11 using exponential smoothing. Assume $F_4 = 80$ and $\alpha = 0.2$. Plot these forecasts on the same graph that you generated in b.

   d. Compare the forecasts that you generated in b and c with the actual demand data plotted in a. Which one seems to be a superior forecasting technique?

33. The following table shows demand for kidney transplants for the past 7 years at the fictitious Crescent General Hospital:

Year	1	2	3	4	5	6	7
Kidney Transplants	38	42	47	51	58	60	63

   a. Compute 3-month moving average forecasts for years 4 to 8.

   b. Compute forecasts for years 4 to 8 using exponential smoothing for two different values of α, 0.5 and 0.7. Assume $F_4 = 51$.

   c. Use the trend-adjusted exponential smoothing method to forecast for years 4 to 8 with $\alpha = 0.5$ and $\beta = 0.2$. Assume that the forecast for year 4 (F_4) is 51 and the trend factor for year 4 is $T_4 = 0$.

   d. Use MSE as the forecast error measure to determine which of the four forecasting techniques is superior.

34. A marketing manager has determined that demand for his company's popular product in a region is a function of the size of the region's population in tens of thousands (x_1), advertising dollars in thousands (x_2), and disposable income in thousands (x_3). Using past data, the manager has developed the following multiple regression model:

$$y_c = 10.3 + 4.1x_1 + 5.3x_2 + 8.5x_3 .$$

   a. Forecast the demand for this product if $x_1 = 5.5$, $x_2 = 20$, and $x_3 = 55$.

   b. In addition to the independent variables, what additional quantitative variables might you include in the model to make it more effective?

35. A manager of a home improvement store has been using the linear trend multiplicative model to predict the demand for his lawn mowers. The quarterly seasonal indices are $S_1 = 0.85$, $S_2 = 0.90$, $S_3 = 1.10$, and $S_4 = 1.00$. The linear trend equation that the manager developed is: $Y_t = 15 + 6t$. The following lawn mower sales have been observed for the most recent nine quarters:

Quarter	1	2	3	4	5	6	7	8	9
Sales	18	33	40	36	24	38	45	42	32

   a. Comment on the effectiveness of the forecasting method used by the manager of the store.

CASE STUDY 13.1 FORECASTING TICKET DEMAND FOR THE SUPER BOWL ················

The 2015 Super Bowl between the New England Patriots and the Seattle Seahawks was a thrilling game that was decided in the final seconds. The relatively short duration of the game, however, contrasted sharply to the weeks of hype and preparation leading up to the contest between the two teams. Nowhere was the frenetic activity felt more than in the ticket sales, particularly the so-called secondary market, which includes organizations such as StubHub (San Francisco, CA), Ticketmaster Entertainment, Inc. (West Hollywood, CA), and Craigslist Inc. (San Francisco, CA). By the last week before the game, the NFL Ticket Exchange, the National Football League's (New York City, NY) official re-sale website, had no tickets for less than US$9,000. The cheapest seats on other sites were essentially the same. This skyrocketing escalation of prices far above face value for tickets took the NFL and other ticket brokers by surprise and led them to examine exactly what went wrong.

In general, every year there is a predictable arc to Super Bowl ticket prices on the secondary market. In the days leading up to the American Football Conference and National Football Conference championship games (to decide who will play in the Super Bowl), ticket prices tend to be high (perhaps three times the face value of the ticket). Once the conference championships have been decided and the Super Bowl opponents determined, brokers expect a price spike as supporters of the Super Bowl teams clamber for a chance to watch their team. Nevertheless, as Super Sunday approaches, a predictable drop in prices occurs as brokers and sellers look to avoid being stuck with unsold tickets and cut prices to sell off their remaining stock.

One challenge for predicting ticket prices comes with determining the teams who make it to the final game. For example, predictions for ticket prices for the 2015 Super Bowl were that they would be lower than usual because the two teams involved—Seattle and New England—had both been to the finals in recent years and it was assumed that their fans were likely feeling some "success fatigue" and a sense that the excitement had worn off.

Yet, in 2015, those predictions did not come true. In fact, not only did the ticket price drop that everyone was anticipating *not* occur, but prices continued to spiral upward as the days passed. Right after the conference championship games were over, tickets were selling for $1,900 to $2,900 (in U.S. dollars) a seat—extremely expensive, but nowhere near where they would end up. At the start of the week before the game, the average price per seat was $6,500 and the least expensive seats were going for $4,200. By Thursday, the cheapest price for a ticket was $7,100, while StubHub alerted the media that "the current average list price for the Super Bowl is $9,484.37, which is up 282.43% since last year at this time ($2,480.06)." And that was for the sites that had tickets. StubHub listed fewer than 300 tickets available, and many of the secondary market sites were posting "no tickets available" announcements on their websites.

What were the forces that caused this completely unanticipated rise in prices and lack of tickets for sale? First, the game was being held indoors. Having a controlled environment is much less risky than playing a football game in early February throughout much of the northern United States. In fact, when Meadowlands Stadium in East Rutherford, New Jersey, hosted the Super Bowl in 2014, rumors of heavy snow and bitter cold helped keep average ticket prices to about $2,500, with several thousand available for purchase through the week before the game. In the case of the Seattle–New England game, the causes of the skyrocketing ticket prices may have been a result of people more than anything else; that is, StubHub accused a handful of large ticket sellers in control of most of the Super Bowl ticket inventory of colluding with each other to manipulate ticket prices, keeping them artificially high while funneling only small numbers onto the secondary market. In this way, they were able to influence supply and subsequent demand for the tickets, pushing prices out of reach for the average football fan.

Even though sports fans were left without tickets, it was the ticket brokers themselves who took the biggest loss. Brokers commonly buy up large blocks of tickets on spec, under the assumption that they can realize profits from the difference between their purchase prices and the price rise they expect to occur. In this case, the going price in the marketplace was much higher than they anticipated, leading to a "short squeeze." That is, because colluders kept a lid on available seats, brokers were forced to pay maximum price for tickets and then hustle to sell them, often for a reduced price, in the days right before the game.

The failure to forecast ticket prices accurately led to a few insiders making high profits, while saddling the majority of ticket brokers with stinging losses.[8]

Questions

1. Given the role that "Mother Nature" plays in forecasting Super Bowl ticket prices, how might you adjust your expectations for ticket costs from year to year, given the location of the event?

2. Consider this case from an ethics perspective. Do you see anything "unethical" with large-block ticket holders hoarding their tickets as long as possible? Why or why not?

CASE STUDY 13.2 ETHICAL FORECASTING: IF YOU TORTURE THE NUMBERS LONG ENOUGH, THEY CAN TELL YOU ANYTHING!

Katie is a brand new intern working for one of the biggest advertising firms in the Midwest, headquartered in Chicago. Getting this internship was a dream come true for her, as she grew up in the Chicago area and has always wanted to work in advertising. Additionally, the hiring rate for productive interns is very high, so this opportunity could lead to a full-time position. As a result, she is highly motivated to do a good job, get noticed, and, hopefully, receive a job offer.

Katie is the junior member of an advertising team that is meeting with a long-term client. The meeting is not going well; in fact, the client has serious reservations about continuing its relationship with the firm as a result of a recently failed advertising campaign the firm developed for the client. The client claims that the advertising was expensive and, in the words of its senior manager, "didn't move the needle one bit. We are still at the same market share rate, so we're out millions with nothing to show for it." The meeting breaks for lunch, with the customer threatening to "end the relationship, unless you can give us something." As the rest of the team leaves the room, Katie's boss signals her to stay back.

Boss: "Katie, I hear that you're pretty good with the statistical packages we use for customer data."

Katie: "Yes, I've been using them for years now."

Boss: "OK, I need you to run me some numbers to show that our ads are really working. Their flat sales could be a result of other issues, an industry-wide pattern, or something else. Just find me something that I can use when they get back from lunch."

Katie returns to her desk and works through her lunch break. The results generally are not good. To her best knowledge, the client's sales really have not moved at all as a result of the advertising campaign. Nevertheless, she notices an interesting phenomenon. In the men's age 18–35 demographic, she finds a big uptick in sales in the weeks right after the hockey playoff games were held in town. Although it is apparent to her that these sales increases are specifically related to those special events, she is pretty sure that she can smooth the data to show a general increase in sales. In fact, aggregating this data across all demographic groups could show some sales improvement that she could link to the advertising campaign, especially if no one on the client's team is good with statistical models.

Katie returns to the conference room 5 minutes before the client returns from lunch and meets up with her frantic boss.

Boss: "Well, what did you find for us?"

Katie: ….

Questions

1. This scenario shows how ethics can influence decision-making with forecasting. Put yourself in Katie's position; how would you respond?

2. Select either the "tell the truth" or the "fix the data" position and defend your reasoning. Why do you believe that ethics does or does not factor into this dilemma? What would you say to someone who took the other position?

VIDEO CASE

Watch this video case to learn about how MPK Foods, a family-owned company that produces seasoning mixes sold to grocery stores, forecasts demand amid seasonal variation.

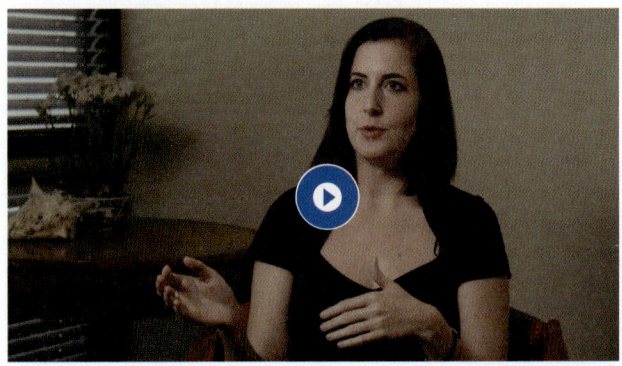

CRITICAL THINKING EXERCISES

The hotel industry is highly competitive. For most companies, margins are low because of high overhead costs, which means that they have to be cost conscious and focus on keeping their rooms occupied. To get maximum competitive advantage, forecasting is essential to improving a hotel's future performance.

a. What types of forecasts do hotels need?

b. What demand forecasting methods would you use for estimating room occupancy?

c. What challenges do hotels face when developing accurate room-occupancy forecasts?

©iStockphoto.com/AlexBrylov

CHAPTER 14

Lean Operations and Supply Chains

LEARNING OBJECTIVES

After studying this chapter, you should be able to:

1. Define lean operations.

2. Describe the philosophy of lean systems.

3. Outline the elements of lean operations systems.

4. Apply lean ideas to service operations.

5. Identify the characteristics of a lean supply chain.

6. Explain why it is so difficult to make global supply chains lean.

7. Discuss how sustainability initiatives can be considered to be an extension of the lean philosophy.

OPERATIONS PROFILE: Lean Operations at Rolls-Royce Indianapolis

Rolls-Royce Holdings plc, headquartered in London, England, is one of the world's leading manufacturers of jet engines for commercial and military uses. The jet engine business has always been highly competitive, especially in periods when fuel costs rise. At such times, airlines are under pressure to reduce costs, and one way they do so is to require suppliers like Rolls-Royce to produce more energy-efficient engines. To maintain its profitability, Rolls-Royce needs to continue to innovate. One critical decision that the company made during such a period was to aggressively move to lean manufacturing.

Since 2000, Rolls-Royce has invested nearly US$100 million in modernizing its manufacturing site, including implementing a series of lean manufacturing initiatives. The initiatives included establishing production levels based on actual customer demand rather than on sales forecasts. A smaller number of parts is warehoused, and engines are produced to order.

To accomplish this change, the company drastically redesigned the plant's operations to improve its flow. The plant adopted a process that involved first gathering from the stockroom all the parts needed to assemble an engine into a kit prior to sending them to the manufacturing line. This practice minimizes unnecessary employee movement and traffic around the plant floor while keeping inventory levels low. The company also improved the lighting and working conditions in the plant and invested in new equipment to accommodate its manufacturing innovations. The overall impact was dramatic: By 2008, the lean plant redesign had enabled Rolls-Royce to demolish more than 850,000 square feet of the facility. As a result of the leaner practices, the space was no longer needed.

The decision by Rolls-Royce to adopt lean operations has paid off handsomely. The company has surpassed Pratt & Whitney (East Hartford, CT) and is now the second-largest supplier of jet engines in the world, behind General Electric (aka GE, Fairfield, CT). "Rolls-Royce has come from a distant number three to a strong number two," said Nick Cunningham, who covers Rolls-Royce for Citigroup Global Markets in London (division of Citigroup Inc., New York, NY).[1] Rolls-Royce's success story illustrates some of the clear advantages that lean operations provide to organizations. In this chapter, we will explore the concept of lean to understand better the philosophy behind lean practices, the steps a firm can take to introduce lean into its operations, as well as the methods to expand lean to supply chains.

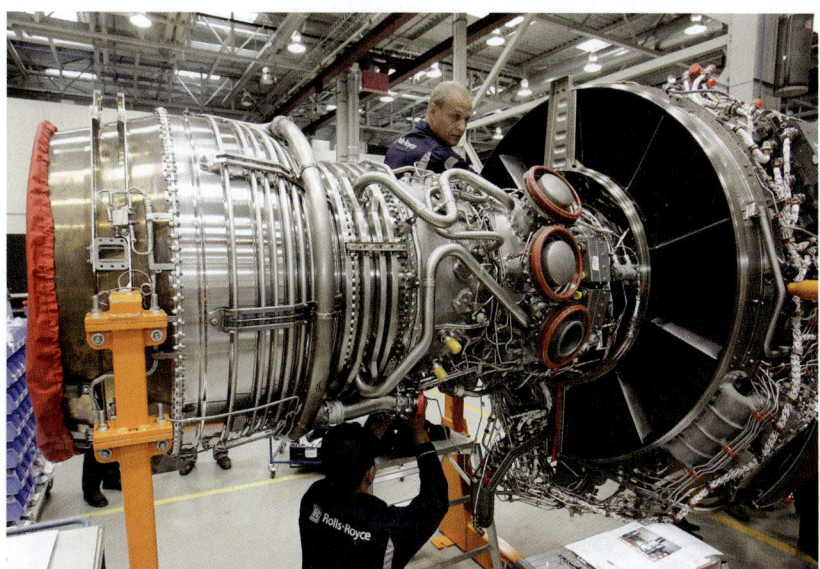

Sean Gallup/Getty Images News/Getty Images

Define lean operations.

Lean philosophy: the belief that any activity or process that does not add value to a product or service wastes resources and, therefore, should be eliminated

Just-in-time (JIT): a system in which customer demand, rather than sales forecasts, dictates production levels

Lean concepts can also be applied in service industries; companies like FedEx utilize lean practices for their delivery management and performance processes.

©iStockphoto.com/jetcityimage

14.1 Introduction to Lean Operations

According to the lean philosophy, which we introduced in Chapter 1, any activity or process that does not add value to the product or service wastes resources and, therefore, should be eliminated. Henry Ford used lean concepts in the assembly lines for his cars in the early 1900s. Just-in-time (JIT) strategies, which we discussed earlier as well, are often a part of lean production. When a company uses a just-in-time strategy, it delays receiving raw materials or inventory from its suppliers until right before they are needed for production. By adopting a just-in-time strategy, the firm reduces its investment in inventory and minimizes the space needed to store raw materials. Products are produced and services are performed only when they are needed.

Lean production and just-in-time concepts became important in the early 1970s, after Tai-ichi Ohno, a longtime employee and executive of Toyota (Toyota Motor Corporation, Toyota City, Japan), used them to propel the automaker to the forefront of its industry. Since then, thousands of companies all over the world have adopted lean production methods to manage both their operations and supply chains. The German automobile manufacturer Porsche AG (Stuttgart, Baden-Württemberg, Germany) is an example. After nearly going bankrupt in the 1990s, lean methods enabled Porsche to move from US$300 million in losses to profitability in just four years. During the last global downturn in 2008, the firm remained one of the most profitable companies in the automobile industry.[2]

Lean operations, however, are just one part of an integrated supply chain. Many individual companies that adopt lean concepts quickly find that whatever gains they can achieve will be limited unless their immediate suppliers and other partners in the supply chain also become lean. From 1990 to 2000, The Boeing Company (Chicago, IL) learned this lesson the hard way, when the company attempted to double its production overnight to respond to an unprecedented demand for new airplanes—without realizing the impact the move would have on the supply chain for the thousands of parts used in the planes. The move resulted in shortages of parts and workers at the assembly stage, forcing Boeing to close its 747 and 737 assembly lines. Ultimately, the company realized a US$1.6 billion loss. In 2001, Boeing revamped its supply chain process through the use of lean manufacturing techniques, which require tighter integration with suppliers and just-in-time delivery of parts.[3]

Global sourcing makes it considerably more difficult to achieve the key components of lean systems, such as the rapid and smooth flow of goods and information as well as the reduction of waste. There are several reasons for this. First, longer lead times and higher inventory levels are needed for global supply chains compared with domestic supply chains. Second, because global supply chains are longer, sales forecasts are rarely accurate and managers sometimes have to contend with significant delays. Nevertheless, applying some lean concepts such as reducing defects and minimizing the orders for changes in parts, assemblies, specifications, engineering drawings, and documents can stabilize these global supply chains and improve the flow of goods. Delta Galil Industries, a private label-clothing manufacturer in Tel Aviv, Israel, has adopted lean supply chain operations to connect its more than 1,000 suppliers, reducing lead times and transactions costs. By contrast, Nissan (Nissan Motor Company Ltd, Yokohama, Japan), in 2010, halted production for three days at four of its Japanese facilities and two American plants because its lean supply chain was mismanaged specifically because Nissan failed to coordinate shipments from its suppliers. Nissan estimated that these stoppages reduced the company's output for 2010 by 15,000 vehicles.[4] Implementing lean systems within a global supply chain may be more expensive and challenging. Yet, it has the potential to produce long-term benefits, making it worth the effort.

The success the manufacturing industry has experienced by adopting lean concepts has also occurred in the service sector. FedEx (FedEx Corporation, Memphis, TN) has employed lean transportation systems in its operations, adopting four "laws of lean" as they apply to delivery management and performance. In 2009, three medical facilities in the comarca del Garraf, near Barcelona, merged into one organization, the Consorci Sanitari del Garraf. As a result of the financial crisis, the health-care organization faced a 17% budget cut and had to find a way to improve its processes and become more efficient. Introducing a wide range of lean methods, it took the Consorci Sanitari del Garraf just one year to improve its processes and develop its human resources to achieve the goals of lean health care: (a) improving the quality of care and patient experience, (b) simplifying tasks for providers, and (c) better use of resources to treat an expanding patient population without adding more doctors and nurses, beds, or equipment.[5] Toyota's lean production system has become the gold standard for U.S. hospitals looking to simplify their processes.[6] In this chapter, we discuss lean systems, including lean supply chains and lean services.

14.2 The Philosophy of Lean Systems

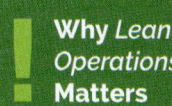

Describe the philosophy of lean systems.

Lean production is not only a methodology but also a philosophy intended to promote respect for people and eliminate waste and inefficiency. In a lean system, assembly-line workers and supervisors take on additional responsibilities. In fact, because they are the firm's best source for spotting problems and ensuring quality, the success or failure of a lean system depends on these workers. Quality at the source is based squarely on the willingness of managers to empower workers to identify quality problems and stop the production line. Consequently, an organization that wants to implement a lean system should create an environment that fosters cooperation, trust, and respect between its workforce and managers. In addition, empowering workers to identify problems during production and make decisions, soliciting their advice for improvements, and having multiskilled employees who can work in different jobs and on different machines can facilitate the implementation of lean systems.

As an example, when Rolls-Royce restructured its jet engine operations into a lean system, the local chapter of the United Auto Workers (UAW)—the principal labor union at the plant—agreed to the proposed changes. In fact, the union not only embraced the lean principles but also did so with so much enthusiasm that the Indianapolis facility is now Rolls-Royce's most productive. This result wouldn't have been possible without the workers and the union committing to the lean philosophy.

The second principle of lean manufacturing is the elimination of waste and inefficiency. Toyota's past president Fujio Cho defined waste as "anything other than the minimum amount of equipment, materials, parts and workers (working time) which are absolutely essential to production." In the original Toyota model, three types of waste were identified by their Japanese names:

1. *Muri* means waste and decreased productivity that result from the unreasonable work managers impose on people and machines because of the poor design of systems. Examples are assignments that require employees to carry excessively heavy weights or engage in dangerous tasks.
2. *Mura* refers to unevenness in the production process, out-of-balance workflows, and uneven workloads. The essence of lean production is to strike a balance between supply and demand, customers and suppliers, workloads and capacity, and so forth. Fluctuations in supply, bottlenecks that result from poor scheduling, or resources that are unavailable may occur if a poor system design leads a production imbalance. This imbalance can lead to excessive wear and tear on equipment, facilities, and people (*muri*), which in turn can create wasteful nonvalue adding (*muda*) activities, such as excess inventories and waiting time.
3. *Muda* is any wasteful activity that does not add value or is unproductive. It also refers to waste that occurs from any variation in output as a result of poorly planned and designed systems. For example, any activity or process that consumes more resources than necessary to produce or deliver the product or service customers actually want is *muda*. Lean approaches are primarily designed to eliminate *muda* from operations.

The ultimate goal of a lean system is to achieve a smooth and rapid flow of materials and work by eliminating nonvalue-adding activities and to improve operations continuously so that products and services have value-added benefits. The extent to which this goal is achieved depends on three factors: eliminating disruptions, keeping the system flexible, and eliminating waste. Table 14.1 on page 504 identifies eight common sources of waste in a company.

Another element in the philosophy of lean operations is commitment to the **Five S (5S)** practices that guide worker behavior and management objectives. The 5S framework is a model for showing how to implement lean practices in any business operation. (Think of the model as a checklist for assessing the quality of a firm's approach to lean.) The 5S's include:

Muri: waste and decreased productivity that result from the unreasonable work managers impose on people and machines because of the poor design of systems

Mura: unevenness in the production process, out-of-balance workflows, and uneven workloads

Muda: any wasteful activity that does not add value or is unproductive

Five S (5S): a model for showing how to implement lean practices in any business operation, including (a) sort and separate, (b) simplify and straighten, (c) shine, (d) standardize, and (e) sustain

TABLE 14.1: Nine Common Sources of Waste[7]

SOURCES OF WASTE	EXAMPLES
1. Waste from overproduction and excess inventory (*mura*)	Producing a product or service before it is actually needed. Overproduction contributes to unnecessary inventory and longer lead times.
2. Waste from waiting time (*muda*)	Production delays that waste the time of personnel. When a product is not moving or being processed, downstream resources are idle.
3. Waste from unnecessary transportation (*muda*)	The excessive movement and handling of a product between processes, which can damage or degrade it without adding value to it. For example, having to deliver inputs to storage facilities prior to their use leads to wasted time and effort, and it increases the likelihood that they will sustain damage.
4. Waste from defective products (*muda*)	Defects in product quality that lead to rework and scrap. Rework leads to additional inspection costs, yield losses, and the loss of goodwill on the part of customers.
5. Waste from inappropriate processing (*muda*)	Using the wrong equipment, tools, or procedures. Using unnecessarily complicated or expensive equipment instead of simpler and flexible machinery will waste money, as do processes that are not streamlined.
6. Waste from the underutilization of workers (*mura*)	The failure to use workers' knowledge and creativity and realize their full potential.
7. Waste from unnecessary motion (*muri*)	Unnecessary efforts, including bending, stretching, lifting, walking, or other movements. Poor machinery placement or the need to move equipment wastes time and leads to injuries.
8. Misguided effort (*muda*)	Manufacturing poorly conceived goods or services that do not meet the demands of customers.

 Lean Practices

1. **Sort and separate.** Sort out and retain everything that is needed for the work area. Separate and remove all unnecessary items (parts, tools, and equipment) or procedures (paperwork, unnecessary checks) from the work area. Doing so will remove clutter, simplify the work space, and make flows more open and orderly.
2. **Simplify and straighten.** Organize and arrange what is left into a logical pattern of work operations or simplified set of motions for the worker.
3. **Shine.** Clean the area daily. Eliminate all forms of contamination, dirt, refuse, or discarded materials.
4. **Standardize.** Make all activities standard and uniform. Eliminate variation from the workflow by establishing operating procedures. Standardize the use of equipment and employee training so that any variations or deviations will be obvious.
5. **Sustain.** Avoid deviating from the first four S's, and embed these practices throughout the company's operations. That is, make sure that all employees remain motivated to sustain the effort, and reward them for their adherence to it.

14.3

Outline the elements of lean operations systems.

Incrementalism: the idea that improvements may not come from any one big fix but from a steady stream of small adjustments

Dependence: the idea that an adjustment to one element in a process will have implications for other elements in the same process

14.3 Elements of Lean Systems

If the critical goal for any operation is to remove waste, the key question is "how?" The first point to remember is that the move to a lean process is ongoing. It is not a one-time activity. The Japanese term for continuous improvement is *kaizen* (see Chapter 5). Kaizen is a perspective that can best be understood if contrasted to the Western saying, "If it ain't broke, don't fix it." In fact, under kaizen, the system can *always* be fixed or improved. The goal of a firm should be to take a critical look at its operations on an ongoing basis and determine what improvements can be made and how they can be accomplished. Improvement may not come from any one big fix but from a steady stream of small adjustments. This is the idea of incrementalism.

Finally, the processes are usually linked together in some way, which means that adjustments to one element in a process (improving one step) will have implications for other steps in the chain. This is the idea of dependence. For example, suppose you work bussing tables in a restaurant, and its managers want to increase the usage rate of those tables. That is, the managers want a great turnover of customers per hour. You may discover a faster way to clear tables (one step in the chain), but unless the next employee in the process (the waiter) can also increase the speed at which he or she takes orders and delivers food, the new clearing approach will not improve the overall speed of the system. In the following sections, we will discuss several different ways to design a lean system. Keep in mind that underlying them all is the principle of kaizen.

Workflow and Throughput

Workflow simply describes any process that consists of a sequence of connected steps or operations necessary to complete a task. For example, the workflow to treating a patient at a hospital emergency room might consist of (a) registering the patient; (b) performing a preliminary evaluation of the person, including taking his or her blood pressure and temperature; (c) having a physician consult with the patient; (d) conducting X-rays and running blood tests; and (e) diagnosing and treating the patient. The more logically and simply we can sequence the workflow sequence, the more repeatable the operations are and the more likely that the system can run efficiently.

Looking at a system's throughput is one way to measure efficiency. **Throughput** is a measure (usually in terms of time or units) of how an order moves from receipt to delivery. Organizations constantly evaluate their throughput to detect inefficiencies or errors that cause delays and add costs. In the case of an emergency room, the hospital strives to eliminate unnecessary delays at any stage that force patients to wait to complete the necessary steps in their treatment. The longer the delays, the more inefficient the process is, and the greater the overall costs to the hospital are. The costs can result from bottlenecks and the dissatisfaction of customers. In other organizations, such as manufacturing firms, delays in throughput can lead to inventory accumulation and storage costs.

Pull Systems Versus Push Systems

Push and pull systems describe different types of throughput in organizations. **Push systems** are systems in which services or products are produced based on forecasts. That is, a certain amount of the good is produced before customers actually demand it. In **pull systems**, by contrast, the product or service is only produced after it is ordered, not in advance. Pull systems characterize the lean philosophy.

To demonstrate, suppose you owned two fast-food restaurants: We'll call them "Instant Burger" and "Custom Burger." Instant Burger prides itself on filling customer orders instantly, with no delays or errors. Instant Burger is located directly across the street from a large plant that employs more than 500 people who each have a 30-minute lunch break. Obviously these people value fast service. You know from experience that you can expect anywhere between 100 and 150 workers to arrive within a 10-minute window of time. The smartest production system in this case would be to cook many hamburgers in advance and have the food prepared and ready for the lunch rush—in other words, to implement a push system. A push system would also help you minimize any variation across the burgers as you prepare them. Timing is also critical: If the burgers are made too early, they will get cold or soggy.

Push systems depend on good planning and stocking the product in advance. Too much food prepared too early leads to waste and will cut into your profit margins. Consequently, you must create a balance between making sure that enough burgers are available to your customers when they want them and not producing so many that they must be thrown out if they are not purchased.

At your other restaurant, Custom Burger, your goal is to provide gourmet hamburgers to customers on an as-ordered basis. Each order is unique and will be filled after it has been placed. This is a pull system. Materials are pulled from inventory, and the burgers are produced only when they are needed. This eliminates a great deal of waste. With a pull system, you purposely sacrifice some delivery speed to minimize waste. A critical issue with pull systems is to pay particular attention to demand and inventory levels. As orders are pulled through the system and produced, inventory levels will dip and must be replenished. Moreover, the use of pull systems ultimately leads to far smaller initial inventory levels, which can make a shortage of it all the more acute.

Deciding whether to use a push or pull system depends on an organization's operating philosophy or type of industry in which it competes. Consider the hair salon industry. In this industry, it is impossible to stockpile hairdos. They are produced and delivered only when they have been ordered. For other businesses, push systems make perfect sense.

Focused Factories

One useful option for eliminating waste and making operations more efficient is the creation of focused factories or specialized plants that are built and operated for

---

Workflow: any process that consists of a sequence of connected steps or operations necessary to complete a task

Throughput: a measure (usually in terms of time or units) of how an order moves from receipt to delivery

Push systems: systems in which services or products are produced based on forecasts

Pull systems: systems in which the product or service is only produced after it is ordered

Determining to use a pull system or a push system depends largely on a company's goals. A fast-food restaurant looking to provide high volumes of the same types of burgers would benefit from a push system while a restaurant that serves highly customizable made-to-order burgers should use a pull system.

©iStockphoto.com/sorendls

a single purpose. For example, a focused factory for Samsung (Ridgefield Park, NJ) might make only LCD televisions rather than the full range of Samsung's electronic products. The narrower focus of these factories can lead to greater efficiencies. Focused factories also do not require as many workers with multiple skills. Toyota, for example, has 12 plants located in the vicinity of Toyota City in Japan. Each one concentrates on building specific models of cars instead of trying to manufacture the full range of Toyota products. By focusing on just a few models, each plant can dramatically improve its throughput.

Value Stream Mapping (VSM)

A company's **value stream** is best understood as the sequence of activities required to design, produce, and provide a good or service, and along which information, materials, and work flow.[8] Value stream mapping (VSM), which is a prerequisite to converting to a lean system, can enable managers, production workers, and suppliers to identify waste and pinpoint the causes of it. The method involves creating a visual map of the production process that shows its cycle time, downtime, work-in-process inventory, movement of materials, and information flow. The map will help a manager visualize both individual activities and the overall state of the system—at the single process level, at the entire plant level, and even across the entire supply chain. The map, in turn, can guide you toward a future desired state and a possible implementation plan. VSM is essentially a communication tool, a business-planning tool, and a mechanism for managing your process change in an efficient manner.

Manufacturing processes that are reasonably routine and standardized are most likely to benefit from value stream mapping. Unlike a typical process flow chart, a VSM is much broader. It shows the big picture of how value is added, not just processes. Consequently, managers can identify sources of wasteful, nonvalue-adding activities and eliminate them.

The first step in VSM is to select the product or service to map. Choose a process that would benefit from implementing leaner, more efficient practices. It's important to define the scope of your map. Identify the start and end points, and make sure you map from one end of the process to the other so you can find the location of the blockages and nonvalue activities. You also need to identify which part of the overall process you need to look at. As an example, if the amount of profit you're generating from each order is falling, then you may want to look at how an entire order is fulfilled. If the volume of orders is falling, then you may want to look at the sales process in more detail. If equipment and resources are used to make multiple products, instead of looking at the manufacturing of one product, you might want to perceive manufacturing as a whole system.

Let's now look at the value stream for an order processing and delivery system. We will create a map of the process of transforming an Internet order into a shipped product. The tasks involved in order processing and delivery are order entry and processing, supplier liaison, inventory management, order picking, packaging, and shipping.

- **Phase 1.** The customer places an order that is received through the firm's order processing system. The order could have been placed by phone, through the Internet, or by some other method. The following figure shows this portion of the map.

Phase 1 of the Value Stream Mapping Process

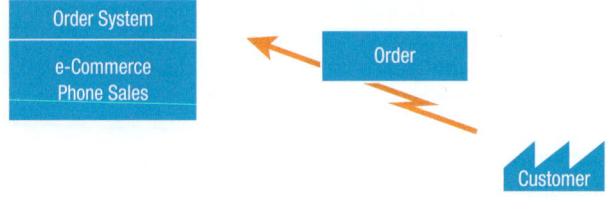

Value stream: the sequence of activities required to design, produce, and provide a good or service, and along which information, materials, and work flow

- **Phase 2.** In the second phase, the order processing system relays the order information to the inventory control system. Assuming there is no available inventory in stock for that item, an order for it is then sent to the supplier. The following figure shows this portion of value stream added onto the previous map.

Phase Two of the Value Stream Mapping Process

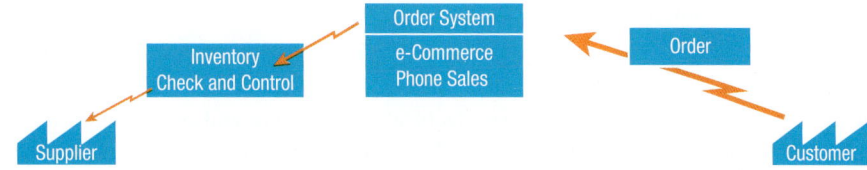

- **Phase 3.** The inventory control system relays the order information to the warehouse for processing. The supplier delivers the order in three weeks, which is stored as inventory (triangle labeled I, for inventory) in the warehouse. The order placed by the customer is then picked, checked for accuracy, packaged, and shipped to the customer. Figure 14.1 shows the fully completed VSM for this operation.

FIGURE 14.1: Completed Value Stream Map[9]

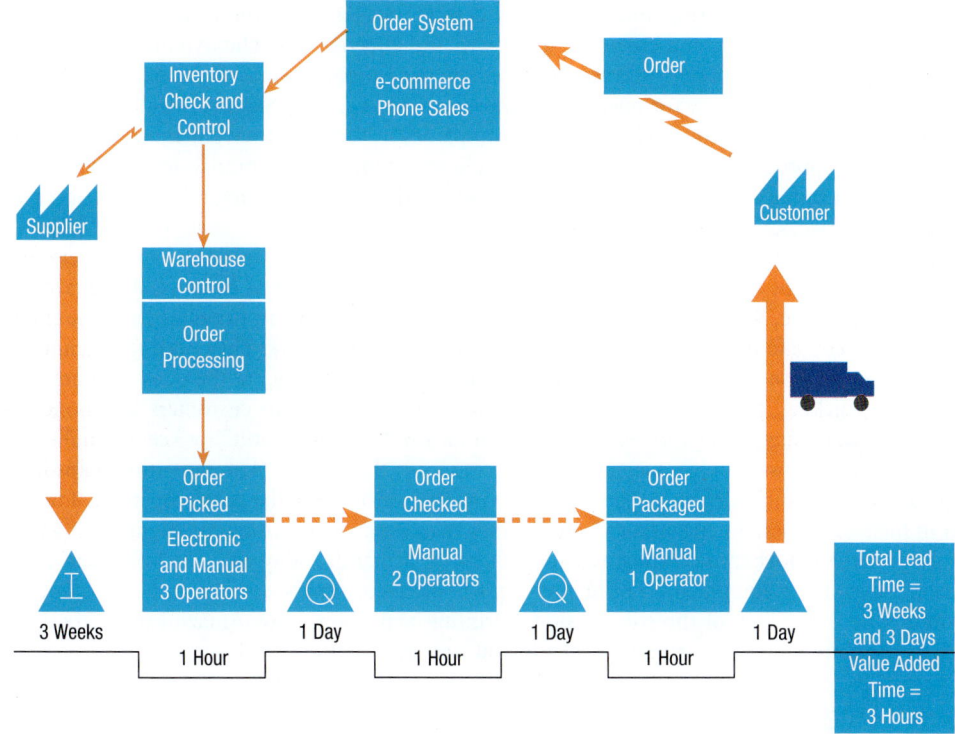

The completion of a value stream map allows you to examine the flow of order placement and processing critically. For example, the full VSM allows you to examine the amount of value-added time as a proportion of the total lead time for order placement and fulfillment. In this example, 24 days (a full three weeks and three days) are needed from the order placement to the receipt of the good. One way of reducing the end lead times of three weeks could be to arrange more frequent orders from the supplier. This would move orders more rapidly through the order processing system and lead to much quicker shipments to customers. The steps that can be used to construct a VSM are presented in Appendix 14.2 to this chapter.

Quality and Lean Systems

Total quality management or TQM, which we discussed in Chapter 5, includes several elements, such as worker responsibility for quality, statistical quality control, the use of fail-safe methods, and systematic or automatic inspection of the manufacturing process. Built-in quality and defective-free processes are absolute prerequisites for lean operations. The use of Six Sigma methodology, improved product design, standard product configurations, and fewer parts reduces the variability in both the product and the process and improves quality.

Lean Six Sigma

Although distinct and separate, the lean manufacturing philosophy and Six Sigma are both vital concepts. Each is required to reduce waste and add value to the end customer. Many leading companies that have used both lean and Six Sigma methods in the past for operational improvements have combined the lean methods and Six Sigma approaches, now referred to as **Lean Six Sigma**, to realize innovations throughout the enterprise that extend beyond operational improvement. The use of Lean Six Sigma in these companies has produced breakthrough innovations resulting in profound impacts on their business performance. More importantly, the use of Lean Six Sigma has eliminated the biggest innovation obstacle in these companies—complacency and unsupportive organizational cultures—by creating an organizational climate in which innovation has become instinctive.[10]

The Lean Six Sigma approach draws on the knowledge, methods, and tools of both the lean and Six Sigma approaches derived from decades of operational improvement, research, and implementation. Although lean approaches focus on reducing cost through optimization of the manufacturing process, Six Sigma focuses on meeting customer requirements and stakeholder expectations and on improving quality by measuring and eliminating defects. Nevertheless, the goal of Lean Six Sigma extends beyond cost cutting and efficiency to growth and effectiveness. The dynamic changes in the competitive global marketplace force companies to change on a massive scale from improvement to *innovation*. Despite its past use for operational improvements, Lean Six Sigma is ideally suited for this step change in target and scope. Many leading companies in the world have demonstrated that the Lean Six Sigma approach can go far beyond the applications for process improvement. These companies have used Lean Six Sigma to innovate in all areas of their businesses including their operations, products and services, and even their business models.[11]

The Six Sigma approach has served as a catalyst for broad-scale innovation in almost every industry, and all firms that have adopted Six Sigma have realized substantial benefits. At Amazon.com (aka Amazon, Seattle, WA), for example, Six Sigma is widely used by an organization that employs thousands of people in its order fulfillment and customer service centers. They need the commitment of all workers at these centers for the program to succeed because they are the ones who are receiving, stowing, picking, packing, and sending packages or responding to customers by phone, chat, or e-mail. Amazon has worked to reinvent the lean idea of "autonomation" by keeping humans for high-value, complex work while using machines to support those tasks. Autonomation helps human beings perform tasks in a defect-free and safe way by only automating the basic, repetitive, low-value steps in their processes. So enthusiastic is Amazon's management regarding Six Sigma that they are exploring ways to move into creating actual products on demand. Today, in some fulfillment centers, Amazon uses printing equipment to print and ship a book to customers within four hours of receiving the order. The technology of three-dimensional printing may soon allow Amazon to create its own products for customers—the ultimate in lean just-in-time production![12]

Quality at the Source

The Japanese word *jidoka*, or quality at the source, means doing it right the first time and stopping production should something go wrong. Workers are personally responsible for the quality of their own work. If someone finds a quality-related problem, he or she is empowered to stop the process by turning on a visual signal. The purpose of stopping the process is to prevent the defective parts from moving forward in a manufacturing facility. Production will not resume until the quality problem is fixed.

To demonstrate how *jidoka* works, assume that a product moves through a sequence of seven manufacturing steps. Also assume that you have found a defective part after completion of all activities in the third step. Unless you stop the assembly line, the defective product will move all the way through the system. Additional work will be done on the product in the fourth, fifth, and sixth steps, before finally coming to the seventh and final manufacturing step. Clearly, the final product that will come off of the assembly line will be defective.

At this point, you have a choice of either discarding the bad product or sending it back through the system for rework. In either case, you incur productivity losses. The time, money, and effort expended by workers after the third manufacturing step are now wasted. Yet, if you stop the assembly line and fix the quality at the source, you solve the problem immediately with little waste, and you send a strong signal to your staff members that they are critical not just to the production process but also to your firm's overall commitment to quality.

Lean Six Sigma: an approach that draws on the knowledge, methods, and tools of both the lean and Six Sigma approaches, derived from decades of operational improvement, research, and implementation, extends beyond cost cutting and efficiency to growth and effectiveness, and is ideally suited for this step change in target and scope.

Jidoka: a Japanese term meaning quality at the source; a production philosophy of doing it right the first time and stopping production should something go wrong

Consider This 14.1:
Calculating Takt Time

Calculating Takt Time

Takt time is simply the cycle time needed to match our production rate to demand for the product.

There is a simple formula for calculating Takt time:

$$\text{Takt time} = (t) \times \frac{(n)}{D}$$

where

    t = Productive operating time per shift

    n = Number of shifts

D = Desired production quantity to meet customers' requirements

Example: Suppose a manufacturing plant that produces widgets needs to produce 900 widgets in 5 days to meet the demands of customers. The plant runs 3 shifts. What is the takt time? Assume that productive operating time per shift is 420 minutes.

Because the customer needs 900 widgets in 5 days, the number of widgets that needs to be produced per day is 900 ÷ 5 = 180 widgets per day. This is the desired production capacity per day. Therefore, the takt time is:

$$\frac{420 \text{ minutes} \times 3 \text{ shifts}}{180 \text{ widgets}} = 7 \text{ minutes per widget}$$

Plant Layouts That Balance Workflow

The goal of a plant layout in lean operations is to design it to achieve a balanced workflow. The plant layout design should also link the internal and external logistics systems to the layout. **Internal logistics systems** are all the management and movement of materials within a manufacturing facility, such as raw materials and parts, work-in-process inventory, and finished goods. **External logistics systems** refer to the collection, transportation, and distribution of goods between suppliers and the plant, as well as between the plant and consumers. This includes managing the external movement of goods through various transportation modes (rail, motor, air, water, or pipeline), their storage in warehouses or distribution centers, and their subsequent distribution.

Stable Schedules

Variations in production volumes are caused by such factors as late deliveries, machine breakdowns, quality problems, and poor worker performance. As a hedge against these problems, companies tend to carry inventory, which can be expensive and is considered a form of waste. Lean production requires that daily production schedules in a repetitive flow environment should be stable for extended time horizons. Schedule stability is accomplished through level schedules, frozen windows, and underutilization of capacity. In a **level schedule**, materials are pulled through the assembly line at a steady rate to allow production activities to respond efficiently to the pull signals. To minimize inventory levels, lean operations tend to underutilize capacity. **Frozen windows** are specific time periods in which production levels cannot be changed. Leveling out the workload or smoothing production to achieve stable schedules, to achieve a steady flow of work, and to eliminate waste is called **uniform plant loading** (or *heijunka*, in Japanese).

Suppose a manufacturing plant produces three types of shoes. The plant's production cycles for each, which are shown in Table 14.2, are referred to as **takt time**. (*Takt* is the German term for rhythm). The essence of lean manufacturing systems is that they operate at a pace, or rhythm, determined by the customer.

Let's assume that for a shoe company, the proportions of sneakers (S), sandals (Sn), and dress shoes (D) demanded are 50%, 25%, and 25%. The takt times for each of these models are:

Dress shoes: 1.0 unit every 6 minutes

Sandals: 1.0 unit every 3 minutes

Sneakers: 1.0 unit every 6 minutes

Suppose the firm knew that it needed to produce footwear in the following quantities every month: sandals (4,000), dress shoes (2,000), and sneakers (2,000). Under a more conventional mass production system, we would most likely order production first to produce all 4,000 sandals, then retool the assembly line to make all the required dress shoes, and finally retool again to make the 2,000 sneakers.

Internal logistics system: all the management and movement of materials within a manufacturing facility, such as raw materials and parts, work-in-process inventory, and finished goods

External logistics system: the collection, transportation, and distribution of goods between suppliers and the plant, as well as between the plant and consumers

Level schedule: a schedule stability method where materials are pulled through the assembly line at a steady rate to allow production activities to respond efficiently to the pull signals

Frozen windows: specific time periods in which production levels cannot be changed

Uniform plant loading: leveling out the workload or smoothing production to achieve stable schedules, to achieve a steady flow of work, and to eliminate waste

TABLE 14.2: Production Cycles and Quantities for Three Types of Footwear Produced at the Same Plant

MODEL	MONTHLY QUANTITY (IN UNITS)	DAILY QUANTITY (IN UNITS)	MODEL CYCLE TIME (IN MINUTES)
Sandals	4,000	200	3
Dress shoes	2,000	100	6
Sneakers	2,000	100	6

Unfortunately, there are problems with this "unleveled" schedule. First, customers do not always buy predictably. The plant will manufacture a certain number of each type of shoe based on forecasted demand. But, as you know, forecasts aren't always accurate. Suppose, for example, the purchases of sneakers unexpectedly jump in one month. Obviously, we don't want to run out of sneakers for customers to buy because it will result in lost sales. If we have not scheduled to handle this increase in orders, we will be forced to produce a larger number of the sneakers and hold them in inventory until they are sold. This increased production of sneakers and the resulting inventory will increase our costs and leave us less time and money to produce sandals and dress shoes. One approach that companies use to handle this predicament is to use safety stock. **Safety stock** is the minimal level of inventory that a company seeks to have on hand at all times to act as a buffer against the mismatch between forecasted and actual demand.

A second problem is the risk of unsold goods. If we cannot sell all the sneakers we produce, we must continue to maintain them in inventory. Third, the use of resources becomes unbalanced. There are different work requirements to make sneakers as compared with sandals (perhaps sneakers take more labor time and materials to produce). So, the plant may need more workers and materials shipments. Our suppliers now must carry larger inventories as well to accommodate our uneven orders. As you can see, even a small change in the demand for sneakers by consumers has a *bullwhip effect* on the entire system. That is, the last-minute change in consumer demand affects so many processes that it gets magnified throughout the production line and the supply chain.

The way to resolve this problem is to have set monthly output rates for all three types of footwear and then make small adjustments to them at the end of the process based on updated demand numbers. Toyota pioneered this practice of a **mixed-model production cycle**. The same mixture of products is produced every day in small quantities. The advantage of a mixed-model production cycle is that several models can be produced initially without a changeover of equipment. The mixed-model production cycle helps smooth out the demand that upstream suppliers face too. An example of a mixed-model production cycle is shown in Table 14.2.[13]

A mixed-model production system may complicate line operations to some extent. Nevertheless, stabilizing the labor requirements for the production process, streamlining and simplifying upstream operations, as well as the inventory, scheduling, and transportation that connect the line with these upstream operations, far outweigh this minor inconvenience.

Faster Setup Times

The changeover of equipment, tools, fixtures, and cleaning—all of which must be done to produce one product or service versus another—reduces a firm's throughput. One way to shorten setup times is to differentiate between internal setups and external setups. Internal setups are activities that require machinery to be stopped or the process to be shut down for the setup work to be completed. External setups refer to work that can be completed outside of the process and do not require machinery to be stopped or the process to be shut down.

Converting internal setup activities into external setup activities can significantly reduce the amount of downtime. This conversion requires some preparation, however. For example, for in an injection molding process, workers could preheat the dies and set the controls for the plastic injection molding machines as an external setup activity. This will reduce the internal setup time. A rule of thumb for setup times is to aim for a change that takes less than 10 minutes. As an example, it takes a race team at the Indianapolis 500 less than one minute to change all four tires and fill a car's fuel tank. This kind of efficiency can only occur after hours of practice. Yet, it also requires a logical flow of all equipment. All tools and materials must be laid out in an orderly way and be sequenced

Takt time: the cycle time needed to match our production rate to demand for the product

Safety stock: the minimal level of inventory that a company seeks to have on hand at all times to act as a buffer against the mismatch between forecasted and actual demand

Mixed-model production cycle: a production method where the same mixture of products is produced every day in small quantities

Internal setups: activities that require machinery to be stopped or the process to be shut down for the setup work to be completed

External setups: work that can be completed outside of the process and does not require machinery to be stopped or the process to be shut down

correctly and within reach when needed. In a factory, the same rules apply: To get setup times to take 10 minutes or less takes time, training, and a careful plan.

Group Technology

Group technology (GT), which we discussed in the context of cellular manufacturing layouts in Chapter 9, is effective in achieving lean production because it addresses the need for this product variety demanded by customers by facilitating customization while reducing costs by standardizing processes.

Kanban Systems

The Japanese term *kanban* means "sign" or "designated place." Kanban systems are manual control systems that use containers and cards. Kanbans are visual signals used to tell workers when it is time to get or make more of something. The production of goods and the delivery of parts are triggered by the demand from a firm's downstream operations. This simple example will demonstrate how a single-card Kanban system works: Your firm, Fly-rite Golf, manufactures premium golf balls. A container with a Kanban card attached holds the amount of rubber compound needed to produce a day's worth of balls. When a downstream user of the rubber compound empties that container, he removes the card and places it on a receiving post. The empty container is then taken to the storage area, refilled, and the card is reattached to the container. The cycle then continues.

Instead of a single card, many companies use a two-card Kanban system. Figure 14.2 shows how a two-card system works. Both production and withdrawal Kanban cards are used. The plant in this example has both a fabrication cell and an assembly line:

1. The container next to the fabrication cell has a production Kanban card, whereas the one near the assembly line has the withdrawal Kanban card.
2. When the last piece of Item A is removed from the container near the assembly line, the withdrawal Kanban card from that container is also removed and placed in the fabrication cell storage area.
3. Next, a worker from the fabrication cell area finds another full container of Item A. She then removes the production Kanban card from that container and attaches the withdrawal Kanban card in its place. The withdrawn Kanban card sends a signal to the assembly cell that the items are ready for use, whereas the production Kanban card that was removed signals the fabrication cell to produce another batch of Item A.

Other visual devices can be used instead of cards, such as flags or bright lights. It is also important to note that use of the Kanban system is not restricted to just a manufacturing facility. It can also be used to coordinate suppliers and manufacturing plants.

Racing pit crews illustrate how fast setup times can make or break an operation.

William West/AFP/Getty Images

FIGURE 14.2: Two-Card Kanban System

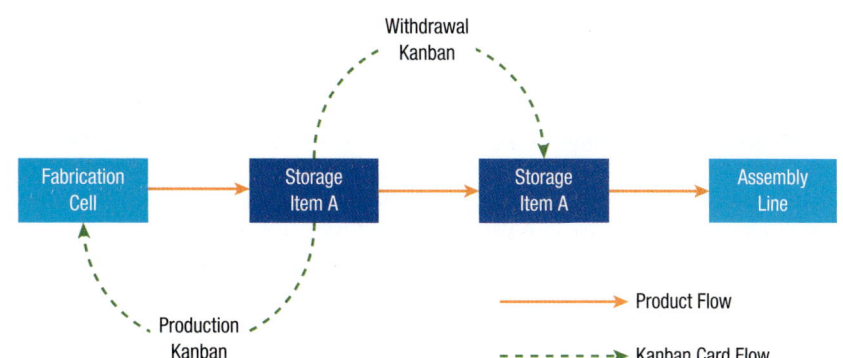

Kanban system: a manual control system that uses visual signals (cards or Kanbans) to tell workers when it is time to get or make more of something

OPERATIONS PROFILE:
Kanban Systems at Dell

Michael Dell founded Dell Computer Corporation (now Dell Inc., Round Rock, TX) in 1984 with only US$1,000 in start-up capital. Since these modest beginnings, the company has grown to be the second largest computer manufacturer in the world, with daily sales of more than US$5 million. Dell factories in the United States, Ireland, Malaysia, China, and Brazil support sales in more than 170 countries.

Customizing Dell's computer products—hardware, software, and networking—to meet the specific needs of each consumer has been one key to the company's success. Dell uses a basic platform for its computers, to which are added the various components each order specifies. Building computers to suit individual consumer orders means that Dell operates with extremely lean inventory levels. Most of the firms' plants carry just eight days of inventory.

Dell uses a pull method for its JIT process, including Kanban systems, to make the assembly process as orderly and efficient as possible. Suppliers and upstream workstations only deliver components when they receive a card (such as an e-mail or an empty order form) informing them of the parts that will be needed for assembly. Dell also employs an integrated Kanban that uses both transport and production Kanban signaling techniques. The transport Kanban works on a daily schedule: Components are produced by suppliers and delivered for each order for that day. The production Kanban outlines when work is to be completed by a particular workstation or cell. Based on that schedule, suppliers can determine at which point in the assembly line the particular components will be needed.

The highly complex nature of Dell's JIT pull system requires that Dell and its suppliers coordinate closely with one another. Although Dell's inventories are lean, they can leave the company's operations vulnerable to supply chain disruptions.[14]

Kanban systems also allow firms to control the flow of resources in a production process by replacing only the parts that have been consumed. When there is schedule stability, it is easy to account for parts and components that are pulled through the assembly line. This is accomplished through an inventory management process known as backflush. During the backflush process, parts that go into each unit of the product are removed from inventory and continually tallied along with the finished units produced. The backflush process ensures supplies remain consistent in the production pipeline. So, instead of ordering supplies in advance by guessing how many of them will be needed in a given period of time, they can be made available just in time.

EXAMPLE 14.1: Orion Manufacturing, Inc. is a fictional producer of a wide assortment of temperature-sensing devices. Although the company's business has been growing at the rate of 15% per year, its operations have been hampered by long lead times and poor on-time delivery. The manager responsible for this product line identified the 10 top-selling products that make up nearly 80% of sensing devices produced in one manufacturing cell. Based on demand history and forecasts, the manager estimated the monthly demand for each of the 10 sensing devices. In addition, he decided to carry two weeks of safety stock in the shipping area for each product.

Consequently, each product was assigned a finished goods Kanban that would hold two weeks' inventory of sensing devices. The number of each sensing device to be produced daily along with the takt time was determined. Next, the number of devices to be produced was multiplied by the production time per product per worker, and the resulting number was further divided by the number of workers in the cell to ensure that enough capacity was available to make the required number of products per day.

The manager also decided that at least 25 units of each product should be produced at a time in the manufacturing cell. A set of Kanban cards with instructions to produce 25 units of a sensing device totaling approximately the number needed for a two-week supply was attached to all of the finished goods Kanbans. As orders to be shipped were filled, the cards were detached and sent to production as a signal to produce sensor devices to replace those that were just shipped.

SOLUTION

Determining the number of Kanban cards and containers is a prerequisite for setting up a Kanban control system. In a finished goods Kanban system, for example, these cards represent the number

Backflush: an inventory management process in which parts that go into each unit of a product are removed from inventory and continually tallied along with the finished units produced

of containers of finished goods that flow back and forth between the production and shipping areas. Because each container represents the production lot size, the containers directly determine the amount of finished goods inventory in the system. **Lot size** refers to the predetermined quantity of an item that is either manufactured or purchased from a supplier.

To determine the correct number of Kanban containers, you need an accurate estimate of the lead time for producing the finished units. The lead time for production consists of the processing time for the container, the waiting time during production, and the transportation time to the shipping area. The number of Kanbans should be sufficient to meet the expected demand during the lead time *plus* any required safety stock. The formula used to calculate the number of Kanbans (K) is:

$$K = \frac{\text{Expected or average demand during the lead time + Safety stock}}{\text{Container quantity size}}$$

$$= \frac{d \times LT + SS}{C}$$

where:

K = the number of kanban card/container sets

d = average number of units demanded per period

LT = Lead time needed for order replenishment

SS = Safety stock expressed in units

C = Quantity size of container

Note: Both lead time and demand must be expressed in the same time units

EXAMPLE 14.2: Let's return to the Orion Manufacturing example. Remember that Orion makes temperature-sensing equipment and uses a Kanban system to pull material through its manufacturing cells. The temperature sensors are made in batches (lot sizes) of 15 units, and the cell that manufactures these devices can replenish an order for a batch of sensors in approximately five hours. The average demand for the sensors is approximately 10 per hour. Orion's managers decided to carry a safety stock of 10% of the average demand during the lead time. How many Kanban sets are needed to manage the replenishment of the temperature sensors?

 Example 14.2

SOLUTION

d = Average number of units demanded per period = 10

LT = Lead time needed for order replenishment = 5 hours

SS = Safety stock expressed in units = 10% of (d × LT) = 0.10 × 10 × 5

C = Container quantity size = 15

K = the number of kanban card/container sets

$$K = \frac{\text{Expected or average demand during the lead time + Safety stock}}{\text{Container quantity size}}$$

$$K = \frac{(10 \times 5) + 5}{15}$$

K = 3.67, or 4 (rounded up)

Orion Manufacturing needs four Kanban card sets and four containers of sensors.

Reduced Inventory

An objective of lean operations is the reduction of inventory to the lowest possible levels: the continuous commitment to finding ways to reduce inventory, not just in the obvious places such as warehouses, but also in other places where inventory can "hide," such as on a firm's plant floor, on carousels, on conveyors, or in transit. Remember that each time you reduce inventory and its locations, you are reducing waste, streamlining operations, and simplifying the steps workers need to take. For

Lot size: the predetermined quantity of an item that is either manufactured or purchased from a supplier

An example of efficient carousel operation like the one used at a Kansas City publishing company.

©iStockphoto.com/Patrick Heagney

example, a Kansas City publisher recently upgraded its sorting operations to include a horizontal carousel system arranged with four carousels per workstation. This setup streamlined the company's order fulfillment processes and minimized its inventory. The system ultimately saved the company 66% in labor costs because employees didn't have to move from shelf to shelf to fulfill orders. Instead they could stand in one place and process them.[15]

Large inventory savings cannot be realized without small and frequent shipments of purchased materials and components from a firm's suppliers. For small and frequent shipments to occur, the firm needs to develop quality standards with its suppliers and demand forecasts so it will have a good sense of the long-run demands that will be placed on its production and distribution systems. This process can be complicated. For example, Target Corporation (aka Target, Minneapolis, MN), a leading retailer, had a partially manual process for tracking inbound shipments. Employees had to input shipments manually into the company's vendor management system, which led them to make transportation decisions with limited information. Target has since implemented a fully automated order-entry system that has made the inbound shipment tracking process much more streamlined and efficient.

Improved Product Designs

Upgrading and improving the design and configuration of products is another element of lean systems. One reason Dell is so successful in shipping personalized orders is its commitment to individualization *and* standardization. That is, although all orders have customized components that are put together for individual customers, the "box" into which they are installed is a standardized unit. In this way, Dell has adopted a standard product configuration with specialized component parts and can therefore reduce the total number of parts it must order from vendors and store them at its assembly sites.

Although the application of lean techniques is used most typically in assembly-line flow processes, it can also be adapted to job-shop production processes. Settings of this type, such as factory machining centers or paint shops, produce a large variety of products in low volumes. The demand for products produced in a job shop isn't as stable as it is for flow operations because the products are customized and depend on different buyers' tastes. Nonetheless, lean techniques can be used in these situations by creating internal demand stability. For example, if demand from downstream production activities can be stabilized by reducing variations in the workflow, then a relatively smoother, just-in-time, and level production schedule can be implemented, and the benefits of lean can be realized.

Apply lean ideas to service operations.

Lean Services

14.4 Lean Services

Lean principles can be used in service industries as well as in manufacturing companies. The more that service delivery systems can be standardized, the easier it is to analyze the process and to identify ways to improve it. McDonald's (Oak Brook, IL), which has long been a leader in standardizing its operations, has adopted lean methods for supplying outlets, training employees, and delivering food to customers.

There are some important principles a service operation should follow to create a lean system. They include:[16]

- *Pinpoint the Value the Service Offers.* To implement lean operations, the service firm must understand the customers' wants and needs. How do customers perceive value in the service exchange? What is it they seek? In lean approaches, the customer determines what value is. For example, a hospital may *assume* it knows what the patient wants during treatment, but it cannot be sure. Value exists only in the eyes of the customer. Taco Bell (subsidiary of Yum! Brands, Inc., Irvine, CA), a fast-food chain, has found that customers want fast delivery, accurate orders, cleanliness, and food served at appropriate temperatures.

OPERATIONS PROFILE:
WIPRO Limited and Lean Software Development

WIPRO Limited (Bangalore, India), the world's largest software development and technology services provider, employs more than 95,000 people. WIPRO relies on lean principles. Lean processes have made it possible to avoid the bottlenecks that had been slowing the company's thousand-plus software development projects it has going on at any point in time.

As part of its lean effort, WIPRO follows these four rules, which are part of Toyota's production system:

- Rule 1: All work shall be highly specified as to content, sequence, timing, and outcome.

- Rule 2: Every customer–supplier connection must be direct, and there must be an unambiguous yes-or-no way to send requests and receive responses.

- Rule 3: The sequence for producing every product and service must be simple and direct.

- Rule 4: Any improvement must be made in accordance with carefully established methods, under the guidance of a teacher or supervisor, at the lowest possible level in the organization.

To implement its lean system, a team of WIPRO's managers visited some lean manufacturing operations to understand how the firm could apply lean principles to its operations. Shortly thereafter, more than half the company's projects were being developed with lean approaches that involved a simple set of practices. Some of these practices are:

- **Using a Simplified Organizational Structure**. WIPRO's project teams are flat. Fewer levels of hierarchy result in fewer delays.

- **Striving for Continuous Improvement**. New ideas and procedures are tested. When they are successful, they are implemented across the organization.

- **Sharing Mistakes**. When mistakes are made on a project, the results are widely shared in a nonthreatening way so they aren't repeated.

- **Specialized Tools**. Project tools and scheduling methods are tested and modified to make them as useful as possible for the types of projects WIPRO undertakes.

The results of WIPRO's lean approach have been very encouraging. Lean principles provide WIPRO with a standard way to tackle new projects, while creating significant savings across its development cycle. WIPRO started slowly, launching 10 pilot projects to see whether the lean approach was a viable option. After receiving encouraging results, the company is now fully committed to lean; in fact, of the 4,000–5,000 projects undertaken yearly by WIPRO, greater than 1,600 are lean projects. The average efficiencies and time and cost savings on new projects are now 20% better than what they used to be and are steadily improving.[17]

- *Identify the Service's Value Stream.* What is a firm's process for designing, developing, providing, and assessing the needs of its customers? How does the supply chain function? Where are the inefficiencies in the system? These critical questions are necessary for understanding the service's value stream. In a lean operation, a company must constantly monitor all the activities required to provide the service and to determine how to streamline and improve the process from the customer's point of view. Customers can identify a company's activities that add value, those that do not affect value, and those that may reduce value. For example, a cable television provider may institute an automated call service to answer technical questions, thinking it is responding to the needs of its customers. Suppose in reality, however, that the firm's technical support personnel simply can't handle the load of calls they are receiving. Perhaps they aren't trained well enough to help frustrated customers quickly. The cable provider may think it is adding value to its product. Nevertheless, it may actually be reducing value because most customers would rather talk to a human being than to an automated call.
- *Improve the Flow of the Service.* Service flow is the manner in which services are delivered to the end user. Lean service firms analyze the flow of their services to find the flaws or delivery delays that prevent the service from proceeding smoothly from the provider to the customer. To speed up its service delivery, Taco Bell remodeled its supply chain, using frequent just-in-time deliveries of preprocessed food products to decrease the firm's inventory and costs and to save space in its restaurants.
- *Be Prepared to Respond to the Pull From Customers.* Service firms have to respond to the needs of the customer at the time of the customer's choosing. Consequently, developing accurate demand forecasts for its services is critical.

- *Pursue Perfection.* The better the first four principles in service delivery are pursued, the greater the probability of satisfying the end user's desire for the highest value at lowest cost. Although perfection can never be achieved, a company can never allow itself to be satisfied with its current state. The idea behind lean systems is that there is always room for improving them.

Southwest Airlines (SWA; Southwest Airlines Co., Dallas, TX) holds the unique distinction of being one of only a handful of steadily profitable airlines during the past decade. In addition, SWA has routinely held the "triple crown awards" of fewest customer complaints, fewest late arrivals, and fewest lost bags. A close look at the airline's approach to operations shows the company is committed to resolving common problems within the airline industry by using innovative techniques some firms might even consider radical. SWA has eliminated services customers don't value. For example, after surveying fliers, the company eliminated in-flight meals. Instead, the company worked harder to provide the services that customers do expect, such as courtesy, on-time departures, and trouble-free travel. Southwest Airlines has been adept at practicing lean service delivery, and the results can clearly be seen in its steady profitability in an extremely difficult industry.

Lean philosophy has helped service providers like SWA develop processes and methods to improve their operations, streamline and cut their costs, and most importantly, satisfy their customers better at the same time. Yet, successful service operations will always be closely linked to how well a firm listens to and satisfies its customers. That is, the continuous improvement strategies that lean methods offer must always be filtered first through the lens of customer needs. Once their needs are understood, they form the goals that will shape the ability of a company to provide effective services in the most efficient way possible.

14.5 Lean Supply Chains

14.5

Identify the characteristics of a lean supply chain.

A lean supply chain is one in which the members work collaboratively to reduce cost and waste by efficiently pulling what is needed to meet the needs of the individual customer. A lean supply chain is a network of integrated organizations in which all of the supply chain partners collectively align their capabilities to meet customer demand effectively. As the Operations Profile box about Wal-Mart (Wal-Mart Stores Inc., Bentonville, AR) demonstrates, expanding lean concepts to the entire supply chain can help its members achieve higher levels of competitiveness as well.

Characteristics of Lean Supply Chain

A Lean Supply Chain

There are three types of flows common to all supply chains: product and service flows, information flows, and financial flows. To build a lean supply chain, the wastes associated with each flow should be identified and eliminated, and the fluctuations smoothed out. As the Wal-Mart box demonstrates, information technologies can successfully link all entities in the network and facilitate the fast and accurate financial flows and information flows. Furthermore, performance metrics and measurement systems should be developed to sustain the efficiency and effectiveness of these flows and for continuous improvement.

Full Collaboration Among the Supply Chain's Partners

The strength and competitive advantages of a lean supply chain result from the synergy and unity of purpose of its partners. Nevertheless, this collective power cannot be achieved without close relationships based on trust and collaboration. These relationships are necessary not only to ensure that the supply chain members can satisfy the customer but also to make each company in the supply chain profitable. These are features of lean relationships:[18]

- *Fewer suppliers.* Fewer suppliers lead to improved communication and cooperation, better control of the process, and more trusting relationships.
- *Interdependency.* In lean supply chains, there is a high degree of interdependence among the members. The result of this interdependence is stability over fixed time with a higher degree of mutually beneficial collaboration. Note that the more complex and critical the final product is, the more serious and permanent the relationships within the supply chain should be. Pfizer, Inc. (New York, NY), for example, will only work with long-term suppliers that have passed its own quality checks and adhere to the company's strategic sourcing processes.

Also, in a lean supply chain, the boundaries of the organizations become blurred, and the entire chain acts as one extended enterprise that works toward common goals.

OPERATIONS PROFILE: Lean Operations at Exempla Lutheran Medical Center

To create and maintain a sterile environment, most hospitals use positive-pressure airflow systems in their surgical rooms. The systems frequently exchange air in the rooms to keep them cool and remove microscopic sources of bacteria. Nonetheless, the sterility of the operating room is compromised when people go in and out during surgical procedures.

Employees of the Exempla Lutheran Medical Center of Denver, Colorado, examined this problem and determined that it often resulted from poor planning prior to the start of surgery. In particular, supplies, instruments, and equipment needed for a procedure were not properly identified in advance and located and placed in the rooms. Instead, as surgeons realized that an instrument was needed, they would ask assistants to leave the room and locate it.

Exempla solved the problem by applying lean principles to the delivery of surgical health care. The medical center developed a streamlined flow process. For example, prior to the start of a surgery, a doctor is now required to supply a list of all instruments, equipment, and other supplies that will likely be needed. These supplies are located in advance and placed in a case cart that is assigned to the surgical room. Missing-item tags attached to the front of the case carts identify which items need to be located and replaced or added prior to the start of a procedure.

The process is especially useful when doctors perform multiple procedures as they are not required to leave the room between operations. Furthermore, the hospital periodically evaluates the doctor's preference list requests as compared with actual usage and eliminates unused or unnecessary items. In this way, doctors and staff constantly review and update their requests. To promote continuous improvement, post-case briefings help to identify problems related to missing equipment or supplies.

Together, these process improvements have led to a 32% reduction in foot traffic in and out of surgical rooms during procedures, and they have dramatically cut down the incidence of surgical-site infections. By employing a lean services philosophy, Exempla Lutheran Medical Center has reduced waste, simplified and improved the flow of its surgical procedures, and adopted continuous improvement practices. These changes have had a positive impact on the hospital staff, but most importantly, they have improved the health-care treatment delivered to patients.[19]

Transparent Information

As much information as possible, including actual and forecasted customer demand, market opportunities, and responsibilities, should be transparent and *shared* among a supply chain's members. Technology that can facilitate a seamless flow of information contributes to the success of lean supply chains. Many information technology (IT) systems used to facilitate information flows within supply chains use **electronic data interchange (EDI)**. EDI improves the exchange of standardized documents such as customer orders, shipment information, and bill payments between computer systems. Electronic Kanbans can be used to generate computerized documents sent to the supply chain members to signal that products and materials need to be pulled.

Companies linked with warehouse management and *radio frequency identification (RFID)* systems can track and trace electronically the materials and products that move among the supply chain members. The IT systems should also provide supply chain partners with real-time information about inventory levels and the status of orders, which are crucial to pull systems. This information helps managers examine historical sales and order information to discover demand patterns and, eventually, to develop accurate forecasts. Last, the information systems in lean supply chains have to play the dual role of maintaining transparency while guarding security. That is, the systems need to provide all of the necessary information to be shared among supply chain partners while securing information that is proprietary, such as patents or other confidential and valuable company information.

The Internet has made developing lean supply chains systems information somewhat easier. Instead of linking all of their separate IT systems, the firms in a supply chain can exchange information over the Internet. Using a joint website that all the firms can easily access, the companies can coordinate their activities. For example, Wal-Mart requires all their suppliers to use their online Retail Link system to coordinate their activities relative to Wal-Mart's needs. The system offers real-time information to vendors on various issues, such as determining which stores are out of stock of particular items or the percentage of Wal-Mart shoppers that buy their product. Often a key supply chain partner (usually the leader) manages and maintains the site.

Electronic data interchange (EDI): technology that facilitates a seamless flow of information to improve the exchange of standardized documents such as customer orders, shipment information, and bill payments between computer systems

OPERATIONS PROFILE: Wal-Mart's
Lean Supply Chain Operations

Wal-Mart is a leader in global supply chain operations, and some of the company's innovations serve as industry standards for organizing and maintaining a lean supply chain.

In the millions of retail firms that still use manual inventory counting and reorder systems, workers must physically walk the aisles of the stores and make an actual count of items on the shelves, compare these numbers to the inventory level, and only then, determine whether to reorder the individual items. From there, the worker fills out a purchase order and telephones the company's central warehouse, where the order is placed.

All of these steps cost the company money in terms of labor, paper supplies, lost sales when customers don't wait for the out-of-stock items to arrive, and excessive inventory holding costs when too much of a good is stocked. Kmart's (subsidiary of Sears Holding Corporation, Hoffman Estates, IL) order entry systems, for example, have been so poor that in the past, the company's stores were forced to rent truck container units and place them in their parking lots to store excess inventory. There was no room inside the stores! In fact, manual reorder systems have historically been so bad that they have led to a whole new retail store category—stores that sell products that were overstocked at other stores. T.J. Maxx (subsidiary of TJX Companies, Framingham, MA), Marshalls (subsidiary of TJX Companies, Framingham, MA), and Big Lots (Big Lots, Inc., Columbus, OH) are examples of stores that take advantage of such overstocked merchandise and resell it at a discount.

Compare this approach with that pioneered by Wal-Mart. When you purchase a new broom from your local Wal-Mart store, the cash register reads the broom's barcode. Within 14 seconds, Wal-Mart's central warehouse is notified that the broom was sold and needs to be replenished. The same system notifies the broom manufacturer that new stock is needed. Even the firms that supply the wood and brush materials (the raw materials for the broom) are notified; and so it goes, right up the supply chain. As a result, Wal-Mart can replenish items on its shelves in less than three days—not from central warehouses to the shelf but directly from the manufacturer to the shelf, which eliminates the need for warehousing space. [20]

Lean Logistics

Lean thinking should be implemented in the logistical flows of a supply chain—from raw materials to the delivery of end products or services. Several lean logistical approaches are:

- *Just-in-Time (JIT) Delivery.* JIT can facilitate a smooth physical flow of goods and materials throughout the entire supply chain. To facilitate JIT delivery, the milk run approach is frequently used. This approach involves routing a supply or delivery vehicle to make multiple pickups or drop-offs at different locations.[21] Supply chain partners in close proximity can easily adopt this approach as long as the demand fluctuations and quantities transported are not too large. The approach has the advantages of minimizing inventory and predictable lead times and of improving inventory visibility and communication among supply chain members.[22]
- *Cross-Docking.* Invented by Wal-Mart, cross-docking is a logistical approach in which goods in incoming shipments are packaged in a way that they can be easily sorted for outgoing shipments. Goods in a warehouse or distribution center that are cross-docked are directly transferred from receiving docks to shipping docks without intermediate storage. Cross-docking can reduce the handling and storage costs of the firms as well as speed up order cycle times and inventory turnover, which can improve the cash flows of the supply chain members.[23]
- *Vendor Managed Inventory (VMI).* In a vendor managed inventory (VMI) system, the management of an item at the customer's site or retail location is entirely the responsibility of the supplier of that item. For example, P&G (Procter & Gamble Co., Cincinnati, OH) manages the inventory of the items it supplies to Wal-Mart in all of its retail locations. VMI incorporates the pull concept, which is used in lean systems, and provides the benefits of improved communication between the supply chain partners and more efficient demand and inventory management in the chain.
- *Third-Party Logistics (3PL).* With increasing globalization, it is almost impossible for individual supply chain members to have their own transportation systems—their own trucks, planes, and so forth—to transport everything they need. Consequently, they rely on third-party logistics (3PL) companies such as FedEx (introduced earlier in the chapter), United Parcel Service, Inc. (aka UPS, Sandy Springs, GA), and DHL Express (division of Deutsche

Post DHL, Bonn, Germany). The members in a supply chain can contract with these 3PL companies to handle many of their logistical needs, which in turn enables them to focus on their core competencies. From a lean perspective, the key advantage of using 3PL providers is the improved and efficient product flows that can be achieved from the point of origin to the point of consumption.

- *Supplier Parks.* The extent to which companies can improve the cost and time associated with logistics is often constrained by the widely separated global locations of the supply chain members. To create a leaner supply chain, one possible option is have suppliers locate near a producer in a supplier park. The physical proximity can improve the efficiency of production and delivery of goods. For example, Nissan announced its intention to spend US$160 million on a 1.5-million square-foot supplier park to locate many of its suppliers close to its Smyrna, Tennessee, plant.[24] Yet, a supplier park is only feasible in situations where there is a high density and concentration of population and manufacturing facilities, and it is more common in countries such as Japan, China, and Taiwan. In geographically large countries such as the United States and Canada, persuading suppliers to relocate near you isn't always feasible.

Approaches to lean logistics will continue to evolve as more and more companies embrace the concept of lean supply chains. Note that lean logistics approaches will work *only* if the supply chain members mutually reinforce and cooperate with each other.

Performance Measurement and Continuous Improvement

Performance metrics can be used to gauge quantitatively how well a supply chain is performing. Time metrics assess the amount of time to process an order, transportation time, and similar variables. Cost metrics assess material and labor costs, the costs associated with returns and repairs, interest, rent, and facilities, transportation, and storage costs. Efficiency metrics evaluate inventory turnover or days of inventory on hand, as well as capacity and capital usage (ROI or cash flow). Effectiveness metrics evaluate the percentage of orders delivered on time and customer satisfaction metrics, such as number of customer complaints and percentage of returned items.[25]

The metrics often used to monitor the performance of lean supply chains are inventory turnover and days of inventory on hand. Nonetheless, several other performance metrics have been developed. An ideal starting point for determining the appropriate performance measurements to use is a value stream map. The value stream map provides a comprehensive view of the entire supply chain, including product and information flows. Using the value stream map, you can identify problem areas and then select relevant performance metrics to improve each.

Nissan decided to open a supplier park near its plant in Smyrna, Tennessee, to cut down on production and delivery costs and increase efficiency in its supply chain.

Bloomberg/Bloomberg

Supplier park: the location of multiple suppliers in close proximity to a producer to create a leaner supply chain

Time metrics: an assessment of the amount of time to process an order, transportation time, and similar variables

Cost metrics: an assessment of material and labor costs, the costs associated with returns and repairs, interest, rent, facilities, transportation, and storage

FIGURE 14.3: Simplified Timeline Chart

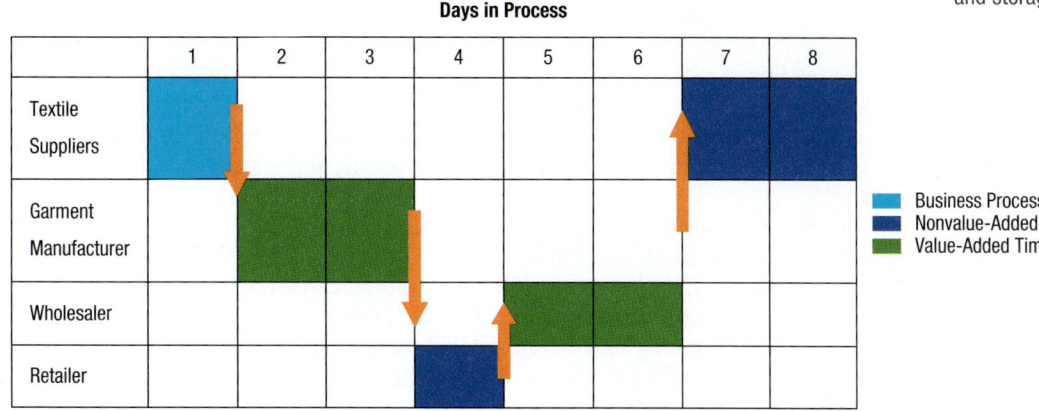

SOURCE: Rivera, L., Wan, H., Chen, F. F., & Lee, W. M. (2007). Beyond partnerships: The power of lean supply chains. In H. Jung, F. F. Chen, & B. Jeong (Eds.), *Trends in supply chain design and management* (p. 249). London, U.K.: Springer.

FIGURE 14.4: Simplified Example of a Cost-Time-Profile Map

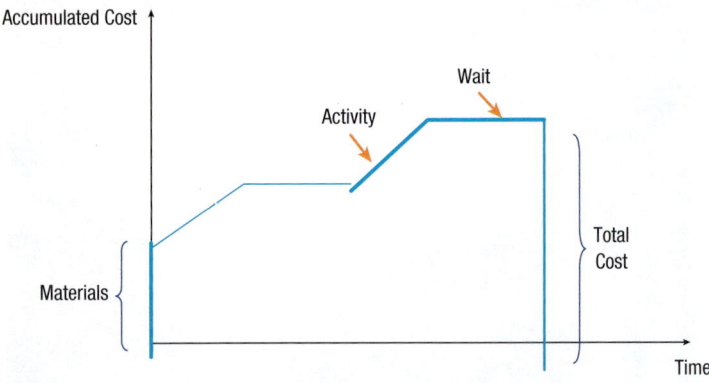

SOURCE: Rivera et al., *op. cit.*

A Global Supply Chain

14.6

Explain why it is so difficult to make global supply chains lean.

Efficiency metrics: the evaluation of inventory turnover or days of inventory on hand, as well as capacity and capital usage (ROI or cash flow)

Effectiveness metrics: the evaluation of the percentage of orders delivered on time and customer satisfaction metrics, such as number of customer complaints and percentage of returned items

Timeline chart: a tool used to track both the value-added and nonvalue-added time a product spends in various production stages

Cost-time-profile map (CTP): a map that tracks the money invested over time in a production process

In addition, a timeline chart, such as the one shown in Figure 14.3, can be used to track both the value-added and nonvalue-added time a t-shirt spends in various production stages. For example, the figure shows that there are two cells where no value-added work is being done on the t-shirt. These cells are indicated in red. The chart shows that the distributor's cycle could be shortened as well as the time the product spends with the contractor before being shipped to the customer. Using the value stream map and the timeline chart in tandem can reveal wastes in the supply chain, identify problem areas, and help pinpoint potential opportunities for improvement.

Neither the value stream map for a product nor its timeline map explicitly provides cost information about the supply chain. To overcome this shortcoming, a cost-time-profile map (CTP), such as the one shown in Figure 14.4, can be constructed. A CTP map tracks the money invested over time in a production process.[26] The advantage is that it provides supply chain managers with insight into the time value of the money invested as working capital, and it enables them to identify problem areas in the supply chain, in terms of both time and costs. For example, activities that provide no value increase the overall production cost. Likewise, the longer a product spends time as inventory represents money that could have been profitably used elsewhere.

The continuous improvement of supply chain performance is an ongoing process. One possible way to improve the performance of a lean supply chain is to develop a future-state value stream map for the chain that is similar to the map for a single firm. To create a future value stream map for a supply chain, begin selecting critical supply chain members that have the greatest impact on the flow of products as well as costs and times. Then construct a value stream map and a timeline map that reflect the desired future state of the lean supply chain, just as you would for a single operation. Implement projects to improve the performance of the lean supply chain, and then repeat the process.[27]

14.6 Lean Global Supply Chains

Global supply chains have many stages and components, and each can increase costs and create risks (or offer opportunities) for every partner. Global supply chains have at least one firm that locates portions of its supply chain in a foreign country. Firms in a global supply chain outsource some of their activities to third-party companies located elsewhere and forge partnerships with firms in other countries through strategic alliances and joint ventures.

Although lean concepts can offer benefits to supply chains, it is often difficult to make global supply chains lean. Why is that so? First, it requires coordination to establish the rapid flow of goods and information in a global supply chain. Achieving this degree of coordination across countries is expensive and difficult. Second, the frequent and often daily deliveries required for JIT inventory management are nearly impossible in a global setting because of long shipping times, infrequent freight connections, unpredictable weather delays, the bureaucracy associated with customs, and labor strikes common in some foreign countries. Third, longer lead times are required, making low inventories hard to achieve, so firms need to carry a greater amount of safety stock to avoid running short on goods. In addition, shipping numerous small quantities of products is less cost effective over long distances. Finally, the lack of face-to-face contact, time-zone differences, and cultural and language barriers can make global communication regarding the design, quality, and scheduling more expensive and less effective.[28]

Despite these obstacles, it is still possible to incorporate certain elements of lean systems in global supply chains. Some trade-offs need to be considered—for example, although JIT production and low inventories may not be feasible, it *is* possible to incorporate certain other features of lean systems such as design-for-manufacturing principles, the reduction of defects, and reduction of engineering change orders. Also, note that not all activities in a global supply chain are of equal importance in the value they add. Supply chain managers need to identify the most critical activities and evaluate the trade-offs of each.

OPERATIONS PROFILE: LESSONS LEARNED
Crocs: Getting Off on the Wrong Foot

Crocs, Inc. (Niwot, CO), the maker of the iconic shoes with quirky colors and styles, was one of the high-profile retailing success stories throughout much of its existence. With steadily increasing sales in 125 countries worldwide and an efficient global supply chain, the company's business strategy seemed to be working. A 2007 Harvard University case study praised Crocs for its flexible supply chain, which allowed it to "adjust to changes in the marketplace" and enabled its rapid and highly profitable growth.

Less than two years later, however, financial auditors at the accounting firm Deloitte (formerly known as Deloitte & Touche, owned by Deloitte Touche Tohmatsu Limited, New York, NY) expressed "substantial doubt" about Crocs. In 2008, the company lost nearly US$200 million, and the slide continued. In 2010, the company's CEO, John Duerden, resigned. The following paragraph, also from Croc's 10-K financial report, clearly summarizes the company's quick rise and fall:

> From our inception [in 2002] through the year ended December 31, 2007, we experienced rapid revenue growth and had difficulty meeting demand for our footwear products. During this period, we significantly increased our production capacity, warehouse space and inventory in an effort to meet demand. This pattern changed in 2008. Our revenue growth moderated and then began to decline during 2008 when compared to 2007. Accordingly, we evaluated our production capacity and operations structure and, in 2008, we discontinued our Canadian manufacturing operations and consolidated our Canadian distribution activities with other existing North American distribution operations, we abandoned certain equipment and molds that represent excess capacity, we discontinued manufacturing operations at our Brazilian manufacturing facility, we decreased our fixed costs by consolidating our global distribution centers and reducing our warehouse space and we reduced our global headcount by approximately 2,000 people over 2008 and into the first quarter of 2009.

How did Crocs move from an industry leader to one in danger of bankruptcy in such a short period of time? According to one expert, Crocs made several supply chain strategy mistakes. The original strategy worked extremely well when actual demand exceeded forecasted demand but not in the opposite situation. In short, the pull strategy was designed to handle order increases but could not when orders dried up.

Some industry experts suspect that the company didn't have real-time knowledge of its retailers' demand and inventory data. So, Crocs may have been a victim of the "bullwhip"—that is, small changes

Boston Globe/Boston Globe/Getty Images

in consumer demand for the shoes resulted in large swings in the demand for the many supplies needed to produce them.

What are the lessons from Crocs' rapid rise and subsequent fall? As one expert noted, "A supply chain that is best-in-class today, within a given set of conditions, can quickly lose its luster tomorrow, under a different set of conditions. The challenge is building supply chains that are robust enough to withstand a broad range of scenarios, and having enough forward visibility to economic changes and supply chain activities so that companies can take preemptive corrective actions."

Since this rocky period for Crocs, the company's performance has fluctuated. Several key acquisitions and a restructuring of its supply chain have brought the firm back to profitability. By correcting many of the original causes of its financial distress, the company then resumed its expansion to more than 600 stores worldwide, while diversifying into nearly 300 product lines for its shoes. Nevertheless, this strategy soon led to its own problems. Analysts grew concerned about the company's retail and supply chain strategies yet again as Crocs was viewed as becoming too stretched. Indeed, the overexpansion in stores and in overseas markets and into product categories including golf and fashion leather boots led the company to admit it spread itself too thin. In 2014, the financial tide seemed to shift against the company once again, with Crocs announcing that financial pressures required it to trim its shoe lines by 30% to 40% and to eliminate its high-end products. It also announced a plan to downsize its Colorado headquarters, and it closed 75–100 stores worldwide and refocused its strategy on its signature plastic molded-shoe business. The company also narrowed its geographic focus to six key markets that represent 70% of its sales: the United States, Japan, China, Korea, Germany, and the United Kingdom. Although Crocs's experience with serious financial turmoil resulted in many hard lessons, it remains to be seen whether the company has the skills and agility to stave off disaster one more time.[29]

Discuss how sustainability initiatives can be considered to be an extension of the lean philosophy.

14.7 Sustainability Issues

Environmentally sustainable practices are a natural extension of lean because the pursuit of lean strategies leads companies toward sustainability initiatives. For example, the lean concept of eliminating waste is also a key objective of sustainability initiatives. Furthermore, lean tools can also be used to solve environmental problems and to reduce a firm's carbon footprint. Thus, sustainability is very much similar to lean practices, in both concept and practice; hence, they can be thought of as an extension of lean to achieve a much broader objective.[30] Both sustainability and lean systems not only share many similarities, but they also have a synergistic relationship. In fact, many companies now believe that lean processes and sustainability initiatives work hand in hand, achieving the same goal of increasing profits. For example, the following lean initiatives that companies adopt will also improve sustainability:[31]

⏵ Sustainability and Lean Systems

- **Fewer product defects:** The lean practice of attempting to minimize product defects means the use of fewer raw materials, less plant space, fewer systems, and less equipment to rework or repair, which leads to less energy consumption.
- **Eliminating overproduction:** This practice is a major focus of lean manufacturing with an emphasis on producing what you need and when you need it. Eliminating overproduction consumes fewer raw materials, uses less energy for production, and eliminates the risk of waste from the accumulation and disposal of excess inventory.
- **Minimizing wasted movement:** The lean principle of minimizing wasted movement among workers through more efficient facility layouts increases worker safety and reduces energy needed for heating, cooling, and lighting.
- **Reducing transportation:** The lean concept of minimizing unnecessary internal or external movement of materials that add no real value to the product can lead to meaningful sustainability results by decreasing energy use and the costs associated with the product.
- **Less excess inventory:** The lean practice of minimizing excess inventory means more efficient use of plant space leading to less energy use, consumption of fewer packaging and raw materials, and reduction in the risk of waste from obsolescence and undiscovered defects.
- **Reduced waiting:** One of the key concepts of lean manufacturing is to reduce waiting time for equipment, information, or materials. The lean practice of synchronizing production processes to reduce waiting can reduce production downtime, thereby leading to less wasted energy.
- **Less over-processing:** The lean practice that every step of a production process adds value to the customer leads to more efficient production processes. As a result, reduced waste lowers a company's environmental and carbon footprint.

Companies that apply lean thinking to their sustainability efforts contribute to the long-term staying power of sustainability initiatives as they add value to the company and its customers.

Application of lean principles minimizes waste and continuously improves operational efficiency. As a result, lean implementation enables a company to reduce operational costs and enhance the value provided to customers. Thus, lean implementation does support a company's desire to act in an ethically responsible manner. Yet, because lean systems force waste elimination and continuous improvement, lean implementation also has ethical implications within the organization as it can cause discomfort and stress among employees dealing with streamlined or modified jobs. Furthermore, applying lean principles may even lead to layoffs of workers with lesser skills or of those working in now redundant roles. One possible way by which a company can overcome this ethical dilemma is to guarantee the jobs of those employees who are dedicated and willing to go through additional training to support lean implementation. A company can also shift employees who lack the necessary skill levels to another position within the company where they can be productive. At a minimum, before implementing lean, a company should give its employees an honest account of the possible consequences of lean implementation.

 SAGE edge™ ....

Visit **edge.sagepub.com/venkataraman** to help you accomplish your coursework goals in an easy-to-use learning environment.

- Mobile-friendly eFlashcards
- Mobile-friendly practice quizzes
- A complete online action plan
- Chapter summaries with learning objectives
- Video and multimedia resources

CHAPTER SUMMARY

14.1 Define what lean operations are. Lean operations, including just-in-time (JIT) practices, are philosophies of continuous improvement. The goal of lean operations is to eliminate waste of any kind, a problem that affects both manufacturing and service organizations.

14.2 Describe the philosophy of lean systems. The first feature of the philosophy of lean systems is to promote respect for people. Consequently, one prerequisite for implementing a lean system is to create an environment that empowers workers and fosters cooperation, trust, and respect between a firm's workforce and managers. Second, to achieve a smooth and rapid flow of materials and work, waste and inefficiency should be eliminated. Finally, the philosophy of lean systems requires commitment to the 5S model that shows how to implement lean practices in any business operation.

14.3 Outline the elements of lean operations systems. Lean systems are based on a pull system of throughput and can include such features as focused factories, value stream mapping, TQM, quality at the source, level scheduling, faster setup times, group technology, plant layouts that balance the workflow, stable scheduling, Kanban systems, reduced inventory, and improved product designs.

14.4 Apply lean ideas to service operations. Lean systems aren't limited to manufacturing operations. A service operation can create a lean system as well by pinpointing the value the service offers, improving the flow of the service, being prepared to respond to the pull from customers, and pursuing perfection.

14.5 Identify the characteristics of a lean supply chain. The lean philosophy is equally critical to enhancing an organization's supply chain and requires four key elements: (1) the full collaboration of all supply chain partners; (2) the use of transparent information; (3) lean logistics, including third-party logistics, vendor-managed inventory, cross-docking, and supplier parks; and (4) performance monitoring.

14.6 Argue why it is so difficult to make global supply chains lean. Difficulties in creating lean global supply chains include the need for high levels of coordination, just-in-time (JIT) delivery, and low inventories as well as the need for frequent and rapid deliveries from suppliers, coordination and information flow, and effective communication. JIT practices are nearly impossible in a global setting because of long shipping times, infrequent freight connections, unpredictable weather delays, the bureaucracy associated with customs, and labor strikes that are common in some foreign countries. The lack of face-to-face contact, time zone differences, and cultural and language barriers can make coordinating global supply chains even more difficult. Once these obstacles are overcome, however, the lean supply chain's advantages can be significant.

14.7 Discuss how sustainability initiatives can be considered an extension of lean. Both sustainability and lean systems share many similarities, and they a have synergistic relationship. Many of the lean initiatives that companies adopt, such as reducing product defects and inventory reduction, will also improve sustainability. In addition, both lean and sustainability initiatives also have the same goal of increasing profits.

KEY TERMS

Backflush   512

Cost metrics   519

Cost-time-profile map (CTP)   520

Dependence   504

Effectiveness metrics   520

Efficiency metrics   520

Electronic data interchange (EDI)   517

External logistics system   509

External setups   510

Five S (5S)   503

Frozen windows   509

Incrementalism   504

Internal logistics system   509

Internal setups   510

Jidoka   508

Just-in-time (JIT)   502

Kanban system   511

Lean philosophy   502

Lean Six Sigma   508

Level schedule   509

Lot size   513

Mixed-model production cycle   510

Muda   503

Mura   503

Muri   503

Pull systems   505

Push systems   505

Safety stock   510

Supplier park   519

Takt time   510

Throughput   505

Time metrics   519

Timeline chart   520

Uniform plant loading   509

Value stream   506

Workflow   505

DISCUSSION AND REVIEW QUESTIONS

1. Explain the three types of waste (*muri*, *mura*, and *muda*) in your own words. Can you think of situations where you have seen each of these types of waste in jobs you have performed?

2. Compare the ideas of lean with the 5S framework. How do they complement each other? How do you see them as distinct approaches?

3. What are the main differences between push and pull systems? Which seems more difficult to manage? Why?

4. Why is production in small lot sizes essential to achieving lean?

5. Why is value stream mapping such a critical first step in a company's move toward a lean approach to operations?

6. What types of production processes are most conducive to developing a value stream map?

7. Lean production requires seven steps be taken. Why, in your opinion, should the first step be designing the process flow?

8. Why is uniform production an important element of lean, and how is it achieved?

9. How are lean thinking and Six Sigma related?

10. What are the advantages of lean services?

11. Which lean approaches work in both lean manufacturing and lean service operations?

12. What are the elements in a lean supply chain? Why are transparent information and full collaboration two critical components of lean supply chains?

13. Discuss briefly the key elements of lean logistics.

14. You are the shift manager of a medium-sized restaurant. You would like to begin taking a lean production approach. Identify three changes you could make to institute a lean approach at the restaurant.

15. Suggest ways in which lean principles can be applied to a hospital.

SOLVED PROBLEM

A hospital is planning to set up a Kanban control system to manage its supply of blood with the regional blood bank. Blood delivery from the regional blood bank to the hospital occurs every day with an order lead time of one day. An order placed at 8:00 am each day will be delivered the next morning. The hospital uses an average of 20 pints a day for each blood type. The hospital maintains a safety stock of 20% over and above its forecasted amount of blood demanded. The regional blood bank delivers blood in five-pint containers. Calculate the number of Kanban sets that the hospital should have.

Solution:

d = average pints of blood demanded per period = 20

LT = lead time needed for order replenishment = 1 day

SS = safety stock expressed in units = 20% of (d × LT) = .20 × 20 × 1 = 4

C = quantity of pints per container = 5

K = number of Kanban card/container sets = ?

$$K = \frac{\text{The expected, or average, demand during the lead time + Safety stock}}{\text{Container quantity size}}$$

$$= \frac{(d \times LT) + SS}{C}$$

$$= \frac{(20 \times 1) + 4}{5}$$

$$= 4.80 \text{ or } 5 \text{ (rounded up)}$$

Note: Both lead time and demand must be expressed in the same time units

The hospital requires five Kanban card sets. Whenever a new container of blood (five-pint size) is opened, the Kanban card is sent to purchasing and an order for a five-pint container of blood will be placed. When the new container of blood is received, the Kanban card will be attached to that container and sent to the blood storage area.

PROBLEMS

1. Sprinkman Inc., a fictional supplier of instrument gauge cluster housings, is planning to use a Kanban control system to control material flow. The first step in this process is to calculate the takt time—the time it takes to produce an item (in this case housing). Given the following information, compute the takt time per house (hint: Compute in seconds the net production time available per day):

   Working shifts per day = 2

   Hours per shift = 8

   Break time per shift = 30 minutes

   Lunch break = 30 minutes

   Demand for housings per day = 1,200 units

2. An autoglass company located in Detroit produces mirrors for automobiles. The company supplies auto mirrors to a nearby Ford (The Ford Motor Company, Dearborn, MI) plant. The demand for mirrors from the Ford plant is 800 mirrors per day. The autoglass company's productive time is 480 minutes:

   a. What is the takt time?

   b. If the total standard operating time required to produce a mirror is 144 seconds, how many workers are needed?

3. What is the takt time for a production system that operates one shift given the following information:

   Total time per shift = 480 minutes

   Coffee breaks = two 20-minute breaks per shift

   Lunch break = 1 hour

   Daily demand = 360 units

4. Given the following information, determine the number of Kanban cards required:

   Demand rate = 800 units per hour

   Lead time = 30 hours

   Container capacity = 1,200 units

   Safety stock = 15%

5. You have the following information:

   Demand rate = 250 units per hour

   Lead time = 15 hours

   Container capacity = 300 units

   Safety stock = 20%

   a. Determine the number of Kanban cards required.

   b. Convert these Kanban cards into the number of hours of demand they represent.

   c. If the container size is reduced from 300 to 150 units, what impact, if any, will it have on inventory levels?

6. You have the following information:

   Demand rate = 500 units per hour

   Lead time = 5 hours

Container capacity = 60 units

Safety stock = 15%

  a.   Determine the number of Kanban cards required.
  b.   Convert these Kanban cards into the number of hours of demand they represent.
  c.   If the lead time is reduced from 5 to 3 hours, what impact, if any, will it have on inventory levels?

7.   A local automotive company delivers five transmissions to the fabrication line every hour. On average, five vehicles are produced every hour and management has decided on a safety stock that equals 40% of the expected demand. Calculate the number of Kanban sets needed.

8.   Megatech Inc. is a fictional producer of airwave scanners for the defense industry. The company is planning to implement a Kanban control system to eliminate waste in the form of unnecessary inventory. After several days of analysis, Jean Costa, the firm's production manager, developed the following data for the manufacturing cell that produces the connectors for the scanners:

   Expected daily demand = 1,500 connectors

   Lead time = 3 days

   Safety stock = 20% of daily demand

   Size of a Kanban container = 450

How many Kanban containers of connectors are needed for this cell?

9.   A U.S. Postal Service office is planning to adopt a pull system. With the current push system, a machine cancels the stamped letters, which are loaded into tubs with 400 letters in each tub. The tubs are then sent to the postal clerks for sorting. The clerks, with the help of an automatic sorting machine, read and key in the zip codes at the rate of 1 tub per 400 seconds. Nevertheless, every now and then, the stamp canceling machine outpaces the sorting operation, causing considerable stress on the clerks. Under the proposed pull system, employees will pull a tub of letters with canceled stamps only when the clerks are ready to sort another tub. Given a safety stock of 20% for the tubs and an average waiting and materials handling time of 20 minutes per tub, calculate the number of tubs that should be circulating between the sorting clerks and the machine canceling area if 100,000 letters are to be sorted during a 10-hour shift.

10.   A bank in New Delhi, India, uses a Kanban system in its check processing facility. Each Kanban container holds 60 checks, requires 25 minutes to be processed, and spends 2.5 hours waiting to be handled. The facility operates 24 hours per day. A safety stock of 25% of the expected daily demand is maintained:

  a.   If 25 Kanban containers are currently in use, what is the expected daily demand of the check processing facility?

  b.   How many containers are needed if the intention is to eliminate all waste in the system completely?

11.   Refer to Table 8.2 as a basis for this problem. This month's master production schedule calls for the production of 180 sandals, 120 dress shoes, and 80 sneakers per eight hour shift.

  a.   What is the average cycle time for each model to achieve the production quota in 8 hours? Hint: Cycle Time = Operating time/desired production.

  b.   If a mixed-model production schedule is used, how many of each model will be produced before the production cycle is repeated?

12.   Dolphin Motors (not a real company) recently installed a mixed-model production line at its plant in Bangalore, India. The sales of its minivans and SUVs have declined in recent months as a result of rising gas prices. The Bangalore plant has the capacity to produce 250 vehicles per day. Dolphin Motors has estimated that monthly demand for its cars is 2,200, for minivans 1,100 per month, and for SUVs 600 per month.

  a.   If a mixed-model production schedule is used, how many of each model will be produced to meet demand?

  b.   How many times per day will the production cycle be repeated?

13.   The Standard Herald Motor Company is a fictional producer of three types of vehicles/cars in a single assembly line: the sedan (S), the hatchback (H), and the SUV (V). The plant manager at Standard Herald wants to implement uniform production and mixed-model scheduling. The company has orders for 800 sedans, 500 hatchbacks, and 300 SUVs next month. The plant operates 25 days per month and has the capacity to produce 200 vehicles per day:

  a.   If a mixed-model production schedule is used, what assembly sequence would the plant manager use?

  b.   How many times per day would the assembly sequence be repeated?

14.   The fictitious Cool Air Inc. assembles three models (A, B, and C) of air conditioners. The production manager at Cool Air plant wants to implement uniform production and mixed-model scheduling. The company has demand forecasts for 500 units of model A, 350 for model B, and 200 units for model C next month. The plant operates 25 days per month and has the capacity to produce 150 air conditioners per day.

  a.   If a mixed-model production schedule is used, what assembly sequence would the production manager use?

  b.   How many times per day would the assembly sequence be repeated?

15.   The same definition of value stream holds true for the office just as it does for the automobile factory, although in an office, it is much harder to see. The easiest value streams to see in an office environment are the ones that are triggered by a piece of paper. Office value streams are by the receipt of a request for a quote, sales order, invoice, job application, benefit claim, procurement request, and so forth. You can then follow the progress of that piece of paper just like you could follow the progress of an automobile being made in a factory. Each activity that occurs in the processing of that piece of paper adds (or subtracts) value just like adding a part to an automobile. For example, processing a job application can have the following activities:

  •   Screening the application
  •   Scheduling a phone interview with the applicant
  •   Conducting a phone interview with the applicant
  •   Scheduling a person-to-person interview with the applicant
  •   Conducting a person-to-person interview with the applicant
  •   Making a hiring decision about the applicant

Each activity occurs in a new hire value stream that produces value in the form of hired employees. It has a specific order in which it must occur. The application screening and phone interviews add incremental value because they assist in improving the quality of candidates selected for the person-to-person interviews.

Create a value stream map for the applicant example. You can use the value stream mapping symbols provided in the appendix.

CASE STUDY 14.1 LEAN GLOBAL SUPPLY CHAINS AND BOEING'S DREAMLINER ....

December 15, 2009, was a watershed day for Boeing, a world leader in the manufacturing of commercial aircraft. On this date, its long-anticipated 787, or Dreamliner, aircraft successfully completed its first test flight. Nearly two years delayed in development, the Dreamliner represented the leading edge of new technology. To maintain fuel efficiency and offer strong operating margins for airlines, the Dreamliner was constructed with carbon-fiber composite materials rather than with the traditional metal frames and outer surface. The innovative design and promised fuel efficiency have led to advance orders for 865 aircrafts from 56 airlines, with a total order book of US$144 billion, more than any other airframe in history. With an expected price tag of US$160 million per aircraft, the Dreamliner is a critical reason that Boeing has been able to maintain its edge in a highly competitive industry. Furthermore, as a clear technological leap forward, Boeing had a great deal riding on the successful release of the Dreamliner, including future profitability and its reputation for quality.

The development of the 787 did not go smoothly. Delays in getting the composite materials and designs right, lead times for qualifying global suppliers, and assorted technological problems not only delayed the launch of the Dreamliner but also forced Boeing to take out-of-pocket losses of more than US$4 billion in the two years leading up to the first test flight. Missed delivery dates also led to automatic penalty clauses being imposed. Some of the airlines that had ordered the Dreamliner asked for price reductions to offset these delays.

Boeing's manufacturing plans for the 787 were nearly as complicated as the aircraft. With greater than 300 global suppliers, Boeing has had to coordinate carefully its components for manufacturing and shipping to its assembly facilities in Seattle, Washington. Boeing's decision to outsource most of the aircraft components, rather than to manufacture them themselves, complicates an already highly integrated, complex process. Huge component parts such as wing assemblies, fuselage sections, and cockpit electronics were manufactured by supply chain partners at plants in Korea, Japan, Italy, South Carolina, and Kansas and were flown or shipped by water to Seattle. Boeing had to coordinate the manufacturing of these components, verify quality, guarantee their on-time delivery, and assemble them in an efficient manner that minimized inventories and bottlenecks. The company's managers projected a schedule in which seven planes a month were assembled. At that pace, it would have taken Boeing more than 10 years just to eliminate its current backlog of orders. Goodrich Corporation (Charlotte, NC) is one of Boeing's key suppliers and the firm contracted to develop the aircraft's brake and thrust reverser systems. The company's CEO, Marshall Larsen, recently noted, "The critical issue is not that Boeing isn't going to have a successful flight test. It's that the Goodriches of the world successfully support Boeing in getting the aircraft into service."[32]

Discussion Questions

1. The quote at the end of this case seems to suggest that the technology of getting this innovative aircraft to fly was the easy part. Discuss why Boeing's real challenges lie in the future rather than in the engineering of a composite aircraft.

2. How does the use of greater than 300 critical global suppliers make Boeing's commitment to lean production so difficult? If the coordination is done poorly, in what ways does Boeing end up seeing its costs skyrocket?

3. How do the philosophies of lean supply chains apply to Boeing's 787 project? Discuss in turn the four keys: (1) transparent information, (2) performance monitoring, (3) lean logistics, and (4) full collaboration.

CASE STUDY 14.2 TAL APPAREL AND JCPENNEY ....

TAL Apparel Limited, a shirt maker in Hong Kong (P.R. China), brings a unique perspective to its approach to solving operations and supply chain problems. In 1947, the company's owner, C.C. Lee, started his first spinning mill in Hong Kong. Over the years, he set up several textile mills, including fabric finishing mills, and by the early 1960s had extended his operations into garment making and founded Textile Alliance Limited (TAL). Since the 1980s, when TAL Apparel Limited was formed, it has been among the foremost innovators in the manufacturing and supply of apparel for some of the best-known companies in North America and Europe.

How big is the company? TAL has established relationships with Banana Republic (division of Gap Inc., San Francisco, CA), Brooks Brothers (New York, NY), L.L. Bean (Freeport, ME), Lands' End (Dodgeville, WI), and Calvin Klein (subsidiary of PVH Corp., New York, NY). TAL's relationship with the retail giant JCPenney (J. C. Penney Company, Plano, TX) is a particularly interesting partnership. Like all major retailers, JCPenney has been under huge pressure to carry lower quantities of goods in stock. It has done this by outsourcing its warehousing and stock replenishment. TAL offered to work with JCPenney to streamline the retailer's operations and take pressure off the firm by handling its reorder operations, forecasting, and inventory management. JCPenney agreed to the arrangement. As a result, JCPenney stores carry almost no extra stock of house-brand dress shirts because TAL collects all point-of-sale data directly from the stores, determines how many replacement shirts to make, and in what styles, colors, and sizes. TAL then sends these quantities directly to the individual stores, bypassing the need for JCPenney to operate large central warehouses.

Suppose, for example, that a JCPenney store in Paramus, New Jersey, sells two white shirts and three blue shirts of a different style on a Saturday, leaving no more blue shirts in stock at the store. TAL's computer system in Hong Kong receives this information instantly and, based on past sales information, calculates the ideal mixture of shirt styles, colors, and sizes for that brand at the Paramus store. Within two days, a factory in Taiwan has received the order to produce and ship the replacement shirts directly to the store.

JCPenney has been willing to maintain this partnership because TAL can instantly do what used to take JCPenney long lead times and extensive warehousing operations to accomplish. Furthermore, because they are linked in real time, any changes in sales generate instant responses. TAL ensures that JCPenney is never without replacement stock.

TAL also removes the guesswork when it comes to forecasting fashion changes and adjusts JCPenney's stock to meet them. TAL's design teams in Dallas and New York can design a new style, give their orders directly to the company's factories in China, and produce 100,000 shirts for a test run in less than four weeks. After analyzing the sales data, it is TAL, not JCPenney, that adjusts the retailer's orders and decides how many of the new shirts to make and ship. With TAL managing the entire process, from design to ordering yarn to manufacturing, the firm can roll out new brands in four months, something that would take JCPenney much longer to accomplish.

The TAL/JCPenney relationship is one that illustrates the positive attributes of lean global supply chains: mutual trust, a commitment to innovative practices, instant information processing, and a philosophy of continuous improvement to streamline the resupply cycle.[33]

Discussion Questions:

1. What are the main advantages of letting a company like TAL manage your inventory and reorder systems? What are the major disadvantages?

2. How does TAL achieve integration in its supply chain? What are the critical success factors that make the supply chain work?

3. How does the partnership with TAL help JCPenney achieve a lean service philosophy?

VIDEO CASE

Watch this video case to learn about how SAGE Publishing cultivates lean systems to make processes more efficient.

CRITICAL THINKING EXERCISES

1. Go to Oracle's (Oracle Corporation, Redwood City, CA) website (https://www.oracle.com/index.html), and read about its software applications for retailers. Thousands of retail and wholesale distribution companies around the world rely on Oracle for maximum flexibility and profitability. How does the software use sales and inventory data to help retailers accomplish lean supply chain operations?

2. Go to GE's website (http://www.ge.com/). How is GE's corporate slogan, "Imagination at Work" consistent with its commitment to Six Sigma? What are the key concepts of Six Sigma as defined by GE?

3. Imagine you work for a company that provides lean operations and logistical solutions for business around the globe. Watch the video, "Kanban Logistics—A Top 3PL Company." What operations management–related job opportunities does the company offer?

APPENDIX 14.1: VALUE STREAM MAPPING SYMBOLS

There are many variations of value stream mapping symbols. The following table shows the most common symbols. You can also create your own symbols for specialized applications:

Process Symbols

This icon represents the supplier when it appears in the upper-left side of the map, which is the usual starting point for material flows. This icon represents a customer when it appears in the upper-right side of the map, which is the usual end point for product flows.

Customer/Supplier

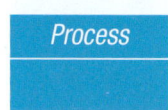

This icon represents a process, operation, machine, or department through which material flows. Instead of indicating every process, which could make the map unwieldy, one icon is typically used to indicate the processes in an entire department. In the case of assembly with several connected workstations, even if some WIP inventory accumulates between machines (or stations), the entire line would show as a single box. If there are separate operations, where one is disconnected from the next, inventory between and batch transfers, then use multiple boxes.

Dedicated Process

This is a process operation, department, or work center that other value stream families share. Estimate the number of operators required for the value stream being mapped, not for the number of operators required for processing all products.

Shared Process

This symbol indicates that multiple processes are integrated in a manufacturing cell. The cells usually process a limited family of similar products or a single product.

Cell

Material Symbols

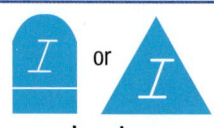

These icons show the inventory between two processes. The amount of inventory is noted beneath the triangle. The icon also represents storage for raw materials and finished goods. If there is more than one inventory accumulation, use an icon for each.

Inventory

Material Symbols

Shipments

This icon can represent the movement of raw materials from suppliers to the firm or the movement of finished goods from the firm to customers.

Push Arrow

This icon represents the pushing of material from one process to the next process.

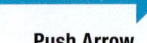

Supermarket

This is an inventory supermarket (Kanban stockpoint). Like a supermarket, a small amount of inventory is available. One or more downstream workers come to the supermarket to pick out what they need. The upstream work center then replenishes the stock in the supermarket. A supermarket reduces overproduction by limiting the total inventory.

Material Pull

Supermarkets connect to downstream processes with this pull icon, which indicates the physical removal of inventory.

MAX=XX

FIFO Lane

This icon is used when processes are connected with a first-in-first-out inventory system that limits input. The icon shows the maximum possible inventory.

Safety Stock

This icon represents safety stock.

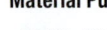

External Shipment

This icon indicates shipments from suppliers or to customers using external transportation.

Information Symbols

Production Control

This icon represents central production scheduling or control department, person, or operation.

Manual Info

A straight, thin arrow shows the general flow of information from memos, reports, or conversations. The frequency of the flow and other information sometimes appear on the symbol as well.

Electronic Info

This wiggle arrow represents an electronic flow of information via an electronic data interchange (EDI), the Internet, intranets, or other electronic medium. It can also indicate the frequency of the information exchange.

Information Symbols

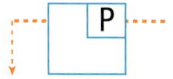

Production Kanban

This icon represents a production Kanban.

Withdrawal Kanban

This icon represents a withdrawal Kanban.

Signal Kanban

This icon is used whenever the on-hand inventory levels in the supermarket between two processes drops to a trigger, or minimum, point. When a triangle Kanban arrives at a supplying process, it signals a changeover and production of a predetermined batch size of the part noted on the Kanban. It is also referred to as one-per-batch Kanban.

Kanban Post

This icon represents a location where Kanban signals reside for pickup. The icon is often used with two-card systems to exchange withdrawal and production Kanban cards.

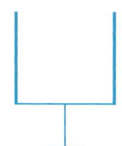

Sequenced Pull

This icon represents a pull system that gives instruction to subassembly processes to produce a predetermined type and quantity of product, typically one unit, without using a supermarket.

Load Leveling

This icon is a tool to batch Kanbans to level out the production volume and mixture of products over a period of time

.MRP/ERP

This icon represents an MRP/ERP or other centralized systems.

Go See

This icon represents the gathering of information through visual means.

Verbal Information

This icon represents verbal or personal information flow.

General Symbols

Kaizen Burst

This icon is used to highlight improvement needs and plan kaizen workshops at specific processes that are critical to achieving a firm's future-state value stream map.

Operator

This icon represents an operator. It shows the number of operators required to process a part family at a particular workstation.

General Symbols

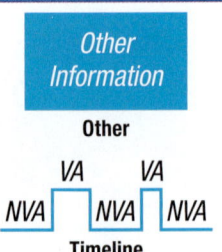

Other

This icon indicates other information needed for the production process.

Timeline

This icon represents a timeline. You can use it to calculate the lead time and the total cycle time.

SOURCE: Adapted from Strategos-International. (n.d.). Value stream & process mapping. Retrieved from http://www.strategosinc.com/value_stream_vs_process_mapping.htm

APPENDIX 14.2: STEPS FOR DEVELOPING A VALUE STREAM MAP

The following steps can be used to develop a VSM:

A. Draw the Current Map

To help you draw the map, gather a team of people who both manage and support the various parts of the value stream. Be sure to include people who actually do the work and not just the managers or team leaders; otherwise, you risk creating a VSM that shows what *should* happen rather than what actually *does* happen:

- Brainstorm with people who are involved, both internally and externally, to determine what is needed to deliver the product or fulfill the customer's needs. Identify the tasks or activities needed to produce the products that meet those needs, and eliminate any tasks that don't need to be done or add value. Some firms video or photograph their systems and then have employees study them to brainstorm ways to eliminate unnecessary activities.
- Put the tasks in order, as much as possible, and include the costs and actual working time required for each task. This will give you a picture of how long it takes and how much it costs to do each task (and, ultimately, the entire, end-to-end process).
- Look at the delays in between stages of the process (for example, the length of time a task sits in someone's inbox), and add in that time.

Depending on your operations, any of these tasks could be the subject of its own value stream map, which is why defining scope is so important.

B. Assess the Current Value Stream

In this step, you analyze whether each activity in the process is adding value. Value-add activities change an item and make it worth more to the customer. Car assembly is a perfect example: As the car body moves along the production line, more and more pieces or assemblies are added, making it more complete. Eventually, it becomes a fully operational vehicle that people will buy. Each step adds value (although clearly the most value is added when the final component is installed!). This is where you can look for lean improvement opportunities:

- At each point in the map, ask yourself, "Does this activity add value?"
- Identify your value-add points.
- Identify your nonvalue-add points (for example, places where there are long lead times, material is stored, or redundant or excessive paperwork is slowing a task).
- Determine which nonvalue-add points are still necessary (for example, for meeting regulatory requirements, addressing other compliance issues, and ensuring worker safety).

C. Create a Future-State Value Stream Map

Map how you want your improved process to look in the future. How will the process work after you've eliminated the waste you identified in the previous step? Follow these tips:

- Ask yourself what your leanest competitor would do.
- Look for similar activities, and see whether there's a way to group them.
- Identify bottlenecks and critical events.
- Look for ways to simplify activities that are complex.
- Confirm that assumptions about adding value align with customers; that is, work to verify that customers actually value each transformation step.
- Look for common forms of waste, such as these:
  - Moving product and materials inefficiently.
  - Using equipment and people unnecessarily.
  - Keeping too much or too little inventory.
  - Performing inefficient quality checks.
  - Stockpiling finished goods.
  - Adding features or conducting processing the customer does not value.

Using these steps, you can critically review current operations with VSM. Here are some opportunities for improvement in the example shown in Figure 14.1:

- Eliminate redundant approvals or move them earlier in the process to prevent unnecessary work.
- Improve the flow of information (paper or electronic). For example, as Figure 14.1 shows, it takes a full day for orders to move from order picking, to checking, to packaging. Through improved communications, it may be possible to streamline this process.
- Restructure warehouse operations for efficiency. The system currently requires three weeks and three days for lead time. Perhaps through improved efficiency, this lead time figure can be trimmed.

D. Create a Plan to Implement the Desired State

When you have identified your objectives, you can develop a plan for change. At this point, many organizations also begin other lean initiatives, such as kaizen and just-in-time processes. Remember, though, that the time you invest in VSM will pay off only if you follow through with the implementation plan. To do so:

- Use the VSM to communicate your goals and objectives.

- Include people on your VSM team, who will work with the new activities. This helps increase their buy-in for the implementation.
- Talk frequently about lean and efficient operations so that it becomes part of your corporate culture.
- Look for ways to reward efficient work and efficiency suggestions.

E. Implement the Plan

Several techniques can be used, but the one that is most frequently used with VSM is a series of kaizen blitzes, each lasting approximately one week.

A kaizen blitz is a focused short-term project in which a cross-functional team makes rapid improvements to a process. The blitz involves observing the existing process, attempting new approaches, and measuring the results. The goal is to move you gradually from the current state to the future state.

F. Review the Results, and Repeat

With the new VSM in place, monitor the new process to see that it is leaner and more efficient than the old process. Choose another process for improvement and repeat the steps listed.

CHAPTER

15

Inventory Management

LEARNING OBJECTIVES

After studying this chapter, you should be able to:

1. Identify the various types of inventory.

2. Describe the types of inventory costs.

3. Examine the role of inventory in an organization's supply chain.

4. Use inventory management measures to determine the efficiency of an inventory system.

5. Illustrate key features in inventory management systems.

6. Identify the causes of the bullwhip effect and other causes of uncertainty in supply chain inventories.

7. Explain how companies can include sustainability and ethical practices in inventory management.

8. Demonstrate the requirements for managing inventory in global supply chains.

9. Describe how service firms apply inventory management methods to their operations.

OPERATIONS PROFILE: Best Buy Moves Inventory Control to Its 1,000 Warehouses

AP Photo/Sue Ogrocki

Best Buy (Richfield, MN) has more than 1,000 stores nationwide and 1,000 mini-warehouses as well. Slow sales and problems with its online shopping system have hampered the company. Part of the problem, the company's executives believe, could be from poor coordination between the company's brick-and-mortar stores and the firm's website.

Best Buy currently ships merchandise from 50 stores to fill orders from online customers. Customers often receive out-of-stock messages on BestBuy.com even though the item in question may be available, resulting in lost revenue annually for a retailer that is struggling to maintain its market share.

Best Buy's (Richfield, MN) chief financial officer, Sharon McCollam, said they have a built-in solution to the problem. Forty percent of the firm's online sales consist of customers who choose to pick up their orders in a store. Why not capitalize on this interaction but in reverse, letting the stores fill and ship orders to customer homes? "When they created the capability to buy online and pick up in stores, they created one inventory," McCollam explained. "It's not clear to me why at that point they did not take it to its ultimate conclusion, which is shipping from the store if you don't have it."

Although logical, experts say a ship-from-store strategy, especially if it involves 1,000 stores instead of just 50, can be complicated. For one thing, a retailer would need software that accurately tracks inventory in real time, said Danny Silverman, the vice president of Catapult Ecommerce (Westport, CT), an e-commerce consulting firm. Situations could occur in which a customer orders an out-of-stock item online and the system says a nearby store has three of those items left. But by the time a store employee looks for the product, the merchandise could have been sold. "You can't say 'we have the product' and then 'never mind,'" said Silverman.

The ship-from-store strategy is only one piece of McCollam's efforts to modernize Best Buy's inventory systems. For example, the retailer ships online orders and store merchandise from separate distribution centers. Remaking its warehouses to fill orders regardless of where customers placed them could boost efficiencies and lower costs. If the plan works, Best Buy estimates it can reduce its cost of goods sold by US$350 million.[1]

Inventory management is a critical element in a firm's operations and supply chain strategy. As the Best Buy example demonstrates, inventory affects customer satisfaction, retailing strategies, and supply chain relationships, with suppliers and distributors. This chapter will examine the important steps in the inventory management process so that we can better understand the benefits and challenges of effective inventory management.

Identify the various types of inventory.

Types of Inventory

15.1 Types of Inventory

All organizations engaged in the manufacturing, sale, or service of products hold inventory in one form or another. Inventories can be in a finished or unfinished state, and they are held for future consumption and sale or for further value-added processing or use by organizations. Companies carry different types of inventory, which are broadly classified into four groups:

- **Raw Materials Inventory.** Raw materials are the basic materials that a manufacturing firm uses to make components, subassemblies, or finished products. Raw materials are typically commodities or extracted materials such as iron ore, minerals, chemicals, and petroleum. The main reason that a manufacturing company holds raw materials inventory is to avoid production disruptions from delays in raw material shipments or a scarcity of them on the world market.
- **Maintenance, Repair, and Operations (MRO) Inventory.** The MRO inventory consists of items that support the production of the main product and are typically purchased from outside suppliers such as nuts and bolts, ball bearings, machine grease or solvents, clamps, or screws.
- **Work-in-Process Inventory.** This category includes materials or semi-finished goods that have had some work done on them but are not completed. In complex and lengthy production processes, the amount of work-in-process inventory held is often high because so much of it is accumulated at different stages of production.
- **Finished Goods Inventory.** This inventory consists of finished products ready for shipment and sale. A company can hold finished goods inventory at its plant or at various stocking points such as distribution centers until it reaches the market and is sold to final customers.

Describe the types of inventory costs.

Inventory Costs

15.2 Inventory Costs

Inventories have economic value and are listed as current assets on a company's balance sheet. They are also typically one of the largest assets held by a company in terms of its monetary value. Maintaining inventories can be expensive. The five major categories of inventory-related costs are as follows: (1) purchase costs, (2) ordering costs, (3) setup costs, (4) holding or carrying costs, and (5) stock-out costs. We discuss each of these next.

Purchase Costs and Ordering Costs

The most obvious and often the largest cost of inventory is the purchase cost or money paid to an upstream supplier for materials or goods purchased. Ordering costs include administrative costs related to determining an order quantity, preparing purchase invoices, inspecting goods received for quality and quantity, and moving goods for temporary storage. These costs also may include import duties. Ordering costs are expressed on a per-order basis and consist of a fixed dollar amount regardless of the order quantity. Consequently, on an annual basis, total ordering costs decrease as the quantity per order increases and the company achieves economies of scale.

Setup Costs

Setup costs are the costs of setting up the machines or changing over production from one item to another. These variable costs include the cost of the personnel needed to set up or change over production as well as the costs of consumable material, such as paper goods and cleaning supplies, used in the tear down and setup. The longer it takes to set up the machines, the higher are the setup costs. As with ordering costs, setup costs also have a fixed cost per production run or setup. Consequently, on an annual basis, total setup costs decrease as the quantity produced per production run increases.

Holding, or Carrying, Costs

When a business stores inventory for any reason, there are costs associated with holding (carrying) it. The components of the holding costs include the variable costs associated with:

- Storage, such as rent for a warehouse and the cost of utilities and personnel to operate it.
- Insurance to protect the inventory and the costs associated with obsolete, stolen, deteriorated, or spoiled inventory.
- Depreciation.
- Taxes (in some states).

Purchase costs: money paid to an upstream supplier for materials or goods purchased

Ordering costs: administrative costs related to determining an order quantity, preparing purchase invoices, inspecting goods received for quality and quantity, and moving goods for temporary storage

Setup costs: the costs of setting up the machines or changing over production from one item to another

Holding costs: the costs associated with holding (carrying) inventory

- Interest costs on the money invested in the inventory as well as the opportunity cost of the money being tied up in inventory when it could have been profitably invested elsewhere.

Holding costs can be expressed as the total carrying cost per unit per time period. This amount can be found by adding all of the individual cost components—the storage, risk, depreciation, taxes, and interest costs—per unit. For example, if on a per-unit, per-period basis, these costs per unit are $1.00, $0.50, $0.25, and $1.00, respectively, then the total inventory cost per unit is $2.75 ($1.00 + $0.50 + $0.25 + $1.00; all in U.S. dollars). Alternatively, holding costs can be expressed as a percentage of the per-unit price per time period. This amount is found by adding up the individual cost components expressed as percentages.

Annual holding costs typically range from 10% to 40% of the value of an item. For example, if the value of an item in inventory is $100, and the cost for holding it is 30% per unit per year, then the annual holding cost for that item per unit is $30 (30% × $100). Holding costs have an inverse relationship with both ordering and setup costs. The higher the order quantity or production quantity per setup, the fewer orders or setups in a year and, hence, the lower annual ordering or setup costs will be. Nevertheless, with higher order or production quantities, your inventory levels in stock tend to be higher, leading to higher carrying costs.

Stock-out Costs

Stock-out costs, also referred to as *shortage costs*, occur when the demand for a product cannot be met because of a shortage of inventory. Stock-out costs are inversely related to carrying costs: The more inventory you carry, the higher your carrying costs will be but the lower your stock-out costs will be. The costs associated with stock-outs can be both tangible and intangible. The tangible costs include lost revenues and profits if the lost sales are permanent and losses in the form of price discounts or rebates that a company has to offer its customers because of delivery delays. Intangible costs of a stock-out can range from the loss of customer goodwill to the permanent loss of customers and future sales. Raw materials stock-outs within a production system can lead to work stoppages and the downtime of labor and equipment. Intangible stock-out costs are more difficult to estimate than other types of inventory costs.

OPERATION MANAGEMENT: LESSONS LEARNED
How Poor Inventory Management Can Lead to Charges of Fraud

In 2011, Acer Inc. (New Taipei, Taiwan), a leading manufacturer of personal computers, took a US$150 million charge against its net income to clear out excess inventory that had been piling up in its Europe, Middle East, and African (EMEA) operations. Company critics charged Acer with fraud and accused the company of deliberately over-shipping products to downstream distributors, allowing inventory levels to build up at their locations, while falsely claiming these higher product volumes as having been purchased. Hiding inventory in a firm's distribution channel can be a way to claim temporarily that your sales revenues are higher and boost a company's stock price. Acer's then CEO, J.T. Wang, acknowledged that the computer maker had stuffed its distribution channel with excess inventory while claiming inventory levels had fallen and the firm's sales were strong. After the discovery of excess inventory, the company issued this statement:

[We] discovered abnormalities in terms of channel inventory stored in freight forwarders' warehouses, and in the accounts receivable from channels in Spain. The investigation

also found areas for vast improvement on managing channel inventory and accounts receivables. [The vendor is to] provide channels with $150 million in sales allowance to clear inventory.

As part of the Acer apology, Wang also agreed to forego his entire salary and performance bonus for the year. The rest of Acer's board accepted a 50% pay cut.[2]

15.3

Examine the role of inventory in an organization's supply chain.

15.3 Inventory Considerations for Supply Chains

Even though it's expensive, companies in a supply chain, whether they are suppliers of raw materials, manufacturers, or retailers, will hold inventories of raw materials, MRO, work-in-progress, or finished goods for several reasons. In this section, we use Comfort Shoes, a fictional manufacturer of shoes and sandals using materials and components purchased from suppliers worldwide, as an example. Figure 15.1 shows the suppliers of three of the materials for making shoes—rubber, leather, and fabric. The shoes produced by the company are then sold through independent retail stores or directly online through the company's website. Customers can buy shoes off the shelf from the retail stores or buy customized shoes that are shipped directly to them. We will now explain why Comfort Shoes holds inventory and, in particular, excess inventory in its supply chain.

Meeting Expected Normal Demand

Meeting Demand

A portion of inventory, called **cycle stock** (or *base stock*), is held to meet a firm's expected, or normal, demand. This is the inventory that a company carries to satisfy its normal cycle of sales orders or production requirements. Cycle stock is received from an upstream supply chain partner, gradually used up, and replenished periodically. For example, suppose the leather supplier ships 10,000 pieces of leather at a time to Comfort Shoes. Because Comfort Shoes cannot use all of this leather at once, it stores the extra as inventory and uses it when it is needed. Over time the company depletes this inventory of leather and then places another order for leather to the supplier. The level of leather in storage rises again, and the cycle of inventory depletion and replenishment continues. The depletion and replenishment of cycle stock follows a sawtooth pattern as shown in Figure 15.2.

Cycle stock inventory will also exist at other points in Comfort Shoes' supply chain. For example, Comfort Shoes' suppliers will also hold their own raw materials cycle stock inventory needed to make the leather, rubber, and fabric pieces that are then sold to downstream customers. Similarly, independent retail stores, which are downstream members in the supply chain, will carry cycle stocks of finished goods to meet the normal expected demand for shoes and sandals from end customers.

Protecting Against Shortages

Companies throughout the supply chain also hold inventory to respond to the uncertainties in demand and supply levels. Unexpected shortages in the supply of critical raw materials can seriously affect

Cycle stock: the inventory that a company carries to satisfy its normal cycle of sales orders or production requirements

FIGURE 15.1: Comfort Shoes' Supply Chain

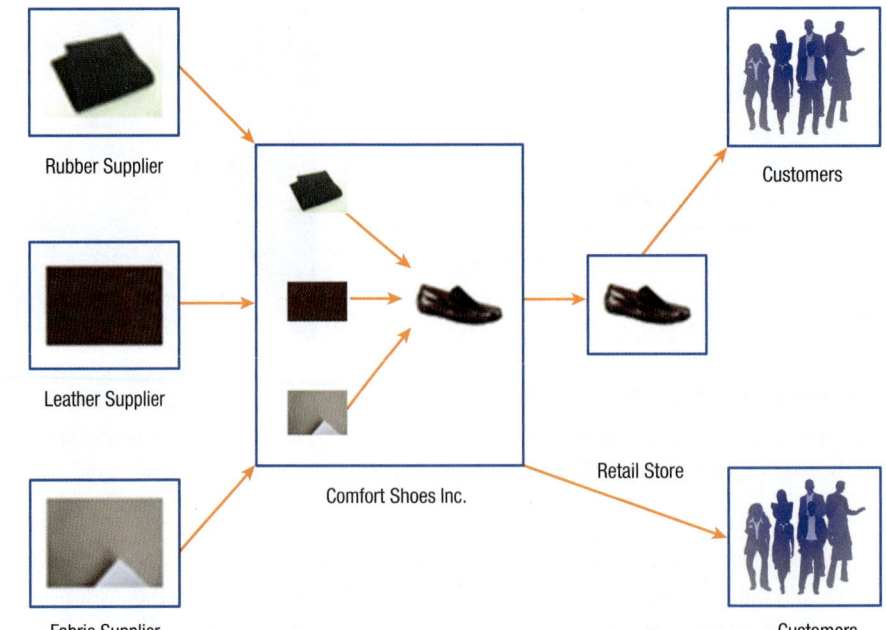

FIGURE 15.2: Cycle Stock Levels at Comfort Shoes

[Chart: "Cycle Stock Levels at Comfort Shoes"]

First Order of Leather Pieces Received

Second Order of Leather Pieces Received

Third Order of Leather Pieces Received

Fourth Order of Leather Pieces Received

Y-axis: Leather Pieces — 10000, 5000, 0

X-axis: Time — 10 Days, 20 Days, 30 Days

Gradual Inventory Depletion Cycle (repeated for each cycle)

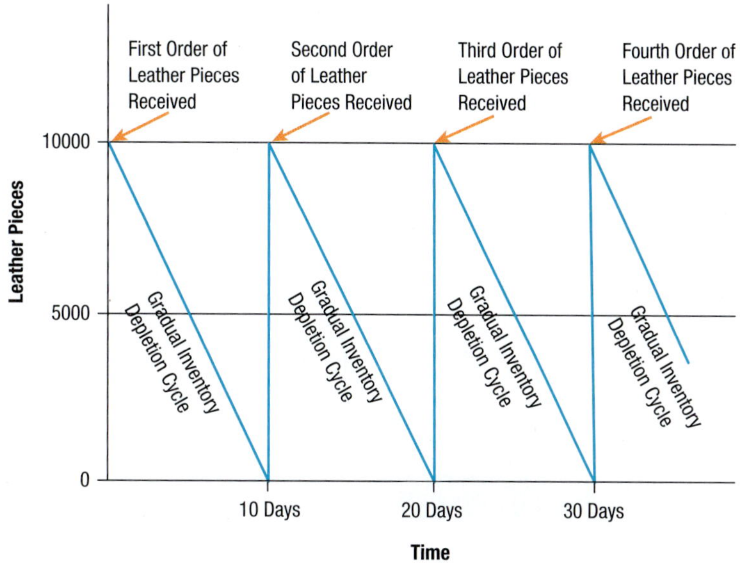

a company's ability to meet demand or disrupt its production runs. Shipping delays can disrupt a company's production activities as well. The extra inventory a company holds to cope with unexpected shortages is called safety stock.

 Product Shortages

Figure 15.2 assumes that the leather supplier delivers the order of 10,000 leather pieces exactly as Comfort Shoes has used up all of its cycle stock. As long as there are no unexpected increases in demand for the company's shoes or shipping delays from the leather supplier, there will be no disruption in the company's production of shoes. Comfort Shoes and its downstream supply chain partners—independent retail stores—will have enough finished shoes and sandals to meet their customers' demand.

Nevertheless, what will happen if there is an unexpected increase in the demand for the company's shoes in the market or there are unanticipated shipping delays from the leather supplier? Should either or both of these scenarios occur, it will cause serious problems for Comfort Shoes and its downstream supply chain activities. Comfort Shoes may be forced to shut down its production lines or its retail stores may run out of their stock of shoes and sandals. Customers' orders may have to be canceled, and shippers, retailers, and customers will have to be notified of delays. Problems such as these are precisely the reason why companies carry safety stock.

Figure 15.3 on page 538 shows what the demand and replenishment pattern would look like if Comfort Shoes decides to carry 500 pieces of leather as safety stock. The safety stock protects Comfort Shoes against stock-outs. Yet, there will also be additional inventory costs related to holding the safety stock.

Receiving Quantity Discounts

Suppliers often offer discounts for purchase volumes above certain amounts. By buying materials in higher volumes, businesses can reduce not only the unit cost of materials but also the costs associated with ordering these materials, including their transportation and delivery costs, and import duties. For example, suppose Comfort Shoes' fabric supplier announces that the price per yard of fabric is US$1 for purchase quantities of less than 500 yards, but it is only US$0.70 for purchase quantities between 500 and 1,000 yards. To take advantage of the lower purchase price, Comfort Shoes may choose to purchase slightly more than 500 yards. This way, the company can take advantage of the price discount without having to increase the costs of holding the excess inventory.

Guarding Against Future Price Increases

Companies commonly buy materials in advance if they expect their prices to increase in the near term for various reasons, such as high demand or turmoil in the markets for them caused by labor strikes, tax increases, governmental instability, and so on. Inventory purchased to guard against uncertainties

FIGURE 15.3: Comfort Shoes' Safety Stock of Leather Pieces

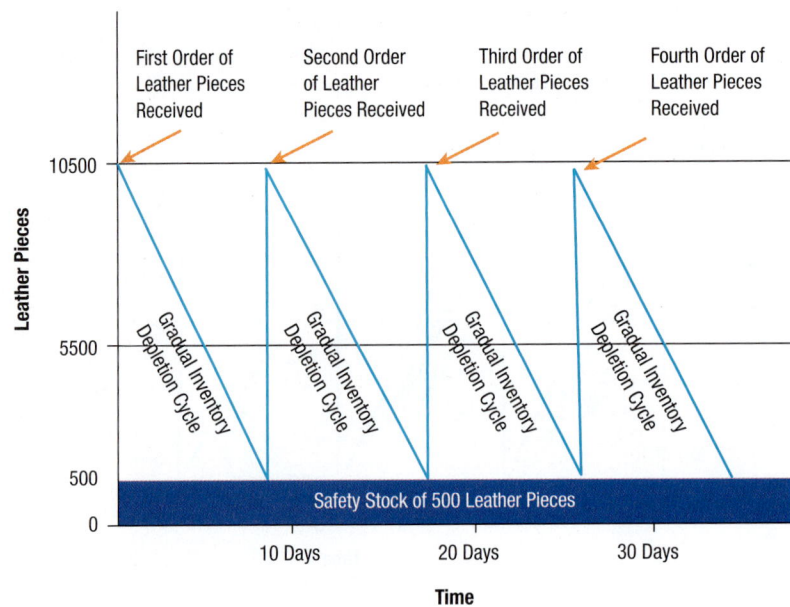

such as these is referred to as **hedge inventory**. For example, a firm that routinely buys gallium (a critical element in manufacturing semiconductors) from China may choose to order extra inventory if political instability has the potential to threaten its supply. Similarly, suppose the leather supplier for Comfort Shoes is located in Italy and there is speculation that the Italian government may increase the tariffs on leather exported from the country. Comfort Shoes may want to purchase additional pieces of leather now and hold them as hedge inventory.

Meeting Sales Increases Caused by Seasonal Demand and Sales Promotions

Companies that produce and sell seasonal products or use sales promotions anticipate a surge in demand for these products. The inventory held in excess of a firm's cycle stock to meet the expected increase in demand is referred to as **anticipation inventory**. For example, if a chain of retail stores Comfort Shoes sells to plans to offer a 20% discount on shoes and sandals, the retailer is likely to hold anticipation inventory to meet the extra demand. Similarly, to meet the anticipated increase in demand from the chain of retail stores, Comfort Shoes will hold additional stocks of leather, rubber, and fabric materials so it can increase production as needed.

Reducing Transportation Costs and Transit Times

Hedge inventory: inventory purchased in advance to guard against uncertainties in pricing

Anticipation inventory: inventory held in excess of a firm's cycle stock to meet the expected increase in demand

Transportation inventories: inventories that are in transit in containers or trucks (also known as pipeline inventories)

Companies can reduce their transportation costs by buying raw materials in bulk and transporting finished goods in full containers or full truckloads. Recall from our discussion in Chapter 11 on logistics that full truckload shipments are cheaper than partial truckload shipments are. In addition, the transit times for full container and truckload shipments are often faster because the goods are shipped directly from their points of origin to their destinations. The transit times are longer for partial shipments because freight forwarders have to wait (sometimes for weeks) for goods from other shippers to fill the containers and truckloads.

Inventories that are in transit in containers or trucks are known as **transportation inventories** (or *pipeline inventories*). The investment in these inventories can be significant in global supply chains because transit times are lengthy. There is a trade-off between in-transit inventory and transportation costs. Faster modes of transportation reduce in-transit inventory and storage costs but have high transportation costs, whereas slower modes of transportation increase in-transit inventory costs but have lower transportation costs. For example, suppose Comfort Shoes is located in Recife, Brazil, and the retail chain is located in the U.S. Midwest. Delivering shoes from Brazil to the United States may take several weeks, and at any given point in time, many shipments could be in the pipeline. One shipment of shoes and sandals might be on an ocean liner en route to the United States, a second shipment may be waiting at a port in Recife, and a third shipment may be on a truck somewhere destined for Chicago and other cities in the Midwest. Consequently, transportation inventories in a global supply chain can often exceed the total combined cycle and safety stock inventories that exist in the rest of the supply chain. In a typical supply chain, it is not uncommon to find several months of inventory accumulating from the time products leave manufacturers' production lines to the time they arrive at the retailers.

Smoothing Out Production Fluctuations

Many raw materials have long lead times. To bridge the gap between upstream production levels and the downstream demand for finished products and to use their production capacities in full, companies carry inventories of both finished products and raw materials. Because these inventories are held to smooth out fluctuations in production, they are called **smoothing inventories**. For example, although the demand for the shoes and sandals produced by Comfort Shoes may vary from day to day, to use its full production capacity, the company may choose to produce at a constant rate of 500 shoes per day. This level-production strategy will smooth out the company's production: Comfort Shoes' inventory of shoes and sandals will build up during periods of slack demand and then diminish during periods of peak demand.

Facilitate Decoupling of Processes

To avoid production disruptions that can result from events such as equipment breakdowns, inventories are often positioned between two process stages so that the two processes can operate independently of each other. This buffer inventory performs a **decoupling** function that enables production to continue temporarily while the production problem at a given process stage is resolved. Decoupling inventories is also prevalent in different supply chain stages to avoid disruptions caused by delayed delivery of raw materials from suppliers or delayed delivery of finished goods to the market by the manufacturers.

15.4 Inventory Management Measures

It should be clear that maintaining the optimum level of inventory is a balancing act—one that requires measurement to control efficiently. Some of the key measures companies use to track how well they are managing their inventories include backorders and lost sales, inventory turnover, days of inventory in stock, order fulfillment lead time, item fill rate, inventory accuracy, and industry benchmarking.

Backorders and Lost Sales

The backorders and lost sales measures tell us the number of times and the number of customers who demanded an item when that item was not in stock. A **backorder** is a customer order a company was unable to meet because the item demanded was not in stock. In this case, however, the customer is willing to wait for the order to be filled in the next scheduled shipment, often for a reduced or discounted purchase price. **Lost sales** occur when a customer doesn't buy the item if that item is not in stock, and the company loses the revenue from the sale of that item.

Inventory Turnover

Inventory turnover is a measure of how frequently a business sells its inventory in a given time period. It is calculated as the ratio of the cost of goods sold to the average investment the firm has in inventory. The formula for inventory turnover measured annually is:

$$\text{Inventory Turnover} = \frac{\text{Annual Cost of Goods Sold}}{\text{Annual Average Inventory Investment}}$$

where the average inventory level for any given period is given by

$$\text{Average Inventory} = \frac{\text{Beginning Inventory} + \text{Ending Inventory}}{2}$$

Therefore, if a company's annual cost of goods sold is US$100,000 and its annual average inventory investment is US$20,000, then its inventory turnover is

15.4
Use inventory management measures to determine the efficiency of an inventory system.

Smoothing inventories: inventories held to smooth out fluctuations in production

Decoupling: a function that enables production to continue temporarily while the production problem at a given process stage is resolved

Backorder: a customer order a company was unable to meet because the item demanded was not in stock

Lost sales: losses in revenue that occur when a customer doesn't buy an item if that item is not in stock

Inventory turnover: a measure of how frequently a business sells its inventory in a given time period

Measuring
Inventory
Management

$$\text{Inventory Turnover} = \frac{\text{Annual Cost of Goods Sold}}{\text{Annual Average Inventory Investment}} = \frac{\$100,000}{\$20,000} = 5$$

This result means that the company sells all of its inventories five times each year.

Inventory turnover is a very useful measure because it can alert managers to potential problems, such as overstocking, product obsolescence, or impending stock-out situations. Generally, the higher a firm's inventory turnover ratio, the less time its inventory spends in storage and, therefore, the more efficient is the firm's use of the inventory. Inventory use is more efficient because the firm is converting its inventory into profits faster, product obsolescence and theft and damage is less of a risk, and the inventory is being refreshed with newer, more up-to-date products. Yet, the ideal inventory turnover ratio varies from industry to industry and depends on a given company's profit margin. For example, products such as wines and spirits have low turnover ratios because they are stored for long periods of time to increase their value. Similarly, companies that sell products with high profit margins also have lower turnover ratios because these products typically require a long time to manufacture or sell. A high inventory turnover rate can also increase a company's risk of stock-outs, backorders, and lost sales.

Days of Inventory in Stock

Days of inventory in stock is the number of days of inventory a firm has on hand to meet its sales. The formula for this measure is:

$$\text{Days of Inventory in Stock} = \frac{\text{Average Inventory in \$}}{\text{Cost of Days's Sales in \$}}$$

where

$$\text{Average Inventory} = \frac{\text{Beginning Inventory} + \text{Ending Inventory}}{2}, \text{and}$$

$$\text{Cost of Day's Sales} = \frac{\text{Annual Cost of Sales}}{365}$$

For example, if at the beginning of the year, a company's inventory is valued at $750,000, its ending inventory is valued at $350,000, and the company's annual cost of sales (obtained from the company's income statement) is $7,300,000 (all in U.S. dollars), then:

$$\text{Average Inventory} = \frac{\text{Beginning Inventory} + \text{Ending Inventory}}{2} = \frac{\$750,000 + \$350,000}{2} = \$550,000$$

and

$$\text{Cost of Day's Sales} = \frac{\text{Annual Cost of Sales}}{365} = \frac{\$7,300,000}{365} = \$20,000$$

Therefore,

$$\text{Days of Inventory in Stock} = \frac{\text{Average Inventory in \$}}{\text{Cost of Day's Sales in \$}} = \frac{\$550,000}{\$20000} = 27.5 \text{ days}$$

Days of inventory in stock: the number of days of inventory a firm has on hand to meet its sales

This result means that the company has enough inventory for 27.5 days to meet its sales. As with the inventory turnover measure, companies strive to achieve the optimal number of days of inventory in stock. If the number of days is too high, it may indicate the firm is overstocked. A low number may imply the firm is at too great a risk of stock-outs and lost sales.

Order Fulfillment Lead Time

Order fulfillment lead time is the average time it takes from the submission of a customer's purchase order until the company delivers the order. A well-managed inventory system will enable a company to shorten the order fulfillment lead time, which in turn will improve the company's cash flow cycle, which is the movement of money into and out of the business. It is the cycle of cash inflows and outflows that determines how solvent a business is. A well-managed inventory system will also enable a company to get its products to customers faster and enhance the firm's reputation for customer service.

Fill Rate

The fill rate is the percentage of customer orders that can be satisfied from inventory in stock. For example, if a customer places an order for 20 units of an item, but the current inventory in stock allows your company to ship only 15 units, your fill rate for the item is 75% (15 / 20). The higher the ratio is, the more effective your inventory management is.

There is a strong relationship between fill rates and the amount of inventory in stock. In general, as inventory is added in steady increments, a firm's fill rate also increases but at a decreasing rate. That is, at some point, it becomes harder and harder to improve the fill rate.

Because it is impossible to predict demand accurately, no business can fill 100% of its orders daily without incurring the risk of overstocking. Most companies have fill rates in the 90% to 95% range. In some industries, fill rates are significantly lower though. For example, in the fashion-apparel industry, fill rates greater than 70% are hard to achieve because new products are introduced frequently, and top-selling fashions sell out quickly.[3]

Inventory Accuracy Rate

Inventory accuracy refers to tracking the discrepancies that exist between all inventory records and the physical state of the inventory. Maintaining accurate inventory records is essential to prevent deterioration in service levels, accounting auditing problems, and financial losses. One of the simplest ways to track inventory accuracy is to calculate the mean absolute deviation between the quantity shown in inventory records and the real quantity that is physically available. To facilitate this calculation, in addition to maintain accurate inventory records, many companies do a physical count of all inventory items in stock on a periodic basis (monthly, quarterly, or annually). Accurate counts can be surprisingly difficult to achieve. Anheuser Busch InBev (Leuven, Belgium) buys millions of tons of rice, barley malt, hops, and yeast each year for brewing its beers, and it must stock millions of empty bottles and aluminum cans, kegs, large quantities of labeling material, and so forth. Keeping accurate records of all of these raw materials as they are used, and where they are in the production process and en route to beer sellers in the supply chain, is complicated. Clearly, a complete physical count in which all raw materials and other production items are counted at one time requires a great deal of effort and may disrupt operations at a plant or facility. Therefore, companies tend to engage in a limited number of physical counts of inventory during a year. With a physical count of inventory, companies can determine the inventory accuracy rate or the percentage accuracy of inventory records.

Companies that typically have more than 95% inventory accuracy often use a procedure called cycle counting. Unlike physical counting, a random sample or subset of inventory in stock in a particular location is counted on a specific day to verify that the inventory accuracy rate is not too far off target. Typically, companies more frequently count items that generate most of their sales and less frequently (perhaps annually) count items that are less profitable or less popular. The advantage of cycle counts is that they are less disruptive to daily operations than a complete physical count is, they provide an ongoing measure of inventory accuracy, and they can be tailored to focus on items with higher values, higher movement volumes, or that are critical to business processes.

In addition to the use of the measures we have discussed, benchmarking can be done to compare a company's inventory measures such as its fill and turnover rates to those of other companies in its industry. Making these comparisons can help a firm gauge whether its inventory management performance meets the industry standard, falls short of it, or exceeds it.

Order fulfillment lead time: the average time it takes from the submission of a customer's purchase order until the company delivers the order

Fill rate: the percentage of customer orders that can be satisfied from inventory in stock

Physical count: determining the real quantity of inventory that is physically available on a periodic basis

Cycle counting: counting a random sample or subset of inventory in stock in a particular location on a specific day to verify that inventory accuracy rate is not too far off target

OPERATIONS MANAGEMENT: LESSONS LEARNED
How Pennsylvania's State Liquor Store System Continues to Mismanage Inventory

Pennsylvania is one of only two states that have not privatized their liquor stores. (Utah is the other state.) Pennsylvania Liquor Control Board (PLCB) officials claim that maintaining the state's control of wine and liquor sales makes them more efficient and responsible in their operations. The evidence, however, does not support this view. Report after report has found that the state's monopoly liquor system is bloated, inefficient, and expensive.

A report issued by Pennsylvania's auditor general found there was widespread mismanagement of the inventory within the system. For example, tens of millions of taxpayers' dollars were spent on a computerized inventory management tool that cost two-and-a-half times more than originally planned and caused widespread shortages at PLCB distribution centers. According to the report, some retail store managers began hoarding some merchandise, leaving other retail stores without that merchandise. The PLCB then demanded purchasers order excessive inventory because of the shortages. Despite the excess inventory, the computerized system automatically ordered yet even more of the items. In some cities, including Scranton and Pittsburgh, the inventory of liquor either doubled or nearly doubled. Much of it had to be moved to non–temperature-controlled trailers because there was no warehouse space in the system to store it.

The PLCB claimed that storing excess inventory in non–temperature-controlled trailers, even though the heat in them exceeded 100 degrees, did not put the inventory at risk of spoilage. Although the auditors' report disputed this, the PLCB continues to deny there was any widespread spoilage and an accurate account of money lost from overheating remains unreported.[4]

15.5

Illustrate key features in inventory management systems.

15.5 Key Features of Effective Inventory Management Systems

The main objectives of inventory management are to provide customers with the right number of products in the right place and at the right time, as well as to keep inventory costs to a minimum. To achieve these goals, operations managers must answer the following questions:

- How much inventory should we order or produce?
- When should we order or produce it?

Several mathematical models can be used to help answers to these questions. A more complete discussion of these models is presented in Chapter 16.

An effective inventory management system will produce reliable demand forecasts and estimates of lead times and inventory costs. It will also classify inventory in a meaningful way, as well as enable the firm to track and monitor its inventories.

Demand Forecasts, Lead Times, and Inventory-Related Cost Information

Effective inventory management requires a forecasting system that provides reliable estimates of customer demand. The firm should have the right amount of inventory and have it when it is needed. Therefore, managers need reliable lead time estimates—estimates of the time it takes to receive materials and goods after placing an order for them. Managers also need to know how variable their demand forecasts and lead times are. Finally, because one of the key objectives of an inventory management system is to minimize inventory costs, a reliable costing system should be in place to give managers accurate estimates of their firms' ordering, setup, holding, and stock-out costs.

Inventory Classification: The ABC Method

Many companies, especially manufacturers, carry thousands of individual items in inventory—items that need to be classified based on their importance to the firm's operations. The ABC classification method, widely used for this purpose, classifies items into A, B, and C categories according to criteria such as their unit costs, value, or the annual revenue they generate for a firm. For example, if the unit cost is the criterion, a department store such as Macy's (Macy's, Inc., Cincinnati, OH) would classify expensive items such as designer clothes and expensive jewelry as A items, vacuum cleaners and dress shoes as B items, and kitchen equipment such as bowls and gadgets and women's accessories as C items. Note that in an ABC classification, an item having low value but high sales volume can also be categorized as an A item.

If annual revenue is the criterion, a firm would do the following to classify its inventory:

1. Calculate the year's sales revenue for each item (units sold × cost per unit).
2. Rank the items in descending order based on revenue.
3. Calculate the revenue generated by each item as a percentage of the firm's total annual revenue, and compute the cumulative percentage of the revenue generated.
4. Place the items that generate approximately 80% of the firm's cumulative annual revenue in the A category.
5. Place the items that generate approximately 15% of the firm's cumulative annual revenue in the B category.
6. Place the items that generate approximately the remaining 5% of the firm's cumulative annual revenue in the C category.

To classify a firm's MRO inventory, the value of the items—what they cost and how many of them are used annually—can be used to categorize them. The ABC classification method also serves as a guide to the cycle counting procedure we discussed earlier. For example, a firm is likely to cycle count A items more frequently than B items, and B items more frequently C items.

EXAMPLE 15.1: Using the ABC classification method, categorize the inventory items in Table 15.1.

 Example 15.1

TABLE 15.1: Example of Inventory Items for ABC Classification

ITEM	ANNUAL SALES (IN UNITS)	UNIT COST (IN U.S. DOLLARS)
1	6,000	1.4
2	2,500	8
3	12,000	20
4	7,000	3
5	8,000	0.7
6	10,000	14
7	4,000	0.7
8	5,500	1.3
9	8,000	4
10	4,000	2.5

SOLUTION

Using the six steps, you would calculate the annual sales value in dollars for each item. In the following Microsoft Excel Microsoft Corporation (Redmond, WA) spreadsheet, column D shows the annual sales value in dollars for each item as well as the firm's total annual sales value in U.S. dollars for all items. The firm's total annual sales in dollars is then employed to figure out the percentage that each item contributes to the total (see column E). Using these percentages of sales in dollars for each item, cumulative percentages are calculated (see column F). Based on these cumulative percentages, the items are then categorized as A, B, or C items (shown in column G).

The solution to this example can be found in an Excel spreadsheet shown in Screenshot 15.1.

ABC classification method: sorting items into A, B, and C categories according to criteria such as their unit costs, value, or the annual revenue they generate for a firm

SCREENSHOT 15.1: Example 1 – ABC Classification

	A	B	C	D	E	F	G
1	Chapter-15-Example-1-ABC Classification						
2				=(B4*C4)		=(E5+F4)	
3	Item	Annual Sales in Units	Unit Cost	Sales in Dollars	Percentage of Total Dollar Sales	Cumulative Percentage	Classification
4	3	12,000	$20.00	240,000	49.286%	49.286%	A
5	6	10,000	$14.00	140,000	28.750%	78.037%	A
6	9	8,000	$4.00	32,000	6.572%	84.608%	B
7	4	7,000	$3.00	21,000	4.313%	88.921%	B
8	2	2,500	$8.00	20,000	4.107%	93.028%	B
9	10	4,000	$2.50	10,000	2.054%	95.082%	C
10	1	6,000	$1.40	8,400	1.725%	96.807%	C
11	8	5,500	$1.30	7,150	1.468%	98.275%	C
12	5	8,000	$0.70	5,600	1.150%	99.425%	C
13	7	4,000	$0.70	2,800	0.575%	100.000%	C
14				$486,950			
15					=(D13/$D$14)		
16							

Inventory Control Systems

There are three basic types of inventory control systems. Each has benefits and drawbacks. Choosing the right inventory control systems depends on the kinds of the products a firm sells and which system provides the most value for the company.

SINGLE-PERIOD SYSTEMS

When a firm uses a single-period system, the entire inventory of a product is ordered at one time—that is, in a single-period—and is not replenished. A company will often use a single-period system when products are seasonal or have a limited shelf life. Newspapers, magazines, Valentine's Day roses, and fresh fish are examples.

With a single-period system, the firm has only one chance to get the quantity right when ordering the product because it has no value after the time it is needed. If too many of the products are ordered but not sold within a specified time period, they may have to be sold at a discounted price, discarded, or hauled away at an additional cost. If the company orders too little, then the company will lose sales because the item isn't in stock. Inventory control for single-period systems are discussed in Chapter 16.

PERIODIC REVIEW SYSTEMS

With periodic review systems (also referred to as *periodic inventory systems*), inventory is physically counted periodically, such as weekly, monthly, or annually, and all reordering takes place at these intervals, which is why this method is also sometimes referred to as a *fixed order interval system*. Periodic inventory systems are best suited for businesses that sell low-volume products or for smaller retail stores, such as college bookstores. After the inventory of each item is counted, a replenishment order for that item is placed. Because periodic review systems do not require stringent monitoring of inventory, they are best suited for the C category of items under the ABC classification scheme.

In a periodic inventory system, inventory isn't monitored between orders. As a result, inventory records don't have to be kept continuously. In addition, because the physical counting and ordering of replacement items occur at the same time, the costs associated with purchasing and ordering them can be minimized because of economies of scale. The biggest drawback of periodic review systems is the lack of direct inventory control between order review periods. For example, a manager might not realize that the stock of an important inventory item is low until later in the period when it's counted. As a result, periodic systems can lead to stock-outs and the need to carry extra safety stock. Inventory control models for periodic review systems are discussed in Chapter 16.

CONTINUOUS REVIEW SYSTEMS

In continuous review systems (also known as *perpetual inventory* or *fixed order quantity* system), inventory levels of every item in stock, including its quantity and availability, are monitored and updated continuously. A continuous review system requires stringent monitoring of inventories because they have high value, and it is best suited for the A category of items under the ABC classification scheme. Information technology tools are used with most continuous review systems.

Single-period system: ordering the entire inventory of a product at one time and it is not replenished

Periodic review systems: a system in which inventory is physically counted periodically and all reordering takes place at these intervals (also referred to as periodic inventory systems or fixed order interval systems)

Continuous review systems: a system in which inventory levels of every item in stock, including its quantity and availability, are monitored and updated continuously (also known as perpetual inventory or fixed order quantity systems)

Consider This:
IKEA's Successful Inventory Management Techniques

The world's largest home furnishing retailer, IKEA (Delft, the Netherlands), has 375 stores in 47 countries. It ranked 46 on the esteemed World's Most Valuable Brands list put out by *Forbes*, and it had net sales of US$36.3 billion in 2016. Each IKEA store is enormous, holding more than 9,500 products. How does IKEA offer so much at such a low price, while always being able to keep items in stock?

Stephen Chernin/Getty Images News/Getty Images

1. IKEA Has a Clear Vision—Its goal is to provide well-designed, functional home furnishings at the lowest possible prices. Its supply chain operations and inventory management practices work together to support this goal. IKEA is so sure of its goals that it commits to a catalog of products that will be stocked for a year at guaranteed prices.

2. Cost Savings in Furniture Design—IKEA designs its products for low manufacturing costs while providing functional performance, efficient distribution, high quality, and low environmental impact. To illustrate, more than 50% of the products are made from sustainable or recycled products. IKEA uses the fewest possible materials to make its furniture, while maintaining quality and durability.

3. Sustainable Supplier Relationships—IKEA depends on getting good prices from its suppliers to keep its own retail prices low. Because IKEA buys products from more than 1,800 suppliers in 50 countries, it is in the position to negotiate prices with suppliers, check material quality, and monitor working conditions within those supplier organizations. IKEA also builds long-term business relationships with suppliers by signing long-term contracts, which allows it to lower the prices of products further.

4. Do-It-Yourself Assembly—Most IKEA furniture is designed and sold in pieces for the customer to assemble, lowering packaging costs. The pieces are packed into flat packages that take up less room in trucks, lowering shipping costs, and maximizing the number of products that can be shipped. This packaging system also takes up less space in warehouse racks, allowing IKEA stores extra room to stock additional items for order fulfillment.

5. Combining Retail and Warehouse Processes—IKEA stores have warehouses on the premises. Customers browse for items on the main showroom floor. They then select the products themselves from shelving within the warehouse part of the store, which features product racks as high as the typical person can reach. After hours, new inventory is moved down to these lower, customer-accessible slots. An additional warehouse that is accessible only to workers contains items too bulky for customers to load without help from the staff.

6. Cost-Per-Touch Inventory Tactic—Retailers know that the more hands that touch the product leads to more costs associated with it. That is, extra costs are incurred whenever the product is handled, shipped, moved, and loaded. To minimize these costs, IKEA allows customers to select and retrieve their own packages. These cost savings are passed along to the customers.

7. In-Store Logistics—IKEA's in-store logistics personnel handle inventory management at its stores by monitoring and recording deliveries, checking delivery notices, sorting and separating the goods, and getting products to the correct sales areas. Overall, they ensure an efficient flow of goods within the stores.

8. High-Flow and Low-Flow Warehouses—IKEA distinguishes between the more popular items, referred to as high-flow items, and the lower selling products by creating separate warehouses for each category. Their high-flow facilities are highly automated and support the continuous storing and retrieval of top-selling goods, whereas the low-flow warehouses are more manual because workers will not be shifting and moving inventory around too much.

These inventory management strategies have made IKEA the world's most successful furniture retailer with low operating costs and high product demand, allowing the company to stay competitive in the industry as it continually seeks more advanced methods to streamline supply chain management.[5]

For example, all major retailers and supermarkets use barcodes. When a product is sold, the barcode, or universal product code (UPC), on the product's package is scanned. The transaction is immediately recorded, and the product's inventory level is instantly updated. When a firm's inventory falls to a predetermined level, which is referred to as the *reorder point*, a new order is placed to replenish it. Determining order quantities and reorder points is discussed in Chapter 16.

Tagging packages with RFID tags has made inventory tracking even more efficient and accurate for companies that handle high volumes of inventory.

©iStockphoto.com/nullplus

The use of **radio frequency identification (RFID)** has further increased the accuracy and efficiency of managing inventory. RFID readers wirelessly detect RFID tags attached to product packages, pallets, boxes, or containers and transmit the information via radio waves to inventory management systems. This ability to track products enables a business to identify and locate any product that is within the range of the RFID reader. RFID is most appropriate for companies that handle and manage large amounts of inventory.

Both active and passive RFID systems can be used for inventory tracking. Active RFID tags have a battery, which is used to run the microchip's circuitry, and the tag broadcasts a signal to a reader in a way that is analogous to the transmission of a cell phone signal to a base station. Passive tags have no battery and draw power from the reader, which sends out electromagnetic waves that induce a current in the tag's antenna. Active tags are useful for tracking high-value goods that need to be scanned over long ranges, such as railway cars on a track, but they can cost a dollar or more each, making them too expensive to put on low-cost items. Many companies prefer passive ultrahigh frequency (UHF) tags, which cost less than 50 cents for large volumes. Their read range isn't as far—often less than 20 feet—but they are far less expensive than active tags and can be disposed of with the product packaging. When active RFID tags are used, inventory movements are monitored by fixed tag scanners located throughout the company's warehouse or storage facility. Whenever an item with an RFID tag passes through the fixed tag scanner, the information related to the item is recorded. When passive RFID tags are used, workers track the movement of inventory with handheld scanners.[6] Large retail chains, such as Wal-Mart (Wal-Mart Stores Inc., Bentonville, AR) and Target (Target Corporation, Minneapolis, MN), as well as companies in other industries, use RFID tags and require their suppliers to. Nonetheless, because of its relatively high cost, the adoption of RFID is still limited.

15.6 Uncertainty in Supply Chain Inventories: The Bullwhip Effect

15.6

Identify the causes of the bullwhip effect and other causes of uncertainty in supply chain inventories.

Radio frequency identification (RFID): technology that allows tags attached to product packages, pallets, boxes, or containers to transmit information via radio waves to readers, allowing companies to wirelessly track inventory

Bullwhip effect: the result of a change in consumer demand that causes a company in a supply chain in close proximity to the consumer (such as a retailer) to order more goods from the immediate upstream supplier (such as a wholesaler or distributor) to meet the demand

Because inventory is an idle asset that consumes space and capital and generates no income, businesses try to avoid holding any more inventory than is absolutely necessary. As we've seen, however, the uncertainties in demand, supply, prices, and lead times can often push companies to hold excessive inventories. In Chapter 14, we talked about a phenomenon called the **bullwhip effect**, which occurs when a change in consumer demand causes a company in a supply chain in close proximity to the consumer (such as a retailer) to order more goods from the immediate upstream supplier (such as a wholesaler or distributor) to meet the demand. The wholesaler or distributor, in turn, orders more goods from the manufacturer. The manufacturer in response to this additional demand from the wholesaler increases the orders for materials from the upstream raw material suppliers. That is, the change in the demand reverberates upstream in the supply chain. For example, if the retailer is running a promotion for the product, and the wholesaler doesn't know it, the wholesaler will think that the demand for the product has increased permanently and increase its inventory accordingly—and the effect will continue up the chain. This effect causes larger and larger demand swings, leading to a massive buildup of buffer inventories and high costs. The bullwhip effect gets its name from the oscillating product demand illustrated in Figure 15.4. Notice how the pattern in the figure is similar to a whip when it's cracked.

The bullwhip effect is not uncommon. When the world economy began recovering from the great recession of 2009–2011, many manufacturers increased their orders with suppliers, leading to progressively greater increases in orders for raw materials to produce new quantities of tier 1 and tier 2 supplies. At the U.S.-headquartered Caterpillar Inc. (Peoria, IL), for example, executives routinely plan for bullwhip effects when placing orders. They have noted that if Caterpillar increases its production by 15%, many of its suppliers would more than double their shipments to the company.[7] That's a dramatic difference, indicating the bullwhip effect is occurring.

Causes of the Bullwhip Effect

To address the inventory buildup that results from the bullwhip effect, companies first need to understand what causes it. There are four major underlying causes for the bullwhip effect.[8]

FIGURE 15.4: The Bullwhip Effect

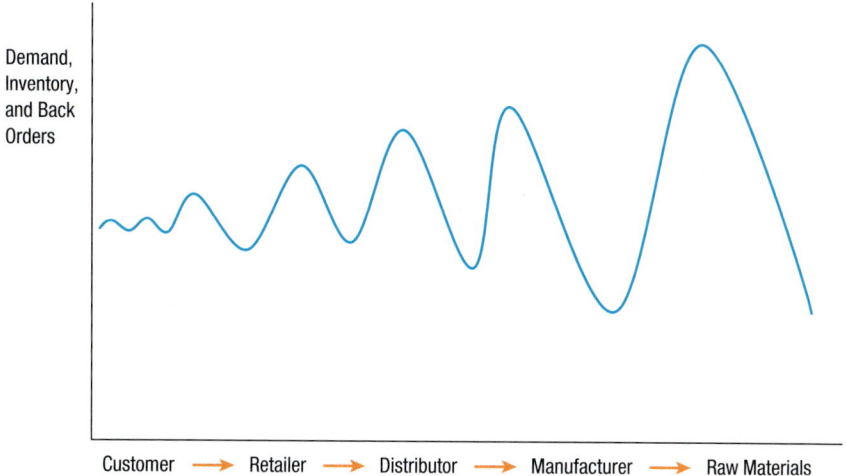

REVISED DEMAND FORECASTS

Every company in a supply chain forecasts product demand for the purposes of production scheduling, capacity planning, inventory control, or material requirements planning. Because forecasts are based on the order histories of their immediate downstream supply chain partners, any increase or decrease in one of their orders sends a signal about future product demand. Consequently, the immediate upstream supply chain members update their demand forecasts and orders accordingly. This ripple effect continues upstream throughout the supply chain. Moreover, because demand forecasts are rarely 100% accurate, each firm in the supply chain is basing its order and production decisions on inaccurate or distorted information. That is, the forecasting errors throughout the chain start to compound, making the problem worse.

The Bullwhip Effect

The bullwhip effect becomes even more pronounced if downstream supply chain members have to hold several weeks of safety stock because the lead times to get it are long. Suppose the drugmaker Pfizer, Inc. (New York, NY), needs to purchase a special chemical but that its supplier requires 90 days to synthesize and refine it. Because of the long lead time, Pfizer will have to stockpile larger quantities of the chemical so that it does not run out before it receives a new shipment.

ORDER ACCUMULATION

Instead of placing frequent orders with their upstream supply chain partners, companies in a supply chain often use **batch ordering** to accumulate or build up demand for products and materials before placing their order. By batch ordering periodically—weekly, biweekly, or monthly—a firm can avoid the increased costs associated with placing frequent orders and goods shipped in partially filled trucks. Order sizes will vary considerably when periodic ordering such as this is used. For example, they may be high in one month and low the next month, amplifying the variability of demand in the supply chain and contributing to the bullwhip effect.

PRICE FLUCTUATIONS

Marketing promotions, such as price discounts, coupons, rebates, and quantity discounts, offered by suppliers cause price fluctuations that also contribute to the bullwhip effect. Many downstream customers will buy products and materials in large quantities when they are discounted. Then, when prices return to normal levels, these customers will stop buying the products because they will have excess inventory on hand. This variation in buying patterns can also lead to a bullwhip effect

RATIONING AND SHORTAGE GAMING

When the demand for a product exceeds its supply, its manufacturer will often ration the sale of it to the firm's immediate customers in the supply chain relative to the size of the order. That is, suppliers ration the amount of a product they will ship to their customers based on the relative order sizes placed historically by their customers. Bigger customers get first priority. More of the product will be shipped to them sooner than to smaller customers. Anticipating the rationing, customers, in turn, will order more of the product to get around the shortage. Eventually, when the demand for the product tapers off, the downstream customers in the supply chain will stop placing orders or cancel their

Batch ordering: ordering inventory periodically to accumulate or build up demand for products and materials before placing an order to avoid the increased costs associated with placing frequent orders and goods shipped in partially filled trucks

existing orders. This ordering pattern is often referred to as gaming and leads to the bullwhip effect because the manufacturer, unable to determine the real demand for the product, will have stockpiled inventories of it.

Strategies for Mitigating the Bullwhip Effect

If managers can thoroughly analyze and understand the causes of the bullwhip effect, they can mitigate it. The innovative strategies that many companies have used to minimize the problem fall into three categories: *information sharing*, *channel alignment*, and *operational efficiency*.[9]

INFORMATION SHARING

Recall that we discussed collaborative planning, forecasting, and replenishment (CPFR) in Chapter 12. If supply chain members share inventory information, then they can coordinate their individual operations and reduce the potential distortion that occurs when each supply chain member updates its forecasts independently. One way retailers make information available is to share their point-of-sales (POS) data with their upstream manufacturers, which helps the manufacturers understand what the real consumer demand is for a given product. Companies such as IBM (International Business Machines Corporation, Armonk, NY), Apple Inc. (Cupertino, CA), and HP Inc. (formerly Hewlett-Packard, Palo Alto, CA) require sellers of their products to provide them with this POS data. Companies that use electronic data interchange (EDI) and the Internet to transmit orders can also facilitate the sharing of timely information among supply chain members. Similarly, downstream supply chain members that have access to inventory information provided by their upstream supply chain members will be less concerned about a product's availability and less likely to game orders.

Using a postponement strategy, which was discussed in an earlier chapter in this textbook, is another way to counter the bullwhip effect. By delaying the final assembly of the product until the more accurate demand information becomes available from the retailer, the manufacturer or distributor can control the buildup of unwanted inventory. For example, Bang & Olufsen A/S (Struer, Denmark), the Danish luxury video and audio product maker, assembles and packages final goods at a separate facility, enabling the company to meet customer-specific demands for features, color, and size without having to overstock inventory. The Benetton Group (aka United Colors of Benetton, Treviso, Italy) has successfully used a postponement strategy in its clothing manufacturing for years. Traditionally, cloth is first dyed and then knitted into garments, which is a lengthy process. Benetton pioneered the idea of knitting garments using bleached yarn and delaying the dying until the last possible moment to ensure that its garments were using popular colors. Before postponement, there were too many garments in colors that the buying public didn't want, while other popular colors quickly sold out. Postponement allowed the company to reduce its unsold stock from 33% to 8%. Benetton's postponement model enables the clothing manufacturer to capitalize on the latest trends while minimizing waste and time spent making garments.[10]

Bang & Olufsen uses a separate facility to assemble its products just before they are sent out to customers. This postponement in assembly allows the company to fulfill custom orders from its customers and offsets the bullwhip effect.

Bloomberg/Bloomberg/Getty Images

CHANNEL ALIGNMENT

Another strategy to prevent information distortion leading to the bullwhip effect is channel alignment or cooperation among supply chain members. When upstream and downstream partners in a supply chain use this strategy, they coordinate pricing, transportation, inventory planning, and the ownership of certain supply chain activities such as warehousing and transportation. A vendor-managed inventory (VMI) is a channel alignment method that mitigates the bullwhip effect caused by forecast updates. With VMI, an upstream supply chain member (such as a manufacturer) has complete access to the demand and inventory information of a downstream supply chain member (a retailer). The upstream supply chain partner uses this information to revise its forecasts and re-supply schedules as consumer demand changes. Companies such as P&G (Procter & Gamble Co., Cincinnati, OH), Texas Instruments Inc. (Dallas, TX), HP, Motorola (Motorola Solutions, Inc., Schaumburg, IL), and Apple regularly use VMI with some of their suppliers and customers. For example, to facilitate

information sharing and diminish the bullwhip effect in its diaper business, P&G uses VMI, both with its supplier 3M (3M Company, Maplewood, MN) and its customer Wal-Mart.

Yet another way to prevent information distortion in a supply chain is disintermediation. When disintermediation is used, an upstream supply chain member such as a manufacturer sells directly to the final consumer, bypassing distributors and retailers. The advantage of this approach is that the manufacturer knows what the demand pattern for its products is. Both Apple and Dell Inc. (Round Rock, TX) use this strategy. Apple sells its products through online shopping, its own retail stores, and maintains a presence within some larger, "big box" stores, like Target and Best Buy. Dell has opted for a nearly exclusive use of online retail channels. Another channel alignment strategy that can be used to control the bullwhip effect is portfolio planning, in which a company signs long-term contracts with one or two suppliers. However, in order to respond quickly to unexpected changes in demand, the firm has a smaller base of suppliers it can contract with on short notice.[11]

To reduce the practice of batch ordering, supply chain partners can work together to provide an upstream supply chain member with the material usage patterns of its immediate downstream customer on a regular schedule. This information enables the supplier to anticipate large batched orders when there is a surge in demand. Recall that one reason that companies in a supply chain use batch ordering and order less frequently is to reduce the high cost of paperwork associated with traditional ordering practices. Nevertheless, the use of EDI greatly reduces the paperwork associated with generating an order. By using EDI, companies such as Nabisco (subsidiary of Mondelēz International, East Hanover, NJ), P&G (already introduced), and General Electric (aka GE, Fairfield, CT) have not only greatly reduced the cost associated with ordering, but they have also enabled their customers to order more frequently.

To reduce batch-ordering practices further and to reap simultaneously the cost advantages of full truck load shipments, manufacturers may have their distributors order an assortment of different products instead of accumulating orders for a single product. P&G and the British retailers Tesco PLC (Hertfordshire, U.K.) and J Sainsbury plc (London, U.K.) use this strategy. Using third-party logistics (3PL), companies can also reduce batching orders by consolidating loads from multiple suppliers located near each other. Yet another approach to controlling the bullwhip effect is to have upstream suppliers coordinate with downstream customers in a supply chain to spread their orders or replenishments evenly over time. For example, P&G coordinates shipments with its retailers by scheduling regular deliveries to all of its retailers evenly throughout a week.

A strategy to mitigate the bullwhip effect caused by marketing promotions and trade discounts leading to price fluctuations is to reduce their frequency. Wal-Mart, for example, is famous for everyday low prices for most of its stock, in part to avoid price fluctuations and allow the company's upstream suppliers to better plan their manufacturing and delivery schedules. In addition, if upstream suppliers allocate products in proportion to past sales records rather than rationing products based on current order sizes, the bullwhip effect that occurs when downstream channel members resort to over ordering during supply shortages can be reduced. During periods of supply shortages, The General Motors Company (aka GM or General Motors, Detroit, MI), Texas Instruments, and Hewlett-Packard have used this strategy. Implementing strict cancellation policies will also discourage buyers from exaggerating their needs and canceling orders.

IMPROVING OPERATIONAL EFFICIENCY

Single-echelon inventory systems, in which each supply chain partner (echelon) sequentially forecasts demand, invariably lead to the bullwhip effect. By contrast, in multi-echelon inventory systems, optimum levels of inventory are determined and updated continuously across the supply chain network based on the demand variability, lead times, delays, and service levels at the higher levels (echelons) in the supply chain. Because upstream supply chain sites operate with better demand and inventory information from downstream sites in multi-echelon inventory systems, operational efficiency improves and there is better control of inventories and the bullwhip effect. Finally, long resupply lead times that aggravate the bullwhip effect can be reduced through improvements in operational efficiency. Such efficiency can be achieved through just-in-time replenishment practices such as continuous replenishment programs (CRPs), quick response (QR), and effective consumer response (ECR). ECR is a collaborative effort used by businesses in the grocery industry to be more responsive to consumer demand and to reduce supply chain costs. Similarly, QR is a collaborative between suppliers and retailers to improve suppliers' order response time. In addition, the use of activity-based costing (ABC) systems that account for inventory cost enable companies to recognize the excessive costs associated with forward buying when trade deals and quantity discounts are offered.

Disintermediation: process when an upstream supply chain member such as a manufacturer sells directly to the final consumer, bypassing distributors and retailers

Portfolio planning: a channel alignment strategy in which a company signs long-term contracts with one or two suppliers

Single-echelon inventory systems: a system in which each supply chain partner sequentially forecasts demand, invariably leading to the bullwhip effect

Multi-echelon inventory systems: a system in which optimum levels of inventory are determined and updated continuously across the supply chain network based on the demand variability, lead times, delays, and service levels at the higher levels in the supply chain

Activity-based costing: a system that accounts for inventory cost and enables companies to recognize the excessive costs associated with forward buying when trade deals and quantity discounts are offered

In summary, companies can effectively counteract the bullwhip effect by thoroughly understanding its underlying causes and by implementing innovating strategies that promote quick flow and sharing of information, forging new organizational relationships with other channel members, and improving operational efficiency.

15.7 Ethical and Sustainability Issues

Explain how companies can include sustainability and ethical practices in inventory management.

Ethics in Inventory Management

Globally, an estimated US$8 trillion of finished goods inventory is sitting idle. This excess inventory is not only a waste of money but also represents an enormous waste of energy and other renewable resources.[12] Environmental awareness and improvements in sustainable supply chain management are forcing companies to manage their inventories in ways that are more sustainable. Let's look at what they are doing:

- *Applying Lean Principles to Inventory Management*

The lean principles discussed in Chapter 14 can be used to manage inventory in ways that are more sustainable. In fact, surveys suggest that well over 30% of companies are adopting lean practices in their inventory management.[13] Lean practices allow organizations to plan their use of scarce or perishable resources better. For example, if a restaurant orders too many vegetables that are not used within a relatively short period of time, the vegetables will spoil and have to be thrown away. Managers can use tools such as value stream mapping and lean Six Sigma to reduce the number of products that do not sell well or that are simply not needed.[14] For example, Amazon.com (aka Amazon, Seattle, WA) has worked to keep its inventory as lean as possible, to save money on inventory holding costs, but also to make sure that it is able to respond to immediate demands from customers. Using Toyota's (Toyota Motor Corporation, Toyota City, Japan) lean methods, robots, an incentivized workforce, and data management systems, Amazon has built an inventory management system that allows it to focus on frequent reordering and rapid response to customer orders. By keeping inventory methods as lean as possible, Amazon contributes to several sustainability goals, including: minimizing wasted movement, less excess inventory, and reduced waiting times.[15]

Utilizing lean principles in inventory management prevents the build-up and waste of inventory with a short shelf life, like produce at a restaurant.

©iStockphoto.com/muratkoc

- *Including Sustainability in the Inventory Classification Scheme*

Including sustainability in a firm's inventory classification scheme can give the company additional insight into the impact of slow-moving goods or idle inventory. For example, the classification scheme could be designed to track the percentage of environmentally friendly products such as biodegradable or recycled materials that the company uses as opposed to materials that harm the environment. Furthermore, the firm can calculate the carbon footprint costs of reordering to minimize reorder deliveries and either order in larger quantities or find greener alternatives. As another example of applying sustainability principles to inventory management, Wal-Mart worked with The Minute Maid Company (Sugar Land, TX) to reorganize its delivery and inventory systems. Now, Minute Maid's Simply Orange Juice goes directly from a production facility in Florida to Wal-Mart distribution centers. Eliminating the intermediate step of delivery to Minute Maid's own distribution centers cut CO_2 emissions by 1,500 metric tons annually and added six days to the shelf life of the orange juice.[16]

- *Using Environmentally Friendly Materials in Product Development and Manufacturing Activities*

By sourcing raw materials that are as environmentally friendly as possible (such as biodegradable materials or recycled materials), companies can ensure that sustainability is at the forefront of their operational and inventory management activities. The Nokia Corporation (Espoo, Finland) has been striving to make 100% of the materials used in its phones recyclable through collection of e-waste.[17]

- *Using State-of-the-Art Technology*

Technologies, such as cloud-based networks that can store data centrally, allow companies to track inventory and then match it with demand. As a result, decisions on inventory allocation can be made when they are actually needed, avoiding build-up of excess inventory, higher handling costs, waste of renewable resources, and expedited shipments.

As in other business decision-making areas, the potential for ethical lapses also exists in inventory management. Some of the ethics problems that occur in inventory management include:[18]

- Misleading buyers about the price of storing inventory for them or the status of their inventory.
- Covering up damaged products that are ready for shipment.
- Manipulating inventory figures and levels when questions about the status of the inventory are raised by outside buyers or auditors or internally by a company's managers or internal auditors. Former executives of the drug store retailer Rite Aid (Rite Aid Corporation, East Pennsboro Township, PA) were convicted of accounting and inventory fraud, by using creative but illegal tactics to inflate Rite Aid's earnings artificially. In one example, the company manipulated inventory levels and, to make higher profits off existing inventory, demanded refunds by reporting incorrectly to its suppliers that large quantities of goods were damaged and outdated.[19]

One way to prevent inventory-related ethics violations from occurring is to establish a **code of ethics**, which are a specific set of professional behaviors and values including confidentiality, accuracy, privacy, and integrity that all company employees must know and strictly abide by. In addition to having a code of ethics, companies should also enforce the standards when ethical violations do occur.

15.8 Global Inventory Management

Demonstrate the requirements for managing inventory in global supply chains.

Global Inventory Management

For companies that are engaged in global sourcing or have offshore manufacturing facilities and suppliers, the sheer complexity of their long, multitiered supply chains, coupled with the need to control and manage their inventories in a global context, can be daunting. The Ford Motor Company (aka Ford, Dearborn, MI), Sony Corporation (Tokyo, Japan), Harley Davidson (Harley Davidson, Inc., Milwaukee, WI), and Wal-Mart have been able to reduce their global pipeline inventories to a certain extent by having their suppliers position inventory close to their facilities to meet tight manufacturing schedules or just-in-time demand requirements. These companies collaborate and share demand information with their suppliers, which in turn can adjust their production and distribution schedules to meet changes in demand.

Some large, global companies are able to reduce their inventory levels by pushing the responsibility for carrying it onto their offshore tier-one, tier-two, and tier-three suppliers. Consequently, there may be very little reduction in the overall inventory levels across the total supply chains of these companies. In fact, research has shown that with globalization and the outsourcing of manufacturing to off-shore companies, the amount of inventory across the supply chain has steadily increased. The increase has occurred because of uncontrollable factors such as long transportation times, congestion at foreign ports, and security issues that inevitably increase inventory levels in global supply chains. Very few global companies are well equipped to address the problem of excess inventory across the global supply chain.[20]

The first requirement for managing inventories in global supply chains is for companies to have a clear understanding of the nature of their business operations (manufacturing, retail, service, and so on) and the impact globalization has on their supply chains. Second, global companies must understand that managing inventories across their supply chain partners abroad requires radically different tools than those used to manage inventories in domestic supply chains. The lack of homogeneity and the disparate computer and software systems that exist among global supply chain partners make gathering meaningful information difficult. For example, although enterprise resource planning (ERP) systems have helped firms effectively manage inventories within their organizations, the systems may be inadequate in the complex global supply chains. Even with improved ERP software that can track inventory and the widespread use of logistics outsourcing (using 3PLs and 4PLs), companies have not been very successful at reducing the amount of inventory they have in their global supply chains. To manage inventory in a global environment effectively, an organization needs to integrate and synchronize its ERP system with its global supply chain.

A strong ERP functionality means that the solutions offered by existing ERP systems should be enhanced with additional business intelligence systems so that relevant information can be collected, transformed, and provided in a timely manner. Achieving full global chain functionality implies the ability to monitor the performance of all tiers of suppliers, track goods and materials through all global sources of supply, manage costs in a complex, multilevel global supply chain environment,

Code of ethics: a specific set of professional behaviors and values including confidentiality, accuracy, privacy, and integrity that all company employees must know and strictly abide and ensure compliance at all components including country, supplier, product, customs, and security. To achieve this integration, companies need to get as close as possible to end customer demand to improve collaborative planning with their supply chain partners. In addition, companies can better manage their global inventories at reasonable costs through the use of technologies, such as cloud computing, which enable companies to access the right information when they need it.

15.9 Service Sector Inventory Management

15.9

Describe how service firms apply inventory management methods to their operations.

 Inventory Management in the Service Sector

Although services are intangible, service-sector companies also hold some tangible goods as inventory. For example, in the hospitality industry, restaurants hold food products and cooking ingredients in their inventories. Similarly, empty rooms in hotels or unoccupied seats in airlines are regarded as unused inventory. In the financial services industry, monetary instruments and funds available for lending can be considered as inventory waiting to be used.[21]

Because services are unique, the particular inventory control methods used will vary depending on the type of service offered. For example, inventory control for the food-service industry poses special challenges because many of the products served are perishable and improper handling can lead to food-borne illnesses. In businesses like restaurants, the focus of an inventory control method is to track the movement of products frequently and proactively. Because items are perishable and need frequent replenishment, on-hand inventory has to be tracked frequently, perhaps hourly or daily rather than weekly or monthly. The batches that items come from should also be apparent so they can be traced should problems occur. For example, when people became ill after dining at Olive Garden and Red Lobster (both owned by Darden Restaurants, Orlando, FL) restaurants in Iowa and Nebraska, the U.S. Food and Drug Administration (FDA) traced the source of the sickness to a parasite known as *Cyclospora* found on the lettuce that was supplied to restaurants in those states by Taylor Farms de Mexico (aka Taylor Fresh Foods, Salinas, CA), a processor of food-service salads.[22] Managing inventory in food-service companies also requires daily monitoring of demand patterns that occur and the expiration dates of perishable items so that the stocks of these can be rotated.[23]

In the airline industry, the inventory of available seats on a plane is typically divided into service classes (such as first, business, or economy class) and booking classes with different prices. Managing seat inventory in an airline involves deciding how many seats will be made available in each fare class. The objective of inventory management in the airline industry is to maximize the total revenues generated by the mixture of fare classes sold for a flight. Service companies, such as airlines and hotels, that have inflexible and expensive capacity with highly perishable inventory (airline seats and hotel rooms) use an approach called yield management (also called *revenue management*) to reduce the excess inventory. Yield management is a variable pricing strategy that enables service companies such as these to control their inventory (seats and rooms) by selling the available inventory to the right customer at the right time for the right price. A more detailed discussion of yield management is presented in Chapter 17.

Effective inventory management is also vital for service organizations in the health-care industry. For example, hospitals have to manage and control complex and diverse inventories of expensive surgical instruments, bed linens, gowns and uniforms, radiology equipment, supplies of drugs, chemicals, and gases. A well-designed inventory management system will enable hospitals to track the use and availability of these items to minimize the potential for loss and theft, and it allows the hospitals to manage more effectively the rotation and replacement of equipment among medical procedures, sterilization, and storage. Hospitals and other health-care organizations also require an effective inventory management system to track the availability of crucial specialty products, such as implantable medical devices (such as aneurysm clips and cerebral spinal fluid shunts) and transplantable organs (hearts or kidneys), to determine what was used on a specific patient for a specific operation. Having this information is vital because in the event the implanted device fails or causes any sort of adverse reaction in the patient, the medical device's history and movement can be traced through the health-care organization's supply chain.

To manage their inventories effectively, service organizations can adopt many of the best practices used in the manufacturing sector. These approaches include improving the demand forecasts for their services, just-in-time or stockless inventory systems, barcodes and RFID technologies for product tracking, and outsourcing the inventory management function to third-party service providers. For example, some hospitals have adopted a stockless inventory system in which much of the management of the hospital's supplies is switched to an outside vendor. By eliminating its storeroom and many of the staffing needs that go along with it, a hospital with a stockless inventory program can realize significant cost savings.

Visit **edge.sagepub.com/venkataraman** to help you accomplish your coursework goals in an easy-to-use learning environment.

- Mobile-friendly eFlashcards
- Mobile-friendly practice quizzes
- A complete online action plan

- Chapter summaries with learning objectives
- Video and multimedia resources

CHAPTER SUMMARY

15.1 Identify various types of inventory. The types of inventory are raw materials inventory, maintenance, repair and operations (MRO) inventory, work-in-process inventory, and finished-goods inventory.

15.2 Describe the types of inventory costs. Maintaining inventories can be expensive. The five most common types of costs associated with inventories are purchase costs, ordering costs, setup costs, holding or carrying costs, and stock-out costs.

15.3 Examine the role of inventory in an organization's supply chain. Organizations in a supply chain hold excess inventory for several reasons: (a) to meet expected normal demand, (b) to protect against shortages, (c) to benefit from quantity discounts, (d) to guard against future price increases, (e) to meet sales increases caused by seasonal demand and sales promotions, (f) to reduce transportation costs and transit times, and (g) to smooth out fluctuations in production requirements.

15.4 Use inventory management measures to determine the efficiency of an inventory system. Some of the key measurements companies use to track how well a firm's inventory is being managed include backorders and lost sales, inventory turnover, order fulfillment lead times, item fill rates, days of inventory in stock, inventory accuracy, and industry benchmarking. Inventory turnover is a measure of how frequently a business sells or replenishes its inventory in a given period.

15.5 Illustrate key features in inventory management systems. Inventory control systems include continuous review systems, periodic review systems, and single-period systems. For continuous review, inventory levels of every item in stock, including its quantity and availability, are monitored and updated on a continuous basis. Periodic review systems physically count inventory periodically, such as weekly, monthly, or annually, and all reordering takes place at these intervals. In a period-review system, inventory is counted on a periodic basis (monthly, quarterly, or annually). One way to improve the management of inventory is to categorize it using the ABC classification method.

15.6 Identify the causes of the bullwhip effect and other causes of uncertainty in supply chain inventories. The bullwhip effect occurs when a small change in the demand for a product downstream in a supply chain reverberates dramatically upstream in the supply chain. The bullwhip effect is caused by revised demand forecasts, order accumulation, price fluctuations, and rationing and shortage gaming. Three methods for mitigating the bullwhip effect are information sharing, channel alignment, and improved operational efficiency.

15.7 Explain how companies can include sustainability and ethical practices in inventory management. Among the strategies to make inventory systems sustainable are (a) applying lean principles in managing inventories, (b) including sustainability into the inventory classification scheme, (c) using environmentally friendly materials in product development and manufacturing, and (d) using technology. There are several ways that ethical lapses may occur in inventory management situations. Ethical violations may occur if firms mislead buyers about the price of storing inventory for them or the status of their inventory, cover up damaged products that are ready for shipment, and manipulate inventory figures and levels when questions about the status of the inventory are raised by outside buyers or auditors or internally by a company's managers or internal auditors.

15.8 Demonstrate the requirements for managing inventory in global supply chains. The first requirement for managing inventories in global supply chains is for companies to have a clear understanding of the nature of their business operations (manufacturing, retail, service, and so on) and the impact globalization has on their supply chains. Second, global companies must understand that managing inventories across their supply chain partners abroad requires radically different tools than the ones used to manage inventories in domestic supply chains.

15.9 Describe how service firms apply inventory management methods to their operations. Although services are intangible, service-sector companies also hold tangible goods as inventory. For example, in the hospitality industry, restaurants carry food products and cooking ingredients in their inventories. Similarly, empty rooms in hotels or unoccupied seats in airlines are regarded as unused inventory. In the financial services industry, monetary instruments and funds available for lending can be considered as inventory waiting to be used.

KEY TERMS

DISCUSSION AND REVIEW QUESTIONS

1. Discuss why inventory management is needed to manage operations and supply chains effectively.

2. Why must companies carry inventory?

3. Identify the various types of inventory, and explain how they contribute to the operations function of an organization.

4. What are the most common types of costs associated with inventory?

5. Why is inventory critical within supply chains?

6. Identify some of the key metrics organizations used to assess how well their inventories are being managed.

7. What are the advantages and disadvantages of physically counting inventory?

8. Use the ABC classification method to categorize the various items at a local grocery store. For example, in what category would fresh fruit and vegetables be listed? Why?

9. Explain the differences among inventory control systems. What are the advantages and disadvantages of each system?

10. Briefly explain the bullwhip effect. Why is it common in batch-ordering situations and for products with seasonal demand?

11. What steps can organizations take to minimize the bullwhip effect?

12. What are some strategies for making inventory systems sustainable?

13. Identify key issues related to managing inventory in the service sector.

SOLVED PROBLEM

1. Kirby Machine Tools wishes to maintain the fictional company's inventory of spare parts. The items, their unit costs, and amount sold annually are shown in Table 15.2. Use the ABC classification method to categorize the items.

TABLE 15.2: Example of Inventory Items for Solved ABC Classification Problem

Inventory Items	Unit Cost (in U.S. dollars)	Annual Sales (in units)
1	70	80
2	380	60
3	40	120
4	90	60
5	40	100
6	30	170
7	20	180
8	300	60
9	620	70
10	10	100

Solution: Using the ABC classification steps discussed in the chapter, in the following Excel screenshot shown, the annual sales in U.S. dollars for each item (column D), the percentage of the total dollar sales the item comprises (column E), and the cumulative percentage of total dollar sales (column F) are calculated. Column G shows how each item is classified as a result.

SCREENSHOT 15.2: Solved Problem 15.1

	A	B	C	D	E	F	G
1	Chapter-15-Solved Problem-1-ABC Classification						
2				=(B4*C4)		=(E5+F4)	
3	Inventory Items	Annual Units sold	Unit Cost	Sales in Dollars	Percentage of Total Dollar Sales	Cumulative Percentage	Classification
4	9	70	$620.00	43,400	38.171%	38.171%	A
5	2	60	$380.00	22,800	20.053%	58.223%	B
6	8	60	$300.00	18,000	15.831%	74.055%	B
7	1	80	$70.00	5,600	4.925%	78.980%	B
8	4	60	$90.00	5,400	4.749%	83.729%	B
9	6	170	$30.00	5,100	4.485%	88.215%	B
10	3	120	$40.00	4,800	4.222%	92.436%	B
11	5	100	$40.00	4,000	3.518%	95.954%	C
12	7	180	$20.00	3,600	3.166%	99.120%	C
13	10	100	$10.00	1,000	0.880%	100.000%	C
14				$113,700			
15					=(D13/$D$14)		
16							

PROBLEMS

1. The text provides a set of inventory management metrics. Suppose you were put in charge of a small clothing store at your local mall specializing in summer and beach wear. Select three of the inventory management metrics from the text, and discuss how you would apply them in your new job.

2. Inventory management in the service sector is a critical function because services often include tangible items as inventory. Discuss how you might manage inventory at a large, multiscreen movie theater. What types of inventory would you need to consider, and how would the nature of this business affect the way you catalogued and managed your inventory?

3. The text discusses four types of inventory. Select a business (not one given in the text), and identify examples of all four classes of inventory as they can be applied to that business.

4. Safety stock is critical for smoothing out potential supply disruptions during reordering. Can you think of some businesses or product categories that require more safety stock than others? (Hint: Why might a pharmaceutical company need large safety stocks of chemicals?)

5. Suppose you were a consultant working for the Wegmans (Wegmans Food Markets, Inc., Rochester, NY) grocery store organization and you were asked to advise the company on steps it could take to make its inventory management practices more sustainable. What steps or actions might you advise Wegmans to consider taking? (Hint: Look up Wegmans on the Internet to get a better sense of the company's operations.)

6. Develop an ABC inventory classification system for a minimum of 20 items at your local Wal-Mart (or a similar general retail store). What criterion did you use for classifying the goods into either the "A," "B," or "C" categories?

7. Lynne Chappell manages the inventory of supplies in a large hospital. To determine which items should be closely monitored, Lynne decided to use the ABC classification scheme to group the items on the basis of their value. As the following table shows, she took a random sample of 20 items and recorded the annual usage and unit cost of each. How should each item be classified?

Inventory Item	Unit Cost (in U.S. dollars)	Annual Usage	Inventory Item	Unit Cost (in U.S. dollars)	Annual Usage
P21	80	800	R82	20	80
A12	400	70	G65	80	70
K43	50	100	L71	220	200
S54	60	90	M94	70	80
C25	50	130	V45	15	60
D76	30	170	T62	30	180
E27	20	200	I17	20	80
F38	300	90	W22	300	90

Inventory Item	Unit Cost (in U.S. dollars)	Annual Usage	Inventory Item	Unit Cost (in U.S. dollars)	Annual Usage
H19	520	120	037	700	85
Q10	10	100	N88	5	100

8. Norman Stark, Inventory analyst at fictional Grimault Industries, is considering the use of the ABC method of classifying inventory so that he can exercise better control over the critical items in the company's inventory. He collected a random sample of ten inventory items, and their unit cost and annual usage are given in the following table. Use the ABC method to classify these inventory items:

Item	Annual Usage (in units)	Unit Cost (in U.S. dollars)
1	6,000	1.4
2	1,500	10
3	11,000	9.5
4	6,500	2.5
5	8,500	0.6
6	7,000	14.5
7	6,000	0.8
8	5,500	1.2
9	8,000	3.5
10	4,000	2.5

9. The financial statements of mythical Reliance Inc. show that in 2012 its beginning inventory balance was $31.82 billion and ending inventory balance was $30.25 billion. The company's cost of goods sold was reported as $290.70 billion (all in U.S. dollars). Calculate the company's inventory turnover ratio for 2012.

10. Refer to problem 3: What is Reliance Inc. days of inventory in stock if in 2013 the company's beginning inventory balance was $30.25 billion, its ending inventory balance was $29.12 billion, and the cost of goods sold was $272.22 billion (again in U.S. dollars)?

11. Hick's Furniture Company (not a real company) sells industrial furniture for office buildings. During the current year, the company reported cost of goods sold on its income statement of $1,650,000. The company's beginning inventory was $2,750,000 and its ending inventory was $3,825,000 (all in U.S. dollars). What is the company's inventory turnover ratio for the current year?

12. Refer to problem 5: Hick's company's inventory valuation was inaccurate. If the company's correct beginning inventory balance is $2,925,000 and its ending inventory was $4,110,000 (again in U.S. dollars), what is the revised inventory turnover ratio? What is the company's days of inventory in stock?

CASE STUDY 15.1 INVENTORY PRESSURES CAUSE TUESDAY MORNING TO ABANDON E-COMMERCE[24]

Although some large discount retailers like T.J. Maxx (subsidiary of TJX Companies, Framingham, MA) and Saks Fifth Avenue OFF 5TH (subsidiary of the Hudson's Bay Company, New York, NY) have relied heavily on e-commerce, the closeout retailer Tuesday Morning (Tuesday Morning Corporation, Dallas, TX) made the decision to shut down its e-commerce site. Instead the firm chose to focus on its brick-and-mortar stores. This decision seemed unusual at a time when most retailers were increasing their online shopping sites.

Nevertheless, maybe Tuesday Morning's decision isn't as unusual as it seems. Unlike discounters, closeout retailers like Tuesday Morning and Big

Lots (Big Lots, Inc., Columbus, OH) buy *closeout* items at wholesale prices from other *retailers* and then sell them at steep discounts. Closeout retailers face challenges that larger retailers don't, namely, ever-changing inventory that moves in and off shelves much too rapidly for them to keep their e-commerce sites updated. Inventory management and e-commerce software have improved, which is why it makes sense for Saks OFF 5TH to enter into this retailer sector. Yet, the best software management systems in the world cannot compensate for rapid inventory turnover. Rather than end up with unhappy online customers and lost revenue, Tuesday Morning is sticking to what it does best.

Questions:

1. Consider a sporting goods store and apply a type A, B, and C classification method to its inventory. What items are likely to turn over often as a result of seasonal demand?

2. Tuesday Morning's business model offers a unique counter-argument for linking e-commerce and inventory management. Can you think of other types of stores or industries in which inventory management problems would be an obstacle to the effective use of an e-commerce retail system?

CASE STUDY 15.2 INVENTORY MANAGEMENT IN THE AGE OF THE ONLINE SHOPPER

Online shoppers have high expectations. Shoppers expect more from online shopping than easy-to-use websites. Successful online retailers are creating online shopping experiences that encourage repeat customers and reward shopper loyalty.

In 2013, UPS (United Parcel Service, Inc., Sandy Springs, GA) conducted a series of studies to gain insight about the shopping behavior of customers. The studies found that customers want to be able to shop anywhere at any time, and they want other services such as the flexibility to choose delivery dates and locations. There are several trends that affect shoppers' delivery expectations:

1. Omnichannel fulfillment. Shoppers want an integrated buying experience across a firm's multiple buying channels (its stores, website, and third-party retailers). According to the UPS study, 44% of online shoppers want the option to buy online and pick up the items at their local store. Another 62% said they wanted the ability to make purchases online and make in-store returns. The study also found that of the shoppers who use the ship-to-store option, 38% of them purchased other items while in the store.

2. Delivery timeframes. Slow or delayed deliveries practices is one of the main reasons consumers do not shop online. Nearly half of online shoppers abandon their online carts before checking out when they find that the products they selected have long shipping times. Furthermore, very few potential customers are willing to pay higher prices for same-day delivery. On the other hand, when customers know how long it will take for their products to arrive, they are surprisingly patient with the retailer (for free shipping, they are willing to wait as long as 7 days for delivery).

3. Customized delivery. Ninety-seven percent of shoppers want order tracking services available so they can instantly determine the status of their order. Whether through e-mail alerts or by accessing the retailer's website, customers demand updated information on the shipping and delivery dates for their orders.

4. Easy return policies. The number of people returning or exchanging orders has grown nearly every year since online shopping became commonplace. Customers expect that returning orders will be "painless" and easily accommodated by online retailers. It also pays off in terms of future sales, with 67% of consumers saying they will shop more often with a retailer if they offer a hassle-free returns policy.

Many of the expectations that online shoppers bring to the retail experience have implications for inventory management, suggesting that firms with fully integrated information and inventory control systems will be better prepared to compete for the growing ranks on online shoppers. Between the steps of integrating upstream inventory, avoiding stock-outs, dealing with the expectations of immediate delivery, and ease of use, today's online systems are critical sources of inventory management. Indeed, the organizations that are best at fully integrating with inventory systems will be best able to compete effectively for online shoppers' business.[25]

Questions:

1. Think of some aspects of inventory management discussed in this chapter (for example, inventory costs or cycle-stock patterns). How does online shopping affect them?

2. How is omnichannel shopping changing the way inventory is managed? How will modern inventory management systems make omnichannel selling easier?

3. Suppose you are working for a local drugstore developing an online shopping site. Think of some products you routinely sell, and apply the ABC classification system to them. How would the ABC classification help you in planning for online sales?

VIDEO CASE

Watch this video case to learn about how SAGE Publishing manages inventory to track book orders, shipments, and returns effectively.

CRITICAL THINKING EXERCISES ....

1. You are the manager of a Macy's store in Buffalo, New York. How would you go about evaluating the impact of inventory shortages?

2. Supermarkets carry a wide range of inventory items that makes managing inventory difficult. The manager of a supermarket in your neighborhood is your friend and seeks your help in calculating inventory turnover because the supermarket is facing severe cash flow problems. How would you go about helping him?

CHAPTER
16

Inventory Control Models

LEARNING OBJECTIVES

After studying this chapter, you should be able to:

1. Describe the Basic Economic Order Quantity (EOQ) model, its assumptions, and use the model to solve problems.

2. Utilize the Economic Production Quantity (EPQ) to solve problems.

3. Solve problems using the EOQ model with quantity discounts.

4. Discuss the various reorder point models, and work typical problems.

5. Explain periodic review systems, and work typical problems.

6. Discuss single period inventory systems, and work typical problems.

OPERATIONS PROFILE: Walgreens Fights to Stay Profitable Through Inventory Management

Walgreens (Walgreens Company, subsidiary of Walgreens Boots Alliance Inc., Deerfield, IL) is now one of the largest drugstore chains in the world, after its 2014 acquisition of the Alliance Boots chain in Europe. It is also in the midst of an attempted US$9 billion dollar takeover of the Rite Aid pharmacy chain. The stock price has fluctuated as a result of attempts to grow through acquisition while keeping a tighter handle on in-store costs. Faced with a profit squeeze through lower drug reimbursement rates from pharmaceutical companies and the U.S. government, Walgreens has sought to find innovative ways to maintain its profitability.

One method for improving the bottom line that Walgreens has adopted is stricter inventory management practices, including ordering and stocking products in its stores. Senior executives recognize that carrying thousands of products on their shelves, particularly slow-moving items, represents a drain on their resources. As a result, the company has been revamping its stores, reducing inventory, and increasing reorder times to best use shelf space. Stores typically pack 22,000 different items on shelves, many of which are lower margin or slower moving products. Walgreens has remodeled its stores to carry some 4,000 fewer items. In total, Walgreens reduced the value of inventory per store by more than 11%. More importantly for the company, these lower inventories have directly contributed to the bottom line, increasing cash flow and keeping the company profitable in the midst of an industry downturn.

Walgreens has long been a leader in inventory management, operating a strategic inventory management system (SIMS) that had previously never been applied to the pharmaceutical sales industry. In using SIMS in combination with its remodeled stores, Walgreens has been able to avoid the twin problems of over- and under-stocking items, while allowing the company to track items to minimize reorder times. Its inventory management system has also helped Walgreens cut customer wait-time in half as products in the store can be quickly identified and located for consumer purchase. All these benefits come from taking an active approach to inventory management and control for greater company profitability.[1]

©iStockphoto.com/patty_c

Introduction

In Chapter 15, we mentioned that the two fundamental questions in inventory management are *how* much to order or produce and *when* to order or produce. The answers depend on the type of inventory control system chosen for the specific products or materials. In this chapter, we discuss several models that tell us how much to order and when to order for each inventory control system discussed in Chapter 15: continuous review systems, periodic review systems, and single-period systems. The inventory control models that we will discuss in this chapter are for independent demand items. These items are typically end or finished products whose demand is determined by external marketing conditions that do not depend on a company's internal operational activities or on the demand for other finished products. Examples of items having independent demand include TVs, cars, and Apple iPhones (Apple Inc., Cupertino, CA). Dependent demand items, on the other hand, are items whose demand depends on the demand for the finished products. These are typically components or materials used in the assembly of the finished product. For example, if the production schedule calls for assembly of 500 motorcycles, then the 1,000 wheels and 1,000 tires that are required to produce the 500 motorcycles are classified as dependent demand items. We will discuss inventory control issues associated with dependent demand items in Chapter 18. Given the uncertainty of demand of independent demand items and the impact they have on customer satisfaction, we will focus our attention on inventory control models for these products.

Master the content.

edge.sagepub.com /venkataraman

⑤SAGE edge™

16.1

Describe the Basic Economic Order Quantity (EOQ) model, its assumptions, and use the model to solve problems.

Inventory Control

16.1 How Much to Order: Continuous Review Systems

We begin our discussion with the question of how much to order or produce if a company uses a continuous review (fixed order) system. Our goal is to arrive at the order or production quantity that will minimize all inventory-related costs. If we are ordering materials from an outside vendor, then the total inventory-related cost on an annual basis is:

Total Annual Cost = Total annual ordering cost + Total annual holding cost + Total annual stock-out cost + Total annual materials purchase cost

If we are producing the product or component in-house, then the total inventory-related cost on an annual basis is:

Total Annual Cost = Total annual setup cost + Total annual holding cost + Total annual stock-out cost + Total annual materials purchase cost

The models described in Sections 16.1 to 16.3 can be used to determine the best order size. These models are the economic order quantity (EOQ) model, the economic production quantity (EPQ) model, and the quantity discount model. Each model depends on a different set of conditions, or assumptions.

Basic Economic Order Quantity (EOQ) model

Basic EOQ Model

In continuous review systems, the **economic order quantity (EOQ)** model is the simplest of the three models to use. The EOQ model applies if we can make the assumptions in Table 16.1.

If all of the assumptions in Table 16.1 are true, then we can remove the stock-out and purchase cost factors from the total cost equation. If shortages are not allowed, then stock-out costs do not exist, and if no quantity discounts are allowed, then the unit purchase price of the materials is constant because it is unaffected by the quantity ordered. Therefore, the total annual cost expression can be simplified to:

Total Annual Cost = Total annual ordering cost + Total annual holding cost

TABLE 16.1: Assumptions of the EOQ Model

Economic order quantity (EOQ): the simplest model for continuous review systems that is used to determine the optimum quantity of materials or product to order from a supplier.

1.	A single product is involved.
2.	The annual demand is known and occurs uniformly throughout the year with a constant demand rate.
3.	The lead time for the receipt of the orders is constant and known.
4.	No shortages are allowed.
5.	The quantity ordered is received all at once in a single delivery.
6.	There are no quantity discounts.

FIGURE 16.1: Inventory Replenishment and Depletion Cycle Patterns Over Time

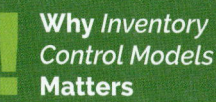

We can drop the purchase cost from the equation because we are not determining the total annual costs of inventory for accounting purposes, such as reporting inventory on the firm's balance sheet or income statement. We are merely determining the costs that are relevant to our decision about how much to order of a particular product. In addition, because the purchase price doesn't change based on how much we order of the product in this case, it doesn't affect our decision.

Suppose an electronics store orders 500 printers from its supplier each time it places an order and that the supplier delivers all of the units at once with a constant lead time of three days. The store's inventory level at the beginning of each cycle jumps from 0 to 500 after delivery. Note that we are allowed to let the inventory level fall to zero at the end of each cycle because we have assumed that the demand and lead times do not vary and that inventory will be replenished with another 500 printers precisely when it falls to zero. As a result, there are no excess inventories or stock-outs.

If the demand for the monitors is constant at 50 units per day, then the inventory cycles of ordering and depletion follow the sawtooth pattern shown in Figure 16.1. In the figure, Q is the quantity ordered, u is the usage rate, and LT is the lead time. Figure 16.1 shows that the inventory level in each cycle falls from a maximum amount of Q to a minimum of zero. Hence, the average inventory level is $\frac{Q}{2}$.

Because the total annual cost is a sum of the total annual ordering costs and the total annual holding costs, the optimal order quantity is an amount that minimizes both. Nevertheless, the ordering costs and holding costs are inversely related. For example, if the order quantity in each order is relatively small, then the average inventory level would be small, resulting in lower annual holding costs. Yet, a small order quantity implies more frequent orders, which will lead to higher annual ordering costs.

Conversely, if the order quantity in each order is large, then fewer orders will be placed during the year, which will result in lower annual ordering costs. Nonetheless, the higher order quantity will cause the average inventory levels to rise, thereby driving up the annual inventory holding costs. Figure 16.2 on page 562 shows the inverse relationship between the number of orders, their sizes, and a firm's average inventory level.

Thus, determining the optimal order quantity requires us to strike a balance between ordering and holding costs; holding costs depend on the firm's average inventory level. To arrive at the optimal order quantity (EOQ), we need to minimize the total annual cost, which is the sum of the total annual ordering cost and the total annual holding cost. We can rewrite this as:

$$TC=\left(\frac{D}{Q}\right)\times S+\left(\frac{Q}{2}\right)\times H$$

where

D = annual demand in units

S = ordering cost per order

H = the holding per unit per year

Q = the order quantity

Why *Inventory Control Models* **Matters**

There are different types of inventory control systems companies can use to manage their inventory. Various models can control inventory for each of these systems. These models provide techniques to determine optimum inventory levels that minimize inventory costs while offering protection against shortages.

FIGURES 16.2: Inverse Relationship Between the Average Inventory Level and Number of Orders

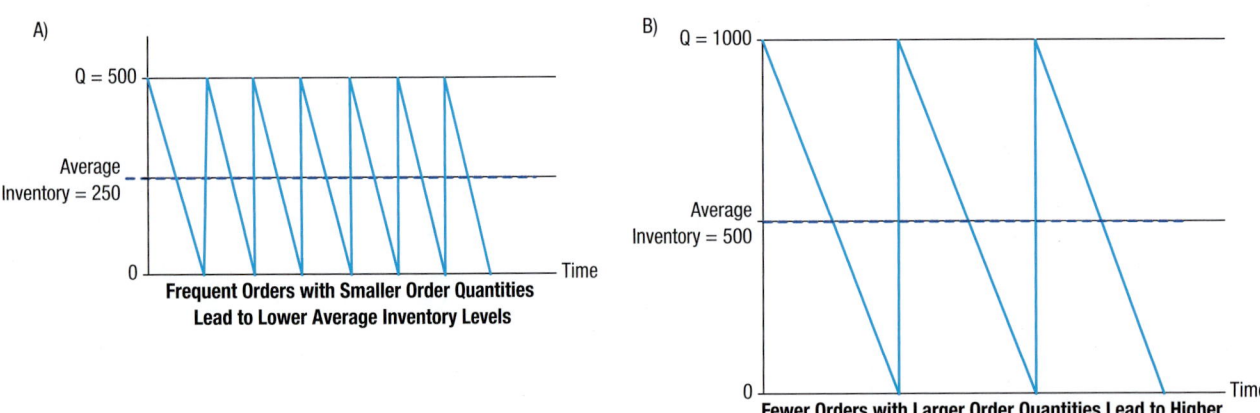

In the total annual cost equation, $\left(\dfrac{D}{Q}\right) \times S$ is the total annual ordering cost obtained by multiplying the total number of orders for materials placed during the year, $\left(\dfrac{D}{Q}\right)$, by the fixed ordering cost per order, S. The total annual holding cost is obtained by multiplying the average inventory level during the year, $\left(\dfrac{Q}{2}\right)$, by the holding cost per unit per year, H. Often the holding cost per unit per period is expressed as a percentage of the purchase price (P). This percentage is called the carrying rate or holding rate (i). Thus, the holding cost (H) is given by:

$$H = i \times P$$

where

   i = the holding rate expressed as a %

   P = the purchase price of the item

The behavior of ordering and holding costs with respect to quantity ordered is shown in Figure 16.3.

In addition to the annual ordering and holding cost curves, the total annual cost (the sum of the annual ordering and holding costs) is also shown in Figure 16.3. Figure 16.3 reveals that minimum cost occurs at the point of intersection of the yearly ordering and holding cost curves. It is also evident from the graph that this point corresponds to the lowest point of the total cost curve. Furthermore, at this optimum intersection point, the total annual ordering cost is equal to the total annual holding cost. Hence, we have

$$\left(\dfrac{D}{Q}\right) \times S = \left(\dfrac{Q}{2}\right) \times H$$

Rearranging terms and solving for Q, we get

$$Q_0 = \sqrt{\dfrac{2 \times D \times S}{H}}$$

Thus, the optimal or economic order quantity, Q_o, is the quantity that minimizes both the yearly ordering and the holding costs. Note that the formula for Q_o can also be derived by using differential calculus, which would require differentiating the total annual cost expression with respect to Q, setting the result equal to zero, and solving for Q_o. Figure 16.3 also shows that if our order quantity is greater than the EOQ (Q_o), then the annual holding costs will be higher than the annual ordering costs. Conversely, if our order quantity is less than the EOQ, then the annual ordering costs will be higher than the annual holding costs. Therefore, conceptually, EOQ occurs at a point where the two costs are equal. The equation for economic order quantity also shows that if the holding costs, H, are high, then our order quantities will be smaller to keep our annual holding costs low. Conversely, if ordering cost per order, S, is high, then our order quantities per order will be larger so that we place fewer orders during the year to keep the annual ordering costs low.

FIGURE 16.3: Effect of Quantity Ordered on Ordering and Holding Costs

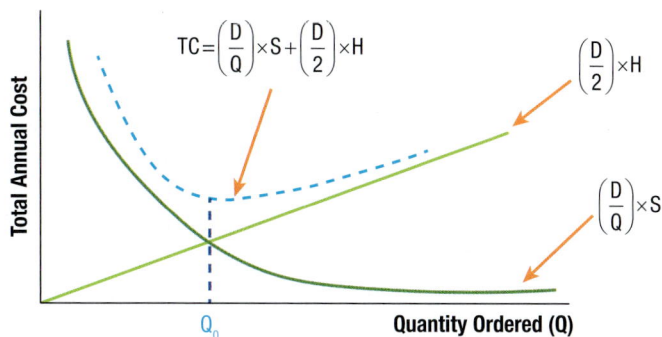

To summarize, holding costs are a linear function of Q, which means that these costs increase if the quantity ordered increases and decrease as the quantity ordered decreases. For example, if the order quantity, Q, is 1,000 units, and the holding costs, H, are US$5 a unit per year, then the average inventory level will be 500 ($\frac{Q}{2}$ = 1,000 / 2), and the total annual holding cost would be 500 × 5 = US$2,500 ($\frac{Q}{2}$ × H). Conversely, if the order quantity (Q) is 2,000 units and the holding costs, H, are US$5 a unit per year, then the average inventory level would be 1,000 ($\frac{Q}{2}$ = 2,000 / 2 = 1,000), and the total annual holding cost will be 1,000 × 5 = US$5,000 ($\frac{Q}{2}$ × H).

On the other hand, for a given annual demand, the ordering costs decrease as the quantity ordered increases. The costs decrease because the larger the quantity in each order, the fewer orders are needed to meet the annual demand requirements. For example, if the annual demand, D, is 10,000 units, and the order quantity (Q) per order is 1,000 units, then there are 10 ($\frac{D}{Q}$ = 10,000 / 1,000 = 10) orders during the year. If the ordering cost per order, S, is US$50 per order, then the total annual ordering cost is US$500 (10 × 50). If the order quantity, Q, per order is 2,000 units, then there are only 5 ($\frac{D}{Q}$ = 10,000 / 2000 = 5) orders during the year, and the total annual ordering cost is US$250 (5 × 50). The reason that ordering costs decrease for larger order sizes is that, unlike holding costs, ordering costs on a per-order basis are less sensitive to changes in order size and remain relatively constant.

EXAMPLE 16.1: A local distributor for a Belgian chocolate manufacturer expects to sell 12,000 cases of chocolate truffles next year. The annual holding costs for the truffles are US$16 per case per year. The ordering cost is US$60 per order. The distributor operates 320 days a year. Given this information:

Example 16.1

1. What is the EOQ?
2. How many orders will there be next year?
3. What is the time between orders?
4. What is the total annual cost of the truffles if they are ordered in EOQ amounts?

SOLUTION

Given:

Annual demand (D) = 12,000 cases

Ordering cost per order (S) = US$60

Annual carrying cost (H) = US$16 per case per year

Number working days during the year = 320

1. What is the EOQ?

$$Q_o = \sqrt{\frac{2 \times D \times S}{H}} = \sqrt{\frac{2 \times 12000 \times 60}{16}} = 300 \, cases$$

Thus, each time the distributor places an order for chocolate truffles, the order quantity will be 300 cases.

2. How many orders will there be next year?

The number of orders per year is given by $\frac{D}{Q_o}$. Thus,

$$\frac{D}{Q_o} = 12,000 / 300 = 40 \text{ orders during the year}$$

3. What is the time between orders?

The time between orders—that is, the length of the order cycle—is:

$$\frac{Q_o}{D} \times \text{Number working days during the year} = (300 / 12,000) \times 320 = 8 \text{ days}$$

Consequently, the distributor will place an order for chocolate truffles every 8 working days.

4. What is the total annual cost of truffles if they are ordered in EOQ amounts?

The total annual cost is (in U.S. dollars):

$$TC = \left(\frac{D}{Q_o}\right) \times S + \left(\frac{Q_o}{2}\right) \times H = \left(\frac{12,000}{300}\right) \times 60 + \left(\frac{300}{2}\right) \times 16 = \$2,400 + \$2,400 = \$4,800$$

Note that the total ordering and holding costs are equal at the EOQ. This is not a coincidence because the EOQ formula was derived by setting these two costs as equal to each other.

The solution to this example can be found in a Microsoft Excel (Microsoft Corporation, Redmond, WA) spreadsheet provided with the study materials for this text.

SCREENSHOT 16.1: Example 16.1

	A	B	C	D	E	F	G	H
1	Chapter 16- Example 1: Basic EOQ Model							
2								
3	Annual Demand	12000						
4	Ordering Cost	$60.00						
5	Carrying Cost	$16.00						
6	Number of working days	320						
7								
8	SOLUTION							
9	EOQ	300			=SQRT((2*$B$3*$B$4)/($B$5))			
10	Total Number of Orders per Year	40.0			=($B$3/$B$9)			
11	Time between orders	8.0			=(($B$9/$B$3)*($B$6))			
12	Total Annual Inventory Cost	$4,800.00			=(($B$3/$B$9)*$B$4+($B$9/2)*($B$5))			
13								

EXAMPLE 16.2: The fictional Kraus Department Store, located in Chicago, Illinois, sells 1,700 coffee-makers per year. The purchase price of each coffeemaker is US$70. The ordering cost is US$90 per order. The holding cost is 30% of the unit purchase price. Compute the economic order quantity and the total annual cost of ordering and holding the inventory of coffeemakers.

SOLUTION

Given:

Annual demand (D) = 1,700 units

Ordering cost per order (S) = US$90

Purchase per unit (P) = US$70

Holding rate (i) = 0.3 per unit per year

Based on this information:

Annual holding cost (H) = the holding rate × the purchase price per unit = i × P

$$= 0.3 \times 70 = \$21 \text{ per unit per year}$$

The optimal order quantity is:

$$Q_o = \sqrt{\frac{2 \times D \times S}{H}}$$

$$= \sqrt{\frac{2 \times 1700 \times 90}{21}} = 120.7 \text{ or } 121 \text{ coffeemakers}$$

The total annual inventory ordering and holding costs at the EOQ are (in U.S. dollars):

$$TC = \left(\frac{D}{Q_o}\right) \times S + \left(\frac{Q_o}{2}\right) \times H$$

$$= \left(\frac{1700}{120.7}\right) \times 90 + \left(\frac{120.7}{2}\right) \times 21$$

$$= \$1267.50 + \$1267.50 = \$2535.00$$

SCREENSHOT 16.2: Example 16.2

	A	B	C	D	E	F	G	H
1	Chapter 16- Example 2: Basic EOQ Model							
2								
3	Annual Demand	1700						
4	Ordering Cost	$90.00						
5	Purchase price per unit	$70.00						
6	Carrying/holding rate per unit per year	0.3						
7	Carrying Cost per unit per year	$21.00	→=($B$5*$B$6)					
8								
9	SOLUTION							
10	EOQ	120.7	→=SQRT((2*$B$3*$B$4)/($B$7))					
11	Total Annual Ordering Cost	1267.5						
12	Total Annual Carrying Cost	1267.5						
13	Total Annual Inventory Cost	$2,535.0	→=(($B$3/$B$10)*$B$4+($B$9/2)*($B$7))					
14								

The ordering cost and holding cost numbers are estimates rather than exact values. As a result, the optimal order quantities we arrive at using the EOQ formula are not precise values but approximate quantities. Therefore, the rounding that we did in the calculations in the example is perfectly valid. Furthermore, as EOQ is fairly robust, the total cost in the neighborhood of EOQ is fairly insensitive to minor deviations in the order quantity from the EOQ amount. That is, even if the actual order quantity differs (within reasonable limits) from the calculated EOQ, the total cost will not increase much and the curve (as shown in Figure 16.3) is relatively flat near the inflection point.

Economic production quantity (EPQ): a model used to determine how much of a product the firm is to produce and when

16.2 Economic Production Quantity (EPQ) Model

The economic production quantity (EPQ) model, developed in 1918, is an extension of the EOQ model. Unlike the EOQ model, which assumes the company will order items from an outside vendor, the EPQ model assumes that the company will produce the items. The EPQ model is therefore used to determine how much of a product the firm should produce and when. The firm, of course, has to meet the demand for the product, but it wants to do so in a way that minimizes costs. For example,

16.2 Utilize the Economic Production Quantity (EPQ) to solve problems.

it does not want to produce an entire year's supply of the product initially because then its holding costs would be high.

Also, unlike the EOQ model, which assumes that a quantity ordered is delivered all at once, the EPQ model does not. The EPQ model assumes units are received incrementally because they are being produced incrementally. Nevertheless, the assumptions of the EPQ model are very similar to those of the EOQ model. The assumptions of the EPQ model are as follows:

TABLE 16.2: Assumptions of the EPQ Model

1. A single product is involved.
2. The demand is known and occurs uniformly and continuously throughout the year.
3. The lead time is constant and is known.
4. No shortages are allowed.
5. There are no quantity discounts.
6. Production runs to replenish inventory occur at regular intervals.
7. During a production run, items are produced continuously at a constant production rate.
8. The quantity ordered is produced incrementally and inventory builds up gradually.
9. The production rate is greater than the demand rate.

If all of these assumptions are true, then the total annual cost associated with the inventory for our purpose of determining what to produce and when is:

Total Annual Cost = Total annual setup cost + Total annual holding cost

Again, we are assuming that the costs of the materials used to produce the product don't change. Consequently, we don't need to include those costs because they have no bearing on our decision about how much to order. In addition, because the product is produced internally, there are no ordering costs. Yet, for each production run during the year, the company incurs setup costs, which are the labor costs related to preparing the necessary equipment, changing tools and fixtures on the equipment, cleaning, and so forth.

The behavior of setup costs with respect to quantity produced is similar to that of ordering cost with respect to quantity ordered in the EOQ model. Specifically, the larger the quantity produced from each production setup, the fewer production runs are needed to meet the demand requirements and, hence, the smaller will be the total annual setup cost. Conversely, the smaller the quantity produced from each production setup, the more frequently production runs are needed to meet the demand requirements and, hence, the larger will be the total annual setup cost.

The chief difference in the EPQ and EOQ models is the average inventory level. Suppose for each production run or setup that 1,000 units are produced. This quantity, however, cannot be produced and delivered all at once. Therefore, let us also assume that goods are produced at a rate of 200 units per day. During the production run, however, there is simultaneously demand for the items produced. Suppose the demand rate is 100 units per day. Table 16.3 tracks the inventory buildup and depletion during a 10-day production and usage cycle.

As Table 16.3 shows, the production process starts producing and delivering the required quantity of 1,000 units at the rate of 200 units per day. At this rate, all of the 1,000 units will be produced in five days, and at the end of day 5, production of this item stops. Nevertheless, demand occurs in

TABLE 16.3: Incremental Inventory Buildup in the EPQ Model

DAY	1	2	3	4	5	6	7	8	9	10
Production rate	200	200	200	200	200					
Usage, or demand rate	100	100	100	100	100	100	100	100	100	100
Inventory in stock	100	200	300	400	500	400	300	200	100	0

FIGURE 16.4: Economic Production Quantity Model

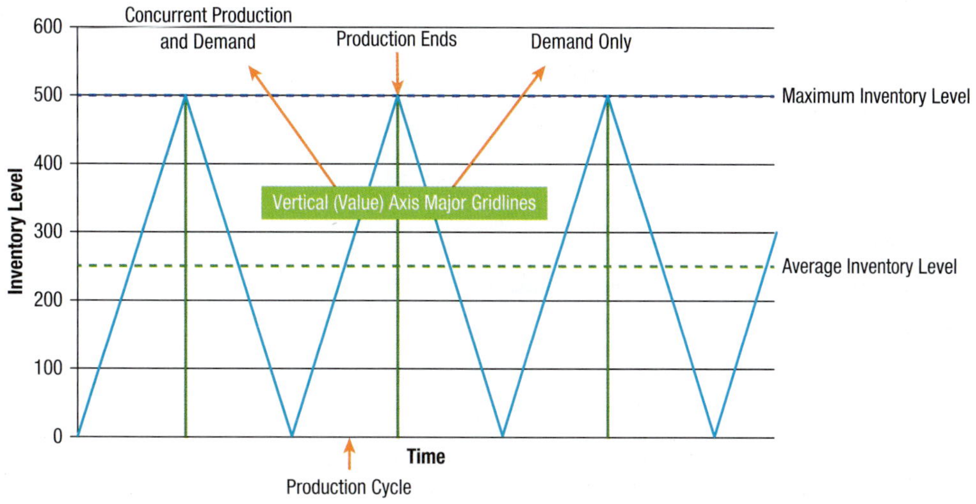

tandem with production at the rate of 100 units per day and continues even after day 5, until all the inventory in stock is used up at the end of day 10. A new production and usage cycle would start on day 11, and the process is repeated. The last row in Table 16.3, inventory in stock, shows the gradual inventory buildup at the rate of 100 (200 –100) units per day until the end of day 5, which is the end of the production run. From day 6 through day 10, the inventory in stock is depleted and is allowed to drop to zero because there are no stock-out costs.

Note in Table 16.3 that the maximum inventory level is 500 units (on day 5) and that the minimum inventory level is zero (on day 10). Hence, the average inventory level during this 10-day production and usage cycle is $(500 - 0) / 2 = 250$ units. If the production and delivery of the 1,000 units had occurred all at once, the average inventory level would have been $(1,000 - 0) / 2 = 500$ units. Clearly, the incremental production results in a lower average inventory level than in the EOQ model. Consequently, the annual inventory holding costs for the EPQ model will be significantly lower than in the corresponding EOQ model. Figure 16.4 is a graph of the EPQ model.

The earlier example can be generalized using variables, as follows:

If the production run size is Q and the production rate is p, then

$$\left(\frac{Q}{p}\right) = \text{the number days of production run}$$

If the demand or usage rate is d, then

$$\left(\frac{Q}{p}\right) \times d = \text{inventory used up or depleted at the end of the production cycle}$$

Because all of the Q units would have been produced and delivered at the end of the production run (represented by the vertical lines in Figure 16.4), we have:

$$[Q - \left(\frac{Q}{p}\right) \times d] = Q \times [1-\left(\frac{d}{p}\right)] = I_{max} = \text{Maximum inventory (the inventory remaining in stock at the end of the production run)}$$

Given that the EPQ model assumes that the minimum inventory level is allowed to fall to zero, we have:

$$\text{Average Inventory} = (\text{maximum inventory} + \text{minimum inventory}) / 2 = \{Q \times [1-\left(\frac{d}{p}\right)]+ 0\} / 2$$

or

$$\text{Average Inventory} = \left(\frac{Q}{2}\right) \times \left[1 - \left(\frac{d}{p}\right)\right] = \frac{Q}{2} \times \left(\frac{p-d}{p}\right)$$

If you substitute the values from the previous numerical example, you will find that 250 units is the average inventory level.

The total annual cost of the EPQ model that we want to minimize to determine the optimum production quantity is:

$$TC = \left(\frac{D}{Q}\right) \times K + \frac{Q}{2} \times \left(\frac{p-d}{p}\right) \times H$$

where

D = the annual demand in units

K = the cost per setup

H = the holding cost per unit per year

Q = the optimal or economic production quantity (EOQ)

p = the production or delivery rate

d = the demand or usage rate

A graph of the total annual costs, setup costs, and holding costs for the EPQ model will be very similar to the graph of the EOQ model in Figure 16.3. Furthermore, for the EPQ model, the total annual cost equation is minimized at the point of intersection of the total setup and holding cost curves. Just as in Figure 16.3, this optimum intersection point also corresponds to the lowest point on the total cost curve. Because the total annual setup cost is equal to the total annual holding cost, we have:

$$\left(\frac{D}{Q}\right) \times K = \frac{Q}{2} \times \left(\frac{p-d}{p}\right) \times H$$

Rearranging terms and solving for Q, we get:

$$Q_{opt} = \sqrt{\frac{2 \times D \times K}{H}} \times \sqrt{\frac{p}{p-d}}$$

Thus, the optimum production quantity or EPQ is Q_{opt} because this is the quantity that minimizes both the yearly setup and holding costs.

EXAMPLE 16.3: Ponting Carpet Mills (not a real company) manufactures a brand called Super Frieze carpets. The setup cost (the cost of setting up the production process) to make Super Frieze carpets is US$20 per setup. The holding cost is US$2.00 per square yard per year, and the annual demand for this carpet is 12,000 square yards per year. The manufacturing facility operates 300 days, and 120 square yards of the carpet are produced per day. Determine the economic production quantity or run size, the length of the production run in days, the number of setups per year, the maximum inventory level, and the total annual cost.

SOLUTION

Given:

Annual demand (D) = 12,000 square yards

Cost per setup (K) = US$20

Carrying cost (H) = US$2.00 per square yard per year

Production rate (p) = 120 square yards per day

Demand rate (d) = Annual demand / Number of working days = 12,000 / 300 = 40 square yards per day

Given the above information:

1. The economic production quantity (EPQ) is:

$$Q_{opt} = \sqrt{\frac{2 \times D \times K}{H}} \times \sqrt{\frac{p}{p-d}}$$

$$= \sqrt{\frac{2 \times 12000 \times 20}{2}} \times \sqrt{\frac{120}{120-40}} = 600 \text{ square yards}$$

Thus, for each production run or setup, Ponting Carpet Mills should produce 600 square yards of the Super Frieze carpet.

2. The length of a production run in days is:

$$\frac{Q_{opt}}{p}$$

$$= \frac{600}{120} = 5 \text{ days}$$

3. The number of production runs or setups annually is:

$$\frac{D}{Q_{opt}}$$

$$= \frac{12,000}{600} = 20 \text{ production runs or setups over the year.}$$

4. The maximum inventory level is:

$$I_{max} = Q_{opt} \times \left(\frac{p-d}{p}\right)$$

$$600 \times \left(\frac{120-40}{120}\right) = 400 \text{ carpets}$$

5. The total annual cost at EPQ is (in U.S. dollars):

$$TC = \left(\frac{D}{Q_{opt}}\right) \times K + [\left(\frac{Q_{opt}}{2}\right) \times \left(\frac{p-d}{p}\right)] \times H$$

$$= \frac{12,000}{600} \times 20 + \left[\left(\frac{600}{2}\right) \times \left(\frac{120-40}{120}\right)\right] \times 2 = \$400 + \$400 = \$800.$$

SCREENSHOT 16.3: Example 16.3

	A	B	C	D	E	F	G	H	I
1	Chapter 16- Example - 3: EPQ Model								
2									
3	Setup Cost	$20							
4	Carrying cost/Yard/Year	$2							
5	Daily Production Rate	120							
6	# of working days	300							
7	Annual Demand	12000							
8	Daily Demand Rate	40	=($B$7/$B$6)						
9									
10	SOLUTION								
11	EPQ	600	=SQRT(((2*$B$7*$B3)/($B$4))*(($B$5)/($B$5-$B$8)))						
12	Length of production run in days	5	=($B$11/$B$5)						
13	Total number of production runs	20	=($B$7/$B$11)						
14	Maximum Inventory	400	=($B$11*($B$5-$B$8)/($B$5))						
15	Total Annual Setup Cost	$400							
16	Total Annual Carrying Cost	$400							
17	Total Annual Inventory Cost	$ 800	=(($B$7/$B$11)*$B$3+($B$11/2)*($B$5-$B$8)/($B$5)*$B$4)						
18									

16.3 EOQ Model with Quantity Discounts

The economic order quantity (EOQ) model assumes there are no quantity discounts, which means that no matter what the order quantity, the unit purchase price of the item remains constant. Consequently, the total annual purchase cost (given by the purchase price per unit × the annual demand) has no impact on the minimum cost point on the total annual cost curve. In reality, however, most sellers offer their buyers quantity discounts, which are price reductions designed to induce buyers to increase their order sizes. Table 16.4 on page 570 shows a quantity discount schedule for an item.

If quantity discounts are offered, then the EOQ may not result in the lowest total annual cost because the EOQ formula considers only the ordering and holding costs and not the quantity discount. The order size that yields the lowest total annual cost may not be the EOQ amount in a given volume range but the minimum quantity in a higher volume range with a lower purchase price. Nevertheless, buying a larger quantity (such as the 2,000 units in Table 16.4) just because it has the

16.3

Solve problems using the EOQ model with quantity discounts.

....

Quantity discounts:
price reductions designed to induce buyers to increase their order sizes

TABLE 16.4: Example of a Quantity Discount Schedule

QUANTITY ORDERED (Q)	UNIT DISCOUNT PRICE (P; IN U.S. DOLLARS)
0 to 499	10.00
500 to 999	9.50
1,000 to 1,999	9.00
2,000 and greater	8.00

 Quantity Discounts

lowest per-unit purchase price ($8.00) might not result in the minimum total annual cost because the holding costs are likely to increase. Therefore, when quantity discounts are available, the buyer must weigh the potential price per-unit savings against the increase in the holding cost. The overall goal for the buyer is to choose the order quantity that will minimize total annual cost, which is now the sum of the yearly holding, ordering, *and* purchase costs. Thus, if quantity discounts are offered:

Total annual cost = Total annual ordering cost + Total annual holding cost
+ Total annual purchase cost

Using the same variable notations we used before, the total annual cost equation when there are quantity discounts is:

$$TC = \left(\frac{D}{Q}\right) \times S + \left(\frac{Q}{2}\right) \times H + P \times D$$

To illustrate the impact that quantity discounts have on the total annual cost and the quantity to be ordered for a product, consider the following values for each variable:

Annual demand (D) = 1,700 units

Ordering cost per order (S) = $90

Holding cost = $21 per unit per year

Purchase per unit (P) = $70 for orders less than 125 units and $65 for orders of 125 units or more

If we ignore the price discounts for the larger orders and calculate the EOQ, we have:

$$Q_o = \sqrt{\frac{2 \times D \times S}{H}}$$
$$= \sqrt{\frac{2 \times 1700 \times 90}{21}} = 120.7, \text{ or } 121 \text{ units when rounded up}$$

The total annual cost for the order quantity that includes the total annual purchase cost is:

$$TC = \left(\frac{D}{Q}\right) \times S + \left(\frac{Q}{2}\right) \times H + P \times D$$
$$= \left(\frac{1700}{120.7}\right) \times 90 + \left(\frac{120.7}{2}\right) \times 21 + 70 \times 1,700$$
$$= \$1,267.60 + \$1,267.35 + \$119,000 = \$121,534.95$$

Yet, because quantity discounts are available, if we increase the order size from the EOQ amount of 120.7 to 125, the purchase price per unit falls to $65. If we choose an order quantity of 125 instead of 120.7, we get the following total annual cost:

$$TC = \left(\frac{1700}{125}\right) \times 90 + \left(\frac{125}{2}\right) \times 21 + 65 \times 1700$$
$$= \$1224 + \$1312.5 + \$110,500 = \$113,036.50$$

Clearly, by increasing the order quantity to 125—the minimum required amount to get the price break—there is a significant reduction in the total annual cost.

When quantity discounts are available, we can determine how much to order by taking the following steps:

1. For each volume range, calculate the EOQ.
2. If the calculated EOQ is feasible (falls within its respective price-volume range), compute the total annual cost. If the feasible EOQ falls within the volume range that has the lowest purchase price, stop. This feasible EOQ is the optimum quantity to order. Otherwise, go to step 3.
3. In addition to the total annual cost calculated for the feasible EOQ in step 2, compute the total annual cost for the minimum quantities in the higher volume ranges with lower purchase prices.
4. Choose the order quantity that has the lowest total annual cost.

There are two scenarios associated with quantity discounts: one in which the holding cost is constant and is expressed in monetary units, and one in which the holding cost is not constant and is expressed as a percentage of the unit price. We will discuss each of these scenarios next, using an example.

EXAMPLE 16.4: Romano Chocolates Boutique, a mythical candy and confectionary store, orders chocolates from a supplier in Belgium. The Belgian supplier offers price discounts for larger orders and uses the volume–price discount schedule shown in Table 16.5. Ordering costs are US$30 per order, and the holding cost is a constant US$15 per case per year. That is, the holding cost per case doesn't drop as more and more of the product is purchased. The holding cost increases at a constant, incremental rate of US$15 per case. The projected annual demand for chocolate is 900 cases. What order quantity will minimize the total cost?

TABLE 16.5: Example of a Quantity Discount With Constant Holding Cost

ORDER QUANTITY (IN CASES)	PRICE PER CASE (IN U.S. DOLLARS)
0 to 49	60.00
50 to 99	55.00
100 or more	50.00

SOLUTION

Step 1. For each volume range, calculate the EOQ.

Because the holding cost per case does not vary with the price, we need to calculate only one EOQ. Given that the annual demand (D) = 900 cases, the ordering cost per order (S) = $30; the holding cost (H) = $15 per case per year, the optimal order quantity (EOQ) is:

$$EOQ = \sqrt{\frac{2 \times D \times S}{H}}$$

$$= \sqrt{\frac{2 \times 900 \times 30}{15}} = 60 \text{ cases}$$

Step 2. If the calculated EOQ is feasible (falls within its respective price–volume range), compute the total annual cost. If the feasible EOQ falls within the volume range that has the lowest purchase price, stop. This feasible EOQ is the optimum quantity to order. Otherwise, go to step 3.

The computed EOQ of 60 cases is feasible for the volume range of 50 to 99 cases, which has a purchase price of $55 per case. Hence, the total annual cost is:

$$TC_{EOQ} = (D/Q_o) \times S + (Q_o/2) \times H + P \times D$$

$$= \left(\frac{900}{60}\right) \times 30 + \left(\frac{60}{2}\right) \times 15 + 900 \times 55$$

$$= \$450 + \$450 + 49,500 = \$50,400$$

Note that the computed EOQ is not feasible for the first and the third volume ranges because it does not fall within those volume ranges. Also, because the computed EOQ of 60 cases does not fall within the volume range with the lowest purchase price, we go to step 3.

Step 3.   In addition to the total annual cost calculated for the feasible EOQ in step 2, compute the total annual cost for the minimum quantities in the higher volume ranges with lower purchase prices.

Next we compute the total annual cost for the next higher minimum quantity, which is 100. The purchase price per case for 100 and more units is $50:

$$TC_{100} = \left(\frac{D}{Q_o}\right) \times S + \left(\frac{Q_o}{2}\right) \times H + P \times D$$

$$= \left(\frac{900}{100}\right) \times 30 + \left(\frac{100}{2}\right) \times 15 + 900 \times 50$$

$$= \$270 + \$750 + 45,000 = \$46,020.$$

Step 4.   Choose the order quantity that has the lowest total annual cost.

Comparing the two total inventory cost values of TC_{EOQ} and TC_{100}, we find the at Q = 100 cases is the optimal order quantity because it has the lowest total annual cost (TC_{100} = $46,020).

The quantity discount for the example with constant holding costs and the three volume range–price schedules is illustrated in Figure 16.5. The figure shows that when the holding cost is constant, the total cost curves have a single minimum point. There is a single minimum point because with a constant holding cost, the differing purchase prices do not affect the holding cost component of the EOQ formula. As a result, the total cost curves for the various purchase prices line up vertically and the minimum point on these cost curves reflects only the total annual cost of ordering and holding inventory associated with EOQ. For simplicity, in Figure 16.5, the three horizontal purchase cost lines for the three volume ranges have been omitted.

FIGURE 16.5: How a Quantity Discount Affects the EOQ When the Holding Cost Is Constant

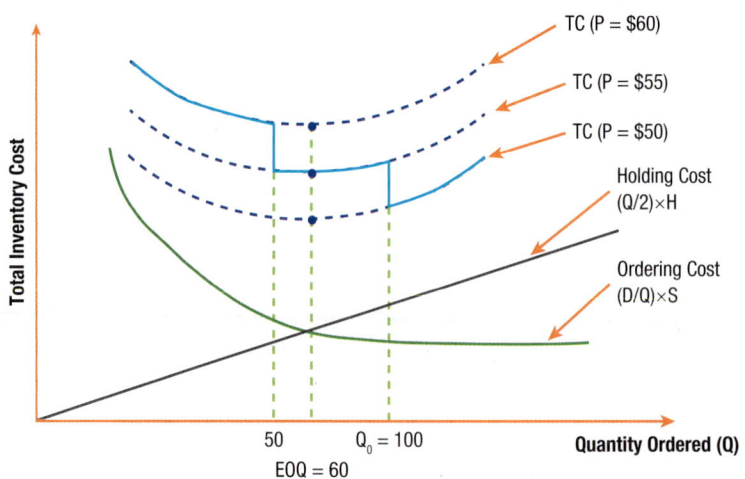

SCREENSHOT 16.4: Example 16.4 – Quantity Discount Model

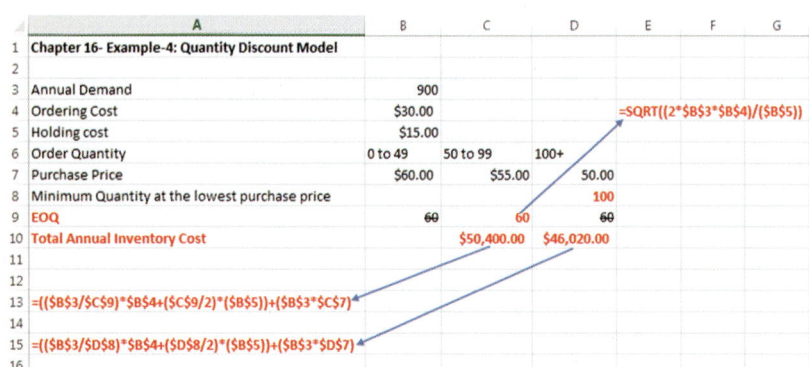

EXAMPLE 16.5: A supplier for fictional Trinity Hospital is offering quantity discounts on catheters. The quantity–price schedule is shown in Table 16.6. The annual demand for the catheters is 1,800 units. The ordering cost is US$48 per order, and the holding cost is 20% of the unit price per year. What order quantity will minimize the hospital's total annual cost?

TABLE 16.6: Example of Quantity Discount for Catheter Orders

ORDER SIZE	PRICE PER CATHETER (IN U.S. DOLLARS)
0 to 99	60.00
100 to 199	54.50
200 or more	48.80

SOLUTION

Step 1. For each volume range, calculate the EOQ.

Because the holding cost is a percentage of the unit price, it will vary with each price. Therefore, we need to calculate an EOQ for each volume–price range.

$$EOQ_{60} = \sqrt{\frac{2 \times D \times S}{H}} = \sqrt{\frac{2 \times 1800 \times 48}{0.2 \times 60}} = 120 \text{ catheters}$$

$$EOQ_{54.50} = \sqrt{\frac{2 \times D \times S}{H}} = \sqrt{\frac{2 \times 1800 \times 48}{0.2 \times 54.5}} = 125.9, \text{ or } 126 \text{ catheter when rounded up}$$

$$EOQ_{48.80} = \sqrt{\frac{2 \times D \times S}{H}} = \sqrt{\frac{2 \times 1800 \times 48}{0.2 \times 48.8}} = 133.06, \text{ or } 131 \text{ catheters when rounded up}$$

Step 2. If the calculated EOQ is feasible (falls within its respective price–volume range), compute the total annual cost. If the feasible EOQ falls within the volume range that has the lowest purchase price, stop. This feasible EOQ is the optimum quantity to order. Otherwise, go to step 3.

Of the three EOQs calculated, $EOQ_{60} = 120$ and $EOQ_{48.80} = 133.06$ are not feasible because they do not fall in the volume ranges of their respective unit prices. For example, the EOQ = 120 calculated for the unit price of $60 is not feasible because for an order quantity of 120 units, the price is $54.50 per unit, not $60. Similarly, the EOQ = 133.06 calculated for the third volume range with a unit price of $48.80 is also not feasible because for an order quantity of 133.06 units, the price will be $54.50 per unit, not $48.80. Hence, the only feasible EOQ is $EOQ_{54.50} = 125.9$ because it falls in the volume range (100 to 199 units) of its respective price, which is $54.50. The total annual cost for the feasible EOQ of 125.9 is:

$$TC_{EOQ} = \left(\frac{D}{Q_o}\right) \times S + \left(\frac{Q_o}{2}\right) \times H + P \times D$$

$$= \left(\frac{1800}{125.90}\right) \times 48 + \left(\frac{125.9}{2}\right) \times (0.20 \times 54.50) + 1800 \times 54.5$$

$$= \$686.26 + \$686.15 + \$98100 = \$99,472.41.$$

The feasible EOQ of 125.9 units, however, does not fall within the volume range that has the lowest purchase price. Therefore, we go to step 3.

Step 3. In addition to the total annual cost calculated for the feasible EOQ in step 2, compute the total annual cost for the minimum quantities in the higher volume ranges with lower purchase prices.

Next, we compute the total cost for the next higher minimum quantity, which is 200. The price per unit in this volume range is $48.80:

$$TC_{200} = \left(\frac{D}{Q_o}\right) \times S + \left(\frac{Q_o}{2}\right) \times H + P \times D$$

$$= \left(\frac{1800}{200}\right) \times 48 + \left(\frac{200}{2}\right) \times (0.2 \times 48.80) + 1800 \times 48.80$$

$$= \$432 + \$976 + \$87,840 = \$89,248.$$

Step 4. Choose the order quantity that has the lowest total annual cost.

Comparing the two total annual cost figures of TC_{EOQ} and TC_{200}, we find the Q = 200 catheters is the optimal order quantity because it has the lowest total annual cost (TC_{200} = $89,248).

Figure 16.6 shows a graph of this example with the holding cost expressed as a percentage of the unit purchase price. As you can see, when the holding costs vary, the total cost curves have different minimum points. The different minimum points occur because with holding costs as a percentage

FIGURE 16.6: How a Quantity Discount Affects the EOQ When the Holding Cost Is Expressed as a Percentage of the Unit Price

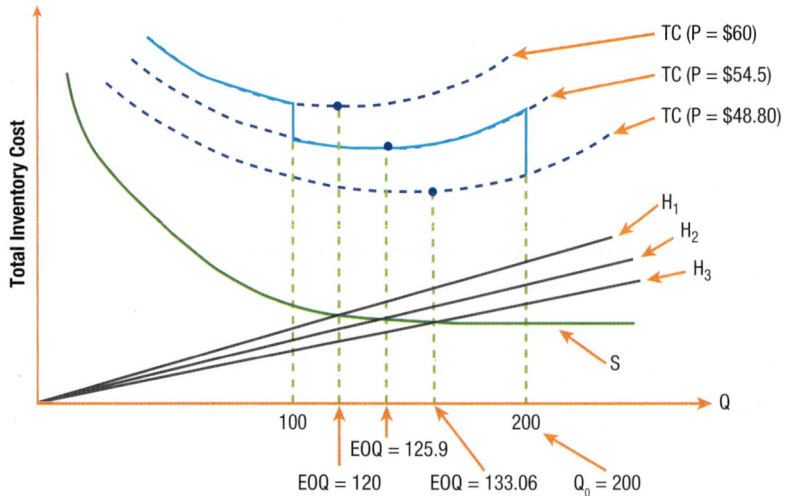

of the purchase price, it has the effect of lowering the holding cost for lower purchase prices. As a result, the minimum point of the total cost curve for each lower purchase price will be located to the right of the minimum point of the previous total cost curve associated with a higher purchase price. For simplicity, the three horizontal purchase cost lines for the three volume ranges have been omitted from the figure.

SCREENSHOT 16.5: Example 16.5 – Quantity Discount Model

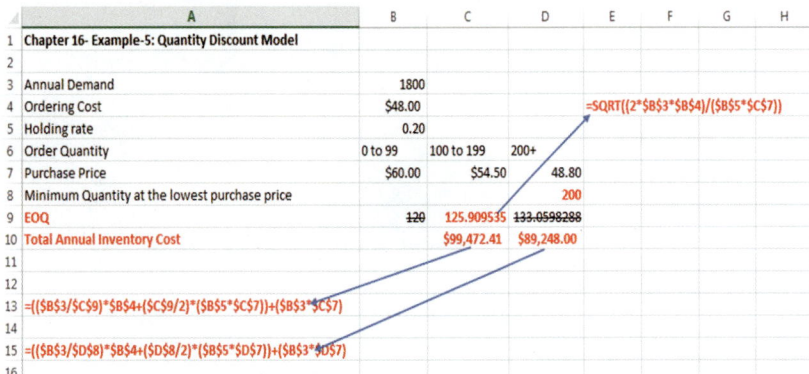

16.4 When to Order: Reorder Point for Continuous Review Systems (EOQ Model)

We will now consider the second inventory control issue for continuous review systems: when to order. Also called the **reorder point**, this inventory level is the amount to which the inventory of an item should fall before the firm places a new order to replenish it. With continuous review systems, the order quantity is fixed. Therefore, the decision of when to place the next order is determined by two variables—the *daily demand rate* and the *lead time*. Based on the assumptions that we make about these two variables, there will be one of four reorder points:

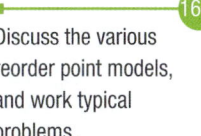

The Reorder Point

16.4

Discuss the various reorder point models, and work typical problems.

1. The reorder point when both the demand and the lead time are constant.
2. The reorder point when the demand is variable and the lead time is constant.
3. The reorder point when the demand is constant and the lead time is variable.
4. The reorder point when both the demand and the lead time are variable.

We will next develop reorder point models for each of these reorder points.

Reorder Point Model for Constant Demand and Constant Lead Time

If both the demand and the lead time are constant, then to determine the inventory level at which to reorder, we need to know the following:

1. The average demand rate ($\bar{d}$) (for example, daily or weekly)
2. The lead time (L) in days or weeks

Given this information, the reorder point (R) is:

$$R = \bar{d} \times L$$

To illustrate this reorder point, assume that our order quantity is Q = 1,000. Under the assumptions of the EOQ model, this is also our maximum inventory level. Demand depletes the inventory at a constant rate and there are no stock-out costs. If, for example, the 1,000 units are depleted to zero in 20 days, then:

The average daily demand rate ($\bar{d}$) = (1,000 − 0) / 20 = 50 units per day

Reorder point: a predetermined level of inventory that signals when a new order is to be placed to replenish it

OPERATIONS MANAGEMENT: LESSONS LEARNED
Inventory Mismanagement Helps Sink Target Canada

In 2015, Target Canada (subsidiary of (Target Corporation, Minneapolis, MN) filed for bankruptcy and liquidated its 133 retail stores across the country. This decision came about only two years after entering the Canadian market in March 2013. When Target announced its intention to open stores across Canada, the news was welcomed by Canadian shoppers, many of whom routinely cross the border to shop in the United States for a variety of products sold at considerably cheaper prices than in Canada. Target's launch was much rockier than anticipated, however, as customers found higher-than-expected prices and a lack of common American brands that were not for sale in the Canadian stores.

One of Target Canada's biggest mistakes was mismanaging its inventory. Products shipped from the United States arrived at the wrong warehouses, resulting in those same products being routed to the wrong stores. Some stores would receive overstocks of products, while others were chronically out of the same goods. Many Target Canada stores were the site of routinely empty shelves. Target attempted to sell essential products like groceries in their stores to encourage customers to develop new buying habits. Unfortunately, along with so many other items, the supplies of essential fresh produce were often delayed or simply never stocked. These continuous shipping and stocking errors served to drive Canadian shoppers, who had looked forward to the stores' opening with anticipation, back to their more familiar Canadian retailers.

What went wrong? Target made several errors in its decision to move into the Canadian market, but one of the most critical was inventory management. For the expansion, Target decided to outsource its logistics

to a Canadian firm, which used an enterprise resource planning (ERP) computer system that needed to integrate with Target's existing software in the United States. Target was so anxious to get the expansion moving forward that it failed to spend enough time testing the systems or training its employees how to use them, resulting in the critical problem of bad data that skewed the reorder points of its products. Target's inventory system was set up to renew purchase orders automatically when they reached their minimum stock level. Yet, once the bad data were in the system, Target started to experience overstocks and stock shortages on many of its retail items. The failure to link its inventory reorder systems successfully with its Canadian logistics partner led to critical mistakes in shipping and inventory management and control, which in less than two years destroyed Target Canada's chances for success and left it with a US$2 billion dollar loss.[2]

If, for example, the lead time, L, equals 3 days, then the reorder point is:

$$R = \overline{d} \times L = 50 \times 3 = 150 \text{ units}$$

This result means that we place our next order for 1,000 units when the inventory level in stock reaches 150 units. These 150 units are needed to meet the average demand of 50 units per day during the lead time of 3 days. Hence,

$$R = \overline{d} \times L = \text{the average demand or expected usage during the lead time.}$$

EXAMPLE 16.6: Romano Chocolates Boutique, the mythical candy and confectionary store introduced earlier, is located in Cary, North Carolina, As mentioned, the company orders chocolates from a supplier in Belgium. The projected annual demand for chocolate is 900 cases of chocolate, and the store is open 300 days during the year. The Belgian supplier takes 10 days to deliver the order from the time an order is placed. If the demand and lead time are assumed to be constant, what is the reorder point?

SOLUTION

Given:

Annual demand (D) = 900 cases

Number of days the store is open = 300

Lead time = 10 days

$$\overline{d} = \text{Annual demand / Number of days the store is open}$$

$$= 900 / 300 = 3 \text{ cases per day}$$

$$R = \overline{d} \times L = 3 \times 10 = 30 \text{ cases}$$

The reorder point is 30 cases, which means that the store places a new order for chocolates when the inventory level in stock falls to 30 cases.

Reorder Point Model for Variable Demand and Constant Lead Time

The reorder point we just discussed assumed that the demand and lead times for a product are constant and known. We will now relax these assumptions so that our model more closely mirrors a real-world scenario. If the demand for the product is not known and is fluctuating, then the greatest risk of running out of inventory occurs during the lead time. Therefore, to reduce the risk of stock-outs, we need to carry additional inventory above the amount needed to meet the average demand during the lead time ($\overline{d} \times L$). This additional inventory is safety stock.

Under conditions of variable demand and constant lead time, the reorder point is:

$$R = \overline{d} \times L + SS$$

where SS is the safety stock.

The reorder point when additional safety stock is carried is shown in Figure 16.7 on page 578. You can see that during the first inventory cycle, despite fluctuating demand, the inventory level of $\overline{d} \times L$ was sufficient given demand and the lead time. Nonetheless, in the second inventory cycle, demand exceeded $\overline{d} \times L$, and additional inventory in the form of safety stock was needed.

The optimum level of safety stock is the minimum amount that will balance the cost of stock-outs against the cost of holding the safety stock. Determining stock-out costs, however, is often difficult because they are intangible costs. Therefore, an approach that companies frequently use is to establish a safety stock that will meet a desired **service level**, which is defined as the *probability* that the demand during the lead time will be met from the inventory in stock. For example, a service level of 95% means that for 95% of the time, the demand during the lead time can be met from the inventory in stock. That is, a service level of 95% implies that the probability of stock-out is 5% (100% – 95%). Probabilistic models are used because they are more realistic—demand and lead times are frequently quite variable.

Only the mean and standard deviation of demand during the lead time are required to determine the reorder point and the associated safety stock. The reorder point is:

$$R = \overline{d} \times L + SS$$

where

$\overline{d}$ = the average daily or weekly demand

L = the lead time in days or weeks

$\overline{d} \times L$ = the average daily or weekly demand × the lead time in days or weeks

= the mean, or average, demand during the lead time.

Service level: the probability that the demand during the lead time will be met from the inventory in stock

FIGURE 16.7: Reorder Point in a Continuous Review System When the Demand Is Variable Demand and the Lead Time Is Constant

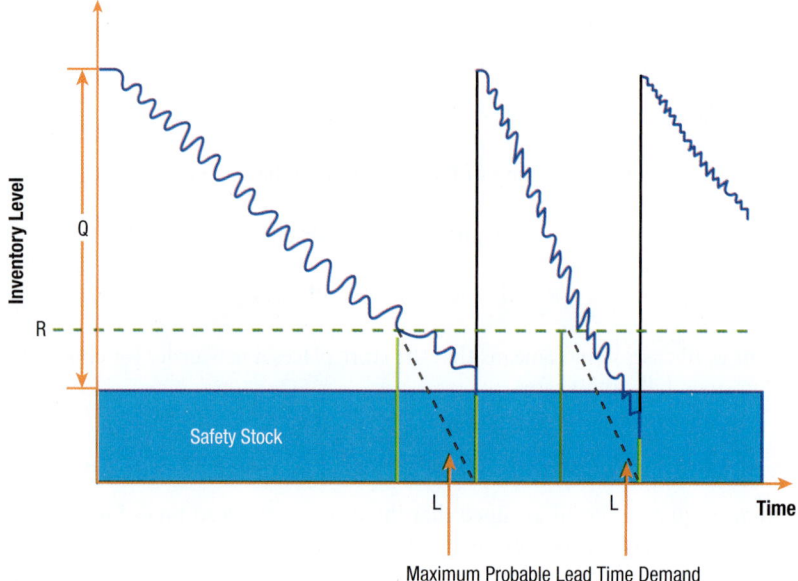

The safety stock, *SS*, is:

$$SS = Z \times \sigma_{dL}$$

where

Z = the number of standard deviations corresponding to the service level

σ_{dL} = the standard deviation of the demand during the lead time

$\quad = \sigma_d \times \sqrt{L}$

L = lead time in days or weeks

σ_d = the standard deviation of the firm's daily or weekly demand

Thus, when the lead time is constant, and the demand fluctuates in a normally distributed way during the lead time, the complete reorder point formula is:

$$R = \bar{d} \times L + Z \times \sigma_d \times \sqrt{L}$$

Once the desired service level is specified, the value of Z that represents the number of standard deviations corresponding to the service level can be obtained from the cumulative standard normal distribution tables. You can also infer from SS equation that the required level of safety stock is determined completely by the level of service and the standard deviation of demand during the lead time. The higher the desired service level, the higher the Z value will be and, hence, the larger the safety stock will be. Similarly, the higher the standard deviation of the demand is during the lead time (σ_{dL}), the larger the safety stock will be. The need for larger safety stocks occurs because higher values of σ_{dL} imply larger demand fluctuations and therefore a higher risk of stock-outs. So, a larger amount of safety stock is needed. Figure 16.8 shows the reorder point when the service level is 95%.

The normal distribution curve in the figure is symmetrical around the average, or mean, value. This distribution means that the inventory level that will meet the average demand during the lead

FIGURE 16.8: Reorder Point When the Service Level Desired Is 95%

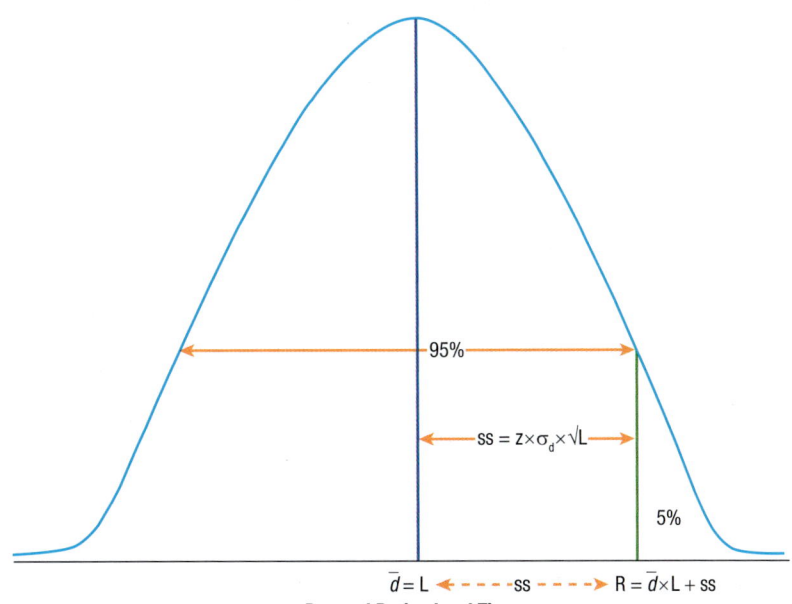

time will provide only a 50% service level. That is, a service level of 50% can be attained with no safety stock. We also know from statistics that if demand during the lead time is normally distributed, then within +1 standard deviation of the average, 34% of the time, the actual demand is greater than the expected or average value. For example, suppose the standard deviation of the demand during the lead time (σ_{dL}) is 50 units. To provide an additional 34% service level (over the 50% provided by $\bar{d} \times L$), 50 ($Z \times \sigma_{dL} = 1 \times 50 = 50$) additional units should be carried as safety stock. These 50 units of safety stock provide protection against stock-outs 34% of the time that actual demand is greater than the expected or average value.

In total, at the reorder point (R = $\bar{d} \times L + SS$), there is enough inventory in stock to protect against stock-outs 84% (50% + 34%) of the time. So, the risk of stock-outs is only 16% (100% – 84%) of the time. Similarly, if we want a service level of 90% (an additional 40% over the 50% provided by $\bar{d} \times L$), then the required safety stock is 64 units ($Z \times \sigma_{dL} = 1.28 \times 50$). The numbers (1 and 1.28) that we used to calculate the safety stock are simply the Z values obtained from the cumulative standard normal distribution table. A sample of Z values for various representative service levels is shown in Table 16.6. In the context of service levels, these Z values are also often referred to as service-level factors.

We assume that demand is normally distributed during the lead time and that service level is specified.

TABLE 16.7: Service-level Factors or Z Values for a Sample of Service Levels

SERVICE LEVEL	50%	80%	85%	90%	93%	95%	97%	98%	99%
Service Factor (Z Values)	0.00	0.84	1.04	1.28	1.48	1.64	1.88	2.05	2.33

EXAMPLE 16.7: Great Lakes Drugs is a fictional pharmaceutical wholesaler to independent drugstores. The company wants to determine an optimal safety stock and reorder point policy for its popular Breathe Easy brand of cold remedy. The lead time for the delivery of Breathe Easy from its manufacturer has averaged a constant four working days. The demand for this product during the lead time is normally distributed with an average daily demand of 30 cases and a daily standard

Service-level factors: another term for Z values in the context of service levels

deviation of 6 cases. If Great Lakes Drugs wishes to provide its customers a service level of 93%, what should the safety stock and reorder point for Breathe Easy be?

SOLUTION

Given:

$$\overline{d} = 30 \text{ cases}$$

$$L = 4 \text{ days}$$

$$\sigma_d = 6 \text{ cases}$$

$$\text{service level} = 93\%$$

Hence, from Table 16.6 (or Appendix A), the service factor or Z value = 1.48. Therefore, the safety stock is:

$$SS = Z \times \sigma_d \times \sqrt{L} = 1.48 \times 6 \times \sqrt{4} = 17.76 \text{ cases}$$

The reorder point is:

$$R = \overline{d} \times L + SS$$

$$= 30 \times 4 + 17.76 = 137.6 \text{ or } 138 \text{ cases}$$

Great Lakes Drugs should place an order for Breathe Easy when the inventory level of the drug drops to 138 cases.

SCREENSHOT 16.6: Example 16.7 – Fixed Order Quantity Reorder Point Model: Variable Demand, Constant Lead Time

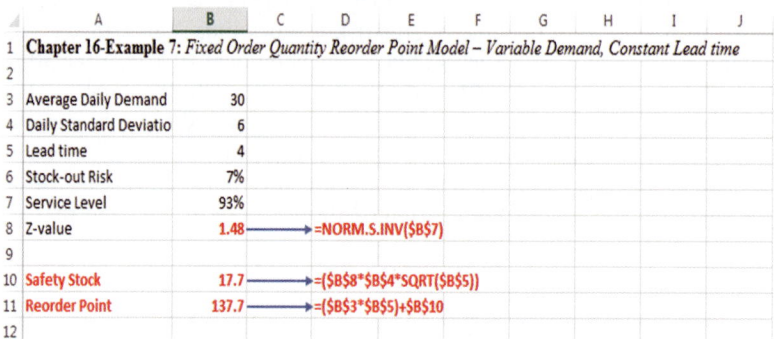

Reorder Point Model for Constant Demand and Variable Lead Time

If demand is constant, but the lead time fluctuates, the reorder point and the associated safety stock for specified service levels can be determined by the following reorder point equation, assuming that the lead times are normally distributed:

$$R = d \times \overline{L} + Z \times d \times \sigma_L,$$

where

    d = the daily or weekly demand

    $\overline{L}$ = the mean, or average, lead time in days or weeks

σ_L = the standard of the lead time in days or weeks

Z = the service factor value for the specified service level (from Appendix A)

EXAMPLE 16.8: The weekly demand for a special brand of tikka masala curry sauce at an Indian restaurant is a constant 60 jars per week. The lead times for the sauce fluctuates in a normally distributed way with a mean of 5 weeks and a standard deviation of 1 week. The restaurant manager, Amisha Patel, is willing to accept a stock-out risk of 3%. Given this information:

1. What are the service level and the corresponding service-level factor (Z) values?
2. What is the reorder point, and how much of the order is the safety stock?

SOLUTION

Given:

Weekly demand, d = 60 jars

Mean or average lead time in weeks, $\overline{L}$ = 5 weeks

Standard of the lead time in days or weeks, σ_L = 1 week

Stockout risk = 3%.

1. Given a stock-out risk of 3%, the corresponding service level is:

$$100\% - 3\% = 97\%$$

For a service level of 97%, the corresponding service factor or Z value from Table 16.6 (or Appendix A) is 1.88.

2. The reorder point is:

$$R = d \times \overline{L} + Z \times d \times \sigma_L$$
$$= 60 \times 5 + 1.88 \times 60 \times 1$$
$$= 300 + 112.8 = 412.8 \text{ or } 413 \text{ jars}$$

Hence, the reorder point is 412.8 or 413 jars, and the safety stock is = 112.8 or 113 jars.

SCREENSHOT 16.7: Example 16.8 – Fixed Order Quantity Reorder Point Model: Constant Demand, Variable Lead Time

	A	B	C	D	E	F	G	H
1	**Chapter 16-Example 8:** *Fixed Order Quantity Reorder Point Model – Constant Demand, Variable Lead time*							
2								
3	Average Daily usage of curry (in jars)	60						
4	Average Lead time in weeks	5						
5	Lead Time Standard Deviation in weeks	1						
6	Stockout risk	3%						
7	Service Level	97%						
8	Z-value	1.88079	→=NORM.S.INV($B$7)					
9								
10	Safety Stock	112.8	→=($B$8*$B$3*$B$5)					
11	Reorder Point	412.8	→=($B$3*$B$4)+$B$10					
12								

Reorder Point Model for Variable Demand and Variable Lead Time

If both the demand and lead times are variable, and assuming that they are independent and are fluctuating in a normally distributed way, then the reorder point and the associated safety stock for specified service levels can be determined by:

$$R = \overline{d} \times \overline{L} + Z \times \sqrt{\left(\overline{L} * \sigma_d^2\right) + \left(\overline{d}^2 \times \sigma_L^2\right)}$$

EXAMPLE 16.9: Tat Hing Hardware Store in Hong Kong (not a real company) sells brushes for electric motors. The daily demand for these brushes follows a normal distribution with a mean of 20 brushes and a standard deviation of 4 brushes. Youngbin Son, the store's manager, orders these brushes from a supplier whose delivery lead time also fluctuates in a normally distributed way with a mean of 8 days and standard deviation of 2 days. Son would like at most a 2% chance of running out of stock during any replenishment period. What is the reorder point and the safety stock for these brushes?

SOLUTION

Given:

$$\overline{d} = 20 \text{ brushes}$$

$$\overline{L} = 8 \text{ days}$$

$$\sigma_L = 2 \text{ days}$$

$$\sigma_d = 4 \text{ brushes}$$

Stock-out risk = 2%

Hence, the service level is 98%. For a service level of 98%, the corresponding service factor, or Z value, from Table 16.6 (or Appendix A) is 2.05:

$$R = \overline{d} \times \overline{L} + Z \times \sqrt{\left(\overline{L} \times \sigma_d^2\right) + \left(\overline{d}^2 \times \sigma_L^2\right)}$$

$$= 20 \times 8 + 2.05 \times \sqrt{(8 \times 16) + (400 \times 4)}$$

$$R = 160 + 85.4 = 245.4 \text{ or } 246 \text{ brushes.}$$

Son should place a replenishment order for brushes when the stock falls to 246 brushes. The safety stock is 85.4 or 86 brushes.

SCREENSHOT 16.8: Example 16.9 – Fixed Order Quantity Reorder Point Model: Variable Demand, Variable Lead Time

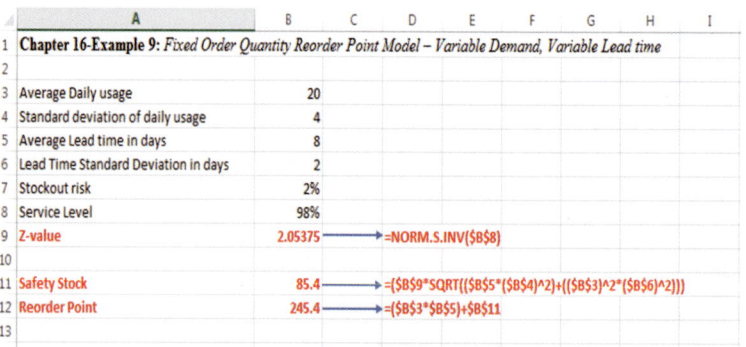

16.5 How Much to Order: Periodic Review Systems

16.5

Explain periodic review systems, and work typical problems.

Recall from Chapter 15 how in a periodic review system (also referred to as a fixed order interval system), replenishment orders are placed at fixed intervals, such as weekly, biweekly, or monthly. The quantity ordered in each period will bring the inventory to a predetermined target level. If we assume that the demand and lead times are constant, then there is no difference between a fixed order interval system and a fixed order quantity system (continuous review system) on the questions of how much and when to order. Nevertheless, if either the demand or the lead time or both vary, then the two models differ. For example, in a fixed order quantity system, the reorder point trigger is *quantity*, whereas in a fixed order interval system, it is *time*. Also, in a fixed order quantity system, fluctuations in the demand or the lead time or both do not affect the quantity ordered but they do affect the timing of when orders should be placed. By contrast, in a fixed order interval system, because the timing of orders is fixed, the quantity to be ordered varies and depends on the inventory that will be needed to cover the demand until the next order is received. In addition, in a fixed order quantity system, safety stock is only needed to absorb demand fluctuations during the lead time. Yet, in a fixed order interval system, a much higher level of safety stock is required because it is needed to buffer demand fluctuations until the next order is received. This timeframe includes the order review period plus the lead time. Figure 16.9 shows the inventory replenishment for a periodic review system when the demand is variable and the lead time is constant.

Companies that produce or sell items with one-time uses and limited shelf lives, such as florists, use single-period inventory systems to determine the optimal ordering amount.

©iStockphoto.com/vgajic

For fixed order interval systems, the predetermined target inventory level (T) should be high enough to meet all demand (except the most unusual and extreme instances) during the review period (RP) and the lead time (L). Specifically, for a given service level, the formula for determining T, when the lead time is constant and the demand fluctuates in a normally distributed way during the review period and the lead time, is:

$$T = \bar{d} \times (RP + L) + SS$$

 Periodic Review

FIGURE 16.9: Inventory Replenishment for a Periodic Review System When the Demand Is Variable and the Lead Time Is Constant

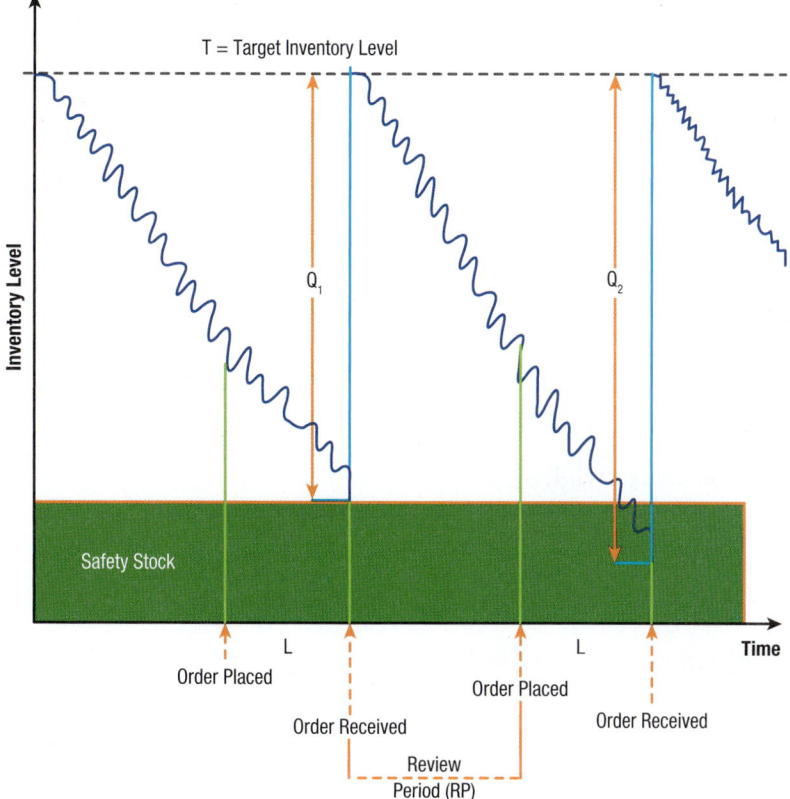

Target inventory level (T): a predetermined inventory level that is established for fixed order interval systems that is high enough to meet all demand

where

$$\bar{d} \times (RP + L) = \text{the average demand during the review period plus the lead time}$$

$$SS = Z \times \sigma_{(RP+L)}$$

In this equation,

$$Z = \text{the number of standard deviations corresponding to the service level}$$

$$\sigma_{(RP+L)} = \text{the standard deviation of demand during the review period plus the lead time}$$

$$= \sigma_d \times \sqrt{RP + L}$$

And in this equation,

$$RP = \text{the review period and L is the lead time}$$

$$\sigma_d = \text{the standard deviation of the daily or weekly demand}$$

Thus, when the lead time is constant and the demand fluctuates in a normally distributed way, the formula for determining the target inventory level, T, is:

$$T = \bar{d} \times (RP + L) + Z \times \sigma_d \times \sqrt{RP + L}$$

EXAMPLE 16.10: A grocery store orders a particular brand of shampoo from the same supplier every 25 days. The lead time for an order is 5 days. The daily demand for the shampoo is approximately normal with a mean of 10 bottles per day and a daily standard deviation of 2 bottles. The desired service level for this shampoo is 95%:

1. What is the target inventory level?
2. What is the average amount of safety stock?
3. If the amount on hand at reorder time is 50 bottles, what should the order quantity be?

SOLUTION

Given:

$\bar{d}$ = 10 bottles

L = 5 days

σ_d = 2 bottles

Order cycle time (OC) = 25 days

Review period = (OC – L) = 25 – 5 = 20 days

Service level = 95%

Hence, from Table 16.6 (or Appendix A), the service-level factor or Z value = 1.64. Therefore:

1. The target inventory level, T, is:

$$T = \bar{d} \times (RP + L) + Z \times \sigma_d \times \sqrt{RP + L}$$

$$= 10 \times (20 + 5) + 1.64 \times 2 \times \sqrt{20 + 5} = 250 + 16.4 = 266.4 \text{ or } 267 \text{ bottles}$$

2. The average safety stock is 16.4 or 17 bottles.
3. The quantity to be ordered, Q, is:

$$Q = T - \text{the amount on hand} = 267 - 50 = 217 \text{ bottles}$$

SCREENSHOT 16.9: Example 16.10 – Fixed Order Interval Model: Variable Demand, Constant Lead Time

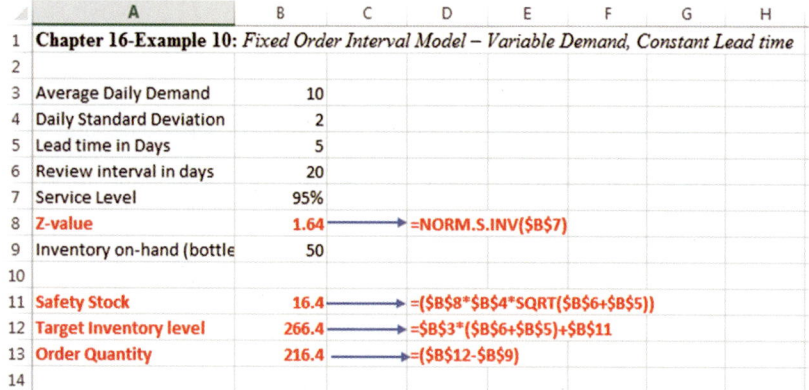

	A	B	C	D	E	F	G	H
1	**Chapter 16-Example 10**: *Fixed Order Interval Model – Variable Demand, Constant Lead time*							
2								
3	Average Daily Demand	10						
4	Daily Standard Deviation	2						
5	Lead time in Days	5						
6	Review interval in days	20						
7	Service Level	95%						
8	Z-value	1.64	→	=NORM.S.INV($B$7)				
9	Inventory on-hand (bottle	50						
10								
11	Safety Stock	16.4	→	=($B$8*$B$4*SQRT($B$6+$B$5))				
12	Target Inventory level	266.4	→	=$B$3*($B$6+$B$5)+$B$11				
13	Order Quantity	216.4	→	=($B$12-$B$9)				
14								

16.6 How Much to Order: Single-Period Inventory Systems

Discuss single period inventory systems, and work typical problems.

Recall from Chapter 15 that single-period inventory systems are used by companies that order seasonal or one-time items such as food and flowers and items with limited shelf lives, such as newspapers or Mother's Day cards. Ordering too much will lead to excess inventory not sold or used. Ordering too little will lead to stock-outs. Consequently, the optimal ordering amount should achieve a balance between stock-out costs and the cost of having excess inventory. Specifically, assuming that demand is normally distributed, the optimal amount is one in which the desired service level is equal to or greater than the following ratio:

$$\text{Service level} = \frac{C_s}{C_s + C_o}$$

where

> C_s = the marginal cost of a shortage, which equals the revenue per unit minus the cost per unit

> C_o = the marginal cost of an overage, which equals the purchase cost per unit minus the salvage value per unit

Note that the service level is the probability that the demand will not exceed the stocking level.

Once the service level is determined, we can determine the appropriate Z value from the cumulative standard normal distribution table (Appendix A). Then, the **optimal stocking level (S$_o$)** is:

$$S_o = \overline{d} + Z \times \sigma_d$$

EXAMPLE 16.11: Kevin Peterson owns a newsstand near a subway station in downtown Chicago. Each day, Kevin sells an average of 100 copies of the *Chicago Sun Times*. The demand for this newspaper is normally distributed with a daily standard deviation of 12 papers. Kevin purchases the newspaper at a cost of $0.75 per paper and sells each for $1.25. On any given day, the *Chicago Sun Times* buys back any unsold newspapers for a refund of $0.40 each (all in U.S. dollars). Kevin wants to determine the optimum number of papers he should order each day.

SOLUTION

optimal stocking level (S$_o$): the optimum inventory level in stock for single-period inventory systems

Given:

> Revenue per unit = $1.25

> Cost per unit = $0.75

Salvage value = $0.40

$\bar{d}$ = 100 papers

σ_d = 12 papers.

Therefore,

C_s = the marginal cost of a shortage = $1.25 – $0.75 = $0.50 per unit

C_o = the marginal cost of an overage = $0.75 – $0.40 = $0.35 per unit

Thus,

$$\text{Service level} = \frac{C_s}{C_s + C_o}$$

$$= \frac{0.50}{(0.50 + 0.35)} = \frac{0.50}{(0.85)} = 0.59 \text{ or } 59\%$$

The Z value that results in a service level of 58.8% is the value that yields a probability of 58.8% in the normal distribution. Appendix A shows that this Z value is approximately 0.22. Hence, the optimum stocking level is:

FIGURE 16.10: Solution to Newspaper Order Problem

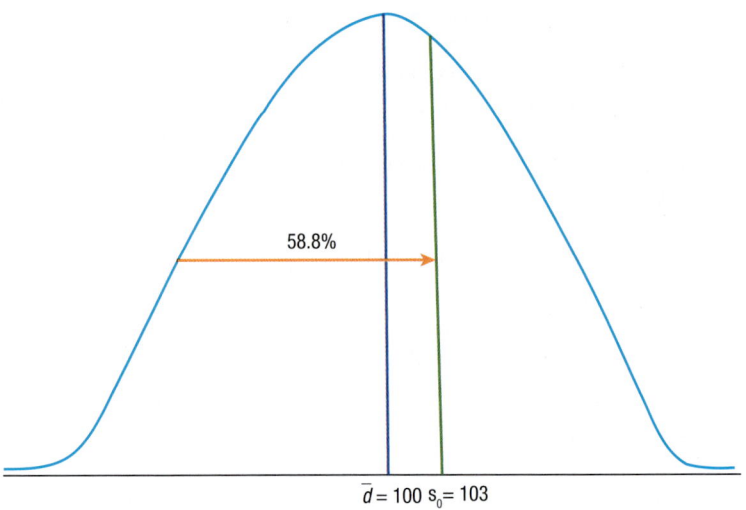

58.8%

$\bar{d}$ = 100 s_o = 103

SCREENSHOT 16.10: Example 16.11—Single Period Order Model: Variable Demand, Constant Lead Time

	A	B	C	D	E	F	G	H
1	Chapter 16-Example 11: Single Period *Order Model – Variable Demand, Constant Lead time*							
2								
3	Average Demand	100						
4	Daily Standard Deviatio	10						
5	Cost per unit	$0.75						
6	Revenue per unit	$1.25						
7	Salvage value	$0.40						
8								
9	Marginal Shortage Cost	$0.50	→=($B$6-$B$5)					
10	Marginal OverageCost	$0.35	→=($B5-$B$7)					
11	Service Level	0.59	→=($B$9/($B$9+$B$10))					
12	Z-value	0.22	→=NORM.S.INV($B$11)					
13	Optimal stocking level	102.2	→=$B$3+ ($B$12*$B$4)					
14								

$$S_o = \bar{d} + Z \times \sigma_d$$

$$= 100 + 0.22 \times 12 = 102.2 \text{ or } 103 \text{ newspapers}$$

Kevin should order 103 copies of the *Chicago Sun Times* each day.

Despite its restrictive assumptions, the EOQ model and its extensions are frequently used by many companies, especially those that deal with large volumes of stock, purchase-to-stock distributors, and make-to-stock manufacturers. These companies typically place multiple orders for their items, have specific order release dates for their products, and have a material requirements planning system for their components. EOQ models are relevant and can be easily applied in manufacturing environments (such as a manufacturer of chemicals) where the end products have a simple structure that requires only a few raw materials and are produced continuously over time at a fairly uniform rate. For such products, production rates are relatively constant over a long time period and economic production run sizes can be easily calculated. Consequently, many materials for these products can be ordered quarterly or annually in bulk in container load, railcar load, or truckload quantities. EOQ models can also be used for items that have a uniform demand such as maintenance, repair, and operating (MRO) inventory items. EOQ models are also applicable in highly repetitive production environments that are characterized by long production runs.[3]

Furthermore, some of the models and methods we discussed in this chapter can be used to make inventory decisions that affect the supply chain and logistics. For example, the EOQ model can be used to select transportation modes by factoring in-transit holding-cost and volume-transportation rates into the total annual cost equation. Similarly, reorder points and stocking levels can be estimated when the demand has a discrete probability distribution rather than a normal distribution. We do not discuss these special applications of EOQ and reorder point.

CHAPTER SUMMARY

16.1 Describe the basic economic order quantity (EOQ) model, its assumptions, and use the model to solve problems. The two fundamental questions in inventory management and control are how much to order or produce, and when to order. The answers depend on the type of inventory control system chosen: continuous review systems, periodic review systems, or single-period order systems. In continuous review systems, the EOQ model is the easiest to use. It is based on six assumptions: a single product is involved; the annual demand is known and occurs uniformly throughout the year with a constant demand rate; the lead time for the receipt of the orders is constant and known; no shortages are allowed; the quantity ordered is received all at once in a single delivery; and there are no quantity discounts.

16.2 Utilize the economic production quantity (EPQ) to solve problems. For continuous systems (fixed order quantity systems), the optimal production quantity is determined by minimizing the total annual costs, which is the sum of the total annual setup and holding costs.

16.3 Solve problems using the EOQ model with quantity discounts. For production systems designed to produce a fixed quantity, the optimal production quantity is determined by minimizing the total annual costs, which is the sum of the total annual setup and holding costs. When quantity discounts are in effect, then the economic order quantity is determined by minimizing the total annual costs, which consists of total annual ordering, holding, and purchase costs.

16.4 Discuss the various reorder point models and their typical problems. Because the order quantity is fixed in continuous review systems, the question of when to order (the reorder point) is determined by the variability in the demand for a product, the lead time, and the desired service level.

16.5 Explain periodic review systems and their typical problems. In periodic review systems (fixed order interval systems), the order interval is fixed, but the quantity ordered varies and depends on fluctuations in the demand and lead time. In such a system, the quantity ordered is an amount that will bring the inventory to a predetermined target level at specific times.

16.6 **Discuss single period inventory systems and their typical problems.** Single-period inventory systems are used for

seasonal or one-time purchases. Ordering too much will lead to excess inventory not sold or used. Ordering too little will lead to stock-outs. The optimal ordering or stocking policy is based on achieving a desired service level that balances the stock-out costs and excess-inventory costs.

KEY TERMS

Economic order quantity (EOQ)   560

Economic production quantity (EPQ)   565

Optimal stocking level (S_0)   585

Quantity discounts   569

Reorder point   575

Service level   577

Service-level factors   579

Target inventory level (T)   583

DISCUSSION AND REVIEW QUESTIONS

1. In the EOQ model, how do we determine the optimum order quantity?

2. What are the major assumptions of the EOQ model, and how do they restrict the model's applicability to real-life inventory issues?

3. How do the demand and the lead time affect reorder points in a continuous review system?

4. What are the differences between the EPQ and the EOQ model?

5. In the EPQ model, what would be the effect if the production rate and the demand rate are equal?

6. A U.S. company that orders brass couplings from a supplier in China noted that the cost of the couplings increases significantly at each reorder cycle. The company uses the EOQ model to determine its order quantity. What alternative approach would you advise

the company to consider to determine the order quantity that will minimize the firm's total inventory cost?

7. When quantity discounts are offered, what factors other than price should be considered?

8. How is the service level related to safety stock?

9. Explain the relationship between the setup time and the average inventory level in the EPQ model. What would be the beneficial effect of reducing setup times?

10. In a continuous review system, how does the variability in both the demand and the lead time affect the target inventory level?

11. In single-period inventory systems, how would a high level of service affect the optimal stocking policy?

SOLVED PROBLEMS

1. KJB Sports Store in Sydney, Australia, (not a real company) sells cricket balls. The store orders the balls from a manufacturer at a cost of US$250 per order. The annual holding cost is 25% of the purchase price, which is US$40 per unit per year. The company has a demand for 20,000 units per year. What is the EOQ, total number of orders required during the year, and the total annual cost (in U.S. dollars)?

Solution:

Given: Annual demand (D) = 20,000 units; Ordering cost per order (S) = $250;

Purchase per unit (P) = $40; Holding rate (i) = 0.25 per unit per year

Given the above information:

Annual holding cost (H) = the holding rate × purchase price per unit

$$= i \times P = 0.25 \times 40 = \$10 \text{ per unit per year}$$

The optimal order quantity (EOQ) is given by:

$$Q_0 = \sqrt{\frac{2 \times D \times S}{H}}$$

SCREENSHOT 16.11: Solved Problem 16.1—EOQ Model

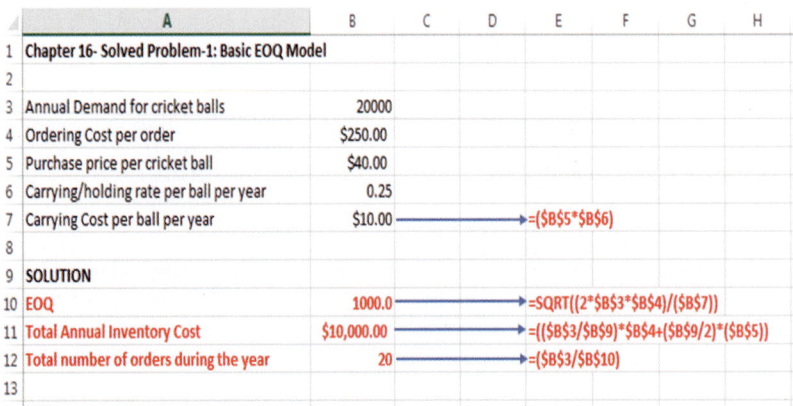

	A	B	C	D	E	F	G	H
1	Chapter 16- Solved Problem-1: Basic EOQ Model							
2								
3	Annual Demand for cricket balls	20000						
4	Ordering Cost per order	$250.00						
5	Purchase price per cricket ball	$40.00						
6	Carrying/holding rate per ball per year	0.25						
7	Carrying Cost per ball per year	$10.00		→=($B$5*$B$6)				
8								
9	SOLUTION							
10	EOQ	1000.0		→=SQRT((2*$B$3*$B$4)/($B$7))				
11	Total Annual Inventory Cost	$10,000.00		→=(($B$3/$B$9)*$B$4+($B$9/2)*($B$5))				
12	Total number of orders during the year	20		→=($B$3/$B$10)				
13								

$$= \sqrt{\frac{2 \times 20000 \times 250}{10}} = 1{,}000 \text{ cricket balls}$$

The total number of orders required during a year is given by:

$$\left(\frac{D}{Q_o}\right) = \left(\frac{20000}{1000}\right) = 20 \text{ orders}$$

The total annual cost of ordering and holding is:

$$TC = \left(\frac{D}{Q_o}\right) \times S + \left(\frac{Q_o}{2}\right) \times H$$

$$= \left(\frac{20000}{1000}\right) \times 250 + \left(\frac{1000}{2}\right) \times 10 = \$5{,}000 + \$5{,}000 = \$10{,}000$$

2. Precision Engineering is a fictional producer of flexible shaft couplings. The company operates 250 days a year and produces couplings at the rate of 120 per day. The demand for these couplings is 80 per day. The annual holding cost is US$4 per coupling, and the production setup cost is US$60 per setup:

    a. Determine the EPQ.

    b. Determine the number of production setups or runs per year.

    c. What is the maximum inventory level?

    d. What are the total annual setup and holding costs (in U.S. dollars)?

Solution:

Given: Demand rate (d) = 80 couplings per day; Number of working days = 250;

Annual demand (D) = 250 × 80 = 20,000; Setup cost per setup (K) = $60;

Holding cost (H) = $4.00 per coupling per year; Production rate (p) = 120 couplings per day;

1. The economic production quantity (EPQ) is:

$$Q_{opt} = \sqrt{\frac{2 \times D \times K}{H}} \times \sqrt{\frac{p}{p-d}}$$

$$= \sqrt{\frac{2 \times 20000 \times 60}{4}} \times \sqrt{\frac{120}{120-80}} = 1{,}341.6 \text{ or } 1{,}342 \text{ couplings}$$

2. The number of production runs or setups annually is:

$$D/Q_{opt} = 20{,}000 / 1{,}342 = 14.9 \text{ or } 15 \text{ production runs or setups over the year.}$$

3. The maximum inventory level is:

$$I_{max} = Q_{opt} \times \left(\frac{p-d}{p}\right)$$

$$= 1342 \times \left(\frac{120-80}{120}\right) = 447.3 \text{ or } 448 \text{ couplings}$$

4. The total annual cost at EPQ is:

$$TC = \left(\frac{D}{Q_{opt}}\right) \times K + \left[\left(\frac{Q_{opt}}{2}\right) \times \frac{(p-d)}{p}\right] \times H$$

$$= \left(\frac{20000}{1342}\right) \times 60 + \left[\left(\frac{1342}{2}\right) \times \left(\frac{120-80}{120}\right)\right] \times 4$$

$$= \$894.43 + \$894.43 = \$1788.86$$

SCREENSHOT 16.12: Solved Problem 16.2—EPQ Model

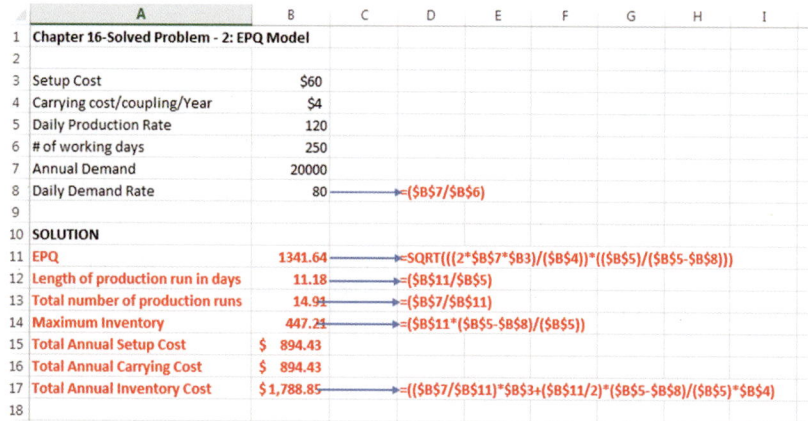

3. Crescent Chemicals, a mythical manufacturer of paint products, produces a special brand of Stormcoat paint. The company operates 277 days a year and produces the specialty paint at the rate of 165 gallons per day. The annual demand for the Stormcoat paint is 9,500 gallons. The annual holding cost is US$1.10 per gallon, and the production setup cost is US$175 per setup.

    1. Determine the EPQ.

    2. Determine the number of production setups or runs per year.

    3. What is the maximum inventory level?

    4. What are the total annual setup and holding costs (in U.S. dollars)?

Solution:

Given: Annual Demand = 9500 gallons; Number of working days = 277;

Demand rate (d) = $\left(\frac{9500}{277}\right)$ = 34. 3 gallons per day; Setup cost per setup (K) = $175;

Holding cost (H) = $1.10 per gallon per year; Production rate (p) = 165 gallons per day;

1. The economic production quantity (EPQ) is:

$$Q_{opt} = \sqrt{\frac{2 \times D \times K}{H}} \times \sqrt{\frac{p}{p-d}}$$

$$= \sqrt{\frac{2 \times 9500 \times 175}{1.10}} \times \sqrt{\frac{165}{165-34.3}} = 1{,}953.5 \text{ or } 1{,}954 \text{ gallons}$$

2. The number of production runs or setups annually is:

$D/Q_{opt} = 9500 / 1{,}954 = 4.86$ or 5 production runs or setups over the year

3. The maximum inventory level is:

$$I_{max} = Q_{opt} \times \left(\frac{p-d}{p}\right)$$

$$= 1{,}954 \times \left(\frac{165-34.3}{165}\right) = 1547.80 \text{ or } 1{,}548 \text{ gallons}$$

The total annual cost at EPQ is:

$$TC = \left(\frac{D}{Q_{opt}}\right) \times K + \left(\frac{Q_{opt}}{2}\right) \times \frac{(p-d)}{p}] \times H$$

$$= \left(\frac{9500}{1954}\right) \times 175 + \left[\left(\frac{1954}{2}\right) \times \left(\frac{165-34.3}{165}\right)\right] \times 1.10$$

$$= \$851.07 + \$851.07 = \$1702.14$$

SCREENSHOT 16.13: Solved Problem 16.3—Nonsymmetrical EOQ Model

	A	B	C	D	E	F	G	H	I
1	Chapter 16-Solved Problem -3: EPQ Model								
2									
3	Setup Cost	$175							
4	Carrying cost/gallon/Year	$1							
5	Daily Production Rate in gallons	165							
6	# of working days	277							
7	Annual Demand in gallons	9500							
8	Daily Demand Rate	34.3		=($B$7/$B$6)					
9									
10	SOLUTION								
11	EPQ	1953.4264		=SQRT(((2*$B$7*$B$3)/($B$4))*(($B$5)/(($B$5-$B$8)))					
12	Length of production run in days	11.838948		=($B$11/$B$5)					
13	Total number of production runs	4.8632494		=($B$7/$B$11)					
14	Maximum Inventory	1547.3975		=($B$11*($B$5-$B$8)/($B$5))					
15	Total Annual Setup Cost	$ 851.07							
16	Total Annual Carrying Cost	$851.07							
17	Total Annual Inventory Cost	$1,702.14		=(($B$7/$B$11)*$B$3+($B$11/2)*($B$5-$B$8)/($B$5)*$B$4)					
18									

4. ABC Ltd., a fictional U.S. paint manufacturing company, buys titanium dioxide from a supplier in Brazil. The company uses approximately 4,800 pounds of the chemical annually. The Brazilian supplier has just announced a price–volume discount, which is shown in the following table. ABC incurs an ordering cost of US$120 per order each time it places an order for titanium dioxide. The holding cost is 20% of the purchase price per pound of the chemical. What is the optimal quantity of titanium dioxide ABC should order from the Brazilian supplier?

Quantity Ordered	Price per Pound (in U.S. dollars)
0 to 999	5.00
1,000 to 1,999	4.80
2,000 or above	4.50

Solution:

1. For each volume range, calculate the EOQ:

$$EOQ_{5.00} = \sqrt{\frac{2 \times D \times S}{H}} = \sqrt{\frac{2 \times 4800 \times 120}{0.2 * 5}} = 1{,}073.3 \text{ or pounds}$$

$$EOQ_{4.80} = \sqrt{\frac{2 \times D \times S}{H}} = \sqrt{\frac{2 \times 4800 \times 120}{0.2 * 4.80}} = 1{,}095.5 \text{ pounds}$$

$$EOQ_{4.50} = \sqrt{\frac{2 \times D \times S}{H}} = \sqrt{\frac{2 \times 4800 \times 120}{0.2 * 4.50}} = 1{,}131.4 \text{ pounds}$$

2. If the calculated EOQ is feasible, compute the total annual cost. If the feasible EOQ falls within the volume range that has the lowest purchase price, stop. This feasible EOQ is the optimum quantity to order. Otherwise, go to step 3.

Out of three EOQs calculated in the previous step, $EOQ_{5.00} = 1{,}073.3$, and $EOQ_{4.50} = 1{,}131.4$ are not feasible because they do not fall in the volume ranges related to their unit prices. Hence, the only feasible EOQ is $EOQ_{4.80} = 1{,}095.5$. It falls in the volume range (1,000 to 1,999 pounds) for its related price (P = $4.80). The total annual cost for the feasible EOQ of 1,095.5 is:

$$TC_{EOQ} = \left(\frac{D}{Q_o}\right) \times S + \left(\frac{Q_o}{2}\right) \times H + P \times D$$

$$= \left(\frac{4800}{1095.5}\right) \times 120 + \left(\frac{1095.5}{2}\right) \times (0.20 \times 4.80) + 4{,}800 \times 4.80$$

$$= \$525.79 + \$525.84 + \$23{,}040 = \$24{,}091.63.$$

The EOQ of 1,095.5, however, does not fall within the volume range that has the lowest purchase price. Therefore, we go to step 3.

3. In addition to the total annual cost calculated for the feasible EOQ in step 2, compute the total annual cost for the minimum quantities in the higher volume ranges with lower purchase prices.

The total cost for the minimum quantity in the next higher volume range (2,000), which has purchase price of \$4.50 per unit, is:

$$TC_{2000} = \left(\frac{D}{Q_o}\right) \times S + \left(\frac{Q_o}{2}\right) \times H + P \times D$$

$$= \left(\frac{4800}{2000}\right) \times 120 + \left(\frac{2000}{2}\right) \times (0.2 \times 4.50) + 4800 \times 4.50$$

$$= \$288 + \$900 + \$21{,}600 = \$22{,}788.$$

4.   Choose that order quantity that has the lowest total annual cost.

Comparing the two total inventory cost figures of TC_{EOQ}, and $TC_{2,000}$, we find at Q = 2,000 pounds is the optimal order quantity because it has the lowest total annual cost ($TC_{2,000}$ = \$22,788).

SCREENSHOT 16.14: Solved Problem 16.4—Quantity Discount Model

5.   For the Kraus Department Store in Example 16.2, let's assume that the daily demand for coffeemakers is normally distributed and that the average daily demand is 20 units with a standard deviation of 3 coffeemakers per day. The lead time for receiving a new order of coffeemakers is 9 days. Determine the reorder point and safety stock if the store wants a stock-out risk equal to 6%.

Solution:

Given: $\bar{d}$ = 20 units; σ_d = 3 units; L = 9 days; Stock-out risk = 6%;

Hence, the service level = (100% − 6%) = 94%;

From Appendix A, the service-level factor or Z value is approximately 1.55.

Therefore, the safety stock is:

$$SS = Z \times \sigma_d \, d \times \sqrt{L} = 1.55 \times 3 \times \sqrt{9} = 13.95 \text{ or } 14 \text{ coffeemakers}$$

The reorder point is:

$$R = \bar{d} \times L + SS$$

$$= 20 \times 9 + 13.95 = 193.95 \text{ or } 194 \text{ coffee makers}$$

Kraus Department Store should place an order for coffeemakers when the inventory level reaches 194 units.

SCREENSHOT 16.15: Solved Problem 16.5—Fixed Order Quantity Reorder Point Model: Variable Demand, Constant Lead Time

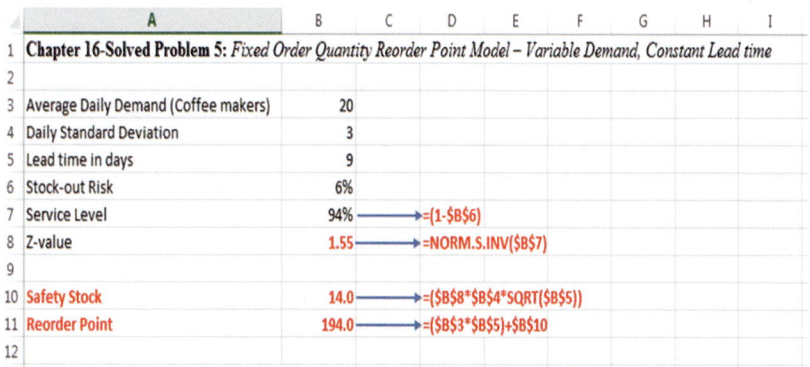

6.   The demand for bars of soap at the mythical Oceanside Motel in Miami is a constant 600 units per day. The lead time to get the bars fluctuates in a normally distributed way and has a mean of 8 days and a standard deviation of 2 days. The manager of the motel wants to maintain a service level of 93%. Given this information:

1.   What is the reorder point?

2.   How many days of supply are in stock at the reorder point?

Solution:

Given: Daily demand, d = 600 bars of soap; Mean, or average, lead time, $\bar{L}$ = 8 days;

Standard deviation of the lead time in days, σ_L = 2 days;
Service level = 93%.

Given a service level of 93%, the corresponding service factor or Z value from Table 16.6 (or Appendix A) is 1.48.

1. The reorder point is:

$$R = d \times \bar{L} + Z \times d \times \sigma_L$$

$$= 600 \times 8 + 1.48 \times 600 \times 2 = 4{,}800 + 1770.9 = 6570.9 \text{ or } 6571 \text{ bars of soap}$$

2. The number of days of supply of bars of soap in stock at the reorder point is:

$$(R/d) = 6571 / 600 = 10.95 \text{ or } 11 \text{ days of supply}$$

SCREENSHOT 16.16: Solved Problem 16.6—Fixed Order Quantity Reorder Point Model: Variable Demand, Constant Lead Time

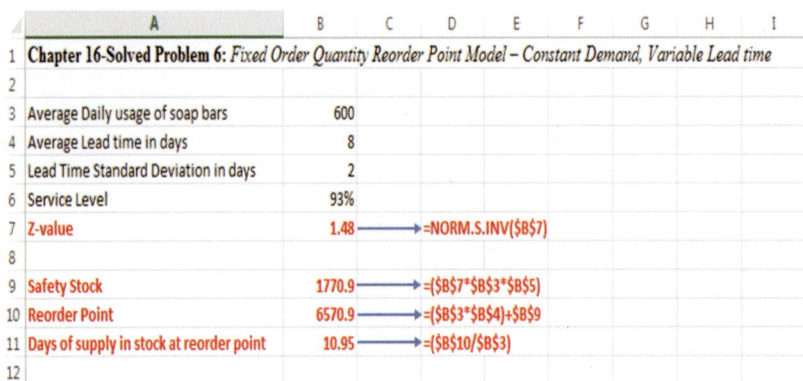

7. The usage rate of a certain type of chemical by a manufacturing company has a mean of 100 pounds per day and a daily standard deviation of 9 pounds per day. The company orders this chemical from a supplier in Houston. The delivery lead time varies with a mean of 10 days and a standard deviation of 2 days. Both the daily demand and the lead time follow an approximate normal distribution. If the manufacturing company wants to provide its customers a 95% service level, what should the reorder point be?

Solution:

Given: $\bar{d}$ = 100 pounds; $\bar{L}$ = 10 days; σ_L = 2 days; σ_d = 9 pounds; Service level = 95%.

For a service level of 95%, the corresponding service factor or Z value from Table 16.6 or Appendix A is 1.65:

$$R = \bar{d} \times \bar{L} + Z \times \sqrt{\left(\bar{L} \times \sigma_d^2\right) + \left(\bar{d}^2 \times \sigma_L^2\right)}$$

$$= 100 \times 10 + 1.65 \times \sqrt{\left(10 \times 9^2\right) + \left(100^2 \times 2^2\right)}$$

$$R = 1{,}000 + 332.3 = 1332.3 \text{ pounds}$$

SCREENSHOT 16.17: Solved Problem 16.7—Fixed Order Quantity Reorder Point Model: Variable Demand, Variable Lead Time

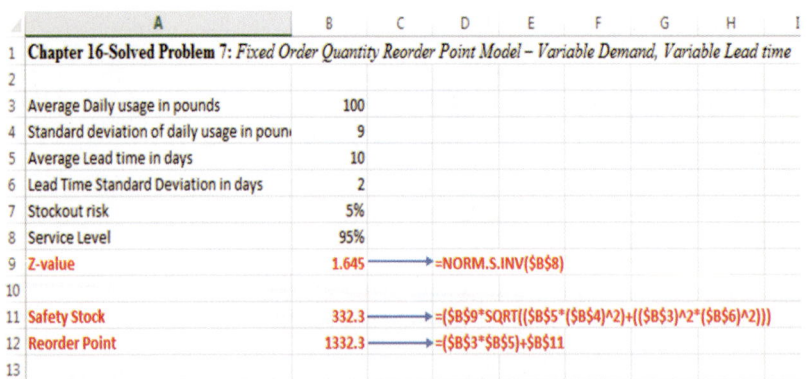

8. A grocery store orders a particular brand of potato chips from a wholesale supplier of food products. The review period is 14 days, and the lead time for order delivery is 3 days. Daily demand for potato chips is approximately normal with a mean of 25 bags per day and a daily standard deviation of 4 bags. The desired service level for the sale potato chips is 95%.

1. What is the target inventory level?

2. What is the average amount of safety stock?

3. If the amount on hand at reorder time is 80 bags, what should the order quantity be?

Solution:

Given: $\bar{d}$ = 25 bags; L = 3 days; σ_d = 4 bags; Review period, RP = 14 days; Service level = 95%.

Hence from Table 16.6 (or Appendix A), the service-level factor or Z value = 1.64. Therefore:

1. The target inventory level, T is:

$$T = \bar{d} \times (RP + L) + Z \times \sigma_d \times \sqrt{RP + L}$$

$$= 25 \times (14 + 3) + 1.64 \times 4 \times \sqrt{14 + 3} = 425 + 27.05$$

$$= 452 \text{ bags}$$

2. The average safety stock is 27 bags.

3. The quantity to be ordered, Q = T − the amount on hand = 452 − 80 = 372 bags.

SCREENSHOT 16.18: Solved Problem 16.8—Fixed Order Interval Model: Variable Demand, Constant Lead Time

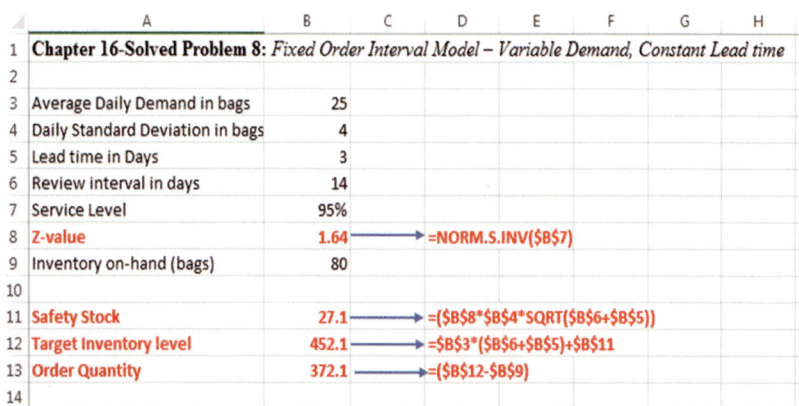

	A	B	C	D	E	F	G	H
1	**Chapter 16-Solved Problem 8:** *Fixed Order Interval Model – Variable Demand, Constant Lead time*							
2								
3	Average Daily Demand in bags	25						
4	Daily Standard Deviation in bags	4						
5	Lead time in Days	3						
6	Review interval in days	14						
7	Service Level	95%						
8	**Z-value**	1.64	=NORM.S.INV($B$7)					
9	Inventory on-hand (bags)	80						
10								
11	**Safety Stock**	27.1	=($B$8*$B$4*SQRT($B$6+$B$5))					
12	**Target Inventory level**	452.1	=$B$3*($B$6+$B$5)+$B$11					
13	**Order Quantity**	372.1	=($B$12-$B$9)					
14								

9. The fictional Sapphire Christmas Tree Company wants to determine how many 8-foot Colorado pine trees it should order for the holiday season. The company buys these trees for US$240 per tree and sells them for US$300 per tree. The demand for them during the season normally distributed with a mean of 90 trees and a standard deviation of 10 trees. Any unsold trees are always eventually sold but at discount of 30%:

1. Determine the service level.

2. What are the service level and the optimal stocking level?

Solution:

Given: Revenue per tree = $300; Cost per tree = $240; Salvage value = (1 -.3) × 300 = $210;

$$\bar{d} = 90 \text{ trees; } \sigma_d = 10 \text{ trees.}$$

Therefore,

C_s = the marginal cost of shortage = $300 − $240 = $60

C_o = the marginal cost of an overage = $240 − $210 = $30

3. The service level is:

$$\text{Service level} = \frac{C_s}{(C_s + C_o)} = \frac{60}{(60 + 30)} = \frac{60}{(90)} = 0.67 \text{ or } 67\%$$

4. The Z value that yields a service level of 66.6% is the value that yields a probability of 66.6% in the normal distribution. From Appendix A, this Z value is approximately 0.43. Hence, the optimum stocking level is:

$$S_o = \bar{d} + Z \times \sigma_d$$

$$= 90 + 0.43 \times 10 = 94.3 \text{ or } 95 \text{ trees}$$

SCREENSHOT 16.19: Solved Problem 16.9—Single-Period Order Model: Variable Demand, Constant Lead Time

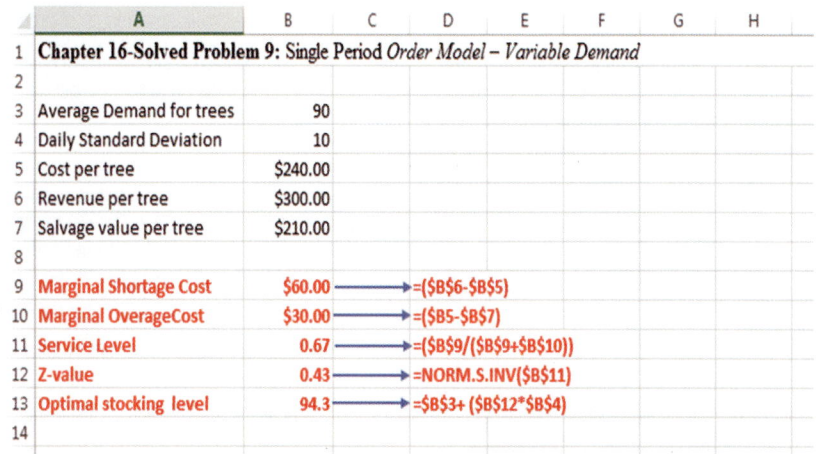

	A	B	C	D	E	F	G	H
1	**Chapter 16-Solved Problem 9:** Single Period *Order Model – Variable Demand*							
2								
3	Average Demand for trees	90						
4	Daily Standard Deviation	10						
5	Cost per tree	$240.00						
6	Revenue per tree	$300.00						
7	Salvage value per tree	$210.00						
8								
9	**Marginal Shortage Cost**	$60.00	=($B$6-$B$5)					
10	**Marginal OverageCost**	$30.00	=($B5-$B$7)					
11	**Service Level**	0.67	=($B$9/($B$9+$B$10))					
12	**Z-value**	0.43	=NORM.S.INV($B$11)					
13	**Optimal stocking level**	94.3	=$B$3+ ($B$12*$B$4)					
14								

PROGRAMS ·

1. Auto Mart is a mythical seller of a variety of automobile parts and accessories. Auto Mart's owner, Jonathan Trott, wishes to determine the optimum order quantity for one of the store's popular wiper blades. The annual demand for the wiper blades is 16,000. The annual holding cost per unit is US$2.50, and the cost to place an order is US$50:

   a. What is the EOQ?

   b. What are the total annual ordering and holding costs (in U.S. dollars)?

2. Refer to problem 1. Assuming that holding cost and order costing remain the same, if annual demand for wiper blades doubles to 32000, does the EOQ also double? Explain your answer with relevant calculations.

3. You're a buyer for fictional Quality Kitchen Appliances. The store has a demand for 1,000 toaster ovens per year. The cost of each toaster oven is US$78. The ordering cost is US$100 per order. The holding cost is 40% of the cost of the oven per unit per year.

   a. What is the optimal order quantity?

   b. How many orders will be placed per year?

   c. What is the total annual cost (in U.S. dollars)?

   d. If the holding cost decreases to 30% of the unit cost of the oven, what effect will it have on EOQ and the total annual cost?

   e. Suppose the store manager purchases 100 ovens per order instead of the EOQ. What impact will the 100-unit order size have on the firm's total annual cost?

4. The Burlap Tire Company is a mythical producer of a brand of tires known as the Snowgrip. The annual demand for this brand of tires at its distribution center is 14,000. The cost of ordering these tires for the distribution center for each order placed is $1,200 per order. The annual holding cost is $8.50 per tire per year (in U.S. dollars):

   a. What is EOQ and the total annual cost at EOQ?

   b. If the company decides to place more frequent orders, then the ordering cost would increase to $1,800 per order. Nevertheless, the increased frequency of orders would decrease the annual holding cost to $6.50 per tire per year. Should the distribution center order tires more frequently?

5. Amco International is a fictional importer of handcrafted leather and reptile skin handbags from India. The Indian company that sells these handbags will ship these handbags only in order sizes of 240 units. The cost of placing an order from this Indian company is US$3,600. The annual demand for these handcrafted bags is 4,800 units. Determine the holding cost per unit that Amco needs to achieve to minimize its total cost.

6. Cannes Croissants (not a real company) wishes to determine the optimum production quantity for its top-selling product, almond croissants. The annual demand for almond croissants is 12,000 units. The setup cost for a production run of the croissants is US$15. The holding cost per unit per year is US$0.50. Production is most efficient when 80 croissants are produced per day. The company operates 300 days during a year

   a. What is the economic production quantity (EPQ)?

   b. How many production runs will there be per year?

   c. What is the maximum inventory level?

   d. What is the total annual cost (in U.S. dollars)?

   e. What is the length of a production run in days?

7. A company manufactures vacuum cleaners. Although the company buys many of the components from outside vendors, it produces in-house HEPA filters at the rate of 600 per day. Vacuum cleaners are assembled daily at the rate of 200 per day. The company operates 300 days a year. The setup cost for a production run of the filters is $50 per setup, and the annual holding costs are $1.50 per filter (in U.S. dollars):

   a. How many filters per run are optimal?

   b. What is the average inventory level for this production size?

   c. How many production setups would there be in a year?

   d. What is the optimal length of production run in days?

   e. What would be the savings in annual inventory cost if setup costs can be reduced to $30 per setup?

8. Park Sung Inc. is a fictional South Korean manufacturer of refrigerators. The company produces at its manufacturing plant in Busan subcomponents for its refrigerators at the rate 275 units per day. The annual usage rate of this subcomponents is 30,000 units. The holding cost is US$3 per unit per year, and the setup cost of producing these subcomponents is US$50 per setup. The company operates its manufacturing facility for 300 days during a year:

   a. What is the economic production quantity (EPQ)?

   b. What is the average inventory level for this optimum production quantity?

   c. How many production setups would there be in a year?

   d. What is the optimal length of production run in days?

   e. What would be the savings in annual inventory cost if setup costs can be reduced to US$40 per setup?

9. The mythical Hacker Microbrewery in Rosenheim, Germany, makes a brand of beer called Golden Eagle, which it bottles and sells in cases to adjoining pubs and stores in Rosenheim. The setup cost of brewing and bottling a batch of beer is US$1,800 per setup. The holding cost of storing a bottle of beer is US$1.50 per year. The annual demand for the Golden Eagle brand of beer is 20,000 bottles. Hacker Microbrewery brews and bottles beer at the rate of 655 bottles per day. The brewery operates 250 days per year:

   a. What is the economic production quantity (EPQ)?

   b. What is the average inventory level for this optimum production quantity?

   c. How many production setups would there be in a year?

   d. What is the optimal length of production run in days?

   e. What would be the savings in annual inventory cost if setup costs can be reduced to $1,500 per setup?

10. Ventura Lumber Mill (not a real company) in Salvador, Brazil, processes 9,000 logs annually and operates 300 days during a year. Ventura's supplier delivers orders to the lumber mill at the rate of 50 logs per day. The cost to Ventura for placing an order to the supplier is US$1,400 per order, and the cost of carrying inventory of logs is US$20 per log per year:

   a. What is the economic production quantity (EPQ)?

   b. What is the average inventory level for this optimum production quantity?

   c. How many production setups would there be in a year?

d. What is the optimal length of production run in days?

e. What would be the savings in annual inventory cost if the holding costs can be reduced to US$18 per log per year?

11. The mythical Owen Distributors has an annual demand of 2,000 units for its handheld security wands. The average cost of the handheld security wand is US$140. Carrying cost is 18% of the unit cost of the security wand. Ordering costs are US$30 per order. If the company orders in quantities of 500 or more, it can get a 6% discount on unit cost of the security wand. Should Owen Distributors take the quantity discount?

12. A printing company uses 2,000 reams of a certain type of paper in a year. The cost of holding one ream of paper in inventory per year US$0.60. The ordering cost per order is US$30.00. The vendor that supplies the paper to the printing company has just announced a quantity discount schedule given in the following table. What is the optimum number of reams to buy at one time?

Quantity Ordered (in reams)	Price per Ream (in U.S. dollars)
0 to 499	8.00
500 to 999	7.20
1,000 to 1,499	6.20
1,500+	5.00

13. A U.S. jewelry store wishes to buy rare green amethyst gemstones. The supplier of the gemstones has announced the quantity discount schedule in the following table. The ordering cost is US$120 per order, and the holding cost is 40% of the unit price per year. The jewelry store is open 300 days a year, and the demand is expected to be 30 gemstones per day. How many of them should the buyer order?

Quantity Ordered	Price per Stone (in U.S. dollars)
0 to 499	55.00
500 to 999	52.00
1, 000 to 1,499	49.00
1,500+	45.00

14. Sun International is a fictional major distributor of hand towels and wash clothes to hotel chains and restaurants. To minimize procurement costs, the company is planning to switch to a supplier overseas. The company has narrowed its choice to two suppliers—one in India and the other in the Philippines. The quantity discount–price schedules offered by both suppliers are given in the following table:

Indian Supplier		Philippines Supplier	
Quantity Ordered	Price per unit (in U.S. dollars)	Quantity Ordered	Price per unit (in U.S. dollars)
0 to 3,999	35.00	0 to 3,999	37.00
4,000 to 7,999	32.00	4,000 to 7,999	34.00
8,000 to 11,999	27.00	8,000 to 11,999	26.00
12,000+	22.00	12,000+	20.00

The annual demand for hand towels and wash clothes is 300,000 units. The cost of placing an order is $320, and it is independent of the supplier chosen or order quantity. The carrying cost is 22% of the item price. Which supplier should Sun International choose to minimize the total costs associated with procurement of these items?

15. Emily Larson is in charge of purchasing surgical supplies for a county hospital. Emily is evaluating two suppliers (suppliers A and B) to purchase forceps for the hospital's surgical use. The quantity–price schedules of both suppliers are given in the following table. The annual demand for forceps is 10,000 units. The ordering cost is US$150 per order, and the carrying cost is 20% of the item's purchase price per unit:

Supplier A		Supplier B	
Quantity Ordered	Price per unit (in U.S. dollars)	Quantity Ordered	Price per unit (in U.S. dollars)
0 to 2,999	10.00	0 to 3,999	11.00
2,000 to 4,999	9.50	4,000 to 7,999	10.50
5,000 to 7,999	8.00	8,000 to 11,999	9.00
8,000+	7.00	12,000+	7.00

a. What is the economic order quantity for each supplier?

b. What quantity should be ordered, and from which supplier?

c. What is the total cost for the quantity ordered in "b"?

d. What additional factors should Emily consider besides total cost?

16. Cheryl Hunter is responsible for maintaining adequate hospital supplies at fictional St. Thomas Hospital. The demand and lead times for syringes are assumed to be constant. During the past year, the daily demand for syringes was 80 units and the lead time from the supplier was 4 days. What is the reorder point?

17. The daily demand for integrated circuit boards by mythical Reliance Computers, which assembles computers, is 80 units. The daily demand is normally distributed and has a standard deviation of 6 units. The lead time from the supplier is a constant 9 days. If Reliance Computers is willing to accept a stock-out risk of 7%, what is the reorder point and how much of the inventory ordered is safety stock?

18. The demand for frozen yogurt at the fictional Garland Ice Cream and Dairy store can be approximated by a normal distribution with a mean of 50 gallons per day and a standard deviation of 6 gallons per day. The lead time from the supplier is a constant 4 days. If the store replenishes its supply of frozen yogurt when the inventory level drops to 220 gallons, what is the safety stock, and how much protection against stock-outs does it provide?

19. The desired service level for a sporting good store's inventory of string bathing suits is 85%. The average demand during the replenishment period is 180 suits with a standard deviation of 30 suits:

a. What is the reorder point?

b. If the store wants to increase its service level to 91% for the suits, what is the reorder point and safety stock?

20. A large law firm uses a constant 50 reams of copier paper per day. The lead time for the paper is approximately normal, averages 9 days, and has a standard deviation of 3 days. What reorder point provides a service level of 90%?

21. Let's return to the Romano Chocolates Boutique, which, as stated, orders chocolates from a supplier in Belgium. Demand for the chocolates is relatively constant at 20 boxes per day. The lead time of these chocolates fluctuates but is normally distributed with a mean of 15 days and a standard deviation of 5 days:

   a. If the desired service level is 50%, what is the reorder point?

   b. What is the reorder point if the desired service level is 95%?

   c. If the standard deviation in the lead time can be reduced from 5 days to 3, what reorder point now provides a 95% service level? How does a 95% service level affect the safety stock?

22. A health food store buys 14-ounce bags of quinoa from a Mexican supplier. The store's daily demand for quinoa is normally distributed with a mean of 30 bags per day and a standard deviation of 4 bags per day. The lead time varies but is normally distributed and has mean of 15 days and a standard deviation of 3 days. If the health food store wants to provide its customers with an 85% service level, what should the reorder point be?

23. An automobile service station uses 900 cases of motor oil annually. The station operates 300 days a year. The order replenishment lead time for motor oil is 4 days with a standard deviation of 4 cases per day. The station has specified an annual service level of 97%:

   a. What is the level of safety stock required assuming that demand during lead time is normally distributed?

   b. If the station decides to hold only 6 six cases of motor oil as safety stock, what is the stock-out risk?

24. The daily usage rate of wheel bearings at a machine shop is normally distributed with a mean of 200 per day and a standard deviation of 15 per day. The lead time fluctuates in a normally distributed way and has a mean of 8 days and a standard deviation of 2 days:

   a. If the machine shop wants to provide its customers with a 95% service level, what should the reorder point be?

   b. If the lead time standard deviation increases to 4 days, what is the probability that the machine shop will run out of stock?

25. A drugstore orders at fixed intervals many of the items it stocks. The store orders a particular brand of cold medicine from a wholesale supplier. The store reviews the stock of the medicine every 25 days and places an order. The lead time is 5 days. The daily demand for the cold medicine is approximately normal with a mean of 10 packages per day and a daily standard deviation of 2.5 packages. If the store wants to maintain a service level of 95%:

   a. What should the target inventory level be?

   b. What is the average amount of safety stock?

   c. If the store has 30 packages of cold medicine on hand at reorder time, what should the order quantity be?

26. A French restaurant's daily demand for pinot noir wine is normally distributed with a mean of 20 bottles and a standard deviation of 3 bottles. The restaurant manager checks its supply every 15 days. The lead time for wine is 5 days and is reasonably constant. A recent periodic review at the restaurant revealed there were 30 pinot noir bottles in stock. The restaurant manager wants to limit his stock-out risk to 3%:

   a. What should the target inventory level be?

   b. What is the order quantity?

27. The manager of a department store uses two types of inventory control systems to manage the inventory of stock keeping units (SKUs) in his store—a continuous review system and a periodic review system. The manager must place replenishment orders for SKU-11 from the continuous review system and SKU-27 from the periodic review system. Although SKU-11 can be ordered any time, SKU-27 can only be ordered every three weeks. The store operates 52 weeks a year, and the weekly demand rates for both SKUs are normally distributed. The following table provides pertinent information on both SKUs:

	SKU-11	SKU-27
Average weekly demand	65 units	100
Standard deviation	5 units per week	8 units per week
Unit cost (in U.S. dollars)	$40	$20
Annual holding rate	35%	15%
Ordering cost (in U.S. dollars)	$100/order	$50/order
Lead time	3 weeks	2 weeks
Desired service level	99%	97%

   a. What is the reorder point for each SKU?

   b. What is the EOQ for SKU-11?

   c. If 80 units of SKU-27 are on hand, what should be the order quantity?

28. A local farm market buys fresh fruits and vegetables from local farmers. It buys peaches from one farmer at a cost of $0.90 per pound and sells it for $2.00 per pound. The demand for peaches during the season is normally distributed with a mean of 40 pounds per day and a daily standard deviation of 5 pounds. At the end of each business day, any unsold peaches are purchased by local restaurants for $0.60 per pound (in U.S. dollars):

   a. Determine the service level.

   b. What is the optimal stocking level for the service level determined in (a)?

29. A bakery must decide how many graduation cakes to prepare for the upcoming weekend. The demand for the cakes can be approximated by a normal distribution with a mean of 8 cakes per day and a standard deviation of 1 cake. The cost to prepare each graduation cake is $35 and can be sold for $63 (in U.S. dollars). Any unsold cakes during the weekend are sold at half the price the following Monday. Typically, half of these cakes get sold at the reduced price, and the other half get donated to a homeless shelter:

   a. Determine the service level.

   b. What is the optimal stocking level for the service level determined in (a)?

30. A small grocery store buys one-gallon bottles of milk from a local dairy farmer. The store buys milk from the dairy farmer at a cost of $2.00 per gallon and sells it for $3.50 per gallon. The demand for milk is normally distributed with a mean of 30 one-gallon bottles per day and a daily standard deviation of 3 bottles. At the end of each business day, any unsold milk is purchased by local restaurants for $1.00 per bottle (in U.S. dollars):

   a. Determine the service level.

   b. What is the optimal stocking level for the service level determined in (a)?

31. Emily Ford, the manager of a college bookstore, purchases polo shirts from a local vendor with the college name and logo printed on them. Emily purchases these t-shirts from the vendor at a cost of US$20 per shirt. The bookstore incurs an ordering cost of US$80 per order, and the annual holding cost is 20% of the purchase cost of a polo shirt. Emily estimates that the demand for the polo shirts for the upcoming year will be 2,000 shirts. The vendor is willing to offer quantity discounts to the bookstore according to the following schedule:

Order Quantity	Discount
0 to 499	0%
500 to 799	3%
700 to 999	4%
1,000+	5%

    Given this quantity discount schedule, what is the optimal quantity of polo shirts that Emily should order, and what would be the total annual cost at this optimal order quantity?

32. Refer to the data in problem 31. If the annual holding cost is a constant $3.50 per shirt per year, compute the optimal order quantity and the total annual cost.

33. A creamery shop sells a special blend of mango and vanilla ice cream. The cost to the shop of making this ice cream is $3.00 per quart and it sells it for $4.50 per quart (in U.S. dollars). The demand for this is normally distributed with a mean of 35 quarts per day and a daily standard deviation of 4 quarts. At the end of each business day, any unsold ice cream is purchased by local restaurants for $1.50 per quart:

    a. Determine the service level.

    b. What is the optimal stocking level for the service level determined in (a)?

34. Daily demand for automotive batteries in an automobile repair shop is normally distributed with a mean of 10 batteries and a standard deviation of 1 battery. The cost of a dissatisfied customer, expedited ordering, and equipment downtime as a result of running out-of-stock is US$400 per battery. The purchase cost is US$250 per battery with no salvage value:

    a. Determine the service level.

    b. What is the optimal stocking level for the service level determined in (a)?

35. A grocery store uses a fixed order cycle policy for ordering the paper towels it sells to the store's customers. Demand for the paper towels is normally distributed with a mean of 50 rolls per day and a daily standard deviation of 3 rolls. The order interval is 12 days with a lead time of three days. The quantity of paper towel rolls in stock at the time of reorder for three order cycles is given in the following table:

Order Cycle	Inventory on Hand
1	35
2	4
3	88

    Determine the order quantity for each of the three order cycles.

CASE STUDY 16.1 WHEN YOUR CUSTOMERS STEER YOU WRONG: WAL-MART'S PROJECT IMPACT DISASTER

Wal-Mart (Wal-Mart Stores Inc., Bentonville, AR) has been known as the iconic store that sells thousands of items at low costs. Over the years, however, one recurring theme from customer complaints was the cluttered feel to its stores, with items stacked and stored nearly everywhere, clothing racks thrust out into the aisles, and a general feeling of (barely) controlled chaos on the shopping floor. In 2008, Wal-Mart decided it was time to listen to its customers and launched "Project Impact," aimed at uncluttering stores through extensive store redesigns to get products out of the way. Wal-Mart spent hundreds of millions of dollars pushing Project Impact across its U.S. locations, and the initial response from its customers was that they loved the changes.

There was just one problem: Sales dropped. In fact, they dropped severely. Customers who supported the redesigned stores and the new, sleeker feel of the shopping environment stopped spending their money at the stores. Wal-Mart removed 15% of inventory from their stores and the response of competitors like Dollar General (Dollar General Corporation, Goodlettsville, TN) and JCPenney (J. C. Penney Company, Plano, TX) was to add shelves and fill up empty wall space with jewelry and electronics counters. Independent estimates suggest that by the time Wal-Mart abandoned Project Impact in 2011 and began restocking their stores to their former, cluttered level, the company had lost nearly US$2 billion in an effort to make its customers happy. In-store sales at Wal-Marts across the United States did not return to pre-remodel levels for nearly three years.[4]

Questions:

1. What does the public's reaction to Wal-Mart's Project Impact suggest about expectations for discount stores?

2. What are the inventory control implications for making drastic changes like Wal-Mart undertook?

3. React to the following statement: "Crowded and cluttered stores send a signal to shoppers that there are bargains to be had. Cluttering store floor space and increasing the height of shelves attracts bargain hunters." Do you agree with this perspective? Why or why not?

4. Discuss how a similar, cluttered approach would be perceived by shoppers at a higher end department store like Nordstrom's (Nordstrom, Inc., Seattle, WA).

VIDEO CASE ....

Learn about how inventory control models help a firm make smart choices about reordering.

CRITICAL THINKING EXERCISES ....

Search for the article, "Five Common Inventory Mistakes and How to Avoid Them" at www.entrepreneur.com.

Investigate the recent history of adidas (adidas Group, Herzogenaurach, Germany) in light of these five common inventory errors. How has adidas's business suffered in recent years, especially relative to the industry leader, Nike (Nike, Inc., Beaverton, OR), and how might better inventory management improve its competitive situation?

Demonstrate your understanding of **inventory control** at Littlefield Labs.

Littlefield Laboratories is a highly automated, state-of-the-art blood testing facility for clinics and hospitals. The lab will operate 24 hours a day for a total of 210 days. You're asked to step in as the operations manager on Day 30, and are tasked with managing the lab's day-to-day inventory of test kits by setting an order quantity and a reorder point. Any inventory remaining when the lab shuts down will be obsolete so you are also tasked with setting the final order for kits near the end of game. Based on historic data you must manage inventory to maximize the lab's profits.

Compete against your classmates to prove your understanding of the chapter concepts:

- LO 16-1: Describe the Basic Economic Order Quantity (EOQ) model, its assumptions, and use the model to solve problems.
- LO 16-4: Discuss various reorder point models, and work typical problems.
- LO 16-6: Discuss single period inventory systems, and work typical problems.

The team with the most cash in hand at the end of the 210-day time frame wins!

©iStockphoto.com/michaeljung

CHAPTER

17

Sales and Operations Planning

LEARNING OBJECTIVES

After studying this chapter, you should be able to:

1. Describe the basic ideas behind sales and operations planning.

2. Describe the benefits of sales and operations planning.

3. Demonstrate the sales and operations planning process and its key features.

4. Compare the options for influencing demand and supply in implementing a sales and operations plan.

5. Identify alternative sales and operations planning strategies for product families.

6. Use the trial-and-error method to develop a sales and operations plan.

7. Explain the benefits of sales and operations planning in supply chains.

8. Describe sales and operations planning for service firms.

9. Detail the importance of sales carbon operations planning.

10. Describe the ethical issues that can arise in sales and operations planning.

OPERATIONS PROFILE: Black Friday Shopping in the United States Spills Over Into the Thanksgiving Holiday

Stan Honda/AFP/Getty Images

Black Friday is the name given to the day after Thanksgiving in the United States, and it is considered the unofficial start to the holiday shopping season. On that day, retail stores across the country offer deep discounts to lure customers and start shoppers on the long consumer spending spree that culminates in Hanukkah and Christmas gift-giving. Black Friday shopping is critical to retailers, with nearly 40% of their annual revenue coming during the narrow time window from Thanksgiving to Christmas. In 2012, Black Friday weekend drew 247 million shoppers, up from 226 million the previous year. Furthermore, 28% of shoppers were at stores by midnight on Black Friday in 2012, compared with 24.4% in 2011. Momentum continues to grow for the Black Friday experience to begin as early as possible. In fact, it is not only shoppers visiting stores who participate in Black Friday sales, e-sales through online retailing continue to grow dramatically on the Monday following the holiday weekend, a day known as Cyber Monday. As a result, either through walking in the front door or accessing shopping websites, the Black Friday experience is a critical opportunity for retailers and one they prepare for carefully.

In recent years, Black Friday has been steadily encroaching on Thanksgiving itself. No longer content to begin opening their stores early Friday morning, many retailers are open on Thanksgiving to allow shoppers to begin the rush for purchases on the holiday itself. Ignoring the disappointment of their own employees and traditionalists who view Thanksgiving as a day for spending time with family, the new holiday shopping patterns promise to be the beginning of a new era in retail, stressing everything from store employees, to shoppers, to retailers, and the other supply chain partners.

Retailers claim they are just responding to the expectations of shoppers who are demanding earlier and earlier access to their stores. In 2012, J. C. Penney Company's (aka JCPenney, Plano, TX) CEO, Ron Johnson, decided that JCPenney would avoid the practice of over-the-top sales and opening stores on Friday morning at 4 am, opting instead for a more reasonable 6 a.m. start to the day. Shoppers deserted them in droves, preferring to shop at competitors who had opened as early as midnight, the night before. A year later, JCPenney, in financial trouble and needing to show solid profits, had no choice but to follow its competition into door-buster prices and early store openings. Likewise, Macy's, Inc. (Cincinnati, OH) blames its decision to open Thanksgiving Day on customers demanding access to their stores. In fact, an American Express (American Express Company, New York, NY) survey found that more and more Americans wanted to do their shopping earlier—27% said they would be done by December 1st. This problem is exacerbated in years when Thanksgiving falls late in the calendar, leaving fewer weeks until Christmas, and putting further demands on companies' sales and operational planning (S&OP) departments. Further, Thanksgiving e-sales have increased 132% over the past 5 years prior to 2017, indicating that Thanksgiving has been growing as a day for online shopping. Given this "shift to shop" mentality, retailers argue that opening their stores on Thanksgiving is simply acceding to the wishes of a public that is already primed and ready to shop on the holiday itself.

Master the content.

edge.sagepub.com
/venkataraman

These increasingly early starts to Black Friday shopping strain retailers' supply chains and the need to coordinate all areas of their operations with suppliers and other delivery partners. Black Friday has traditionally created a strong need to develop clear sales and operational planning goals. With the gradual loss of the Thanksgiving Day of rest and relaxation, future S&OP activities will become increasingly complicated to coordinate supplier deliveries with changing expectations from a growing U.S. shopping population.[1]

17.1

Describe the basic ideas behind sales and operations planning.

17.1 The Basics of Sales and Operations Planning

In Chapter 1, we noted that a company's operations function interfaces not only with the other internal functions (marketing, finance, R&D, etc.) of the company, but also with groups and organizations (the company's supply chain partners) outside of the firm. To effectively manage a company's operations, the managers must establish cross-functional cooperation within their own company and with other businesses or partners in the supply chain. We have stressed the roles of *cross-functional cooperation* and *supply chain integration* throughout this book, particularly in creating effective and efficient operations for success in the marketplace. In this chapter, we extend these themes of cross-functional cooperation and the coordination and integration of supply chain activities by applying them to the execution of a company's tactical plans. In Chapter 1, we stated that decisions in operations and supply chain management occur on three levels: the *strategic*, the *tactical*, or the *operational* level. Most of our discussions so far have focused on operations and supply chain decisions that are strategic and have a long-term orientation. We have considered tactical decisions in Chapter 14 on lean operations and supply chains and in Chapter 15 on inventory management. We now turn our attention to tactical decisions that relate to sales and operations planning (S&OP). Sales and operations planning (S&OP), also known as aggregate planning, integrates customer-focused marketing plans for new and existing products with supply chain management. For the medium time frame (often viewed as 6 weeks to 18 months in the future), the sales and operations planning process attempts to match the company's supply of resources efficiently to market demand expectations. S&OP integrates the specific, tactical plans in every business area (sales, marketing, R&D, manufacturing, sourcing, and finance) into a single set of plans that is well-aligned with the overall company strategy.[2] Thus, it gives a complete picture of forecasted demand, supply capacity, and corresponding financial information. S&OP is performed at least once each month and is reviewed by management at an aggregate (product family) level. It provides management with the ability to direct the company's business strategically to achieve a competitive advantage. By integrating the vision, strategy, and financial and tactical plans of a business into one unified operating plan, S&OP enables a company to best allocate its critical resources: people, capacity, materials, time, and money. As the information generated by S&OP impacts the entire supply chain, companies should share this information with their supply chain partners, who can provide valuable inputs to make the S&OP plan more meaningful.

Companies lose billions of dollars every year from either stock-outs or excess inventory that are caused by the imbalance between supply and demand. In such cases, companies need to offer deep promotional discounts. Factors such as changing demand patterns, new product introductions, or product promotions can cause mismatches between supply and demand and make the process of demand and supply planning a challenge. Specifically, companies and their supply chain partners need to implement a sales and operations planning process to manage the following problems caused by the mismatch between supply and demand:

Sales and operations planning (S&OP): the integration of customer-focused marketing plans for new and existing products with supply chain management (also known as aggregate planning)

Aggregate planning: see sales and operations planning (S&OP)

Improper calculations of supply or demand can leave companies with too little or too much inventory, occasionally necessitating deep discounts in prices.

Paul Ellis/AFP/Getty Images

- Disruptions in supply that cause delays in production and on-time delivery.
- Excess inventories and obsolete products.
- Material and product shortages that lead to increased expediting, stock-outs, lower profits, and loss of customers.
- Poor resource use or lack of resources when needed.
- Production and supply chain bottlenecks that result in unacceptable lead times.
- Lack of coordination and poor collaboration between internal or external stakeholders.

All of these problems affect a company's financial performance, customer service, and the ability to achieve strategic goals. Companies that have an effective sales and operations planning process possess the agility to better manage their products and promotional planning, minimize unwanted inventory buildup, and improve revenues. For example, by implementing an enterprise-wide sales and operations process as part of an overall supply chain improvement initiative, a leading food manufacturer saved more than US$20 million per year. Similarly, by implementing sales and operations planning, a consumer electronics company gained a better understanding of the fluctuations in supply and demand and, as a result, was able to reduce its inventory level by 17%. These companies were able to improve their performance by implementing a well-coordinated operating plan to support their customer demand, business plan, and strategy.[3]

Sales and Operations Planning

17.2 Benefits of Sales and Operations Planning

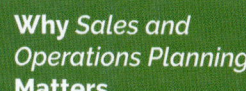

Describe the benefits of sales and operations planning.

Companies that have an effective and well-integrated S&OP process are able to reap the following benefits:

- *Achieve a greater understanding of demand and supply across the company through better alignment of supply and demand.*

By bringing together the company's marketing, finance, sales, and operations departments, and the supply chain partners, the sales and operations planning process can continuously monitor customer demand, the firm's current production capacity, and the supplies needed to meet that demand. When the separate departments collaborate, the improved communication leads to the most up-to-date and accurate insights into market demand. With this clearer knowledge, the S&OP process can then provide the means to create the required supply, capacity, and production plans to meet market demand. The net result is that companies have a complete picture of forecasted demand, supply capacity, and the corresponding financial information required to develop business plans and achieve the company's strategic goals. For example, Brown-Forman Corporation (Louisville, KY), a U.S.-based company that manufactures wines and spirits, believes its S&OP process enables it to better align supply and demand with its business requirements, build better internal communications, and plan activities to meet customers' needs.[4]

> **Why *Sales and Operations Planning* Matters**
>
> Sales and operations planning (S&OP) is a planning process that bridges the gap between long-term strategic plans and short-term operational plans. S&OP plans match the company's aggregate supply of resources with the aggregate demand for its products, which can improve revenues, decrease costs, and increase customer satisfaction.

- *Improve revenues, decrease costs, and increase customer satisfaction.*

Many companies that have implemented a well-defined S&OP process have reported improved revenues, decreased costs, and improved customer service. S&OP helps reduce problems such as stock-outs and the high operational costs associated with major swings in inventory and service levels caused by promotional campaigns by proactively managing supply and demand. For example, by implementing S&OP, a global fashion apparel manufacturer reduced problems in its supply chain, such as long lead times, excess inventories, high forecast errors, and missed or incorrect product deliveries. The S&OP process enabled the company to use a cross-functional collaborative approach to forecasting and to make better decisions on production sourcing and inventory by evaluating service and lead time trade-offs. As a result, the company's revenues and profits increased and its inventory costs plummeted.[5] Similarly, a major medical company with plants and distribution centers in North America, Europe, and Asia implemented a company-wide S&OP process in conjunction with lean manufacturing practices. Over time, the combination of lean and S&OP processes enabled the company to achieve customer service levels above 98% and inventory reductions of more than US$100 million.[6]

- *Improve the product life cycle management process.*

We discussed the product life cycle in Chapter 4. Companies recognize that, over time, their products begin to lose their appeal to customers and must either be updated or improved to maintain their viability. Coordinating the internal activities of R&D, production, and marketing with the external supplier activities enables a company to launch new products in a timely manner. In addition, with an effective S&OP process, poorly performing product lines are reviewed so that necessary product phase-outs can be carefully planned to minimize the high costs associated with excess inventories or stock-outs. A reason for the success of Eli Lilly and Company (Indianapolis, IN), the global pharmaceutical company, is that it possesses one of the most productive new product development pipelines

An Unusual
Strategy

in its industry. The company attributes its ability to successfully launch all of its new products in a very complex environment without adding significant cost, resources, or inventories to its S&OP process. Eli Lilly believes that its S&OP process enables it to carefully plan and execute the launch of its new products in many markets. Although Eli Lilly's product portfolio grew rapidly, the company was still able to maintain a customer service rating close to 98% while simultaneously reducing its inventory by US$500 million.[7]

- *Improve financial performance.*

Involving a company's finance department in its S&OP process ensures that the supply and demand plans are viewed in financial terms of revenue, margins, and working capital requirements. This approach results in a plan that ensures that the S&OP plan contributes to the firm's revenue and profit margin targets and that the company's budgets are consistent and feasible in terms of resource requirements needed to implement the plan. At Procter & Gamble Co. (Cincinnati, OH), the S&OP process has helped the company to optimize its use of resources to achieve better financial results. In the company's monthly S&OP meetings, besides allocating and aligning company resources to a single set of sales and supply plans, the financial implications of the plan are evaluated as well as its impact on supply and demand.[8]

- *Foster communication between departments.*

One of the biggest benefits of the S&OP process is that it fosters unhindered communication among different departments of the company. As a result of this open conversation, the different stakeholders bring their own individual perspectives to the S&OP plan. For example, the finance department shares its perspective in terms of revenues, margins, and working capital; marketing members share their views on customers, sales, channels, and brands; and the manufacturing and logistics members share their concerns on production and capacity constraints and supply sources. The net result of this communication is the creation of a single information systems platform in which all the departments can see the same data at the same time from their own perspective and can develop their individual plans (production, marketing, or financial) that are well-aligned with the overall business strategy. For example, the improved communication facilitated by the S&OP process has enabled ExxonMobil Chemical (Exxon Mobil Corp., Irving, TX) to create and work with a single information system that allows the company to better align its supply plans with the company's worldwide business strategy, improving customer response times and saving the company millions of dollars in the process.[9]

Sales and Operations Plan: Inputs and Outputs

Figure 17.1 shows some key internal inputs to a company's S&OP. Demand forecasts, capacity constraints, and corresponding outputs such as the sales plan or operations plan and the departments responsible for providing and producing these inputs and outputs are all part of this schematic. In addition, other important outputs from a sales and operations plan include a finance plan, human resources plan, and inventory plan. Figure 17.1 also shows some key elements of both the sales plan

TABLE 17.1: Objectives of Sales and Operations Planning

- Arrive at a consensus for managing the mismatch between supply and demand.
- Establish greater accountability for the individual plans (sales plan, operations plan, financial plan) developed by the various functional groups.
- Determine the total resource capacity needed for the planning time frame (6 weeks to 18 months).
- Develop a minimum cost strategy for effectively meeting demand.
- Establish a company-wide game plan to allocate resources efficiently to meet the aggregate demand for product groups or families over the medium-term time horizon.
- Develop a supply plan that balances the conflicting needs and constraints of the supply chain partners.
- Coordinate supply chain partners.
- Establish communication among various stakeholders, including finance, marketing, production, and suppliers.

FIGURE 17.1: Sales and Operations Plan: Key Inputs and Outputs

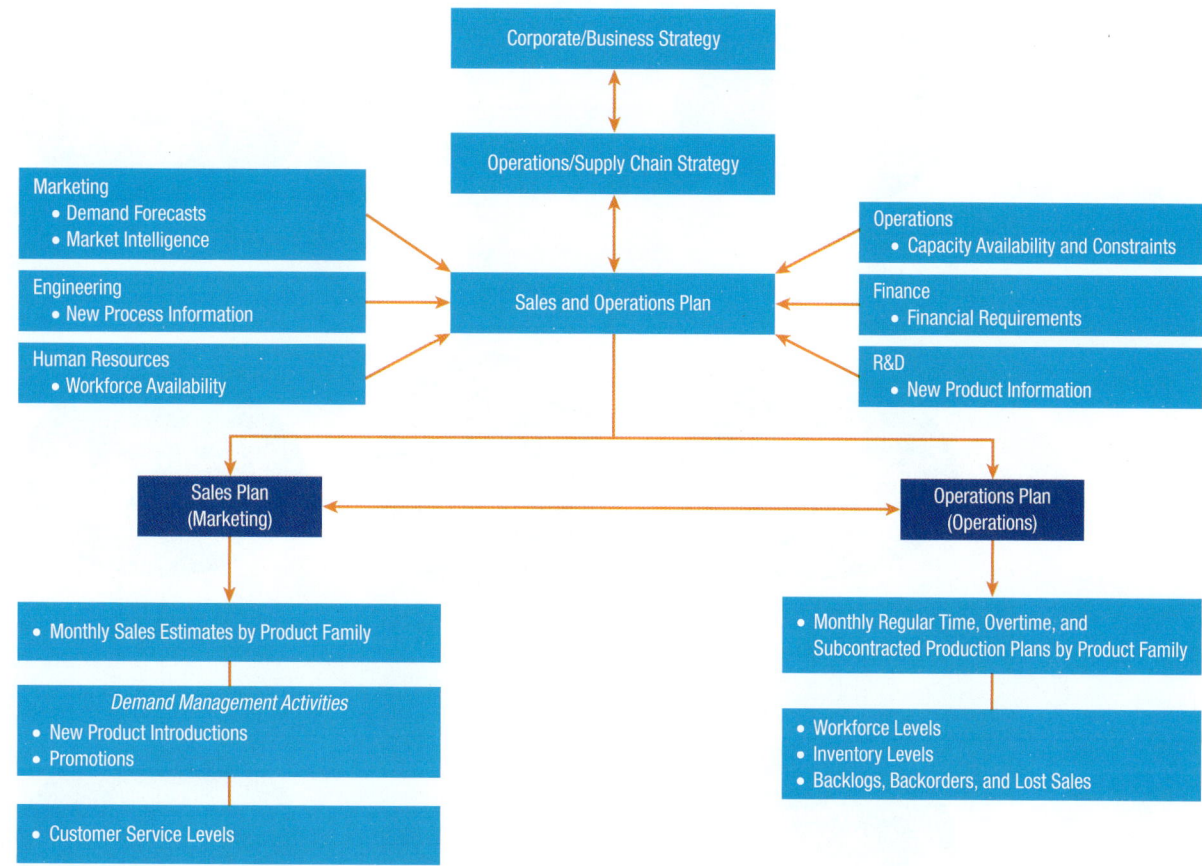

and the operations plan. The double-headed arrows show that the development of the S&OP and the other functional plans are an iterative process that requires extensive exchange of information and revisions among the various functional groups.

17.3 Framework of the Sales and Operations Planning Process

There are six stages in the process of developing an S&OP plan. Figure 17.2 shows a framework of integrated and interdependent business planning and reviews. The reviews verify that the tactical plans created by the S&OP process support the overall company strategy. Developing the process framework is critical to forging the necessary consensus among the company's stakeholders through collaboration and information sharing. Through this framework, top managers can understand and analyze the various alternatives, and it gives them the foundation for developing the tactical plans necessary to effectively satisfy demand with an integrated and responsive supply chain. The six-stage review process begins with data gathering, followed by demand and supply planning, and financial reviews. S&OP is a continuous, monthly planning process, with a planning time frame that depends on the nature of the business. It can take from 12 months to 24 months to complete the process. For example, because of the longer time frames needed to produce wines and spirits, Brown-Forman develops and implements both strategic and tactical supply chain planning processes. To develop demand, near-term inventory, and production plans, the company's S&OP process creates an 18-month consensus forecast.[10]

Let us consider each stage of the S&OP framework in Figure 17.2 on page 606.

Data Gathering

The success of the S&OP process depends on the quality and reliability of the data collected and assembled from the various departments within the organization. As demand, supply, new product, and financial data are reviewed as part of the S&OP process, it is critical to interpret and organize

17.3

Demonstrate the sales and operations planning process and its key features.

The Planning Process

FIGURE 17.2: Sales and Operations Planning Process Framework

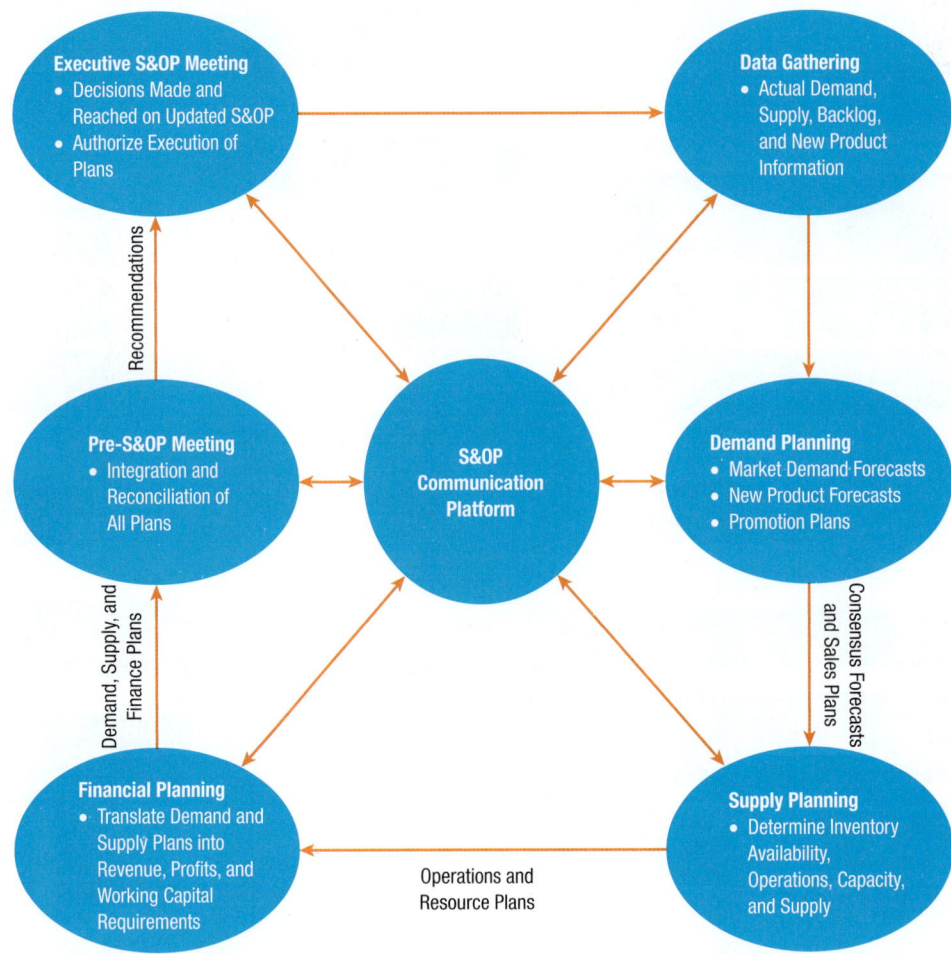

the data so that a homogeneous measure can be used for analysis. One possible approach to preparing a homogeneous measure is to collect the supply and demand data for product families and then combine the family data into aggregate demand and supply data. The S&OP process typically makes projections for a 24-month planning horizon. Hence, both historical and planned data should be collected and presented in a monthly report. Examples of the kind of data collected, shown in Figure 17.2, include monthly data on actual demand, supply, backlog (unfilled orders), and new product information. In addition, the company collects financial data and performance measurement data. Because almost every organization uses some kind of computerized data management system, such as enterprise resource planning (ERP), to manage their operations, these systems are the source of additional S&OP support data from accounting, purchasing, and inventory control.[11]

Demand Planning

The goal of the *demand planning* stage is to reach a consensus among the various stakeholders on various demand scenarios, the products that will be sold, and the revenues that will be generated for each product line in each month of the planning horizon. To arrive at such a consensus and improve forecast accuracy, all the demand planning stakeholders (sales, marketing, finance, product development, and supply chain) discuss factors such as competition, new product introductions, and other market conditions that may influence demand. In the case of new product introductions, the demand planning team should also predict how the new products will affect the firm's market by considering pricing and profit margins, the additional demand that will be generated, the cannibalization of sales of existing products, and so on. Ultimately, the participants in the demand planning team arrive at an estimate of the total demand requirements from all market sources by using quantitative forecasts, input from sales and marketing, and what-if analysis of the different possible customer orders and

OPERATIONS PROFILE: Problems in Predicting and Planning for Demand: The Pharmaceutical Industry

Companies developing and manufacturing pharmaceuticals in the United States make up a multi-billion-dollar industry. Planning operations is challenging for pharmaceutical companies because the process of manufacturing and distributing medicines is complex and highly risky. Accurately predicting new drug introductions and likely demand for these formulations is difficult because there are multiple critical stakeholders and numerous qualifications steps. In addition, there is no guarantee that the drug, once introduced, will be commercially successful. According to current estimates, for every drug that reaches a pharmacy, somewhere between 5,000 and 10,000 other medicines fail to reach the commercialization stage. Furthermore, only 21.5% of drug candidates entering clinical trials actually achieve Food and Drug Administration (FDA) approval for sale. Thus, a drug qualification stage that costs pharmaceutical companies, on average, US$37 billion of their US$100 billion R&D budgets still faces heavy odds of failure.

The annual supply chain spending for drugs under clinical trials can weigh heavily on the company's bottom line, accounting for 20% or more of the annual R&D budget. It is common for pharmaceutical firms to spend millions of dollars to produce the supplies needed for just one clinical trial for one drug. Should the drug fail at the clinical trial stage, every dollar that was spent on manufacturing, packaging, and distribution is lost. Further, all unused materials must be properly destroyed at disposal facilities. For example, CoTherix, Inc. (South San Francisco,

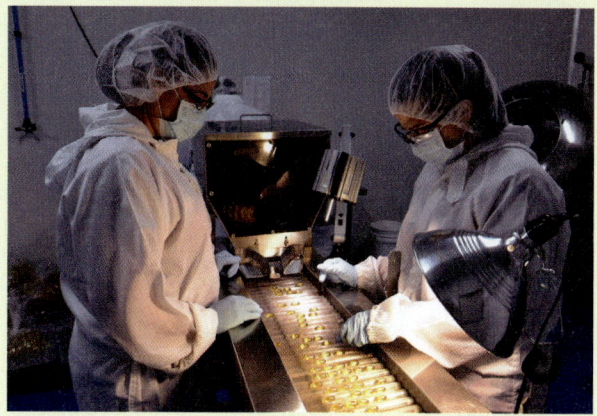

Bloomberg/Bloomberg/Getty Images

CA) estimated its costs to be US$126,000 just to destroy an obsolete drug that was valued at US$1.5 million. As a result of large R&D budgets, the high likelihood of clinical trial failure, and the excessive costs for disposing of inventories of outdated drugs, demand planning in the pharmaceutical industry, while critical to profitability, is also extremely complex and requires detailed analysis and coordination of the planning activities within marketing, finance, R&D, and the manufacturing functions. Getting demand planning correct is difficult, but the alternative is hugely expensive.[12]

market conditions that affect demand. The final output of this stage is a single demand plan that has the agreement of all the stakeholders of the S&OP process, which is then passed on to the supply team responsible for the next phase of supply planning.[13]

Supply Planning

After the completion of a consensus demand forecast, the next stage of S&OP is supply planning. The supply planning team typically consists of personnel from purchasing, inventory management, production, warehousing, and logistics. The objective of this phase of planning is to ensure that there is sufficient manufacturing and distribution capacity to meet the demand forecasts. During this stage, decisions are also made on whether outsourcing is needed to acquire additional capacity. Specifically, the supply planning team will

- Proactively resolve imbalances between expected demand and available capacity and resources.
- Identify capacity constraints and alternatives to overcome them.
- Develop a procurement plan.
- Evaluate both past and future capacity utilization.

The pre-S&OP meeting gives key stakeholders the opportunity to set priorities, resolve imbalances, and align their goals to conceive of a S&OP plan to recommend to senior management.

©iStockphoto.com/annebaek

- Maximize the use of resources such as production, storage, and transportation capacities, workers, and materials.

The output of the supply planning stage includes a capacity plan that roughly verifies whether there is sufficient capacity available to meet demand, a procurement plan, and an assessment of the estimated costs of these plans. The information generated during this stage is used as the primary input to the subsequent planning phases and decisions.[14]

Financial Planning

The financial feasibility of the demand and supply plans developed in the previous stages is now evaluated in terms of return on assets (ROA), revenue, profit margin, and working capital requirements. By conducting what-if analyses for possible demand scenarios and their impact on the various financial measures, supply and demand is rebalanced by taking into account potential supply problems and constraints. The revised set of plans generated in this financial planning phase serves as input to the next stage, the pre-S&OP meeting.

Pre-S&OP Meeting

In the pre-S&OP meeting, representatives from the demand, supply, and financial planning teams, and other relevant stakeholders, discuss and resolve any imbalances between supply and demand and ensure that the supply plan has been validated by the financial planning team. That is, the separate demand, supply, and financial plans are reconciled to develop a master plan that integrates these plans. The participants in this meeting also discuss and set priorities for the company's strategic initiatives. The final outcome of this stage is a recommendation to senior management on a sales and operations plan that includes both the trade-offs and the financial and nonfinancial implications of the plan.

Executive S&OP Meeting

The participants in this meeting include senior executives from finance, sales, marketing, purchasing, operations, planning, logistics, and from other functional groups as needed. In this meeting, the senior executives review all previous demand and supply plans, financial plans, and strategic business objectives, and they address any unresolved issues from previous meetings. If there are imbalances, the participants discuss alternatives and options to resolve them. During this meeting the senior executives set the strategic direction on capacity, availability of raw materials, and new business opportunities, and the group comes to a consensus on the sales and operations plan. The executive team authorizes the execution of a single sales and operations plan, which becomes the operating plan for each function within the company.[15]

Top-Down Versus Bottom-Up: How Should S&OP Planning Proceed?

Two planning approaches can be used for developing a sales and operations plan using the framework presented in Figure 17.2. The two approaches are top-down planning and bottom-up planning.

- *Top-down planning.*

The top-down approach to sales and operations planning is the simplest because it is driven by a single aggregate sales forecast. It is most appropriate if a firm produces a combination of products and services that require similar resources or if it produces essentially the same mix of products and services from one period to the next. Top-down planning is based on the assumption that management can create accurate tactical plans based on the overall aggregate forecast and then divide the resources across the individual products and services during the subsequent detailed operational planning and control activities.

- *Bottom-up planning.*

Bottom-up planning is used by those companies whose mix of product and service offerings changes from period to period or by companies whose resource requirements vary greatly across the product

Supply planning: ensuring that there is sufficient manufacturing and distribution capacity to meet the demand forecasts

Financial planning: evaluating the financial feasibility of the demand and supply plans developed in the previous stages of S&OP planning in terms of return on assets (ROA), revenue, profit margin, and working capital requirements

Top-down planning: assuming that management can create accurate tactical plans based on the overall aggregate forecast and then divide the resources across the individual products and services during the subsequent detailed operational planning and control activities

Bottom-up planning: planning used when management calculates the resource requirements for each individual set of products or services and then combines them to get an overall picture of resource requirements and service mix offerings. In cases like these, a single aggregate sales forecast is not useful for determining the resource requirements. Therefore, the bottom-up planning approach is used when management calculates the resource requirements for each individual set of products or services and then combines them to get an overall picture of resource requirements.

17.4 Options for Influencing Demand and Supply in Sales and Operations Planning

Compare the options for influencing demand and supply in implementing a sales and operations plan.

The primary focus of the sales and operations planning process is to balance supply and demand in the face of demand uncertainty. To achieve this balance, managers can attempt to influence demand or supply while developing sales and operations planning strategies. Table 17.2 presents the options for influencing demand and supply.

Options to Influence Demand

Influencing Demand

The options to influence demand are intended to manipulate the demand side of the sales and operations plan, and hence, their use is a more proactive way to match supply and demand. We describe the options listed in Table 17.2.

- *Price.*

In S&OP, when there is a mismatch between supply and demand, planners can use price as a variable to balance the two. For example, to smooth out demand for seasonal items such as air conditioners, retailers offer them at a much lower price during the winter months to push sales of any excess inventories left over from the previous summer (peak demand). Similarly, hotels, airlines, and movie theaters offer lower rates during off-peak periods, as for night-time travel and matinee shows. The Four Seasons Hotels Ltd. (Toronto, Ontario, Canada) offers steep discounts at their ski resort in Whistler, British Columbia, and at their property in Scottsdale, Arizona, during the summer to boost otherwise low demand. The use of price differentials is to shift demand to those slack periods to reduce the excess capacity (rooms and seats), matching demand more closely with available supply. The opportunity cost of using price to shift demand from peak to slack periods, however, is lost profit during peak demand periods because of the lack of sufficient capacity to meet demand during these periods.

- *Advertising and promotions.*

Advertising and sales promotions are often used to influence demand for products or services. Nevertheless, although sales promotions are short-term efforts that reduce price as a way to increase demand, advertising is an investment to improve demand for the company's products over the long run by adding value to a company's brand. Both options are intended to increase the customers' value perceptions of the product or service. Whereas sales promotions increase the perception of value of the product or service by reducing the cost, advertising increases value perception through a comparison of the benefits of a company's product or service relative to its cost.[16] Both advertising and promotions can be used in S&OP to influence demand so that it closely matches available capacity. Yet, the success from using either of these options depends on when they are used and the extent of customer response. For example, if sales promotions efforts are not timed properly, the sudden surge in demand may stress a company's production capacity to a point that it will be unable to meet the market demand for the product.

TABLE 17.2: Options to Influence Demand and Supply

OPTIONS TO INFLUENCE DEMAND	OPTIONS TO INFLUENCE SUPPLY
• Price • Advertising and promotion • Back orders and reservations systems • Developing counter-seasonal products and services	• Varying the workforce size • Use of overtime or slack time • Use of inventories • Use of part-time workers • Use of subcontracting

- *Backorders and reservation systems.*

A backorder is a customer order that a company accepts in one period but promises to deliver at a later point in time. During peak demand periods, when there is maximum stress on production capacity, companies can use backorders to shift demand to a later period. Some backorders are unavoidable, as when the firm has insufficient capacity at the time the customer places the order. Backorders also may be planned because the company wants to even out its capacity utilization across several periods. Backorders can be a viable tactic for shifting demand to a different period as long as the customer is willing to wait for the delivery of the order at a later period. Otherwise, the inability to fill an order when demanded can result in a lost sale. Service organizations, such as hotels and airlines, try to smooth demand by using advance reservation systems to avoid sudden surges in demand caused by walk-in customers. Reservation systems allow a company to allocate or partition demand across several time periods. The disadvantage can be a lost sale if the customer cancels the reservation or does not show up.

- *Developing counter-seasonal products and services.*

Many companies that offer seasonal products and services (for example, lawn mowers, winter coats, or ski vacations) have to contend with excess capacity during the off seasons. One S&OP option available to these companies to deal with excess capacity and bridge the gap between supply and demand during the off seasons is to produce or deliver counter-seasonal products and services. For example, companies that produce lawn mowers to meet demand during the summer months can also manufacture snow blowers. Similarly, retailers who sell cold weather products such as fireplaces and gas logs for the winter seasons can also offer counter-seasonal services or products such as lawn mowing and lawn care products. The purpose of developing counter-seasonal products and services is to shift demand to a new set of products and services that can be developed and produced using existing capacity.

Options to Influence Supply

Companies also can take actions to influence the supply or capacity portion of the sales and operations plan. These options are reactive or passive approaches to manipulating the supply side of the sales and operations plan to react to a change in demand that has occurred.

- *Varying the workforce size.*

In the face of fluctuating demand, one option that planners can use to match supply and demand is to change the size of the workforce by hiring and firing workers. Although this option has the advantage of matching production rates to demand, it has several disadvantages. Hiring and firing workers incurs costs to train or supervise new workers or separation costs in the form of severance pay or provision for certain benefits when laying-off workers. Another problem is that productivity and quality may suffer initially until the new workers become fully trained. Union regulations may restrict excessive use of hiring and firing workers and may lead to labor problems. Finally, laying-off workers may lower the morale of existing workers and reduce the cohesion of groups of workers.

- *Use of overtime or slack time.*

The use of overtime or idle times enables planners to vary the production rate to match demand while maintaining a constant workforce. Nonetheless, using overtime is a costly option. In some firms, work rules mandate significantly higher pay for non-salary employees and excessive use of overtime can lead to worker fatigue, resulting in lower productivity and quality. Finally, there is often a limit on the amount of overtime that can be used, and it is not a viable option to meet large increases in demand. Use of slack or idle time when demand is low can also be an expensive process if the company cannot absorb the costs of the idle time.

- *Use of inventories.*

When the production capacity is greater during low demand periods, managers make full use of existing production capacity to build inventories. The excess inventory is then used up to meet demand during the peak demand periods. Although building inventories makes full use of available production capacity, it can be expensive because it increases capital investment and the holding costs associated with storage, insurance, handling, obsolescence, and pilferage.

- *Use of part-time workers.*

Many retail and service organizations that have seasonal demands for their products and services use part-time workers. Examples are department stores, supermarkets, restaurants, hotels, and tax preparation companies, such as H&R Block, Inc. (Kansas City, MO). The advantage of this option is to temporarily increase capacity at a relatively low cost because seasonal work involves low to moderate worker skill levels. The disadvantage, however, is that part-time workers may not show the same dedication as the full-time workers to improve productivity and quality.

- *Use of subcontracting.*

During peak demand periods, planners can smooth production temporarily by acquiring additional capacity through subcontracting. The option involves hiring an outside firm to produce the product or service that the company itself is unable to produce because of insufficient capacity. The biggest disadvantages of subcontracting are loss of control over the output produced, quality problems, and higher costs. In addition, the subcontractor may be a competing firm with conflicting interests.

17.5 Sales and Operations Planning Strategies

Given these options for manipulating supply and demand, and regardless of the planning approach used (top-down or bottom-up), companies usually employ one of the three basic strategies to create S&OP plans at the product family level. These strategies are level, chase, or mixed strategies.

Level Strategy

The aim of a **level strategy** (also known as level scheduling) is to maintain a constant production rate. In addition, it is desirable to keep the workforce level constant. A level strategy is appropriate for manufacturing organizations that have stable market demand or production levels, where the decision to change production levels can be expensive, whereas the cost of holding inventory is low. By using a level production strategy, companies maintain constant production and workforce levels and they use inventories to bridge the gap between demand and production (supply). Automobile companies, such as Nissan Motor Company Ltd. (Yokohama, Japan) and Toyota Motor Corporation (Toyota City, Japan) and many oil companies employ this strategy. These companies continuously produce the same quantity of goods every period, calculated based on the total demand for these goods. For example, let us assume that a company's aggregate demand for a product over a 6-month period is 45,000 units, and there are a total of 150 working days in this period. By using a level production strategy, the company will produce 300 units per day (45,000 / 150). The level strategy offers several advantages. Because there is no need for frequent workforce changes, workers tend to be highly skilled and experienced. Further, the company can enjoy lower turnover, higher morale, and lower absenteeism of its

Companies that experience seasonal peaks in demand may look for part-time workers to boost their capacity and meet the increased demand. This model is most effective for jobs that require little training as part-time workers may not be able to provide the same level of quality and productivity as full-time employees.

©iStockphoto.com/Lauri Wiberg

17.5

Identify alternative sales and operations planning strategies for product families.

 Strategies

FIGURE 17.3: Level Production Strategy in Sales and Operations Planning

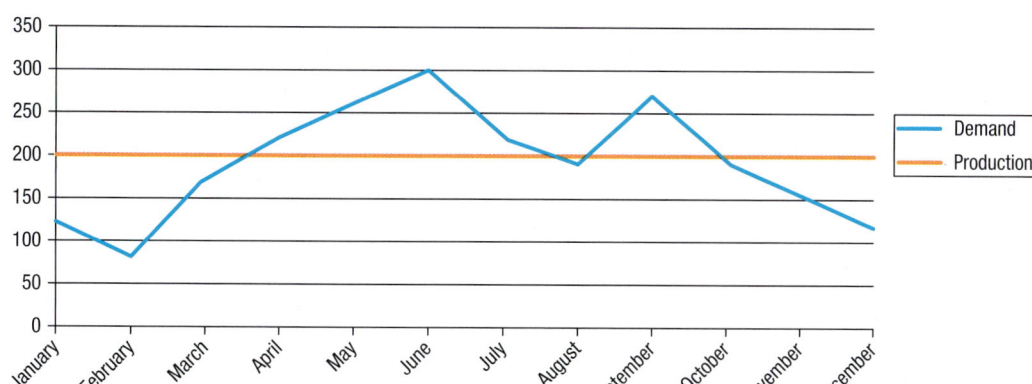

Level strategy: maintaining constant production and workforce levels and using inventories to bridge the gap between demand and production (supply). Also known as level scheduling

employees. The major disadvantage of this strategy is the higher cost of inventories during periods of slack demand. As production remains constant regardless of demand, inventory builds up during the slack months, and hence, the associated inventory costs can be considerable. Figure 17.3 represents the level production strategy. If demand is less than the constant production output, inventory builds up. On the other hand, if demand is greater than the constant production output, inventory in stock is used up to meet the excess demand. Note that in this scenario, in any given period, if there is unusually high demand and there is not sufficient inventory in stock, a stock-out situation may occur. If demand equals the production output, then the inventory level remains constant.

Chase Strategy

Companies that need to meet demand that fluctuates from one time period to another use the **chase strategy**. To do so, the firm manipulates its workforce to meet demand. Firms using this strategy employ the options of hiring and laying off workers, overtime work, subcontracting, and part-time workers to meet demand. In this demand-matching strategy, production is geared toward producing whatever amount of goods is needed to meet demand. For example, a typical restaurant starts preparing meals only after the customer places an order, thereby matching actual production with customer demand. On the other hand, The Hershey Company (Hershey, PA), the chocolate maker, uses the chase strategy at its manufacturing facility. Demand for chocolate is typically high during the winter months and low during the summer months. The location of Hershey's manufacturing facility enables the company to hire local farmers who are underemployed during the winter months as factory workers to increase production to meet demand. The farmers are laid off during the spring and summer months when demand drops and they, in turn, can resume their farming work in the fields.

An advantage of the chase demand strategy is that it offers companies flexibility in the use of capacity to meet demand fluctuations. In addition, as supply is matched to demand from period to period, inventory levels are kept low, minimizing inventory holding costs associated with cost of capital, warehousing, depreciation, insurance, taxes, obsolescence, and shrinkage. These reductions in inventory levels free up cash for the company for other operational activities, such as the purchase of raw materials and components. The major disadvantages of the chase strategy are higher costs associated with hiring, training, and layoffs, and low employee morale. Figure 17.4 shows the chase strategy.

Mixed Strategy

The **mixed strategy** is a hybrid strategy that combines the advantages of both the level strategy and the chase strategy. Most firms find that using a mixed strategy, which enables them to select options that influence both the demand for and supply of their products, achieves a sales and operations plan that has lower costs and meets the organizational goals and objectives better than either of the pure strategies used independently.

Choosing a Strategy

A company's choice of a particular strategy depends on company policies and the degree of resource flexibility required. These two factors may restrict the available options that influence demand or

Chase strategy: a demand-matching strategy in which production is geared toward producing whatever amount of goods is needed to meet demand

Mixed strategy: a hybrid strategy that combines the advantages of both the level strategy and the chase strategy, enabling firms to select options that influence both the demand for and supply of their products

FIGURE 17.4: Chase Production Strategy in Sales and Operations Planning

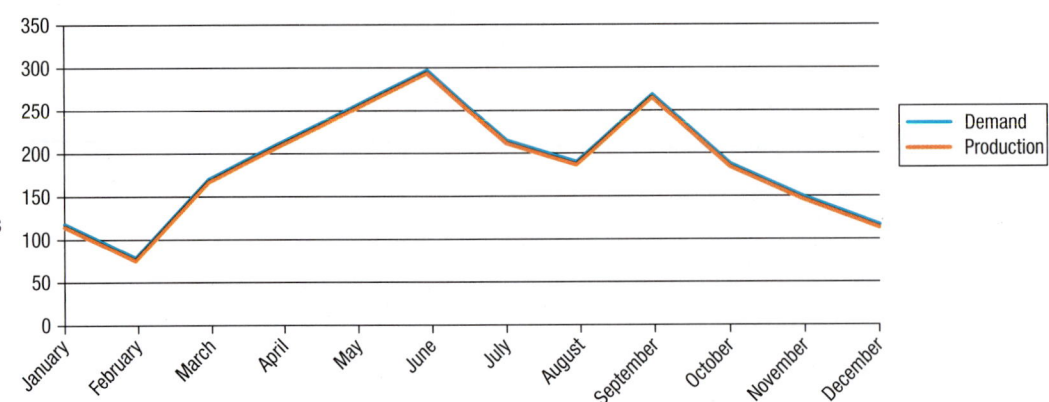

supply that the company can use in its sales and operations plan. For example, company policy may prohibit worker layoffs except under extreme conditions. Similarly, union contracts may limit employment of part-time workers. Likewise, proprietary aspects of manufacturing the product and product quality may deter the company from using subcontractors. Finally, companies that are designed for high and steady output volume (such as the sugar or oil refineries) have very little process flexibility and, hence, may not be able to use the chase strategy. Therefore, sales and operations planners should attempt to match supply and demand at the minimum cost within the firm's policy and process limitations.

17.6 Methods for Sales and Operations Planning

Several techniques can be used to create a sales and operations plan. These techniques range from informal trial-and-error approaches, such as simple tables or graphs, to more advanced mathematical techniques, including optimization techniques such as linear decision rules (LDR) or the transportation method of linear programming.

Optimization methods: These methods attempt to optimize a company's objective, such as maximizing profits or minimizing costs, given constraints such as scarce productive resources (availability of raw materials or skilled labor). Linear programming, mixed integer programming, and goal programming are some of the more frequently used optimization techniques. Linear programming is an optimization technique in which the objective and constraint functions are linear and the variables are continuous. Linear programming is discussed in more detail in Module A. For sales and operations planning, a special case of linear programming known as the transportation method can be used to obtain optimum aggregate plans that can enable planners to balance capacity and demand at the lowest possible cost. The major drawback of linear programming is the restrictive assumption of linearity that is not representative of many real-world aggregate planning situations. Linear decision rule is another optimization approach that can be used to create aggregate plans. In this technique, the total production cost (consisting of labor, overtime and slack time, hiring and layoff, and inventory costs) is represented by a single quadratic cost function, which is minimized using calculus. The process yields two linear equations—one to determine the optimum production plan for each period and the other to determine the optimum workforce plan for each period.

Management coefficients model: The management coefficients model, formulated by E. H. Bowman, is a formal decision model that is based on past managerial performance and experience but does not have any explicit cost functions. The model assumes that managers make sound decisions, even in the absence of explicit costs. The method analyzes past production planning decisions using the statistical technique of regression to determine the relationship between relevant variables such as demand and workforce levels that can be used for future production planning decisions.[17]

Simulation: Simulation methods use search decision rules to find the appropriate combination of production and workforce levels that will minimize costs. The method requires computer programs and overcomes some restrictive assumptions of linear programming, such as linearity of cost, but does not guarantee optimum solutions.

Planners can use a general procedure for developing a sales and operations plan, no matter which method is used, that includes the following:

1. Determine the expected demand (sales forecasts) for each period of the planning horizon.
2. Determine the resources and capacities required for each period of the planning horizon. These capacities include regular time, overtime, and subcontracting, and they should match demand. In top-down planning, the sales forecasts are aggregated into a single set of planning values and then translated into the necessary resources required in terms of labor hours or machine hours. In bottom-up planning, the individual products and services not only have varying resource requirements, but the mix also varies from one period to the next. Therefore, in bottom-up planning the resource requirements for each product or service must be determined individually then aggregated across all products and services to get an estimate of the overall resource requirements. Other than this major difference in determining capacities and resources, the remaining steps for both planning approaches are identical.
3. Identify constraints such as company, departmental, or union policies and any requirements, such as maintaining a certain safety stock level, a reasonably stable workforce, backorder policies, overtime policies, and other process-related constraints specific to individual industries.

17.6

Use the trial-and-error method to develop a sales and operations plan.

Linear programming: an optimization technique in which the objective and constraint functions are linear and the variables are continuous

Transportation method: a special case of linear programming that can be used to obtain optimum aggregate plans that can enable planners to balance capacity and demand at the lowest possible cost

Linear decision rule: an optimization approach that can be used to create aggregate plans in which the total production cost is represented by a single quadratic cost function, which is minimized using calculus

Management coefficients model: a formal decision model based on past managerial performance and experience. The model uses the technique of regression analysis of past production decisions made by managers

Simulation: a method that uses search decision rules to find the appropriate combination of production and workforce levels that will minimize costs

4. Determine unit costs of regular time, overtime, and subcontracting production. In addition, determine the costs associated with holding inventories, backorders, or hiring and layoffs. Also, estimate intangible costs, such as the costs associated with loss of customer goodwill, although they are difficult to measure.

5. Develop alternative sales and operations plans using chase, level, and mixed strategies and compute the total cost of each strategy.

6. Choose the least-cost plan that best satisfies objectives.

We will demonstrate next how sales and operations plans are developed for each of the basic chase, level, and mixed strategies using the trial-and-error approach. Interested students can use the more advanced mathematical techniques such as the transportation method (presented in Module B) to develop a sales and operations plan.

Developing a Sales and Operations Plan: Trial-and-Error Method

The trial-and-error approaches to developing a sales and operations plan are easy to use and understand. They involve constructing spreadsheets and graphs that enable planners to manipulate a few options used to adjust demand or supply in the S&OP to see how the projected demand requirements match the available capacity. The only major disadvantage of trial-and-error approaches is that they do not guarantee an optimum sales and operations plan. We will demonstrate the application of the trial-and-error approach to developing a sales and operations plan for each of the three basic strategies—level, chase, and mixed—in the following example. This example, and all other examples and problems in this chapter, are based on the following assumptions:

- Regular time output capacity remains constant for all periods regardless of the number of working days in any given period.
- Cost is a linear function of unit cost and the number of units.
- Sufficient inventory, subcontracting, and other supplemental capacity options exist to accommodate any changes in output requirements.
- Unit costs are independent of the quantity produced and, hence, all costs associated with decision alternatives can be represented by a lump sum.
- Reasonable cost estimates for the various options can be made, and these costs are assumed to remain constant for a given planning horizon.
- Production occurs at a uniform rate throughout each period and inventories are also accumulated and depleted at a uniform rate.
- Backlogs, when allowed, are assumed to exist for the entire period.

Example 17.1

EXAMPLE 17.1: Himalayan Sports Inc. is a fictional manufacturer of different lines of skis that are sold through major sports equipment retailers. The company's marketing team has estimated the aggregate demand for its ski product line for the upcoming year (see Table 17.3).

TABLE 17.3: Demand for Skis for Himalayan Sports

MONTH	DEMAND (IN PAIRS OF UNITS)	MONTH	DEMAND (IN PAIRS OF UNITS)
Jan	9,000	July	1,000
Feb	7,000	Aug	1,200
Mar	5,000	Sept	1,600
Apr	4,000	Oct	3,000
May	2,000	Nov	5,700
June	1,500	Dec	7,000

Planning Values for Skis (all in U.S. dollars)

- Regular time production cost: $300/pair of skis.
- Overtime production cost: $360/pair of skis.

- Subcontracting cost: $420/pair of skis.
- Average monthly inventory holding cost: $10/pair of skis per month.
- Average labor hours required to produce a pair of skis: 4 hours.
- Maximum regular time production capacity per month: 10,000 pairs of skis.
- Maximum allowable overtime production per month: 500 pairs.
- Number of worker-hours per month: 160 hours.
- Hiring cost per worker: $500.
- Layoff cost per worker: $300.
- Current workforce level: 100 workers.

Given this information, find the following:

a. Develop a production plan using a level production strategy. Assume a beginning inventory level at the start of January to be 9,000 pairs of skis.
b. Develop a production plan using a chase production strategy. Vary the workforce size to adjust to variations in demand. Assume that the beginning inventory is zero in January.
c. Develop a production plan using a mixed production strategy for a constant workforce level of 25 workers. Use only overtime and subcontracting to absorb variations in demand. Assume that the beginning inventory is zero in January.

SOLUTION

a. Level production strategy.

In a level production strategy, the regular time production quantity per period is held constant, and inventories are used to absorb variation in demand.

Step 1: Calculate the average monthly forecasted demand.

$$(9,000 + 7,000 + 5,000 + 4,000 + 2,000 + 1,500 + 1,000 + 1,200 + \\ 1,600 + 3,000 + 5,700 + 7,000) / 12 = 4,000$$

This is the planned constant monthly regular time production level.

Step 2: Calculate the number of workers required to meet the production level.

Because each worker takes 4 hours to produce a pair of skis and works 160 hours per month, the number of pairs of skis produced by each worker in a month is given by: 160 / 4 = 40 pairs.

As the number of pairs of skis to be produced each month using a level production strategy is 4,000 pairs, we need: 4,000 / 40 = 100 workers.

As the current workforce level is 100 workers, we have enough workers to meet the required production levels each month.

Step 3: Calculate ending inventory and the average inventory levels at the end of each period.

Ending inventory level at the end of each period is given by:

Ending inventory = Inventory level at the beginning of each period + production in that period − forecasted demand in that period

Note: The inventory level at the beginning of each month is the ending inventory level in the previous month.

The average inventory level at the end of each month is given by:

Average inventory = (Beginning inventory + Ending inventory) / 2

In this example, for the month of January, beginning inventory = 9,000; regular time production = 4,000; and the forecasted demand is 9,000. Therefore,

Ending inventory level for January = 9,000 + 4,000 − 9,000 = 4,000 and

$$\text{Average inventory level for January} = (9{,}000 + 4{,}000) / 2 = 6{,}500$$

Step 4: Calculate the regular time production and inventory holding costs for each period.

The regular time production costs and inventory holding costs for each period are given by:

$$\text{Regular time production cost} = \text{Regular time production} \times \text{Regular time cost/unit}$$

$$\text{Inventory holding cost} = \text{Inventory holding cost/unit/period} \times \text{Average inventory level}$$

In this example, for the month of January, as the regular time cost/unit = $300; inventory holding cost/unit/period = $10; and the average inventory level = 6,500, we have (all in U.S. dollars):

$$\text{Regular time production cost} = 4{,}000 \times \$300 = \$1{,}200{,}000$$

$$\text{Inventory holding cost} = \$10 \times 6{,}500 = \$65{,}000$$

Step 5: Calculate the total cost of the level production plan.

The total cost for the level plan is given by:

$$\text{Total cost} = (\text{Sum of the regular time production costs for all periods} +$$
$$\text{Sum of the inventory holding costs for all periods})$$

For Example 17.1, the total cost is given by:

$$\text{Total cost} = (4{,}000 \times \$300) \times 12 + (6{,}500 \times \$10 + \ldots + 10{,}500 \times \$10) = \$15{,}167{,}000$$

The results of all of the calculations using these steps for the level production plan are shown in Screenshot 17.1.

SCREENSHOT 17.1: Level Production Strategy Example

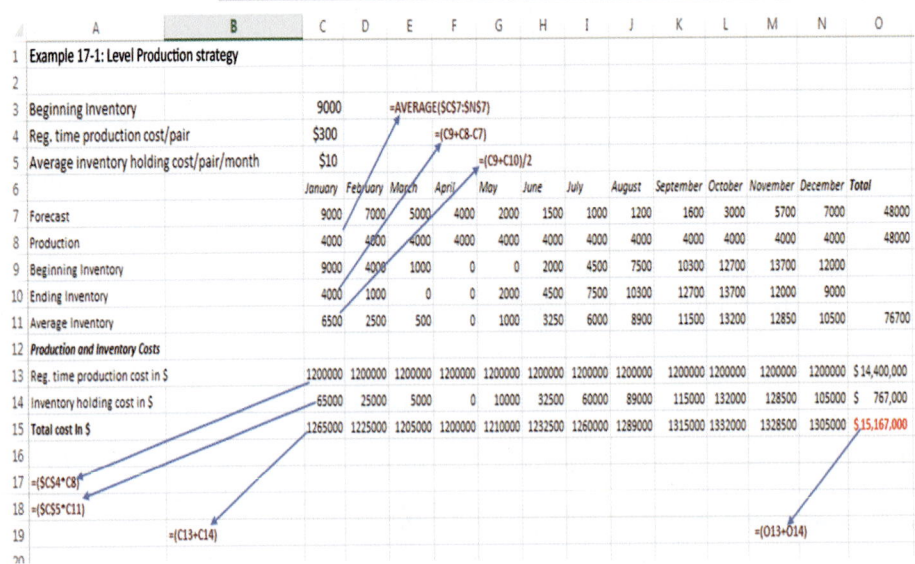

Figure 17.5 shows how the cumulative forecast deviates from the cumulative level of production.

FIGURE 17.5: Cumulative Graph of the Level Production Strategy for Skis

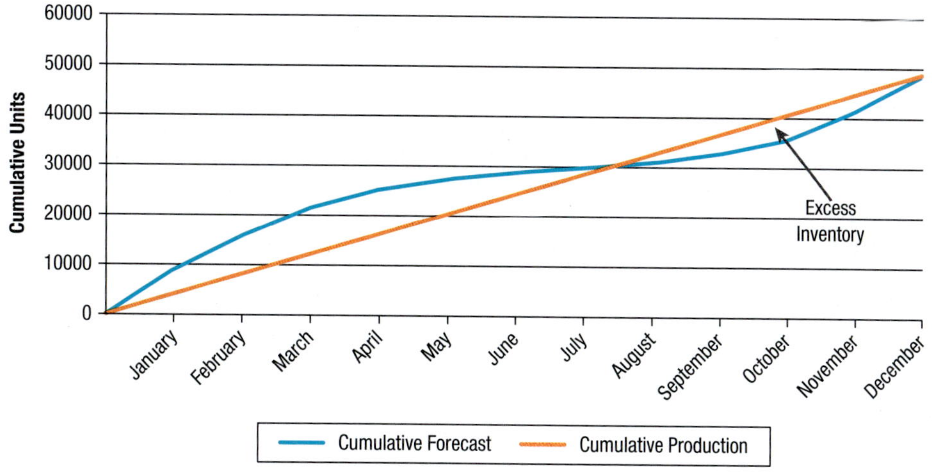

b. Chase production strategy.

In a pure chase production strategy, production levels are adjusted by varying the workforce levels period by period to meet demand. The following steps are used to develop a chase production strategy.

STEP 1: COMPUTE THE NUMBER OF WORKERS NEEDED FOR EACH PERIOD.
The number of workers needed for each period is calculated as follows:

$$\text{Number of workers needed} = \text{Net production required/production per worker}$$

For Example 17.1, because the demand in January is 9,000 pairs of skis and because we have no inventory on hand at the beginning of January, 9,000 pairs of skis should be produced for that month. Also, as it takes a worker 4 hours to produce a pair of skis, and each worker works for 160 hours each month, the number of skis that each worker can produce in a given month is 160 / 4 = 40 pairs. Hence:

$$\text{Number of workers needed} = 9{,}000 / 40 = 225$$

STEP 2: COMPUTE THE NUMBER OF WORKERS TO BE HIRED OR FIRED.
The number of workers to be hired or fired is computed by determining the difference between the number of workers required in each period and the number of workers available in that period. If this difference is positive, we will hire additional workers; if it is negative, then we will layoff some existing workers. In Example 17.1, as we require 225 workers and the current workforce level is 100, we need to hire additional workers. Thus,

$$\text{Number of workers hired for January} = 225 - 100 = 125 \text{ workers}$$

STEP 3: COMPUTE THE REGULAR TIME PRODUCTION COST AND HIRING AND FIRING COST FOR EACH PERIOD.

$$\text{Regular time production cost} = \text{Regular time production} \times \text{Regular time cost/unit}$$
$$\text{Hiring cost} = \text{Number of workers hired} \times \text{Hiring cost/worker}$$
$$\text{Firing cost} = \text{Number of workers fired} \times \text{Firing cost/worker}$$

Using these formulas, given that the regular time cost/unit = $300 and the hiring cost/worker = $500, the regular time production and hiring costs for the month of January in Example 17.1 are (in U.S. dollars):

$$\text{Regular time production cost} = 9,000 \times \$300/\text{pair} = \$2,700,000$$

$$\text{Hiring cost} = 125 \times \$500/\text{worker} = \$62,500$$

STEP 4: CALCULATE THE TOTAL COST OF THE CHASE PRODUCTION PLAN.

The total cost for the chase plan is given by:

Total cost = (Sum of the regular time production costs for all periods + Sum of the hiring costs for all periods + Sum of the firing costs for all periods)

For Example 17.1, the total cost is given by:

$$\text{Total cost} = (9,000 \times \$300 + 7,000 \times \$300 + \ldots + 5,700 \times \$300 + 7,000 \times \$300) +$$
$$(125 \times \$500 + \ldots + 175 \times \$500) + (0 \times \$300 + 50 \times 300 + \ldots + 0 \times 300) = \$14,597,500$$

The results of all of the calculations using these steps for the chase production plan are shown in Screenshot 17.2.

SCREENSHOT 17.2: Chase Production Strategy

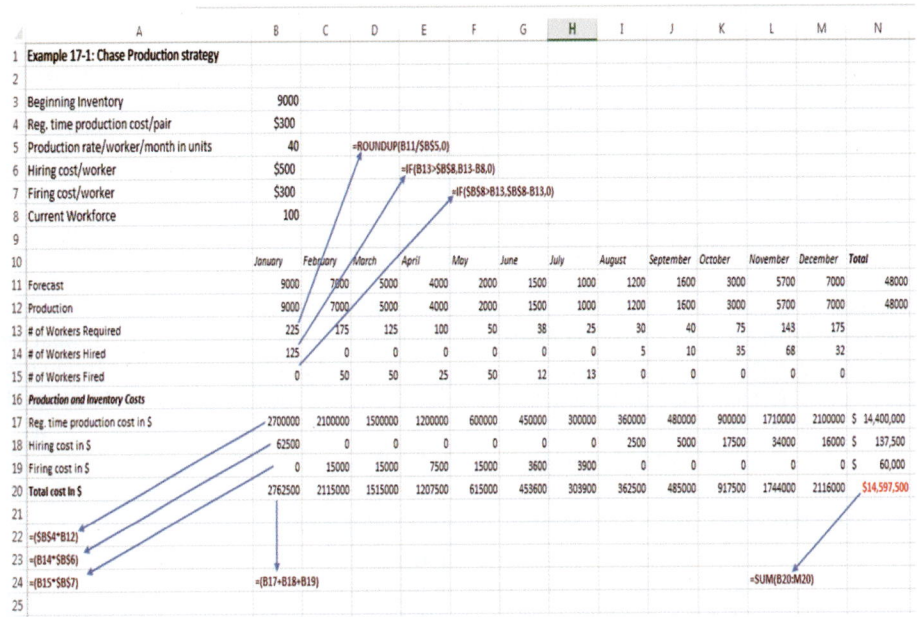

c. Mixed production strategy.

In this strategy, we will hold the workforce level constant at 25 workers but use overtime and subcontracting to absorb demand variations. The steps for developing this plan are given as follows.

STEP 1: DETERMINE THE REGULAR TIME, OVERTIME, AND SUBCONTRACTED PRODUCTION REQUIRED FOR EACH PERIOD.

For Example 17.1, because each worker can produce only 40 units each month, and the workforce size is 25 workers, we have

$$\text{Regular time production} = 40 \times 25 = 1,000 \text{ pairs each month}$$

Because the expected demand in January is 9,000, the remaining production requirements of 8,000 (9,000 − 1,000) pairs can only be met through overtime and subcontracted production. Note, we will use the overtime option first as it has a lower per unit cost than subcontracting. Yet, because the maximum overtime production allowable is only 500 units, production using subcontracting is given by:

$$\text{Subcontracted production} = \text{Monthly demand requirements} - \text{Regular time production} -$$
$$\text{Overtime production} = 9,000 - 1,000 - 500 = 7,500$$

STEP 2: COMPUTE THE REGULAR TIME PRODUCTION, OVERTIME, AND SUBCONTRACTING COSTS FOR EACH PERIOD.

For Example 17.1, for the month of January (in U.S. dollars):

$$\text{Regular time production cost} = 1,000 \times \$300/\text{pair} = \$300,000$$

$$\text{Overtime production cost} = 500 \times \$360/\text{pair} = \$180,000$$

$$\text{Subcontracting cost} = 7,500 \times \$420/\text{pair} = \$3,150,000$$

STEP 3: CALCULATE THE TOTAL COST OF THE MIXED PRODUCTION PLAN.

The total cost for the mixed production plan is given by:

$$\text{Total cost} = (\text{Sum of the regular time production costs for all periods} + \\ \text{Sum of overtime costs for all periods} + \text{Sum of subcontracting costs for all periods})$$

For Example 17.1, the total cost is given by:

$$\text{Total cost} = (1,000 \times \$300 \times 12) + (500 \times \$360 + \ldots + 500 \times \$360) + \\ (7,500 \times \$420 + 5,500 \times \$420 + \ldots + 5,500 \times \$420) = \$18,408,000$$

The results of all calculations using these steps for the mixed production plan are shown in Screenshot 17.3.

SCREENSHOT 17.3: Mixed Production Strategy

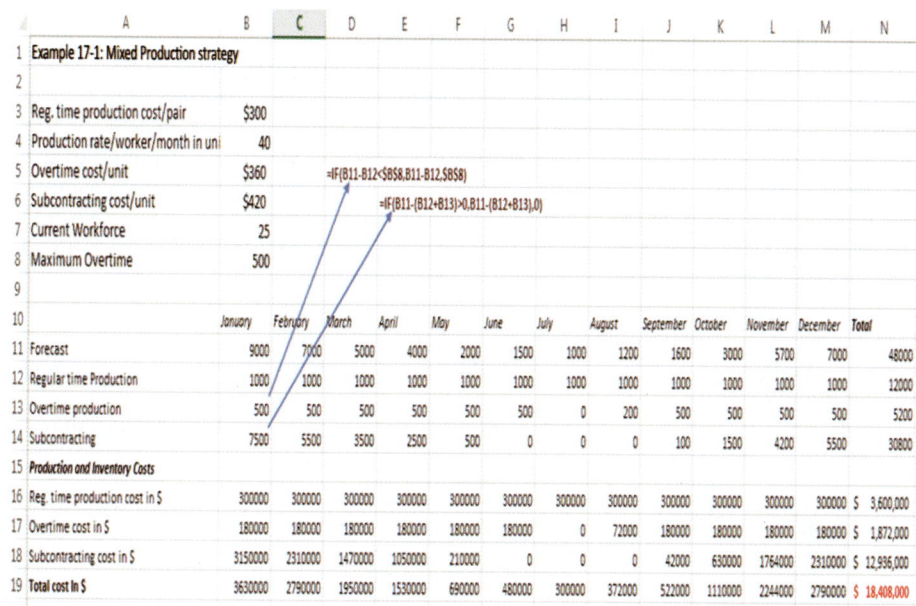

	A	B	C	D	E	F	G	H	I	J	K	L	M	N
1	Example 17-1: Mixed Production strategy													
2														
3	Reg. time production cost/pair	$300												
4	Production rate/worker/month in uni	40												
5	Overtime cost/unit	$360		=IF(B11-B12<$B$8,B11-B12,$B$8)										
6	Subcontracting cost/unit	$420		=IF(B11-(B12+B13)>0,B11-(B12+B13),0)										
7	Current Workforce	25												
8	Maximum Overtime	500												
9														
10		January	February	March	April	May	June	July	August	September	October	November	December	Total
11	Forecast	9000	7000	5000	4000	2000	1500	1000	1200	1600	3000	5700	7000	48000
12	Regular time Production	1000	1000	1000	1000	1000	1000	1000	1000	1000	1000	1000	1000	12000
13	Overtime production	500	500	500	500	500	500	0	200	500	500	500	500	5200
14	Subcontracting	7500	5500	3500	2500	500	0	0	0	100	1500	4200	5500	30800
15	**Production and Inventory Costs**													
16	Reg. time production cost in $	300000	300000	300000	300000	300000	300000	300000	300000	300000	300000	300000	300000	$ 3,600,000
17	Overtime cost in $	180000	180000	180000	180000	180000	180000	0	72000	180000	180000	180000	180000	$ 1,872,000
18	Subcontracting cost in $	3150000	2310000	1470000	1050000	210000	0	0	0	42000	630000	1764000	2310000	$ 12,936,000
19	**Total cost in $**	3630000	2790000	1950000	1530000	690000	480000	300000	372000	522000	1110000	2244000	2790000	$ 18,408,000

17.7 Sales and Operations Planning for Supply Chains

S&OP plays a critical role in effectively managing supply chains. The S&OP process requires inputs from various supply chain partners, and its outputs affect supply chain performance. For example, good forecasts are required for the effective demand planning stage of the S&OP process. As we discussed in Chapter 13, such forecasts can be created if the upstream and downstream supply chain partners work together. In addition, if the supply chain partners are involved during the supply planning stage of the S&OP process, upstream supply chain partners are aware of constraints (such as the availability of sufficient supplier capacity) that have an impact on developing an effective supply plan. Just as inputs from supply chain partners are critical to

17.7

Explain the benefits of sales and operations planning in supply chains.

Manufacturing highly
seasonal products like ice
cream require sales and
operations planning to inform
their supply chain decisions.

©iStockphoto.com/&#169 Leonid
Shcheglov

S&OP in the
Supply Chain

S&OP, the outputs from the S&OP process are also of immense value to the company's upstream and downstream supply chain partners. The production plans generated from a company's S&OP process serve as demand inputs to the company's upstream suppliers, and they also serve as supply constraints to the company's downstream customers. Sales and operations planning attempts to anticipate problems that could have a negative impact on supply chain performance by eliminating the inefficiencies in the supply chain. For example, if a company's sales and operations plan calls for significant increases in manufacturing output, planners can use this information to evaluate the impact this increase in the company's production output would have on its distribution channels. The result of this evaluation may lead the company to advise its downstream supply chain partners to increase the size of their warehouse and production workers to handle the increases in goods traffic and to explore other options such as hiring a larger logistics company to facilitate increased shipping and materials handling. This advance planning will not only help the company to reduce its costs and improve service to its customers, but it also will enhance the efficiency of its supply chain.

As an example, think of the role of S&OP in a large ice cream manufacturing company and its supply chain. The highly seasonal demand for ice cream has a ripple effect throughout its supply chain, from its customers through distributors to manufacturers, and to the suppliers of raw materials. Peak demand for ice cream typically occurs during the summer months, and demand for ice cream falls in the winter. Because of the highly seasonal demand for ice cream and the high capital investment required, building a manufacturing facility just to meet the peak demand in the summer months is a costly and probably unattractive option. In addition, on the supply side, an ice cream manufacturer will need raw materials such as cream, condensed milk, butterfat, sugar, flavorings, eggs, and additives such as emulsifiers and stabilizers, all with the potential for shortages or uncertain delivery. To prevent these potential problems, ice cream manufacturers use sales and operations planning to determine production and inventory levels. As a sales and operations planning strategy, ice cream manufacturers can build up the inventory of ice cream products during the slower winter months for sale in the peak summer months when demand is greater than the capacity of the manufacturing facility. In addition, the manufacturing facility may operate 24 hours per day in three shifts including weekends during the peak summer months, whereas the plant may operate only one shift from Monday to Friday during the winter. Clearly, by taking into account both the demand variability and the inputs across the supply chain, sales and operations planning can enable an ice cream manufacturer and its supply chain to reduce costs and maximize profits.

Because S&OP affects the entire supply chain, there are benefits to linking the S&OP process to the operations of the company's supply chain partners.

1. Coordinating the S&OP process across the supply chain can improve overall supply chain performance by improving efficiency and reducing procurement, manufacturing, and logistics costs. For example, by working with the suppliers, the company may decide to adopt a level production plan because under such a plan the supplier is willing to offer more favorable prices because material orders to the suppliers become more stable.
2. Involving supply chain partners in the S&OP process reduces the level of uncertainty in the supply chain, because the partners can use the output information generated from the process to better plan their own operations.
3. During the demand planning stage of the S&OP process, involving supply chain partners can pave the way for a collaborative planning, forecasting, and replenishment (CPFR) process, which, in turn, will improve forecast accuracy.
4. Research has shown that when members of the supply chain functions (purchasing, manufacturing, and logistics) of an organization are involved in the S&OP process, significant reductions in inventory are achieved.[18]
5. Linking the company's S&OP process to the rest of the supply chain improves overall supply chain agility or "the ability to recalibrate plans in the face of market, demand and supply volatility and deliver the same cost or comparable cost, quality and customer service."[19]

In summary, given demand forecasts for each period of the planning horizon, the goal of S&OP is to determine production, inventory, and capacity levels for each period that will maximize both the firm's and its supply chain's performance over the planning horizon. To achieve this goal, all supply chain stages should work together in developing the sales and operations plan.

Global Sales and Operations Planning

In an integrated global market, an accurate S&OP process is necessary to respond to the demands of a constantly changing supply and market conditions. This means that a global marketplace requires a consolidated sales and operations plan, unlike the past S&OP processes, which had been operating within independent functional groups. Nevertheless, developing such a consolidated plan in a global business environment can be very difficult. Some challenges of global sales and operations planning include:[20]

- Proliferation of product lines, because global customers demand greater product variety, and products with shorter life cycles.
- Differences in business practices across multiple geographical regions, with executives from different countries and all of the cultural and regional differences.
- Global customers have higher expectations of quality, service, and cost.
- Higher product demand volatility caused by swings in demand in emerging economies such as Brazil, Russia, India, and China.
- Need to reduce high inventory levels caused by poor forecasts or lack of production flexibility.
- Longer supply chains that require creation of regional or global planning centers.
- Given geographically dispersed multiple planning systems, there is a need to provide an S&OP framework that strikes the right balance between consistency and flexibility. In other words, the framework should be standardized enough to be used by all divisions in the company and yet flexible enough to accommodate the needs of local businesses.[21]

To meet these challenges and stay in close touch with global customers, many multinational companies have developed or partnered with a geographically dispersed set of local sales companies that provide the products, services, and leadership through regional or global centers of excellence. Such global operations, however, require global S&OP processes that must respond to the new requirements and challenges of operating through a combination of local, cluster, regional, and global levels.[22]

The basic stages of the global S&OP process remain the same as those presented in Figure 17.2. Yet, because the different functions in a global business may be separated by distances and time zones, global sales and operations plans have different requirements.[23]

- A global sales and operations plan must be able to balance differing stakeholder needs and goals. For example, the global S&OP process should be able to reconcile the conflicting needs of sales, which might want high service levels, and manufacturing plants, which may want to minimize minimum operating costs, within a global region against the needs of similar departments in other regions in which the firm operates.
- A global sales and operations plan must be able to deal with differing processes and technologies. Different global regions may differ in the levels of sophistication in processes and technologies used. For example, locations in North America may use advanced processes and technologies such as integrated ERP systems, whereas regions in Southeast Asia may still be using only basic spreadsheet software. Global S&OP processes should be able to deal with such differences in business maturity levels among global regions.
- Formal communication channels should be part of a sales and operations plan. In a global business, different functional units may be located in different geographically dispersed global locations, and the same personnel may not be involved in all S&OP meetings. Effective communication is important to coordinate the various groups.
- The global sales and operations plan must be able to reconcile product allocations. Within each global market region and across global markets, the global S&OP process should be able to allocate products to meet demand and load factories across the supply chain.

The entire global S&OP process should be managed as a single whole process, even though the different functions (manufacturing, sales, finance, etc.) may be operating from geographically dispersed locations. All the different stages (demand planning, sales planning, etc.) of the S&OP process have to be fully integrated in such a manner that each step adds value. To ensure such integration of the

Global sales and operations planning: a consolidated sales and operations planning approach that can respond to frequently changing global supply and market conditions

Consider This 17.1:
Global Sales and Operations Planning: The World Has Changed

S&OP has been in use for more than 20 years; nevertheless, much has changed in that time, most notably, the shift to a globalized economy. S&OP has become a more important management tool for multinational firms for many reasons.

- Companies have grown through mergers and acquisitions, creating more complex global organizations. Their business units are located in geographically dispersed locations.

- Product lines have become more complex. Companies produce greater quantities and varieties (modifications) of new products that are often invisible to the planning teams in the different operations functions.

- Retailers are demanding of service levels, quality, and cost. In particular, larger retailers such as Wal-Mart Stores Inc. (Bentonville, AR) can pressure suppliers to meet their desired price and customer service expectations.

- Holding excessive product and raw material stock is costly. It is necessary to have a plan to manage stock so that critical supplies are not simply targeted for reduction without full consideration as to why and when they are needed.

- The global marketplace is more volatile than domestic markets. Product demand in some parts of the world is stable and predictable, whereas growth in emerging economies of the world creates swings in demand that must be forecasted and managed.

- Supply chains have become longer and more complex than in the past. With many links in the supply chain around the world, each step (supplier) must be carefully managed and companies must coordinate their activities with the requirements of upstream suppliers and downstream manufacturers.[24]

global S&OP process, the entire global supply chain should operate on a single agreed-upon estimated demand figure. In other words, the suppliers of critical components should develop production plans to support the company's S&OP process and provide planners with advance information on capacity constraints or potential (or real) shortages of critical raw materials. Finally, supplier plants with common production capabilities should communicate with each other to optimize production within the global supply network.

Similarly, finance provides global S&OP planners with information on capital expenditure planning and budgeting activities. This information enables planners to make appropriate capital investment decisions and determine working capital budgets necessary to fund appropriate stock levels of finished goods and raw materials throughout the supply chain. In addition, the planning team of the global S&OP process can meet to resolve any imbalances between supply and demand. It is also worth noting that there is no "one size fits all" S&OP model that can be used by all global companies. The particular global S&OP model that a company selects will be unique to that business and will be dictated by the company's strategic direction, available technology, the nature of its products (high or low value), volume of demand (high or low), its supply chain structure, and the desired span of control. A company's choice of a global business model is a decision that requires the company to spend time evaluating its business and the internal and external challenges the company is currently facing or likely to face in the future.[25]

The S&OP process spans the entire business, so it is important that during the implementation phase of a global S&OP the company take the following actions:[26]

- Involve a broad range of senior stakeholders to enlist their support.
- Given the complex structure of a global company with multiple layers of demand and supply, it is critical to identify the decision makers within the firm who have the responsibility and authority for making the different decisions both on the demand side and on the supply side of the global business.
- In addition to securing agreement on a "single number" forecast, the company should ensure all plans (sales, financial, and operations plans) of the sales and operations planning process are well aligned. Any mismatch among these plans will require last-minute stop-gap measures that will eventually lead to a vicious circle of failure and cost escalation. For example, there is a mismatch of plans if the sales group expects to sell distinctly unique products whereas the

operations group plans to produce standardized products. The resulting mismatch of these plans will eventually lead to customer dissatisfaction and increases in production costs.

- Because stakeholders in a global company represent diverse interests, it is likely that stakeholders will have conflicting business objectives. Therefore, it is critical to align key performance indicators across the various divisions and multiple layers of the global company so that they produce the best results for the global company as a whole.
- A successful global S&OP requires the support of senior executives of the company. Given the enormous challenges inherent in designing and implementing a global S&OP, without the support of top management, any S&OP initiative is bound to fail.

Benefits of Global S&OP

Companies that have an effective global S&OP realize the following benefits:

- Reduced inventory.

Companies with a well-integrated S&OP typically have only 25 to 30 days of inventory as safety stock, whereas companies with a poor S&OP have upward of 60 days of safety stock.

- Increased forecast accuracy.

Companies using S&OP have well-integrated plans that include customers and suppliers, which lead to greater forecast accuracy and reduction in supply uncertainty. These companies have reduced expedited costs caused by rush orders and have increased sales and a greater market share.

- Full use and optimization of the supply chain.

A strong global S&OP fully uses the network of all the manufacturing plants to optimize production—achieved through a process that can be monitored, controlled, and managed—to achieve flexible manufacturing capacity, and to drive collaboration between the global company and its supply chain partners. Process visibility, flexibility, and collaboration enable the global company to eliminate redundant production and waste by making the proper trade-offs by using techniques such as inventory optimization and postponement.

- Improvements in communication, accountability, empowerment, and teamwork.
- Improved customer relationships as a result of better visibility and planning.

In the final analysis, for businesses operating in the global marketplace, an integrated global S&OP process also can provide increased cash flow and the competitive edge needed to succeed in global markets.

17.8 Sales and Operations Planning in Service Industries

Sales and operations planning for service businesses faces a unique set of challenges for many reasons.

- Services cannot be inventoried.

Because most services are perishable, companies in the service industry do not have the ability, as manufacturers do, of stockpiling inventory during periods of low demand. Any unused capacity is wasted and cannot be reserved for later use. For example, an empty hotel room or an empty airline seat cannot be held as inventory and sold at a later time when demand may be higher. Even those service businesses, such as florists and restaurants, where the service provided is accompanied by tangible goods, inventories can be held only for very short periods because many goods, such as flowers or food, are perishable.

- Services have high demand variability.

Demand for services is variable and, hence, is much more difficult to predict. Demand for services can fluctuate not only from day to day but also from hour to hour. For example, restaurants may

17.8 Describe sales and operations planning for service firms.

 S&OP for Services

Many cities often subcontract work to landscaping firms, pool maintenance companies, or private contractors that employ and supply part-time help.

©iStockphoto.com/JFsPic

experience short periods of high demand followed by periods of low demand. Regardless of the level of demand, a successful service company must meet that demand quickly.

- Capacity is difficult to predict.

Because demand for a service varies from period to period and from customer to customer, the processing requirements for services vary, and this variability makes it difficult to predict service capacity requirements. For example, the number of registered nurses that a hospital may need on any given day depends not only on the number of patients but also on the type of patient care required. Similarly, hospitals need to have doctors available to provide emergency services in addition to their regularly scheduled appointments.

- Service capacity must be made available at the right place and at the right time.

As customers from geographically dispersed locations demand services, service businesses need to see that appropriate service capacity is available in these locations when needed. This demand for service capacity coverage is precisely the reason why banks have branches and ATMs located throughout a geographic region.

- Shortage of skilled labor.

Labor is the most important resource constraint in services. Although demand variability in many service businesses can be met by the use of unskilled labor, lack of skilled labor can be a serious problem for service companies. For example, universities may find it difficult to recruit and retain instructors in technical fields, such as engineering or computer sciences, because demand for their skills is so strong that they are sought by both public sector and private sector organizations.

Companies in the service section often use mixed S&OP strategies that combine the options to influence capacity and demand. Nevertheless, the focus of S&OP strategies in the service sector is primarily on workforce schedules, in contrast to production plans in the manufacturing sector. Recall that services are typically much more labor intensive than manufacturing and, therefore, constraints in the form of availability of labor resources can exist. Yet, labor is flexible and workers can perform different tasks. Consequently, labor can be an advantage in sales and operations planning.

The various mixed strategies that can be used in S&OP for services can broadly be classified into the following two categories:

a. The use of options to control capacity to match demand.

Many service organizations vary the size of their workforce to match demand. The following options are available to these companies in formulating their S&OP strategies:

- Maintain a permanent small-to-medium-level regular time workforce throughout the year, but use overtime or hire additional full-time or part-time workers during periods of peak demand. Many companies in the retail, hospitality, and health-care industries use this option to match capacity to demand.
- Maintain a small level of staff over the year and subcontract all additional work, including part-time help. For example, parks and recreation departments in many cities often subcontract work to landscaping firms, pool maintenance companies, or private contractors that employ and supply part-time help.
- Use the strategy of annualized hours. Under the annualized hours strategy, employees of a service company are hired as contractors to work for a certain number of hours (say 2,000 hours) per year for a fixed sum of money. During peak demand periods, employees may be

Annualized hours strategy: a strategy in which employees of a service company are hired as contractors to work for a certain number of hours per year for a fixed sum of money

asked to work more than the contracted hours; during low demand periods they are asked to work fewer hours. When employees work beyond their annual contracted hours, they receive overtime pay. The advantage of this strategy to the company is lower labor costs and increased flexibility. The employees, in turn, enjoy the greater security offered by a steady income, with no fear of layoffs. Many companies in the German retail industry use the annualized hours strategy.[27]

b. The use of options to influence demand to match available capacity.

Like companies in the manufacturing sector, service businesses can also use options to influence demand by setting prices and offering promotions. Service companies, such as airlines and hotels, that have inflexible and expensive capacity with highly perishable products (airline seats and hotel rooms) use an approach called yield management (also called *revenue management*) to match demand with available capacity. The objective of yield management is for the company with capacity constraints to maximize revenue from its service operations, while at the same time providing the desired level of service to the right customer at the right time and at the right price. Some of the techniques of the yield management strategy include:

- Overbooking. Airlines and hotels routinely overbook customers beyond their existing capacity of seats and rooms to compensate for customers who cancel their reservations or fail to show up. The companies have determined that their costs of offering customers incentives for shifting flights or changing hotel plans is more cost efficient than having empty seats on a flight or having unused hotel rooms.
- Adjusting prices to augment demand. The yield management systems used by airlines and hotels are designed to routinely and automatically adjust prices to augment demand to sell unused capacity. Similarly, lower prices are offered to customers who are price sensitive, but are indifferent to the time (peak versus off-peak times) at which they are willing to receive services (e.g., lower airline prices for flights during off-peak times).
- Using different fare classes to partition demand. Service companies such as airlines, hotels, sports stadiums, and concert halls offer different classes of seats (premium and economy) with different price structures. The challenge for sales and operations planners is to allocate optimum capacities to these different fare classes to maximize revenue while accommodating customers with varying time and price sensitivities.

To summarize, the techniques of yield management attempt to match the time and price at which services are provided to the customers' willingness to pay for that level of service at the time at which it is offered.

17.9 Sustainable S&OP: Sales Carbon Operations Planning (SCOP)

Companies throughout the world are under pressure to incorporate sustainability into their business practices. Because of the involvement of a company's internal and external stakeholders, the sales and operations planning process provides an ideal entry point for incorporating sustainability. The sales carbon operations planning (SCOP) process, which incorporates sustainability into S&OP, is intended not only to cover carbon emissions but also the management and reduction of the economic and environmental impact of greenhouse gas emissions. Extending an S&OP process to SCOP does not expand the size or complexity of the current S&OP process. It forces the company to broaden its view of the systems and processes to change the focus to the triple bottom lines (economic, social, and environmental) of sustaining a business as shown in Figure 17.6 on page 626.

Additional Features and Functions of SCOP

A company has to perform several additional tasks and functions, listed as follows, to adopt SCOP:[28]

a. New product development. The SCOP process identifies and evaluates the environmental impact through all the stages of the new product development process, from design to disposal. This evaluation will affect all other operational and supply chain decisions of production, procurement, and logistics to be made before release of the new product to production and subsequent product launch to market.

Yield management: an approach for service companies with capacity constraints to maximize revenue from their service operations, while at the same time providing the desired level of service to the right customer at the right time and at the right price

17.9

Detail the importance of sales carbon operations planning.

Sales carbon operations planning: a process that incorporates sustainability into S&OP, intended not only to cover carbon emissions but also the management and reduction of the economic and environmental impact of greenhouse gas emissions

FIGURE 17.6: Sales Carbon Operations Plan Framework

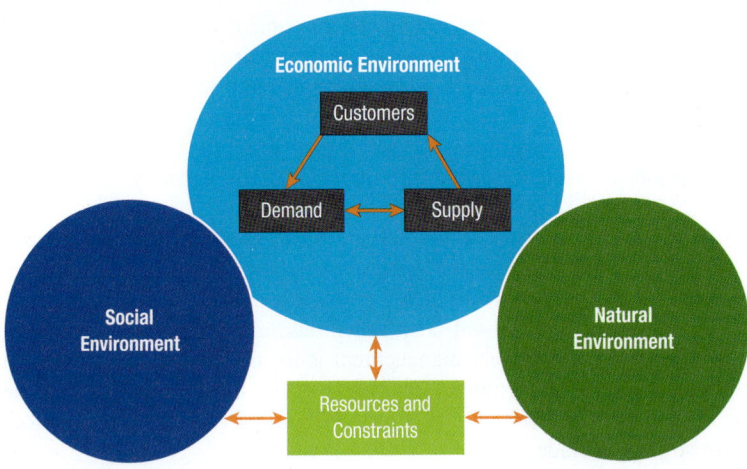

SOURCE: Sustainable Manufacturing Consulting. (2009). Sales carbon operations planning: A business process for the clean economy. *Sustainable Manufacturing Consulting*. Retrieved from http://www.sustainablemanufacturing.biz/media//DIR_17101/SCOP_White_Paper.pdf.

 Sales Carbon Operations Planning

b. Impact on existing products. The goal of SCOP for existing products is to improve forecast accuracy and quantify costs associated with forecast errors. The purpose is to reduce or eliminate waste, and therefore costs, caused by inaccurate forecasts. In addition, the SCOP process attempts to prolong the life of existing products through repair, remanufacture, and upgrades, thereby postponing product obsolescence and the need to turn out new products as quickly.

c. Demand planning. In the SCOP process, there is an increased emphasis on responding to customers' expectations of providing a clean, sustainable value chain. Hence, the SCOP process includes activities that attempt to reduce the environmental impact of excessive inventory, frequent shipments, and excessive production. Remember that excessive inventories of unsold goods must be warehoused, managed in an environmentally safe way, and maintained. All of these lead to higher costs and energy use. In addition, the demand planning phase of SCOP focuses on identifying new sources of revenue that can result from reducing the carbon emissions.

d. Supply planning. Supply planning and procurement activities focus on the location and selection of suppliers, logistics, and modes of transportation based on their ability to reduce carbon emissions. In this stage, there is also an increased emphasis on recycling, reusing, and selling excess inventories.

e. Operations planning. During this stage of the SCOP process, the firm engages in activities that use energy efficiently, use renewable energy sources, and minimize waste in production processes.

Benefits of SCOP

Companies that adopt SCOP can achieve short-term and long-term benefits:[29]

- SCOP reduces the risks and costs associated with the scarcity of raw materials and reduced availability of energy sources.
- SCOP offers the ability to attract new capital from investors interested in sustainability.
- The design of green products and the adoption of new technologies or operational processes as a result of SCOP will attract new customers or avoid the loss of existing customers.
- SCOP results in sources or opportunities for increased revenue from new projects produced to reduce carbon emissions and from integrating sustainability principles throughout the company's supply chain.
- SCOP increases quality and innovation in addition to reducing costs.

17.10 Ethical Issues

17.10 Describe the ethical issues that can arise in sales and operations planning.

The discussion on SCOP in the previous section emphasizes the importance of ethical behavior of companies in relation to the environment. The SCOP process, which includes activities that attempt to reduce the environmental impact of excessive inventory, frequent shipments, and excessive production are a form of ethical behavior. In addition, because one of the primary activities of S&OP is acquiring

OPERATIONS PROFILE: Sustainable S&OP: Matching Up Industries to Save Energy

With extremely high temperatures required to heat limestone, cement is a product with a heavy carbon footprint. Nonetheless, the drive to use more industrial waste and renewable energy in cement production may actually be the motivation needed to create a form of *industrial symbiosis* (a situation in which one company's refuse becomes another's raw material), accelerating our progress toward a zero-waste world.

A critical component in cement is a porous, pebbly, calcium product known as clinker. Manufacturing clinker, which traditionally makes up about 90% of cement, is the most energy-intensive part of the product. Changing limestone to clinker needs temperatures of up to 1,500°C, which means burning large amounts of fuel. As a result, an important step in reducing cement's carbon footprint is to increase the energy efficiency of cement plants and find alternative fuels to power furnaces. Additionally, a second substantial source of emissions comes from the chemical conversion process itself, during which calcium carbonate is extracted from the limestone, generating large amounts of carbon dioxide.

Cement makers cannot solve these emission problems simply by finding ways to increase their plant and fuel efficiency; instead, the key seems to be alternatives to manufacturing clinker. The benefits of this option are important. First, cement made with less clinker reduces the fuel needed to power the kilns. Second, cement that has a lower proportion of clinker has generated lower emissions from the chemical decomposition of limestone.

A range of materials can be used to replace clinker. These include active minerals derived from industrial waste—such as slag from steel mills and fly ash, a byproduct of power plant coal combustion—as well as naturally active materials such as volcanic ash. The technology behind co-processing is well understood. The bigger challenge, however, is to create the infrastructure and industry collaborations that encourage the trading of waste between waste producers and cement producers.

"Our process allows us to use waste as fuel and integrate that into the product without any risk to health," said Raul Quintal, director of operations planning and performance at Cemex S.A.B. de C.V. (Monterrey, Mexico), one of the world's largest cement producers. For those in the waste management sector, cement kilns—with their high temperatures—provide a safe way of destroying unwanted and often hazardous materials, helping solve public health and safety challenges.

"[Co-processing] is a pretty elegant piece of industrial ecology," said Raj Sapru, director of advisory services at Business for Social Responsibility,

Inc. (San Francisco, CA), a U.S.-based business association and advisory group. As new facilities are planned, using waste materials in cement could also influence location selection when deciding where to build a cement plant. The key is to support efficiency across operations in different industries, requiring extensive planning for co-processing ventures. That is, when choosing between locations for developing new plants, one critical issue in the future will be the location of other, partner industrial plants, whose waste products can be conveniently shipped to the new plants as a fuel source.

Co-processing offers a unique opportunity for pursuing sustainability in operations, but it requires careful planning, testing for alternative materials that can serve as fuel sources, mapping out of supply routes and resource needs, and developing long-term supply plans. Though complicated in the short term, using a co-processing strategy for manufacturing can go far to reducing the carbon footprint of plants worldwide, making them more efficient, more interdependent, and a source of cleaner products.[30]

Businesses and their supply chains throughout the world are under increasing pressure from the public and private sectors to engage in activities that will not harm the environment. Factors such as increasing energy and commodity prices, global warming, and a strong demand from company stakeholders for sustainable products and processes makes sustainable manufacturing a necessity. The best way to incorporate sustainability within a company and its supply chain is through the S&OP process, because it brings together all the relevant stakeholders to act in unison to meet customer expectations. In addition, adopting a SCOP framework has been made much easier as many business software and ERP systems are now offering sustainability functionality by including carbon management and carbon accounting tools. For example, CAD packages such as SOLIDWORKS and Sustainability Xpress include life cycle assessment (LCA) and carbon footprint calculations during the design and R&D of new products.

Sales and operations planning is a critical planning process for any company. Although a company can reap numerous benefits if it has an effective S&OP process in place, the consequences of poor sales and operations planning are enormous. These include waste of resources, unwanted inventory, excessive use of overtime and other supplemental resources, frequent expediting of orders, and poor order fulfillment rates. These problems ultimately lead to poor customer service and adversely affect the company's bottom line. Furthermore, if sales and operations planning activities are not well-aligned and integrated, small problems quickly escalate into major challenges, which, in turn, have a negative impact on the company's ability to compete and its overall performance.

Ethics in S&OP

human resources to meet expected demand, it is important that companies pay close attention to the type of human resources acquired and how these resources are used. For example, the use of child, forced, or prison labor violates ethical principles. Hiring practices used to support S&OP should ensure that no one is denied employment because of gender, ethnic origin, or religious affiliation. S&OP decisions should ensure that employees work in a safe and healthy environment.

As described in the Operations Profile at the beginning of this chapter, many retail organizations have felt forced to expand their stores' hours to attract Black Friday shoppers. This policy has caused ordinary store workers to sacrifice their Thanksgiving holiday. In 2013, Kmart (Sears Holding Corporation, Hoffman Estates, IL), for example, opened at 6 am on Thanksgiving morning and stayed open for 42 hours straight. This operating decision created a significant worker backlash against retail employers. For example, one online petition at change.org asked Target Corporation (Minneapolis, MN) to "give Thanksgiving back to families" and delay its planned 9 pm Thanksgiving opening. Even though the petition collected 376,000 signatures, the company refused to change its opening time. Similarly, a "boycott Black Thursday" Facebook (Menlo Park, CA) site quickly generated over 140,000 likes. On the other hand, large retailers, including Costco Wholesale Corporation (Issaquah, WA); Nordstrom, Inc. (Seattle, WA); The Home Depot, Inc. (Atlanta, GA); and Marshalls (TJX Companies, Framingham, MA), all publicly announced their intention of staying closed on Thanksgiving to provide their workers with time to be with their families. This situation is just one example of how organizations facing sales and operations planning challenges have factored in (or refused to consider) the role of ethics in their decision-making processes.

$SAGE edge™

Visit edge.sagepub.com/venkataraman to help you accomplish your coursework goals in an easy-to-use learning environment.

- Mobile-friendly eFlashcards
- Mobile-friendly practice quizzes
- A complete online action plan

- Chapter summaries with learning objectives
- Video and multimedia resources

CHAPTER SUMMARY

17.1 Describe the basic ideas behind sales and operations planning. Sales and operations planning (S&OP), also known as aggregate planning, integrates customer-focused marketing plans for new and existing products with supply chain management. For the medium time frame (often viewed as 6 weeks to 18 months in the future), the sales and operations planning process attempts to match the company's supply of resources efficiently to market demand expectations by integrating the specific, tactical plans in every business area (sales, marketing, R&D, manufacturing, sourcing, and finance) into a single set of plans that aligns with the company's overall strategy.

17.2 Describe the benefits of sales and operations planning process. Sales and operations planning (S&OP) is a medium-term planning process that bridges the gap between the long-term strategic planning and the short-term operational plans. It is a structured collaborative process that generates a single sales and operation plan to match supply and demand. It is also known as aggregates planning, as the sales and operations plan is expressed in aggregate terms. The objective of the S&OP process

is to generate plans for production levels, employment levels, and inventory levels at the minimum cost. An effective sales and operations plan can improve revenues, decrease costs, and increase customer satisfaction.

17.3 Demonstrate the sales and operations planning process and its key features. The S&OP process is demonstrated in Figure 17.2 to consist of a variety of elements. Several organizational functions (e.g., marketing, engineering, operations) offer their input to help develop the sales and operations plan. This plan is then used as a medium-term planning device to develop sales plans for marketing, including demand management activities, monthly sales estimates, and expected customer service levels. It is also used to develop the operations plan, including developing workforce and inventory levels, anticipating backlogs, and creating workflow charts for employees, which include overtime and regular hours to complete all assignments.

17.4 Compare the options for influencing demand and supply in implementing a sales and operations plan. To match supply and demand, planners can employ options that influence demand or supply in their sales and operations planning strategies. To influence demand, the firm can use price, advertising and promotion, backorders and reservation systems, and production of counter-seasonal products and services. To influence supply, the firm can vary its workforce size, use overtime or slack time, build inventories, hire part-time workers, and subcontract.

17.5   Identify alternative sales and operations planning strategies for product families. Three basic strategies can be used to create product family-level sales and operations plans: level, chase, and mixed strategies. In the level strategy, the production output rate and workforce levels are held constant. Variations in demand are balanced by inventory and generation of backorders. In a chase strategy, workforce levels are changed through hiring and layoffs to compensate for variations in demand. A mixed strategy is a hybrid of the level and chase strategies.

17.6   Use the trial-and-error method to develop a sales and operations plan. A variety of techniques can be used in the task of developing a sales and operations plan. These techniques include informal trial-and-error approaches and mathematical techniques such as the linear decision rule (LDR), the transportation method of linear programming, the management coefficients model, and simulation. For this chapter, we demonstrate the use of trial-and-error as a method for developing a sales and operations plan.

17.7   Explain the benefits of sales and operations planning in supply chains. Companies that have an effective global S&OP realize the following benefits: (1) reduced inventory; (2) increased forecast

accuracy; (3) full use and optimization of the supply chain; (4) improvements in communication, accountability, empowerment, and teamwork; and (5) improved customer relationships as a result of better visibility and planning.

17.8   Describe sales and operations planning for service firms. Sales and operations planning for businesses in the service sector poses some unique challenges because most service companies are unable to carry inventory. The focus of S&OP strategies in the service sector is primarily on workforce schedules because services are more labor intensive and labor resources provide the flexibility to satisfy a variety of service requirements.

17.9   Detail the importance of sales carbon operations planning. Sales carbon operations planning (SCOP) is an extension of S&OP that integrates sustainability into the traditional sales operations plan. A sustainable sales and operations plan offers a number of benefits including risk mitigation, increased revenues, and the manufacture of green products.

17.10   Describe the ethical issues that can arise in sales and operations planning. Because one of the primary activities of S&OP is acquiring human resources to meet expected demand, it is important that companies pay close attention to the type of human resources acquired and how these resources are used. For example, the use of child, forced, or prison labor violates ethical principles. Hiring practices used to support S&OP should ensure that no one is denied employment because of gender, ethnic origin, or religious affiliation. S&OP decisions should ensure that employees work in a safe and healthy environment.

KEY TERMS

Aggregate planning   602

Annualized hours strategy   624

Bottom-up planning   608

Chase strategy   612

Financial planning   608

Global sales and operations planning   621

Level strategy   611

Linear decision rule   613

Linear programming   613

Management coefficients model   613

Mixed strategy   612

Sales and operations planning (S&OP)   602

Sales carbon operations planning   625

Simulation   613

Supply planning   608

Top-down planning   608

Transportation method   613

Yield management   625

DISCUSSION AND REVIEW QUESTIONS

1.   What is sales and operations planning (S&OP), and why is it important to companies in many industries?

2   What are the major differences between the level and chase S&OP planning strategies?

3.   List some industries or situations where each of the three basic S&OP strategies is appropriate?

4.   The objective of S&OP is to minimize total cost. What are the major cost categories of this total cost?

5.   What are the problems that S&OP planners face in an environment of high demand uncertainty? What decision options do they have in such an environment?

6.   A company currently uses the level strategy for implementing its sales and operations plan. The company recently introduced several new products into the market that have significantly increased the

cost of holding inventory. Discuss the impact of this change on the company's sales and operations planning strategy.

7.   Holding inventories is not an option for many service businesses. How does this impact sales and operations planning for these businesses?

8.   Discuss some of the S&OP strategies that service companies can use.

9.   What are the benefits of coordinating a company's S&OP process with its supply chain partners? What are the challenges?

10.   What are some of the unique challenges and requirements of global sales and operations planning?

11.   What are some of the issues that companies should address in implementing a global sales and operations plan?

12.   What is sales carbon operations planning (SCOP)? How is it different from the typical S&OP process?

SOLVED PROBLEM ....

Cool Air Inc., a fictitious manufacturer of air conditioners, has estimated the demand for its air conditioners for the upcoming year in Table 17.4.

TABLE 17.4: Cool Air Demand for Air Conditioners

Month	Jan	Feb	Mar	Apr	May	Jun	Jul	Aug	Sept	Oct	Nov	Dec
Working Days	22	20	23	22	24	22	23	17	21	22	20	20
Forecast	700	850	900	1,000	1,250	1,350	1,450	1,300	1,000	880	720	600

a. Use a level production strategy if Cool Air has 25 full-time employees whose regular time production rate is two air conditioners per day and costs of $200/unit. Use inventory and backorders to absorb variations in demand. Inventory carrying cost is $10/unit per month and backorder cost is $20 per unit per month.

b. Use a chase production strategy. Hiring and training an employee costs $400. The per-employee layoff cost is $300. Current workforce size is 25 full-time employees.

c. Use a mixed production strategy with a constant force of 20 employees per month. Use inventory, overtime, and subcontracting to absorb demand variations. Regular time production cost is $200 per unit. Overtime is limited to 30% of regular time production and costs $300/unit. Subcontracting is also limited to 500 units per month and costs $350/unit. Inventory carrying cost is $10/unit per month. Ignore employee idle time.

d. Which plan has the minimum total cost (in U.S. dollars)? Comment on the drawbacks of this plan.

Solution:

a.   Level production strategy.

The regular time production rate per day (2 units/day) and the number of regular time workers (25) are held constant. Nevertheless, as the number of working days varies each month, inventories are used to absorb variation in demand.

Step 1: Calculate the regular time production quantity each month.

The regular time production quantity for January is given by:

Production rate per day × Number of regular time workers × Number of working days in January

$$= 25 \times 2 \times 22 = 1,100 \text{ units}$$

Similarly, for the regular time production for February

$$= 25 \times 2 \times 20 = 1,000 \text{ units}$$

and so on.

The regular time production quantities for the remaining months are shown in Screenshot 17.4.

Step 2: Calculate ending inventory and the average inventory levels at the end of each month.

Ending inventory level at the end of each period is given by:

Ending inventory = Inventory level at the beginning of each period + Production in that period – Forecasted demand in that period

Note: The inventory level at the beginning of each month is the ending inventory level in the previous month.

The average inventory level at the end of each month is given by:

Average inventory = (Beginning inventory + Ending inventory) / 2

For the previous example, for the month of January, beginning inventory = 0, regular time production = 1,100, and the forecasted demand is 700. Therefore,

Ending inventory level for January = 0 + 1,100 – 700 = 400, and the

Average inventory level for January = (0 + 400) / 2 = 200

Ending and average inventory levels for the remaining months are shown in Screenshot 17.4.

Note: The negative values of ending inventory for August and September represent backorders. Therefore, if the average inventory calculated for any of these months shows a negative value, set the average inventory value for that month as zero.

Step 3: Calculate the regular time production costs, inventory holding costs, and backorder costs for each month.

These costs are given by:

Regular time production cost = Regular time production × Regular time cost/unit

Inventory holding cost = Inventory holding cost/unit/month × Average inventory level

Backorder Cost = Backorder cost/unit/month × number of units backordered

For this problem, for the month of January, as the regular time cost/unit = $200, inventory holding cost/unit/period = $10, average inventory level = 200, backorder cost/unit/month = $20, and the number of units backordered = 0, we have (in U.S. dollars):

Regular time production cost = 1,100 × $200 = $220,000

Inventory holding cost = $10 × 200 = $2,000

Backorder cost = $20 × 0 = $0

Similar cost calculations are performed for the remaining months, and the costs are shown in Screenshot 17.4.

Step 4: Calculate the total cost of the level production plan.

The total cost for the level plan is given by:

Total cost = Sum of the regular time production costs for all periods + Sum of the inventory holding costs for all periods + Sum of the backordering costs for all periods

SCREENSHOT 17.4: Solved Problem 17.1a: Level Production Strategy

	A	B	C	D	E	F	G	H	I	J	K	L	M	N
1	**Solved Problem 17-1a: Level Production strategy**													
2														
3	Beginning Inventory	0												
4	Reg. time production cost/unit	$200												
5	Average inventory holding cost/unit/month	$10												
6	Workforce Size	25		=($B$6*$B$7*B$12)			=(B14+B13-B11)		=(B14+B15)/2					
7	Production Rate/employee/day	2												
8	Backorder Cost in $/unit/month	$20												
9														
10		*January*	*February*	*March*	*April*	*May*	*June*	*July*	*August*	*September*	*October*	*November*	*December*	***Total***
11	Forecast	700	850	900	1000	1250	1350	1450	1300	1000	880	720	600	12000
12	# of working days	22	20	23	22	24	22	23	17	21	22	20	20	
13	Production	1100	1000	1150	1100	1200	1100	1150	850	1050	1100	1000	1000	12800
14	Beginning Inventory	0	400	550	800	900	850	600	300	-150	-100	120	400	
15	Ending Inventory	400	550	800	900	850	600	300	-150	-100	120	400	800	
16	Average Inventory	200	475	675	850	875	725	450	75	-125	10	260	600	5070
17	***Production and Inventory Costs***													
18	Reg. time production cost in $	220000	200000	230000	220000	240000	220000	230000	170000	210000	220000	200000	200000	$2,560,000
19	Inventory holding cost in $	2000	4750	6750	8500	8750	7250	4500	750	0	100	2600	6000	$ 51,950
20	Backorder Cost in $	0	0	0	0	0	0	0	3000	2000	0	0	0	$ 5,000
21	**Total cost In $**	222000	204750	236750	228500	248750	227250	234500	173750	212000	220100	202600	206000	$2,616,950
22														
23	=($B$4*B13)													
24	=IF(B16>0,($B$5*B16),0)													
25	=IF(B15>0,0,($B$8*(-B15)))													
26	=(B18+B19+B20)											=(N18+N19+N20)		

For problem 17.1a, the total cost is given by:

Total cost = (1,100 × $200 + 1,000 × 200 +.... + 1,000 × 200) + (200 × $10 + ... + 600 × $10) + (0 × $20 +...+ 150 × $20 + 100 × $20 +...+ 0) = **$2,616,950**

The results of all of the calculations using these steps for the level production plan are shown in Screenshot 17.4.

b. Chase strategy.

In a pure chase production strategy, production levels are adjusted by varying the workforce levels period by period to meet demand in each period. The following steps are used to develop a chase production strategy.

Step 1: Compute the number of workers needed for each period.

The number of workers needed for each period is calculated as follows:

Number of workers needed = Net production required / Production per worker

For problem 17.1b, as the demand in January is 700 units of air conditioners, and as we have no inventory on hand at the beginning of January, 700 units should be produced for that month. Also, each worker produces 2 units per day, and given 22 working days in January, the number of workers needed for that month is given by:

Number of workers needed for January = 700 / (2 × 22) = 15.9 or 16 workers

Similarly, the number of workers needed for February is given by:

Number of workers needed for February = 850 / (2 × 20) = 21.25 or 22 workers

The number of workers required for the remaining months is calculated in the same manner and is shown in Screenshot 17.5.

Step 2: Compute the number of workers to be hired or fired.

The number of workers to be hired or fired is computed by determining the difference between the number of workers required in each month and the number of workers available in that month. If this difference is positive, we will hire additional workers; if it is negative, then we will lay off some of the existing workers. In problem 17.1b, as we require 16 workers in January, and the current workforce level is 25, we need to lay off 9 (25 – 16) of the workers currently employed. Thus:

Number of workers fired in January = 25 – 16 = 9 workers

In February, we require 22 workers and we have only 16 workers (from January), we need:

Number of workers hired in February = 22 – 16 = 6 workers

The number of workers hired or fired for the remaining months is calculated in the same manner and is shown in Screenshot 17.5.

Step 3: Compute the regular time production cost and hiring and firing cost for each period.

Regular time production cost = Regular time production × Regular time cost/unit

Hiring cost = Number of workers hired × Hiring cost/worker

Firing cost = Number of workers fired × Firing cost/worker

Using these formulas, given that the regular time cost/unit = $200, hiring cost/worker = $400, and the layoff cost/worker = $300, the regular time production

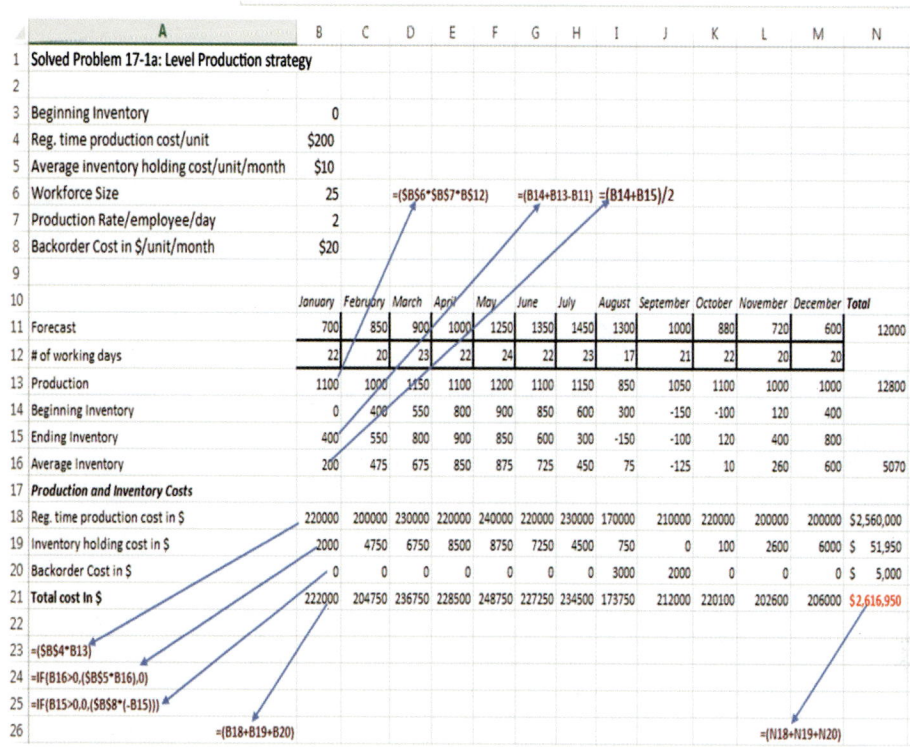

SCREENSHOT 17.5: Solved Problem 17.1b: Chase Production Strategy

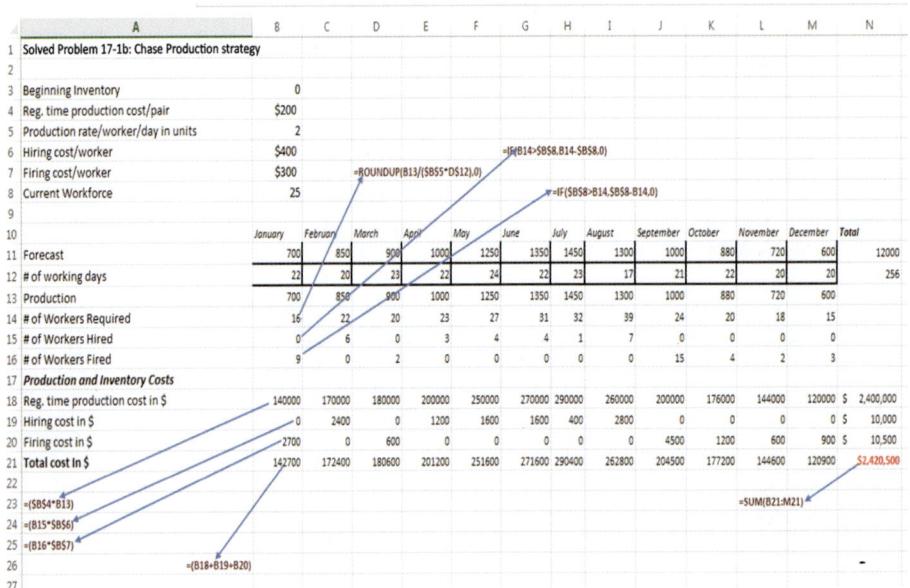

costs, hiring costs, and layoff costs for the month of January in problem 17.1b are (in U.S. dollars):

$$\text{Regular time production cost} = 700 \times \$200/\text{unit} = \$140,000$$

$$\text{Hiring cost} = 0 \times \$400/\text{worker} = \$0$$

$$\text{Layoff cost} = 9 \times \$300 = \$2,700$$

The regular time production costs, hiring costs, and layoff costs for the remaining months are calculated in the same manner and are shown in Screenshot 17.5.

Step 4: Calculate the total cost of the chase production plan.

The total cost for the chase plan is given by:

Total cost = Sum of the regular time production costs for all periods + Sum of the hiring costs for all periods + Sum of the firing costs for all periods

For problem 17.1b, the total cost is given by:

Total cost = (700 × $200 + 850 × $200 + ...+ 720 × $200 + 600 × $200)
+ (0 × $400 + 6 × $400.... +
7 × $400...+ 0 × $400) + (9 × $300 + 0 × $300 + ...+ 3 × $300) =
$2,420,500

The results of all of the calculations using these steps for the chase production plan are shown in Screenshot 17.5.

C.   Mixed strategy.

In this strategy, we will hold the workforce level constant at 20 workers, but use only inventory, overtime, and subcontracting to absorb demand variations. The steps for developing this plan using these options are given as follows.

Step 1: Determine the regular time, overtime, and subcontracted production required for each period.

For problem 17.1c, each worker can produce only 2 units per day, and the workforce size is 20 workers. Given 22 working days in January, we have for January:

$$\text{Regular time production} = 2 \times 22 \times 20 = 880 \text{ units}$$

For January, as the expected demand is only 700, no additional production using overtime and subcontracting will be required. There is, however, (880 − 700) = 180 units of ending inventory in January, which will be the beginning inventory for February.

For the month of February with 20 working days, we have:

$$\text{Regular time production} = 2 \times 20 \times 20 = 800 \text{ units}$$

$$\text{Ending inventory} = 180 + 800 - 850 = 130 \text{ units}$$

Continuing with similar calculations, you will find in Screenshot 17.6 that no additional production using overtime and subcontracting will be required until May. For the month of May, however:

$$\text{Regular time production} = 2 \times 20 \times 24 = 960 \text{ units}$$

As the forecast for May is 1,250 units, additional production using overtime and/or subcontracting will be required. Note, we will use the overtime option first as it has a lower per-unit cost than the subcontracting option. Yet, since the maximum overtime production allowable is only up to 30% of regular time production, and the beginning inventory for May is 30 units:

$$\text{Overtime production} = \text{Min } \{0.3 \times 960, (1250 - 30 - 960)\} = \text{Min } \{288, 260\} = 260 \text{ units}$$

The combined inventory on hand, regular time, and overtime production in May is enough to meet the forecasted demand. Therefore, no subcontracted production is required.

Similarly, for the month of June we have:

$$\text{Regular time production} = 2 \times 20 \times 22 = 880 \text{ units}$$

As the forecast for June is 1,350 units, additional production using overtime and/or subcontracting will be required. Again, we will use the overtime option first as it has a lower per unit cost than the subcontracting option. Nevertheless, since the maximum over-time production allowable is only up to 30% of regular time production, and the beginning inventory for June is 30 units:

$$\text{Overtime production} = \text{Min } \{0.3 \times 880, (1250 - 0 - 880)\} = \text{Min } \{264, 370\} = 264 \text{ units}$$

SCREENSHOT 17.6: Solved Problem 17.1c: Mixed Production Strategy

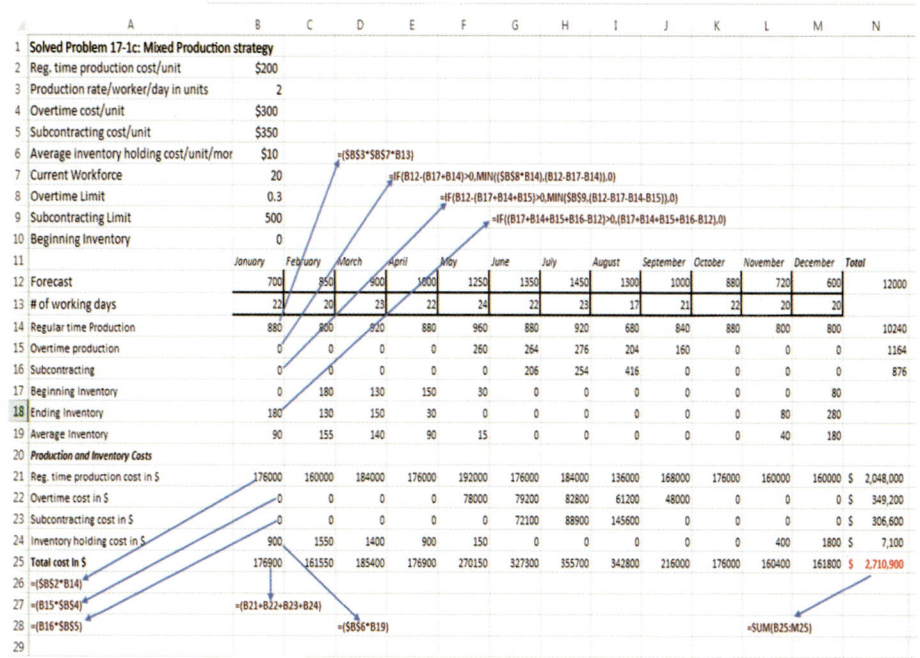

As the combined regular time and overtime production in June (880 + 264 = 1,144 units) is not enough to meet the forecasted demand, subcontracted production is required. Hence, the remaining units produced using the subcontracting option is given by:

Subcontracted production = Monthly demand requirements –
Regular time production –
Overtime production = 1,350 – 880 – 264 = 206 units

Screenshot 17.6 shows the results of these computations for all the months.

Step 2: Compute the regular time production, overtime, subcontracting, and inventory holding costs for each period.

For the month of January (in U.S. dollars):

Regular time production cost = 880 × $200/unit = $300,000

Overtime production cost = 0 × $300/unit = $0

Subcontracting cost = 0 × $350/unit = $0

Inventory holding cost = Average inventory × Holding cost/unit/month = 90 × 10 = $900

Screenshot 17.6 shows the results of these computations for all the remaining months.

Step 3: Calculate the total cost of the mixed production plan.

Total cost = Sum of the regular time production costs for all months + Sum of overtime costs for all months + Sum of subcontracting costs for all months + Sum of inventory holding costs for all months

For problem 17.1c, the total cost is given by:

Total cost = {(880 × $200 + ...+ 800 × $200) + (0 × $300 + ...+ 260 × $300........ + 0 × $360) + (0 × $350 + ...+ 206 × $350 + ...+ 0 × $350) + (90 × $10 +....... + 180 × $10) = **$2,710,900**

The results of all of the calculations using these steps for the mixed production plan are shown in Screenshot 17.6.

d. Among the three plans, the plan to choose is the chase strategy as it has the minimum total cost. Yet, the major drawback of this strategy is loss of employee morale and lack of loyalty caused by the frequent changes in the workforce.

PROBLEMS

1. Sales and operations planning (S&OP) has been referred to as the means for bringing together a company's marketing, finance, sales, and operations departments for fully integrated business development. Using the example of a local restaurant, how would S&OP help with their overall operations and coordination? Give specific examples.

2. Why is demand planning so difficult for a company to perform? Use the example of a video game developer. How would they use demand planning prior to the anticipated launch of a new product? How would their demand planning differ for the launch of an updated version of an existing product?

3. Suppose you were in charge of product purchasing for the men's sportswear department of a large department store in the suburbs of Chicago. How might you use top-down and bottom-up planning for your S&OP? What would likely be some of the advantages and disadvantages of each approach?

4. You have just been put in charge of a golf equipment store in the western New York region and are interested in employing some "demand influencing options" for boosting sales. Please give examples of how you would employ different options (e.g., price, advertising and promotions, etc.) for improving demand.

5. You have been named manager for a Mexican-themed restaurant at a vacation hot spot in the Dominican Republic. Your highest volume season is typically from mid-November to late March. How might you use various "supply influencing options" for improving capacity and sales planning at the restaurant? Go through each option from the textbook (e.g., varying the workforce size, use of inventories, etc.) and discuss how each option could be used to improve the efficiency of your operations.

6. Given the following forecast and cost information, determine the total cost of a plan that uses regular time production output of 600 units per month, overtime is used when needed up to a maximum of 60 units per month, and subcontracting is used if additional units are needed to meet the forecast:

Month	1	2	3	4	5	6
Forecast	570	600	630	650	670	690

Regular time cost = $40 per unit

Overtime cost = $60 per unit

Subcontracting cost = $80 per unit

Holding cost = $10 per unit per month

Note: Holding costs for each month are calculated on the average inventory level and in U.S. dollars.

7. Given the following forecast and cost information, determine the total cost of a chase plan that uses regular time production output of 400 units per month, overtime is used when needed up to a maximum of 40 units per month, and subcontracting is used if additional units are needed to meet the forecast:

Month	1	2	3	4	5	6
Forecast	430	400	440	450	480	480

Regular time cost = $50 per unit

Overtime cost = $65 per unit

Subcontracting cost = $75 per unit

8. Refer to the data in problem 6. If backorders are allowed, determine the total cost of a plan if overtime is limited to 40 units per month and subcontracting is limited to 20 units per month. Backordering costs are $30 per unit.

9. The manager of a company that produces compressors for refrigerators has developed the following forecast for compressor demand:

Month	1	2	3	4	5	6	7
Forecast	140	155	150	145	155	145	130

The company has a regular time capacity to produce 140 compressors each month, and the regular and overtime costs of production per compressor are $50 and $70, respectively. Develop a chase plan that matches the forecast and compute the total cost of this plan.

10. Develop a level production plan for the compressor demand forecast in problem 9 by using overtime, inventory, and backlogs to absorb demand fluctuations. Inventory holding costs are $10 per month per compressor and backlog costs are $80 per compressor per month.

11. Refer to Example 17.1. Suppose the company's manufacturing plant was shut down during February and March due to a labor strike. Nonetheless, demand for those 2 months still had to be met. The company had the options of using subcontracting and backorders to meet demand. A maximum of 1,000 pairs of skis can be subcontracted and a maximum of 1,000 pairs of skis can be backordered for those 2 months. The cost of backorders is $30/pair/month. All other planning values given in Example 17.1 remain the same. Develop a least-cost sales and operations plan for the 12-month planning horizon.

12. Refer to Example 17.1. Suppose process reengineering initiatives have enabled the company to reduce the number of worker hours required to produce a pair of skis to 3 hours. Develop a least-cost sales and operations plan using a level strategy of regular time production of 3,000 units per month. Use a combination of subcontracting, overtime, inventory, and backorders to absorb the variations in demand. Assume a beginning inventory of 4,000 at the beginning of January and a backorder cost of $30/pair/month. All other planning values given in Example 17.1 remain the same.

13. Refer to Solved Problem 17.1. Suppose Cool Air Inc. has a maximum regular time production capacity of 900 air conditioners per month for the months of January through October and only 600 air conditioners in November and December. Use a level strategy of maximum regular time production each month, and use overtime and subcontracting to absorb demand variations. No backlogs are allowed and ending inventory should be zero at the end of December. Overtime usage is limited to a production of 300 units per month and subcontracting to 200 units per month. Inventory carrying cost is $10/unit per month; regular time production cost is $200/unit; overtime costs are $300/unit; and subcontracting costs are $350/unit (all in U.S. dollars). Ignore employee idle time.

14. Refer to Solved Problem 17.1. Use a chase production strategy. Yet, the number of full-time employees hired or fired is restricted to 5 employees per month. During peak demand periods, the company has the option of using overtime to meet any excess demand. Overtime cost is $300/unit. Hiring and training an employee costs $400. The per-employee layoff cost is $300. The current workforce size is 25 full-time employees. Compute the total cost of this plan.

15. PharmaTech, Inc., a fictional manufacturer of pharmaceutical products and medical supplies located in Zurich, Switzerland, uses sales and operations planning to set production, workforce, and inventory levels for its annual planning horizon. Among the variety of items the company produces, one of the items used for S&OP planning is a standard emergency medical kit that contains medical products that can be used to treat a variety of injuries. The demand for this item fluctuates due to seasonal illnesses and the differing ordering policies used by the various hospitals. The average regular time production rate of this kit by a worker at PharmaTech is 800 kits per month. The regular time production cost is $10 per kit and $12 per kit if overtime production is used. Production of these kits can also be subcontracted to external vendors at $15 per kit. Inventory carrying costs are $3 per kit per month. Overtime is limited to 50% of regular production, but there is no production limit if subcontracting is used. The high skill level required in production of these kits means that newly hired workers require extensive training and, therefore, hiring costs are $1,200 per worker. Firing costs per worker are also high at $1,000/worker (all in U.S. dollars). PharmaTech currently has 40 full-time workers. The forecast of demand for these medical kits for the first 6 months of next year is given as follows:

Month	January	February	March	April	May	June
Forecast	20,000	30,000	45,000	20,000	25,000	50,000

Develop a 6-month aggregate production plan for PharmaTech using:

a. A pure chase strategy.
b. A pure level strategy using a constant workforce of 40 full-time workers.
c. A mixed strategy where the production rate is kept constant at 30,000 kits per month. Demand during peak periods is met using overtime and subcontracting as needed.

16. Excelsior Clay Works, a fictional manufacturer of a variety of high-quality glazed clay roof tiles in Kerala, India, has the following composite demand forecasts (in hundreds of units):

Month	Jan	Feb	Mar	Apr	May	Jun	Jul	Aug	Sep	Oct	Nov	Dec
Work days	22	20	23	22	24	22	23	17	21	22	20	20
Forecast	200	300	350	600	450	150	190	260	360	490	340	160

Additional Planning Data

Hiring cost: $400 per worker hired.

Firing cost: $200 per worker fired.

Regular time cost: $100 per worker per day.

Overtime cost: $150 per worker per day.

Idle time cost: $60 per worker per day.

Inventory carrying cost: $10 per hundred units/month

Backorder cost: $20 per hundred units (based on shortages at the end of the month).

Productivity rate: 100 units per worker per day.

Workforce size at the beginning of January: 20 workers.

Beginning inventory at the beginning of January: 0 units.

Develop a sales and operations plan using the following three strategies and find the total cost of each of the strategies:

a. A level strategy of constant workforce with inventories and backorders to meet demand variations.
b. A chase strategy with the options of hiring and firing workers.
c. A mixed strategy keeping the workforce size constant at 20 and by using overtime and idle time to absorb changes in demand.

17. Kate Russell, the plant manager of a furniture manufacturing company, is in the process of developing a sales and operations plan for the upcoming year. She has obtained a forecast of expected demand for the 12 months of the planning horizon, given in the following table. Demand is seasonal and is relatively high in months 5, 6, and 7:

Periods	1	2	3	4	5	6	7	8	9	10	11	12
Forecasts	160	140	190	160	270	320	360	250	170	150	130	180

The manufacturing plant currently has 20 full-time employees, each of whom can produce 10 units of output per month at a cost of $8 per unit. Inventory carrying cost is $4 per unit per month, and backlog cost is $10 per unit per month (in U.S. dollars). Kate is planning to hire two temporary workers to work during the peak demand months of 5, 6, and 7. Each temporary worker would cost an additional $300 for each month they work. You are asked to assist Kate in developing the following two sales and operations plans. Determine the total cost of each plan:

a. Use the full-time employees as needed for regular time production. In addition, hire the two temporary workers for periods 5, 6, and 7. Use up to 30 units of subcontracting per month to meet any excess demand at a cost of $15/unit. Also, backlogs in any given month cannot exceed 70 units. Assume no beginning inventory at the start of month 1, and there should be no ending inventory at the end of month 12.

b. Keep the regular time output constant at 200 units per month. Use up to 30 units of subcontracting when needed. No temporary workers are hired. There are no restrictions on backlogs.

18. Medaas Electronics is a fictional producer of laser printers. The company's production planner, Christian Medaas, has developed the following cost data (in U.S. dollars):

Regular time cost: $80 per printer.

Overtime cost: $120 per printer.

Subcontracting cost: $140 per printer.

Inventory carrying cost: $10 per printer per month.

For the next 6 months, the forecasted demand and the available capacity for printers are given in the following table:

Demand	3,000	3,200	1,800	2,700	3,400	2,200
Regular Time Capacity	2,500	2,700	1,000	2,000	2,600	1,700
Overtime Capacity	500	500	300	500	500	500
Subcontracting Capacity	600	600	600	600	600	600

Christian Medaas has 600 printers in stock at the beginning of the planning period. Develop a least-cost production plan. No backorders are permitted.

19. Reagan Health Foods Inc. is a fictional producer of protein drinks. The company's production planner has developed the following demand forecast (in cases) for the first 6 months of 2016: 3,500; 4,600; 5,800; 7,600; 6,700; and 4,700, as well as the following cost data (in U.S. dollars):

Regular time cost: $15 per case.

Overtime cost: $22 per case.

Subcontracting cost: $25 per case.

Inventory carrying cost: $2 per case per month.

Backlog cost: $10 per case per month.

Using this information, develop aggregate plans for the following three scenarios and compute the total cost of each plan:

a. Use a level production strategy and use overtime when needed.

b. Use a combination of overtime, inventory, and subcontracting to absorb demand variations. Use a maximum of 600 cases of overtime and 400 cases of subcontracting.

c. Use a combination of overtime (700 cases maximum), inventory, and backlogs (if necessary). There should be no backlogs at the end of the planning period.

20. Montague Furniture Corporation is a fictional chair manufacturer located in Pampanga, Philippines. They make two types of rattan bamboo chairs— Rocking Chair and Windsor Chair. Both chairs are manufactured in the same factory and require the same amount of equipment and labor resources. You also have the following additional data (in U.S. dollars):

Regular time production cost = $400 per chair.

Overtime production cost = $550 per chair.

Subcontracting cost = $25 per case.

Labor hours required to make each chair = 4.2 hours.

Labor hours available each month = 200 hours per worker.

Cost of hiring a worker = $300.

Cost of each worker layoff = $400.

Monthly carrying cost = $20 per chair.

The company begins the next planning horizon of 12 months with 30 workers and 0 chairs in inventory. The forecasted demand for both types of chairs is given in the following table:

Month	Rocking Chair	Windsor Chair
January	700	1,220
February	730	1,550
March	745	1,700

Month	Rocking Chair	Windsor Chair
April	690	2,070
May	540	2,250
June	420	2,400
July	870	1,700
August	770	1,310
September	910	1,890
October	830	1,640
November	400	890
December	780	1,460

a. Develop a level production plan for the 12-month planning period. Use overtime, subcontracting, and inventory to absorb demand variations.
b. Develop a chase production plan by hiring and laying off workers.
c. Which plan yields the lowest cost?

21. A company's production planner for the company's popular product has developed the following demand forecast and the per-unit regular time production cost information for the first 6 months of 2016. Due to seasonal factors, the cost of regular time production is not constant. Overtime can be used up to a maximum of 100 units each month at 150% of the regular time production cost for that month. Production of units can be subcontracted at a cost of $150 per unit. The inventory holding cost is $5 per unit per month. The inventory level at the beginning of the planning horizon is 100 units and the inventory level at the end of the planning horizon should be zero. No backlogs are allowed:

Month	1	2	3	4	5	6
Forecast	1,200	1,300	900	700	1,500	1,700
Production cost in $ per unit	90	95	100	105	100	100

Using this information, develop aggregate plans for the following three scenarios and compute the total cost of each plan:

a. Use a level production strategy and use overtime when needed.
b. Use a combination of overtime, inventory, and subcontracting to absorb demand variations.
c. Use a chase production strategy.
d. Which plan yields the lowest cost?

CASE STUDY 17.1: COORDINATING SALES AND OPERATIONS PLANNING FOR THE NEXT BIG THING: THE CASE OF THE SONY PS4 LAUNCH[31]

In autumn 2013, Sony Corporation (Tokyo, Japan) launched the long-anticipated successor to its PlayStation family of game consoles. Since its release in 2006, gamers made the PlayStation 3 one of the most successful and longest-lived game consoles in history. The PS4 was announced in February and formally introduced in mid-November. If initial demand was any indicator of success, the PS4 appeared to be an instant hit: more than one million of the units were purchased in the first 24 hours of its release in the United States and Canada.

The release did not go off without a hitch, however. "A noteworthy portion of the customer reviews for the console on Amazon were negative," Nick Wingfield pointed out in the *New York Times*. "As of Sunday afternoon, one version of the PS4 had just over 1,800 reviews on Amazon, and about 500 of the reviewers gave a 1-star rating, the lowest possible on Amazon. Many of those people wrote that their consoles stopped functioning after a short period of playing or didn't work at all." Some users reported problems with the PlayStation Network, several users had broken HDMI cords, others had problems ejecting disks, and still others saw the "ominous Red Line of Death"—a system error indicator of a terminally damaged machine. Sony maintained that these problems occurred in just 0.4% of the total shipped

PlayStation 4 units; in other words, though the negative publicity was loud, a minority of users had problems with the new system.

The reaction of this vocal minority of disgruntled users of the PlayStation 4 illustrates the importance of not only staying out ahead of demand expectations through careful operations planning and supply chain management, but also managing customer reactions to the system. Dissatisfied customers will share their grievances on social media to make their concerns known and known right away. Sony's response was to stay on top of this situation through those same social media channels to which complainers flock. A page on its own community pages, for example, directly addressed the "blinking blue light" system error message that so many users complained about, offering symptoms, possible causes, and solutions. In short, managing the supply chain for sales and operations planning now also includes the need to carefully monitor and manage the customer interaction and online communication.

What does Sony anticipate for the PlayStation 4's down the road? The company expects to sell 20 million PS4 consoles by 2017. Although overall sales of videogame systems have been in a continuous slump since 2008, as a result of competition from games offered on mobile devices and social networking sites, game console manufacturers, including Sony and Microsoft Corporation (Redmond, WA), are experiencing robust sales of their latest offerings (the PS4 and Xbox One respectively), suggesting that, after nearly a decade of playing games on the same old consoles, there is pent-up demand for these new systems, provided Sony and Microsoft continue to do a careful job of planning to support the successful launch of their next-generation game systems.

Questions

1. How has social media made the S&OP process more complex?

2. How can e-commerce help and hurt the coordination of sales and operations planning forecasts?

3. Why is the challenge of managing customer relations a critical issue to integrate into the S&OP process?

VIDEO CASE ....

Watch this video case to learn about how the Rockefeller Gastropub uses customer-focused plans to manage seasonal changes and new promotions.

CRITICAL THINKING EXERCISES ....

Consider a restaurant and a manufacturer of electronic products. Discuss the advantages and disadvantages these two companies face in developing and implementing their sales and operations plans.

CHAPTER
18

Master Scheduling and Material Requirements Planning

LEARNING OBJECTIVES

After studying this chapter, you should be able to:

1. Compose a master schedule and identify its functions.

2. Explain the conditions under which MRP is appropriate, its inputs, processing, and outputs, as well as its benefits and limitations.

3. Discuss the role that sustainability and ethics play in MRP systems.

OPERATIONS PROFILE: Managing Materials and Production at Rolls-Royce

TIM Graham/Getty Images News/Getty Images

Rolls-Royce Holdings plc (London, U.K.) is the world's second-largest manufacturer of aircraft engines and, because of its favored position within the industry, it is expected to double production of engines by 2018. Among other contracts, Rolls-Royce is the sole supplier of engines for the Airbus (Airbus SAS, Blagnac, France) A350 and A380 aircraft, and one of two prime suppliers for Boeing's (The Boeing Company, Chicago, IL) successful 787 Dreamliner. By some estimates, Rolls-Royce holds 54% of the supplier market share among the wide-body aircraft engine providers.

Producing jet engines efficiently requires attention to detail. Rolls-Royce's largest engine is the Trent 1000, a 9-foot wide giant with 66 turbine blades spinning at 13,500 rpm, generating 74,000 pounds of thrust each and, at takeoff, capable of pulling in 1.25 tons of air every second. These are the engines used to power the largest aircraft in the world. The Trent 1000 has 18,000 components, and each engine is manufactured to withstand the extraordinary performance demands placed on it. Not only is there a huge parts list for each engine, but the process for manufacturing many of these components is difficult. For example, each high-pressure turbine blade is grown from a single crystal of a Rolls-Royce alloy in a vacuum furnace. As it grows, it incorporates a complex series of air passages to cool the blade. Then it needs external cooling holes created by accurate laser drilling. On top of the blade assembly is a thermal barrier coating that is stronger than that used to make the tiles on the space shuttle. Furthermore, each blade remains in the high-pressure turbine, where the gas temperature is at least 400 degrees *above* the melting point of the blade's alloy. It sits in a disk that rotates at more than 10,000 rpm, and the force on the blade root is equivalent to hanging a London double-decker bus from its tip. Every time the plane takes off, this single blade achieves the same horsepower as a Formula 1 racing car, and yet it can travel 10 million miles before it needs replacing. Each component of the engine, in addition to each blade, is painstakingly produced and carefully checked for flaws or potential problems. Because safety and reliability are so critical to the engine, any signs of problems in a part lead to immediate scrapping and, in some cases, a reassessment of the production process itself to maintain production standards.

To manage the supply chain and materials flow for Trent engine production, the company's supply chain managers must coordinate deliveries of materials, parts, and subassemblies from hundreds of worldwide suppliers so that these components are on site and ready to be used when production orders arrive. Because Rolls is looking to dramatically increase production of the Trent series at its manufacturing facilities in Bristol, U.K., and Singapore, it is under considerable pressure to find ways to reduce production and supply chain costs over the next several years. One reason Rolls-Royce has to cut costs is that its current product margins are well below those of its nearest competitor, General Electric (Fairfield, CT), and Rolls-Royce has announced plans to increase profitability through cost-cutting and making its supply chain more responsive. The key to the success of this venture, however, will be maintaining the flow of materials for the Trent family of engines, the driver of Rolls-Royce's expected future success.[1]

18.1

Compose a master
schedule and identify
its functions.

Master Scheduling

18.1 Master Scheduling

In Chapter 1, we noted that for operations and supply chain management, there are three categories of decisions: *strategic, tactical,* and *operational* (see Figure 1.6). Our discussions in this chapter will focus on decisions that must occur at the operational level. The sales and operations plan that we discussed in Chapter 17 established production and resource levels in aggregate terms (such as product families, standard labor and machine hours, or dollar units) for the medium term. Although aggregate planning is critical for operations management, it does not provide the detailed material and resource plans needed to produce or acquire individual products and components. To meet short-run demand and to facilitate production, it is necessary that the aggregate units established by sales and operations planning (S&OP) should be *disaggregated,* or broken down, first into requirements for finished product and then into materials, labor and machine capacity, and inventory requirements. These operational plans are made in the medium-term to short-term time frames of the planning hierarchy and are listed as follows:

1. Master scheduling.
2. Material requirements planning.
3. Capacity requirements planning.
4. Detailed scheduling.

These tasks follow a sequence that can be presented in the framework shown in Figure 18.1. The sequence of four operational planning and control tasks follow sales and operations planning. These tasks have to be performed within the constraints established by the sales and operations plan. In this chapter, we will discuss the first three tasks in the sequence: master scheduling, material requirements planning, and capacity requirements planning. Detailed scheduling is discussed in Chapter 19.

FIGURE 18.1: Hierarchical Framework for Operational Planning

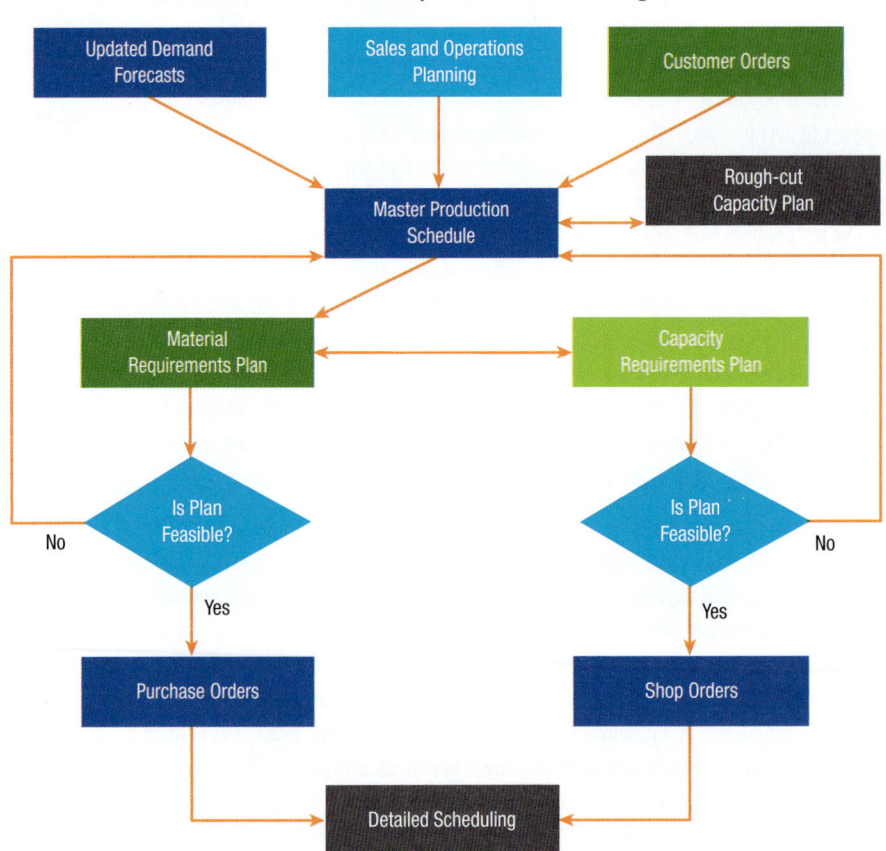

Master scheduling leads to a manufacturing plan that determines the quantity of each end item to be produced in specific periods during the short-range planning horizon. The master schedule is essential for all operations planning and control decisions. The master schedule sets the production quantities required to meet demand from every possible source in an organization, such as final customers, warehouses, and requirements from other plants in a multi-plant environment. Preparation of the company's master schedule requires coordination with many of its functional areas, such as marketing, operations, and senior management. Master scheduling allows sales and marketing to make realistic delivery commitments to distribution centers and final customers. It enables the operations functions to determine whether sufficient production capacity is available to meet demand. If capacity is inadequate, the master schedule provides advance information to both the operations and marketing functions to find alternative capacity sources or to negotiate different delivery options with customers. Furthermore, the master schedule provides top management with timely information so that it can determine whether the company's strategic objectives will be met or whether a change in the business plan is needed. By taking into account both actual customer orders and updated demand forecasts, available capacity, inventory levels, and so forth, the master schedule determines what end products or major subassemblies the company will produce and when. As shown in Figure 18.1, it serves as the link between the higher level S&OP and the short-term material and capacity requirements plans and detailed scheduling. Specifically, the master schedule breaks down (or disaggregates) the aggregate production levels set for product families into specific end products to be produced in specific time periods over a time-phased schedule. This output of individual production quantities of the end items to be produced at various points of the short-term planning horizon is called the **master production schedule (MPS)**.

Master Scheduling Inputs, Processing, and Outputs

The inputs to the master schedule are the beginning inventory levels of the product, forecasts of demand for each period of the master schedule planning time frame, and customer orders for each period of the schedule (quantities committed to customers). Using these inputs, the master scheduling process begins with an initial calculation of projected on-hand inventory for each period of the schedule horizon. These calculations will show when (in which periods of the schedule) the available on-hand inventory will become zero or fall below the required safety stock level, and therefore require additional production. This is the period in which predetermined production quantities will be scheduled, and this quantity and timing of production is called the master production schedule (MPS). This predetermined production quantity is often referred to as a **lot size** and is defined as "the amount of a particular item that is ordered from the plant or a supplier or issued as a standard quantity to the production process."[2]

There are various lot-sizing techniques that can be used to determine production quantities in the master scheduling process. The appropriate choice depends on the demand pattern for the specific product. For example, for products that have a stable demand, the fixed-order quantity lot-sizing techniques of EOQ and EPQ, discussed in Chapter 16, are appropriate. Nevertheless, there are other situations in which we cannot assume stable demand because there are fluctuations due to seasonal needs or changes in customer tastes or expectations. In such situations, there are other variable lot-sizing techniques that can be used. The outputs of this master scheduling process are period-by-period projected on-hand inventory, scheduled production requirements (MPS), and any uncommitted inventory that is physically on hand, referred to as **available-to-promise (ATP) inventory**. The availability of ATP inventory will enable the company's marketing function to generate new customer orders and commit to realistic delivery dates. Let us consider an example to illustrate the inputs, process, and outputs of master scheduling.

EXAMPLE 18.1: Prepare a master production schedule for the Just Plowing Company, a fictitious manufacturer of snow blowers. The demand forecast for these snow blowers for each week of an 8-week schedule is 60 units. The production lot size is 80 units, and production is scheduled in those weeks when the projected on-hand inventory becomes negative (that is, when there are shortages). In addition, the company has the following committed customer orders for the first 4 weeks: 65, 45, 30, and 18. Assume a beginning inventory of 5 snow blowers. Construct a master schedule for the 8-week time horizon.

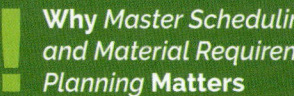

Why *Master Scheduling and Material Requirements Planning* **Matters**

Efficient operational plans can result in the twin benefits of reducing costs and satisfying customers. Aggregate resources specified by S&OP plans are translated into a master production schedule, which is a manufacturing plan for producing the end products. This approach leads to the development of a plan for acquiring the needed materials and capacity to support production of the end products.

Master scheduling: the process that determines the quantities of each end item to be produced in specific periods during a specific planning horizon. The master schedule is essential for all operations planning and control decisions. The master schedule sets the production quantities required to meet demand from every possible source in an organization, such as final customers, warehouses, and requirements from other plants in a multi-plant environment

Master production schedule (MPS): individual production quantities of the end items to be produced at various periods of a given planning horizon

Lot size: the amount of a particular item that is ordered from the plant or a supplier or issued as a standard quantity to the production process

Available-to-promise (ATP) inventory: uncommitted inventory that is physically on hand that can be realistically promised for new customer order deliveries

 Example 18.1

SOLUTION

INPUTS
The inputs to the master schedule for this example are beginning inventory, the forecasts of demand for each of the 8 weeks, and the customer orders for the first 4 weeks. These inputs are shown in Table 18.1.

TABLE 18.1: Partial Master Scheduling Record for the Just Plowing Company Snow Blowers

Beginning inventory in week 1 = 5 units.

WEEK	1	2	3	4	5	6	7	8
Forecast	60	60	60	60	60	60	60	60
Customer Orders	65	45	30	18				

PROCESS
The first step in the master scheduling process is to calculate the projected on-hand inventory for each week of the 8-week schedule until it becomes negative (the limit specified in this example). When the projected on-hand inventory in any week becomes negative, production for that week is scheduled for the given lot-size quantity (MPS = 80 units). No production is scheduled in a period as long as the on-hand inventory in that period is above the specified limit of zero. The following formula is used to calculate the projected on-hand inventory:

$$\text{Projected on-hand inventory} = I_{t-1} + MPS_t - \text{Maximum }(CO_t, F_t)$$

where

I_{t-1} = Ending inventory from week t – 1

MPS_t = Production quantity (lot size) scheduled in week t

CO_t = Customer orders (committed) in week t

F_t = Forecasted demand in week t

For week 1 in our example, the ending inventory from the previous week is the beginning inventory in week 1, or 5 units. As indicated in the formula, we will choose the maximum (larger) of the customer order or forecast in week 1, which is the customer order of 65 units. Because the projected on-hand inventory in week 1 will become negative, production for the lot-size quantity (MPS = 80) should be scheduled in week 1. We use the customer orders because these are actual committed orders as opposed to the estimate of demand given by the forecasted figure. Using forecasts in periods where the customer orders are larger will overestimate the inventory levels in those periods. Therefore,

$$\text{Projected on-hand inventory in week 1} = I_0 + MPS_1 - \text{Maximum }(CO_1, F_1)$$
$$= 5 + 80 - 65 = 20$$

Similarly, for week 2, as the ending inventory from week 1 is 20 units and the larger of the customer order or forecast is the forecast quantity of 60 units, the projected on-hand inventory will become negative. Therefore, production for the MPS quantity of 80 units should also be scheduled for week 2. Note that we use the forecast value (the larger quantity) in this case because it is likely that the customer orders booked in week 2 may not reflect all of the demand that will eventually occur in that week. Thus,

$$\text{Projected on-hand inventory in week 2} = I_1 + MPS_2 - \text{Maximum }(CO_2, F_2)$$
$$= 20 + 80 - 60 = 40$$

Similar calculations are performed for the remaining weeks, and the results are shown in Table 18.2. The projected on-hand inventory that we calculate in preparing a master schedule is a conservative estimate of what the inventory levels will be at the end of each week, based on available information on demand forecasts and customer orders.

TABLE 18.2: Partial Master Scheduling Record for the Just Plowing Company Snow Blowers

Beginning inventory in week 1 = 5 units.

WEEK	1	2	3	4	5	6	7	8
Forecast	60	60	60	60	60	60	60	60
Customer Orders	*65	45	30	18				
MPS	80	80	80	—	80	80	80	—
Projected On-Hand Inventory	20	40	60	0	20	40	60	0

* In computing projected on-hand inventory, the value of customer orders is used because it is greater than the forecasted value.

Note that in Table 18.2, no production was scheduled for weeks 4 and 8 because the inventory from the previous week (3 and 7) of 60 units was sufficient to meet the forecasted demand of 60 units.

The next step in the master scheduling process is to calculate the available-to-promise (ATP) inventories, which are uncommitted inventories that are available to meet any potential future customer orders. For example, at the beginning of week 1, suppose the marketing department asks the master scheduler, the person responsible for developing and implementing the master schedule, whether it should continue to generate additional customer orders for snow blowers. To determine the answer, the master scheduler needs to know if there are any additional uncommitted inventories of snow blowers that are physically available. The formulas for calculating ATP are as follows:

For the first week of the master schedule:

$$ATP_t = I_{t-1} + MPS_t - \sum_{i=t}^{k-1} CO_i$$

For all subsequent weeks in which an MPS is scheduled,

$$ATP_t = MPS_t - \sum_{i=t}^{k-1} CO_i$$

where

I_{t-1} = Ending inventory from week t – 1

MPS_t = Production quantity (lot size) scheduled in week t

$\sum_{i=t}^{k-1} CO_i$ = Sum of all customer orders from week 1 until the next scheduled MPS in week k

Let us calculate ATP using these formulas for Example 18.1. For week 1, the ending inventory from the previous week is 5 units and MPS is 80 units. Because another MPS for 80 units has been scheduled in week 2, the sum of all customer orders until the next MPS (week 2, or k = 2) is the customer order of 65 units in week 1. Therefore,

$$ATP_1 = I_0 + MPS_1 - \sum_{i=1}^{2-1} CO_i = I_0 + MPS_1 - CO_1 = 5 + 80 - 65 = 20 \text{ units}$$

For week 2, because the next MPS occurs in week 3 (k = 3), we have

$$ATP_2 = MPS_2 - \sum_{i=2}^{3-1} CO_i = MPS_2 - CO_2 = 80 - 45 = 35 \text{ units}$$

For week 3, because the next MPS occurs in week 5 (k = 5), we have

$$ATP_2 = MPS_3 - \sum_{i=3}^{5-1} CO_i = MPS_3 - (CO_3 \bullet CO_4) = 80 - (30 + 18) = 32 \text{ units}$$

We can perform ATP calculations for the remaining weeks in a similar manner. The results are shown in Table 18.3.

TABLE 18.3: Complete Master Scheduling Record for the Just Plowing Company Snow Blowers

WEEK*	1	2	3	4	5	6	7	8
Forecast	60	60	60	60	60	60	60	60
Customer Orders	65	45	30	18				
MPS	80	80	80	0	80	80	80	0
Projected On-Hand Inventory	20	40	60	0	20	40	60	0
Available-to-Promise	20	35	32	—	80	80	80	—

*Beginning inventory in week 1 = 5 units.

Note that in Table 18.3, for weeks 4 and 8, as no production quantity is scheduled (MPS = 0), the ATP records for those weeks are left blank. Also, for weeks 5, 6, and 7, as there are no customer orders, the entire 80 units of production scheduled is ATP, the uncommitted inventories available for meeting customer orders. Yet, when sales representatives accept customer orders for these weeks, the values would be entered in the master schedule, and the values for both the projected on-hand inventories and ATPs would be updated.

Functions of the Master Schedule

Functions of a
Master Schedule

The master schedule is the basis for all short-term operations planning and control activities. It performs the following functions.

DISAGGREGATION OF THE SALES AND OPERATIONS (AGGREGATE) PLANS

The sales and operations plan sets the overall, aggregate, medium-term production output levels, set for product families or expressed in dollar volumes. Nonetheless, medium-term plans are future forecasts of expectations. As these medium-term plans become current, the aggregate plans need to be broken down (disaggregated) into specific quantities of end items to be produced or actual services to be offered. This disaggregation process is performed by the master schedule within the resource constraints (such as labor and machine hours or materials) established by aggregate plans. For example, suppose that Just Plowing Company in Example 18.1 has an aggregate plan that calls for a product family of 300 snow blowers in January and 400 in February. Just Plowing Company's family of snow blowers consists of single-stage electric snow blowers, single-stage gas snow blowers, two-stage gas snow blowers, and tractor-mounted snow blowers. Thus the 300 and 400 aggregate snow blowers to be produced in the months of January and February must be translated into specific types of snow blowers to be produced for each of these months. During the master scheduling process, the planners disaggregate the product families prior to actually purchasing the required materials and parts, scheduling production, and planning for the inventory requirements for each type of snow blower. Table 18.4 shows the master schedule for the four types of snow blowers that flow from the aggregate plan for a family of snow blowers.

Although aggregate plans have a longer time horizon (typically between 12 and 18 months), the master schedule disaggregates only a portion of the aggregate plan. That is, the breakdown of the aggregate plan in the master scheduling process occurs in stages with a time horizon that may range from 4 to 13 weeks. For instance, the Just Plowing Company in our example would likely revise its master schedule at the end of January to reflect changes that may occur in forecasts or customer orders for February, and it may include any planned production for March.

EVALUATION OF CAPACITY REQUIREMENTS

The outcome of the master scheduling process is a tentative master schedule. To establish the feasibility of this tentative master schedule, it is critical that there are sufficient capacities of labor, suppliers, and production and warehouse facilities. The process of verifying that sufficient capacity resources are

TABLE 18.4: Disaggregation of the Aggregate Plan by the Master Schedule

MONTH	JANUARY				FEBRUARY			
Aggregate Plan Total quantity of snow blowers	300				400			
Weeks	1	2	3	4	5	6	7	8
Master Schedule Type of snow blower to be produced								
Single-stage electric snow blower	50					50		
Single-stage gas snow blower		50		50		50		50
Two-stage gas snow blower			100		100		100	
Tractor-mounted snow blower				50				50

available to meet the capacity requirements of the tentative master schedule is called *rough-cut capacity planning* (RCCP). During the RCCP process, the capacity available for each key resource is compared with the amount of each resource required to meet the tentative master scheduling requirements.

GENERATION OF MATERIAL REQUIREMENTS

The master schedule specifies what and how many end products are to be produced and when. Once the master schedule is set, it initiates the next planning stage of material requirements planning (MRP). For example, the fictional Just Plowing Company is planning to manufacture 100 units of its two-stage gas snow blower in the third week of January (see Table 18.4). To verify that the required units of snow blowers can be produced, materials and critical parts must first be purchased from a vendor or produced in-house. The MRP for purchase or production of materials and components will be discussed in Section 18.3.

FACILITATION OF INFORMATION PROCESSING

The effectiveness of a master schedule depends on how well it interfaces with the other functional areas of a company, such as operations and marketing. By providing up-to-date information on capacity availability, inventory, and production schedules, the master schedule enables production to effectively use its capacity and marketing to meet its customer demand. In addition, by providing timely information when customer demand cannot be met by existing capacity, a master schedule enables production and marketing to negotiate with customers to defer due dates on order deliveries. By generating these exception reports, the master schedule provides top management the necessary information to determine whether corporate objectives will be achieved.

Master Schedule Planning Horizon and Replanning

The appropriate time intervals and planning horizons used in master scheduling are determined by the type, volume, and component lead times of the products being produced. For products whose purchase or production lead times are short and can be assembled quickly, the master schedule has weekly time intervals and the planning horizon typically ranges from 4 to 13 weeks (monthly to quarterly). On the other hand, for complex products, such as jet engines or medical devices, the purchase, production, and assembly lead times of the components and the product are long. As a result, the master schedule typically operates using monthly "time buckets" (the time intervals used for MRP planning) and the planning horizon can range from several months to more than a year.

As the planning process progresses over time, customer orders are met, and new demand information is generated, the master schedule needs to be updated. This updating is done on a rolling schedule, where the impact of the actual transactions on the master schedule is captured from one period to the next. For instance, after week 1, Just Plowing Company (in Example 18.1) would update its master schedule for snow blowers by developing a schedule for weeks 2 through 9. Similarly, after capturing the actual transactions in week 2, the master schedule would be updated to cover weeks 3 through 10 and so on.

Material requirements planning (MRP): a computer-based system that translates the end item requirements of the master schedule into subassemblies, components, and raw materials. Given the due date, MRP works backward by using lead times and other information to determine when and how much of the materials to order

Rolling schedule: updating the schedule when moving forward in time by capturing the impact of actual transactions on the master schedule from one period to the next

As an example of a make-to-order product, Lamborghini's Veneno Roadster has a 750 horsepower engine, goes from 0 to 60 in 2.9 seconds, and costs $4.5 million. The company plans to make only nine of them in 2015.

Claudio Villa/Getty Images News/ Getty Images .

Achieving Master Schedule Stability

A stable master schedule will lead to more orderly purchasing of components and production schedules. Planners have to be aware that frequent changes to a master schedule, particularly the early portions of the schedule, can be disruptive. These changes often reduce the efficiency of the production process. On the other hand, a rigid master schedule with too few opportunities to make changes may suggest that the company is not responding to customer demand, leading to poor customer service and the increased costs from excess inventory. Therefore, companies need to strike an appropriate balance between flexibility and rigidity by preparing a stable master schedule. Companies with an effective master schedule use the process of *time fencing* to achieve this stability. In the time fencing approach, the master schedule time horizon is divided into three portions: frozen time fence, slushy time fence, and flexible time fence (Figure 18.2).

The frozen time fence describes the portion of the master schedule in which no changes to the schedule can be accommodated unless a senior executive requests such changes. The time fence is considered frozen because delivering new customer orders is virtually impossible this quickly without resorting to very costly options, such as expedited procurement of materials, expedited production and shipping, or postponing the delivery date of another customer order. The length of the frozen time fence typically encompasses the cumulative lead times needed to procure the materials for the product, produce the item, and ship the end product. In the slushy time fence portion, changes to the master schedule may require trade-offs, but because the timeframe is further out into the future, these trade-offs are usually less disruptive. The master scheduler typically has the authority to accept new customer orders in this stage. Order entries in this stage are initiated as long as the required materials and components are readily available or can be procured, and the master scheduler is reasonably confident that the required order delivery dates can be met. The flexible time fence is that portion of the master schedule time horizon that is farthest out in the future. In this time window, the company can easily accommodate cancellations of existing orders and fill new customer orders. The customer order delivery dates during this stage are tentative and will be confirmed at a later date when these orders enter the frozen portion of the master schedule. Time fencing and rules are key features of the master scheduling process and should be strictly adhered to and communicated throughout the company for the process to be effective.

Relationship Between the Master Schedule and the Production Environment

In Chapter 9, we found that, depending on the degree of customization, manufacturing processes can be classified into four categories: make-to-stock (MTS), assemble-to-order (ATO), make-to-order (MTO), and engineer-to-order (ETO). A company's approach to master scheduling will vary depending on which of the four production environments it operates within:

- In a *make-to-stock* (MTS) production environment in which standardized products such as soft drinks, cereals, or light bulbs are produced repetitively in high volume, master scheduling is conducted at the finished or end-product level. The focus of master scheduling will be on producing the finished goods to meet the inventory and customer service target levels. The production process used to produce these items can be a continuous, repetitive, or batch process.

Frozen time fence: the portion of the master schedule in which no changes to the schedule can be accommodated unless a senior executive requests such changes

Slushy time fence: changes to the master schedule may require trade-offs, but because the timeframe is further out into the future, these trade-offs are usually less costly and disruptive

Flexible time fence: the portion of the master schedule time horizon that is farthest out in the future and changes can be easily accommodated

FIGURE 18.2: Time Fences in Master Scheduling

WEEK								
1	2	3	4	5	6	7	8	9
Frozen Time Fence			Slushy Time Fence			Flexible Time Fence		

- In an *assemble-to-order* (ATO) environment, typical of products such as computers or high-priced sports cars where the product is often assembled after receiving the customer order, master scheduling occurs in two stages. At the first stage, the master scheduling process focuses on producing standardized modules or major subassemblies of the product based on forecasted demand. At the second stage of the process, after receiving the customer orders, a final assembly schedule focuses on assembling modules or subassemblies into different configurations of the finished products that will meet the specific customer requirements. For example, you can order an automobile with or without a sunroof, an option, or a fast-food restaurant can assemble a hamburger for you with or without cheese.

This heat-exchange boiler has been custom-built for an oil refinery and is an example of an engineer-to-order product.

Rui Saraiva / Alamy Stock Photo

- In a *make-to-order* (MTO) environment, production begins only after an actual customer order is received for a specific product. In this environment, as products are produced to meet specific customer requirements, the focus of the master scheduling process is to acquire required raw materials to produce the product to meet customer requirements, allow sufficient lead time, and reach customer service targets. Examples of products produced in a make-to-order environment include airplanes or luxury yachts.
- In an *engineer-to-order* (ETO) environment, products are custom-designed and built to very specific customer requirements. These products have a unique engineering design and require significant customization. The firm may need to purchase new or unique materials to manufacture them. Companies operating in an ETO environment typically have high product variety and low volumes of product demand. In such project-oriented production processes, project networks, Gantt charts, and project milestones are used to facilitate master scheduling. Examples of ETO products include large industrial engines and centrifugal slurry pumps that are used in the mining industry.

18.2 Material Requirements Planning

Once the master schedule is set, the next stage of operational planning decisions is material requirements planning (MRP; see Figure 18.1). MRP is vital for companies that produce finished products from purchased or manufactured components because they need a systematic method of planning for their material and capacity requirements. Recall that the MPS record in the master schedule shows the *quantities* of independent demand items to be produced in the various time periods. It is now necessary to plan for the production or purchase of components and materials (dependent demand items) required to produce the final products. This is the task of the MRP system. MRP is a computerized ordering and scheduling system that converts the end-product requirements specified by the MPS record of the master scheduling system into time-phased requirements for raw materials, components, and subassemblies. Beginning with due dates for the end items, and using information about lead times and inventory, MRP works backward to determine the quantity and timing for acquiring dependent demand items. Specifically, MRP determines:

1. What components and materials are needed for the final products and the quantities required to produce, fabricate, or assemble those end items.
2. When (on what date) these components and materials should be ordered from an outside supplier or produced from an in-house production facility.

Thus, the MRP system, by using the end-item requirements generated by the master schedule, triggers the lower level requirements for components and materials, which are then scheduled (usually weekly) so that purchasing, fabrication, and assembly can be set to produce the products when they are needed. **Time phasing** is the process of scheduling and describing the receipt of inventories of materials, components, subassemblies, and finished products as they are needed over time. With time phasing logic, as materials, components, and subassemblies are to be made available only when they are needed, the MRP system keeps inventory levels low. Hence, MRP is not only a production planning and

18.2

Explain the conditions under which MRP is appropriate, its inputs, processing, and outputs, as well as its benefits and limitations.

Material Requirements Planning

Time phasing: the process of scheduling and describing the receipt of inventories of materials, components, subassemblies, and finished products as they are needed over time

scheduling system but also an inventory control system. It is most useful in production environments in which different products that have a complex manufacturing sequence are produced. Specifically, MRP works best in manufacturing environments in which demand for many components and subassemblies (dependent demand items) depends on the demands of final products (independent demand items). On the other hand, it is not very useful in a job-shop or when continuous processes are tightly linked.

MRP Terminology

Before we discuss MRP in detail, it is helpful to define some terms used in an MRP record or data file:

- *Gross requirements*: The total expected requirements for raw materials, components, subassemblies, or finished goods from all sources regardless of the amount of on-hand inventory. Gross requirements should also include parts used for service and maintenance.

- *Net requirements*: These are amounts actually needed. They are obtained by subtracting the item's on-hand inventory from the gross requirements.

- *Parent and component items*: A parent is an assembly composed of a group of basic parts or components. A parent at one level of the product structure hierarchy can be a component of a higher level parent.

- *MRP explosion*: The process of breaking down or exploding the requirements of a parent item at one level into its component requirements at the next level. The purpose is to plan and schedule the purchase or production of each of these components individually.

- *Time phasing*: It is the process of scheduling to produce or purchase the right amounts of components or materials as they are needed over time. The time phasing logic is critical to an MRP system, because it makes products available only in those time periods in which they are needed, not before or after.

- *Time buckets*: The time intervals used for MRP planning. Time buckets are usually measured in weeks, but they can be as long as months, depending on the parent-component lead time sequence, which is the cumulative time required to acquire the components and produce or assemble the parent item.

- *Lead-time offset*: The elapsed time between placing an order for production or purchase of an item and the receipt of that item.

- *Scheduled receipt*: It is the time at which materials that have already been ordered (open orders) from a vendor or an in-house production facility will be received. MRP will show both the quantity and projected time of the receipt of these orders.

- *On-hand inventory:* This is the projected available inventory for an item at the beginning of each period. On-hand inventory includes inventory leftover from the previous period and any scheduled receipts.

- *Lot size*: The quantity of an order for an item that is either purchased from a vendor or produced in an in-house production facility.

- *Planned order receipt*: An order quantity that is expected to be received at a specified future date. Unlike scheduled receipts, planned order receipts are orders that have not yet been released.

- *Planned order release*: The date at which an order quantity for an item will be released to a vendor or an in-house production facility. It is derived from planned order receipts by taking into account the lead time required for delivery of the item.[3]

MRP Inputs, Process, and Outputs

Figure 18.3 shows an overview of the MRP system and identifies the major inputs and the outputs generated. We will discuss each of these topics in more detail.

MRP INPUTS

The three major inputs to an MRP system are the quantities generated in the master production schedule, the bill of materials file, and the inventory status file.

FIGURE 18.3: Overview of an MRP System

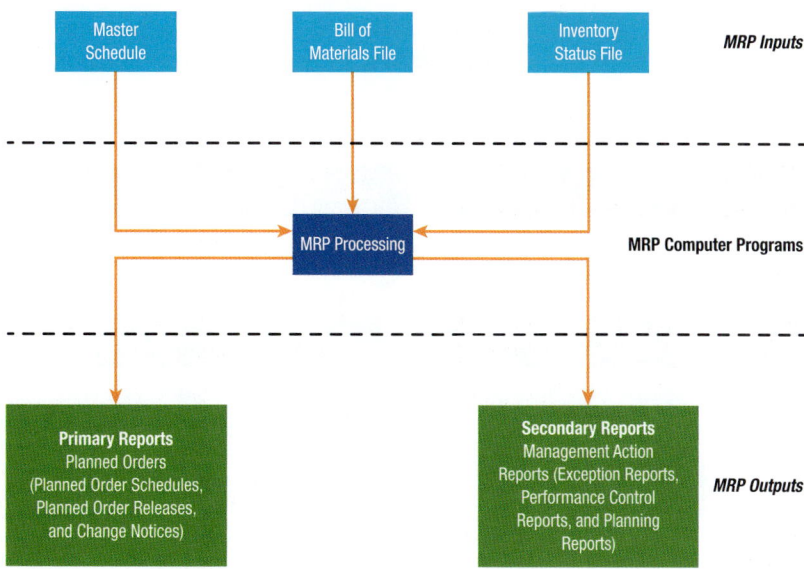

THE MASTER SCHEDULE

The first and primary input to an MRP system is the master schedule. Recall that the master production schedule (MPS) record specifies what end items are to be produced, in what quantities they are to be produced, and when they are needed. The MPS quantities are calculated based on information from several sources, such as forecasts and customer orders for end products, warehouse orders, interplant orders, and safety stock requirements. Given these inputs for end-item requirements and their lead times, the MRP system converts these requirements into individual time-phased component and material requirements.

THE BILL OF MATERIALS FILE

A bill of materials (BOM) file is a computerized data file that contains the complete listing of all assemblies, subassemblies, parts and components, and raw materials needed and the manufacturing and assembly sequence to produce one unit of a finished product. Thus, each finished product has its own unique BOM file. A BOM file is organized as a hierarchy with the finished product at the top of the hierarchy. Each subsequent level of the hierarchy shows the quantities of each item needed to produce one unit of the parent item above it.

The BOM file assigns each component a unique part number and identifies products in a very precise and unambiguous manner, and, as a result, the component requirements to produce each product are clearly delineated. The BOM file facilitates MRP processing by expanding or exploding the end item into its components. A product structure tree is a useful way to represent the BOM file that shows the product hierarchy and the explosion into its parts. A product structure tree represents the components and subassemblies required to assemble an end product. Figure 18.4 on page 652 shows a product structure tree for a wheelbarrow, and Figure 18.5 shows a more sophisticated bill of materials (BOM) structure for a children's wagon. Note the extensiveness of the BOM file for even a relatively simple product such as a wagon and consider how much more expansive the BOM file would be for more sophisticated, larger, or more technical products.

Let us examine the product structure for a wheelbarrow shown in Figure 18.4. You can see that the end-product wheelbarrow, the subassemblies, and components are all identified by unique part numbers (WB999, 1070, 1022, etc.). In addition, the tree also shows the quantities required to assemble each parent item. For example, to assemble the wheelbarrow, we require one can of paint, one wheel assembly, one handlebar assembly, and one box. Similarly, each wheel assembly requires one axle, one wheel, and two bearings. Each handlebar assembly requires two bars and two grips, and, finally, each wheel requires one tire. These subassembly and component requirements are listed with a product structure code in a hierarchy beginning with zero for the end product, one for the next level, and so on.

Bill of materials (BOM): a computerized data file that contains the complete listing of all assemblies, subassemblies, parts and components, and raw materials needed and the manufacturing and assembly sequence to produce one unit of a finished product

Product structure tree: a way to represent the BOM file that shows the product hierarchy and the explosion into its parts

FIGURE 18.4: Product Structure Tree for a Wheelbarrow

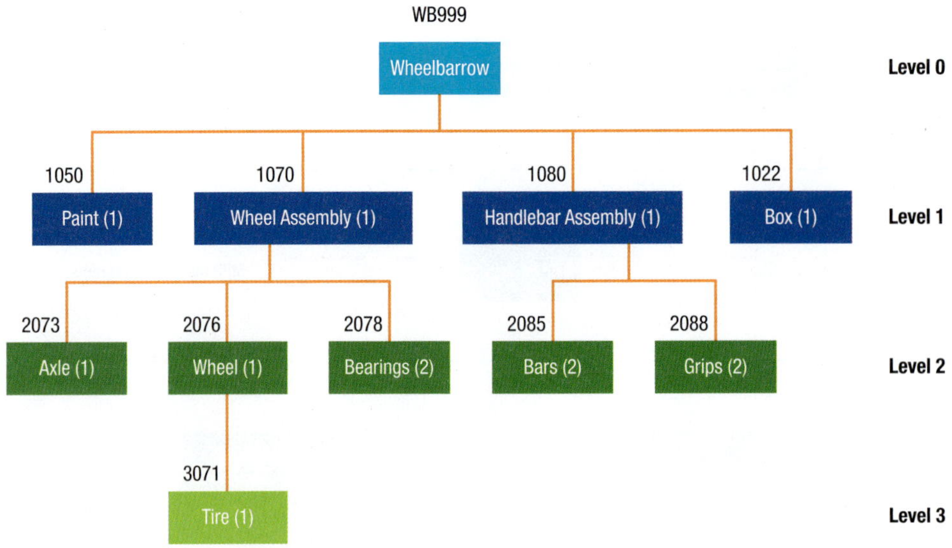

FIGURE 18.5: Bill of Materials for Wagon Production

Component ID	Description	Type	Total Qty	UM	Fixed Qty	Overage %
1080-000	Red Wagon	BOM	1	EA	☐	0
8720-010	Sheet Metal. 10 gauge. 2.5 x 4. stainless	Item	1	EA	☐	0
8110-010	Paint. Red	Item	0.25	GAL	☐	0
1081-100	Front Undercarriage Assembly	BOM	1	EA	☐	0
1081-110	Wheel Assembly - Front	BOM	1	EA	☐	0
1081-200	Bracket. front. steering	Item	1	EA	☐	0
1081-240	Axel Rod. 15 inch	Item	1	EA	☐	0
1081-250	Axel cap, red	Item	2	EA	☐	0
1081-260	Wheel Standard. metal hub. rubber tire	Item	2	EA	☐	0
1081-130	Handle Assembly	BOM	1	EA	☐	0
1081-220	Handle Bar. metal	Item	1	EA	☐	0
1081-230	Handle Grip. metal	Item	1	EA	☐	0
8420-010	Bolt 1/4 x 1. stainless	Item	1	EA	☐	0
8430-010	Nut. 1/4. stainless	Item	1	EA	☐	0
8440-010	Washer. 1/4. stainless	Item	1	EA	☐	0
8410-020	Cotter Pin. 2 inch. stainless	Item	1	EA	☐	0
8420-010	Bolt 1/4 x 1. stainless	Item	2	EA	☐	0
8430-010	Nut. 1/4. stainless	Item	2	EA	☐	0
8440-010	Washer. 1/4. stainless	Item	2	EA	☐	0
1081-120	Wheel Assembly - Rear	BOM	1	EA	☐	0
1081-210	Bracket. rear	Item	1	EA	☐	0
1081-260	Wheel Standard. metal hub. rubber tire	Item	2	EA	☐	0
1081-250	Axel cap, red	Item	2	EA	☐	0
1081-240	Axel Rod. 15 inch	Item	1	EA	☐	0
8420-010	Bolt 1/4 x 1. stainless	Item	8	EA	☐	0
8440-010	Washer. 1/4. stainless	Item	8	EA	☐	0
8430-010	Nut. 1/4. stainless	Item	8	EA	☐	0
1081-270	Decal Set. wagon	Item	1	EA	☐	0

SOURCE: Reprinted from http://3.bp.blogspot.com/-H-X1520sVGl/T5dla15Bgol/AAAAAAAAw8/secWkmZclPo/s1600/Bill+of+Material+Setup.png

The quantities of materials at each level in the product structure tree refer only to the amounts needed to complete the assembly at the next higher level. This type of hierarchical arrangement of materials is called *low-level coding*, which defines the sequence in which all materials are planned in an MRP run. In low-level coding, a particular material or component may be used in several products and may appear in more than one level of the product structure hierarchy. By entering products in this way, the total requirements for a material are grouped at the lowest level in which the material appears.

As a result, the total requirements for any given material or component will only be planned after all assemblies or products in which it occurs have been planned and determined.

EXAMPLE 18.2: The final assembly of a chair requires a leg assembly, a seat, and a back assembly. Each leg assembly requires two legs and a cross bar. Each back assembly requires two side rails, one cross bar, and three back supports. Given this information:

 a. Construct a product structure tree for the chair using low-level coding.

 b. Determine the quantities of assemblies and components that will be required to assemble 10 chairs, given the following on-hand inventory:

Leg assemblies = 2; back assembly = 1; legs = 4; cross bars = 6; side rails = 4; and back supports = 10.

SOLUTION

 a. The product structure tree for the finished chair is shown in Figure 18.6.

FIGURE 18.6: Product Structure Tree for a Chair

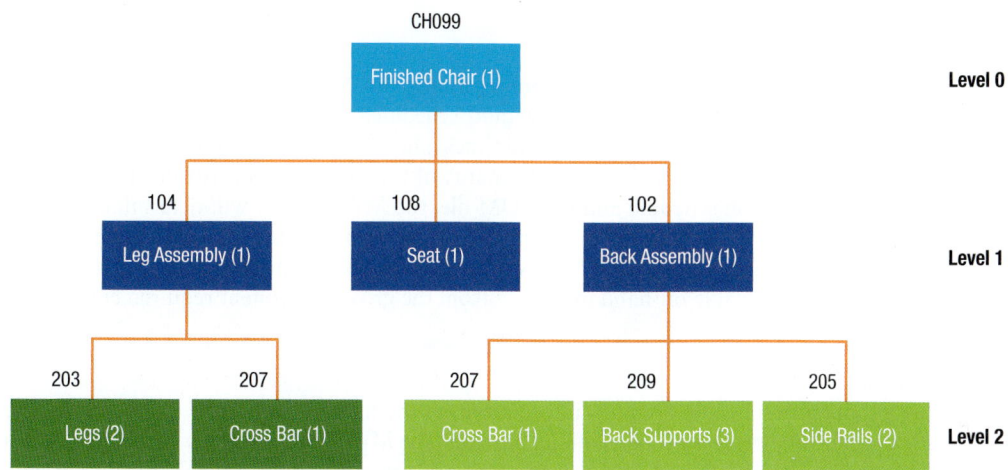

 b. The product structure tree for 10 finished chairs, given the amounts of on-hand inventory, is shown in Figure 18.7.

FIGURE 18.7: Product Structure Tree for Example 18.2b

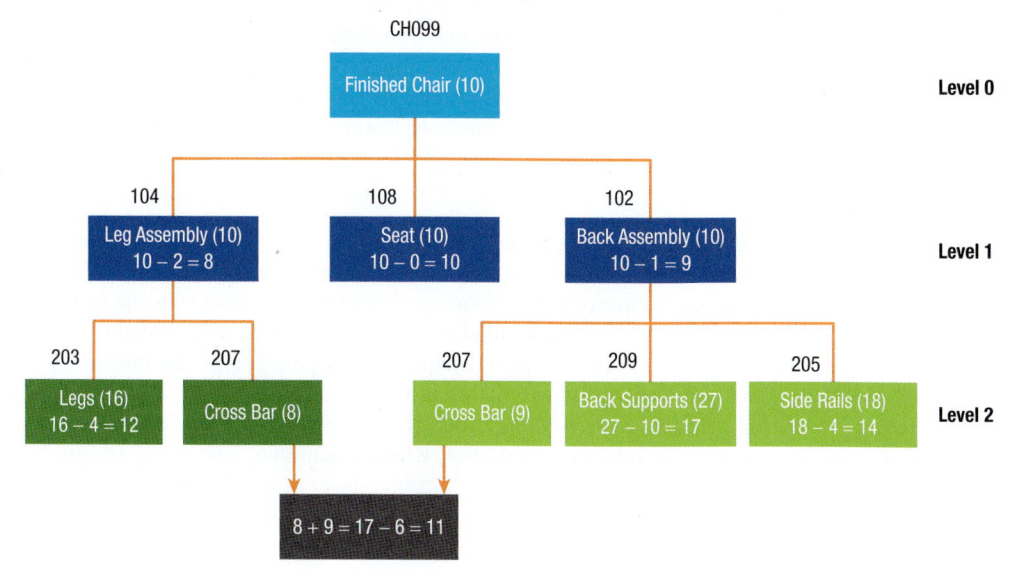

Thus, given the amounts of on-hand inventory, 10 finished chairs will require

Leg assemblies: 8

Seats: 10

Back assemblies: 9

Legs: 12

Cross bars: 11

Back supports: 17

Side rails: 14

This example demonstrates that the bill of materials (BOM) file reflects the composition of a product. Therefore, it is important that the BOM file is accurate. In determining quantity requirements of components for product assembly, errors in any level of the product structure tree are magnified because of the multiplication process. Without accurate BOM records, it is impossible to determine exact material and component requirements needed for the effective functioning of an MRP system.

c. *The inventory status file.*

The third input to an MRP system is the inventory status file, which contains the records of all items in inventory, including on-hand inventory and scheduled receipts. The inventory status file also contains information about the supplier, lead times, and lot size policy for each item. As materials are received in inventory or withdrawn, the status of the inventory records must be updated. From the master production schedule and the BOM file, the MRP system will determine the gross component requirements of materials and components for each production level. Based on the inventory status file, the MRP system determines the net requirements for each component or material by subtracting the available on-hand inventory from the gross component requirements (just as we did in Example 18.2).

MRP PROCESS

The master production schedule provides information on the number of units required for an end product for specific time periods of the planning horizon. The MRP system accepts these end-product requirements from the master schedule and then gathers information from the BOM file on the components needed to assemble the end product. In addition, the MRP system also accesses information on the available inventory for both finished products and the various components. Using this information, the MRP system calculates the gross and net requirements of all components and materials at each level of the product structure tree. This process, which we referred to as MRP explosion, begins with the end product—the top level of the product structure tree. The net requirements of the parent-level item are first determined before moving down to the next level of the hierarchy, representing subassemblies and components. After determining the component requirements at each lower level, taking into account lead time, the MRP system determines the dates for ordering materials so that they arrive when needed. Note that planned order releases for components at one level in turn generate requirements for materials at the next immediate lower level. Let us illustrate the MRP processing logic with an example.

Inventory status file: contains the records of all items in inventory, including on-hand inventory and scheduled receipts

MRP explosion: the process by which the MRP system calculates the gross and net requirements of all components and materials at each level of the product structure tree

EXAMPLE 18.3: Suppose a firm producing wheelbarrows has customer orders with delivery due dates of 50 in week 1, 70 in week 4, 70 in week 6, and 40 in week 8. Refer back to Figure 18.4 for the product structure tree for a wheelbarrow. The product structure tree shows that the subassemblies required for each wheelbarrow are one handlebar assembly and one wheel assembly. Each wheel assembly requires one tire. Prepare a material requirements plan for the handlebar assemblies, wheel assemblies, and tires for an 8-week planning horizon. The end-item master schedule for the customer orders for wheelbarrows, and the order quantities, lead times, scheduled receipts, and on-hand inventories for the handlebar assemblies, wheel assemblies, and tires, are given in Table 18.5.

TABLE 18.5: End-Item Master Schedule for Wheelbarrows: Customer Orders

WEEK	1	2	3	4	5	6	7	8
Customer Orders	50			70		70		40

SUBASSEMBLY/COMPONENT	ORDER QUANTITY	LEAD TIME (IN WEEKS)	ON-HAND INVENTORY
Handlebar assemblies*	200	3	120
Wheel assemblies	300	4	200
Paint	300	1	250
Box	200	1	250
Tires	500	1	100

* A shipment of 200 handlebar assemblies is scheduled to be received at the beginning of week 3.

SOLUTION

Step 1: Begin with the time-phased end-item requirements from the master schedule. The requirements for wheelbarrows obtained from the master schedule are: 50 in week 1, 70 in week 4, 70 in week 6, and 40 in week 8.

Step 2: By using the information from the product's BOM file and the inventory status file, explode the net end-item requirements into gross and net requirements for components in a level-by-level manner into a time-phased schedule. Remember that net requirements are the gross requirements minus on-hand inventory plus any scheduled receipts.

We will use the product structure tree for a wheelbarrow (Figure 18.4), which provides its BOM information, to conduct the MRP explosion process.

From Figure 18.4 and the on-hand inventory information, we determine the gross and net requirements for handlebar assemblies, wheel assemblies, paint, box, and tires. One unit of a wheelbarrow requires one handlebar assembly and one wheel assembly, one paint, and one box. Because there are no inventories in stock for wheelbarrows and we need to produce 50 units of wheelbarrows in week 1, we compute the level 1 subassembly requirements of handlebar and wheel assemblies as shown:

WEEK 1: LEVEL 1 REQUIREMENTS: HANDLEBAR ASSEMBLIES

Each wheelbarrow requires one handlebar assembly. Therefore, to satisfy the required 50 wheelbarrows, the gross requirements for:

$$\text{Handlebar assemblies: } 50 \times 1 = 50$$

Since we already have 120 handlebar assemblies on hand, the net requirements are 0.

WEEK 1: LEVEL 1 REQUIREMENTS: WHEEL ASSEMBLIES

Each wheelbarrow requires one wheel assembly. To satisfy the requirements for 50 wheelbarrows, the gross requirements for:

$$\text{Wheel assemblies: } 50 \times 1 = 50$$

Since we already have 200 wheel assemblies on hand, the net requirements are 0.

Similarly, as we have 250 units of paint and 250 boxes on hand, the net requirements for these level 1 items are zero for the entire 8-week planning horizon.

The MRP explosion process for week 1 stops at level 1 because all requirements to assemble the 50 wheelbarrows have been met. Consequently, it is not necessary to activate the material plans for the lower level components (levels 2 and 3), because all the higher level requirements of the parent items have been met. At the end of week 1, assuming that the customer orders of 50 wheelbarrows have been delivered, the on-hand inventories of the relevant products, subassemblies, and components are: wheelbarrows = 0; handlebar assemblies = 120 – 50 = 70; and wheel assemblies = 200 – 50 = 150.

The week 1 material requirements plans for handlebar assemblies and wheel assemblies are calculated next.

HANDLEBAR ASSEMBLIES

TABLE 18.6: End-Item Master Schedule for Wheelbarrows: Customer Orders

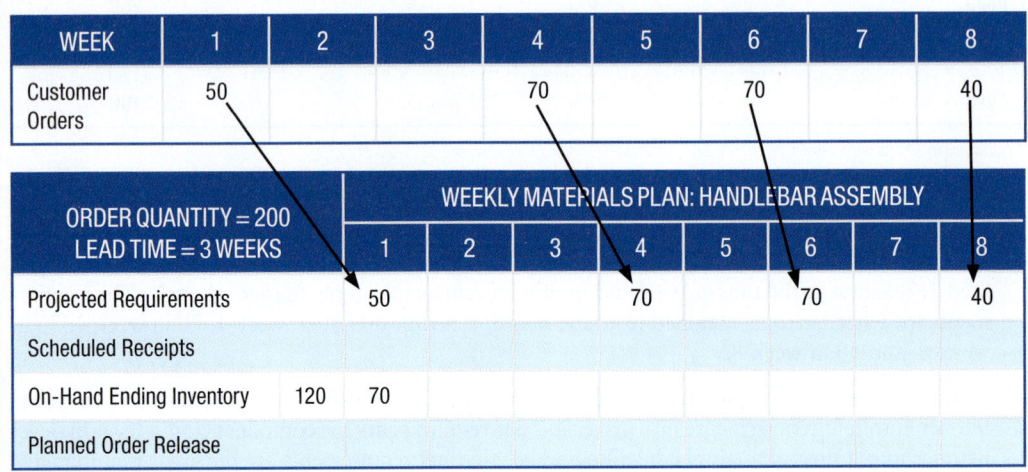

WHEEL ASSEMBLIES

TABLE 18.7: End-Item Master Schedule for Wheelbarrows: Customer Orders

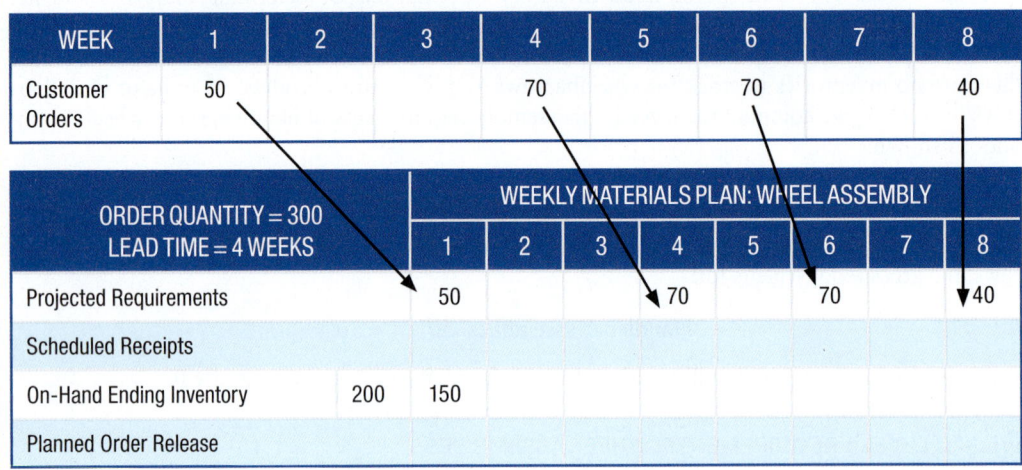

WEEKS 2 TO 8: LEVEL 1 REQUIREMENTS: HANDLEBAR ASSEMBLIES

There is no demand for wheelbarrows in weeks 2 and 3, and, therefore, the materials plan for handlebar assemblies remains unchanged except for the scheduled receipt of 200 handlebar assemblies at the beginning of week 3. With this additional inventory of 200 handlebar assemblies, no further changes (other than in the on-hand inventory record) will occur in the materials plan for handlebar assemblies for the remaining weeks of the 8-week planning horizon. The updated materials plan for handlebar assemblies for the entire 8-week planning horizon is given in Table 18.8.

TABLE 18.8: Updated Materials Plan for Handlebar Assembly

ORDER QUANTITY = 200 LEAD TIME = 3 WEEKS	WEEKLY MATERIALS PLAN: HANDLEBAR ASSEMBLY							
	1	2	3	4	5	6	7	8
Projected Requirements	50			70		70		40
Scheduled Receipts			200					
On-Hand Ending Inventory	120	70	70	270	200	200	130	130	90
Planned Order Release								

WEEKS 2 TO 8: LEVEL 1 REQUIREMENTS: WHEEL ASSEMBLIES

There is no demand for wheelbarrows in weeks 2 and 3, therefore, the materials plan for wheel assemblies remains unchanged for these two weeks. There is a demand for 70 wheel assemblies in weeks 4 and 7. Nevertheless, the on-hand inventory of 150 units is sufficient to meet those requirements. The updated partial materials plan for wheel assemblies for the first 7 weeks of the 8-week planning horizon is given in Table 18.9.

TABLE 18.9: Updated Materials Plan for Wheel Assembly

ORDER QUANTITY = 300 LEAD TIME = 4 WEEKS	WEEKLY MATERIALS PLAN: WHEEL ASSEMBLY							
	1	2	3	4	5	6	7	8
Projected Requirements	50			70		70		40
Scheduled Receipts								
On-Hand Ending Inventory	200	150	150	150	80	80	10	10	-30
Planned Order Release								

Step 3: If the net requirement for any end item, subassembly, or component cannot be met, then a planned order release should be generated by taking into account the lead-time offset. In other words, the date at which an order quantity for an item will be released to a vendor or an in-house production facility should be set after taking into account the lead time required for delivery of the item when it is needed.

Note that in week 8 we have a demand for 40 wheel assemblies. Thus, given that wheel assemblies have a lead time of 4 weeks, an order release for the lot size of 300 units should have been placed at the beginning of week 4. If it were not, there will not be enough wheel assemblies in stock to meet the requirement of 40 units in week 8. To correct this potential shortfall, we will set a planned order release of 300 units at the beginning of week 4. The updated materials plan for wheel assemblies for the entire 8-week planning horizon that reflects these changes is shown in Table 18.10.

TABLE 18.10: Updated Materials Plan for Wheel Assembly for Full 8 Weeks

ORDER QUANTITY = 300 LEAD TIME = 4 WEEKS	WEEKLY MATERIALS PLAN: WHEEL ASSEMBLY							
	1	2	3	4	5	6	7	8
Projected Requirements	50			70		70		40
Scheduled Receipts								300
On-Hand Ending Inventory	200	150	150	150	80	80	10	10	270 ~~-30~~
Planned Order Release				300				

Step 4: Generate requirements for lower level components based on the planned order releases for the parent item at the immediate higher level.

WEEK 1 TO 8: LEVEL 3 REQUIREMENTS: TIRES

We now prepare the materials plan for tires, which is at level 3 of the product structure hierarchy. Because we met the requirements for the tires' higher level parent items during the first 2 weeks of the 8-week planning horizon, the materials plan for this component was not activated. Nevertheless, the planned order release of 300 wheel assemblies in week 4 generates the requirement for wheels (level 2), and, in turn, the requirement for tires (level 3). Because tires have a delivery lead time of 1 week and should be available at the beginning of week 4 to be ready for the wheel assembly, a planned order release of 500 units (order quantity lot size) should be placed at the beginning of week 3. The complete material requirements plan for the 8-week planning horizon is shown in Table 18.11.

TABLE 18.11: Complete Materials Requirements Plan

ORDER QUANTITY = 300 LEAD TIME = 4 WEEKS	WEEKLY MATERIALS PLAN: WHEEL ASSEMBLY							
	1	2	3	4	5	6	7	8
Projected Requirements	50			70		70		40
Scheduled Receipts								300
On-Hand Ending Inventory 200	150	150	150	80	80	10	10	270 -30
Planned Order Release				300				

ORDER QUANTITY = 500 LEAD TIME = 1 WEEK	WEEKLY MATERIALS PLAN: TIRES							
	1	2	3	4	5	6	7	8
Projected Requirements				300				
Scheduled Receipts				500				
Projected On-Hand Inventory 100	100	100	100	300 -200	300	300	300	300
Planned Order Release			500					

The computations and steps in the MRP process require simple arithmetic, and although they can be cumbersome, they are not complicated. Yet, if a product has a complex structure, as is the case when a given component is used in different stages of the production of an end item or used by multiple end items, the BOM file must be exploded carefully. In Example 18.3, suppose the order quantity of 300 wheel assemblies needed in period 6 also includes 100 wheel assemblies for another end product (for example, a garden tractor). The planned order releases need to account not only for the wheel assemblies required for the wheelbarrows, but also for those required for the garden tractors. In situations in which a component is required in different parent items, the **pegging capability** of the MRP system can identify the particular parent item that has generated the component requirements for that item. In addition, the MRP system's pegging capability will enable managers to identify which end products would be most affected as a result of problems such as late deliveries or poor quality. The MRP process appears simple enough when applied to a single end item. Nonetheless, a typical firm produces many different end products, and each may have its own unique set of components. Creating material requirements plans for all these end items will require a computerized MRP system in which all the MRP records (on-hand inventory, scheduled receipts, and planned order releases) can be quickly and efficiently updated as changes and rescheduling occur.

Pegging capability: can identify the particular parent item that has generated the component requirements for that item

MRP OUTPUTS

MRP systems can generate a range of outputs that can be classified into two categories: primary reports and secondary reports (see Figure 18.3). The three primary output reports are the planned order schedules, the planned order releases, and changes to planned orders.

Planned order schedules: These are schedules that delineate the quantity and timing of future material orders.

Planned order releases: These reports authorize the execution of the planned orders.

Changes to planned orders: Changes to planned orders might include cancellations of orders or revisions of the order quantity or due dates.

The three secondary output reports are performance control reports, planning reports, and exception reports.

Performance control reports: These are reports that managers can use to track problems such as missed delivery dates and stock-outs to evaluate MRP system performance. These reports also provide information to assess the manufacturing system's cost performance.

Planning reports: These are reports that can be used to forecast future inventory requirements. They may also include purchase commitments and other information that can be used to evaluate future material requirements.

Exception reports: These reports call managers' attention to major problems such as overdue and late orders, excessive scrap rates, reporting errors, and requirements for nonexistent parts.

Because the MRP system has the capability to generate a wide range of reports, users can tailor the system to create reports that will address their specific needs.

Other Considerations in MRP

In addition to the main features of inputs, processing capabilities, and outputs of an MRP system, managers should be aware of other MRP system parameters. These include the MRP planning horizon and replanning frequency, lead times, safety stock, and lot-size considerations.

 MRP Considerations

CHANGING THE PLANNING HORIZON AND REPLANNING OF THE MRP SYSTEM

The MRP planning horizon can be 10, 26, or even 52 weeks. The actual planning horizon will depend on the type of company and the sorts of products produced. At a minimum, however, the planning horizon should exceed the cumulative lead times of the longest time sequence of any parent-component relationship. For example, let's assume that it takes 2 weeks to assemble components B and C to get end-product A. If the lead time to produce component B in house is 4 weeks and the lead time to get component C from a vendor is 12 weeks, then the MRP planning horizon should be at least greater than 14 (12 + 2) weeks.

When the MRP system is run, orders are released and components and products are produced and assembled. Nevertheless, the MRP system is dynamic; as time passes, the status of existing orders changes. For example, some of the current orders will have been completed and some may have been delayed because of late deliveries of raw materials and components, changes in order quantity, and so forth. In addition, new orders will have arrived and have to be processed. As a result, over time, the MRP document must be replanned and updated. Updating the MRP document, like the master schedule, is also done on a rolling basis. To demonstrate, consider the material requirements plan for wheel assemblies in the wheelbarrow example (Example 18.3). After creating the initial plan for weeks 1 to 8 and moving forward in time, the status of the orders for wheel assemblies will change and the MRP records will need updating. Assuming the MRP records are updated weekly, the next MRP schedules for wheel assemblies would be for weeks 2 through 9, 3 through 10, and so on.

Replanning and updating of MRP records can be done using either a **regenerative system** or a **net-change system**. In a regenerative MRP system, updating or replanning the MRP records is performed periodically (most commonly every week). All the changes (new orders, cancelled orders, delays, etc.) that occurred in a given period are identified and a new MRP plan is prepared by exploding the bill of materials for each item in a level-by-level manner. Regenerative MRP systems are suitable for production systems that are relatively stable and have the advantage of lower processing costs. The main disadvantage is the time lag between the availability of information and the time in which that information can be incorporated into the material requirements plan.

In a net-change MRP system, replanning is done continuously, whenever changes occur in the MRP records. For example, if a vendor delays delivery of an item, that information is entered into the system to reflect the change in the MRP record. Unlike the regenerative system, the entire production plan is not regenerated, but only the changes in the bill of materials of the affected item are exploded in a level-by-level manner. The net-change approach works best for production systems that

Planned order schedules: schedules that delineate the quantity and timing of future material orders

Planned order releases: reports that authorize the execution of the planned orders

Regenerative system: a system in which the updating or replanning of the MRP records is performed periodically, most commonly every week

Net-change system: a system in which replanning is done continuously, whenever changes occur in the MRP records

Companies may choose to hold safety stock of their inventory to anticipate uncertainties in supply and demand.

©iStockphoto.com/stockvisual

have frequent changes. Its main advantage is that it provides managers with up-to-date information of the MRP records for planning and control. The primary disadvantage is the increased processing that arises from continuously updating the system and the instability caused by frequent changes to the MRP records. This instability in the MRP system, often referred to as nervousness, can be disruptive for the purchasing and production departments. MRP system nervousness means minor changes initiated at the higher level MRP records or the master schedule cause significant changes to MRP plans.

One possible approach to reduce this instability is to make the minor changes that occur in the system on a periodic basis, while updating only major changes on a continuous basis. Another approach that can be used to reduce MRP system nervousness is to use firm planned orders. These orders are not changed automatically when conditions change; they require approval from a senior manager. In addition, the pegging capability of the MRP system is a tool that managers can use to locate the parent item that caused the changes to the requirements and decide whether a change to the MRP schedule is necessary.

LEAD TIMES

When scheduling order releases, the MRP system uses planned instead of actual lead times. Nevertheless, the actual lead times are not always the same as the planned lead times. When there is a difference in lead times, delivery of materials can sometimes be expedited without affecting job priorities and their due dates. If expediting is not possible, then the actual lead times should be input into the MRP system so that all affected jobs can be replanned.

SAFETY STOCKS

MRP is a planning system for dependent demand items. Although the demand for dependent demand items is fairly predictable because there is relatively less uncertainty about the time in which they'll be needed and the number of items to order, they typically do not require a safety stock. Yet, if there is supply or demand uncertainty for these items and the expected cost of running out of stock of these items is high, then it makes sense to hold safety stock for such items anywhere within the MRP system. Examples of the uncertainty of dependent demand items include late deliveries of materials ordered from a supplier, power outages or work stoppages at the warehouse, or delivery of poor quality items from a supplier. There may also be unexpected increases in customer demand for the end items. To protect against uncertainty, safety stocks are typically held for end items or for component items produced at bottleneck operations. If the uncertainty is associated with supply or production lead times, then MRP systems can use safety lead time to minimize the uncertainty. When safety lead time is incorporated into an MRP system, shop orders or purchase orders are released and scheduled for delivery or completion before they are needed.

LOT-SIZING CONSIDERATIONS

In MRP, purchase or shop orders must specify a discrete quantity (lot size) to purchase or produce. In Chapter 16, we noted that for independent demand items, managers typically use economic order or production quantity (EOQ or EPQ) lot-sizing techniques. The primary objective of choosing a lot-sizing technique for both independent and dependent demand items is to minimize ordering, set up, or carrying costs. Nonetheless, for MRP that deals with dependent demand items, because the demand for these items is lumpy or predictable, managers have to choose from a wider array of lot-sizing techniques because no one particular method has a clear cost advantage over the others. The basic distinction among the different methods is that some generate a fixed-order quantity, whereas others allow order quantities to vary from one (purchase or shop) order to the next.

The economic order quantity (EOQ), which is a fixed-order quantity lot-sizing technique, can be used in MRP systems if the demand for the material and components over the planning horizon is fairly uniform. This sort of demand pattern is typical of lower level items that are common to several parent items. Yet, because most products or components in an MRP system have discontinuous and non-uniform demand, EOQ is generally not a suitable lot-sizing technique. The imbalance between supply and demand will lead to unnecessarily excessive inventories and higher holding costs. As an example, let's consider the demand for an MRP item shown in Table 18.12.

Nervousness: instability in the MRP system

Firm planned orders: orders that are not changed automatically when conditions change, usually requiring approval from a senior manager

Safety lead time: a strategy to combat uncertainty associated with supply or production lead times

TABLE 18.12: Demand for MRP Item

WEEK	1	2	3	4	5	6	7	8
Demand		100						180

Let us further assume that we use the EOQ lot-sizing technique for this item with an order size of 300 units. If we also assume that our beginning inventory at the start of week 1 is zero and an order of 300 units was placed earlier and received during week 1, we have the situation shown in Table 18.13.

This table shows that by using the EOQ lot-sizing technique, we are holding unwanted excess inventories for this item in weeks 2 through 7, resulting in higher inventory carrying costs.

For items with discontinuous and sporadic demand, the lot-for-lot lot-sizing technique is the simplest of the variable-order quantity techniques. In this technique, the amount ordered or produced is the same as the demand requirements for the MRP items. As a result, holding costs for these types of items are virtually eliminated, thereby minimizing inventory investments. The major disadvantages of this technique are that the ordering or setup costs tend to be high because of the varying order sizes and increased order frequency, and a new setup is required for each production run. For example, a firm that manufactures solar panels has a high initial setup cost. Using the lot-for-lot ordering technique will require a new production setup every time there is a demand for this product, which can result in very high overall production cost. Nevertheless, if the firm could reduce ordering and setup costs per order or setup, then the lot-for-lot technique would be the best minimum cost lot-sizing technique. For the demand pattern shown in the table, the lot-for-lot ordering technique would be a better lot-sizing technique than EOQ, because the firm would order 100 units to cover the demand for the MRP item in week 2 and 180 units to meet demand in week 8. By doing so, the on-hand inventory throughout the planning period will be minimized.

TABLE 18.13: EOQ Lot-Sizing Impact

WEEK	1	2	3	4	5	6	7	8
Demand		100						180
Receipts	300							
On-Hand Inventory	300	200	200	200	200	200	200	20

Another variable-order lot-sizing technique that can be used for MRP items is the fixed-period ordering technique. In this technique, orders for the MRP items are placed at fixed periods. Because the order interval or the point in time at which an item is ordered is fixed, the quantity ordered varies depending on changes in demand and fluctuations in lead times. The fixed-period ordering technique covers the demand for a fixed number of periods with one order or setup. The simplest rule for the fixed-period ordering technique is to order every two periods. For example, consider the demand pattern for an MRP item as shown in Table 18.14.

TABLE 18.14: Demand Pattern for MRP Item

WEEK	1	2	3	4	5	6	7
Demand	80	100	70	50	4	120	6

For this demand pattern, using a 2-week rule of fixed-period ordering, we would order 180 units to cover the demand for weeks 1 and 2 and 120 units to cover demands for weeks 3 and 4. Continuing with the 2-week rule, we can order 124 units to cover the demands for weeks 5 and 6. Yet, because the demand for week 7 is only six units, we combine the demands for weeks 5, 6, and 7 and order 130 units. The major advantage of this lot-sizing technique is that stock is automatically delivered and fluctuations in demand are absorbed in any given period. The disadvantages are the costs associated with carrying excess inventory if demand is lower than expected or the risk of stock-outs if there are large, unexpected increases in demand.

Lot-for-lot: lot-sizing technique used for items with discontinuous and sporadic demand; it is the simplest of the variable-order quantity techniques in which the amount ordered or produced is the same as the demand requirements for the MRP items

Fixed-period ordering: lot-sizing technique in which orders for the MRP items are placed at fixed periods

Yet another popular lot-sizing technique is the part-period balancing (PPB) heuristic. In PPB, both order (or production) quantity and time between orders (or setups) are allowed to vary. The focus of this approach is to select the number of periods covered by an order or setup such that the holding cost over the covered horizon is approximately equal to the ordering or setup cost. Let us illustrate PPB with an example.

Consider an MRP item that is to be produced in house with the net requirements shown in Table 18.15. Assume that the production cost per setup to produce this item is $100 and per-unit inventory holding cost is $1/week (in U.S. dollars).

TABLE 18.15: Net Requirements for MRP Item

WEEK	1	2	3	4	5	6	7	8	9	10
Net Requirements	30	50	20	60	60	20	30	50	30	40

Part-period is the number of parts in a lot multiplied by the number of periods those parts are carried in inventory. For example, 20 parts carried for one period, 10 parts carried for two periods, and 5 parts carried for four periods all represent a 20 part-period and incur the same inventory carrying cost. The objective in PPB lot sizing is to determine the lot-size quantity and point when parts will be scheduled for production over the 10-week planning horizon. The criterion for this determination is that the setup costs and carrying cost should be approximately equal.

TABLE 18.16: Calculating Lot Size Using PPB Over Periods 1 to 4 of the Planning Horizon

PERIODS COMBINED	LOT SIZE (CUMULATIVE NET REQUIREMENTS)	SETUP COST	PART-PERIODS	INVENTORY CARRYING COST (IN U.S. DOLLARS)
1	30	$100	0	$0 \times \$1 = 0$
1, 2	80	$100	50×1	$50 \times \$1 = \$50$
1, 2, 3	100	$100	$50 \times 1 + 20 \times 2$	$90 \times \$1 = \$90$
1, 2, 3, 4	160	$100	$50 \times 1 + 20 \times 2 + 60 \times 3$	$270 \times \$1 = \$270$

The best solution is the third option: produce 100 parts in week 1, because with this solution the carrying cost ($90) is closest to the setup cost ($100). The lot size of 100 units will cover the net requirements for weeks 1, 2, and 3. Table 18.17 continues this example over the next four periods (weeks 4–7).

TABLE 18.17: Calculating Lot Size Using PPB Over Periods 4 to 7 of the Planning Horizon

PERIODS COMBINED	LOT-SIZE (CUMULATIVE NET REQUIREMENTS)	SETUP COST	PART-PERIODS	INVENTORY CARRYING COST (IN U.S. DOLLARS)
4	60	$100	0	$0 \times \$1 = 0$
4, 5	120	$100	60×1	$60 \times \$1 = \$60$
4, 5, 6	140	$100	$60 \times 1 + 20 \times 2$	$100 \times \$1 = \$100$
4, 5, 6, 7	170	$100	$60 \times 1 + 20 \times 2 + 30 \times 3$	$190 \times \$1 = \$190$

The best solution is the third solution, which is to produce 140 parts in week 4 because the carrying cost ($100) is equal to the setup cost ($100). The lot size of 140 units will cover the net requirements for weeks 4, 5, and 6. Finally, Table 18.18 extends the example for periods 7–10.

The best solution is the third solution, which is to produce 110 parts in week 7 because the carrying cost ($110) is closest to the setup cost ($100). The lot size of 110 units will cover the net requirements for weeks 7, 8, and 9. Assuming no information is available on the net requirements after week 10, a lot size of 40 units will be scheduled for production in week 10.

The final MRP production schedule is given in Table 18.19.

Part-period balancing (PPB): lot-sizing technique in which both order (or production) quantity and time between orders (or setups) are allowed to vary. The focus of this approach is to select the number of periods covered by an order or setup such that the holding cost over the covered horizon is approximately equal to the ordering or setup cost

TABLE 18.18: Calculating Lot Size Using PPB Over Periods 7 to 10 of the Planning Horizon

PERIODS COMBINED	LOT-SIZE (CUMULATIVE NET REQUIREMENTS)	SETUP COST	PART-PERIODS	INVENTORY CARRYING COST
7	30	$100	0	0 × $1 = 0
7, 8	80	$100	50 × 1	50 × $1 = $50
7, 8, 9	110	$100	50 × 1 + 30 × 2	100 × $1 = $110
7, 8, 9, 10	150	$100	50 × 1 + 30 × 2 + 40 × 3	230 × $1 = $230

TABLE 18.19: Final MRP Production Schedule

WEEK	1	2	3	4	5	6	7	8	9	10
Net Requirements	30	50	20	60	60	20	30	50	30	40
Planned Order Receipts	100			140			110			40

The main advantage of PPB for lot sizing is that, like EOQ, it attempts to find a minimum cost solution by balancing ordering or setup costs and inventory carrying cost. Unlike EOQ, in PPB both the order quantity and the period number of lot sizing varies. Consequently, it is also effective for the items whose demand is unstable, whereas EOQ is suitable only for those items whose demand is stable.

Potential Benefits and Drawbacks of MRP

The benefits of MRP systems for manufacturers include reduction in inventory costs, the ability to track material requirements, and greater efficiency of capacity.

INVENTORY BENEFITS
Because MRP systems place more emphasis on the timing of the order placement for materials and components rather than quantity ordered, inventories of these materials and components are made available only when they are needed. Consequently, production managers can minimize in-process inventories and their associated carrying costs.

ABILITY TO TRACK MATERIAL REQUIREMENTS
An MRP system gathers the information on end-item requirements provided by the master schedule, available inventories from the inventory status file, and the information on subassemblies and components needed to produce the end product and the manufacturing sequence from the BOM file. Using this information and through explosion, MRP systems can accurately track material requirements. In addition, with a backflushing capability, which is accurate reporting of completed items, MRP systems can accurately track component and material requirements and use. In backflush, an end item's BOM is exploded to determine the quantities of component parts, material, and subassemblies that were used to make the item. In a material backflush transaction, when a shop order is received, the material required for that shop order is issued automatically. For example, if each printed circuit board requires two transistors, then a shop order of 200 printed circuit boards requires 400 transistors. Therefore, a shop order receipt of 100 printed circuit boards would automatically prompt a backflush of 200 transistors (100 received / 200 ordered × 400 required). Thus, in single-issue transactions or for low-cost, high-volume items, a backflushing transaction can save time but still capture the material use on a shop order.

Backflushing: enables accurate reporting of completed items. In a backflush, an end item's BOM is exploded to determine the quantities of component parts, material, and subassemblies that were used to make the item

One benefit of using MRP systems is the ability to track material requirements. Utilizing backflushing can track material use in addition to saving time placing orders.

©iStockphoto.com/microgen

Benefits of MRP

CAPACITY BENEFITS

MRP systems enable production managers to effectively use capacity by allocating production time efficiently among the various products, balancing workloads across departments, and planning for future capacity needs.

In addition to these benefits, many manufacturing employees use the information provided by MRP outputs. In addition to production planners and production managers, plant supervisors rely on the output of MRP systems to issue work orders and maintain production schedules. Similarly, the performance and exception reports provided by the MRP system enable purchase managers to monitor supplier performance in meeting delivery commitments and the quality of materials supplied. Finally, with the information provided by the output of the MRP system, customer service representatives can make commitments on delivery dates to customers.

There are also several potential drawbacks in using MRP systems. The MRP system is only as good as the inputs it receives. That is, if the master schedule and bill of materials are not accurate, if lead time estimates are poor, or if inventory records have not been maintained, then using an MRP system can lead to serious problems, such as missing parts, excessive order quantities, schedule delays, and missed delivery dates. Another potential drawback of an MRP system is that it can be difficult, time consuming, and costly to implement. Many companies have encountered employee resistance to MRP implementation because workers may be unwilling to abandon old habits of sloppy record keeping and hoarding parts in case of inventory shortages. For an MRP implementation to be successful, all employees who will use the system should receive adequate training and education and should be assured that they will be better served and benefit from the new system.

Integrating MRP and JIT Systems

Both MRP and just-in-time (JIT) systems control production and inventory levels in a manufacturing enterprise. (JIT systems are discussed in Chapter 14.) Nevertheless, there are differences between the two systems. First, whereas MRP systems have the required materials and components available when needed for the production of finished goods based on forecasted requirements, JIT systems focus on detailed scheduling of production in response to actual orders. JIT systems rely on the timely delivery of exactly the right raw materials in the right quantities to the right place to allow for production as orders are received. Second, MRP is suited for batch or job-shop production, and it has the ability to adjust material and component requirements in response to changing demand. JIT, on the other hand, is a system that is best suited for a repetitive production process that produces similar products that have stable demand. Third, an MRP system is a computerized information system that requires accurate and timely information on end-product requirements, whereas the emphasis of JIT systems is on shop floor physical operations. Fourth, the main function of an MRP system is parts scheduling without regard to available capacity on the shop floor, whereas the main function of a JIT system is operations scheduling, given finite capacity on the shop floor. Finally, an MRP system can readily adapt to changes in the production environment and is better equipped than a JIT system to respond to production fluctuations. In a JIT system, unanticipated demand for products may hamper production because there is a lack of sufficient capacity. Table 18.20 summarizes the major differences between these two systems.[4]

Despite the differences, both MRP systems and JIT systems offer several benefits. Both systems reduce waste in production processes, improve inventory levels, and prevent lost production time. Therefore, an integrated MRP and JIT system that incorporates the best attributes of each can provide

TABLE 18.20: Differences Between MRP and JIT Systems

FEATURES	MRP SYSTEM	JIT SYSTEM
Main characteristic	Computerized information system	Shop floor physical operations
Main function	Parts scheduling without regard to capacity	Operations scheduling
Shop floor work authorization	Push system	Pull system
Rates of output	Variable or level	Level, stable
Capacity required	Capacity requirements planning	Flexible
Forms of control	Middle management	Shop floor line workers

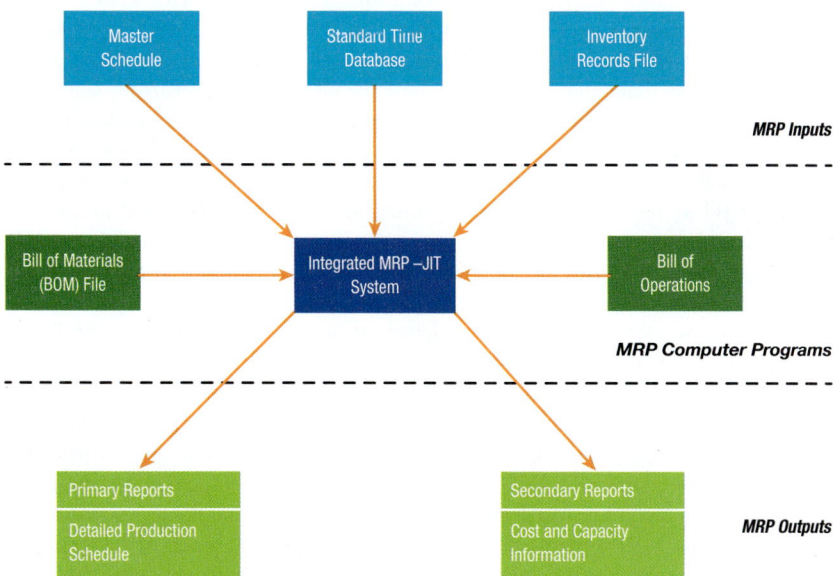

SOURCE: Ho, J. C., & Chang, Y. L. (2001). Integrated MRP and JIT framework. *Computers & Industrial Engineering. 41*:173–185.

a more effective manufacturing system than either alone and can address the changing needs of companies in the manufacturing sector. Specifically, by combining the best planning features of an MRP system and the best execution features of a JIT system, manufacturing companies will have a more efficient and effective production system.

Figure 18.8 shows the arrangement of an integrated MRP and JIT system.

Of the five major inputs to the integrated system shown in Figure 18.8, three—the master schedule, the BOM file, and the inventory records file—are exactly the same as those in an MRP system. The master schedule specifies the requirements for the end item or independent demand item for each period. The BOM file includes the parts, the quantities needed, and the manufacturing sequence for producing a parent item. The inventory records file provides current information on the on-hand inventory and the fixed or constant portion of the production lead time for each part. The integrated system requires two more inputs—bill of operations and standard time database. The bill of operations file provides information on the number of operations and the precedence among these operations in the production process. It also specifies the machines that perform the operations. Finally, the standard time database provides information on machine capacity, machine time cost per unit, operation process time, and setup time. The primary output of the integrated system is a detailed production schedule, which specifies the individual work centers that will perform specific operations on specific parts in specific time periods. The secondary output is a set of reports that includes detailed cost and capacity utilization information.[5]

The features of the integrated system are as follows:[6]

1. Just as in MRP systems, the system is triggered by the requirements for a higher level parent item provided by the master schedule.
2. Similar to JIT systems, the demand for this parent item pulls or triggers the last operation for this item. To schedule operations such as this one, decision rules need to be embedded in the integrated system.
3. The scheduling of the last operation of this parent item triggers all preceding operations for the lower level children of the parent item until all operations required to produce the parent item specified by the master schedule are scheduled. This scheduling process resembles MRP explosion as the final operation required to produce the parent item triggers the scheduling of all child items in the product hierarchy.

The integrated system is similar to an MRP system because it is also a computerized information system. As in MRP processing, the integrated system also uses the product explosion and time phasing. Nevertheless, unlike MRP, the integrated system will provide a detailed day-to-day schedule. Also, whereas MRP uses predetermined lead times that are fixed, the lead times in the integrated system are derived from the schedule and can be adjusted. Third, the time buckets or periods defined in the integrated system are much shorter (typically a day or a shift) as compared with weekly time buckets commonly found in MRP processing. Finally, the integrated system includes total production cost as part of its output, whereas MRP systems provide no such cost information. Thus, the integrated system generates measurements that can be used to evaluate the effectiveness of various solutions obtained by using different decision rules. The integrated system is also similar to a JIT system in the sense that it is also a pull system because the operations scheduling process is triggered by downstream operations required to produce a higher level parent item. Yet, although the integrated system provides a formal daily schedule, a JIT system does not. Also, the integrated system can be used in both repetitive processes and batch processes because it does not require level production schedules as JIT systems do. Finally, the integrated system uses decision rules to generate schedules that attempt to minimize total production cost, whereas JIT systems do not.[7]

There are several ways to facilitate the implementation of an integrated system. First, the planned order releases to the shop floor from the MRP system can be modified by using finite capacity scheduling systems. These scheduling systems will ensure that we take into account the finite capacity available at the various work centers and, therefore, can obtain a realistic and finite production schedule. Second, the MRP time buckets, which are often weekly, should be reduced to a bucketless MRP system, in which material requirements are specified on a daily basis or by shift. It might be preferable to use hourly time buckets. In fact, to reduce lead times and increase material flows, many companies are now switching to bucketless MRP systems to accommodate the pull approach of JIT systems on the shop floor. Third, by using a manufacturing supermarket, which is an inventory stocking location right on the shop floor, the integrated system can achieve the pull approach of a JIT system. Having such an inventory stocking location pulls materials needed for production from the stocking location as and when needed. As parts and materials in the supermarket are used up, they are replenished as needed. Fourth, by defining the proper Kanban levels of the JIT system, maintaining the data integrity in the MRP system, having the right mix of products flow through the process to maximize efficiency, and minimizing inventory at each stage of production, the firm can achieve a balanced flow of materials through each stage of the production process. Finally, by using backflushing to enter material changes in the system, material use can be calculated from the production of the final product. Backflushing will facilitate the implementation of the JIT approach because it reduces the amount of paperwork by eliminating the need to collect detailed usage information on the shop floor.

MRP in the Service Sector

MRP also has applications for the production and delivery of services, although its use is less prevalent than in manufacturing firms. MRP is also useful for service companies or service items that have dependent demand. For example, in a hospital, the demand for a specific surgical procedure will generate demand for surgical items (dependent demand items) specifically required for that surgical procedure. In fact, many hospitals use MRP to purchase preassembled surgical kits from suppliers because of the complexity involved in acquiring so many diverse items.

Similarly, in an international airport, the scheduled arrival and departure times of an aircraft will trigger marshaling services required to direct and tow the aircraft to the specific arrival gate; ramp services, such as toilet cleaning and gas refueling; and cabin services, such as catering, cleaning, and garbage removal, prior to the departure time of that aircraft. To effectively perform these services, airports use MRP principles. Similar to a BOM file, a service firm creates a bill of service file that will show the time units required to perform each service. Because there are no inventories in services, the MRP schedule will have one row for each required and scheduled airport service activity; the columns will show the required and scheduled time buckets.

In the hospitality industry, hotel chains such as Marriott International, Inc. (Bethesda, MD) use MRP systems when renovating their hotel rooms. The MRP system allows the hotel to plan for the acquisition and timely delivery of dependent demand items such as the number of mattresses and bed frames, mirrors, tables, televisions and phones, and bathroom fixtures so that the room renovations can be completed on time. Restaurants typically use MRP systems because the ingredients and

Bucketless: MRP system in which material requirements are specified on a daily basis or by shift

Manufacturing supermarket: inventory stocking location right on the shop floor

Servicing aircraft includes unglamorous jobs like pumping lavatory waste from bathrooms.

Jim West / Alamy Stock Photo

FIGURE 18.9: Product Structure Tree for Veal Parmigiana at Luigi's Ristorante

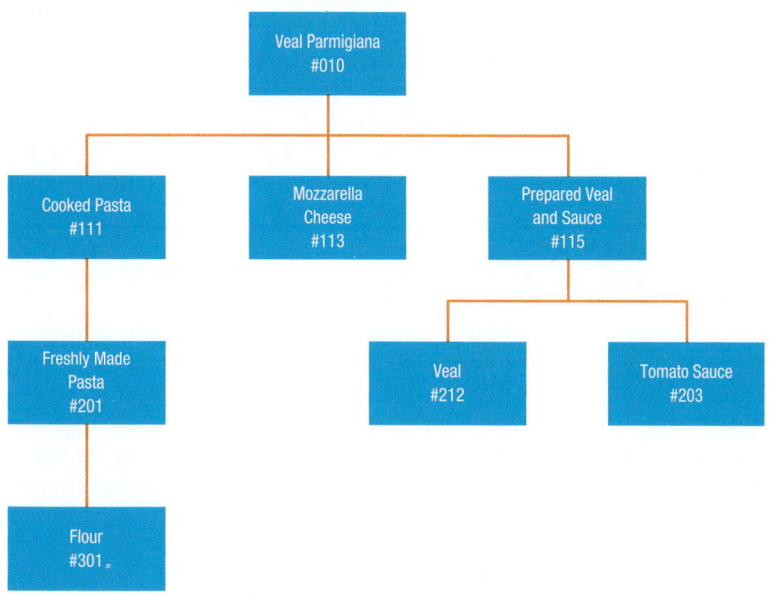

side dishes for a meal, such as vegetables, spices, meat, pasta, and bread, are dependent demand items. The end-item master schedule would be the meals or entrées, and we could construct a separate product structure tree and BOM file for each unique entrée prepared (see Figure 18.9 and Table 18.21). Furthermore, as the preparation time for each meal would vary, and would require different kitchen workers, MRP processing in labor-intensive service industries such as a restaurant would also require a **bill of labor or bill of resources file (BOL or BOR)**. A bill of labor file or bill of resources file shows the operations and the sequence in which they have to be performed and the key resources, such as the type of labor and labor hours, that will be required to perform each operation.

MRP principles can also be applied in higher education services such as a university to schedule, load, and control student course enrollments. By using inputs such as the master curriculum schedule for the department, a bill of courses file, and a student records file (MRP inputs similar to the master schedule, BOM file, and inventory records files), the necessary number of required courses can be scheduled and each of these courses can be loaded based on student priorities. By applying MRP principles to course scheduling, university administrators can improve student service and faculty utilization.[8]

TABLE 18.21: Bill of Materials File for Veal Parmigiana at Luigi's Ristorante

PART NUMBER	DESCRIPTION	QUANTITY	MEASURE	UNIT COST (IN U.S. DOLLARS)	TOTAL COST (IN U.S. DOLLARS)	LABOR HOURS
#111	Cooked Pasta					.20
#113	Mozzarella Cheese	10	Oz.	0.15	1.50	
#115	Prepared Veal and Sauce					.35
#201	Fresh Pasta	14	Oz.	0.21	2.94	
#203	Tomato Sauce	6	Oz.	0.40	2.40	
#203	Veal	8	Oz.	0.85	6.80	
#301	Flour	10	Oz.	0.08	0.80	
Total BOM					$14.44	.55

Bill of labor or bill of resources file (BOL or BOR): shows the operations and the sequence in which they have to be performed and the key resources that will be required to perform each operation

When MRP principles are applied to determine requirements for production and delivery of services it can be considered service requirements planning (SRP). Just like MRP, an SRP system uses information from BOM files, bills of labor, and existing orders to convert the master schedule for end services and component services. Just as in MRP, orders are released for services, and services are rescheduled if due dates cannot be met. Using BOM files, SRP determines what materials are needed and when, and after factoring the lead times for materials receipt, purchase orders are generated. Similarly, SRP will determine the service operations that are needed, when they are needed, and the time required to complete each operation. The system will generate work schedules to complete these operations.[9]

Discuss the role that sustainability and ethics play in MRP systems.

Issues in MRP

18.3 Ethical and Sustainability Issues

The role that sustainability and ethics play in the manufacturing process continues to grow in importance. Nevertheless, manufacturing strategies and sustainability are interrelated. Surveys conducted in the year 2000 found that 90% of U.S. manufacturers had environmental strategies that were aimed at reducing the negative impact of their operations on the environment. Since then, government policies and public concern for slowing the release of greenhouse gases and reducing the use of diminishing resources has made sustainability part of the manufacturing process. More and more organizations recognize their ethical obligation to operate and produce goods and services in ways that minimize environmental damage.

Government actions and pressure from investors and consumers have caused companies to reexamine their manufacturing and service operations in light of sustainability.

1. Government agencies enforce regulations on environmental conditions that affect manufacturing practices. For example, in the United States, the Environmental Protection Agency (EPA) has tightened requirements limiting the release of carbon-based particulate, altering the manner in which companies use energy.
2. Investors are wary of the environmental liabilities of companies they are considering funding. Firms that have a reputation for environmentally unsound behavior are finding it difficult to obtain funding because investors fear that local and national government agencies will place sanctions on unsustainable practices or levy fines.
3. Consumers seek proof of environmental responsibility in the products and services they purchase. Products, such as coffee, that are labeled fair trade or eco-friendly demonstrate a concern for the environment that appeals to potential buyers.

This chapter has described manufacturing as the center of the supply chain function and the MRP process as a way to improve the manufacturing function. Because MRP ultimately determines how much gets made (what machines are used and how often they are turned on), what raw materials are ordered (who supplies our raw materials for production), and what orders are filled in what order (where the goods are going once they leave the factory), companies must recognize that the MRP systems they employ have a dual obligation to be efficient and promote sustainability.

When it was originally conceived, MRP operated under very different competitive and market conditions than it currently faces. That is, companies operated for years in a "push and promote" manner, where the primary goal was to produce lots of products as cheaply and efficiently as possible. These "push" strategies are aimed at creating large quantities of standardized products based on forecasts. Marketing departments then focused on convincing potential buyers of the value of these products. The problem with this approach is that it can be wasteful—it ignores sustainability concerns by making excess products or failing to streamline operations and conserve scarce resources. Because MRP systems focus on controlling production flows in manufacturing and service settings, they allow companies to integrate environmental issues such as purchasing materials made from recycled products or reconfiguring bill of materials (BOM) files to eliminate unnecessary steps or hazardous materials.

Rethinking the way that goods and services are produced to account for ethical and sustainable operations is not only good for society at large but it can save firms money and manufacturing time. MRP systems are a critical feature in ethical manufacturing management because they not only allow organizations the opportunity to be mindful of the need for sustainability but also offer concrete means, through organizing materials purchases and use, to put these concerns into action.[10]

Service requirements planning (SRP): MRP principles applied to determine requirements for production and delivery of services

Visit **edge.sagepub.com/venkataraman** to help you accomplish your coursework goals in an easy-to-use learning environment.

- Mobile-friendly eFlashcards
- Mobile-friendly practice quizzes
- A complete online action plan

- Chapter summaries with learning objectives
- Video and multimedia resources

CHAPTER SUMMARY

18.1 Compose a master schedule and identify its functions. The aggregate production and resource levels established by the sales and operations plan act as constraints to subsequent operational plans and should be disaggregated to provide the detailed material and resource plans needed to produce or acquire individual products and components. The first step of this disaggregation is the process of master scheduling. The master scheduling process leads to a manufacturing plan that determines the quantity of each end item to be produced in specific periods of the short-range planning horizon. The process determines the production quantities required to meet demand from every possible source of an organization including end customers, warehouses, and requirements from other plants in a multi-plant environment. Among the functions of the master schedule are disaggregation of the sales and operations (aggregate) plans, evaluation of capacity requirements, generation of material requirements, and facilitation of information processing.

18.2 Explain the conditions under which MRP is appropriate, its inputs, processing, and outputs, as well as its benefits and limitations. The master scheduling process leads to a manufacturing plan that determines the quantity of each end item to be produced in specific periods of the short-range planning horizon. The process determines the production quantities required to meet demand from every possible source of an organization including end customers, warehouses, and requirements from other plants in a multi-plant environment. Once the master schedule is set, material requirements planning (MRP) can be employed as a method for scheduling production and inventory control for products that are demand dependent. MRP depends on accurate requirements for all products, a master schedule, inventory and lead times, and purchasing records.

The inputs for an MRP system include the master schedule, inventory status file, and bill of materials (BOM) file, which is used to create a product structure tree. Processing in an MRP system starts with a master production schedule, which provides information on the number of units required for an end product for specific time periods of the planning horizon. The MRP system accepts these end-item requirements from the master schedule and then gathers information from the BOM file on the components needed to assemble the end product. In addition, the MRP system also gets information on the available inventory for both the finished products

and the various components. The MRP system then calculates the gross and net requirements of all components and materials at each level of the product structure tree. This process is referred to as MRP explosion. The outputs of the MRP system include planned order schedules, planned order releases, changes to planned orders, performance control reports, planning reports, and exception reports.

Benefits of MRP Systems:

1. Inventory benefits. Production managers can minimize in-process inventory levels and their associated carrying costs.

2. Ability to track material requirements. MRP gathers the information on end-item requirements provided by the master schedule, available inventories from the inventory status file, and the information on subassemblies and components needed to produce the end product and the manufacturing sequence from the BOM file.

3. Capacity benefits. MRP systems enable production managers to use capacity by efficiently allocating production time among the various products, balancing workloads across departments, and planning for future capacity.

Problems with MRP systems arise if the master schedule and bill of materials are not accurate, if lead time estimates are poor, or if inventory records have not been maintained. Using an MRP system in these cases can lead to problems such as missing parts, excessive order quantities, schedule delays, and missed delivery dates. An MRP system can be difficult, time consuming, and costly to implement. Many companies have encountered employee resistance to MRP implementation.

18.3 Discuss the role that sustainability and ethics play in MRP systems. Organizations are increasingly recognizing their ethical obligation to operate and produce goods and services in ways that minimize environmental damage. In a variety of ways, government actions and pressure from investors and consumers have caused companies to reexamine their manufacturing and service operations in light of sustainability. Furthermore, because MRP systems focus on controlling production flows in manufacturing and service settings, they allow companies to integrate environmental issues such as purchasing materials made from recycled products or reconfiguring bill of materials (BOM) files to eliminate unnecessary steps or hazardous materials.

KEY TERMS

DISCUSSION AND REVIEW QUESTIONS

1. What are the immediate inputs to the master scheduling process?

2. What are the outputs from the master scheduling process?

3. Define available-to-promise (ATP).

4. Discuss briefly the different functions of the master schedule.

5. Describe the time fencing concept used to achieve stability in the master schedule.

6. How does the master scheduling process differ for the various production environments?

7. What are some of the guidelines for effectively managing and controlling the performance of a master schedule?

8. What is the difference between independent and dependent demand? Explain the difference with an example.

9. What are the inputs to an MRP system? What information is provided by each of these inputs?

10. Describe the time phasing logic in MRP.

11. Describe the process of MRP explosion.

12. Explain the pegging capability of the MRP system.

13. What are the key outputs from the MRP process?

14. What are the differences between a regenerative and a net-change MRP system?

15. What is the meaning of "nervousness" in an MRP system? Describe its impact and the mitigation approaches that can be taken.

16. Describe briefly the different lot-sizing approaches used in MRP.

17. Discuss briefly the benefits and limitations of an MRP system.

18. Discuss the key features and advantages of an integrated MRP–JIT system.

19. Explain how MRP can be applied in the following service businesses: (a) a hospital and (b) aircraft scheduling.

20. Suppose you were in charge of your company's MRP system and received a memo from the CEO stating the need to "search diligently" for ways to improve manufacturing sustainability. Explain how MRP can be used to promote sustainable operations and give three specific actions that you would support, through MRP, to enhance your company's sustainability policies.

SOLVED PROBLEMS

1. Diamond Equipment Inc. is a fictitious manufacturer of lawn mowers, garden tractors, and snow blowers. The company has developed a forecast of demand for each week for an 8-week planning horizon, which is given in Table 18.22.

TABLE 18.22: Demand Forecast for 8-Week Planning Horizon

Week	1	2	3	4	5	6	7	8
Forecast	60	85	110	90	120	45	55	80

In addition, the company has the following committed customer orders for the first four weeks: 70, 60, 35, and 20. The company assembles lawn mowers in lot sizes of 100 mowers per production run. Production is scheduled in those weeks when the projected on-hand inventory falls below 10 mowers (safety stock). The company has a beginning inventory of 60 mowers at the start of the planning horizon. Develop a master schedule for the 8-week time horizon.

Solution:

Step 1: Develop a partial master schedule that includes available data.

TABLE 18.23: Partial Master Scheduling Record for the Lawn Mowers

Week	1	2	3	4	5	6	7	8
Forecast	60	85	110	90	120	45	55	80
Customer Orders	70	60	35	20				
MPS Lot Size: 100 units								
Projected On-Hand Inventory = 60								
Available-to-Promise								

Step 2: Calculate the projected on-hand inventory. Schedule production if the projected on-hand inventory falls below the 10 units of safety stock.

Projected on-hand inventory $= I_{t-1} + MPS_t - \text{Maximum} (CO_t, F_t)$, where

$I_{t-1} =$ Ending inventory from week $t - 1$

$MPS_t =$ Production quantity (lot size) scheduled in week t

$CO_t =$ Customer orders (committed) in week t

$F_t =$ Forecasted demand in week t

For week 1, the beginning inventory is 60 units. The larger of the customer order or forecast in week 1 is the customer order of 70 units. Since the projected on-hand inventory in week 1 will fall below the required 10 units of safety stock, production for the lot-size quantity (MPS = 100) should be scheduled in week 1. Thus,

$$\text{Projected on-hand inventory in week 1} = I_0 + MPS_1 - \text{Maximum} (CO_1, F_1)$$

$$= 60 + 100 - 70 = 90$$

Similarly, for week 2, as the ending inventory from week 1 is 90 units and the larger of the customer order or forecast is the forecast quantity of 85 units, the projected on-hand inventory will fall below the required 10 units. Therefore, production for the MPS quantity of 100 units should also be scheduled for week 2. Thus,

$$\text{Projected on-hand inventory in week 2} = I_1 + MPS_2 - \text{Maximum} (CO_2, F_2)$$

$$= 90 + 100 - 85 = 105$$

For week 3,

$$\text{Projected on-hand inventory in week 3} = I_2 + MPS_3 - \text{Maximum} (CO_3, F_3)$$

$$= 105 + 100 - 110 = 95$$

Similar calculations are performed for the remaining weeks, and the results are shown in Table 18.24.

TABLE 18.24: Master Scheduling Record for the Lawn Mowers (Remaining Weeks)

Week	1	2	3	4	5	6	7	8
Forecast	60	85	110	90	120	45	55	80
Customer Orders	70	60	35	20				
MPS Lot Size: 100 units	100	100	100	100	100		100	100
Projected On-Hand Inventory = 60	90	105	95	105	85	40	85	105
Available-to-Promise								

Step 3: Calculate available-to-promise (ATP).

The formulas for calculating ATP is as follows:

For the first week of the master schedule,

$$ATP_t = I_{t-1} + MPS_t - \sum_{i=t}^{k-1} CO_i$$

For all subsequent weeks in which an MPS is scheduled,

$$ATP_t = MPS_t - \sum_{i=t}^{k-1} CO_i$$

where

$I_{t-1} =$ Ending inventory from week $t - 1$

$MPS_t =$ Production quantity (lot size) scheduled in week t

$\sum_{i=t}^{k-1} CO_i =$ Sum of all customer orders from week t until the next scheduled MPS in week k

For week 1, the beginning inventory is 60 units, and MPS is 100 units. Since another MPS for 100 units has been scheduled in week 2, the sum of all customer orders until the next MPS (k = 2) is the customer order of 70 units in week 1. Therefore,

$$ATP_1 = I_0 + MPS_1 - \sum_{i=1}^{2-1} CO_i = I_0 + MPS_1 - CO_1 = 60 + 100 - 70 = 90 \text{ units}$$

For week 2, since the next MPS occurs in week 3 (k = 3), we have

$$ATP_2 = MPS_2 - \sum_{i=2}^{3-1} CO_i = MPS_2 - CO_2 = 100 - 60 = 40 \text{ units}$$

For week 3, since the next MPS occurs in week 4 (k = 4), we have

$$ATP_3 = MPS_3 - \sum_{i=3}^{4-1} CO_i = MPS_3 - CO_3 = 100 - 35 = 65 \text{ units}$$

For week 4, since the next MPS occurs in week 5 (k = 5), we have

$$ATP_4 = MPS_4 - \sum_{i=4}^{5-1} CO_i = MPS_4 - CO_4 = 100 - 20 = 80 \text{ units}$$

ATP calculations for the remaining weeks are performed in a similar manner. Nevertheless, since there are no customer orders for the remaining weeks, all of the MPS quantities scheduled are treated as ATP. The final master schedule is shown in Table 18.25.

TABLE 18.25: Final Master Scheduling Record for the Lawn Mowers

Week	1	2	3	4	5	6	7	8
Forecast	60	85	110	90	120	45	55	80
Customer Orders	70	60	35	20				
MPS Lot Size: 100 units	100	100	100	100	100		100	100
Projected On-Hand Inventory = 60	90	105	95	105	85	40	85	105
Available-to-Promise	90	40	65	80	100		100	100

2. Assembling a wooden cabinet requires a top panel, a bottom panel, a back panel, two side panels, two doors, four shelves, and two shelf supports. Assembling each door requires two hinges, one handle, one magnet, and eight screws. Each side panel requires two door catches and two screws. The bottom panel requires four legs, and assembling the back panel to the top, bottom, and side panels requires 12 screws. Construct a product structure tree for this wooden cabinet, and show the level of the end product, subassemblies, and components in the product hierarchy using low-level coding.

Solution:

The complete product structure tree for the wooden cabinet using low-level coding is shown in Figure 18.10.

FIGURE 18.10: Complete Product Tree Structure

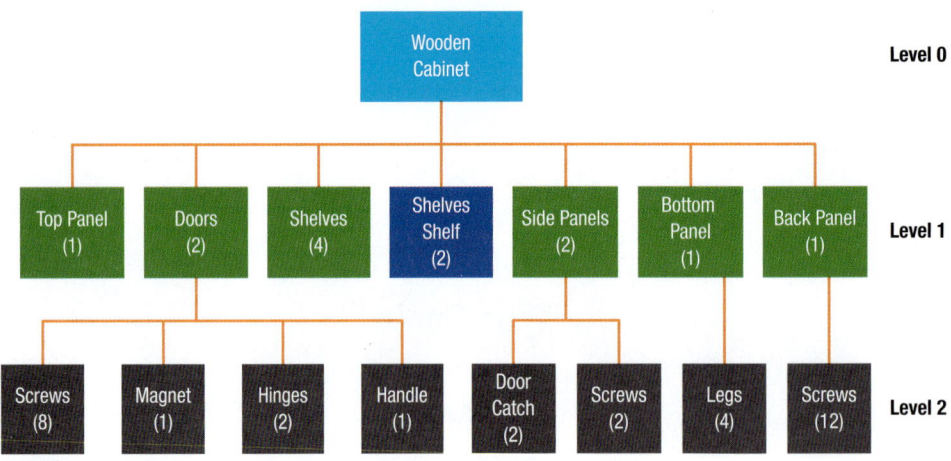

3. Refer to Example 18.2. The product structure tree for assembling a chair developed for that example is reproduced in Figure 18.11.

FIGURE 18.11: Product Structure Tree for Chair Assembly

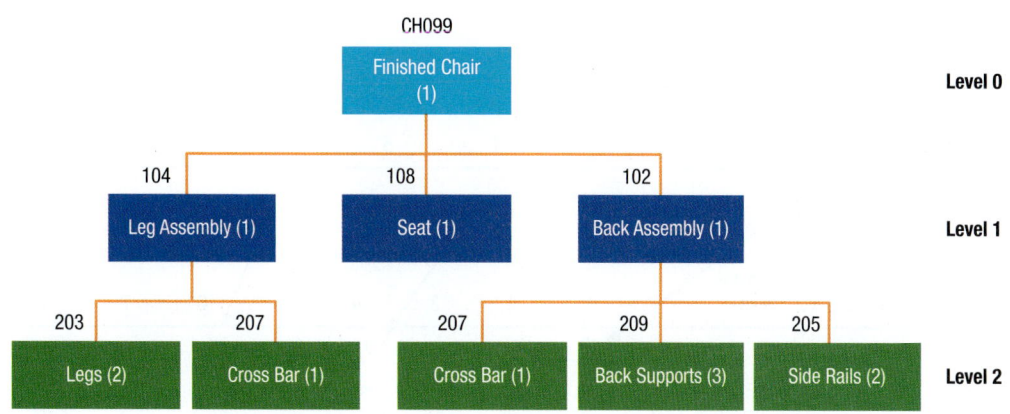

Suppose the firm that assembles this chair receives customer orders with delivery due dates of 40 in week 1, 80 in week 4, 80 in week 6, and 50 in week 8. Based on Figure 18.11, some of the subassemblies required for each chair are one leg assembly and one back assembly. Each back assembly and leg assembly also require one cross bar each. Assume that the lead times for assembling the chair from Level 1 subassemblies are negligible and that there are no safety stock requirements. Develop a material requirements plan for the leg assemblies, back assemblies, and cross bars for an 8-week planning horizon. The end-item master schedule for the customer orders for chairs, and the order quantities, lead times, scheduled receipts, and on-hand inventories for the leg assemblies, back assemblies, and cross bars, are given in Table 18.26.

TABLE 18.26: End-Item Master Schedule for Chairs: Customer Orders

Week	1	2	3	4	5	6	7	8
Customer Orders	40			80		80		50

Subassembly/Component	Order Quantity	Lead Time in Weeks	On-Hand Inventory
Leg assemblies*	Lot-for-lot	1	100
Back assemblies	Lot-for-lot	2	100
Cross bars	200	1	200

Solution:

Step 1: Generate requirements for Level 1 items based on the master schedule requirements for the Level 0 item (chair). We compute the Level 1 requirements for leg and back assemblies as shown in Tables 18.27 and 18.28.

TABLE 18.27: Weeks 1 Through 8: Leg Assemblies

Weeks 1 through 8: Level 1 Requirements: Leg Assemblies

End-Item Master Schedule for Chairs: Customer Orders

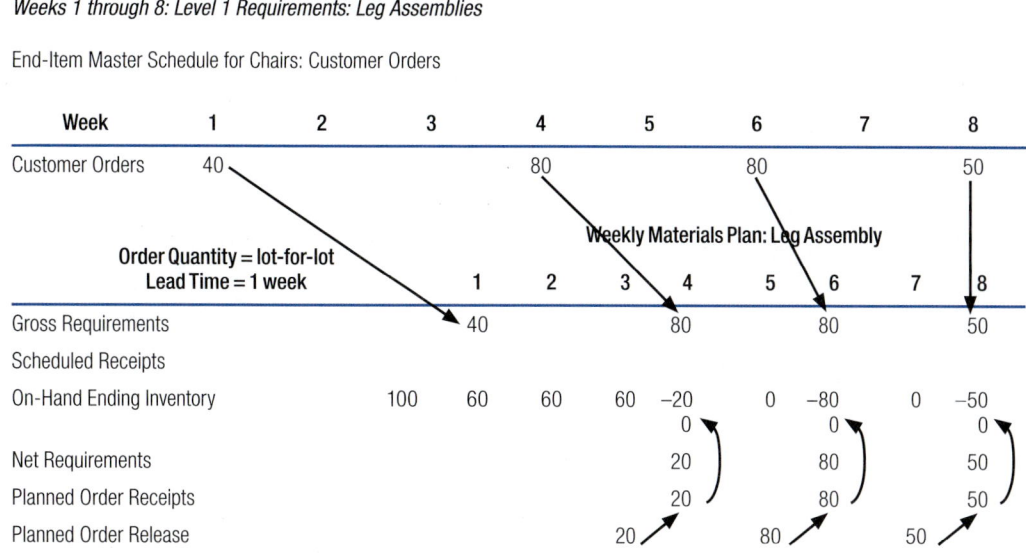

TABLE 18.28: Weeks 1 Through 8: Back Assemblies

Weeks 1 through 8: Level 1 Requirements: Back Assemblies

End-Item Master Schedule for Chairs: Customer Orders

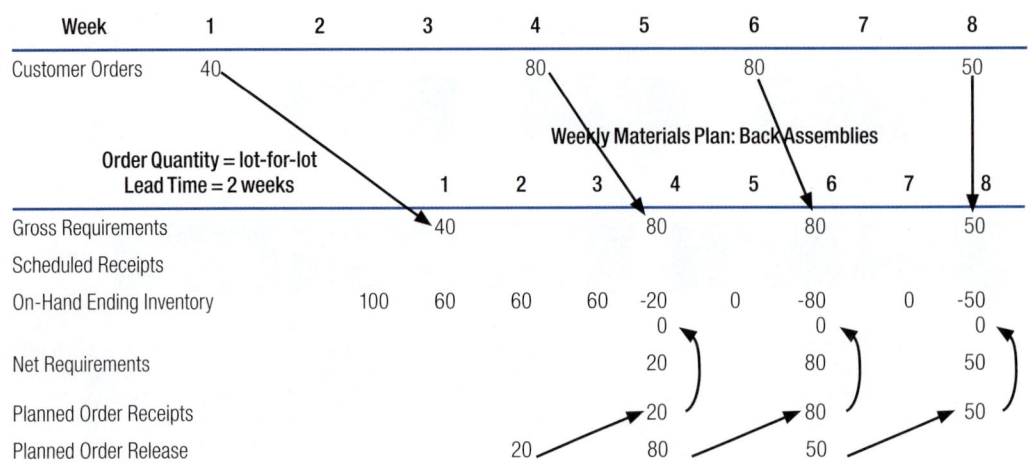

Week	1	2	3	4	5	6	7	8
Customer Orders	40				80		80		50

Weekly Materials Plan: Back Assemblies

Order Quantity = lot-for-lot
Lead Time = 2 weeks

	1	2	3	4	5	6	7	8
Gross Requirements			40		80		80		50
Scheduled Receipts								
On-Hand Ending Inventory	100	60	60	60	-20 / 0	0	-80 / 0	0	-50 / 0
Net Requirements					20		80		50
Planned Order Receipts					20		80		50
Planned Order Release			20		80		50		

Step 2: Generate requirements for lower-level components based on the planned order releases for the parent item at the immediate higher level. We compute the level-two requirements for cross bars based on the planned order releases for leg and back assemblies as shown in Table 18.29.

TABLE 18.29: Weeks 1 Through 8: Cross Bars

Weeks 1 Through 8: Level 2 Requirements: Cross Bars

Planned Order Releases for Back Assemblies

	1	2	3	4	5	6	7	8
Planned Order Releases			20		80		50	

Planned Order Releases for Leg Assemblies

Week	1	2	3	4	5	6	7	8
Planned Order Releases		20		80		50		

Weekly Materials Plan: Cross Bars

Order Quantity = 400
Lead Time = 1 week

	1	2	3	4	5	6	7	8
Gross Requirements			20	20	80	80	50	50	
Scheduled Receipts								
On-Hand Ending Inventory	200	200	180	160	80	0	-50 / 150	100	
Net Requirements							50		
Planned Order Receipts							200		
Planned Order Release						200			

4. Flex Shoes, a mythical shoe company, uses MRP to manufacture shoes and sneakers. Anita Kohli, the firm's operations manager, wants to make a decision on the best lot-sizing rule to use to minimize the total costs associated with MRP-generated orders. Anita selects the firm's popular brand of running shoes as a test case and collected the following data over an 8-week period (see Table 18.30).

TABLE 18.30: Running Shoe Orders

Week	1	2	3	4	5	6	7	8
Gross Requirements	50	60	40	80	30	70	40	30

Ordering cost = $100/order; carrying cost/pair = $2; beginning inventory = 50 shoes; lead time = 1 week (in U.S. dollars).

How would you help Anita to determine which of the following lot-sizing techniques to choose?

Lot-for-lot, EOQ, fixed-period ordering (2-week), part-period balancing.

a. Lot-for-lot rule.

TABLE 18.31: Lot-Sizing Techniques - Lot-for-Lot Rule

Product: Running Shoes Low-Level Code: 0 Lead Time: 1 week Lot Size: lot-for-lot	Week							
	1	2	3	4	5	6	7	8
Gross Requirements	50	60	40	80	30	70	40	30
Scheduled Receipts								
Projected On-Hand Inventory = 50	0	0	0	0	0	0	0	0
Net Requirements		60	40	80	30	70	40	30
Planned Order Receipts		60	40	80	30	80	40	30
Planned Order Releases	60	40	80	30	70	40	30	

Total cost = (# of orders × ordering cost/order) + (projected on-hand inventory × carrying cost)
For the lot-for-lot rule,
Total Cost = 7 × 100 + 0 × 2 = $700

b. Economic order quantity (EOQ) rule.

Recall from our discussion in the supplement to Chapter 12 that the formula for EOQ is given by:

$$\sqrt{\frac{2 \times D \times S}{H}}$$

where D is the annual demand, S is the ordering cost per order, and H is the carrying or holding cost. For this problem, instead of the annual demand (D), we will use the average demand (d) for the 8-week period (in U.S. dollars):

$$\bar{d} = (50 + 60 + 40 + 80 + 30 + 70 + 40 + 30) / 8 = 400 / 8 = 50$$

$$EOQ = \sqrt{\frac{2 \times 50 \times 100}{2}} = 70 \text{ units (approximately)}$$

TABLE 18.32: Lot-Sizing Techniques – EOQ Rule

Product: Running Shoes Low-Level Code: 0 Lead Time: 1 week Lot Size: EOQ	Week							
	1	2	3	4	5	6	7	8
Gross Requirements	50	60	40	80	30	70	40	30
Scheduled Receipts								
Projected On-Hand Inventory = 50	0	10	40	30	0	0	0	0
Net Requirements		70	30	40	30	70	30	30
Planned Order Receipts		70	70	70		70	70	
Planned Order Releases	70	70	70		70	70		

Total Cost = 5 × 100 + (10 + 40 + 30) × 2 = $660

c.   2-week fixed-period ordering.

In this technique, the order quantity will be the sum of the gross requirements for 2 weeks and we will order every 2 weeks as shown in Table 18.33.

TABLE 18.33: Lot-Sizing Techniques – 2-Week Fixed-Period Ordering

Product: Running Shoes Low-Level Code: 0 Lead Time: 1 week Lot Size: 2-week fixed-period ordering	Week							
	1	2	3	4	5	6	7	8
Gross Requirements	50	60	40	80	30	70	40	30
Scheduled Receipts								
Projected On-Hand Inventory = 50	0	40	0	30	0	70	30	0
Net Requirements		60		80		70		
Planned Order Receipts		100		110		140*		
Planned Order Releases	100		110		140*			

*Note: Our planned order release in the period will be 140 units, which will cover the gross requirements for 3 weeks (6, 7, and 8) instead of 2 weeks.
Total Cost = 3 × 100 = (40 + 30 + 70 + 30) × 2 = $640

d.   Part-period balancing rule.

The objective for this rule is to determine the order quantity that has the setup costs and carrying cost approximately equal. We start from period 2 as the on-hand inventory is enough to meet the requirements in period 1 (see Table 18.34).

TABLE 18.34: Calculating Lot Size Using PPB Over Periods 2 to 4 of the Planning Horizon

Periods Combined	Lot Size (cumulative net requirements)	Setup Cost (in U.S. dollars)	Part-Periods	Inventory Carrying Cost (in U.S. dollars)
2	60	$100	0	0 × $2 = 0
2, 3	100	$100	40 × 1	40 × $2 = $80
2, 3, 4	180	$100	40 × 1 + 80 × 2	200 × $2 = $400

The best solution is the second solution, which is to have a planned receipt of 100 pairs of shoes in week 2, as for this solution the carrying cost ($80) is closest to the setup cost ($100). The lot size of 100 units will cover the net requirements for weeks 2 and 3.

TABLE 18.35: Calculating Lot Size Using PPB Over Periods 4 to 6 of the Planning Horizon

Periods Combined	Lot Size (cumulative net requirements)	Setup Cost (in U.S. dollars)	Part-Periods	Inventory Carrying Cost (in U.S. dollars)
4	80	$100	0	0 × $2 = 0
4, 5	110	$100	30 × 1	30 × $2 = $60
4, 5, 6	180	$100	30 × 1 + 70 × 2	170 × $2 = $340

The best solution is the second solution, which is to have a planned receipt of 110 pairs of shoes in week 4, as for this solution the carrying cost ($60) is closest to the setup cost ($100). The lot size of 110 units will cover the net requirements for weeks 4 and 5 (see Table 18.35).

TABLE 18.36: Calculating Lot Size Using PPB Over Periods 6 to 8 of the Planning Horizon

Periods Combined	Lot Size (cumulative net requirements)	Setup Cost (in U.S. dollars)	Part-Periods	Inventory Carrying Cost (in U.S. dollars)
6	70	$100	0	0 × $2 = 0
6, 7	110	$100	40 × 1	40 × $2 = $80
6, 7, 8	140	$100	40 × 1 + 30 × 2	100 × $2 = $200

Order quantity of 110 will cover the demand for weeks 6 and 7, and an order of 30 units in week 7 will cover the requirements for week 8 (Table 18.36). The PPB solution is shown in Table 18.37.

TABLE 18.37: Lot-Size Solution Using the Part-Period Balancing Rule

Product: Running Shoes Low-Level Code: 0 Lead Time: 1 week Lot Size: PPB	Week							
	1	2	3	4	5	6	7	8
Gross Requirements	50	60	40	80	30	70	40	30
Scheduled Receipts								
Projected On-Hand Inventory = 50	0	40	0	30	0	70	0	0
Net Requirements		60		80		70		30
Planned Order Receipts		100		110		110		30
Planned Order Releases	100		110		110		30	

Total Cost = 4 × 100 + (40 + 30 + 70) × 2 = $680

Anita should use the 2-week fixed-period ordering lot-size rule as it has the lowest total cost.

PROBLEMS

1. Visual Optics Inc. (a fictitious company) produces a premium line of women's sunglasses. The company has prepared a 10-week forecast for these sunglasses, given in the following table. In addition, the company has actual customer orders of 120, 90, 60, and 30 units for the first four weeks, and 120 and 80 in weeks 8 and 9 of the 10-week planning horizon. These sunglasses are assembled in lot sizes of 200 units. The company currently has an on-hand inventory of 130 of these sunglasses. Prepare a time-phased master scheduling record.

Week	1	2	3	4	5	6	7	8	9	10
Forecast	100	90	100	120	70	85	50	60	40	70

2. Complete the master production schedule based on the following information:

Week	1	2	3	4	5	6	7	8
Forecast	120	100	130	110	140	140	170	180
Customer Orders	110	100	75	50	32	11	5	0
Projected On-Hand Inventory								
MPS								
Available-to-Promise (ATP)								

Additional Information:

On-hand inventory: 160

Schedule production whenever projected on-hand inventory drops below 30

MPS lot size: 300

3. Complete the master production schedule based on the following information:

Week	1	2	3	4	5	6	7	8	9
Forecast	320	100	30	110	40	240	290	60	410
Customer Orders	60	50	80	20	60	60			
Projected On-Hand Inventory									
MPS Released									
MPS Due									
Available-to-Promise (ATP)									

Additional Information:

On-hand inventory: 600

Schedule production whenever projected on-hand inventory drops below 30

MPS lot size: 300

Production lead time or lead time for MPS releases: 1 week

4. Given the product structure tree below for end-product P,

    a. Determine the number of units of S, T, U, and V needed if 10 units of end-product P are to be assembled.

    b. What is the low-level code for T?

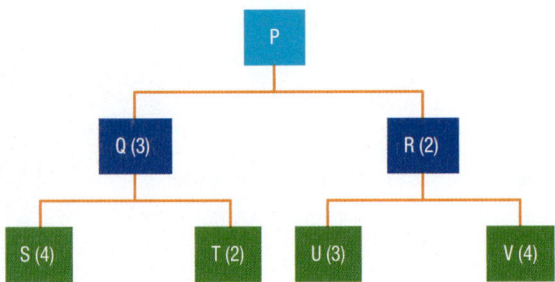

5. Draw a product structure tree for a rolling cart using the low-level coding scheme.

Item	Components
Rolling Cart	Top, leg assembly, frame
Top	
• Sheet steel	Sheet steel
Leg Assembly	Legs (4), casters (4)
• Legs	
• Casters	Wheel, ball bearing, axle, caster frame
• Wheel	
• Ball Bearing	
• Axle	
• Caster frame	
Frame	Bars (4)
• Bars	

6. The components needed to assemble an end product, their lead times, and the amount of their on-hand inventories are presented in the following table. The product structure tree of the end product is also given as follows:

Item	End Product	J	K	L	M	N	O	P	Q
Lead Time (in weeks)	1	1	2	3	2	1	2	1	1
On-Hand Inventory	0	5	10	20	15	25	30	10	0

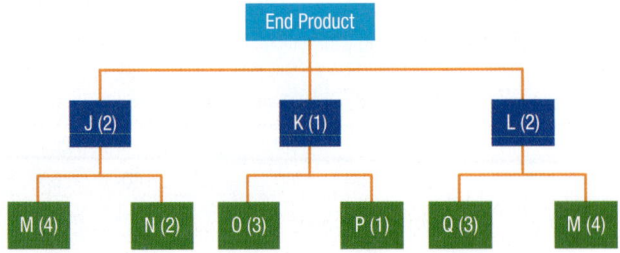

Given this information:

    a. If 15 units of the end product are to be assembled, how many units of M and O are needed?

    b. If an order for the end product is to be shipped at the beginning of week 12, what is the latest week by which work on that order has to be started and still be shipped on time?

Note: You do not have to develop a material requirements plan to answer these questions.

7. Refer to problem 6. If 70 units of the end product are required at the beginning of week 8, develop material requirements plans for subassemblies J and L as well as component M. Subassemblies J and L are assembled in quantities to meet the net requirements, and component M is ordered from a supplier in lot sizes of 300 units. Use the information provided in problem 6 for lead times and on-hand inventories.

8. Dickinson Sports Equipment Inc. is a mythical manufacturer of a variety of sports goods. The bill of materials for one of its popular products, a sidewalk skateboard, is made up of a fiberglass board and two wheel assemblies. Each wheel assembly requires two wheels, one spindle, one wheel mount stand, and two locknuts. Given this information:

   a. Draw a product structure tree using low-level coding and indicate the quantities for each component.
   b. Determine the gross requirements for each subassembly and components to assemble 60 sidewalk skateboards.
   c. If 60 sidewalk skateboards are to be assembled, compute the net requirements if there are 10 fiberglass boards, 20 wheel assemblies, and 15 spindles in stock.

9. Refer to problem 8. You are the production planner at Dickinson Sports Equipment Inc. The lead times for assembling the skateboard and for assembling or acquiring the various subassemblies and components are as follows: skateboard (1 week), fiberglass board (2 weeks), wheel assembly (2 weeks), wheel mount stand (3 weeks), wheels (1 week), spindle (3 weeks), and locknut (1 week). Given this information, if an order for the skateboard is to be shipped at the beginning of week 10, what is the latest week by which work on that order has to be started and still be shipped on time?

10. Refer to the following product structure tree. At the beginning of week 7, 100 units of P are to be assembled. Component S is ordered in lot sizes of 300 units, and one such order is scheduled to arrive at the beginning of week 3. The lead time for assembling Q from S and T is 1 week, and the lead time for S is 2 weeks. There are 60 units of Q and 30 units of S currently in stock. Given this information:

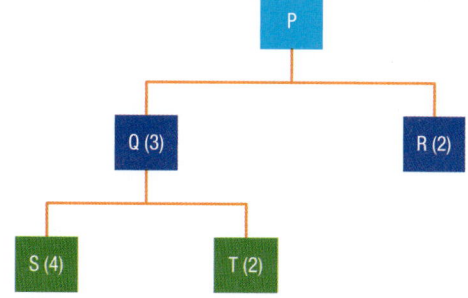

   a. Prepare a material requirements plan for S.
   b. Assume that in week 5 that the quantity of P needed in week 7 has been changed from 100 to 90. If all the planned order releases through week 4 have been executed, how many units of Q and S will be on hand at the end of week 7?

11. Refer to problems 8 and 9. If the master schedule calls for 70 sidewalk skateboards to be assembled at the beginning of week 10, prepare a material requirements plan for all subassemblies and components. Assume no inventories are on hand and a lot-for-lot lot-sizing rule.

12. The following product structure tree is for a step stool:

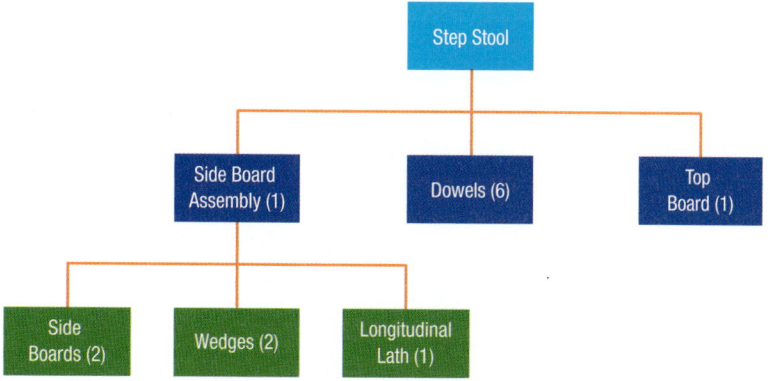

A company that assembles step stools wants to ship 110 units at the beginning of week 4, 140 units at the beginning of week 5, and 200 units at the beginning of week 7. A scheduled receipt of 100 top boards will arrive at the beginning of week 4. Additional information on lead times for assembly and purchase of components and on-hand inventories is given in the following table:

Item	Lead time (in weeks)	On-hand inventory
Step stool	1	10
Top board	1	20
Dowels	1	300
Side board assembly	1	20
Side boards	2	0
Wedges	1	0
Longitudinal lath	2	0

Prepare a material requirements plan using lot-for-lot ordering.

13. Assembling a pair of scissors requires a straight blade assembly, a bent blade assembly, and a screw. Each straight blade assembly requires a straight blade and a straight blade grip. Each bent blade assembly requires a bent blade and a bent blade grip. There is demand for 800 pair of scissors on day 8. There are on-hand inventories of 100 straight blade assemblies, 50 bent blade assemblies, 300 front blades, 200 bent blades, 100 straight blade grips, 50 bent blade grips, and 500 screws. Lead time for assembling scissors is 1 day, and delivery lead times for straight blades and straight blade grips are 2 days, 3 days for bent blades and bent blade grips, and 1 day for screws. Given this information:

   a. Construct a product structure tree for a pair of scissors.
   b. Assuming a lot-sizing rule of lot-for-lot, prepare a material requirements plan.

14. Complete the MRP records for component K.

Component K Low-Level Code: 1 Lead Time: 2 weeks Lot Size: 200	Week								
	1	2	3	4	5	6	7	8	9
Gross Requirements	55	75	80	120	65	50	70	40	35
Scheduled Requirements		200							
Projected On-Hand Inventory = 50									
Planned Order Receipts									
Planned Order Releases									

15. Complete the MRP records for end-product P.

Product P Low-Level Code: 0 Lead Time: 1 week Lot Size: 2-week fixed-period ordering	Week									
	1	2	3	4	5	6	7	8	9	10
Gross Requirements	60	90	60	130	65	75	100	40	85	55
Scheduled Requirements										
Projected On-Hand Inventory = 200										
Planned Order Receipts										
Planned Order Releases										

16. Component X has the following weekly demand requirements:

Week	1	2	3	4	5	6	7	8	9	10
Demand	60	90	60	130	65	75	100	40	85	55

The ordering cost for this item is $50/order and holding cost is $2/unit/week (in U.S. dollars). To develop a material requirements plan for this component, which of the following lot-sizing techniques will yield the lowest total cost?

   a. EOQ.
   b. 2-week fixed-period ordering.
   c. Lot-for-lot.
   d. Part-period balancing (PPB).

17. Component K has the following weekly demand requirements:

Week	1	2	3	4	5	6	7	8	9
Demand	60	90	60	130	65	75	100	40	85

The ordering cost for this item is $100/order and holding cost is $1/unit/week (in U.S. dollars). To develop a material requirements plan for this component, which of the following lot-sizing techniques will yield the lowest total cost?

   a. EOQ.
   b. 2-week fixed-period ordering.
   c. Lot-for-lot.
   d. Part-period balancing (PPB).

18. The following table is a partial master schedule:

Week	1	2	3	4	5	6	7	8
Forecast	240	240	225	225	200	200	210	210
Customer Orders	190	196	240	99	145	78	92	50
MPS								

Lot Size: 400 units

Projected On-Hand Inventory = 300

Available-to-Promise

   a. Complete the master schedule records. Show all calculations.
   b. Suppose a customer cancels an order of 60 units in week 3, what effect would it have on the projected on-hand inventory and the available-to-promise record for that week?
   c. Complete the projected on-hand inventory and available-to-promise records of the master schedule shown in the following table:

Week	1	2	3	4	5	6	7	8
Forecast	110	60	110	60	110	60	110	60
Customer Orders	80	60	120	85	55	30	130	40
MPS	110	60	110	60	110	60	110	60

Projected On-Hand Inventory = 40

Available-to-Promise

19. A finished product R is assembled from two units of S and two units of Q. Production of S requires two units of K, three units of L, and one unit of M. Q is produced from two units of X and three units of Z.

   a. Construct a product structure tree for R.
   b. Assuming zero inventories on hand, how many Zs are needed to produce 90 units of R?
   c. If the finished product R takes 2 weeks to assemble, the subassemblies S and Q take 3 weeks, and the components K, L, M, X, and Z take 1 week, when should the order for Z be released if 90 units of R are required by week 8?

20. Refer to problem 19. Using the information provided in that problem and the following data, prepare an MRP table for finished product R.

Week	1	2	3	4	5	6	7	8	9
Gross Requirements	20	25	35	85	70	95	55	70	80

The minimum production lot size for R is 60. Assume no beginning inventory.

21. Refer to problem 19. Using the information provided in that problem and the following data, prepare an MRP table for subassembly Q.

Week	1	2	3	4	5	6	7	8	9
Gross Requirements	80	55	75	85	100	140	80	100	90

- The lot size for Q is in multiples of 70.
- There are 140 units of Q on hand at the beginning of week 1.
- There is a scheduled receipt of 70 units of Q in week 2.

22. Refer to the product structure tree and the following data:

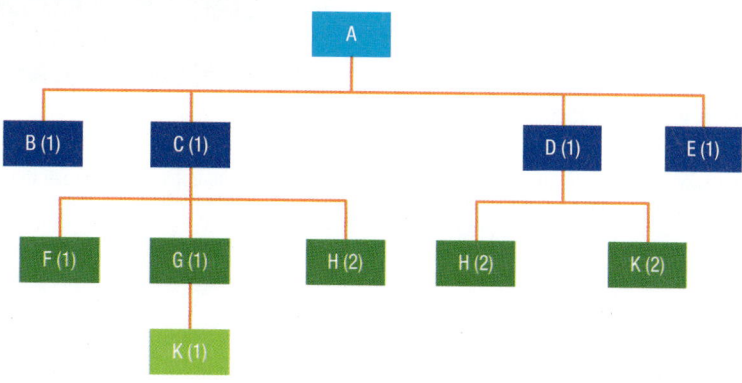

Week		10	11	12	13	14	15
Gross Requirements for A		90	80	100	50	90	70

Item	A	B	C	D	E	F	G	H	K
On-Hand Inventory	0	90	70	70	60	65	80	30	0
Lead Time (in weeks)	1	1	2	2	1	1	2	1	1

Based on this product structure tree and the data provided, develop a gross and net requirement plan for subassemblies C and D.

23. Refer to problem 22. Given the data and the product structure tree provided in that problem, develop a material requirements plan for all the nine items.

CASE STUDY 18.1 BRINGING ORDER TO A CHAOTIC RESTAURANT

Amy Peters, the co-owner of a restaurant in Stamford, Connecticut, has been feeling the pressure. When *Vistas* opened last year, it was the culmination of years of hard work learning the demanding culinary trade, working late nights, and suffering her share of disappointments along the way. Finally, after years of working in various positions within other restaurants, Amy found a business partner who shared her dreams. Together, they launched *Vistas* to considerable fanfare in the local community, with Amy running the business side of the venture and her partner serving as the executive chef. The restaurant had a large and diverse menu and the largest wine cellar outside of New York City. The future looked bright indeed.

Less than 10 months after the opening, Amy found running a restaurant of her own to be less than she had hoped for. In particular, patronage was down and repeat customers were simply no longer coming, in spite of praise for the quality of the food and competitive prices. This behavior was puzzling, because there seemed to be no obvious reason why people were not frequenting the restaurant as much in recent months. As Amy started scanning online rating services like Yelp (San Francisco, CA), she started noticing a pattern. Customer comments were generally positive, although there was one intriguing thread that seemed to run through many of the customer comments: "If you want to enjoy the widest menu options, make sure to arrive early."

Amy was curious about this opinion, and one Saturday night she made a point of staying until closing to get a sense of what was happening. She was dismayed to discover that by 9 pm, almost half of the advertised entrees were no longer available, as the kitchen had run out of stock. When she questioned her partner, the chef, he admitted that they had no good idea of how many ingredients to order and, to cut down on expenses, he preferred to underestimate food service orders rather than carry too much in the freezer. He also was unsure of the amounts and types of food products that they needed to keep in stock to make many of their specialty dishes. Amy realized that they had to do a better job with materials management if they were to stay in business, but she didn't know what the next steps should be. Where should they start?

Questions

1. How would materials management allow Amy and her partner to better organize and coordinate deliveries and maintain critical stocks of food for service?

2. Construct a hypothetical product structure tree and bill of materials file for a single restaurant dish (e.g., a turkey dinner with mashed potatoes, green beans, and apple pie for dessert). How would a product structure tree help Amy and *Vistas* to stay in business?

VIDEO CASE

Watch this video case to learn about how Rolls-Royce uses material requirements planning to meet their business needs.

CRITICAL THINKING EXERCISES

Interview the registrar of your university to learn about the course scheduling process. Based on this interview, write a report on how MRP principles can be applied to improve the efficiency of the course scheduling process.

©iStockphoto.com/andresr

SUPPLEMENT FOR CHAPTER

18

Capacity Requirements Planning, MRP II, ERP, and DRP

LEARNING OBJECTIVES

After studying this supplement, you should be able to:

1. Describe the features of a CRP system.

2. Identify the features of an MRP II system and its benefits.

3. Describe an ERP system and its common modules, its benefits, and its drawbacks.

4. Identify the effects of MRP, MRP II, and the ERP systems on supply chains.

5. Describe the features of a DRP system.

6. Describe how ERP systems can promote sustainability.

OPERATIONS PROFILE: Callaway Golf Uses ERP to Keep Swinging

Callaway Golf Company (Carlsbad, CA) has been a leading manufacturer of golf equipment, including apparel, for more than 30 years. With a global workforce and a complicated and lengthy supply chain for its products, Callaway has invested heavily in enterprise resource planning (ERP), as it has worked to integrate and systematize its wide-ranging operations. Consider Callaway's newest driver, the XR series. That product alone has a supply chain that is nearly 51,000 miles long, which is twice the circumference of the earth. Coordinating the design department, research and development teams, raw material producers, and the manufacturing and warehousing locations is an extremely complicated undertaking and one, without ERP, the company would not be able to accomplish as effectively.

As industry sales have remained relatively flat since 2010, club makers have been forced to work harder to find competitive advantages. Callaway needed to adopt faster methods for product innovation while working to contain costs. That is, it had to become more efficient and get new products to the market more quickly. It was through its ERP system that Callaway has been able to gain the competitive advantage it sought. Their ERP links together all important supply chain functions, including raw material orders and monitoring, coordinating with licensee factories in China and shipping firms to get the clubs to their necessary locations on time. Other systems within their ERP allow Callaway employees to update sales, inventory, and other key reports rapidly. They are even putting ERP to use as a workforce management system, allowing them to monitor hiring and training, safety compliance, and other regulatory requirements.

The golf industry has been stagnant for the past several years and profits have slipped for all major companies in the industry. Callaway has placed a huge bet on the use of ERP as a means to make its new product development and manufacturing processes more efficient and better in tune with the buying public. As the world's largest manufacturer of golf clubs, it has held a key position in the industry for several years, attributing much of its competitive success to its willingness to use the latest technology and supply chain methods to stay on top.[1]

Companies make capacity planning decisions for long-term, medium-term, and short-term time frames, as we discussed in Chapter 7. The focus of Chapter 7 was on long-term capacity planning decisions, but our interest here is on capacity planning decisions for the medium-term, which companies achieve through *capacity requirements planning* (CRP). CRP enables a company to analyze the capabilities of its operations system to determine whether the company has enough capacity to meet a proposed production schedule for a specified time frame. By doing so, a company can plan to acquire additional resources to bridge the gap between available and required capacities.

In this supplement, we will also discuss three important extensions of the traditional MRP system: manufacturing resource planning (MRP II), enterprise resource planning (ERP), and distribution requirements planning (DRP). Whereas MRP's primary concern is planning for materials required for production, MRP II goes further and focuses on the coordination of all activities related to production, including materials, finance, and human resources. The goal of MRP II is to provide consistent data to all participants involved in various stages of the production process. DRP, which is similar to MRP, is used by companies to plan and control systematically their logistics and product distribution activities. ERP systems go beyond MRP and MRP II and provide a real-time integrated view of a company's core business processes, including other functions, such as marketing and human resource management. Through information sharing, ERP systems tie together the critical components of an organization to achieve cross-functional collaboration. As a result, ERP systems enable companies to minimize errors in production and other related transactions.

Manufacturing resource planning (MRP II): the coordination of all activities related to production by providing consistent data to all participants involved in various stages of the production process

Distribution requirements planning (DRP): a system used by companies to systematically plan and control their logistics and product distribution activities through generating a time-phased inventory replenishment plan to manage and minimize inventories in the supply chain

Describe the features
of a CRP system.

**Master the
content.**

edge.sagepub
.com/venkataraman

▶ Capacity
Requirements
Planning

18S.1 Capacity Requirements Planning (CRP)

A capacity requirements planning system operates in tandem with the MRP system (see Figure 18.1). Capacity refers to the productive capability of a facility per unit of time. Capacity planning decisions begin with long-range capacity decisions, which may include designing the initial facility layout, followed by aggregate planning (resource planning) and rough-cut capacity planning (RCCP). In aggregate planning, operations managers determine aggregate resources such as gross labor hours, floor space, and machine hours. RCCP allows managers to modify their existing resource levels to execute the master schedule. As the long-term plans become current, capacity decisions for the medium time frame are concerned with determining that sufficient resources such as labor or machinery are available to execute planned orders and do specific jobs as required by the MRP system. Capacity planning for the medium time range is called capacity requirements planning or CRP. Capacity decisions in the short term are referred to as capacity control, which we discuss in Chapter 19.

This sequence of production planning and control activities is also referred to as priority and capacity planning and control decisions. Figure 18S.1 shows the relationship among these activities. In a manufacturing environment, priority planning activities are primarily concerned with order due dates, and it is the responsibility of the master scheduling and MRP system to be sure that production and purchase orders are issued with valid due dates to meet the end customer order due dates. Priority control activities are accomplished through detailed scheduling (see Chapter 19). Detailed scheduling activities control priorities by dispatching rules that determine start and end dates for jobs, authorization, and follow-up and monitor purchase orders placed to suppliers. The capacity planning activities operate in tandem with the priority planning activities and include resource planning, rough-cut capacity planning, and capacity requirements planning (CRP). Capacity control is primarily concerned with making sufficient capacity available to execute jobs identified by detailed scheduling. Capacity control is accomplished by finite scheduling through the use of techniques such as input–output control.

Capacity requirements planning (CRP) is the process of making a more detailed comparison of the available and required capacity by projecting resource requirements for labor, equipment, and other production needs. The CRP system accepts the planned production or shop orders released by the MRP system and converts them to labor and machine standard hours of **load** required on the various work centers. A load is the amount of planned work scheduled and actual work assigned to a production

FIGURE 18S.1: Interrelationships Among Priority and Capacity Planning and Control Activities

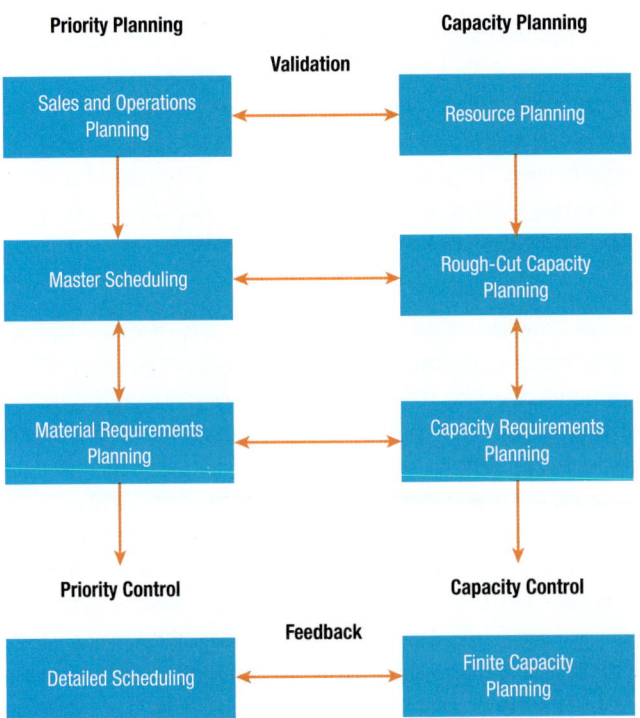

Load: the amount of planned work scheduled and actual work assigned to a production facility for a specific period of time

SOURCE: Adapted from Bihun and Musolf, *Capacity Management Certification Review Course*, 1985.

facility for a specific period of time. Note the difference between capacity and load. Whereas capacity is the rate at which work is completed at a particular work center, load represents the orders waiting to be processed in that work center. If the flow of orders (load) to a work center exceeds its existing capacity, then work-in-process inventory builds up at the work center. On the other hand, if capacity of the work center is greater than that required, then the load on the work center may become stable or even decline. In the context of a CRP system, a load represents the setup time plus run time required from a specific work center. CRP attempts to ensure the feasibility of the tentative MRP schedule so that the capacity availabilities required for executing the shop orders can be met.

A computerized CRP system uses the data file from the MRP system and calculates loads for the company's various work centers that approximately balance the available capacities in these work centers. Specifically, CRP compares the loads required from the various work centers due to current and future shop orders against the capacity available in each work center for each time period. The goal of CRP is to regulate both the flow of work orders and work center capacities to achieve a steady flow of work with minimal load backup. Nevertheless, if available capacities are not in balance with what is required, changes need to be made either to available capacities, by increasing capacity through overtime or subcontracting, or the production requirements imposed by the master schedule on the MRP system have to be modified. CRP systems, like MRP systems, are most useful for job shop or batch production processes. CRP, in particular, is most conducive for job shop production. Job shops are most suitable because, unlike other types of production, they simultaneously process numerous jobs with different routings, quantities, due dates, priorities, and material and resource requirements, and hence, planning and allocating the limited capacity available is necessary.

The key inputs to a CRP system are

- planned order releases from the MRP system;
- load information from the work center status file, which provides information on available equipment and personnel capacities;
- routing information from the shop routing file, which provides information on the sequence of tasks required to manufacture a product;
- job times; and
- any changes that will modify capacity, provide alternative routings, or change planned orders.

The CRP system processing is initiated by the explosion by the MRP system of the master schedule end-item requirements into tentative planned shop orders for components. Using the information from the work center status and shop routing files, the CRP system converts these tentative planned shop orders into standard hours of load on the appropriate workers and equipment. Computing standard hours of load is accomplished by multiplying each period's production quantity requirements by standard labor or equipment requirements per unit, or both. For example, let's assume that 200 units of component X are scheduled for production in the fabrication work center. Let us further assume that each unit of X requires a labor standard time of 2 hours per unit and machine standard time of 1 hour per unit. Based on this information, the 200 units of X convert into the following standard labor and machine hours of load requirements in the fabrication work center.

Labor: 200 × 2 hours/unit = 400 standard labor hours

Machine: 200 × 1 hour/unit = 200 standard machine hours

These load requirements can now be compared with the available capacity in the fabrication work center to determine the extent to which component X requires available capacity. For example, if the fabrication work center has 400 labor hours and 150 machine hours, then all of the available labor capacity will be needed to meet the labor requirements for this component. Yet, as 200 machine hours are required and only 150 hours of machine capacity are available, the facility is overloaded in terms of machine capacity. Therefore, to meet this shortfall in machine load requirements, it may be

 Capacity and Load

necessary to schedule overtime, purchase more machining equipment, or even outsource the work to a shop with excess capacity to get the work done. If capacity cannot be increased by these or any other means, full production of component X may have to be rescheduled.

As you can see from this example, CRP loads all the work centers without regard to the actual capacity available in the work center. This type of loading is called **infinite loading**. The advantage of infinite loading is that it enables planners to see the impact that the planned order releases will have on the capacity required at the work centers. Consequently, if capacity needs to be increased, managers can now make decisions about alternative approaches such as using overtime or delaying selected orders to balance the loads on the work centers. The second type of loading is called **finite loading**. In this case, loading limits are set on the amount of load assigned to each work center per period. Finite loading is typically done using computerized loading systems. In reality, because CRP is a medium-term plan, it uses the infinite loading approach to load the work centers as it gives managers advance notice about potential capacity underloads and overloads. As a result, managers have the time to make decisions about alternative approaches for increasing or decreasing capacity. In fact, the CRP process goes beyond infinite loading because it is an iterative planning and replanning process. The iterative process continues until it achieves a realistic load on the work centers. Finite loading, on the other hand, will not work well in a CRP system because, by limiting the capacity availability at work centers, it forces changes all the way up to MRP, including revisions to the master schedule. For the medium time range, finite loading does not provide the best solution to scheduling problems. It is best suited for the short-range capacity control decisions.

The key outputs of the CRP system are load projection reports on key work centers. Figure 18S.2 shows a hypothetical loading profile for a work center.

Figure 18S.2 shows a 13-week time horizon for the expected loads (resource usage) for jobs currently in production, for planned order releases, and for future expected orders. With this type of load profile, planners can determine if there will be sufficient capacity to meet these resource requirements. If there is sufficient capacity, then the planned order releases of the MRP system are verified and become shop orders and a portion of the master schedule that has generated these resource requirements can be frozen. On the other hand, if the load projection reports show underloads or overloads in specific work centers, planners can attempt to balance the loads by using alternative job routings, using safety stocks, and altering or eliminating lot sizes. For example, in the load profile shown in week 5, the combined resource requirements for current production and planned order releases exceed available capacity. Nevertheless, it appears that by moving some jobs to the immediately preceding or following periods, the firm can meet the resource requirements in period 5. Similarly, the apparent overloads in weeks 9 and 10 can also be adjusted by moving jobs to adjacent periods. In addition, managers can also use **lot splitting**, which is the division of a single lot into two or more sublots and then simultaneously processing each sublot on identical (or very similar) work centers as separate lots. Lot splitting compresses lead times and reduces overloads. It is also possible to increase capacity through overtime, transferring employees from other work centers or by subcontracting some of the work. If none of these alternatives can balance the loads, then the master schedule needs to be revised and the entire MRP and CRP processes have to be repeated until a viable production schedule can be generated. Note that if a master schedule has to be revised, then the manager may have to reassign

Infinite loading: the process of loading all the work centers without regard to the actual capacity available in the work center

Finite loading: the process of setting loading limits on the amount of load assigned to each work center per period

Lot splitting: the division of a single lot into two or more sublots and the simultaneous processing of each sublot on identical (or very similar) work centers as separate lots

FIGURE 18S.2: Loading Profile for a Hypothetical Work Center

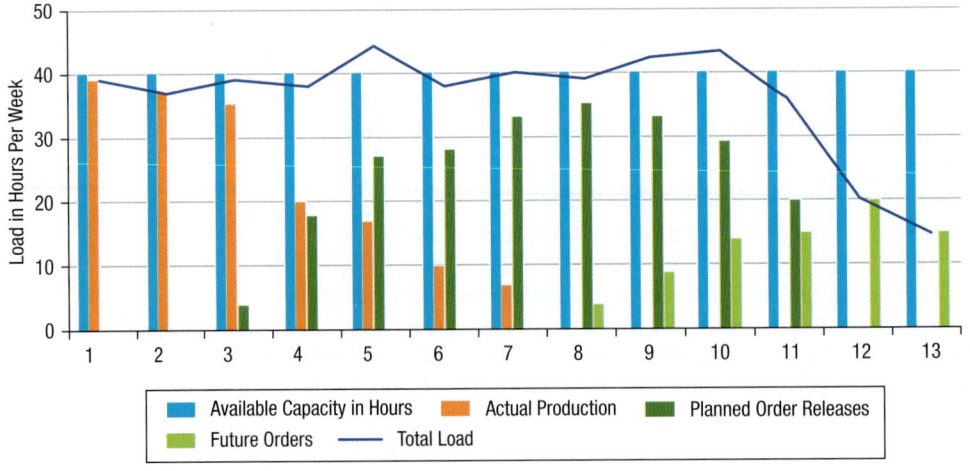

priorities on some customer orders because some customer orders may be completed later than originally planned. To be viable and useful, the load reports generated by the CRP system should include complete information on actual, planned, and released orders. They also should be current and should be based on valid priorities, and they should facilitate future planning.

The CRP system is equal in importance to the master scheduling and MRP systems. Without the CRP system to manage capacity needs, all the efforts expended by master scheduling and MRP systems are fruitless. Despite the advantages, CRP systems have certain limitations. First, CRP is primarily applicable to job shop production. Second, it requires large amounts of input data. Finally, it does not show the effect of master schedule revisions on achieving load balances.[2]

18S.2 Manufacturing Resource Planning (MRP II)—An Extension of MRP

When MRP was first introduced in the late 1960s, it was an **open loop MRP system**. In such a system, the MRP plans and schedules developed assumed infinite capacity and on-time, correct delivery of materials ordered by the suppliers. Yet, it had no provision for feedback. Consequently, when changes, such as a change in demand, occurred, it was impossible to maintain valid schedules by adjusting the production plans. The use of open loop MRP systems led to excessive replanning, delayed deliveries to customers and from suppliers, and escalated costs, and caused other shop floor disruptions. Nonetheless, advances in information technology have made it possible for companies to upgrade their open loop MRP system to a **closed loop MRP system**. Figure 18S.1 showed the structure of a closed loop MRP system. The closed loop system has a provision for feedback that enables plans generated by the system to be checked and adjusted. By synchronizing material purchase and component production plans with the master schedule and by providing feedback on manufactured items and materials on hand, a closed loop MRP system enables plans to be adjusted according to capacity and other requirements. Through its feedback capability, the closed loop MRP system overcomes the fundamental weakness of the open loop material requirements planning system.

Manufacturing resource planning (MRP II) is an extension of the closed loop MRP system. In fact, Figure 18S.1 can be modified to reflect the structure of MRP II by adding modules such as financial and human resources planning, and cost and revenue inputs (Figure 18S.3 on page 690). Whereas MRP is concerned with only planning and acquiring the materials needed for production, MRP II expands those capabilities by integrating additional data—employee, machinery, and financial resources—essential for the successful operation of a manufacturing plant. By centralizing, integrating, and processing real-time information, MRP II creates detailed production schedules to coordinate the arrival of components with resources such as machine and labor availability. MRP II adds value at every phase, beginning with the purchase of materials, all the way through the manufacturing facility to the shipping dock where the product is packaged and sent to the end customer. This value stream includes production planning, machine capacity scheduling, demand forecasting and analysis modules, and quality tracking tools. MRP II also has tools to track employee attendance, labor contribution, and productivity.[3]

MRP II systems begin with MRP, which allows for the input of sales forecasts from sales and marketing. These forecasts, in turn, determine the demand for raw materials. The master schedule initiates both MRP and MRP II systems. MRP allows for the coordination of raw materials purchasing, whereas MRP II facilitates the development of a detailed production schedule that accounts for machine and labor capacity and for scheduling the production runs according to the arrival of materials. Thus, the MRP II system integrates the master schedule, MRP, and the CRP systems. An MRP II output is a final labor and machine schedule.[4]

MRP II systems offer a number of benefits to organizations that employ them. These benefits are better inventory control, more efficient scheduling, and improved relationships with suppliers. MRP II helps the design and engineering function to improve design control, quality, and quality control. It aids the finance and accounting functions by reducing working capital for inventory, by improving cash flow through quicker deliveries, and by generating accurate inventory records.[5]

Because MRP II performs more functions than the traditional MRP system, it requires several additional inputs. One such input is the bill of resources, which identifies the key resources, such as labor, machinery, tools, space, and materials, needed to produce one unit of a product. By using the bill of resources, MRP II can alert work centers of potential shortages that can occur at specific times. With this advance notice, managers can take corrective action, such as hiring additional workers. With the help of the embedded CRP module, MRP II can track machine loads and project machine capacity shortages, which may signal a need for acquiring more machines or hiring a subcontractor.

18S.2

Identify the features of an MRP II system and its benefits.

Manufacturing Resource Planning

Open loop MRP system: developing MRP plans and schedules by assuming infinite capacity and on-time, correct delivery of materials ordered by the suppliers

Closed loop MRP system: a system that enables plans to be adjusted according to capacity and other requirements by synchronizing material purchase and component production plans with the master schedule and by providing feedback on manufactured items and materials on hand

FIGURE 18S.3: Addition of Open Loop Inputs to an MRP System

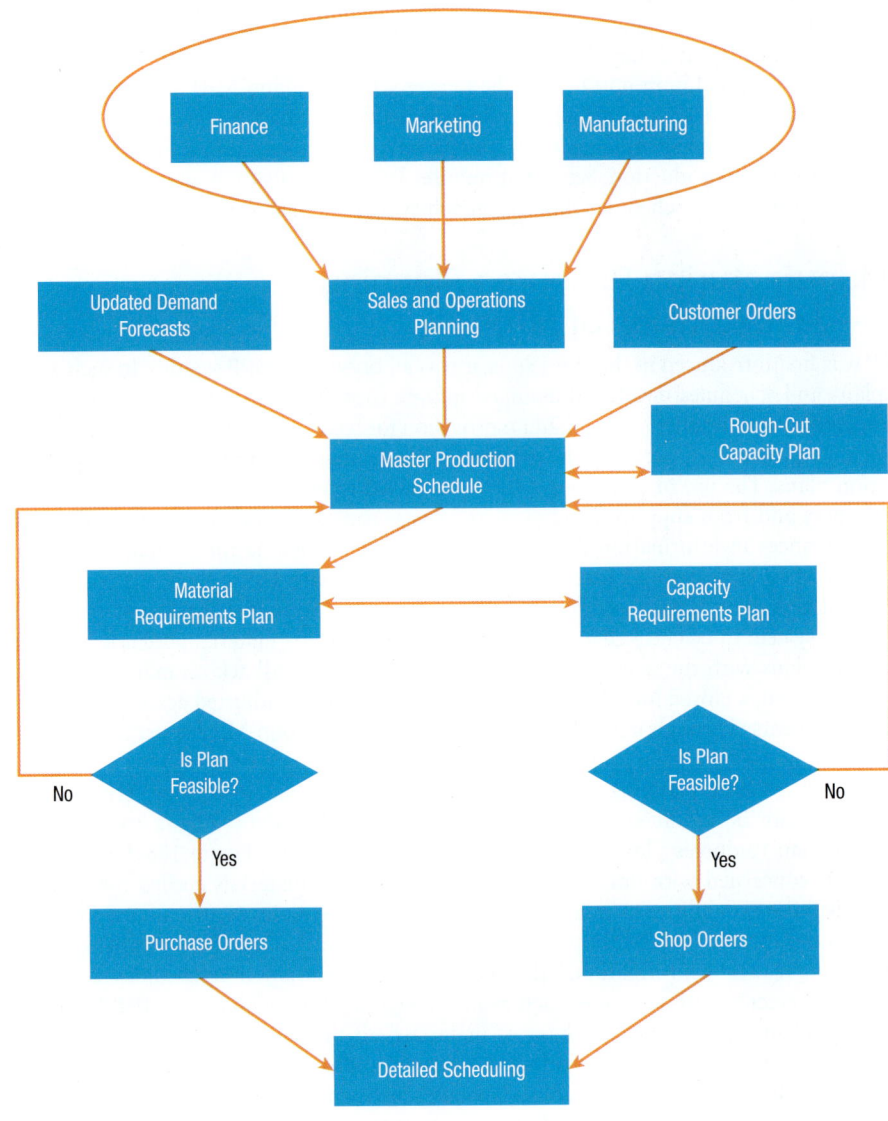

To aid financial planning, MRP II creates a cash flow forecast by calculating the cost and payment dates of all planned order releases for components resulting from MRP explosion. This cash flow forecast, in addition to payments to suppliers, also includes cash outflows associated with wages, power consumption, and other consumables associated with production. Furthermore, MRP II simplifies the budgeting process by projecting cash outflows for a year or more. It also organizes financial expenditures by expense category or by work center.

Many large companies, such as The Ford Motor Company (Dearborn, MI) and Caterpillar Inc. (Peoria, IL), use MRP II capabilities to run their manufacturing operations. Nevertheless, as a comprehensive, computer-based system, MRP II is expensive and can be scaled up to include many submodules, including those for materials handling, production process scheduling, reorders, and machine scheduling. Not all companies will need all of these modules or components of the MRP II system. Therefore, depending on the needs of the company and how it plans and controls its business, MRP II systems can be customized to some extent by adding only those modules that the company needs.

18S.3 Describe an ERP system and its common modules, its benefits, and its drawbacks.

18S.3 Enterprise Resource Planning (ERP)

MRP II overcomes many limitations of the traditional MRP systems by integrating the manufacturing process with tasks such as capacity planning, demand management, production scheduling, and distribution. Yet, even MRP II is geared primarily to serve the needs of the manufacturing function within

Consider This 18S.1:
Electronic Medical Records Bring Together Patients and Their Health Care Providers

A popular trend in the health care industry is the development and use of electronic medical records (EMR) as a means to digitize and make more readily available a patient's health information. Historically, patients who had to seek services from multiple providers (primary care physician, hospital, specialty practices, and follow-up care facilities) and coordinate with their insurance company were required to either physically carry their own medical information or rely on doctor's offices to fax or transport large paper files. Electronic medical records technology integrates all aspects of patient information, including past care, prescription drug orders, lab results, X-rays, and treatment protocols into a comprehensive document that allows all health care providers full access to enhance patient care.

Among the advantages of fully integrated EMR are the following:

- Compared with paper records, digital patient record systems can add information management tools so providers can more efficiently organize, interpret, and react to data.

- EMR software can provide clinical reminder alerts while connecting experts for health care decision support.

- EMR can allow medical researchers to analyze aggregate data for both care management and research.

- The more interactive the system, the more it will prompt doctors to collect additional information. These prompts help doctors focus on issues they might have missed through their normal clinical procedures.

- EMR is the future of health care because it provides critical data that inform clinical decisions, and they help coordinate care between all providers in the health care system.

- EMR systems focus on the total health of the patient. They are built to share information with other health care providers, such as laboratories and specialists, so they contain information from all the clinicians involved in the patient's care.

- The information moves with the patient—to the specialist, the hospital, the nursing home, the next state, or even across the country.

Electronic medical records systems serve a similar function to organizations employing ERP systems. Their goal is open communication, linking all relevant sources of information together to allow health-care professionals to fashion a complete picture of the individual patient. This holistic perspective encourages better communication among health-care professionals, medical facilities, and patients themselves, proving once again that when it comes to maintaining our health, the more information we can collect and organize, the better health care we can provide.[6]

a company. Its data and processes are not fully integrated with the company's other functions, such as marketing, finance, and human resources. In today's intensely competitive, global marketplace, businesses must operate more efficiently and effectively by sharing and integrating information across the different organizational units. Until the mid-1990s, however, information in most companies was often dispersed across many computer systems housed in different organizational functions. Although each of these "information islands," such as MRP and MRP II, did a good job of supporting a specific business activity, such as manufacturing, the lack of integrated information hindered enterprise-wide performance.

 Enterprise Resource Planning

The overwhelming need for information sharing and integration both within the organization and with major stakeholders led to the development of *enterprise resource planning* (ERP) systems. ERP is an enterprise-wide information system that enables companies to

1. Integrate and automate the flow of information across all departments within a company.
2. Standardize business processes, enabling coordination of all resources and activities within the business enterprise.
3. Use a centralized database with a common computing platform to provide all users with a unified, consistent, uniform environment.

With ERP, a company can more than simply integrate the data and processes of all its functions (accounting, finance, marketing, and manufacturing), it can also facilitate information sharing across organizational units and geographic locations, as well as with its customers and suppliers. The core of an ERP system is a common centralized database shared by all applications; therefore, data need to be entered into an ERP system only once. Any data entered into the system, such as a customer order entry, ripple through the enterprise, changing inventory, production schedules, accounts payable, balance sheet, materials reordering, and shipping schedules. For example, suppose that Adidas

(adidas Group, Herzogenaurach, Germany) receives an order for 10,000 pairs of soccer shoes from its European retail store network NEO. This information is instantly available to the company's production department and work begins to fill the order. Simultaneously, the accounting department generates invoices and shipping notifies NEO stores of the expected date of delivery of the soccer shoes. Meanwhile, where needed, new stocks of shoe materials are being ordered from suppliers to replenish the dip in inventories caused by the order. The entire process is transparent and representatives from both Adidas and affected NEO stores can check the status of the order at any time.

Although the actual modules in an ERP software package will vary from one ERP vendor to another, Figure 18S.4 shows the most common modules.[7]

- *Manufacturing Module*: This module improves the efficiency of manufacturing. It is in this module that most of the product differentiation, including industry-specific functionality, is incorporated. This module typically provides forecasting, master scheduling, MRP II (including CRP), product data management (PDM), work order management, and shop floor control.
- *Human Resources Management (HRM):* This module has applications for managing human resources, such as performance management, payroll, time and labor tracking, benefits administration, compensation management, payroll tax calculations, employee recruitment, and planning workforce needs.
- *Supply Chain Management (SCM):* Applications commonly included in this module are demand management, distribution management, inventory management, warehouse management, procurement, sourcing, and order management.
- *Finance and Accounting:* This module includes applications such as general ledger entry, compiling accounts receivable and accounts payable, billing, and fixed asset management. It also typically includes tools for financial management such as creating and adhering to budgets, cash flow management, expense management, risk management, and tax management.
- *Customer Relationship Management (CRM):* This module enables companies to improve customer service by providing the necessary tools to fulfill customers' orders, respond to customers' service needs, and create marketing campaigns. Typical applications included in this module provide customers with sales quotes, place orders, schedule orders, print shipping labels and invoices, generate leads, manage direct mailing campaigns, and create sales literature.

In addition to these five modules, many ERP packages include a business intelligence (BI) module. The tools from this module enable all enterprise personnel to share and analyze the data collected from the various ERP applications to make informed decisions. Many organizations have adopted ERP systems after they became available in the late 1990s. As a result, there are more than 150 ERP vendors. Among these many ERP vendors, SAP SE (Walldorf, Germany), Oracle Corporation (Redwood City, CA), The Sage Group plc (Newcastle upon Tyne, U.K.), Infor (New York City, NY), and Microsoft Corporation (Redmond, WA) are the market leaders; they accounted for 53% of total ERP market revenues in 2013.[8]

FIGURE 18S.4: Common Modules in an ERP System

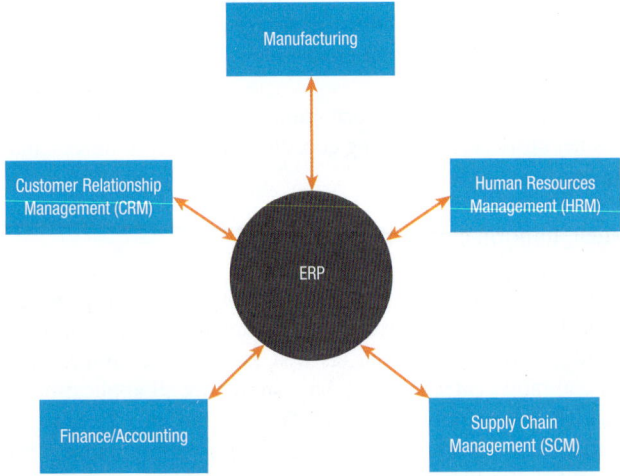

Benefits and Limitations of ERP

Consolidating the data from ERP software creates a number of organizational benefits, including

Benefits of Using
an ERP

- Significant reductions in operating, administrative, and inventory costs.
- Improvements in communication, productivity, and efficiency from integration and information sharing among various departments.
- Elimination of the problem of coordinating and synchronizing changes between many systems.
- Provision of a real-time, enterprise-wide view of the business for faster and more effective decision making.
- Reductions in production and delivery lead times.

The biggest limitation of adopting an ERP is that it is expensive. In fact, the total cost of a full ERP system implementation can cost several million dollars. Another disadvantage is that eliminating the functional boundaries within the company created by ERP information flow can create problems of accountability and confusion about lines of responsibility.

ERP for Service Industries

In many industries, the types of services provided to end customers constantly change and they often must be customized. As a result, using ERP systems for a service business can be very complex because service businesses have unique needs, challenges, and requirements. Businesses in the service sector have to first assess their operations' needs before selecting a specific ERP package. Service ERP systems are designed to improve efficiency and match supply of resources with the demand for services, outsourcing, financial performance, and the management and estimation of projects. Service ERP systems typically include modules that provide back-office support, customer relationship management, time management, expense management, resource management, and project management.

Nevertheless, depending on the service offered, other additional industry-specific functions may be included in the ERP system. For example, for businesses offering professional services, such as law firms, architectural firms, engineering companies, or consultant groups, the ERP system often includes financial management tools to manage payroll and accounts payable and receivable; track expenses; and produce financial reports. On the other hand, firms in the health care, catering, hospitality, and distribution sectors require an ERP system that has functions unique to those markets. Despite these differences, service companies do have some common requirements that are typically offered in ERP packages, such as accounting and billing capabilities, quality control, and customer relationship management.

18S.4 Impact of MRP, MRP II, and ERP on Supply Chains

18S.4
Identify the effects of
MRP, MRP II, and ERP
systems on supply
chains.

Resource Planning
and the Supply Chain

All three systems (MRP, MRP II, and ERP) have varying degrees of influence on a company's supply chain. For example, a company's MRP system focuses on ensuring that the right components are available on hand at the right time to assemble their products such as computers or cars. The advance notice of the need for parts and components provided by an MRP system enables manufacturers to coordinate their production needs with their suppliers. In general, MRP systems have the following beneficial effects on a company's supply chain performance.[9]

- *Improved on-time delivery*: The ability of the MRP system to provide better visibility on future needs for materials and components enables a company to schedule purchase orders with suppliers well in advance of the dates when they are actually needed. As a result, suppliers can improve their on-time delivery performance.
- *Improved quality performance*: The advance lead times that MRP provides for the acquisition of materials and parts enables a company to improve the quality of its products by allowing sufficient time to select quality suppliers.
- *Improved supplier relations*: The time phasing that the MRP system provides indicates when the parts and components will be needed in a given planning horizon. As a result, suppliers are better prepared to make the requested on-time deliveries. Hence, a company's relationship with its suppliers improves as there are fewer expedited and last-minute rush orders.

- *Improved availability of sufficient supplier capacity*: With the availability of a planned purchase order release schedule, a company through regular communication with suppliers can assess if there is sufficient supplier capacity to meet the requirements of the planned purchase order release schedule. If sufficient capacity is not available, then the company has the time to explore other alternatives, such as multi-sourcing and other suppliers.
- *Improved accuracy of capacity plans*: By determining the capacity required from suppliers to meet future orders, a company can generate valid supplier capacity plans to contract blocks of capacity required from suppliers, instead of placing orders for specific parts and components.
- *Reduced paperwork*: Improved supplier relations facilitated by the MRP system can pave the way for long-term contracts with suppliers. Such long-term contracts will reduce paperwork through simpler forms of authorization for delivery and shipment, rather than generating frequent formal purchase orders.

SUMMARY ON MRP, MRP II, AND ERP

Although MRP was primarily concerned with materials, MRP II focused on the integration of all aspects of the manufacturing process, including materials, capacity, finance, and human resources. MRP II systems, if implemented successfully, can enhance and redesign business processes to eliminate non-value-added activities and allow companies to focus on core and truly value-added activities. Thus, MRP II completely incorporates the company's internal supply chain to help integrate the core

OPERATIONS MANAGEMENT: LESSONS LEARNED
Surviving an ERP System Disaster

Although there is strong evidence to support the value of ERP systems throughout a wide variety of manufacturing organizations worldwide, the path to success has not always been smooth. In fact, for some famous companies, ERP planning and implementation mistakes have led to enormous costs—in money and reputation. Consider just some examples.

Lumber Liquidators

When Lumber Liquidators, Inc. (Toano, VA), the discount flooring chain, completed implementation of its ERP software in 2010, it was disappointed by the results. Although overall sales had continued to increase throughout the multi-year implementation of the system, lower productivity led to an estimated $12 million to $14 million in unrealized net sales, according to the company. Net income fell nearly 45% to $4.3 million. Executives at Lumber Liquidators attribute these productivity declines to the time employees had to spend learning the new systems. Although their previous systems were flexible and easy to use, the new ERP software was much more structured and did not easily adjust to specific circumstances.

Marin County Alleges Fraud

In 2010, Marin County in California sued its ERP provider, SAP, for $35 million, alleging, among other charges, that the company misrepresented the quality and usefulness of the ERP software they installed, used the installation process as a training ground for inexperienced workers, and routinely over-billed for work the county claims was badly done. At one point, Marin County went so far as to charge the consultant and ERP developers under the auspices of the federal RICO (Racketeer Influenced and Corrupt Organizations) Act, which would have trebled

the damages. These charges were subsequently dismissed by a judge. After threatening to cancel the project and return to their old legacy systems, the two sides eventually settled their differences in 2013.

Hewlett-Packard's Lost Customers

In 2004, Hewlett-Packard (HP Inc., Palo Alto, CA) made the decision to switch to a new ERP system. Although they anticipated that the rollout would require a transition period, they were unprepared for just how bad the outcome would be. Shortly after the new ERP was installed, HP discovered that approximately 20% of their orders were not going through. Fixing this error took time and created a huge server backlog that HP was unprepared to handle. HP's customers began switching to their competitors when it became clear that the ERP problems were having an impact on order fulfillment. By the time the system was fixed, it had cost the company approximately $160 million in revenue and also damaged its reputation.

What have these lessons meant for hundreds of other companies as they decide to implement ERP systems? First, *plan for potential issues.* Companies that have successfully introduced ERP have set aside time and resources for unexpected problems. Second, *engage a third-party support firm.* Buying directly from an ERP vendor may result in getting the system the vendor wants your firm to have, not necessarily the best system for your firm's needs. A neutral, third-party consultant can work between the ERP vendor and your firm, tailoring the ERP to the organization.

Although most companies using ERP systems have profited from their installation and use, knowing the pitfalls of the implementation process helps to see what *not* to do.[10]

business processes of an entire company into a single software and hardware system. Both MRP and MRP II systems, however, focus on the efficiency and integration of manufacturing or the activities of a company's internal supply chain. Integration of other components of a company's external supply chain, including upstream suppliers, distribution, transportation, and the downstream customers, are largely ignored. It is precisely to overcome these limitations that efforts were undertaken that led to the evolution of ERP.

The impact of ERP systems on supply chains has been more pervasive and beneficial than MRP and MRP II systems. In addition to integrating data within the enterprise, ERP solutions with their customizable web services enable companies to quickly connect with suppliers, logistics providers, and customers and share most of the critical data in real time. The unique ability of ERP systems to integrate external business processes and connect applications across multiple systems in a cost-effective manner makes it possible for manufacturers to respond quickly to changing customer and supplier demand. In addition, ERP systems have inventory management tools that facilitate better forecasting and planning, and as a result, supply and inventory levels can be fine-tuned to customer demand. With ERP systems, the availability of real-time data gives users faster access to the tasks and critical business intelligence information needed to optimize the supply chain.[11]

Although ERP systems have a number of positive influences on supply chains, they still do not provide data on all of the real-time changes in the supply chains. For example, when changes (including changes in forecasts or delayed production or shipments) occur in supply chains, ERP systems are not able to immediately capture these changes, nor take them into consideration. ERP systems make effective supply chain plans, but they fall short of expectations when it comes to supply chain execution.

Today's supply chains are complex, with thousands of parts and with suppliers geographically dispersed, which make transit times less predictable. Furthermore, in the absence of real-time information about the location and status of shipments, supply chain managers are unable to make decisions that will optimize supply chain performance. MRP, MRP II, and ERP technologies enhanced operations and supply chain performance by integrating data and disparate systems. Advances in information use as a means to make the operations discipline even more efficient will be a hallmark of future efforts.[12]

18S.5 Distribution Requirements Planning (DRP)

One area of the supply chain in which MRP practices have been applied successfully is logistics. Companies in a supply chain that are involved in logistics activities needed a systematic and detailed approach for planning and controlling product distribution. This need led to the development of distribution requirements planning (DRP), also referred to as distribution resource planning. DRP is a powerful and widely used technique by companies that are involved in all phases of a supply chain. DRP generates a time-phased inventory replenishment plan to manage and minimize inventories in the supply chain. The underlying idea behind a DRP system is that by generating accurate forecasts of demand, time-phased delivery schedules can be developed. DRP and its procedures are similar to those of MRP. The DRP process typically begins at the retail level (the farthest point of the outbound supply chain network). At this point, gross requirements consist of expected demand, which is a combination of actual customer orders and forecasted demand. As with MRP, the scheduled receipts are the goods the retailer expects to receive from orders that already have been released, whereas goods that have already been received and entered represent on-hand inventory. Net requirements are calculated by subtracting scheduled receipts and on-hand inventory from gross requirements. Based on the retailer's lot-sizing and safety stock policies, planned order releases (offset by the required lead times) are generated to cover the net requirement for some designated future periods. The planned order releases generated by the retailer becomes the gross requirements for the next level down the supply chain (wholesaler or manufacturer), and the process continues. DRP is a pull system because demand at the retail level pulls inventory and shipments through the supply chain. Figure 18S.5 on page 696 illustrates the DRP process. In addition to projecting stock replenishments, if DRP is extended to include projections for resources, such as labor, material handling facilities, and storage space, then it is called distribution resource planning.

Companies that use DRP realize several benefits. They can manage inventory with maximum efficiency and have adequate levels of stock on hand. In addition, as the DRP system generates supply plans based on the forecasted demand, production and material flows will be uninterrupted. As a result, the production process becomes more effective and cost efficient, and the companies can meet promised due dates, leading to satisfied customers. Finally, as DRP carefully monitors inventory stock levels, procurement processes become more efficient because they experience fewer problems (such as non-availability of stock) and procurement procedures become less costly.[13]

18S.5

Describe the features of a DRP system.

Distribution Requirements Planning

FIGURE 18S.5: DRP System

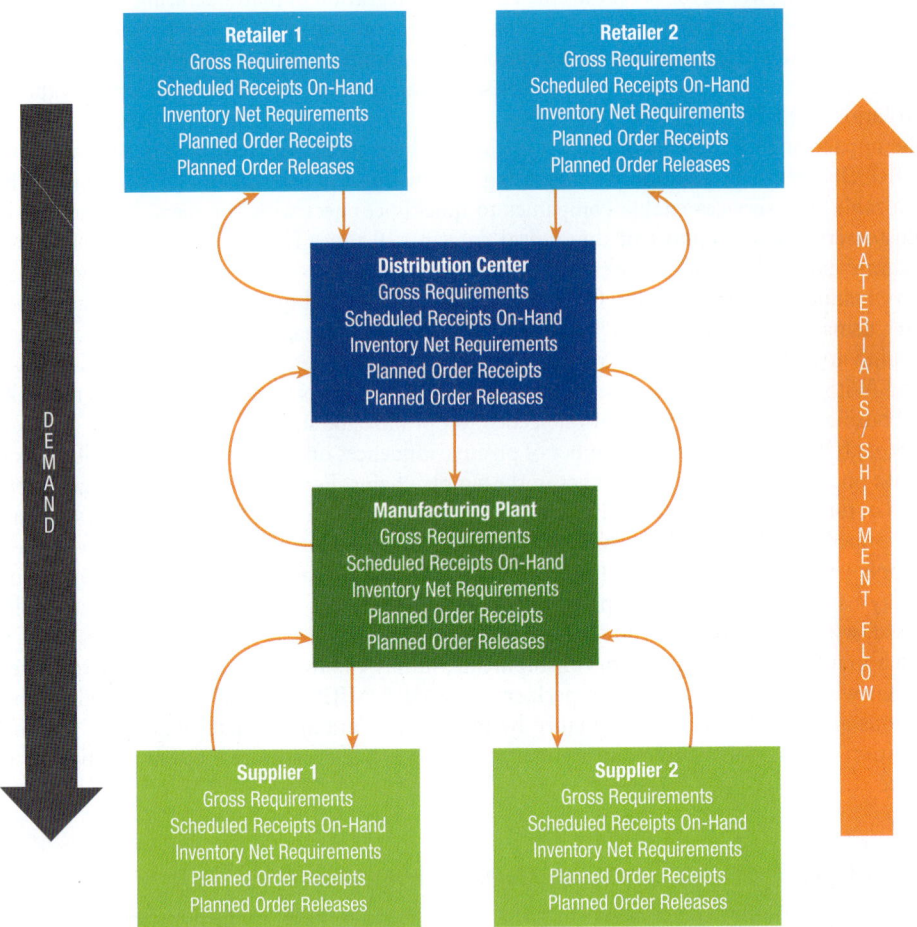

18S.6 Sustainability Issues

18S.6

Describe how ERP systems can promote sustainability.

ERP Systems and Sustainability

Using ERP systems to promote greater sustainability is a new application for the technology. We typically think of ERP functions as an effective means to integrate information flows across all departments; standardize business processes to coordinate resources, inventories, and manufacturing schedules; and create a centralized database. Nevertheless, creative use of the technology offers additional advantages that organizations are only recently beginning to exploit. The integration of all facets of an enterprise can contribute to a manufacturer's sustainability efforts. For example, in determining what products to make and how to assign materials costs, some firms are reassessing the true costs of manufacturing by including environmental costs. As a result, when calculating production runs or deciding which machinery or production facilities to use, firms can now compare the carbon footprints of newer facilities, modern equipment, or locations and choose those that are less likely to add to the environmental costs of production.

Standard ERP business modules such as SCM (supply chain management), MRP II (manufacturing resource planning), FRM (finance resource management), HRM (human resource management), and CRM (customer relationship management) can be integrated to support data from the many environmental sources that are affected by manufacturer activity. These are some decisions firms can make to embed sustainability in ERP calculations and scheduling:

1. What products to make? What are the true costs of a product when we consider the added expense of carbon "offsets"; that is, the reduction in emissions of carbon dioxide or greenhouse gases to compensate for an emission made elsewhere by a supply chain partner?
2. When should we schedule production? How can we optimize the production master schedule to take advantage of lower emissions, lower carbon generation, or more efficient plants and machinery? For example, if we schedule production at night, can we take advantage of hydroelectric power rather than gas or coal-fired power from the energy grid?

3. What processes maximize both efficiency and sustainability? Are some specific machines more energy efficient than others?
4. Where should we manufacture our products? Do some plants operate in areas that are powered by wind or solar power rather than gas-powered electricity?

Factoring in the additional costs related to sustainable operations is not always straightforward. The typical cost accounting or materials maintenance module for an ERP system does not automatically accommodate these important, additional considerations. Vendors and users of ERP systems will need to consider how to rework their calculations for fixed assets, order entry, job costing, production scheduling, logistics, transportation management, and many more applications to pursue sustainability. Nevertheless, it is encouraging to note that ERP can be applied to more than an organization's bottom line. Making the best use of ERP should also result in positive benefits for society's bottom line.[14]

Visit **edge.sagepub.com/venkataraman** to help you accomplish your coursework goals in an easy-to-use learning environment.

- Mobile-friendly eFlashcards
- Mobile-friendly practice quizzes
- A complete online action plan

- Chapter summaries with learning objectives
- Video and multimedia resources

SUPPLEMENT SUMMARY

18S.1 Describe the features of a CRP system. Capacity planning for the medium time range is called capacity requirements planning or CRP. A computerized CRP system uses the data file from the MRP system and calculates loads for the company's various work centers that approximately balance the available capacities in these work centers. Specifically, CRP compares the loads required from the various work centers by current and future shop orders against the capacity available in each work center for each time period. The goal of CRP is to regulate both the flow of work orders and work center capacities to achieve a steady flow of work with minimal load backup. The key inputs to a CRP system are planned order releases from the MRP system; load information from the work center status file; routing information from the shop routing file; job times; and any changes that will modify capacity, provide alternate routings, and change planned orders. The key outputs of the CRP system are load projection reports on key work centers.

18S.2 Identify the features of an MRP II system and its benefits. Manufacturing resource planning (MRP II) extends the closed loop MRP system by adding modules such as financial and human resources planning and cost and revenue inputs. Although MRP is concerned with only planning and acquiring the materials needed for production, MRP II goes beyond that by integrating additional data—employee, machinery, and financial resources—essential for the successful operation of a manufacturing plant. By centralizing, integrating, and processing real-time information, MRP II creates detailed production schedules to coordinate the arrival of component materials with resources such as machine and labor availability.

18S.3 Describe an ERP system and its common modules, its benefits, and its drawbacks. ERP is an enterprise-wide information system that enable companies to (1) integrate and automate the flow of information across all departments within a company;

(2) standardize business processes, enabling the coordination of all resources and activities within the business enterprise; and (3) use a centralized database with a common computing platform to provide all users with a unified, consistent, uniform environment. An ERP system typically contains the following modules: manufacturing module, human resources management (HRM), supply chain management (SCM), finance/accounting, and customer relationship management (CRM). ERP software creates a number of organizational benefits, including (1) significant reductions in operating, administrative, and inventory costs; (2) improvements in communication, productivity, and efficiency from integration and information sharing among the various departments; (3) elimination of the problem of coordinating and synchronizing changes between many systems; (4) provision of a real-time, enterprise-wide view of the business that facilitates faster and more effective decision making; and (5) reductions in production and delivery lead times. The biggest limitations of adopting an ERP are that it is expensive and may require constant updating and system monitoring.

18S.4 Identify the effects of MRP, MRP II, and ERP systems on supply chains. MRP, MRP II, and ERP systems affect supply chains by (1) improving on-time delivery, (2) improving quality performance, (3) improving supplier relations, (4) ensuring availability of sufficient supplier capacity, (5) contracting for capacity, and (6) reducing paperwork.

18S.5 Describe the features of a DRP system. Companies in a supply chain that are involved in logistics activities needed a systematic and detailed approach for planning and controlling product distribution. DRP is a powerful and widely used technique by companies that are involved in all phases of a supply chain. DRP generates a time-phased inventory replenishment plan to manage and minimize inventories in the supply chain. The underlying idea behind a DRP system is that, by generating accurate forecasts of demand, time-phased delivery schedules can be developed. DRP and its procedures are similar to those of MRP. The DRP process typically begins at the retail level (the farthest point of the outbound supply chain network).

18S.6 Describe how the ERP system can promote sustainability. Companies can use the ERP system to promote sustainability by embedding sustainability into ERP calculations and scheduling.

Integrating sustainability into ERP systems can be achieved by factoring in the additional costs of producing products and using efficient plants and equipment that have low carbon emissions, by scheduling production at a time when energy sources that have low carbon emissions are available, and by operating plants in regions where wind or solar power is available.

KEY TERMS

Closed loop MRP system   689

Distribution requirements planning (DRP)   685

Finite loading   688

Infinite loading   688

Load   686

Lot splitting   688

Manufacturing resource planning (MRP II)   685

Open loop MRP system   689

DISCUSSION AND REVIEW QUESTIONS

1. What are the key inputs and outputs of the capacity requirements planning system?

2. Describe briefly how the capacity planning process works.

3. Describe the differences among MRP, MRP II, and ERP systems.

4. What are some key features of an ERP system?

5. Discuss briefly the common modules included in an ERP system.

6. What are the key benefits and limitations of an ERP system?

7. What are the key features of a DRP system?

8. How can ERP contribute to sustainable business practices?

SOLVED PROBLEM

A work center has two machines and two operators. The work center operates on two shifts and each operator works one shift at 8 hours per shift. The efficiency and utilization rates of the two machines and operators at this work center are 92% and 85%, respectively. Table 18S.1 presents the work order to be completed in this work center on Friday of this week along with the information on the number of units to be produced, setup time, and the run time for each work order. Is there sufficient capacity available in this work center to complete all work orders? If not, what options would you suggest to mitigate the capacity overload?

TABLE 18S.1: Work Orders to Be Completed

Work Order #	# of Units	Setup Time (in minutes)	Run Time (in minutes/unit)
501	200	7	0.10
610	800	12	0.09
702	4,000	5	0.20
800	7,000	16	0.15

Solution:

The available capacity in this work center on Friday of this week is given by:

$$2 \text{ machines} \times 2 \text{ shifts} \times 8 \text{ hours/shift} \times 92\% \text{ efficiency} \times 85\% \text{ utilization} = 25.024 \text{ hours}$$
$$= 25.024 \times 60 \text{ minutes} = 1{,}501 \text{ minutes}$$

The required capacity or projected load in this work center is given in Table 18S.2.

TABLE 18S.2: Required Capacity for the Work Center

Work Order #	# of Units	Setup Time (in minutes)	Run Time (in minutes/unit)	Total Time = Setup Time + (run time × # of units)
501	200	7	0.10	7 + (0.10 × 200) = 27
610	800	12	0.09	12 + (0.09 × 800) = 84
702	4,000	5	0.20	5 + (0.20 × 4,000) = 805
800	5,000	16	0.14	16 + (0.14 × 5,000) = 716
				Total time = 1,632 minutes

The work center will have a capacity overload of 131 minutes on Friday of this week. Some options to reduce the overload are to increase the efficiency of the work center by reducing setup time or to have the operators work overtime. Screenshot 18S.1, done in Microsoft Excel (Microsoft Corporation, Redmond, WA), gives the solution to this problem.

The solution to this example can be found in an Excel spreadsheet provided with the study materials for this text.

SCREENSHOT 18S.1: Solved Problem 18S.1

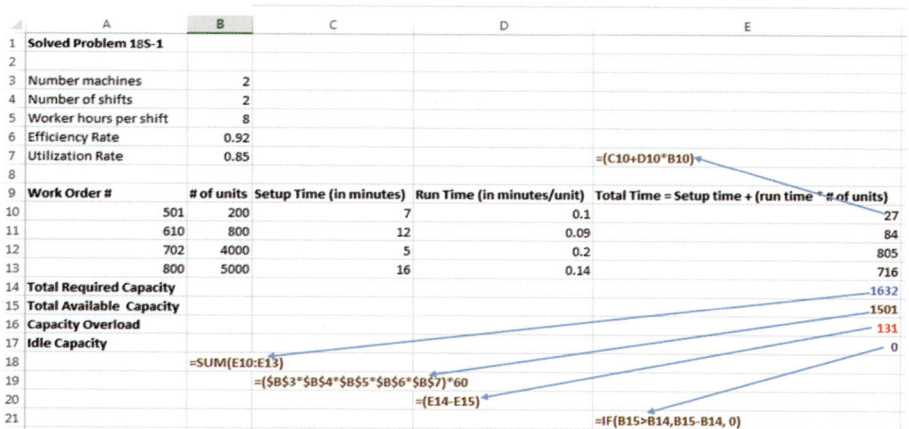

PROBLEMS

1. A company that manufactures roofing materials for houses has the following demand forecasts for the next 4 weeks.

Week	1	2	3	4
Material Forecast (in tons)	60	70	50	80

The company's available capacities for labor and machines and their production work standards are also given as follows:

	Labor	Machine
Production Work Standard (in hours per ton)	6	4
Weekly Available Capacity (in hours)	450	300

What is the capacity utilization for each resource for each of the next 4 weeks?

Do you anticipate capacity-related problems in any of the 4 weeks? What are your recommendations to address the problems?

2. Orion Manufacturing Inc., a fictional company, has scheduled production of the following three of its products for the 4 weeks of January as shown in the following table:

	Week			
Product	1	2	3	4
A	70	120	200	160
B	25	35	75	55
C	30	20	70	90

The two key work centers for producing these three products are fabrication and assembly. The fabrication work station has capacity efficiency and utilization rates of 90% and 95%. The efficiency and utilization rates of the assembly work station are 94% and 90%. The standard hours per unit of time required for the three products in each of the two work centers are given in the following table:

Product	Fabrication	Assembly
A	0.3	0.4
B	0.2	0.25
C	0.1	0.2

If each work center is available for 8 hours, 5 days a week, determine the work load per week in each work center in January.

3. Firebird Bicycle Company, a fictional company, produces three brands of bicycles: Racing, Mountain, and Cruiser bicycles. The master schedule in the following table shows the demand requirements for the month of March for the three brands of bicycles. The standard labor hours per unit required for each brand in the two key work centers of welding and assembly are also given in the second table:

Master Schedule Requirements

Brand	Demand Requirements
Racing bicycles	100
Mountain bicycles	150
Cruiser bicycles	200

Standard Labor Hours per Unit in Each Work Center

Brand	Welding	Assembly
Racing bicycles	0.6	1.7
Mountain bicycles	1.0	1.9
Cruiser bicycles	0.5	1.3

Assuming an 8-hour work day and 20 working days in the month of March, how many workers would be needed in each work center to meet the master schedule requirements? If there is a capacity overload or underload in any of the work centers, what are some approaches you would take to level capacity?

4. Nerula Bakeries, a fictional bakery, has the following demand requirements for its specialty cakes in the month of June.

Specialty Cake	Demand Requirements
Graduation cake	100
Anniversary cake	70
Wedding cake	50

The labor skill requirements for making specialty cakes are high, and the process involves two critical operations—baking and decorating. The time required for each operation varies depending on the type of specialty cake. The standard labor hours per unit of skilled labor required for the three types of specialty cakes vary and are given in the following table:

Standard Labor Hours per Unit for Each Operation

Specialty Cake	Baking	Decorating
Graduation cake	1.0	2.0
Anniversary cake	3.0	6.0
Wedding cake	5.0	9.0

Assuming an 8-hour work day with two shifts and 30 working days in the month of June, how many skilled workers would the bakery need to meet the demand requirements? If there is a capacity overload or underload in any of the work centers, what are some approaches you would take to level capacity?

5. The manufacturing sequence for two products that a company produces involves fabrication, assembly, and painting operations. Each operation requires 2 days to completely process a production lot before it can be moved to the next department. The processing times (in hours per unit) for both products at each of the three departments in terms of both labor and machine resources are given in the following table:

	Fabrication		Assembly		Painting	
	Labor	Machine	Labor	Machine	Labor	Machine
Product P	2	2	1	1.5	1	1
Product K	2	1	2	1	1.5	0.5

The available labor and machine capacities at each department are 800 hours of labor and 600 hours for each day of a 5-day work week. For the upcoming work week, the company has developed the following production schedule for the two products.

Product	Monday	Tuesday	Wednesday	Thursday	Friday
P	400	300	200	200	100
K	400	100	300	200	100

Assuming no setup or change-over time, determine the capacity requirements for each product and the total load for each of the three departments for each day of the 5-day work week.

6. An air compressor assembly department has four employees who each work 40 hours a week. The processing time for assembling an air compressor is 3 hours. Given the information provided in the following table:

a. Determine the available capacity and develop a load profile for the air compressor assembly.

b. As a capacity planner, what problems related to capacity do you see and what are your recommendations to solve the problems?

Week	1	2	3	4	5	6	7	8
Planned order releases	80	70	30	45	60	50	55	70
Processing load in hours								
Available capacity in hours								

7. Dorian Furniture Inc., a fictional furniture manufacturer, has established the following production schedule for the next 4 weeks for three of its furniture products:

	Week			
Product	1	2	3	4
Dresser	40	70	120	90
Dining table	20	30	50	65
Chair	90	100	140	60

The two critical work centers for manufacturing these products are sanding and painting. The sanding work center has efficiency and utilization rates of 96% and 92%, respectively. Similarly, the painting work center has efficiency and utilization rates of 92% and 96%, respectively. The time required (in hours) for each furniture product at each work center is given in the following table:

Work Center	Dresser	Dining Table	Chair
Sanding	0.75	0.5	0.3
Painting	1.0	0.75	0.5

Assuming each work center is available for 40 hours a week, determine the capacity and load profile for each work center for each week.

8. A work center has two machines and two operators. The work center operates on two shifts and each operator works one shift at 8 hours per shift. The efficiency and utilization rates of the two machines and operators at this work center are 95% and 90%, respectively. The following table presents the work order to be completed in this work center on Friday of this week along with the information on the number of units to be produced, setup time, and the run time for each work order. Is there sufficient capacity available in this work center to complete all work orders? If not, what options would you suggest to mitigate the capacity overload?

Work Order #	# of Units	Setup Time (in minutes)	Run Time (in minutes/unit)
702	300	8	0.15
520	700	15	0.10
650	3,500	7	0.30
830	7,500	20	0.20

9. Given the following product structure tree, master production schedule, and routing and work standards information:

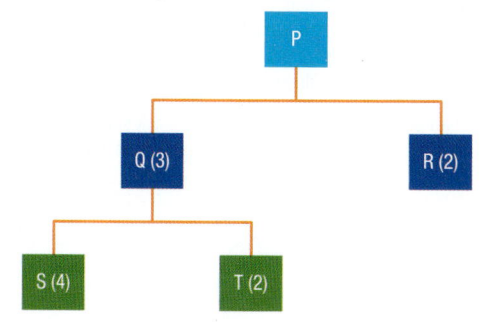

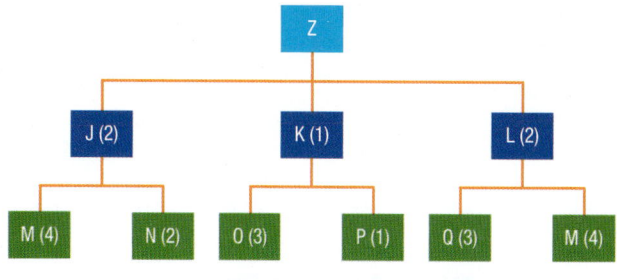

Master Production Schedule

Week	1	2	3	4	5	6
Product P	120	140	90	180	80	80

Routing and Work Standards

Number of Operations Required	Item	Work Station	Standard Hours of Work per Unit
5	T	Lathing	0.6
15	T	Shearing	0.5
10	S	Lathing	0.7
20	R	Milling	1.0
10	Q	Drilling	2.0
30	P	Assembly	0.5

a. Develop a load projection report for each of the five work stations.
b. Balance the loads. Discuss the implications of shifting the work to other periods.

10. Given the following product structure tree, master production schedule, and routing and work standards information:

Master Production Schedule

Week	1	2	3	4	5	6
Product Z	100	100	120	160	130	70

Routing and Work Standards

Number of Operations Required	Item	Work Station	Standard Hours of Work per Unit
5	M	Heat Treating	0.5
10	M	Machining	0.6
15	Q	Machining	1.7
20	P	Heat Treating	1.0
25	O	Machining	1.5
30	N	Heat Treating	0.5
35	J	Heat Treating	0.9
40	K	Machining	0.8
45	L	Heat Treating	0.4
50	Z	Assembly	1.0

a. Develop a load projection report for each of the three work stations.
b. Balance the loads. Discuss the implications of shifting the work to other periods.

CASE STUDY 18S.1 THINKING OUTSIDE THE BOX: ENTERPRISE TRAINING AT GENERAL MILLS

With nearly 40,000 employees worldwide and US$17 billion in annual revenue, General Mills, Inc. (Golden Valley, MN) has devoted a lot of effort to training its employees. With regard to supply chains, the business operates 31 manufacturing plants across North America staffed with workers who need to be trained for highly specialized operational and technical jobs in the production facilities. The challenge lies in providing training that is of similar content and quality across all the plants. When left to individual work sites, there is a potential that some workers will receive in-depth supply chain training, whereas others will only be taught the rudiments. Employees often preferred different methods of training delivery. Some chose to learn by shadowing a co-worker in a production line and observing how job tasks were done before performing them unattended, and others asked for more hands-on demonstrations and instruction. "Because the training was tracked manually on a plant-to-plant basis, it was hard to even identify what the variations were," said Ron McGuire, Training and Development Manager at General Mills. "Adopting a standardized tracking system would make those variations more readily visible to training administrators who could then better understand where the variations exist and what countermeasures they could take to start working toward a standard process."

In a creative move, General Mills adopted an offshoot of ERP software to standardize the manner in which training is conducted, success measured, and results reported across all their plant locations. The software consisted of a consistent global system that all training managers were taught and that was then used as a guide for their standardized learning system. Among the advantages of the global system are the ability to pull up immediate information on the current status of training, exception reports in cases where training methods need modifications, and follow-up documentation for tracking training methods and needed changes when manufacturing processes are changed.

Through a web-based interface, General Mills' supply chain employees can now register for online classes or hands-on instruction and take online assessments. Meanwhile, those in charge of site training can more easily track and review training history, including verifying that all critical training has been successfully undertaken. The manufacturing plants can jointly supervise and ensure the regulatory and safety training that their employees must take every month. Although these topics change monthly, General Mills' enterprise system created a way to standardize the topics throughout the plants and the way each plant runs the training—whether with classroom instruction, pop quizzes, online assessments, management training, or a combination. "Rather than have training administrators or HR employees manually gather information by combing through spreadsheets, piles, or handwritten data on sign-in sheets, and forwarding it up the chain, now we have better reporting and a more effective way of tracking training," said McGuire.[15]

Questions

1. Enterprise training represents just one more example of the types of enterprise-wide initiatives companies use their ERP systems to support. Can you think of other types of enterprise-wide processes these systems could influence positively?

2. How can enterprise systems be used to track safety documentation or other records routinely required by governmental agencies?

CRITICAL THINKING EXERCISES

Visit the websites of the two major ERP vendors, SAP and Oracle, and answer the following questions.

1. What are the features of SAP's ERP system?

2. What are the features of Oracle's ORDBMS system?

3. In terms of ERP functionality, how do these two vendors differ?

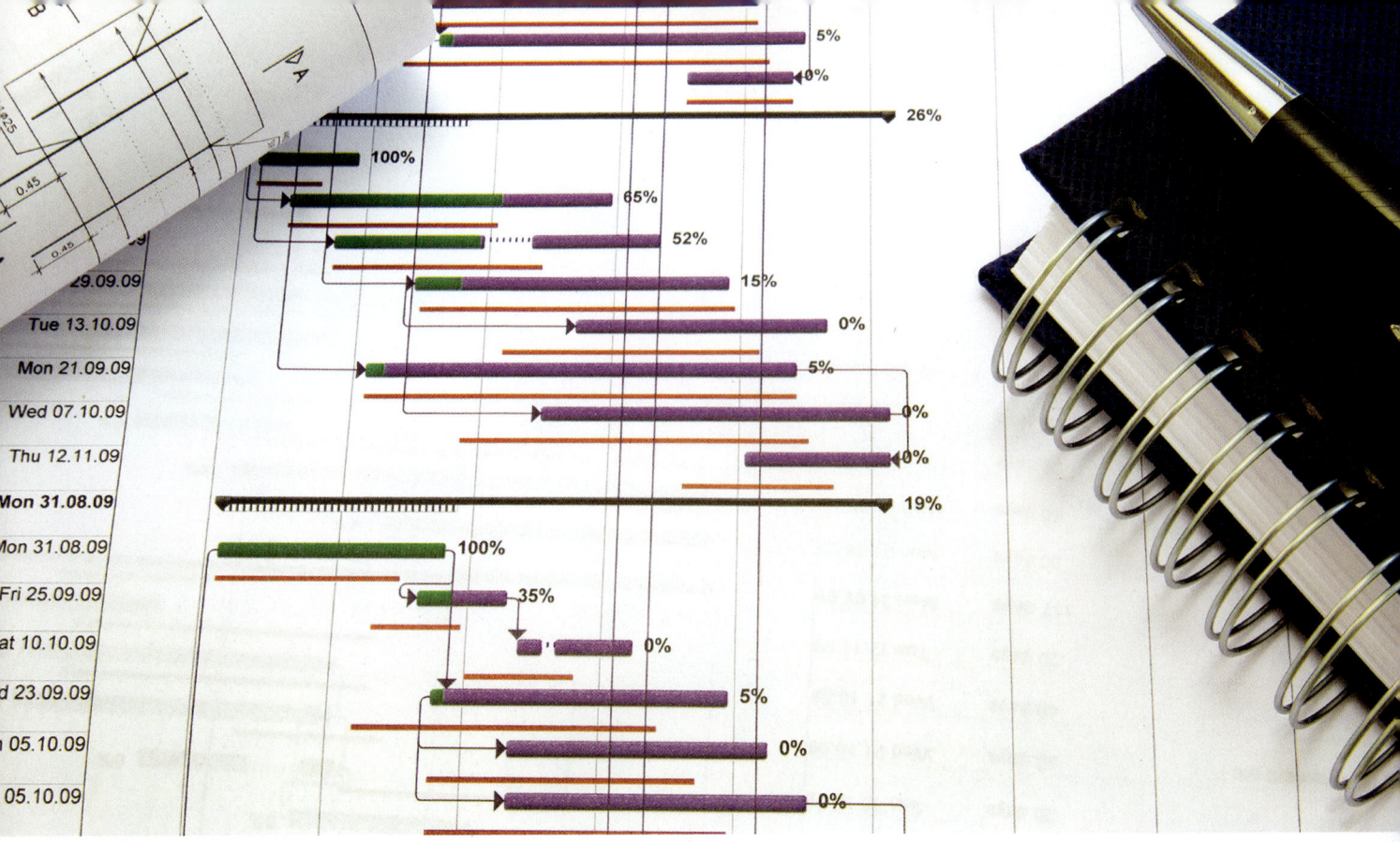

CHAPTER
19

Detailed Scheduling

LEARNING OBJECTIVES

After studying this chapter, you should be able to:

1. Define detailed scheduling.

2. Demonstrate the main types of scheduling and show when each type should be employed.

3. Explain why scheduling is complex.

4. Describe the scheduling methods used in service organizations.

5. Describe supply chain scheduling.

6. Explain how companies can make scheduling decisions to promote sustainability.

OPERATIONS PROFILE: Scheduling at Walt Disney World: FastPass and Waiting for Rides

Walt Disney World (WDW), located in Orlando, Florida (The Walt Disney Company, aka Disney, Burbank, CA), is the largest single-site employer in the United States, with greater than 3,700 job classifications and more than 66,000 employees working at the parks on any given day. For guests, the popularity of WDW is stronger than ever: In 2015, 20.5 million guests visited the Magic Kingdom, 11.8 million visited EPCOT, 10.8 million guests passed through the turnstiles at Disney's Hollywood Studios, and another 10.9 million visited Animal Kingdom. Since opening in 1971, Walt Disney World remains one of the most popular vacation destinations in the world.

The parks' popularity is a challenge for WDW, however, because management must find ways to enhance its guests' experience. Capacity on the theme and thrill rides is limited by the constraints of the size and frequency of the rides. Each attraction inside a Disney theme park has a maximum number of guests that the attraction can handle on any particular day. For example, a ride-through attraction like the Haunted Mansion may be able to carry 2,000 guests per hour of operation. During a 12-hour operating day, 24,000 guests can experience this attraction. Similarly, a live theatrical show with a theater capacity of 3,000 guests that has five shows during the day has a capacity of 15,000 guests. But when a popular park averages 100,000 visitors each day, the guests' dreams of thrill rides quickly meet the reality of ride capacity. In fact, research suggests that the average Disney guest in a single day can go on just nine rides. On an average day, the ticket price for an adult is US$105, making the Disney experience expensive. Disney has tried to make it less frustrating, however. One way it improved wait times and ride scheduling was to introduce the FastPass system in 1999. In 2014, it offered a new version called FastPass+ (FP+), which at an estimated cost of more than US$1 billion completely replaced the old system. The new system uses a virtual reservation approach, centralized reservation machines, and radio-frequency identification (RFID) guest bracelets, rather than the old paper ticket dispenser kiosks.

When FastPass is installed on an attraction, a certain number of seats in the theater, on the ride vehicles, and so on, are set aside. The remaining seats are made available on a stand-by basis to other park guests. At the beginning of the operating day, the enabled attraction's wait is preset at a given time (for example, 45 minutes). The number of FastPasses available is then evenly divided into time intervals (usually five minutes, but sometimes as little as three minutes). Similar to making a dinner reservation at a restaurant, FastPass+ allows you to make a reservation to ride an attraction at a Disney theme park. You can request a specific time, such as 7:30 PM, or you can let the FastPass+ system suggest some times. Each FastPass+ ride reservation lasts for an hour, although reservation windows for shows may be shorter. Thus, if you make a FastPass+ reservation to ride Space Mountain at 7:30 PM, you have until 8:30 PM to use it or change it to something else. Just like a restaurant reservation, your FastPass+ may be canceled if you don't show up on time.

Despite the advantages of the FastPass+ system, customers complain that it is not without problems. For guests staying at a Disney resort, it is possible to book FP+ reservations from a tablet or smartphone to plan out park days in advance; yet, the system will only allow guests to make a total of three FP+ reservations each day and there is a tiered system in place for the most popular rides. That is, guests can make a reservation at EPCOT for Soarin or Test Track but not for both. Another significant concern is the large amount of personal information that Disney collects from those registering on the FastPass+ website. Disney patrons may wonder whether refusal to register on the website (and pass along personal information) limits their accessibility of the FastPass+ system.

Overall, Disney's FastPass+ system has been a highly effective means of allowing the park and its guests to schedule their time to make each day an enjoyable experience and to maximize the number of rides that guests can enjoy, while helping Disney employ efficient short-term scheduling methods that improve capacity planning and the delivery of its unique brand of service.[1]

19.1 What Detailed Scheduling Is

In the hierarchy of decisions made in the field of operations, detailed scheduling is the final step before the actual production of the product or delivery of the service. Figure 19.1 shows the hierarchical sequence of decisions for both manufacturing and service organizations. These decisions range from system design decisions (product and service design, long-term capacity planning, etc.) through sales and operations planning to detailed scheduling.

Scheduling is the process of making specific resources such as labor, equipment, and facilities to produce a product or deliver a service available. As detailed scheduling is the last set of decisions in the sequence, these decisions are subject to the constraints established by the higher level planning decisions in the hierarchy. Consequently, scheduling decisions are typically narrow in scope and have short-term time horizons. Every business, whether it is in the manufacturing or service sector, has to set schedules. United Airlines (United Continental Holdings, Inc., Chicago, IL), for example, in addition to scheduling daily departures and arrivals of its aircrafts, also has to schedule pilots and flight attendants. Similarly, GE Transportation (Chicago, IL) at its Erie, Pennsylvania, plant schedules workers, components, and equipment for the production of its locomotives. Each semester, universities prepare schedules to assign classrooms for students and instructors. Each day, hospitals set schedules for surgery, patient admissions, doctors, and nurses, and for other support services such as security, maintenance, cleaning, and meal preparation. Professional services such as lawyers, barbers, doctors, and dentists must schedule appointments for their clients and patients.

To construct an operations schedule, managers have to balance several conflicting goals. Hence, the objectives of scheduling are to achieve the necessary trade-offs among these goals to ensure that

- Resources such as equipment, labor, and facilities are used effectively.
- Productivity is increased by maximizing the flow of goods and services through the facility.
- Customer waiting time, work-in-process inventories, processing times, and thus overall costs are minimized.

19.2 Types of Scheduling for Manufacturers

The function of scheduling differs depending on whether the manufacturer uses a project, line (continuous or repetitive flow), or intermittent (batch or job shop) production process. In this chapter, we will discuss scheduling for line and intermittent production processes. Project scheduling is discussed in Chapter 3.

FIGURE 19.1: Hierarchy of Operations Decisions

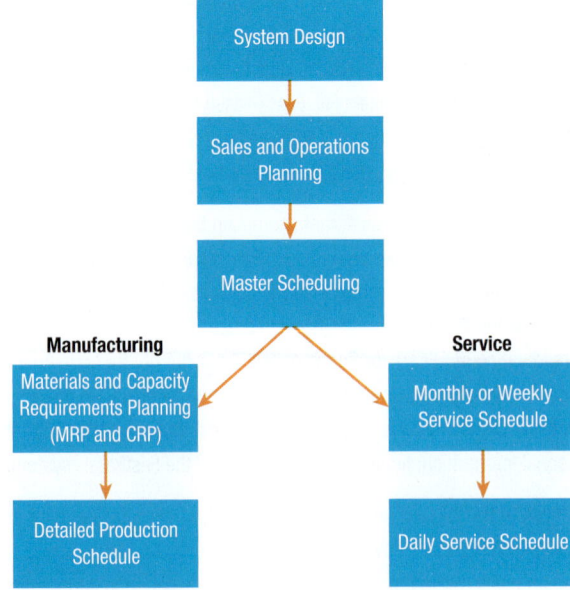

Line Process Scheduling

Line processes are high-volume production processes that typically produce standardized products and require identical or similar operations. Examples of such production processes are automobile assembly lines, petroleum and sugar refineries, and cafeteria lines. We discussed the characteristics of these systems in Chapter 8. Scheduling for these systems is often referred to as flow-shop schedul-ing. Because of the highly repetitive nature of production in these systems, many of the scheduling decisions such as the loading of the work centers and sequencing operations are predetermined when these production systems are designed. Recall from our discussion in the supplement to Chapter 8 that the main goal of such systems is to balance the line so that there is an equal amount of work among the various stations. Consequently, the focus of scheduling decisions for such high-volume systems is also to have a highly balanced production system that facilitates high utilization of labor and equipment and the maximum possible rate of output.

In line processes, if only one product is produced, scheduling is straightforward and relatively easy because the production line will be used only to the extent needed for the production of that single product. In reality, however, line flow processes are rarely devoted to the production of a single product. For example, an automobile manufacturer produces several models of cars with varying features such as four-door and two-door sedans; 4-cylinder, V-6, or V-8 engines; sunroofs or closed roofs; and leather or fabric seats. In line flow processes like these that produce multiple but similar products, scheduling is complicated. The reason is that scheduling has to take into account the slightly different changes in materials, parts, and processing requirements. In such cases, runout time calculations are used to determine a schedule that allocates the capacity of the line among the several products. The following steps should be used to schedule multiple products through a line flow process:

Step 1: In a line flow process used to produce multiple products, the key issue in scheduling is the changeover time in switching production from one product to another. In Chapter 16, in discussing economic production, we saw that lot sizes minimize changeover (setup) costs and inventory carrying costs. Hence, the first requirement in scheduling multiple products in a line process is to calculate the economic or optimum production lot sizes for each product.

Step 2: Once the optimum production lot sizes are determined, the next step is to determine when each product should be produced. This is the heart of the scheduling problem: What should the sequence of products be in the assembly line? Scheduling in such cases is based on a rule that considers the current inventory levels of each product in relation to its future demand rate. A way to express this relationship is to schedule lots by calculating the runout times for each product. The formula for calculating runout times is

$$r_i = \frac{I_i}{d_i}$$

where

r_i = runout time for the ith product

I_i = current inventory level in units for the ith product

d_i = demand in units per period for ith product

Step 3: After calculating the runout times for each product, the next step is to schedule the first lot of that product that has the lowest runout time (r_i). The next step is to recalculate the runout times assuming the first lot has been completed, and the process is repeated until several lots of the products have been scheduled. That is, products are scheduled through the line sequentially by applying the equation, while updating inventory quantities.

Intermittent Process Scheduling

In an intermittent process, a firm produces a variety of products in relatively low volumes. In intermittent processes such as job shops, products are made to

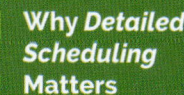

Why *Detailed Scheduling* Matters

Scheduling involves the allocation of labor, equipment, and facilities to produce a product or deliver a service. Operations managers must balance several conflicting goals to increase productivity and minimize overall costs through reducing customer waiting time, work-in-process inventories, and processing times.

Flow-shop scheduling: a form of line process scheduling in which many scheduling decisions are predetermined when the production systems are designed

Runout time: calculations that are used to determine a schedule that allocates the capacity of the line among the several products

Serving food in a cafeteria is a good illustration of line process scheduling.

©iStockphoto.com/ monkeybusinessimages

In the same way that dams are used to regulate the flow of water, input-output control scheduling is meant to maintain a steady flow of job queues.

©iStockphoto.com/poplasen

order and each order has unique material and processing requirements, processing sequence, and processing time. Because of these varying product requirements and because the firm's schedules cannot be established before the receipt of actual job orders, job-shop scheduling is considerably more complex than line process scheduling. The primary problem in intermittent process scheduling is how to manage the queues of work-in-process inventories that build up at each work center as jobs wait for these work centers to become available. To minimize the size of these queues, schedulers need to address the following three issues: input–output control, loading, and sequencing.

INPUT–OUTPUT CONTROL

Input–output control is concerned with regulating inputs to a work center in relation to output and available capacity so that the queues and waiting times of jobs can be managed and kept under control. In the absence of input–output control, jobs may be slow to arrive at a work center (low input), leading to underused facilities and low utilization of labor and equipment. Conversely, too much input will overload facilities, which then causes long customer delivery times. To manage queues effectively, input–output control attempts to balance input and output rates to and from a work center by controlling job processing times, capacity utilization, and inventories. A simple example of input–output control is the use of dams in rivers to control water flow. The reservoirs created by dams impound the water that flows in. The aim is not only to prevent floods but also to regulate the outflow that provides water for irrigation, human consumption, and other needs. Input–output control monitors the work flowing through a work center by comparing the planned input and planned output for a work center with the actual inputs to and outputs from that work center. The planned input to a work center is determined by the capacity planning techniques used by the company and is based on the expected arrival of jobs at a particular work center. The planned output is determined based on available staffing levels, hours to be worked, and so forth. All data for the purposes of input–output control are expressed in standard hours. An input–output control report shows the backlog of work waiting to be processed and the deviations of actual inputs and outputs from the planned values. Table 19.1 shows a sample input–output report for a hypothetical work center. In Table 19.1, the backlog for each period is calculated by adding or subtracting the difference

Input–output control: regulating inputs to a work center in relation to output and available capacity so that the queues and waiting times of jobs can be managed and kept under control

TABLE 19.1: Sample Input–Output Report for a Hypothetical Work Center*

		WEEK				
		1	2	3	4	5
Planned input		70	70	60	60	60
Actual input		90	66	55	58	65
Deviation		+20	−4	−5	−2	+5
Cumulative deviation		+20	+16	+11	+9	+14
Planned output		75	75	70	70	70
Actual output		80	70	65	65	69
Deviation		+5	−5	−5	−5	−1
Cumulative deviation		+5	0	−5	−10	−11
Actual backlog	15	25	21	11	4	0

NOTE: The values in the table are processing times expressed in standard hours.

between the current period's actual output and that period's actual input, from the previous period's backlog. For example, for week 1, the difference between the actual output and the actual input is –10 (80 – 90). Because the actual output is less than the actual input, this additional backlog of 10 hours is added to the previous period's backlog of 15 to arrive at a backlog of 25 hours (15 + 10) for week 1. Similarly, for week 2, the actual backlog is 21 (25 – 4) as the difference between the actual output and the actual input is +4 (70 – 66), which reduces the backlog from the previous period by four hours.

The backlog and deviation values such as those in Table 19.1 will enable managers to identify possible sources of problems and take the necessary corrective actions.

LOADING

The second scheduling decision to be made for intermittent processes is loading. Loading is the assignment of jobs to work or processing centers. Managers must decide which specific jobs to assign to the various machines in work centers. Loading decisions are straightforward if a job can be processed exclusively in a specific work center. The decision, however, is more complex if there is a variety of jobs to be processed and there are several work centers capable of performing the required jobs. The objectives of loading decisions are to minimize processing and setup time or costs, minimize idle time in the work centers, or minimize the time it takes to complete the required work. In making loading decisions, managers use the total hours required or number of jobs to be completed to get an approximate idea of when orders can be delivered or whether capacity will be exceeded. A precise schedule or an exact order of job sequence is not prepared at this point. Rather, managers use tools such as Gantt charts or the assignment method to load work centers.

GANTT CHARTS

Gantt charts (see Chapter 3) are visual tools that can be used to make decisions in intermittent processes. They are easy to construct and understand, and managers can quickly see the current status of a work center or planned loading situations. For scheduling decisions, two types of Gantt charts can be used: Gantt load charts and Gantt schedule charts.

Gantt load charts show the loads on the various work centers, equipment, or facilities as well as the associated idle times. By revealing the relative loads on the various work centers or machines in the production system, Gantt load charts enable managers to make the required adjustments or changes. Gantt load charts, however, have some limitations. First, they do not show production fluctuations or variability that can be caused by unexpected machine breakdowns or human errors and, therefore, require job rework. Second, the chart must be updated periodically to reflect new job arrivals and revised time estimates. Figure 19.2 is an example of a Gantt load chart.

In the Gantt load chart in Figure 19.2, both the lathing and the painting work centers are fully loaded for the week. Note that the shearing and the assembly work centers are idle on Monday and Wednesday as no jobs are scheduled. Also, the lathing work center is unavailable on Wednesday, the shearing work center is unavailable on Friday, and the painting work center is unavailable on Thursday because of preventive maintenance.

A Gantt schedule chart, a common project scheduling tool, is also used to monitor jobs in progress. It shows which jobs are on schedule and which are ahead or behind schedule. For example, let us assume that a refrigerator parts manufacturer has three jobs in progress, one each for KitchenAid and Maytag (both manufactured by the Whirlpool Corporation, Benton Charter Township, MI) as well as for GE (General Electric, Fairfield, CT). The Gantt schedule chart in Figure 19.3 on page 710 indicates progress status of these three jobs. The colored bars in the figure show the actual progress of these jobs. The blue lines represent scheduled activity times for these jobs.

Gantt Charts

Assignment method: a method applied to situations in which various resources must be allocated to activities on a one-to-one basis

FIGURE 19.2: Sample Gantt Load Chart

Work Center	Day of the Week				
	Monday	Tuesday	Wednesday	Thursday	Friday
Lathing	Job 540	Job 540	✕	Job 541	Job 541
Shearing	Unscheduled	Job 610	Job 540	Job 540	✕
Assembly	Job 460	Job 460	Unscheduled	Job 540	Job 610
Painting	Job 350	Job 350	Job 460	✕	Job 540

Processing ▮ (blue)
Unscheduled ▮ (black)
Unavailable (e.g., maintenance) ✕

FIGURE 19.3: Gantt Schedule Chart for a Refrigerator Parts Manufacturer

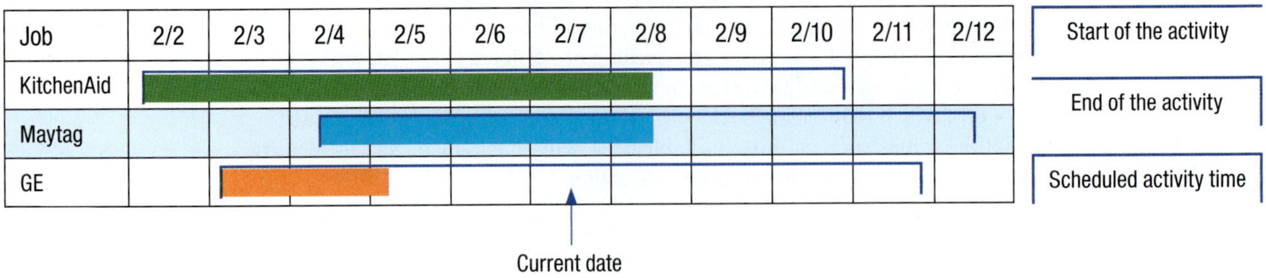

In the Gantt schedule chart, the KitchenAid job is ahead of schedule and the Maytag job is on schedule. Nevertheless, the GE job is behind schedule as work has been completed only through February 5th.

THE ASSIGNMENT METHOD

The assignment method is a special case of a group of problems known as linear programming problems (LPs). Linear programming is a technique used to optimize an objective (such as maximizing profits or minimizing cost) under certain constraints, such as availability of resources. Module A presents a more detailed discussion of linear programming. The assignment method is applied to situations in which various resources must be allocated to activities on a one-to-one basis. Examples of such problems are assigning workers to jobs, jobs to machines, and sales representatives to market regions. The objective of the assignment is to minimize the cost or time involved in the process or to maximize the profit or sale. Note that in assignment problems, only one job can be assigned to one machine or only one sales representative to a market region. Example 19.1 illustrates the assignment method.

EXAMPLE 19.1: A factory supervisor has three workers available and three jobs to be completed. The supervisor has to decide which job should be given to which worker (load jobs). The following table shows the costs incurred in performing each job by each worker. The supervisor wants to make this assignment to minimize the total cost, under the constraint that only one job can be assigned to one worker:

JOB	WORKER (IN U.S. DOLLARS)		
	1	2	3
A	13	16	8
B	10	12	13
C	11	14	9

SOLUTION: The assignment procedure involves performing a series of subtractions and additions of the values in the table to find the lowest opportunity cost. The effect of these calculations is that we will get a series of zeros in the table, implying that these assignments will involve zero opportunity cost.

STEP 1: ROW REDUCTIONS

Subtract the minimum value in each row from all other values in that row. For example, the minimum value in the first row is $8. Subtracting this number from all other values in that row gives us 13 – 8 = 5, 16 – 8 = 8, and 8 – 8 = 0. Similar calculations are performed for the other rows, and the resulting table after the row reductions is as follows:

JOB	WORKER (IN U.S. DOLLARS)		
	1	2	3
A	5	8	0
B	0	2	3
C	2	5	0

STEP 2: COLUMN REDUCTIONS

Now subtract the minimum value in each column from all other values in that column. For example, in the row-reduction table, the minimum value in the first column is $0. Subtracting this value from all others in that column gives us 5 − 0 = 5, 0 − 0 = 0, and 2 − 0 = 2. Similar calculations are performed for the other columns, and the resulting table after the column reductions is as follows:

JOB	WORKER (IN U.S. DOLLARS)		
	1	2	3
A	5	6	0
B	0	0	3
C	2	3	0

STEP 3: CROSS OUT THE ZEROS IN THE TABLE BY USING THE MINIMUM NUMBER OF HORIZONTAL AND/OR VERTICAL LINES

The resulting table after performing the row and column reductions is an opportunity cost matrix. Cross out all zeros in the table by drawing the minimum number of horizontal or vertical lines:

JOB	WORKER		
	1	2	3
A	$5	$6	$0
B	$0	$0	$3
C	$2	$3	$4

STEP 4: CHECK FOR AN OPTIMUM SOLUTION

In Step 3, if the number of lines required to cross out all zeros in the table equals the number of rows or columns, stop. We have arrived at an optimum solution. Jobs can be assigned to those workers who have zeros in their cells. Otherwise, modify the opportunity cost matrix by subtracting the minimum uncrossed value in the table from all other uncrossed values in that table. Add that same minimum value to those values in the cells that are at the intersections of the lines drawn. All other values in the table remain unchanged. In this example, there are three columns and three rows (workers and jobs), and we needed only two lines to cover the zeros. Therefore, we have not arrived at an optimum solution. Hence, we subtract the minimum uncovered value ($2) from all other uncovered values in the table: 2 − 2 = 0, 5 − 2 = 3, 6 − 2 = 4, and 3 − 2 = 1. We will now add the same minimum number ($2) to the value in the cell that is at the intersection of the two lines: 3 + 2 = 5. The resulting table after performing all these calculations is as follows:

JOB	WORKER		
	1	2	3
A	$3	$4	$0
B	$0	$0	$5
C	$0	$1	$4

STEP 5: REPEAT STEPS 3 AND 4 UNTIL YOU GET AN OPTIMUM SOLUTION

As described in Step 3, we draw a horizontal line to cross out the zero that appears in the previous table.

We needed three lines to cover all zeros in this matrix. That number of lines equals the number of rows or columns, and an optimum solution has been reached. Thus, we assign Job A to Worker 3, Job B to Worker 2, and Job C to Worker 1.

Note that we could have assigned Job B to Worker 1 but that solution would have left us with no assignment for Job C.

	WORKER		
JOB	1	2	3
A	$3	$4	~~$0~~
B	~~$0~~	~~$0~~	~~$5~~
C	~~$0~~	~~$1~~	~~$4~~

BACKWARD AND FORWARD SCHEDULING

One difficulty in scheduling is that many jobs compete for the same limited resources. Consequently, one of the key challenges that managers have in scheduling is how to meet the due dates for completion required for specific jobs. To address this challenge, managers can use one or both of the following scheduling techniques: backward scheduling and forward scheduling.

Backward scheduling begins with the due date for each job and loads the processing requirements for these jobs at each work center by proceeding backward in time. Managers use backward scheduling to determine in advance the capacity required at each work center for each time period to complete the jobs by the due dates. In addition to scheduling in manufacturing firms, backward scheduling is used in many service companies and for individual projects. Backward scheduling can be used to schedule surgeries in hospitals and to plan an event such as a wedding.

Forward scheduling begins with the current date for those jobs that have known processing requirements, and it loads the jobs forward in time. The processing time is accumulated against each work center. The objective of forward scheduling is to determine the approximate completion time for each job and the capacity required in each time period. In many made-to-order manufacturing processes and services, forward scheduling is used to determine whether early delivery due dates requested by customers can be met. In reality, however, businesses use a combination of the forward and backward scheduling techniques by loading some jobs forward and others backward in time to strike a balance between available capacity and the need to meet customer due dates. Figure 19.4 shows the backward and forward scheduling techniques.

LOADING APPROACH IN SCHEDULING

In our discussion of CRP in the supplement to Chapter 18, we discussed two loading approaches, infinite and finite loading. At the CRP stage, infinite loading is the more appropriate approach to load the work centers. At the scheduling stage, however, to avoid exceeding capacity, finite loading is the preferred approach because it takes into account the actual processing times of jobs and the available capacity at each work center. By using the finite loading approach, managers can determine detailed

Backward scheduling: a scheduling process used to determine in advance the capacity required at each work center for each time period to complete the jobs by the due dates by beginning with the due date for each job and loading the processing requirements for these jobs at each work center by proceeding backward in time

Forward scheduling: a scheduling process used to determine the approximate completion time for each job and the capacity required in each time period by beginning with the current date for those jobs that have known processing requirements and then loading the jobs forward in time

FIGURE 19.4: Backward and Forward Scheduling

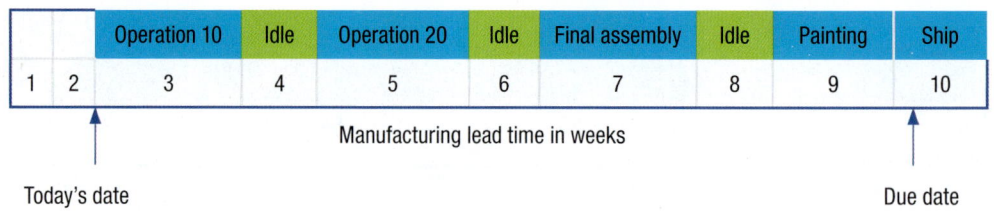

a. Backward Scheduling

b. Forward Scheduling

schedules for each job through each work center based on available work center capacities and other jobs that have already been scheduled. Finite loading provides managers with a set of start and finish dates for each operation at each work center based on the finite capacity limits at that work center. The drawback of finite loading is that schedules may have to be revised frequently because of factors such as processing delays at work centers, addition of new jobs or cancellation of existing jobs, or machine breakdowns.

SEQUENCING

The machines and work centers that will be used to perform specific jobs are determined by loading decisions. Nevertheless, when several jobs are assigned to a work center, managers need to determine the exact order or priority in which to process these jobs. The process of determining the exact order or priority of job processing is called sequencing. Sequencing decisions are made to schedule individual jobs through the various work centers. If all jobs to be scheduled require approximately the same amount of processing time and the work centers have relatively light loads, then sequencing jobs is fairly straightforward. Yet, if the work centers are heavily loaded and if jobs require varying processing times with some relatively lengthy jobs, then accurate sequencing is critical. Without an exact order of job processing activities, costs may escalate as a result of idle time on work centers and lengthy queues of jobs waiting for facilities to become available. Therefore, to come up with an efficient sequence of job processing, managers schedule jobs based on certain prescribed priority rules.

Priority rules are simple decision rules that are used to select jobs for the next operation to control the flow of work as jobs progress through a single process, machine, or work center. The following priority rules are commonly used for sequencing individual jobs:

- **First Come, First Served:** The job that arrives first at a work center or machine will be processed first and completed.
- **Shortest Processing Time:** Jobs are ranked according to their processing times, and the job with the shortest processing time will be processed first and completed.
- **Earliest Due Date:** Jobs are ranked according to their due dates, and the job that has the earliest due date is processed first and completed.
- **Longest Processing Time:** Jobs are ranked according to their processing times, and the job with the longest processing time will be processed first and completed.
- **Critical Ratio (CR):** For all jobs, an index number, which is a ratio of the time remaining until the due date to the work or processing time remaining, is calculated. The job that has the lowest critical ratio is processed first and completed:

$$\text{Critical ratio} = \frac{\textit{Time remaining}}{\textit{Work remaining}} = \frac{\textit{Due date} - \textit{Today's date}}{\textit{Processing time remaining}}$$

Note: Based on this formula:

- If the time remaining is greater than the work remaining, then CR > 1 and the job is ahead of schedule.
- If the time remaining is equal to the work remaining, then CR = 1 and the job is on schedule.
- If the time remaining is less than the work remaining, then CR < 1 and the job is behind schedule.

The critical ratio is a dynamic sequencing rule that gives priority to those jobs that most urgently need work so that orders can be completed by the due date and shipped on schedule. As you can see from the formula, if a job gets farther and farther behind schedule, its critical ratio progressively falls lower and lower. The critical ratio can be applied for scheduling in make-to-stock and make-to-order production systems. By computing critical ratio indices, a manager can determine the relative status of jobs, dynamically track their progress, and automatically revise priorities and schedules as changes occur both in demand and job progress.

To make the scheduling problem more manageable, the use of the priority rules requires the following assumptions:

- The set of jobs to be processed is known and does not change; that is, existing jobs are not canceled and no new jobs arrive.
- Setup times and processing times of jobs are known and do not vary.
- Setup times are independent of job processing sequence.
- There are no unexpected interruptions in job processing, such as machine breakdowns or accidents.

Sequencing: the process of determining the exact order or priority of job processing

Priority rules: simple decision rules that are used to select jobs for the next operation to control the flow of work as jobs progress through a single process, machine, or work center

First come, first served: a priority rule that specifies the job that arrived first at a work center or machine will be processed first and completed

Shortest processing time: a priority rule that ranks jobs according to their processing times and the job with the shortest processing time will be processed first and completed

Earliest due date: a priority rule that ranks jobs according to their due dates, and the job that has the earliest due date is processed first and completed

Longest processing time: a priority rule that ranks jobs according to their processing times and the job with the longest processing time will be processed first and completed

Critical ratio (CR): a priority rule that specifies an index number can be calculated for all jobs. The job that has the lowest critical ratio is processed first and completed

In actual practice, however, these assumptions are not realistic, because jobs do get canceled and new jobs arrive. Therefore the schedule has to be revised. The priority rules can be evaluated based on the following performance criteria:

- *Average or mean job flow time*: Job flow time is the total length of time that a job spends at a work center or shop from the point of arrival to the point at which the job leaves the work center or shop. This total length of time includes the actual processing time, transportation time, and any waiting time at the shop or work center. The average or mean job flow time for a group of jobs is the total flow time for all the jobs divided by the number of jobs.
- *Average or mean number of jobs in the system*: This is a surrogate measure for the average work-in-process inventory in the system and is computed using the following formula:

$$\text{Average number of jobs} = \frac{\text{Total flow time}}{\text{Makespan}}$$

where makespan is the total time needed to complete a group of jobs starting with the first job until the completion of the last job.

- *Average job tardiness*: This is the time that the completion of an actual job exceeds its due date.

In a job shop, based on the sequencing rule selected, managers generate working documents known as dispatch lists that show the sequence of work to be done at each work center. These dispatch lists are revised frequently (daily or for each shift) as conditions change in the shop.

EXAMPLE 19.2: Susan Burke is the manager of a custom furniture job shop. She has five jobs, shown in the following table, that are waiting to be processed through a work center. Susan wants to know what the exact sequence of job processing should be. Help Susan determine the exact sequence for processing these jobs, the average flow time, the average job tardiness, and the average number of jobs in this work center, for each of the following priority rules and compare the relative performance of these priority rules for the three performance criteria. Assume that the jobs have arrived in the order shown in the table:

a. First come, first served (FCFS)

b. Shortest processing time (SPT)

c. Earliest due date (EDD)

d. Longest processing time (LPT)

JOB	PROCESSING TIME (IN DAYS)	DUE DATE (IN DAYS FROM TODAY'S DATE)
A	3	8
B	9	17
C	5	5
D	11	18
E	6	16

SOLUTION

First come, first served: The sequence is A-B-C-D-E. The calculations involved in calculating the performance measures are shown as follows:

JOB	PROCESSING TIME (IN DAYS)	FLOW TIME (IN DAYS)	DUE DATE (IN DAYS FROM TODAY'S DATE)	TARDINESS (IN DAYS; FLOW TIME −DUE DATE; 0 IF NEGATIVE)
A	3	3	8	0
B	9	12	17	0

Job flow time: the total length of time that a job spends at a work center or shop from the point of arrival to the point at which the job leaves the work center or shop

Makespan: the total time needed to complete a group of jobs starting with the first job until the completion of the last job

JOB	PROCESSING TIME (IN DAYS)	FLOW TIME (IN DAYS)	DUE DATE (IN DAYS FROM TODAY'S DATE)	TARDINESS (IN DAYS; FLOW TIME −DUE DATE; 0 IF NEGATIVE)
C	5	17	5	12
D	11	28	18	10
E	6	34	16	18
	34	94		40

Note from these calculations that the flow time is the cumulative processing times and the sum total of the processing times is makespan.

Dividing the sum total of the cumulative processing times by the number of jobs gives the average flow time. Thus for the FCFS rule,

$$\text{Average flow time} = \frac{Sum\,total\,of\,cumulative\,processing\,times}{Number\,of\,jobs} = \frac{94}{5} = 18.8\,days$$

Similarly,

$$\text{Average tardiness} = \frac{Sum\,total\,of\,tardiness\,in\,days}{Number\,of\,jobs} = \frac{40}{5} = 8\,days$$

and

$$\text{Average number of jobs in the work center} = \frac{Sum\,total\,of\,cumulative\,processing\,times}{Number\,of\,jobs} = \frac{94}{34} = 2.76$$

Shortest processing time: The sequence of jobs is A-C-E-B-D. The calculations involved in calculating the performance measures are shown as follows:

JOB	PROCESSING TIME (IN DAYS)	FLOW TIME (IN DAYS)	DUE DATE (IN DAYS FROM TODAY'S DATE)	TARDINESS (IN DAYS; FLOW TIME − DUE DATE; 0 IF NEGATIVE)
A	3	3	8	0
C	5	8	5	3
E	6	14	16	0
B	9	23	17	6
D	11	34	18	16
	34	82		25

For the SPT rule,

$$\text{Average flow time} = \frac{Sum\,of\,cumulative\,processing\,times}{Number\,of\,jobs} = \frac{82}{5} = 16.4\,days$$

$$\text{Average tardiness} = \frac{Sum\,total\,of\,tardiness\,in\,days}{Number\,of\,jobs} = \frac{25}{5} = 5\,days$$

and

$$\text{Average number of jobs in the work center} = \frac{Sum\,total\,of\,cumulative\,processing\,times}{Makespan} = \frac{82}{34} = 2.41$$

Earliest due date: The sequence is C-A-E-B-D. The calculations involved in calculating the performance measures are shown as follows:

JOB	PROCESSING TIME (IN DAYS)	FLOW TIME (IN DAYS)	DUE DATE (IN DAYS FROM TODAY'S DATE)	TARDINESS (IN DAYS; FLOW TIME – DUE DATE; 0 IF NEGATIVE)
C	5	5	5	0
A	3	8	8	0
E	6	14	16	0
B	9	23	17	6
D	11	34	18	16
	34	84		22

For the EDD rule,

$$\text{Average flow time} = \frac{\textit{Sum of cumulative processing times}}{\textit{Number of jobs}} = \frac{84}{5} = 16.8 \, \text{days}$$

$$\text{Average tardiness} = \frac{\textit{Sum total of tardiness in days}}{\textit{Number of jobs}} = \frac{22}{5} = 4.4 \, \text{days}$$

and

$$\text{Average number of jobs in the work center} = \frac{\textit{Sum total of cumulative processing times}}{\textit{Makespan}} = \frac{84}{34} = 2.47$$

Longest processing time: The sequence is D-B-E-C-A. The calculations involved in calculating the performance measures are shown as follows:

JOB	PROCESSING TIME (IN DAYS)	FLOW TIME (IN DAYS)	DUE DATE (IN DAYS FROM TODAY'S DATE)	TARDINESS (IN DAYS; FLOW TIME – DUE DATE; 0 IF NEGATIVE)
D	11	11	18	0
B	9	20	17	3
E	6	26	16	10
C	5	31	5	26
A	3	34	3	31
	34	122		70

For the LPT rule,

$$\text{Average flow time} = \frac{\textit{Sum of cumulative processing times}}{\textit{Number of jobs}} = \frac{122}{5} = 24.4 \, \text{days}$$

$$\text{Average tardiness} = \frac{\textit{Sum total of tardiness in days}}{\textit{Number of jobs}} = \frac{70}{5} = 14 \, \text{days}$$

and

$$\text{Average number of jobs in the work center} = \frac{\textit{Sum total of cumulative processing times}}{\textit{Makespan}} = \frac{122}{34} = 3.59$$

The following table compares the relative performance of the four priority rules across the three performance criteria:

PRIORITY RULE	AVERAGE FLOW TIME (IN DAYS)	AVERAGE TARDINESS (IN DAYS)	AVERAGE NUMBER OF JOBS IN THE WORK CENTER
FCFS	18.8	8	2.76
SPT	16.4	5	2.41
EDD	16.8	4.4	2.47
LPT	24.4	14	3.59

For Example 19.2, the SPT rule has the best performance because it has the lowest value for two of the three measures. The ranking of the other priority rules is: EDD, FCFS, and LPT.

EXAMPLE 19.3: Blake Miller has five jobs waiting to be processed through his grinding and polishing work center. The due dates for these jobs and their remaining processing time in days are given in the following table. Suggest a sequence of job processing for the grinding and polishing work center using the critical ratio rule. Today is day 20.

Job	DUE DATE (IN DAYS)	PROCESSING TIME REMAINING (IN DAYS)
A	25	5
B	30	6
C	24	8
D	28	6
E	23	5

SOLUTION

We compute the critical ratios for the five jobs using the following formula:

$$\text{Critical ratio} = \frac{Time\ remaining}{Work\ remaining} = \frac{Due\ date - Today's\ date}{Processing\ time\ remaining}$$

The results of these computations are shown in the following table:

JOB	DUE DATE (IN DAYS)	PROCESSING TIME REMAINING (IN DAYS)	CRITICAL RATIO
A	25	5	$\frac{25-20}{5} = 1.0$
B	30	6	$\frac{30-20}{6} = 1.67$
C	24	8	$\frac{24-20}{8} = 0.5$
D	28	6	$\frac{28-20}{6} = 1.33$
E	23	5	$\frac{23-20}{5} = 0.6$

Based on the critical ratios, the current sequence of job processing is C-E-A-D-B. Both jobs C and E have critical ratios of less than 1.0 and have to be expedited to meet their due dates. Job C, which has the lowest critical ratio, has the highest priority and should be scheduled first followed by job E. Job A is on schedule, and jobs B and D have some slack. After job C is completed, we should recompute the critical ratios for the remaining four jobs to determine whether their priorities have changed.

Sequencing N Jobs Through Two Machines: Johnson's Rule

The priority rules discussed earlier are appropriate when jobs have to be sequenced through a single process, machine, or work center. Nevertheless, in reality, most production environments have multiple processes and a production manager has to use techniques that identify an optimal sequence for processing any number of jobs through more than one process, machine, or work center. For sequencing N jobs through two machines, processes, or work centers in the same order, Johnson's rule provides the most efficient method. The rule yields minimum processing time for sequencing N jobs through two machines, processes, or work centers for situations where

- The same processing sequence must be maintained on either processes, machines, or work centers.
- There are no in-process inventory storage problems.
- There are no overriding individual job priorities.

The objective of Johnson's rule is to minimize makespan—the total amount of time spent together on the two processes, machines, or work centers. Four steps are necessary to implement Johnson's rule.

Step 1: List all jobs along with their processing times on the work centers or machines for both processes.

Step 2: Find the jobs with the minimum processing times in both work centers or machines (t_{i1}, t_{i2}).

Step 3a: If the minimum processing time is in the first process, machine, or work center, then place the associated job in the first available place in the sequence. Go to Step 4.

Step 3b: If the minimum processing time is in the second process, machine, or work center, then place the associated job in the last available place in the sequence. Go to Step 4.

Step 4: Remove assigned jobs from further consideration. Return to Step 1 until all jobs are assigned.

 Example 19.4

EXAMPLE 19.4: A group of five jobs needs to go through a two-machine flow shop. The first operation involves grinding, and the second is deburring. Use Johnson's rule to find the optimum sequence of jobs that will minimize the total completion time for these jobs:

Job	PROCESSING TIME (IN HOURS)	
	GRINDING	DEBURRING
A	3.5	4.5
B	4.8	1.6
C	2.3	5.1
D	5.9	4.1
E	3.2	2.8

SOLUTION

1ST ITERATION

Step 1: The table shows all the five jobs along with their processing times on the two machines. The unscheduled jobs are A-B-C-D-E.

Step 2: Find the job with the minimum processing time.

The job with the minimum processing time of 1.6 hours is B.

Step 3b: Because the minimum processing time is in the second machine, deburring, job B is placed last in the sequence:

				B

Step 4: Remove job B from further consideration. Go to Step 1.

2ND ITERATION

Step 1: The remaining unscheduled jobs are A-C-D-E.

Step 2: Find the job with the minimum processing time.

The job with the minimum processing time of 2.3 hours is C.

Step 3a: Because the minimum processing time is in the first machine, grinding, job C is placed first in the sequence.

C				B

Step 4: Remove job C from further consideration. Go to Step 1.

3RD ITERATION

Step 1: The remaining unscheduled jobs are A-D-E.

Step 2: Find the job with the minimum processing time.

The job with the minimum processing time of 2.8 hours is E.

Step 3b: Because the minimum processing time is in the second machine, deburring, job E is placed in the last available place in the sequence:

C			E	B

Step 4: Remove job E from further consideration. Go to Step 1.

4TH ITERATION

Step 1: The remaining unscheduled jobs are A-D.

Step 2: Find the job with the minimum processing time.

The job with the minimum processing time of 3.5 hours is A.

Step 3a: Because the minimum processing time is in the first machine, grinding, job A is placed in the first available place in the sequence:

C	A		E	B

Step 4: Remove job A from further consideration. Go to Step 1.

The only remaining job is D, and it goes in the only available (third) place in the sequence. The final schedule is:

C	A	D	E	B

The following chart shows the total completion time of the five jobs and the idle time (in dark blue) at each of the two machines:

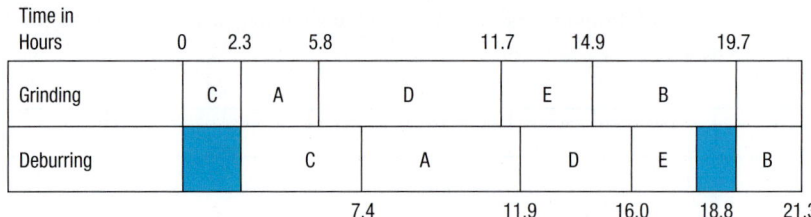

Time in Hours	0	2.3	5.8		11.7	14.9		19.7	
Grinding		C	A	D		E	B		
Deburring			C		A		D	E	B
			7.4		11.9		16.0	18.8	21.3

Thus the total time to complete the five jobs in the two machines (the makespan) is 21.3 hours. The deburring machine has to wait 2.3 hours for the first job and 0.9 hours for the completion of job B in the first machine (grinding).

19.3 Why Scheduling Is Complex

19.3

Explain why scheduling is complex.

In the discussions and examples presented so far, we have made several assumptions such as constant setup and processing times. These simplifications were intended to demonstrate the basic ideas behind scheduling concepts and techniques. In practice, however, such assumptions are usually unrealistic. For example, most setup and processing times and job priorities vary frequently, and machines setup times depend on the order of job processing. In addition, in a job shop, the high variety and low volume of jobs that require processing through shared resources require schedule changes and disruptions are inevitable. It is impossible to analyze the many alternatives and job permutations to arrive at an optimal schedule. Fortunately, software programs make real-time scheduling possible.

Computerized short-term scheduling, often referred to as **finite capacity scheduling (FCS)**, removes many of the drawbacks of rule-based scheduling. By providing interactive computing and graphic output, the ability to monitor events, and the collection of real-time information, the scheduler can make instantaneous changes to the schedule. In addition, FCS systems have many additional capabilities, such as simulations, that give the scheduler the ability and flexibility to respond to changes in job order priorities and changes in labor or machine. FCS systems, like manual scheduling systems, require the same data such as the output from the MRP and CRP systems, shop routing files, due dates, available work center capacities, and resource requirements. Nevertheless, because the output from the MRP and CRP systems is based on infinite loading of work centers, these systems assume no capacity constraints. FCS systems, however, generate realistic schedules by refining these requirements based on the finite capacities currently available at the work centers and the most updated job orders. There are many FCS software systems such as advanced planning and scheduling (APS) systems and manufacturing execution systems (MES). For example, SAP (SAP SE, Walldorf, Germany) uses an APS scheduling software known as the Advanced Planner and Optimizer (APO), and the scheduling software used by i2 Technologies, Inc. (Farmers Branch, TX) is known as the Factory Planner.

There are numerous steps that managers can take to mitigate scheduling problems. First, the due dates set for order delivery should be as realistic as possible and should take existing loads on work centers and available work center capacities into account. Second, when there are significant differences in job processing times, lot splitting can be used for large orders. Third, if increasing the operational capacity in the manufacturing facility is not feasible, then scheduling should be first based on the capacity of the operations that are bottlenecks. The scheduling of the other operations that do not cause bottlenecks should then be subject to the constraints imposed by the bottleneck operations. One such approach that attempts to minimize the complexity of scheduling problems by focusing on bottlenecks is the **theory of constraints**, which was developed by Eli Goldratt.[2]

Theory of Constraints

In a scheduling context, the basic premise of the theory of constraints is that resource use in a manufacturing process is typically uneven, and to achieve a balanced flow of work through the process, the bottleneck resource (or constraining resource) should be controlled. Specifically, the bottleneck resource should never be kept idle either because of nonproductive activities such as setups or because there is a wait for materials or work to arrive. The bottleneck operation should always be fully staffed and should be the focus of any automation or productivity improvement efforts. After scheduling production of the bottleneck operation, all nonproductive resources should be used to support the bottleneck operation. That is, production should be synchronized based on the requirements of the bottleneck operation.

Finite capacity scheduling (FCS): computerized short-term scheduling that allows the scheduler to make instantaneous changes to the schedule

Theory of constraints: the assumption that resources used in a manufacturing process are typically uneven, and to achieve a balanced flow of work through the process, the bottleneck resource (or constraining resource) should be controlled

OPERATIONS MANAGEMENT: LESSONS LEARNED
Fixing Manufacturing Processes at Hitachi Tools

Hitachi Tool Engineering, Ltd. of Japan uses technology to design and manufacture cutting tools that it sells to other manufacturing firms. Although the firm is internationally known for the quality of the tools it produces at its main plant, the company faces stiff competition in the industry, with competitors launching new products every six months and customers continuously demanding newer and higher quality tools. The key to successful competition in the industry is improving efficiency, while maintaining the highest standards for quality.

After failing in its initial attempt to implement lean processes, Hitachi Tool Engineering began using the theory of constraints in just one plant in Japan. In particular, Hitachi introduced the drum-buffer-rope (DBR) system for improving the workflow (throughput) on the factory floor. The net results were improvements in due dates, significant reductions in work-in-process inventory and lead times, and a 20% increase in product output with the same labor force. Other supply chain improvements and benefits followed as reduced lead times and better responsiveness led to improved cash flow for Hitachi's key distributors, which enabled the company to secure more business with these distributors.[3]

©iStockphoto.com/KathyDewar

Hitachi's managers have since extended the introduction of theory of constraints to nonmanufacturing functions, and it is becoming the common company culture in its manufacturing plants located in different countries.

Achieving this synchronization requires the use of the **drum-buffer-rope (DBR)** method. The DBR is a planning and scheduling method that assumes that within any manufacturing system there are a limited number of scarce resources, and they control the overall output of that system. These scarce resources (bottleneck resources), referred to as the *drum*, control the output rate of the manufacturing process and dictate the pace of all other non bottleneck resources. Therefore, to maximize the output, all planning and scheduling decisions should be focused on exploiting the drum. To maximize the use of the drum and to protect it against any disruptions such as idle time, a small amount of inventory referred to as the *buffer* is kept ahead of the drum or the bottleneck operation. The *rope* is the mechanism that synchronizes or subordinates all other resources and decisions to the activities of the drum to maximize its effectiveness. For example, after the drum resource has been scheduled for production, material releases and shipping are connected to it, using the buffer offset. Materials are released at the same rate as the drum can consume them. Orders are shipped at the rate of drum production. The advantage of the DBR approach is that it provides a scheduling solution that maximizes the output rate, reduces lead times, and minimizes the need for holding excess inventory. In addition, use of the DBR approach enables the manufacturer to improve its on-time delivery performance, while minimizing schedule disruptions that require expediting.

To maximize the performance of the bottleneck operation, Goldratt also developed a system of varying batch sizes. He suggested two different ways to assess batch sizes: the process batch and the transfer batch. A **process batch** is the lot-size quantity of a product processed at a work center. A **transfer batch** is the quantity of units that is transported from one work center to the next. In general, the transfer batch size should be less than the process batch size. In synchronized manufacturing systems, where materials and resources are moved systematically through all stages of manufacturing in tandem with market demand, the transfer batch size generally should be kept as small as possible to ensure a smooth and rapid flow of materials. The process batch size should be allowed vary based on the requirements of the production process, and for bottleneck operations, it should be large so that resources would be used fully, eliminating the need for setups. At bottleneck work centers, especially those with significant setup times, small transfer batches should be used to eliminate the waiting time of the bottleneck operation and to ensure a smooth and rapid flow of materials through the process.

 Video:
Theory of Constraints

Drum-buffer-rope (DBR): a planning and scheduling method that assumes that within any manufacturing system there are a limited number of scarce resources and that they control the overall output of that system

Process batch: the lot-size quantity of a product processed at a work center

Transfer batch: the quantity of units that is transported from one work center to the next

Theory of constraints aims to achieve a balanced flow through the manufacturing process with the overall goal of maximizing the output rate of the process as a whole. Five steps can be used to implement the theory of constraints, beginning with the bottleneck operation:

1. Identify the constraints. (Identify the bottleneck operations or resources. They are the weakest links in the chain.)
2. Exploit the constraints. (Plan how to make full use of these limiting or constraining resources or operations.)
3. Subordinate all other nonconstraining resources or operations to the decisions made in the first two steps.
4. Elevate the constraints. (Find ways to eliminate or overcome the constraints that are limiting performance.)
5. If the identified constraint is "broken" (that is, if it is no longer a constraint), then go back to step 1 to identify the next-highest constraint.

Theory of constraints uses three performance measures to evaluate whether the effectiveness of the improvements made has enabled the system to make more money:

a. Increased throughput

b. Reductions in inventory

c. Reductions in operating expense

The application of theory of constraints is not limited to just manufacturing processes. The theory also applies to service firms. Many businesses including the 3M Company (Maplewood, MN), The Boeing Company (Chicago, IL), Bank One Corporation (Chicago, IL), Abbott Laboratories (Lake Bluff, IL), and American Express (New York, NY) use theory of constraints to manage their operations.

19.4 Scheduling in the Service Sector

19.4
Describe the scheduling methods used in service organizations.

Scheduling considerations for service organizations have many different concerns from manufacturing organizations. The two main types of service scheduling are for appointments and reservations.

©iStockphoto.com/Rudyant Wijaya

Up to this point in the chapter, we have addressed the challenge of scheduling in manufacturing settings. Nonetheless, many service-based organizations face their own set of complicated scheduling challenges. Most of the scheduling techniques that we have described for use in manufacturing do not transfer to the service environment because of some unique characteristics typically not encountered in the manufacturing environment:

a. Unlike manufacturers that can use inventories to smooth out demand fluctuations, it is not possible to store or inventory services.

b. The fluctuating demand for services and the need to customize services for individual customers make scheduling services more difficult.

c. Services may be difficult to schedule because they are typically labor intensive and often require employees with specialized skills.

d. Service schedules are constrained by legal requirements and union contracts that dictate the number of hours that employees can work in a given time period.

The particular approach that service businesses such as hospitals, banks, retail stores, restaurants, hotels, and airlines choose depends on whether scheduling involves customers, employees, or equipment. In service businesses in which scheduling involves very little customer contact, as is the case in back-office operations such as tax preparations and processing loan requests in banks, work is scheduled in batches with the objective of maximizing labor efficiency. When scheduling customers for specific services, then scheduling is typically done through appointment or reservation systems.

APPOINTMENT SYSTEMS

Doctors' offices, hospitals, and attorneys typically use **appointment systems** to schedule patient visits, surgeries, and client meetings. The purpose of an appointment system is to minimize customer or client waiting time while maximizing the labor and capacity utilization of the service system. In a hospital, for example, the best appointment system would be one that minimizes both customer waiting time and the doctor's idle time. Even with an appointment system, scheduling in these service businesses can be problematic because some patients fail to show up or arrive late and there are variations in the length of contact time with the service provider that can delay other patient appointments. Many hospitals and doctors' offices use computer software systems to schedule and manage their patient appointments.

Video: Scheduling in the Service Sector

RESERVATION SYSTEMS

Many service businesses such as hotels, restaurants, airlines, and resorts use **reservation systems** to schedule and manage customer demand for their services. Using computerized systems, these businesses can maximize customer satisfaction by smoothing out demand for their services in any given time, thereby minimizing unnecessary customer waiting time and making sure that the internal staff resources are available and deployed to provide each guest with an enjoyable experience. For example, ABACUS is a central reservation system that many airlines such as Lufthansa (Deutsche Lufthansa AG, Cologne, Germany), Air France (Société Air France, S.A., Tremblay-en-France, France), and Singapore Airlines (Singapore Airlines Limited, Singapore, Singapore) use to manage passenger reservations on their flights.

WORKFORCE SCHEDULING

Thus far we have focused the discussion of scheduling services on managing the demand side of services, that is, customers. We will now look at scheduling the supply or capacity side (the workforce) of service providers to meet the demand for their services. Among the many resources that an organization has at its disposal, the most flexible resource is its workforce. For example, a company can alter its workforce levels through hiring and firing or alter its workforce capacity through overtime, additional shifts, or hiring part-time workers. For service businesses, in particular, this workforce flexibility is extremely useful for dealing with the highly variable demands that these companies face. Nevertheless, this inherent flexibility has also made day-to-day scheduling decisions highly complex, as is the case for service organizations such as hospitals, airlines, and police departments that operate 24 hours a day with multiple shifts. Scheduling the workforce for these businesses is constrained by union and federal rules and regulations, workers' skill levels, number of hours that they can work, vacation days, and so forth. Typically, employees in these service organizations work on a cyclical basis. That is, they work for a certain number of days or shifts during a week and then have days off, and the pattern is repeated in subsequent weeks.

United and American Airlines, Inc. (Fort Worth, TX) are just two examples of air travel companies that use mathematical programming models to schedule their ticket agents and flight crews. Yet, most service businesses use decision rules to develop their workforce schedules that involve a cyclical pattern of work assignments. We will describe one such simple scheduling procedure for a service business that operates seven days a week, but each employee works five days a week and then has two consecutive days off.

DECISION RULES FOR WORKFORCE SCHEDULING WITH TWO CONSECUTIVE DAYS OFF

Step 1: Determine the daily workforce requirements for all seven days of a given week, and enter these staffing requirements in a table.

Step 2: Identify the two consecutive days that have the *lowest total workforce requirements,* and highlight these two days. Assign these two days off to the first employee. If there is a tie, give preference to Saturday–Sunday pairs or break the tie arbitrarily.

Step 3: There is now *one* employee working the remaining five days of the week. Set up a new row in the table for the second employee by subtracting 1 from the daily requirements of the previous row, except for the highlighted days or any day that has a zero value.

Step 4: In the newly created second row, identify and highlight the two consecutive days that have the lowest total requirement, and assign to the second employee these two days off.

Step 5: Repeat steps 3 and 4 until all workforce requirements are met.

Example 19.5 illustrates how this procedure can be applied to set a workforce schedule

Appointment systems: a scheduling system for service organizations that minimizes customer or client waiting time while maximizing the labor and capacity utilization of the service system by designating specific times for clients to arrive

Reservation systems: a scheduling system for service organizations that uses computerized systems to maximize customer satisfaction by smoothing out demand for their services in any given time

EXAMPLE 19.5: The Chief of Police of Millcreek Township, Jennifer Taylor, wants to construct a workforce schedule for her department's police officers using a standard 5-day work week with two consecutive days off. Jennifer's objective is to minimize the total amount of excess capacity. The staffing requirements for the second week of January are given in the following table:

DAY	MONDAY	TUESDAY	WEDNESDAY	THURSDAY	FRIDAY	SATURDAY	SUNDAY
Number of police officers required	7	5	9	10	11	4	3

SOLUTION

Step 1: Determine the daily workforce requirements for seven days of a given week.

The daily requirements for police officers are given in the table.

Step 2: Identify the two consecutive days that have the *lowest total workforce requirements* and highlight these two days. Assign these two days off to the first employee. If there is a tie, give preference to Saturday–Sunday pairs or break the tie arbitrarily.

The two consecutive days with the lowest police officer requirements of 4 and 3 are Saturday and Sunday. We will assign the first police officer these two days off as highlighted in the following table:

DAY	MONDAY	TUESDAY	WEDNESDAY	THURSDAY	FRIDAY	SATURDAY	SUNDAY
Officer –1	7	5	9	10	11	**4**	**3**

Step 3: As we now have *one* police officer working Monday through Friday, create a new row for the second police officer by subtracting 1 from the daily requirements of the row in the previous table, except for the highlighted days or any day that has a zero value. The table with the newly created row is as follows:

DAY	MONDAY	TUESDAY	WEDNESDAY	THURSDAY	FRIDAY	SATURDAY	SUNDAY
Officer – 1	7	5	9	10	11	**4**	**3**
	6	4	8	9	10	**4**	**3**

Step 4: In the newly created second row, the two consecutive days that have the lowest total requirements are Saturday and Sunday, and hence, we assign the second police officer also Saturday and Sunday off.

DAY	MONDAY	TUESDAY	WEDNESDAY	THURSDAY	FRIDAY	SATURDAY	SUNDAY
Officer – 1	7	5	9	10	11	**4**	**3**
Officer – 2	6	4	8	9	10	**4**	**3**

Step 5: Repeat steps 3 and 4 until all workforce requirements are met.

After going through a series of iterations by repeating steps 3 and 4, we have the assignments for all the police officers as shown:

DAY	MONDAY	TUESDAY	WEDNESDAY	THURSDAY	FRIDAY	SATURDAY	SUNDAY
Officer – 1	7	5	9	10	11	**4**	**3**
Officer – 2	6	4	8	9	10	**4**	**3**

DAY	MONDAY	TUESDAY	WEDNESDAY	THURSDAY	FRIDAY	SATURDAY	SUNDAY
Officer – 3	5	3	7	8	9	**4**	**3**
Officer – 4	**4**	**2**	6	7	8	4	3
Officer – 5	4	2	5	6	7	**3**	**2**
Officer – 6	**3**	**1**	4	5	6	3	2
Officer – 7	3	1	3	4	5	**2**	**1**
Officer – 8	2	**0**	**2**	3	4	2	1
Officer – 9	1	0	2	2	3	**1**	**0**
Officer – 10	**0**	**0**	1	1	2	1	**0**
Officer – 11	0	0	0	0	1	**0**	**0**

Jennifer needs 11 police officers to meet the staffing needs. The final schedule is as shown in the following table. In the table, X represents a working day and O is a day off:

FINAL SCHEDULE								
POLICE OFFICER	**MON**	**TUE**	**WED**	**THURS**	**FRI**	**SAT**	**SUN**	**TOTAL**
Officer – 1	X	X	X	X	X	O	O	
Officer – 2	X	X	X	X	X	O	O	
Officer – 3	X	X	X	X	X	O	O	
Officer – 4	O	O	X	X	X	X	X	
Officer – 5	X	X	X	X	X	O	O	
Officer – 6	O	O	X	X	X	X	X	
Officer – 7	X	X	X	X	X	O	O	
Officer – 8	X	O	O	X	X	X	X	
Officer – 9	X	X	X	X	X	O	O	
Officer – 10	O	X	X	X	X	X	O	
Officer – 11	X	X	X	X	X	O	O	
Capacity	7	8	10	11	11	4	3	54
Requirements	7	5	9	10	11	4	3	49
Idle Capacity	0	3	1	1	0	0	0	5

Example 19.5 shows that solving a workforce scheduling problem even for small workforce levels can be computationally cumbersome. Large-scale workforce scheduling requires computerized scheduling systems. Many workforce scheduling software systems are available either as stand-alone systems or as part of the larger ERP package. For example, SAP Workforce Management facilitates employee planning and scheduling the retail companies. This module:[4]

- Performs the complex process of creating optimum employee schedules.
- Effectively balances the retail location's work scheduling strategy with the goals of the organization, customer expectations, and employees' career needs.
- Creates the best possible floor schedule by balancing staffing needs, employee skill levels, payroll requirements, employee availabilities, and workplace rules.

19.5 Scheduling for Supply Chains

Describe supply chain scheduling.

Supply Chain Scheduling

So far, we have discussed detailed or operational schedules that can effectively minimize costs, minimize makespan, or meet customer due dates for individual companies with different types of production processes. In reality, however, the ability of these individual companies to meet these performance measures really depends on the scheduling decisions made by the upstream and downstream partners of their supply chains. For example, consider a simple supply chain consisting of a supplier, a manufacturer, a distributor, and several retailers. The distributor, who manages the finished goods in the supply chain hierarchy, consolidates the finished goods produced by the manufacturer and delivers them to the various retailers to meet the demands of end customers. The manufacturer has the responsibility of producing these finished goods and will use a production schedule with large production lot sizes to optimize its production costs. If this manufacturer's production schedule is imposed on the distributor, the downstream supply chain partner, then the distributor will incur a higher inventory holding cost. Conversely, if the distributor imposes on the manufacturer what it perceives as an optimal distribution schedule, then the manufacturer may incur higher production costs.[5]

A similar conflict is likely between the supplier and the manufacturer, if each of these supply chain members attempts to develop a detailed schedule to optimize its individual company performance. Let us say, for example, that the supplier attempts to deliver the parts ordered by the manufacturer by the due date. To improve its scheduling flexibility and capacity utilization, the manufacturer would like to receive parts earlier rather than later. Yet, because of production capacity constraints and orders from other customers, the supplier may have to prioritize its production scheduling decisions of certain parts. That is, the supplier is faced with challenge of coordinating its scheduling decisions with its batch production and delivery requirements. The manufacturer in the supply chain who has to meet the needs of downstream customers faces a similar problem. The manufacturer, however, cannot begin to make any of its production scheduling decisions until the upstream supplier has made its production and delivery decisions on the parts ordered by the manufacturer. You can clearly see that it may be mutually beneficial if both the supplier and the manufacturer develop schedules that incorporate the needs and total costs of both parties.[6] Therefore, to protect against this suboptimal performance of the supply chain, scheduling decisions made by any member of the supply chain should be coordinated with the decisions of the other supply chain partners. The process of achieving this coordination is called **supply chain scheduling**.

The purpose of supply chain scheduling is to analyze the scheduling problems throughout a supply chain that includes suppliers, manufacturers, distributors, and third-party logistics providers and to coordinate the schedules of all of the supply chain members. This coordination is accomplished through information sharing and cooperation among members of the supply chain and by developing and implementing joint scheduling models for the whole supply chain. Through supply chain scheduling, companies can not only shorten their lead time and improve customer service levels, but also they can lower the operations cost of the entire supply chain. Unlike other supply chain management strategies such as electronic data interchange (EDI) and quick response (QR), supply chain scheduling requires a company to take into account the capacity limitations of upstream suppliers before making its scheduling decisions.

Effective supply chain scheduling requires close relationships among supply chain partners where there can be free exchange of data such as capacity availability and order backlogs across the various stages of the supply chain. Supply chain scheduling can be successfully implemented in companies such as Zara (Coruña, Spain), the European garment retailer, which have vertically integrated supply chains. Nevertheless, in many global supply chains in which the suppliers and customers are geographically dispersed in various countries, the coordination required to accomplish effective supply chain scheduling can be much more difficult. Despite this difficulty, supply chain scheduling is a relatively new field of study and many global companies are exploring various approaches to achieving the coordination required among their global supply chain partners to improve their supply chain scheduling performance.

Supply chain scheduling: the process of coordinating scheduling decisions made by any member of a supply chain with the decisions of other supply chain partners

19.6 Ethical and Sustainability Issues

The traditional scheduling methods used in the manufacturing and logistics industries focus on performance indicators such as makespan and meeting customer delivery due dates with the goal of improving profits. These scheduling performance measures, however, ignore the negative impact that manufacturing and transportation operations can have on the environment if proper care is not taken to consider a broader set of goals besides meeting due dates and maximizing profits. Side effects, such as excessive carbon emissions and other undesirable by-products generated by these operations, can lead to serious concerns about the detrimental consequences of a too narrow focus on scheduling. In recent years, however, the sustainability aspects of manufacturing and logistics systems have come under greater scrutiny, largely as a result of declining natural resources, environmental deterioration, and regulatory pressures. Consequently, companies in these sectors have been forced to pay more attention to the environmental impact of their operational and supply chain decisions.[7]

From a sustainability perspective, one key area of concern for many manufacturing firms is energy consumption. Scheduling decisions made by these companies can play a vital role in improving the energy efficiency of their manufacturing operations. For example, in addition to using state-of-the-art production equipment, by carefully scheduling production such that the peak electrical power consumption of the manufacturing plant is limited to specific hours of the day or seasons of the year, energy consumption can be made more efficient. Similarly, in the transportation sector, by introducing alternative fuel vehicles such as hybrids or electric transports, companies have been able to reduce the emission of greenhouse gases and other air pollutants. In addition, by properly scheduling these new types of vehicles by taking into account their specific refueling requirements, firms can also contribute directly to the reduction and control of the carbon footprint of transportation. For companies in the manufacturing and logistics sector that are exploring possible approaches to implementing sustainability, their operations schedules can provide numerous opportunities.

In the service sector, scheduling hospital employees has been problematic. For many hospital employees, particularly doctors and nurses, balancing their work hours and personal life has been a huge challenge. Many hospital residents work 30 hours straight, and such heavy workloads can lead to burnout and can have a negative impact on the quality of life. Scheduling has also been a thorny issue in restaurant settings as well. Many restaurant employees work double shifts or work early-morning shifts immediately after late-night shifts. Such a pattern of scheduling that overworks the employees raises the issue of whether these service companies are conducting their business in an ethically responsible manner. Also, the strategy of yield management used by airlines and hotels for scheduling fixed capacity raises the question of whether the strategy results in price discrimination because these service companies charge different customers different prices for providing the same service. Many customers believe that it is unethical to penalize them for the timing of the use of the company services from circumstances beyond their control. In the final analysis, scheduling decisions raise several sustainability issues for companies in both the service and the manufacturing sector. Those companies that can make scheduling decisions in an ethically responsible manner and in a ways that protects people and the environment can reap in the long run the benefits of such actions in the marketplace.

Explain how companies can make scheduling decisions to promote sustainability.

Issues in Schedudling

Energy consumption, particularly with regards to transportation, is a major concern of organizations today. Utilizing clean energy sources and using strategic scheduling techniques can reduce an organization's carbon footprint.
©iStockphoto.com/Ken Graff

Visit **edge.sagepub.com/venkataraman** to help you accomplish your coursework goals in an easy-to-use learning environment.

- Mobile-friendly eFlashcards
- Mobile-friendly practice quizzes
- A complete online action plan
- Chapter summaries with learning objectives
- Video and multimedia resources

CHAPTER SUMMARY

19.1 **Define scheduling.** Scheduling involves allocating specific resources such as labor, equipment, and facilities to produce a product or deliver a service. As scheduling is constrained by the higher level planning decisions, it is typically narrow in scope and has short-term time horizons. Scheduling requires operations managers to balance several conflicting goals so that resources are used effectively, productivity is increased, and overall costs are minimized through reductions in customer waiting time, work-in-process inventories, and processing times.

19.2 **Demonstrate the main types of scheduling and show when each type should be employed.** Manufacturers use different methods for scheduling, depending on their specific types of operations. Line process scheduling is used for high-volume production processes that typically produce standardized products and require identical or similar operations. Because of the highly repetitive nature of production in these systems, many scheduling decisions are predetermined when these production systems are designed. In intermittent process scheduling, a firm produces a variety of products in relatively low volumes. Products are made to order, and each order has its unique material and processing requirements, processing sequence, and processing time. Because of these varying product requirements and because the firm's schedules cannot be established before the receipt of actual job orders, job-shop scheduling is considerably more complex than line process scheduling is. The primary problem in intermittent process scheduling is how to manage the queues of work-in-process inventories that build up at each work center as jobs wait for these work centers to become available. The challenges of line process scheduling and intermittent process scheduling require the application of various scheduling tools for the most efficient application of resources.

19.3 **Explain why scheduling is complex.** Scheduling is complex because setup and processing times and job priorities vary frequently, and machines setup times depend on the order of job processing. Furthermore, in job-shop scheduling, schedule changes and disruptions occur frequently as a result of the high variety and low volume of jobs that require processing through shared resources.

Given the innumerable alternatives and job permutations, it is impossible to analyze all of them in real time to arrive at an optimal schedule. Fortunately, the availability of many computer programs that provide interactive computing and graphic output, the ability to monitor events, and the collection of real-time information makes real-time scheduling possible.

19.4 **Understand the alternative scheduling methods within the service sector.** Scheduling for services poses different challenges than does scheduling for processes in manufacturing firms, and it requires different techniques. For example, appointment systems and reservation systems are all methods for scheduling services. Finally, workforce scheduling represents a significant challenge in applying a supply (or a capacity) side approach to the scheduling problem.

19.5 **Describe supply chain scheduling.** Supply chain scheduling depends on the scheduling decisions made by upstream and downstream partners in the supply chain, making it highly complex and subject to both expected and unexpected constraints from supply chain partners. Supply chain scheduling is the process of coordinating scheduling decisions made by any member of the supply chain with the decisions of the other supply chain partners. Such coordination achieved through information sharing and cooperation among supply chain members can improve overall supply chain performance.

19.6 **Explain how companies can make scheduling decisions to promote sustainability.** A component of scheduling that is rarely considered is the manner in which sustainability plays a part in the scheduling decision; that is, how can an organization develop schedules that are efficient but also maximize sustainability goals? Manufacturing companies, for example, can reduce energy consumption by using state-of-the-art production equipment and by limiting peak electric power consumption to specific hours of the day or seasons of the year. Similarly, transportation companies can reduce the emission of greenhouse gases and other air pollutants by introducing alternative fuel vehicles such as hybrids or electric transports. To promote sustainability, service organizations such as hospitals and restaurants should develop employee schedules that ensure that employees are not overworked and that they are able to balance their work hours and personal life.

KEY TERMS

Appointment systems 723	Flow-shop scheduling 707	Process batch 721
Assignment method 709	Forward scheduling 712	Reservation systems 723
Backward scheduling 712	Input–output control 708	Runout time 707
Critical ratio (CR) 713	Job flow time 714	Sequencing 713
Drum-buffer-rope (DBR) 721	Johnson's rule 718	Shortest processing time 713
Earliest due date 713	Longest processing time 713	Supply chain scheduling 726
Finite capacity scheduling (FCS) 720	Makespan 714	Theory of constraints 720
First come, first served 713	Priority rules 713	Transfer batch 721

DISCUSSION AND REVIEW QUESTIONS

1. Explain the scheduling technique used when multiple products have to be scheduled in a line process.

2. Why is job-shop scheduling considerably more complex?

3. What is input–output control, and why is it an important scheduling technique for job shops?

4. Describe Gantt charts and how they are useful in job shop scheduling.

5. Define backward loading and forward loading. What is the purpose of using each of these loading techniques?

6. What is sequencing? Explain how each of the five commonly used priority rules works in sequencing individual jobs.

7. List the assumptions made in the use of the five priority rules.

8. Describe briefly the three criteria used to evaluate the performance of the priority rules.

9. Explain when Johnson's rule can be used as a scheduling technique.

10. What is finite capacity scheduling (FCS), and what are its features?

11. Explain how applying the principles of the theory of constraints can minimize the complexity of scheduling.

12. Explain the drum-buffer-rope concept.

13. What is the difference between a process batch and a transfer batch?

14. In what ways is scheduling for services different from scheduling in the manufacturing environment?

15. What is yield management and what ethical issues does an organization have to deal with in using this scheduling strategy?

16. What is supply chain scheduling, and what are its key features and benefits?

17. Describe some of the sustainability and ethical issues that organizations have to contend with in making scheduling decisions.

SOLVED PROBLEMS

1. The following table provides information on planned and actual inputs and outputs of an automotive service center in terms of standard hours of work. The beginning backlog is 15 standard hours of work. Determine the cumulative deviation and the backlog for each period:

Week	1	2	3	4	5
Planned input	25	25	25	25	20
Actual input	26	28	20	23	25
Planned output	25	25	25	25	24
Actual output	25	23	24	25	25

Solution: Screenshot 19.1 is a Microsoft Excel (Microsoft Corporation, Redmond, WA) spreadsheet that shows the solution to this problem.

SCREENSHOT 19.1: Solved Problem – Input–Output Control

	A	B	C	D	E	F	G
1	Chapter 19–solved Problem 19.1: Input-Output Control						
2					=(D6-D5)		
3							
4	**Week**		1	2	3	4	5
5	Planned input		25	25	25	25	20
6	Actual input		26	28	20	23	25
7	Deviation		1	3	-5	-2	5
8	Cumulative Deviation		1	4	-1	-3	2
9							
10	Planned output		25	25	25	25	24
11	Actual output		25	23	24	25	25
12	Deviation		0	-2	-1	0	1
13	Cumulative Deviation		0	-2	-3	-3	-2
14	Actual Backlog	15	16	21	17	15	15
15							
16	Note						
17	Rows highlighted in green show values input by the user						
18	Rows highlighted in red show values calculated by Excel		=B14+(C6-C11)				

2. Murali Aromatics Inc. (not a real company) makes four types of aromatic oils used by massage therapists, hotels, and spas. Production of these oils requires the raw materials to go through a distillation process. The distillation machines used for the process are not identical, and the production of some aromatic oils is better suited to some machines. Given the following production time in minutes per ounce, determine the optimal assignment of aromatic oil to distillation machine:

	Machines			
Product	A	B	C	D
Sandalwood oil	18	12	15	20
Lavender oil	10	17	10	15
Chamomile oil	17	15	16	13
Jasmine oil	12	12	10	16

Solution:

Step 1: Subtract the minimum value in each row from all other values in that row. The results are shown in the following table:

	Machines			
Product	A	B	C	D
Sandalwood oil	6	0	3	8
Lavender oil	0	7	0	5
Chamomile oil	4	2	3	0
Jasmine oil	2	2	0	6

Step 2: Using the table obtained from row reductions, subtract the minimum value in each column from all other values in that column. The resulting table is as follows:

	Machines			
Product	A	B	C	D
Sandalwood oil	6	0	3	8
Lavender oil	0	7	0	5
Chamomile oil	4	2	3	0
Jasmine oil	2	2	0	6

Step 3: The resulting table after performing the row and column reductions is our opportunity cost matrix. Cross out all zeros in the table by drawing the minimum number of horizontal or vertical lines as follows:

	Machines			
Product	A	B	C	D
Sandalwood oil	6	0	3	8
Lavender oil	0	7	0	5
Chamomile oil	4	2	3	0
Jasmine oil	2	2	0	6

Step 4: In Step 3, as the number of lines required to cross out all zeros (4) in the table were equal to the number of rows or columns, an optimum solution has been reached. Thus, we assign

Sandalwood oil to distillation machine B

Lavender oil to distillation machine A

Chamomile oil to distillation machine D

Jasmine oil to distillation machine C

Note that we could have assigned lavender oil to distillation machine C, but that solution would have left us with no optimum assignment for jasmine oil. This assignment is the most optimum solution in terms of production efficiency.

3.   James Peck, a house remodeling contractor, has five jobs waiting to be processed. The job processing times and due dates, both expressed in days, are presented in the following table. Assume jobs arrived in the order shown in the table:

Job	Processing Time (in days)	Due Date (in days from today's date)
A	7	24
B	14	17
C	17	28
D	4	18
E	11	26

a. Determine the exact sequence for processing these jobs using the following priority rules: 1) FCFS, 2) SPT, 3) EDD, 4) LPT, and 5) Critical Ratio (CR).

b. Compare the relative performance of these priority rules for the three performance criteria of average flow time, average job tardiness, and average number of jobs in this work center.

Solution:

a. The sequence of job processing for each priority rule is as follows:

      First Come First Served: A-B-C-D-E

      Shortest Processing Time: D-A-E-B-C

      Earliest Due Date: B-D-A-E-C

      Longest Processing Time: C-B-E-A-D

Critical Ratio: We compute the critical ratios for the five jobs using the following formula:

$$\text{Critical ratio} = \frac{Time\ remaining}{Work\ remaining} = \frac{Due\ date - Today's\ date}{Processing\ time\ remaining}$$

The result of these computations are shown in the following table:

Job	Due Date (in days)	Processing Time Remaining (in days)	Critical Ratio
A	24	7	$\frac{24-0}{7}=3.4$
B	17	14	$\frac{17-0}{14}=1.21$
C	28	17	$\frac{28-0}{17}=1.65$
D	18	4	$\frac{18-0}{4}=4.50$
E	26	11	$\frac{26-0}{11}=2.36$

Based on the critical ratios, the sequence of job processing is B-C-E-A-D.

b. The Excel solution for the various sequencing rules of this problem along with their performance measures are shown in the following series of screenshots (Screenshot 19.2–19.6). The Excel procedure is to highlight the input data table and then to use the "sort" option from the "Data" menu in the tool bar. You will sort by first come, first served; shortest processing time; earliest due date; longest processing time; and lowest critical ratio.

FCFS: A-B-C-D-E

SCREENSHOT 19.2: First Come, First Served

	A	B	C	D	E	F
3	FCFS	A-B-C-D-E				
4	Job	Processing time	Flow time	Due date	Tardiness in days	
5					(flow time – due date), 0 if negative	
6						
7	A	7	7	24	0	
8	B	14	21	17	4	
9	C	17	38	28	10	
10	D	4	42	18	24	
11	E	11	53	26	27	
12	TOTAL	53	161		65	
13	*Average flow time*	32.2				
14	*Average tardiness*	13				
15	*Average number of jobs in the system*	3.04				
16						

SPT: D-A-E-B-C

SCREENSHOT 19.3: Shortest Processing Time

	A	B	C	D	E	F
17	SPT	D-A-E-B-C				
18	Job	Processing time	Flow time	Due date	Tardiness in days	
19					(flow time – due date), 0 if negative	
20	D	4	4	18	0	
21	A	7	11	24	0	
22	E	11	22	26	0	
23	B	14	36	17	19	
24	C	17	53	28	25	
25	TOTAL	53	126		44	
26	*Average flow time*	25.2				
27	*Average tardiness*	8.8				
28	*Average number of jobs in the system*	2.38				
29						

EDD: B-D-A-E-C

SCREENSHOT 19.4: Earliest Due Date

	A	B	C	D	E	F
30	EDD	B-D-A-E-C				
31	Job	Processing time	Flow time	Due date	Tardiness in days	
32					(flow time – due date), 0 if negative	
33	B	14	14	17	0	
34	D	4	18	18	0	
35	A	7	25	24	1	
36	E	11	36	26	10	
37	C	17	53	28	25	
38	TOTAL	53	146		36	
39	*Average flow time*	29.2				
40	*Average tardiness*	7.2				
41	*Average number of jobs in the system*	2.75				
42						

LPT: C-B-E-A-D

SCREENSHOT 19.5: Longest Processing Time

	A	B	C	D	E	F
43	LPT	C-B-E-A-D				
44	Job	Processing time	Flow time	Due date	Tardiness in days	
45					(flow time – due date), 0 if negative	
46	C	17	17	28	0	
47	B	14	31	17	14	
48	E	11	42	26	16	
49	A	7	49	24	25	
50	D	4	53	18	35	
51	TOTAL	53	192		90	
52	*Average flow time*	38.4				
53	*Average tardiness*	18				
54	*Average number of jobs in the system*	3.62				
55						

CR: B-C-E-A-D

SCREENSHOT 19.6: Critical Ratio

	A	B	C	D	E	F
55						
56					=(D60-0)/B60	
57	CR	B-C-E-A-D				
58	Job	Processing time	Flow time	Due date	Tardiness in days	Critical Ratio
59					(flow time – due date), 0 if negative	
60	B	14	14	17	0	1.2
61	C	17	31	28	3	1.6
62	E	11	42	26	16	2.4
63	A	7	49	24	25	3.4
64	D	4	53	18	35	4.5
65	TOTAL	53	189		79	
66	*Average flow time*	37.8				
67	*Average tardiness*	15.8		=IF((C60-D60)>0, (C60-D60),0)		
68	*Average number of jobs in the system*	3.57				

The following table shows the relative performance of the five priority rules across the three different metrics:

Priority Rule	Average Flow Time	Average Tardiness	Average Number of Jobs in the Work Center
FCFS	32.2	13	3.04
SPT	25.2	8.8	2.38
EDD	29.2	7.2	2.75
LPT	38.4	18	3.62
CR	37.8	15.8	3.57

For the previous example, the SPT rule has the best performance on two of three measures followed by EDD.

The solution to this example can be found in an Excel spreadsheet provided with the study materials for this text.

4. Jessica Lange's wood furniture repair and restoration shop has the following jobs to be completed. The wood furniture restoration process involves two operations that need to be performed in the following order: sanding and then painting. The time required to complete each of these five jobs varies depending on the type of furniture and the extent of repair and refinishing work involved. The processing time in hours for each of these two operations for each job is given in the table:

Job	Sanding	Painting
A	7	9
B	12	6
C	8	4
D	10	8
E	5	9

a. Find the optimum sequence of job processing that will minimize the makespan time.

b. Draw a Gantt chart of the schedule, and determine the idle time at the painting work center.

Solution: 4a. Find the optimum sequence

1st iteration

Step 1: All five jobs along with their processing times on the two machines are given in the previous table. The unscheduled jobs are A-B-C-D-E.

Step 2: Find the job with the minimum processing time.

The job with the minimum processing time of 4.0 hours is C.

Step 3b: As the minimum processing time is in the second work center, painting, job C is placed in the last available place in the following sequence as shown:

Step 4: Remove job C from further consideration. Go to Step 1.

2nd iteration

Step 1: The remaining unscheduled jobs are A-B-D-E.

Step 2: Find the job with the next minimum processing time.

The job with the next minimum processing time of 5.0 hours is E.

Step 3a: As the minimum processing time is in the first work center, sanding, job E is placed in the first available place in the following sequence as shown:

E				C

Step 4: Remove job E from further consideration. Go to Step 1.

3rd iteration

Step 1: The remaining unscheduled jobs are A-B-D.

Step 2: Find the job with the next minimum processing time.

The job with the next minimum processing time of 6.0 hours is B.

Step 3b: As the minimum processing time is in the second work center, painting, job B is placed in the last available place in the following sequence as shown:

E			B	C

Step 4: Remove job B from further consideration. Go to Step 1.

4th iteration

Step 1: The remaining unscheduled jobs are A-D.

Step 2: Find the job with the next minimum processing time.

The job with the next minimum processing time of 7.0 hours is A.

Step 3a: As the minimum processing time is in the first work center, sanding, job A is placed in the first available place in the following sequence as shown:

E	A		B	C

Step 4: Remove job A from further consideration. Go to Step 1.

As the only remaining job is D, it goes to the only available (third) place in the sequence and the final schedule is:

E	A	D	B	C

4b. Draw a Gantt chart of the schedule, and determine the idle time in the painting work center.

Thus, the total time to complete the five jobs in the two machines, that is, the makespan, is 46 hours. The painting work center has to wait 5 hours for job E and 5 hours for the completion of job C in the sanding work center. These idle times in the painting work center are shown in blue shaded cells. The total idle time in the painting work center is 10 hours.

5. The manager, Ravi Teja, of Heritage Fresh Grocery Store wants to develop a workforce schedule for his store employees using a standard 5-day work schedule. The store is open 24 hours a day, 7 days a week. Ravi's objective is to minimize the total amount of slack capacity. The staffing requirements for the first shift of next week are given in the following table. Ravi wants to give his employees two consecutive days off. Note that if a tie occurs in assigning consecutive days off, break the tie arbitrarily:

Day	Mon	Tue	Wed	Thurs	Fri	Sat	Sun
Employees required	3	4	6	5	6	8	7

Solution: Using the steps demonstrated in example 5, the workforce schedule is developed as shown:

Day	Mon	Tue	Wed	Thurs	Fri	Sat	Sun	Assignment
Employee-1	**3**	**4**	6	5	6	8	7	M-T pair has the lowest requirement. Assign employee-1 M-T off
Employee-2	**3**	**4**	5	4	5	7	6	M-T pair has the lowest requirement. Assign employee-2 M-T off
Employee-3	**3**	**4**	4	3	4	6	5	There is three-way tie (M-T, W-Th, and Th-F) for the lowest requirement. We break the tie aribitrarily, and assign employee-3 M-T off
Employee-4	3	4	**3**	**2**	3	5	4	There is two-way tie (W-Th, and Th-F) for the lowest requirement. We break the tie aribitrarily, and assign employee-4 W-Th off
Employee-5	2	3	3	**2**	**2**	4	3	Th-F has the lowest requirement, hence we assign employee-5 Th-F off
Employee-6	**1**	**2**	2	2	2	3	2	There is two-way tie (M-T, and S-M) for the lowest requirement. We break the tie aribitrarily, and assign employee-6 M-T off
Employee-7	1	2	**1**	**1**	1	2	1	There is three-way tie (W-Th, Th-F, and S-M) for the lowest requirement. We break the tie arbitrarily, and assign employee-7 W-Th off
Employee-8	**0**	1	1	1	0	1	**0**	S-M has the lowest requirement, hence we assign employee-8 S-M off

The final employee schedule for the store's first shift is given in the following table:

Employee	Mon	Tue	Wed	Thurs	Fri	Sat	Sun	Total
				Final Schedule				
Employee-1	0	0	X	X	X	X	X	
Employee-2	0	0	X	X	X	X	X	
Employee-3	0	0	X	X	X	X	X	
Employee-4	X	X	0	0	X	X	X	
Employee-5	X	X	X	0	0	X	X	
Employee-6	0	0	X	X	X	X	X	
Employee-7	X	X	0	0	X	X	X	
Employee-8	0	X	X	X	X	X	0	
Capacity	3	4	6	5	7	8	7	40
Requirements	3	4	6	5	6	8	7	39
Idle Capacity	0	0	0	0	1	0	0	1

PROBLEMS

1. The following table provides information on planned and actual inputs and outputs of an automotive service center in terms of standard hours of work. The beginning backlog is 14 standard hours of work. Determine the cumulative deviation and the backlog for each period:

Week	1	2	3	4	5
Planned input	30	30	30	30	20
Actual input	32	34	25	28	25
Planned output	30	30	30	30	25
Actual output	30	28	28	30	22

2. Given the following data on planned and actual inputs and outputs of a machine shop in terms of standard hours of work, determine the cumulative deviation and the backlog for each period. The beginning backlog is 10 standard hours of work:

Week	1	2	3	4	5
Planned input	180	180	200	200	190
Actual input	190	180	185	205	198
Planned output	180	180	200	200	190
Actual output	185	175	196	210	190

3. Given the following data on planned and actual inputs and outputs of work center 4 of a tool and die shop in terms of standard hours of work, determine the cumulative deviation and the backlog for each period. The beginning backlog is 15 standard hours of work:

Week	1	2	3	4	5
Planned input	55	60	65	70	70
Actual input	45	55	60	65	70
Planned output	55	60	65	70	70
Actual output	55	55	60	65	70

4. An elite logistics company wants to determine the optimum assignment of its fleet of trucks to delivery routes. The objective is to minimize total cost. The cost data in hundreds of dollars for the various truck-route combinations are given in the following table. Develop an assignment that will minimize total cost:

	Route (in U.S. dollars)			
Truck	1	2	3	4
A	9	13	8	5
B	10	11	7	6
C	12	6	14	9
D	8	9	10	12

5. Virat Kohli, the hospital administrator at mythical Trinity Hospital, wants to assign nurses beginning a shift in the oncology ward of the hospital. The time required for patient care varies from one patient to the next based on the type of care, experience, and skill level of the nurses. Given the following patient roster and time estimates in hours required by each nurse for each patient, develop an efficient assignment of nurses to patients:

	Time Required (in hours)			
Patient	Nurse-1	Nurse-2	Nurse-3	Nurse-4
Sharma	2	3	1	4
Singh	1	4	2	5
Brown	3	5	4	2
Warner	5	1	3	3

6. Refer to problem 5. Two weeks after assigning the nurses, Virat Kohli of Trinity Hospital wanted to focus on the patient satisfaction with the care they received from the nurses. Accordingly, he asked the patients to evaluate the quality of care they received and their preferences for nurses on a scale of 0 to 100. The following table shows the scores that each nurse received from the patients. Use the assignment method to reassign the nurses to the highest possible patient satisfaction ratings:

	Patient Satisfaction Ratings			
Patient	Nurse-1	Nurse-2	Nurse-3	Nurse-4
Sharma	90	96	85	87
Singh	92	75	97	88
Brown	91	93	80	85
Warner	94	80	55	95

7. Susan Inskeep is the plant manager of an electronic manufacturing plant. The plant's current product line has five electronic components that can be processed in five machines. The productive ratings of these machines vary depending on the component they are assigned for processing. The following table has the time in minutes required to process each of these components in each of these machines. Develop an optimum assignment of components to machines:

	Processing Time (in minutes)				
Component	Machine-1	Machine-2	Machine-3	Machine-4	Machine-5
A121	19	11	14	15	21
B85	13	8	15	10	15
C144	12	15	13	16	13
C105	15	12	10	17	18
A62	14	11	8	14	12

8. The Chief of Police, Karen Stanley, of the Make Believe Police Department needs to assign five detective squads to five pending criminal cases. Karen wants to come up with an optimum assignment that will minimize the total time it takes to conclude the cases. Data on past performance of each detective squad to complete each case assigned in terms of average number of days is presented in the following table:

	Average Completion Time (in days)				
Detective Squad	Case-1	Case-2	Case-3	Case-4	Case-5
A	15	8	4	8	28
B	21	8	13	7	32

Detective Squad	Average Completion Time (in days)				
	Case-1	Case-2	Case-3	Case-4	Case-5
C	11	4	5	6	20
D	9	12	8	13	20
E	14	24	25	27	9

Use the assignment method to solve the problem.

If squad D cannot be assigned to case-5 as a result of a conflict of interest, solve the problem given this new constraint.

9. The following jobs are waiting to be processed at a work center. Assume that the jobs arrived today and are listed in the order in which they have arrived.

Job	Processing Time (in days)	Due Date (in days)
A	15	22
B	12	17
C	9	16
D	8	19
E	21	25

Sequence the jobs using the following priority rules: FCFS, EDD, SPT, LPT, and CR.

For each of the rules, determine the average flow time, the average job tardiness, and the average number of jobs in this work center.

Based on your answers, is one rule better than the others? Discuss.

10. Ross Barber is a senior at Pennsylvania State University pursuing a dual degree in marketing and supply chain management. Ross is overwhelmed because he has several assignments to be completed in the upcoming weeks. The estimated time required to complete these assignments and their due dates are given in the following table. Today is March 1:

Assignments	Estimated Time for Completion (in days)	Due Date
Business ethics case	6	March 21
Term project	12	March 17
MRP project in SAP	5	March 30
Term paper	22	April 5
Statistical analysis project	17	April 2

What sequencing rule should Ross use if he wants to complete as many assignments as possible on time?

How would the sequence that Ross comes up with change if he is interested in minimizing the average tardiness of his assignments?

11. A local tool and die shop has the following jobs to be processed. Today is day 120:

Job	Date Job Arrived	Processing Days Required	Job Due Date
A	100	25	130
B	90	30	140
C	95	40	170
D	120	50	170
E	110	20	180

Using the critical ratio rule, determine the sequence in which the jobs should be processed.

12. An engine repair shop has the following jobs waiting to be processed. Jobs are listed in the order in which they arrived:

Job	Date Job Arrived	Processing Days Required	Job Due Date
A-101	180	25	250
B-206	190	35	270
C-310	192	15	245
D-285	195	21	300
E-405	200	23	280

Use the following sequencing rules to determine the order in which the jobs should be processed: FCFS, EDD, SPT, and LPT.

For each of these rules, determine the average flow time, the average job tardiness, and the average number of jobs in this work center.

Based on your answers, is one rule better than the others? Discuss.

13. A machining center has the following small jobs from five of its customers. The jobs are listed in the order in which they were received. Each job requires a certain amount of setup time in addition to its processing time. Job names refer to the names of the customers. Note that the job completion time is the sum of the total processing time for each job and its setup time:

Job	Processing Time (in hours per unit)	Number of Units	Setup Time	Due Date (in hours)
Patel	0.14	50	1.0	5
Smith	0.20	17	1.6	11
Lopez	0.15	15	0.75	13
Garcia	0.30	45	0.5	23
Chen	0.10	90	1.0	17

Use the following sequencing rules to determine the order in which the jobs should be processed: FCFS, EDD, SPT, and CR.

For each of these rules, determine the average flow time, the average job tardiness, and the average number of jobs in this machining center.

14. Use Johnson's Rule to obtain the optimum sequence of job processing for the following jobs through a two-machine flow shop. Each job must follow the sequence of job processing—machine-1 first, followed by machine-2. All job times listed are in hours:

Job	Machine-1	Machine-2
A	2.80	4.50
B	4.00	1.70
C	2.50	3.30
D	5.50	3.70
E	4.00	1.50

15. A local bakery makes custom cakes for special events such as weddings and graduation. Making cakes is a two-step process of baking and decorating. The bakery has received eight orders, and the times required in hours for baking and decorating for each order are given in the following table:

Cake Order	Baking	Decorating
A	3	4
B	1	2
C	4	7
D	2	4
E	5	10
F	2	6
G	5	7
H	6	13

Determine a sequence that will minimize the makespan time.

Construct a chart of the resulting sequence, and determine the idle time in the decoration process.

16. A publisher has eight book manuscripts to be processed through two operations in the following order: printing first and then binding. Processing times in hours for these two operations for each of the book manuscripts are given in the following table. Determine the sequence that will minimize the makespan time for processing these eight book manuscripts. What is the total idle time in the binding operation work center?

Book	A	B	C	D	E	F	G	H
Printing	17	5	6	8	12	5	4	7
Binding	4	7	12	7	8	6	5	4

17. A machine shop has seven jobs to be processed through two work centers in the following order: milling and then grinding. The start and finish times in hours for each job for each operation are given in the following table:

Job	Milling		Grinding	
	Start	Finish	Start	Finish
S	0	3	3	6
T	3	7	7	10
U	7	11	11	14
V	11	16	16	21
W	16	19	21	24
X	19	22	24	26
Y	22	24	26	30

Determine a sequence that will minimize the total completion time of all jobs.

18. A local painting firm has contracted five interior house painting jobs. The extent of work involved will vary as the houses are of different sizes, have different painting requirements, and are in different states of repair. Each painting job will have to go through a two-step process of preparation (old paint removal, cleaning, and priming), and then painting. The following table shows the time requirements in days for each operation for each house. The job names refer to the names of the clients whose houses need to be painted:

Job	Preparation	Painting
Tendulkar	5	3
Deshmukh	4	7
Patterson	4	2
Robbins	6	8
Zhao	2	5

a. Determine a sequence that will minimize the makespan time.

b. Construct a Gantt chart, and determine the total idle time for the painting operation.

19. Shila Nathan, the hospital administrator for a hospital in Chennai, India, has to devise for the coming week a workforce schedule for nurses in the orthopedic department of the hospital. The daily requirements of nurses for the week are given in the following table:

Day	Monday	Tuesday	Wednesday	Thursday	Friday	Saturday	Sunday
Nurses required	4	4	5	6	5	4	4

Help Shila create a workforce schedule that will meet the daily requirements with the minimum of nurses while ensuring that each nurse gets two consecutive days off.

20. Amy Campbell, the manager of a restaurant in Istanbul, Turkey, needs help scheduling her wait staff for next week. The amount of wait staff needed for each day of the week is given in the following table:

Day	Monday	Tuesday	Wednesday	Thursday	Friday	Saturday	Sunday
Wait staff required	3	4	5	5	6	5	4

Help Amy create a workforce schedule that will meet the daily requirements with the minimum of wait staff while ensuring that each wait staff member gets any two days off.

Revise the schedule so that each wait staff member gets two consecutive days off.

21. Mary Dexter needs help scheduling volunteers working at a soup kitchen in Chicago. Develop a schedule that will meet the demand requirement with the constraint that each volunteer will work only four days a week:

Day	Monday	Tuesday	Wednesday	Thursday	Friday	Saturday	Sunday
Volunteers required	5	4	3	4	7	5	3

22. Use the assignment method to determine the optimum assignment of workers to jobs, given the following profit information. Compute the total profit of this assignment:

	Jobs (in U.S. dollars)			
Workers	**1**	**2**	**3**	**4**
A	10	12	8	9
B	9	10	7	8
C	13	9	15	10
D	7	11	10	14

23. Given the following data on planned and actual inputs and outputs of an automobile service center in terms of standard hours of work, determine the cumulative deviation and the backlog for each period. The beginning backlog is 10 standard hours of work:

Day	**1**	**2**	**3**	**4**	**5**
Planned input	55	60	65	70	70
Actual input	45	55	60	65	70
Planned output	55	60	65	70	70
Actual output	55	55	60	65	70

24. Shyam Nathan, a hospital administrator, needs help scheduling the nurses of his hospital for next week. The amount of nurses needed for each day of the week is given in the following table:

Day	**Monday**	**Tuesday**	**Wednesday**	**Thursday**	**Friday**	**Saturday**
Nurses required	2	3	6	4	7	4

Help Shyam create a workforce schedule that will meet the daily requirements with the minimum of nurses while ensuring that each nurse gets any two days off.

Revise the schedule so that each nurse gets two consecutive days off.

25. A machine shop has seven jobs to be processed through a two-step process. The processing times in hours for each job for each operation are given in the following table. Determine the job sequence that will minimize the total time required to complete the jobs:

	Step 1	**Step 2**
Job	**Processing Time**	**Processing Time**
R	1.50	1.70
K	1.00	1.40
L	2.40	1.20
M	1.90	1.70
N	1.80	2.00
O	2.00	1.55
P	1.60	1.70

26. Virender Sehwag, the manager of a homeless shelter, wants to develop a staffing schedule for volunteers working at the shelter given the following requirements. Determine a volunteer schedule with the minimum number of volunteers needed to meet the daily requirements. Give volunteers any two days off:

Day	**Monday**	**Tuesday**	**Wednesday**	**Thursday**	**Friday**	**Saturday**	**Sunday**
Volunteers required	3	4	4	2	5	6	6

27. Sunil Roberts, the manager of a restaurant, wants to develop a staffing schedule given the following employee requirements. Determine an employee schedule with the minimum number of employees needed to meet the daily requirements. Give employees two consecutive days off, not including Sundays:

Day	**Monday**	**Tuesday**	**Wednesday**	**Thursday**	**Friday**	**Saturday**
Employees required	3	3	5	4	6	4

28. A service center has the planned and actual inputs and outputs (in standard hours of work) shown in the following table. Given a beginning backlog of 13 standard hours of work, compute the actual backlog of work each day:

Day	1	2	3	4	5
Planned input	30	30	30	30	25
Actual input	28	32	25	26	31
Planned output	30	30	30	30	27
Actual output	30	28	29	30	28

29. Given the following processing times and due dates for six jobs, determine the optimum sequence using the following rules: FCFS, SPT, EDD, and CR.

Job	Processing Time (in hours)	Due Date (in hours)
A	2.5	6
B	1.0	5
C	3.5	17
D	4.0	21
E	1.5	3
F	5.0	19

30. Another machine shop has five jobs to be processed through three operations: lathing, grinding, and drilling. The hours required to process these jobs for each of the three operations are shown in the following table:

Job	Lathing	Grinding	Drilling
A	4	2	5
B	1	3	6
C	2	3	2
D	2	4	1
E	5	2	0

a. Sequence the jobs using the SPT and the LPT rules.

b. Prepare a Gantt chart for each operation for each rule.

c. Which rule is preferable, and why?

CASE STUDY 19.1 TELLING UMPIRES WHERE TO GO! ·····················

Ross Davis is a member of his county sheriff department's softball team. Every summer, the team plays about 20 games against other teams in its league that represent fire stations, other police departments, and religious groups. The biggest challenge in scheduling the games has been a lack of available umpires. With 14 teams in the league and only 6 umpires, it is tricky scheduling the softball games around the township.

Ross is responsible for scheduling the umpires. Last year, he was told that the umpires would like to work consecutive nights, when possible,

but not more than four times each week. The staffing requirements for umpires for a typical week of the season are given in the table below.

Questions:

1. How can you use workforce scheduling methods to schedule the umpires this coming summer?

2. Can you think of other situations where workforce scheduling can be applied in your life?

Day	Monday	Tuesday	Wednesday	Thursday	Friday	Saturday	Sunday
Umpires required	1	2	3	1	4	4	1

VIDEO CASE

Watch this video case to learn about how the Rockefeller Gastropub manages scheduling in various ways to make sure they are well-staffed and prepared to meet customer demand.

CRITICAL THINKING EXERCISES

1. Visit a local bank and write a report on how you would use the drum-buffer-rope concept to alleviate the bottleneck problems (if any) that the bank faces in providing effective customer service.

2. Search the Internet and choose three computerized planning and scheduling software programs. Write a brief summary on the features of each of these software systems.

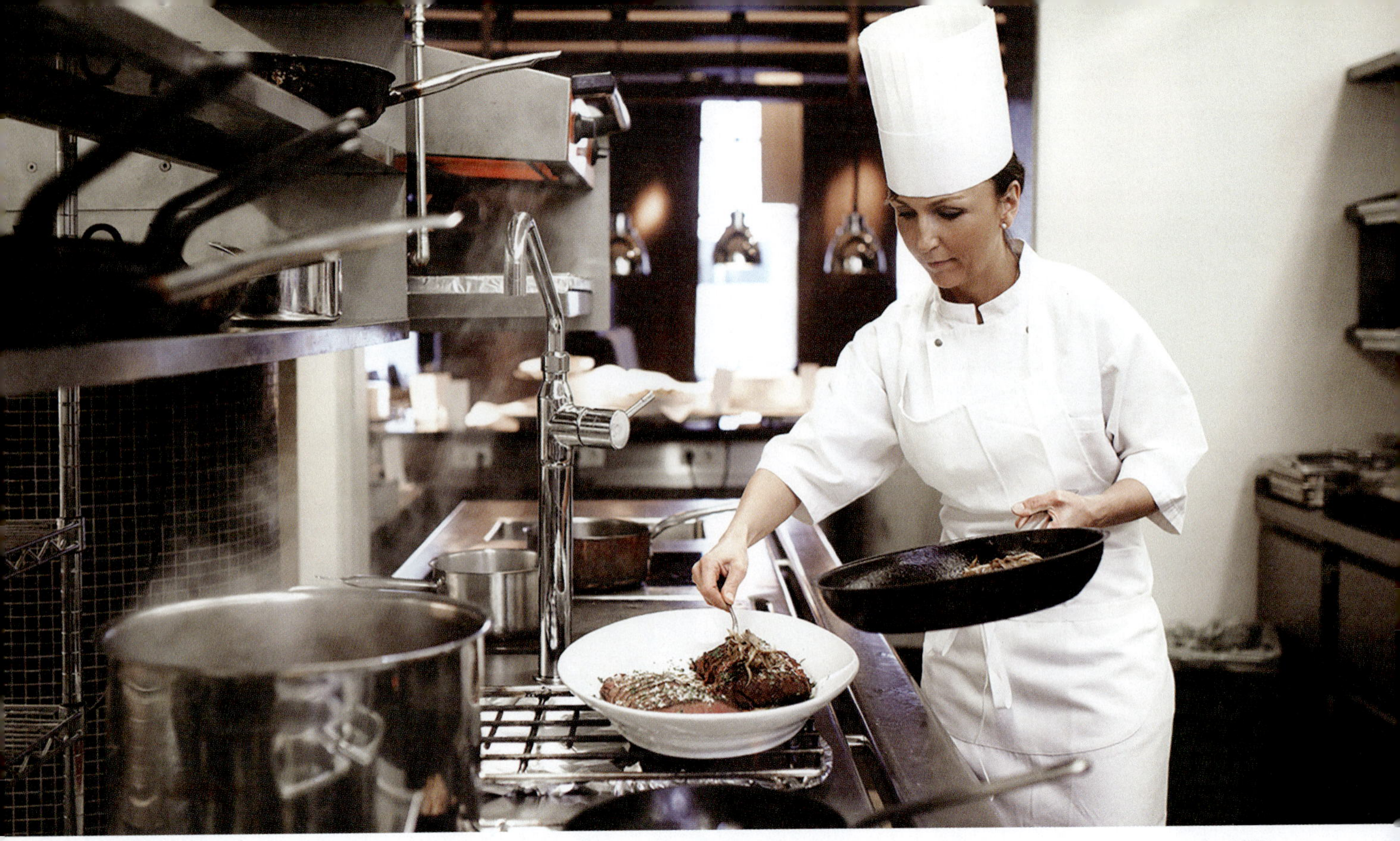

©iStockphoto.com/STEEX

MODULE A Linear Programming

LEARNING OBJECTIVES

After studying this module, you should be able to:

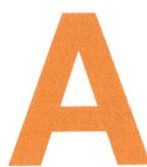

1. Identify the critical features of linear programming (LP) and explain why it is critical for business operations success.
2. Solve LP problems with both maximization and minimization objectives, using graphical methods and Excel Solver.
3. Perform sensitivity analysis on solutions to LP problems.
4. Apply LP to other problems, including product mixture, blending, and personnel scheduling situations.

OPERATIONS PROFILE: Using Linear Programming in the Restaurant Industry

One of the most disappointing sentences that a restaurant customer can hear is, "I'm sorry, we're out of that menu item." It is an admission of failure: a failure of the restaurant's planning and preparation. As a result, restaurant managers go to extremes to have the right quantities of the necessary ingredients on hand at the beginning of the evening before customers start arriving. Not having the right ingredients available means not having a sufficient number of the critical menu items that can maximize profit.

To have the right ingredients on hand, restaurants routinely employ algebraic techniques like linear programming (LP) to their menu planning to optimize meal production. For example, managers can determine the cost of preparing different menu items to decide how many of each menu item to prepare for optimal profit. On the other hand, if they discover that the kitchen has only half its supply of chicken and vegetable stock for soups, they can only prepare half their usual amount of "ready soup" in advance. Linear programming also helps the restaurant stay on budget (and, therefore, maintain profitability). Critical cost constraints are factored into the menu calculations to make sure that the day's budget can support the different menu options in the right quantities. Developing these sometimes complicated, but always critical, menu-planning formulas is important for efficient and profit-maximizing restaurants.[1]

Introduction

The decisions that operations and supply chain managers make often are about the effective use of limited company resources to achieve certain objectives. The limited availability of resources, usually referred to as constraints, can apply to labor, materials, time, equipment, energy, or money. Some examples of such constraints include the number of pilots available when scheduling airline flights or the advertising dollars budgeted for a marketing campaign. In addition to the limited availability of resources, constraints can also affect the right mixture of ingredients or materials in a product. Manufacturing a pharmaceutical drug, for example, requires carefully measured quantities of various chemical compounds. Linear programming is a mathematical modeling technique that managers can use in making decisions that involve optimizing an objective, such as maximizing profits or minimizing cost, subject to constraints such as limited resource availability. Linear programming has been applied in a variety of industries to various problems. Table A.1 lists some of these applications.

Consider some specific examples based on the categories in Table A.1. Credit Suisse, an international investment bank and financial institution headquartered in Zurich, Switzerland, can use linear programming in working with customers who are seeking to maximize returns on their investment portfolios. By identifying combinations of investment options (treasury securities, short-term notes, consumer and commercial loans, and long-term bonds), Credit Suisse can structure a portfolio that maximizes returns while avoiding unnecessary risks. United Airlines (United Continental Holdings, Inc., Chicago, IL) faces very different problems for which linear programming is useful. United Airlines and its regional partners operate more than 5,000 flights each day. The challenge of scheduling flight crews across their international and domestic departures to make sure that each flight has a fully rested and effective crew at the aircraft when needed is a logistics challenge for which linear programming allows optimal solutions.

Constraints: the limited availability of resources

TABLE A.1: Linear Programming Applications

PROBLEM TYPE	LP APPLICATION
Crew scheduling	To determine an optimal schedule for airline pilots and ground personnel
Financial planning	To determine the optimum investment portfolio that will achieve certain returns while minimizing investment risks
Diet	To determine the best combination of food items (such as in hospital and school cafeterias) that will meet all nutritional requirements at the minimum cost
Production planning	To determine the supply of resources (labor, machines, etc.) needed to meet demand for the intermediate time frame at the minimum cost
Assignment	To determine optimum assignment of jobs to machines or workers
Vehicle routing (traveling salesperson)	To determine the shortest route from a source to destination (such as the shortest route for FedEx* and UPS** to deliver packages)
Transportation	To determine the shipment of goods from multiple sources to multiple destinations (such as shipment of crude oil from different oilfields to different refineries) to minimize transportation costs
Call routing	To determine the best way to route telephone calls (such as from Chicago to New York or from Seattle to Houston)
Product mixture	To determine the optimum mixture of products to produce either to maximize profits or minimize costs, given resource constraints

* FedEx (FedEx Corporation, Memphis, TN).
** United Parcel Service, Inc. (aka UPS, Sandy Springs, GA).

A.1 Features of a Linear Programming (LP) Problem

All linear programming problems have four distinct features:

1. *Objective Function*
   Every LP problem will have an objective that needs to be either maximized or minimized, such as the maximization of profits or the minimization of costs. For example, in determining the combination of products to produce and sell, a company may choose profit maximization as its objective. Similarly, after determining the appropriate shipment routes for its goods, a company may choose the objective of minimizing its transportation costs. Note that the objective for an LP problem need not necessarily be expressed in monetary units; it can also be in other metric units, such as minimizing employee travel time or customer waiting times. The objective of an LP problem expressed mathematically is referred to as an **objective function.**

2. *Decision Variables*
   The **decision variables** in linear programming are alternative courses of action, for example, determining the number of products to produce or the number of shipping routes for transporting goods from the available alternative choices. These variables are under the control of the decision maker, who can use LP to decide what would be the best way to allocate the resources among these alternative courses of action to achieve the stated objective.

3. *Constraints*
   If there were no restrictions or limitations on the availability of resources, LP would not be needed as a decision-making tool. In reality, however, resources *are* scarce and decisions have to be made within the limitations imposed by this scarcity. For example, for a product mixture problem, the decision to produce the number of units of each product to maximize profits has to be made within a set of resource limitations such as capacity and raw materials available. It is the presence of these resource limitations, referred to as constraints, that makes LP such a powerful decision-making tool. These resource constraints are modeled in LP mathematically as inequalities or equalities.

Objective function:
the objective of an LP problem expressed mathematically

Decision variables:
variables in an LP model such as production levels, purchase quantities, and shipping routes that are under the control of the decision maker

4. *Linearity*

The last requirement of a linear programming problem is that the objective function and the constraints have linear relationships. That is, the effect of changing a decision variable is proportional to its magnitude. Although this requirement of linearity may seem overly restrictive, many real-world business problems can be formulated in this manner. Nevertheless, there are also many real-world problems that cannot be formulated as a linear program because either the objective function or one or more of the constraints are nonlinear. For such nonlinear problems, there are other advanced solution methods that are available, but they are not discussed in this module because they are beyond the scope of this book.

Linear Programming

Formulating a Linear Programming Problem

Example A.1 illustrates the steps for using LP to determine the optimal product mix.

EXAMPLE A.1: Enrobe Textiles Inc.[a] is a small clothing manufacturer that produces men's polo shirts and pants. The production manager, Zhang Wei, uses two primary resources: sewing machine hours and cutting machine hours. For next month's production of shirts and pants, Mr. Wei can schedule up to 300 hours of sewing machine time and up to 240 hours of cutting machine time. Production of each polo shirt requires 3.0 hours of sewing time and 1.0 hour of cutting time. Each pair of pants requires 2.0 hours of sewing time and 2.0 hours of cutting time. Based on the analysis of cost and sales figures, Mr. Wei estimates that each polo shirt will yield a profit of $5 and each pair of pants will generate a profit of $7. Enrobe's objective is maximizing profits.[b]

SOLUTION

We first organize the information given in the example as shown in Table A.2.

TABLE A.2: Enrobe Textiles Inc. Data

	PROFITS/UNIT	SEWING TIME/UNIT (IN HOURS)	CUTTING TIME/UNIT (IN HOURS)
Polo Shirts	$5	3.0	1.0
Pants	$7	2.0	2.0
Total Time Available (in hours)		300	240

Step 1: Define the decision variables.

We begin by first defining the decision variables, which are the alternative courses of action available to the decision maker. The production manager, Zhang Wei, has to choose the number of polo shirts, the number of pairs of pants, or a combination of the two to be produced. Because these numbers will vary and are under Zhang Wei's control, we define the decision variables as

$$X_1 = \text{number of polo shirts to be produced}$$

$$X_2 = \text{number of pairs of pants to be produced}$$

Step 2: Define the objective function.

Because each polo shirt yields $5 in profits, if Zhang produces 20 shirts, Enrobe earns $100 ($5 × 20) in profits, and if Zhang produces 50 shirts, Enrobe earns $250 ($5 × 50) in profits. Similarly, if Zhang produces 100 pairs of pants, Enrobe earns $700 ($7 × 100) in profits. Because Zhang wants the best production combination of polo shirts and pants that will maximize profits, he defines the objective function as follows:

$$\text{Maximize profit} = \$5X_1 + \$7X_2$$

Linear relationship: the effect of changing a decision variable is proportional to its magnitude

---

[a] Unless otherwise stated, in the Examples, Solved Problems, and Problems, fictional company names are used.
[b] Unless otherwise stated, all currency is in U.S. dollars.

Step 3: Define the constraints.

Enrobe cannot produce an unlimited number of polo shirts and pairs of pants because production of these two products requires the use of two scarce resources: sewing time and cutting time. There are only 300 hours of sewing time and 240 hours of cutting time available. Hence, the number of polo shirts and pairs of pants that can be produced is *constrained* by the available number of hours of these two resources, also suggesting that there is also a limit on the amount of profits that can be made. The constraint function is formulated as follows:

As each polo shirt requires 3 hours of sewing time, if Zhang produces 100 polo shirts, then Enrobe will use 300 hours (3×100) of sewing time. Therefore, if he produces X_1 polo shirts, the sewing time used for producing polo shirts will be $3X_1$. Similarly, because each pair of pants requires 2 hours of sewing time, producing 50 pairs of pants will use 100 (2×50) hours of sewing time. Thus, if he produces X_2 pairs of pants, the sewing time used for producing pants will be $2X_2$. Remember, though, that the sum of sewing time used for producing both polo shirts and pants cannot exceed 300 hours. The mathematical expression of sewing time constraint is shown as follows:

Sewing time constraint:

$$3X_1 + 2X_2 \leq 300 \text{ (hours of sewing time available)}$$

The cutting time constraint is expressed as follows:

Cutting time constraint:

$$X_1 + 2X_2 \leq 240 \text{ (hours of cutting time available)}$$

There is one other set of constraints in LP problems: The decision variables have to be nonnegative. That is, the number of polo shirts and pairs of pants that Enrobe chooses to produce should be greater than or equal to zero:

$$X_1 \text{ and } X_2 \geq 0$$

The complete LP equation is

$$\text{Maximize profit} = \$5X_1 + \$7X_2$$

subject to

$$3X_1 + 2X_2 \leq 300 \text{ (hours of sewing time available)}$$

$$X_1 + 2X_2 \leq 240 \text{ (hours of cutting time available)}$$

$$X_1 \text{ and } X_2 \geq 0$$

where

$$X_1 = \text{number of polo shirts to be produced}$$

$$X_2 = \text{number of pairs of pants to be produced}$$

Solving Linear Programming Problems: The Graphical Method

For solving simple linear programming problems involving two decision variables, the graphical approach can be used. Nevertheless, for more complex LP problems with more than two decision variables, the two-dimensional graphical approach is not appropriate. Complex problems will require more sophisticated solutions. We will examine some of these approaches in Section A.4 of this module. Here, we use the graphical solution approach to solve Example A.1.

STEPS FOR SOLVING EXAMPLE A.1

Step 1: Draw a two-dimensional graph by plotting one decision variable on the X-axis and the other on the Y-axis.

We plot decision variable X_1 (polo shirts) on the X-axis and X_2 (pairs of pants) on the Y-axis as shown in Figure A.1.

FIGURE A.1: Plot of the Decision Variables

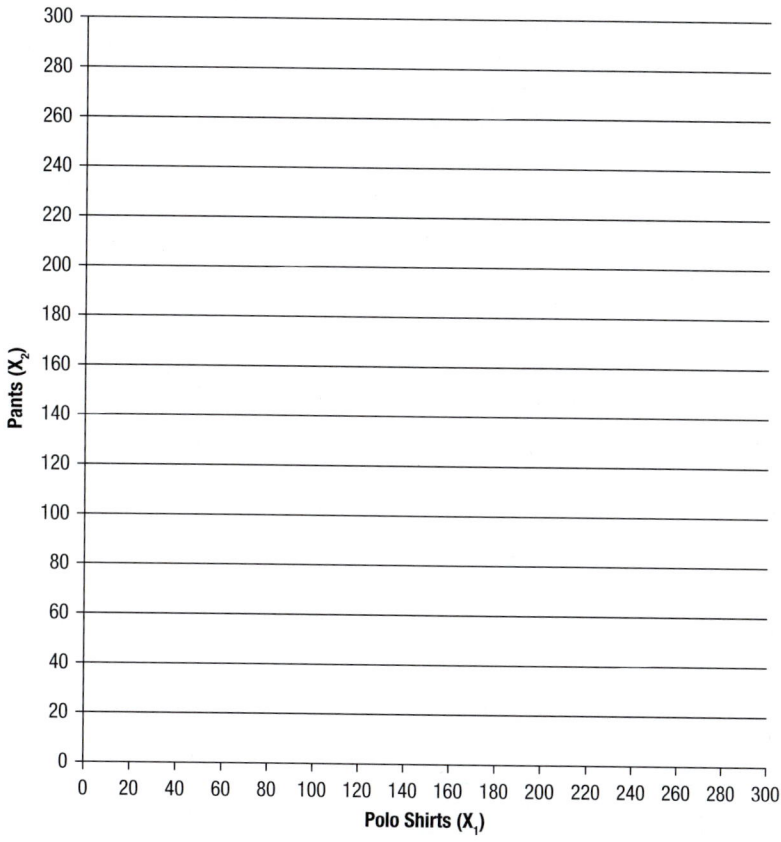

Step 2: Plot the constraints on the graph with the decision variables, and identify the feasible region.

For Example A.1, we can graph each constraint separately and then plot both constraints together. To plot the constraints, we first need to convert the inequalities into equalities as follows:

Sewing Time Constraint: $3X_1 + 2X_2 = 300$

Cutting Time Constraint: $X_1 + 2X_2 = 240$

Because both equations are now the equations for a straight line, we plot the line for the sewing time constraint as follows.

Set $X_2 = 0$ and solve for X_1. This is the value of the point at which the line will intersect the horizontal axis. The calculation is

$$3X_1 + 2X_2 = 300$$

Setting $X_2 = 0$, we have

$$3X_1 + 2 \times 0 = 300$$

$$3X_1 = 300$$

$$X_1 = 100$$

Similarly, setting $X_1 = 0$ and solving for X_2 gives us the value of the point at which the line will intersect the vertical axis. The calculations are

$$3X_1 + 2X_2 = 300$$

$$3 \times 0 + 2X_2 = 300$$

$$2X_2 = 300$$

$$X_2 = 150$$

By joining these two points on the horizontal axis ($X_1 = 100$) and the vertical axis ($X_2 = 150$), we get the straight line for the sewing time constraint, which is plotted in Figure A.2.

FIGURE A.2: Plot of the Sewing Time Constraint

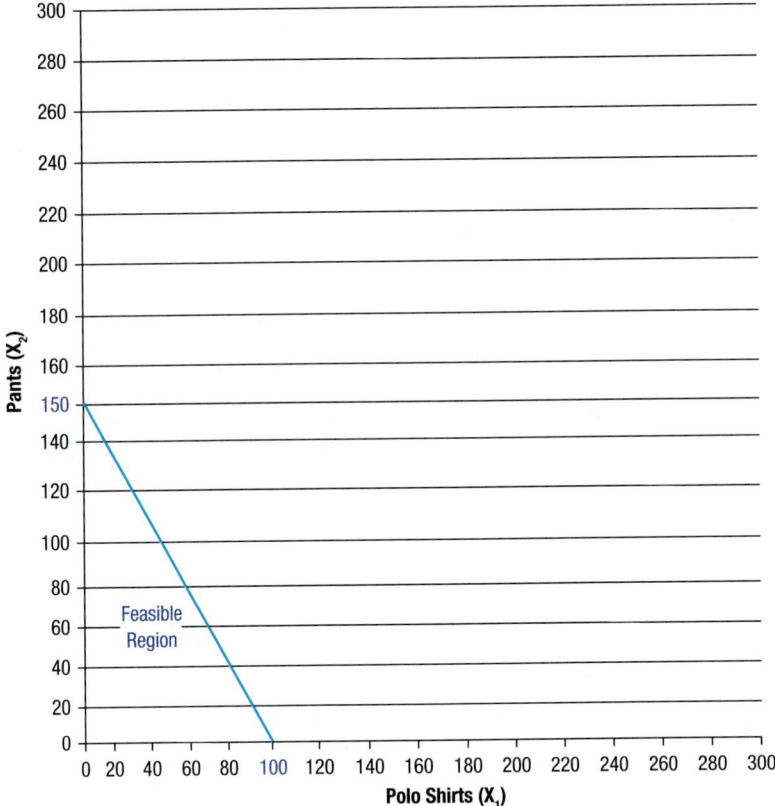

In Figure A.2, the area bounded by the straight line represents the feasible region. That is, based on the constraint imposed by the sewing time available, the area bounded by the straight line represents the feasible combination of X_1 (polo shirts) and X_2 (pairs of pants) that can be produced. The feasible region suggests that although we can always sew fewer combinations of shirts and pants, we cannot sew more than what is indicated by the boundary line.

We similarly plot the line for the cutting time constraint as follows.

Set $X_2 = 0$ and solve for X_1. This is the value of the point at which the line will intersect the horizontal axis. The calculations are

$$X_1 + 2X_2 = 240$$

Setting $X_2 = 0$, we have

$$X_1 + 2 \times 0 = 240$$

$$X_1 = 240$$

Similarly, setting $X_1 = 0$ and solving for X_2 gives us the value of the point at which the line will intersect the vertical axis. The calculations are

$$X_1 + 2X_2 = 240$$

$$1 \times 0 + 2X_2 = 240$$

$$2X_2 = 240$$

$$X_2 = 120$$

By joining these two points on the horizontal axis ($X_1 = 240$) and the vertical axis ($X_2 = 120$), we get the straight line for the cutting time constraint, which is plotted in Figure A.3.

FIGURE A.3: Plot of the Cutting Time Constraint

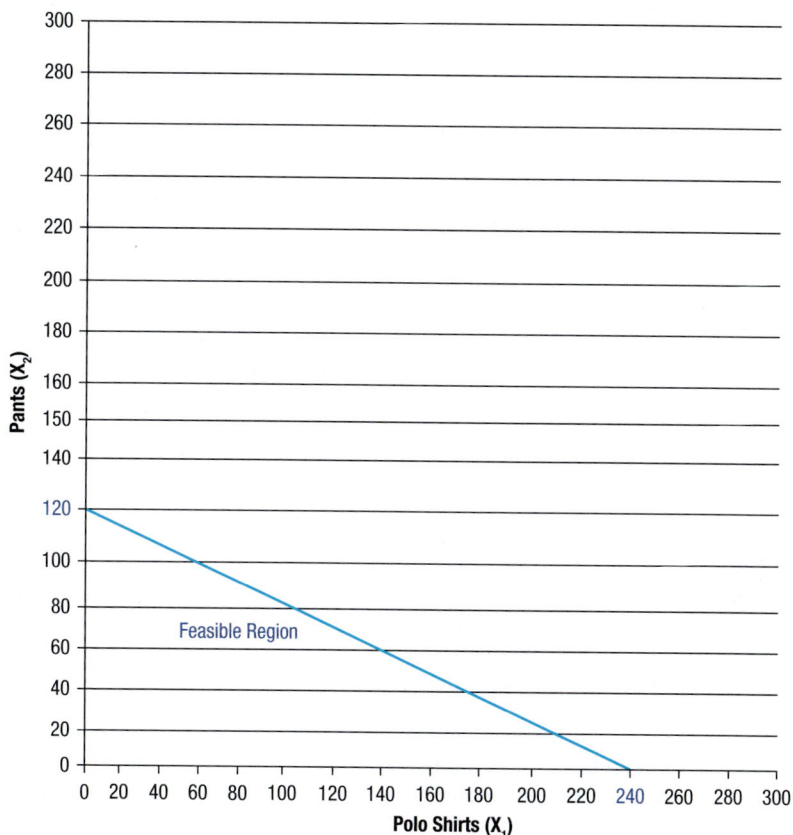

In Figure A.3, the area bounded by the straight line represents the feasible region. Based on the constraint imposed by the cutting time available, the area bounded by the straight line represents the feasible combination of X_1 (polo shirts) and X_2 (pairs of pants) that can be produced.

Because a feasible solution to the LP problem is one that will satisfy both constraints, we must combine Figures A.2 and A.3. Figure A.4 on page 752 shows the graph that plots both the sewing and cutting time constraints.

In Figure A.4, the feasible solution region that satisfies both the sewing and cutting time constraints is the area bounded by the solid lines.

FIGURE A.4: Feasible Solution Region for the LP Problem

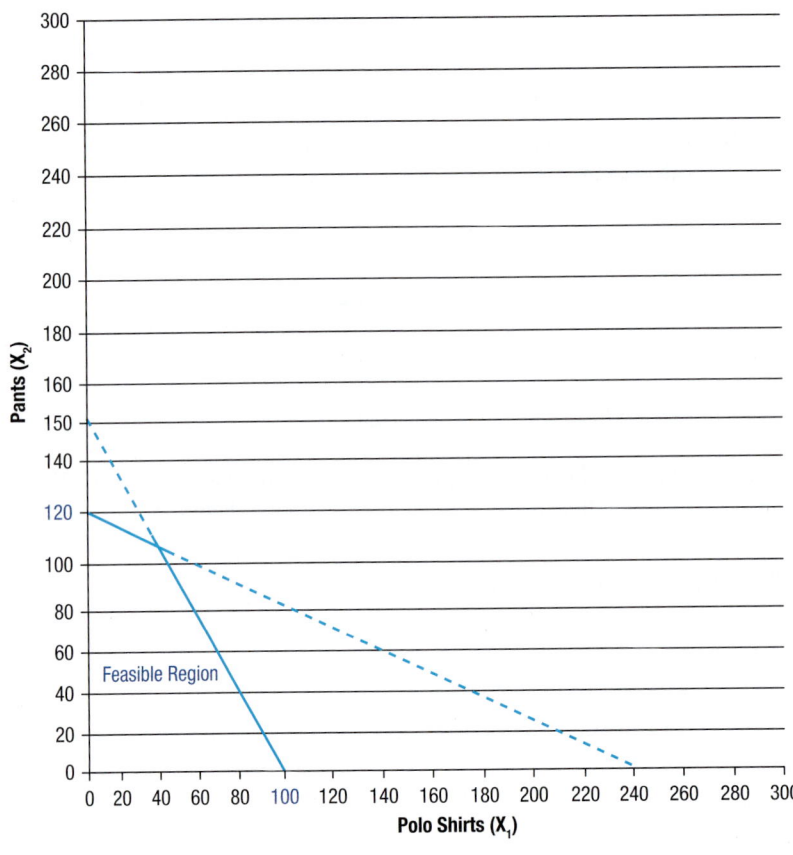

Typically the feasible solution region for an LP problem is defined by the constraints as they form the boundary lines of the feasible solution region. Occasionally, however, there may be constraints in an LP problem that do not affect the boundaries of the feasible solution region. Such constraints are referred to as redundant constraints. A constraint becomes redundant if there are other constraints in the problem that are more restrictive. Also, the addition or removal of a redundant constraint does not alter the feasible solution region. For example, let us assume that Enrobe Textiles Inc. in Example A.1 has added to its problem an additional packaging constraint of the form: $X_1 + X_2 \leq 280$.

When we plot this additional constraint as shown in Figure A.5, you can see the feasible solution region (defined by the sewing and cutting time constraints) remains unaffected. The packaging time constraint is a redundant constraint that plays no role in defining the feasible solution region, and hence, it plays no role in our search for the optimal solution to the problem.

Step 3: Finding the optimal solution to the LP problem.

Once the feasible solution region has been determined, the next step is to solve the LP problem for an optimum solution. Among the many available solution approaches, we will apply the corner point solution method and the iso-profit line method to solve the Enrobe Textiles Inc. problem.

METHOD 1: CORNER POINT SOLUTION METHOD

According to the mathematical theory underlying LP problems, the optimal solution, which in Example A.1 will be the values of X_1 and X_2 that yield the maximum profits, to an LP problem will occur at one of the *corner points* or *extreme points* of the feasible region. Therefore, we examine each corner point occurring at the boundaries of the feasible solution region. The four corners or extreme points of Example A.1 labeled O, A, B, and C of the four-sided polygon represent the feasible solution region shown in Figure A.6.

The next step is to substitute the values of X_1 and X_2 at each corner point into the objective function equation. The values of X_1 and X_2 at each corner point are determined by finding the coordinates of these points on the graph. The optimum solution is the corner point whose values of X_1 and X_2

Redundant constraints: constraints in an LP problem that do not affect the boundaries of the feasible solution region

Corner point solution method: a process in which each corner point occurring at the boundaries of the feasible solution region is examined to determine the optimal solution

Iso-profit line method: a method by which parallel profit lines are plotted in the LP graphical solution approach to determine the maximum profit solution to LP problems with profit maximization objective

FIGURE A.5: Example of Redundant Constraints in LP Problems

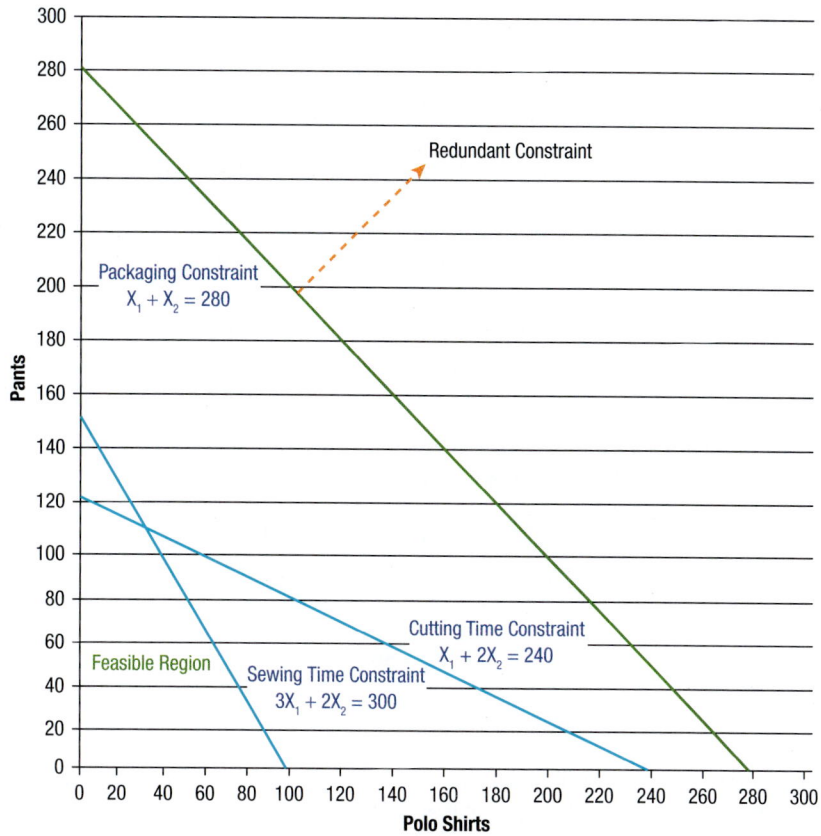

FIGURE A.6: Four Extreme Points of the Feasible Solution Region

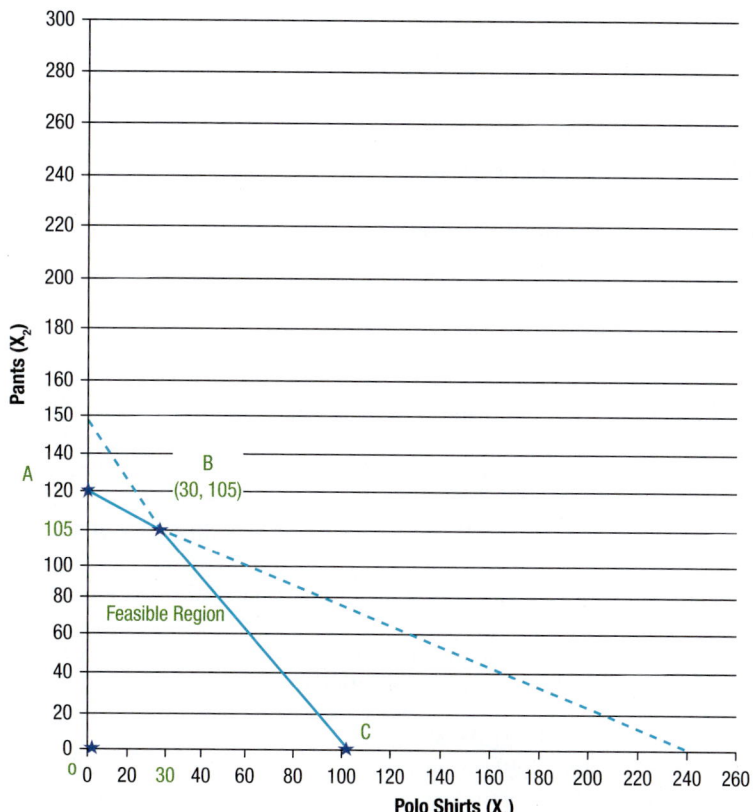

yield the maximum profits. The procedure and calculations involved in determining the optimal solutions are shown as follows:

$$\text{Corner Point O: } X_1 = 0 \text{ and } X_2 = 0$$

$$\text{Corner Point A: } X_1 = 0 \text{ and } X_2 = 120$$

$$\text{Corner Point C: } X_1 = 100 \text{ and } X_2 = 0$$

To determine the coordinates of corner point B accurately, we need to solve for the intersection point of the two constraint lines. This is done algebraically using these equations:

$$3X_1 + 2X_2 = 300 \text{ (Sewing Time Constraint)}$$

$$X_1 + 2X_2 = 240 \text{ (Cutting Time Constraint)}$$

To arrive at the optimum solution, we solve these two equations simultaneously by subtracting the cutting time constraint equation from the sewing time constraint equation:

$$3X_1 + 2X_2 - (X_1 + 2X_2) = 300 - 240$$

$$3X_1 + 2X_2 - X_1 - 2X_2 = 60$$

$$2X_1 = 60$$

$$X_1 = 30$$

Using this procedure enabled us to eliminate one decision variable (X_2) and solve for the other (X_1). We now substitute the value determined above for $X_1 = 30$ into one of the original constraint equations and solve for X_2. By substituting the value of $X_1 = 30$ into the second equation, we have

$$30 + 2X_2 = 240$$

$$2X_2 = 240 - 30 = 210$$

$$X_2 = 105$$

Thus, the coordinates of the corner point B are

$$\text{Corner Point B: } X_1 = 30 \text{ and } X_2 = 105$$

We next substitute the values of X_1 and X_2 into the objective function equation:

$$\$5X_1 + \$7X_2$$

$$\text{Corner Point O: } X_1 = 0 \text{ and } X_2 = 0 \quad \text{Profits} = \$5 \times 0 + \$7 \times 0 = \$0$$

$$\text{Corner Point A: } X_1 = 0 \text{ and } X_2 = 120 \quad \text{Profits} = \$5 \times 0 + \$7 \times 120 = \$840$$

$$\textbf{Corner Point B: } X_1 = 30 \textbf{ and } X_2 = 105 \quad \textbf{Profits} = \$5 \times 30 + \$7 \times 105 = \$885$$

$$\text{Corner Point C: } X_1 = 100 \text{ and } X_2 = 0 \quad \text{Profits} = \$5 \times 100 + \$7 \times 0 = \$500$$

Because the corner point B yields the maximum profits of $885, the product mixture of $X_1 = 30$ polo shirts and $X_2 = 105$ pairs of pants is the optimal solution to Example A.1.

METHOD 2: ISO-PROFIT LINE SOLUTION METHOD

In this method, we begin by choosing an arbitrary value of profits that is feasible. Specifically, we let profits equal some value that does not violate any of the constraints. For Enrobe Textiles Inc., let us choose a profit level of $350. The objective function can now be written as

$$\$5X_1 + \$7X_2 = 350$$

We can plot this profit line on the graph in Figure A.4. We first determine the values of X_1 and X_2 by following the same procedure that we used to plot the constraint lines. We will first let $X_2 = 0$ and solve for X_1. These values will give the point at which the profit line intersects the horizontal axis:

$$\$5X_1 + \$7 \times 0 = 350$$

$$\$5X_1 = 350$$

$$X_1 = 70$$

Next we will let $X_1 = 0$ and solve for X_2 to determine the point at which the profit line intersects the vertical axis:

$$\$5 \times 0 + \$7X_2 = 350$$

$$\$7X_2 = 350$$

$$X_2 = 50$$

By connecting these two points on the horizontal and vertical axes, we get a line that yields a profit of $350. Figure A.7 shows the plot of this line (black dashed).

Note that all points on this profit line represent feasible solutions that will yield a profit of $350. We can also see from Figure A.7 that the profit line of $350 is not optimum because it does not produce the maximum profits. There is room for improvement in profits. Hence, as Figure A.8 shows, we can graph three more profit lines, each one yielding a higher profit than the previous one. By following the same procedure that we used to plot the $350 profit line, we draw a series of profit lines representing profits of $490, $885, and $1120. The plots of the lines are shown in Figure A.8. on page 756.

Notice in Figure A.8 that all of the profit lines are parallel to each other and, hence, the profit lines are referred to as iso-profit lines. You can also see from Figure A.8 that as we move further away from the origin, profits go up. Remember, however, that we cannot assume the profits continue to increase because profits are limited by resource constraints (cutting and sewing time). Thus, to find the optimum solution point, we draw a series of profit lines that are parallel to each other. The profit line that just touches one corner point of the feasible solution space is the optimum solution at that point. Furthermore, it is only at that point that a feasible solution to the problem is possible. All other points

FIGURE A.7: Profit Line of $350 Plotted for Enrobe Textiles Inc.

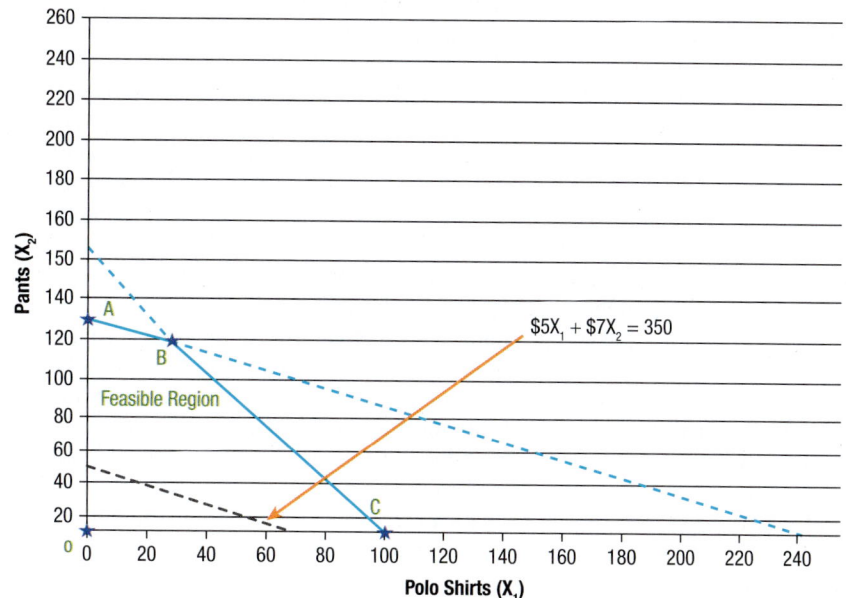

FIGURE A.8: Plot of the Iso-Profit Lines for Enrobe Textiles Inc.

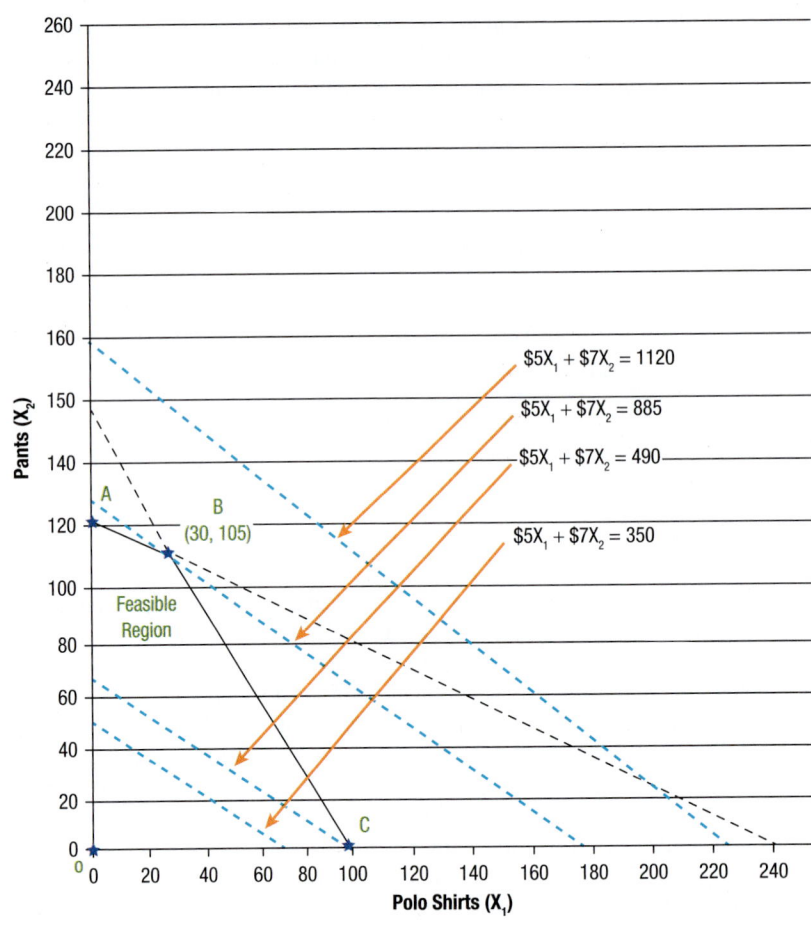

on that profit line represent infeasible solutions. For example, the line representing profits of $1,120 is not achievable because it falls outside the feasible solution region. Thus, for Enrobe Textiles Inc., corner point B is the unique optimum solution point with the product mixture of X_1 = 30 polo shirts and X_2 = 105 pairs of pants yielding the maximum profits of $885.

When the LP problem has only two variables, it is much easier to plot the objective function, and the iso-profit line method can be used to identify easily the corner point that provides the optimum solution. Nevertheless, when the LP problem has more than two decision variables, the graphical method is not appropriate and, hence, the iso-profit line method cannot be used. In such cases, the corner point method is the appropriate technique for determining the optimal solution.

There may also be instances in which the iso-profit line is parallel to one of the constraints that defines the boundaries of the feasible solution region. In such cases, every combination of values of the decision variables that falls on that segment of the constraint line that just touches the feasible solution region represents an optimum solution to the problem. That is, there may be **multiple optimum solutions** to the problem. Yet, even in such cases, the optimum solution is still one corner point—the end points of that segment of the constraint line that just touches the feasible region—although there will be two corner points representing the optimum solution.

The constraints that form the corner points at the boundaries of the feasible solution region are known as **binding constraints**. It is these binding constraints that limit the values of the decision variables, which in turn limit the objective function values. Unless the binding constraints are relaxed (making them less restrictive), an improved solution will not be possible. In Example A.1, by increasing the available sewing time and cutting time (the available resources represented by the right-hand-side values of these constraints), an improved solution in the form of increased profits is possible. If, however, the packaging time constraint (which is a redundant constraint) shown in Figure A.5 is a nonbinding constraint, increasing the right-side value of this constraint will have no effect on the objective function value.

Multiple optimum solutions: every combination of values of the decision variables that falls on that segment of the constraint line that just touches the feasible solution region

Binding constraints: constraints that form the corner points at the boundaries of the feasible solution region and limit the values of the decision variables, which in turn limit the objective function values

Furthermore, for binding constraints at optimality, the right-hand- and the left-hand-side values should be equal. That is, when the optimal values of the decision variables are substituted into the left-hand-side of the binding constraint equations, the resulting values should be equal to the right-hand-side values of those constraints. For nonbinding constraints, however, when the optimal values of the decision variables are substituted into the left-hand-side of those binding constraint equations, the resulting values will not be equal to the right-hand-side values of those constraints. At optimality, if the left-hand-side values are greater than the right-hand side, then we have a surplus. Conversely, if the left-hand-side values are less than the right-hand side, then we have slack. Thus, slack is the amount by which the left-hand-side values are less than the right-hand-side values and can only occur in constraints that have a < inequality sign. Similarly, surplus is the amount by which the left-hand-side values are greater than the right-hand-side values, and can only occur in constraints that have a > inequality sign.

Solving Problems With Minimization Objective Using LP

In addition to maximizing an objective such as profits, many real-life business situations also have minimization objectives, such as minimizing cost or minimizing total number of employees used on any one day or for any work shift. For example, a bank may wish to set a work schedule for its tellers that will effectively meet the demand for their services while minimizing the total number of tellers required. Similarly, a farmer who is planning to fertilize a field prior to planting a crop may want to decide which combination of fertilizers to use that will minimize the total cost of fertilizing. Similar to problems with a maximization objective, by making some minor changes in the problem formulation, linear programming can also be used to solve problems with minimization objectives. Solving minimization LP problems can also be done graphically by first determining the feasible solution space, and then by using the corner point method or the iso-cost line method. The iso-cost line method is similar to the iso-profit line method except that instead of plotting profit lines, we will plot the cost lines on the graph. Example A.2 illustrates an LP minimization problem.

EXAMPLE A.2: To fertilize his vegetable farm prior to planting, a farmer, Raju Reddy, needs to decide which brand of fertilizer to choose from two available fictional bio-fertilizer brands—Nitro Plus and Phosphate Max. Each brand contains two main ingredients, nitrogen and phosphate, in specific amounts per bag, as shown in the table.

BRAND	INGREDIENTS	
	NITROGEN (IN POUNDS/BAG)	PHOSPHATE (IN POUNDS/BAG)
Nitro Plus	8	6
Phosphate Max	4	8

Raju Reddy's vegetable farm requires at least 32 pounds of nitrogen and 48 pounds of phosphate. Nitro Plus costs $7 per bag, and Phosphate Max costs $9. Raju Reddy needs to decide the number of bags of each brand of fertilizer to buy that will minimize the total cost of fertilizing his farm. Use linear programming to solve Raju Reddy's problem.

SOLUTION

Step 1: Define the decision variables.

We begin by first defining the decision variables, which are the alternative courses of action available to the decision maker. In this example, Raju Reddy has to decide on the number of bags of each brand of fertilizer to buy. Hence the decision variables are

$$X_1 = \text{Number of bags of Nitro Plus to be purchased}$$

$$X_2 = \text{Number of bags of Phosphate Max to be purchased}$$

Surplus: the amount by which the left-hand-side values are greater than the right-hand-side values

Slack: the amount by which the left-hand-side values are less than the right-hand-side values

Iso-cost line method: a method by which parallel cost lines are plotted in the LP graphical solution approach to determine the least cost solution to LP problems with cost minimization objective

Step 2: Define the objective function.

Raju Reddy's objective is to minimize the total cost of fertilizing his vegetable farm. If Raju Reddy purchases 20 bags of Nitro Plus, the cost would be \$140 (\$7 × 20). Similarly, if he purchases 12 bags of Phosphate Max, the cost would be \$108 (\$9 × 12). Raju wants to purchase the right combination of Nitro Plus and Phosphate Max that will minimize total costs, and so the objective function for this problem is defined as follows:

$$\text{Minimize total cost} = \$7X_1 + \$9X_2$$

Step 3: Define the constraints.

The constraints in this problem are the minimum amounts of nitrogen and phosphate required to fertilize the vegetable farm effectively. Raju needs at least 32 pounds of nitrogen and 48 pounds of phosphate. Thus, if he buys 4 bags of Nitro Plus, there will be 32 pounds (4 × 8) of nitrogen, and if he buys 6 bags of Phosphate Max, then there will be 24 pounds (6 × 4) of nitrogen. Raju, however, has to purchase that combination of fertilizer bags that contain nitrogen that is either equal to or greater than 32 pounds. Similarly, he has to purchase that combination of fertilizer bags containing phosphate that is either equal to or greater than 48 pounds. Thus, if Raju purchases X_1 bags of Nitro Plus and X_2 bags of Phosphate Max, the two ingredient constraints can be written as

$$8X_1 + 4X_2 \geq 32 \text{ pounds of nitrogen}$$

$$6X_1 + 8X_2 \geq 48 \text{ pounds of phosphate}$$

As in Example A.1, the final constraint in LP problems is that the decision variables have to be non-negative. That is, the number of fertilizer bags of Nitro Plus and Phosphate Max that Raju chooses to purchase should be greater than or equal to zero:

$$X_1 \text{ and } X_2 \geq 0$$

The complete LP equation for Example A.2 is

$$\text{Minimize total cost} = \$6X_1 + \$8X_2$$

subject to these constraints

$$8X_1 + 4X_2 \geq 32 \text{ pounds of nitrogen}$$

$$6X_1 + 8X_2 \geq 48 \text{ pounds of phosphate}$$

$$X_1 \text{ and } X_2 \geq 0$$

where

$$X_1 = \text{number of bags of Nitro Plus to be purchased}$$

$$X_2 = \text{number of bags of Phosphate Max to be purchased}$$

Solving Linear Programming Minimization Problems: The Graphical Method

STEPS FOR SOLVING EXAMPLE A.2

Steps 1 and 2: Draw a two-dimensional graph by plotting one decision variable on the X-axis and the other on the Y-axis. Plot the constraints on the graph with the decision variables, and identify the feasible region.

For Example A.2, we plot decision variable X_1 (bags of Nitro Plus) on the X-axis and X_2 (bags of Phosphate Max) on the Y-axis. We graph each constraint separately and then combine them into a

graph that will show both constraints plotted together. To plot the constraints, we first need to convert the inequalities into equalities as shown:

$$\text{Nitrogen requirement constraint: } 8X_1 + 4X_2 = 32 \text{ pounds of nitrogen}$$

$$\text{Phosphate requirement constraint: } 6X_1 + 8X_2 = 48 \text{ pounds of phosphate}$$

Both equations are now written as equations for a straight line. We plot the line for the nitrogen requirement constraint as follows.

Set $X_2 = 0$ and solve for X_1. The result is the value of the point at which the line will intersect the horizontal axis. The calculations are

$$8X_1 + 4X_2 = 32$$

Setting $X_2 = 0$, we have

$$8X_1 + 4 \times 0 = 32$$
$$8X_1 = 32$$
$$X_1 = 4$$

Similarly, setting $X_1 = 0$ and solving for X_2 will give us the value of the point at which the line will intersect the vertical axis. The calculations are

$$8X_1 + 4X_2 = 32$$
$$8 \times 0 + 4X_2 = 32$$
$$4X_2 = 32$$
$$X_2 = 8$$

By joining these two points on the horizontal axis ($X_1 = 4$) and the vertical axis ($X_2 = 8$), we get the straight line for the nitrogen requirement constraint. The resulting plots of the nitrogen constraint are shown in Figure A.9.

FIGURE A.9: Plot of the Nitrogen Requirement Constraint

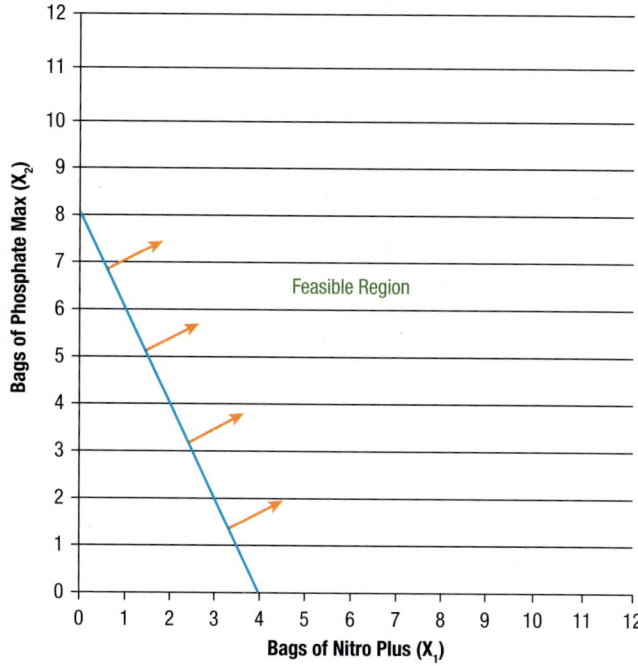

In Figure A.9, the area above the line (as shown by the arrows) represents the feasible region. Based on the constraint imposed by the minimum requirements of the nitrogen ingredient, the area above the straight line represents the feasible combination of X_1 (Nitrogen Plus) and X_2 (Phosphate Max) that should be purchased.

We similarly plot the line for the phosphate requirement constraint as follows.

Set $X_2 = 0$ and solve for X_1. The result is the value of the point at which the line will intersect the horizontal axis. The calculations are

$$6X_1 + 8X_2 = 48$$

Setting $X_2 = 0$, we have

$$6X_1 + 8 \times 0 = 48$$

$$6X_1 = 48$$

$$X_1 = 8$$

Similarly, setting $X_1 = 0$ and solving for X_2 gives us the value of the point at which the line will intersect the vertical axis. The calculation is

$$6X_1 + 8X_2 = 48$$

$$6 \times 0 + 8X_2 = 48$$

$$8X_2 = 48$$

$$X_2 = 6$$

By joining these two points on the horizontal axis ($X_1 = 8$) and the vertical axis ($X_2 = 6$), we get the straight line for the phosphate requirement constraint plotted in Figure A.10.

In Figure A.10, the area above the line (shown by the arrows) represents the feasible region. Based on the constraint imposed by the minimum requirements of the phosphate ingredient, the area above the straight line represents the feasible combination of X_1 (Nitrogen Plus) and X_2 (Phosphate Max) that should be purchased.

Because a feasible solution to the LP problem is one that will satisfy both constraints, we will combine Figures A.9 and A.10. Figure A.11 shows the graph of the plot of both the nitrogen and phosphate requirement constraints.

Step 3: Finding the optimal solution to the LP problem.

Given that we identified the feasible solution space, the next step is to solve the LP problem for an optimum solution. As in Example A.1, we will apply the corner point solution method and the iso-profit line method to solve Raju Reddy, fertilization problem.

METHOD 1: CORNER POINT SOLUTION METHOD

As we know, the optimal solution to an LP problem will occur at one corner or extreme point of the feasible space. Therefore, we will examine each corner point occurring at the boundaries of the feasible solution space in Figure A.11. The values of X_1 and X_2 will yield the minimum costs at one corner point of the feasible solution space. The three corner or extreme points in Example A.2 are labeled as A, B, and C of the feasible solution space, as shown in Figure A.12 on page 762. Unlike the maximization problem in Example A.1, in this case, we are only concerned with the three corners (A, B, and C) because there is no valid fourth corner to investigate.

We can substitute the values of X_1 and X_2 at each corner point into the objective function equation. The values of X_1 and X_2 at each corner point are determined by finding the coordinates of these points on the graph. The optimum solution is that corner point whose values of X_1 and X_2 yields the minimum costs. The values for determining the optimal solutions are

Corner Point A: $X_1 = 0$ and $X_2 = 8$

Corner Point C: $X_1 = 8$ and $X_2 = 0$

FIGURE A.10: Plot of the Phosphate Requirement Constraint

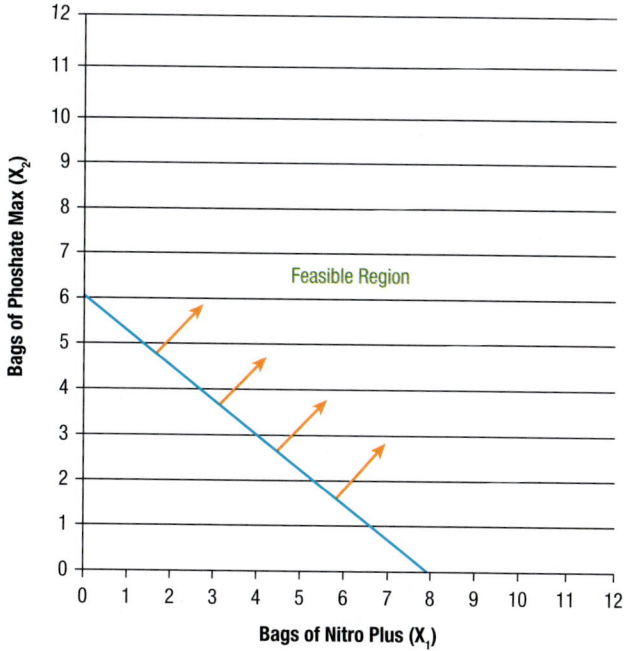

FIGURE A.11: Plot of the Feasible Solution Region

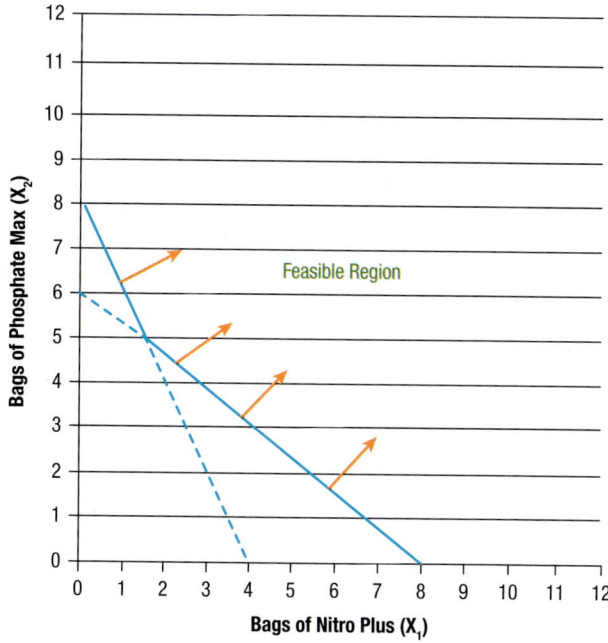

To determine the coordinates of corner point B accurately, we solve for the intersection point of the two constraint lines. This is an algebraic procedure using simultaneous equations:

$$8X_1 + 4X_2 = 32 \text{ (Nitrogen Requirement Constraint)}$$

$$6X_1 + 8X_2 = 48 \text{ (Phosphate Requirement Constraint)}$$

To solve for these two equations simultaneously, we first multiply the nitrogen requirement constraint equation by 2 to get a modified nitrogen requirement constraint equation. The purpose of this

FIGURE A.12: Three Extreme Points of the Feasible Solution Space

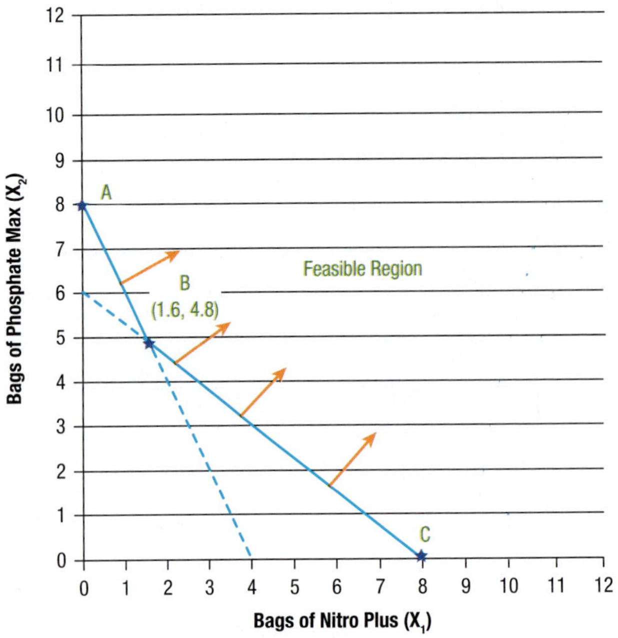

intermediate step is to bring the coefficients of one variable to equality. By doing so, we can perform arithmetical operations (add or subtract) to eliminate that variable and solve for the other:

$$(8X_1 + 4X_2) \times 2 = 32 \times 2$$

$$16X_1 + 8X_2 = 64$$

We now subtract the phosphate requirement constraint equation from the modified nitrogen requirement constraint equation:

$$16X_1 + 8X_2 - (6X_1 + 8X_2) = 64 - 48$$

$$16X_1 + 8X_2 - 6X_1 - 8X_2 = 16$$

$$10X_1 = 16$$

$$X_1 = 1.6 \text{ bags}$$

We've eliminated one decision variable (X_2) and can solve for the other (X_1). We now substitute the value determined above for $X_1 = 1.6$ into one of the original constraint equations and solve for X_2. By substituting the value of $X_1 = 1.6$ into the second equation, we have

$$6 \times 1.6 + 8X_2 = 48$$

$$8X_2 = 48 - 9.6 = 38.4$$

$$X_2 = 4.8 \text{ bags}$$

Thus, the coordinates of corner point B are

Corner Point B: $X_1 = 1.6$ and $X_2 = 4.8$

We next substitute the values of X_1 and X_2 into the objective function equation: $\$7X_1 + \$9X_2$

Corner Point A: $X_1 = 0$ and $X_2 = 8$ Costs = $\$7 \times 0 + \$9 \times 8 = \$72$

Corner Point B: $X_1 = 1.6$ and $X_2 = 4.8$ Costs = $7 \times 1.6 + \$9 \times 4.8 = \$54.40$

Corner Point C: $X_1 = 8$ and $X_2 = 0$ Costs = $7 \times 8 + \$9 \times 0 = \$56$

Because corner point B yields the minimum cost of $54.40, Raju should purchase $X_1 = 1.6$ bags of Nitro Plus and $X_2 = 4.8$ bags of Phosphate Max, which is the optimal solution to the problem. In reality, the fractional values may have to be rounded up because the store selling the products will probably require Raju to round up and purchase 2 bags of Nitro Plus and 5 bags of Phosphate Max.

METHOD 2: ISO-COST LINE SOLUTION METHOD

In this method, we begin by choosing an arbitrary value of costs for the objective function that is feasible. That is, we let the objective function equal some value that does not violate any of the constraints. For Example A.2, let us start by choosing a cost level of $81. The objective function can now be written as

$$\$7X_1 + \$9X_2 = 81$$

We can plot this cost line on the graph in Figure A.12. To do so we determine the values of X_1 and X_2 by following the same procedure that we used to plot the constraint lines. We first let $X_2 = 0$ and solve for X_1. This calculation gives the point at which the cost line intersects the horizontal axis:

$$\$7X_1 + \$9 \times 0 = 81$$

$$\$7X_1 = 81$$

$$X_1 = 11.571$$

Next we will let $X_1 = 0$ and solve for X_2 to determine the point at which the cost line intersects the vertical axis:

$$\$7 \times 0 + \$9X_2 = 81$$

$$X_2 = 9$$

By connecting these two points on the horizontal and vertical axes, we get a line that yields a cost of $81. Figure A.13 shows the plot of this line (dashed).

FIGURE A.13: Plot of the Cost Line of $81

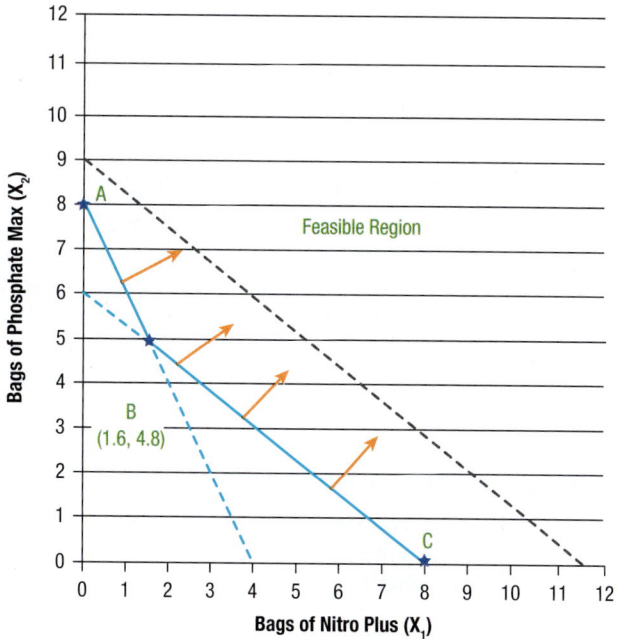

FIGURE A.14: Plot of the Iso-Cost Lines

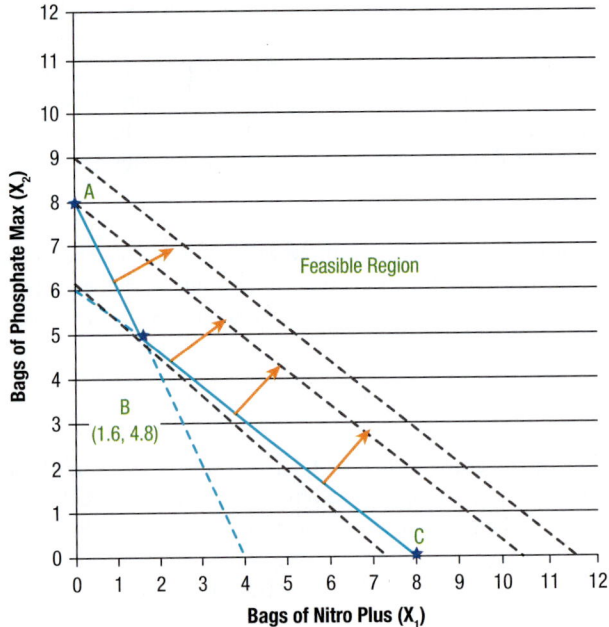

Note that all points on this profit line represent feasible solutions that will yield a cost of $81. Nevertheless, the cost line of $81 is not optimum as it does not minimize the farmer's costs. Hence, in Figure A.14, we will graph two more cost lines that are parallel to the cost line of $81. Each of these additional cost lines has a lower cost than the previous one. The plot of the lines is shown in Figure A.14.

Because all of the cost lines from Figure A.14 are parallel to each other, they are referred to as iso-cost lines. You can also see from Figure A.14 that as we move toward the origin, costs will decrease. The cost line that just touches one corner point of the feasible solution space is the optimum solution point. Furthermore, it is only at that point that a feasible solution to the problem is possible. All other points on that cost line represent infeasible solutions. Thus, for Raju Reddy's fertilization problem, corner point B is the unique optimum solution point. Because corner point B yields the minimum cost of $54.40, Raju should purchase X_1 = 1.6 bags of Nitro Plus and X_2 = 4.8 bags of Phosphate Max.

The Simplex Method of Linear Programming

Simplex method: an algorithm that provides a systematic way of examining the corner or extreme points of the feasible region of more complex LP problems to determine the optimal value of the objective function

The graphical solution method discussed in the previous section can be used for linear programming problems having two variables. Nevertheless, for real-world problems involving more than two variables or having a large number of constraints, other computer-based approaches should be used. One such method is called the simplex method developed by George Dantzig in 1946. The simplex method is an algorithm that provides a systematic way of examining the corner or extreme points of the feasible region of more complex LP problems to determine the optimal value (maximum profits or minimum cost) of the objective function. Many computer programs, including Microsoft Excel's Solver (Microsoft Corporation, Redmond, WA) tool, can be used to solve linear programming problems with the simplex method. The actual algebraic steps of the simplex method are beyond the scope of this book; for details on this method, refer to an operations research or management science textbook.

A.2 Solving Linear Programming Problems Using Excel

 Solve LP problems with both maximization and minimization objectives, using graphical methods and Excel Solver.

Excel provides an excellent means for solving linear programming problems. To demonstrate, we can use the Solver tool in Excel to solve the Enrobe Textiles Inc. problem (Example A.1). Screenshot A.1 shows the Excel spreadsheet for this example.

SCREENSHOT A.1: Excel Spreadsheet for the Enrobe Textiles Inc. Problem

Linear Programming
in Excel

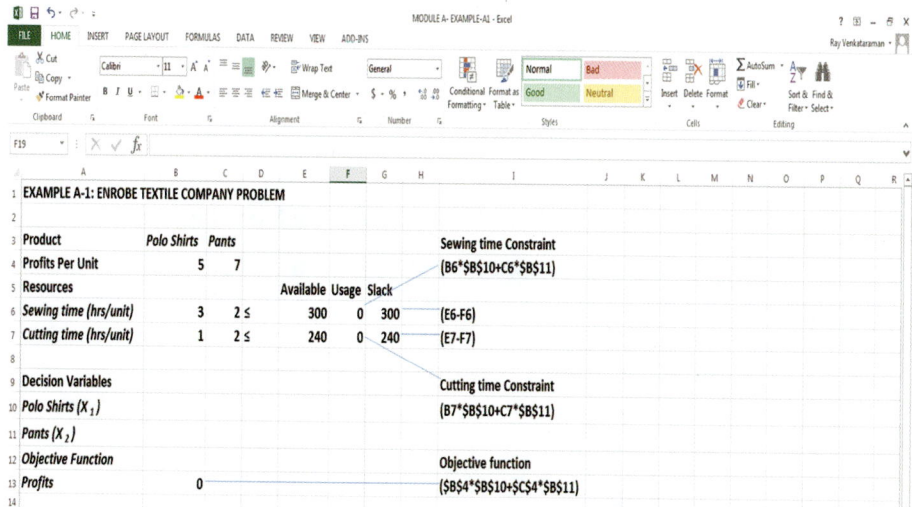

In the spreadsheet, the values of the decision variables (polo shirts and pairs of pants) are in cells B10 and B11, and the value of the objective function (profits) is in cell B13. Because the problem has not yet been solved, these cells are empty. The spreadsheet also shows the formulas embedded in cells B13, F6, and F7 for the objective function and the two constraints of sewing time and cutting time, respectively.

Before solving the problem, the Solver tool needs to be activated through the following steps:

Step 1: From the toolbar at the top of the Excel (Version 2013) screen, click "Add-ins."

Step 2: From the "Add-ins" menu, select "Solver."

Once the Solver tool has been activated, click on the "Data" tab on the tool bar, and then click on "Solver." The window for the "Solver Parameters" will appear as shown in Screenshot A.2.

SCREENSHOT A.2: Excel Solver Parameters Window

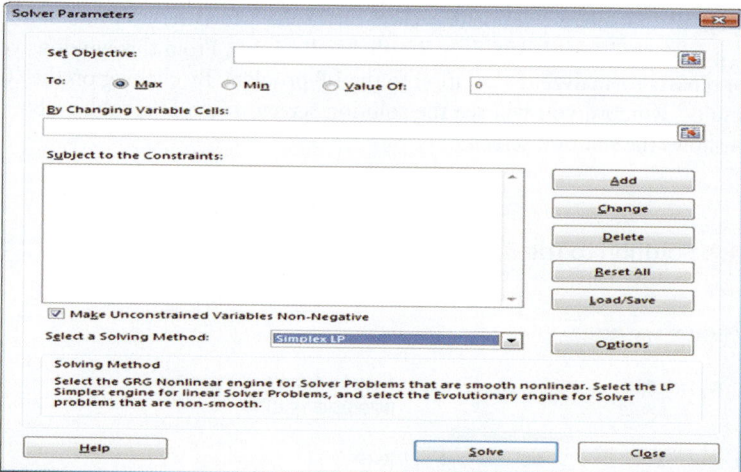

The Excel Solver Parameters window is currently blank. We need to input the following information:

1. In the "Set Objective" row, input the cell reference that contains our objective function, which is cell B13 in Example A.1.
2. Click on the "Max" button because we are maximizing our objective function.
3. In the "By Changing Variable Cells" row, we input the cell references for the decision variables, which are cells B10 and B11.

Using Excel Solver for Linear Programming

4. To input the model constraints, click on the "Add" button. This will activate a new window for adding the constraints. For the example, cell references F6, F7, and E6, E7 will be added as shown in Screenshot A.3.
5. In the row for "Select a Solving Method," choose Simplex LP.

The complete model with all the inputs is shown in Screenshot A.3.

SCREENSHOT A.3: Excel Solver Parameters Window With All Model Inputs

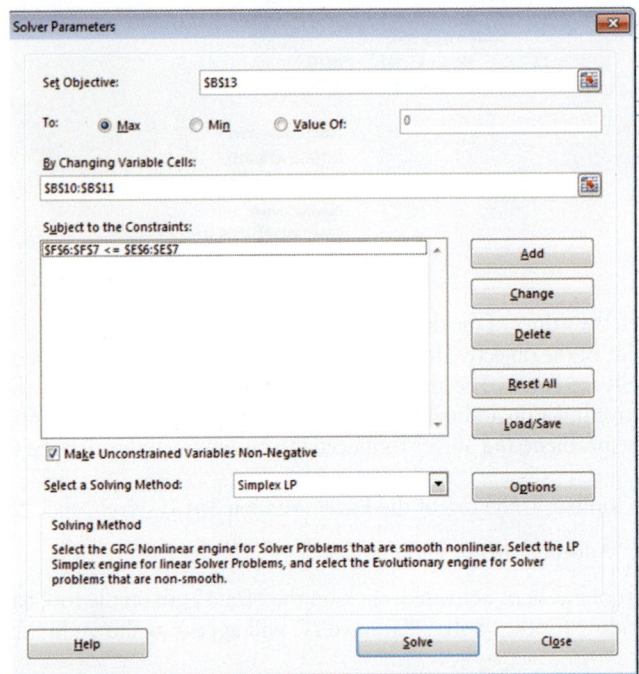

After entering all the solver parameters, click on "Solve" to determine the solution to the LP problem. First, a new window titled "Solver Results" will appear. From this window, you can choose several types of reports to analyze the solution to the LP problem. By clicking on the "OK" button in the "Solver Results" window, you will see the solution screen to the LP problem. For Example A.1, Screenshot A.4 shows the solution screen.

SCREENSHOT A.4: Solution to the Enrobe Textiles Inc. Problem

	A	B	C	D	E	F	G	H	I
1	EXAMPLE A-1: ENROBE TEXTILE COMPANY PROBLEM								
2									
3	Product	Polo Shirts	Pants						Sewing time Constraint
4	Profits Per Unit	5	7						(B6*$B$10+C6*$B$11)
5	Resources				Available	Usage	Slack		
6	Sewing time (hrs/unit)	3	2 ≤		300	300	0		(E6-F6)
7	Cutting time (hrs/unit)	1	2 ≤		240	240	0		(E7-F7)
8									
9	Decision Variables								Cutting time Constraint
10	Polo Shirts (X_1)	30							(B7*$B$10+C7*$B$11)
11	Pants (X_2)	105							
12	Objective Function								Objective function
13	Profits	885							($B$4*$B$10+$C$4*$B$11)
14									

Notice in Screenshot A.4 that we arrived at the same solution using the graphical method. An Excel spreadsheet of the solution to the minimization LP problem (Example A.2) appears in Screenshot A.5.

SCREENSHOT A.5: Solution to Raju Reddy's Fertilizer Purchase Problem

	A	B	C	D	E	F	G	H	I
1	EXAMPLE A-2: Raju Reddy's Fertilzer Purchase Problem								
2									
3	Fertilizer	NitroPlus	Phosphate Max						Nitrogen Requirement Constraint
4	Cost Per Bag	7	9						(B6*$B$10+C6*$B$11)
5	Ingredients				Required	Present	Surplus		
6	Nitrogen (lbs/bag)	8	4 ≥		32	32	0		(E6-F6)
7	Phosphtae(lbs/ba)	6	8 ≥		48	48	0		(E7-F7)
8									
9	Decision Variables								Phosphate Requirement Constraint
10	Nitro Plus (X_1)	1.6							(B7*$B$10+C7*$B$11)
11	Phosphate Max (X_2)	4.8							
12	Objective Function								Objective function
13	Costs	54.4							($B$4*$B$10+$C$4*$B$11)

A.3 Sensitivity Analysis

A key assumption of all linear programming models is that the input parameters such as the objective function coefficients and the right-hand-side values of the constraints are assumed to be constant. In real-life decisions, however, the values of these parameters are estimates at best. Therefore, in addition to the optimal solution obtained by solving an LP problem, managers need to know what would be the impact of changes to the input parameter values, such as the objective function coefficients or the right-hand-side values of the constraint equations, or both. In essence, managers are asking, how sensitive is the current optimal solution to changes in the input parameter values? Answering this question is the purpose of sensitivity or post-optimality analysis.

Although a trial-and-error approach can be used to evaluate the impact of these changes, it is not a very efficient way to resolve the entire LP model every time that an input parameter is changed. Fortunately, all LP software packages have the capability of generating sensitivity analysis reports that provide information on the range of values of the problem parameters within which the current optimal solution will not be affected.

Screenshot A.6 is the sensitivity analysis report generated by Excel Solver for the Enrobe Textiles Inc. problem. This report has two major components: a variable cells table and a constraints table. By using these tables, managers can answer several what-if questions regarding the current optimal solution and the input parameters. Note that in interpreting this report, the values refer to changes to one input parameter value at a time, while the others are held constant. The values in the report do not reflect concurrent changes in several input parameter values.

Changes in the Objective Function Coefficient

In Screenshot A.6, the variable cells table shows the impact of changes to the current objective coefficients of $5 and $7 of the decision variables—polo shirts and pairs of pants. Changes in the objective function coefficients of these decision variables do not affect the feasible solution region, but they do affect the slope of the iso-profit lines. The allowable increase and allowable decrease columns of Screenshot A.6 show the extent to which the profit per unit of the decision variables can be changed without affecting the current optimal solution. For example, as long as the profit per unit of polo shirts is within the range of $3.5 to $10.5, the current optimal solution will not change. Note, however, that changing the value of the objective function coefficient will change the total profits. Suppose, for example, that the profit per unit of polo shirts is changed from $5 to $6. By implementing this change, profits will increase from $885 to $915, but the values of the decision variables in the original optimum solution will not change. The values still are $X_1 = 30$ and $X_2 = 105$. Similarly, decreasing the profit per unit of pants $7 to $5 will decrease total profits to $675, but the values of the decision

A.3

Perform sensitivity analysis on solutions to LP problems.

Linear Programming Sensitivity Analysis

Sensitivity or post-optimality analysis: the determination of how sensitive the current optimal solution is to changes in the input parameter values

SCREENSHOT A.6: Sensitivity Analysis Report for the Enrobe Textiles Inc. Problem

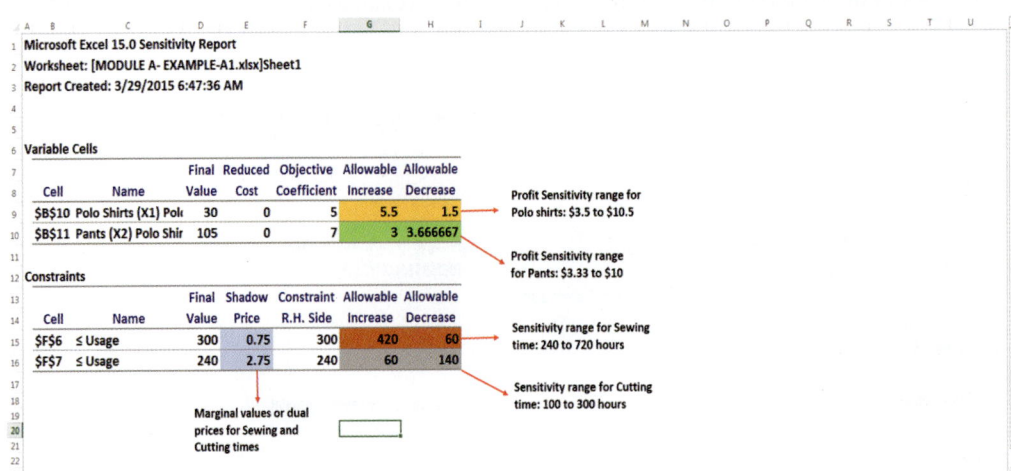

variables will still be $X_1 = 30$ and $X_2 = 105$, and the original optimum solution is still valid. Specifically, the range of profits per unit within which the current solution will remain optimum is $3.5 to $10.50 for polo shirts and $3.33 to $10 for pants. This range of values of the objective function within which the optimal values of the decision variables will not change is known as the **range of optimality**. Beyond this range, however, the current solution will no longer be optimal.

Changes in the Right-Hand-Side Values of the Resource Constraints

Changes in the right-hand values of the constraints result from changes in resource availability. Note that changing the right-hand value of a constraint will change the feasible solution region and, quite often, the optimum solution, unless it is a redundant constraint. For example, if the available sewing time is increased from 300 to 310 hours, the new optimal solution will be $X_1 = 35$ and $X_2 = 102.5$ for a total profit of $892.50. Note, however, that the optimum solution point is still corner point B. This new optimal solution is shown graphically in Figure A.15. Thus, increasing the sewing time resource by 10 hours increases profit by $7.50 or by $0.75 per hour. This change of $0.75 per hour in profits is called the **shadow price or dual price**. This shadow price of $0.75 represents the extent to which profits will improve if an additional hour of sewing time (the right-hand value of the constraint) is made available. Similarly, the shadow price of $2.75 (shown in Screenshot A.4) represents the improvement in the objective function value if an additional hour of cutting time is made available. Conversely, a decrease of one hour of sewing time will reduce profits by $0.75 and a reduction of one hour of cutting time will reduce profits by $2.75, respectively.

The shadow prices are valid as long as the available resources stay within a certain range. Enrobe Textiles Inc. cannot indefinitely keep on increasing its sewing and cutting time resources and make infinite profits. That is not realistic, and the shadow price of $0.75 will only hold for a certain range of available sewing time. This range is given in the allowable increase and allowable decrease columns of the constraints table in Screenshot A.6. For the sewing time resource, the allowable increase is 420 hours and the allowable decrease is 60 hours. Thus, the shadow price of $0.75 is valid as long as the available sewing time is between 240 hours (300 – 60) and 720 hours (300 + 420). Similarly, the shadow price of $2.75 for the cutting time constraint is valid as long as the available cutting time is between 100 hours (240 – 140) and 300 hours (240 + 60). This limited range over which the shadow price remains constant is called the **range of feasibility**.

A.4 Additional Linear Programming Models

The LP models that we have discussed so far are fairly simple because they have just two variables and two constraints. Most real-life problems are considerably more complex with many variables and numerous constraints. Let us consider more complex linear programming models.

Range of optimality: the range of values of the objective function within which the optimal values of the decision variables will not change

Shadow price or dual price: the price associated with a resource that indicates how much more profit would be earned by increasing the amount of the resource by one unit. Conversely, it is the price one would be willing to pay for acquiring an additional unit of that resource

Range of feasibility: the limited range over which the shadow price remains constant

 A.4

Apply LP to other problems, including product-mixture, blending, and personnel scheduling situations.

FIGURE A.15: Sensitivity Analysis of the Resource Availability of Enrobe Textiles Inc.

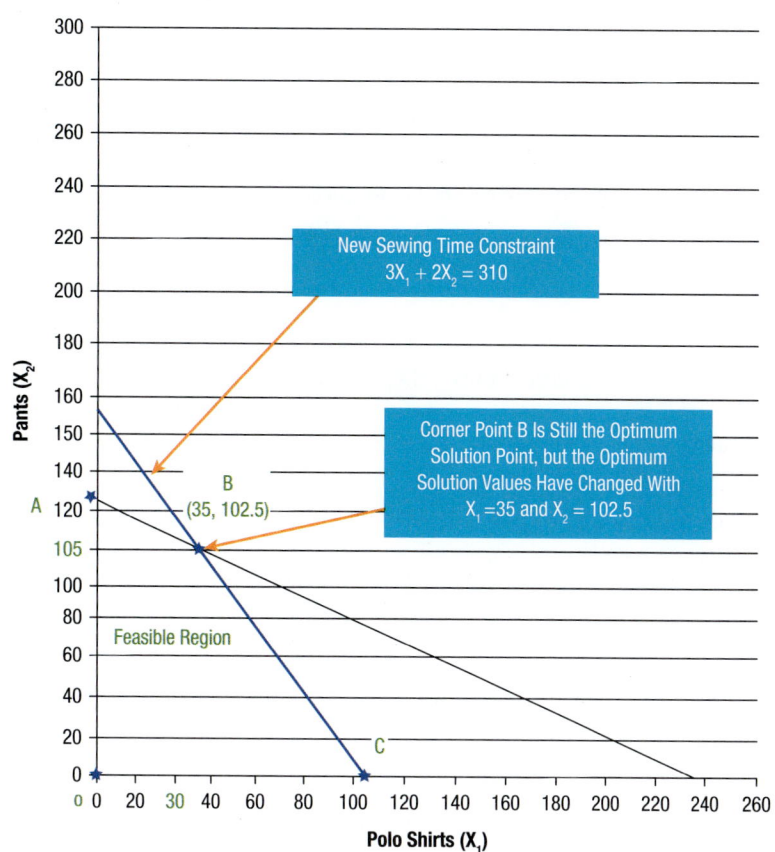

EXAMPLE A.3

Diamond Plywood Inc. manufactures four types of plywood panels. Each product must go through the following operations: patching, grading, gluing, and baking. The time in hours required for each operation for each panel, the total capacity available for each these operations in a given month, and the profit contributions per panel are given in the following table. In addition, the minimum production requirements for these panels to meet demand are also given in the table. Use linear programming to solve this problem with the objective of profit maximization:

PLYWOOD PANEL	OPERATION				PROFIT	MINIMUM PRODUCTION REQUIREMENTS
	PATCHING	GRADING	GLUING	BAKING		
Soft	0.6	1	1.5	1	$8	120
Hardwood	1.0	2.5	4	2	$12	150
Tropical	2.0	3.5	4	3	$18	200
Aircraft	2.5	5	6	4	$30	300
Total Capacity Available (in hours)	2,500	3,500	5,000	4,000		

SOLUTION

Define the Decision Variables

X_1 = number of soft plywood panels to be produced

X_2 = number of hardwood plywood panels to be produced

X_3 = number of tropical plywood panels to be produced

X_4 = number of aircraft plywood panels to be produced

Define the Objective Function

$$\text{Maximize Profits} = 8X_1 + 12X_2 + 18X_3 + 30X_4$$

Define the Constraints

$$0.6X_1 + 1X_2 + 2X_3 + 2.5X_4 \leq 2{,}500 \quad \text{(Hours of patching time available)}$$

$$1X_1 + 2.5X_2 + 3.5X_3 + 5X_4 \leq 3{,}500 \quad \text{(Hours of grading time available)}$$

$$1.5X_1 + 4X_2 + 4X_3 + 6X_4 \leq 5{,}000 \quad \text{(Hours of gluing time available)}$$

$$1X_1 + 2X_2 + 3X_3 + 4X_4 \leq 4{,}000 \quad \text{(Hours of baking time available)}$$

$$X_1 \geq 120 \text{ soft plywood panels}$$

$$X_2 \geq 150 \text{ hardwood plywood panels}$$

$$X_3 \geq 200 \text{ tropical plywood panels}$$

$$X_4 \geq 300 \text{ aircraft plywood panels}$$

$$X_1, X_2, X_3, X_4 \geq 0$$

EXAMPLE A.4

Sai Coffee Shop sells its customers two blends of coffee to its customers: regular blend and premium blend. The shop uses three different types of coffee beans to produce these blends: Hawaiian, Ethiopian, and Colombian. The mixing requirements for each blend, their revenues per pound of sales, and the costs per pound of the different types of beans are given in the following table. Customer demand per week is at least 120 pounds for the regular blend and 100 pounds for the premium blend. If the shop's objective is to maximize the total profits from the sales of the different blends of coffee, formulate the problem as a linear programming problem:

BLEND	BLENDING REQUIREMENTS	REVENUE/ POUND
Regular	At least 40% Ethiopian, at most 20% Colombian, and no more than 30% Hawaiian	$7.00
Premium	At least 25% Hawaiian, at least 25% Ethiopian, and at least 30% Colombian	$9.00

BEANS	COST/POUND
Hawaiian	$4.00
Ethiopian	$5.00
Colombian	$6.00

SOLUTION

Define the Decision Variables

X_{ij} = Pounds of coffee beans i used in blend j, where i = H, E, or C, and j = R if regular and P if premium.

Thus:

X_{HR} = number of pounds of Hawaiian beans in regular blend

X_{ER} = number of pounds of Ethiopian beans in regular blend

X_{CR} = number of pounds of Colombian beans in regular blend

X_{HP} = number of pounds of Hawaiian beans in premium blend

X_{EP} = number of pounds of Ethiopian beans in premium blend

X_{CP} = number of pounds of Colombian beans in premium blend

Define the Objective Function

$$\text{Maximize Profits} = \$7 \times (X_{HR} + X_{ER} + X_{CR}) + \$9 \times (X_{HP} + X_{EP} + X_{CP}) - \$4 \times (X_{HR} + X_{HP}) - \$5 \times (X_{ER} + X_{EP}) - \$6 \times (X_{CR} + X_{CP})$$

Define the Constraints

$$X_{HR} \leq 0.3 \times (X_{HR} + X_{ER} + X_{CR})$$

$$X_{ER} \geq 0.4 \times (X_{HR} + X_{ER} + X_{CR})$$

SCREENSHOT A.7: Excel Solution to Example A.4: Blending Problem

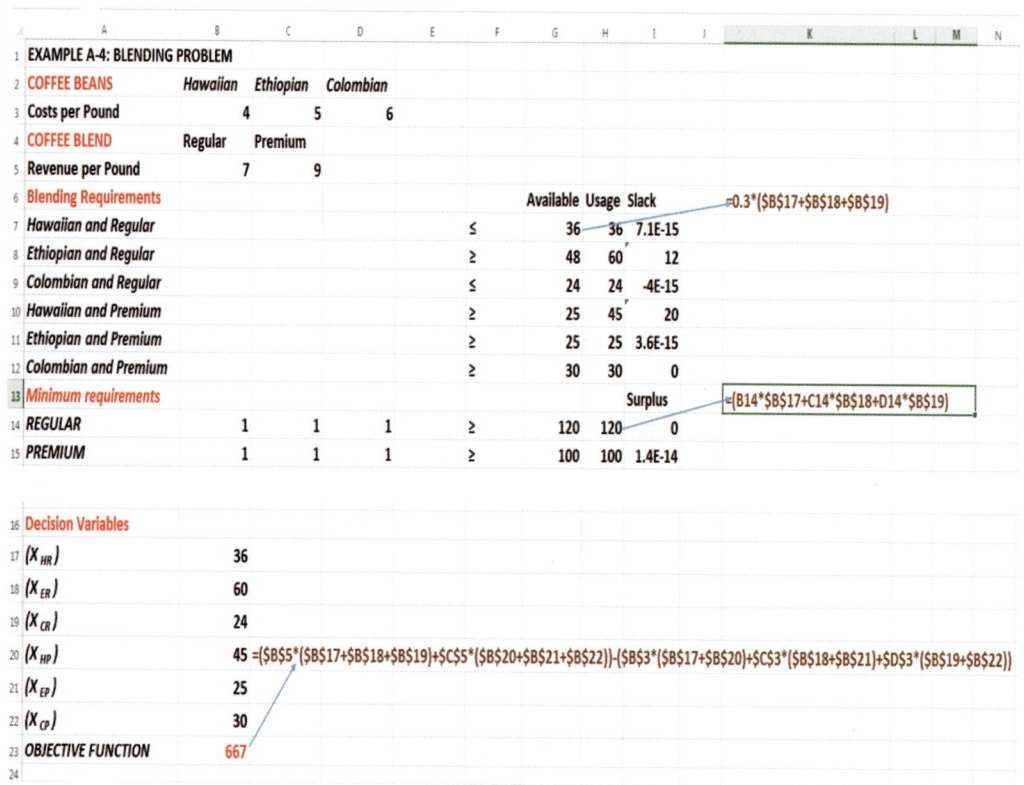

$$X_{CR} \leq 0.2 \times (X_{HR} + X_{ER} + X_{CR})$$

$$X_{HP} \geq 0.25 \times (X_{HP} + X_{EP} + X_{CP})$$

$$X_{EP} \geq 0.25 \times (X_{HP} + X_{EP} + X_{CP})$$

$$X_{CP} \geq 0.3 \times (X_{HP} + X_{EP} + X_{CP})$$

$$(X_{HR} + X_{ER} + X_{CR}) \geq 120$$

$$(X_{HP} + X_{EP} + X_{CP}) \geq 100$$

$$(X_{HR}, X_{ER}, X_{CR}, X_{HP}, X_{EP}, X_{CP}) \geq 0$$

An Excel spreadsheet and an embedded Excel file of the solution to this problem are given in Screenshot A.7.

EXAMPLE A.5

Maureen Nair, hospital administrator for Trinity Hospital, would like to set up a workforce schedule for its registered nurses. Maureen wants a work schedule that will use the minimum number of nurses without affecting the quality of patient care. Nurses are needed for patient care on a continuous, 24-hour basis. Each nurse will work for eight consecutive hours. The minimum number of nurses needed to provide adequate patient care in six four-hour time intervals are provided in the following table:

TIME INTERVAL	MINIMUM NUMBER OF NURSES REQUIRED
00–04	7
04–08	8
08–12	22
12–16	26
16–20	18
20–24	12

NOTE: Both 00 and 24 clock times refer to midnight.

Use a linear programming model to find the minimum number of nurses needed, while meeting the minimum requirements of nurses for each of the four-hour time slots.

SOLUTION

Maureen assumes that each nurse reporting for work will start working at the beginning of the four-hour time slot. In other words, the starting times are 00, 04, 08, 12, 16, and 20. Nevertheless, any nurse starting work at the beginning of any time interval will work for eight consecutive hours. Thus, a nurse who starts his or her work at midnight will work until 8 in the morning.

Define the Decision Variables

X_1 = number of nurses working between 00 and 04

X_2 = number of nurses working between 04 and 08

X_3 = number of nurses working between 08 and 12

X_4 = number of nurses working between 12 and 16

X_5 = number of nurses working between 16 and 20

X_6 = number of nurses working between 20 and 24

Define the Objective Function

Minimize: $X_1 + X_2 + X_3 + X_4 + X_5 + X_6$

Define the Constraints

$$X_6 + X_1 \geq 7$$

$$X_1 + X_2 \geq 8$$

$$X_2 + X_3 \geq 22$$

$$X_3 + X_4 \geq 26$$

$$X_4 + X_5 \geq 18$$

$$X_5 + X_6 \geq 12$$

$$X_1, X_2, X_3, X_4, X_5, X_6 \geq 0$$

An Excel spreadsheet screenshot and an embedded Excel file of the solution to Example A.5 are given as follows:

	A	B	C	D	E	F	G	H	I	J	K
1	EXAMPLE A-5: PERSONNEL SCHEDULING PROBLEM										
2								=($B$12+$B$17)			
3	*Time Interval*										Surplus
4	00-04	1	0	0	0	0	1 ≥		7	7	0
5	04-08	1	1	0	0	0	0 ≥		8	8	0
6	08-12	0	1	1	0	0	0 ≥		22	22	0
7	12-16	0	0	1	1	0	0 ≥		26	27	1
8	16-20	0	0	0	1	1	0 ≥		18	18	0
9	20-24	0	0	0	0	1	1 ≥		12	12	0
10											
11	*Decision Variables*							=($B16+$B17)			
12	X_1	7									
13	X_2	1									
14	X_3	21									
15	X_4	6									
16	X_5	12									
17	X_6	0									
18	*Objective Function*		=SUM($B12:$B17)								
19	*Number of Nurses*	47									

$SAGE edge™ ···

Visit **edge.sagepub.com/venkataraman** to help you accomplish your coursework goals in an easy-to-use learning environment.

- Mobile-friendly eFlashcards
- Mobile-friendly practice quizzes
- A complete online action plan

- Chapter summaries with learning objectives
- Video and multimedia resources

MODULE SUMMARY

A.1 Identify the critical features of linear programming (LP), and explain why it is critical for business operations success.
There are four critical features of linear programming. The objective of an LP problem expressed mathematically is referred to as an objective function. Every linear programming problem will have an objective that needs to be either maximized or minimized, such as the maximization of profits or the minimization of costs. Additionally, the decision variables are alternative courses of action. These variables are under the control of the decision maker who can use LP to decide what would be the best way to allocate the resources among these alternative courses of action to achieve the stated objective. Linear programming problems also include constraints. Constraints arise because resources are scarce and decisions have to be made within the limitations imposed by this scarcity. The last requirement of a linear programming problem is that the objective function and the constraints have linear relationships. That is, the effect of changing a decision variable is proportional to its magnitude.

The decisions that operations and supply chain managers make often deal with the effective use of limited company resources to achieve certain objectives. The limited availability of resources, usually referred to as constraints, can be in the form of labor, materials, time, equipment, energy, money, and so forth. Linear programming is a mathematical modeling technique that managers can use in decisions that involve optimizing an objective (such as maximizing profits or minimizing cost) subject to constraints such as limited resource availability. Linear programming has been applied in a variety of industries to address a variety of problems.

A.2 Solve LP problems with both maximization and minimization objectives, using graphical methods and Excel Solver. A variety of business problems with both profit maximization and cost

minimization objectives can be formulated and solved using the linear programming technique. Simple LP problems can be solved using the graphical approach. This approach is useful because it is relatively straightforward to apply, and it is intuitively appealing. Nevertheless, for more complex LP problems that involve more than two decision variables, the two-dimensional graphical approach is not appropriate. Complex problems will require more sophisticated solution approaches. There are a variety of software tools that allow us to formulate and solve more complex linear programming problems that involve multiple variables and constraint functions. Excel Solver is a good application software tool for solving these problems.

A.3 Perform sensitivity analysis on solutions to LP problems. A key assumption of all linear programming models is that the input parameters such as the objective function coefficients and the right-hand values of the constraints are assumed to be constant. In real-life decisions, however, the values of these parameters are estimates. Managers seek to determine how sensitive a current optimal solution is to changes in the input parameter values. Therefore, in addition to the optimal solution obtained by solving an LP problem, sensitivity analysis lets managers know what would be the impact of changes to the input parameter values, such as the objective function coefficients or the right-hand values of the constraint equations, or both.

A.4 Apply LP to other problems, including product mixture, blending, and personnel scheduling situations. Linear programming can be applied to more complex situations than simple profit or cost maximization or minimization using two variables, such as problems involving product mixture, blending, and personnel scheduling. As these problems have several variables and constraints, solving them requires tools such as Excel Solver.

KEY TERMS

Binding constraints   756

Constraints   745

Corner point solution method   752

Decision variables   746

Iso-cost line method   757

Iso-profit line method   752

Linear relationship   747

Multiple optimum solutions   756

Objective function   746

Range of feasibility   768

Range of optimality   768

Redundant constraints   752

Sensitivity or post-optimality analysis   767

Shadow price or dual price   768

Simplex method   764

Slack   757

Surplus   757

DISCUSSION AND REVIEW QUESTIONS

1. State the conditions under which linear programming can be used as a decision-making tool.

2. What does the term "linear" refer to in linear programming?

3. How is the feasible solution region defined on the graph of a linear programming model?

4. Discuss briefly the steps involved in formulating a linear programming model.

5. What are the steps to be followed in the graphical method of solving linear programming problems?

6. What are the limitations of the graphical method of solving linear programming problems?

7. What do iso-profit and iso-cost lines refer to in the graphical approach to solving linear programming problems?

8. What does moving the objective function line to the boundaries of the feasible solution space mean in a maximization linear programming problem?

9. What does the term *shadow price* mean in the linear programming sensitivity analysis output obtained using Excel Solver?

10. What do the terms *allowable increase* and *allowable decrease* refer to in the linear programming sensitivity analysis output obtained using Excel Solver?

11. What are some possible effects that adding an additional constraint can have on the feasible solution space and the optimal values of a linear programming solution?

SOLVED PROBLEMS ·

1   An appliance manufacturer produces two models of TVs—A and B. Each unit of Model A requires six hours of fabrication, three hours of assembly, and two hours of packaging. Each unit of Model B requires three hours of fabrication, nine hours of assembly, and two hours of packaging. The manufacturer has only 900 hours of fabrication, 720 hours of assembly, and 400 hours of packaging. Model A contributes $80 to profits, and Model B contributes $60 to profits. Formulate the problem as a linear programming model, and solve the problem using the graphical approach.

Define the Decision Variables

A = number of units of Model A TVs to be produced

B = number of units of Model B TVs to be produced

Define the Objective Function

Maximize Profits = $80A + $60B

Define the Constraints

6A + 3B ≤ 900 (Hours of fabrication time available)

3A + 9B ≤ 720 (Hours of assembly time available)

2A + 2B ≤ 400 (Hours of packaging time available)

A, B ≥ 0

Solution

The graphical solution to this problem with the plot of the constraints and the iso-profit lines is shown in Figure A.16. The feasible solution region is bounded by the polygon OPQR. The corner points of the feasible solution region and their coordinates are

$$O: (0, 0)$$
$$P: (0, 80)$$
$$R: (150, 0)$$

The coordinates for Q are obtained by solving the following two constraint equations simultaneously:

$$6A + 3B = 900$$
$$3A + 9B = 720$$

Multiplying the first equation by 3, we get

$$18A + 9B = 2700$$

Subtracting the second equation from the third equation, we get

$$18A + 9B - 3A - 9B = 2700 - 720$$
$$15A = 1980$$
$$A = 132$$

Substituting the value of A in the first equation and solving for B, we get

$$B = 36$$

Thus, the coordinates for Q are (132, 36).

Substituting the values of A and B of the corner points into the objective function 80A + 60B, we get

$$O: 80 \times 0 + 60 \times 0 = \$0$$
$$P: 80 \times 0 + 60 \times 80 = \$4,800$$
$$R: 80 \times 150 + 60 \times 0 = \$12,000$$
$$Q: 80 \times 132 + 60 \times 36 = \$12,720$$

Hence, Q is the optimum solution point. We will produce 132 units of Model A and 36 units of Model B for a total profit of $12,720. Also, note that the packaging constraint is a redundant constraint that does not participate in defining the feasible solution region. Screenshot A.7 shows the solution to this problem in Excel Solver.

FIGURE A.16: Graphical Solution to the TV Models Production Problem

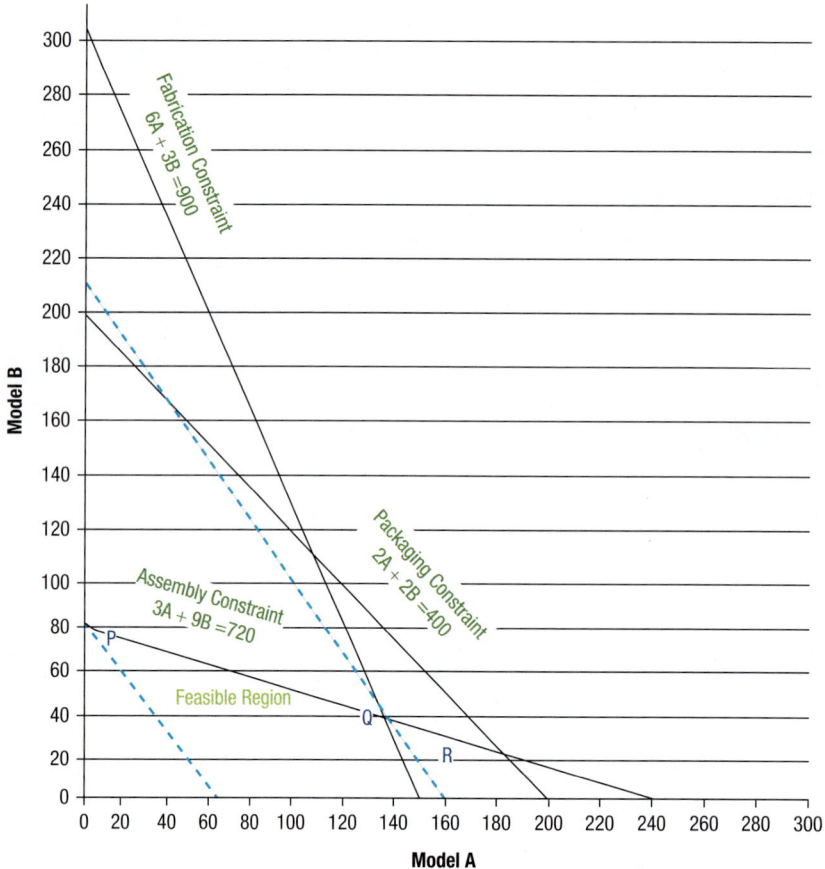

SCREENSHOT A.7: Excel Solver Solution to TV Model Product Mixture Problem

	A	B	C	D	E	F	G	H	I
1	Solved Problem-1: TV PRODUCTION PROBLEM								
2									
3	Product	MODEL A	MODEL B						Fabrication time Constraint
4	Profits Per Unit	80	60						(B6*$B$10+C6*$B$11)
5	Resources				Available	Usage	Slack		
6	Fabrication time (hrs/unit)	6	3 ≤		900	900	0		
7	Assembly time (hrs/unit)	3	9 ≤		720	720	0		
8	Packaging time (hrs/unit)	2	2 ≤		400	336	64		Assembly time Constraint
9	Decision Variables								(B7*$B$10+C7*$B$11)
10	TV MODEL (A)	132							Packaging time Constraint
11	TV MODEL (B)	36							(B8*$B$10+C8*$B$11)
12	Objective Function								Objective function
13	Profits	12720							($B$4*$B$10+$C$4*$B$11)
14									

2. Hard Wicke High School is trying to determine a nutritional diet to feed its students. The school would like to offer some combination of milk and beans. The school's objective is to minimize cost, subject to meeting the minimum nutritional requirements of protein, calcium, and calories. The cost and nutritional content of each food, along with the minimum nutritional requirements, are shown as follows. Formulate this diet problem as a linear programming model, and solve using the graphical method:

Nutrient	Kidney Beans	Tofu	Minimum Daily Requirement
Cost per pound	$0.90	$1.50	
Calcium in units per pound	15	6	30
Protein in units per pound	10	10	40
Calories in units per pound	3	9	18

Solution

Define the Decision Variables

K = Number of pounds of kidney beans to purchase

T = Number of pounds of tofu to purchase

Define the Objective Function

Minimize Cost = $0.90K + $1.50T

Define Constraints

$15K + 6T \geq 30$ (units of calcium)

$10K + 10T \geq 40$ (units of protein)

$3K + 9T \geq 18$ (units of calories)

$K, T \geq 0$

Graphical Solution

The graphical solution to this problem with the plot of the constraints and the iso-cost lines is shown in Figure A.17.

FIGURE A.17: Graphical Solution to the School Diet Problem

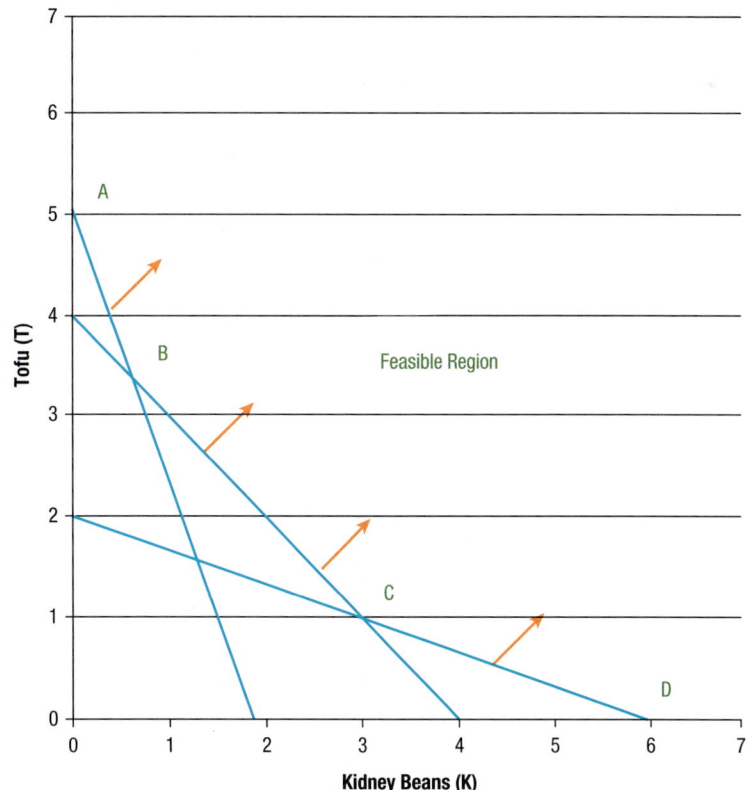

The corner points of the feasible solution region are A, B, C, and D with coordinates A: (0, 5) and D: (6, 0). The values for the coordinates of corner points B and C are obtained by solving for the following constraint equations simultaneously. For B, we solve the following two equations simultaneously:

$$15K + 6T = 30$$

$$10K + 10T = 40$$

Multiplying the first equation by 2, and the second equation by 3, we get

$$30K + 12T = 60$$

$$30K + 30T = 120$$

Subtracting the third equation from the fourth equation, we get

$$30K + 30T - 30K - 12T = 60$$

$$18T = 60$$

$$T = 10/3$$

Substituting the value of $T = 10/3$ in the first equation and solving for K, we get

$$K = 2/3$$

Thus, the coordinates for B are (2/3, 10/3).

For C, we solve the following two equations simultaneously:

$$10K + 10T = 40$$

$$3K + 9T = 18$$

Multiplying the second equation by 3, and the fifth equation by 10, we get

$$30K + 30T = 120$$

$$30K + 90T = 180$$

Subtracting the sixth equation from the seventh, we get

$$30K + 90T - 30K - 30T = 60$$

$$60T = 60$$

$$T = 1$$

Substituting the value of $T = 1$ in the first equation and solving for K, we get

$$K = 3$$

Thus, the coordinates for C are (3, 1).

Substituting the coordinate values of K and T of the corner points into the objective function

$$\text{A: } \$0.90 \times 0 + \$1.50 \times 5 = \$7.50$$

$$\text{B: } \$0.90 \times (2/3) + \$1.50 \times (10/3) = \$5.60$$

$$\textbf{C: \$0.90} \times \textbf{3 + \$1.50} \times \textbf{1 = \$4.20}$$

$$\text{D: } \$0.90 \times 6 + \$1.50 \times 0 = \$5.40$$

The optimum solution is point C: The school should buy 3 pounds of kidney beans and one pound of tofu daily for a total cost of $4.20. Screenshot A.8 shows the solution to this problem in Excel Solver.

SCREENSHOT A.8: Excel Solver Solution to the School Diet Problem

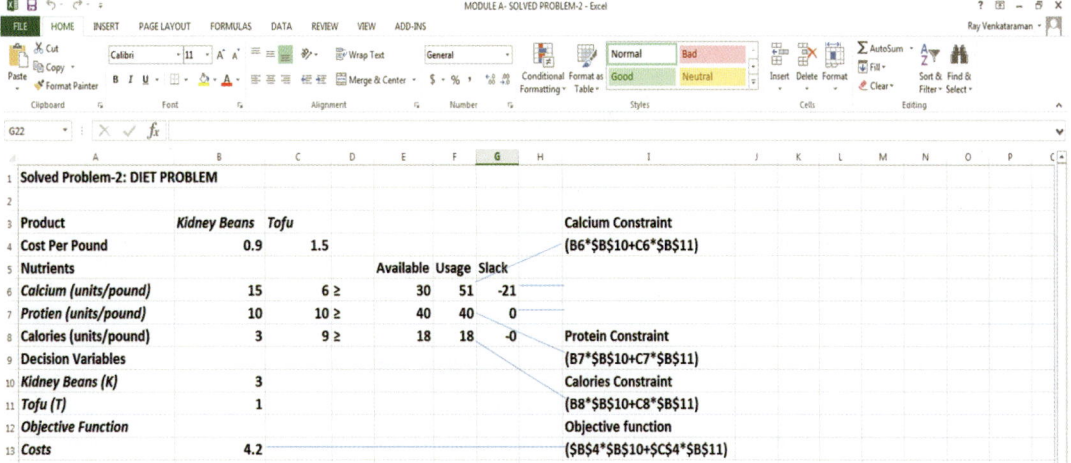

PROBLEMS

1. Solve the following linear programming problem using the graphical method:

   Maximize Profits = $8S + $12T

   Subject to

   $$2S + 4T \leq 16$$

   $$10S + 8T \leq 40$$

   $$S, T \geq 0$$

2. Consider the following linear programming model:

   Maximize Profits = $6X + $5Y

   Subject to

   $$3X + 2Y \leq 24 \text{ (hours of fabrication time)}$$

   $$2X + 4Y \leq 40 \text{ (hours of assembly time)}$$

   $$X, Y \geq 0$$

   a. What are the optimal solution values of the decision variables?

   b. How much slack does each constraint have, and what do these values mean?

3. Solve the following linear programming problem using the graphical method:

   Minimize Costs = $4X_1 + 6X_2$

   Subject to

   $$8X_1 + 4X_2 \geq 40 \text{ (ounces of ingredient A)}$$

   $$4X_1 + 12X_2 \geq 36 \text{ (ounces of ingredient B)}$$

   $$2X_1 + 4X_2 \leq 24 \text{ (ounces of ingredient C)}$$

   $$X_1, X_2 \geq 0$$

4. Consider the following linear programming model:

   Minimize Costs = $2P + $3R

   Subject to

   $$2.5P + 4R \geq 100 \text{ (units of calcium)}$$

   $$7.5P + 3R \geq 120 \text{ (units of calories)}$$

   $$2P + 6R \geq 90 \text{ (units of protein)}$$

   $$R \geq 5 \text{ (ounces)}$$

   $$P, R \geq 0$$

   a. What are the optimal solution values of the decision variables?

   b. How much surplus or slack does each constraint have, and what do these values mean?

5. Refer to Example A.3.

   a. Solve this product mixture problem using Excel Solver. What are the optimum solution values?

   b. Interpret the "allowable increase" and "allowable decrease" values for the objective function coefficients.

   c. Interpret the values of the shadow prices and the "allowable increase" and "allowable decrease" values for the right-hand-side values of the constraints.

6. Refer to Example A.4.

   a. Solve this blending problem using Excel Solver. What are the optimum solution values?

   b. Interpret the "allowable increase" and "allowable decrease" values for the objective function coefficients.

   c. Interpret the values of the shadow prices and the "allowable increase" and "allowable decrease" values for the right-hand-side values of the constraints.

7. Refer to Example A.5.

   a. Solve this personnel scheduling problem using Excel Solver. What are the optimum solution values?

   b. Interpret the "allowable increase" and "allowable decrease" values for the objective function coefficients.

   c. Interpret the values of the shadow prices and the "allowable increase" and "allowable decrease" values for the right-hand-side values of the constraints.

8. Kiran More, a farmer in India, has 20 acres of farming land to grow wheat and rice. Kiran has a limited amount of money and can spend only $3,200 to plant the crops. The cost of planting an acre of wheat is $400, and the cost to plant an acre of rice is $200. Kiran wants to plant at least 10 acres and has to plant the crops within 24 hours. An acre of wheat takes two hours to plant, and an acre of rice 3 hours to plant. If the profit is $800 per acre of wheat and $600 per acre of rice and the objective is to maximize profits:

   a. Formulate this problem as a linear programming problem.

   b. Solve this problem using the graphical method, and provide the optimal solution values of all variables.

9. A copper extraction company in South Africa extracts copper from two sources: P and N. For optimum capacity utilization, the extraction company's plant should process at least four tons of copper ore per day. The cost per ton to process the ore from source P is $16, and the cost per ton to process the ore from source N is $8. As the company has only a limited amount of cash available, processing cost cannot exceed $64 per day. In addition, because of governmental regulations, the amount of ore extracted from source N should be less than or equal to twice the amount of ore extracted from source P. If the ore from source P yields 3 ounces of copper per ton, and the ore from source N yields 4 ounces of copper per ton, and the objective is to maximize the amount of copper extracted:

   a. Formulate this problem as a linear programming problem.

   b. Solve this problem using the graphical method, and provide the optimal solution values of all variables.

10. A fertilizer manufacturer has orders for 900 tons of a certain fertilizer from Chicago, Illinois, and 600 tons from Omaha, Nebraska. The company has 1,050 tons of this fertilizer in a warehouse in Springfield, Missouri, and 1,200 tons in a warehouse in Madison, Wisconsin. It costs $10 to ship a ton of the fertilizer from Springfield to Chicago, and the cost to ship a ton from Springfield to Omaha is $20. The shipping cost per ton is $8 from Madison to Chicago, but it costs $15 per ton to ship from Madison to Omaha. If the fertilizer manufacturer's objective is to minimize the total shipping costs from each warehouse to each destination:

    a. Formulate this problem as a linear programming problem.

    b. Solve this problem using Excel Solver, and provide the optimal solution values of all variables.

11. A cattle rancher in Australia wants to determine a least-cost diet to feed the cattle on his ranch. The diet, however, must contain certain minimum amounts of the following four essential nutrients: fat, carbohydrates, protein, and calcium. These components can be found in three types of cattle food, A, B, and C. The amount of every nutrient in ounces per pound of these cattle foods is shown in the following table:

	Nutrients in Ounces per Pound				
Cattle Food	Fat	Carbohydrates	Protein	Calcium	Cost per Pound
A	150	150	300	100	$3.00
B	100	200	150	200	$5.00
C	200	100	300	150	$4.00

The cattle daily diet must be a mixture of at least 400 ounces of fat, 600 ounces of carbohydrates, 2,000 ounces of protein, and 1,600 ounces of calcium.

a. Formulate this problem as a linear programming problem.

b. Solve this problem using Excel Solver, and provide the optimal solution values of all variables.

12. A furniture manufacturer produces high-quality end tables and chairs using mahogany wood. An end table produced by the furniture manufacturer yields a profit of $15 per table, and each chair yields a profit of $20. During any given week of production, resources in the form of 100 hours of skilled labor and 400 square feet of mahogany wood are available. Each end table requires 4 hours of skilled labor and 16 square feet of mahogany wood. Each chair requires 6 hours of skilled labor and 12 square feet of mahogany. Formulate this product mixture problem as a linear programming model, and solve the problem using the graphical method. How many end tables and chairs should be produced to maximize profits? What is the maximum profit for the optimal solution?

13. Duke Manufacturing produces both baseballs and cricket balls on a weekly basis. The resources needed to produce baseballs and cricket balls are leather, cutting, and dyeing time, as well as sewing and packaging time. Each baseball requires 0.5 square feet of leather, and each cricket ball requires 0.4 square feet of leather. The cutting and dyeing time and the sewing and packaging time for each product and its profit contribution per unit are given in the following table:

	Hours Required per Ball		
Product	Cutting and Dyeing	Sewing and Packaging	Profit per Unit
Baseball	1	2	$8
Cricket Ball	2	3	$12

Each week a total of 400 hours of cutting and dyeing time and 480 hours of sewing and packaging time are available. In addition, the company has 4,800 square feet of leather available each week. Formulate this problem as a linear programming model, and solve using the graphical method. What are the optimal number of baseballs and cricket balls that Duke Manufacturing should produce, and what is the value of profits at optimality?

14. Elixir Juice Company produces four types of juice cocktails: mango juice, orange juice, pine apple juice, and a mixed fruit juice. Elixir Juice receives the required ingredients to make these juice cocktails every day, and sells them to grocery stores. The cost of these ingredients per gallon and their amounts available in gallons each day are given in the table below. Note 1 gallon = 4 quarts:

Ingredients	Amount Available (in gallons each day)	Cost per Gallon
Mango concentrate	2500	$3.00
Orange concentrate	1500	$1.50
Pineapple concentrate	2000	$2.00
Purified water	7000	$0.12

In addition, Elixir Juice receives each day up to 5000 pounds of pure cane sugar that costs $0.50 per pound. The mango juice cocktail is 30% mango concentrate and 70% water, and uses 10 ounces of sugar per gallon of the cocktail produced. Orange juice cocktail per gallon has 40% orange concentrate, 60% water, and 6 ounces of sugar. The pineapple juice cocktail per gallon has 45% pineapple concentrate, 55% water, and 8 ounces of sugar. The mixed juice blend has equal parts of mango, orange, pineapple, and water, and uses 4 ounces of sugar per gallons of juice produced. The juices are bottled in glass containers that costs $0.10 each. The costs of labor for making and packaging these juice cocktails are: $0.25 per quart for the mango juice cocktail, $0.20 per quart for the orange juice cocktail, $0.22 per quart for the pineapple juice cocktail and $0.30 per quart for the missed fruit juice blend. The daily demand requirements for these products are at least: 8,000 quarts of mango juice cocktail and 5,000 quarts of the orange juice cocktail, 7000 quarts of pineapple juice cocktail, and 6000 quarts of the mixed fruit juice blend. The total daily production capacity is 43,000 quarts. Elixir Juice sells to retail stores mango juice cocktail at $1.18 per quart, orange juice cocktail at $0.77 per quart, pineapple juice cocktail at $1.03 per quart, and mixed juice cocktail at $1.15 per quart. Formulate a linear programming model that specifies the daily production schedule that will maximize profit.

15. A gold mining company extracts gold from mine A and mine B. Both mines produce three grades of gold: high, medium, and low. The cost to mine a ton of gold from mine A is $300, and from mine B, it is $200. Mine A yields 4 tons of high-grade gold for each day of operation, and mine B yields 3 tons. Both mines yield 2 tons each of medium-grade gold each day. The yield each day for low-grade gold is 5 tons from mine A and 8 tons from

mine B. The company has contracted with a gold processor to supply at least 6 tons of high-grade gold, 4 tons of medium-grade gold, and 12 tons of low-grade gold. How many tons of gold from both mines must be extracted each day to minimize the total cost subject to the above constraints?

16. Deluxe Chemicals produces two types of photo developing chemicals—D78 and R45. The cost to produce D78 is $2, and for R45, it is $1. Based on next month's forecasts of demand for these chemicals, Deluxe Chemicals Management has decided to produce at least 40 gallons of D78 and 30 gallons of R45. Production of both these chemicals requires the use of a highly perishable raw material. The company has 120 pounds of this raw material in stock, which needs to be used within the next 10 days to avoid spoilage. Hence, Deluxe Chemicals has decided to produce both the products D78 and R45 within the next 10 days and plans to use all of the 120 pounds of the perishable raw material. Each gallon of D78 requires 2 pounds of this raw material, and R45 requires 1 pound. Formulate this problem as a linear programming model with a cost minimization objective, and solve using the graphical method.

17. Karen Stanley, the fictional superintendent of education of Erie County, Pennsylvania, has the responsibility of assigning students to three high schools in her county and to provide bus transportation to several of the students living in various suburbs. Karen has partitioned Erie County into several school districts to develop a plan that will minimize the total number of student miles traveled by bus. The following table has data on the location of the three high schools, the number of high-school-age students living in each school district, and the distance in miles from each school district to each high school. The "0" in the table implies that a student living in a school district where the high school is located can walk to school and will not need bus transportation.

	Distance to School in Miles			
School District	Millcreek High School	Fairview High School	Harborcreek High School	Number of Students
Erie	2	5	7	600
Millcreek	0	3	8	700
Fairview	3	0	16	600
Harborcreek	8	16	0	500
Northeast	15	20	5	300

The capacity of each high school is 930 students.

a. Formulate this problem as a linear programming problem with the objective of minimizing the total number of student miles traveled by bus.

b. Solve the problem using Excel Solver.

18. Asean Aromatics, a manufacturer of perfumes and aromatic oils in India, has three manufacturing plants in Trichy, Vijayawada, and Mysore, and warehouses in Chennai, Cochin, and Vizag. The following table shows the shipping costs per hundred gallons between each manufacturing plant and warehouse, and the production capabilities (in hundreds of gallons) of each plant and the capacities (in hundreds of gallons) of each warehouse. The company would like to keep the warehouses filled to capacity to ensure most demand requirements are met.

To / From	Chennai	Cochin	Vizag	Production Capacity
Trichy	$30	$50	$70	10
Vijayawada	$40	$60	$40	8
Mysore	$30	$40	$60	7
Warehouse Capacity	12	8	5	

a. Formulate this problem as a linear programming model. (Hint: Let X_{ij} = 100s of gallons of the product to be shipped from plant i to warehouse j.)

b. Solve the problem using Excel Solver.

19. Filbeck Investments manages the money invested by several wealthy clients. The company tailors its investment strategy based on the client's risk tolerance and desire for the return on investment. Sanath Kumar, an investor, has authorized Filbeck Investments to invest $1 million in stocks and bonds. Each unit of stock fund costs $60 and yields an annual rate of return of 9%. Each unit of bond fund costs $90 and yields an annual rate of return of 3%. Sanath Kumar wants to minimize the risk associated with his investments, but he wants his investments to generate at least $50,000 in annual income.

Based on the risk analysis conducted by the company, stocks have a risk index of 7, and bonds have a risk index of 2. The higher the risk index is, the riskier the investment. Sanath Kumar has also instructed Filbeck Investments that at least $400,000 be invested in bonds.

a. Formulate this problem as a linear programming model with the objective of minimizing the total risk index for the portfolio.

b. Solve the problem to determine the units to be invested in each fund and the annual income generated by the optimal investment strategy.

c. What would be the optimum portfolio if Sanath Kumar's objective is to maximize annual return on investments?

20.   Tasty Eateries is a restaurant that is open 24 hours a day. Restaurant employees report for work at 2 A.M., 6 A.M., 10 A.M., 2 P.M., 6 P.M., and 10 P.M. The employees work on eight-hour shifts, and the following table shows the minimum number of employees needed for each of the six time intervals:

Time Interval	Minimum Number of Employees Required
2 A.M.–6 A.M.	4
6 A.M.–10 A.M.	10
10 A.M.–2 P.M.	16
2 P.M.–6 P.M.	11
6 P.M.–10 P.M.	14
10 P.M.–2 A.M.	5

Formulate a linear programming model that will minimize the number of employees needed for the restaurant while meeting the minimum requirements of employees for each of the four-hour time intervals.

CASE STUDY A.1 HAPPY HOUR, HAPPY PROFITS

While attending college, Ross Tylman worked as a bartender at a local restaurant to pay his way through school. Far from finding the work tedious, he enjoyed the time he spent with the wait staff, customers, and the restaurant's managers; so much so, in fact, that upon graduation, he decided that he wanted to open his own bar in that same college town. He secured funding from family members, friends, and a local bank and set out to make his fortune. Ross realizes that he owes money to his family and is determined to pay them back as quickly as possible.

Ross currently offers three drink options: beer, wine, and mixed drinks. Beer and wine are the easiest to serve in a short time but have the lowest profit margins. Mixed drinks take longer to make but have a higher profit margin. His cost per unit (bottle) for beer is $1.85; for a glass of wine, it is $2.50, and for mixed drinks, it is $3.00. He has $7,000 in cash available to purchase the beer, wine, and mixed drinks. Ross can serve one bottle of beer in 1 minute, a glass of wine in 2 minutes, and a mixed drink in 5 minutes. For each beer

Ross sells, he can make $2.15; his unit profit for a glass of wine is $3.10, and each mixed drink earns him a profit of $4.25. His bar is open for 90 hours each week. To meet his financial obligations such as rent on the bar facilities and other interest payments, Ross has calculated that he has to sell at least 1,000 bottles of beer, 900 glasses of wine, and at least 500 mixed drinks per week.

Ross's goal is to maximize his weekly profit. What is the best combination of drinks that will allow Ross to maximize profit from his bar's sales?

Questions:

1.   Set up Ross's challenge as a linear programming (LP) problem. Identify the critical decision variables, objective function, and constraints.

2.   What is the optimal combination of drinks that Ross must sell to maximize his profits each week?

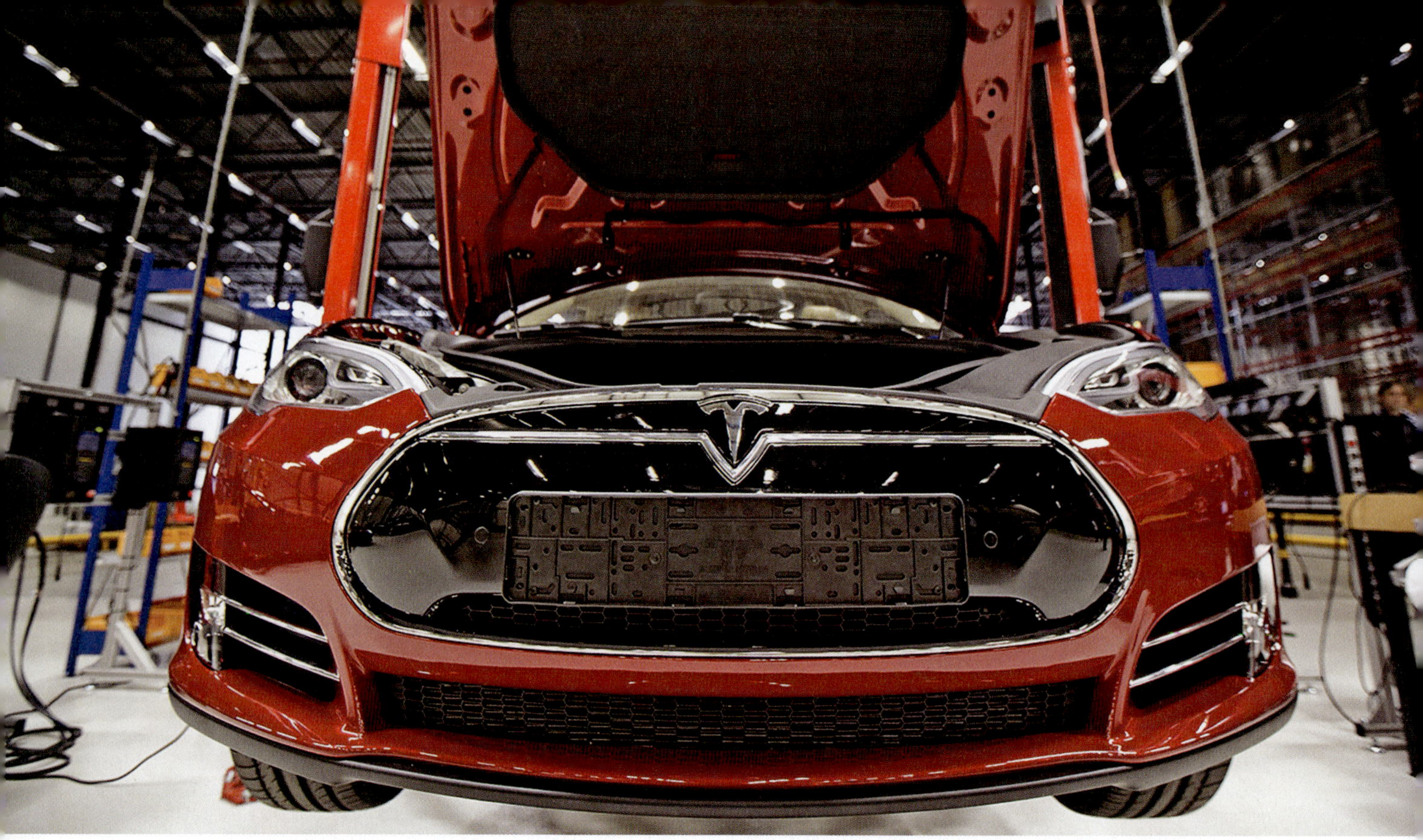

AFP/AFP/GETTY Images

MODULE
B

The Transportation Models

OPERATIONS PROFILE: Tesla and the Challenge of Locating a Battery Factory

Tesla Motors, Inc. (Palo, Alto, CA), developer of the iconic Model S electric sports car, unveiled plans to create a "gigafactory" to produce batteries to power its automobiles. The plan was introduced by Tesla's owner, Elon Musk, who called the proposed battery plant the world's largest, leading to hiring 6,500 new workers and creating thousands of ancillary jobs in the process. Musk's plan is to build a factory that will cover 10 million square feet of space with a manufacturing capacity sufficient to produce 35 gigawatt hours of batteries per year. To put this in perspective, Tesla's closest competitor in producing car batteries is Nissan's (Nissan Motor Company Ltd, Yokohama, Japan) battery factory in Tennessee, which employs only 300 workers and can turn out 4.8 gigawatt hours of batteries. In setting its sights on building the world's largest battery factory, Tesla and Elon Musk are gambling that there is growing demand for electric cars. Musk's plan is for the plant to start producing batteries by 2017, eventually ramping up to full production by 2020.

Tesla's first car, the Tesla Model S, is a fully electric powered sports car that has generated huge publicity for its performance, styling, and quality. *Consumer Reports* magazine gave the car a rating of 99, its highest score ever. Selling for more than $80,000 per car, however, has limited the market for the Tesla Model S to the very affluent.[a] As a result, Tesla has already announced plans for a midpriced car, the Gen III, which is expected to have a starting price of around $35,000. Tesla's challenge lies in reducing the cost of its batteries. The 85 kilowatt-hour battery pack for the Model S can cost more than $25,000, and for a midpriced car to be a possibility, Tesla has to find a way to lower battery costs. Its initial target is a 30% reduction.

With the promise of such a massive factory and the thousands of jobs the project would bring, several western states were actively competing to be the host site for the structure. Officials in Arizona, Nevada, New Mexico, and Texas have all promised tax breaks, the opportunity for Tesla to open its own retail stores statewide, and many other incentives for Tesla to agree to build in their state. When Tesla announced that it would open its factory in Sparks, Nevada, the company cited its proximity to profitable California markets, favorable tax incentives, and access to various modes of transportation for Tesla's supply chain and shipping. Tesla broke ground in late 2014 and work moved rapidly to construct the giant factory.

Tesla, with sales of slightly more than 50,000 cars in 2015, is already the largest buyer of lithium-ion battery cells in the world. Its plans to sell 500,000 vehicles means that its own demand would be greater than the demand for every laptop, mobile phone, and tablet sold in the world. Tesla executives believe that they need the plant to guarantee future supplies of the millions of battery cells required, at the reduced costs that come from economies of scale and logistics savings. As we will see in this module, by using the transportation model, Tesla can identify the best location for its new factory, which will enable the company to minimize both the inbound and outbound distribution costs of its batteries.[1]

B.1: Formulating and Solving the Transportation Problem

In supply chain network design, the location of factories, warehouses, and distribution centers is a strategic decision that has important cost implications. Consequently, companies devote time and resources in considering and evaluating alternatives to choose the one that is most suitable for them. In Chapter 8 on

B.1

Formulate and solve the transportation problems using both manual methods and the Excel Solver, and interpret the solutions.

---

[a]Unless otherwise stated, all currency is in U.S. dollars.

Transportation model:
a special case of linear
programming problems in
which the objective is to
minimize the total cost of
transporting goods from
the various supply origins
to the different demand
destinations

**Northwest corner
rule:** involves first
allocating shipping units
at the northwest (top
left-hand) corner of the
transportation matrix
and then proceeding
systematically by making
allocations of shipping
units to cells along either
a row or column until the
bottom right-hand corner
of the matrix is reached
(that is, we make enough
allocations of shipping
units to reach an initial
feasible solution)

**Matrix least cost
method:** an initial
feasible solution to the
transportation problem
is obtained by allocating
shipments beginning
with the route that has
the lowest unit cost of
transportation

**Stepping stone
method:** the term
stepping stone refers
to the occupied cells in
the initial solution of the
transportation matrix,
which are used in arriving
at an improved solution

supply chain design and location planning, we saw that a company needs to consider several quantitative and qualitative factors and use a variety of techniques to choose the right location for the company. One such quantitative technique is the transportation model.

Many companies have multiple plants or sources of supply (origins) and multiple demand locations (destinations) for their goods and services. To improve profit margins, companies need to reduce the costs of transportation that they incur as their goods are physically moved from the manufacturing plants to the final consumers through the various channels of distribution (wholesalers, retailers, distributors, etc.). The Ford Motor Company (aka Ford, Dearborn, MI), for example, has eight assembly plants within United States but thousands of dealers who demand the company's cars, trucks, and SUVs. For Ford and many other companies, the transportation model can provide an optimal distribution plan that will help the company reduce its distribution costs. Specifically, the transportation model can aid companies in minimizing the overall costs of transportation and distribution from the various supply sources to the demand destinations. The transportation model helps managers to make decisions about the location of their plants or supply sources relative to the demand destinations and about the number of units of a particular product that should be transported from each supply origin to each demand destination to satisfy the demand for the company's product.

The transportation model is a special case of linear programming problems in which the objective is to minimize the total cost of transporting goods from the various supply origins to the different demand destinations. The model is often classified under linear programming problems because the relationship between the variable transportation costs and the number of units shipped is assumed to be linear; that is, the more units we ship, the higher the transportation costs are likely to be. Also, our discussion of the transportation model in this module assumes that there is an existing supply–demand or distribution network. Thus, when we consider adding a new supply or demand location, such as a factory or distribution center, in addition to allocating shipments to that new location, the allocation of shipments among existing supply and demand locations will also change, and our overall mixture of products to be shipped to our distribution centers will change. The new location chosen among available alternatives will be the one that minimizes the total distribution or transportation costs for the entire system.

To solve transportation problems, we should first set up the problem as a transportation matrix. By doing so, we can summarize all the relevant data and track all the necessary computations. The next step is to arrive at an initial feasible solution to the problem. Among the number of methods available to establish an initial feasible solution, we will discuss two of them, the northwest corner rule and the matrix least cost method. Once an initial solution is established, we will use the stepping stone method to progress from the initial feasible solution to an optimal solution to the problem

The Northwest Corner Rule

Arriving at an initial feasible solution using the northwest corner rule involves first allocating shipping units at the northwest (top left-hand) corner of the transportation matrix and then proceeding systematically by making allocations of shipping units to cells along either a row or column until the bottom right-hand corner of the matrix is reached (that is, we make enough allocations of shipping units to reach an initial feasible solution). The application of the rule involves the following steps:

1. Begin at the top left-hand or northwest corner of the transportation matrix allocate as many units to this cell as possible until either the supply is exhausted or the demand requirements are met.
2. Exhaust the capacity from each supply location (row) before moving down to the next supply location.
3. Exhaust the requirements from each demand location (column) before moving right to the next demand location.
4. Repeat steps 2 and 3 until all available supply capacity is exhausted and demand requirements are met.

We will next discuss the matrix least cost method, which is yet another method that can be used to arrive at an initial feasible solution to a transportation problem.

Matrix Least Cost Method

With the matrix least cost method, an initial feasible solution to the transportation problem is obtained by allocating shipments beginning with the route that has the lowest unit cost of transportation. As the overall objective is to minimize total cost, this method is intuitively more appealing and has better rationale than the northwest corner rule. As a result, this method reduces the number of computations and the time required to determine the optimal solution. The steps for this method are as follows:

1. Begin with the cell in the transportation matrix that has the lowest per unit cost. In case of any ties among cells for the lowest cost, break the ties arbitrarily.
2. Allocate to this cost cell the maximum number of units allowable given available capacity or demand requirements. Eliminate the row or column that exhausts the supply or meets the demand requirements by this allocation from further consideration.
3. From the remaining available cells in the matrix, choose the one that has the next lowest per unit cost and repeat step 2.
4. Repeat step 3 until all units have been allocated.

After we arrive at an initial feasible solution to the transportation problem by using either the northwest corner rule or the matrix least cost method, we will use the stepping stone method to find an improvement to the initial feasible solution. The stepping stone method is an iterative process that will enable us to move from an initial feasible solution to finding an optimal solution to the transportation problem.

Stepping Stone Method

One method that can be used to determine the optimality of the initial solution, and if it is not optimal, to improve the current solution is the stepping stone method. The term *stepping stone* refers to the occupied cells in the initial solution of the transportation matrix, which are used in arriving at an improved solution. The steps involved in using the stepping stone method are as follows:

The Stepping Stone Method

1. Select an empty cell in the initial basic feasible solution (Figure B.3 or B.4) to be evaluated.
2. Beginning at this empty cell, draw a closed path back to that cell using only horizontal and vertical moves, ensuring that turning corners occurs only on occupied cells. Stepping over any occupied or unoccupied cell is allowed.
3. Beginning with a plus (+) sign for the empty cell being evaluated, place alternating minus (–) and plus (+) signs on the corner cells of this closed path.
4. Calculate an improvement index that is a value obtained to determine whether there is an improvement in cost by choosing another route. It is calculated by first summing up the unit costs in the cells with a plus sign, and then from the resulting total, subtract the sum obtained by adding the unit costs in cells containing a minus sign.
5. Repeat steps 1 through 4 to calculate an improvement index for all unoccupied cells. If all the improvement indices have values greater than or equal to zero, then the current solution is optimal. If not, the current solution can be improved and the total transportation costs can be decreased further.
6. If any of the improvement indices has a negative value, then refer to the closed path that produced the negative improvement index. Select the cell with a minus sign that has the smallest shipment quantity.
7. To obtain an improved solution, add the smallest quantity found in step 6 to all the cells with a + sign in the closed path. Subtract the same quantity from all the cells with a – sign. All other cells are left unchanged.
8. This new improved solution may or may not be optimum. Steps 1 through 5 should be repeated to test each unoccupied cell in the new solution matrix. The process stops when all improvement indices computed have a value greater than or equal to zero, which indicates that an optimum solution has been reached. A nondegenerate optimum solution must satisfy the following two conditions:

   i. All supply should be exhausted and all demand requirements must be met.
   ii. The number of cells with positive allocations should be equal to $R + C - 1$, where R is the number of rows and C is the number of columns in the transportation matrix.

We will discuss the concept of degenerate solutions in Section B.2 of this module.

EXAMPLE B.1: Figure B.1 shows the structure of the transportation problem for Orion Electronics.[b] Orion has three supply locations with respective production capacities of an electronic component (Denver, Milwaukee, and Columbia) and three demand locations with their demand requirements for that electronic component. For example, the Denver plant is capable of producing 1,000 units per month and the demand at the Los Angeles warehouse facility 3,000 units per month. The numbers above the arrows in Figure B.1 represent the shipping cost per unit in dollars.

FIGURE B.1: Structure of the Transportation Problem

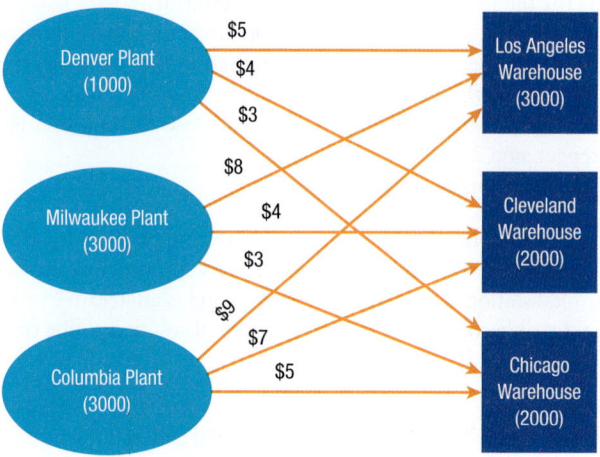

Given the various alternatives of possible allocation of shipments from the three supply locations to the three demand locations, the transportation model will help us to determine the optimal distribution plan that will minimize the total shipment or transportation costs.

To use the transportation model, we need the following information:

1. All supply locations (origins) and the production capacities at each supply location per period.
2. All demand locations (destinations) and the demand requirements at each destination per period.
3. The distribution or transportation cost of shipping one unit from each origin to each destination.

Use of the transportation model also requires the following major assumptions:

1. Capacity at each supply location or origin is limited.
2. The demand requirements at each destination are known.
3. Regardless of their origin or destination, the items shipped are the same (homogeneous).
4. Regardless of the number of units shipped, the shipping cost per unit remains the same.
5. Between each origin and destination, the mode of transportation being used does not change, and there is only one route used.

Given these assumptions, let us now look at the steps involved in the transportation modeling process to arrive at an optimal shipping plan for Orion Electronics Company.

SOLUTION

Step 1: Using the information available on capacities and demand requirements for the various origins and destinations, and the shipping cost per unit for each route, set up a transportation table or matrix.

Using the information displayed in Figure B.1, we can set up a transportation table for Orion Electronics Company as shown in Figure B.2.

---

[b]Unless otherwise stated, in the Examples, Solved Problems, and Problems, fictional company names are used.

FIGURE B.2: Transportation Matrix for Orion Electronics

TO FROM	LOS ANGELES	CLEVELAND	CHICAGO	PRODUCTION CAPACITY
Denver	$4	$3	$2	1,000
Milwaukee	$7	$3	$2	3,000
Columbia	$8	$6	$4	3,000
Demand Requirement	3,000	2,000	2,000	**7,000**

Unbalanced Transportation Problems

In Figure B.2, the cells in the production capacity column represent the capacity available (constraint) at each supply or origin location. The cells in the demand requirement row represent the unit's demand at each of the demand or destination location. The numbers in the inset of each cell are the shipping cost per unit of the product shipped. Note that the cell highlighted in red represents the total demand and supply. In this example, because the total number of units demanded (7,000) is equal to the total number of supply units available, it is called a **balanced transportation problem**. If the total number of supply units available is greater than the demand requirements or vice versa, then the problem is labeled as an **unbalanced transportation problem**. For now, our focus will be on solving a balanced transportation problem.

Step 2: Develop an initial basic feasible solution.

Several methods can be used to obtain the initial basic feasible solution. We will apply the two most popular methods to obtain an initial basic feasible solution: the northwest corner rule and the matrix least cost method.

We will apply the northwest corner rule steps to the Orion Electronics Company:

1. Allocate 1,000 units to the top left-hand corner cell (the Denver to Los Angeles cell) to exhaust the supply from Denver.
2. Allocate 2,000 units from Milwaukee to Los Angeles to meet the demand requirements for Los Angeles.
3. Allocate 1,000 units from Milwaukee to Cleveland to exhaust the supply from Milwaukee.
4. Allocate 1,000 units of supply available from Columbia to Cleveland to meet the demand requirements for Cleveland.
5. Allocate the 20,00 units of the supply available from Columbia to Chicago to meet the demand requirements for Chicago and to exhaust the supply available from Columbia.

As all supply has been exhausted and all demand requirements have been met, we have an initial feasible solution using the northwest corner rule for Orion Electronics, as shown in Figure B.3 on page 790.

Given that we know the shipping cost per unit of our product, the total cost of this initial shipping allocation is $35,000 and can be calculated as shown in Table B.1 on page 790.

The advantage of the northwest corner rule is that it allows us to find an initial feasible solution to the transportation problem, but we wish to find an initial solution that satisfies all constraints without regard to the relative shipping costs of those orders. For example, note in Figure B.3 that two thirds of the units shipped to Los Angeles came from a much more expensive source—Milwaukee. Likewise, we selected the Columbia plant as the shipping source for New York even though the cost per unit was twice as expensive compared with shipping from Denver or Milwaukee. That is, the northwest corner rule generates feasible solutions but not necessarily an optimum least cost solution. To generate an optimum solution, we need to use other approaches, such as the stepping stone method discussed in Step 3.

Balanced transportation problem: a problem in which the total number of units demanded is equal to the total number of supply units available

Unbalanced transportation problem: a problem in which the total number of supply units available is greater than the demand requirements or vice versa

FIGURE B.3: Transportation Matrix With an Initial Feasible Solution for Orion Electronics Using the Northwest Corner Rule

TO FROM	LOS ANGELES	CLEVELAND	NEW YORK	PRODUCTION CAPACITY
Denver	$4 1,000	$3	$2	1,000
Milwaukee	$7 2,000	$3 1,000	$2	3,000
Columbia	$8	$6 1,000	$4 2,000	3,000
Demand Requirement	3,000	2,000	2,000	**7,000**

TABLE B.1: Transportation Cost for the Initial Shipping Allocation Using the Northwest Corner Rule

FROM	TO	UNITS SHIPPED	COST PER UNIT	TOTAL COST
Denver	Los Angeles	1,000	$4	$4,000
Milwaukee	Los Angeles	2,000	$7	$14,000
Milwaukee	Cleveland	1,000	$3	$3,000
Columbia	Cleveland	1,000	$6	$6,000
Columbia	Chicago	2,000	$4	$8,000
Total				$35,000

Let us now apply the matrix least cost method to find an initial basic feasible solution to the Orion Electronics example:

1. The Milwaukee–Chicago and the Denver–Chicago cells have the lowest per unit cost of $2. We will choose the Milwaukee–Chicago cell.
2. We will allocate the maximum allowable 2,000 units to that cell. This allocation meets the demand requirements for Chicago, so we will eliminate that column from further consideration as shown by the line crossing out that column in Figure B.4.
3. The cells with the next lowest per unit cost are the Denver–Cleveland and Milwaukee–Cleveland cells with per unit cost of $3. Again, we will the break the tie arbitrarily and allocate the maximum allowable 1,000 units to the Denver–Cleveland cell. This allocation exhausts the supply available from Denver. Eliminate that row from further consideration as shown by the green line crossing out that row in Figure B.4.
4. We will now choose the Milwaukee–Cleveland cell, which also has a cost of $3 per unit. We will allocate the remaining 1,000 units of supply available to that route. This allocation exhausts the supply available from Milwaukee, so we can eliminate that row from further consideration, as shown by the blue line crossing out that row in Figure B.4. This allocation also meets the demand requirements for Cleveland. Let's eliminate that column from further consideration, as shown by the line crossing out that column in Figure B.4.
5. The only remaining unallocated cell is the Columbia–Los Angeles cell with per unit cost of $8. Allocating 3,000 units of supply available to that cell exhausts the supply available from Columbia and meets the demand requirements for Los Angeles. Eliminate that column and row as shown by the black lines crossing out that column and row in Figure B.4. All supply available has been exhausted, and all demand requirements have been met.

FIGURE B.4: Transportation Matrix With an Initial Basic Feasible Solution for Orion Electronics Using the Matrix Least Cost Method

TO \ FROM	LOS ANGELES	CLEVELAND	CHICAGO	PRODUCTION CAPACITY
Denver	$4	$3	$2	1,000
		1,000		
Milwaukee	$7	$3	$2	3,000
		1,000	2,000	
Columbia	$8	$6	$4	3,000
	3,000			
Demand Requirement	3,000	2,000	2,000	**7,000**

The total cost of this initial shipping allocation is $34,000 as shown in Table B.2. This initial solution is better than the one obtained by the northwest corner rule because it saves us $1,000.

TABLE B.2: Transportation Cost for the Initial Shipping Allocation Using the Matrix Least Cost Method

FROM	TO	UNITS SHIPPED	COST PER UNIT	TOTAL COST
Denver	Cleveland	1,000	$3	$3,000
Milwaukee	Chicago	2,000	$2	$4,000
Milwaukee	Cleveland	1,000	$3	$3,000
Columbia	Los Angeles	3,000	$8	$24,000
Total				$34,000

Step 3: Find an optimal solution using the stepping stone method.

Once we have an initial feasible solution, the next step is to determine whether that initial solution is optimal. Our task now is to apply the eight steps of the stepping stone method to the Orion Electronics Example. Let's use our initial solution (Figure B.3) obtained using the northwest corner rule to illustrate the method.

1st iteration

Steps 1 and 2: We will begin with the Denver–Cleveland route (unoccupied cell; refer to Figure B.3). We will trace a closed path using only the currently occupied cells.

Step 3: Beginning with a + sign for the empty cell being evaluated (Denver-Cleveland in this case), place alternating – and + signs on the corner cells of this closed path as shown in Figure B.5.

The reason for placing alternate + and - signs is that to find an improved solution, we are trying to determine whether choosing the Denver–Cleveland route would reduce the transportation cost. Thus, by placing a + sign, we are indicating that we are shipping one more unit of the product in this route. Nevertheless, by shipping this one additional unit from Denver to Cleveland, we are increasing the total units shipped from Denver to 1,001, which is more than 1,000 units of capacity available at that supply location. Therefore, we reduce the units shipped from Denver to Los Angeles by 1 unit (from 1,000 to 999) to meet the capacity constraints at Denver. The minus sign in the Denver–Los Angeles cell indicates this reduction in units shipped as we move left in the closed path from the Denver–Cleveland cell.

By shipping one less unit from Denver to Los Angeles, we are falling short of meeting the demand requirement for Los Angeles by 1 unit (from 3,000 to 2,999). Hence, moving down the closed path to the Milwaukee–Los Angeles cell and increasing the units shipped in that route by 1 (from 2,000 to 2,001) will bring us back to the original demand requirement for Los Angeles. Yet, by shipping this one additional unit from Milwaukee to Los Angeles, we are increasing the total units shipped from Milwaukee to 3,001, which is more than 3,000 units of capacity available at the Milwaukee location. Therefore, we move right in the closed path to the Milwaukee–Cleveland route and place a – sign to reduce the units shipped in that route by 1 unit (from 1,000 to 999) to meet the capacity constraints at Milwaukee. Note that we had increased the total units shipped to Cleveland to 2,001 when we decided to evaluate the Denver–Cleveland route by shipping 1 unit in that route. The reduction of a one-unit shipment in the Milwaukee–Cleveland route also reduces the total units shipped to Cleveland to the original demand requirement of 2,000 units. The evaluation of the Denver–Cleveland cell (route) is represented schematically in Figure B.5.

FIGURE B.5: Evaluation of the Denver–Cleveland Cell

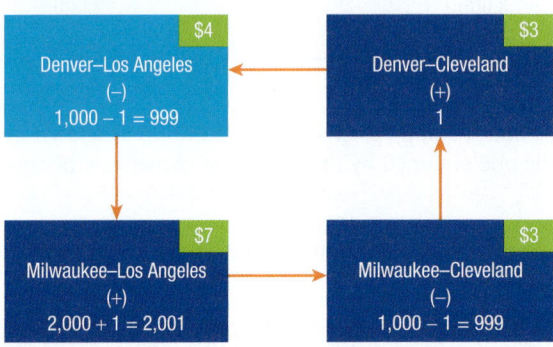

FIGURE B.6: Transportation Matrix for the Evaluation of the Denver–Cleveland Route for Orion Electronics Using the Stepping Stone Method

TO / FROM	LOS ANGELES	CLEVELAND	CHICAGO	PRODUCTION CAPACITY
Denver	$4	$3	$2	1,000
	1,000–	+		
Milwaukee	$7	$3	$2	3,000
	2,000+	–1,000		
Columbia	$8	$6	$4	3,000
		1,000	2,000	
Demand Requirement	3,000	2,000	2,000	**7,000**

Step 4: We calculate an improvement index for the Denver–Cleveland cell (route) by first summing the unit costs in the cells with a plus sign in the closed path, and from the resulting sum, subtracting the sum obtained by adding the unit costs in cells containing a minus sign. The results are:

$$(3 + 7) - (3 + 4) = +3$$

The result of +3 tells us that for every additional unit shipped in the Denver–Cleveland route, the total transportation cost will increase by $3 from the current level of $35,000.

Since the improvement index has a positive value, we go to Step 5.

FIGURE B.7: Transportation Matrix for the Evaluation of the Denver–Chicago Route for Orion Electronics Using the Stepping Stone Method

TO \ FROM	LOS ANGELES (L)	CLEVELAND (CL)	CHICAGO (C)	PRODUCTION CAPACITY
Denver (D)	$4 1,000–	$3	$2 +	1,000
Milwaukee (M)	$7 2,000+	$3 1,000	$2	3,000
Columbia (CO)	$8	$6 +1,000	$4 –2,000	3,000
Demand Requirement	3,000	2,000	2,000	**7,000**

Step 5: Because the improvement index for the Denver–Cleveland route was positive, we will conduct a second iteration and repeat Steps 1 through 4 to calculate an improvement index for another unoccupied cell of the initial solution matrix obtained using the northwest corner rule.

2nd Iteration

Steps 1–3: We will now evaluate the Denver–Chicago cell (route). We will trace a closed path using only the currently occupied cells, and beginning with + sign for the empty cell being evaluated, place alternating "–" and "+" signs on the corner cells of this closed path as shown in Figure B.7.

Step 4: We can calculate an improvement index for the Denver–Chicago (route) by first summing the unit costs in the cells with a plus sign in the closed path, and from the resulting sum, subtracting the sum obtained by adding the unit costs in cells containing a minus sign. The results are:

$$(2 + 7 + 6) - (4 + 3 + 4) = +4$$

The positive value of the improvement indicates that the Denver–Chicago route is also not an attractive option as it will increase the total costs by $4 for every unit shipped.

Step 5: Because the improvement index for the Denver–Chicago route was positive, we will conduct a third iteration and repeat Steps 1 through 4 to calculate an improvement index for another unoccupied cell of the initial solution matrix obtained using the northwest corner rule.

3rd Iteration

Steps 1–4: We will now evaluate the Milwaukee–Chicago cell (route). We will trace a closed path using only the currently occupied cells, and beginning with + sign for the empty cell being evaluated, place alternating "–" and "+" signs on the corner cells of this closed path and calculate an improvement index as shown:

Milwaukee–Chicago Index: (MC + CLCO) – (MCL + COC) = (2 + 6) – (3 + 4) = +1

Step 5: Because the improvement index for the Milwaukee–Chicago route was also positive, we will conduct a fourth iteration and repeat Steps 1 through 4 to calculate an improvement index for another unoccupied cell of the initial solution matrix obtained using the northwest corner rule.

4th Iteration

Steps 1–4: We will now evaluate the Columbia–Los Angeles cell (route). We will trace a closed path using only the currently occupied cells, and beginning with + sign for the empty cell being evaluated, place alternating "–" and "+" signs on the corner cells of this closed path and calculate an improvement index as shown:

Columbia–Los Angeles Index: (COL + MCL) – (ML + COCL) = (8 + 3) – (7 + 6) = –2

The negative value of –2 for the Columbia–Los Angeles route means that for each unit shipped via that route, the total transportation costs are reduced by $2. Therefore, we go to Step 6.

Step 6: From the closed path for Columbia–Los Angeles route, we will select the cell with a minus sign that has the smallest shipment quantity. The cell with a minus sign that has the smallest quantity of 1,000 units is the Columbia–Cleveland route, so we select the Columbia–Cleveland cell. The transportation matrix with the closed path for the Columbia–Los Angeles cell is shown in Figure B.8.

FIGURE B.8: Transportation Matrix for the Columbia–Los Angeles Route

TO / FROM	LOS ANGELES (L)	CLEVELAND (CL)	CHICAGO (C)	PRODUCTION CAPACITY
Denver (D)	$4 1,000	$3	$2	1,000
Milwaukee (M)	$7 2,000–	$3 +1,000	$2	3,000
Columbia (CO)	$8 +	$6 –1,000	$4 2,000	3,000
Demand Requirement	3,000	2,000	2,000	**7,000**

Step 7: To obtain an improved solution, we will add the smallest quantity of 1,000 units found in the previous step to all the cells with a + sign in the closed path and subtract the same quantity from all the cells with a – sign. All other cells are left unchanged. The results are shown in Figure B.9.

FIGURE B.9: Transportation Matrix With an Improved Solution in the Second Iteration of the Stepping Stone Method

TO / FROM	LOS ANGELES (L)	CLEVELAND (CL)	CHICAGO (C)	PRODUCTION CAPACITY
Denver (D)	$4 1,000	$3	$2	1,000
Milwaukee (M)	$7 1,000	$3 2,000	$2	3,000
Columbia (CO)	$8 1,000	$6	$4 2,000	3,000
Demand Requirement	3,000	2,000	2,000	**7,000**

The total cost for this improved solution is (1000 × 4 + 1000 × 7 + 2000 × 3 + 1000 × 8 + 2000 × 4) = $33,000. This is a reduction of $2,000 from the total cost of $35,000 for the initial feasible solution.

Step 8: This new improved solution may or may not be optimum. Steps 1 through 5 should be repeated to test each unoccupied cell in the new solution matrix.

5th Iteration

Steps 1–4: In Figure B.9, we will now evaluate the Milwaukee–Chicago route. We will trace a closed path using only the currently occupied cells, and beginning with + sign for the empty cell being evaluated, place alternating "–" and "+" signs on the corner cells of this closed path and calculate an improvement index as shown:

$$(MC + COL) - (ML + COC) = (2 + 8) - (7 + 4) = -1$$

Step 6: From the closed path for the Milwaukee–Chicago route, we will select the cell with a minus sign that has smallest shipment quantity. The cell with a minus sign that has the smallest quantity of 1,000 units is the Milwaukee–Los Angeles route, so we select the Milwaukee–Los Angeles cell. The transportation matrix with the closed path for the Milwaukee–Chicago cell is shown in Figure B.10.

FIGURE B.10: Transportation Matrix for the Milwaukee–Chicago Route

TO / FROM	LOS ANGELES (L)	CLEVELAND (CL)	CHICAGO (C)	PRODUCTION CAPACITY
Denver (D)	$4	$3	$2	1,000
	1,000			
Milwaukee (M)	$7	$3	$2	3,000
	1,000–	2,000	+	
Columbia (CO)	$8	$6	$4	3,000
	1,000+		2,000–	
Demand Requirement	3,000	2,000	2,000	**7,000**

Step 7: To obtain an improved solution, we will add the smallest quantity of 1,000 units found in the previous step to all the cells with a "+" sign in the closed path and subtract the same quantity from all the cells with a minus sign. All other cells are left unchanged. The results are shown in Figure B.11.

FIGURE B.11: Transportation Matrix With an Improved Solution in the Third Iteration of the Stepping Stone Method

TO / FROM	LOS ANGELES (L)	CLEVELAND (CL)	CHICAGO (C)	PRODUCTION CAPACITY
Denver (D)	$4	$3	$2	1,000
	1,000			
Milwaukee (M)	$7	$3	$2	3,000
		2,000	1,000	
Columbia (CO)	$8	$6	$4	3,000
	2,000		1,000	
Demand Requirement	3,000	2,000	2,000	**7,000**

The total cost for this improved solution is (1000 × 4 + 2000 × 3 + 1000 × 2 + 2000 × 8 + 1000 × 4) = $32,000. This is a reduction of an additional $1,000 from the total cost of $33,000 obtained from the second iteration.

Step 8: This new improved solution is the optimum solution as the improvement index values for all unoccupied cells in Figure B.10 are positive. Also, we have reached a nondegenerate optimum

> solution as all supply has been exhausted and all demand requirements have been met, and the number of cells with positive allocations is 5, which is equal to R + C − 1 (3 + 3 − 1 =5), where R is the number of rows and C is the number of columns in the transportation matrix.

For relatively small problems, the stepping stone method will enable us to arrive at an optimum solution by reducing transportation costs through a series of iterative steps. Nevertheless, it is time-consuming to calculate each potential reduction by hand and can be even more complicated for large matrices with several production facilities and points of destination. As a result, for large real-life problems, Microsoft Excel (Microsoft Corporation, Redmond, WA) and other computerized methods will allow us to determine the optimal solution to such problems quickly.

Solving Transportation Problems Using Excel (Version 2013)

The procedure for solving transportation problems using Excel Solver is almost identical to the steps used for solving linear programming problems described in Module A. The only difference in balanced transportation problems is that all of the constraints (except the non-negativity constraints of the decision variables) should set as an = sign in the Excel Solver dialogue. For the Orion Electronics example, Screenshot B.1 shows the model formulation and solution in Excel.

SCREENSHOT B.1: Orion Electronics Company Transportation Model Formulation and Solution in Excel

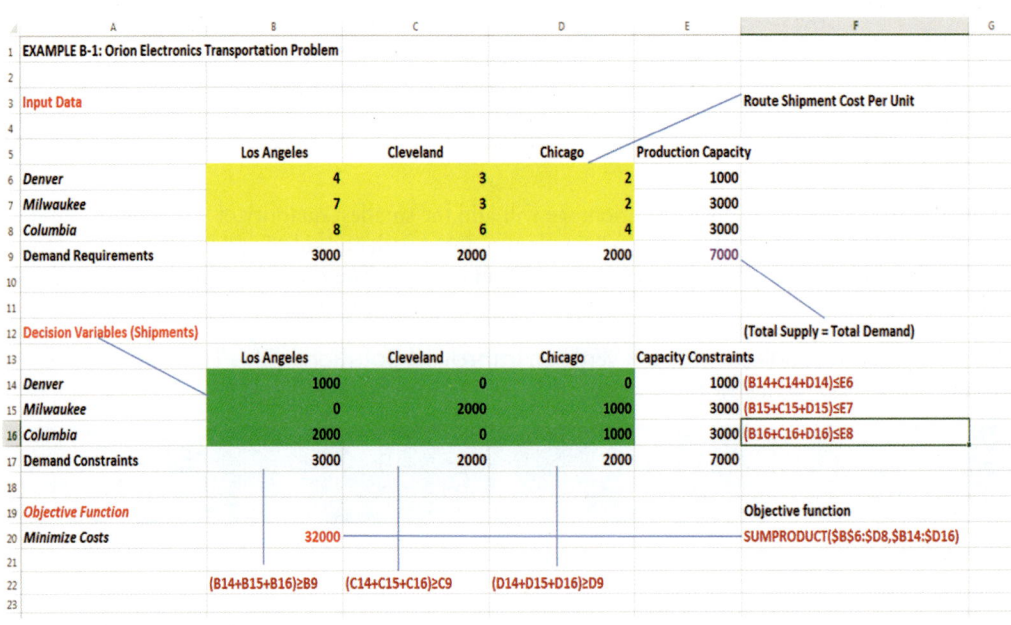

Dummy supply sources: a fictitious supply source created to arrive at a balanced transportation problem (i.e., total demand = total supply)

Dummy demand destinations: a fictitious demand destination created to arrive at a balanced transportation problem (i.e., total demand = total supply)

B.2

Apply transportation modeling to other situations.

B.2. Additional Issues in Transportation Modeling

In real-life transportation problems, we commonly encounter two situations. The first case is a situation in which total demand is not equal to total supply, and the second case is a condition called degeneracy, which occurs when too few shipping routes are used.

Unequal Supply and Demand

The discussion of transportation models thus far has assumed that we have a balanced transportation problem. In effect, we have assumed that the total supply or capacity from all the origins is equal to the total demand requirements from all the destinations. If this condition is not met, as would be the case if total supply is greater than demand or demand is greater than supply, then we have an unbalanced transportation problem. To model and solve an unbalanced transportation problem, we need to convert the unbalanced problem to a balanced one. We do so by adding dummy supply sources or dummy demand destinations in the transportation matrix. A dummy supply source or a dummy demand destination is a fictitious supply source or a fictitious demand destination created to arrive at

Using Dummy Demand Destinations

a balanced transportation problem (i.e., total demand = total supply). For example, if the total supply is greater than the total demand, then we will add a dummy demand destination to capture the excess surplus. If the total demand is greater than the total supply, then we will make the supply exactly equal to the surplus demand by adding a dummy supply source. Because these demand locations were created for modeling convenience and no units will be shipped in these routes, we will assign zero per unit costs to the cells of these dummy locations. We demonstrate the use of dummy variables in Example B.2 by creating a dummy demand destination.

EXAMPLE B.2: Orion Electronics has decided to increase its production capacity from 1,000 units to 2,500 units. Reformulate the transportation problem in Example B.1, and solve the problem using Excel Solver.

SOLUTION

The increase in supply of electronic components from Denver makes the total supply (8,500) greater than the total demand (7,000). As a result, the transportation problem of Orion Electronics has now become unbalanced. To reformulate this problem as a balanced transportation problem, we first add a dummy demand destination column with demand requirements of 1,500 units. The new balanced transportation matrix is presented in Figure B.12.

FIGURE B.12: Revised Transportation Matrix for Orion Electronics With a Dummy Destination

TO / FROM	LOS ANGELES	CLEVELAND	CHICAGO	DUMMY DESTINATION	PRODUCTION CAPACITY
Denver	$4	$3	$2	$0	2,500
Milwaukee	$7	$3	$2	$0	3,000
Columbia	$8	$6	$4	$0	3,000
Demand Requirement	3,000	2,000	2,000	1,500	8,500

As in Example B.1, we next apply the northwest corner rule to get an initial feasible solution. Figure B.13 shows the results.

FIGURE B.13: Transportation Matrix With an Initial Feasible Solution Using the Northwest Corner Rule for the Revised Transportation Problem of Orion Electronics

TO / FROM	LOS ANGELES	CLEVELAND	CHICAGO	DUMMY DESTINATION	PRODUCTION CAPACITY
Denver	$4 2,500	$3	$2	$0	2,500
Milwaukee	$7 500	$3 2,000	$2 500	$0	3,000
Columbia	$8	$6	$4 1,500	$0 1,500	3,000
Demand Requirement	3,000	2,000	2,000	1,500	8,500

The total cost for this initial solution is: 2,500 × ($4) + 500 × ($7) + 2,000 × ($3) + 500 × ($2) + 1500 × ($4) + 1,500 × ($0) = $26,500.

The optimum solution to this problem can then be obtained by applying the stepping stone method or by using Excel Solver. Spreadsheet B.2 shows the optimum solution to this problem obtained using Excel Solver. The optimum solution is:

Denver to Los Angeles: 2,500 units

Milwaukee to Cleveland: 2,000 units

Milwaukee to Chicago: 1,000 units

Columbia to Los Angeles: 500 units

Columbia to Chicago: 1,000 units

Columbia to Dummy Destination: 1,500 units

Note that no actual shipments will be made in the route involving the dummy destination. The total cost for this initial solution is:

2,500 × ($4) + 2,000 × ($3) + 1,000 × ($2) + 500 × ($8) + 1,000 × ($4) + 1,500 × ($0) = $26,000

SCREENSHOT B.2: Optimum Solution to the Orion Electronics Transportation Problem With a Dummy Destination

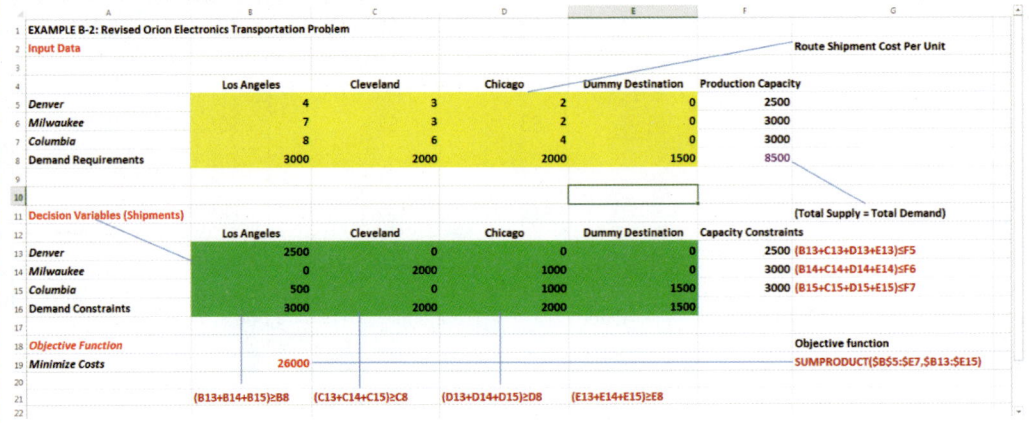

Degeneracy

Degeneracy is a condition that occurs when the solution to a transportation problem has occupied routes (cells) that are less than the (number of origins + the number of destinations – 1). As we noted, our final solution to the balanced transportation problem of Orion Electronics (Figure B.11) is a non-degenerate optimum solution because the number of occupied routes (cells), which is 5, is equal to the number of rows (3) + the number of columns (3) – 1, which is also 5.

Nevertheless, if you refer to Figure B.4 (which is reproduced as Figure B.14), the initial feasible solution using the matrix least cost method, the solution is degenerate because the number of occupied routes (cells) equals 4, which is less than (number of rows (3) + the number of columns (3) -1), which is 5.

In transportation problems, degeneracy occurs when one of the occupied routes (cells) fully exhausts the supply from a source and meets the demand requirements for a destination. For example, in Figure B.14, the occupied Columbia–Los Angeles route fully exhausts the supply from Columbia (3,000 units) and meets the demand requirements for Los Angeles (3,000 units).

Degeneracy: a condition that occurs when the solution to a transportation problem has occupied routes (cells) that are less than the (number of origins + the number of destinations – 1)

FIGURE B.14: Transportation Matrix With a Degenerate Initial Solution for the Orion Electronics Company Problem Using the Matrix Least Cost Method

TO \ FROM	LOS ANGELES	CLEVELAND	CHICAGO	PRODUCTION CAPACITY
Denver	$4	$3	$2	1,000
		1,000		
Milwaukee	$7	$3	$2	3,000
		1,000	2,000	
Columbia	$8	$6	$4	3,000
	3,000			
Demand Requirement	3,000	2,000	2,000	**7,000**

The problem that degeneracy creates is that when we apply the stepping stone method, it is impossible to trace a closed path for one or more of the unoccupied cells or routes. To overcome the problem of degeneracy, we need to create an artificially occupied cell. This can be done by placing a 0 or a negligible amount representing a fictitious shipment in one of the currently unoccupied cells. By doing so, we treat that unoccupied cell as occupied. It is important, however, that we carefully choose the unoccupied cell that will be treated as an occupied cell. We should choose that unoccupied cell that will allow us to close all possible stepping stone paths. A closer look at Figure B.14 shows that if we treat the currently unoccupied Milwaukee–Los Angeles cell as artificially occupied, all stepping stone paths for the other unoccupied cells can be closed. This procedure is shown in Figure B.15.

 Degeneracy

Note that we also want to make sure that we avoid creating an artificial cell that will end up with a negative sign when we trace a closed path. To create an artificially occupied cell, some experimentation will be required because not every unoccupied cell will permit us to draw a closed path. The solution in Figure B.15 is now a nondegenerate initial solution and an optimum solution can now be obtained using the stepping stone method.

Solving the transportation problem is a critical challenge for operations and supply chain managers within organizations that seek to identify the best possible mixture of routes among their production

FIGURE B.15: Transportation Matrix by Creating an Artificially Occupied Cell to Overcome Degeneracy

TO \ FROM	LOS ANGELES	CLEVELAND	CHICAGO	PRODUCTION CAPACITY
Denver	$4	$3	$2	1,000
		1,000		
Milwaukee	$7	$3	$2	3,000
	0	1,000	2,000	
Columbia	$8	$6	$4	3,000
	3,000			
Demand Requirement	3,000	2,000	2,000	**7,000**

facilities and storage locations. As this module has demonstrated, the steps involved in creating the optimal (cost-effective) solution can be time-consuming and tricky, but finding the best solution is a necessary activity for maximizing the organization's supply chain. The better we understand the rules and steps in transportation problems, the more value we can add to our companies as they seek the best and lowest cost means to get products from their point of origin to their final destinations.

Visit **edge.sagepub.com/venkataraman** to help you accomplish your coursework goals in an easy-to-use learning environment.

- Mobile-friendly eFlashcards
- Mobile-friendly practice quizzes
- A complete online action plan
- Chapter summaries with learning objectives
- Video and multimedia resources

MODULE SUMMARY

B.1 **Formulate and solve the transportation problems using both manual methods and the Excel Solver, and interpret the solutions.** In supply chain network design, the location of factories, warehouses, and distribution centers is a strategic decision that affects costs. Consequently, companies spend a significant amount of time and resources in considering and evaluating alternatives to choose the one that is most suitable for them. Specifically, the transportation model can aid companies in minimizing the overall costs of transportation and distribution from the various supply sources to the demand destinations by making decisions about the location of their plants or supply sources relative to the demand destinations and decisions about how many units of a particular product should be transported from each supply origin to each demand destination, to satisfy the existing demand for the company's products.

The transportation model is a special case of linear programming problems in which the objective is to minimize the total cost of transporting goods from the various supply origins to the different demand destinations. The model is often classified as a linear programming problem because the relationship between the variables transportation costs and the number of units shipped is assumed to be linear. There are important decision rules that must be applied to the transportation problem. The transportation model requires the following assumptions:

a. Capacity at each supply location or origin is limited.

b. The demand requirements at each destination are known.

c. Regardless of their origin or destination, the items shipped are the same (homogeneous).

d. Regardless of the number of units shipped, the shipping cost on a per unit basis remains the same.

e. Between each origin and destination, the mode of transportation being used does not change, and there is only one route used.

Two methods that can be used to obtain the initial basic feasible solution are the northwest corner rule and the matrix minimum cost method. The advantage of the northwest corner rule is that it allows us to find an initial feasible solution to the transportation problem. It emphasizes finding an initial solution that satisfies all constraints without regard to the relative shipping costs of those orders. The northwest corner rule generates feasible solutions but not necessarily an optimum least cost solution. The objective of the matrix minimum cost method is to minimize total cost, making this method more intuitively appealing. This method also reduces the number of computations and the time required to determine the optimal solution.

The stepping stone method is intended to generate improved solutions for transportation problems. The model begins with an initial feasible solution, and it is then used to determine whether that initial solution is optimal. The term *stepping stone* refers to the occupied cells in the initial solution of the transportation matrix, which are used in arriving at an improved solution.

Excel Solver offers a means for finding optimal solutions to the transportation problem. The procedure for solving transportation problems using Excel Solver is almost identical to the steps used for solving linear programming problems (see Module A).

B.2 **Apply transportation modeling to other situations.** If a transportation problem is not balanced, it has to be converted into a balanced situation by adding dummy supply sources or dummy demand destinations in the transportation matrix. A transportation problem is degenerate if one of the occupied routes (cell) fully exhausts the supply from a source and meets the demand requirements for a destination. If degeneracy exists, it is impossible to apply the stepping stone method and it is impossible to trace a closed path for one or more of the unoccupied cells or routes. To overcome the problem of degeneracy, we need to create an artificially occupied cell.

KEY TERMS

DISCUSSION AND REVIEW QUESTIONS

1. Why are transportation models treated as a special case of linear programming models?

2. What are the three pieces of information required to formulate a transportation model?

3. What are the five major assumptions required for transportation modeling?

4. What is the difference between a balanced and an unbalanced transportation problem?

5. List the four "steps" of the northwest corner rule.

6. List the four "steps" of the matrix least cost method.

7. Why does the matrix least cost method gives a better initial solution than the northwest corner rule does?

8. What is the implication of getting a negative value of improvement index for a closed path?

9. For a balanced transportation problem, what are the two criteria for a nondegenerate optimum solution?

10. What does the term *degeneracy* mean in the context of transportation modeling, and what problems does it create in applying the stepping stone method?

11. Can the structure of transportation models be applied to other operations management situations? If the answer is "yes," provide some examples.

12. In the stepping stone method, what is the rationale for placing alternate + and − signs around the closed path?

13. Why do we create dummy supply sources or dummy demand destinations in transportation modeling problems?

SOLVED PROBLEMS

1. Excelsior Furniture Inc., located in Europe, manufactures office furniture. The company currently has factories in Hamburg, Germany, and Vienna, Austria. The company ships its office furniture products for distribution to retail stores to warehouses in Paris, Amsterdam, and Milan. Because the demand for one of the company's popular products, office desks, is expected to increase in the coming years, Excelsior has decided to open a third factory in Berne, Switzerland. Relevant data on production and shipping costs, as well as expected demand for the company's office desks, and the production capacities of the three factories are given in Table B.3. Use the transportation model to develop a least cost production and shipping plan for Excelsior.

TABLE B.3: Data on Production and Shipping Costs, Production Capacities, and Expected Demands for Excelsior Furniture Inc.

To / From	Paris	Amsterdam	Milan	Production cost/ Unit	Production Capacity
Hamburg	$9	$5	$4	$9	1,500
Vienna	$10	$5	$4	$7	900
Berne	$8	$7	$6	$8	1,600
Expected Demand	1,400	1,700	900		

Solution:

We begin by setting up a transportation matrix (Figure B.16) showing the cells (routes) for the three factories and three warehouses. The per unit cost in each cell (route) shown in Figure B.16 is the sum of the production and shipping costs per unit for that factory-to-warehouse route.

FIGURE B.16: Transportation Matrix Showing Unit Costs for Excelsior Furniture

To / From	Paris	Amsterdam	Milan	Production Capacity
Hamburg	$18	$14	$13	1,500
Vienna	$17	$12	$11	900
Berne	$16	$15	$14	1,600
Warehouse Demand	1,400	1,700	900	4,000

As demonstrated for Example B.1, we next apply the northwest corner rule to get an initial feasible solution. The results are shown in Figure B.17.

FIGURE B.17: Transportation Matrix With an Initial Solution for Excelsior Furniture Using Northwest Corner Rule

To From	Paris	Amsterdam	Milan	Production Capacity
Hamburg	$18 1,400	$14 100	$13	1,500
Vienna	$17	$12 900	$11	900
Berne	$16	$15 700	$14 900	1,600
Warehouse Demand	1,400	1,700	900	4,000

The total cost for this initial feasible solution is:

$$1400 \times \$18 + 100 \times \$14 + 900 \times \$12 + 700 \times \$15 + 900 \times \$14 = \$60,500$$

We next compute the improvement indices using the stepping stone method for all the unoccupied cells (routes) in Figure B.16 to determine whether an improved solution is possible. These computations are shown as follows:

$$\text{Hamburg–Milan: } +13 - 14 + 15 - 14 = 0$$

$$\text{Vienna–Paris: } +17 - 12 + 14 - 18 = +1$$

$$\text{Vienna–Milan: } +11 - 12 + 15 - 14 = 0$$

$$\text{Berne–Paris: } +16 - 15 + 14 - 18 = -3$$

As the Berne–Paris route decreases the total cost by $3 for each unit shipped in that route, we want to get an improved solution by shipping as many units as possible (700 units in this case) in this currently unused route. This improved solution is shown in Figure B.18.

FIGURE B.18: Transportation Matrix With an Improved Solution for Excelsior Furniture

To From	Paris	Amsterdam	Milan	Production Capacity
Hamburg	$18 700	$14 800	$13	1,500
Vienna	$17	$12 900	$11	900
Berne	$16 700	$15	$14 900	1,600
Warehouse Demand	1,400	1,700	900	4,000

The total cost for this improved solution is:

$$700 \times \$18 + 800 \times \$14 + 900 \times \$12 + 700 \times \$16 + 900 \times \$14 = \$58,400$$

This is an improvement over the initial solution as there is a cost reduction of $2,100. Nevertheless, this improved solution may or may not be optimum. Therefore, we need to test the currently unused routes in Figure B.17 by computing the improvement indices for these unused routes.

$$\text{Hamburg–Milan: } +13 - 14 + 16 - 18 = -3$$

Vienna–Paris: $+17 - 12 + 14 - 18 = +1$

Vienna–Milan: $+11 - 14 + 16 - 18 + 14 - 12 = +3$

Berne–Amsterdam: $+15 - 16 + 18 - 14 = +3$

As the Hamburg–Milan route shows a cost reduction of \$3 per unit shipped, we ship as much as possible (700 units in this case) in this unused route. The results are shown in Figure B.19.

The total cost for this improved solution is:

$$800 \times \$14 + 700 \times \$13 + 900 \times \$12 + 1400 \times \$16 + 200 \times \$14 = \$56,300$$

FIGURE B.19: Transportation Matrix With a Second Improved (Optimal) Solution for Excelsior Furniture

To \ From	Paris	Amsterdam	Milan	Production Capacity
Hamburg	$18	$14 / 800	$13 / 700	1,500
Vienna	$17	$12 / 900	$11	900
Berne	$16 / 1,400	$15	$14 / 200	1,600
Warehouse Demand	1,400	1,700	900	4,000

Evaluating the currently unused routes in Figure B.18 by computing the improvement indices for these unused routes, we have

Hamburg–Paris: $+18 - 16 + 14 - 13 = +3$

Vienna–Paris: $+17 - 16 + 14 - 13 + 14 - 12 = +4$

Vienna–Milan: $+11 - 13 + 14 - 12 = 0$

Berne–Amsterdam: $+15 - 14 + 13 - 14 = 0$

As all improvement indices are positive or zero, the solution in Figure B.19 is the optimum solution. Incidentally, this transportation problem has multiple optimum solutions. For example, solving this problem using Excel Solver yields another optimum solution with the same cost of \$56,300. This solution is presented in Screenshot B.3.

SCREENSHOT B.3: Another Optimum Solution to Excelsior Furniture Transportation Problem

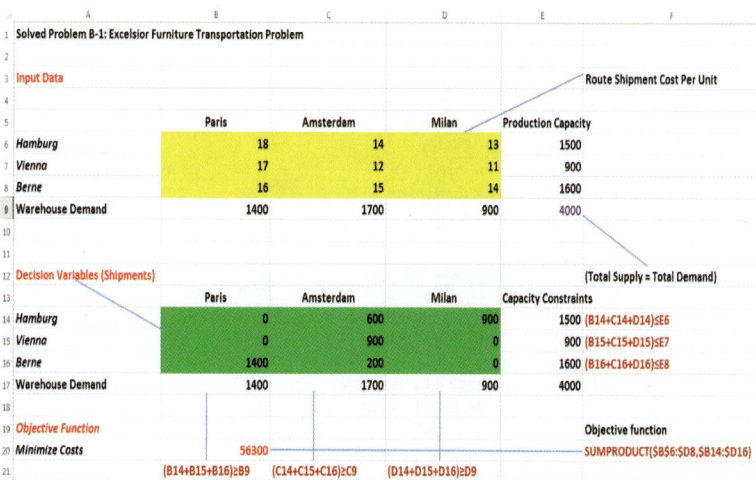

2.   We have discussed in this module that transportation problems belong to a special class of linear programming models. Reformulate the Excelsior Furniture problem as a linear programming model.

Solution: Using the data in Figure B.16, we formulate the LP problem as follows:

$$\text{Minimize Cost} = \$18X_{HP} + \$14X_{HA} + \$13X_{HM} + \$17X_{VP} + \$12X_{VA} + \$11X_{VM} + \$16X_{BP}$$

$$+ \$15X_{BA} + \$14X_{BM}$$

Subject to:

$$X_{HP} + X_{HA} + X_{HM} \leq 1{,}500 \text{ (production capacity at Hamburg)}$$

$$X_{VP} + X_{VA} + X_{VM} \leq 900 \text{ (production capacity at Vienna)}$$

$$X_{BP} + X_{BA} + X_{BM} \leq 1{,}600 \text{ (production capacity at Berne)}$$

$$X_{HP} + X_{VP} + X_{BP} \geq 1{,}400 \text{ (Paris demand requirements)}$$

$$X_{HA} + X_{VA} + X_{BA} \geq 1{,}700 \text{ (Amsterdam demand requirements)}$$

$$X_{HM} + X_{VM} + X_{BM} \geq 900 \text{ (Milan demand requirements)}$$

$$X_{HP}, X_{HA}, X_{HM}, X_{VP}, X_{VA}, X_{VM}, X_{BP}, X_{BA}, X_{BM} \geq 0, \text{ where}$$

The decision variables are:

$$X_{HP} = \text{number units shipped from Hamburg to Paris}$$

$$X_{HA} = \text{number units shipped from Hamburg to Amsterdam}$$

$$X_{HM} = \text{number units shipped from Hamburg to Milan}$$

$$X_{VP} = \text{number units shipped from Vienna to Paris}$$

$$X_{VA} = \text{number units shipped from Vienna to Amsterdam}$$

$$X_{VM} = \text{number units shipped from Vienna to Milan}$$

$$X_{BP} = \text{number units shipped from Berne to Paris}$$

SCREENSHOT B.4: Sensitivity Analysis Report for the Excelsior Furniture Company Problem

	A	B	C	D	E	F	G	H
1	Microsoft Excel 15.0 Sensitivity Report							
2	Worksheet: [MODULE B- Solved Problem-B1.xlsx]Sheet1							
3	Report Created: 11/11/2015 5:53:02 AM							
4								
5								
6	Variable Cells							
7				Final	Reduced	Objective	Allowable	Allowable
8		Cell	Name	Value	Cost	Coefficient	Increase	Decrease
9		$B$14	Hamburg Paris	0	3	18	1E+30	3
10		$C$14	Hamburg Amsterdam	600	0	14	1	0
11		$D$14	Hamburg Milan	900	0	13	0	14
12		$B$15	Vienna Paris	0	4	17	1E+30	4
13		$C$15	Vienna Amsterdam	900	0	12	0	1E+30
14		$D$15	Vienna Milan	0	0	11	1E+30	0
15		$B$16	Berne Paris	1400	0	16	3	16
16		$C$16	Berne Amsterdam	200	0	15	0	1
17		$D$16	Berne Milan	0	0	14	1E+30	0
18								
19	Constraints							
20				Final	Shadow	Constraint	Allowable	Allowable
21		Cell	Name	Value	Price	R.H. Side	Increase	Decrease
22		$B$17	Warehouse Demand Paris	1400	16	1400	0	1400
23		$C$17	Warehouse Demand Amsterdam	1700	15	1700	0	200
24		$D$17	Warehouse Demand Milan	900	14	900	0	200
25		$E$14	Hamburg Capacity Constraints	1500	-1	1500	200	0
26		$E$15	Vienna Capacity Constraints	900	-3	900	200	0
27		$E$16	Berne Capacity Constraints	1600	0	1600	1E+30	0

X_{BA} = number units shipped from Berne to Amsterdam

X_{BM} = number units shipped from Berne to Milan

In addition to Screenshot B.3, which shows the Excel Solver solution to this problem, Screenshot B.4 presents the sensitivity analysis of the solution to this problem.

PROBLEMS

1. For the following transportation problem, use the northwest corner rule to find an initial feasible solution and then the stepping stone method to find an optimum solution:

To / From	A	B	C	Capacity
1	$7	$5	$8	30
2	$5	$2	$7	40
3	$9	$6	$8	80
Demand	100	30	20	150

2. For the following transportation problem, use the matrix least cost method to find an initial feasible solution and then the stepping stone method to find an optimum solution:

To / From	A	B	C	Capacity
1	$3	$3	$4	14
2	$3	$2	$7	16
3	$2	$4	$5	18
Demand	12	15	21	38

3. For the following transportation problem, use the northwest corner rule to find an initial feasible solution and then the stepping stone method to find an optimum solution:

To / From	A	B	C	Capacity
1	$7	$4	$4	27
2	$9	$5	$6	25
3	$8	$6	$5	23
Demand	24	25	26	75

4. An electronics company has manufacturing plants at locations A, B, and C. The company ships a computer component manufactured in these plants to warehouses at locations X, Y, and Z. Unit shipping costs in $, plant capacities, and demand requirements from the warehouses are given in the following table:

To / From	X	Y	Z	Capacity
A	15	19	11	300
B	13	7	17	260
C	25	23	15	190
Warehouse Demand	280	220	250	750

a. Use the northwest corner rule to find an initial basic feasible solution. What is the total cost?

b. Use the matrix least cost method to find an initial basic feasible solution. What is the total cost?

c. Use the stepping stone method to find the optimal solution. What is the total cost?

5. J & K Timber Supply Company ships oak flooring from three of its mills in Jodhpur, Bhopal, and Nagpur to three warehouses in Chennai, New Delhi, and Chandigarh. Shipping costs in $ per ton, mill capacities, and demand requirements from the warehouses are given in the following table:

To From	Chennai	New Delhi	Chandigarh	Mill Capacity (in tons)
Jodhpur	$5	$5	$4	30
Bhopal	6	4	5	45
Nagpur	5	4	5	35
Warehouse Demand (in tons)	35	35	40	110

   a. Use the northwest corner rule to find an initial basic feasible solution. What is the total cost?

   b. Use the matrix least cost method to find an initial basic feasible solution. What is the total cost?

   c. Use the stepping stone method to find the optimal solution. What is the total cost?

6. A trucking company has to move 120 tons of concrete from three supply sources (A, B, and C) to three road construction project sites (X, Y, and Z). Shipping costs in $ per truck load, supply capacities, and demand requirements from the project sites are given in the following table:

To From	X	Y	Z	Capacity (in truck loads)
A	$6	$11	$11	40
B	21	31	21	45
C	6	9	11	35
Demand (in truckloads)	50	40	30	120

   a. Use the northwest corner rule to find an initial basic feasible solution. What is the total cost?

   b. Use the matrix least cost method to find an initial basic feasible solution. What is the total cost?

   c. Use the stepping stone method to find the optimal solution. What is the total cost?

7. The following transportation matrix provides an initial feasible solution to a transportation problem. Perform *one iteration* of the stepping stone method to find an improved solution. What is the reduction in total cost of this improved solution?

To From	Dallas	Erie	Fargo	Capacity
Cleveland	$10 400	$4	$12	400
Calgary	$18 100	$12 600	$8 0	700
Tucson	$12	$10 100	$14 800	900
Demand	500	700	800	2,000

8. The following transportation matrix provides an initial feasible solution to a transportation problem. Perform *one iteration* of the stepping stone method to find an improved solution. What is the reduction in total cost of this improved solution?

To From	W	X	Y	Z	Capacity
1	$8 200	$3	$2	$5	200
2	$10 200	$7 200	$6 200	$8	600
3	$9	$4	$4 100	$7 200	300
Demand	400	200	300	200	1,100

9. Refer to Example B.1. Reformulate the Orion Electronics Company transportation problem as a linear programming model.

10. Refer to problem 5. Reformulate that transportation problem as a linear programming model.

11. Cool Air Inc. currently manufactures room air conditioners in its Chicago and Baton Rouge plants. The company ships its air conditioners to three warehouses in Boston, Tucson, and Denver. As a result of increasing demand for the company's air conditioners, Hari Prasad, the company owner, is planning to build a new plant. He has narrowed down his choices to two possible new locations—Cleveland and Atlanta. The estimated production capacity of both the new plants will be 300 air conditioners. The total cost per unit of production and shipping from Cleveland to the three warehouses are $50, $60, and $100, and from Atlanta, the costs are $80, $70, and $100. Production capacities for the existing plants and the demand requirements from the three warehouses, as well as the total costs per unit (includes production and shipping costs) for each of the current routes are given in the following table. Which new location (Cleveland or Atlanta) should Hari Prasad select as the location for the company's new plant? (Hint: *A dummy variable is needed to solve the problem.*)

Plant	Warehouse			Capacity
	Boston	Tucson	Denver	
Chicago	$110	$90	$70	200
Baton Rouge	$120	$70	$80	150
Demand	160	250	190	

12. National Energy Inc. supplies natural gas to customers to three counties in Pennsylvania—Erie, Franklin, and Venango. National Energy receives natural gas from three suppliers—Energy Efficient, Northeast Gas, and Western Gas. Expected demand for natural gas for the upcoming winter season are as follows: Erie County: 500 units; Franklin County: 300 units; and Venango County: 400 units. The supplies of natural gas available from the three suppliers are as follows: Energy Efficient: 400 units; Northeast Gas: 350 units; and Western Gas: 500 units. The cost of distribution per unit of natural gas (in $000) varies depending on the location of the suppliers and is given in the following table. Develop an optimum distribution plan, and compute the total cost:

From \ To	Erie	Franklin	Venango	Supply available
Energy Efficient	11	13	14	400
Northeast Gas	13	15	12	350
Western Gas	20	17	15	500
Demand	500	400	400	

13. Ranbaxy Chemicals produces a synthetic resin that is manufactured in two of the company's plants in Colorado Springs and Dayton. Four distributors from Buffalo, Atlanta, New Orleans, and Seattle belonging to different industries have placed orders that exceed the combined capacity of the company's two plants. Although the production and distribution costs vary between the two plants and the location of the customer, contractual agreements between the company and the distributors prevents Ranbaxy chemicals from selling its product only to the highest bidder. After factoring in prices, production, and distribution costs, the company has determined the profit contribution per unit between the various plant-distributor alternatives, which are given in the following table. Determine an optimum distribution plan that will maximize profits for Ranbaxy Chemicals.

From \ To	Buffalo	Atlanta	New Orleans	Seattle	Capacity
Colorado Springs	$45	$43	$40	$50	4,500
Dayton	$ 47	$40	$36	$47	5,000
Demand	1,500	4,000	3,500	2,000	

14. Pennington Hardwood Lumber Supplier has three lumber mills in San Jose, Dayton, and Boston that manufacture pre-cut hardwood. These pre-cut hardwood are shipped to building warehouses in Cleveland, Orlando, Denver, San Diego, and New York for further distribution. The following table shows the production capacity in tons of pre-cut hardwood at each mill, the number of tons of hardwood required at each of the building warehouse, and the shipping costs (in $ per ton). Solve this transportation problem to minimize total costs using Excel Solver.

From \ To	Cleveland	Orlando	Denver	San Diego	New York	Mill Capacity (in tons)
San Jose	$15	$21	$13	$10	$22	45
Dayton	3	11	9	21	7	50
Boston	4	12	10	25	5	35
Demand (in tons)	25	20	35	20	30	130

15. Refer to problem 14. Reformulate that transportation problem as a linear programming model.

16. Neptune Enterprises manufactures central processing units (CPUs) for a line of personal computers. Currently, the CPUs are manufactured in three existing plants in Raleigh, Akron, and Cedar Rapids. The company is considering adding a fourth plant in one of two locations: Mobile or Atlanta. Relevant data on shipping costs, capacities, and demand requirements for both the existing plants and destinations, and the proposed plants and destinations are given in the following tables. In which location should the fourth plant be added?

	Destinations			
Existing Plants	Miami	Seattle	Houston	Capacity
Raleigh	$22	$19	$23	350
Akron	$27	$29	$22	250
Cedar Rapids	$24	$27	$24	200
Demand	310	290	400	

	Destinations			
Proposed Plants	Miami	Seattle	Houston	Capacity
Mobile	$30	$31	$31	200
Atlanta	$28	$30	$32	200

17. Consider the following transportation matrix that has an initial feasible solution obtained using the northwest corner rule. It is impossible to apply the stepping stone method to this matrix in its current form. What is the term used to label this condition? How would you overcome this condition to apply the stepping stone method? Apply the necessary fix and solve the problem using the stepping stone method to get an optimum solution:

To From	Dallas	Erie	Fargo	Capacity
Cleveland	$9 400	$6	$10	400
Calgary	$20	$10 700	$8 200	900
Tucson	$14	$16	$15 600	600
Demand	400	700	800	2,000

18. The following transportation matrix provides a degenerate initial feasible solution to a transportation problem. Apply the necessary fix to overcome the degenerate condition, and perform *one iteration* of the stepping stone method to find an improved solution. What is the reduction in total cost of this improved solution?

To From	W	X	Y	Z	Capacity
1	$7 200	$4	$3	$6	200
2	$9 200	$8 200	$5	$7	400
3	$8	$5	$4 300	$6 200	600
Demand	400	200	300	200	1100

19. You have been hired as a consultant by a refrigerator manufacturer to evaluate the freight costs of motors needed for assembly of the company's refrigerators. Relevant data on plant capacities, warehouse demands, and shipping cost per unit between each plant and warehouse are provided in the following table:

To From	Warehouse					Capacity
	A	B	C	D	E	
Plant-1	$10	$9	$12	$8	$6	1,200
Plant-2	7	12	9	5	7	1,500
Plant-3	6	5	8	4	9	900
Plant-4	13	7	10	8	5	1,100
Plant-5	8	11	6	10	12	1,300
Demand	1,400	800	1,700	1,400	900	6,000 / 6,200

a. Use the matrix least cost method to first find an initial feasible solution and then the stepping stone method to find the least cost optimum solution.

b. Verify the least cost solution found in a) by resolving the above problem using Excel Solver.

20. Refer to problem 19. Reformulate that transportation problem as a linear programming model.

CASE STUDY B.1 PLANT LOCATION FOR TRU-BLADE SKI COMPANY ···················

The Tru-Blade Ski Company makes downhill skis and snowboards for recreational winter sport enthusiasts. Business has been growing rapidly, and the firm has outgrown its single factory location, in Pocatello, Idaho. Tru-Blade has warehouses in five locations: Burlington, Vermont; Eureka, California; Denver, Colorado; Philadelphia, Pennsylvania; and Montreal, Canada. Managers have forecast that a new production plant with a capacity of 10,000 units per month will soon be needed, and they have decided to consider where such a plant should be located. They have narrowed their list to two possible locations—Portland, Oregon, and Cleveland, Ohio—and have identified empty

factory buildings that would require minimal conversion costs. The following two tables give the capacities, forecasted demand, and shipping costs associated with these options.

You are a supply chain expert hired by Tru-Blade to help its managers make this location decision. For the alternative plant locations, determine the shipping patterns that will minimize total transportation costs. Where should the new plant be located? Why?

Plant	Capacity (skis per month)	Warehouse	Demand (skis per month)
Pocatello	12,000	Burlington	6,000
New Plant	10,000	Eureka	3,500
		Denver	8,000
		Philadelphia	1,500
		Montreal	3,000
Total	22,000	Total	22,000

	Shipping Cost to Warehouse (per pair of skis)				
Plant	Burlington	Eureka	Denver	Philadelphia	Montreal
Pocatello	$8.00	$3.00	$4.00	$7.00	$6.00
Portland (option 1)	$10.00	$3.00	$5.00	$8.00	$7.00
Cleveland (option 2)	$5.00	$8.00	$6.00	$3.00	$4.00

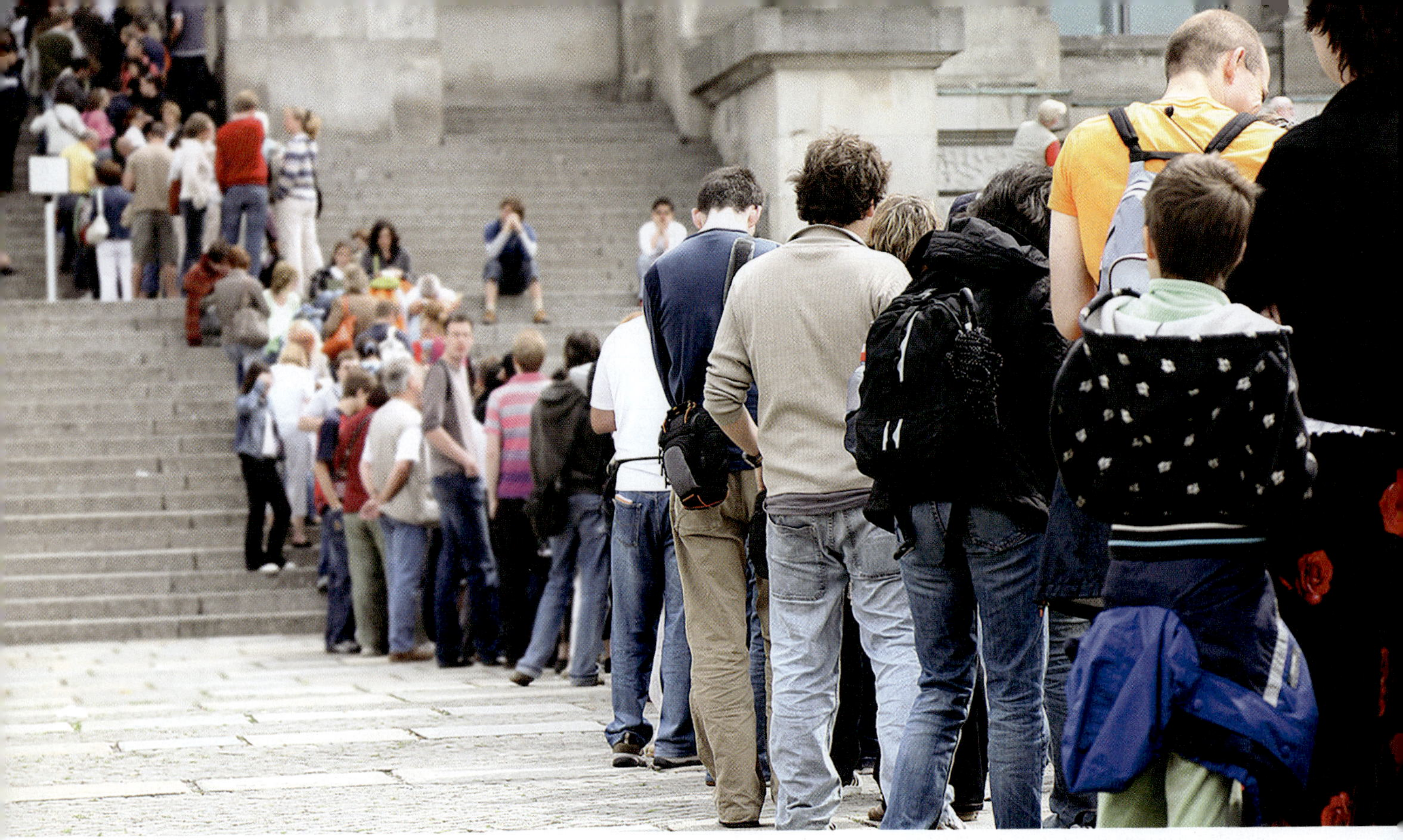

©iStockphoto.com/TommL

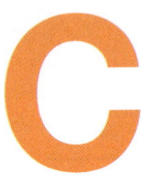

MODULE C Waiting Line Models

LEARNING OBJECTIVES

After studying this module, you should be able to:

1. Identify the various cost implications and the key features of waiting lines.
2. Employ the various queuing models and understand when and how to use them to calculate optimal queuing solutions, including the psychology underlying waiting lines.

OPERATIONS PROFILE: How Some Companies Deal With Waiting Lines

Some years ago, executives at a Houston airport sought to resolve passenger complaints about the long waits at the baggage claim. They did so by hiring additional workers and increasing the number of baggage handlers working on each shift. Sure enough, the average wait time fell to eight minutes, well within industry standards and comparable with other major airports. Nevertheless, the customer complaints continued. At this point, the executives examined the customer deplaning process more carefully. They found that it took passengers a minute to walk from their arrival gates to baggage claim and seven more minutes to get their bags. Roughly 88% of a passenger's time was spent standing around waiting for luggage.

The airport implemented an alternative solution: Instead of reducing wait times even more, it moved the arrival gates further away from the main terminal and routed bags to the outermost carousel. Passengers now had to walk six times longer to get their bags. Complaints dropped to near zero.

This problem with waiting lines is found not only in a small subset of the manufacturing and service industries, but also in everyday life for shoppers and customers. Waiting for a cable TV technician to arrive ("sometime between 8:00 a.m. and noon") or standing in line at a supermarket with fewer cashiers are common and familiar examples. The boredom from unoccupied time also leads to the popularity of impulse-buy items, which earn supermarkets approximately $5.5 billion annually.[a] Tabloid magazines, candy, and other special deals offer relief from interminable waiting.

Other than taking full advantage of waiting customers with impulse purchase items at hand, many organizations are finding ways to reduce their customers' perception of waiting times to improve their satisfaction. Sometimes the means for speeding up waiting times can be calculated and handled through more efficient operations. At other times, the best means for improving perceived waiting times is to understand the consumer's psychology when it comes to waiting lines. That is why The Walt Disney Company (aka Disney, Burbank, CA), for example, one of the best organizations in the world at applying queuing theory models and psychology in its theme parks, takes the science of waiting lines so seriously. Disney has learned over time that beating expectations makes people happy. That is, people who wait for less time than they anticipated are more satisfied than are those who wait longer than expected. To apply this idea, Disney always overestimates wait times for rides, so that its guests are pleasantly surprised when they ascend *Expedition Everest* ahead of schedule. Disney also knows that people forced to wait are usually more concerned with how long a line is rather than with how fast it's moving. Given a choice between a slow-moving short line and a fast-moving long one, a consumer will often opt for the former, even if the waits are identical. This is why Disney typically hides the length of its lines by wrapping them around buildings, moving them through short displays, and keeping guests' lines of sight as short as possible.[1]

C.1. Introduction to Waiting Line Models

Waiting lines of customers at service facilities such as grocery stores, theme parks, fast food restaurants, automobile service stations, and doctors' offices or waiting lines of products in a manufacturing facility waiting to be processed are all common occurrences in everyday life. In addition to these examples of customers physically waiting in line for service, waiting lines can also be nonphysical such as waiting online in which the server cannot accommodate all those trying to

C.1

Identify the various cost implications and the key features of waiting lines.

---

[a] Unless otherwise stated, all currency is in U.S. dollars.

access the website. Waiting in line occurs, even in underloaded facilities, for several reasons. First, customers arrive at a service facility at random rather than at predictable intervals. Second, the time it takes to service a customer varies as each customer's need for service is often unique. Third, the waiting time for a given customer depends on the number of people waiting for service ahead of that customer. Fourth, the design of the service system itself has an impact on waiting times. For example, in systems where customer arrivals can be prescheduled and the service time required from customer to customer is relatively constant, then waiting lines tend to be minimal. Just-in-time (JIT) and lean production systems attempt to minimize waiting times by eliminating variability in arrival and service rates. In the context of waiting lines for this module, we will use the term *customer* in its broadest sense. Customers can be people or inanimate objects, such as machines or products, or computer processes, telephone calls, and so forth. Anything that has the potential to wait for processing or service is a customer.

Cost Implications of Managing Waiting Lines

 Costs and Waiting Lines

The primary objective of managing waiting lines is to minimize their total costs throughout any service or manufacturing facility. This total cost has two components: the cost related to customer waiting time and the cost related to capacity.

COST RELATED TO CUSTOMER WAITING TIME

In a service context, waiting lines form whenever the customer demand for a service exceeds the ability of that facility to provide that service in a given time interval. Similarly, in manufacturing facilities, waiting lines of work-in-process inventory begin to form at bottleneck workstations or when machines break down. Regardless of why waiting lines form, they cause tangible and intangible costs. Tangible costs include wages that must be paid to workers while the facility remains idle (perhaps because of machine repair or lack of parts) and lost productivity. Tangible costs may also include cost of materials used while waiting; for example, airplanes will continue to consume fuel as they wait at a terminal for gates to become available or for clearance to take off. Intangible costs include lost sales because customers decided not to wait and received service from a competitor, and loss of goodwill as a result of customer dissatisfaction.

CAPACITY-RELATED COSTS

Costs related to capacity are incurred to maintain existing facility capacity or add additional capacity to provide the required service. For example, supermarkets tend to have more stations open at busier times of the day or week, a doctor's office may expand the size of the existing facility to accommodate increased patient demand, or an automobile service shop such as Jiffy Lube (Jiffy Lube International, Inc., Houston, TX) may increase the number of bays for providing services such as oil and filter change.

In waiting line systems, because many of the costs are intangible or difficult to estimate and quantify, managers typically decide what level of service to offer (i.e., they determine an acceptable waiting time) and then establish the facility capacity to provide that level of service. Note, however, in waiting line systems, the cost of service levels provided and capacity-related costs are inversely related. For example, a low level of service often results in longer waiting lines, which could lead to higher customer dissatisfaction. Conversely, a high level of service means lower waiting time costs because of reductions in customer dissatisfaction, but they also result in higher capacity-related costs from the additional capacity needed to provide that high service level. Because of the inverse relationship between customer waiting time costs and capacity-related costs, managers must strike a balance between these two costs to arrive at an optimal level of service to provide and establish the optimum capacity needed to provide that service. Because long waiting lines increase waiting time costs and adversely affect the company's quality image and adding more capacity increases capacity-related costs, many companies train their employees to deliver services demanded by customer faster and more efficiently. Figure C.1 plots the behavior patterns of costs associated with a waiting line system.

Characteristics of Waiting Lines

The study and analysis of waiting lines or queues is part of a branch of mathematics known as **queuing theory**.[2] A **queue** represents a certain number of customers waiting for service at a facility. Queuing theory is a part of an operations manager's toolbox in making business decisions about resources needed to provide a service, and it has many applications. It is used in analysis and design of waiting lines in grocery stores, hospitals, telecommunications, factories, retail stores, and offices.[3]

Queuing theory: a part of an operations manager's toolbox in making business decisions about resources needed to provide a service, and it has many applications. It is used in analysis and design of waiting lines in grocery stores, hospitals, telecommunications, factories, retail stores, and offices

Queue: a certain number of customers waiting for service at a facility

FIGURE C.1: Optimum Service Level and Costs for Waiting Line Systems

Queuing Theory

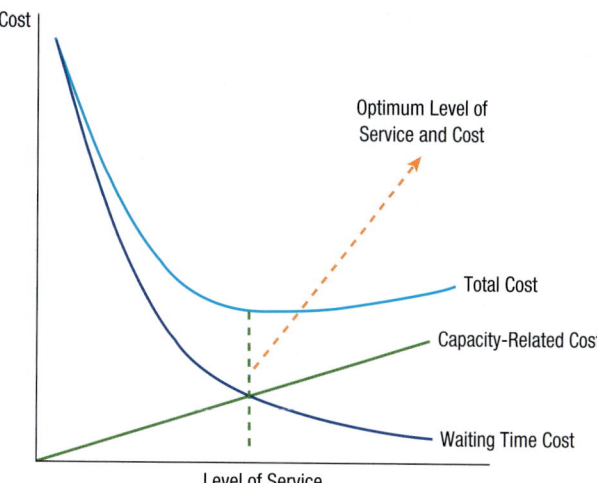

In queuing theory, a mathematical model of a waiting line system is constructed so that the lengths of the queues and the associated waiting times in those queues can be predicted. There are many different queuing models. To arrive at meaningful results, it is important to select the correct model to represent the waiting line system to be analyzed. The choice of the correct model depends on the characteristics of the given waiting line system analyzed: customer population, arrival pattern, queue size and discipline, service system structure, and service pattern.

Customer Population

The population of customers that potentially needs service can be considered as arriving either from a limited (finite) population or from an unlimited (infinite) population. Examples of a limited population source may be the number refrigerators to be repaired by a repair technician or the number of patients assigned to a nurse in the gynecology ward of a hospital. The population is limited in the sense that the number of patients that might need care at any given time cannot exceed the number of patients assigned to that nurse. An infinite or unlimited population source, on the other hand, theoretically represents systems that potentially have a large number of possible customers. Examples of such systems are toll booths on expressways, banks on busy streets, movie theaters, theme parks, or help desks for Apple Inc. (Cupertino, CA) customer support. Whenever the population source is assumed to be infinite, the potential number of arriving customers requiring service significantly exceeds the capacity of the system providing that service. Nevertheless, relative to the size of the population, the number of customers requiring service at any given point in time is relatively small.

Arrival Pattern

The arrival pattern is the way customers arrive at the service system. Although in some cases customers will arrive at a service system at some prescheduled times (by making an appointment), typically arrivals at most service facilities are random with random intervals between two adjacent arrivals. Random arrivals means that the exact time when a customer will arrive cannot be predicted and the arrivals of customers are independent of each other. A key element of arrival pattern is the arrival rate, which is the number of customer arrivals per unit of time. The arrival rate is a discrete random variable, a variable whose outcomes take on numerical values that can be counted. It can be estimated by analyzing the past data of arrivals to the waiting line system. For example, if 45 customers arrive at a teller window in a bank during a nine-hour period, then the average arrival rate is five customers per hour. Note, however, that the actual number of customers arriving at this teller booth could vary from one hour to the next. For example, from 10:00 to 11:00, there could be no customers arriving at the booth, but 15 may arrive during the lunch hour of 12:00 to 1:00. In waiting line problems, the arrival rate is typically described by a discrete probability distribution known as the Poisson distribution. The mathematical expression for the Poisson distribution is given by:

$$P(x) = \frac{e^{-\lambda} \lambda^x}{x!}$$

Limited (finite) population: examples of a limited population source may be the number refrigerators to be repaired by a repair technician or the number of patients assigned to a nurse in the gynecology ward of a hospital. The population is limited in the sense that the number of patients that might need care at any given time cannot exceed the number of patients assigned to that nurse

Unlimited (infinite) population: theoretically represents systems that potentially have a large number of possible customers. Examples of such systems are toll booths on expressways, banks on busy streets, movie theaters, theme parks, or help desks for Apple customer support

Discrete random variable: a variable whose outcomes take on numerical values that can be counted

Poisson distribution: the mathematical expression for the Poisson distribution is given by:

$$P(x) = \frac{e^{-\lambda} \lambda^x}{x!}$$

where

$P(x)$ = probability of x arrivals

x = number of arrivals per unit of time

λ = expected or average arrival rate

e = 2.7183 (a constant which is the base of the natural logarithms)

where

P(x) = probability of x arrivals

x = number of arrivals per unit of time

λ = expected or average arrival rate

e = 2.7183 (a constant which is the base of the natural logarithms)

Let us illustrate the use of this formula with an example. Assume the average arrival rate, λ = 3 customers per hour; then the probability of no customer arriving (x = 0) in any random hour is given by:

$$P(x) = \frac{e^{-\lambda}\lambda^x}{x!} = P(0) = \frac{2.7183^{-3}3^0}{0!} = 0.05 \text{ or } 5\%$$

Thus, the probability that no customers will arrive in any random hour is 5%. We can similarly calculate probabilities for other arrivals rates by setting x = 0, 1, 2, 3, etc. These probability values can be easily computed by using the table in Appendix A that provides the values of $e^{-\lambda}$ in the formula. Figure C.2 shows the Poisson distribution for a value of λ = 3.

Figure C.2 shows that if the average arrival rate (λ) = 3 customers per hour, then the probability that 5 customers will arrive in any given hour is 10% and the probability that 9 customers will arrive in any given hour is almost zero.

In the queuing models that we will discuss in this module, we will make several key assumptions about the arrival pattern. We will assume that the customers will patiently wait in line for their turn to receive service, will not switch lines (*jockey*), will not leave the waiting line (*renege*), or will not refuse to join the line (*balk*). In reality, however, many of these assumptions do not hold as customers do grow impatient while waiting in line and leave the line without receiving service. Furthermore, we know from our own experience that when waiting lines are long, customers often refuse to join the line.

Another important concept in analyzing arrival patterns is interarrival time, which is the elapsed time between one customer arrival and the next. Interarrival time is a **continuous random variable**, a variable whose numerical outcomes can be measured. In waiting line models, the variable interarrival time is assumed to follow a probability distribution known as the **negative exponential distribution**, which is a probability distribution that describes the time between events in a process in which events occur continuously and independently at a constant average rate.

Queue Size and Discipline

Queue size can be either infinite or finite. As stated earlier, in an infinite queue, the length or size of the queue is potentially unlimited; for example, an interstate toll booth stop can have a waiting line of cars that extend to any size or length. Likewise, the customer support phone line for GE Appliances (General Electric, Fairfield, CT) can be of potentially infinite length. Capacity constraints limit the size or length of a finite queue. For example, the drive-through window at Taco Bell (subsidiary of Yum! Brands, Inc., Irvine, CA) has the capacity to handle only a limited number of cars within a given time period before the queue overflows into the streets.

Continuous random variable: a variable whose numerical outcomes can be measured

Negative exponential distribution: a probability distribution that describes the time between events in a process in which events occur continuously and independently at a constant average rate

FIGURE C.2: Example of Poisson Distribution of the Number of Customer Arrivals

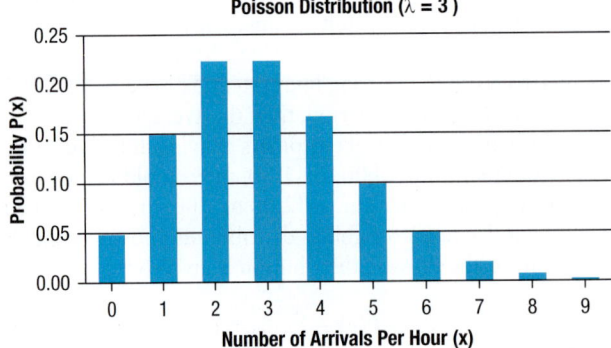

Queue discipline refers to the order in which customers waiting in line receive service at the facility. Although there are different types of queue disciplines, the most common is first come, first served; that is, the first customer in the queue is the first to receive service. There are, however, other waiting line systems where the first come, first served rule may be preempted. For example, in a code blue event at a hospital emergency room, the heart attack patient is in a more critical condition and will get treated first regardless of when that patient joined the queue. Similarly, computer programs that generate company paychecks at the end of every month may create paychecks based on priority scheduling (that is, the boss gets paid first). Other queue disciplines are (a) last in, first out; (b) prior appointments; (c) alphabetical order of last names; and (d) random order. The last-in, first-out queue discipline typically occurs in waiting line systems that involve processing by machines. For example, a server in a telecommunications system may process message signals queued for transmission over a telecommunications channel using a last-in, first-out queue discipline.

Service System Structure

Service system structure is the design or structure of the service system. Service systems are classified by the number of channels or servers and by the number of phases. The number of channels refers to the total number of counters, service bays, or other providers that are part of the system, for example, the number of teller windows open at any given time. The number of phases refers to the number of service stops that each customer must make in sequential servers to complete the required service. We will discuss four basic service system structures in Section C2. There are, however, many more complex queuing system structures that are beyond the scope of this book. Figure C.3 presents the four basic service system structures based on the number of channels and phases.

Of the four basic structures presented in Figure C.3, the single-channel, single-phase structure is the simplest. In this case, there is only one server and one phase in the waiting line service system, for example, an optometrist's office with only one optometrist serving a single waiting line of customers. In a single-channel multiphase structure, the customer joins a single waiting line but receives service

FIGURE C.3: Basic Service Structures

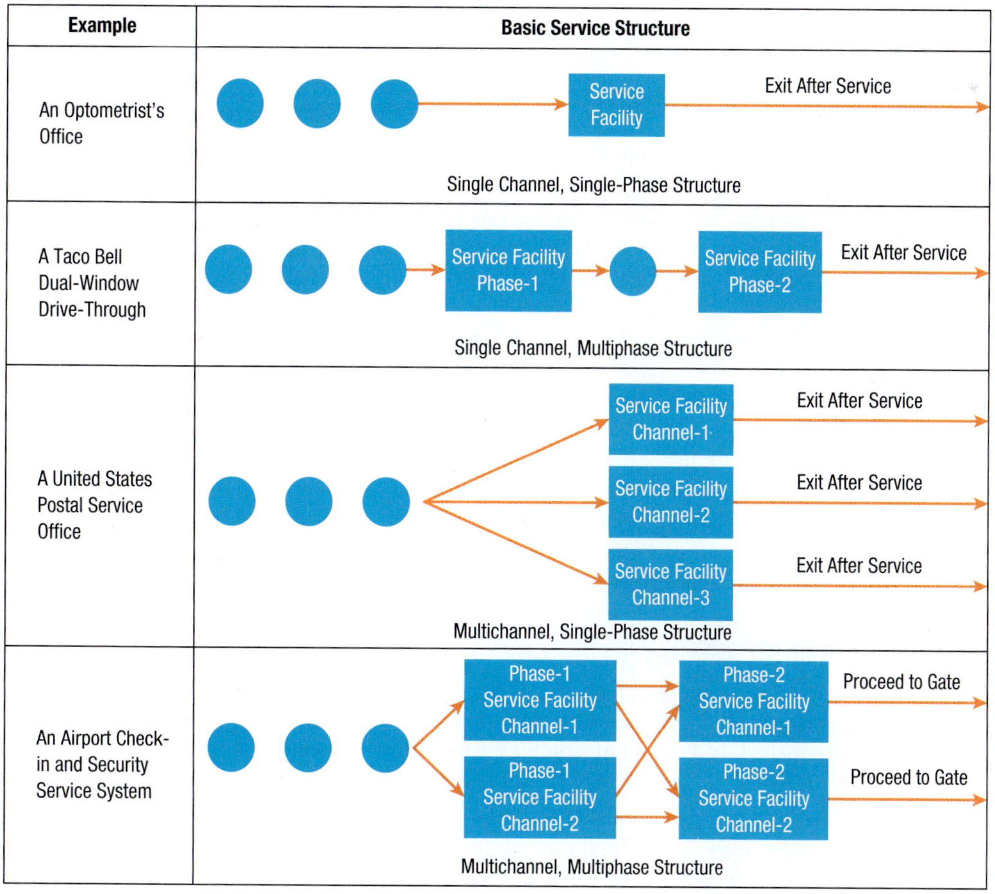

Queue discipline: the order in which customers waiting in line receive service at the facility

in multiple phases. Taco Bell uses such a system in which the customers waiting in a single line receive service in sequential phases, by first placing an order and paying for food in one service booth and then by collecting food in a second service booth.

An example of a multichannel single-phase service structure is a U.S. Postal Service office. In this structure, multiple servers (postal clerks) provide service to customers waiting in a single line. Finally, in a multichannel, multiphase structure, multiple servers provide service to customers in multiple phases. For example, at airports, multiple ticket counters first enable traveling customers to check in their baggage and receive boarding passes. Then in a subsequent phase, traveling customers join the queue for security screening where multiple security booths are available to provide service.

Service Pattern

A service represents an activity that consumes time, and in its broadest sense, services can be performed on real people or on inanimate objects, such as machines and products. In analyzing service in waiting line systems, we need to distinguish between **service rate** and **service time**. Service rate, which is the number of customers served per unit of time, like arrival rate, is also a discrete random variable. Like arrival rate, service rate is also assumed to follow a discrete Poisson probability distribution. Service time, on the other hand, resembles interarrival time, in that it is a continuous random variable and it is also assumed to follow a probability distribution known as the negative exponential distribution. In analyzing service times, service must also be expressed as a rate (e.g., units per hour or per month) to be consistent with arrivals, which are also expressed as a rate. With regard to service rate, a key assumption that we make in the queuing models we discuss in this module is that the service rate is greater than the arrival rate. Otherwise, the waiting line would grow infinitely long. Note that although service time is typically a random variable, it can also be constant in cases where automated machines, such as an automatic carwash, provide service to customers. In such cases, it takes more or less the same amount of time to service each customer. The mathematical expression for the negative exponential probability distribution representing service times is given by:

$$P \text{ (service time > t)} = e^{-\mu t}$$

where

P (service time > t) = probability that service exceeds time t

t = any value of service time

μ = expected or average service rate, i.e., the average number of customers served per unit of time

e = 2.7183 (a constant that is the base of the natural logarithms)

The following example illustrates how to use this formula. Let us assume the average number of customers served per hour, i.e., the average service rate, μ, is 2 customers per hour. The probability that the service exceeds 9 minutes (service time > 0.15 hour) for any customer is then given by:

$$P \text{ (service time > 0.15)} = e^{-\mu t} = 2.7183^{-2 \times 0.15} = 0.74 \text{ or } 74\%$$

This means that given an average service rate of 2 customers served per hour, the probability that it will take more than 9 minutes to service any given customer is 74%.

We can similarly calculate probabilities for other service times exceeding a given value, such as t = 0.3, 0.45, 1, etc. Figure C.4 shows the negative exponential distribution of service times for a value μ = 2. Notice that, given an average service rate of 2 customers served per hour, the probability that it will take more than one hour to service any given customer is 14%, and the probability that it will take more than 2.3 hours is almost zero.

Service rate: the number of customers served per unit of time

Service time: a continuous random variable that is also assumed to follow a probability distribution known as the negative exponential distribution

Measuring Performance of Waiting Line Systems

Managers use a variety of queuing models to balance waiting line costs against the cost of providing service (capacity-related costs). All queuing models make several restrictive assumptions that in practice can rarely be satisfied. In fact, many complex waiting line systems cannot be solved at all, and in such cases, the only technique that may be applied is simulation—a topic that we will discuss in Module D. Despite these limitations, queuing models are useful from a practical standpoint as they provide a solution to the problem of finding an optimum number of servers by balancing the costs of providing service against the costs associated with waiting for the service.

FIGURE C.4: Example of Negative Exponential Distribution of Service Times

Queuing models can calculate many measures of waiting line system performance for different waiting line systems. The most commonly used measures are:

1. Average number of customers in the waiting line system (waiting and being served).
2. Average number of customers waiting in line.
3. Average time a customer spends in the waiting line system (waiting time plus service time).
4. Average time a customer spends waiting in line for service.
5. Capacity utilization factor for the system.
6. Probability that no customers are in the waiting line system, that is, the service facility is idle.
7. Probability that a particular number of customers is in the waiting line system.

C.2 Queuing Models

Managers can choose from a variety of queuing models. We will, however, discuss four basic models that are most commonly used. Each of the four models has the following four common assumptions:

1. Arrival rates have a Poisson probability distribution
2. A single service phase
3. First-in, first-out (FIFO) queue discipline
4. The waiting line system operates under a steady-state condition; that is, the average arrival and service rates remain stable during analysis

C.2

Employ the various queuing models and understand when and how to use them to calculate optimal queuing solutions, including the psychology underlying waiting lines.

Model I: Single-Channel or Single-Server Queuing Model

The single-channel queuing model is the simplest and the most frequently encountered waiting line model, in which there is a single service station that will serve a queue of customers waiting in a single line. The notation used in queuing theory to identify this model is *M/M/1*. The first M refers to the Poisson distribution of arrival rates, the second M refers to the Poisson distribution of service rates, and the number 1 refers to a single channel or server. Remember, as we discussed in an earlier section of this module, if the service rate forms a Poisson distribution, then the service times have a negative exponential distribution.

Queuing Models

MODEL ASSUMPTIONS:

1. Arrival rates have a Poisson probability distribution.
2. Arrivals are from an infinite (unlimited) population source, and every arrival waits for its turn to be served.
3. Average arrival rates remain constant over time, and each arrival is independent of all others.
4. Service times follow a negative exponential probability distribution, vary from one customer to the next, and are independent of each other.

TABLE C.1: Formulas to Measure Performance of the Single-Line, Single-Server Model

λ = Average number of arrivals per unit of time

μ = Average number of customers or objects served per unit of time

$\rho = \dfrac{\lambda}{\mu}$ = Capacity utilization for the system

L_s = Average number of customers in the waiting line system (waiting and being served) = $\dfrac{\lambda}{\mu - \lambda}$

L_q = Average number customers waiting in line (queue) = $\dfrac{\lambda^2}{\mu(\mu - \lambda)}$

W_s = Average time a customer spends in the system (waiting time plus service time) = $\dfrac{1}{\mu - \lambda}$

W_q = Average time a customer spends waiting in line for service = $\dfrac{\lambda}{\mu(\mu - \lambda)} = \dfrac{Lq}{\lambda}$

P_0 = Probability that no customers are in the waiting line system, that is, the service facility is idle = $(1 - \dfrac{\lambda}{\mu})$

P_n = Probability that exactly n customers are in the waiting line system = $(\dfrac{\lambda}{\mu})^n \times P_0 = (\dfrac{\lambda}{\mu})^n \times (1 - \dfrac{\lambda}{\mu})$

5. The size of the queue is infinite, and the queue discipline is FIFO.
6. Arrival and service rates are known, and the arrival rate is less than the service rate.

If these assumptions hold, then the formulas required to measure the performance of Model I can be constructed and are given in Table C.1.

EXAMPLE C.1: Customers at the Golden Beach Amusement Park[b] arrive at the rate of 15 customers per hour. The entry booth to the park is staffed by one theme park employee. The mean service time at the booth to provide service to each customer is 3 minutes. The arrival rate of customers follows a Poisson distribution and the service time at the booth follows a negative exponential distribution. Determine each of the following performance measures:

a. Capacity utilization for the system.

b. Percentage of time the employee at the service booth will be idle.

c. Average number customers waiting in line (queue).

d. Average time a customer spends in the system (waiting time plus service time).

e. Probability that five customers are in the system.

SOLUTION

Since the arrival rate λ = 15 per hour, to be consistent, the service time should be converted into an hourly service rate, that is, customers served per hour. This conversion is done (as shown) by restating the service time in hours and then by taking the reciprocal of the resulting value:

(3 minutes per customer / 60 minutes per hour) = 1 / 20 = 1 / μ
Thus, μ = 20.

a. Capacity utilization for the system (ρ):

$$\rho = \frac{\lambda}{\mu} = 15/20 = 0.75 \text{ or } 75\%$$

b. Percentage of time the employee at the service booth will be idle:

$$= 1 - \rho = 1 - 0.75 = 0.25 \text{ or } 25\%$$

Note: This also means that the probability that no customers are in the waiting line system, P_0, is also 25%.

---

[b]Unless otherwise stated, in the Examples, Solved Problems, and Problems, fictional company names are used.

c. Average number customers waiting in line (L_q):

$$L_q = \frac{\lambda^2}{\mu(\mu - \lambda)} = \frac{15^2}{20(20 - 15)} = 2.25 \text{ customers}$$

d. Average time a customer spends in the system (W_s):

$$W_s = \frac{1}{\mu - \lambda} = = \frac{1}{20 - 15} = 0.20 \text{ hours, or 12 minutes}$$

e. Probability that exactly n = 5 customers are in the waiting line system (P_5):

$$P_5 = (\frac{\lambda}{\mu})^5 \times P_0 = (\frac{15}{20})^5 \times (1 - \frac{15}{20}) = 0.059 \text{ or } 5.9\%$$

All of the queuing models discussed in this model can be solved using Microsoft Excel (Redmond, WA). Screenshot C.1 shows the Excel solution to Example C.1.

SCREENSHOT C.1: Excel Solution to Example C.1: The Single-Server (M/M/1) Model

	A	B	C	D	E	F	G
	Module C-Example C-1: Single Server Model						
	Input Data						
	Arrival Rate (λ)		15	customers per hour			
	Average Service time		3	minutes per customer			
	Service rate (μ)		20	customers per hour			
	Performance Measures						
	Capacity utilization for the system (ρ)	0.75			=(B4/B6)		
	Probability that no customers are in the system (P₀)	0.25			=(1-(B4/B6))		
	Average number customers waiting in line (L_q)	2.25			=((B4)^2/(B6*(B6-B4)))		
	Average time a customer spends in the system (W_s)	0.2			=(1/(B6-B4))		
	Probability of exactly 5 customers in the system (P_5)	0.059			=((B4/B6)^5*B11)		

EXAMPLE C.2: The owner of the Golden Beach Amusement Park, Lara Brown, is interested in computing the per day total cost of the waiting line system for entry into the amusement park. She has estimated that the cost of customer waiting time associated with dissatisfied customers and loss of goodwill is $12 per hour. The employee at the service booth in the park is paid $8 an hour. Assume that the park is open 10 hours per day. Given the above information and the data in Example C.1, calculate:

a. Average customer waiting time cost per day in the queue.

b. Total expected costs per day for the waiting line system.

SOLUTION

To compute the average customer waiting time cost in the queue, we should first compute the average time a customer spends waiting in line for service (W_q). This given by:

$$W_q = \frac{\lambda}{\mu(\mu - \lambda)} = \frac{L_q}{\lambda} = \frac{2.25}{15} = 0.15 \text{ hour per customer}$$

Given an average of 15 customer arrivals per hour, the average number of customer arrivals per day to the park is 15 × 10 = 150 customers. Thus, the average total number of hours customers wait for entry into the park per day is:

0.15 × 150 = 22.5 hours

a. The average customer waiting time cost in the queue is:

22.5 × $12 = $270.

In addition to the above cost, the only other cost that Lara Brown has to compute is the capacity-related cost associated with the service booth employee for the park. This is the hourly salary of $8 paid to the employee. Hence the total capacity related cost per day is $8 × 10 hours = $80. Thus

b. Total expected costs per day for the waiting line system is:

Total expected costs per day = average customer waiting time cost per day + capacity related cost per day

$$= \$270 + \$80 = \$350.$$

Screenshot C.2 shows the Excel solution to Example C.2.

SCREENSHOT C.2: Excel Solution to Example C.2: The Single-Server (M/M/1) Model

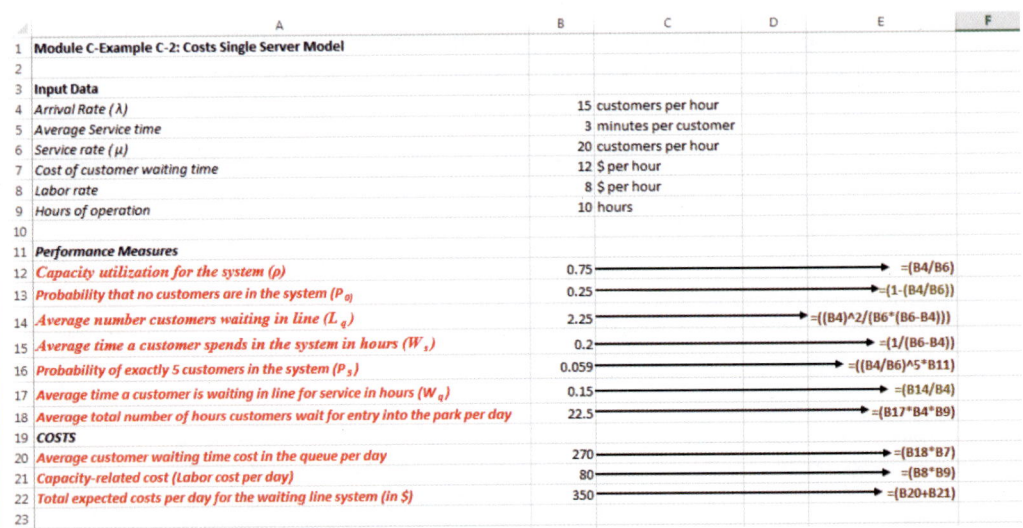

	A	B	C	D	E	F
1	Module C-Example C-2: Costs Single Server Model					
2						
3	**Input Data**					
4	Arrival Rate (λ)	15	customers per hour			
5	Average Service time	3	minutes per customer			
6	Service rate (μ)	20	customers per hour			
7	Cost of customer waiting time	12	$ per hour			
8	Labor rate	8	$ per hour			
9	Hours of operation	10	hours			
10						
11	**Performance Measures**					
12	Capacity utilization for the system (ρ)	0.75			=(B4/B6)	
13	Probability that no customers are in the system (P_0)	0.25			=(1-(B4/B6))	
14	Average number customers waiting in line (L_q)	2.25			=((B4)^2/(B6*(B6-B4)))	
15	Average time a customer spends in the system in hours (W_s)	0.2			=(1/(B6-B4))	
16	Probability of exactly 5 customers in the system (P_5)	0.059			=((B4/B6)^5*B11)	
17	Average time a customer is waiting in line for service in hours (W_q)	0.15			=(B14/B4)	
18	Average total number of hours customers wait for entry into the park per day	22.5			=(B17*B4*B9)	
19	**COSTS**					
20	Average customer waiting time cost in the queue per day	270			=(B18*B7)	
21	Capacity-related cost (Labor cost per day)	80			=(B8*B9)	
22	Total expected costs per day for the waiting line system (in $)	350			=(B20+B21)	
23						

Model II: Single-Channel or Server, Constant Service Rate Queuing Model

For some service systems, such as an automatic carwash or amusement park rides, the assumption of constant service times (instead of the negative exponential distribution) is valid. In waiting line facilities like these, service is provided in fixed cycles (for example, the service time to wash every car in an automatic carwash can be fixed at a constant 5 minutes). Unlike the M/M/1 model that assumes variability in both arrival and service rates, the assumption of constant service rate cuts the average number of customers waiting in line (L_q) and the average waiting time in the queue (W_q) by half. The notation used in queuing theory for this model is M/D/1. The letter M refers to Poisson distribution of arrival rates, the letter D refers to constant service rate, and 1 refers to a single channel or server. The formulas for the M/D/1 model are given in Table C.2.

TABLE C.2: Formulas to Measure Performance of the M/D/1 Model

$$L_q = \text{Average number customers waiting in line (queue)} = \frac{\lambda^2}{2\mu(\mu - \lambda)}$$

$$W_q = \text{Average time a customer spends waiting in line for service} = \frac{\lambda}{2\mu(\mu - \lambda)}$$

$$L_s = \text{Average number of customers in the system} = L_q + \frac{\lambda}{\mu}$$

$$W_s = \text{Average time a customer spends in the system} = W_q + \frac{1}{\mu}$$

EXAMPLE C.3: An automatic carwash with a single bay takes a constant four minutes to wash a car. Cars on a Friday afternoon arrive at the rate of 12 per hour. The arrival rate of cars tends to follow a Poisson distribution. Compute:

a. The average number of cars waiting in line for the carwash.

b. The average time cars spend in the system (waiting in line plus the wash).

SOLUTION

Given $\lambda = 12$ per hour and $\mu = 15$ per hour. (The service time for each car is 4 minutes, and so the facility can process 15 cars in 60 minutes.)

a. The average number of cars waiting in line for the wash (L_q):

$$L_q = \frac{\lambda^2}{2\mu(\mu - \lambda)} = \frac{12^2}{2 \times 15 \times (15 - 12)} = 1.6 \text{ cars}$$

b. The average time cars spend in the system (W_s):

$$W_s = W_q + \frac{1}{\mu} = \frac{\lambda}{2\mu(\mu - \lambda)} + \frac{1}{\mu} = \frac{12}{2 \times 15 \times (15 - 12)} + \frac{1}{15} = 0.2 \text{ or } 12 \text{ minutes}$$

Screenshot C.3 shows the Excel solution to Example C.3.

SCREENSHOT C.3: Excel Solution to Example C.3: The Single-Server (M/D/1) Model

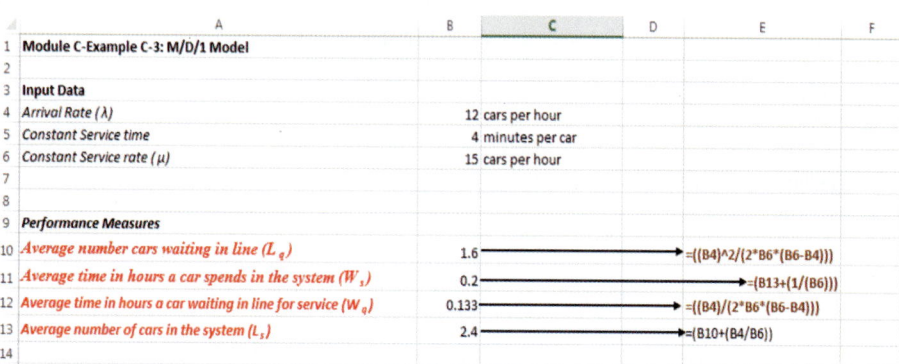

Model III: Multiple-Channel or Multiple-Server Queuing Model

In many real-life situations, we can find waiting line systems in which service is provided to customers in a single phase with multiple servers. In such systems, we still assume that customers wait in a single line and receive service from the first available servers on a first-come, first-served basis. Examples of such waiting line systems can be found in banks, the post office, or security screening at airports. All the assumptions that we made for the M/M/1 model still hold. In addition, we also assume that all the servers perform at the same average rate. The letter S in the M/M/S notation refers to multiple servers. The equations that can be used to compute the various performance measures for the M/M/S system are presented in Table C.3.

TABLE C.3: Formulas to Measure Performance of the M/M/S Model

S = Number of open channels
λ = Average number of arrivals per unit of time

(Continued)

TABLE C.3: *(Continued)*

μ = Average number of customers or objects served per unit of time

n = Number of customers in the queuing system

ρ = Capacity utilization for the system = $\dfrac{\lambda}{S\mu}$

P_0 = Probability that no customers are in the waiting line system, that is, the service facility is idle

$$P_0 = \frac{1}{\left[\sum_{n=0}^{S-1}\dfrac{1}{n!}\left(\dfrac{\lambda}{\mu}\right)^n\right] + \dfrac{1}{S!}\left(\dfrac{\lambda}{\mu}\right)^S \dfrac{S\mu}{S\mu-\lambda}}$$

P_n = Probability that n customers are in the waiting line system

$$P_n = \begin{cases} \dfrac{1}{S!S^{n-s}}\left(\dfrac{\lambda}{\mu}\right)^n P_0 & \text{for } n > S \\[2ex] \dfrac{1}{S!}\left(\dfrac{\lambda}{\mu}\right)^n P_0 & \text{for } n \geq S \end{cases}$$

P_w = Probability that an arriving customer must wait for service

$$P_w = \frac{1}{S!}\left(\frac{\lambda}{\mu}\right)^S \frac{S\mu}{S\mu-\lambda}\; P_0$$

L_s = Average number of customers in the waiting line system (waiting and being served)

$$L_s = \frac{\lambda\mu\left(\frac{\lambda}{\mu}\right)^S}{(S-1)!(S\mu-\lambda)^2}\; P_0 + \frac{\lambda}{\mu}$$

W_s = Average time a customer spends in the system (waiting time plus service time)

$$W_s = \frac{Ls}{\lambda}$$

L_q = Average number customers waiting in line (queue) = $L_s - \dfrac{\lambda}{\mu}$

W_q = Average time a customer spends waiting in line for service = $W_s - \dfrac{1}{\mu} = \dfrac{Lq}{\lambda}$

EXAMPLE C.4: Lara Brown, the owner of the Golden Beach Amusement Park, has decided to open a second entry booth and hire another employee to service customers entering the amusement park. Customers arrive at the rate of 15 per hour and will wait in a single line until one of the two employees is available to provide service. Each employee at each service booth takes an average of 3 minutes to provide service to a customer. The arrival rate of customers follows a Poisson distribution, and the service time at the booth follows a negative exponential distribution:

a. Compute the performance measures listed in Table C.3 for this multichannel waiting line system.

b. If the cost of customer waiting time associated with dissatisfied customers and loss of goodwill is $12 per hour and each employee at the service booth in the park is paid $8 an hour, compute the average customer waiting time cost per day in the queue, and the total expected costs per day for the waiting line system. Assume that the park is open 10 hours per day.

SOLUTION

Given:

S = Number of open channels = 2

λ = Average number of arrivals per hour = 15

μ = Average number of customers served per hour = 3 / 60 = 20

P_0 = Probability that no customers are in the waiting line system is:

$$P_0 = \cfrac{1}{\left[\sum_{n=0}^{S-1}\dfrac{1}{n!}\left(\dfrac{\lambda}{\mu}\right)^n\right] + \dfrac{1}{S!}\left(\dfrac{\lambda}{\mu}\right)^S\dfrac{S\mu}{S\mu-\lambda}}$$

$$P_0 = \cfrac{1}{\left[\sum_{n=0}^{2-1}\dfrac{1}{n!}\left(\dfrac{15}{20}\right)^n\right] + \dfrac{1}{2!}\left(\dfrac{15}{20}\right)^2\dfrac{2\times20}{2\times20-15}} = \cfrac{1}{\left[1+\left(\dfrac{15}{20}\right)\right] + \dfrac{1}{2}\times\dfrac{225}{400}\times\dfrac{40}{25}} = 0.45$$

P_3 = Probability that 3 customers are in the waiting line system. Because n > S, we have:

$$P_3 = \frac{1}{S!S^{n-s}}\left(\frac{\lambda}{\mu}\right)^n P_0 = \frac{1}{2!2^{3-2}}\left(\frac{15}{20}\right)^3 * 0.45 = 0.0474$$

P_w = Probability that an arriving customer must wait for service:

$$P_w = \frac{1}{S!}\left(\frac{\lambda}{\mu}\right)^S\frac{S\mu}{S\mu-\lambda} P_0 = = \frac{1}{2!}\left(\frac{15}{20}\right)^2\frac{2\times20}{2\times20-15}\times 0.45 = 0.2025$$

L_s = Average number of customers in the waiting line system (waiting and being served):

$$L_s = \frac{\lambda\mu\left(\frac{\lambda}{\mu}\right)^S}{(S-1)!(S\mu-\lambda)^2}P_0 + \frac{\lambda}{\mu} = \frac{15\times20\times\left(\dfrac{15}{20}\right)^2}{(2-1)!\times(2\times20-15)^2}\times 0.45 + \frac{15}{20} = 0.8715$$

W_s = Average time a customer spends in the system (waiting time plus service time):

$$W_s = \frac{Ls}{\lambda} = \frac{0.8715}{15} = 0.0581 \text{ hours or } 3.5 \text{ minutes}$$

L_q = Average number customers waiting in line = $L_s - \dfrac{\lambda}{\mu}$ = $0.8715 - \dfrac{15}{20} = 0.1215$

W_q = Average time a customer spends in line = $\dfrac{Lq}{\lambda} = \dfrac{0.1215}{15} = 0.008$ hours (0.486 minutes)

We will now compute the costs for this multichannel waiting line system: Average customer waiting time cost per day in the queue, and the total expected costs per day for the waiting line system.

The average customer waiting time cost in the queue:

Given an average of 15 customer arrivals per hour, the average number of customer arrivals per day to the park is:

15 × 10 = 150 customers

Since the average time a customer spends waiting in line for service is W_q = 0.008 hour per customer, the average total number of hours customers wait for entry into the park per day is:

0.008 × 150 = 1.2 hours

Thus, the average customer waiting time cost in the queue is:

1.2 × $12 = $14.40

In addition to this cost, the only other cost that Lara Brown has to compute is the capacity-related cost associated with the service booth employees for the park. This is the hourly salary of $8 paid to each employee. Hence, the total capacity-related cost per day is 2 × $8 × 10 hours = $160. Thus, the total expected cost per day for the waiting line system is:

Average customer waiting time cost per day + capacity related cost per day

= $14.40 + $160.00 = $174.40

You can see from the solution to Example C.4 that the expected total costs for the two-channel waiting line system are about half of that for a the single-channel system (Example C.2). Also, note that the formulas for the performance measures for a multichannel queuing system are significantly more complex than they are for single-channel system. We illustrated the use of these formulas by solving Example C.4 primarily for the purpose of completeness. Instead of going through the cumbersome calculations, you can use Table C.4 to determine the values of L_q and P_0 for selected values of λ, μ, and M. Once L_q and P_0 are known, the values of the other performance measures can be easily computed. Screenshot C.4 shows the Excel solution to Example C.4.

SCREENSHOT C.4: Excel Solution to Example C.4: The Multiple-Server (M/M/S) Model

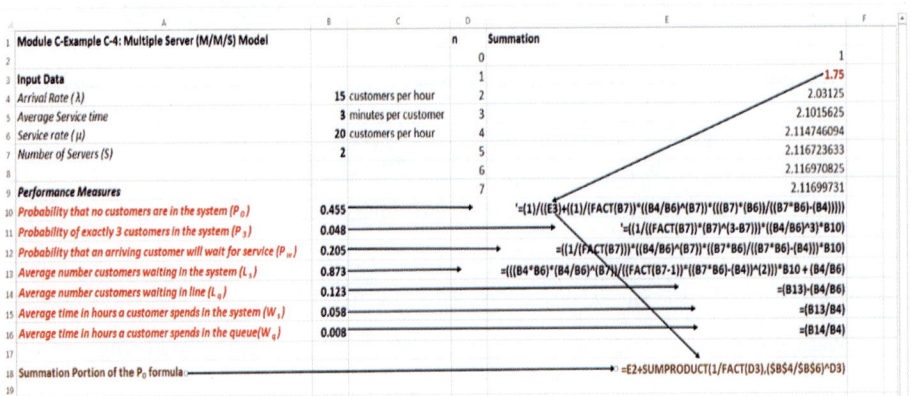

You can see from Example C.4 and its calculations that formulas in multiple-server models are considerably more complex (particularly for L_q and P_0) than are the formulas in single-server models.

Little's Law

 Little's Law

Little's law is a simple and commonly used theorem in queuing theory. The law makes very few assumptions except that the system is at a steady state. Steady state means that the number of customers or objects in a waiting line system is the same as the number of customers or objects leaving the system—the arrival rate is equal to the service rate. Except for this steady state assumption, Little's law does not make any other assumptions, such as about the probability distribution of customer arrivals or service times, number of servers in the queuing system, or about the queue discipline (such as FIFO). Little's law can be written as:

$$L = \lambda \times W$$

where

L = average number of customers or objects in the queuing system

W = average waiting time in the system for a customer or an object

λ = average number of customers/objects arriving per unit time, or the arrival rate

This relationship is so simple and general that it can be applied to many different queuing systems. For example, let us assume that at an oil and filter change shop, customers arrive at the rate of 8 per hour and wait for an average of 0.5 hour in the shop. Applying Little's law, we have:

$$L = \lambda \times W = 8 \times 0.5 = 4$$

The result shows that the average number of customers in the shop at any given time will be 4. Now, let us assume that the shop wants to increase its business through advertising and promotion campaigns to double the customer arrival rate from 8 to 16 per hour. Applying Little's law, we have:

$$L = \lambda \times W = 16 \times 0.5 = 8$$

This result tells us that the shop must now either increase its capacity to accommodate an average of 8 customers or reduce the waiting time in the system from an average of 0.5 to 0.25 hour. Little's law

Little's law: a simple and commonly used theorem in queuing theory. It makes very few assumptions except that the system is at a steady state

TABLE C.4: L_q and P_o Values for M = 1 to 6 and Selected Values of λ/μ

	POISSON ARRIVALS AND EXPONENTIAL SERVICE TIMES											
	NUMBER OF SERVERS, M											
	1		2		3		4		5		6	
λ/μ	L_q	P_o	L_q	P_o	L_q	P_o	L_q	P_o	L_q	P_o	L_q	P_o
0.10	0.011											
0.15	0.026	0.850	0.001	0.860								
0.20	0.050	0.800	0.002	0.818								
0.25	0.083	0.750	0.004	0.778								
0.30	0.129	0.700	0.007	0.739								
0.35	0.188	0.650	0.011	0.702								
0.40	0.267	0.600	0.017	0.667								
0.45	0.368	0.550	0.024	0.633	0.002	0.637						
0.50	0.500	0.500	0.033	0.600	0.003	0.606						
0.55	0.672	0.450	0.045	0.569	0.004	0.576						
0.60	0.900	0.400	0.059	0.538	0.006	0.548						
0.65	1.207	0.350	0.077	0.509	0.008	0.521						
0.70	1.633	0.300	0.098	0.481	0.011	0.495						
0.75	2.250	0.250	0.123	0.455	0.015	0.471						
0.80	3.200	0.200	0.152	0.429	0.019	0.447						
0.85	4.817	0.150	0.187	0.404	0.024	0.425	0.003	0.427				
0.90	8.100	0.100	0.229	0.379	0.030	0.403	0.004	0.406				
0.95	18.050	0.050	0.277	0.356	0.037	0.383	0.005	0.386				
1.00			0.333	0.333	0.045	0.364	0.007	0.367				
1.10			0.477	0.290	0.066	0.327	0.011	0.332				
1.20			0.675	0.250	0.094	0.294	0.016	0.300	0.003	0.301		
1.30			0.951	0.212	0.130	0.264	0.023	0.271	0.004	0.272		
1.40			1.345	0.176	0.177	0.236	0.032	0.245	0.006	0.246		
1.50			1.929	0.143	0.237	0.211	0.045	0.221	0.009	0.223		
1.60			2.844	0.111	0.313	0.187	0.060	0.199	0.012	0.201		
1.70			4.426	0.081	0.409	0.166	0.080	0.180	0.017	0.182		
1.80			7.673	0.053	0.532	0.146	0.105	0.162	0.023	0.165		
1.90			17.587	0.026	0.688	0.128	0.136	0.145	0.030	0.149	0.007	0.149
2.00					0.889	0.111	0.174	0.130	0.040	0.134	0.009	0.135
2.10					1.149	0.096	0.220	0.117	0.052	0.121	0.012	0.122

(Continued)

TABLE C.4: (Continued)

	POISSON ARRIVALS AND EXPONENTIAL SERVICE TIMES											
	NUMBER OF SERVERS, M											
	1		2		3		4		5		6	
λ/μ	L_Q	P_0	L_Q	P_0	L_Q	P_0	L_Q	P_0	L_Q	P_0	L_Q	P_0
2.20					1.491	0.081	0.277	0.105	0.066	0.109	0.016	0.111
2.30					1.951	0.068	0.346	0.093	0.084	0.099	0.021	0.100
2.40					2.589	0.056	0.431	0.083	0.105	0.089	0.027	0.090
2.50					3.511	0.045	0.533	0.074	0.130	0.080	0.034	0.082
2.60					4.933	0.035	0.658	0.065	0.161	0.072	0.043	0.074
2.70					7.354	0.025	0.811	0.057	0.198	0.065	0.053	0.067
2.80					12.273	0.016	1.000	0.050	0.241	0.058	0.066	0.060
2.90					27.193	0.008	1.234	0.044	0.293	0.052	0.081	0.054
3.00							1.528	0.038	0.354	0.047	0.099	0.049
3.10							1.902	0.032	0.427	0.042	0.120	0.044
3.20							2.386	0.027	0.513	0.037	0.145	0.040
3.30							3.027	0.023	0.615	0.033	0.174	0.036
3.40							3.906	0.019	0.737	0.029	0.209	0.032
3.50							5.165	0.015	0.882	0.026	0.248	0.029
3.60							7.090	0.011	1.055	0.023	0.295	0.026
3.70							10.347	0.008	1.265	0.020	0.349	0.023
3.80							16.937	0.005	1.519	0.017	0.412	0.021
3.90							36.859	0.002	1.830	0.015	0.485	0.019
4.00									2.216	0.013	0.570	0.017
4.10									2.703	0.011	0.668	0.015
4.20									3.327	0.009	0.784	0.013
4.30									4.149	0.008	0.919	0.012
4.40									5.268	0.006	1.078	0.010
4.50									6.862	0.005	1.265	0.009
4.60									9.289	0.004	1.487	0.008
4.70									13.382	0.003	1.752	0.007
4.80									21.641	0.002	2.071	0.006
4.90									46.566	0.001	2.459	0.005
5.00											2.938	0.005

can be applied to subsystems within a larger system. For example, in the oil and filter shop, there is an average of 6 cars waiting in queue (L_q) at the bay. Given a λ of 8 cars arriving per hour we have:

$$L_q = \lambda \times W_q$$

or

$$W_q = L_q / \lambda = 6/8 = 0.75 \text{ or } 45 \text{ minutes of average waiting time in the queue}$$

Little's law also can be used to determine the average inventory levels in inventory control systems. Suppose a unit of an item stays in an inventory system for an average of 7 days. If the demand rate for this item is 10 units per day, then the average inventory level for this item in the inventory system should be:

$$L = \lambda \times W = 10 \times 7 = 70 \text{ units}$$

These examples illustrate that Little's law can be applied to a wide variety of queuing model situations, except the finite population model, which we discuss next.

Model IV: Finite Population Queuing Model

The three queuing models that we have discussed thus far assume that customer or object arrival to the waiting line system is from an unlimited population of potential customers. There are, however, some waiting line systems in which the number of customers arriving at the service facility originates from a population that has only a limited number of potential customers. Some examples of a finite population of potential customers include several processes to be run by a computer, a certain number of machines assigned for repair to a technician in a maintenance and repair shop, or a group of patients assigned to a nurse for patient care in a hospital. In each of these examples, the size of the population of potential customers—number of processes, number of machines, and number of patients—is finite. For example, the nurse in a hospital may be responsible for providing care for 12 patients; thus, the size of the calling population is 12. Note that there may be more than one nurse (server or channel) on the medical ward or service area in question. For example, depending on the extent of care required for the 12 patients, another nurse may be assigned to provide patient care.

The finite population queuing model, like the infinite population models, also assumes that the arrival rates have a Poisson distribution and the service times have a negative exponential probability distribution. The significant difference between the two models is that in the case of a finite calling population model, the length of the queue has an *impact* on the arrival rate. That is, the arrival rate is *dependent* on the length of the queue. As the length of the queue increases, the arrival rate decreases because there are now fewer customers in the population requiring service. At the limit, when all the potential customers are waiting in line for service at the same time, the arrival rate is zero as there are no more customers to be served in the population.

Let us illustrate the concept of the impact on arrival rate with an example. Assume that 1 of the 12 patients assigned to a nurse requires care (service). The size of the population of patients is now reduced to 11, and the probability that 1 of the remaining 11 patients requiring care is different from the probability of 1 out of 12—the original population size. If 2 patients require care, then there are only 10 remaining patients and the probability of yet another patient requiring care will again change. Conversely, when a patient is cared for and returned to the population, the finite patient population size increases, and the probability of a patient requiring care changes again. Because the formulas required for computing the performance measures of a finite population queuing model are complex, finite population queuing tables that have been developed, along with simple formulas, are used to analyze such systems. Table C.5 presents some of the key formulas required for analyzing the finite population queuing model. Note that the notation used in this model differs from that in the three infinite population queuing models. Also, Table C.6 on page 828 displays a portion of the published finite population queuing tables that provide data to be used for the formulas in Table C.5 for a population of size N = 5.[4]

To use Table C.6 to compute the values for the formulas in Table C.5, we follow these steps:

Step 1: For a given population size, N, and the number service channels, M, compute the value of X, the service factor using the formula given in Table C.5:

$$X = T/ (T + U)$$

TABLE C.5: Notation and Formulas for the Performance Measures of a Finite Population Queuing Model

---

Notation

D = Probability that a customer or object will have to wait in queue

F = Efficiency Factor = 1 – Percentage of customers or objects waiting in queue

H = Average number of customer or objects being served

J = Average number of customers or objects not in queue or in service

L = Average number of customers or objects waiting for service

M = Number of service channels

N = Number of potential customers

T = Average service time

U = Average time between customer or object service requirements per customer/object

W = Average time a customer or object waits in line

X = Service factor

Performance Measures

Service factor: $X = \dfrac{T}{T+U}$

Average number waiting: $= L = N(1-F)$

Average waiting time: $W = \dfrac{L(T+U)}{N-L} = \dfrac{T(1-F)}{T+U}$

Average number running: $J = NF(1-X)$
Average number being served: $H = FNX$
Number in Population: $N = J + L + H$

SOURCE: Adapted from Peck, L. G., & Hazelwood, R. N. (1958). *Finite queuing tables.* New York: Wiley.

TABLE C.6: Finite Queuing Tables for a Population of N = 5

X	M	D	F	X	M	D	F	X	M	D	F	X	M	D	F
.012	1	0.48	.999	.050	1	.198	.989	.070	2	.027	.999	.120	2	.076	.995
									1	.275	.977		1	.456	.927
.019	1	.076	.998	.052	1	.206	.988	.075	2	.031	.999	.125	2	.082	.994
									1	.294	.973		1	.473	.920
.025	1	.100	.997	.054	1	.214	.987	.080	2	.035	.998	.130	2	.089	.933
									1	.313	.969		1	.489	.914
.030	1	.120	.996	.056	2	.018	.999	.085	2	.040	.998	.135	2	.095	.993
					1	.222	.985		1	.332	.965		1	.505	.907
.034	1	.135	.995	.058	2	.019	.999	.090	2	0.44	.988	.140	2	.102	.992
					1	.229	.984		1	.350	.960		1	.521	.900
.036	1	.143	.994	.060	2	.020	.999	.095	2	.049	.997	.145	3	.011	.999
					1	.237	.983		1	.368	.955		2	.109	.991
													1	.537	.892
.040	1	.159	.993	.062	2	.022	.999	.100	2	.054	.997	.150	3	.012	.999
					1	.245	.982		1	.386	.950		2	.115	.990
													1	.568	.877
.042	1	.167	.992	.064	2	.023	.999	.105	2	.059	.997	.155	3	.013	.999
					1	.253	.981		1	.404	.945		2	.123	.989
													1	.568	.877

X	M	D	F	X	M	D	F	X	M	D	F	X	M	D	F
.044	1	.175	.991	.066	2	.024	.999	.110	2	.065	.996	.160	3	.015	.999
					1	.260	.979		1	.421	.939		2	.130	.988
													1	.582	.869
.046	1	.183	.990	.068	2	.026	.999	.115	2	.071	.995	.165	3	.016	.999
					1	.268	.978		1	.439	.933		2	.137	.987
													1	.597	.861
.170	3	.017	.999	.260	3	.058	.994	.360	4	.017	.998	.540	4	.085	.989
	2	.145	.985		2	.303	.950		3	.141	.981		3	.392	.917
	1	.611	.853		1	.811	.695		2	.501	.880		2	.806	.708
									1	.927	.542		1	.991	.370
.180	3	.021	.999	.270	3	.064	.994	.308	4	.021	.998	.560	4	.098	.986
	2	.161	.983		2	.323	.944		3	.163	.976		3	.426	.906
	1	.638	.836		1	.827	.677		2	.540	.863		2	.831	.689
									1	.941	.516		1	.993	.357
.190	3	.024	.998	.280	3	.071	.993	.400	4	.026	.977	.580	4	.113	.984
	2	.117	.980		2	.342	.938		3	.186	.972		3	.461	.895
	1	.665	.819		1	.842	.661		2	.579	.845		2	.854	.670
									1	.952	.493		1	.994	.345
.200	3	.032	.998	.290	4	.007	.999	.420	4	.031	.997	.600	4	.130	.981
	2	.194	.976		3	.079	.992		3	.211	.966		3	.497	.883
	1	.986	.801		2	.362	.932		2	.616	.826		2	.875	.652
					1	.856	.644		1	.961	.471		1	.998	.308
.210	3	.032	.998	.300	4	.008	.999	.440	4	.037	.996	.650	4	.179	.972
	2	.211	.973		3	.086	.990		3	.238	.960		3	.588	.850
	1	.713	.783		2	.382	.926		2	.652	.807		2	.918	.608
					1	.869	.628		1	.969	.451		1	.998	.308
.220	3	.036	.997	.310	4	.009	.999	.460	4	.045	.995	.700	4	.240	.960
	2	.229	.969		3	.094	.989		3	.266	.953		3	.678	.815
	1	.735	.765		2	.402	.919		2	.686	.787		2	.950	.568
					1	.881	.613		1	.975	.432		1	.999	.286
.230	3	.041	.997	.320	4	.010	.999	.480	4	.053	.994	.750	4	.316	.944
		.247	.965		3	.103	.988		3	.296	.945				.777
		.756	.747		2	.422	.912		2	.719	.767				.532
					1	.892	.597		1	.980	.415				
.240	3	.046	.996	.330	4	.012	.999	.500	4	.063	.992	.800	4	.410	.924
	2	.265	.960		3	.112	.986		3	.327	.936		3	.841	.739
	1	.775	.730		3	.442	.904		2	.750	.748		2	.987	.500
					2	.442	.904		2	.985	.399				
					1	.902	.583								
.250	3	.052	.995	.340	4	.013	.999	.520	4	.073	.991	.850	4	.522	.900
	2	.284	.955		3	.121	.985		3	.359	.927		3	.907	.702
	1	.794	.712		2	.462	.896		2	.779	.728		2	.995	.470
					1	.911	.569		1	.988	.384				

SOURCE: Adapted from Peck, L. G., & Hazelwood, R. N. (1958). *Finite queuing tables*. New York: Wiley.

where

T is the average service time

U is the average time between customer service requirements

Step 2: For computed value X in Step 1 and the given value of M, locate the values of D and F in Table C.6.

Step 3: Using the values of N, M, X, D, and F, compute the performance measures needed using the formulas in Table C.5.

Step 4: Compute relevant costs if needed to make a decision.

EXAMPLE C.5: M & J Machine Shop specializes in repair and maintenance of industrial grinding machines. Dan Hacker, the only repair technician, has been assigned five identical grinding machines for repair and maintenance. The machines break down after about 25 hours of use, and the breakdowns have a Poisson probability distribution. It takes Dan Hacker about five hours to repair a machine, and the repair times are found to follow an exponential distribution. Machine downtime costs the company $200 an hour, and Dan Hacker is paid $40 an hour. Determine whether the M & J shop needs a second repair technician.

SOLUTION

Given: N = 5, M = 1, U = 25 hours, T = 5
   Therefore,

Step 1:

$$X = \frac{T}{T+U} = \frac{5}{5+25} = \frac{1}{6} = 0.166 \text{ (close to 0.165 for determining the values of D and F)}$$

Step 2:

For N = 5, M = 1, and X = 0.165, D = 0.597, and F = 0.861

For N = 5, M = 2, and X = 0.165, D = 0.137, and F = 0.987

Step 3: To determine whether the shop needs another repair technician, we first have to determine the average number of machines that will break down. To do so, we need to determine J, the average number of machines working, that is, that are not waiting for repair or in service for both M = 1 and 2.

The average number of machines working, J = N × F × (1 − X)

For M = 1: J = 5 × 0.861 × (1 − 0.165) = 3.59

For M = 2: J = 5 × 0.987 × (1 − 0.165) = 4.12

Step 4: Compute the relevant costs associated with having one or two repair technicians available to make the appropriate decision. These computations are shown as follows.

NUMBER OF TECHNICIANS (M)	AVERAGE NUMBER OF MACHINES DOWN (N − J)	AVERAGE COST PER HOUR OF DOWNTIME (N − J) × $200	COST PER HOUR FOR TECHNICIANS ($40 PER HOUR)	TOTAL COST PER HOUR
1	5 − 3.59 = 1.41	1.41 × $200 = $282	$40	$322
2	5 − 4.12 = 0.88	0.88 × $200 = $176	$80	$256

The M & J Machine shop should hire a second repair technician. By doing so the shop will reduce cost by $66 per hour.

Other Considerations in Waiting Line Systems

In real life, many waiting line systems have features of the four basic models that we have discussed in this module. Nevertheless, in practice, there are many complex waiting line systems that require more complex queuing models and mathematical formulas than those we have presented. For example, potential airline passengers have to go through multichannel, multiphase waiting line systems before they can board a plane. Similarly, in a university's course registration process for a semester, students go through a first-come, first-served priority queuing procedure, with graduating senior students getting the first choice of courses and class hours over other students. Also, although the assumptions of Poisson and exponential probability distributions for arrival rates and service times are usually valid for many real-world waiting line systems, other probability distributions (such as a normal distribution) also exist for arrival rates and service times in many practical waiting line systems.

Virtual Queuing

Managers develop performance measures for waiting line systems for the sole purpose of designing a service system that can balance the capacity-related costs against the expected costs associated with customers waiting in line. Yet, there are many real-life service organizations in which costs are less important than providing quick service. For example, paramedics, police, and fire departments are expected to have enough capacity to respond quickly to customer demand for service. Nonetheless, such service providers often have excess capacity that leads to extended periods of underutilization of employee resources.

Waiting in lines is a pervasive phenomenon in everyday life, both for individuals and for businesses. Despite their best efforts to provide sufficient capacity, service providers realize that it is not possible to reduce the length of waiting lines or to provide quicker service beyond a point. Therefore, to reduce customer dissatisfaction associated with long waits, many service providers recognize that, in addition to the science of queuing theory and waiting line models, important perceptual and psychological steps can be taken to minimize the appearance of excessive waits and, therefore, minimize customer dissatisfaction. In fact, the case at the end of this module refers to the psychology of waiting lines and steps to ease the burdens of perceived excessive waiting. Ultimately, organizations need to adopt a combination of techniques to offer the highest possible level of service, despite the need for queuing and waiting lines.

Visit edge.sagepub.com/venkataraman to help you accomplish your coursework goals in an easy-to-use learning environment.

- Mobile-friendly eFlashcards
- Mobile-friendly practice quizzes
- A complete online action plan
- Chapter summaries with learning objectives
- Video and multimedia resources

MODULE SUMMARY

C.1 Identify the various cost implications and features of waiting lines. The primary objective of managing waiting lines is to minimize their total costs throughout any service or manufacturing facility. This total cost is composed of the cost related to customer waiting time and capacity-related cost. The costs related to customer waiting time are tangible and intangible. Tangible costs include wages that must be paid to workers while the facility remains idle and the costs associated with lost productivity. Tangible costs may also include cost of materials used while waiting. Intangible costs include lost sales because customers decided not to wait and received service from a competitor, and costs associated with loss of goodwill as a result of customer dissatisfaction. Capacity-related costs include those costs incurred to maintain existing facility capacity or add additional capacity to provide the required service.

A queue represents a certain number of customers waiting for service at a facility. In queuing theory, a mathematical model of a waiting line system is constructed to predict the lengths of the queues and the associated waiting times in those queues. Several queuing models are available, and to ensure meaningful analysis and results, it is important that the correct model is chosen to represent the waiting line system to be analyzed. The choice of the correct model depends on the following key features of the given waiting line system analyzed: customer population, arrival pattern, queue size and discipline, service system structure, and service pattern.

C.2 Employ the various queuing models and understand when and how to use them to calculate optimal queuing solutions, including the psychology underlying waiting lines. This module identified several assumptions, including:

a. Arrival rates have a Poisson probability distribution.

b. Service times have a negative exponential distribution.

c. First-in, first-out (FIFO) queue discipline.

d. All models assume that the waiting line system is operating under a steady state condition. In other words, the average arrival and service rates remain stable during analysis.

Three common queuing models are (1) the single-channel or single-server queuing model, (2) the single-channel or single-server, constant service rate queuing model, and (3) the multiple-channel or multiple-server queuing model.

The single-channel or single-server queuing model is the simplest and the most frequently encountered waiting line problem, in which there is a single service station that will serve a queue of customers waiting in a single line. The single-channel or single-server, constant service rate queuing model is similar to the first model, but it assumes constant service times. In the multiple-channel or multiple-server queuing model, service is provided to customers in a single phase with multiple servers. In such systems, we still assume that customers wait in a single line and receive service from the first available servers on first-come, first-served basis.

Ultimately, waiting lines and queuing theory represent a challenge that is as much psychological as it is computational. As a result, and despite their best efforts to provide sufficient capacity, service providers realize that it is not possible to reduce the length of waiting lines or provide faster service beyond a point.

Therefore, to reduce customer dissatisfaction associated with long waits, many service providers recognize that there are important perceptual and psychological steps that can be taken to minimize the appearance of excessive waits and, therefore, to minimize customer dissatisfaction. These steps may involve deliberate distractions or other means to minimize the psychological feelings of delay and the dissatisfaction that subsequently accompanies these perceptions.

KEY TERMS

Continuous random variable   814

Discrete random variable   813

Limited (finite) population   813

Little's law   824

Negative exponential distribution   814

Poisson distribution   813

Queue discipline   815

Queue   812

Queuing theory   812

Service rate   816

Service time   816

Unlimited (infinite) population   813

DISCUSSION AND REVIEW QUESTIONS

1. List some reasons why waiting lines occur.

2. What are some of the undesirable consequences of a waiting line?

3. What are the cost implications of managing waiting lines?

4. List the four key features of a waiting line system.

5. The following are some real-world waiting line systems. Indicate whether it is a single- or multichannel, single-phase or multiphase, the queue discipline, and whether the calling populations is limited or unlimited:

   a. A small drug store

   b. A machine repair shop

   c. Getting a driver's license

   d. Beauty salon

   e. Laundromat

6. For most waiting line systems, the first-come, first-served (FCFS) rule is the most frequent assumption of queue discipline. Give some examples of waiting line systems where this assumption would not be appropriate.

7. Give some examples of single-channel waiting line systems with constant service times.

8. Which of the two performance measures is larger: L_s or L_q? Explain.

9. What are the common performance measures calculated for evaluating waiting line systems?

10. What does the term "steady state" mean in the context of a waiting line system?

11. Define in your own words "Little's Law." Why is it applicable to a wide variety of queuing systems?

12. What are some factors you should consider (in addition to choosing a queuing model) in managing real-world waiting lines?

13. Choose a waiting line system that you commonly encounter in your daily life. How would you improve that system by using the knowledge gained from this module?

SOLVED PROBLEMS

1. O'Hare International Airport in Chicago has one airline agent to serve at each gate for checking in passengers on standby, answering questions, and rerouting passengers and so forth. At one of the United Airlines (United Continental Holdings, Inc., Chicago, IL) gate that is most frequently used, in any given day, passengers arrive at the desk of that gate at an average rate of 50 per hour. The average time that the airline agent takes to serve a passenger is 0.8 minutes. Assuming that the arrival rate has a Poisson and the service time has an exponential distribution, compute ρ, P_0, Lq, W_s, P_5, and Wq for this waiting line system, and comment on the quality of service.

Solution:

Since the arrival rate $\lambda = 50$ per hour, to be consistent, the service time should be converted into an hourly service rate, that is, passengers served per hour. This is done (as shown) by restating the service time in hours and then by taking the reciprocal of the resulting value:

(0.8 minutes per customer/60 minutes per hour) = 0.8 / 60 = $1/\mu$. Thus, μ = 60 / 0.8 = 75 passengers per hour:

a. Capacity utilization for the system (ρ):

$$\rho = \frac{\lambda}{\mu} = 50/75 = 0.67 \text{ or } 67\%$$

b. Probability no passengers are in the system = P_0 = Percentage of time the agent at the gate will be idle:

$$P_0 = 1 - \rho = 1 - 0.67 = 0.33 \text{ or } 33\%$$

c. Average number passengers waiting in line (L_q):

$$L_q = \frac{\lambda^2}{\mu(\mu - \lambda)} = \frac{50^2}{75(75 - 50)} = 1.33 \text{ passengers}$$

d. Average time a passenger spends in the system (W_s):

$$W_s = \frac{1}{\mu - \lambda} = \frac{1}{75 - 50} = 0.04 \text{ hours or 2.4 minutes}$$

e. Probability that exactly n = 5 customers are in the waiting line system (P_5):

$$P_5 = (\frac{\lambda}{\mu})^5 \times P_0 = (\frac{50}{75})^5 \times (1 - \frac{50}{75}) = 0.044 \text{ or 4.4\%}$$

f. Average time a passenger spends waiting in line for service (W_q), which is given by:

$$W_q = \frac{\lambda}{\mu(\mu - \lambda)} = \frac{Lq}{\lambda} = \frac{1.33}{50} = 0.0267 \text{ hours or 1.6 minutes per passenger}$$

Given that the average passenger waiting time at the system is less than 3 minutes, the quality of service is quite good. Nevertheless, there is 33% idle capacity in the system.

Screenshot C.5 shows the Excel solution to Solved Problem C.1.

SCREENSHOT C.5: Solved Problem C.1: Airport Gate Single-Server Problem

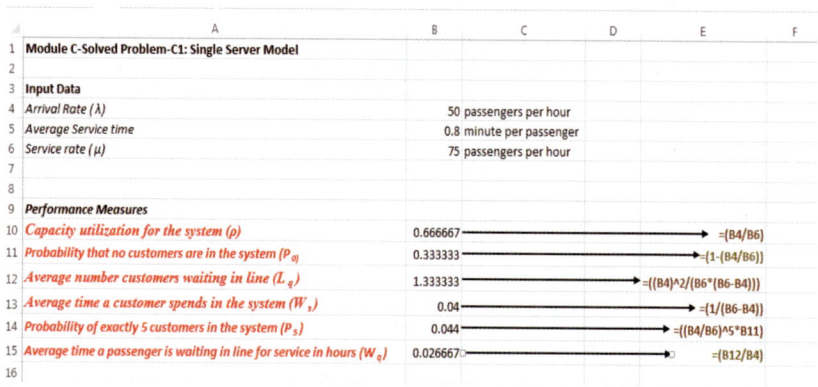

2. Refer to Solved Problem C.1. The management of United Airlines is interested in computing the per day total cost of the waiting line system at this gate in O'Hare International Airport. It has estimated that the cost of passenger waiting time associated with a dissatisfied passenger and loss of good will is $50 per hour and the gate agent is paid $20 an hour. Assume that the gate is open 12 hours per day. Given this information and the data in Solved Problem C.1, compute:

    a. Average customer waiting time cost per day in the queue

    b. Total expected costs per day for the waiting line system

Solution:

a. To compute the average passenger waiting time cost in the queue, we use the average time a passenger waits in line for service (W_q), computed in Solved Problem C.1:

$W_q = 0.0267$ hours per passenger

Given an average of 50 passenger arrivals per hour, the average number of passenger arrivals per day to the gate is 50 × 12 = 600 passengers. Thus, the average total number of hours passengers wait for service at the gate per day is:

0.0267 × 600 = 16 hours

Thus, the average customer waiting time cost in the queue is:

16 × $50 = $900

In addition to this cost, the only other cost that has to be computed is the capacity-related cost associated with the gate agent. This is the hourly salary of $20 paid to the agent. Hence, the total capacity-related cost per day is $20 × 12 hours = $240. Thus:

b. Total expected costs per day for the waiting line system is:

Total expected costs per day = average passenger waiting time cost per day + capacity related cost per day

= $900 + $240 = $1,040

Screenshot C.6 shows the Excel solution to Solved Problem C.2.

SCREENSHOT C.6: Solved Problem C.2: Airport Gate Single-Server Problem Cost

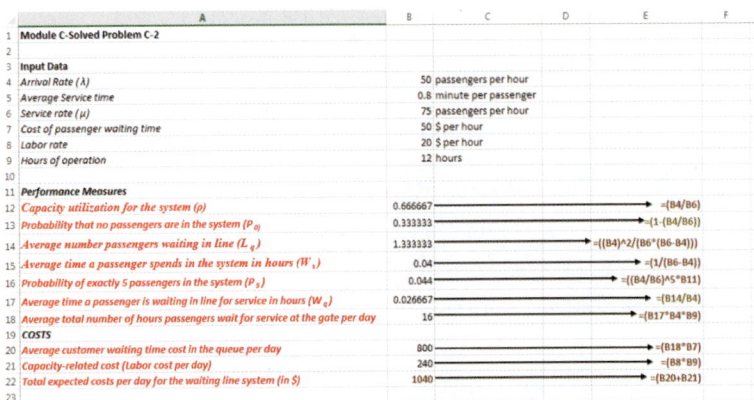

3. The manager of an indoor waterpark resort has installed a new tumbling waterslide. It takes the children a constant 2.4 minutes to complete the slide one at a time. Children arrive to play at the waterslide gate at an average rate of 22 per hour. The arrival rate has a Poisson probability distribution. The manager wants to know the average number of children in the waiting line and the average waiting time for a child to play the waterslide game.

Solution:

Given: $\lambda = 22$ per hour; $\mu = 25$ per hour (service time for each child is 2.4 minutes; hence, 25 children in 60 minutes):

a. The average number of children waiting in line to play in the waterslide (L_q):

$$L_q = \frac{\lambda^2}{2\mu(\mu-1)} = \frac{22^2}{2 \times 25 \times (25-32)} = 3.2 \text{ or 4 children}$$

b. The average time a child waits in the line (W_q):

$$W_q = \frac{\lambda}{2\mu(\mu-1)} = \frac{22}{2 \times 25 \times (25-22)} = 0.147 \text{ or 8.8 minutes}$$

Screenshot C.7 shows the Excel solution to Problem C.3.

SCREENSHOT C.7: Solved Problem C.3: Water Slide Game With Constant Service Time

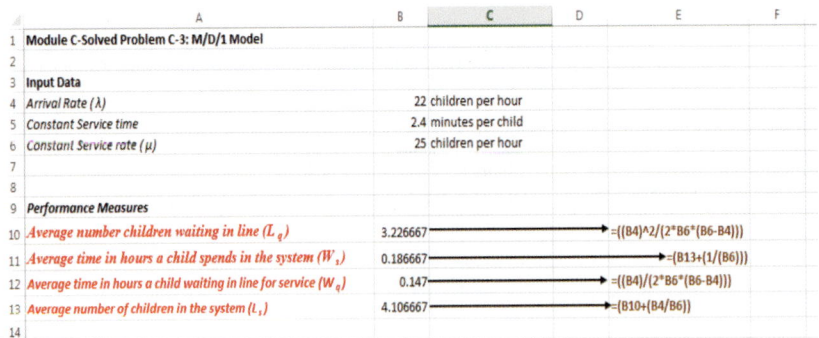

4. The Unemployment Office in Erie County, Pennsylvania, has two service booths to assist unemployed individuals to register and file for unemployment compensation. Arriving customers form a single line and are served by the first available service agent of the office. Customers arrive at the average rate of 40 per hour. Each service agent can provide service to customers at the average rate of 25 per hour. Assume that both arrival rate and service rate have a Poisson probability distribution. Determine the probability that there are no customers in the waiting line system, the average number of customers waiting in line, and the average waiting time in the queue.

Solution:

Given:

S = Number of open channels = 2

λ = Average number of arrivals per hour = 40

μ = Average number of customers served per hour = 25

P_0 = Probability that no customers are in the waiting line system is:

$$P_0 = \cfrac{1}{\left[\sum_{n=0}^{S-1}\dfrac{1}{n!}\left(\dfrac{\lambda}{\mu}\right)^n\right] + \dfrac{1}{S!}\left(\dfrac{\lambda}{\mu}\right)^S \dfrac{S\mu}{S\mu-\lambda}}$$

$$P_0 = \cfrac{1}{\left[\sum_{n=0}^{2-1}\dfrac{1}{n!}\left(\dfrac{40}{25}\right)^n\right] + \dfrac{1}{2!}\left(\dfrac{40}{25}\right)^2 \dfrac{2\times25}{2\times25-40}} = \cfrac{1}{\left[1+\left(\dfrac{40}{25}\right)\right] + \dfrac{1}{2}\times\dfrac{1600}{625}\times\dfrac{50}{10}} = 0.111 \text{ or } 11.1\%$$

L_q = Average number of customers in the line waiting:

$$L_q = \cfrac{\lambda\mu\left(\dfrac{\lambda}{\mu}\right)^S}{(S-1)!(S\mu-\lambda)^2}\,P_0 = \cfrac{40\times25\times\left(\dfrac{40}{25}\right)^2}{(2-1)!\times(2\times25-40)^2}\times0.111 = 2.84$$

W_q = Average time a customer spends in queue

$$W_q = \frac{Lq}{\lambda} = \frac{2.84}{40} = 0.071 \text{ hours (4.26 minutes)}$$

Screenshot C.8 shows the Excel solution to Solved Problem C.4.

SCREENSHOT C.8: Solved Problem C.4: Unemployment Office Problem With Multiple Servers

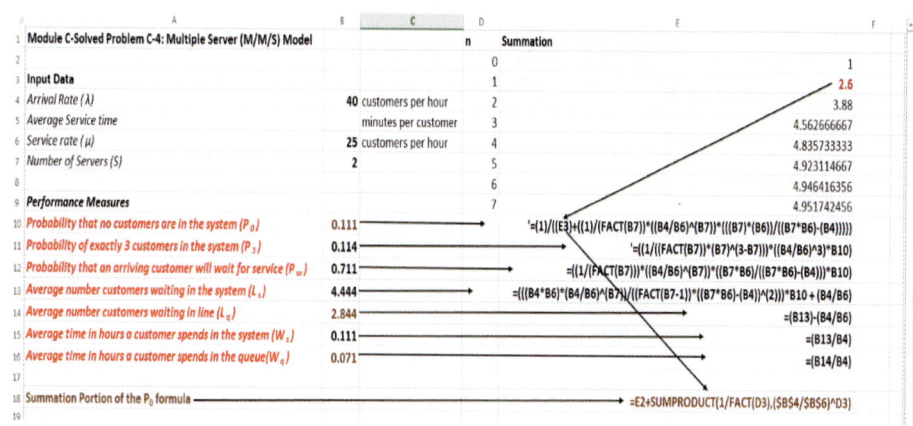

5. Ruth Tailor is a fictional full-time math tutor at the learning resource center at Penn State University. She has 5 students assigned to her for tutoring. Ruth works 40 hours a week. A student visits her for tutoring at an average of every 12 hours, and the interarrival time has an exponential distribution. Ruth tutors only one student at a time, spends an average of 2 hours tutoring a student, and the tutoring time has an exponential distribution. The other students who need tutoring spend their time studying while waiting in the reception area of the learning resource center. What is the waiting time for a student before he or she can meet with Ruth?

Solution:

Given: $N = 5$; $M = 1$; $U = 12$ hours; and $T = 2$

Therefore:

$$X = \frac{T}{T+U} = \frac{2}{2+12} = \frac{1}{14} = 0.071 \text{ (close to 0.070 for determining the values of D and F)}$$

For $N = 5$, $M = 1$, $X = 0.070$, and $F = 0.977$

Average waiting time: $W = \dfrac{L(T+U)}{N-L} = \dfrac{T(1-F)}{T+U} = \dfrac{2(1-0.977)}{2+12} = 3.28 \text{ hours}$

PROBLEMS

1. A grocery store in a small town has a single check-out counter to service its customers. Customers wait in a single line at the checkout counter and are served on a first-come, first-served basis. On average, 25 customers per hour arrive at the checkout counter and customer arrivals are assumed to have a Poisson distribution. The employee at the checkout counter can serve the customers at an average rate of 30 customer per hour, with the service time being described by a negative exponential distribution. Determine:

   a. Capacity utilization for the system

   b. Average number customers waiting in line (queue)

   c. Average time a customer spends in the system (waiting time plus service time)

   d. Probability that five customers are in the system

2. The student recreation center of a state university has only one coffee shop. Students arrive at the coffees shop at an average rate of 35 per hour according to a Poisson distribution. The only employee at the coffee shop takes an average of 90 seconds to service one student. Determine the following:

   a. Capacity utilization for the system

   b. Average number students in the queue

   c. Average time a student spends in waiting in the queue

   d. Average time a student spends in waiting in the system

3. The local driver license center uses a single-server, single-line, single-phase system when processing license renewals. Customers arrive at the facility according to a Poisson distribution at the rate of 10 customers per hour. The time to process a license renewal is an average of 4 minutes per customer with the service times following a negative exponential distribution. The manager of the license center, Jonathan Trott, is concerned with the center's waiting line system. He cannot understand why waiting lines form at the license center when the average service rate is greater than the average arrival rate. The customers come from an infinite population, patiently wait for their turn in the queue, and are served on a first-come, first served basis. Jonathan Trott would like you analyze the Center's waiting line system. What are your findings and conclusion about the center's waiting line system?

4. Refer to the data in Problem C.2. The owner of the coffee shop at the student recreation center, Amanda Murdock, is interested in computing the per day total cost of the waiting line system at the coffee shop. She has estimated that the cost of waiting time associated with a dissatisfied student and loss of good will is $15 per hour and the employee at the coffee shop is paid $10 an hour. Assume that the shop is open 10 hours per day. Given this information and the data in Problem C.2, compute:

   a. Average customer waiting time cost per day in the queue

   b. Total expected costs per day for the waiting line system

5. An automatic roller coaster ride at an amusement park takes a constant 2 minutes to complete a ride. Customers arrive at the automatic roller coaster ride facility at the rate of 25 per hour. The arrival rate of customers tend to follow a Poisson distribution. Compute:

   a. The average number of customers waiting in line for the ride

   b. The average time customers spend in the system (waiting in line plus the ride)

   c. The average number of customers in the system

6. Amanda Murdock, the owner of the coffee shop at the student recreation center in Problem C.2, to reduce the student waiting time at the coffee shop has decided to install an automatic coffee vending machine outside her shop. Amanda charges $2.50 per cup of coffee at the vending machine. The service time at the vending machine is a constant 60 seconds per student. The arrival rate of students is Poisson distributed and is an average of 45 students per hour. Determine:

   a. Average number students in the queue.

   b. Average time a student spends in waiting in the queue

   c. Amanda realized that operating the vending machine at $2.50 per cup was not profitable. Hence, she decided to raise the price to $3 per cup but reduced the service time to 45 seconds per cup. Nevertheless, because of the higher price, the arrival students dropped to 30 per hour. What are the average number students in the queue, and the average time a student spends in waiting in the queue now?

7. The Canara Bank drive-in teller window can serve a customer at an average of 4 minutes per customer. Service time has a negative exponential distribution. Customers arrive in their cars at a rate (Poisson distributed) of 12 per hour and form a single waiting line:

   a. Determine the average waiting time, the average queue length, and the probability that there is no customer in the system.

b. If Canara Bank decides to open a second drive-in teller window with the same service rate as the first one, how will your answers to part a change?

8. Neptune Manufacturing Inc. makes soaps in an assembly line process. One of the machines on the line is an automatic soap press that has single assembly line feeding into it. Partially completed units of soap arrive at the press every 3 minutes and are assumed to have a negative exponential distribution. The processing time of the soap press is a constant 2.4 minutes for each partially completed unit of soap. Compute L_q, W_q, L_s, and W_s.

9. Jonathan Trott, the manager of the driver license center in Problem C.3, has decided to open another service counter to improve the license renewal processing service. The time to process a license renewal in the second server, like the first server, is also an average of 4 minutes per customer with the service times following a negative exponential distribution. Because of the availability of a second service booth, the arrival rate of customers has now increased to an average of 24 customers per hour (Poisson distributed). Determine the following:

a. Probability that no customers are in the waiting line system

b. Average number customers waiting in line (queue)

c. Average time a customer spends in the system (waiting time plus service time)

d. Probability that five customers are in the system

e. Probability that an arriving customer must wait for service

10. Refer to the data in Problem C.3. Jonathan Trott, the manager of the driver license center, is interested in computing the per day total cost of the waiting line system at the center. He has estimated that the cost of waiting time associated with a dissatisfied customer and loss of good will is $35 per hour and the employee at the center with a single server is paid $20 an hour. Assume that the shop is open 10 hours per day. Given this information and the data in Problem C.3, compute:

a. Average customer waiting time cost per day in the queue

b. Total expected costs per day for the waiting line system

c. Refer to Problem C.9. If the estimated that the cost of waiting time associated with a dissatisfied customer and loss of good will is $35 per hour and each employee at each of the two servers is paid $20 an hour, answer the questions in parts a) and b).

d. Based on your answers to b) and c), should Jonathan Trott use a single server or two servers?

11. A local pharmacy has the following pertaining to prescription requests and service times on a typical Monday:

Time Period	Prescription Request Rate per Hour	Service Time to Fill Each Prescription (in minutes)	Number of Pharmacists
Morning	12	4	2
Afternoon	18	3	3
Evening	25	2	3

a. Determine for each time period the probability that there are no customers in the waiting line system.

b. Determine for each time period the average number of prescriptions in the queue.

c. Determine for each time period the average time a prescription spends in the system (waiting time plus filling time).

d. Determine for each time period the maximum queue length for a probability of 95%.

12. The Donghai Bridge of China is a 20.2-mile-long toll bridge stretching from Shanghai to the Yangshan offshore water port. Currently, there are six exact-change toll booths, each staffed by an employee of the toll bridge system. Cars arrive at the toll bridge at the rate of 8 cars per minute, form a single lane, and use the first available toll booth. The service rate at each toll booth is also 8 cars per minute. Determine P_0, L_q, W_q, L_s, and W_s for the toll bridge system.

13. The Gulf Shipping Company in Dubai, UAE, has four terminal docks in its warehouse. Arriving trucks form a single line and use one of the four available docks for loading and unloading of the cargo. Truck arrivals are Poisson distributed, and the average arrival rate of truck is 8 trucks per hour. The loading/unloading times of cargo have a negative exponential distribution, and the average time to load/unload a truck is 20 minutes.

a. Compute P_0, L_q, W_q, L_s, and W_s for this terminal dock waiting line system.

b. If the average cost of loading/unloading a truck per terminal dock is $100 an hour, and the average waiting time cost of a truck is $150 an hour, compute the total expected cost per day. Assume a 10-hour working day.

14. Refer to Problem C.13. The management of the shipping company wants to reduce the average service time per terminal dock to 15 minutes per truck by adding a fifth terminal dock. Assume the arrival rate of trucks and the relevant costs per hour are the same as given in Problem C.13.

a. Compute P_0, L_q, W_q, L_s, and W_s for this new terminal dock waiting line system.

b. Compute the total expected cost per day for this new system, and compare it with the four-dock system in Problem C.13.

15. A large hotel receives telephone calls to its switchboard at an average rate of 50 calls per hour according to a Poisson distribution. The switchboard is staffed by three operators, and the service rate for each of the three operators is an average of 20 calls per hour, with exponential service times. Calculate the following performance measures for the switchboard service system:

a. The average utilization of the help desk

b. The probability that there are no calls to the system

c.   The average number of calls waiting in line

d.   The average time a call spends waiting in line

e.   The average time a call spends in the system

f.   The average number of calls in the system

16.   A service technician for a laser printer manufacturer services five customers who have bought five large printers from the company. Each of these printers requires repair and maintenance work after 25 hours of use. Assume that the time between two successive repairs has a negative exponential distribution. The service technician takes an average of 3 hours to service a printer, and the service times also follow a negative exponential distribution. Printer downtime costs the company $200 per hour, and the service technician is paid $30 an hour. Should the company hire a second technician?

17.   A drilling department Orion Manufacturing Inc. has five drill press machines and has one repair technician to service these machines. Each drill press operates for an average of 10 hours (negative exponentially distributed) before requiring maintenance work. It takes the service technician about two hours to repair a machine, and the repair times are found to follow a negative exponential distribution. Machine downtime costs the company $150 an hour, and the service technician is paid $35 an hour. Determine whether Orion Manufacturing needs a second repair technician.

18.   The registration desk at the exclusive Le Meridien Hotel has four staff agents to check in the hotel guests. Guests arrive at the registration desk at an average rate of 40 per hour (Poisson distributed) and form a single line and wait for service from the next available agent. The average time for an agent to check in a guest is 5 minutes, and the service time has a negative exponential distribution. Each service agent is paid $15 an hour, and the cost of customer dissatisfaction and loss of good will as a result of excessive waiting times is $25 an hour. Determine how effective the present guest check-in system is at the hotel and whether an additional server (fifth service agent) is needed to improve service.

19.   Passengers at the Sahar International Airport arrive at a security gate at the rate of 40 passengers per hour (Poisson distributed) and form a single line waiting for a security check at one of the two available security gates. Each service gate on the average takes 2.4 minutes to service a passenger, and the service times have a negative exponential distribution:

a.   Compute the average waiting time and the average number of passengers in the waiting line.

b.   On any given time of the day, passenger traffic varies significantly at the security gates. There may be no passenger traffic at certain times of the day, but it can be as high as 80 passengers per hour during flight take-off times. Design the security server system for the maximum level of passenger traffic.

20.   A local department of motor vehicles has an automated photographic machine that imprints the photographic image on to the license card including the lamination of the complete card. Drivers arrive at the photographic machine according to a Poisson distribution at an average rate of 12 per hour. The machine takes a constant 4 minutes to print and laminate a complete license. Determine:

a.   The average number of drivers waiting in line for the machine

b.   The average time a driver spends in the system (waiting in line plus the service)

CASE STUDY C.1 THE PSYCHOLOGY OF WAITING IN LINES ....

Although much has been written about and calculated for the most efficient ways to minimize waiting lines and to reduce the losses from queuing, there is an equally important, but often overlooked issue, which is how waiting affects those stuck in queues. As FedEx (FedEx Corporation, Memphis, TN) noted years ago: "Waiting is frustrating, demoralizing, agonizing, aggravating, annoying, time consuming and incredibly expensive."[5] Consequently, there is a branch of psychology devoted to analyzing the waiting line problem and to considering how people typically respond to the requirement that they wait, sometimes for excessive periods of time, in lines. In reflecting on what modern psychological theory can teach us about customers and waiting lines, David Maister, a psychologist who has studied the psychological effects of waiting, formulated a set of principles to help businesses minimize the negative consequences of forcing customers to wait. He proposed that it is first critical to understand a simple idea as it pertains to customers: $S = P - E$.

In this equation, S stands for satisfaction, P for perception, and E for expectation. If you expect a certain level of service and perceive the service reviewed to be higher, you are a satisfied client. If you perceive the same level as before, but you expected a higher level, you are disappointed and, consequently, a dissatisfied client. Remember that both P and E are psychological ideas; they are not quantifiable but represent the attitudes of customers. As a result, all efforts that a company can make to improve P, the perception of the service encounter, are going to result in satisfied customers.

In applying Maister's ideas about waiting, business should consider the following psychological attributes of waiting:

1.   **Occupied time goes by faster than unoccupied time does.** Time spent aimlessly waiting seems to drag on interminably. If, instead, customers can be engaged (or occupied) in some manner while they are waiting, they are less likely to feel that their time has been wasted. Disney is masterful at minimizing perceived waiting time for rides at their theme parks by providing a series of entertaining and engaging displays all along the waiting lines. The cost of these displays can sometimes run well over hundreds of thousands of dollars, but Disney knows that it is worth it to keep their customers occupied.

2.   **People want to get going.** Uno Pizzeria & Grill (aka Unos, Chicago, IL) is famous for its deep-dish pizza, and lines form early to get a table at its flagship downtown restaurant. In fact, because deep-dish pizza takes so long to cook, customers can wait in line for well over an hour. That's why Unos hands out menus in advance and offers waiting customers the opportunity to order drinks from the bar while they wait. Unos recognizes that letting people start early goes a long way toward improving their satisfaction.

3.   **The more the uncertainty, the longer the wait seems to take.** When waiting on standby at an airline counter or hoping to be one of

the first 50 customers to enter a department store for special deals on Black Friday, we naturally became anxious. Will they run out of the on-sale televisions I desire? Will I make my flight or not? The more information that people can be given, the less anxious they will be and the shorter the wait they will perceive. For example, at Toys "R" Us, Inc. (Wayne, NJ), an employee may leave the store and walk along the waiting line offering advance purchase tickets to the first 100 customers waiting for a new videogame console, thereby eliminating their anxiety.

4. **Uncertain waits seem to last longer than do known, finite waits.** Seemingly endless waits at doctor's offices are frustrating, particularly when the receptionist clearly has no idea of how long the wait is likely to be. On the other hand, when all persons entering the doctor's office are informed immediately that, "Due to an emergency, the doctor will be running 30 minutes late today," their perception of the wait immediately improves. With a finite end in sight, waiting is not so stressful.

5. **Unexplained waits seem to take longer than do waits that are explained to us.** A corollary to point 4 suggests that when consumers lack knowledge of why a delay is occurring, their view of waiting is more negative. Think of roadwork occurring on an interstate highway, further ahead where you cannot see it. When traffic is stopped and there is no explanation for the cause, the perception is that the waiting time seems to drag along. On the other hand, smartphones accessing Uber cars (Uber Technologies, Inc., San Francisco, CA) for a pickup can track, using GPS, the exact location of the scheduled ride and observe the driver's real-time status as the car heads to our location.

6. **Unfair waits seem to take longer than do waits we perceive are equable.** Watch a crowd waiting to get into a trendy nightclub as people are forced to queue behind a velvet rope. Over time, it may be possible for them to estimate how much longer before it is their turn to enter the club. Now, observe the reaction when a VIP guest skirts the line and walks directly to the bouncer at the front. When some customers are allowed to bypass the wait assigned to everyone else, it serves to make other waiting guests feel that their queuing time is much longer. In other situations, we know that many people will wait twice as long for fast food, provided the establishment uses a first-come, first-served, single-queue ordering system as opposed to a multiqueue setup. Anyone who's ever had to choose a line at a grocery store knows how unfair multiple queues can seem; invariably, you wind up kicking yourself for not choosing the line next to you that appears to be moving twice as fast!

7. **Waiting by yourself feels longer than does waiting with a group.** When we feel isolated in our wait, as in the case of waiting for a take-out order at a restaurant or in a doctor's office, we tend to perceive the waiting time as significantly longer than situations where a firm makes the wait more group-based. So, for example, if Disney assigns sets of 50 riders to a special prep room in advance of their ride experience, they perceive the wait as shorter and less burdensome than they do when they lack a sense of camaraderie.

No one relishes waiting and the more that organizations seek ways to minimize waits (improving perceptions of the waiting), the greater is customer satisfaction and by implication, the better customers are pleased with (and more loyal to) those organizations over time.[6]

Questions for Discussion:

1. What does this case suggest about the way in which operations and queuing models must also address the psychology of waiting lines in formulating methods for minimizing wait?

2. Think of a long wait that you experienced in the past week. How would one or more of these attributes of waiting have improved your perception of the wait and increased your satisfaction with the service encounter?

3. Suppose you were hired to manage the operations flow at a local restaurant as the front-end manager. The most common complaint that the restaurant receives is the long wait times to get a table, and overall profitability is starting to suffer as a result of lower patronage rates. Employ at least four of these attributes in redesigning the front end to increase customer satisfaction.

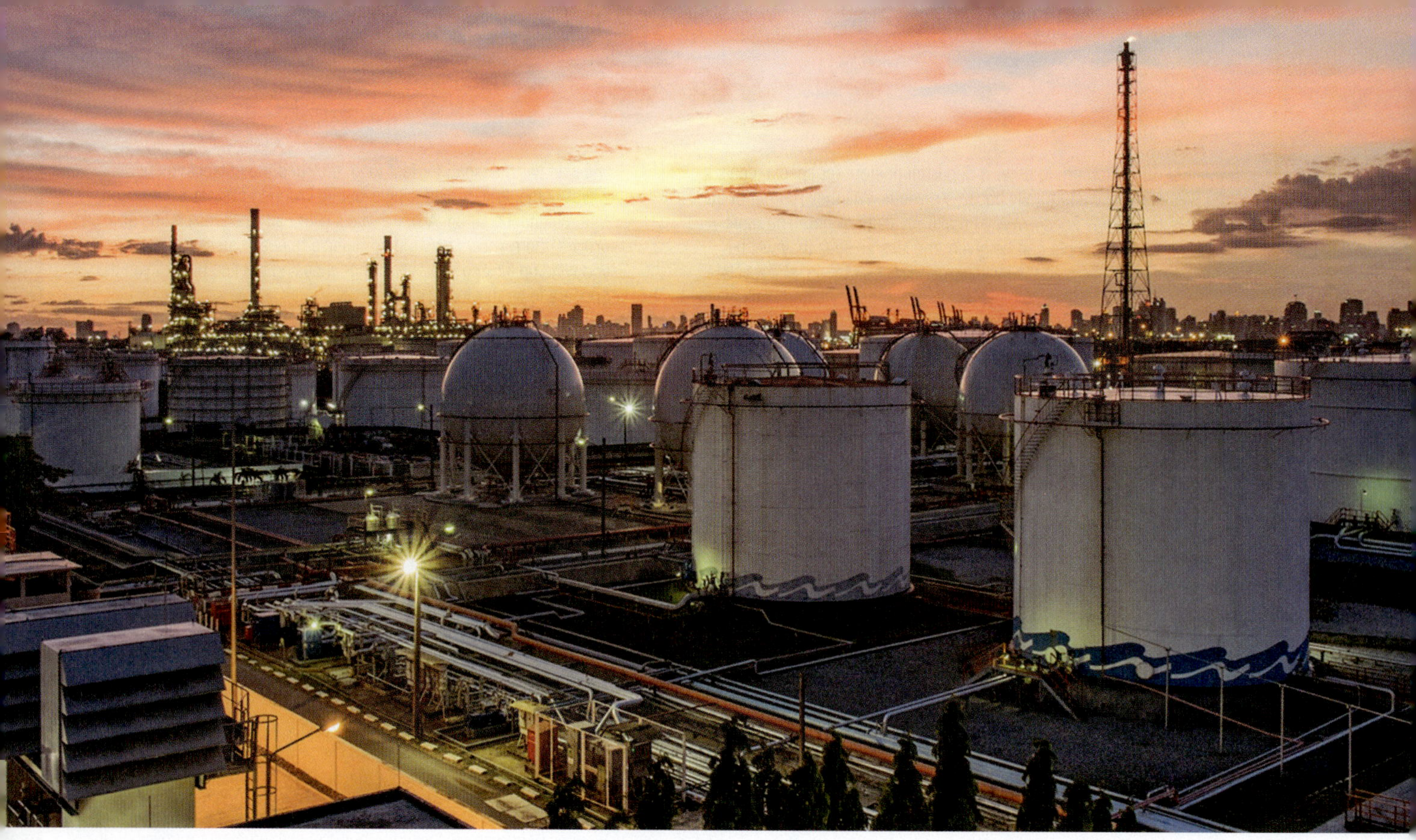

©iStockphoto.com/Kawinnings

MODULE
D

Simulation

OPERATIONS PROFILE: Using Simulation to Answer the "What If?" Questions in the Oil Business

ExxonMobil Chemical (Exxon Mobil Corp., Irving, TX) is one of the largest companies in the world, involved in oil and gas exploration, drilling, refining, transportation, and retail sales. In 2015, its revenues approached $260 billion.[a] The company possesses billions of dollars in assets across its value chain, including drilling rigs for exploration, refineries for production, tank farms for storing chemicals and refined products, super tankers to transport its products, and retail gas and other outlets to bring its products directly to consumers. Every step of this incredibly complicated value chain must be managed by itself but also in relation to links up the chain and downstream. For example, a decision to close a refinery temporarily for annual maintenance must consider the production capacity and availability of alternative refineries that allow its products to flow to customers without any supply disruptions. The decision to spend $1 billion on a new floating oil rig for exploration in the Gulf of Mexico is complicated, especially when new technologies like hydraulic fracturing (or "fracking") have driven down the global price of oil in 2016 to below $50 a barrel.

Some "what if?" questions Exxon Mobil considered when making supply chain decisions include political realities and potential instabilities in countries where it drills, weather and climate patterns and its impact on transportation, changes to currency exchange rates, potential for gas well fires and other disasters, and so forth. Because Exxon Mobil must carefully manage this supply chain, it uses a computer simulation to run complex "alternative" decision models, testing the best responses for various possible situations and their outcomes. Spending millions of dollars on super-computers and complex simulation models is an expense that Exxon Mobil is happy to undertake, especially since implementing untested models could be financially, politically, and environmentally devastating.[1]

D.1 Introduction to Simulation

Simulation is the act of duplicating the operation of a real-world process or system over time.[2] Because the simulation approach can be applied to a wide variety of real-world problems, it is a popular step for companies to take when testing processes and solving problems. Whenever it is impossible, cost prohibitive, or impractical to use any other approach for problem-solving, simulation is typically the only option that can be used. By using the simulation modeling approach, an analyst can evaluate the performance of an existing or proposed system or process over time and draw conclusions about the behavior of the actual system or process. Simulation can be used to show the real impact of alternative conditions and courses of action on the system under study. Many real-life problems that have been analyzed using simulation include:

- Production scheduling
- Employee/worker scheduling
- Analysis of waiting line systems
- Inventory planning and control
- Design of plant layout and distribution systems
- Space flight launches
- Sales processes
- Project management training and analysis

Figure D.1 shows a schematic representation of a simulation study.

See in Figure D.1 how the simulation process is iterative in nature. As conditions change, the altered system will lead to new simulation studies, to be repeated as necessary. It is also important to note that the simulation process is

D.1

Explain the concept of simulation, its advantages, and the key steps in developing a simulation model.

Simulation: the act of duplicating the operation of a real-world process or system over time

---

[a]Unless otherwise stated, all currency is in U.S. dollars.

FIGURE D.1: Schematic of a Simulation Study

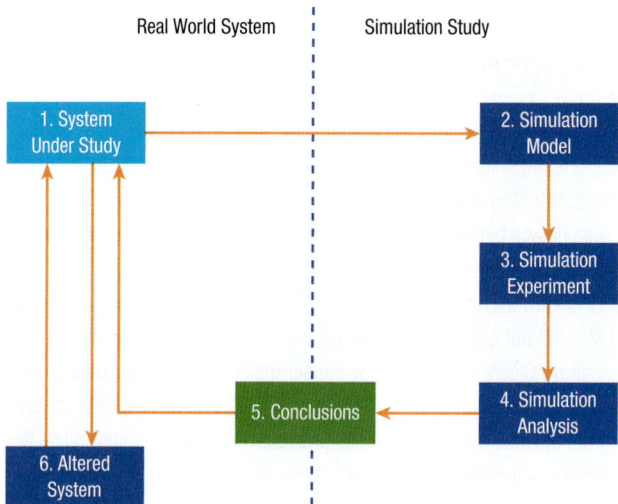

Real World System   Simulation Study

1. System Under Study

2. Simulation Model

3. Simulation Experiment

4. Simulation Analysis

5. Conclusions

6. Altered System

SOURCE: Maria, A. (1997). Introduction to modeling and simulation. *Proceedings of the 1997 Winter Simulation Conference.* Retrieved from http://www.inf.utfsm .cl/~hallende/download/Simul-2-2002/Introduction_to_Modeling_and_Simulation.pdf

not automatic or simple; at each stage depicted in Figure D.1, the intervention of the experienced simulation analyst will be needed. The steps for using simulation are as covered in the following section.

Steps for Using Simulation

STEP 1: DEVELOP A MODEL THAT REPRESENTS THE REAL-LIFE SYSTEM OR PROCESS THAT IS TO BE STUDIED AND ANALYZED

Modelling and Simulation

Although most simulation modeling approaches involve the use of abstract mathematical models, there are also examples of physical simulation. When physical simulation is used, physical objects replace the actual objects. One example is building a model aircraft for wind-tunnel studies to simulate the performance of a real aircraft design; another is using simulators to create the conditions of weightlessness to mirror what will occur during space flights. In this module, however, we will focus on using mathematical models for simulating operations management subsystems or processes that represent the actual system or process. The mathematical model is a description of a system using mathematical concepts. Although an abstraction of reality, mathematical models should capture the key features, behaviors, or functions of the real system or process. Even though the mathematical models represent the system itself, the simulation process captures the operation of the system over time.

STEP 2: DEFINE THE PROBLEM

The analyst must clearly define the specific problems or shortcomings of the existing system or process that will be addressed by the simulation study. He or she must also identify what the changed system will require to overcome these shortcomings, including performance measures, key input variables, and the quantitative criteria that will be used to compare alternative courses of action. In addition, the analyst should also know whether the simulation model will be used to make a one-time decision (such as for a capital expenditure) or over a period of time to make routine decisions (such as air traffic scheduling). Finally, the analyst must know who will be the end-user of the simulation model.[3]

STEP 3: FORMULATE THE MATHEMATICAL MODEL

Physical simulation: the act of duplicating the operation of a real-world process or system over time using physical objects to replace the actual objects

It is important to note that the model does not have to match the real system exactly. Nevertheless, it should abstract the essential features of the problem or system that is being studied. While constructing the model, the analyst must include the basic assumptions that characterize the system. The analyst should start with a simple model and progressively make the model more complex, but only to the extent required to accomplish the objectives of the study. If you are simulating a waiting line system, the model should include only as many channels as are required for the study, and should make the appropriate assumptions about the probability distributions of arrival and service rates.

STEP 4: GATHER THE DATA NEEDED FOR THE STUDY

While building the early model, it is helpful to begin collecting the needed input data on all the relevant variables of the model. The collected data must be examined to see whether they fit known theoretical probability distributions. We know from past research and from practical experiences on waiting lines that the arrival rate of a customer to a service facility may follow a Poisson distribution. Data collection is often the most time-consuming phase of a simulation study, and as the model complexity changes, the input data required may also change.

STEP 5: TRANSLATE THE MODEL TO COMPUTERIZED SIMULATION SOFTWARE

Since modeling most real-world systems requires extensive data storage and involves complex computations, these models must be programmed in a computerized simulation language. Depending on the nature of the problem to be addressed, the analyst must choose the appropriate simulation language (some examples include Arena, GPSS/H, and ProModel) or they can use a special-purpose simulation software package.

STEP 6: VERIFY AND VALIDATE THE MODEL

Model verification involves ensuring that the model behaves as intended, whereas validation, which is typically achieved through statistical analysis, is the process of ensuring that the model is a reasonably robust and accurate reflection of the real-world system that is being studied.

STEP 7: EXPERIMENT AND ANALYZE

Experimentation involves testing alternative courses of action by choosing alternative models, and executing the simulation repeatedly as necessary. After executing these simulation runs, the analysis phase focuses on statistically comparing the performance of the various alternatives with that of the real system.

STEP 8: DOCUMENT AND RECOMMEND

Documentation consists of preparing a detailed written report of the simulation study. This report includes the objectives of the simulation study, model assumptions, the input variables, the results, and the implications of the study. Finally, the best course of action is recommended and justified.

Advantages and Disadvantages of Simulation

Simulation is a popular tool used by managers from a wide variety of organizations because of its many advantages. As we will discuss in this module, some of the main advantages include:

 Using Simulation

- Simulation can be used to study the behavior of a system without the expensive alternative of actually building it.
- Many real-world complex problems that do not lend themselves to analysis using mathematical models can be studied using simulation. Furthermore, simulation results are generally more accurate than analytical models are.
- Simulation enables managers to perform "What-If" analysis. As a result, several decision alternatives and their impact can be assessed quickly.
- Simulation models do not make restrictive assumptions that typically do not hold in real-world scenarios. In analyzing waiting line systems, simulation does not require the user to make any assumptions about the probability distribution of arrival rates and service times. Instead, it will work with any user-defined probability distribution.
- Simulation performed using computers can quickly analyze the impact of a policy decision in a real-life situation that typically is observed over several years.
- Simulation is a flexible tool and can be quickly adapted as conditions in the problem environment change.

The main disadvantages of simulation include:

- Developing complex simulation models can be time consuming and expensive.
- For simulation models to produce meaningful results, the analyst must provide the appropriate input and must replicate the conditions and constraints of the real-life problem as accurately as possible.
- Because each simulation model is specifically developed to analyze a specific problem, the model, results, or the conclusions, cannot be transferred to other problems.

D.2

Describe Monte Carlo simulation, and set up and solve operations problems using Monte Carlo simulation, by hand and using Excel.

Monte Carlo simulation: a probabilistic simulation technique that involves selecting numbers randomly from a known probability distribution to be used in simulation trials

Cumulative probability distribution: a distribution of probability values that shows that a random variable such as demand has a probability less than or equal to a specified value. Given a column of probability values associated with each value of the random variable, it is computed by adding the probability associated with each demand value to the cumulative probability value in the previous column

Random numbers: a sequence of numbers that is uniformly distributed over a defined interval or range, for which it is not possible to predict their future values based on their past or current values

D.2 Monte Carlo Simulation

Decision makers for real-world problems have to contend with uncertain circumstances or unpredictable events. A production planner trying to decide production levels for the products in his facility has to contend with the variable nature of demand. A restaurant has to contend with the random nature of customer arrivals to their location and still schedule wait staff as efficiently as possible. Because of the presence of random variables (such as uncertain demand), it is impossible to solve many real-life problems using analytical methods. In such cases, the only option that a decision maker has is to use a simulation, specifically **Monte Carlo simulation**. Monte Carlo simulation is a probabilistic simulation technique, and in its narrowest sense, it can be defined as a technique that involves selecting numbers randomly from a known probability distribution to be used in simulation trials. The term "Monte Carlo" was coined because the basic principle underlying the number selection process is identical to that of a roulette wheel or dice you might find in a casino in Monaco.

Monte Carlo simulation was introduced in the 1940s by a group of scientists working on the Manhattan Project, which resulted in the first atomic bomb. They used Monte Carlo simulation to compute reliable probabilities that enabled them to estimate the amount of uranium, a scarce raw material, needed for testing. Since then, Monte Carlo methods have been applied to solve a wide range of problems in science, engineering, and businesses in almost every industry. Some examples of how companies use Monte Carlo simulation include:[4]

- The General Motors Company (aka GM or General Motors, Detroit, MI), P&G (Procter & Gamble Co., Cincinnati, OH), Pfizer, Inc. (New York, NY), Bristol-Myers Squibb Company (New York, NY), and Eli Lilly and Company (aka Lilly, Indianapolis, IN) use simulation to estimate the average return on and the risk factor associated with introducing new products. At GM, this information is used by the CEO to determine which products come to market.
- GM also uses simulation to forecast net income for the corporation, predict structural and purchasing costs, and determine the company's susceptibility to different kinds of risk, such as interest rate changes and exchange rate fluctuations.
- Lilly uses simulation to determine the optimal plant capacity for each drug they produce.
- P&G uses simulation to model and optimally hedge foreign exchange risk.
- Sears (Sears, Roebuck & Co., Hoffman Estates, IL) uses simulation to determine how many units of each product line should be ordered from suppliers.
- Oil and drug companies use simulation to value real options, such as the value of an option to expand, contract, or postpone a project.
- Financial planners use Monte Carlo simulation to determine optimal investment strategies for their clients' retirement.

Monte Carlo simulation comprises the following five steps:

1. Generate a probability distribution for the various possible values of key random variables.
2. Compute a **cumulative probability distribution** for each random variable.
3. Assign an interval of **random numbers** for each potential value of the random variable.
4. Generate random numbers by using a random number table or a computer.
5. Simulate a series of trials, and analyze the results.

The steps of Monte Carlo Simulation are illustrated in Example D.1.

EXAMPLE D.1: The manager of a large electronics store that sells televisions and other related accessories wants to determine how many LED TVs to order each day. The key random variable is the average demand for LED TVs each day, which will determine the average daily revenue the store will generate. The average price of an LED TV is $800. Based on past sales records, the manager has determined the demand distribution for the past 100 days shown in Table D.1. Use Monte Carlo simulation to determine how many LED TVs to order each day.

TABLE D.1: Demand Distribution for LED TVs

DEMAND FOR LED TVs	FREQUENCY OF OCCURRENCE (IN DAYS)
0	15
5	30
10	40
20	10
25	5
	Total = 100 days

SOLUTION

Step 1: Generate a probability distribution for the possible values of key random variables.

Table D.1 shows that demand for 0 LED TVs occurs 15 out of 100 days. Hence, the probability of demand for 0 LED TVs is 15 / 100 or 15%. The probabilities for the other possible values of the random variable, demand, are calculated in a similar manner and are shown in Table D.2.

TABLE D.2: Demand Probability Distribution for LED TVs

DEMAND FOR LED TVs	FREQUENCY OF OCCURRENCE (IN DAYS)	PROBABILITY OF DEMAND
0	15	15 / 100 = 0.15
5	30	30 / 100 = 0.30
10	40	40 / 100 = 0.40
20	10	10 / 100 = 0.10
25	5	5 / 100 = 0.05
	Total = 100 days	100 / 100 = 1.00

Step 2: Compute a cumulative probability distribution for each random variable.

We next compute the cumulative probabilities for the demand random variable as shown in Table D.3. The process of computing cumulative probabilities is found by adding the probability associated with each demand value to the cumulative probability value in the previous column.

TABLE D.3: Cumulative Demand Probability Distribution for LED TVs

DEMAND FOR LED TVs	FREQUENCY OF OCCURRENCE (IN DAYS)	PROBABILITY OF DEMAND	CUMULATIVE PROBABILITY
0	15	15 / 100 = 0.15	0.15
5	30	30 / 100 = 0.30	0.15 + 0.30 = 0.45
10	40	40 / 100 = 0.40	0.45 + 0.40 = 0.85
20	10	10 / 100 = 0.10	0.85 + 0.10 = 0.95
25	5	5 / 100 = 0.05	0.95 + 0.05 = 1.00
	Total = 100 days	100 / 100 = 1.00	

Step 3: Assign an interval of random numbers for each potential value of the random variable.

Monte Carlo simulation is initiated by randomly generating demand. This is done by assigning an interval of random numbers associated with the probability of each potential value of demand: the random variable. For Example D.1, we can generate a series of 100 two-digit random numbers (e.g., 00, 01, 02 …… 99) by a process that ensures that each random variable has an equal chance of being selected. We use two-digit random numbers because the frequency distribution has maximum values in two digits. We next partition these 100 random numbers into intervals that reflect the probabilities of the potential values that the demand random variable can take on. Since there is a 15% probability that the demand will be for 0 LED TVs, we could assign the first 15 two-digit random numbers out of the 100 selected. The order in which you assign the random numbers does not matter as long as you assign 15 two-digit random numbers to represent 0 demand. Similarly, we assign 30 random numbers to reflect the probability of 30% demand for five LED TVs and so on. The results of assigning random number intervals associated with the probabilities of the potential values of the demand random variable are shown in Table D.4. Note that the width of each random interval corresponds to the probability associated with that demand value.

TABLE D.4: Random Number Intervals for LED-TV Demand Values

DEMAND FOR HD TVs	FREQUENCY OF OCCURRENCE (IN DAYS)	PROBABILITY OF DEMAND	CUMULATIVE PROBABILITY	RANDOM NUMBER INTERVALS
0	15	15 / 100 = 0.15	0.15	00 to 14
5	30	30 / 100 = 0.30	0.15 + 0.30 = 0.45	15 to 44
10	40	40 / 100 = 0.40	0.45 + 0.40 = 0.85	45 to 84
20	10	10 / 100 = 0.10	0.85 + 0.10 = 0.95	85 to 94
25	5	5 / 100 = 0.05	0.95 + 0.05 = 1.00	95 to 99
	Total = 100 days	100 / 100 = 1.00		

Step 4: Generate random numbers by using a table of random numbers or a computer.

The process of generating the random numbers can be done manually, such as by spinning a roulette wheel, by using a table of random numbers, or by using a computer program. For small simulation problems that can be done manually, we can use a random number table such as Table D.5. For large simulation problems, generating the needed random numbers is best done by computer programs.

TABLE D.5: Table of Two-Digit Random Numbers

```
56 74 93 83 39 69 06 44 81 70 50 11 28 29 26 36 07 93 07 66 91 89 20 27 33 16 65 94 80 49 14 19 58 13 22 49
68 09 35 10 84 36 79 77 31 95 29 02 09 59 10 31 20 55 49 93 35 82 67 60 82 15 43 84 61 79 24 14 71 75 37 76
86 02 82 43 60 61 58 67 12 25 39 97 22 21 52 59 64 48 96 25 11 81 46 50 90 45 53 80 73 40 66 15 15 68 84 08
62 00 60 07 41 91 41 63 51 87 54 98 67 87 99 91 14 46 75 90 92 10 56 46 03 06 69 81 18 34 13 74 65 66 63 72
44 57 71 02 54 52 83 64 69 53 01 57 16 12 77 55 95 76 59 85 05 72 71 47 47 99 16 40 94 58 18 65 99 22 00 95
83 18 12 56 25 46 57 49 72 05 06 48 51 69 14 78 34 64 27 39 76 92 71 32 23 24 21 31 02 88 02 61 12 84 15 22
27 11 59 15 74 44 36 14 53 34 17 43 63 30 30 05 79 31 74 98 26 90 24 96 04 54 31 26 15 50 44 88 30 77 89 81
04 10 38 79 82 00 19 09 66 96 32 71 08 97 77 37 55 56 53 62 33 20 34 92 17 16 47 54 59 43 91 20 06 75 41 45
85 40 48 75 95 35 61 37 10 63 06 03 57 22 55 28 36 86 36 58 46 81 76 20 62 09 94 86 09 41 70 11 87 05 51 41
98 01 64 02 13 28 08 69 86 87 84 94 39 52 65 24 49 47 78 85 91 75 23 52 38 07 72 77 16 71 80 07 00 67 93 42
42 94 11 35 89 27 87 33 68 17 68 90 78 13 81 25 93 14 25 18 40 73 01 16 19 37 83 73 29 33 95 08 45 60 40 01
92 93 89 99 70 83 97 29 80 79 10 90 96 80 28 84 43 39 04 82 21 03 85 12 32 99 98 73 74 26 42 67 21 58 18 65
99 22 00 95 83 18 12 56 25 46 57 49 72 05 06 48 51 69 14 78 34 64 27 39 76 92 71 32 23 24 21 31 02 88 02 61
12 84 15 22 27 11 59 15 74 44 36 14 53 34 17 43 63 30 30 05 79 31 74 98 26 90 24 96 04 54 31 26
```

Step 5: Simulate a series of trials, and analyze the results.

In this step, we simulate a series of trials by selecting a random number for each trial from Table D.5. Take note of the random interval in Table D.4 in which the selected random number falls. The demand value that corresponds to that interval is the outcome of the first simulated trial or experiment.

Suppose you chose the random number 73 from Table D.5. That number falls in the random number interval of 45 to 84 in Table D.4, which corresponds to a demand of 10 LED TVs.

Assume that the manager of the electronics store wants to simulate 15 days of demand for L ED TVs.

To generate these 15 days of demand, begin at the top left-hand corner of Table D.5 and continue across the row. Note the random number and the daily demand that corresponds to that number. The results are shown in Table D.6.

TABLE D.6: Simulated Demand Values

DAY	RANDOM NUMBER	SIMULATED DEMAND
1	56	10
2	74	10
3	93	20
4	83	10
5	39	5
6	69	10
7	06	0
8	44	5
9	81	10
10	70	10
11	50	10
12	11	0
13	28	5
14	29	5
15	26	5
		Total = 110

Thus, the average demand for LED TVs for this 15-day simulation trails is:

$$\text{Average simulated demand} = 115 / 15 = 7.67 \text{ LED TVs}$$

We can also calculate the expected demand for LED TVs (the long run average) as follows:

$$\text{Expected Demand} = \sum_{i=0}^{25} D_i \times P(D_i)$$

$$= (0 \times 0.15 + 5 \times 0.30 + 10 \times 0.40 + 20 \times 0.10 + 25 \times 0.05) = 8.75 \text{ LED TVs}$$

Observe the average demand obtained from the simulation trials is fairly close to the expected demand. In fact, if the simulation trials are repeated a large number of times, the average simulated demand and the expected demand would be nearly equal. Nevertheless, it is important to note that this example is simplistic, meant to illustrate the fundamental principles of a simulation study. Drawing any definitive conclusions about the nature of demand for LED TVs based on this simple example would be unwise.

Simulation Using Excel

The simulation that we performed manually in Example D.1 for LED TVs was not time consuming as there were only 15 trials. Yet, if the problems are complex or require thousands of trials, then the simulation procedure cannot be performed manually. For complex problems, simulations are performed using computers that can handle large numbers of trials. Computer simulation models can be developed using general-purpose programming languages such as Fortran or C++ or special-purpose simulation languages such as GPSS or Arena. We will, however, use Microsoft Excel (Microsoft

Corporation, Redmond, WA) spreadsheets to illustrate how to develop a computer simulation model. We will demonstrate the Excel procedure for Example D.1.

EXAMPLE D.1 USING EXCEL

Step 1: Generate a probability distribution for the possible values of key random variables

The random variable demand for LED TVs and its frequency occurrences are entered in Cells A4 through B8.
 To compute probabilities of demand:

Enter the formula "= (B4/$B$9)" in cell C4, and copy it to cells C5 to C8.

Step 2: Compute a cumulative probability distribution for each random variable

To compute cumulative probabilities of demand:

Enter the formula "=C4" in cell D4.
Enter the formula "= (D4+C5)" in cell D5, and copy it to cells D6 to D8.

An Excel screenshot of steps 1 and 2 is shown in Screenshot D.1.

SCREENSHOT D.1: Steps 1 and 2 of Excel Simulation: Input Data

	B	C	D	E	F	G
	\multicolumn{6}{l}{Module D-Simulation-Example-D1}
	Demand for HD TVs	Frequency of occurrence in days	Probability of Demand	Cumulative Probability		
	0	15	0.15	0.15	→=D4	
	5	30	0.30	0.45	→=(E4+D5)	
	10	40	0.40	0.85		
	20	10	0.10	0.95		
	25	5	0.05	1.00		
	Total	100	1			
				=(C4/$C$9)		
	=(A4+D4)					

Step 3: Enter the number of the simulation trials, and generate a random number for each trial

Enter numbers 1 to 15 in cells H4 to H18 to represent the 15 simulated days of demand.
Since Excel can generate random numbers between 0 and 1, cover cells I4 to I18 and type in the formula "= RAND()" in cell I4, and then hit the "Ctrl" and "Enter" keys. This procedure will generate the random numbers required for the 15 simulation trials as shown in Screenshot D.2.

SCREENSHOT D.2: Step 3 of Excel Simulation: Generating Random Numbers

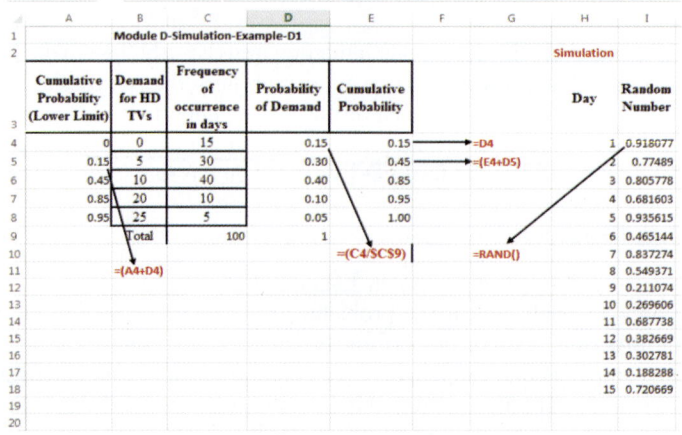

- Note that the numbers we used when we solved this example manually were whole numbers between 0 and 99. This was done for illustrative purposes. Computers programs like Excel, however, typically generate random numbers in the interval 0 and 1. To generate normally distributed random numbers for a given mean and standard deviation, we use the following formula:

$$\text{NORMINV}(RAND(), mean, standard\ deviation)$$

- For example, to generate a normally distributed random number for a distribution that has a mean of 8 and a standard deviation of 2, we use the following formula:

$$\text{NORMINV}(RAND(), 8, 2)$$

- We will insert this formula in a single cell and copy to as many cells as we want to generate normally distributed random numbers.

- The random numbers we generated in cells I4 to I18 will change every time we recalculate anything on the spreadsheet. To have the same random numbers that you generated the first time, follow these steps:

    1. First cover the cells I4 through I18, and then copy these cells using the right mouse button.

    2. Next, click the "Paste Special" on the menu, and then choose the "Values" option. Click "OK."

This procedure will lock the random numbers already in place.

Step 4: Generate the simulated values of demand for each random number

Follow these steps to generate the simulated values of demand:

1. Insert a new column titled "Cumulative Probability (lower limit) to the left of the "Demand for LED TVs" column.
2. In cell A4 under this new column, enter 0. In cell A5, enter the formula "A4+D4". Now copy this formula to cells A6 to A8.
3. In cell J4, enter the formula "= VLOOKUP(I4,$A$4:$B$8,2,TRUE). Copy this formula to cells J5 through J18.

This procedure will generate the simulated demand values in cells J4 to J18 as shown in Screenshot D.3.

SCREENSHOT D.3: Step 4 of Excel Simulation: Simulating Demand Values

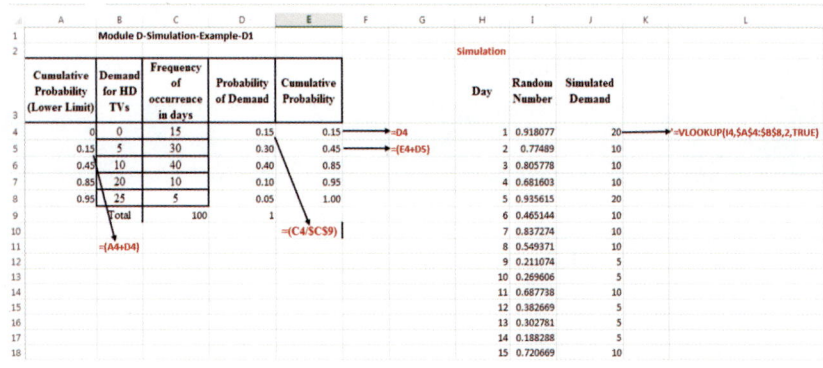

The VLOOKUP function in column J will look up the random number generated in column I, compare it with the "Cumulative Probabilities (Lower Limit)" in cells A4 through A8, and generate the correct demand values from cells B4 to B8. For example, the random number in Cell I4 is 0.918077. The VLOOKUP function will look down the "Cumulative Probabilities (Lower Limit)" column of the lookup table ($A$4:$B$8). When it finds the value of 0.95, it will retrieve the value from the cell in the immediate preceding row of column B ("Demand for LED TVs"). This demand value is 20, which is in cell B7. Thus, any random number that has value less than 0.95, but is greater than 0.85, will simulate a demand value of 20.

Step 5: Compute the average daily simulated demand

Type "AVERAGE(J4:J18)" in cell J19. The value is 1.8. Screenshot D.4 shows the final results of the simulation for Example D.1 using Excel.

 Note that the average value of 9.67 is higher than the 7.67 that we obtained earlier using manual simulation. This is because Excel generated a different stream of random numbers than the one we generated using the table of random numbers.

SCREENSHOT D.4: Step 5 of Excel Simulation: Final Simulation Results

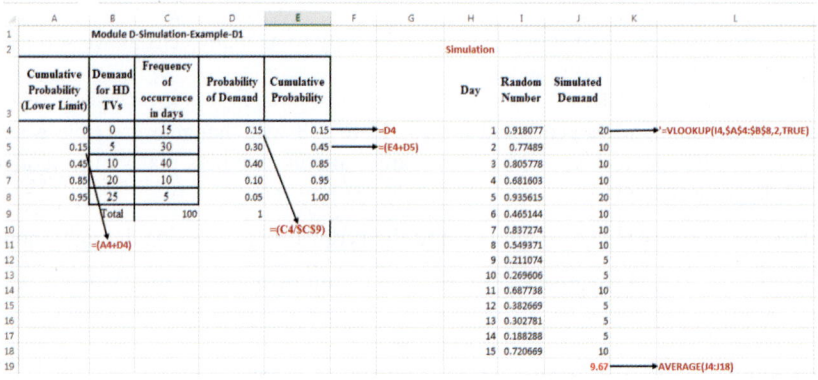

Inventory Simulation

Inventory Simulation

In Chapter 16, we discussed several inventory models that had many restrictive assumptions, including constant demand and constant lead times. None of these assumptions hold true for real-world inventory problems, and therefore, many of the inventory models that we discussed may not be applicable. Using simulation may be the only alternative for such intractable real-world inventory problems. Example D.2 illustrates how simulation can be used to solve inventory problems when both demand and lead times fluctuate.

EXAMPLE D.2: Daily demand for microwave ovens at Orion Electronics Store varies and the replenishment lead time of microwave reorders from the supplier is also variable.[b] Ryan Smith, the store manager, would like to establish an inventory policy of ordering 12 microwave units whenever the inventory level drops to 6. The replenishment lead time varies by 1, 2, or 3 days, which means that if the replenishment lead time is 2 days, an order placed on Monday will arrive on Thursday. Ryan would like to test this inventory policy using simulation. Based on the past 200 days of daily demand, Ryan has developed probability distributions for demand along with the frequency of occurrences. Similarly, based on the

TABLE D.7: Demand and Lead Time Frequency Distribution for Microwave Ovens

DEMAND FOR MICROWAVE OVENS	FREQUENCY OF OCCURRENCE (IN DAYS)	LEAD TIME FOR MICROWAVE OVENS	FREQUENCY OF OCCURRENCE (IN DAYS)
0	20	1	20
1	40	2	50
2	70	3	30
3	60		
4	20		
5	10		
	Total = 200		Total = 100

---

[b]Unless otherwise stated, in the Examples, Solved Problems, and Problems, fictional company names are used.

past 100 replenishment orders, he has developed probability distributions for lead times along with its frequency of occurrences. These data are given in Table D.7. Ryan also knows that any unmet demand for the microwave ovens as a result of inventory shortages will be lost sales. Assuming a beginning inventory of 8 units of microwave ovens, conduct a 10-day simulation experiment.

SOLUTION

We follow the steps that we used in the manual simulation of demand for HD TVs in Example D.1.

Steps 1 to 3: For this example D.2, the results of the first 3 steps of calculating the probabilities, cumulative probabilities, and establishing random intervals for both the random variables demand and lead time are given in Tables D.8 and D.9.

TABLE D.8: Probability, Cumulative Demand Probability Distribution, and Random Number Intervals for Microwave ovens

DEMAND FOR MICROWAVE OVENS	FREQUENCY OF OCCURRENCE (IN DAYS)	PROBABILITY OF DEMAND	CUMULATIVE PROBABILITY	RANDOM NUMBER INTERVAL
0	20	0.10	0.10	00 to 09
1	40	0.20	0.30	10 to 29
2	70	0.35	0.65	30 to 64
3	50	0.25	0.90	65 to 89
4	10	0.05	0.95	90 to 94
5	10	0.05	1.000	95 to 99
	Total = 200	1.00		

TABLE D.9: Probability, Cumulative Probability Distribution, and Random Number Intervals for Lead Times

LEAD TIME	FREQUENCY	PROBABILITY	CUMULATIVE PROBABILITY	RANDOM NUMBER INTERVAL
1	30	0.3	0.3	00 to 29
2	50	0.5	0.8	30 to 79
3	20	0.2	1.00	80 to 99
	Total = 100	1.00		

Steps 4 and 5: We use the random number table (Table D.5) to generate the needed random numbers. To generate the 10 days of simulated demand, we will begin at the top left-hand corner of Table D.5 and go down that column, noting the random number and daily demand that corresponds to that number. Similarly, whenever an order is placed, to generate the simulated lead times, we will begin at the top right-hand corner of Table D.5 and go down that column, noting the random number and the lead time that corresponds to that number. Note that selection of the starting point to choose a stream of random numbers is arbitrary. For simulating lead times, we chose the top right-hand corner as the starting point so as not to mirror our selection of random numbers for simulated demand. The results are shown in Table D.10. The entire 10-day simulation process for this inventory problem is presented in Table D.10.

TABLE D.10: Orion Electronics Inventory Simulation

DAY	ORDER RECEIPT	BEGINNING INVENTORY	RANDOM NUMBER	SIMULATED DEMAND	ENDING INVENTORY	LOST SALES	ORDER PLACED?	RANDOM NUMBER	SIMULATED LEAD TIME
1		8	56[a]	2	6	0	YES[b]	49[c]	2
2		6	14	1	5	0	NO[d]		
3		5	82	3	2	0	NO[d]		
4	12[e]	14	96	5	9	0	NO		
5		9	67	3	6	0	YES	60	2
6		6	83	3	3	0	NO		
7		3	83	3	0	0	NO		
8	12	12	02	0	12	0	NO		
9		12	04	0	12	0	NO		
10		12	53	2	10	0	NO		
					Total = 65				

[a] Random number that corresponds to the first simulated demand. As the random number 56 falls within 30 to 69 of the random number interval in Table D.8, the corresponding simulated demand is 2 units.

[b] First order was placed as the ending inventory hits the reorder point level of 6 units.

[c] Random number that corresponds to the first simulated lead time. As the random number 49 falls within 30 to 79 of the random number interval in Table D.9, the corresponding simulated lead time is 2 days.

[d] No orders were placed on days 2 and 3 as there is an outstanding order that was placed on day 1 that has not yet arrived.

[e] Order placed on day 1 for an order quantity of 12 units was received on day 4 at the expiration of the two-day lead time.

Populating Table D.10 was done one day at a time, beginning with day 1. On day 1 as the beginning inventory was 8 units and the simulated demand was 2 units, the ending inventory was $8 - 2 = 6$ units. As all units demanded were met on day 1, there were no lost sales. Nevertheless, as the ending inventory reached the reorder point level of 6 units, an order for 12 units was placed on day 1. That order was scheduled to be received on day 4 at the expiration of the simulated lead time of 2 days. Other rows in Table D.10 were completed using the same logic.

From the results obtained in Table D.10, we can calculate per day the average ending inventory level, average number of orders placed, and the average lost sales:

Average ending inventory = 69 / 10 = 6.9 units per day

Average number of orders placed = 2 / 10 = 0.2 orders per day

Average lost sales = 0 / 10 = 0

If we assume that the ordering cost of placing an order for the microwave oven is \$20/order, the holding cost is per oven per day is \$5, and the cost of each lost sale is \$15; then:

Inventory holding cost/day = (holding cost/oven/day) × Average ending inventory

= \$5 × 6.9 = \$34.50

Ordering cost/day = (ordering cost per order) × (average number of orders placed per day) = \$20/order × 0.2 = \$4.00 per day

Shortage cost/per day = (cost of each lost sale) × (average lost sales per day) = \$15 × 0 = 0

Hence:

Total daily inventory cost = \$34.50 + \$4.00 + \$0.00 = \$38.50

If Ryan Smith, the store manager of Orion Electronics, thinks that the total daily inventory cost incurred is too high using a 10-day simulation, he can extend the simulation to significantly more days (perhaps 100) before drawing any conclusions about his current inventory policy. Using a computer, he can conduct 1,000 days of simulation trials, and test alternative inventory policies that entail different order quantities and reorder points. In fact, Ryan should simulate all possible combinations of order quantities and reorder points using extended simulation runs, and then choose that combination of order quantity and reorder point that yields the lowest cost.

Screenshot D.5 shows the Excel simulation results for Example D.2. Note that the results obtained differ from the ones obtained from the simulation performed manually because Excel generated different sets of random numbers. In fact, the results obtained from Excel simulation is worse than those obtained manually as both the average inventory and lost sales values are higher in Excel simulation. This is precisely the reason why no conclusion can be drawn without a significant number of simulation trials.

SCREENSHOT D.5: Results of Inventory Simulation Using Excel

Module D-Simulation-Example-D2-Inventory Simulation

Order Quantity	12
Reorder point	6
B.Inventory	8

Cumulative Probability (Lower Limit)	Demand for Microwave Ovens	Frequency of occurrence in days	Probability of Demand	Cumulative Probability
0	0	20	0.10	0.10
0.10	1	40	0.20	0.30
0.30	2	70	0.35	0.65
0.65	3	50	0.25	0.90
0.90	4	15	0.08	0.98
0.98	5	5	0.03	1.00
	Total	200	1.00	

Simulation

Day	Order Receipt	B.Inventory	DemandR.N	Simulated Demand	E.Inventory	Lost Sales	Order Placed	Lead Time R.N.	Simulated Lead time
1		8	0.72744356	3	5	0	YES	0.653292185	2
2		5	0.99885831	5	0	0	NO		
3		0	0.87465121	3	0	3	NO		
4	12	12	0.49180144	2	10	0	NO		
5		10	0.24715045	1	9	0	YES	0.287969533	1
6		9	0.5788519	2	7	0	NO		
7	12	19	0.47197782	2	17	0	NO		
8		17	0.25859043	1	16	0	NO		
9		16	0.15331794	1	15	0	NO		
10		15	0.33055291	2	13	0	NO		
TOTAL					92	3			

Cumulative Probability (Lower Limit)	Lead time for Replenishment Orders	Frequency	Probability	Cumulative Probability
0.00	1	30	0.30	0.30
0.30	2	50	0.50	0.80
0.80	3	20	0.20	1.00
	Total	100	1.00	

Average Ending Inventory = 9.2
Average number of orders = 0.2
Average number of lost sales = 0.3

Sheet1

Simulation of Waiting Line Systems

In Module C, we discussed the assumptions that we had to make about arrival and service rates and noted that their probability distributions were restrictive. For most real-world waiting line problems, these assumptions do not hold. To solve such problems, simulation is the best approach we can use. Example D.3 illustrates the use of simulation for a small grocery store and its associated waiting line system. In this example, we make no assumption about the probability distribution of arrival and service rates, so none of the queueing models in Module C can be used to solve this problem. Let us then use simulation to generate the optimal solution.

 Waiting Line Simulation

EXAMPLE D.3: Customers arrive at the single checkout counter of a small grocery store at a rate of between 1 and 5 minutes. The service time at the checkout counter for each customer varies between 1 and 6 minutes. The probability distributions of interarrival times and service times are given in Table D.11 on page 854. Analyze this waiting line system by simulating the arrival and service times of 10 customers, assuming that the first customer arrives at time 0.

SOLUTION

We will follow the five steps of Monte Carlo simulation to solve this waiting line problem.

Steps 1 to 3: For Example D.3, the results of the first 3 steps of calculating the probabilities, cumulative probabilities, and establishing random intervals for both the random variables interarrival and service times are given in Tables D.12 and D.13.

TABLE D.11: Interarrival and Service Time Probability Distribution of Customers of a Grocery Store

INTERARRIVAL TIME	PROBABILITY	SERVICE TIME	PROBABILITY
1	0.10	1	0.10
2	0.20	2	0.20
3	0.40	3	0.30
4	0.20	4	0.15
5	0.10	5	0.15
		6	0.10
Total = 1.00			Total = 1.00

TABLE D.12: Probability, Cumulative Probability Distribution, and Random Number Intervals for Interarrival Times

INTERARRIVAL TIMES	PROBABILITY OF DEMAND	CUMULATIVE PROBABILITY	RANDOM NUMBER INTERVAL
1	0.10	0.10	00 to 09
2	0.20	0.30	10 to 29
3	0.40	0.70	30 to 69
4	0.20	0.90	69 to 89
5	0.10	1.00	90 to 99
Total = 1.00			

TABLE D.13: Probability, Cumulative Probability Distribution, and Random Number Intervals for Service Times

SERVICE TIMES	PROBABILITY OF DEMAND	CUMULATIVE PROBABILITY	RANDOM NUMBER INTERVAL
1	0.10	0.10	00 to 09
2	0.20	0.30	10 to 29
3	0.30	0.60	30 to 59
4	0.15	0.75	60 to 74
5	0.15	0.90	75 to 89
6	0.10	1.00	89 to 99
Total = 1.00			

Steps 4 and 5: We will use the random number table, Table D.5, to generate the needed random numbers. To generate the interarrival times of 10 customers, begin at the top of the second corner of Table D.5, go down the column, and note the random number and the interarrival time that corresponds to that number. Similarly, to generate customer service times, begin from the top right-hand corner of Table D.5, go across that row, and note down the random number and the service time that corresponds to that number. The results are shown in Table D.14. The entire 10-day simulation process for this waiting line problem is also presented in Table D.14.

TABLE D.14: Simulation of the Grocery Store Waiting Line System

CUSTOMER	RANDOM NUMBER	SIMULATED INTERARRIVAL TIME (IN MINUTES)	ARRIVAL TIME	RANDOM NUMBER	SIMULATED SERIVICE TIMES (IN MINUTES)	TIME SERVICE BEGINS	WAITING TIME IN QUEUE	TIME SERVICE ENDS	TIME CUSTOMER IS IN THE SYSTEM	SERVER IDLE TIME
1		–	0	49	3	3	0	3	3	0
2	74	4	4	80	5	4	0	9	5	1
3	19	2	6	94	6	9	3	15	9	0
4	15	2	8	65	4	15	7	22	11	0
5	25	2	10	16	2	22	12	24	14	0
6	87	4	14	33	3	24	10	27	13	0
7	64	3	17	27	2	27	10	29	12	0
8	18	2	19	20	2	29	10	31	12	0
9	61	3	22	89	6	31	9	37	15	0
10	54	3	25	91	6	37	12	43	18	0
Total		25			39		73		112	1

- As the first customer was assumed to arrive at time 0, service begins immediately and finishes at time unit 3. The first customer was in the waiting line system for:

$$\text{(Waiting time + Service time)} = 0 + 3 = 3 \text{ minutes}$$

- The second customer arrives at time unit 4. But since the first customer left the checkout counter at time unit 3, the system has been idle for 1 minute (4 – 3). This is shown in the last cell of the second row. The second customer's service time is 5 minutes and leaves the system at time unit 9:

$$\text{(arrival time + service time} = 4 + 5 = 9)$$

- The third customer arrives at the sixth time unit. Nevertheless, since the service provided for the second customer ends only at the ninth time unit, the service for the third customer can only start at the ninth time unit. Hence, the waiting time for the third customer is:

$$\text{(Time service begins – Arrival time)} = \text{Waiting time, or } 9 - 6 = 3 \text{ minutes}$$

Subsequent rows in the table are completed in a similar manner. From the simulation results shown in Table D.14, we can calculate the following key performance measures for this grocery store waiting line system:

$$\text{Average waiting time per customer} = \frac{Total\ Waiting\ Time}{Number\ of\ Customers} = \frac{73\ minutes}{10} = 7.3 \text{ minutes/customer}$$

$$\text{Average service time per customer} = \frac{Total\ Service\ Time}{Number\ of\ Customers} = \frac{39\ minutes}{10} = 3.9 \text{ minutes/customer}$$

$$\text{Average total time in the system time per customer} = \frac{Total\ Time\ in\ the\ system}{Number\ of\ Customers} = \frac{112\ minutes}{10}$$
$$= 11.2 \text{ minutes/customer}$$

Probability that a customer has to wait in the queue
$$= \frac{Total\ number\ of\ customer\ Waiting\ in\ queue}{Number\ of\ Customers} = \frac{8}{10} = 80\%$$

From the results obtained from our simulation of 10 customers, it appears that customers' waiting time in the queue is high. Yet, no definitive conclusion can be drawn about this waiting line system unless simulation is extended to significantly more customer trials. Simulating 10 customers shows an average of 7.3 minutes average waiting time; were we to simulate 200–300 customers, we might find somewhat different results.

Visit **edge.sagepub.com/venkataraman** to help you accomplish your coursework goals in an easy-to-use learning environment.

- Mobile-friendly eFlashcards
- Mobile-friendly practice quizzes
- A complete online action plan

- Chapter summaries with learning objectives
- Video and multimedia resources

MODULE SUMMARY

D.1 Explain the concept of simulation, its advantages, and the key steps in developing a simulation model. Simulation involves building physical or analytical/mathematical models that attempt to duplicate real-world systems or problems. By doing so, the simulation process enables a manager to study and analyze the real-world system without actually building it. The wide range of business applications for which simulation can be applied also illustrates just how valuable the process can be. Some of the many applications for simulation include production scheduling, employee/worker scheduling, analysis of waiting line systems, inventory planning and control, design of plant layout and distribution systems, and sales processes.

There are eight key steps in developing a simulation model. These steps include (1) develop a model that represents the real-life system or process that is to be studied and analyzed; (2) define the problem; (3) formulate the mathematical model; (4) gather the data needed for the study; (5) translate the model to computerized simulation software;

(6) verify and validate the model; (7) experimentation and analysis; and (8) documentation and recommendation.

D.2 Describe Monte Carlo simulation, and set up and solve operations problems using Monte Carlo simulation, by hand and using Excel. Although simple problems and systems can be studied through manual simulation, most real-world problems and systems are complex and, therefore, require computer simulation models. The Monte Carlo simulation approach uses random numbers to represent key random variables such as demand, lead time, arrival rates, and services times. These variables are then simulated in a series of trials to examine policy decisions. Although simpler examples can be solved by manually using Monte Carlo simulation, for larger problems that are more complex or involve more variables, it is often necessary to employ software tools to solve such problems using Monte Carlo simulation. Excel is a popular choice for solving problems using Monte Carlo simulation, as we demonstrated throughout this module.

KEY TERMS

Cumulative probability distribution 844	Physical simulation 842	Simulation 841
Monte Carlo simulation 844	Random numbers 844	

DISCUSSION AND REVIEW QUESTIONS

1. What is simulation, and why is it a widely used tool for solving real-world problems?

2. Provide some examples of real-world problems that have been studied using simulation.

3. What steps should a manager follow in using the simulation tool?

4. What is Monte Carlo simulation?

5. What role do random numbers play in the Monte Carlo simulation process?

6. Provide examples of how some companies use Monte Carlo simulation.

7. List the five basic steps of the Monte Carlo simulation technique.

8. To draw meaningful conclusions about the simulation study of a real-world system, a large number of simulation trials is required. Why?

9. What are the advantages of computer simulations (compared to manual simulations) in analyzing real-world problems?

10. Why simulation may be the only choice (instead of other analytical tools) that a manager may have in studying inventory ordering policies and waiting line problems?

11. List the disadvantages of simulation.

SOLVED PROBLEM

Tom Daly, owner of an automobile tire store, has a certain brand of radial tires for which the probability distribution of demand per day and the probability distribution of the lead time, developed from past records, are as shown in the following tables. Tom Daly would like to establish an inventory policy of ordering 30 radial tires whenever the inventory level drops to 15. The replenishment lead time that varies by 1, 2, 3, or 4 days means that if the replenishment lead time is 3 days an order placed on Monday will arrive on Friday. Tom would like to test this inventory policy using simulation. Tom also knows that any unmet demand for radial tires as a result of inventory shortage will incur a backorder cost. Backorders will be filled the day when there is inventory in stock. The costs associated with ordering, holding inventory, and backorders are given here. Assuming a beginning inventory of 20 radial tires, conduct a 20-day Monte Carlo simulation experiment and compute the total inventory costs for this simulation study.

TABLE D.15: Daily Demand Probability Distribution for Radial Tires

Daily Demand	1	2	3	4	5	6	7	8	9	10
Probability	0.05	0.08	0.12	0.25	0.20	0.15	0.05	0.05	0.03	0.02

TABLE D.16: Lead Time Probability Distribution for Radial Tires

Lead Time (in days)	1	2	3	4
Probability	0.20	0.30	0.40	0.10

Ordering cost per order = $60

Holding cost per unit per day = $2

Backorder cost = $30 per day

Solution:

Using the five basic steps of Monte Carlo Simulation, begin solving this problem by developing cumulative probability distributions and assigning two-digit random number intervals for both the demand and lead-time random variables. These results are shown in Tables D.17 and D.18.

TABLE D.17: Cumulative Demand Probability Distribution and Random Number Intervals for Radial Tires

Demand for Radial Tires	Probability of Demand	Cumulative Probability	Random Number Interval
1	0.05	0.05	00 to 04
2	0.08	0.13	05 to 12
3	0.12	0.25	13 to 24
4	0.25	0.50	25 to 49
5	0.20	0.70	50 to 69
6	0.15	0.85	70 to 84
7	0.05	0.90	85 to 89
8	0.05	0.95	90 to 94
9	0.03	0.98	95 to 97
10	0.02	1.00	98 to 99
Total	1.00		

TABLE D.18: Cumulative Lead Time Probability Distribution and Random Number Intervals for Radial Tires

Lead Time	Probability	Cumulative Probability	Random Number Interval
1	0.20	0.20	00 to 19
2	0.30	0.50	20 to 49
3	0.40	0.90	50 to 89
4	0.10	1.00	90 to 99
Total	1.00		

Use the random number table in Table D.5 to generate the needed random numbers. To generate the 20 days of simulated demand, begin at the top left-hand corner of Table D.5 and go across that row and note the random number and the daily demand that corresponds to that number. Similarly, whenever an order is placed, generate the simulated lead times by beginning at the top right-hand corner of Table D.5, going down that column, and noting the random number and the lead time that corresponds to that number The results and the entire 20-day simulation process for this inventory problem are presented in Table D.19.

TABLE D.19: Radial Tires Inventory Simulation

Day	Order Receipt	Beg. Inv.	R.N.	Simulated Demand	End. Inv.	Backorders	Order Placed	R.N.	Simulated LT
1		20	56[a]	5	15	0	YES[b]	49[c]	2
2		15	74	6	9	0	NO[d]		
3		9	93	8	1	0	NO[d]		
4	30[e]	31	83	6	25	0	NO		
5		25	39	4	21	0	NO		
6		21	69	5	16	0	NO		
7		16	06	2	14	0	YES	60	3
8		14	44	4	10	0	NO		
9		10	81	6	4	0	NO		
10		4	70	6	0	2[f]	NO		
11	30	30	50	5	23[g]	0	NO		
12		23	11	2	21	0	NO		
13		21	28	4	17	0	NO		
14		17	29	4	13	0	YES	48	2
15		13	26	4	9	0	NO		
16		9	36	4	5	0	NO		
17	30	35	07	2	33	0	NO		
18		33	93	8	25	0	NO		
19		25	07	2	23	0	NO		
20		23	66	5	18	0	NO		
Total					302	2	3		

[a] Random number that corresponds to the first simulated demand. As the random number 56 falls within 50 to 69 of the random number interval in Table D.16, the corresponding simulated demand is 5 tires.
[b] First order was placed as the ending inventory hits the reorder point level of 15 tires.
[c] Random number that corresponds to the first simulated lead time. As the random number 49 falls within 20 to 49 of the random number interval in Table D.17, the corresponding simulated lead time is 2 days.
[d] No orders were placed on days 2 and 3 as there is an outstanding order that was placed on day 1 that has not yet arrived.
[e] Order placed on day 1 for an order quantity of 30 tires was received on day 4 at the expiration of the 2-day lead time.
[f] Denotes back order of 2 tires as the demand for 6 tires exceeds the inventory in stock of 4 tires.
[g] Denotes the ending inventory after the backorder of 2 tires was filled along with the current demand of 5 tires on day 11.

Populating Table D.19 was done one day at a time beginning with day 1. On day 1 as the beginning inventory was 20 tires and the simulated demand was 5 tires, the ending inventory was 20 − 5 = 15 tires. As all units demanded were met on day 1, there were backorders. Nevertheless, as the ending inventory reached the reorder point level of 15 tires, an order for 30 tires was placed on day 1. That order was scheduled to be received on day 4 at the expiration of the simulated lead time of 2 days. Other rows in Table D.19 were completed using the same logic.

Table D.19 also shows the total ending inventory level, total number of orders placed, and the total back orders.

Total ending inventory = 302 tires

Total number of orders placed = 3

Total back orders = 2 tires

Given the ordering cost of placing an order for radial tires is $60/order, the holding cost per tire per day is $2, and the cost of each backordered tire is $10, we have:

Total inventory holding cost = (holding cost/oven/day) × total ending inventory = $2 × 302 = $604.00

Total ordering cost = (ordering cost per order) × (total number of orders placed) = $60/order × 3 = $180.00

Total backorder cost = (cost of each backorder) × (backorder cost/tire/day) = $10 × 2 = $20

Hence, the total inventory for the 20-day period is:

Total inventory cost = $604.00 + $180.00 + $20.00 = $804.00

PROBLEMS

1. The interarrival time of cars at a toll booth on an interstate expressway is defined by the following probability distribution:

Interarrival Time (in minutes)	1	2	3	4
Probability	0.25	0.35	0.30	0.10

   a. Simulate the arrival of cars at the toll booth for 15 arrivals, and compute the average interarrival time.

   b. Using a different stream of random numbers from those used in (a), compute the average interarrival time by simulating the arrival of cars at the toll booth for 30 minutes.

   c. What conclusions can you draw by comparing the results obtained in (a) and (b).

2. Refer to problem D.1. The service time for each car arriving at this toll booth is between 1 and 5 minutes. The probability distribution of service times is given in the following table. Using the same data for interarrival times given in problem D.1., simulate the arrival and service times of 15 cars, assuming that the first car arrives at time 0:

Service Time (in minutes)	1	2	3	4	5
Probability	0.20	0.40	0.20	0.15	0.05

   a. Compute for each car the average waiting time in queue, the average service time, and the average total time in the toll booth system.

   b. What is the probability that a car waits in the queue?

3. The time between emergency calls at the 9-1-1 emergency call service of a Pennsylvania township has the following probability distribution. The 9-1-1 service sends emergency responders 24 hours per day, 7 days per week:

Time Between Emergency Calls (in hours)	1	2	3	4	5	6	7	8
Probability	0.10	0.15	0.20	0.20	0.15	0.10	0.06	0.04

   a. From the probability distribution, compute the expected value of the time between calls.

   b. Using a random number table, simulate the emergency calls for 2 days. (Hint: Use a "running" or cumulative, hourly clock), and compute the average time between calls.

   c. Compare the values obtained in (a) and (b). Provide an explanation for the different results.

4. Refer to Example D.2. Ryan Smith, the Orion Electronics store manager, would like to try an alternative inventory policy of ordering 15 microwave units whenever the inventory level drops to 5. Also, any unmet customer demand will be backordered and the backorders will be filled immediately when there is inventory in stock. The ordering cost of placing an order for the microwave oven is $20/order, the holding cost per oven per day is $5, and the cost of each backorder per day per oven is $15:

   a. Using the same data for beginning inventory, daily demand, and lead times given in Example D.2, conduct a 20-day inventory simulation.

   b. Compute the total inventory cost for this inventory simulation.

5. The Neptune Manufacturing Company has a process that requires four machines to manufacture a product. The number of machines that will break down in any given week varies and the time to repair a machine is also a random variable. Both the random variables of machine breakdowns and repair times have probability distributions given in the following tables:

Machine Breakdowns per Week	0	1	2	3	4
Probability	0.20	0.30	0.30	0.15	0.05

Repair Time (in hours)	1	2	3	4
Probability	0.20	0.40	0.30	0.10

   a. By using different streams of random numbers for breakdowns and repair times, simulate the repair time for 15 weeks and compute the average repair time.

   b. If the cost of machine downtime and repairing the machine is $100, what is the average weekly breakdown cost?

6. The Gulf Shipping Company in Dubai, UAE, unloads cargo from ships arriving daily on a first-come, first-served basis. Ships that are not unloaded on the day they arrive are unloaded the following day. Nevertheless, ships that are waiting to be unloaded cost money. The arrival rates of ships and the daily unloading rates are random variables with no known probability distributions. The manager of the Port of Dubai wants to improve the efficiency of the waiting line system and decides to conduct a simulation study to analyze cargo ship arrivals, unloading of cargo, and delays that occur in the Port. Based on last year's data, the port manager has compiled the data given in the following table:

Number of Daily Ship Arrivals	0	1	2	3	4	5
Probability	0.10	0.20	0.25	0.30	0.10	0.05

Daily Unloading Rates of Ships	1	2	3	4	5
Probability	0.15	0.25	0.35	0.15	0.10

a.   Conduct a 20-day simulation trial of ship arrivals and unloading of cargo.

a.   Based on the simulation results, compute the daily average number of ship arrivals, daily average number of ships unloaded, and the average number ships waiting to be unloaded till the next day.

7. The administrator of emergency ward of Trinity Hospital has to decide the number of doctors to be made available to treat patients arriving at the facility every night. The number of doctors required varies with the type of emergency, which are classified as minor, routine, and critical. A minor emergency will require one doctor, whereas the routine and critical emergencies require will require 2 and 4 doctors, respectively. Both the arrival rates of patients to the emergency ward and the type of emergency are random variables with no known probability distribution. Yet, the administrator of the emergency ward was able to determine from past hospital records the following probability distributions for the two random variables:

Arrival Rate of Patients	0	1	2	3	4	5	6	7
Probability	0.05	0.10	0.15	0.20	0.25	0.10	0.10	0.05

Type of Emergency	Minor	Routine	Critical
Probability	0.20	0.50	0.30

a.   Conduct a 15-night simulation trial of patient arrivals and emergency type for the emergency ward of Trinity Hospital.

b.   Compute the average number of patient arrivals each night, the average number of each type of emergency each night, and the maximum number of doctors needed for any given night.

8. Champion Electronics Warehouse sells a certain brand of headsets that it orders from Reliance Electronics in Japan. The probability distribution of demand per week for the headsets and the probability distribution of the replenishment lead time for the headset orders placed, which were developed from past records, are as shown in the following tables. Champion would like to establish an inventory policy of ordering 20 headsets whenever the inventory level drops to 5 units. The replenishment lead time that varies by 1, 2, 3, or 4 weeks means that if the replenishment lead time is 2 weeks, an order placed on week 1 will arrive at the beginning of week 4. Any unmet customer demand for headsets as a result of inventory shortage will be lost with a lost sales cost of $200. The costs associated with ordering headsets and holding inventory are $70 per order and $20 per headset per week. Assuming a beginning inventory of 8 headsets, conduct a 10-week Monte Carlo simulation experiment and compute total inventory costs for this simulation study:

Weekly Demand	1	2	3	4	5	6	7	8	9	10
Probability	0.05	0.08	0.12	0.25	0.20	0.15	0.05	0.05	0.03	0.02

Lead Time per Week	1	2	3	4
Probability	0.20	0.30	0.40	0.10

9. A satellite TV network provider receives calls for technical assistance from customers at its call center. The interarrival time between calls is a random variable and varies between 1 and 5 minutes. The call center has two technical personnel, Tom and Harry, to provide technical assistance to calling customers. As a result of his experience, Tom can provide faster service to customers than Harry can. The probability distributions of arrival times and service times of Tom and Harry are given in the following tables:

Time Between Calls (in minutes)	1	2	3	4	5
Probability	0.20	0.25	0.35	0.15	0.05

Tom's Service Time (in minutes)	1	2	3	4	5
Probability	0.15	0.25	0.35	0.15	0.10

Harry's Service Time (in minutes)	3	4	5	6	7
Probability	0.25	0.35	0.20	0.15	0.05

a. Conduct a 20-caller simulation study of this call center study.

b. Compute average customer waiting time, average time the customer is in the system, and the average service time of Tom and Harry.

10. A grinding machine has two bearings that fail periodically. The probability distribution of the life of both bearings is identical and is shown in the following table:

Life of the Bearing (in hours)	800	900	1,000	1,100	1,200	1,300	1,400	1,500	1,600	1,700
Probability	0.05	0.08	0.12	0.25	0.20	0.15	0.05	0.05	0.03	0.02

When a bearing fails, a repair technician is called to replace the failed bearing with a new bearing. The service time it takes to remove the failed bearing and install a new bearing is a random variable that has a probability distribution shown in the following table:

Service Time (in minutes)	5	10	15	20
Probability	0.20	0.40	0.30	0.10

The repair technician charges an hourly rate of $40 for his service. The downtime costs on the grinding machine as a result of a failed bearing is $1,000 per hour. Management has decided to replace both bearings even if only one of the two fails. Conduct a simulation study of 10 trials of bearing replacement, and compute the total cost.

CASE STUDY D.1 STAYING AHEAD OF THE DEMAND FOR ICE CREAM

The Millers Ice Cream store in Bar Harbor, Maine, is one of the most popular tourist destinations in the downtown area. Bar Harbor is the definition of a seasonal attraction, with most of its crowds and foot traffic occurring during the busy summer months, from Memorial Day to Labor Day. During this time, Bar Harbor receives thousands of visitors each week and business at the ice cream store is brisk. On the other hand, once the summer season ends, foot traffic quickly drops off and the shop settles in for the slower fall and winter seasons. In past years, Millers has not done a good job estimating demand for its products and as a result have often ended the season with a large inventory of ice cream that will not keep well for the next summer. Millers even has a problem with estimating demand during the hot summer months. If too much ice cream is ordered each time, Millers must rent extra storage freezers. Ordering too little ice cream means lost sales or high shipping rates to rush extra supplies to the store.

This summer, the owner's nephew, Pat, has returned from his university's business school with better knowledge of simulation and has set about organizing the ordering system to make it more efficient. After going through the past year's sales records, Pat determined that the majority of sales came from ice cream cones and decided to use simulation to estimate the demand for the upcoming summer. Because of the short summer, he chose to analyze sales each two-week period (the typical time between reordering ice cream). His analysis found the following:

Based on this information:

1. Calculate the probability of demand for ice cream across each increment.

2. Using random numbers, simulate demand values across the 14-day period.

3. Calculate the average daily simulated demand for ice cream.

Optional:

4. Use Excel to calculate average daily simulated demand for ice cream.

Demand for Ice Cream Cones	Frequency of Occurrence (in days)
100	2
150	3
200	5
250	3
300	1

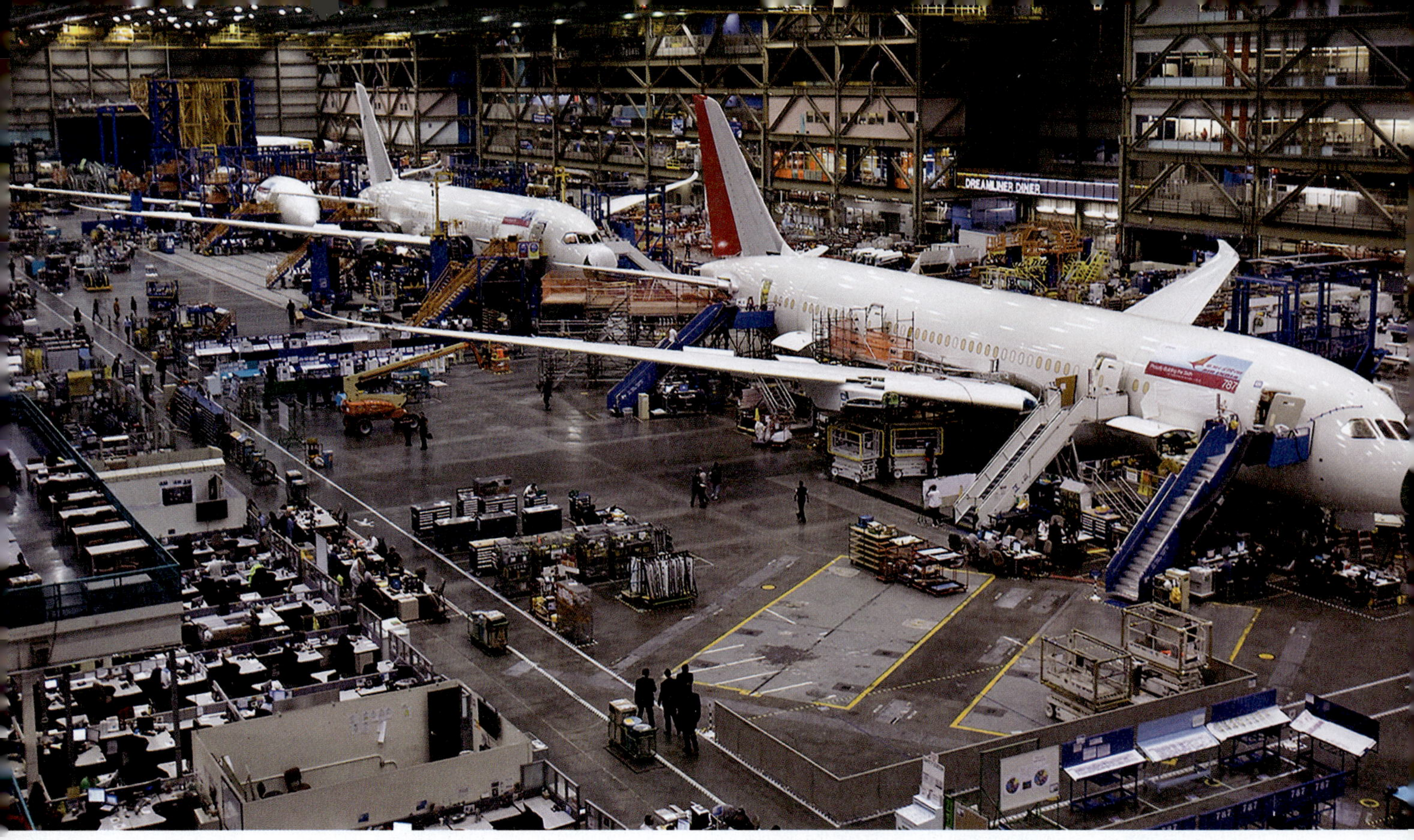

Bloomberg/Bloomberg/Getty Images

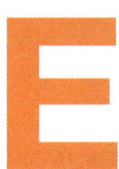

MODULE E Learning Curves

LEARNING OBJECTIVES

After studying this module, you should be able to:

1. Define the concept of learning curves.
2. Identify the various ways to apply learning curves for operations processes.
3. Apply various approaches to solving learning curve problems.
4. Implement learning curves for cost estimation problems.
5. Discuss the advantages and limitations of learning curves.

OPERATIONS PROFILE: Boeing: Relying on Learning Curves for Cost Analysis and Pricing Decisions

Learning curves have a self-evident name: We (people and companies) often learn at predictable rates. If can determine just how quickly we learn, we can make accurate predictions about factors like construction costs, parts and labor rates, and subsequently, optimal pricing for our products. Learning curves were first used by the aircraft industry in the 1930s. The Boeing Company (Chicago, IL) pioneered the discipline when it discovered that the cost to build new airplanes was highly predictable and followed a declining curve.

It might cost $100 million to build the first model of a new airplane, $80 million to build the second, $64 million to make the fourth, $51 million for the eighth, and so on, with the unit cost falling 20% at every doubling of volume before reaching a plateau—say $15 million—past which the product cannot be produced any cheaper.[a] Learning curves help us understand that the planes get cheaper to build as the company learns how to build them more efficiently. Workers work faster, make fewer mistakes, and waste less material.

Plotting these production costs against units of production yields a learning curve that slopes from the upper left to the lower right. The steeper the curve, the faster the person, project team, or company is learning to produce an item or service.

This information can be crucial for a company like Boeing. It knows it can't price its new airplane at $100 million or even $50 million, but it can make a profit by pricing it at $25 million each. This aggressive, lower figure recognizes that manufacturing the first half dozen or so aircrafts in a new model will be expensive and lead to overall losses, but low prices also discourage rivals like Airbus SAS (Blagnac, France) or Bombardier Inc. (Montreal, Quebec, Canada) from entering the market, while motivating the plant assembly personnel to ramp up production and work more efficiently and quickly, cutting the costs to the point where a $25 million price tag will result in a strong profit. When will the company reach a break-even level of production, how much will it have lost up to that point, and how much profit will it make on planes built after that? Learning curves can help answer those kinds of questions.

Boeing Moves Down the Learning Curve Average Days in Final Assembly

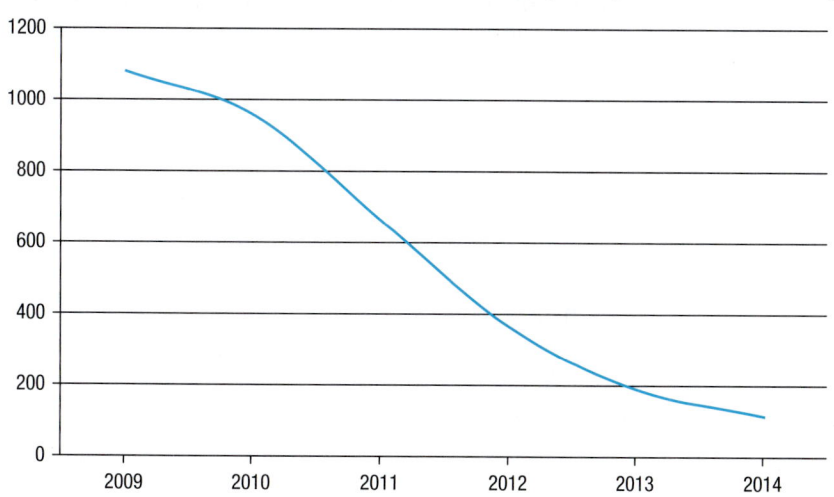

SOURCE: Adapted from AirInsight.com. (2014, November 7). Boeing and the 787 learning curve. Retrieved from http://airinsight.com/2014/11/07/boeing-787-learning-curve/#.VVns5_IVhBd

---

[a]Unless otherwise stated, all currency is in U.S. dollars.

This information is important for the latest model aircraft that Boeing has introduced: the 787. Although technical challenges and leading edge materials initially delayed the learning curve and led to significant losses in the early years for the airplane, in the past three years, overall costs are steadily decreasing. From the start of production at the Everett, Washington, plant, it now takes 40 days to push a new 787 out the door. On the other hand, at the Columbia, South Carolina, plant, the learning curve still lags to a 56-day process. By the turn of the decade, Boeing expects to split production equally between the two plants, with each building seven airplanes a month. Once the two main plants can match production of the 787 at the faster rate, Boeing executives anticipate the program will become stable and highly profitable.[1]

E.1 What Are Learning Curves?

E.1

Define the concept of learning curves.

 Learning Curves

Typically, as workers repeat their tasks, their performance improves. Specifically, when an activity is performed repeatedly, the time required to perform it steadily decreases. This is because workers learn to perform the task more accurately and efficiently with each repetition. Learning curves capture this phenomenon. Learning curves show that as the production rate for an item doubles, the processing time per unit of that item decreases by a constant percentage. In fact, some research supports the idea that performance improves by a fixed percentage each time production doubles.[2]

The extent of improvement and the number of repetitions required to achieve a significant improvement in performance, however, depends on the nature and complexity of the task performed. For activities that are fairly complex and take a long time to complete, such as ship building or aircraft assembly, performance improvements occur over a longer time span. On the other hand, for short, routine or repetitive activities, minor improvements may be realized after only a few repetitions. Hence, learning curve tools are most useful for measuring performance improvements for nonroutine and complex jobs that require several repetitions and a long time to complete. For routine and repetitive jobs of short duration, such as in repetitive manufacturing or mass production processes, learning curves are of little use. Figure E.1 shows the basic learning curve relationship between the number of repetitions or units produced and the time required per repetition or unit.

Note that in Figure E.1, the curve flattens out after the number of repetitions or units produced reach a certain point. This flattening suggests that after a certain point, no further learning occurs, each subsequent repetition or unit produced takes the same amount of time, and the system has reached a steady state. Learning, and hence improvement in performance, will not occur indefinitely and the curve will never touch the horizontal axis; in other words, the time per repetition or unit produced will never be zero. Furthermore, the time reduction per repetition will steadily decrease as the number of repetitions or units produced increases. Once the system reaches a steady state, no further reduction in time per repetition or unit occurs. Figure E.2 illustrates this behavior of learning curves.

As mentioned, as the number of repetition units of an item produced doubles, the processing time per unit of that item decreases by a constant percentage. This constant percentage is typically in the 10% to 20% range. The convention used to describe learning curves is in terms of the complement of their improvement rates. Thus, an 80% learning curve means that there will be a 20% (100% − 80%)

Learning curves: a principle that shows that as the production rate for an item doubles, the processing time per unit of that item decreases by a constant percentage

FIGURE E.1: Learning Curve Relationship

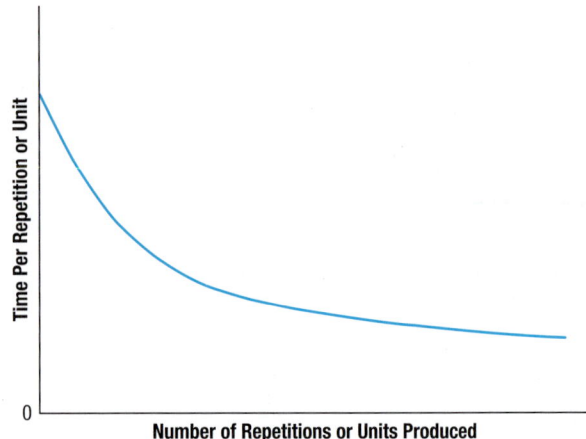

FIGURE E.2: End of Learning or Improvement

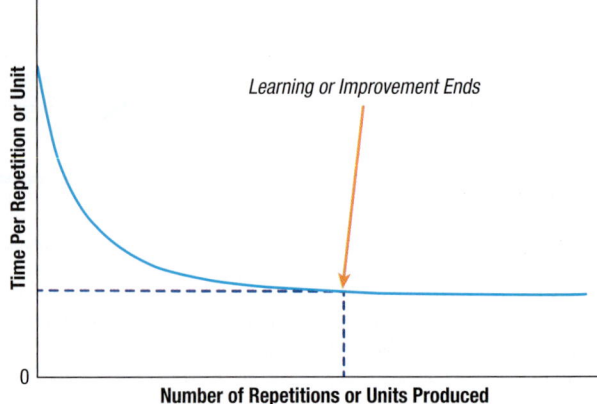

decrease in unit time as the number of repetitions or units produced doubles. Similarly a 10% improvement is denoted by a 90% learning curve, and so on.

E.2 Applications of Learning Curves

Identify the various ways to apply learning curves for operations processes.

Using the Concept of Learning Curves

The learning curve is a powerful concept and is applicable to all processes that involve learning. Although uses of learning curves were known as early as 1885, they were first applied in the aircraft industry in 1936. In an article published in the *Journal of Aeronautical Sciences*, Theodore Paul Wright described the impact of learning on the cost of producing an airplane. Specifically, he showed that as the number of planes produced increased, the direct labor cost of producing those airplanes decreased.[3] Since then, the concept of learning curves has been applied in a wide variety of manufacturing and service organizations, including electronics, automotives, construction, aerospace, chemical, steel, hospitals, restaurants, and software companies. It is important to note, however, that it is much easier to apply learning curves in areas such as manufacturing where the outputs are physical products. It can be more challenging to apply learning curves in the service industry where the outputs are often intangible and therefore more difficult to measure. In addition to its broad applications in the manufacturing and service sectors, learning curves have been found to be useful in specific areas that include:

- *Workforce planning and scheduling*
  Learning curves can help operations managers to plan their workforce levels. Given known learning rates and initial production output rates, managers can use learning curves to determine the number of workers needed and when they are needed to meet planned production level targets.

- *Cost estimation and budgeting*
  Learning curves can enable managers to create cost estimates for labor and materials. During the initial stages of production, the per unit labor cost will be high and material usage will be low as a result of the low volume of output. Nevertheless, as learning occurs, the increased productivity will reduce per unit labor costs and increase the material usage rate. Knowledge of such learning curve effects will help managers to develop more accurate estimates of labor and material costs that will be incurred during production cycles.

- *Procurement negotiations in supply chains*
  The procurement of complex items such as drill rigs, aircraft, or special-purpose machines typically involve negotiated purchasing. Although the direct labor cost for the initial units produced of such made-to-order items will be high, these costs are bound to decrease as more of these specialized items are produced as a result of the effects of learning curves. Understanding learning curves will enable procurement specialists to determine the number of units of the specialized item that they plan to order, and then negotiate with the supplier based on the order size. Increasingly, procurement contracts are coming to reflect the impact of learning curves for repetitive operations. In the automotive industry, the manufacturer of hydraulic cylinders may be given a contract for the first year to provide cylinders at a price of $24 each. Each subsequent year, the cost of the cylinder sold to the automobile maker is priced at $1 less, under the assumption that learning curves will allow the cylinder manufacturer to produce the product at a steadily lower cost. Learning curves are factored into the value of long-term contracts.

- *New product pricing*
  Understanding learning curve effects can help managers to set appropriate prices for new products. As our Boeing example illustrated, although the initial cost of producing a new product will be high, managers armed with the knowledge of learning curves realize that production costs will decrease as the production levels for the new product increase over time. As a result, managers can price their product lower than the initial cost of making the product, and once the learning curve effect kicks in, the product can be produced for less than its selling price. Learning curve effects enable managers to pursue aggressive pricing strategies to penetrate new markets and still be profitable in the long run.

Several companies use learning curves and reap the benefits from its effects. We noted in our profile on Boeing at the beginning of this module that they use learning curves for capacity analysis, resource requirements planning, cost-reduction proposals, and estimations of production-line performance. Similarly, numerous hospitals use learning curves to evaluate the efficiency and effectiveness of medical procedures and the use of technologies.

E.3

Apply various
approaches to
solving learning
curve problems.

E.3 Approaches to Solving Learning Curve Problems

There are three possible approaches to solving learning curve problems: arithmetic approach, logarithmic formula approach, or by using a table of learning curve coefficient values.

Arithmetic Approach

Solving a Learning
Curve Problem

The arithmetic approach is the simplest of the three approaches and is based on the assumption that as production doubles, the per unit production time declines by a constant percentage, often referred to as the learning rate. Assume that it takes 200 labor hours to produce the first unit of a product and that the learning rate for this production process is 70%. Using the arithmetic approach, Table E.1 shows the labor hours required to produce the second, fourth, eighth, 16th, and the 32nd unit.

Table E.1 shows that as production doubles, the time required to produce the doubled unit declines but by a decreasing margin. The time required to produce the second unit is 60 hours (200 – 140) less than the first unit. Similarly, the time required to produce the fourth unit is 32 hours (140 – 98) less than the second unit, and so on. This illustrates the behavior of learning curves shown in Figure E.1. One major limitation of the arithmetic approach is that it is only suitable for estimating the number of hours required to produce the nth unit, where n is a doubled value. This approach cannot be used to find the time required to produce the intermediate units such as the third, fifth, or seventh unit. The logarithmic approach, which we discuss in the next section, provides the flexibility to estimate the time required to produce any unit value of production.

TABLE E.1: Arithmetic Approach to Estimate Learning Curve Effects

nTH UNIT PRODUCED	TIME ESTIMATE IN HOURS FOR THE nTH UNIT
1	200
2	(200 × 0.70) = 140
4	(140 × 0.70) = 98
8	(98 × 0.70) = 68.6
16	(68.6 × 0.70) = 48.02
32	(48.02 × 0.70) = 33.614

Logarithmic Approach

The logarithmic approach uses the following formula to determine the number of direct labor hours required to produce the nth unit:

$T_n = T_1 \times n^b$ where

T_n = the time required to produce the nth unit

T_1 = the time required to produce the first unit

b = ln (learning rate) / ln (2), where "ln" stands for natural logarithm

To use the formula to determine the time required to produce the nth unit (T_n), you need to know the time required to produce the first unit (T_1) and the learning rate. Alternatively, to determine the time required to produce the first unit (T_1), you need to know the time required to produce the nth unit (T_n), and the learning rate.

EXAMPLE E.1: Trinity Hospital[b] just completed its first kidney transplant, a procedure that took 40 hours. During the month of May, the hospital has four more kidney transplants scheduled. Based on other similar procedures that the hospital has conducted, the hospital estimates that it has an 85% learning rate. Estimate the time it will take to complete:

---

[b]Unless otherwise stated, in the Examples, Solved Problems, and Problems, fictional company names are used.

a.   The third transplant

b.   The fifth transplant

c.   The total time required for all five transplants

SOLUTION

Given: T_1 = 40 hours; learning rate = 85%

Hence, b = ln (learning rate) / ln (2) = b = ln (0.85) / ln (2) = (−0.1625 / 0.693) = −0.234

As, $T_n = T_1 \times n^b$

a.   The time required for the third transplant is:

$$T_3 = 40 \times 3^{(-0.234)} = 40 \times 0.773 = 30.92 \text{ hours}$$

b.   The time required for the fifth transplant is:

$$T_5 = 40 \times 5^{(-0.234)} = 40 \times 0.686 = 27.44 \text{ hours}$$

c.   The total time required for all five transplants is:

$$T_1 + T_2 + T_3 + T_4 + T_5$$

$$T_1 = 40 \text{ hours}$$

$$T_2 = 40 \times 2^{(-0.234)} = 40 \times 0.850 = 34.00 \text{ hours}$$

$$T_3 = 40 \times 3^{(-0.234)} = 40 \times 0.773 = 30.92 \text{ hours}$$

$$T_4 = 40 \times 4^{(-0.234)} = 40 \times 0.723 = 28.92 \text{ hours}$$

$$T_5 = 40 \times 5^{(-0.234)} = 40 \times 0.686 = 27.44 \text{ hours}$$

Therefore:

$$T_1 + T_2 + T_3 + T_4 + T_5 = 40.00 + 34.00 + 30.92 + 28.92 + 27.44 = 161.28$$

The Microsoft Excel (Microsoft Corporation, Redmond, WA) solution to Example E.1 is shown in Screenshot E.1. Note that Screenshot E.1 shows the various formulas (highlighted) used in learning curve calculations.

SCREENSHOT E.1: Trinity Hospital Kidney Transplant Learning

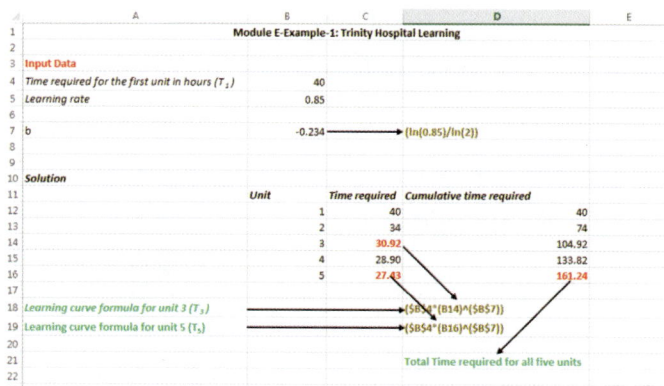

Use of Table of Learning Curve Coefficient Values

The third approach to solving learning curve problems is to select **learning curve coefficient** values from a table and use them in the following formula. For any given value of the learning rate, and n, the number of repetitions of the task or units produced:

Time required nth repetition or produce the nth unit:

$$T_n = T_1 \times \text{Unit time coefficient value}$$

and

Total or cumulative time required to produce n units

Total time = T1 × **Total time coefficient value**

Both learning curve coefficient values can be obtained from a table like Table E.2. For various repetitions of a task or units produced (n), and for a given learning rate, Table E.2 shows two coefficient values (C_n). The first value is the unit time coefficient value, which is the value (n^b) in the original learning curve formula. The second value is the total time coefficient value, which is the cumulative or total time required to complete a given number of repetitions of a task or produce a given number of units of an item.

The use of Table E.2 is illustrated in Example E.2.

EXAMPLE E.2: Purple Airlines has ordered 28 small jet aircrafts from Prince Aeronautics, Inc. Prince Aeronautics has estimated that the first aircraft will require 360 days of direct labor to manufacture and assemble. From past experience on the production of similar aircrafts, Prince Aeronautics estimates that the learning rate is 75%. Estimate the number of days of direct labor:

   a.   For the 15th jet aircraft

   b.   For all 28 jet aircrafts

   c.   The average number of days for the 28 jets

SOLUTION

Given: $T_1 = 360$ days; Learning rate = 75%

   a.   For the 15th jet aircraft

From Table E.2, for $n = 15$ and learning rate of 75%:

Unit time coefficient value = 0.325

Number of days required to produce the 15th unit:

$$T_{15} = 360 \times 0.325 = 117 \text{ days}$$

   b.   Total or cumulative time required to produce 28 units

From Table E.2, for $n = 28$ and learning rate of 75%

Total time coefficient value = 10.955

Number of days required to produce all 28 jet aircrafts

Total time = 360 × 10.955 = 3,943.8 days of direct labor

   c.   The average number of days for the 28 jets

The average number of days for the 28 jets = Total time / n

= 3,943.8 / 28 = 140.85 or 141 days

Unit time coefficient value: the time required to complete a particular repetition of a task or produce a particular unit of an item

Total time coefficient value: the cumulative or total time required to complete a given number of repetitions of a task or produce a given number of units of an item

Considerations for Employing Learning Curves

Regardless of the method employed for estimating learning curves, there are some factors to consider when applying them to various production settings. First, it is important to note that different production features will affect the degree of learning that takes place (i.e., the learning rate). A fully automated line will have a learning curve of 100% because, in effect, no learning need take place. When people are removed from the production process through the full automation of a manufacturing

TABLE E.2: Learning Curve Coefficients (Unit Time and Total Time Multipliers)

UNIT NUMBER	70%		75%		80%		85%	
	UNIT TIME	TOTAL TIME	UNIT TIME	TOTAL TIME	UNIT TIME	TOTAL TIME	UNIT TIME	TOTAL TIME
1	1.000	1.000	1.000	1.000	1.000	1.000	1.000	1.000
2	.700	1.700	.750	1.750	.800	1.800	.850	1.850
3	.568	2.268	.634	2.384	.702	2.502	.773	2.623
4	.490	2.758	.562	2.946	.640	3.142	.723	3.345
5	.437	3.195	.513	3.459	.596	3.738	.686	4.031
6	.398	3.593	.475	3.934	.561	4.299	.657	4.688
7	.367	3.960	.446	4.380	.534	4.834	.634	5.322
8	.343	4.303	.422	4.802	.512	5.346	.614	5.936
9	.323	4.626	.402	5.204	.493	5.839	.597	6.533
10	.306	4.932	.385	5.589	.477	6.315	.583	7.116
11	.291	5.223	.370	5.958	.462	6.777	.570	7.686
12	.278	5.501	.357	6.315	.449	7.227	.558	8.244
13	.267	5.769	.345	6.660	.438	7.665	.548	8.792
14	.257	6.026	.334	6.994	.428	8.092	.539	9.331
15	.248	6.274	.325	7.319	.418	8.511	.530	9.861
16	.240	6.514	.316	7.635	.410	8.920	.522	10.383
17	.233	6.747	.309	7.944	.402	9.322	.515	10.898
18	.226	6.973	.301	8.245	.394	9.716	.508	11.405
19	.220	7.192	.295	8.540	.388	10.104	.501	11.907
20	.214	7.407	.288	8.828	.381	10.485	.495	12.402
21	.209	7.615	.283	9.111	.375	10.860	.490	12.892
22	.204	7.819	.277	9.388	.370	11.230	.484	13.376
23	.199	8.018	.272	9.660	.364	11.594	.479	13.856
24	.195	8.213	.267	9.928	.359	11.954	.475	14.331
25	.191	8.404	.263	10.191	.355	12.309	.470	14.801
26	.187	8.591	.259	10.449	.350	12.659	.466	15.267
27	.183	8.774	.255	10.704	.346	13.005	.462	15.728
28	.180	8.954	.251	10.955	.342	13.347	.458	16.186
29	.177	9.131	.247	11.202	.338	13.685	.454	16.640
30	.174	9.305	.244	11.446	.335	14.020	.450	17.091
35	.160	10.133	.229	12.618	.318	15.643	.434	19.294
40	.150	10.902	.216	13.723	.305	17.193	.421	21.425

system, there is no need to consider learning curve effects. For more complicated manual assembly problems where workers are responsible for multiple steps or complex assembly processes, the learning rate may be 75% or lower. For subassemblies or production "kitting" (see Chapter 14 on Lean Systems), the learning rate may reach 80% to 90%.

A second factor to consider is that a company may decide to first conduct work sampling on its production assemblies to examine the various assembly or manufacturing systems and to determine where the greatest opportunities for learning, and applying learning curves, are centered. Different systems throughout the factory will yield different opportunities for learning and different shapes of learning curves. Selecting production processes that offer the fastest opportunities for meaningful learning will allow these organizations to apply learning curves most effectively.

Finally, it is also important to note that to be the most effective, learning curves should be applied to production lines that have stabilized—that is, lines that are fully functional—rather than production lines that are still being modified or improved. Applying the learning curve to the first unit produced on a line requires that the line be fully functioning. If we use the first unit from a process that is still being adjusted, we cannot be certain of worker learning rates or when the production time is truly stabilized.

E.4

Implement learning curves for cost estimation problems.

E.4 Learning Curves in Cost Estimation

Cost estimation, particularly for labor hours, often assumes a uniform rate at which work is done. When performing multiple activities, the amount of time necessary to complete the first activity is not significantly different from the time necessary to complete the nth activity. In software development, it is considered standard practice to estimate each activity cost independently of other related activities with which the programmer is involved. Therefore, in the case of a programmer required to complete four work assignments, each involving similar but different coding activities, many cost estimators will simply apply a direct, multiplicative rule-of-thumb estimate:

Cost of activity		Number of times activity is repeated		Total cost estimate
($8,000)	×	(4)	=	$32,000

Learning Curves and Cost Estimation

If each actual coding sequence is likely to take approximately 40 hours of work, we can create the more formal direct cost budget line for this resource. Assuming an overhead rate of 0.60 and a cost per hour for the programmer's services of $35/hour, we can come up with a direct billing charge of:

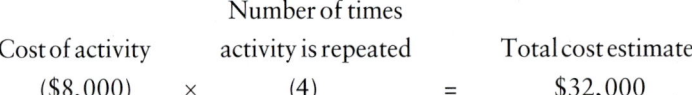

Wage		Unit		Overhead Rate		Hours / Unit		
($35 / hr)	×	(4 iterations)	×	(1.60)	×	(40 hours)	=	$8,960

Although this rule of thumb is simple, it may also be simplistic. We now know from learning curves that the time necessary to do a coding routine the fourth time will not take as long as it took to do it the first time. Therefore, it is reasonable to assume that the time needed (and thus the cost) for the fourth iteration should be shorter than the earlier iterations.

To see how **learning curves** affect cost estimation, apply the learning curve formula to the software coding routine scenario. Return to the discussion where we tried to determine the true cost for the senior programmer's time. Recall that the first linear estimate, in which no allowance was made for the learning curve effect, was found to be:

$$(\$35 / hr)(4\ iterations)(1.60)(40\ hours) = \$8,960$$

Now we can apply additional information to this cost estimate in the form of learning-rate effects. Suppose, for example, that the programmer's learning rate for coding is 0.85. The steady state time (T_4) for the fourth iteration ($n = 4$) to code the sequence is 40 hours. Our estimate of the time needed for the first coding iteration is:

$$b = \ln 0.85 / \ln 2 = -0.1625 / 0.6931 = -0.2345$$

As, $T_n = T_1 \times n^b$, we have

$$40 = T_1 \times (4)^{-0.2345}$$

$$T_1 = 40 / (4)^{-0.2345} = 55.37\ hours$$

The first unit would take 15.37 hours longer than the steady state 40 hours. For this programming example, we can determine the appropriate unit and total time multipliers for the calculated initial unit time by consulting Table E.2, the table of learning curve coefficients (multipliers) for $n = 1$. We can also calculate unit and total time multipliers by identifying the unit time multipliers from 1 to 3 units of production (coding sequences) with a learning rate of 0.90. We use the units 1 to 3 because we assume that by the fourth iteration, the programmer has reached the steady state time of 40 hours. From Table E.2, the total time multiplier for three iterations at the learning rate of 85% is 2.623. Therefore, the time needed to code the first three sequences is:

$$\text{Total time for the first three sequences} = 40 \times 2.623 = 104.92 \text{ hours}$$

Because the steady state time of 40 hours occurs for the final coding iteration, the total coding time required for all four sequences is given as:

$$104.92 + 40 = 144.92$$

The more accurate direct labor cost for the coding activities is:

Wage	Overhead	Rate	Total Hours
($35/hr)	×(1.60)	× 144.92	= $8,115.52

Compare this figure with the original value of $8,960 we had calculated the first time, which over-stated the programming cost by $844.48. The second figure, which includes an allowance for learning curve effects, represents a more realistic estimate of the time and cost required for the programmer to complete the project activities.

In some industries, it is possible to chart the cost of repetitive activities to accurately adjust cost estimation for learning curves. Note the curve relating time (or cost) against activity repetition shown in Figure E.1. The learning curve effect shows savings in time as a function of the sheer repetition of activities found in many business processes and projects. Using the table of multipliers, the savings in revising cost estimates downward to account for learning curve effects can be significant. Budgets must be adjusted for activities in which learning curve effects are likely to occur, and these effects must be factored into cost estimates of activities.

EXAMPLE E.3: A construction firm wants to estimate the direct labor cost of a worker who will be asked to perform multiple iterations of tasks of a similar nature (e.g., fitting, riveting, and squaring). The worker must do a total of 15 of these activities to reach the steady state. The time estimated to perform the 15th iteration (the steady state) is 1 hour, and the construction firm knows from past experience the learning rate for this highly repetitive activity is 70%. The cost of labor is $35 an hour. Using this information, calculate:

a. The estimated time necessary to complete the first activity

b. The direct total labor cost for 15 iterations of these activities

SOLUTION

Given: Learning Rate = 0.70; T_{15} = 1 hour; Direct labor cost = $35/hour

a. The estimated time necessary to complete the first activity:

$$b = \ln 0.70 / \ln 2 = -0.3567 / 0.6931 = -0.5146$$

$$\text{As, } T_n = T_1 \times n^b, \text{ we have:}$$

$$T_{15} = 1 = T_1 \times (15)^{-0.5146}; \text{ Hence, } T_1 = 1 / (15)^{-0.5146} = 4.03 \text{ hours}$$

The solution can also be obtained by using Table E.2 as follows: for $n = 15$ and a learning rate of 70%:

$$\text{Unit time coefficient value} = 0.248$$

$$T_{15} = 1 = T_1 \times 0.248$$

Hence:

$$T_1 = 1 / 0.248 = 4.03$$

b. The direct total labor cost for 15 iterations of these activity

From Table E.2, for $n = 15$, and a learning rate of 70%:

Total time coefficient value = 6.274

Hence, the number of hours required for all 15 iterations of these activities is:

Total time = $T_1 \times 6.274 = 4.03 \times 6.274 = 25.28$ hours

For a labor cost of $35 per hour, the total labor cost is:

Total labor cost = $25.28 \times \$35 = \$884.80$

Discuss the advantages and limitations of learning curves.

E.5. Limitations of Learning Curves

Although learning curves can be applied to a wide variety of business processes, they do have some limitations. These limitations include the following:

- Learning rates differ from company to company, from industry to industry, and by the complexity of the tasks performed. Therefore, each company should determine the learning rates for each of its business operations using empirical data.
- Learning curve calculations provide only estimates of actual times; as conditions change, estimates must be revised.
- In learning curves calculation, the times estimates for subsequent repetitions of an activity or unit production are based on the time it takes to perform the first iteration of the activity or the first unit produced. It is vital that this base time is accurate and valid. Revisions to the base estimate may be needed as subsequent times for the activity revisions or units produced become available.
- Even though learning curves level off in the long run, changes to workers or job design may alter the trajectory of learning curves, causing a temporary upward spike in the curve.
- Learning curves have limited use in mass production situations as the improvements that occur through learning are negligible.
- If a worker is not motivated or bored by conducting repetitive tasks, then very little learning occurs. Additionally, if a worker's interest drops as the project near its end, the learning process may prematurely level off.
- Learning curves are mostly applicable to direct labor and materials. They may not be of much use for indirect labor or materials.

Challenges of Learning Curves

Visit edge.sagepub.com/venkataraman to help you accomplish your coursework goals in an easy-to-use learning environment.

- Mobile-friendly eFlashcards
- Mobile-friendly practice quizzes
- A complete online action plan
- Chapter summaries with learning objectives
- Video and multimedia resources

MODULE SUMMARY

E.1 Define the concept of learning curves. The phenomenon of reduction in time required to perform an activity when that activity is repeatedly performed by a worker is called the concept of learning curves.

E.2 Identify the various ways to apply learning curves for operations processes. Applications of the concept of learning curves are prevalent in both manufacturing and service organizations. In addition, learning curves can be applied in operations and supply chain processes such as workforce planning and scheduling, cost estimation and budgeting, procurement negotiations in supply chains, and new product pricing.

E.3 Apply various approaches to solving learning curve problems. Problems involving learning curves can be solved using three

approaches. These are the arithmetic approach, the logarithmic formula approach, or by using a table of learning curve coefficient values.

E.4 Implement learning curves for cost estimation problems. In many business processes and projects, the learning curve effect shows savings in time as a function of the sheer repetition of activities. Therefore, cost estimates of activities and budgets can be revised to account for savings as a result of learning curve effects.

E.5 Discuss the advantages and limitations of learning curves. Although learning curves can be applied to a wide variety of business processes in both manufacturing and service organizations, they do have some limitations. Some of these limitations include the need to estimate learning rates using empirical data, the accuracy of activity time estimates, changes in learning due job redesign, and so forth.

KEY TERMS

Learning curves   864

Learning rate   866

Total time coefficient value   868

Unit time coefficient value   868

DISCUSSION AND REVIEW QUESTIONS

1. Explain the learning curve phenomenon.
2. Why are learning curve effects not particularly significant in mass production systems?
3. What are the factors that determine the extent to which learning occurs?
4. Why is it easier to apply the learning curve concepts in a manufacturing rather than in a service setting?
5. Discuss some of the areas where applications of learning curve concepts have been found useful.
6. Discuss why more learning occurs at a 70% learning rate than at an 80% rate.
7. Why do learning curves flatten out as the number of repetitions of task increases?
8. What are some limitations of learning curves?
9. What factors might cause a learning curve to peak upward as the number of repetitions increase?
10. Can you think of some circumstances where a manager may want no learning to occur?

SOLVED PROBLEMS

1. A software project that requires the coding services of a senior programmer to complete 14 coding sequences that are relatively similar. It is estimated that the programmer's learning rate is 85% and that the first coding sequence is likely to take her 20 hours to complete:

    a. Using the learning curve formula, estimate the time required to code the 14th sequence.

    b. Estimate the total time required to complete all 14 sequences. (Hint: Use Table E.2.)

Solution:

$$Given: T_1 = 20 \text{ hours}; n = 14; \text{Learning rate} = 0.85$$

Recall that the learning curve formula for calculating the time required to produce the nth of output is represented as:

$$T_n = T_1 \times n^b$$

where

$$T_n = \text{the time required to produce the } n\text{th unit}$$

$$T_1 = \text{the time required to produce the first unit}$$

$$b = \ln (\text{learning rate}) / \ln (2), \text{ where "ln" stands for natural logarithm}$$

a. Time required to code the 14th sequence:

$$b = \ln 0.85 / \ln 2 = -0.1625 / 0.6931 = -0.2345$$

$$T_{14} = 20 \times (14)^{-0.2345} = 10.77 \text{ hours}$$

b. Total time required to complete all 14 sequences

From Table E.2, for $n = 14$, and a learning rate of 85%, the total time coefficient value = 9.331.

Hence, the number of hours required for all 14 iterations of these activities is:

$$\text{Total time} = T_1 \times 6.274 = 20 \times 9.331 = 186.62 \text{ hours}$$

2. Tri-Ocean Cruise lines located in southern India is planning to purchase four small ships from Smooth Sailing Shipyard. The shipyard has estimated that it will take the company 90,000 hours to build the fourth ship. The shipyard also knows based on its prior experience in building ships that its learning rate is 80%. The cost per labor hour of work in the ship yard is $45. Using this information, calculate:

   a. The estimated time required to build the first ship

   b. The direct total labor cost that shipyard will incur for building the four ships for Tri-Ocean Cruise Lines

Solution:

Given: Learning rate = 0.80; T_4 = 90,000 hours; Direct labor cost = $45/hour

a. The estimated time required to build the first ship:

$$b = \ln 0.80 / \ln 2 = -0.2231 / 0.6931 = -0.3219$$

$$\text{As, } T_n = T_1 \times n^b, \text{ we have:}$$

$$T_4 = 90,000 = T_1 \times (4)^{-0.3219}; \text{ Hence, } T_1 = 90,000 / (4)^{-0.3219} = 140,619.5 \text{ hours}$$

The solution may also be obtained by using Table E.2. From Table E.2, for $n = 4$ and a learning rate of 80%:

$$\text{Unit time coefficient value} = 0.640$$

$$T_4 = 1 = T_1 \times 0.640$$

hence,

$$T_1 = 90000 / 0.640 = 140,625 \text{ hours (slight difference from the solution as a result of rounding)}$$

b. The direct total labor cost for building four ships

From Table E.2, for $n = 4$ and a learning rate of 80%:

$$\text{Total time coefficient value} = 3.142$$

Hence, the number of hours required to build all four ships is:

$$\text{Total time} = T_1 \times 3.142 = 140,625 \times 3.142 = 441,843.75 \text{ hours}$$

For a labor cost of $45 per hour, the total labor cost is:

$$\text{Total labor cost} = 441,843.75 \times \$45 = \$19,882,968.75$$

PROBLEMS ···

1. A contractor for the Department of Defense (DoD) is manufacturing a component for the hydraulic systems of jet fighter planes. The direct labor time estimate for the production of the first unit of that component is 200 hours. The company based on the past production of similar components has estimated a 75% learning rate. Estimate the direct labor hours required for the 80th and the last component.

2. A software company hires a new programmer to write the coding sequences for a software project. It is estimated that the new programmer will take 30 hours to write the first coding sequence. Assuming a learning rate of 90%, calculate:

   a. The estimated time required to code the 5th coding sequence

   b. The total time required for all five coding sequences

3. The clerical employees of an insurance company process claims and the process has an 84% learning rate. The learning in this process reaches a steady state (i.e., no additional learning takes place) after the 50th claim, and the time estimate to process this claim is 22 minutes. What is the time estimate to process the first claim?

4. A new electronic component produced for an oil drill rig took 40 hours for the production of the first unit. If the production process has an 85% learning rate, calculate:

   a. The estimated time required to produce the first five units

   b. The time estimate for producing the 25th unit

5. It took MegaTech, Inc., 100,000 labor-hours to produce the first of several oil-drilling rigs for Antarctic exploration. Your company, Natural Resources, Inc., has agreed to purchase the fifth (steady state) oil-drilling rig from MegaTech's manufacturing yard. Assume that MegaTech experiences a learning rate of 80%. At a labor rate of $35 per hour, what should you, as the purchasing agent, expect to pay for the fifth unit?

6. Problem E.5 identified how long it should take to complete the fifth oil-drilling platform that Natural Resources plans to purchase. How long should all five oil-drilling rigs take to complete?

7. Suppose that you are assigning costs to a major project to be undertaken this year by your firm, DynoSoft Applications. One particular coding process involves many labor-hours but highly redundant work. You anticipate a total of 200,000 labor-hours to complete the first iteration of the coding and a learning curve rate of 70%. You are attempting to estimate the cost of the 20th (steady state) iteration of this coding sequence. Based on this information and a $60 per hour labor rate, what would you expect to budget as the cost of the 20th iteration? The 40th iteration?

8. Assume you are a project cost engineer calculating the cost of a repetitive activity for your project. There are a total of 20 iterations of this activity required for the project. The project activity takes 2.5 hours at the 15th iteration when it reaches the steady state and the learning rate is 75%. Calculate the initial output time for the first unit produced. What is the total time estimate for all 20 iterations?

9. Timothy Moore, an IRS auditor, wants to determine the approximate learning rate for processing tax returns. He has recorded the following times (in minutes) for the first seven tax returns:

Tax Returns	1	2	3	4	5	6	7
Time in Minutes	50	43	39	37	36	34	34

   a. Determine the approximate learning rate by using the learning curve formula.

   b. Based on your answer to part a, what is the average processing time per tax return, assuming that 20 tax returns have to be processed?

10. An operations manager claims that one of the production processes he oversees has a learning rate of 88%. One of the new components produced in this production process has the following completion times (in minutes) for the first five units: 55, 45, 40, 37, and 35:

   a. Is the manager's claim of 88% learning rate valid? Support your answer with appropriate calculations.

   b. If the manger's claim is not valid, what is the correct learning rate? By using this learning rate, compute the total time estimate to produce 30 units.

11. Alert Corporation produces a new home security system with a built-in surveillance camera. It took the company 82 hours to produce the first unit, and the company has a learning rate of 75%:

   a. How long will it take the company to produce the 15th unit?

   b. Compute the total time required for the first 15 units.

   c. If Alert Corporation incurs a direct labor cost of $40 an hour, what would be the total labor cost for units 16 through 20?

12. Orion Electronics produces electronics components. As a result of the increasing demand for this component, the company hires three new skilled workers. The following table lists the time it takes in hours for each of these workers to produce first two units of the electronic component. If the steady state time to produce this component is 12 hours, how many repetitions will be required for each worker to reach the steady state?

Worker	1st unit	2nd unit
Jordan	20	18
Pippen	22	19
Johnson	24	20

13. The housekeeping department hires a new maid, Donna Hunter, to clean the hotel's guest rooms. Donna took 90 minutes for her first iteration of cleaning a room and 75 minutes for the second iteration. If the time required to clean a room at the steady state is 45 minutes, how many iterations would Donna need to reach the steady state?

14. An Operations Management consultant, Dr. Varun Gupta, has been asked to prepare a new SAP-based (SAP SE, Walldorf, Germany) ERP system training course that will be taught yearly at a local company. It takes Varun 7 hours to prepare his lectures the first time he teaches the course. If the steady state time to prepare the lectures for this course is one hour, and if Varun reaches this steady state during his 10th year of lecture preparation, what is Varun's implied learning rate?

15. Prince Aerospace Inc. builds small commuter aircrafts for sale to various customers. The company has a skilled workforce of 15. The total labor time contributed by each worker of this work force is 2,200 hours per year. Prince Aerospace has contracted with a regional airline company to build a small jet aircraft. It is estimated that building the first jet aircraft will take 8,000 hours to complete. Based on past experience of building aircrafts, the company believes its learning rate to be 80%:

   a. How many jet aircrafts can Prince Aerospace build in one year?

   b. Through additional training, if the company can increase the learning rate of workers to 75%, how many aircrafts can the company make now?

16. SuperTech Enterprises contracts with both regional and national airline companies to service the hydraulic systems of their aircrafts. The company has to prepare a new service contract to service the hydraulic systems of an airline company's large aircrafts. Based on similar work done in the past, the company estimates that the time required to service the first of these hydraulic systems is 8 direct labor hours and the job has a 75% learning rate:

   a. Estimate the total time required to service 15 hydraulic systems.

   b. If the actual time to service the fifth hydraulic system was 6.5 hours, what is the actual learning rate?

17. Clear Site Inc. is a manufacturer of night vision devices. The company is about to bid on a new night vision goggle for the military. The product uses state-of-the-art infrared illuminator technology. Clear Site's learning rate for producing such products is estimated to be 70%. The time it will take to produce the first unit of this new night vision goggles is 60 hours. The contractual requirements call for a delivery 35 of these goggles:

   a. What is the total time estimate to produce the 35 units?

   b. What would be the average time to produce each of these goggles?

   c. If each worker at Clear Site assigned to this project works 160 hours per month, how many workers should be assigned to this project to complete it in a month?

18. Refer to Problem E.16. Using the data in Problem E.16:

   a. How long will it take to service the 10th hydraulic system?

   b. How long will it take to service hydraulic systems 10 through 15?

   c. If SuperTech pays its workers $45 per direct labor hour, what would be the total cost to service all 15 hydraulic systems?

19. A firm has a training program for assembling computers. The firm closely monitors the progress of the trainees, and those who cannot meet the standard of a assembling a computer in the 5th repetition within 5 hours or less are reassigned to other jobs. The firm currently has three trainees— Theresa, Eric, and Nicole—who have completed two repetitions of computer assembly.

   Theresa took 11 hours for the first assembly and 9 hours for second. Eric took 10 and 9 hours for the first and second repetitions, and Nicole had times of 12 and 9 hours. Which of the trainees will be reassigned to other jobs? Support your conclusions with the necessary calculations.

20. Refer to Problem E.17. The direct labor cost to produce a night vision goggle is $30 per hour. Job setup costs and direct material costs are $40, and material costs are $15 per goggle. The overhead charge for producing the goggles is at 60% of labor, material, and setup costs. Clear Site sells the goggles for $200 per unit. Clear Site's learning rate is 70%:

   a. What is the unit cost for 25 units, given that the first unit took 60 hours to produce?

   b. How many units should be sold for Clear Site to breakeven (Total revenue = Total cost)?

CASE STUDY E.1 ESTIMATING THE COST OF A DRILLING PLATFORM ·······················

Spar Solutions, Inc. (SSI) is an engineering and fabrication firm that specializes in manufacturing drilling rigs for deep water oil exploration. SSI produces a special drilling platform called the Spar Hull, which resembles a giant cylindrical hull that floats on the surface of the water, is anchored in place with giant chain and anchor systems, and is capped with the drilling platform, including derricks, workers' quarters, and office space. Spar hulls can be more than 100 feet in diameter and comprise more than 20,000 tons of steel. A spar hull design is extremely stable and, although expensive, is resilient and capable of being deployed in locations where standard off-shore drilling platforms cannot be used.

SSI is headquartered on the west coast of Finland in a town called Pori. The shipyard where they design and build the spar hulls is capable of only producing one hull at a time. Because of long lead times, a 6-month building cycle, and the potential for currency fluctuations, they will only backorder one hull in their queue. Your engineering and design team has traveled to Pori to negotiate a contract for the design and construction of one of their specialized hulls. Because the technology is fairly constant across fabrications, you know that it took SSI about 100,000 labor hours to manufacture the first spar hull five years ago. Your company is interested in purchasing the next hull that will be available, which is the 7th in their product line.

1. Use the learning curve table in the module, and assume that SSI experiences a learning rate of 80%. Given an overall labor rate of $4,500 per hour for design and fabrication, what should you, as the manager in charge of the final contract price, be willing to pay for the 7th unit?

2. Suppose your purchase had to be delayed for three years. What would you pay for the 10th unit if you assume a steady state unit value of 10 and a learning rate of 70%

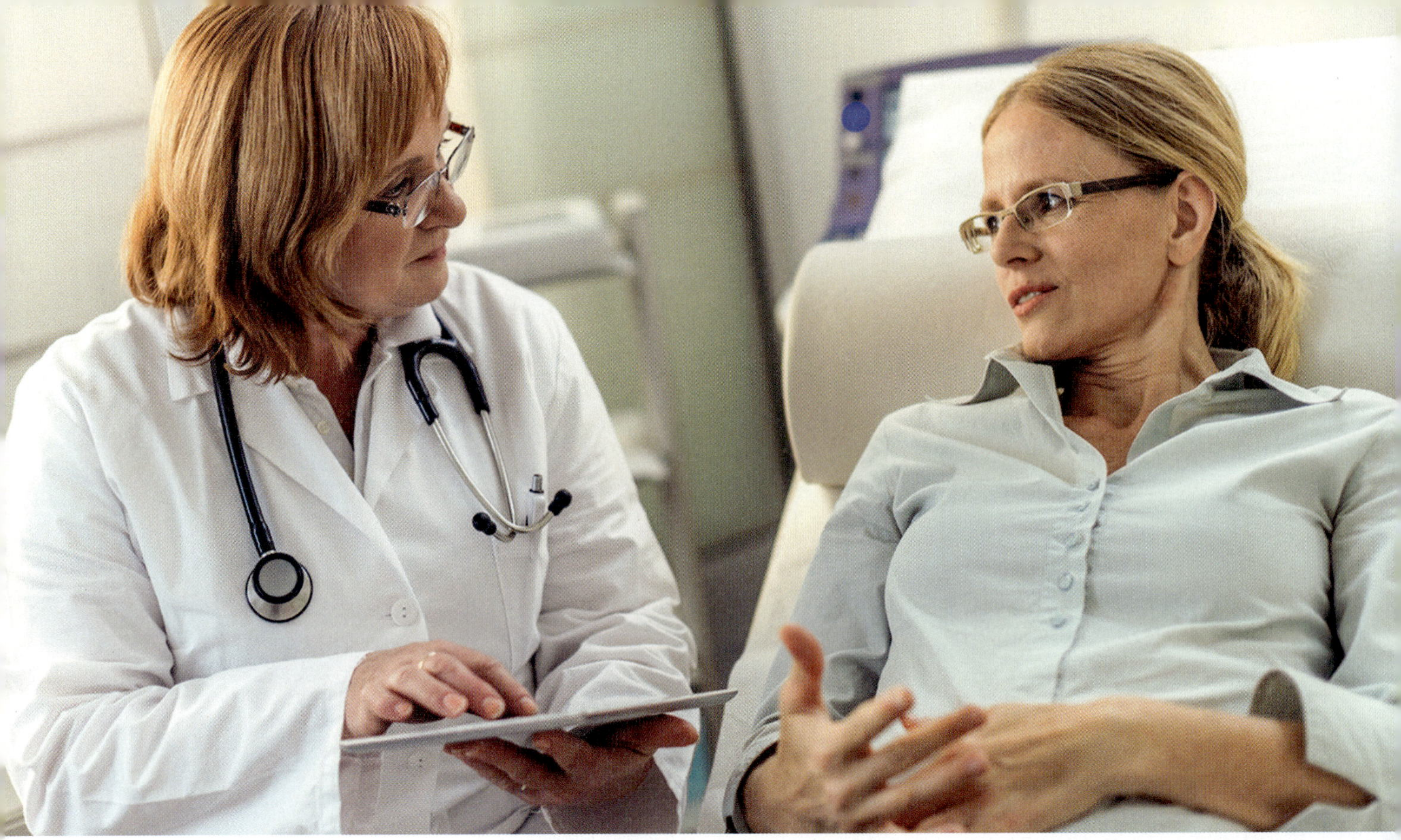

©iStockphoto.com/vm

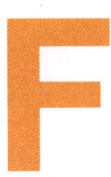

MODULE F

Decision-Making Tools

LEARNING OBJECTIVES

After studying this module, you should be able to:

1. Explain the importance of following a systematic process to make operations and supply chain management decisions.
2. Define the elements in the decision-making process.
3. Appraise the different environments, or categories, under which decision are made.
4. Solve decision-making problems under certainty, uncertainty, and risk.
5. Use decision trees and sensitivity analyses to make sequential decisions.

OPERATIONS PROFILE: Decision-Making Tools for Health Care Choices

With changes to health-care plans and options available to U.S. consumers under the Affordable Health Care Act (officially Patient Protection and Affordable Care Act of 2010, P.L. 111-148), those shopping for health-care options face a much broader variety of decisions that must be made about finding health-care. At the same time, information is more readily available and more widely used by the American public as a basis for its health-care decisions. This combination of choices and search options has created a challenging environment in which to consider the ways that decision-making methods can be applied. A recent survey indicated that consumers consider selecting a health plan and care options one of the most complex decisions they face. Among the decisions that consumers face are choices between:

- Health-care plans: Many employers offer multiple plans with different benefits and restrictions. Which type of medical insurance plan is the most valuable in terms of cost and available services (e.g., HMO vs. PPO)?
- Health-care providers: In many locations, multiple doctors, medical practices, and hospitals are viable choice alternatives for health-care consumers. Consumers have to make choices that give them the best access to health-care providers, consider qualifications and capabilities of medical practices, and consider the location of offices and emergency facilities.
- Treatment options: The Internet has made a wealth of information available to consumers looking for quick and viable treatment options. According to a survey, more than 80% of Internet users have looked online for information related to their health, diet, lifestyles, or treatment options. WebMD, Mayoclinic.com, health insurance websites, and other online services offer numerous tips on healthy lifestyles, treatment options, and service providers.

Despite the increased use of decision support tools for making health-care–related decisions, most consumers are hampered by several problems with making informed choices. Many consumers who use the Internet to make health-care decisions have low levels of literacy about their health-care options, or they engage in limited Internet searches that miss critical information. Other problems include a lack of trust in sources of health-care information (e.g., unwillingness to trust insurance companies who provide the information) as well as the inability to understand the information itself. As a result, making accurate decisions about health-care is a challenge that most consumers will continue to face.[1]

F.1 Using a Systematic Decision-Making Process

Operations and supply chain managers use a systematic decision-making process to make strategic long-term and short-term decisions. Although using a systematic approach won't guarantee these decisions will be the "right" ones, it greatly improves the chances that they will be.

The systematic decision-making process operations and supply chain managers rely on consists of seven steps:

1. *Define the problem or challenge as clearly and concisely as possible.* This includes identifying causes and factors that were responsible for the problem occurring in the first place.
2. *Define the specific and measurable objectives the decision needs to accomplish.* "Reducing the defect rate of a manufacturing process by 5% over the next three months" would be an example of a specific and measurable objective.

F.1
Explain the importance of following a systematic process to make operations and supply chain management decisions.

Systematic Decision Making

3. *Determine the best decision-making tool to use.* It could be using the tools and techniques covered in this supplement. Or, it could be building a business case, or relying on simple guesswork or rules-of-thumb. The choice of tool depends on the nature of the problem, its complexity, environmental factors, and the time and cost needed to implement the tool.

4. *Generate as many alternative solutions as possible.* Generate all possible solutions, which should be collectively exhaustive and mutually exclusive.

5. *Evaluate each alternative solution.* Weigh the cost and time related to selecting and implementing each alternative.

6. *Choose and implement the best alternative solution.* Pick the alternative that best meets your criteria in terms of the objectives to be achieved, cost, and time incurred, and then implement it in a timely way.

7. *Monitor the results.* Evaluate the results to determine whether the desired objectives were achieved in the established timeframe.

F.2

Define the elements in the decision-making process.

F.2 Elements in the Decision-Making Process

Any decision-making situation comprises the following four elements:

- *Decision Alternatives*: The actions the decision maker can take to address or solve the problem.
- *States of nature*: Future events or occurrences that can take place that are beyond the control of the decision maker.
- *Consequences*: The outcomes that result given the actual decision made and the state of nature that occurs.
- *Payoffs*: The values (monetary or nonmonetary) the decision maker places on each combination of actual decisions and states of nature. Payoffs can be positive or negative.

Elements of Decision Making

Let's look at a simple scenario to show how these elements come into play. Suppose you are getting ready to leave for work in the morning and discover that the weather forecast predicts rain. The *actual decision* that you have to make is whether or not to carry a raincoat. The impact of the specific decision you make (to carry or not to carry a raincoat) depends on whether or not it rains (the *state of nature*). The possible *consequences* of your decision include staying dry or getting wet and the burden of having to carry a raincoat or not. Depending on the decision that you make for a given state of nature, the monetary/nonmonetary payoffs can be:

States of nature: future events or occurrences that can take place that are beyond the control of the decision maker

Payoff: the positive or negative values (monetary or nonmonetary) a decision maker places on each combination of actual decisions and states of nature

Decisions under certainty: decisions made when the state of nature is known

Decisions under uncertainty: decisions made when there are not only multiple states of nature but they are also unpredictable and the decision maker cannot even make an educated guess about the chances, or probabilities, of their occurring

- *No raincoat and no rain*: You incur no cost for dry cleaning your suit later and no burden of carrying a raincoat.
- *No raincoat and rain*: You incur a cost for dry cleaning your suit later but no burden of carrying a raincoat.
- *Raincoat and no rain*: You incur no cost for dry cleaning your suit later, but you were burdened by carrying a raincoat,
- *Raincoat and rain*: You incur no cost for dry cleaning your suit later, but you were burdened by carrying a raincoat.

F.3 Categorizing Decisions

Depending on the degree of certainty about the states of nature, every decision-making situation can be classified into one of three categories:

- **Decisions under certainty**: In this case you know without a doubt what the state of nature is going to be. Nevertheless, even under the assumption of certainty, determining the payoffs for each alternative may not be straightforward, particularly if the outcomes are expressed in terms that may not be directly comparable because they are both monetary and nonmonetary. When choosing a flat screen TV, certainly we want to compare their prices, but we also look at other factors such as their screen resolutions, brand reputations, and technology types (e.g., LCD vs. LED). In such a case, a single overall measure of the payoffs for the outcomes has to be calculated so they can be directly compared.
- **Decisions under uncertainty**: In this case, there are not only multiple states of nature but they are also unpredictable and the decision maker cannot even make an educated guess about the chances, or probabilities, of their occurring. These are typically the most common types of

decisions organizations face. A company's decision to introduce a new product into a market is an example of a decision under uncertainty because the company cannot predict if the product will succeed or not if there is total uncertainty about future economic conditions, competition, consumer preferences, and so forth.

- **Decisions under risk:** This scenario falls between the two extremes of certainty and uncertainty. The decision maker, although not certain, is aware of the chances, or probabilities, of the various states of nature occurring. As an example, assume that a company is planning to build a new manufacturing facility in a foreign country to produce and market its products in that country. Let us further assume that the success or failure of this venture depends on the demand for the products produced in this facility. If the company estimates that there is a 70% probability of high demand for its products produced from this facility, then the company is facing a situation of having to make a decision under risk. The risk element in this situation is the 30% probability of low demand because if the company builds the facility and demand for its products turns out to be low, then the company suffers a loss.

The category of the decision you have to make will dictate the decision-making technique you use.

Appraise the different environments, or categories, under which decision are made.

Categorizing Decisions

F.4 Techniques for Making Decisions Under Certainty, Uncertainty, and Risk

Several techniques can be used to analyze decisions that must be made under certain, uncertain, and risky conditions. Let's look at these tools using an example.

Solve decision-making problems under certainty, uncertainty, and risk.

EXAMPLE F.1: Pegasus Textiles operates a factory in Sharjah, United Arab Emirates.[a] The company has experienced steady sales growth over the past two years and could grow substantially if the firm receives orders for its products from overseas apparel stores. Because the company's existing factory doesn't have the capacity to meet the future demand the company could experience, it is considering three options: (1) expanding the existing factory, (2) building another small factory, or (3) building a large factory. Expanding the existing factory will generate $3 million in profits if the future demand is low but $4 million in profits if demand is high.[b] If a second small factory is built and the demand is low, the profits will be $2.5 million. Nevertheless, profits will be $5 million if the demand turns out to be high. Building a large factory will generate a profit of $10 million if the demand is high, but the company will lose $4 million if the demand turns out to be low. What should the company do under each of the following decision scenarios: certainty, uncertainty, and risk?

To begin with, let's put this information into a table called a payoff matrix (Table F.1), which shows the payoff for each combination of decision and state of nature.

TABLE F.1: Payoff Matrix

DECISION ALTERNATIVE	STATE OF NATURE	
	LOW DEMAND	HIGH DEMAND
Expand current facility	$3 million	$4 million
Build small factory	$2.5 million	$5 million
Build large factory	−$4 million	$10 million

Technique for Making Decisions Under Certainty

First, let's treat Pegasus Textiles's dilemma as a decision that can be made under the conditions of certainty. In other words, we know with certainty what the state nature is going to be. Since we know this, we simply choose the alternative in the matrix with the highest payoff for that state of nature. If we know the demand is going to be low, we will expand the existing factory because doing so

Decisions under risk: this scenario falls between the two extremes of certainty and uncertainty. The decision maker, although not certain, is aware of the chances, or probabilities, of the various states of nature occurring

---

[a]Unless otherwise stated, in the Examples, Solved Problems, and Problems, fictional company names are used.

[b]Unless otherwise stated, all currency is in U.S. dollars.

will result in the highest payoff ($3 million) for this state of nature. By contrast, if we know that the demand will be high, then we will build a large factory, which will result in a payoff of $10 million.

Techniques for Making Decisions Under Uncertainty

Making Decisions Under Uncertainty

If we aren't sure what the states of nature (in this case, demand) will be or what their probabilities of occurring are, we cannot estimate them with any degree of precision. We are therefore in the position of having to solve the problem under conditions of uncertainty. There are several approaches to solving problems under these conditions, each with advantages and drawbacks. We will now solve the Pegasus Textiles's problem using each of them to demonstrate how they differ.

THE LAPLACE CRITERION

According to the Laplace criterion, if the probabilities of the states of nature are unknown, we should assume they are equal, and the different decision alternatives should be evaluated using the expected value of their payoffs. The expected value (EV) is the weighted average of the values of all possible outcomes of the decision. In other words, the expected value is the average payoff that would be realized if the decision were to be repeated many times. The weights used are the probabilities associated with the various states of nature.

If there are n mutually exclusive and collectively exhaustive states of nature with probabilities of occurrence P_1, P_2, P_3, and P_n and, if a given decision alternative has outcomes x_1, x_2, x_3, and x_n, then the EV associated with this decision is:

$$EV = \sum_{i=1}^{n} x_i \times P_i$$

$$EV = x_1 \times P_1 + x_2 \times P_2 + x_3 \times P_3 + \ldots\ldots\ldots + X_n \times P_n$$

The decision would be to choose the alternative with the maximum expected value. For the Pegasus example, however, we have only two possible states: low demand and high demand. Assuming equal likelihoods for these two states, we would expect that the probability of low demand is 0.5 and the probability of high demand is 0.5; that is, each state has a 50/50 chance of occurring:

$$EV_{expand} = (\$3 \text{ million} \times 0.5) + (4 \text{ million} \times 0.5) = \$3.5 \text{ million}$$

$$EV_{small} = (\$2.5 \text{ million} \times 0.5) + (5 \text{ million} \times 0.5) = \$3.75 \text{ million}$$

$$EV_{large} = (-\$4 \text{ million} \times 0.5) + (10 \text{ million} \times 0.5) = \$3.0 \text{ million}$$

Using the Laplace criterion solution, the company would receive the highest expected payoff by building the small factory. Note that if the payoffs are in monetary terms, the expected value of the payoffs is often referred to as the *expected monetary value or EMV*.

THE MAXIMIN CRITERION

A decision maker may use the maximin criterion when the negative impact of making the wrong decision is so high that he or she chooses that alternative that guarantees at least the minimum payoff. For example, during an economic downturn, people generally take a more conservative approach to investing by buying CDs and savings bonds rather than by buying stocks, which are a riskier investment.

To our original payoff matrix, we've added a column to Table F.2 that shows the minimum payoff for each decision alternative Pegasus Textile is facing.

Laplace criterion:
a decision-making approach used when the probabilities of the states of nature are unknown and assumed as equal. The different decision alternatives should be evaluated using the expected value of their payoffs

Expected value (EV):
the weighted average of the values of all possible outcomes of the decision, or the average payoff that would be realized if the decision were to be repeated many times

Maximin criterion:
a decision-making approach used when the negative impact of making the wrong decision is so high that he or she chooses that alternative that guarantees at least the minimum payoff

TABLE F.2: Pegasus Textile Payoff Matrix for Maximin Criterion

	STATE OF NATURE		
DECISION ALTERNATIVE	LOW DEMAND	HIGH DEMAND	MINIMUM PAYOFF
Expand factory	$3 million	$4 million	**$3 million**
Build small factory	$2.5 million	$5 million	$2.5 million
Build large factory	−$4 million	$10 million	−$4 million

The decision that should be made based on the maximin criterion is to expand the current factory because $3 million is the maximum of the minimum payoffs shown in the last column; that is, this amount is the best of the worst payoffs.

THE MAXIMAX CRITERION

The maximax criterion is the exact opposite approach of the maximin criterion. In this case, the decision maker is optimistic about the future events and their outcomes. Therefore, the decision maker identifies the maximum payoff associated with each decision and then chooses the maximum of the maximum payoffs, or the best of the best. To use this approach, we've taken our original payoff matrix and added a maximum payoff column in Table F. 3 for each of Pegasus Textiles's decision alternatives.

The decision based on the maximax criterion is to a build a large factory because $10 million is the highest payoff of the maximum payoffs.

TABLE F.3: Pegasus Textile Payoff Matrix for Maximax Criterion

DECISION ALTERNATIVE	STATE OF NATURE		MAXIMUM PAYOFF
	LOW DEMAND	HIGH DEMAND	
Expand factory	$3 million	$4 million	$4 million
Build small factory	$2.5 million	$5 million	$5 million
Build large factory	−$4 million	$10 million	**$10 million**

THE HURWICZ CRITERION

The Hurwicz criterion is a decision-making approach that attempts to find a compromise between the two extremes posed by the pessimistic maximin criterion and the optimistic maximax criterion. By applying a certain percentage weight (α) to the most optimistic outcome, and ($1 - \alpha$) to the most pessimistic outcome, the Hurwicz criterion strikes a balance between the two. The coefficient α is often called the "coefficient of realism" because it moderates the unbridled optimism of the maximax approach. The coefficient's mirror image ($1 - \alpha$) is the coefficient of pessimism, which eliminates some of the risk of the maximin approach. A weighted average is computed for every decision alternative by weighting its maximum payoff by α and its minimum payoff by ($1 - \alpha$). The steps for the Hurwicz criterion are as follows:

1. Select a value for α – the coefficient of realism.
2. For every decision alternative (i), compute a Hurwicz weighted average (H_i):

$$H_i = \alpha \times (\text{maximum payoff}) + (1 - \alpha) \times (\text{minimum payoff})$$

3. Choose the decision alternative that has the highest weighted average of the positive-flow payoffs and the lowest weighted average of the negative-flow payoffs.

You can see in the formula if we set $\alpha = 1$, then the Hurwicz criterion reduces to the maximax decision rule, and at $\alpha = 0$, it becomes the maximin decision criterion.

Let's now solve Pegasus Textiles's dilemma using the Hurwicz criterion. Suppose we select a weight of 0.7 for α. In other words, we believe there is a 70% chance that the high demand (optimistic) state will occur. Recall that the payoffs in Pegasus Textiles's payoff matrix are as follows:

TABLE F.4: Pegasus Textile Payoff Matrix for the Hurwicz Criterion

DECISION ALTERNATIVE	STATE OF NATURE		MAXIMUM PAYOFF	MINIMUM PAYOFF
	LOW DEMAND	HIGH DEMAND		
Expand factory	$3 million	$4 million	$4 million	$3 million
Build small factory	$2.5 million	$5 million	$5 million	$2.5 million
Build large factory	−$4 million	$10 million	$10 million	−$4 million

Maximax criterion: a decision-making approach used when the decision maker is optimistic about the future events and their outcomes, identifies the maximum payoff associated with each decision, and chooses the maximum of the maximum payoffs

Hurwicz criterion: a decision-making approach that attempts to find a compromise between the two extremes posed by the pessimistic maximin criterion and the optimistic maximax criterion by applying a certain percentage weight (α) to the most optimistic outcome, and ($1 - \alpha$) to the most pessimistic outcome

Plug the maximum and minimum payoffs into the formula for the Hurwicz criterion to get the following results for each alternative:

$$H_{expand} = 0.7 \times (\$4 \text{ million})] + (1 - 0.7) \times (\$3 \text{ million}) = \$3.7 \text{ million}$$

$$H_{small} = 0.7 \times (\$5 \text{ million}) + (1 - 0.7) \times (\$2.5 \text{ million}) = \$4.25 \text{ million}$$

$$H_{large} = 0.7 \times (\$10 \text{ million}) + (1 - 0.7) \times (-\$4 \text{ million}) = \textbf{\$5.8 million}$$

The decision Pegasus Textiles should make based on the Hurwicz criterion is to a build a large factory because it has the highest weighted average of the positive-flow payoffs. We can redo the computations for different values of α. For example, we could lower the values of α to see the effect of a greater degree of pessimism on the decision.

THE MINIMAX REGRET CRITERION

The minimax regret criterion incorporates the concept of regret into decisions made under uncertainty. "Regret" in this context is the *opportunity cost,* or loss, to the decision maker for making a nonoptimal decision for a given state of nature. It is the difference between the best payoff for a given state of nature and the payoff associated with the actual decision made for that particular state of nature. The goal of the minimax regret criterion is to minimize the regret, or loss, associated with making a nonoptimal decision.

For this approach, we need to identify the maximum regret associated with each decision and incorporate that information into our original payoff matrix. We then choose the decision that has the lowest maximum-regret value.

For positive-flow payoffs such as revenues, profits, income, and so on:

1. Identify the maximum payoff for each state of nature in the payoff matrix.
2. Take each maximum payoff and subtract from it the values in the matrix associated with that payoff's state of nature.

For negative-flow payoffs such as costs, losses, expenditures, and so on:

1. Identify the minimum payoff for each state of nature in the payoff matrix.
2. Subtract from each maximum payoff the original values in the matrix associated with that payoff's state of nature.

To apply the minimax regret criterion to the Pegasus Textiles scenario, first identify the maximum payoff for each state of nature in the payoff matrix. Recall from our previous matrixes that these values are as follows:

$$\text{Maximum payoff for low demand} = \$3 \text{ million}$$

$$\text{Maximum payoff for high demand} = \$10 \text{ million}$$

Next, subtract from each maximum payoff the original values in the matrix associated with that payoff's state of nature. These calculations are as follows:

TABLE F.5: Pegasus Textile Regret Calculations for Using the Minimax Criterion

DECISION ALTERNATIVE	STATE OF NATURE	
	LOW DEMAND	HIGH DEMAND
Expand factory	$3 – $3 = $0 million	$10 – $4 = $6 million
Build small factory	$3 – $2.5 = $0.5 million	$10 – $5 = $5 million
Build large factory	$3 – (–$4) = $7 million	$10 – $10 = $0 million

Minimax regret criterion: a decision-making approach that attempts to minimize the regret, or loss, associated with making a nonoptimal decision

TABLE F.6: Regret Table

DECISION ALTERNATIVE	STATE OF NATURE		MAXIMUM REGRET
	LOW DEMAND	HIGH DEMAND	
Expand factory	$0 million	$6 million	$6 million
Build small factory	$0.5 million	$5 million	**$5 million**
Build large factory	$7 million	$0 million	$7 million

Based on these computations, we can create a "regret table." It shows the calculations we just did for each low- and high-demand scenario as well as the maximum regret associated with each decision alternative. We want to choose the alternative with the lowest maximum-regret value because it will result in the lowest opportunity cost. (Note that a maximum regret value of "0" means "no regrets," so any decision associated with that value would be the best choice.)

Looking at the last the column, the decision alternative that has the minimum ($5 million) of the maximum regret values is the "build small factory" alternative, which is the decision Pegasus Textiles should choose based on the minimax regret criterion. See Screenshot F.1 of the solutions to the previous example using Microsoft Excel (Microsoft Corporation, Redmond, WA).

SCREENSHOT F.1: Results for Pegasus Textile Example for Decisions Under Uncertainty

	A	B	C	D	E	F	G	H	I	J	K
1	Module F-Example-1										
2											
3		States of Nature					Regret table				
4	Decision Alternatives	Low Demand	High demand	Maximum	Minimum		Low Demand	High demand	Maximum Regret		
5	Expand	3000000	4000000	4000000	3000000		0	6000000	6000000		
6	Build Small	2500000	5000000	5000000	2500000		500000	5000000	5000000		
7	Build Large	-4000000	10000000	10000000	-4000000		7000000	0	7000000		
8											
9	HURWICZ CRITERION										
10	ALPHA =	0.7									
11	1-ALPHA=	0.3									
12	Expand	3700000									
13	Build Small	4250000									
14	Build Large	5800000									
15											
16	LAPLACE CRITERION										
17		States of Nature									
18	Decision Alternatives	Low Demand (0.5)	High demand (0.5)								
19	Probabilities	0.5	0.5	EMV							
20	Expand	3000000	4000000	3500000							
21	Build Small	2500000	5000000	3750000							
22	Build Large	-4000000	10000000	3000000							
23											
24		BEST PAYOFF	DECISION								
25	LAPLACE CRITERION =	3750000	BUILD SMALL								
26	MAXIMIN CRITERION =	3000000	EXPAND								
27	MAXIMAX CRITERION =	10000000	BUILD LARGE								
28	HURWICZ CRITERION =	5800000	BUILD LARGE								
29	MINIMAX REGRET CRITERION =	5000000	BUILD SMALL								
30											

PROS AND CONS OF THE TECHNIQUES USED TO MAKE DECISIONS UNDER UNCERTAINTY

Several decision-making methods can be used under uncertainty. Which one of them should Pegasus Textiles—and operations and supply chain managers in general—use? Both the maximax and maximin criteria are flawed in that they exclude most of the information available in the payoff matrix. Both ignore three out of the six pieces of information available in Pegasus Textiles's payoff matrix: The maximin criterion ignores the payoffs associated with the "high demand" state of nature, whereas the maximax criterion ignores the payoffs associated with the "low demand" state of nature. The Hurwicz criterion approach is an improvement compared with the maximax and maximin criteria because all of the data in the payoff matrix are taken into consideration. Nevertheless, if there are more than two states of nature, then the Hurwicz criterion will omit part of the information in the payoff matrix. For example, if there are three states of nature and three decision alternatives, then the Hurwicz criterion will ignore three of the intermediate payoffs out of the total 9 (33%) pieces of information.

The Laplace criterion, unlike the previous three criteria, takes all of the information available in the matrix into consideration. Therefore, it is a good method to use as long as it's reasonable to assume that the states of nature are equally likely to occur. Yet, it's not a good method to use when the underlying states of nature are not equally probable. For example, even if you know nothing about the game of basketball, in a matchup between the Miami Heat and a high school basketball team, it would be a serious error to assume it's equally likely either team can win. So, if you were making a bet on one of the teams, using the Laplace criterion could cost you quite a bit of money. Using the minimax regret criterion would be superior to using the maximax, maximin, and perhaps even the Hurwicz criteria because the regret concept includes more relevant problem information: actual monetary losses plus unrealized potential profits. Consequently, the minimax regret criterion leads to a more informed decision than do the maximax, maximin or the Hurwicz criteria. Despite these merits, the minimax regret criterion still does not use all of the available information in the payoff matrix. Because the approach assumes that the decision maker is either risk averse or risk neutral, it ignores the maximum payoffs that could be realized if the decision maker were a risk taker. The criterion also ignores the probabilities associated with the possible states of nature.

Techniques for Making Decisions Under Risk

Risk is the potential that a decision made will lead to undesirable outcomes. For example, when you invest in stocks, there is a risk that the value of the stocks will drop and you will lose your investment. Similarly, launching new products is risky because often the demand anticipated for them does not materialize. Whenever there is uncertainty about future events, there is risk. Nonetheless, unlike the case of total uncertainty, decision-making under risk assumes that although there is uncertainty about the various states of nature, the decision maker can estimate the likelihood or probability of the occurrence of each state of nature. The greater the degree of uncertainty there is, the higher is the risk of making the wrong decision. In risky situations, managers try to answer three questions before making a decision:

1. What can go wrong if a particular decision alternative is chosen?
2. What is the likelihood or probability of that happening?
3. What will be the impact or outcome of that decision?

In addition, the states of nature must be mutually exclusive and collectively exhaustive, and the sum of the probabilities of these states of nature must be equal to 1. Mutually exclusive events are events that cannot occur at the same time; collectively exhaustive events are the only events that can occur. In a single toss of a coin, the events—heads and tails—are not only mutually exclusive but also collectively exhaustive. Once the probabilities associated with the various states of nature are estimated, the decision maker then calculates the EV associated with each decision alternative. Once the expected values for all decision alternatives are calculated, the decision criterion is to choose that decision that has the highest expected value. We will now illustrate how to make decisions under risk using an example.

EXAMPLE F.2: Greer Chemicals, Inc., is a paint product manufacturer, and one of the company's manufacturing plants is experiencing a substantial increase in demand. The future demand for the products could be low, medium, or high with the probabilities estimated to be 20%, 50%, and 30%, respectively. The firm is considering three possible courses of action: (1) subcontracting the needed additional capacity; (2) building a new plant; or (3) doing nothing and continuing operations as usual. The company wants to determine the financial impact associated with the three decision alternatives under the varying levels of demand. Given the following payoff matrix, what decision should the firm's managers make?

TABLE F.7: Payoff Matrix for Greer Chemicals, Inc.

	DEMAND		
DECISION ALTERNATIVE	LOW (20%)	MEDIUM (50%)	HIGH (30%)
Subcontract additional capacity	$8 million	$40 million	$70 million
Build a new plant	−$60 million	$20 million	$110 million
Do nothing	$15 million	$30 million	$85 million

SOLUTION

Because the probabilities of the various demand scenarios are available, this is a problem of decision-making under risk. Hence, we should compute the expected values for the three decision alternatives and choose the one that has the maximum EV:

$$\text{EV}_{\text{subcontract}} = (\$8\text{ million} \times 0.2) + (\$40\text{ million} \times 0.5) + (\$70\text{ million} \times 0.3) = \$42.6\text{ million}$$

$$\text{EV}_{\text{build}} = (-\$60\text{ million} \times 0.2) + (\$20\text{ million} \times 0.5) + (\$110\text{ million} \times 0.3) = \$31.0\text{ million}$$

$$\text{EV}_{\text{do nothing}} = (\$15\text{ million} \times 0.2) + (\$30\text{ million} \times 0.5) + (\$85\text{ million} \times 0.3) = \textbf{\$43.5 million}$$

The decision the company should make is to do nothing because this decision has the highest EV.

If the firm's managers can get perfect information from an economic forecaster about what the demand for the products will be, they can make the best possible decision. If the expert predicts the demand will be high, then the decision maker would opt to build the new plant because this alternative has the highest payoff at $110 million; if the expert predicts the demand will be low, then the decision maker would choose the "do nothing" alternative because its payoff is the highest at $15 million.

Before hiring this expert, the decision maker should investigate the value of this additional information. Furthermore, even with perfect information, if this decision-making scenario were repeated a large number of times, the probabilities outlined in the table wouldn't change: Only 30% of the time will the demand be high. The remaining 50% and 20% of the time, there will be medium and low demand, respectively. In other words, even though perfect information is available to the decision maker to make the correct decision, each state of nature will occur only a certain portion of the time. Think again about flipping a coin. Even if someone could tell you with 100% certainty that it will come up heads, the next time you flip the coin, the probability of it coming up heads will still be 50%, just as it was the first time you flipped the coin. Consequently, the payoffs associated with each decision using perfect information must be weighted by its corresponding probability. Thus, the decision maker needs to compute the expected value of this additional information, commonly labeled as the expected value of perfect information (EVPI). EVPI is the difference between the expected value of the decision with perfect information and the expected value of the decision without perfect information. It is the maximum amount a decision maker should pay for additional information that gives perfect information as to the state of nature:

$$\text{EVPI} = \text{EV with perfect information} - \text{EV without perfect information}$$

We can compute EVPI for the previous example. If perfect information is available as to the nature of demand, then we have the following best monetary payoffs associated with the various decisions as shown in Table F.8.

TABLE F.8: Best Decision for Greer Chemicals Inc. for Each State of Nature

STATE OF NATURE	BEST MONETARY PAYOFF	DECISION ALTERNATIVE
Low Demand	$15 million	*Do nothing*
Medium Demand	$40 million	*Subcontract additional capacity*
High Demand	$110 million	*Build a new plant*

Using the information in Table F.8 and the probability values of 0.2, 0.5, and 0.3 associated with low, medium, and high demand, respectively, we can now compute the expected value of the decision with perfect information:

$$\text{EV with perfect information} = (\$15\text{ million} \times 0.2) + (\$40\text{ million} \times 0.5) + (\$110\text{ million} \times 0.3)$$

$$= \$56\text{ million}$$

The expected value of the decision without perfect information is the expected value of the decision that we made under conditions of risk, which was $43.5 million. Recall that this was the amount the company would earn by choosing the "do nothing" option. Therefore:

Expected value of perfect information (EVPI): the difference between the expected value of the decision with perfect information and the expected value of the decision without perfect information

$$\text{EVPI} = \text{EV with perfect information} - \text{EV without perfect information}$$

$$= \$56 \text{ million} - \$43.5 \text{ million}$$

EVPI = $12.5 million

The maximum value of the perfect (additional) information the expert can provide about the nature of the demand (states of nature) is $12.5 million. The amount the decision maker should pay to purchase this information should definitely be less than $12.5 million. See Screenshot F.2 of the solutions to the previous example using Microsoft Excel.

SCREENSHOT F.2: Results in Excel for the Greer Chemicals Inc. Example

	A	B	C	D	E	F
1	MODULE F- EXAMPLE-2					
2						
3	DEMAND	LOW	MEDIUM	HIGH		
4	PROBABILITIES	0.2	0.5	0.3		
5						
6						
7						
8	PAYOFF TABLE (Payoff values are in millions of $)					
9			Demand			
10	Decision	Low	Medium	High	EMV	
11	Subcontract additional capacity	8	40.00	70.00	42.6	
12	Build a new plant	(60)	20.00	110.00	31	
13	Do nothing	15	30.00	85.00	43.5	
14						
15			Demand			
16		Low	Medium	High		
17	Best Monetary Payoff	15	40	110		
18	EV WITH PERFECT INFORMATION =	56				
19	EV WITHOUT PERFECT INFORMATION =	43.5				
20	EV OF PERFECT INFORMATION (EVPI) =	12.5				
21						

Another approach that we can use to compute EVPI is by using the **expected regret** approach. Let's use this approach to compute EVPI for Greer Chemicals. Recall the steps needed to create a regret table are as follows:

For positive-flow payoffs such as revenues, profits, and income:

1. Identify the maximum payoff for each state of nature in the payoff matrix.
2. Take each maximum payoff and subtract from it the values in the matrix associated with that payoff's state of nature.

For negative-flow payoffs such as costs, losses, expenditures, etc.:

1. Identify the minimum payoff for each state of nature in the payoff matrix.
2. Take each maximum payoff and subtract from it the values in the matrix associated with that payoff's state of nature.

Greer Chemical's regret table is shown in Table F. 9.

TABLE F.9: Regret Table for Greer Chemicals

	DEMAND		
DECISION ALTERNATIVE	LOW (0.2)	MEDIUM (0.5)	HIGH (0.3)
Subcontract additional capacity	(15 − 8) = $7 million	(40 − 40) = $0 million	(110 − 70) =$ 40 million
Build a new plant	(15− (−60)) = $75 million	(40 − 20) = $20 million	(110 − 110) = $0 million
Do nothing	(15 − 15) =$0 million	(40 − 30) = $10 million	(110 − 85) = $25 million

We can now compute the expected regret for each alternative:

Subcontract additional capacity: $(7 \times 0.2) + (0 \times 0.5) + (40 \times 0.3) = 13.4$ million

Build a new plant: $(75 \times 0.2) + (20 \times 0.5) + (0 \times 0.3) = 25.0$ million

Do nothing: $(0 \times 0.2) + (10 \times 0.5) + (25 \times 0.3) = 12.5$ million

Expected regret: the expected value of regret associated with each decision

The lowest expected regret is $12.5 million, which is the same value of the EVPI that we calculated earlier and is associated with the alternative "do nothing." Using the regret table and calculating the expected regrets shows us that the value associated with the minimum expected regret is also the expected value of perfect information (EVPI).

PROS AND CONS OF THE TECHNIQUE USED TO MAKE DECISIONS UNDER RISK

Although the expected value concept provides valuable information about choices made under risk, the approach suffers from significant limitations. First, it assumes that the decision maker is rational and will choose the optimum decision with the highest expected value. In reality, however, the decision maker is often not rational. The person may be overly influenced by psychological factors such as fear and anxiety associated with taking risks or the cost of making the decision. The expected value approach for decision-making under risk does not take into consideration these irrational factors. Second, the expected value approach also ignores elements other than monetary payoffs, including the impact on the quality of life or the current monetary status of the decision maker. People who live on fixed incomes or are facing bankruptcy may not make the rational choice determined by the expected value approach because they perceive the downside risk as simply too high.

F.5 Techniques for Making Sequential Decisions

Using a payoff matrix to compute the expected values of a decision is appropriate as long as a single decision has to be made at a given point in time. Nevertheless, if a sequence of decisions must be made over a period of time, then using a payoff matrix approach is not sufficient.

F.5
Use decision trees and sensitivity analyses to make sequential decisions.

Decision Trees

When sequential decisions need to be made, a **decision tree** similar to the one in Figure F.1 should be used. The key features of a decision tree are as follows:

Decision Trees

- The tree is drawn from left to right
- A square node (□) in the tree represents a decision point.
- Branches (–) from a square node represent decision alternatives.
- A circle node (○) represents a chance event—an uncertain event whose occurrence cannot be predicted.
- Branches (–) from a circle node represent states of nature.
- After drawing the tree, it is analyzed from right to left.
- The decision criterion is to choose that initial decision that has the highest expected value.

CONSTRUCTING AND ANALYZING A DECISION TREE

To construct a decision tree and analyze it, take the following four steps:

Step 1: Begin the tree with the initial decision to be made.

Designate the first decision to be made with a square node, starting on the left. For each possible initial decision alternative, draw a line (branch) emanating out from the square node. Label each decision alternative along its line.

Step 2: Expand the tree.

If the problem requires you to make another decision, draw another square node for each decision alternative. If the alternative leads to a chance event or the outcome is uncertain, draw a circle. If you drew a circle, draw lines out from it to represent the states of nature. If you drew a square, draw lines emanating from it to represent additional decision alternatives.

Decision tree: a technique used for making sequential decisions that allows the decision maker to map each possible decision alternative visually to determine the best decision

Step 3: Evaluate the tree and expand it again as necessary.

Evaluate the tree to ensure all possible states of nature and decisions are represented. If they are not, go back to Step 2 and continue to expand the tree. If all possible states of nature and decisions are represented, then write the payoff associated with each decision sequence to the right of the tree for each sequence from the initial decision point.

FIGURE F.1: Simple Decision Tree

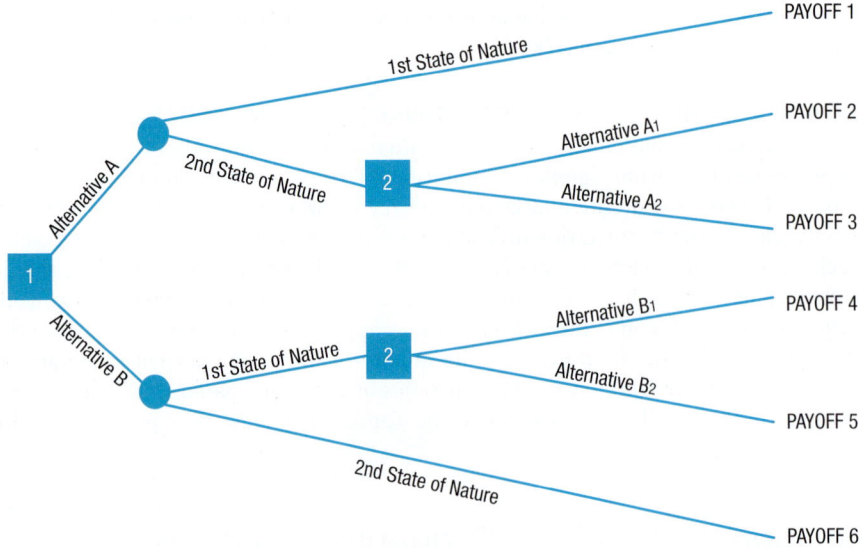

Step 4: Analyze the tree and make a decision.

After you have placed all possible states of nature, decisions, and payoffs on the tree, consider each decision path and its final payoff. Next, eliminate any paths that are clearly suboptimal or not viable. Starting from the right of the decision tree, calculate the expected payoffs for the remaining paths by working backward to each decision point along its path until you reach the initial decision point at the left of the tree. The initial decision alternative that led to the expected payoff is the best choice.

EXAMPLE F.3: Murali Aromatics, which manufactures essential oils and aromatic compounds used in perfumes, must decide on the type of facility it should build. Initially the company is considering either (a) building a large facility or (b) building a small facility. The firm's managers estimates that the probability of low demand to be 0.30, and the probability of high demand to be 0.70. If the firm builds a small facility and the demand turns out to be low, then the payoff will be $30,000. If the demand turns out be high, the firm can either subcontract some work and realize a payoff of $100,000, or expand the small facility and realize a payoff of $120,000. If the company builds a large facility initially and the demand turns out to be low, then the firm will lose $100,000. By contrast, if the demand is high, the company will realize a payoff of $200,000.

Our challenge is to determine the optimal course of action by constructing and analyzing a decision tree.

Step 1: Begin the tree with the initial decision to be made.

First, as Figure F.2 shows, we begin constructing the tree with an initial decision point along with the firm's alternatives of building a small or a large facility.

Step 2: Expand the tree.

Each of these alternatives leads to a chance event of uncertain demand with two possible states of nature: low and high demand. Therefore, our second step is to expand the tree by incorporating these events and states of nature.

Step 3: Evaluate the tree and expand it again as necessary.

If a small facility was built initially and the demand turned out to be high, the company has the additional alternatives of subcontracting work or expanding the existing facility. Our third step is to expand the tree again by including this extra information in the diagram. We also need to include the payoff associated with each decision beginning from the initial decision. Once this done, our tree is complete.

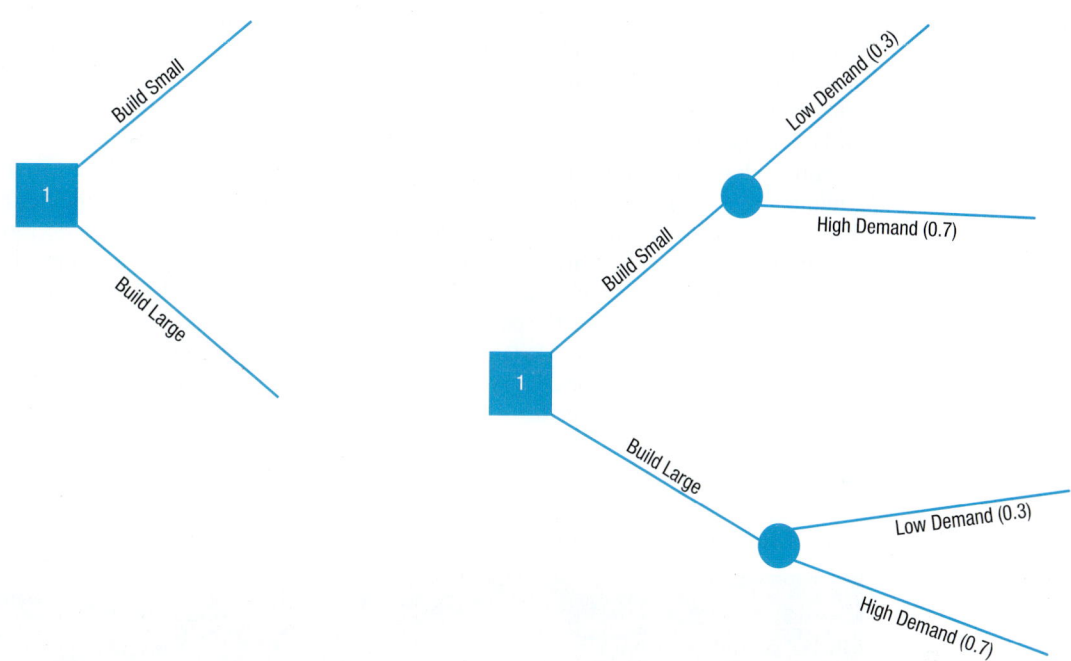

FIGURE F.2: Initial Decision Alternatives for the Tree

FIGURE F.3: Expanded Tree With States of Nature

Step 4: Analyze the tree and make a decision.

Our fourth step is to analyze the tree and make a decision. Starting from the right side of the tree, we calculate the expected values of the payoffs by working backward to each decision point along its path until we reach the initial decision point at the left of the tree. We will choose that decision option that has the maximum expected payoff. Nevertheless, if the company built a small facility initially and demand turned out to be high, then the best second decision to be made is to expand the small facility because it has a higher payoff than subcontracting. We will prune the "subcontract" branch to indicate that it is not a viable decision option.

$$EV_{\text{build large}} = (-\$100,000 \times 0.3) + (\$200,000 \times 0.7) = \$110,000$$

$$EV_{\text{build small}} = (\$300,000 \times 0.3) + (\$120,000 \times 0.7) = \$93,000$$

The company's initial decision should be to build the large facility because it has the highest expected value ($110,000). The final decision tree along with the expected values is shown in Figure F.5.

FIGURE F.4: Expanded Tree With Additional Decision Alternatives

FIGURE F.5: Completed Decision Tree for Murali Aromatics

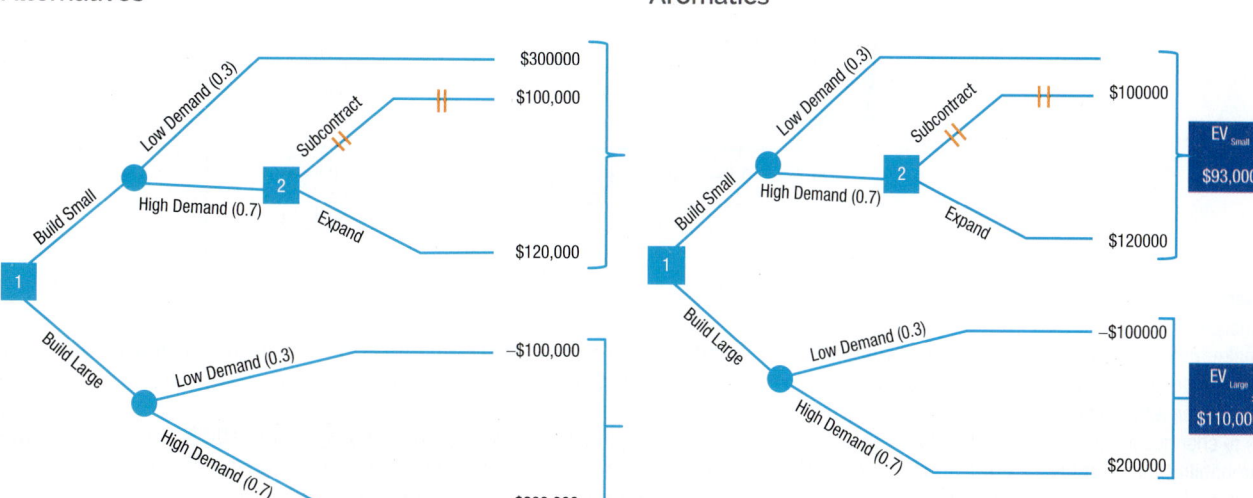

Sensitivity Analysis for Decision Trees

In decision-making scenarios under uncertainty or risk, the values of the probabilities of the various states of nature and the payoffs associated with them are either unknown or estimates. Nevertheless, instead of single-point estimates, it is often more useful to have a range of values for the estimates. In other words, if decision makers can determine how sensitive an alternative is to changes in the values of these variables, they are in a much better position to make a sound decision.

Although it is impossible to consider all of the combination of values these variables can take, at a minimum, you can conduct a **sensitivity analysis** of their estimated probabilities of occurring. In this case, a sensitivity analysis will provide a range of values over which one decision alternative is preferred to others. If there are only two states of nature, a sensitivity analysis involves constructing a graph and then using simple algebra to determine the range of probability values. In addition, the algebraic calculations provide the end points for the range of values.

Using the information for Murali Aromatics, we will demonstrate how to conduct a sensitivity analysis. First, we will use the company's assessment of the probability that the "high demand" state of nature will occur. We can perform sensitivity analysis for low demand in a similar way.

Step 1: Present the information on the decision alternatives, states of nature, and payoffs in a payoff matrix.

TABLE F.10: Payoff Matrix for Murali Aromatics

	STATE OF NATURE	
DECISION ALTERNATIVE	LOW DEMAND	HIGH DEMAND
Subcontract	20	100
Build new facility	−100	200
Do nothing	30	70

Payoffs in thousands ($).

Step 2: Construct a graph with probability values from 0 to 1 on the x-axis.

Label the *x*-axis as P (High Demand), which represents probability of high demand. Draw two *y*-axes—one on the left for the low-demand payoff values and the other on the right for the high-demand payoffs. The graph with these labels is as follows in Figure F.6.

FIGURE F.6: Graph of Demand Probabilities

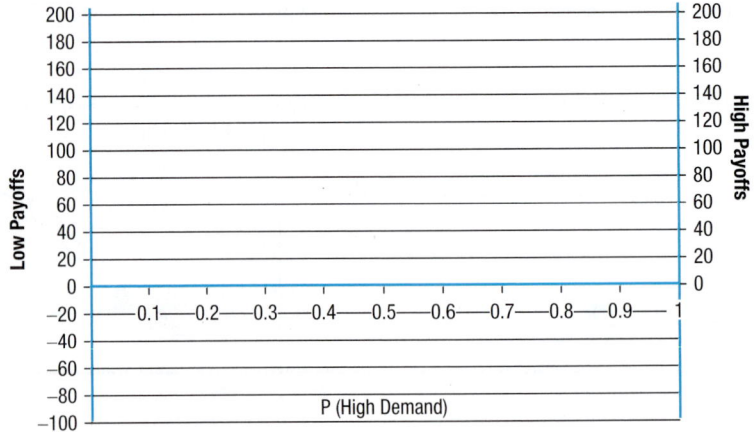

Sensitivity analysis: analysis a decision maker conducts to determine how sensitive a decision alternative is to changes in the probability values of the states of nature

Step 3: For each decision alternative, plot the payoff value for low demand on the left vertical axis, and the payoff value for high demand on the right vertical axis.

If the probability of high demand is 0 and the probability of low demand is 100%, then for the subcontracting option, the value of 20 from our payoff matrix is the point on the left vertical axis we would plot. By contrast, if the probability of high demand is 100%, then, as the matrix shows, the company's payoff for subcontracting would be 100. Consequently, we would plot this point on the right vertical axis. Connect the points associated with the low and high payoffs for subcontracting with a straight line. Similarly, for the "Build new" and "Do nothing" alternatives, the payoffs for low and high demand are plotted on the left and right vertical axes, respectively. The graph with these modifications is shown in Figure F.7.

FIGURE F.7: Graph With Decision Alternatives Plotted

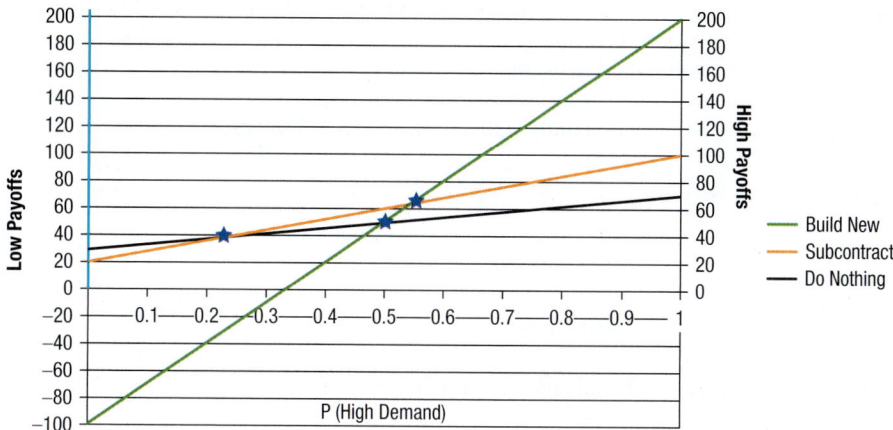

Step 4: We have three intersection points on the graph: one for the intersection of the lines for the "Build new" and "Do nothing" options; the second for the intersection of the "Build new" and "Subcontracting" options; and the third, for the "Do nothing" and "Subcontract" options.

To identify the values of these intersection points, we need to determine the equations for these three straight lines. Recall that the equation for a straight line is:

$$Y = mX + c$$

where

c = the y-intercept (the point at which the line intersects the y-axis at $X = 0$)

m = the slope of the line given by $(Y_2 - Y_1) / (X_2 - X_1)$

In our example, the X-values are the probability values labeled P (High Demand), which can vary from 0 to 1. To calculate the slope of each line, we determine the value of the payoff on the left vertical axis when the P (High Demand) = 0, and the value of the payoff on the left vertical axis when the P (High Demand) = 1. Thus, the equations for the three lines representing the three alternatives are:

Subcontract: $(100 - 20) / (1 - 0) \times$ Probability (High Demand) + 20

$= 80 \times$ P (High Demand) + 20

Build New: $(200 - (-100)) / (1 - 0) \times$ Probability (High Demand) + (-100)

$= 300 \times$ P (High Demand) - 100

Do Nothing: $(70 - 30) / (1 - 0) \times$ Probability (High Demand) + 30

$= 40 \times$ P (High Demand) + 30

At the intersection point of any two lines representing the decision alternatives, the payoffs are equal. We set the equations for these two lines as being equal to each other. Thus, for the intersection point of the "Subcontract" and "Build new" options, we have:

$$80 \times \text{P (High Demand)} + 20 = 300 \times \text{P (High Demand)} - 100$$

Rearranging the terms, we have:

$$120 = 220 \times P \text{ (High Demand)}$$

or

$$P \text{ (High Demand)} = 120 / 220 = 0.545$$

This means that there is no difference between subcontracting or building a new facility if the P (High Demand) = 54.5% because both alternatives yield the same payoff. The same type of interpretation would apply for the other two intersection points.

For the "Do nothing" and "Build new" options, we have:

$$40 \times P \text{ (High Demand)} + 30 = 300 \times P \text{ (High Demand)} - 100$$

Rearranging the terms, we have:

$$130 = 260 \times P \text{ (High Demand)}$$

or:

$$P \text{ (High Demand)} = 130 / 260 = 0.50$$

Finally, for the "Do nothing" and "Subcontract" options, we have:

$$40 \times P \text{ (High Demand)} + 30 = 80 \times P \text{ (High Demand)} + 20$$

Rearranging the terms, we have:

$$10 = 40 \times P \text{ (High Demand)}$$

or:

$$P \text{ (High Demand)} = 10 / 40 = 0.25$$

The probabilities associated with the three intersection points are shown in Figure F.8.

Based on the calculations and the graph in Figure F.8, we can draw the following conclusions:

1. If the P (High Demand) > 0.545, choose the "Build new facility" alternative.
2. If the P (High Demand) is between 0.25 and 0.545, choose the "subcontract" alternative.
3. If the P (High Demand) < 0.25, choose the "Do nothing" alternative.
4. If the P (High Demand) is between 0.50 and 0.545, choose the "subcontract" alternative as it has a higher payoff than "Do nothing" and "Build new facility" alternatives.

Conducting a sensitivity analysis on the states of nature provides valuable information about the range of probabilities over which different alternatives should be chosen.

FIGURE F.8: Graph of Sensitivity Analysis of the Decisions

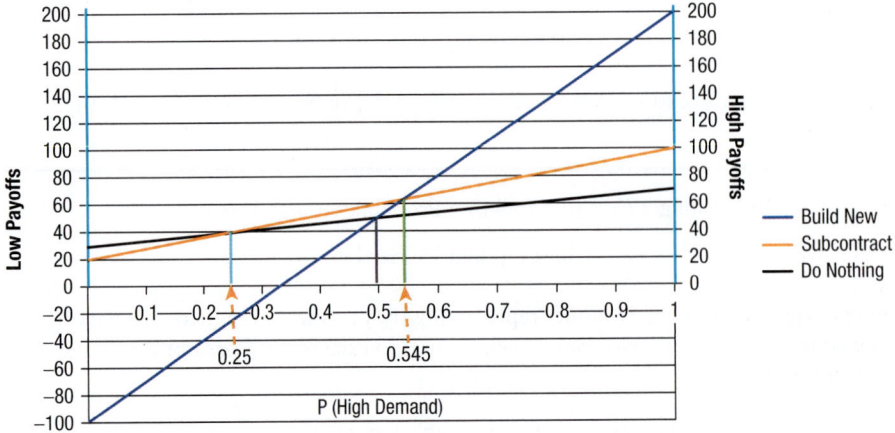

Although we used the various decision-making tools discussed in this supplement for capacity planning problems, these tools can be used in any decision-making situation that involves uncertainty about the states of nature. In fact, these decision-making tools are extensively used for tackling many real-life problems across diverse organizational functions, including the areas of operations and supply chain management, marketing and finance, and in industries such as health-care, banking, manufacturing, and others.

Visit **edge.sagepub.com/venkataraman** to help you accomplish your coursework goals in an easy-to-use learning environment.

- Mobile-friendly eFlashcards
- Mobile-friendly practice quizzes
- A complete online action plan

- Chapter summaries with learning objectives
- Video and multimedia resources

MODULE SUMMARY

F.1 **Explain the importance of following a systematic process to make operations and supply chain management decisions.** Decision analysis is the art and science of formal decision-making. It is often used to make decisions in many areas of business including operations, finance, marketing, and so forth. Decision analysis offers both individuals and organizations a framework, specific methodologies and tools to identify and analyze uncertain events, risk factors, and possible outcomes to reach optimal decisions.

F.2 **Define the elements in the decision-making process.** Any decision-making situation comprises the following four elements: (1) the *decision alternatives* that can be taken to address the problem; (2) the *states of nature,* which consist of future events or conditions beyond the control of the decision maker; (3) the *consequences* of the decision made and the state of nature that occurs; and (4) the decision's monetary or nonmonetary *payoffs.*

F.3 **Appraise the different environments, or categories, under which decision are made.** Decisions can be made under a variety of different environments, including, first, *decisions under certainty*—situations where we know without a doubt what the state of nature is going to be. Second are *decisions under uncertainty*—in which there are not only multiple states of nature but they are also unpredictable and the decision maker cannot even make an educated guess about the chances, or probabilities, of their occurring. These are typically the most common types of decisions organizations face. Finally, the

third category is *decisions under risk*—a scenario that falls between the two extremes of certainty and uncertainty. The decision maker, although not certain, is aware of the chances, or probabilities, of the various states of nature occurring.

F.4 **Solve decision-making problems under certainty, uncertainty, and risk.** When you know with certainty what the state nature is going to be, simply choose the alternative in the matrix with the highest payoff for that state of nature. When you are uncertain about what the state of nature will be, the Laplace criterion, maximin criterion, maximax criterion, Hurwicz criterion, or minimax regret criterion can be used. Under conditions of risk, the expected value decision-making approach should be used.

F.5 **Use decision trees and sensitivity analyses to make sequential decisions.** When sequential decisions need to be made, a decision tree should be used. Begin the tree with the initial decision to be made. Then expand it for different alternatives. After all possible states of nature, decisions, and payoffs have been placed on the tree, consider each decision path and its final payoff. In decision-making scenarios under uncertainty or risk, the values of the probabilities of the various states of nature and the payoffs associated with them are either unknown or estimates. Nevertheless, instead of single-point estimates, as a decision maker, you can use a range of values for the estimates to determine how "sensitive" an alternative is to changes in the values of these variables.

KEY TERMS

Decision tree   889

Decisions under certainty   880

Decisions under risk   881

Decisions under uncertainty   880

Expected regret   888

Expected value (EV)   882

Expected value of perfect information (EVPI)   887

Hurwicz criterion   883

Laplace criterion   882

Maximax criterion   883

Maximin criterion   882

Minimax regret criterion   884

Payoff   880

Sensitivity analysis   892

States of nature   880

DISCUSSION AND REVIEW QUESTIONS ···

1. What are the two key reasons for poor decisions?

2. List and explain briefly the steps in the decision-making process.

3. List and explain the four elements of a decision.

4. Discuss the three decision-making categories.

5. Define the following decision-making criteria:

   a. Laplace criterion

   b. Maximin criterion

   c. Maximax criterion

   d. Hurwicz criterion

   e. Minimax regret

6. What is the expected value concept?

7. Why is sensitivity analysis a useful tool for making decisions under uncertainty?

8. When are decision trees an appropriate tool to use in the decision-making process?

9. What are some criticisms of the Hurwicz and the Laplace criteria?

10. In evaluating several capacity planning alternatives using EV, a manager arrives at a virtual tie between two alternatives. What are some additional factors he should consider to break the tie?

11. When is it appropriate to use the expected value approach as a decision criterion? When is it not appropriate?

12. List some ways by which the tools of decision analysis can be used to promote potentially unethical behavior?

SOLVED PROBLEMS ··

1. Miller Snow Blowers, located in western New York, manufactures industrial-strength loader mounted snow blowers that can withstand rigorous conditions, including packed ice, snow, and road debris. The owner of the company, Larry Miller, is planning to expand the capacity of his factory to meet the peak demand for snow blowers during the upcoming winter season. From years of experience, Larry knows there is a direct association between winter weather and the demand for snow blowers. A winter with heavy snow should generate a high demand, and a moderate or warm winter will likely generate a medium or low demand. Larry is considering three possible capacity options: (1) a large expansion, (2) a small expansion, or (3) a subcontracting option. Larry is concerned that if he opts for a large expansion when the winter season has only light snow, he will suffer a loss. He has estimated the payoffs for the different combinations of decision alternatives and states of nature, and they are listed in Table F.11.

TABLE F.11: Payoff Matrix for Miller Snow Blowers

Decision Alternative	State of Nature		
	Heavy Snowfall	Medium Snowfall	Light Snowfall
Large expansion	$60,000	$20,000	($40,000)
Small expansion	$25,000	$15,000	($5,000)
Subcontract	$8,000	$6,000	$2,000

a. Which alternative should be selected under the maximax criterion?

b. Which alternative should be selected under the maximin criterion?

c. Which alternative should be selected under the Laplace criterion?

d. Which alternative should be selected under the Hurwicz criterion? Assume the value for $\alpha = 0.6$.

e. Which alternative should be selected under the minimax regret criterion?

Solution:

a. Maximax Criterion

If he uses the maximax criterion, Larry should choose the maximum of the maximum returns ($60,000), which corresponds to the large expansion.

TABLE F.12: Payoff Matrix for Miller Snow Blowers Using Maximax and Maximin Criteria

Decision Alternative	State of Nature			Maximum Return	Minimum Return
	Heavy Snowfall	Medium Snowfall	Light Snowfall		
Large expansion	$60,000	$20,000	($40,000)	$60,000	($40,000)
Small expansion	$25,000	$15,000	($5,000)	$25,000	($5,000)
Subcontract	$8,000	$6,000	$2,000	$8,000	$2,000

b. **Maximin Criterion**

Using the maximin criterion, Larry should choose the maximum of the minimum returns ($2,000), which corresponds to the decision to subcontract.

c. **Laplace Criterion**

For the Laplace criterion, we assume that each state of nature is equally likely to occur. So, for this example, the probability of each state of nature is one third. Next, we calculate the expected value for each alternative by finding the average value of the three payoffs for it. To do this, we sum up the payoffs and then divide that sum by three:

$$\text{Large Expansion: } (\$60,000 + \$20,000 - \$40,000) / 3 = \$40,000 / 3 = \$13,333.33$$

$$\text{Small Expansion: } (\$25,000 + \$15,000 - \$5,000) / 3 = \$35,000 / 3 = \$11,666.67$$

$$\text{Subcontract: } (\$8,000 + \$6,000 + \$2,000) / 3 = \$16,000 / 3 = \$5,333.33$$

Larry should choose the large expansion because it has highest expected value, which is $13,333.33.

d. **Hurwicz Criterion**

For the Hurwicz criterion, we proceed as follows:

Identify the maximum and the minimum payoff for each alternative:

TABLE F.13: Payoff Matrix for Miller Snow Blowers Using the Hurwicz Criterion

| Decision Alternative | State of Nature | | | | |
	Heavy Snowfall	Medium Snowfall	Light Snowfall	Maximum Return	Minimum Return
Large expansion	$60,000	$20,000	($40,000)	$60,000	($40,000)
Small expansion	$25,000	$15,000	($5,000)	$25,000	($5,000)
Subcontract	$8,000	$6,000	$2,000	$8,000	$2,000

Select a value for α, which in this example is 0.6. Therefore $1 - \alpha = 0.4$.

For every decision alternative (i), compute a Hurwicz weighted average (H_i).

$$H_i = \alpha \times (\text{maximum payoff}) + (1 - \alpha) \times (\text{minimum payoff})$$

$$H_{\text{expand large}} = 0.6 \times (\$60,000) + (1 - 0.6) \times (-\$40,000) = \mathbf{\$20,000}$$

$$H_{\text{expand small}} = 0.6 \times (\$25,000) + (1 - 0.6) \times (-\$5,000) = \$13,000$$

$$H_{\text{subcontract}} = 0.6 \times (\$8000) + (1 - 0.6) \times (\$2,000) = \$5,600$$

The decision based on the Hurwicz criterion is the large expansion because it has the highest weighted average of the positive-flow payoffs.

e. **Minimax Regret Criterion**

For this criterion, we compute the regret associated with each decision in the original payoff matrix:

TABLE F.14: Regret Table

| Decision Alternatives | States of Nature | | |
	Heavy Snowfall	Medium Snowfall	Light Snowfall
Large expansion	$60,000 – $60,000 = $0	$20,000 – $20,0000 = $0	$ 2,000 – (–$40,000) = $42,000
Small expansion	$ 60,000 – 25,000 = $35,000	$20,000 – $15,000 = $5000	$2000 – (–$5,000) = $7000
Subcontract	$60,000 – $8000 = $52,000	$20,000 – $6000= $14,000	$2,000 – $2,000 = $0

Next, for each decision, we identify the maximum regret associated with that decision. These regret values are:

Large expansion: $42,000

Small expansion: $35,000

Subcontract: $52,000

Using this criterion, Larry should choose the decision that has the minimum of the maximum regrets, which is the small expansion. See Screenshot F.3 of the solutions to the previous problem using Microsoft Excel.

SCREENSHOT F.3: Excel Solution to the Miller Snow Blowers Problem of Decisions Under Uncertainty

	A	B	C	D	E	F	G	H	I	J	K	L
1	MODULE F-SOLVED PROBLEM-1											
2												
3		States of Nature							Regret table			
4	Decision Alternatives	Heavy Snow fall	Medium Snow fall	Light Snow fall	Maximum	Minimum		Heavy Snow fall	Medium Snow fall	Light Snow fall	Maximum Regret	
5	Expand Large	60000	20,000	-40000.00	60000	-40000		0	0	42000	42000	
6	Expand Small	25,000	15,000	-5,000	25000	-5000		35000	5000	7000	35000	
7	Subcontract	8000	6000	2,000	8000	2000		52000	14000	0	52000	
8												
9	HURWICZ CRITERION											
10	ALPHA =	0.6										
11	1-ALPHA=	0.4										
12	Expand Large	20000										
13	Expand Small	13000										
14	Subcontract	5600										
15												
16	LAPLACE CRITERION											
17		States of Nature										
18	Decision Alternatives	Heavy Snow fall	Medium Snow fall	Light Snow fall								
19	Probabilities	1/3	1/3	1/3	EMV							
20	Expand Large	60000	20,000	-40000.00	13333							
21	Expand Small	25,000	15,000	-5,000	11667							
22	Subcontract	8000	6000	2,000	5333							
23												
24		BEST PAYOFF	DECISION									
25	MAXIMAX CRITERION =	60000	EXPAND LARGE									
26	MAXIMIN CRITERION =	2000	SUBCONTRACT									
27	LAPLACE CRITERION =	13333	EXPAND LARGE									
28	HURWICZ CRITERION =	20000	EXPAND LARGE									
29	MINIMAX REGRET CRITERION =	35000	EXPAND SMALL									
30												

2. In Solved Problem F.1, Larry Miller, while evaluating the various decision options, was also able to estimate the probabilities of the nature of the snowfall that could occur in the upcoming winter season. His probability estimates were heavy snowfall: 0.5; medium snowfall: 0.3; and light snowfall: 0.2:

a. What decision should Larry make now?

b. If Larry wants to use the services of a meteorologist to gather additional information about the nature of the snowfall, what is the maximum amount he should pay for these services?

Solution:

a. Because the probabilities for the states of nature are known, this problem now is one of decision-making under risk. The revised payoff table with the new information is shown in Table F.15.

TABLE F.15: Revised Payoff Matrix for Miller Snow Blowers With Probability Estimates

	State of Nature		
Decision Alternative	Heavy Snowfall (0.5)	Medium Snowfall (0.3)	Light Snowfall (0.2)
Large expansion	$60,000	$20,000	($40,000)
Small expansion	$25,000	$15,000	($5,000)
Subcontract	$8,000	$6,000	$2,000

This is a problem of decision-making under risk. So, based on the meteorologist's probabilities, Larry must first compute the expected value associated with each decision:

Large expansion: ($60,000 × 0.5) + ($20,000 × 0.3) + (−$40,000 × 0.2) = $28,000

Small expansion: ($25,000 × 0.5) + ($15,000 × 0.3) + (−$5,000 × 0.2) = $16,000

Subcontract: ($8,000 × 0.5) + ($6,000 × 0.3) + ($2,000 × 0.2) = $6,200

Larry should choose the large expansion because its expected value is the highest.

b. What's meteorologist's advice worth? Let's calculate it:

$$EVPI = EV \text{ with perfect information} - EV \text{ without perfect information}$$

Since perfect information about the nature of the snowfall is available, then we have the following best monetary payoffs and decisions associated with the various snowfall scenarios, as shown in Table F.16.

TABLE F.16: Best Decision for Miller Snow Blowers for Each State of Nature

State of Nature	Best Monetary Payoff	Decision
Heavy snowfall	$60,000	Expand Large
Medium snowfall	$20,000	Expand Large
Light snowfall	$2,000	Subcontract

Using this information and the probability values of 0.6, 0.3, and 0.2 associated with high, medium, and light snowfalls, respectively, we can compute the expected value of the decision with perfect information as follows:

$$EV \text{ with perfect information} = (\$60,000 × 0.5) + (\$20,000 × 0.3) + (\$2,000 × 0.2) = \$36,400$$

The EV *without* perfect information is $28,000. Recall that this amount corresponds to the large expansion we determined Larry should make in part (a) of this problem. Therefore, the EVPI is:

$$EVPI = EV \text{ with perfect information} - EV \text{ without perfect information} = \$36,400 - \$28,000$$

$$= \$8,400$$

The maximum amount that Larry should pay the meteorologist to purchase the additional information about the nature of snowfall is $8,400.

See Screenshot F.4 for the solutions to the previous problem using Microsoft Excel.

SCREENSHOT F.4: Excel Solution for Miller Snow Blowers Problem of Decisions Under Risk

3. A hotel owner is planning to expand her facility. She has two alternatives: Expand on a large scale or expand on a smaller scale. If she chooses to expand on a smaller scale, she may have to expand again in four years. The success or failure of her decision depends on the nature of the hotel's demand. The probability of high demand for the hotel is 0.60. Expanding large now will yield profits of $400,000 if the demand is high and of $80,000 if the demand is low. Expanding small will yield profits of $120,000 if the demand is low. If the demand turns out be high after a small expansion, the

owner can opt for further expansion or do nothing. A later expansion will yield a profit of $250,000. Doing nothing at that point will a yield profit of $150,000:

a. Which alternative should the hotel owner choose?

b. Perform sensitivity analysis for the probability of high demand occurring.

Solution:

a. The problem requires sequential decisions be made. Consequently, we need to construct a decision tree like the one in Figure F.9.

FIGURE F.9: Decision Tree for the Hotel Owner's Facility Expansion Problem

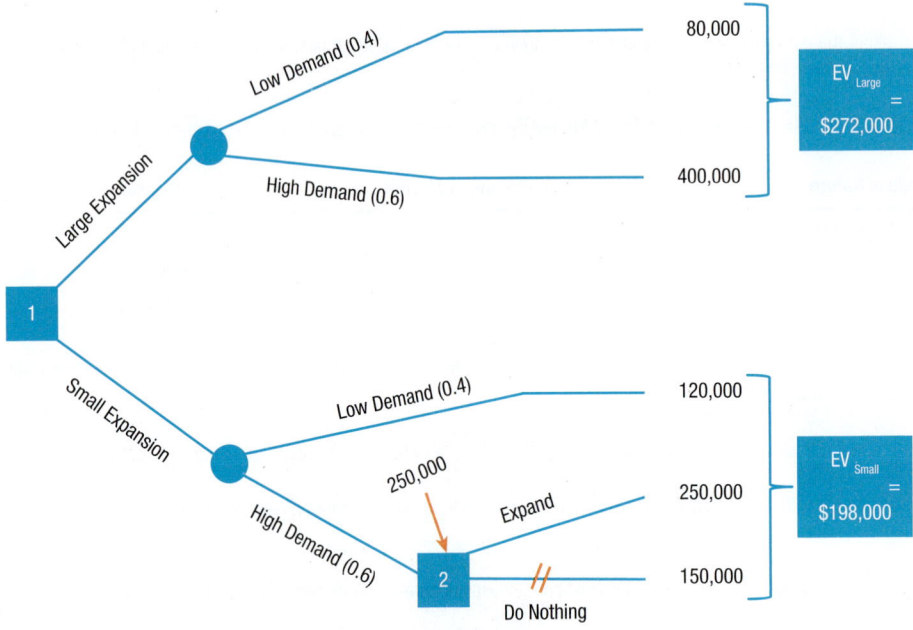

First we calculate the EV for the large expansion:

$$EV_{large} = (\$80,000 \times 0.4) + (\$400,000 \times 0.6) = \$272,000$$

If the demand is high, then we are better off further expanding the facility because doing so has a higher payoff than doing nothing. Hence, we choose to expand and prune off the "Do Nothing" branch in the decision tree.

Next, we calculate the expected value of the small expansion:

$$EV_{small} = (\$120,000 \times 0.4) + (\$250,000 \times 0.6) = \$198,000$$

The hotel owner's decision should be to expand large because it has the higher EV ($272,000).

b. The payoff matrix for this problem is shown in Table F.17.

TABLE F.17: Hotel Facility Expansion Payoff Matrix

Decision Alternative	Low Payoff	High Payoff
Expand Large	$80,000	$400,000
Expand Small	$120,000	$250,000

Using the information in Figure F.9, we construct a graph for the two decision alternatives in Figure F.10.

As Figure F.10 shows, the probability associated with the intersection point is 0.21.

We will algebraically determine the value for the P (high demand) at the point intersection of the two lines:

FIGURE F.10: Graph of Sensitivity Analysis of the Decisions

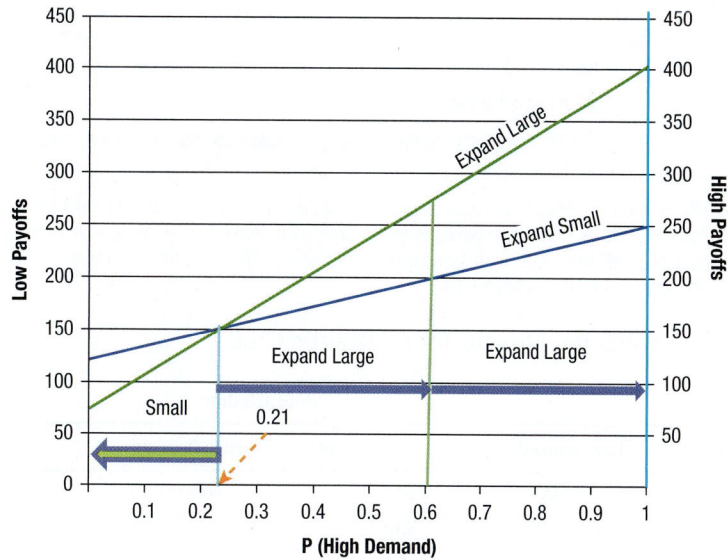

Expand Large: $(400 - 80) / (1 - 0) \times$ P (High Demand) + 80

$$= 320 \times \text{P (High Demand)} + 80$$

Expand Small: $(250 - 120) / (1 - 0) \times$ P (High Demand) + 120 = 130 × P (High Demand) + 120

Where the two lines intersect, the payoffs of the two alternatives are equal. So, we set the equations for these two lines as being equal to each other:

$$320 \times \text{P (High Demand)} + 80 = 130 \times \text{P (High Demand)} + 120$$

Rearranging the terms and solving for P (High Demand), we have:

$$\text{P (High Demand)} = 40 / 190 = 0.21$$

Therefore, as long as the P (High Demand) < 0.21, the hotel owner should opt for small expansion. If it is > 0.21, then she should expand large. Thus, the decision to "expand large" is fairly insensitive to changes to the original estimate of P (High Demand) of 0.6. It would only change if the probability of high demand falls below 0.21.

PROBLEMS ··

1. Ayush Pharmaceuticals, an Indian manufacturer of health-care products, is planning to expand its capacity to produce a new line of ayurvedic and herbal products. Nevertheless, the president of the company, Girija, is unsure about the nature of demand for this new product line. She is considering three possible capacity alternatives: Do nothing, expand the company's existing plant, or subcontract the production of the products. The estimated profits (in $) for the three alternatives under three different demand scenarios are provided in Table F.18. What decision would Girija select if the decision is made using:

    TABLE F.18

Decision Alternative	State of Nature		
	Low Demand	Medium Demand	High Demand
Do nothing	$ 40,000	$ 60,000	$80,000
Expand	−$30,000	$100,000	$160,000
Subcontract	$10,000	$70,000	$100,000

    a. The Laplace criterion

    b. The maximin criterion

    c. The maximax criterion

   d.   Hurwicz criterion ($\alpha = 0.6$)

   e.   The minimax regret

2.   Refer to Problem 1. After examining the past history of sales for similar products, Girija was able to estimate the probabilities for the three demand scenarios as: P (low) = 0.3; P (medium) = 0.4; and P (high) = 0.3.

   a.   What is the EV for each alternative, and which one is the best?

   b.   If Girija hires an expert from the health-care industry to get additional information about the demand for ayurvedic products, how much is this information worth?

3.   Miles Diller, the owner of the athletic club The Muscle Toner, is planning to expand the size of the club to meet the growth in demand he anticipates. His options for expanding the facility are to do nothing, make a moderate expansion, make a large expansion, or build a second facility that's bigger than the current one. There could be small, moderate, high, or no growth in demand. The net profits for the various combinations of alternatives and demand scenarios are shown in the payoff matrix in Table F.19.

TABLE F.19: Payoff Matrix For Muscle Toner Athletic Club

Decision Alternative	State of Nature			
	Low Demand	Medium Demand	High Demand	No Change
Do nothing	$5,000	$10,000	$20,000	$0
Moderate expansion	$10,000	$30,000	$70,000	−$20,000
Large expansion	−$20,000	$60,000	$100,000	−$50,000
New facility	−$40,000	$90,000	$160,000	−$100,000

What decisions would Miles select if he uses the Hurwicz ($\alpha = 0.4$) and minimax regret decision criteria?

4.   Refer to Problem 3. After consulting with various fitness facilities in his state and examining demographic data, Miles was able to estimate the following demand probabilities: P (Low) = 0.2; P (Medium) = 0.3; P (High) = 0.4; and P (No change) = 0.1.

   a.   What is the EV for each alternative, and which one is the best?

   b.   If Miles hires an expert to get additional demand information, how much is it worth?

5.   The Great Western University bookstore buys textbooks two months prior to the beginning of each semester. The store manager, Heidi Strong, uses departmental data and past student registration records to determine the number of textbooks to order from publishers. Pre-registration records show that currently 100 students are enrolled in various sections of a required introductory supply chain management course. Historically, however, there has been a considerable amount of variability in these enrollment numbers. Heidi, based on her experience, has determined the probabilities of selling the following number of textbooks for the course.

TABLE F.20: Probability Distribution of Books for Great Western University Book Store

Number of units	80	90	100	110	120
Probability	0.10	0.20	0.25	0.30	0.15

The bookstore purchases this book for $100 a copy and sells it the students for a price of $140. The publisher will buy back any unsold textbooks and, after deducting restocking and shipping costs, provide the bookstore a refund of $45 per textbook:

   a.   Construct a payoff matrix for Heidi.

   b.   To achieve the highest EV, how many copies of the textbook should Heidi initially order from the publisher?

6.   Sun Screen Inc., a U.S.-based manufacturer of solar panels, is planning to build a new manufacturing facility in one of five possible locations: Mexico, India, China, Greece, or Argentina. The cost of building a facility will vary, depending on the country's economic, social, and political climate and currency exchange rates. As Table F.21 shows, Sun Screen has estimated the cost (in millions of U.S. dollars) of building a facility in each country under two different economic climates. The probability of a favorable climate is 0.55, and the probability of an unfavorable one is 0.45.

TABLE F.21: Probabilities Associated With States of Nature

Country	Economic, Social, and Political Climate	
	Favorable	Unfavorable
Mexico	$20.0	$22.0
India	$16.0	$21.0
China	$17.0	$25.0
Greece	$14.0	$18.0
Argentina	$19.0	$20.0

Values are in millions.

Determine the best lowest-cost decision using the following decision criteria:

a. The Laplace criterion

b. The maximin criterion

c. The maximax criterion

d. The Hurwicz criterion ($\alpha = 0.4$)

e. The minimax regret criterion

Because the table consists of costs instead of revenues, the reverse logic applies. In other words, instead of the option with the highest value, the firm will want to choose the option with the lowest cost value. For example, the maximax criterion becomes the minimin criteria, which means you will choose the minimum of the minimum costs, and so on.

7. AMCO International, a major apparel retail company, has several stores in the United States and in countries throughout the globe. It imports most of its apparel products and garments from overseas suppliers. To improve its global supply chain operations, the company wants to contract with a single supplier located in one of the major ports around the world who can supply the majority of the apparel products it needs. The company is considering five major garment and apparel suppliers in the following major port cities: Chennai, India; Chittagong, Bangladesh; Manila, Philippines; Shanghai, China; and Jakarta, Indonesia. AMCO International has estimated the future profits (or loss) it may achieve will depend on a variety of future conditions (states of nature) including market conditions, exchange rates, quality of second and third tier suppliers, security issues, port capacity, and ship and container availability. These future conditions can be classified into three categories: status quo (no change), favorable, and unfavorable. Table F.22 summarizes the payoffs (in $ millions) from each of the overseas supplier for the three different states of nature.

TABLE F.22: Payoff Matrix for AMCO International

Decision Alternative	States of Nature		
	Status Quo	Favorable	Unfavorable
Chennai	$38	$75	−$40
Chittagong	$22	$45	−$17
Manila	$27	$60	−$23
Shanghai	$37	$70	−$44
Jakarta	$40	$55	−$32

Determine the best choice of supplier for each of the following decision criteria:

a. The Laplace criterion

b. The maximin criterion

c. The maximax criterion

d. The Hurwicz criterion ($\alpha = 0.3$)

e. The minimax regret criterion

8. Refer to Problem 7. After consulting with economists, government officials, and other supply chain experts, the vice president of supply chain for AMCO international was able to estimate the following probabilities for the three different states of nature:

P (Status Quo) = 0.2; P (Favorable) = 0.5; P (Unfavorable) = 0.3

a. What is the EV for each supplier, and which one is the best?

b. If AMCO hires a global supply chain expert to get additional information about the three different states of nature, how much is this information worth?

9. Michael Brusco has inherited a large amount of money from his aunt. He wants to invest this money for two years and is considering several short-term investment alternatives. The returns on his investment will largely depend on the state of the economy in the next two years. The various investment alternatives and their returns are given in Table F.23.

TABLE F.23: Payoff Matrix for Michael Brusco

Decision Alternative	States of Nature (Economic Conditions)		
	Stable	Favorable	Unfavorable
Stocks	$500,000	$800,000	−$300,000
Bonds	$230,000	$350,000	−$100,000
Money market fund	$110,000	$150,000	$50,000
Real estate	$300,000	$500,000	−$170,000
Hedge fund	$420,000	$650,000	−$220,000

Determine the best investment alternative for each of the following decision criteria:

a.   The Laplace criterion

b.   The maximin criterion

c.   The maximax criterion

d.   The Hurwicz criterion ($\alpha = 0.3$)

e.   The minimax regret criterion

10. Refer to Problem 9. After consulting with economic professors of his alma mater, Penn State University, Mike Brusco was able to estimate the following probabilities for the three different states of nature: P (Stable Economy) = 0.3; P (Favorable Economy) = 0.5; and P (Unfavorable Economy) = 0.3.

a.   What is the expected value for each investment alternative, and which one is the best?

b.   If Mike hires a financial/economic analyst to get additional information about the three different states of nature, how much is this information worth?

11. Scary Toys, Inc. must decide how to promote a new singing Zombie doll. Initially, the company must decide whether to market the doll or test market it first. Following the test marketing, the firm must decide whether to abandon the doll or nationally distribute it. If the product is a success, it will increase the company's profits by $400,000. By contrast, a failure will reduce the company's profits by $120,000. Abandoning the product will not affect the firm's profits. The test marketing will cost Scary Toys an additional $12,000. If no test marketing is conducted, the probability of the product's success is judged to be 0.40. The estimated probability of a favorable test-marketing result is 0.50. The probability that the product will be a success if its test marketing is favorable is 0.80. The probability that the product will be a success if its test marketing is unfavorable is 0.10. Construct a decision tree and analyze it to determine the optimal course of action.

12. Ozgun Demirag, the owner of a high-end U.S. apparel store, Feminine Fashions, is planning to open another facility in her hometown of Izmir, Turkey. Demirag can open a large store, a small store, or, to hedge her bets, she could open a medium-sized store. The market for high-end apparel in Izmir could be favorable or unfavorable. If the market is favorable, a large store will earn Ozgun a payoff of $200,000. Nevertheless, if the market is unfavorable, she will suffer a net loss of $180,000. If she opens a medium-sized store and the market is unfavorable, her loss will be $100,000. By contrast, a favorable market for a medium-sized store will generate a payoff of $140,000. A small store with a favorable market will result in a payoff of $ 60,000 but a payoff of −$20,000 if the market is unfavorable. The probability of a favorable market is 0.60 and that of an unfavorable market is 0.4:

a.   What should Ozgun decide? Analyze the problem using a decision tree.

b.   Perform a sensitivity analysis for the P (Unfavorable Market) to provide a range of probability values where one decision alternative would be preferred over the other two.

c.   If Ozgun hires an expert in the apparel industry in Turkey to get information about whether or not the market will be favorable, how much should Ozgun pay for the information?

13. Kumar Electronics is planning to introduce a new line of electronic products it plans to market and sell in India. Sanjay Kumar, the owner, is trying to decide whether to build a small or large manufacturing facility in his hometown of Jodhpur. High demand for the new line of products and a large facility will generate a net profit of $600,000. Building a small facility and then experiencing high demand will provide a net profit of $250,000. Yet, if a large facility is built and the demand turns out to be low, Sanjay will lose $200,000. A small facility and low demand will result in a net profit of $100,000. The probability of the demand being low is 0.4, and the probability of it being high is 0.6:

a.   Analyze the problem using a decision tree.

b.   Perform a sensitivity analysis for the P (High Demand) to help Sanjay make a decision.

c.   What would be the EVPI if Sanjay can hire a market research analyst to get additional information about the demand for his company's electronic products?

14. Refer to Problem 12. Ozgun Demirag is now considering whether to conduct a test-marketing program before opening any type of store in Izmir, Turkey. The test-marketing program will cost $10,000. If she initially decides to conduct such a program, the probability that it will yield favorable results is 0.5. By contrast, if the test-marketing results are favorable, the probability of a favorable market is now 0.85, regardless of the size of the store Ozgun plans to open. On the other hand, if the results are unfavorable, then the probability of a favorable market drops down to 0.15. If Ozgun decides not to conduct a test-marketing program to begin with, then the payoffs and probabilities of a favorable and unfavorable market is the same as in Problem 8.

Note: Conducting the program will reduce each payoff for the various alternatives in Problem 8 by $10,000.

a.   Given this new information, revise the decision tree you constructed for Problem 8.

b.   Analyze the revised decision tree to advise Ozgun about the decision she should make.

15. Refer to Problem 13. In the previous decision situation, the owner, Sanjay Kumar, decided to build a small facility. After operating the facility for a year, Sanjay realized that the market-growth potential for his company's new line of electronic products during the next eight years was significant. The initial decision that Sanjay has to make now is whether to expand the existing facility or purchase land to build a new facility three years into the future if the market growth continues to remain favorable. The probability of favorable market growth is 0.6. Favorable market growth after expanding the current facility will provide a payoff of $500,000. No market growth after the expansion will lead to a payoff of −$100,000. If the initial decision is to purchase land, and the market growth continues to remain favorable, Sanjay can build a second facility or sell the land. Building a second facility under favorable market-growth conditions will provide the company a payoff of $1,000,000. Selling the land under these conditions will generate a $400,000 payoff. Nevertheless, if the market growth is not favorable, Sanjay has the option of selling the purchased land for $170,000. Or, he can build a warehouse that will give him a payoff of $300,000. Depending on the options Sanjay chooses, the company will incur the following costs:

- Initial expansion: $100,000
- Land purchase: $150,000

- Building a second facility: $250,000
- Building a warehouse: $120,000

What should Sanjay do? Analyze the problem using a decision tree.

16. Medaas Oil Company located in Stavanger, Norway, is considering making a bid for an oil exploration contract to be awarded by the Norwegian government. Megan Medaas, the Chief Financial Officer of the company, has decided to a make a bid for $120 million. The cost of preparing the proposal for the bid is $3 million. The probability of winning the contract with this bid is 65%. If the company wins the contract, it can choose to use one of the three methods for extracting oil: use an innovative method, use the existing method, or subcontract. The probabilities of finding oil for each of the three methods with varying degrees of success are given in Tables F.24–F.26.

TABLE F.24: Payoff Matrix for Medaas Oil Company Using the Innovative Method

Result	Probability	Payoff (in $ miilions)
Highly Successful	0.40	$800
Moderately Successful	0.50	$400
Failure	0.10	−$200

TABLE F.25: Payoff Matrix for Medaas Oil Company Using the Existing Method

Result	Probability	Payoff (in $ miilions)
Highly Successful	0.45	$400
Moderately Successful	0.35	$250
Failure	0.20	−$60

TABLE F.26: Payoff Matrix for Medaas Oil Company Using Subcontracting

Result	Probability	Payoff (in $ millions)
Highly Successful	0.50	$300
Moderately Successful	0.40	$150
Failure	0.10	−$100

Instead of bidding for the oil contract, Megan also has the option of partnering with another oil company in an alternative new venture. This option has a guaranteed payoff of $60 million. What should Megan do? Analyze the problem using a decision tree.

17. Elite Shipping Inc., a third-party logistics provider, in Chennai, India, is planning to build a new warehouse to accommodate the increasing demand for its warehousing services. Mr. Venkatesh, the CEO of the company, is not able to decide whether to build a small-, large-, or medium-size warehouse as future demand for the company's warehousing services is uncertain. If a small warehouse is built and demand is low, the company will have a net payoff of $600,000. Nevertheless, if demand turns to be high, the company has the option of expanding the existing warehouse or leasing additional warehousing facility. Expansion will provide a net payoff of $700,000, while the leasing option will have a net payoff of $400,000. If a medium-sized facility is built and demand turns out to be low, then the company will make $300,000. On the other hand, if demand turns out to be high, the net payoff will be $1 million.

Building a large warehouse to begin with will have a net payoff of $3 million if demand is high. If demand turns out to be low, then by building a large warehouse, the company will incur a loss of $800,000. The probability of high demand is 60%. What decision should Venkatesh make? Analyze the problem using a decision tree.

18. Refer to Problem 17. Although Mr. Venkatesh of Elite Shipping has estimated the payoffs associated with the various warehouse options, he is not willing to assign probabilities to the two states of nature associated with demand. Information about the payoffs and the two states of nature given in Problem 15 is presented in Table F.27.

a. For each alternative, plot the payoff value lines on a graph for P (low demand).

b. If the goal is to maximize expected payoffs, for what range of P (low demand) would the alternative building small would be the best choice?

c. If the goal is to maximize expected payoffs, is there any alternative that is not appropriate? Explain.

TABLE F.27: Payoff Matrix for Elite Shipping

Warehousing Alternatives	States of Nature	
	Low Demand	High Demand
Small	$600,000	$700,000
Medium	$300,000	$1,000,000
Large	−$800,000	$3,000,000

19. Refer to Problem 12. Ozgun Demirag of Feminine Fashions is reluctant to assign probabilities to the different states of nature (market conditions). She asks for your help in determining which alternative among the three types of stores—small, medium, or large store—she should build for a range of probabilities of favorable market conditions, i.e., P (Favorable Market). Help Ozgun make a decision by performing a sensitivity analysis for P (Favorable Market).

20. Refer to Problem 13. Sanjay Kumar of Kumar Electronics is reluctant to assign probabilities to the different states of nature (demand). He asks for your help in determining which alternative among the two types of plants—a small or large facility—he should build for a range of probabilities of low demand, i.e., P (Low demand). Help Sanjay to make a decision by performing a sensitivity analysis for P (Low demand).

21. Asean Aromatics, a manufacturer of perfumes and aromatic oils, is planning to introduce three new perfumes: Lavender Mist, Jasmine Dreams, and Sandalwood Delight. Nevertheless, the president of the company, Capt. Muralidharan is unsure about the nature of demand for this new product line of perfumes. The estimated annual profits (in $) for the three new perfumes under four different demand scenarios are provided in Table F.28. What decision would Capt. Muralidharan select if the decision is made using:

    a. The Laplace criterion

    b. The maximin criterion

    c. The maximax criterion

    d. Hurwicz criterion ($\alpha = 0.6$)

    e. The minimax regret

TABLE F.28: Payoff Matrix for Asean Aromatics

Decision Alternative	State of Nature (Demand)			
	Low	Average	Good	Excellent
Lavender Mist	$50,000	$60,000	$80,000	$110,000
Jasmine Dreams	−$40,000	$90,000	$130,000	$150,000
Sandalwood Delight	$20,000	$80,000	$100,000	$120,000

22. Refer to Problem 21. After extensive discussion with an economics professor from his alma mater, Capt. Muralidharan has decided that reasonable probabilities for the various demand scenarios are 0.10 for low, 0.30 for average, 0.40 for good, and 0.20 for excellent demand:

    a. Which perfume will yield the maximum expected profits?

    b. Compute the expected value of perfect information, and interpret it.

23. Patagonia, designer of outdoor clothing and sports equipment, is planning to introduce a new brand of ski jackets: Ultra lite and Feather lite. The probabilities for the various possible states of nature associated with these two new products and the expected payoffs for each combination of decision and states of nature are provided in the decision tree diagram in Figure F.11. Determine the new jacket ski that will have the highest expected payoff.

FIGURE F.11:

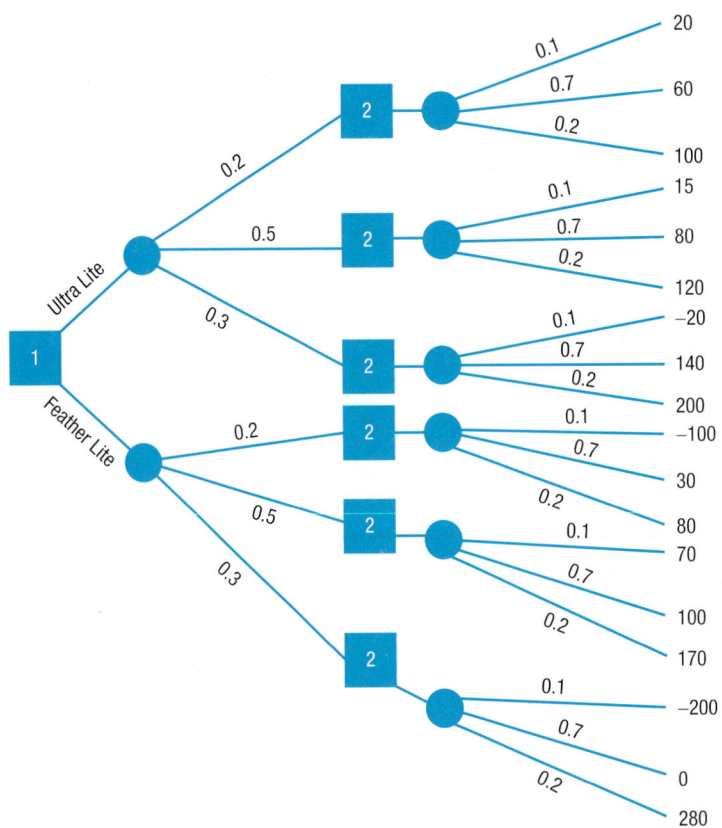

24. Sunshine Health Club is planning to build a new athletics and recreation facility and is debating which of the service feature alternatives (shown in Table F.29) to include in addition to the usual features of a health club such as a weight room, aerobics room, locker rooms and showers, and offices. Customer demand for these features (which is uncertain) determines their profitability. The payoffs associated with each of these service feature alternatives for three different demand scenarios are also given in Table F.29.

TABLE F.29: Payoff Matrix for Sunshine Health Club

Service Features	Demand		
	Low	Moderate	High
Swimming Pool	−$60,000	$30,000	$100,000
Running Track	$10,000	$25,000	$55,000
Child-care Center	$22, 000	$32,000	$45,000
Indoor Basket Ball court	−$20,000	$22,000	$48,000
Sauna	−$15,000	$5,000	$17,000
Food Court	−$35,000	$15,000	$75,000

Determine the best decision for the health club using each of the following criteria:

a. The Laplace criterion

b. The maximin criterion

c. The maximax criterion

d. Hurwicz criterion ($\alpha = 0.6$)

e. The minimax regret

25. Refer to Problem 24. The Sunshine Health Club hired an economist to estimate for each service feature the probabilities of occurrence for the three different states of nature (demand). These probabilistic estimates are given in Table F.30.

TABLE F.30: Probabilities for Each Combination of Service Feature and State of Nature

Service Features	Demand		
	Low	Moderate	High
Swimming Pool	0.20	0.30	0.50
Running Track	0.25	0.45	0.30
Child-care Center	0.10	0.50	0.40
Indoor Basket Ball court	0.12	0.38	0.50
Sauna	0.05	0.25	0.70
Food Court	0.20	0.50	0.30

a. Which decision will yield the maximum expected profits?

b. Compute the expected value of perfect information, and interpret it.

CASE STUDY F.1 GERBER PRODUCTS COMPANY: THE PROBLEM

The Gerber Products Company (subsidiary of Nestlé Group, Fremont, MI), the well-known maker of baby products, was facing a set of critical choices about whether to continue using the plastic known as polyvinyl chloride, commonly known as PVC. PVC is a composite plastic material used in numerous household, commercial, and medical products including food storage containers, toys, and medical tubing. To make PVC pliable for use, chemical plasticizers called *phthalates* are added to soften the plastic. In late 1998, the environmental group Greenpeace announced that it had conducted scientific testing on the effects of phthalates on lab rats and found them to cause cancer. Greenpeace claimed its testing showed that the chemical leeches from the plastic over time and was particularly worrisome when it was used in products small children suck or chew on. Phthalates have been used in the plastics industry for several decades with no known cases of them causing health problems. Nevertheless, Greenpeace's press release, which was strategically timed to coincide with the holiday shopping season, was immediately picked up by television networks. The show *20/20* did an entire segment on the possible health risks of phthalates.

Gerber's problems got worse when attention focused specifically on products made for oral use by children, including pacifiers, nipples, and other feeding products. Gerber, which is the largest producer of these products in the United States, faced a serious strategic decision. Should it continue using phthalates, which had been so critical to the development of its many products but could be carcinogenic, or invest heavily in new technologies to eliminate phthalates from its product line? The choices were risky and involved significant costs—societal and legal costs as well as monetary costs. The company clearly needed a strategy for effectively analyzing the alternatives and selecting the best option.

Questions:

1. Frame this situation as a decision. What are the strategic choices that Gerber faces as a result of these circumstances?

2. Suppose you were a senior manager at Gerber when this issue came to light. What are the critical choices you need to make? What are the potential risks and costs for:

a. Ignoring the potential problem.

b. Responding with the decision to end the use of all phthalates in your production processes immediately.

CASE STUDY F.2 GERBER PRODUCTS COMPANY: THE SOLUTION

In dealing with the phthalates issue, Gerber's managers had to evaluate all of the information it had, determine its various options, weigh the consequences of each action, and decide on the best one. The firm knew that all scientific evidence indicates that phthalates are completely safe. Nevertheless, in the wake of the Greenpeace announcement, the Consumer Product Safety Commission (CPSC) decided to issue its own press release expressing doubts about phthalates. A month before Christmas, the commission informed Gerber it intended to issue a press release advising parents of the potential dangers of phthalates, specifically naming Gerber as one of the biggest companies making products containing phthalates.

Gerber was faced with two choices, both of which had significant drawbacks. The firm could (1) proactively address the problem by removing phthalates from its products regardless of the public's response to the Greenpeace report, or (2) it could wait for the CPSC's announcement and monitor public response before deciding on a course of action. The CSPC's report suggested the agency either was likely to issue a recall of all products containing phthalates or it would merely post a notification expressing concern about phthalates; in which case, the public's reaction could be minimal. Given these two initial alternatives, Gerber came up with eight possible outcomes on its decision tree.

Respond Proactively. If Gerber reacted proactively by discontinuing use of all phthalates, and the report simply issued a warning, there was an 80% chance that the public would react favorably to Gerber's responsiveness, causing sales to jump relative to competing firms that responded more slowly. A possible revenue increase of $l million was therefore entered into the decision tree. With a proactive response and a favorable CSPC report, Gerber also predicted there would be a 20% chance its sales would decline by $1 million because of the nature of the press coverage.

If the report were more strongly negative, resulting in a recall, and Gerber responded proactively, the company believed that there was a 25% probability it could preserve its current sales and a 75% probability that sales would fall by $1.25 million.

Respond Reactively. Four more alternatives were judged possible in the event that Gerber decided to wait for the press release before taking action. With a favorable report and a delayed response, the firm figured there would be a 25% chance that sales would remain flat and a 75% chance that sales would decline by $2 million.

The worst-case scenario was if Gerber were to remain nonresponsive, and the CSPC issued a recall. In that case, Gerber predicted there was a 20% probability that it could still increase its sales by approximately $.5 million at the expense of companies that were less prepared for the report. Nevertheless, Gerber predicated there was an 80% probability it would lose a significant amount of sales (approximately $5 million) by remaining passive. Gerber's decision tree is shown in Figure F.12.

The EV calculations for the tree are as follows:

I. Respond Proactively

1. Favorable report, sales increase: $1 million

2. Favorable report, and sales decline: −$1 million

$$EV_1 = (\$1 \text{ million} \times 0.8) + (-\$1 \text{ million} \times 0.2) = \$600{,}000$$

3. Unfavorable report, sales increase: $0

4. Unfavorable report, sales decline: −$1.25 million

FIGURE F.12

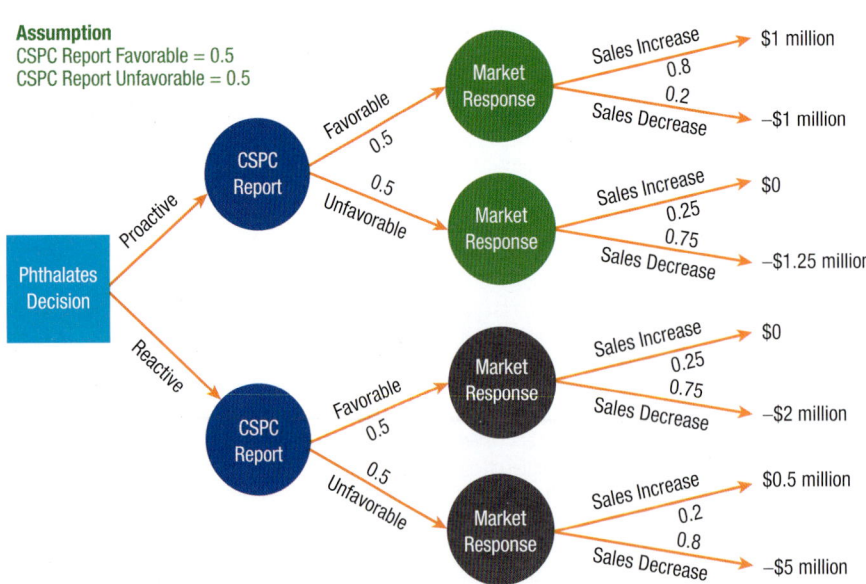

$$EV_2 = (\$0 \times 0.25) + (-\$1.25 \text{ million} \times 0.75) = -\$937,500$$

$$EV_{\text{respond proactively}} = (EV_1 \times 0.5) + (EV_2 \times 0.5)$$

$$= (\$600,000 \times 0.5) + (-\$937,500 \times 0.5)$$

$$= -\$168,750$$

II.   Respond Reactively

5.   Favorable report, sales increase: $0

6.   Favorable report, sales decline: −$2 million

$$EV_1 = (\$0 \times 0.25) + (-\$2 \text{ million} \times 0.75) = -\$1.5 \text{ million}$$

7.   Unfavorable report, sales increase: $0.5 million

8.   Unfavorable report, sales decline: −$5 million

$$EV_2 = (\$0.5 \text{ million} \times 0.2) + (-\$5 \text{ million} \times 0.8) = -\$3,900,000$$

$$EV_{\text{respond reactively}} = (EV_1 \times 0.5) + (EV_2 \times 0.5)$$

$$= (-\$1,500,000 \times 0.5) + (-\$3,900,000 \times 0.5) = -\$2,600,000$$

Based on the decision tree and the expected values of the alternatives it calculated, Gerber concluded that its best option was to respond proactively without waiting for the CPSC's report. Then, Gerber hoped for a favorable report. This would give the company a strategic advantage over its competitors that had failed to take action. Nevertheless, the CPSC, U.S. Food & Drug Administration, and American Council on Science and Health (ACSH) ultimately approved phthalates for use in toys and other products. In fact, an ACSH panel of scientists and physicians reinforced the benefits of using phthalates in medical applications. Nonetheless, Gerber's decision to respond proactively was based on a rational decision-making process and the best information the firm had. Because it is impossible to accurately predict outcomes, often the best choices still cost money.[2]

Questions

1.   This case illustrates an example of the fact that sometimes the "best" alternative is the one that minimizes costs; in other words, the optimal solution is the one that isn't profitable itself but keeps a firm from losing too much money as a result of a bad decision choice. Can you think of another circumstance where an organization faced a similar decision that involved minimizing the negative payoff? (Hint: Think of industries with significant pollution of environmental hazard concerns.)

2.   Given the fact that, ultimately, the government found that phthalates were not harmful, was Gerber's decision to respond proactively a good one or a bad one? Why? Can an organization afford to wait until full information is available about potential health risks?

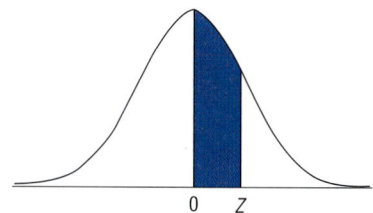

TABLE A. Areas under the normal curve, 0 to z

z	.00	.01	.02	.03	.04	.05	.06	.07	.08	.09
0.0	.0000	.0040	.0080	.0120	.0160	.0199	.0239	.0279	.0319	.0359
0.1	.0398	.0438	.0478	.0517	.0557	.0596	.0636	.0675	.0714	.0753
0.2	.0793	.0832	.0871	.0910	.0948	.0987	.1026	.1064	.1103	.1141
0.3	.1179	.1217	.1255	.1293	.1331	.1368	.1406	.1443	.1480	.1517
0.4	.1554	.1591	.1628	.1664	.1700	.1736	.1772	.1808	.1844	.1879
0.5	.1915	.1950	.1985	.2019	.2054	.2088	.2123	.2157	.2190	.2224
0.6	.2257	.2291	.2324	.2357	.2389	.2422	.2454	.2486	.2517	.2549
0.7	.2580	.2611	.2642	.2673	.2703	.2734	.2764	.2794	.2823	.2852
0.8	.2881	.2910	.2939	.2967	.2995	.3023	.3051	.3078	.3106	.3133
0.9	.3159	.3186	.3212	.3238	.3264	.3289	.3315	.3340	.3365	.3389
1.0	.3413	.3438	.3461	.3485	.3508	.3531	.3554	.3577	.3599	.3621
1.1	.3643	.3665	.3686	.3708	.3729	.3749	.3770	.3790	.3810	.3830
1.2	.3849	.3869	.3888	.3907	.3925	.3944	.3962	.3980	.3997	.4015
1.3	.4032	.4049	.4066	.4082	.4099	.4115	.4131	.4147	.4162	.4177
1.4	.4192	.4207	.4222	.4236	.4251	.4265	.4279	.4292	.4306	.4319
1.5	.4332	.4345	.4357	.4370	.4382	.4394	.4406	.4418	.4429	.4441
1.6	.4452	.4463	.4474	.4484	.4495	.4505	.4515	.4525	.4535	.4545
1.7	.4554	.4564	.4573	.4582	.4591	.4599	.4608	.4616	.4625	.4633
1.8	.4641	.4649	.4656	.4664	.4671	.4678	.4686	.4693	.4699	.4706
1.9	.4713	.4719	.4726	.4732	.4738	.4744	.4750	.4756	.4761	.4767
2.0	.4772	.4778	.4783	.4788	.4793	.4798	.4803	.4808	.4812	.4817
2.1	.4821	.4826	.4830	.4834	.4838	.4842	.4846	.4850	.4854	.4857
2.2	.4861	.4864	.4868	.4871	.4875	.4878	.4881	.4884	.4887	.4890
2.3	.4893	.4896	.4898	.4901	.4904	.4906	.4909	.4911	.4913	.4916
2.4	.4918	.4920	.4922	.4925	.4927	.4929	.4931	.4932	.4934	.4936
2.5	.4938	.4940	.4941	.4943	.4945	.4946	.4948	.4949	.4951	.4952
2.6	.4953	.4955	.4956	.4957	.4959	.4960	.4961	.4962	.4963	.4964
2.7	.4965	.4966	.4967	.4968	.4969	.4970	.4971	.4972	.4973	.4974
2.8	.4974	.4975	.4976	.4977	.4977	.4978	.4979	.4979	.4980	.4981
2.9	.4981	.4982	.4982	.4983	.4984	.4984	.4985	.4985	.4986	.4986
3.0	.4987	.4987	.4987	.4988	.4988	.4989	.4989	.4989	.4990	.4990

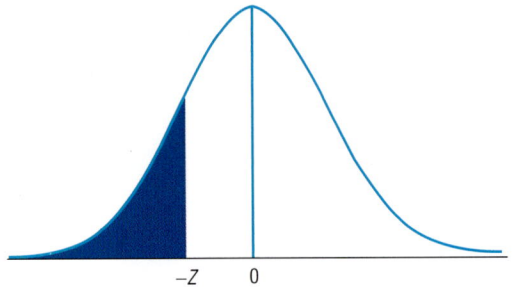

TABLE B1. Areas under the standardized normal curve, from –∞ to –z

.09	.08	.07	.06	.05	.04	.03	.02	.01	.00	z
.0002	.0003	.0003	.0003	.0003	.0003	.0003	.0003	.0003	.0003	−3.4
.0003	.0004	.0004	.0004	.0004	.0004	.0004	.0005	.0005	.0005	−3.3
.0005	.0005	.0005	.0006	.0006	.0006	.0006	.0006	.0007	.0007	−3.2
.0007	.0007	.0008	.0008	.0008	.0008	.0009	.0009	.0009	.0010	−.31
.0010	.0010	.0011	.0011	.0011	.0012	.0012	.0013	.0013	.0013	−3.0
.0014	.0014	.0015	.0015	.0016	.0016	.0017	.0018	.0018	.0019	−2.9
.0019	.0020	.0021	.0021	.0022	.0023	.0023	.0024	.0025	.0026	−2.8
.0026	.0027	.0028	.0029	.0030	.0031	.0032	.0033	.0034	.0035	−2.7
.0036	.0037	.0038	.0039	.0040	.0041	.0043	.0044	.0045	.0047	−2.6
.0048	.0049	.0051	.0052	.0054	.0055	.0057	.0059	.0060	.0062	−2.5
.0064	.0066	.0068	.0069	.0071	.0073	.0075	.0078	.0080	.0082	−2.4
.0084	.0087	.0089	.0091	.0094	.0096	.0099	.0102	.0104	.0107	−2.3
.0110	.0113	.0116	.0119	.0122	.0125	.0129	.0132	.0136	.0139	−2.2
.0143	.0146	.0150	.0154	.0158	.0162	.0166	.0170	.0174	.0179	−2.1
.0183	.0188	.0192	.0197	.0202	.0207	.0212	.0217	.0222	.0228	−2.0
.0233	.0239	.0244	.0250	.0256	.0262	.0268	.0274	.0281	.0287	−1.9
.0294	.0301	.0307	.0314	.0322	.0329	.0336	.0344	.0351	.0359	−1.8
.0367	.0375	.0384	.0392	.0401	.0409	.0418	.0427	.0436	.0446	−1.7
.0455	.0465	.0475	.0485	.0495	.0505	.0516	.0526	.0537	.0548	−1.6
.0559	.0571	.0582	.0594	.0606	.0618	.0630	.0643	.0655	.0668	−1.5
.0681	.0694	.0708	.0721	.0735	.0749	.0764	.0778	.0793	.0808	−1.4
.0823	.0838	.0853	.0869	.0885	.0901	.0918	.0934	.0951	.0968	−1.3
.0985	.1003	.1020	.1038	.1056	.1075	.1093	.1112	.1131	.1151	−1.2
.1170	.1190	.1210	.1230	.1251	.1271	.1292	.1314	.1335	.1357	−1.1

(Continued)

.09	.08	.07	.06	.05	.04	.03	.02	.01	.00	z
.1379	.1401	.1423	.1446	.1469	.1492	.1515	.1539	.1562	.1587	−1.0
.1611	.1635	.1660	.1685	.1711	.1736	.1762	.1788	.1814	.1841	−0.9
.1867	.1894	.1922	.1949	.1977	.2005	.2033	.2061	.2090	.2119	−0.8
.2148	.2177	.2206	.2236	.2266	.2296	.2327	.2358	.2389	.2420	−0.7
.2451	.2483	.2514	.2546	.2578	.2611	.2643	.2676	.2709	.2743	−0.6
.2776	.2810	.2843	.2877	.2912	.2946	.2981	.3015	.3050	.3085	−0.5
.3121	.3156	.3192	.3228	.3264	.3300	.3336	.3372	.3409	.3446	−0.4
.3483	.3520	.3557	.3594	.3632	.3669	.3707	.3745	.3783	.3821	−0.3
.3859	.3897	.3936	.3974	.4013	.4052	.4090	.4129	.4168	.4207	−0.2
.4247	.4286	.4325	.4364	.4404	.4443	.4483	.4522	.4562	.4602	−0.1
.4641	.4681	.4721	.4761	.4801	.4840	.4880	.4920	.4960	.5000	−0.0

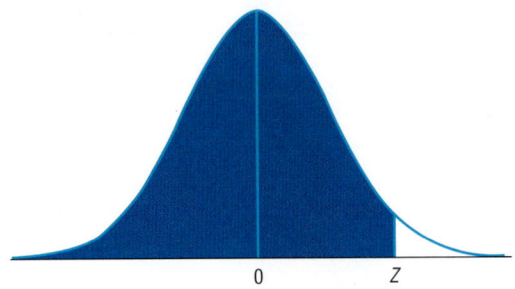

TABLE B2. Areas under the standardized normal curve, from −∞ to +z

z	.00	.01	.02	.03	.04	.05	.06	.07	.08	.09
.0	.5000	.5040	.5080	.5120	.5160	.5199	.5239	.5279	.5319	.5359
.1	.5398	.5438	.5478	.5517	.5557	.5596	.5636	.5675	.5714	.5753
.2	.5793	.5832	.5871	.5910	.5948	.5987	.6026	.6064	.6103	.6141
.3	.6179	.6217	.6255	.6293	.6331	.6368	.6406	.6443	.6480	.6517
.4	.6554	.6591	.6628	.6664	.6700	.6736	.6772	.6808	.6844	.6879
.5	.6915	.6950	.6985	.7019	.7054	.7088	.7123	.7157	.7190	.7224
.6	.7257	.7291	.7324	.7357	.7389	.7422	.7454	.7486	.7517	.7549
.7	.7580	.7611	.7642	.7673	.7703	.7734	.7764	.7794	.7823	.7852
.8	.7881	.7910	.7939	.7967	.7995	.8023	.8051	.8078	.8106	.8133
.9	.8159	.8186	.8212	.8238	.8264	.8289	.8315	.8340	.8365	.8389
1.0	.8413	.8438	.8461	.8485	.8508	.8531	.8554	.8577	.8599	.8621
1.1	.8643	.8665	.8686	.8708	.8729	.8749	.8770	.8790	.8810	.8830
1.2	.8849	.8869	.8888	.8907	.8925	.8944	.8962	.8980	.8997	.9015
1.3	.9032	.9049	.9066	.9082	.9099	.9115	.9131	.9174	.9162	.9177
1.4	.9192	.9207	.9222	.9236	.9251	.9265	.9279	.9292	.9306	.9319
1.5	.9332	.9345	.9357	.9370	.9382	.9394	.9406	.9418	.9429	.9441
1.6	.9452	.9463	.9474	.9484	.9495	.9505	.9515	.9525	.9535	.9545
1.7	.9554	.9564	.9573	.9582	.9591	.9599	.9608	.9616	.9625	.9633
1.8	.9641	.9649	.9656	.9664	.9671	.9678	.9686	.9693	.9699	.9706
1.9	.9713	.9719	.9726	.9732	.9738	.9744	.9750	.9756	.9761	.9767
2.0	.9772	.9778	.9783	.9788	.9793	.9798	.9803	.9808	.9812	.9817
2.1	.9821	.9826	.9830	.9834	.9838	.9842	.9846	.9850	.9854	.9857
2.2	.9861	.9864	.9868	.9871	.9875	.9878	.9881	.9884	.9887	.9890
2.3	.9893	.9896	.9898	.9901	.9904	.9906	.9909	.9911	.9913	.9916
2.4	.9918	.9920	.9922	.9925	.9927	.9929	.9931	.9932	.9934	.9936
2.5	.9938	.9940	.9941	.9943	.9945	.9946	.9948	.9949	.9951	.9952
2.6	.9953	.9955	.9956	.9957	.9959	.9960	.9961	.9962	.9963	.9964

(Continued)

z	.00	.01	.02	.03	.04	.05	.06	.07	.08	.09
2.7	.9965	.9966	.9967	.9968	.9969	.9970	.9971	.9972	.9973	.9974
2.8	.9974	.9975	.9976	.9977	.9977	.9978	.9979	.9979	.9980	.9981
2.9	.9981	.9982	.9982	.9983	.9984	.9984	.9985	.9985	.9986	.9986
3.0	.9987	.9987	.9987	.9988	.9988	.9989	.9989	.9989	.9990	.9990
3.1	.9990	.9991	.9991	.9991	.9992	.9992	.9992	.9992	.9993	.9993
3.2	.9993	.9993	.9994	.9994	.9994	.9994	.9994	.9995	.9995	.9995
3.3	.9995	.9995	.9995	.9996	.9996	.9996	.9996	.9996	.9996	.9997
3.4	.9997	.9997	.9997	.9997	.9997	.9997	.9997	.9997	.9997	.9998

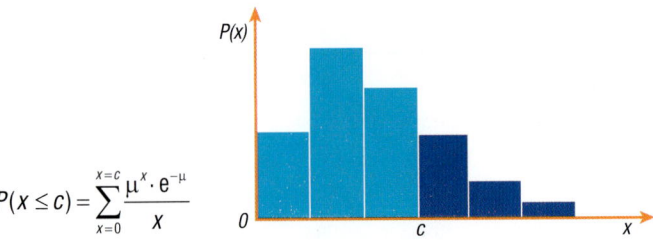

$$P(x \le c) = \sum_{x=0}^{x=c} \frac{\mu^x \cdot e^{-\mu}}{x}$$

TABLE C. Cumulative Poisson probabilities

μ\x	0	1	2	3	4	5	6	7	8	9
0.05	.951	.999	1.000							
0.10	.905	.995	1.000							
0.15	.861	.990	.999	1.000						
0.20	.819	.982	.999	1.000						
0.25	.779	.974	.998	1.000						
0.30	.741	.963	.996	1.000						
0.35	.705	.951	.994	1.000						
0.40	.670	.938	.992	.999	1.000					
0.45	.638	.925	.989	.999	1.000					
0.50	.607	.910	.986	.998	1.000					
0.55	.577	.894	.982	.998	1.000					
0.60	.549	.878	.977	.997	1.000					
0.65	.522	.861	.972	.996	.999	1.000				
0.70	.497	.844	.966	.994	.999	1.000				
0.75	.472	.827	.960	.993	.999	1.000				
0.80	.449	.809	.953	.991	.999	1.000				
0.85	.427	.791	.945	.989	.998	1.000				
0.90	.407	.772	.937	.9.87	.998	1.000				
0.95	.387	.754	.929	.984	.997	1.000				
1.0	.368	.736	.920	.981	.996	.999	1.000			
1.1	.333	.699	.900	.974	.995	.999	1.000			
1.2	.301	.663	.880	.966	.992	.998	1.000			
1.3	.273	.627	.857	.957	.989	.998	1.000			
1.4	.247	.592	.833	.946	.986	.997	.999	1.000		
1.5	.223	.558	.809	.934	.981	.996	.999	1.000		
1.6	.202	.525	.783	.921	.976	.994	.999	1.000		
1.7	.183	.493	.757	.907	.970	.992	.998	1.000		

(Continued)

μ\x	0	1	2	3	4	5	6	7	8	9
1.8	.165	.463	.731	.891	.964	.990	.997	.999	1.000	
1.9	.150	.434	.704	.875	.956	.987	.997	.999	1.000	
2.0	.135	.406	.677	.857	.947	.983	.995	.999	1.000	
2.2	.111	.355	.623	.819	.928	.975	.993	.998	1.000	
2.4	.091	.308	.570	.779	.904	.964	.988	.997	.999	1.000
2.6	.074	.267	.518	.736	.877	.951	.983	.995	.999	1.000
2.8	.061	.231	.470	.692	.848	.935	.976	.992	.998	.999

TABLE C. (concluded)

μ\x	0	1	2	3	4	5	6	7	8	9	10	11	12	13	14	15	16	17	18	19	20
3.0	.050	.199	.423	.647	.815	.916	.966	.988	.996	.999	1.000										
3.2	.041	.171	.380	.603	.781	.895	.955	.983	.994	.998	1.000										
3.4	.033	.147	.340	.558	.744	.871	.942	.977	.992	.997	.999	1.000									
3.6	.027	.126	.303	.515	.706	.844	.927	.969	.988	.996	.999	1.000									
3.8	.022	.107	.269	.474	.668	.816	.909	.960	.984	.994	.998	.999									
4.0	.018	.092	.238	.433	.629	.785	.889	.949	.979	.992	.997	.999									
4.2	.015	.078	.210	.395	.590	.753	.868	.936	.972	.989	.996	.999	1.000								
4.4	.012	.066	.185	.359	.551	.720	.844	.921	.964	.985	.994	.998	.999	1.000							
4.6	.010	.056	.163	.326	.513	.686	.818	.905	.955	.980	.992	.997	.999	1.000							
4.8	.008	.048	.143	.294	.476	.651	.791	.887	.944	.975	.990	.996	.999	1.000							
5.0	.007	.040	.125	.265	.441	.616	.762	.867	.932	.968	.986	.995	.998	.999	1.000						
5.2	.006	.034	.109	.238	.406	.581	.732	.845	.918	.960	.982	.993	.997	.999	1.000						
5.4	.005	.029	.095	.213	.373	.546	.702	.822	.903	.951	.978	.990	.996	.999	1.000						
5.6	.004	.024	.082	.191	.342	.512	.670	.797	.886	.941	.972	.988	.995	.998	.999	1.000					
5.8	.003	.021	.072	.170	.313	.478	.638	.771	.867	.929	.965	.984	.993	.997	.999	1.000					
6.0	.003	.017	.062	.151	.285	.446	.606	.744	.847	.916	.957	.980	.991	.996	.999	.999	1.000				
6.2	.002	.015	.054	.134	.259	.414	.574	.716	.826	.902	.949	.975	.989	.995	.998	.999	1.000				
6.4	.002	.012	.046	.119	.235	.384	.542	.687	.803	.886	.939	.969	.986	.994	.997	.999	1.000				
6.6	.001	.010	.040	.105	.213	.355	.511	.658	.780	.869	.927	.963	.982	.992	.997	.999	.999	1.000			
6.8	.001	.009	.034	.093	.192	.327	.480	.628	.755	.850	.915	.955	.978	.990	.996	.998	.999	1.000			
7.0	.001	.007	.030	.082	.173	.301	.450	.599	.729	.830	.901	.947	.973	.987	.994	.998	.999	1.000			
7.2	.001	.006	.025	.072	.156	.276	.420	.569	.703	.810	.887	.937	.967	.984	.993	.997	.999	.999	1.000		
7.4	.001	.005	.022	.063	.140	.253	.392	.539	.676	.788	.871	.926	.961	.980	.991	.996	.998	.999	1.000		
7.6	.001	.004	.019	.055	.125	.231	.365	.510	.648	.765	.854	.915	.954	.976	.989	.995	.998	.999	1.000		
7.8	.001	.004	.016	.048	.112	.210	.338	.481	.620	.741	.835	.902	.945	.971	.986	.993	.997	.998	.999	1.000	
8.0	.000	.003	.014	.042	.100	.191	.313	.453	.593	.717	.816	.888	.936	.966	.983	.992	.996	.998	.999	1.000	
8.2	.000	.003	.012	.037	.089	.174	.290	.425	.566	.692	.796	.873	.926	.960	.979	.990	.995	.998	.999	1.000	
8.4	.000	.002	.010	.032	.079	.157	.267	.400	.537	.666	.774	.857	.915	.952	.975	.987	.994	.997	.999	1.000	
8.6	.000	.002	.009	.030	.070	.142	.246	.373	.509	.640	.752	.849	.909	.949	.973	.986	.993	.997	.999	1.000	
8.8	.000	.002	.007	.024	.062	.128	.226	.348	.482	.614	.729	.822	.889	.935	.964	.981	.990	.995	.998	.999	1.000
9.0	.000	.002	.006	.021	.055	.116	.207	.324	.456	.587	.706	.803	.876	.926	.959	.978	.989	.995	.998	.999	1.000
9.5	.000	.001	.004	.015	.040	.089	.165	.269	.392	.522	.645	.752	.836	.898	.940	.967	.982	.991	.996	.998	.999

Chapter 1

3. A company usually outsources work to take advantage of specialized skills, cost efficiencies, or operational flexibility they may be lacking. India has low labor costs, many English speakers, and an educated workforce.

9. The 2015–2016 World Economic Forum report ranks, from most to least competitive, Bangladesh 107, Nigeria 124, Venezuela 132. The Bangladesh company has survived in a more competitive environment and would likely be a more robust company to work with.

11. Multiple layers of first- and second-tier suppliers provide some measure of insurance against supply chain disruptions and unanticipated demand but require more coordination and complicate communication.

13. Retailers, companies, and consumers that buy your products require relationship management costs, coordination of promotion, and channels of distribution.

Chapter 2

1. Corporate strategy addresses improving economic performance of the firm and value creation for the shareholders. It can be argued that the triple bottom line takes a longer term and more inclusive perspective of value that is not as easily quantified but no less impactful than traditional measures.

3. Boeing's customers include airlines and the flying public. Their core competencies include designing and customizing aircraft and multisourcing. Boeing's operational critical success factors are flexibility (each plane is a snowflake) and coordination of a complex international supply chain. Their product factors recognize that they are dealing with a mature high tech product where traceability is mandated by regulatory agencies. This product must deliver value to industry customers that have historically had thin margins.

5. a. The threat of war between Pakistan and India might impact choices for outsourcing services; b. A significant drop in oil prices could delay implementation of green/sustainability initiatives; c. Price deflation in the European Union may cheaper imports, so increased outsourcing a possibility; d. New federal regulations limiting fossil fuel use could accelerate green/sustainability initiatives; e. Demographic changes leading to fewer young people entering the workforce could delay implementation of system requiring extensive training or social media components; f. New federal legislation mandating health-care coverage for firms employing 50 or more full-time workers might be an incentive to downsize via outsourcing or automation.

7a. Week 7. b. Different floor layouts, different tiles used, accessibility of power, water, or other resources.

9. a. *US Labor* = 8.33; *India Labor* = 5.14
   US Materials = 14.71; *India Materials* = 15.00
   US Equipment = 3.01; *India Equipment* = 2.69

   Differences in labor productivity may be driven by workforce skill or education and equipment productivity may be a result of plant modernization, plant layout or the general level of prices in each country.

   b. *US Multifactor* = 3.01
   India Multifactor = 2.69

   Multifactor productivity gives a complete picture and compensates for substitution effects of labor versus capital.

11. 1.46

13. a. 12.5 units/hour b. 25 units/hour c. .38 units/$

15.

	% Change
Labor productivity (units/labor hour)	13.79%
Machine productivity (units/machine hour)	−8.33%
Material productivity (units/pound)	22.22%
Energy productivity (units/BTU)	51.72%

Energy productivity shows the greatest improvement in productivity.

17. 1.625 $/*hour* or 0.11 $/$

Chapter 3

5.

	Consequences		
Likelihood	Low	Medium	High
High			Competitor first to market.
Medium			Technical failure
Low		Budget cut	Loss of lead programmer

Answers will vary for strategies to mitigate each risk.

7. 8.5

9.

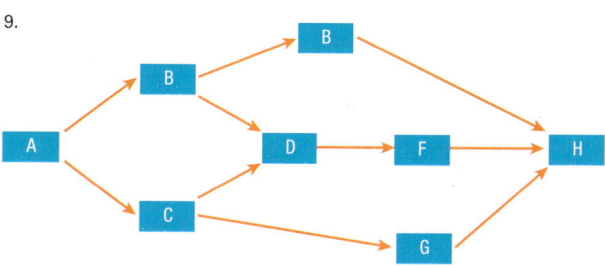

11.

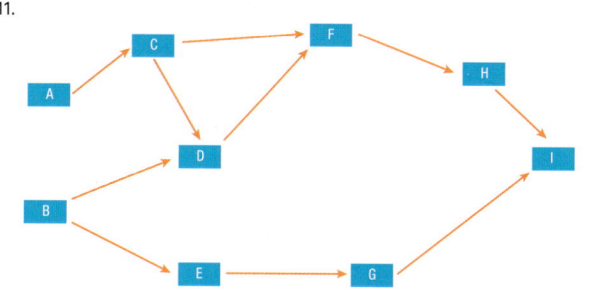

13a. 19

b. Activity B LF: 12 Activity B LS: 7; Activity C LF: 12 Activity C LS: 10; Activity D LF: 19 Activity D LS: 12

c. Activity C has 4 days of slack.

15. Critical path: ADGIJ. The other two paths are ACFHJ and ABEHJ.

17a,b.

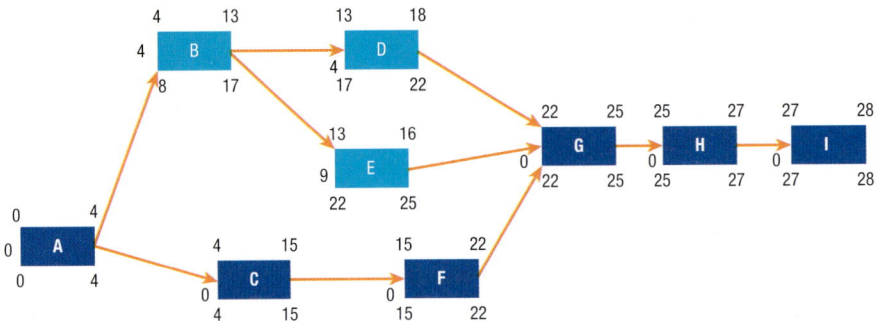

17c. Extending B and D both by 5 days far exceeds the slack for that path. The critical path would shift to ABDGHI = 4+14 +10+3+2+1=34 days.

19a.

Activity	T_E
A	4
B	6
C	4
D	12
E	7
F	9
G	5

19b.

Activity	Variance
A	1
B	0.69
C	0.25
D	1.78
E	2.25
F	2.78
G	0.69

19c. The project duration is 22 weeks.

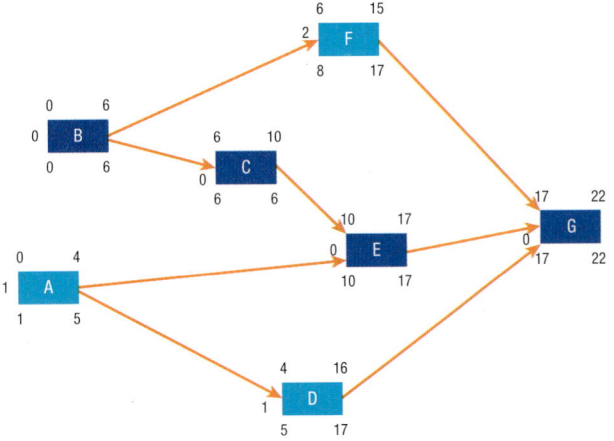

19d. The critical path is BCEG. Other paths are BFG with a slack of 2, AEG with a slack of 1, and ADG with a slack of 1.

21.

Activity	Variance
A	1.00
B	0.69
C	1.00
D	0.69
E	1.78
F	1.00
G	0.69
H	1.78
I	2.78
J	0.44

Activity I has the highest variance of 2.87.

23.

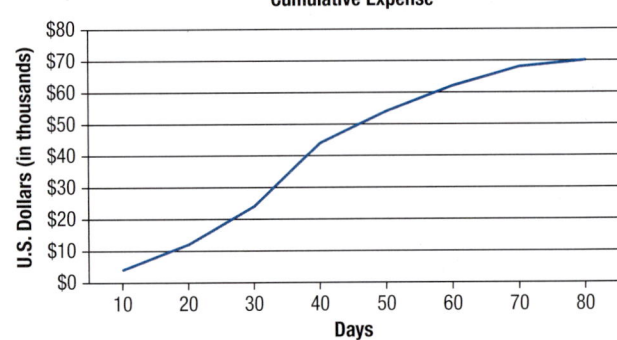

25a.

	5	10	15	20	25	30	35	40	45
Monthly	4	7	12	24	34	12	6	4	2
Monthly Cumulative	4	11	23	47	81	93	99	103	105

25b.

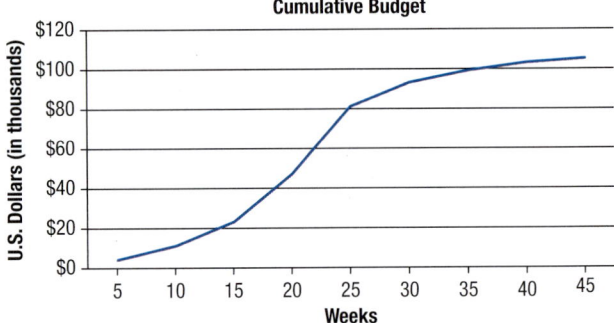

Chapter 3 Supplement

1.   a. 0.067 b. 0.5 c. 0.93 d. 18.29
3a.   P(completed within 50 days) = 0
      P(completed within 70 days) = 0.75
      P(completed within 90 days) = 1.00
3b. 74.98 *days*
5a.

Activity	TE
A	4
B	6
C	4
D	12
E	7
F	9
G	5

5b. Project total length = 22 weeks

Activity	Slack
A	1
B	0
C	0
D	1
E	0
F	2
G	0

5c. Critical path is BCEG; Paths ADG and AEG are 21 weeks and have 1 week slack, path BFG has 2 weeks slack.

5d. Burst activities are A & B, Merge activities are E & G

5e. 0.78

5f. 27.96 *weeks*

7a.

Activity	T_E
A	4.00
B	6.00
C	4.00
D	12.00
E	7.00
F	9.00
G	5.00

7b.

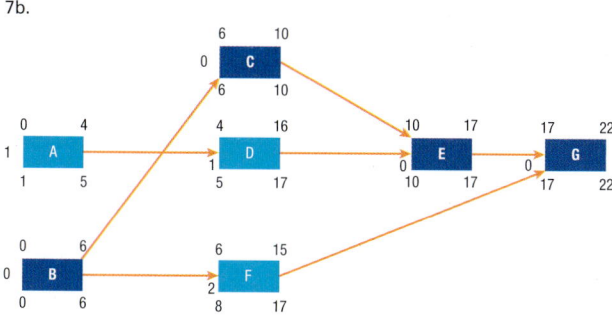

7c. Critical path: BCEG. Alternative paths: ADEG (slack = 1) and BFG (slack = 2)

7d. Burst activity: B. Merge activities: E and G.

7e. 0.78

7f. 27.88

9a. Project duration: 25 weeks. Activities C and F have 4 weeks of slack time. Critical path: ABDEG.

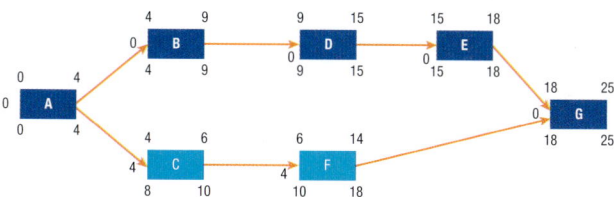

9b. To reduce the project duration as inexpensively as possible, expedite activities on the critical path starting from least expensive to most expensive. The first action should be to reduce activity D by two weeks at $2,000 per week. Then reduce activity E by one week for $2,500 and activity G by one week for $2,500.

9c. 21 weeks.

9d. The next purchases would be to reduce B by one week for $3000 and A by one week for $4000 to bring the project down to 19 weeks.

11. Planned Value (PV) = 98
Earned Value (EV) = 54
SPI = 0.55
Estimated Time to Completion = 21.78 months

Actual Cost of Work Performed (AC) = 94
Cost Performance Index (CPI) = 0.57
Estimated Cost to Completion = $438,600

13. a. **Schedule Variances**
Planned Value (PV) = 32
Earned Value (EV) = 22
SPI = 0.69
Estimated Time to Completion = 13.1 months

b. **Cost Variances**
Actual Cost of Work Performed (AC) = 37
Cost Performance Index (CPI) = 0.59
Estimated Cost to Completion = $168,000

15. SPI = 1.067; Estimated time to completion = 14.06.81 months

Chapter 4

1.

Customer Requirements	Technical Requirements	Frame material	Lens material	Crush proof case	Assemble with screws	Polarized lenses	Your company
Customer Requirements	Ratings						
Aesthetics	1	▲					G
Reduce glare	4		★			●	G
Adjustable	6	●			●		F
Take prescription lenses	5		★				G
Unbreakable	3	★	●	★			P
Target Values		Carbon fiber	glass	500 psi min	phillips	Unified glare rating	

3.

Customer Requirements	Technical Requirements	Boeing 737	Flight crew	Ground support	Snacks	Website	Your company
Customer Requirements	Ratings						
On time arrival	2	▲	★	★			G
Low cost	1	●	●	●	●	★	G
Peanuts	4				★		F
Fun attendants	5		★				G
Clean planes	3			★	▲		G
Target Values		30 yr max age	Internal score	Clean and fuel in 30 minutes	Free	1 sec load	

Chapter 4 Supplement

1. 0.71
3. A = 0.9025 B = 0.913 C = 0.94 D = 0.985. D is most reliable.

5.
Cost of System A:	$6462.50
Cost of System B:	$10,305.00
Cost of System C:	$11,000.00
Cost of System D:	$12,225.00

From a cost perspective, system A should be chosen.

7. *Availability* = 75.76% Bobbie should purchase a new printer.
9. *Availability* = 95.2%

Chapter 5

1.

Dimension	Premium	Low-Price
Reliability	Higher levels of compensation and training for workers result in better outcomes on service requests.	Workers tend to be less-skilled and training may be lacking resulting in inconsistent outcomes.
Responsiveness	Staffing levels are higher, so phones are answered more quickly, items can be delivered more quickly	Skeleton crew present, room deliveries are delayed if multiple residents need things simultaneously
Assurance	More seasoned workers know their system well and can convey this level of comfort to guests.	Assurance may be assumed by newer workers and therefore not passed on to customers.
Empathy	Workers at these properties may make the connection between empathy and gratuities, which are likely to be larger than at lower priced properties.	Workers may not know how to get things done or may exhibit little empathy for the types of problems faced by their customers.
Tangibles	Furnishings and fixtures of high quality	Inexpensive, older furnishings and fixtures

5. The advantage of Six Sigma is the reliance on using data to make decisions about how to remove causes of defects and to minimize process variation. Six Sigma relies on understanding the needs of the customer and addressing problems in an employee-driven fashion. Since defects and errors tend to be expensive in air traffic control, it would be wise to try to eliminate as many as possible. The stakes are smaller for a bakery, but they too could benefit from such a program.

Chapter 6

1.

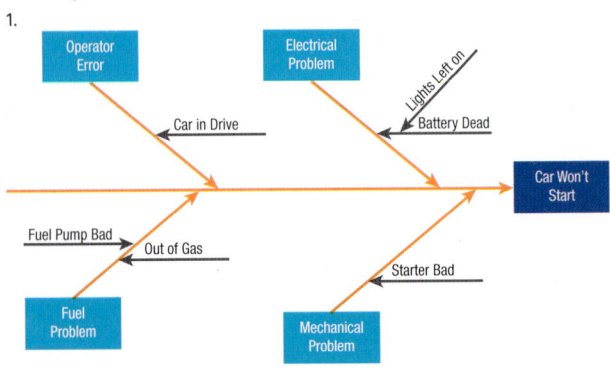

3.

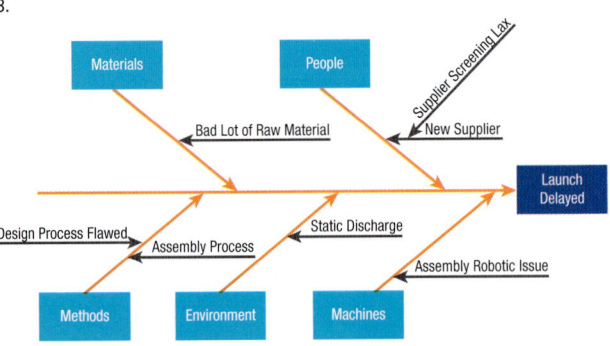

5a.

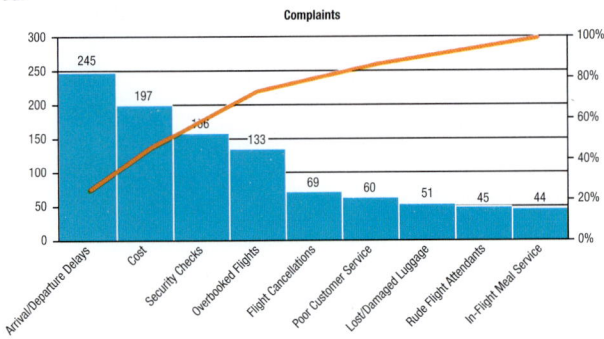

5b. The two most common complaints are airport delays and price, so efforts to improve should be focused here.

7.

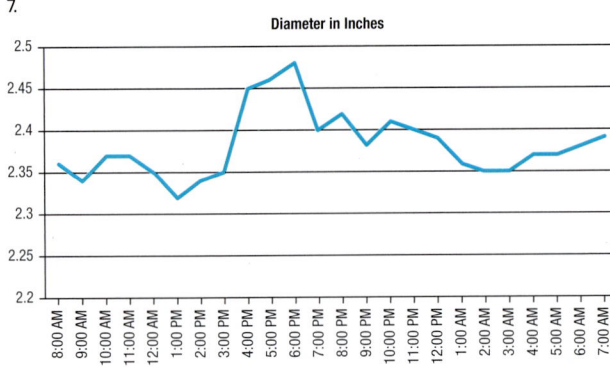

The process produces within the stated specifications of 2.3 to 2.5 inches.

9.

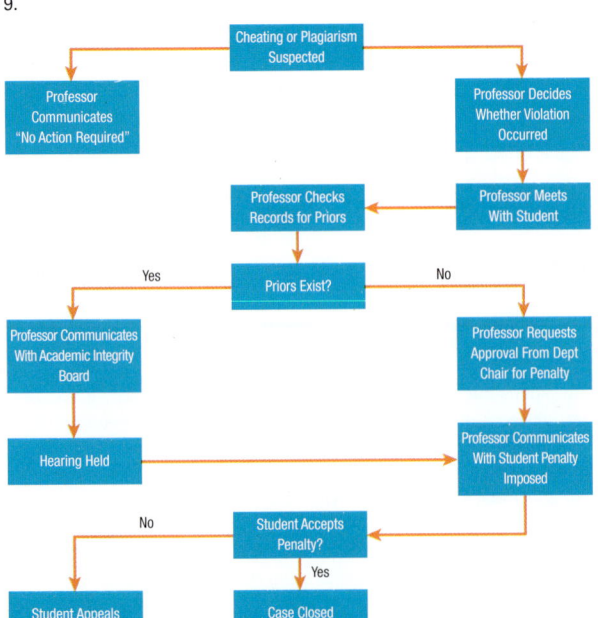

11a.

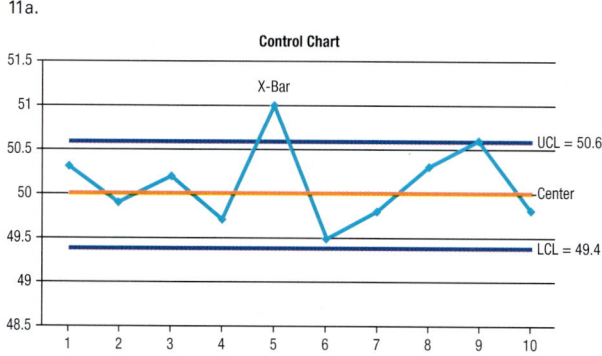

11b. The process is out of control for sample 5.

13a.

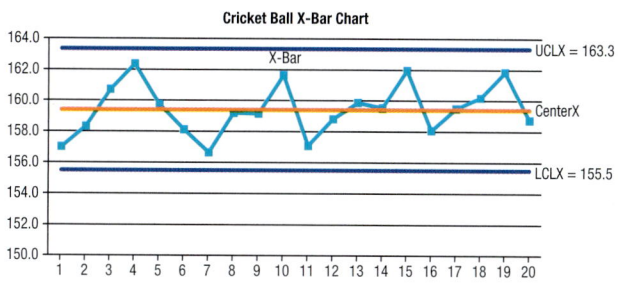

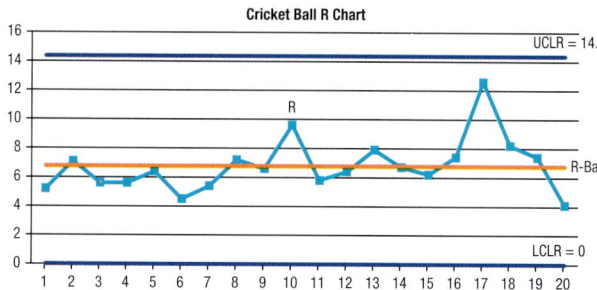

13b. The process was not in control throughout May. The sample mean of 164 violates the upper control limit of the mean chart.

13c. A larger sample size would result in tighter control = 15.8, so the mean chart would still show an out of control situation in May.

15a. A c chart is appropriate because the defects are being counted over a consistent window of opportunity.

b.

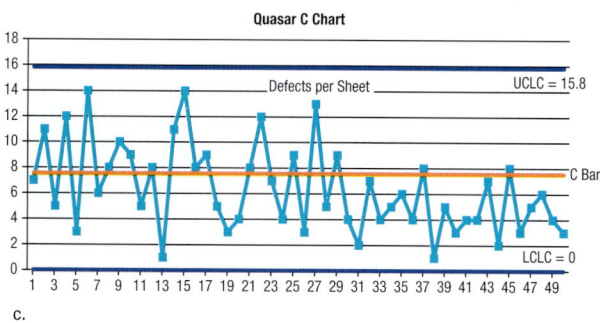

c.

15c. The process is in control, but is close to violating the rule about 8 successive points on one side of the center line. There appears to be a lower defect rate after process improvements were made.

17.

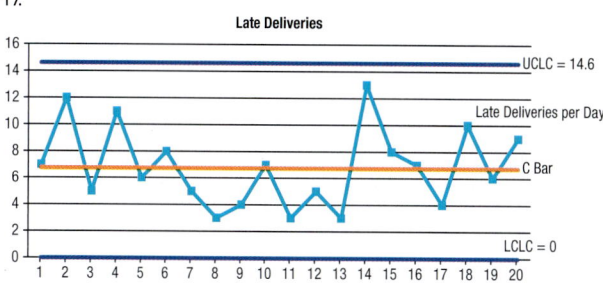

19a. A p-chart is appropriate because the data are binomial and have a variable sample size.

b.

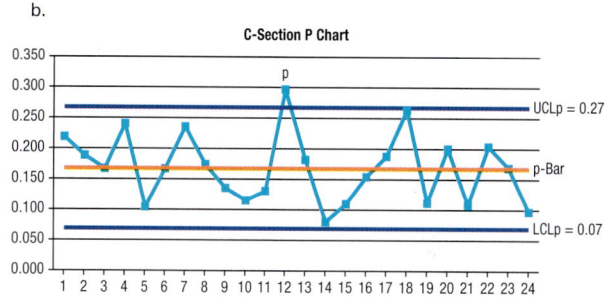

19c. Since the sample size is variable, the average sample size of 56.875 was used in the standard deviation formula to determine the standard deviation of 0.0496.

The process exceeds the upper control limit once, on week 12.

21. $C_P = 0.4$

$C_{PK} = 0.4$

The process is assumed to be centered, so C^{PK} and C^P are identical. Process capability is low.

23. *Loss* = k86.69

The high standard deviation contributes more to the loss parameter of 86.69, about 83% of that value, so the delivery service should strive for greater consistency first.

25a.

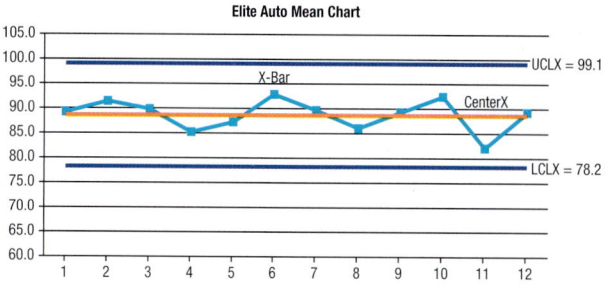

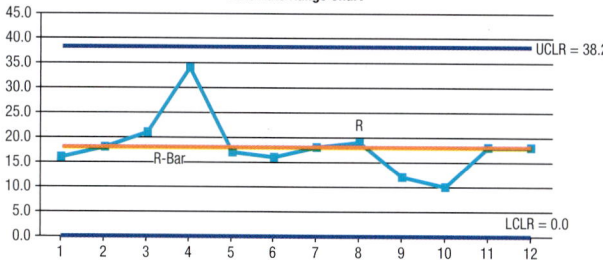

25b. The manager can achieve a customer rating score between 90 and 96 in some cases, but are far from being able to consistently hit this level of performance.

27.

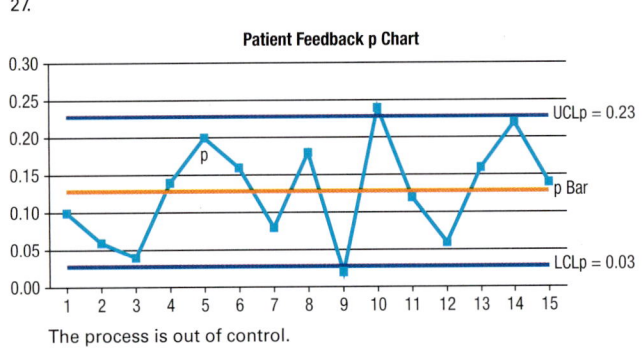

The process is out of control.

29a.

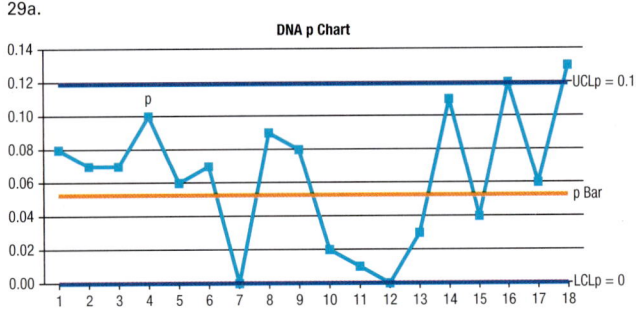

29b. The last four samples show a process that is out of control.

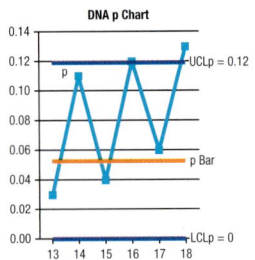

Chapter 7

1. Capacity Ultilization = 72%; Capacity Efficiency = 90%
   The manager might schedule maintenance and changeovers during a different part of the day to increase effective capacity. The manager should balance output with demand; overproduction of a perishable product can be costly.
3. Capacity Ultilization = 67%; Capacity Efficiency = 77%
5. 19.61 *loans / wk*
7. a. Station B b. 336 units c. Increase capacity of Station B by 1.5 units/hour to equal capacity with stations A and C. d. 420 units.
9. a. Machine II b. 2 Machine IIs
11. Milling = 41, 584; Sawing = 30,360; Assembly = 94,674
13. 3,000 *units*
15. a. Assembly b. 600 units/month
17. Increasing assembly by 10%
19. Design capacity = 3,000 units/day; Effective capacity = 2,700 units/day; Actual output = 2,484 units/day; Capacity Utilization = 83%; Capacity Efficiency = 92%

Chapter 8

1. Arlington Heights
3. Bangalore

5a. Singapore
5b. If Communication Infrastructure has a weight of zero, then India has the highest score at 6.0.
9a.

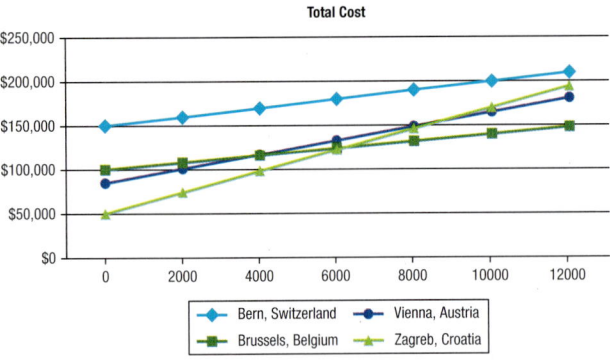

9b. Zagreb 0-6,250, Brussels 6,250 and up
9c. Brussels
11. x-coordinate = 9.12; y-coordinate = 10.31
13. x-coordinate = 8.23; y-coordinate = 7.08
15. a. x-coordinate = 20.67; y-coordinate = 62.39 b. Frankfurt c. If the center of gravity yields a feasible location, then it presents a minimal total distance traveled.
17. a. x-coordinate = 15.10; y-coordinate = 33.71 b. Tumkur c. Answers will vary depending on infrastructure and assumptions inherent in the center of gravity method.
19. a. Raleigh b. Raleigh c. Raleigh

Chapter 9

5. A mass production environment attempts to achieve smooth rapid flow of materials through the production area. The focus would be on high utilization of workers and equipment with minimal transportation between adjacent processing steps.
7. A product process design strives for low unit costs, high efficiency, and high volume of production generally with minimal customer interaction or customization. A service process design for a business like a hospital is traditionally not focused on speed, but has a high degree of customization and customer interaction

Chapter 9 Supplement

1.

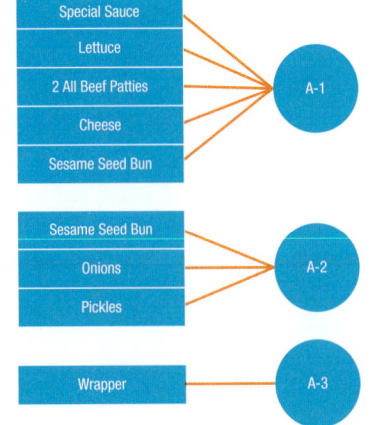

3.

Step	Distance (ft)	Time (sec)	Symbols	Description
1	0	2	→ □ ⊘ □ Δ	Select courses online
2	0	1	→ ⊘ ○ □ Δ	Submit course requests online
3	0	0.005	→ □ ⊘ □ Δ	System prerequisite check
4	0	0.005	→ ⊘ ○ □ Δ	System registration hold check
5	0	0.005	→ □ ⊘ □ Δ	Generate bill for tuition and fees
6	0	2,419,243	→ □ ○ □ Δ	Pay bill

5. a. Process A b. 4,000 units

7. a. Intermittent b. Repetitive c. 30,769

9. a. $68,200 b. $62,600

11. The current layout requires 41,970 feet of travel. An improved layout, which keeps department 1 in room 1, but moves department 4 to room 2, department 6 to room 3, department 2 to room 4, department 3 to room 5, and department 5 to room 6, has only 35,160 feet of travel.

13.

	Customer Movements					
FROM/TO	Electronics	Men's	Boys	Girls'	Women's	Infants
Electronics	–	50				
Men's	70	–	30	20		
Boys	50	30	–	40		
Girls'	20		30	–	50	
Women's	10	40	50	60	–	50
Infants				40		–

15a. Cycle time is 9 minutes

Most following tasks rule CT=9

Station	1	2	3	4	5	6
Tasks	A	B C	D E	F	H	G I
Work Time	8	5 4	5 4	9	9	6 3
Idle	1	0	0	0	0	0

Balance Efficiency = 54/55 = 98.2%

15b.

Ranked positional weight rule CT=9

Station	1	2	3	4	5	6
Tasks	A	B C	D E	F	H	G I
Work Time	8	5 4	5 4	9	9	6 3
Idle	1	0	0	0	0	0

Balance Efficiency = 54/55 = 98.2%

15c. The efficiencies are identical.

17a. 12 *min/unit*

17b.

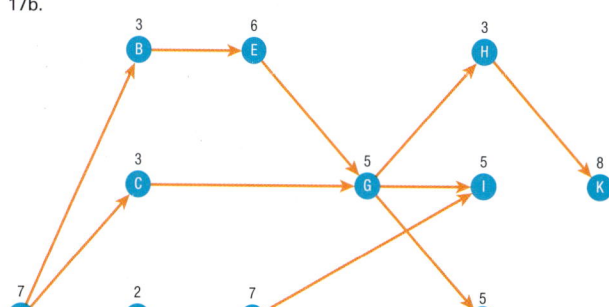

17c. 5 *stations*

17d.

Most following tasks rule

Station	1	2	3	4	5	6	
Task	A, B, D	C, E	G, F	H, J	I	K	Σ
Work	7, 3, 2	3, 6	5, 7	3, 5	5	8	54
Idle	0	3	0	4	7	4	12

17e.

Ranked positional weight rule

Station	1	2	3	4	5	
Task	A, B, D	E, C	G, F	H, K	J, I	Σ
Work	7, 3, 2	6, 3	5, 7	3, 8	5, 5	54
Idle	0	3	0	1	2	6

17f. Balance efficiency for most following task rule: 75%. Balance efficiency for ranked positional weight rule = 90%

17g. Ranked positional weight rule.

19.

Department 1	Department 2	Department 3
Department 6	Department 5	Department 4

21a.

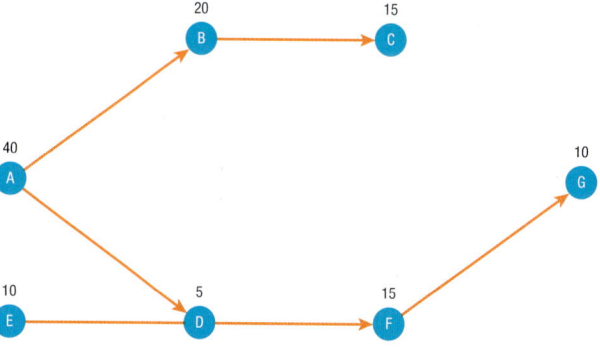

21b. Total time to assemble one unit = 115 minutes
CT = 40 *minutes/unit*

21c.

Most following tasks			Efficiency=115/120=95.83%
Station	1	2	3
Task	A	E, D, B	F, C, G	Σ
Work	40	10, 5, 20	15, 15, 10	115
Time	0	5	0	5

21d. Two workers must be assigned to Task A.

23a.

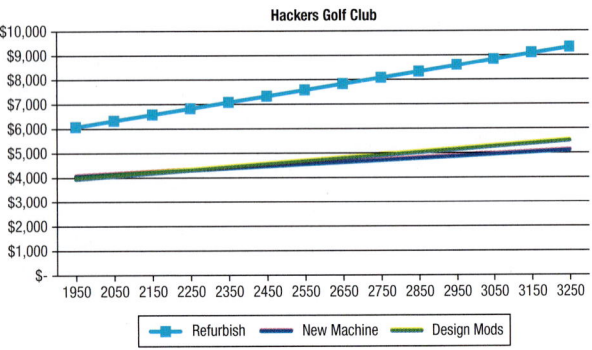

23b. The new machine is the lowest cost alternative.

23c. From 2000 to 2250, Design Modification is least expensive, and from 2250 to 3000, New Machine is least expensive.

Chapter 10

5. Of the five types of supplier risks identified, the implementation risk and the performance risk are of greatest concern. Implementation risk can be mitigated by rapid identification and selection of new suppliers. Performance risk can be mitigated by continuous monitoring of suppliers and their host countries for early warning signals of political unrest, bankruptcy, labor strikes, instability in the region or in their suppliers.

7. Potential supplier: China and Vietnam with scores of 65 and 59, respectively

    Preferred suppliers: Singapore with a score of 81

Chapter 11

1a. Pipeline; pipelines are used for fluids as an inexpensive and safe medium.

b. Air; the distance, need for speed, and low weight to value ratio.

c. Water; both are port cities, time is not crucial.

d. Truck; short distance between the cities with good flexibility.

3. Cross-docking is a system where truck bays on opposite sides of a warehouse are served by supplier trucks and customer trucks. Bulk from a shipment from one supplier truck is parsed to many customer trucks that serve different customer locations. Cross-docking provides a way for deliveries to be managed quickly and inexpensively. Cross-docking would be used to bring produce from the StayFresh produce supplier in one side of the building and transfer one crate of bananas to each of the seven trucks on the opposite side for that day's delivery. Paper products, canned goods and would each come from one truck on the supplier side and some portion sent to each truck bound for a grocery store.

Chapter 12

1. Economic factors would include whether you have the capital necessary for such a venture and whether a base of customers exists in the area that can afford your offerings. A technological factor is whether your supply chain can reliably bring fresh produce quickly to your restaurant.

3. Amazon Prime has free shipping for tangible products and offers on-demand delivery of a wide variety of entertainment. It also permits customers to schedule constant use items for periodic deliveries, removing the need to take time to place an order.

Chapter 13

1ab.

Week	Auto Demand	MA3	AD_{MA3}	WMA	AD_{WMA}
1	9				
2	11				
3	8				
4	12	9.333	2.67	9.00	6.33
5	10	10.333	0.33	10.70	10.37
6	13	10.000	3.00	10.40	7.40
7	7	11.667	4.67	12.00	7.33
8	12	10.000	2.00	9.10	7.10
9		10.667		10.60	

1c. The moving average of three periods is more accurate based on the MAD calculation.

1d. 12

3. a. 4.47 b. 4.56 c. α = .2

5. a. 69.9 b. 68.8
    c. The MSE for the exponential smoothing approach is 91.65 and for the trend adjusted exponential smoothing is 90.59. The bias for the exponential smoothing approach is .93 and for the trend adjusted exponential smoothing is 0.19.

7. a. 27 b. 463

9. a. 292.68 b. 332.62 c. The trend line approach is more accurate.

11a. Simple average

Day	Seasonal Indices
Monday	0.79
Tuesday	0.68
Wednesday	0.62
Thursday	0.65
Friday	1.10
Saturday	1.93
Sunday	1.22

11b.

Day	Unadj SI	Adj SI
Mon	0.80	0.80
Tue	0.69	0.69
Wed	0.61	0.61
Thu	0.65	0.65
Fri	1.11	1.12
Sat	1.91	1.92
Sun	1.21	1.22
Σ	6.99	7.00

13a. There is a slight upward trend.

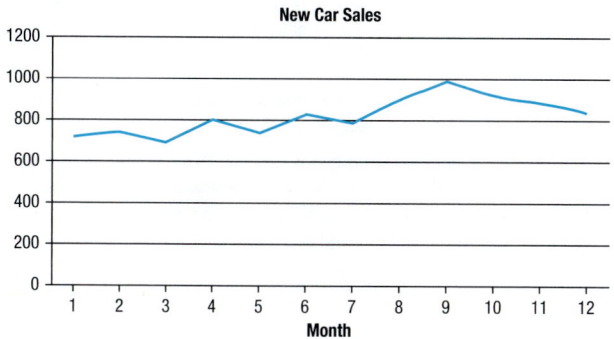

New Car Sales

13b.

Period	New Car Sales	Seasonal Indexes	Deseasoned
1	720	0.85	847.1
2	742	0.85	872.9
3	695	0.65	1069.2
4	798	0.9	886.7
5	740	0.85	870.6
6	830	1	830.0
7	785	0.96	817.7
8	900	1.2	750.0

Period	New Car Sales	Seasonal Indexes	Deseasoned
9	990	1.3	761.5
10	920	1.3	707.7
11	890	1.35	659.3
12	840	1.35	622.2

c. *Sales* = 988.06 − 27.7 *Period*

d. January 2015 = 627.8
   February 2015 = 600.0

e. January 2015 = 533.6; February 2015 = 510.0

15a.

Quarter	Demand	Adjusted Seas Ind	Adj Demand
Jan–Mar	370	0.76	486.84
Apr–Jun	550	0.97	567.01
Jul–Sep	770	1.49	516.78
Oct–Dec	420	0.78	538.46

b. *Forecast* = 473.83 + 14.63 *Quarter* c. 722.55 d. 563.59

17. a. *Enrollment* = 9795.49−0.0985 *Tuition* b. 8,908.8 c. The model explains almost 83% of the variation and demonstrates a strong positive linear relationship. The standard error of the estimate is about 7% of the average of the dependent variable.

19a

Regression Statistics

Multiple R	0.993
R Square	0.987
Adjusted R Square	0.984
Standard Error	1.696
Observations	12

ANOVA	df	SS	MS	F	Significance F
Regression	2	1903.04	951.52	330.98	3.75E-09
Residual	9	25.87	2.87		
Total	11	1928.92			

	Coefficients	Std Error	t Stat	P-value	Lower 95%	Upper 95%
Intercept	−5.21	1.80	−2.89	0.02	−9.28	−1.13
Personal Income (in $000)	0.52	0.07	7.28	0.00	0.36	0.69
Advertising	−0.06	0.07	−0.84	0.42	−0.22	0.10

19b. b_0 is the level of sales in the absence of advertising and personal income. It is difficult to purchase a car without personal income and the data set does not contain any observations with a value of personal income near 0, so the b_0 value is not very meaningful. The coefficient b_1 is the incremental change in sales attributable to one more unit, in this case one thousand dollars, of personal income. The coefficient b_2 is the incremental change in sales derived from one additional unit of advertising, in this case $1000.

19c. Multiple R is the multiple correlation coefficient, which provides some sense of how strong the linear relationship is between the model and the actual data. R Squared is the percentage of the variation in sales predicted by the level of income and advertising expenditures. We explain 98.7% of sales variation using these two variable and the correlation is very strong.

19d. 39,363.8

21.

Month	Demand	Forecast	Signal
1	1772	1774	−2/2= −1.00
2	1790	1780	8/6=1.33
3	1796	1792	12/5.33=2.25
4	1783	1794	1/6.75=0.15
5	1775	1772	0.67
6	1770	1764	1.67
7	1765	1758	2.77
8	1777	1779	2.67

Month	Demand	Forecast	Signal
9	1782	1765	4.65
10	1794	1782	5.95
11	1755	1768	3.92
12	1779	1795	1.75

The approach shows two out of the twelve forecasts exceed the +4 MAD limit

23a. *Sales* = 4857.845 − 47.326 *Price* + 5.3581 *Promotion*

27a.

23b. For every unit increase of the Price variable, the value of Sales drops by 47.326 units. For every unit increase of the Promotion variable, the value of Sales increases by 5.3581 units.

23c. $Y = 7,917$

25. a. *Final Score* = 45.152 + 0.535 *Homework Problems* b. *Final Score* = 76.735 c. $R^2 = 0.788$; $r = 0.888$; $s_{yx} = 5.406$

The number of homework problems explains 78.8% of the variation of the course score. The two variables exhibit a strong positive correlation, so most values fall along a straight line with a positive slope. The difference between the predicted and actual course score is 5.4.

Regression Statistics

Multiple R	0.893
R Square	0.797
Adjusted R Square	0.772
Standard Error	827.671
Observations	10

ANOVA	df	SS	MS	F	Significance F
Regression	1	21520380	21520379.6	31.41482	0.0005073
Residual	8	5480312	685039.001		
Total	9	27000692			

	Coefficients	Std Error	t Stat	P-value	Lower 95%	Upper 95%
Intercept	−905.90	614.17	−1.48	0.18	−2322.17	510.37
Age of the truck (in years)	546.33	97.47	5.60	0.00	321.56	771.11

If the truck is 7 years old the maintenance cost is −905.9 + 546.33(7) = $2,918.43.

27b.

Regression Statistics

Multiple R	0.822
R Square	0.676
Adjusted R Square	0.635
Standard Error	1046.204
Observations	10

ANOVA	df	SS	MS	F	Significance F
Regression	1	18244342.95	1.8E+07	16.6684	0.00352
Residual	8	8756348.646	1094544		
Total	9	27000691.6			

	Coefficients	Std Error	t Stat	P-value	Lower 95%	Upper 95%
Intercept	168.003	599.310	0.280	0.786	−1214.008	1550.013
Number of Miles Driven	0.120	0.029	4.083	0.004	0.052	0.188

A truck driven 32,300 miles will have maintenance costs of 168+0.12(32,300=$4,055.18.

27c. All measures in the table demonstrate that Age is a better predictor of maintenance cost than Miles. The correlation and variance explained are higher and the standard error of the estimate is lower.

27d. The forecasts in parts a) and b) are statistically significant, but the multiple regression forecast performs better in terms of explained variance, correlation, and standard error.

Statistic	Age	Miles
R_2	.797	.676
r	.893	.822
S_{xy}	827.67	1046.2

Model	Prediction	R_2	r	S_{xy}
Age	$2,918	.797	.893	827.67
Miles	$4,055	.676	.822	1046.2
Age & Miles	$3,658	.836	.914	607.73

29. a. $MAD_{F1} = 5.67$; $MAD_{F2} = 5.44$ b. $MSE_{F1} = 45.44$ $MSE_{F2} = 38.78$;
    c. $MAPE_{F1} = 7.017$ $MAPE_{F2} = 6.517$
    d. Convenience and ease of computation are important, but ultimately the ability to help the forecaster distinguish the best forecast from among the possibilities is the most important criterion.

31. a. $F_9 = 332.75$; b. $F_9 = 336.6$; c. $F_9 = 334.7$

33. a. Year 4 = 42.33; Year 5 = 46.67; Year 6 = 52.00; Year 7 = 56.33; Year 8 = 60.33;
    b. $\alpha = .5$ Year 4 = 51; Year 5 = 51; Year 6 = 54.5; Year 7 = 57.3; Year 8 = 60.1
    $\alpha = 7$ Year 4 = 51; Year 5= 51; Year 6 = 55.9; Year 7 = 58.8; Year 8 = 61.7

33c.

Year	Expon$_{\alpha=.5}$	Trend$_{\beta=.2}$	Trend Adj Smoothing
4	51	0	51+0=51
5	51	.2(51-51)+.8(0)=0	51+0=51
6	54.5	.2(54.5-51)+.8(0)=0.7	54.5+.7=55.2
7	57.3	.2(57.3-54.5)+.8(0)=1.11	57.3+1.11=58.36
8	60.1	.2(60.1-57.3)+.8(0)=1.46	60.1+1.46=61.59

33d. The mean squared error of 12.83 for periods 5-7 is lowest for the exponential smoothing $\alpha=.5$ model.

35. A plot of the actual and forecasted sales indicates this model works well.

Chapter 14

1. Takt = 42 seconds

3. Takt = 63.33 seconds

5. a. 15 b. 18 hours c. There will be no difference in the total amount of system inventory.

7. 2

9. 14

11. a. 1.26 min/pair b. 20 cycles/day

13. a. 3 Sedans, 2 Hatchbacks and 1 SUV for a total of 6 cars produced in a cycle b. 33.3 cycles/day

15.

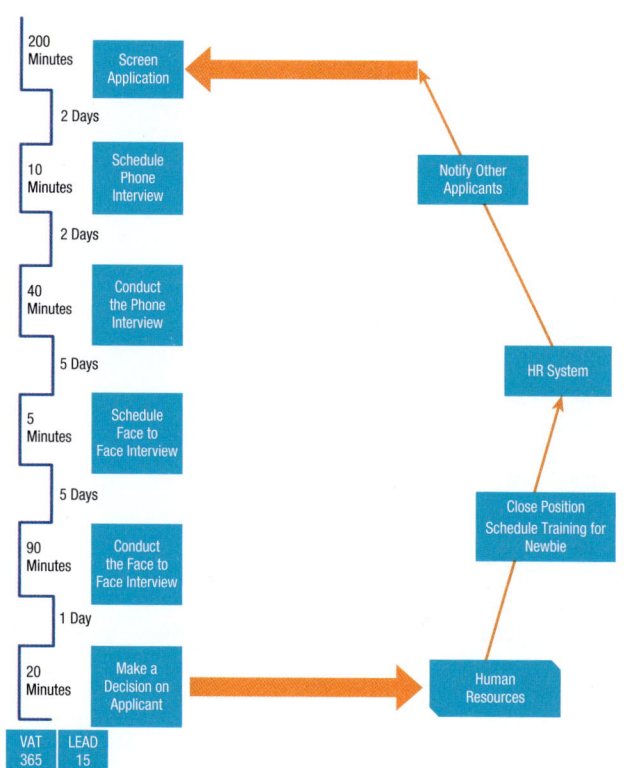

Chapter 15

1. The metrics discussed include backorders and lost sales, turnover, days of inventory in stock, inventory accuracy, order fulfillment lead time, and fill rate. A small clothing store is more likely to use the first four of these metrics. The manager could track backorders and lost sales to adjust the reorder point for each item. Turnover would help a manager determine whether order quantities were appropriate and which items sell well or poorly. Days of inventory in stock also provides the manager a measure of whether each item is selling well and how order levels might be adjusted.

7.

Inventory Item	Category
P21	C
A12	B
K43	A
S54	B
C25	C
D76	B
E27	C
F38	B
H19	A
Q10	C

9. 9.367

11. 0.502

Chapter 16

1. a. 800 b. $2000

3. a. 80.06 b. 12.49 c. $2498 d. 92.45; $2163.30; Order quantity increases as it becomes less expensive to hold inventory. The total cost drops. e. $2560; total cost increases

5. 600

7. a. 2450 b. 816.5 c. 24.5 d. 4.08 e. $552

9. a. 7394.48 b. 3245.67 c. 2.7 d. 11.29 e. $848

11. 500 magic wands per order.

13. 1500 gemstones per order

15. a. Supplier A = 8000 Supplier B = 12,000 b. 12,000 units per order from Supplier B c. $78,525 d. Emily should consider speed and reliability of delivery and quality of the goods.

17. $R = 746.6$; Safety stock = 26.6

19. a. $R = 211.09$ b. $R = 220.22$; Safety stock = 40.22

21. a. 300 b. 464 c. $R = 398$; Safety stock drops 66 units

23. a. 15.04 b. 77.4%

25. a. 322.5 b. 22.5 c. 292.5

27. a. SKU-11: 801; SKU-27: 533.64 b. 219.7 c. 453.6

29. a. $0.\overline{8}$ b. 9.22

31. 1000 units for $40,060

33. a. 0.5 b. 35

35. $Q = T - \text{on hand}_{35} = 734.1$; $Q = T - \text{on hand}_4 = 765.1$; $Q = T - \text{on hand}_{88} = 681.1$

Chapter 17

7. $139,100

9.

Month	1	2	3	4	5	6	7
Forecast	140	155	150	145	155	145	130
Regular	140	140	140	140	140	140	130
Overtime		15	10	5	15	5	

Total Cost = $139,100

11.

Month	Forecast	Beginning Inventory	Regular Output	Overtime
Jan	9000	9000	10000	0
Feb	7000	10000	0	0
Mar	5000	3000	0	1000
Apr	4000	−1000	8000	0
May	2000	3000	10000	0
Jun	1500	11000	10000	0
Jul	1000	19500	0	0
Aug	1200	18500	0	0
Sep	1600	17300	0	0
Oct	3000	15700	0	0
Nov	5700	12700	0	0
Dec	7000	7000	0	0

Total Cost = $13,007,000

13.

Month	Forecast	Beginning Inventory	Regular Output	Overtime	Subcontracting
Jan	700	0	900	0	0
Feb	850	200	900	0	0
Mar	900	250	900	0	0
Apr	1000	250	900	300	0
May	1250	450	900	300	0
Jun	1350	400	900	300	0
Jul	1450	250	900	300	0
Aug	1300	0	900	300	100
Sep	1000	0	900	100	0
Oct	880	0	900	0	0
Nov	720	20	600	100	0
Dec	600	0	600	0	0

Total Cost = $2,603,200

15a.

	January	February	March	April	May	June	Total
Forecast	20000	30000	45000	20000	25000	50000	190000
Regular Production	20000	29600	44800	20000	25000	50000	
Overtime Production units		400	200		200	400	
# of Workers Required	25	37.5	56.25	25	31.25	62.5	
# of Workers Hired	0	12	19	0	6	31	
# of Workers Fired	15	0	0	31	0	0	
Workers on Payroll	25	37	56	25	31	62	
Costs							
Reg. time cost in $	200000	296000	448000	200000	250000	500000	$1,894,000
Overtime cost in $	$0	$4,800	$2,400	$0	$2,400	$4,800	$ 14,400
Hiring cost in $	0	14400	22800	0	7200	37200	$ 81,600
Firing cost in $	15000	0	0	31000	0	0	$ 46,000
Total cost In $	$215,000	$315,200	$473,200	$231,000	$259,600	$542,000	**$2,036,000**

15b.

	January	February	March	April	May	June	Total
Forecast	20,000	30,000	45,000	20,000	25,000	50,000	190,000
Regular Production	20,000	29,600	44,800	20,000	25,000	50,000	
Production	32,000	32,000	32,000	32,000	32,000	32,000	192,000
Beginning Inventory	0	12,000	14,000	1,000	13,000	20,000	
Ending Inventory	12,000	14,000	1,000	13,000	20,000	2,000	
Average Inventory	6,000	13,000	7,500	7,000	16,500	11,000	61,000

	January	February	March	April	May	June	Total
Production and Inventory Costs							
Reg. time production cost in $	320,000	320,000	320,000	320,000	320,000	320,000	$1,920,000
Inventory holding cost in $	60,000	130,000	75,000	70,000	165,000	110,000	$610,000
Backorder Cost in $	0	0	0	0	0	0	$0
Total cost In $	380,000	450,000	395,000	390,000	485,000	430,000	**$2,530,000**

15c.

	January	February	March	April	May	June	Total
Forecast	20,000	30,000	45,000	20,000	25,000	50,000	190,000
Regular Production	30,000	30,000	30,000	30,000	30,000	30,000	180,000
Overtime Production units		0	5,000		0	5,000	10,000
Beginning Inventory	0	10,000	10,000	0	10,000	15,000	
Ending Inventory	10,000	10,000	0	10,000	15,000	0	
Average Inventory	5,000	10,000	5,000	5,000	12,500	7,500	45,000
Production and Inventory Costs							
Reg. time production cost in $	300,000	300,000	300,000	300,000	300,000	300,000	$1,800,000
Overtime production cost in $	0	0	60,000	0	0	60,000	$120,000
Holding Cost	15,000	30,000	15,000	15,000	37,500	22,500	$135,000
Total cost In $	315,000	330,000	375,000	315,000	337,500	382,500	**$2,055,000**

17a.

	1	2	3	4	5	6	7
Forecast	160	140	190	160	270	320	360
Regular Production	200	200	200	200	220	220	220
Overtime Units							140
Workers on Payroll	20	20	20	20	22	22	22
# of Workers Hired					2	2	2
# of Workers Fired							
Beginning Inventory	0	40	100	110	150	100	0
Ending Inventory	40	100	110	150	100	0	0
Average Inventory	20	70	105	130	125	50	0
Production and Inventory Costs							
Reg. time production cost in $	$1,600	$1,600	$1,600	$1,600	$1,760	$1,760	$1,760
Holding Cost	$80	$280	$420	$520	$500	$200	$0
Overtime Cost	$0	$0	$0	$0	$0	$0	$21,000
Temporary Worker Cost	$0	$0	$0	$0	$600	$600	$600
Total cost In $	$1,680	$1,880	$2,020	$2,120	$2,860	$2,560	$23,360

	8	9	10	11	12	Total
Forecast	250	170	150	130	180	2480
Regular Production	200	200	200	200	200	2460
Overtime Units	50					190
Workers on Payroll	20	20	20	20	20	
# of Workers Hired						
# of Workers Fired	2					
Beginning Inventory	0	0	30	80	150	

	8	9	10	11	12	Total
Ending Inventory	0	30	80	150	170	
Average Inventory	0	15	55	115	160	
Production and Inventory Costs						
Reg. time production cost in $	$1,600	$1,600	$1,600	$1,600	$1,600	$19,680
Holding Cost	$0	$60	$220	$460	$640	$3,380
Overtime Cost	$7,500	$0	$0	$0	$0	$28,500
Temporary Worker Cost	$0	$0	$0	$0	$0	$1,800
Total cost In $	$9,100	$1,660	$1,820	$2,060	$2,240	**$53,360**

17b.

	1	2	3	4	5	6
Forecast	160	140	190	160	270	320
Regular Production	200	200	200	200	200	200
Subcontracting amount				0	30	30
Workers on Payroll	20	20	20	20	20	20
# of Workers Hired					0	0
# of Workers Fired						
Beginning Inventory	0	40	100	110	150	110
Ending Inventory	40	100	110	150	110	20
Average Inventory	20	70	105	130	130	65
Production and Inventory Costs						
Reg. time production cost in $	$1,600	$1,600	$1,600	$1,600	$1,600	$1,600
Holding Cost	$80	$280	$420	$520	$520	$260
Backlog Cost	$0	$0	$0	$0	$0	$0
Subcontracting Cost	$0	$0	$0	$0	$450	$450
Temporary Worker Cost	$0	$0	$0	$0	$0	$0
Total cost In $	$1,680	$1,880	$2,020	$2,120	$2,570	$2,310

	7	8	9	10	11	12	Total
Forecast	360	250	170	150	130	180	2480
Regular Production	200	200	200	200	200	200	2400
Subcontracting amount	20	0					80
Workers on Payroll	20	20	20	20	20	20	
# of Workers Hired	0						
# of Workers Fired		0					
Beginning Inventory	20	−120	−170	−140	−90	−20	
Ending Inventory	−120	−170	−140	−90	−20	0	
Average Inventory	−50	−145	−155	−115	−55	−10	
Production and Inventory Costs							
Reg. time production cost in $	$1,600	$1,600	$1,600	$1,600	$1,600	$1,600	$19,200
Holding Cost	$0	$0	$0	$0	$0	$0	$2,080
Backlog Cost	$1,200	$1,700	$1,400	$900	$200	$0	$5,400
Subcontracting Cost	$300	$0	$0	$0	$0	$0	$1,200
Temporary Worker Cost	$0	$0	$0	$0	$0	$0	$0
Total cost In $	$3,100	$3,300	$3,000	$2,500	$1,800	$1,600	**$27,880**

19a.

	January	February	March	April	May	June	Total
Forecast	3500	4600	5800	7600	6700	4700	32900
Regular	5483	5483	5483	5483	5483	5483	32898
Overtime	0	0	0	0	1	1	2
Subcontracting	0	0	0	0	0	0	0
Beginning Inventory	0	1983	2866	2549	432	−784	
Ending Inventory	1983	2866	2549	432	−784	0	
Average Inventory	991.5	2424.5	2707.5	1490.5	−176	−392	7046
Production and Inventory Costs							
Reg. time production	$82,245	$82,245	$82,245	$82,245	$82,245	$82,245	$493,470
Overtime	$0	$0	$0	$0	$22	$22	$44
Subcontracting	$0	$0	$0	$0	$0	$0	$0
Holding Cost	$1,983	$4,849	$5,415	$2,981	$0	$0	$15,228
Backorder Cost	$0	$0	$0	$0	$7,840	$0	$7,840
					Total Cost		$516,582

19b. In the absence of a limit on regular capacity, the plan for part a remains the lowest cost.

	January	February	March	April	May	June	Total
Forecast	3500	4600	5800	7600	6700	4700	32900
Regular	5483	5483	5483	5483	5483	5483	32898
Overtime	0	0	0	0	1	1	2
Subcontracting	0	0	0	0	0	0	0
Beginning Inventory	0	1983	2866	2549	432	−784	
Ending Inventory	1983	2866	2549	432	−784	0	
Average Inventory	991.5	2424.5	2707.5	1490.5	−176	−392	7046
Production and Inventory Costs							
Reg. time production	$82,245	$82,245	$82,245	$82,245	$82,245	$82,245	$493,470
Overtime	$0	$0	$0	$0	$22	$22	$44
Subcontracting	$0	$0	$0	$0	$0	$0	$0
Holding Cost	$1,983	$4,849	$5,415	$2,981	$0	$0	$15,228
Backorder Cost	$0	$0	$0	$0	$7,840	$0	$7,840
					Total Cost		$516,582

19c. In the absence of a limit on regular capacity, the plan for part a remains the lowest cost.

	January	February	March	April	May	June	Total
Forecast	3500	4600	5800	7600	6700	4700	32900
Regular	5483	5483	5483	5483	5483	5483	32898
Overtime	0	0	0	0	1	1	2
Subcontracting	0	0	0	0	0	0	0
Beginning Inventory	0	1983	2866	2549	432	−784	
Ending Inventory	1983	2866	2549	432	−784	0	
Average Inventory	991.5	2424.5	2707.5	1490.5	−176	−392	7046
Production and Inventory Costs							
Reg. time production	$82,245	$82,245	$82,245	$82,245	$82,245	$82,245	$493,470
Overtime	$0	$0	$0	$0	$22	$22	$44

	January	February	March	April	May	June	Total
Subcontracting	$0	$0	$0	$0	$0	$0	$0
Holding Cost	$1,983	$4,849	$5,415	$2,981	$0	$0	$15,228
Backorder Cost	$0	$0	$0	$0	$7,840	$0	$7,840
					Total Cost		$516,582

21a.

Month	1	2	3	4	5	6	Totals
Forecast	1200	1300	900	700	1500	1700	7300
Production Cost in $/unit	90	95	100	105	100	100	
Overtime Cost in $/unit	135	142.5	150	157.5	150	150	
Subcontracting Cost in $/unit	150	150	150	150	150	150	
Inventory Holding Cost $/unit	5	5	5	5	5	5	
Beginning Inventory	100	100	0	300	800	500	
Regular Output	1200	1200	1200	1200	1200	1200	7200
Overtime Output							0
Subcontracting Output							0
Ending Inventory	100	0	300	800	500	0	
Average Inventory	100	50	150	550	650	250	
Cost Calculations							
Regular Output Cost	$108,000	$114,000	$120,000	$126,000	$120,000	$120,000	$708,000
Overtime Output Cost	$0	$0	$0	$0	$0	$0	$0
Subcontract Output Cost	$0	$0	$0	$0	$0	$0	$0
Holding Cost	$500	$250	$750	$2,750	$3,250	$1,250	$8,750
Total Cost	$108,500	$114,250	$120,750	$128,750	$123,250	$121,250	$716,750

21b.

Month	1	2	3	4	5	6	Totals
Forecast	1200	1300	900	700	1500	1700	7300
Production Cost in $/unit	90	95	100	105	100	100	
Overtime Cost in $/unit	135	142.5	150	157.5	150	150	
Subcontracting Cost in $/unit	150	150	150	150	150	150	
Inventory Holding Cost per unit	5	5	5	5	5	5	
Beginning Inventory	100	0	0	100	400	0	
Regular Output Level	1000	1000	1000	1000	1000	1000	6000
Overtime Output Level	100	200			100	350	750
Subcontracting Output Level		100				350	450
Ending Inventory	0	0	100	400	0	0	
Average Inventory	50	0	50	250	200	0	
Cost Calculations							
Regular Output Cost	$90,000	$95,000	$100,000	$105,000	$100,000	$100,000	$590,000
Overtime Output Cost	$13,500	$28,500	$0	$0	$15,000	$52,500	$109,500
Subcontracting Output Cost	$0	$15,000	$0	$0	$0	$52,500	$67,500
Holding Cost	$250	$0	$250	$1,250	$1,000	$0	$2,750
Total Cost	$103,750	$138,500	$100,250	$106,250	$116,000	$205,000	$769,750

21c.

Month	1	2	3	4	5	6	Totals
Forecast	1200	1300	900	700	1500	1700	7300
Production Cost in $/unit	90	95	100	105	100	100	
Overtime Cost in $/unit	135	142.5	150	157.5	150	150	
Subcontracting Cost in $/unit	150	150	150	150	150	150	
Inventory Holding Cost per unit	5	5	5	5	5	5	
Beginning Inventory	100	0	0	0	0	0	
Regular Output Level	1100	1300	900	700	1500	1700	7200
Overtime Output Level	0	0			0	0	0
Subcontracting Output Level		0				0	0
Ending Inventory	0	0	0	0	0	0	
Average Inventory	50	0	0	0	0	0	
Cost Calculations							
Regular Output Cost	$99,000	$123,500	$90,000	$73,500	$150,000	$170,000	$706,000
Overtime Output Cost	$0	$0	$0	$0	$0	$0	$0
Subcontracting Output Cost	$0	$0	$0	$0	$0	$0	$0
Holding Cost	$250	$0	$0	$0	$0	$0	$250
Total Cost	$99,250	$123,500	$90,000	$73,500	$150,000	$170,000	$706,250

21d. The chase strategy is the lowest cost approach

Chapter 18

1.

Week	1	2	3	4	5	6	7	8	9	10
Forecast	100	90	100	120	70	85	50	60	40	70
Customer Orders	120	90	60	30				120	80	
Projected On-hand Inventory	210	120	20	100	30	145	95	175	95	25
MPS	200			200		200		200		
Available-to-Promise (ATP)	60			170		200		80		

3.

Week	1	2	3	4	5	6	7	8	9
Forecast	320	100	30	110	40	240	290	60	410
Customer Orders	60	50	80	20	60	60			
Projected On-hand Inventory	280	180	100	290	230	290	300	240	130
MPS Released			300		300	300		300	
MPS Due				300		300	300		300
Available-to-Promise (ATP)	410			220		240	300		

5.

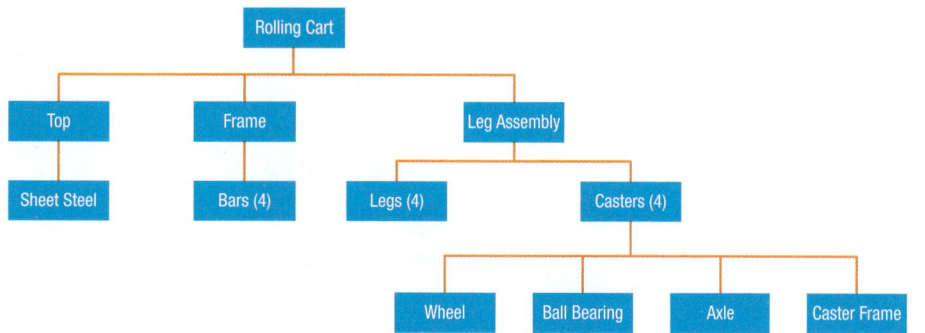

7.

Product: End Product
Low level code: 0
Lead time: 1 week
Lot size: L4L

	1	2	3	4	5	6	7	8
Gross Requirements						70		
Scheduled Receipts								
Projected on Hand = 0								
Net Requirements						70		
Planned Order Receipts						70		
Planned Order Releases					70			

Product: Subassembly J
Low level code: 1
Lead time: 1 week
Lot size: L4L

	1	2	3	4	5	6	7	8
Gross Requirements					140			
Scheduled Receipts								
Projected on Hand = 5					5			
Net Requirements					135			
Planned Order Receipts					135			
Planned Order Releases				135				

Product: Subassembly L
Low level code: 1
Lead time: 3 weeks
Lot size: L4L

	1	2	3	4	5	6	7	8
Gross Requirements					140			
Scheduled Receipts								
Projected on Hand = 20					20			
Net Requirements					120			
Planned Order Receipts					120			
Planned Order Releases		120						

Product: Component M
Low level code: 2
Lead time: 2 week
Lot size: L4L

	1	2	3	4	5	6	7	8
Gross Requirements		480		540				
Scheduled Receipts								
Projected on Hand = 15		15	135	135				
Net Requirements		465		405				
Planned Order Receipts		600		600				
Planned Order Releases		600						

There is a planned order release of 600 in week 0 for Component M.

9. Week 4

11.

Product: Skateboard
Low level code: 0
Lead time: 1 week
Lot size: L4L

	1	2	3	4	5	6	7	8	9	10
Gross Requirements										70
Scheduled Receipts										
Projected on Hand = 0										
Net Requirements										70
Planned Order Receipts										70
Planned Order Releases									70	

Product: Board
Low level code: 1
Lead time: 2 weeks
Lot size: L4L

	1	2	3	4	5	6	7	8	9	10
Gross Requirements									70	
Scheduled Receipts										
Projected on Hand = 0										
Net Requirements									70	
Planned Order Receipts									70	
Planned Order Releases							70			

Product: Wheel Assembly
Low level code: 1
Lead time: 2 weeks
Lot size: L4L

	1	2	3	4	5	6	7	8	9	10
Gross Requirements									140	
Scheduled Receipts										
Projected on Hand = 0										
Net Requirements									140	
Planned Order Receipts									140	
Planned Order Releases							140			

Product: Wheel
Low level code: 2
Lead time: 1 week
Lot size: L4L

	1	2	3	4	5	6	7	8	9	10
Gross Requirements							280			
Scheduled Receipts										
Projected on Hand = 0							0			
Net Requirements							280			
Planned Order Receipts							280			
Planned Order Releases						280				

Product: Spindle
Low level code: 2
Lead time: 3 weeks
Lot size: L4L

WEEK	1	2	3	4	5	6	7	8	9	10
Gross Requirements							140			
Scheduled Receipts										
Projected on Hand = 0							0			
Net Requirements							140			
Planned Order Receipts							140			
Planned Order Releases				140						

Product: Mount Stand
Low level code: 2
Lead time: 3 weeks
Lot size: L4L

WEEK	1	2	3	4	5	6	7	8	9	10
Net Requirements							140			
Planned Order Receipts							140			
Planned Order Releases				140						

Product: Locknut
Low level code: 2
Lead time: 1 week
Lot size: L4L

WEEK	1	2	3	4	5	6	7	8	9	10
Gross Requirements							280			
Scheduled Receipts										
Projected on Hand = 0							0			
Net Requirements							280			
Planned Order Receipts							280			
Planned Order Releases						280				

Product: Mount Stand
Low level code: 2
Lead time: 3 weeks
Lot size: L4L

WEEK	1	2	3	4	5	6	7	8	9	10
Gross Requirements							140			
Scheduled Receipts										
Projected on Hand = 0							0			

13a.

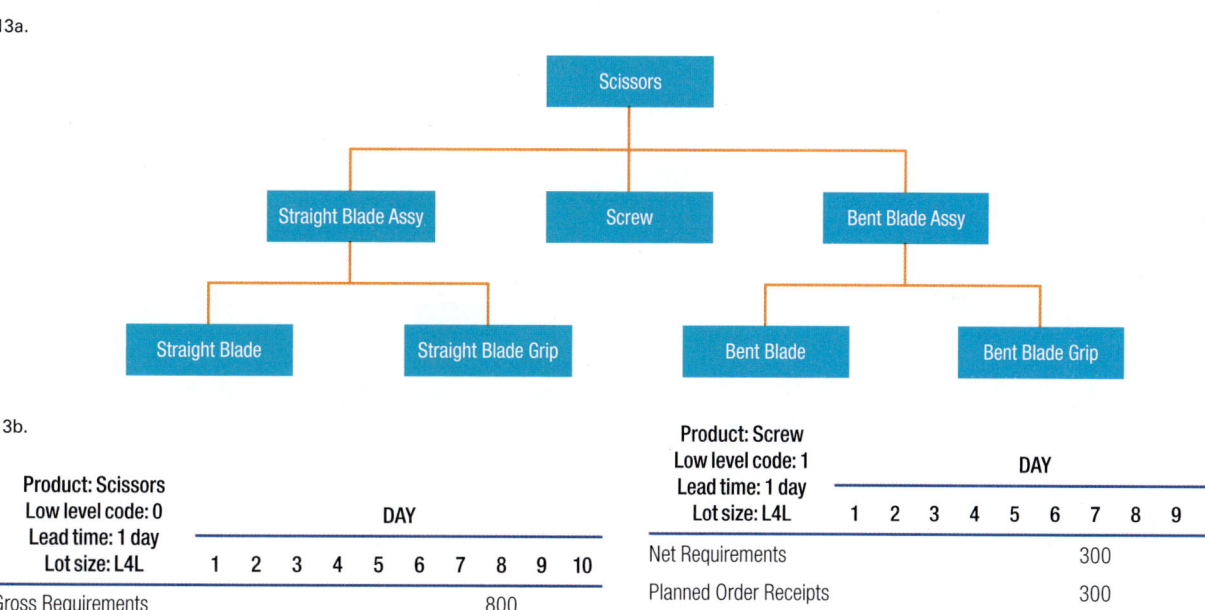

13b.

Product: Scissors
Low level code: 0
Lead time: 1 day
Lot size: L4L

DAY	1	2	3	4	5	6	7	8	9	10
Gross Requirements								800		
Scheduled Receipts								0		
Projected on Hand = 0								0		
Net Requirements								800		
Planned Order Receipts								800		
Planned Order Releases							800			

Product: Screw
Low level code: 1
Lead time: 1 day
Lot size: L4L

DAY	1	2	3	4	5	6	7	8	9	10
Gross Requirements							800			
Scheduled Receipts							0			
Projected on Hand = 500							500			

Product: Screw
Low level code: 1
Lead time: 1 day
Lot size: L4L

DAY	1	2	3	4	5	6	7	8	9	10
Net Requirements							300			
Planned Order Receipts							300			
Planned Order Releases						300				

Product: Straight Blade Assy
Low level code: 1
Lead time: 0 day
Lot size: L4L

DAY	1	2	3	4	5	6	7	8	9	10
Gross Requirements							800			
Scheduled Receipts										
Projected on Hand = 100	100	100	100	100	100	100	100			
Net Requirements							700			
Planned Order Receipts							700			
Planned Order Releases							700			

Product: Straight Blade
Low level code: 2
Lead time: 2 days
Lot size: L4L

	1	2	3	4	5	6	7	8	9	10
Gross Requirements							700			
Scheduled Receipts										
Projected on Hand = 300	300	300	300	300	300	300	300			
Net Requirements							400			
Planned Order Receipts							400			
Planned Order Releases					400					

Product: Straight Blade Grip
Low level code: 2
Lead time: 2 days
Lot size: L4L

	1	2	3	4	5	6	7	8	9	10
Gross Requirements							700			
Scheduled Receipts										
Projected on Hand = 100	100	100	100	100	100	100	100			
Net Requirements							600			
Planned Order Receipts							600			
Planned Order Releases					600					

Product: Bent Blade Assy
Low level code: 1
Lead time: 0 day
Lot size: L4L

	1	2	3	4	5	6	7	8	9	10
Gross Requirements							800			
Scheduled Receipts										
Projected on Hand = 50	50	50	50	50	50	50	50			
Net Requirements							750			
Planned Order Receipts							750			
Planned Order Releases							750			

Product: Bent Blade
Low level code: 2
Lead time: 3 days
Lot size: L4L

	1	2	3	4	5	6	7	8	9	10
Gross Requirements							750			
Scheduled Receipts										
Projected on Hand = 200	200	200	200	200	200	200	200			
Net Requirements							550			
Planned Order Receipts							550			
Planned Order Releases				550						

Product: Bent Blade Grip
Low level code: 2
Lead time: 3 days
Lot size: L4L

	1	2	3	4	5	6	7	8	9	10
Gross Requirements							750			
Scheduled Receipts										
Projected on Hand = 50	50	50	50	50	50	50	50	50		
Net Requirements							700			
Planned Order Receipts							700			
Planned Order Releases				700						

15.

Product P
Low level code: 0
Lead time: 1 week
Lot size: Two-week fixed period ordering

	1	2	3	4	5	6	7	8	9	10
Gross Requirements	60	90	60	130	65	75	100	40	85	55
Scheduled Receipts										
Projected on Hand = 200	200									
Net Requirement										
Planned Order Receipts		150		195		175		180		
Planned Order Releases	150		195		175		180			

17. EOQ

19a.

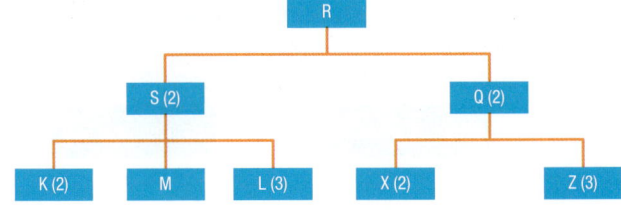

b. 540 c. Week 2

21.

Product: Subassembly Q
Low level code: 1
Lead time: 3 weeks
Lot size: L4L

	1	2	3	4	5	6	7	8	9
Gross Requirements	80	55	75	85	100	140	80	100	90
Scheduled Receipts		70							
Projected on Hand = 140	140	130	75	0	55	25	25	15	55
Net Requirements	0		0						
Planned Order Receipts				140	70	140	70	140	70
Planned Order Releases	140	70	140	70	140	70			

Chapter 18 Supplement

1.

Week	Material Forecast (in tons)	Labor Needed	Machine Needed	Labor Utilization	Machine Utilization
1	60	60x6=360	60x4=240	360/450=80%	240/300=80%
2	70	70x6=420	70x4=280	420/450=93%	280/300=93%
3	50	50x6=300	50x4=200	300/450=67%	200/300=67%
4	80	80x6=480	80x4=320	480/450=107%	320/300=107%

Capacity will be exceeded in week 4. Since roofing materials can be inventoried, one solution would be to make some of week 4's anticipated demand during week 3.

3. 2 welding workers and 5 assembly workers.
There is a significant round up in the assembly area of half a worker. It might be less expensive to hire five workers to work ten hour days. Workers might be cross trained to fill in where needed whether in assembly or welding.

5. Total load by department for each product

Product	Input	Monday	Tuesday	Wednesday	Thursday	Friday	Total
P	Labor	1600	1200	800	800	400	4800
	Machine	1800	1350	900	900	450	5400
K	Labor	2200	550	1650	1100	550	6050
	Machine	1000	250	750	500	250	2750

Total load for each of the departments

Fabrication		Assembly		Painting	
Labor	Machine	Labor	Machine	Labor	Machine
4600	3500	3400	2900	2850	1750

7.

Hours Needed	1	2	3	4
Sanding	67	97.5	157	118
Painting	100	142.5	227.5	168.75

Capacity at Sanding=35.328 hours=Capacity at Painting. Dorian will not be able to meet demand.

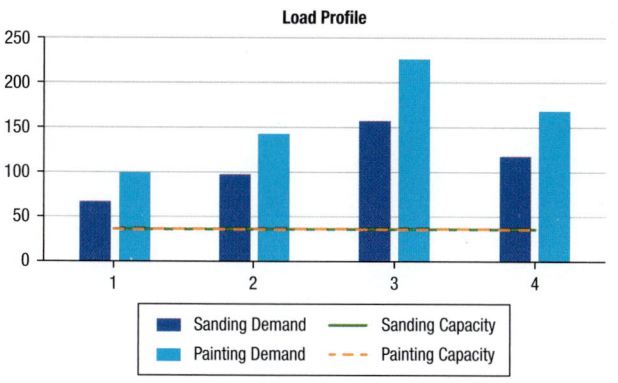

Load Profile

9.

Master Production Schedule

Week	1	2	3	4	5	6
Product P	120	140	90	180	80	80
Q(3)	3(120)=360	420	270	540	240	240
R(2)	2(120)=240	280	180	360	160	160
S(4)	4(360)=1440	1680	1080	2160	960	960
T(2)	2(360)=720	840	540	1080	480	480

Operation	1	2	3	4	5	6
Lathing	1440	1680	1080	2160	960	960
Shearing	360	420	270	540	240	240
Milling	240	280	180	360	160	160
Drilling	720	840	540	1080	480	480
Assembly	360	420	270	540	240	240

Week 4 is the highest demand week for all work stations, but weeks 5 & 6 have the lowest demands during the period. If some percentage, like 30–40%. of the demand in week 4 could be evenly distributed between 5 & 6, the load would be more even across the six periods.

Chapter 19

1.

Week	1	2	3	4	5
Input Deviation	2	4	−5	−2	5
Input Cumulative Deviation	2	6	1	−1	4
Output Deviation	0	−2	−2	0	−3
Output Cumulative Deviation	0	−2	−4	−4	−7
Output Actual Backlog	16	22	19	17	20
Output Beginning Backlog	14				

3.

Week	1	2	3	4	5
Input Deviation	−10	−5	−5	−5	0
Input Cumulative Deviation	−10	−15	−20	−25	−25
Output Deviation	0	−5	−5	−5	0
Output Cumulative Deviation	0	−5	−10	−15	−15
Output Actual Backlog	5	5	5	5	5
Output Beginning Backlog	15				

5. A total of 5 hours is the optimal assignment.

	Time required in hours			
Patient	Nurse-1	Nurse-2	Nurse-3	Nurse-4
Sharma			Assign	
Singh	Assign			
Brown				Assign
Warner		Assign		

7. The optimal assignment has a total time of 55 minutes.

	Processing time in minutes				
Component	Machine-1	Machine-2	Machine-3	Machine-4	Machine-5
A121		Assign			
B85				Assign	
C144	Assign				
C105			Assign		
A62					Assign

9ab.

Rule	Sequence	Avg. Flow Time	Avg. Tardiness	Avg # Jobs
FCFS	ABCDE	37.4	19	2.88
EDD	CBDAE	33.6	15.2	2.58
SPT	DCBAE	32.6	15	2.51
LPT	EABCD	45.4	26.4	3.49
CR	EBACD	44.8	25.8	3.45

9c. SPT shows superior performance across all metrics

11. ABDCE.

13.

Rule	Sequence	Avg. Flow Time	Avg. Tardiness	Avg # Jobs
FCFS	PSLGC	21.4	7.6	2.68
EDD	PSLCG	20.6	6.8	2.58
SPT	LSPCG	18.6	7.4	2.33
CR	PGCSL	27.8	14.2	3.48

15a. Optimal sequence is BDFACEGH

15b. The only idle time in the decorating process is the one hour at the start of the sequence.

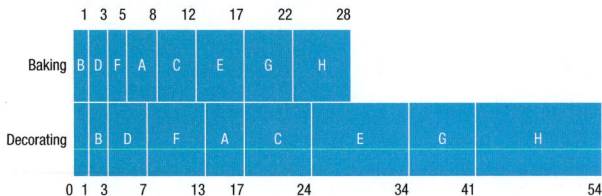

17. YSWVUTX

19.

Day	Monday	Tuesday	Wednesday	Thursday	Friday	Saturday	Sunday
Nurses Required	4	4	5	6	5	4	4
Anand	X	X	X	X	X		
Vineeth			X	X	X	X	X

Day	Monday	Tuesday	Wednesday	Thursday	Friday	Saturday	Sunday
Poorvik	X	X	X	X	X		
Rakshmi			X	X	X	X	X
Shethal	X	X	X	X			X
Swathi	X	X			X	X	X
Gejo			X		X		

21.

Day	Monday	Tuesday	Wednesday	Thursday	Friday	Saturday	Sunday
Volunteers Req'd.	5	4	3	4	7	5	3
A	X			X	X	X	
B	X	X			X	X	
C				X	X	X	X
D	X	X	X		X		
E				X	X	X	X
F	X	X	X		X		
G	X	X	X	X			
H					X	X	X

23.

Week	1	2	3	4	5
Input Cumulative Deviation	−10	−15	−20	−25	−25
Output Cumulative Deviation	0	−5	−10	−15	−15
Actual Backlog	0	0	0	0	0
Beginning Backlog	10				

25. KRPNMOL

27.

Day	Monday	Tuesday	Wednesday	Thursday	Friday	Saturday
Employees Req'd.	3	3	5	4	6	4
A		X	X	X	X	
B			X	X	X	X
C		X	X	X	X	
D	X	X			X	X
E	X			X	X	X
F	X		X			X
G			X		X	

29.

Rule	Sequence
FCFS	ABCDEF
EDD	EBACFD
SPT	BEACDF
LPT	FDCAEB
CR	EAFCBD

Module A

1. Maximum occurs at S=1.333,
    T=3.333, Profit=$50.67

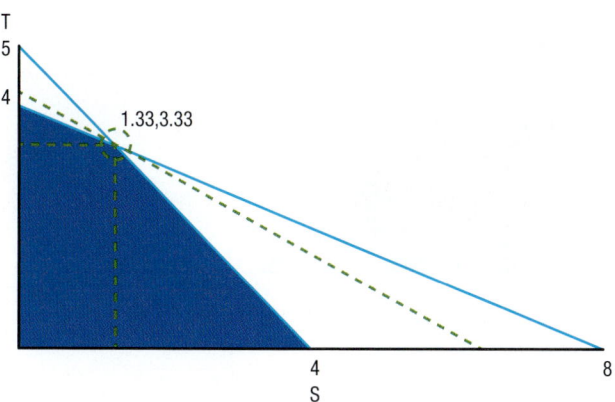

5a. 925 Soft, 150 Hardwood, 200 Tropical, and 300 Aircraft for a total profit of $21,800.

5bc. The Hardwood coefficient in the objective function is 12 and has an allowable increase of 8 and an allowable decrease of infinity. Hardwood panel is being produced only in the minimum quantity required by the constraint (at least 150 units). It doesn't matter how unprofitable Hardwood is, as long as Diamond must produce 150 units, they will do so. The allowable increase of 8 means that for a profit contribution from 8 up to 20, Diamond will produce 150 units of Hardwood. If the objective function coefficient exceeds 20, then the optimal quantity of Hardwood will change (in this case, increase above 150 units). Softwood is the opposite case, it is a profitable product so Diamond wants to make as much as it possibly can. If the objective coefficient increases beyond the level of 8, Diamond would still make it at the expense of the other products. If the coefficient drops by more than 2, down to below $6, then Diamond will not make 925 units of this product.

7a. The optimal schedule is

Time Interval	Workers starting this shift
00–04	7
04–08	1
08–12	21
12–16	5
16–20	13
20–24	0

Based on this system of equations

$Min\ Z = x_1 + x_2 + x_3 + x_4 + x_5 + x_6$

subject to:

$x_1 + x_2 \geq 8$
$x_2 + x_3 \geq 22$
$x_3 + x_4 \geq 26$
$x_4 + x_5 \geq 18$
$x_5 + x_6 \geq 12$
$x_6 + x_1 \geq 7$

7b. The allowable increase and decrease values for the objective function coefficients provide a valid range for the reduced cost

3. The optimal solution is X_1=4.2, X_2=1.6 for Cost=$26.4

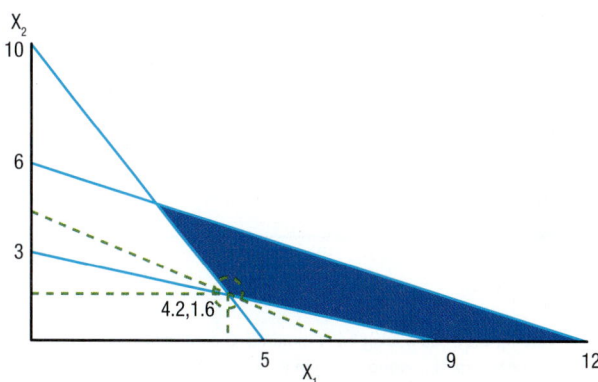

entries. In the objective function, all coefficients are 1; counting the number of workers for any shift more than twice will result in a different schedule but identical number of workers.

7c. Shadow prices are the marginal values for one additional unit of the right hand side. If the RHS of the original constraint is increased by 1 unit, the value of the objective function at optimality changes by the value of the shadow price as long as that increase or decrease is within the allowable increase and decrease. Changes in RHS values outside the allowable increases and decreases will not be a direct multiplier of the shadow prices.

9a. $Max\ Z = 3P + 4N$

subject to:

$P + N \geq 4$
$16P + 8N \leq 64$
$-2P + N \leq 0$

9b.

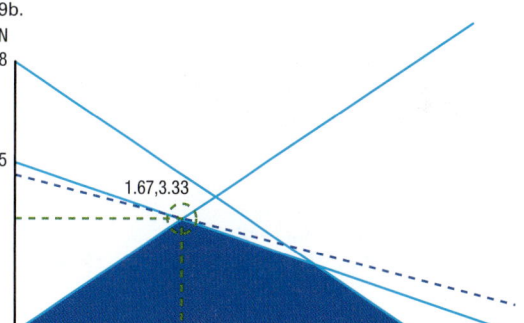

The optimal extraction solution is to mine 1.6666 tons of P and 3.3333 tons of N.

11a. $Min\ Cost = \$3A + \$5B + \$4C$

subject to:

$150A + 100B + 200C \geq 400$
$150A + 200B + 100C \geq 600$
$300A + 150B + 300C \geq 2000$
$100A + 200B + 150C \geq 1600$

11b. 1.8 units of B and 4.266 units of C make a feed that meets these requirements while costing $41.067 per pound

A13.

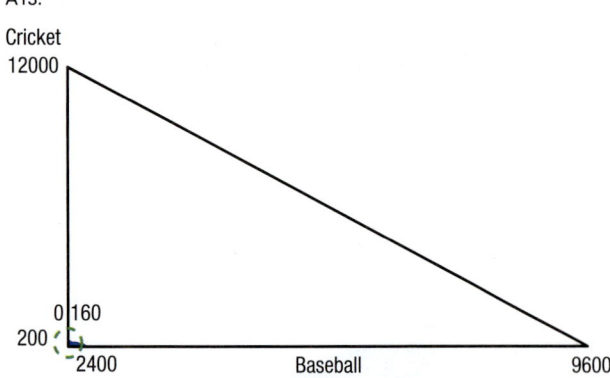

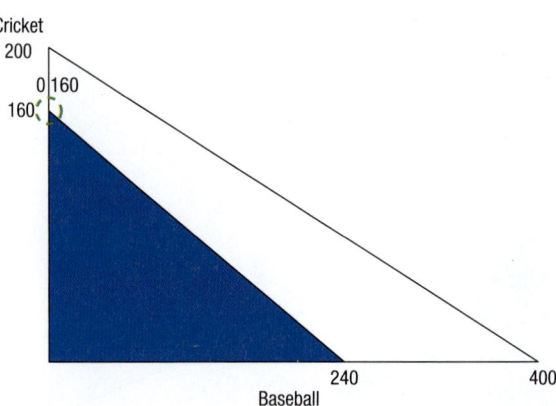

Producing only 160 cricket balls maximizes profit at $1920. The leather constraint is nonbinding in a big way. The same graph without the nonbinding leather constraint is:
The cutting and dyeing constraint is also nonbinding, but is less so than the leather constraint.

15. Min Cost = $300X_{HighA} + $300X_{MedA} + $300X_{LowA} + $200X_{HighB} +
$200X_{MedB} + $200X_{LowB}

S.T.

$$X_{HighA} + X_{HighB} \geq 6$$
$$X_{MedA} + X_{MedB} \geq 4$$
$$X_{LowA} + X_{LowB} \geq 12$$
$$X_{HighA} \leq 4$$
$$X_{HighB} \leq 3$$
$$X_{MedA} \leq 2$$
$$X_{MedB} \leq 2$$
$$X_{LowA} \leq 5$$
$$X_{LowB} \leq 8$$

X_{HighA} = 3 tons; X_{MedA} = 2 tons; X_{LowA} = 4 tons
X_{HighB} = 3 tons; X_{MedB} = 2 tons; X_{LowB} = 8 tons
Total cost = $5300

This problem has no feasible solution; the daily requirements for both high grade ore and low grade ore far exceed the mines' capacity.

17. This objective function and constraints seeks to assign all students to the three high schools in such a way as to minimize total distance traveled.

a. Min Distance = $2x_{EM} + 0x_{MM} + 3x_{FM} + 8x_{HM} + 15x_{NM}$
$+5x_{EF} + 3x_{MF} + 0x_{FF} + 16x_{HF} + 20x_{NF} + 7x_{EH} + 8x_{MH} + 16x_{FH} + 0x_{HH} + 5x_{NH}$
subject to:
$$x_{EM} + x_{MM} + x_{FM} + x_{HM} + x_{NM} \leq 800$$
$$x_{EF} + x_{MF} + x_{FF} + x_{HF} + x_{NF} \leq 800$$
$$x_{EH} + x_{MH} + x_{FH} + x_{HH} + x_{NH} \leq 800$$
$$x_{EM} + x_{EF} + x_{EH} = 600$$
$$x_{MM} + x_{MF} + x_{MH} = 700$$
$$x_{FM} + x_{FF} + x_{FH} = 600$$
$$x_{HM} + x_{HF} + x_{HH} = 500$$
$$x_{NM} + x_{NF} + x_{NH} = 300$$

b. Solver cannot satisfy all constraints, there are more total students (2700) in the district than the three high schools can accommodate (2400).

19a. Min Risk = $7S + 2B$
subject to:
$60S + $90B = $1,000,000$
$90B \geq $400,000$
$5.4S + $2.7B \geq $50,000$

b. 11,111.1 bonds

c. Max Return = $5.4S + $2.7B$
subject to:
$60S + $90B = $1,000,000$ This formulation buys 5,555,5 stocks
$90B \geq $400,000$
$5.4S + $2.7B \geq $50,000$

and 7,407.4 bonds

Module B

1. $1020

3. $9170

5. a. $520 b. $520 c. $485

7. $400

9. Min Cost = $5DL + $4DCl + $3DCh + $8ML + $4MCl$
$+$3MCh + $9CoL + $7CoCl + $5CoCh$
subject to:
$$DL + DCl + DCh = 1000$$
$$ML + MCL + MCh = 3000$$
$$CoL + CoCl + CoCh = 3000$$
$$DL + ML + CoL = 3000$$
$$DCl + MCl + CoCl = 2000$$
$$DCh + MCh + CoCh = 2000$$

All variables ≥ 0

11. Cleveland

13. $386,000

15. Min Cost = $15SjCl + $21SjOr + $13SjDe + $10SjSd + $22SjNy +$
$$3DaCl + $11DaOr + $9DaDe + $21DaSd + $7DaNy +$
$$4BoCl + $12BoOr + $10BoDe + $25BoSd + $5BoNy$
subject to:
$$SjCl + SjOr + SjDe + SjSd + SjNy = 45$$
$$DaCl + DaOr + DaDe + DaSd + DaNy = 50$$
$$BoCl + BoOr + BoDe + BoSd + BoNy = 50$$
$$SjCl + DaCl + BoCl = 25$$
$$SjOr + DaOr + BoOr = 20$$
$$SjDe + DaDe + BoDe = 35$$
$$SjSd + DaSd + BoSd = 20$$
$$SjNy + DaNy + BoNy = 30$$
all variables ≥ 0

17. The condition is degeneracy and it can be overcome by creating an artificially occupied cell that allows a complete path to be traced. Placing a negligible amount in the Calgary-Dallas route permits application of the stepping stone method. The optimum solution costs $18,600.

19a. The matrix is unbalanced, so a dummy source must be added as Plant 6 with a capacity of 200.

From	To	Warehouse					Capacity
		A	B	C	D	E	
Plant-1		400	400	400			1200
Plant-2		1000			500		1500
Plant-3					900		900
Plant-4			200			900	1100
Plant-5				1300			1300
Plant-6			200				200
Demand		1400	800	1700	1400	900	6200
							6200

19b. $37,800

Module C

1. a. 0.83 b. 4.17 c. 0.2 d. 0.07

3. The system's utilization is 66% and if all customers had appointments 6 minutes apart and took exactly 4 minutes per customer, there would be no waiting line. However, there is variability in the arrival and service process, so there will be times when lines form and other times when the server is idle for several minutes.

5. a. 2.08 b. 0.12 c. 2.92

7a. $W_q = 0.27$; $L_q = 3.2$; $P_0 = .2$

7b. $W_q = 0.01$; $L_q = 0.15$; $P_0 = 0.43$

9. a. $P_0 = .11$; b. $L_q = 2.84$; c. $W_s = 0.19$; d. $P_5 = .07$; e. $P_{n>0} = 0.89$

11.

Time Period	λ	μ	S	11a: P_0	11b: L_q	11c: W_s	11d: Lq_{max}
Morning	12	15	2	.54	.06	.05	2
Afternoon	18	20	3	.40	.03	.05	2
Evening	25	30	3	.43	.02	.03	3

13. $P_0 = .06$; $L_q = 0.76$; $W_q = 0.09$; $L_s = 3.42$; $W_s = .43$

Labor cost=$100x10=$1000; Waiting cost=.43x10x8x150=$5160; System cost=$6160

15. a.utilization=0.83; b. P_0=0.04; c. L_q=3.51; d. W_q=0.07; e. W_s=0.12; f. L_s=6.01

17. A second technician is needed.

19a. W_q=0.07; L_q=2.84

19b. If the service time remains 2.4 minutes, the system will need a minimum of 4 servers so the system service rate can exceed the customer arrival rate at the maximum rate of 80 per hour. With four servers the L_q = 2.39 and W_q = 1.8 minutes.

Module D

1a. Answers will vary but should approach 2.25

1b. Answers will vary but should approach 2.25

1c. This is a very small sample, but the averages should be approximately equal

3a. 3.89

3c. This is a small sample so the simulated values should be different from the computed values in part a.

5a.

Day	Random Number	Break downs	Random Number	Repair Time	Random Number	Repair Time	Random Number	Repair Time	Random Number	Repair Time
1	56	2	74	2	19					
2	14	0								
3	82	3	15	1	25	1	87	2		
4	96	4	64	2	18	1	61	2	54	1
5	67	2	62	2	22	1				
6	83	3	69	2	94	3	8	1		
7	83	3	99	3	78	2	34	1		
8	2	0								
9	4	0								
10	53	2	93	3	58	1				
11	57	2	43	1	11	1				
12	8	0								

Day	Random Number	Break downs	Random Number	Repair Time	Random Number	Repair Time	Random Number	Repair Time	Random Number	Repair Time
13	42	1	99	3						
14	95	4	69	2	12	1	12	1	31	1
15	32	1	33	1						

Average repair time is 1.62 hour b. $280.

7a.

Day	Rand #	Patient Arrivals	Rand #	Rand #	Rand #	Rand #	Rand #	Rand #	Rand #	Highest Rand #	# Doctors
1	3	0								0	0
2	20	2	66	73						73	4
3	35	3	23	19	90					90	4
4	25	2	28	46						46	2
5	29	2	66	57						66	2
6	78	5	78	30	2	17	31			78	4
7	16	2	54	96						96	4
8	72	4	83	47	80	52				83	4
9	75	5	81	20	89	36	15			89	4
10	61	4	88	68	59	0				88	4
11	32	3	59	72	11					72	4
12	14	1	18							18	1
13	15	2	14	12						14	1
14	94	6	29	65	27	96	35	42		96	4
15	49	3	68	39	79					79	4

7b. The average number of patient arrivals each night is 2.65. Using just the maximum injury as an indicator, there are 3.2 doctors needed each night with a maximum of 4 on several nights. If each patient need multiple doctors and the doctors are not allowed to switch from one patient to the next, then the maximum number of doctors needed is 14 on night 14 and the average number needed is 6.87.

9a.

Call	Rand #	Call Interarrival	Arrival Time	Rand #	Tom Time	Rand #	Harry Time	In Queue	Tom Ready	Harry Ready
1	25	1	1	60	2				3	
2	10	1	2			65	4			6
3	42	1	3	0	1	56	3		4	
4	99	4	7			91	5			12
5	87	3	10	18	1				11	
6	10	1	11	27	1				12	
7	47	2	13			69	4			17
8	56	2	15	40	2				17	
9	54	2	17	21	1				18	
10	21	1	18	27	1				19	
11	80	3	21			46	3			24
12	27	1	22	36	1				23	
13	94	3	25			46	3			28
14	46	2	27	13	1				28	
15	58	2	29	94	4				33	
16	38	1	30			7	3			33
17	97	4	34	73	2				36	

Call	Rand #	Call Interarrival	Arrival Time	Rand #	Tom Time	Rand #	Harry Time	In Queue	Tom Ready	Harry Ready
18	33	1	35			47	3			38
19	68	2	37	45	2				39	
20	75	2	39			31	3			42

9b. There is no customer waiting in this simulation. Customers are in the system only for actual call time, which averages 2.5 minutes. Tom averages 1.58 minutes per call while Harry averages 3.44 minutes per call.

Module E

1. 32.45

3. 58.85

5. $2,084,731

7. 20th iteration = $2,568,567; 40th iteration = $1,798,060

9. a. 0.864 b. 32.05

11. a. 26.65 b. 600.16 c. $4949

13. 14

15. a. 5 b. 6

17. a. 607.98 b. 17.371 c. 4

19.

Trainee	1st unit	2nd unit	LC	5th Unit	Reassigned
Theresa	11	9	.82	$T_n = T_1 \times n^b = 11 \times 5^{\ln(.82)/\ln(2)} = 6.94$	Yes
Eric	10	9	0.9	$T_n = T_1 \times n^b = 10 \times 5^{\ln(.9)/\ln(2)} = 7.82$	Yes
Nicole	12	9	0.75	$T_n = T_1 \times n^b = 12 \times 5^{\ln(.75)/\ln(2)} = 6.15$	Yes

Module F

1. a. Expand $76,666 b. Do Nothing $40,000 c. Expand $160,000
   d. Expand $84,000 e. Subcontract $60,000

3. The Hurwicz selection is Moderate Expansion

5a.

Demand	80	90	100	110	120	Probability
			Order Quantity			
80	$3,200	$2,650	$2,100	$1,550	$1,000	0.10
90	$3,200	$3,600	$3,050	$2,500	$1,950	0.20
100	$3,200	$3,600	$4,000	$3,450	$2,900	0.25
110	$3,200	$3,600	$4,000	$4,400	$3,850	0.30
120	$3,200	$3,600	$4,000	$4,400	$4,800	0.15

Each sold book results in $40 profit, each ordered, but unsold book results in a loss of $55.

5b. 100.

7. a. Chennai $24.33 b. Chittagong –$17 c. Chennai $75 d. Manila $1.90
   e. Manila $15

9. a. Stocks $333.33 b. Money Market $50 c. Stocks $800 d. Money Market $80 e. Hedge Fund $270

11.

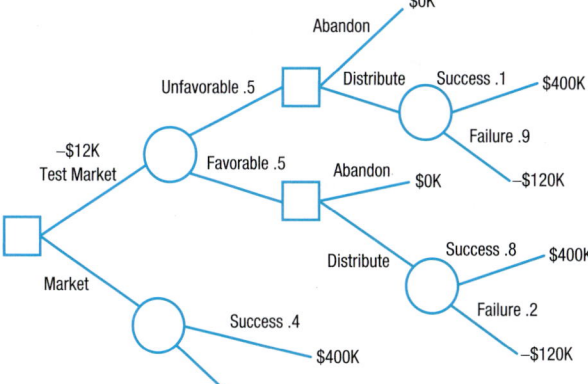

Going directly to market has a value of $88
The test market branch has a value of $148 to distribute after a favorable test and a value of $0 to distribute after an unfavorable test. Weighting these as 0.5 each yields a value of $74, less an initial outlay of $12, for an initial value of $62 to go to a test market. Thus, going directly to market is the best choice at an expected value of $88,000.

13a. The optimal choice is build large, which has an expected value of $280,000.

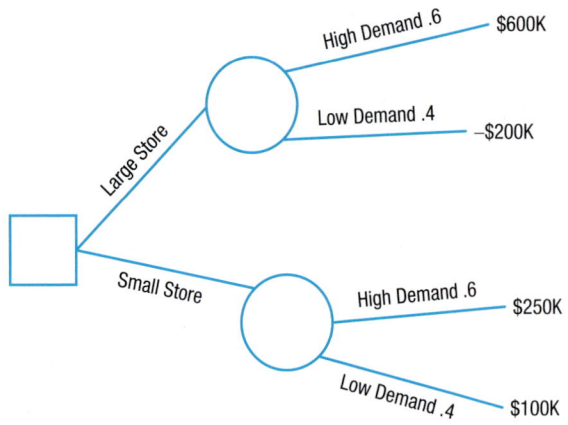

b.

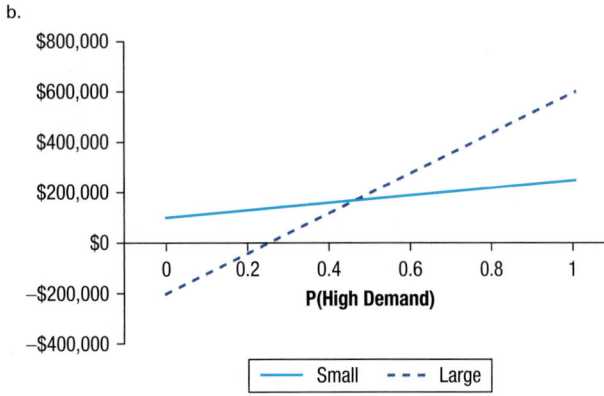

Small demand = 150,000X+100,000 & Large demand = 800,000X-200,000

Intersection point is 0.46. From P(High demand) = 0 to 0.42, build small, and from P(High demand) 0.42 to 1, build large.

c. $120,000

15.

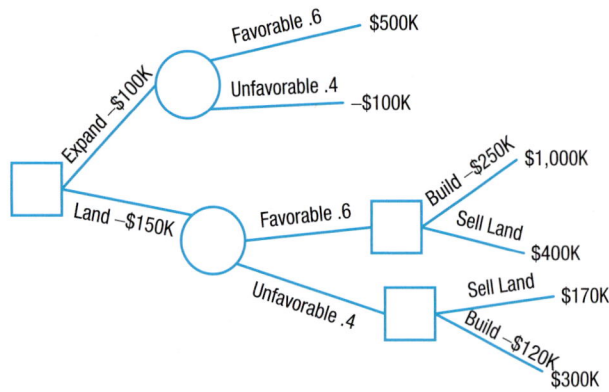

Sanjay should buy land.

17.

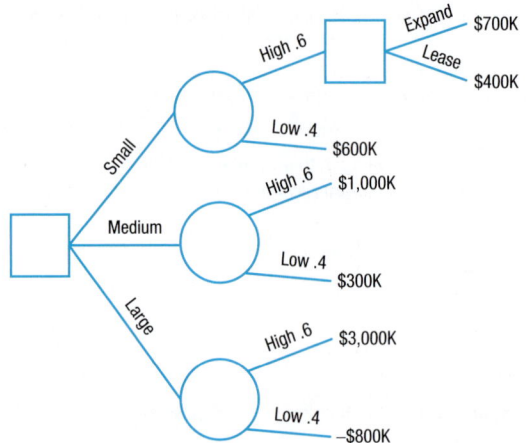

Venkatesh should build a large warehouse.

19.

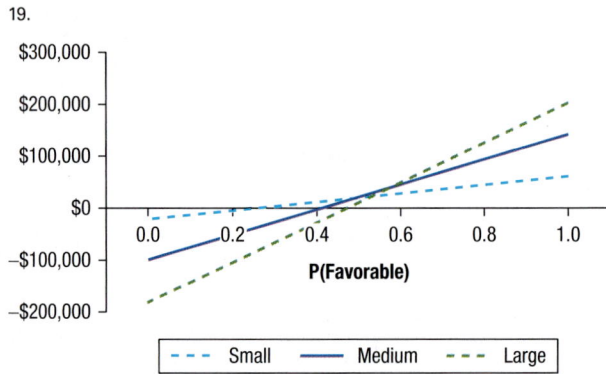

Small & Medium lines cross at 80,000X-20,000=240,000X-100,000 → X=0.5; if P(Favorable Market) is 0.5 or less, build small. Medium and Large lines cross at 240,000X-100,000=380,000X-180,000 → X=.5714. If P(Favorable) exceeds 0.5714, the build Large. Between P(Favorable)=0.5 and 0.57, build medium.

21. a. Jasmine $82.5 b. Lavender $50 c. Jasmine $150 d. Lavender $86 e. Sandalwood $30

23. Ultra Lite has the highest expected payoff.

25 a. Swimming pool
b. The perfect information decision for Low demand is Running Track at 2,500. The perfect information decision for Moderate demand is Child care center at $16,000. The perfect information decision for High demand is Swimming pool at $50,000. The total is $68,500, but the likelihoods sum to 1.25

ABC classification method. sorting items into A, B, and C categories according to criteria such as their unit costs, value, or the annual revenue they generate for a firm

Activity network. a diagram that illustrates how activities should best be sequenced

Activity on arrow (AOA). a type of activity network that uses arrows to represent the activities and nodes separating the arrows as events that indicate the completion of one task prior to the beginning of the next

Activity on node (AON). a type of activity network that uses nodes to represent the individual project activity and the path arrows to represent the sequencing of tasks from node to node through the network

Activity slack. the amount of time an activity may be delayed from its early start (ES) without delaying the finish of the project. Activity slack is defined as Activity Slack = LS − ES (or LF − EF)

Activity-based costing. a system that accounts for inventory cost and enables companies to recognize the excessive costs associated with forward buying when trade deals and quantity discounts are offered

Actual cost of work performed (AC). the cumulative total cost of completing the project's work packages

Actual output. also called *actual capacity*, the capacity that can be achieved given all production factors, not just regular changes in the production process

Adaptive manufacturing. a process that combines lean and agile manufacturing with flexible manufacturing systems to adapt production in response to changing market conditions

Additive model. a model of combining trends and seasonal components in which the seasonal indices are added to the projected trend data to create a combined forecast

Aggregate planning. also known as sales and operations planning (S&OP), is the process of matching supply and demand at the minimum total cost

Agile manufacturing. the ability of an organization to respond quickly to market changes with a set of processes, tools, and training available as needed

Annualized hours strategy. a strategy in which employees of a service company are hired as contractors to work for a certain number of hours per year for a fixed sum of money

Anticipation inventory. inventory held in excess of a firm's cycle stock to meet the expected increase in demand

Appointment systems. a scheduling system for service organizations that minimizes customer or client waiting time while maximizing the labor and capacity utilization of the service system by designating specific times for clients to arrive

Appraisal costs. the costs of measuring and inspecting products and services and the processes used to produce them

Assemble-to-order (ATO). a hybrid of the MTS and MTO methods in which the basic parts and components of a product are standardized, have already been manufactured, and are kept in stock until an order is received, when they are quickly assembled based on the customer's requirements

Assembly chart. a chart that maps how a product's parts go together and the order in which they are assembled, sometimes called a *gozinto* chart

Assembly drawing. an enlarged view of a product that shows all of its parts and subassemblies

Assignment method. a method applied to situations in which various resources must be allocated to activities on a one-to-one basis

Attribute. a quality characteristic that is counted using whole numbers and often categorized using either/or measures

Availability. the percentage of the time that the system or equipment is operating properly when it is needed for use

Available-to-promise (ATP) inventory. uncommitted inventory that is physically on hand that can be realistically promised for new customer order deliveries

Backflush. an inventory management process in which parts that go into each unit of a product are removed from inventory and continually tallied along with the finished units produced

Backflushing. enables accurate reporting of completed items. In a backflush, an end item's BOM is exploded to determine the quantities of component parts, material, and subassemblies that were used to make the item

Backhaul. the return journey of the trucks to their origins after the freight is delivered if the trucks are empty, resulting in the shipper paying a higher rate for the transportation of the product

Backorder. a customer order a company was unable to meet because the item demanded was not in stock

Backward pass. the process of labeling the activity nodes in a network to determine the project's critical path and the total slack time for each activity

Backward scheduling. a scheduling process used to determine in advance the capacity required at each work center for each time period to complete the jobs by the due dates by beginning with the due date for each job and loading the processing requirements for these jobs at each work center by proceeding backward in time

Balance efficiency. the measure of how well a process uses the time available to complete it

Balance of trade. the net difference between the monetary value of exports and imports of that country during a specific period

Balanced scorecard. a performance measurement system and a strategic planning and management system that allows managers to align a firm's activities with the vision and strategy of the organization, improve the firm's internal and external communications, and track and monitor the firm's performance against its strategic goals

Balanced transportation problem. a problem in which the total number of units demanded is equal to the total number of supply units available

Bargaining surplus. any difference in value to be gained between the buyer and the supplier

Batch ordering. ordering inventory periodically to accumulate or build up demand for products and materials before placing an order to avoid the increased costs associated with placing frequent orders and goods shipped in partially filled trucks

Batch process. a process that is selected to produce a moderate variety of products in moderate volumes in groups or batches

Benchmarking. the process of comparing the quality of your company's products or services and its processes with those companies considered to be world leaders in quality

Beta testing. field testing done to obtain valuable feedback on a product

Bill of labor or bill of resources file (BOL or BOR). shows the operations and the sequence in which they have to be performed and the key resources that will be required to perform each operation

Bill of lading. a document that delineates the terms of the contract between the shipper and the transportation company, indicating who has the title to the goods and who has the contractual agreement with the carrier, and serves as a receipt for the goods

Bill of materials (BOM). a computerized data file that contains the complete listing of all assemblies, subassemblies, parts and components, and raw materials needed and the manufacturing and assembly sequence to produce one unit of a finished product

Binding constraints. constraints that form the corner points at the boundaries of the feasible solution region and limit the values of the decision variables, which in turn, limit the objective function values in the graphical solution method to linear programming problems

Black Belt. employees who have received Six Sigma training and, along with Master Black Belts, tackle broader quality issues, such as improving entire operations and processes

Blanket purchase order. a purchase order used for long-term purchases made on multiple delivery dates scheduled over a period of time

Bottleneck. a limit or constraint on the workflow in an operation

Bottom-up planning. planning used when management calculates the resource requirements for each individual set of products or services and then combines them to get an overall picture of resource requirements

Breakeven analysis. a technique that is used to determine the production quantity at which total revenues are equal to total costs and net profits are equal to zero

Bucketless. MRP system in which material requirements are specified on a daily basis or by shift

Budgeted cost at completion (BAC). the total budget for a project at its completion

Bulk breaking. the process in which a warehouse (typically a distribution center) receives a large bulk shipment of goods from a single supplier and then splits (or breaks) it into individual orders for shipment and local delivery to multiple buyer destinations

Bullwhip effect. the result of a change in consumer demand that causes a company in a supply chain in close proximity to the consumer (such as a retailer) to order more goods from the immediate upstream supplier (such as a wholesaler or distributor) to meet the demand

Business process management (BPM). a management approach that focuses on continuously improving the efficiency of business processes through innovation, flexibility, and the seamless integration of technology

Business process reengineering (BPR). the radical redesign of a firm's existing workflows and resources to reduce operational costs and better meet the needs of customers and support a firm's overall mission

Business-unit strategy. a strategy that establishes how each business unit should compete within its particular industry or market

Buyback contract. an agreement that includes a buyback or returns clause that allows the supplier to buy back some of the buyer's unsold inventory up to a specified amount at an agreed-upon price (also known as a returns contract)

Capacity. the maximum amount of output an operation is capable of producing in a given time period

Capacity control. analyzing a facility's existing capacity relative to its weekly production schedules, also called capacity planning in the short term

Capacity cushion. the extra capacity added in anticipation of future increases in demand for products and services

Capacity efficiency. a measure of how well the available effective capacity is being used to produce the actual output

Capacity gap. the difference between the capacity required and capacity available

Capacity planning. the process of determining the capacity that an operations system will need to meet this demand effectively

Capacity requirements planning (CRP). the process of doing a more detailed comparison of the available capacity and the required capacity, for the medium time frame, by projecting your resource requirements for labor, equipment, and so forth

Capacity utilization. a measure of the extent to which the capacity designed and installed is actually used

Capacity-reservation contract. an agreement where the manufacturer has the option of reserving additional production capacity with the supplier to be exercised in the future as needed

Carrier. a transportation company responsible for transporting goods or people via land, sea, or air

Cash-in-advance. this method enables the seller, or exporter, to avoid all risk and receive payment before the ownership of the goods is transferred to the foreign buyer

Cause-and-effect diagram. a quality management tool that can be used to analyze and identify the root causes of problems in a process, also known as the fishbone diagram

C-chart. an attribute control chart that is used to monitor countable occurrences

Cellular manufacturing layout. a popular hybrid layout in which a self-contained production unit (within the larger plant) is completely responsible for producing a product or process

Centered moving average method. a method for calculating seasonal indices in which moving averages for each season are centered

Center-of-gravity method. a quantitative technique used to determine the location of a single warehouse or distribution center at the center of movement within a geographic area to minimize its distribution costs

Central limit theorem. a theorem that states that as the size of a sample gets larger and larger, its distribution also approaches the normal distribution, even if the underlying population from which the samples were collected is not normally distributed

Certificate of origin. a document that specifies the country in which the goods in a particular shipment were manufactured or processed

Chase strategy. a demand-matching strategy in which production is geared toward producing whatever amount of goods are needed to meet demand

Check sheet. chart used to record and collect quality-related data that helps identify the frequency and timing of problem occurrences

Closed loop MRP system. a system that enables plans to be adjusted according to capacity and other requirements by synchronizing material purchase and component production plans with the master schedule and by providing feedback on manufactured items and materials on hand

Clustering. a phenomenon where several companies in the same industry are located in the same area because of a concentration of critical resources in a particular region

Code of ethics. a specific set of professional behaviors and values including confidentiality, accuracy, privacy, and integrity that all company employees must know and strictly abide

Coefficient of determination. the proportion of variation explained by regression

Collaborative forecasting. the process of gathering information from within and outside of the organization to forecast the demand for a product

Collaborative planning, forecasting, and replenishment (CPFR). a process that enhances the integration and efficiency of supply chains through collaboration between supply chain partners on activities such as demand planning and forecasting, inventory management, and information sharing

Commercial invoice. a customs declaration document provided by an exporter of goods that crosses international borders

Common carrier. a transportation firm hired by the general public for interstate transportation

Common cause variations. variations in quality that arise from random natural differences

Competitive bidding. the process of allowing interested suppliers to review a company's RFP or RFQ electronically and submitting a bid for the job

Competitive strengths. *See* core competencies

Computer-aided design (CAD). part of a larger computer application known as computer-aided engineering (CAE), which refers to the broad range of software that helps engineers design new products electronically rather than drawing by hand

Computer-aided manufacturing (CAM). an application of programmable automation in manufacturing processes that uses computer software and hardware to control machine tools and other related machinery

Computer-aided process planning (CAPP). a technological application that involves the use of computer technology to assist in planning the processes required to manufacture a part or product

Computer-integrated manufacturing (CIM). a technological application in which a manufacturing plant uses computers to control all processes

Concurrent engineering. a new product development approach in which tasks are performed in parallel and every aspect of product development is considered early in the process, also sometimes referred to as simultaneous engineering or integrated product development (IPD)

Consignee. the buyer of goods and receiver of freight shipments

Consignor. the seller of goods

Constraints. the limited availability of resources

Continuous flow process. a process that is selected when very large volumes of a highly standardized product are to be produced

Continuous random variable. a variable whose numerical outcomes can be measured

Continuous review systems. a system in which inventory levels of every item in stock, including its quantity and availability, are monitored and updated continuously (also known as perpetual inventory or fixed order quantity systems)

Contract carrier. a for-hire transportation company that provides transportation for one or a limited number of shippers under a specific contract but does not serve the general public

Contract warehouse. a warehouse that charges clients a fee for leasing their facilities for a longer term where clients have to pay despite whether the space is used

Control chart. a tool used in statistical process control to monitor and control the consistency, or stability, of a process

Core competencies. the activities at which a firm excels or strives to excel

Corner point solution method. an approach in linear programming in which each corner point occurring at the boundaries of the feasible solution space is examined to determine the optimal solution

Corporate social responsibility (CSR). the process of incorporating the interests of the public into a company's core business

Corporate strategy. a strategy formulated by an organization's top managers and board of directors that attempts to address the fundamental question of what industries and markets the organization should enter and compete in

Correlation coefficient. a statistic that measures the strength of the relationship between two variables, and takes on a value between -1 and $+1$

Cost metrics. an assessment of material and labor costs, the costs associated with returns and repairs, interest, rent, facilities, transportation, and storage

Cost of goods sold (COGS). expenses incurred from purchasing the supplies used to make products

Cost of poor quality (COPQ). additional production and material expenses incurred as a result of scrap and rework

Cost performance index (CPI). the earned value divided by the actual, cumulative cost of the work performed to date (EV/AC). This value allows us to calculate the projected budget to completion

Cost-plus contracts. an agreement that allows a supplier to be paid in full for all reasonable expenses incurred up to a preset limit as well as an additional sum so that the supplier realizes a profit on the transaction

Cost-time-profile map (CTP). a map that tracks the money invested over time in a production process

Crashing. the process of speeding up a project's remaining activities to move its completion date forward

Critical path. the sequence of activities in a network that defines the overall length of the project (the longest individual path)

Critical ratio (CR). a priority rule in intermittent process scheduling that specifies an index number that can be calculated for all jobs. The job that has the lowest critical ratio is processed first and completed

Critical success factors (CSFs). strategic factors unique to a specific industry

Critical-to-quality (CTQ). the specific, measurable characteristics of a product or service that customers say are necessary for their satisfaction

Cross docking. a process in which materials from incoming transportation carriers are unloaded and directly loaded on outbound carriers intended for different destinations

Cross-docking warehouse. a warehouse where incoming shipments from various suppliers are sorted and batched and then delivered to buyers, spending little or no time in storage

Cumulative probability distribution. a distribution of probability values that shows that a random variable such as demand has a probability less than or equal to a specified value. Given a column of probability values associated with each value of the random variable, it is computed by adding the probability associated with each demand value to the cumulative probability value in the previous row

Cumulative sum error (CSE). the sum of the differences between the actual and the forecasted demand values

Customer management. the process of interfacing with individuals or companies that buy and use finished products

Customer profitability analysis (CPA). the process of allocating revenue and costs to specific customer segments or individual customers to determine the profitability of those segments or individual customers

Customer-focused supply chain management (CFSCM). a management method in which every supply chain member is linked to the customer, requiring collaborative relationships throughout the supply chain

Customs-house broker. a service provider that oversees the movement of goods through customs and verifies that accompanying documents are complete and accurate

Cycle counting. counting a random sample or subset of inventory in stock in a particular location on a specific day to verify that inventory accuracy rate are not too far off target

Cycle stock. the inventory that a company carries to satisfy its normal cycle of sales orders or production requirements

Cycle time. the time required for the line to produce one unit to achieve an output rate that allows a firm to meet its demand requirements

Cyclical variations. wave-like oscillations in demand about the trend line caused by changes in economic or business cycles, such as boom or recession or as a result of changes in political conditions

Damped trend. a pattern in which the level of demand increases initially and levels off in the long term

Days of inventory in stock. the number of days of inventory a firm has on hand to meet its sales

Decision tree. a technique used for making sequential decisions that allows the decision maker to map each possible decision alternative and probable future events visually to determine the best decision

Decision variables. variables in an LP model such as production levels, purchase quantities, and shipping routes that are under the control of the decision maker

Decisions under certainty. decisions made when the state of nature is known

Decisions under risk. this scenario falls between the two extremes of certainty and uncertainty. The decision maker, although not certain, is aware of the chances, or probabilities, of the various states of nature occurring

Decisions under uncertainty. decisions made when there are not only multiple states of nature but they are also unpredictable and the decision maker cannot even make an educated guess about the chances, or probabilities, of their occurring

Decoupling point. *See* push–pull boundary

Decoupling. a function that enables production to continue temporarily while the production problem at a given process stage is resolved

Degeneracy. a condition that occurs when the solution to a transportation problem has occupied routes (cells) that are less than the (number of origins + the number of destinations − 1)

Delivery safety. the ability of companies to deliver products to customers without loss or damage

Delphi method. a qualitative method that attempts to eliminate or minimize the problem of bias in the opinion of a single expert by using a panel of experts to generate forecasts

Demand forecasting. the process of estimating the demand for a firm's products in the future

Demand management. the process of first determining accurately what the customer wants, and then coordinating the processes and procedures both

within the firm and across its supply chain to meet that demand quickly and efficiently

Demand planning. the process of accurately forecasting the demand for a company's products and services well into the future to give the company and its supply chain partners a basis for all the planning needed to acquire the supplies to meet that demand

Dependence. the idea that an adjustment to one element in a process will have implications for other elements in the same process

Dependent demand. demand for a part or component that depends on the demand for the end product

Dependent or predicted variable. a variable that is affected by an independent or predictor variable

Design capacity. the maximum rate of output achieved by an operation, a process, or a manufacturing or service facility that is producing under ideal conditions

Design for disposal, remanufacturing, and recycling (DFDRR). a process that determines the parts of a product to be designed for refurbishing and reuse, and the parts to be designed that are to be discarded, broken down, and recycled

Design for logistics. the process of designing a product so that it can be transported easily through the supply chain

Design for manufacturing and assembly (DFMA). a process that reduces the number of parts in a product, making it easier to manufacture and assemble and less expensive to produce

Design for reliability (DFR). a process that encompasses the range of tools and practices that describes how, when, and in what order an organization needs to deploy them to design reliable products

Design for supply chain. the process of designing a product so that it matches up well with the capabilities of a firm's supply chain members

Design of experiments (DOE). the process of conducting design experiments and using their statistical results to identify a product's optimum configuration, or design

Design specification limits. numerical maximum and minimum values within which the outputs produced by a process are expected to fall to be considered as having acceptable quality to the customer, also known as tolerance limits

Deterministic estimation. a duration estimation that assumes that sufficient information from historical records or the opinion of experts is available to make this determination with a reasonable degree of accuracy

Devaluation. a reduction in the value of currencies

Direct materials purchase. the purchase of materials that are directly incorporated to the production of finished goods and include most raw materials and components

Direct-shipment design. a transportation network design in which each supplier sends shipments directly to each of the buying firm's locations

Discrete random variable. a variable whose outcomes take on numerical values that can be counted

Diseconomies of scale. an increase in the volume of output beyond a point at which the cost per unit increases

Disintermediation. process when an upstream supply chain member such as a manufacturer sells directly to the final consumer, bypassing distributors and retailers

Disruptive innovation. a product or service that creates new and often unexpected markets through offering a totally new set of value propositions

Distribution requirements planning (DRP). a system used by companies to systematically plan and control

their logistics and product distribution activities through generating a time-phased inventory replenishment plan to manage and minimize inventories in the supply chain

Documentary collections. a mode of payment in which a bank used by the seller sends the required shipment documents to the buyer's bank, along with instructions for payment

Drum-buffer-rope (DBR). a planning and scheduling method that assumes that within any manufacturing system there are a limited number of scarce resources and that they control the overall output of that system

Dummy demand destinations. a fictitious demand destination created to arrive at a balanced transportation problem (i.e., total demand = total supply)

Dummy supply sources. a fictitious supply source created to arrive at a balanced transportation problem (i.e., total demand = total supply) e = 2.7183 (a constant which is the base of the natural logarithms)

Earliest due date. a priority rule that ranks jobs according to their due dates, and the job that has the earliest due date is processed first and completed

Early finish time (EF). the earliest possible date on which an activity can be completed. Early finish is defined as ES + activity duration = EF

Early start time (ES). the earliest possible date on which an activity can start, based on the beginning and ending times for previous activities in the network

Earned value (EV). the real budgeted cost, or "value," of the work actually performed to date

Earned value management (EVM). a method to calculate the value generated by the project as well as the budgeted and actual costs at a certain point time

Economic order quantity (EOQ). the simplest model for continuous review systems that is used to determine the optimum quantity of materials or product to order from a supplier. It induce buyers to increase their order sizes

Economic production quantity (EPQ). a model used to determine how much of a product the firm is to produce and when

Economic value. the traditional bottom line of economic performance

Economies of scale. a decrease in the cost per unit of output as the volume of output increases

Effective capacity. the capacity that can be achieved given the actual changes in product mixture, machines, and equipment that require periodic maintenance, scheduling changes, and workers who take time off for lunch, absences, and other needs

Effectiveness. how well the task accomplished its intended purpose

Effectiveness metrics. the evaluation of the percentage of orders delivered on time and customer satisfaction metrics, such as number of customer complaints and percentage of returned items

Efficiency metrics. the evaluation of inventory turnover or days of inventory on hand, as well as capacity and capital usage (ROI or cash flow)

Efficiency. how economically resources, particularly time and money, were used to complete an activity

Electronic data interchange (EDI). technology that facilitates a seamless flow of information to improve the exchange of standardized documents such as customer orders, shipment information, and bill payments between computer systems

Electronic service quality (e-SQ). the level of success or failure of companies that deliver services electronically

Engineer-to-order (ETO). a method in which products are designed, manufactured, and assembled to the customer's specifications from start to finish

Enterprise resource planning (ERP). an information system that integrates information across all departments of an organization, as well as facilitates and manages the flow of information across all functions within an enterprise and to its external stakeholders

Environmental value. the value created by sustainable practices

Error sum of squares. a measure of the variation not explained by the regression model but resulting from other factors or variables

Exception management. the continuous monitoring of shortages or sudden changes in the quality of materials

Expected regret. the expected value of regret associated with each decision

Expected value (EV). the weighted average of the values of all possible outcomes of the decision, or the average payoff that would be realized if the decision were to be repeated many times

Expected value of perfect information (EVPI). the difference between the expected value of the decision with perfect information and the expected value of the decision without perfect information

Expert opinion. the intuition or the experienced judgment of experts

Exponential growth/decline. examples of nonlinear trends

Exponential smoothing. a forecasting method in which the next period's forecast is a weighted average of all previous observations that gives progressively less weight to older observations

Export management company. a service provider that helps companies that lack the resources or expertise to ship their products abroad themselves

Export packers. a service provider that provides the necessary packaging services for export shipments

Export trading company. a service provider that helps domestic companies locate potential importers of their products and provides services such as preparing export documents that meet the foreign government's import requirements and arranging for transportation

External failure costs. the costs that result from defects or quality problems after the product or service has been delivered to the customer

External logistics system. the collection, transportation, and distribution of goods between suppliers and the plant, as well as between the plant and consumers

External setups. work that can be completed outside of the process and does not require machinery to be stopped or the process to be shut down

External variation. product variations caused by environmental conditions, such as temperature, humidity, or dust

Factor rating method. the process of evaluating the various location alternatives by rating relevant factors

Fifth-party logistics providers (5PL). e-business solutions, including developing information systems for managing and tracking shipments through the supply chain

Fill rate. the percentage of customer orders that can be satisfied from inventory in stock

Financial planning. evaluating the financial feasibility of the demand and supply plans developed in the previous stages of S&OP planning in terms of return on assets (ROA), revenue, profit margin, and working capital requirements

Finite capacity scheduling (FCS). computerized short-term scheduling that allows the scheduler to make instantaneous changes to the schedule

Finite loading. the process of setting limits on the amount of load assigned to each work center per period

Firm planned orders. orders that are not changed automatically when conditions change, usually requiring approval from a senior manager

First come, first served. a priority rule that specifies the job that arrived first at a work center or machine will be processed first and completed

Five S (5S). a model for showing how to implement lean practices in any business operation, including (a) sort and separate, (b) simplify and straighten, (c) shine, (d) standardize, and (e) sustain

Fixed automation. the process of producing a product or component in a fixed sequence of operations

Fixed-period ordering. lot-sizing technique in which orders for the MRP items are placed at fixed periods

Fixed-position layout. a layout type in which the product remains stationary in the plant

Fixed-price contract. an agreement in which set prices are not subject to any change regardless of changes in the external environment

Flexible automation. the process of using high-cost, general-purpose machines to produce a variety of products in low volumes or in small batches

Flexible manufacturing system (FMS). a processing method that can produce parts, allow changes to be made to products being manufactured, and handle varying levels of production

Flexible time fence. portion of the master schedule time horizon that is farthest out in the future and changes can be easily accommodated

Flow time. the time required to produce an item completely if only one unit is being produced at a time

Flow-shop scheduling. a form of line process scheduling in which many scheduling decisions are predetermined when the production systems were designed

Forecasting errors. the deviations of actual demand from the forecast

Forward pass. the process of fully labeling the activity nodes in a network to determine the earliest times each activity can begin and the earliest it can be completed

Forward scheduling. a scheduling process used to determine the approximate completion time for each job and the capacity required in each time period by beginning with the current date for those jobs that have known processing requirements and then loading the jobs forward in time

Fourth-party logistics providers (4PL). a company that integrates and assembles the resources, capabilities, and technology not only for its own organization but also for other 3PL providers to design, build, and implement comprehensive supply chain solutions

Frozen time fence. the portion of the master schedule in which no changes to the schedule can be accommodated unless a senior executive requests such changes

Frozen windows. specific time periods in which production levels cannot be changed

Fulfillment centers. firms hired by large companies to handle their order fulfillment process to save time and focus on their core business

Full truckload (FTL). the transportation of freight that fills the full delivery-load capacity of a truck

Functional strategies. Strategies that coordinate and integrate the activities and resources within each functional area of a company

Gantt chart. a diagram that links project activities to a schedule, usually a calendar

Geographic information system (GIS). a computerized system that can store, relate, and display data collected from a physical environment or a geographical location

Global freight forwarder. a service provider that performs international shipment functions

Global platform. a set of standards and practices that allows companies geographically dispersed around the globe to share information, developments, products and components, payment methods, and other relevant information

Global product development (GPD). the process of introducing innovative new products, using an integrated, collaborative global team of engineers, that exceed customer expectations while maximizing the financial and operational productivity of the product development process

Global sales and operations planning. a consolidated sales and operations planning approach that can respond to frequently changing global supply and market conditions

Green Belt. employees who have received Six Sigma training and typically solve lower level quality problems, such as reducing minor process variations

Group technology (GT). a parts coding and classification system in which parts or products with similar characteristics are grouped into families

Hedge inventory. inventory purchased in advance to guard against uncertainties in pricing

Histograms. a vertical bar chart that shows the frequency of occurrences of values

Historical life-cycle analogy. a method used to forecast demand for a new product or service that is similar to existing products

Holding costs. the costs associated with holding (carrying) inventory

House of quality (HOQ). a planning diagram that resembles a house used for capturing accurate and verifiable data from the customer in the first phase of the QFD process

Hurwicz criterion. a decision-making approach that attempts to find a compromise between the two extremes posed by the pessimistic maximin criterion and the optimistic maximax criterion by applying a certain percentage weight (α) to the most optimistic outcome, and ($1 - \alpha$) to the most pessimistic outcome

Hybrid layout. a layout type that combine the advantages of the three basic layout types, also known as a combination layout

Import quota. another type of trade barrier that limits the quantity of certain goods that can be imported to a country in a given period of time

Inbound portion. elements of a supply chain that consist of local or foreign suppliers of product ideas, designs, basic raw materials and components, transportation links, and warehouses that end with the internal operations of the company

Incrementalism. the idea that improvements may not come from any one big fix but from a steady stream of small adjustments

Independent demand. an item whose demand is unrelated to the demand of any other product or item

Independent events. components that, when working or failing, in no way affect the probability that another will work or fail

Independent or predictor variable. a variable that, when changed, causes an effect on a dependent or predicted variable.

Indirect materials purchase. the purchase of materials not directly used in the finished product but that support their production

Industrial Robot. a versatile machine that can perform routine tasks such as cutting and boring, welding, assembly, and materials handling without any human intervention

Infinite loading. the process of loading all the work centers without regard to the actual capacity available in the work center

Innovation. the process of implementing new ideas or changes that create value for customers

Input–output control. regulating inputs to a work center in relation to output and available capacity so that the queues and waiting times of jobs can be managed and kept under control

Inspection. a quality control technique used to determine whether products, processes, and services conform to quality by measuring, examining, and testing them against specified requirements

Integrated logistics management (ILM). the practices used to control the movement of products (and the associated costs) so there is a continuous and uninterrupted flow of materials and products from suppliers to manufacturers to the final consumers

Intermodal transportation. a newer mode of transportation in which freight stored in containers is carried by two or more other modes of transportation

Internal failure costs. the costs that result from defects or quality problems before the product or service is delivered to the customer

Internal logistics system. all the management and movement of materials within a manufacturing facility, such as raw materials and parts, work-in-process inventory, and finished goods

Internal setups. activities that require machinery to be stopped or the process to be shut down for the setup work to be completed

Internal variation. product variations caused by the wear and tear of production equipment as it ages

International Organization for Standardization (ISO). The world's largest developer and publisher of international standards, created in 1947 and based in Geneva, Switzerland. The ISO has representatives from various national standards organizations that reach a consensus on the international standards prior to their publication.

Inventory status file. contains the records of all items in inventory, including on-hand inventory and scheduled receipts

Inventory turnover. a measure of how frequently a business sells its inventory in a given time period

Irregular variations. unusual variations in demand caused by uncommon factors

Iso-cost line method. a method by which parallel cost lines are plotted in the LP graphical solution approach to determine the least cost solution to LP problems with cost minimization objective

Iso-profit line method. a method by which parallel profit lines are plotted in the LP graphical solution approach to determine the maximum profit solution to LP problems with profit maximization objective

Jidoka. a Japanese term meaning quality at the source; a production philosophy of doing it right the first time and stopping production should something go wrong

Job flow time. the total length of time that a job spends at a work center or shop from the point of arrival to the point at which the job leaves the work center or shop

Job-shop process. a process that is selected when the processing requirements are intermittent and different for each product because it is unique and produced in low volumes or sporadically

Johnson's rule. a method for sequencing N jobs through two machines, processes, or work centers in the same order to minimize makespan

Joint venture. a strategic alliance in which two firms create an independent company by sharing their resources and capabilities

Just-in-time (JIT). a system in which customer demand, rather than sales forecasts, dictates production levels

Kaizen. a Japanese term for continuous improvement of the quality of a firm's products, services, and processes

Kanban system. a manual control system that uses visual signals (cards or Kanbans) to tell workers when it is time to get or make more of something

Keiretsu network. a strategic alliance common among Japanese businesses in which manufacturers and their suppliers of raw materials and components form a coalition

Lagging strategy. the process of increasing capacity only when there is a sizeable increase in demand

Laplace criterion. a decision-making approach used when the probabilities of the states of nature are unknown and assumed as equal. The different decision alternatives should be evaluated using the expected value of their payoffs

Late finish time (LF). the latest possible date an activity can be completed without delaying the project's completion. Late finish is defined as LS + activity duration = LF

Late start time (LS). the latest possible date that an activity may begin without delaying the project completion

Layout. the physical arrangement of work and storage areas, departments, or equipment within the confines of some physical structure such as a plant, office, warehouse, or a service facility

Lead time. the total time it takes a supplier to both produce a product and deliver it after it's been ordered

Leading indicators. variables such as the number of housing starts in the economy, number of unemployment insurance claims, inventory changes, and stock prices used to track cyclical fluctuations

Leading strategy. the process of increasing capacity in anticipation of future increases in demand for products or services

Lean manufacturing. a management philosophy that originated in the 1990s based on Toyota's production system that states that any activity or process that does not add value to the product or service is a waste and, therefore, should be eliminated

Lean philosophy. *See* lean manufacturing

Lean production. *See* lean manufacturing

Lean Six Sigma. an approach that draws on the knowledge, methods, and tools of both the lean and Six Sigma approaches, derived from decades of operational improvement, research, and implementation, extends beyond cost cutting and efficiency to growth and effectiveness, and is ideally suited for this step change in target and scope.

Learning curves. a principle that shows that as the production rate for an item doubles, the processing time per unit of that item decreases by a constant percentage

Learning rate. the assumption that as production doubles, the per unit production time declines by a constant percentage

Least-squares method. a method used to draw the line of best fit in linear regression analysis

Less-than-truckload (LTL). the transportation of freight that does not fill the full delivery-load capacity of a truck

Letter of credit (LC). a document issued by a bank that authorizes the exporter (seller) to draw a specified sum of money, usually after the receipt by the bank of certain documents such as bill of lading, invoice, packing list, or certificate of origin as proof of delivery within a specified time

Level capacity plan. the process of producing products at a steady rate and then storing them until they are demanded

Level schedule. a schedule stability method where materials are pulled through the assembly line at a steady rate to allow production activities to respond efficiently to the pull signals

Level strategy. maintaining constant production and workforce levels and using inventories to bridge the gap between demand and production (supply). Also known as level scheduling

Life cycle. the stages of a project's development. conceptualization, planning, execution, and termination

Limited (finite) population. examples of a limited population source may be the number refrigerators to be repaired by a repair technician or the number of patients assigned to a nurse in the gynecology ward of a hospital. The population is limited in the sense that the number of patients that might need care at any given time cannot exceed the number of patients assigned to that nurse

Line balancing. assigning production tasks in such a way that the time required to complete them is approximately equal across workstations

Linear decision rule. an optimization approach that can be used to create aggregate plans in which the total production cost is represented by a single quadratic cost function, which is minimized using calculus

Linear programming. an optimization technique in which the objective and constraint functions are linear and the variables are continuous

Linear regression analysis. a predictive technique that models the relationship between a dependent variable and one or more independent variables

Linear relationship. the effect of changing a decision variable is proportional to its magnitude

Linear trend multiplicative method. a method in which the seasonal indices are expressed as percentages and the combined forecast is expressed as percentage adjustments of the underlying linear trend

Linear trend. a pattern in which demand either increases or decreases in successive periods

Line-haul cost. the cost of moving goods from the point of origin to the final destination point

Little's law. a simple and commonly used theorem in queuing theory. It makes very few assumptions except that the system is at a steady state

Load. the amount of planned work scheduled and actual work assigned to a production facility for a specific period of time

Logistics. the activities needed to transport, warehouse, and distribute products

Logistics outsourcing. a practice in which third-party logistics providers perform some or all of the logistics functions for a company

Longest processing time. a priority rule that ranks jobs according to their processing times and the job with the longest processing time will be processed first and completed

Lost sales. losses in revenue that occur when a customer doesn't buy an item if that item is not in stock

Lot size. the predetermined quantity of an item that is either manufactured or purchased from a supplier

Lot splitting. the division of a single lot into two or more sublots and the simultaneous processing of each sublot on identical (or very similar) work centers as separate lots

Lot-for-lot. lot-sizing technique used for items with discontinuous and sporadic demand; it is the simplest of the variable-order quantity techniques in which the amount ordered or produced is the same as the demand requirements for the MRP items

Maintainability. the ease with which an equipment or system can be repaired or serviced

Makespan. the total time needed to complete a group of jobs starting with the first job until the completion of the last job

Make-to-order (MTO). a manufacturing method in which products are manufactured only after receiving a customer's order

Make-to-stock (MTS). a manufacturing method used for products that typically require little or no customization, are produced in large volumes, and are stored as inventory for future use

Management coefficients model. a formal decision model based on past managerial performance and experience. The model uses the technique of regression analysis of past production decisions made by managers

Manufacturing resource planning (MRP II). the coordination of all activities related to production by providing consistent data to all participants involved in various stages of the production process

Manufacturing supermarket. inventory stocking location right on the shop floor

Mass customization process. a process that allows a firm to produce customized products at the speed, volume, cost, and quality of repetitive or continuous flow process configurations

Mass customization. the mass production of individually customized products through the use of components assembled in several different configurations

Master Black Belt. employees who have received the most statistical Six Sigma training and serve as in-house coaches to Black Belts and Green Belts, checking to see that Six Sigma efforts are applied consistently across an organization

Master production schedule (MPS). individual production quantities of the end items to be produced at various periods of a given planning horizon

Master scheduling. the process that determines the quantities of each end item to be produced in specific periods during a specific planning horizon. The master schedule is essential for all operations planning and control decisions. The master schedule sets the production quantities required to meet demand from every possible source in an organization, such as final customers, warehouses, and requirements from other plants in a multi-plant environment

Matching strategy. the process of increasing capacity in small increments to keep pace with increases in demand

Material requirements planning (MRP). a computer-based system that translates the end item requirements of the master schedule into subassemblies, components, and raw materials. Given the due date, MRP works backward by using lead times and other information to determine when and how much of the materials to order

Matrix least cost method. an initial feasible solution to the transportation problem is obtained by allocating shipments beginning with the route that has the lowest unit cost of transportation

Maximax criterion. a decision-making approach used when the decision maker is optimistic about the future events and their outcomes, identifies the maximum payoff associated with each decision, and chooses the maximum of the maximum payoffs

Maximin criterion. a decision-making approach used when the negative impact of making the wrong decision is so high that he or she chooses that alternative that guarantees at least the minimum payoff

Mean absolute deviation (MAD). the average of the sum of the absolute differences between the actual and the forecasted demand values

Mean absolute percentage error (MAPE). a measure of the absolute error as a percentage of the actual demand

Mean chart. a control chart to monitor if the average value of the process variable is around target

Mean squared error (MSE). the average of the sum of the squared differences between the actual and the forecasted demand values

Mean time between failures (MTBF). the reliability of a product or component expressed as the average length of time elapsed before the product or component fails

Mean time to repair (MTTR). a quantitative metric for maintainability

Milk run. a delivery system in which a single truck picks up shipments from several suppliers and the goods are delivered to a single location

Minimax regret criterion. a decision-making approach that attempts to minimize the regret, or loss, associated with making a nonoptimal decision

Mixed strategy. a hybrid strategy that combines the advantages of both the level strategy and the chase strategy, enabling firms to select options that influence both the demand for and supply of their products

Mixed-model production cycle. a production method where the same mixture of products is produced every day in small quantities

Modular design. an approach in which independently created units called *modules* can be combined with others and easily rearranged, replaced, or interchanged to create different products

Monte Carlo simulation. a probabilistic simulation technique that involves selecting numbers randomly from a known probability distribution to be used in simulation trials

Moving average. a short-term time series forecasting method in which the average of the most recent demand periods are used to predict demand in the future period

MRP explosion. the process by which the MRP system calculates the gross and net requirements of all components and materials at each level of the product structure tree

Muda. any wasteful activity that does not add value or is unproductive

Multichannel marketing systems. systems that allow customers to purchase products and have them delivered in different ways

Multi-echelon inventory systems. a system in which optimum levels of inventory are determined and updated continuously across the supply chain network based on the demand variability, lead times, delays, and service levels at the higher levels in the supply chain

Multiple linear regression. a predictive technique that models the relationship between a dependent variable and several independent variables

Multiple optimum solutions. every combination of values of the decision variables that falls on that segment of the constraint line that just touches the feasible solution region in the LP graphical solution method

Multiple-channel or multiple-server queuing model. waiting line systems in which service is provided to customers with multiple servers

Multiple-sourcing strategy. a plan to contract with several suppliers to ensure that backup supplies are available

Multiplicative model. a model of combining trends and seasonal components in which the seasonal indices are expressed as percentages and the combined forecast is expressed as percentage adjustments of the underlying trend

Mura. unevenness in the production process, out-of-balance workflows, and uneven workloads

Muri. waste and decreased productivity that result from the unreasonable work managers impose on people and machines because of the poor design of systems

Muther's grid. a visual layout representation that shows a relationship rating in which symbols or letters represent the relationships between departments

Naïve approach. a forecasting method in which it is assumed that the demand in the next period will be the same as it is in the current period

Negative exponential distribution. a probability distribution that describes the time between events in a process in which events occur continuously and independently at a constant average rate

Negotiation. a process in which a buyer and supplier bargain on the contractual terms of a purchase, such as its price, payment terms, and delivery

Nervousness. instability in the MRP system

Net-change system. a system in which replanning is done continuously, whenever changes occur in the MRP records

New product development (NPD). the overall process of strategy, organization, concept generation, product and marketing plan creation and evaluation, and commercialization of a new product

Nonlinear trend. a pattern in which demand either increased or decreases irregularly

Northwest corner rule. involves first allocating shipping units at the northwest (top left-hand) corner of the transportation matrix and then proceeding systematically by making allocations of shipping units to cells along either a row or column until the bottom right-hand corner of the matrix is reached (that is, we make enough allocations of shipping units to reach an initial feasible solution)

Numerically controlled (NC) machines. machines that are programmed with a specific set of instructions that tell the machines the details of the operations to be performed

Objective function. the objective of an LP problem expressed mathematically

Offshoring. sourcing from overseas or getting work done in a foreign country

Online reverse auctions. an e-procurement solution for selecting suppliers in which suppliers compete for the buyer's business by offering their products or services at lower and lower prices

Open account. a payment method in which goods are shipped and delivered before payment is made

Open loop MRP system. developing MRP plans and schedules by assuming infinite capacity and on-time, correct delivery of materials ordered by the suppliers

Open office layout. a layout type that opens up the traditional workplace by lowering or eliminating cubicle walls, relocating private offices, and taking advantage of mobile technology by creating alternative workspaces in alcoves, bistro areas, lounges, cafeterias, and outdoor plazas

Operations management (OM). the process of managing the system of designing, producing, and delivering goods or services that add value throughout the supply chain and benefit the final consumer

Operations strategies. strategies that use an organization's resources efficiently to gain a competitive edge in the marketplace by achieving key operations objectives related to product quality, delivery, flexibility, cost, service, and innovation. These strategies should outline the vision and road map for a firm's operational decision-making

Operations strategy. a strategy that uses the company's operational resources effectively to help it achieve a competitive advantage.

Optimal stocking level (S_o). the optimum inventory level in stock for single-period inventory systems

Order cycle time consistency. a metric for reliable customer service

Order delivery completeness. the ability of a company to deliver the orders placed by customers fully and completely

Order fill rate. the percentage of customer orders that can be fully and completely filled from items in stock

Order fulfillment lead time. the average time it takes from the submission of a customer's purchase order until the company delivers the order

Order fulfillment. the process by which a company responds to customer orders

Order loser. a qualifying criterion a firm fails to meet

Order qualifier. a competitive criterion (core competence) that must be present in a product for it to be a viable competitor in the marketplace

Order winner. a competitive criterion (core competence) of a product that causes a customer to choose it instead of a competitor's product

Ordering costs. administrative costs related to determining an order quantity, preparing purchase invoices, inspecting goods received for quality and quantity, and moving goods for temporary storage

Outbound portion. elements of a supply chain that begin when the organization delivers its output to its immediate customers in the supply chain and may consist of globally dispersed wholesalers, retailers, distribution centers, and transportation companies, the consumer, and companies that facilitate the return of products or their disposal

Outsourcing. contracting with a third party or an external company to manufacture a good or deliver a service

$$P(x) = \frac{e^{-\lambda} \lambda^x}{x!}$$

$P(x) = $ $P(x) = $ Probability of x arrivals

Package or parcel carriers. common carriers that specialize in shipments weighing less than 150 pounds

Parameter design. an approach to design that focuses on determining the optimal design of a product and the processes used to produce it so as to minimize variations

Pareto chart. a graph that helps identify the relatively few, but most critical, causes of problems

Pareto chart. a vertical bar chart where the bars are arranged in decreasing height from left to right; the height of an individual bar represents how often a particular problem has occurred

Part-period balancing (PPB). lot-sizing technique in which both order (or production) quantity and time between orders (or setups) are allowed to vary. The focus of this approach is to select the number of periods covered by an order or setup such that the holding cost over the covered horizon is approximately equal to the ordering or setup cost

Payoff. the positive or negative values (monetary or nonmonetary) a decision maker places on each combination of actual decisions and states of nature

P-chart. an attribute control chart that is used to monitor the fraction, or proportion, of defects or errors in a product or service

P-diagram. a diagram that identifies the various factors that have an effect on the design and performance of a product or process

Pegging capability. can identify the particular parent item that has generated the component requirements for that item

Periodic review systems. a system in which inventory is physically counted periodically and all reordering takes place at these intervals (also referred to as periodic inventory systems or fixed order interval systems)

Physical count. determining the real quantity of inventory that is physically available on a periodic basis

Physical simulation. the act of duplicating the operation of a real-world process or system over time using physical objects to replace the actual objects

Plan, Do, Study, and Act (PDSA) cycle. a visual, circular representation of total quality management that illustrates the never-ending process of continuous improvement

Planned order releases. reports that specify when an order quantity for an item will be released to a vendor or an in-house production facility

Planned order schedules. schedules that delineate the quantity and timing of future material orders

Planned purchase order. a purchase order for purchases to be made on approximate dates at specified quantities when inventories run low.

Planned value (PV). a cost estimate of the budgeted resources scheduled across the project's life cycle (cumulative baseline)

Point of postponement (POP). the point that divides the supply chain into the supplier side and the customer side

Points of indifference. the intersection of two lines on a breakeven analysis graph that show the point at which total costs of two processes are identical

Poisson distribution. the mathematical expression for the Poisson distribution is given by:

$P(x) = $

where

$P(x) = $ Probability of x arrivals
$x = $ number of arrivals per unit of time
$\lambda = $ Expected or average arrival rate
$e = 2.7183$ (a constant which is the base of the natural logarithms)

Poka yoke. a Japanese term that means "fail-safing" or "mistake-proofing," referring to any mechanism or device that can help an equipment operator avoid mistakes in a manufacturing process.

Portfolio planning. a channel alignment strategy in which a company signs long-term contracts with one or two suppliers

Precedence diagramming. sometimes called *network diagramming*, the process of creating a chart that shows precedence relationships among project's activities and indicates how they should logically be coordinated with one another

Precedence relationships. the relationship between two or more tasks that requires certain tasks to be done before others

Prevention costs. the costs incurred to prevent defects and errors from occurring before manufacturing the product or delivering the service

Primary packaging. the material that covers and holds the product and is in direct contact with its contents

Priority rules. simple decision rules that are used to select jobs for the next operation to control the flow of work as jobs progress through a single process, machine, or work center

Private warehouse. a warehouse owned and operated by firms producing or owning the goods

Probabilistic estimation. a duration estimation that assigns probabilities to a range of time estimates for each activity

Process. a collection of interrelated tasks that convert specific inputs into specific outputs

Process batch. the lot-size quantity of a product processed at a work center

Process capability analysis. a technique used to determine whether a process is able to meet a set of design specification limits, or normal level of variations, that reflect the customer's requirements for a product or service

Process capability index (C_p). a measure of how well a procees meets its specification limits

Process centering capability index (C_{pk}). a measure of how well the process is centered between the design specification limits

Process chart. a diagram that uses graphics to show all activities related to a process, including its inputs and outputs, decision points such as approvals and exceptions, and any cross-functional relationships

Process control chart. a graphic used to monitor outputs from a process to determine that the process is operating within established control limits

Process design. the most cost-effective way to achieve the transformation of inputs to outputs to produce goods or services that satisfy customers' needs and achieve the firm's sustainability goals while accommodating the firm's technological and managerial constraints

Process flowchart. a graphical representation of the steps in a process and its flow

Process layout. a layout type that is used when a firm produces low volumes of products using job-shop or batch production processes, often referred to as a functional layout

Process selection. the decisions of selecting the kind of process that can give a firm a competitive advantage in terms of speed to market, responsiveness to customers, and cost savings

Process simulation. a technique that provides a dynamic view of a process using computers, multiple inputs, work centers, and processing techniques to help operations managers look at the variability of a process under different conditions

Process strategy. the strategy a firm opts to take in producing goods and services determined by the availability and mixture of labor, equipment, and automation

Product development cycle time. the time it takes to conceptualize a new good or service, produce it, and make it available to customers

Product layout. a layout type that is used for repetitive or continuous flow processes used to produce a highly standardized product with high and constant demand, also referred to as a straight-line layout

Product life-cycle management (PLCM). a marketing concept that refers to managing the business side of the product during its lifecycle, particularly its costs and sales performance

Product lifecycle management (PLM). a strategic, company-wide business approach that spans all aspects of a product's life cycle and supply chain, focusing on the engineering aspects of a product throughout its useful life

Product platform. a set of subsystems and components that form a common structure from which a family of products can be efficiently developed and produced

Product profiling. a way to evaluate the alignment of the needs of a company's markets with its processes through identifying the key product and service dimensions of a market to uncover misalignments that can occur over time

Product structure tree. a way to represent the BOM file that shows the product hierarchy and the explosion into its parts

Productivity. the ratio of outputs (goods and services) produced to the inputs used

Productivity index. the ratio of productivity measured in a particular time period to the productivity measured in a base period

Program evaluation and review technique (PERT). a project scheduling technique that uses probabilities by applying a weighted average of optimistic, pessimistic, and most likely estimates to derive an expected duration for a project

Project. a unique venture with a beginning and an end, conducted by people to meet established goals within certain cost, schedule, and quality parameters

Project charter. a document that identifies the project's objective, expected timeline, budget, scope, and the key personnel involved in the effort

Project management. the application of knowledge, skills, tools, and techniques to project activities to meet the project requirements

Project process. a process that is selected when the product is unique and typically produced one at a time to the customer's specifications

Project risk. any event that can negatively affect the viability of a project based on the formula:

$$\text{Project Risk} = (\text{Probability of Event}) \times (\text{Consequences of Event})$$

Project scheduling. the process of converting a project's goals into a logical method for completing them on time

Project success. a project's success is evaluated by the elements that characterize it. These elements are time (adherence to schedule), cost (adherence to budget), quality, and customer satisfaction

Public warehouse. a warehouse that charges clients a certain fee to store their goods, depending on the volume of warehouse space used and any additional warehouse services that the clients desire

Pull systems. systems in which the product or service is only produced after it is ordered

Purchase costs. money paid to an upstream supplier for materials or goods purchased

Purchase order. a form that includes the terms and conditions specified in the contract between the buyer and supplier and authorizes the supplier to produce and ship the item and send the invoice to the buying company afterward

Push systems. systems in which services or products are produced based on forecasts

Push–pull boundary. the interface between the parts of a supply chain that can be managed using a push approach and the parts that can be managed as a pull system

Quadruple constraint. a modern iteration of triple constraints that considers the goal of satisfying a customer or client. The elements of quadruple constraint are time, cost, quality, and customer satisfaction

Qualitative method. a forecasting method based on intuition, judgment, or informed opinions of experts in the industry, used if no measurable, reliable, historical, or statistical data are available

Quality. a product's fitness for use depending on the price the customer is willing to pay for it

Quality assurance (QA). a set of procedures to improve a product's quality or a service's quality before it is delivered

Quality circle. a concept introduced by Kaoru Ishikawa in 1962, which advocates volunteer groups of employees meeting regularly to identify and solve quality and production problems related to their work

Quality control (QC). a process to monitor quality of a product or service after it is produced or delivered

Quality function deployment. a method that translates customers' wants and needs into product or service features, to prioritize those features, and to set development targets for the product or service

Quantitative method. a forecasting method based on measurable, historical data and evidence that shows past demand is indicative of its future demand

Quantity discounts. price reductions designed to induce buyers to increase their order sizes

Quantity-flexibility contract. an agreement in which the buyer has the flexibility to change the quantity purchased based on the buyer's updated demand forecasts for the product

Queue discipline. the order in which customers waiting in line receive service at the facility

Queue. a certain number of customers waiting for service at a facility

Queuing theory. a part of an operations manager's toolbox in making business decisions about resources needed to provide a service, and it has many applications. It is used in analysis and design of waiting lines in grocery stores, hospitals, telecommunications, factories, retail stores, and offices

Radio frequency identification (RFID). technology that allows tags attached to product packages, pallets, boxes, or containers to transmit information via radio waves to readers, allowing companies to wirelessly track inventory

Random numbers. a sequence of numbers that is uniformly distributed over a defined interval or range, for which it is not possible to predict their future values based on their past or current values

Random variations. all other variations in demand not accounted for by any of the four classifications of trend, seasonality, cycle, and irregular variations

Range chart. a control chart that monitors the variability within samples

Range of feasibility. the limited range over which the shadow price remains constant

Range of optimality. the range of values of the objective function within which the optimal values of the decision variables will not change

Rapid prototyping. quickly creating a miniature version of a product or a mock-up of a product using new technology based on methods that are designed to create virtual reality games

Redundancy. the duplication of critical components, by which duplicate systems operate in parallel with the original component

Redundant constraints. constraints in an LP problem that do not affect the boundaries of the feasible solution region

Regenerative system. a system in which the updating or replanning of the MRP records is performed periodically, most commonly every week

Regression sum of squares. a measure of the difference between the mean Y and the predicted or computed value of Y using regression

Relationship rating. a technique developed by Richard Muther used to design new layouts or change old ones based on qualitative criteria

Reliability. the probability that a component, product, or system can perform its intended function over a period of time under a given set of normal operating conditions of its use

Reorder point. a predetermined level of inventory that signals when a new order is to be placed to replenish it

Repetitive process. a process that is selected when a high volume of standardized products needs to be produced

Request for proposal (RFP). a document prepared by a buying company and sent to potential suppliers detailing the specifications for the product being purchased, its quality requirements, delivery and service requirements, evaluation criteria, pricing, and shipping and payment terms

Request for quotation (RFQ). *See* request for proposal

Reservation systems. a scheduling system for service organizations that uses computerized systems to maximize customer satisfaction by smoothing out demand for their services in any given time

Revenue-sharing contract. an agreement where the supplier and the buyer or manufacturer share the revenue generated from the sale of the products

Reverse engineering. a process in which a firm dismantles a competitors' existing products to see how they work and whether they can be improved

Reverse logistics. activities such as managing product returns, repairing and remanufacturing products, and disposing or recycling of packaging material

Risk management. the process of anticipating and figuring out how to respond to a project's risks prior to beginning the project

Robust product design. an approach to product or service design in which minor variations caused by various factors in a production process do not adversely affect how a product performs

Rolling schedule. updating the schedule when moving forward in time by capturing the impact of actual transactions on the master schedule from one period to the next

Rough-cut capacity planning (RCCP). the process of doing a rough check of production plans and schedules to determine whether the required capacity and the available capacity are in balance

Route sheet. a document that describes the sequence of different operations, places, or people involved in a process

Runout time. calculations that are used to determine a schedule that allocates the capacity of the line among the several products

Safety lead time. a strategy to combat uncertainty associated with supply or production lead times

Safety stock. the minimal level of inventory that a company seeks to have on hand at all times to act as a buffer against the mismatch between forecasted and actual demand

Sales and operations planning (S&OP). the integration of customer-focused marketing plans for new and existing products with supply chain management (also known as aggregate planning)

Sales carbon operations planning. a process that incorporates sustainability into S&OP, intended not only to cover carbon emissions but also the management and reduction of the economic and environmental impact of greenhouse gas emissions

Sampling distribution. how the values in a sample are distributed on the chart

Scatter diagram. a graph that shows the extent and direction of the relationship between two variables

Schedule performance index (SPI). the earned value to date divided by the planned value of work scheduled to be performed (EV/PV). This value allows us to calculate the project's schedule to completion

Scope creep. a situation in which project specifications are continually modified or improved as new ideas emerge or new technical solutions become possible

Scope management. the process of determining the best way in which the project's goals can be accomplished given its constraints

S-curve. the typical shape of a project's status graphically plotted against time

Seasonal indices. factors that capture the seasonal contribution to demand in each period during the year

Seasonal variations. periodic, fairly short-term fluctuations in demand often caused by human activities or weather

Secondary packaging. outer wrappings that envelop and protect primary packages

Sensitivity analysis. analysis a decision maker conducts to determine how sensitive a decision alternative is to changes in the probability values of the states of nature

Sensitivity or post-optimality analysis. the determination in the LP technique of how sensitive the current optimal solution is to changes in the input parameter values

Sequencing. the process of determining the exact order or priority of job processing

Service blueprint. a tool for analyzing processes that have high service content by specifying how the service will be provided

Service failure. the result of an organization's failure to meet customers' expectations for service performance

Service level. the probability that the demand during the lead time will be met from the inventory in stock

Service rate. the number of customers served per unit of time

Service recovery. an effort by the organization to appease dissatisfied customers such as offering them refunds, credits, discounts, apologies, or free items or services

Service requirements planning (SRP). MRP principles applied to determine requirements for production and delivery of services

Service support. the process of interfacing with suppliers that provide the company with support

Service system design matrix. a tool that establishes the relationship among three key factors of service. (1) the degree of contact between the consumer and the service provider, (2) the opportunity for sales, and (3) the service system's production efficiency

Service time. a continuous random variable that is also assumed to follow a probability distribution known as the negative exponential distribution

Service-level factors. another term for Z values in the context of service levels

Servicescape. the physical surroundings in which a service is assembled and delivered and the seller and customer interact

SERVQUAL. a gap analysis model that uses surveys to determine the gaps that exist between the services that the customers expected to receive and what they actually received

Setup costs. the costs of setting up the machines or changing over production from one item to another

Shadow price or dual price. the price associated with a resource that indicates how much more profit

would be earned by increasing the amount of the resource by one unit. Conversely, it is the price one would be willing to pay for acquiring an additional unit of that resource

Shipper's export declaration. a document completed by the shipper of goods and shows the value, weight, destination, and other features of export shipments

Shipper's letter of instructions. a document required by the carrier or certain logistics service providers to obtain the authorization to issue and sign the air waybill on behalf of the shipper

Shortest processing time. a priority rule that ranks jobs according to their processing times and the job with the shortest processing time will be processed first and completed

Simple averaging method for seasonality. a method for calculating seasonal indices by dividing the average demand for each season by the average total demand to arrive at the seasonal indices for each month

Simplex method. an algorithm that provides a systematic way of examining the corner or extreme points of the feasible region of more complex LP problems to determine the optimal value of the objective function

Simulation. a method that uses search decision rules to find the appropriate combination of production and workforce levels that will minimize costs

Simulation. the act of duplicating the operation of a real-world process or system over time

Single-channel or single-server queuing model. the simplest and the most frequently encountered waiting line model, in which there is a single service station that will serve a queue of customers waiting in a single line

Single-echelon inventory systems. a system in which each supply chain partner sequentially forecasts demand that invariably leads to the bullwhip effect

Single-period system. ordering the entire inventory of a product at one time and it is not replenished

Single-sourcing strategy. a plan to contract with a single supplier when purchasing a particular item, enhancing the cooperation between the buyer and the supplier

Six Sigma. the methodology of improving quality through reducing the number of defects in a given process

Slack. the amount by which the left-hand-side values are less than the right-hand-side values in LP constraints

Slushy time fence. time frame in which the master schedule may be accommodated with trade-offs, but because the timeframe is further out into the future, these trade-offs are usually less costly and disruptive

Smoothing inventories. inventories held to smooth out fluctuations in production

Social value. the value that results when the well-being of workers and other stakeholders is taken into account

Special cause variations. variations in quality that are not normally present in the process and can be attributed to unique or assignable causes

Spend analysis. an examination of what products and suppliers a company spends the most money on, and if the company is getting what has been promised for the money spent

Splintering. the practice of breaking traditional supply chains into smaller and more agile supply chains that can better respond to higher levels of business complexity, save money, and improve customer service

Stage-Gate® approach. a method that helps prevent runaway, over-budget product development cycles by

dividing new projects into stages (or phases), with gates separating consecutive stages

Standard error of the estimate. a measure of the variation of the actual (observed) y values from the predicted y values ($\hat{y}$)

Standard purchase order. a purchase order used for one-time purchases

States of nature. future events or occurrences that can take place that are beyond the control of the decision maker

Stepping stone method. the term *stepping stone* refers to the occupied cells in the initial solution of the transportation matrix, which are used in arriving at an improved solution

Stock-out costs. also referred to as shortage costs, are costs incurred when the demand for a product cannot be met because of a shortage of inventory

Strategic capacity planning. the process of capacity planning for the long term that requires managers to forecast demand over several years and looking at demand and growth trends as well as at cyclical demand patterns

Strategic profit model (SPM). a model that provides a visual representation of an organization's financial performance in terms of its return on investment and return on assets (also known as the DuPont model)

Supplier management. a business process that enables a company to identify and select the best possible suppliers and negotiate the best possible prices for the resources it purchases from them

Supplier park. the location of multiple suppliers in close proximity to a producer to create a leaner supply chain

Supplier scorecard. a form that contains measures used to evaluate the performance of suppliers

Supply chain scheduling. the process of coordinating scheduling decisions made by any member of a supply chain with the decisions of other supply chain partners

Supply chain. a sequence of interconnected organizations that helps develop, produce, distribute, and sell a product to the final consumer

Supply planning. ensuring that there is sufficient manufacturing and distribution capacity to meet the demand forecasts

Supply warehouses. part of a manufacturing plant used for the long-term storage of goods

Supply-base optimization. the process of determining the best number of suppliers to purchase from

Surplus. the amount by which the left-hand-side values are greater than the right-hand-side ones in LP constraints

Sustainability. the use of methods, systems, and materials that won't deplete resources or harm natural cycles

Sustaining innovation. a product or service targeted toward an existing market that can be radical or incremental in nature

Synchronous manufacturing. a manufacturing strategy that adds process flexibility by synchronizing customers' orders with the tasks performed at the various workstations

Taguchi Methods. used to reduce variation in a process through robust product design

Taguchi-loss function. a process created by Genichi Taguchi in the 1980s that tracks the financial loss to society as a result of poor quality designs

Takt time. the cycle time needed to match our production rate to demand for the product

Target inventory level (T). a predetermined inventory level that is established for fixed order interval systems that is high enough to meet all demand

Target market. the potential set of consumers who might buy a product

Tariffs. taxes levied on specific items exported from or imported to a country

Technology management. the process of continuously looking for ways to improve the design of facilities and engineering of processes to make production more efficient

Temporal aggregation. the process of combining customer orders over a period of time

Terminal. a facility where freight is moved between trucks

Terms of sale. the rights and obligations of each party in the transport of goods

Tertiary packaging. the grouping of secondary packaging for the purposes of protecting bulk handling products during storage and transportation

Theory of constraints. the assumption that resources used in a manufacturing process are typically uneven, and to achieve a balanced flow of work through the process, the bottleneck resource (or constraining resource) should be controlled

Third-party logistics providers (3PL). a service provider hired by a company to perform all of the company's logistics functions

Third-party quality assurance services. independent firms that manage supplier-related activities for other firms, located in the same country in which their suppliers are located

Throughput. a measure (usually in terms of time or units) of how an order moves from receipt to delivery

Time metrics. an assessment of the amount of time to process an order, transportation time, and similar variables

Time phasing. the process of scheduling and describing the receipt of inventories of materials, components, subassemblies, and finished products as they are needed over time

Time series. is a sequence of regular intervals over a period of time

Time-based competition. a strategy intended to reduce the time required to conceptualize, develop, manufacture, market, and deliver products so as to gain a competitive advantage

Timeline chart. a tool used to track both the value-added and nonvalue-added time a product spends in various production stages

Time-phased budget. a budget that identifies the correct sequencing of tasks and the points in the project when budgeted money is likely to be spent as those tasks are completed

Tolerances. *See* Design specification limits

Top-down planning. planning approach in which management creates accurate tactical plans based on the overall aggregate forecast and then divide the resources across the individual products and services during the subsequent detailed operational planning and control activities

Total cost of ownership (TCO). the overall costs (both direct and indirect) associated with purchasing, transporting, handling, inspecting, storing and insuring the products, and then disposing of them

Total landed cost. the total cost of making and delivering the product so that it generates revenue

Total quality management (TQM). a management philosophy that focuses on continuously improving the quality of a company's products and processes

Total sum of squares. a measure of the variation of the actual Y-values around the mean Y

Total time coefficient value. the cumulative or total time required to complete a given number of repetitions of a task or produce a given number of units of an item

Tracking signals. upper and lower control limits used to determine whether the forecasting errors related to a method are within these limits

Transfer batch. the quantity of units that is transported from one work center to the next

Transportation infrastructure owners. publicly or privately owned transportation entities or owners of infrastructure, railroads, and the pipelines that are operated by companies in the private sector

Transportation inventories. inventories that are in transit in containers or trucks (also known as pipeline inventories)

Transportation method. a special case of linear programming that can be used to obtain optimum aggregate or distribution plans that can enable planners to balance capacity and demand at the lowest possible cost

Transportation model. a special case of linear programming problems in which the objective is to minimize the total cost of transporting goods from the various supply origins to the different demand destinations

Trend. the long-term movement (increasing or decreasing) of data over time

Trend-adjusted exponential smoothing. a variation of simple exponential smoothing that includes a trend factor, a weighted measure of the change between the current forecast and the next period's forecast

Triple bottom line. three performance targets that measure sustainability. the (a) economic value it provides its shareholders and the (b) environmental and (c) social value the company creates

Triple constraint. elements that characterize a project and are used to evaluate its success. time (adherence to schedule), cost, and quality

Unbalanced transportation problem. a problem in which the total number of supply units available is greater than the demand requirements or vice versa

Uniform plant loading. leveling out the workload or smoothing production to achieve stable schedules, to achieve a steady flow of work, and to eliminate waste

Unit time coefficient value. the time required to complete a particular repetition of a task or produce a particular unit of an item

Unit-to-unit variation. product variations caused by variations in the materials, processes, or equipment used to produce a product

Unlimited (infinite) population. theoretically represents systems that potentially have a large number of possible customers. Examples of such systems are toll booths on expressways, banks on busy streets, movie theaters, theme parks, or help desks for Apple customer support

U-shaped layout. a compact layout in the shape of a U that allows workers to handle jobs in multiple workstations, gives workers an unobstructed view of the entire line, and allows workers to travel efficiently between workstations

Value analysis (VA). analysis conducted to improve, at a minimum cost, the functionality of a product without affecting its existing functions and standards

Value chain. *See* supply chain

Value engineering (VE). analysis conducted to improve the value of all components used to develop a product from its design to its final delivery

Value stream mapping (VSM). a process-mapping technique used to analyze and design the flow of materials and information across multiple processes

Value stream. the sequence of activities required to design, produce, and provide a good or service, and along which information, materials, and work flow

Variable. a quality characteristic that is measured on a continuous, or incremental, scale

Vendor managed inventory (VMI). a system that allows a vendor firm to track and manage the inventory of all its products in all of its buyer locations

Warehouse management system (WMS). technologies used to track products, control inventory, and improve order picking and loading as well as unloading-dock logistics

Weighted moving average. a short-term time series forecasting method in which forecasters assign more weight to most recent values in the time series if they feel that these values reflect how the actual demand will behave in the near future

Work breakdown structure (WBS). a process of breaking down a project's overall mission into step-by-step tasks

Work center. a part of a production facility where all activities related to a particular phase of the production process are performed

Work packages. activities that comprise the deliverables of a project

Workflow. any process that consists of a sequence of connected steps or operations necessary to complete a task where

Yield management. an approach for service companies with capacity constraints to maximize revenue from its service operations, while at the same time providing the desired level of service to the right customer at the right time and at the right price

λ = Expected or average arrival rate

Chapter 1

1. U.S. Bureau of Labor Statistics. (2010). *Charting international labor comparisons* (p. 24). Washington, DC: Author.
2. Jacoby, D. (2008, May/June). Can Western manufacturers beat the competition? *APICS Magazine*, pp. 40–44.
3. Careers-in-Business. (n.d.). *Careers in operations management: Facts and trends*. Retrieved from http://www.careers-in-business.com/omfacts.htm
4. Aurora, N. (n.d.). Career avenues in service operations management. *Operations Crossing*. Retrieved from http://www.operationscrossing.com/article/280010/Career-Avenues-in-Service-Operations-Management/
5. (a) Careers-in-Business. (n.d.). *Careers in operations management*. Retrieved from http://www.careers-in-business.com/om.htm. (b) Careers-in-Business. (n.d.). *Careers in operations management: Facts and trends*. Retrieved from http://www.careers-in-business.com/omfacts.htm
6. (a) Careers-in-Business. (n.d.). Homepage. Retrieved from http://www.careers-in-business.com/. (b) Council of Supply Chain Management Professionals. (n.d.). *Starting your supply chain management career*. Retrieved from http://www.careersinsupplychain.org/
7. Economypedia.com. Retrieved June 16, 2015, from http://www.economypedia.com/wiki/index.php?title=Goods_and_services
8. Russell, R. S., & Taylor, B. W. III. (2011). *Operations management: Creating value along the supply chain* (7th ed., p. 2). Hoboken, NJ: Wiley.
9. Sincavage, J. R., Haub, C., & Sharma, O. P. (2010, May). Labor costs in India's organized manufacturing sector. *Monthly Labor Review*, pp. 3–22.
10. Russell & Taylor, *op. cit.*, p. 2.
11. Adapted from Russell & Taylor, *op. cit.*, p. 4.
12. Russell & Taylor, *op. cit.*, p. 2.
13. Global supply chain management: Shifting strategies: A roundtable overview. Retrieved January 23, 2013, from http://www.pdf-finder.com/Global-Supply-Chain-Management%3A-Shifting-Strategies.html
14. (a) Rohwedder, C. (2004, February 24). Style and substance: Making fashion faster as knockoffs beat originals to market, designers speed the trip from sketch to store. *Wall Street Journal*, p. B1. (b) Rohwedder, C., & Johnson, K. (2008, February 20). Pace-setting Zara seeks more speed to fight its rising cheap-chic rivals. *Wall Street Journal*. Retrieved from http://online.wsj.com/article/SB120345929019578183.html. (c) Walters, D. (2006). Effectiveness and efficiency: The role of demand chain management. *The International Journal of Logistics Management*, *17*(1), 75–94. (d) Capell, K. (2008, October 9). Zara thrives by breaking all the rules. *BusinessWeek*. Retrieved from http://www.bloomberg.com/news/articles/2008-10-08/zara-thrives-by-breaking-all-the-rules
15. Wakabayashi, D. (2014, November 20). Inside Apple's broken sapphire factory. *Wall Street Journal*, pp. B1 and B4.
16. Iakovaki, A., & Srai, J. S. (2009). *Service supply chain integration in multi-organization networks: New approaches to service network design*. Cambridge, England: Institute for Manufacturing, University of Cambridge. Retrieved February 9, 2013, from http://www.ifm.eng.cam.ac.uk/cim/symposium2009/. . ./16_iakovaki.pdf
17. Poor quality nearly short circuits electronics company. (1993, February). *Productivity*, 1–3.
18. Malik, Y., Niemeyer, A., & Ruwadi, B. (2011, January). Building the supply chain of the future. *McKinsey Quarterly*. Retrieved from https://www.mckinseyquarterly.com/Building_the_supply_chain_of_the_future_2729
19. Ellis, S. (2010, March 4). Top 10 predictions for Global supply chains. *MaterialHandling&Logistics (MHL) News*. Retrieved from http://mhlnews.com/global-supply-chain/top-10-predictions-global-supply-chains
20. Managing global supply chains: McKinsey global survey results. (2008). *McKinsey Quarterly*. Retrieved from http://www.supplychainbrain.com/content/nc/general-scm/global-supply-chain-mgmt/single-article-page/article/managing-global-supply-chains-mckinsey-global-survey-results/
21. Ellis, *op. cit.*
22. Malik et al., *op. cit.*
23. Retrieved from http://www.arch.wsu.edu/09%20publications/sustain/defnsust.htm
24. Clark, L. (2011, March 11). McDonald's makes sustainable commitment. *Supply Management*. Retrieved from http://www.cips.org/supply-management/news/2011/march/mcdonalds-makes-sustainable-commitment/
25. Hamm, S. (2006, August 21). A passion for the planet. *Bloomberg Businessweek*. Retrieved from http://www.bloomberg.com/news/articles/2006-08-20/a-passion-for-the-planet
26. (a) China-Window.com. (n.d.). *Multinational companies adjust strategies to China*. Retrieved from http://www.china-window.com/china_market/china_industry_reports/multinational-companies-a.shtml. (b) Waldmeir, P. (2010, July 21). Multinationals in China: Right city, Right sector. *Financial Times*. Retrieved from http://blogs.ft.com/beyond-brics/2010/07/21/multinationals-in-china-right-city-right-sector/ (Registration required to access article.)
27. (a) Wailgum, T. (2008, August 22). Nintendo Wii shortage: Shrewd marketing or flawed supply chain? *CIO Magazine*. Retrieved from http://www.cio.com/article/2434123/supply-chain-management/nintendo-wii-shortage--shrewd-marketing-or-flawed-supply-chain-.html. (b) Newman, J. (2010, February 10). Wii's old supply problems are new again. *Technologizer*. http://technologizer.com/2010/02/10/wiis-old-supply-problems-are-new-again/. (c) Richter, F. (2014, June 11). Sony trumps Nintendo in shrinking console market. *Statista*. Retrieved from https://www.statista.com/chart/2345/video-game-console-sales/. (d) Alabaster, J. (2013). Wii U pre-orders are strong so Nintendo expects shortages this year. *PCWorld*. Retrieved from http://www.pcworld.com/article/2013080/wii-u-pre-orders-are-strong-so-nintendo-expects-shortages-year.html

Chapter 2

1. Siegfried, M. (2011). Ripe for change. *Inside Supply Management*, *22*(3), 22. Retrieved from http://www.ism.ws/pubs/ISMMag/ismarticle.cfm?ItemNumber=21481
2. Salazar, C., & Bajak, F. (2013, March 26). Peru declares oil contamination emergency in remote Amazon region. *The Huffington Post*. Retrieved August 11, 2014, from http://www.huffingtonpost.com/2013/03/26/peru-oil-contamination-emergency_n_2955630.html
3. Penfield, P. (2008). Generating for the environment, drive down costs while helping Mother Nature. *APICS Magazine*, *18*(6).
4. EPA. (n.d.). *Life-cycle assessment*. Retrieved August 11, 2014, from http://www.epa.gov/sustainability/analytics/life-cycle.htm
5. Verisk Maplecroft. (2014, December 3). *Human rights risk atlas 2015*. Retrieved from http://maplecroft.com/portfolio/new-analysis/2014/12/03/human-rights-deteriorating-most-ukraine-thailand-turkey-due-state-repression-civil-unrest-maplecroft-human-rights-risk-atlas/
6. Bussey, J. (2012, January 13). The anti-Kodak: How a U.S. firm innovates and thrives. *Wall Street Journal*, pp. B1 and B4.
7. Inman, R. A. (n.d.). Thought leader strategy. *Reference for Business*. Retrieved from http://www.referenceforbusiness.com/management/Ob-Or/Operations-Strategy.html
8. Inman, R. A., *op. cit.*
9. Mitsubishi Motors North America, Inc. (n.d.). *Mission statement*. Retrieved from http://www.mitsubishimanufacturing.com/about/mission/index.asp
10. Garvin, D. A. (1987, November–December). Competing on the eight dimensions of quality. *Harvard Business Review*, pp. 101–109.
11. *American Machinist*. (2006, March 24). On-time delivery, the competitive advantage. Retrieved from http://www.americanmachinist.com/304/News/Article/False/13638/
12. R&R Engineering Co. (n.d.). Company information. *Thomasnet.com*. Retrieved from http://www.thomasnet.com/profile/118755/r-r-engineering-co.htm
13. Hill, T. (2000). *Manufacturing strategy: Text and cases* (3rd ed.). Homewood, IL: Irwin.
14. Eisenstein, P. A. (2010, May 27). Buick may owe its survival to China. *NBCNews.com*. Retrieved from http://www.nbcnews.com/id/37361381/ns/business-autos/#.V4T9ErgrKUk
15. Marching orders for your company. Retrieved August 11, 2014, from http://clarification.wordpress.com/2008/01/21/marching-orders/
16. "Marching orders for your company," *op. cit.*
17. Metters, R., King-Metters, K., Pullman, M., & Walton, S. (2006). *Successful service operations management*. Mason, OH: Thomson South-Western.
18. Design to Improve Life. Retrieved July 7, 2014, from http://www.designtoimprovelife.dk/index.php?option=com_content_custom&view=article&id=418:creating-hospitals-of-the-future&catid=23:danish-cases&Itemid=194
19. Productivity concepts and measures. *Encyclopedia of Management*. Retrieved from http://www.enotes.com/management-encyclopedia/productivity-concepts-measures
20. Ojasalo, K. (2003, June 22). Customer influence on service productivity. *SAM Advanced Management Journal*, *68*(3), 14.
21. (a) Ojasalo, *op. cit.* (b) Balle, L. (n.d.). How to improve service productivity and customer service. *eHow.com*. Retrieved from http://www.ehow.com/how_8314817_improve-service-productivity-customer-service.html#ixzz1WdB2ABbY
22. (a) Illing, D. (2015, April 17). Addressing the ultra-large container ship challenge. *Journal of Commerce*. Retrieved November 9, 2015, from http://www.joc.com/maritime-news/container-lines/addressing-ultra-large-container-ship-challenge_20150417.htm. (b) Campo-Flores, A., & McWhirter, C. (2015, April 30). Bigger ships snarl U.S. ports. *Wall Street Journal*, pp. A1 and A10.
23. Adapted from p. 47 of Chopra, S., & Meindl, P. (2007). *Supply chain management* (3rd ed.). New York, NY: Pearson-Prentice-Hall.

24. Chopra & Meindl, *op. cit.*
25. Chopra & Meindl, *op. cit.*
26. Ferrer, J., & Karlberg, J. (2006, May). Supply chain management: How to build a successful global operations model. *Outlook Journal.*
27. Nuclear Energy Institute. (n.d.). U.S. nuclear operators employ multiple safeguards to cope with power outages. Retrieved from http://safetyfirst.nei.org/industry-actions/u-s-nuclear-operators-employ-multiple-safeguards-to-cope-with-power-outages/
28. Charlton, A. (2011, March 28). Nuclear industry touts safety of new reactors. *Chicago Sun Times.* Retrieved from http://www.suntimes.com/news/world/4544806-418/nuclear-industry-touts-safety-of-new-reactors.html
29. Bohlander, G. W., & Snell, S. A. (2010). *Managing human resources* (15th ed.). Mason, OH: South-western Cengage Learning.
30. Murphy, M. (2011, January 11). Reinforcing the supply chain. *The Wall Street Journal*, p. B6.
31. Ferrari, B. (2009, March 4). Another data point for supply chain sustainability strategies [Blog post]. *Supply chain matters.* Retrieved from http://www.theferrarigroup.com/supply-chain-matters/?s=Another+data+point+for+supply+chain+sustainability+ strategies
32. Bowman, R. J. (2011, April 11). Another disaster, another supply-chain disruption. Will we ever learn? *SupplyChainBrain.* Retrieved from http://m.supplychainbrain.com/content/index.php?id=3861&tx_ ttnews[cat]=4&tx_ ttnews[tt_news]=10867&tx_ ttnews [backPid]= 3860&cHash=9e2d445d14

Chapter 3

1. (a) Bowman, Z. (2010). Nissan Leaf owners have rapid response system lying in wait. *Autoblog.com.* Retrieved from http://www.autoblog.com/2010/11/24/nissan-leaf-owners-have-rapid-response-system-lying-in-wait/. (b) Ramsey, M. (2010, November 23). Nissan Leaf claims 99 MPG. *Wall Street Journal*, p. B8. (c) Voelker, J. (2010, December 2). GM confirms, yes, we're losing money on every Volt we build. *Green Car Reports.* Retrieved from http://www.greencarreports.com/blog/1052107_gm-confirms-yes-were-losing-money-on-every-volt-we-build. (d) Welsh, J. (2010, November 24). Nissan Leaf gets 99-MPG rating from EPA, Volt still waiting. *Wall Street Journal.* Retrieved from http://blogs.wsj.com/drivers-seat/2010/11/24/nissan-leaf-gets-99-mpg-rating-from-epa-volt-still-waiting/
2. Buchanan, D. A., & Boddy, D. (1992). *The expertise of the change agent: Public performance and backstage activity.* London, England: Prentice-Hall.
3. Zwikael, O., & Smyrk, J. (2011). *Project management for the creation of organisational value.* London, England: Springer.
4. Project Management Institute. (2013). *Project management body of knowledge* (5th ed.). Newtown Square, PA: Author.
5. (a) Feickert, A. (2008). *The Marines' expeditionary fighting vehicle (EFV): Background and issues for Congress.* Washington, DC: Congressional Research Service, Library of Congress. Retrieved from http://www.dtic.mil/cgi-bin/GetTRDoc?Location=U2&doc=GetTRDoc.pdf&AD=ADA486513. (b) Hodge, N. (2010, August 27). Marines question craft needed to hit the beach. *Wall Street Journal*, p. B8. (c) Merle, R. (2007, February 7). Problems stall Pentagon's new fighting vehicle. *The Washington Post.* Retrieved from http://www.washingtonpost.com/wp-dyn/content/article/2007/02/06/AR2007020601997.html. (d) Ackerman, S. (2010, August 17). Senate may finally sink Marines' swimming tank. *Wired.* Retrieved from http://www.wired.com/dangerroom/2010/09/senate-may-finally-sink-marines-swimming-tank/. (e) *Defense Industry Daily.* (2015, July 27). Marine APCs: Peregrinations of the EFV to ACV to MPC to ACV 1.1. Retrieved from http://www.defenseindustrydaily.com/the-usmcs-expeditionary-fighting-vehicle-sdd-phase-updated-02302/
6. Project Management Institute, *op. cit.*
7. Martin, M. G. (1998). Statement of work: The foundation for delivering successful service projects. *PMNetwork, 12*(10), 6–7.
8. Martin, M. (2008). *Federal statements of work: A practical guide.* Vienna, VA: Management Concepts.
9. Larson, E. W., & Gray, C. F. (2011). *Project management: The managerial process* (5th ed.). New York, NY: McGraw-Hill.
10. Pinto, J. K., & Rouhiainen, P. (2001). *Building customer-based project organizations.* New York, NY: Wiley.
11. Gohring, N. (2007, July 5). Microsoft opens Vancouver office as immigration workaround. *itbusiness.ca.* Retrieved from http://www.itbusiness.ca/it/client/en/Home/News.asp?id=44187
12. Duhigg, C., & Bradsher, K. (2012, January 21). How the U.S. lost out on iPhone work. *The New York Times.* Retrieved from http://www.nytimes.com/2012/01/22/business/apple-america-and-a-squeezed-middle-class.html?_r=1
13. Muller, J. (2004, February 1). Counterfeiting cars in China. *Forbes.* Retrieved from http://www.nbcnews.com/id/4131724/ns/business-forbes_com/t/counterfeiting-cars-china/#.V4VZPLgrKUI
14. Pinto, J. K. (2010). *Project management: Achieving competitive advantage* (2nd ed.). Upper Saddle River, NJ: Prentice-Hall.
15. (a) Riemer, S., & Meyer, S. (2009, October 15). Integrating sustainability in project management—A practical approach. *Strategies to Sustainability.* (b) Tiron-Tudor, A., & Ioana-Maria, D. (2013). Project success by integrating sustainability in project management. In G. Silvius & J. Tharp (Eds.), *Sustainability integration for effective project management* (pp. 1069127). Hershey, PA: IGI Global.
16. Harder, A., & Ailworth, E. (2016, June 2). Fossil fuels' unpopularity leaves a mark. *Wall Street Journal*, pp. B1–B2.
17. Martin, 1998, *op. cit.*
18. (a) Camp, N. (2013, June 26). Three stages to every project—pre-production, production, and post-production [Blog post]. *The Video Effect.* Retrieved from http://www.thevideoeffect.tv/2013/06/26/video-pre-production-and-post-production/. (b) Rhyne, C. C. (2008). Looking behind the scenes. *Project Management Institute.* Retrieved from http://www.pmi.org/learning/project-management-motion-picture-industry-7121

Chapter 3 Supplement

1. (a) Cox, C. (2015, June 2). £1bn Manchester Airport transformation: Super-sized terminal, faster security, more passengers, more routes. *Manchester Evening News.* Retrieved from http://www.manchestereveningnews.co.uk/news/greater-manchester-news/manchester-airport-expansion-plan-security-9370929. (b) Cox, C. (2016, February 24). Impressive fly-through video shows how Manchester Airport will look after £1bn transformation. *Manchester Evening News.* Retrieved from http://www.manchestereveningnews.co.uk/news/greater-manchester-news/impressive-fly-through-video-shows-10946668
2. Pinto, J. K. (2010). *Project management: Achieving competitive advantage* (2nd ed.). Upper Saddle River, NJ: Prentice-Hall.
3. Brandon, D. M. Jr. (1998). Implementing earned value easily and effectively. *Project Management Journal, 29*(2), 11–18.

Chapter 4

1. (a) American Pet Products Association (APPA). (n.d.). Pet industry market size & ownership statistics. Retrieved from http://www.americanpetproducts.org/press_industrytrends.asp. (b) Brady, D., & Palmeri, C. (2007, August 6). The pet economy. *BusinessWeek*, pp. 45–54.
2. Stables, J. (2016, February 17). Best fitness trackers 2016: Jawbone, Misfit, Fitbit, Garmin and more., *WAREABLE.* Retrieved from http://www.wareable.com/fitness-trackers/the-best-fitness-tracker
3. Ecostrategy Group. Retrieved October 7, 2014, from http://www.ecostrategygroup.com/top10reasons.pdf
4. Osborn, A. (2002, August 23). New from McDonald's: The McAfrika burger (don't tell the 12m starving). *The Guardian.* Retrieved from http://www.theguardian.com/world/2002/aug/24/famine.andrewosborn
5. The Topic Lounge. Retrieved October 10, 2014, from http://www.thetopiclounge.com/fashion-target-market-examples/
6. (a) Moran, L. (2012, March 13). "It's like calling a shoe the Al Qaeda": Outrage as Nike names new trainer after British Black and Tans who cracked down on Irish in 1920s (just in time for St Paddy's Day!). *Daily Mail.* Retrieved from http://www.dailymail.co.uk/news/article-2114278/St-Patricks-Day-themed-Nike-trainers-named-British-Black-Tans-cause-outrage.html#ixzz1qbNHaMwJ. (b) *FoxNews.com.* Nike apologizes for unofficial names of 'Black and Tan' sneaker. (2012, March 13). Retrieved from http://www.foxnews.com/world/2012/03/13/nike-apologizes-for-unofficial-name-black-and-tan-sneaker/
7. Matthews, D. (2015, March 11). Why the Apple Watch won't sell. *Forbes.* Retrieved from http://www.forbes.com/sites/danmatthews/2015/03/11/why-the-apple-iwatch-wont-sell/
8. ASME website. Newsletters & Magazine page. Retrieved from http://memagazine.asme.org/Articles/2010/September/Safety_First.cfm
9. Ecostrategy Group, *op. cit.*
10. Christensen, C. (n.d.). Key concepts—disruptive innovation. Retrieved from http://www.claytonchristensen.com/key-concepts/
11. Belliveau, P., Griffin, A., & Somermeyer, S. (2002). *The PDMA toolbook 1 for new product development.* New York, NY: Wiley.
12. ISA. Retrieved October 13, 2014, from http://www.isa.org/InTech Template.cfm?Section=InTech &template=/ContentManagement/ContentDisplay.cfm&Content ID=20067
13. Cooper, R. G. (1990). Stage-gate systems: A new tool for managing new products - conceptual and operational model. *Business Horizons, 33,* 44–54.
14. (a) *Illy Issimo* gives coffee lovers two new tastes of lower calorie

decadence anytime, anywhere. (n.d.). *BusinessWire.* Retrieved from http://www.businesswire .com/news/home/20110516006794/ en/illy-issimo-Coffee-Lovers-Tastes-Calorie-Decadence. (b) Moye, J. (2013, March 6). The next big thing. How Coke's venturing and emerging brands team stays one step ahead of tomorrow's thirsts. *The Coca-Cola Company.* Retrieved from:http://www. coca-colacompany.com/stories/ the-next-big-thing-how-cokes-venturing-emerging-brands-unit-stays-a-step-ahead-of-tomorrows-thirsts

15. Technical Change Associates. (n.d.). Value engineering/value analysis. Retrieved from http:// www.technicalchange .com/value-engineering-value-analysis.html

16. HubPages. (2010). DFMA design for manufacturing and assembly. Retrieved from http:// hubpages.com/hub/DFMA

17. Realisoft R&D Staff. (n.d.). Design for reliability: Overview of the process and applicable techniques. *Reliability Edge,* 8(2). Retrieved from http://www .reliasoft.com/newsletter/v8i2/ reliability.htm

18. New Mako boats embrace classic 'V' design for reliability, handling. (2011, November 7). *LoneStar Outdoor News.* Retrieved from http://www .lsonews.com/component/ content/article/17-products/1861-alan-clemons

19. American Cleaning Institute. (n.d.) Some facts about cleaning product disposal. Retrieved from http://www.cleaninginstitute .org/sustainability/some_facts_ about_.aspx

20. American Cleaning Institute. (n.d.) Some facts about cleaning product disposal. Retrieved from http://www.cleaninginstitute .org/sustainability/some_facts_ about_.aspx

21. Lutz, R. (2003). *Guts: Eight laws of business from one of the most innovative business leaders of our time.* Hoboken, NJ: Wiley.

22. Time-based competition. (n.d.). *Reference for Business.* Retrieved from http://www .referenceforbusiness.com/ management/Str-Ti/Time-Based-Competition.html

23. Vitez, O. (n.d.). Product platform strategy. *eHow.* Retrieved from http://www.ehow.com/ facts_7166004_product-platform-strategy.html

24. Siemens. (n.d.). CAD / computer-aided design. Retrieved from https://www.plm.automation. siemens.com/en_us/plm/cad .shtml

25. Khemani, H. (2008, September 10). Benefits of using CAD software in your organization. *Bright Hub Engineering.* Retrieved from http://www .brighthub.com/engineering/ mechanical/articles/879. aspx#ixzz1Tz1MO6mg

26. Pinto, J. K. (2010). *Project management: Achieving competitive advantage* (2nd ed.). Upper Saddle River, NJ: Prentice-Hall.

27. PTC.com. (n.d.). Gaining competitive advantage through global product development. White Paper. Retrieved from http://www.aia-aerospace. org/assets/smc_wp-competitiveadvantage.pdf

28. PTC.com, *op. cit.*

29. ptc. (n.d.). Overcoming the challenges of globablized product development. *CAD Software Blog.* Retrieved May 12, 2012, from http://creo.ptc. com/2011/05/11/overcoming-the-challenges-of-globalized-product-development/

30. Pinto, *op. cit.*

31. Ryan, V. (2004). Colours and cultures. Retrieved from http:// www.technologystudent.com/ despro2/colcul1.htm

32. Brand culture failures: Kellogg's in India [Blog post]. (2006, November 15). *Brand failures – and lessons learned!* Retrieved from http://brandfailures.blogspot. com/2006/11/brand-culture-failures-kelloggs-in.html

33. (a) Rohwedder, C. (2004, February 24). Style and substance: Making fashion faster as knockoffs beat originals to market, designers speed the trip from sketch to store. *Wall Street Journal,* p. B1. (b) Rohwedder, C., & Johnson, K. (2008). Pace-setting Zara seeks more speed to fight its rising cheap-chic rivals. *Wall Street Journal.* Retrieved from http://online.wsj.com/article/ SB120345929019578183.html. (c) Walters, D. (2006). Effectiveness and efficiency: The role of demand chain management. *The International Journal of Logistics Management,* 17(1), 75–94. (d) Capell, K. (2008, October 7). Zara thrives by breaking all the rules. *BusinessWeek.* Retrieved from http://www.bloomberg.com/ news/articles/2008-10-08/zara-thrives-by-breaking-all-the-rules

34. Kong and Allan. (2007, July 17). Supply chain processes in new product development. Retrieved from http://www.kongandallan .com/en/us_pdf/SCPNPD0707U .pdf

35. Kong and Allan, *op. cit.*

36. *Transforming an Indian manufacturing company: The Rane Brake Linings case.* (2006). Working Paper. Krannert School of Management, Lafayette, IN.

37. (a) Davies, G. (2011, July 21). What is service design. Retrieved from http:// EzineArticles.com/6442437. (b) Lin, Y., Shi, Y., & Zhou, L. (2010). Service supply chain: Nature, evolution, and operational implications. In G. Huang et al. (Eds.), *DET2009 Proceedings* (AISC 66, pp. 1189–1204). Berlin, Germany: Springer-Verlag.

38. Hayhow, M. (2014, February 3). Six principles of service design to help you reach your customer. *Moz.com.* Retrieved from https://moz.com/blog/ applying-service-design-online

39. Enotes.com. (n.d.). Product design. Retrieved October 10, 2014, from http://www.enotes. com/management-encyclopedia/ product-design

40. Ichida, T., & Voigt, E. C. (1996). *Product design review: A method for error-free product development.* New York, NY: Productivity Press.

41. Ramey, J. (2016, January 6). Report: VW struggling with fix for U.S. diesels. *Autoweek.* Retrieved from http://autoweek.com/article/ vw-diesel-scandal/report-vw-struggling-fix-us-diesels

42. Buick Pressroom. (2011, October 18). Buick Verano sets high standard for seat comfort [Press release]. Retrieved from http:// media.buick.com/media/us/ en/buick/vehicles/verano/2012. detail.html/content/Pages/news/ us/en/2011/Oct/1018_verano.html

43. Meador, R. (2015, March 6). Bowing to pressure, 3M agrees to reshape its sustainable forestry policies, *Minnpost.* Retrieved from https://www.minnpost.com/ earth-journal/2015/03/bowing-pressure-3m-agrees-reshape-its-sustainable-forestry-policies

44. Institute of Engineers, Australia. (n.d.). Design: The importance of project planning and design in moving toward sustainability. Retrieved from http://www .engineersaustralia.org.au/sites/ default/files/shado/Representation/ Policy%20Positions/ Sustainability/Design.pdf

45. Dewick, P., & Pietikainen, A. (2008). Integrating sustainability into the innovation process. Paper presented at the International Association for Management of Technology conference. CERAM Business School, Nice, France.

46. Terlop, S. (2011, August 30). Coaxing miles from a Chevy redesign. *Wall Street Journal,* pp. B1–B2.

Chapter 4 Supplement

1. Martin, H., & Masunaga, S. (2015, July 8). United Airlines blames grounding of hundreds of flights on computer glitch. *Los Angeles Times.* Retrieved from http://www.latimes.com/ business/la-fi-united-flights-grounded-20150708-story.html

2. Hope, B., Strumpf, D., & Vaishampayan, S. (2015, July 9). Glitch freezes big board for hours. *Wall Street Journal,* pp. A1–A2.

3. Weibull.com. (2003, April). Relationship between availability and reliability. *Reliability HotWire, 26.* Retrieved from http://www.weibull.com/ hotwire/issue26/relbasics26.htm

Chapter 5

1. Foulkes, N. (2016, January 17). Louis Vuitton watch qualifies for the Seal of Geneva. *Financial Times.*

2. Kotelnikov, V. (n.d.). Quality management—A prerequisite of your market success. Retrieved from http://www.1000ventures. com/business_guide/mgmt_ quality.html

3. Garvin, D. A. (1987, November–December). Competing on the eight dimensions of quality. *Harvard Business Review,* pp. 101–109.

4. Newport, J. P. (2011, March 19). The quiet importance of sound. *Wall Street Journal.* Retrieved from http://www.wsj.com/articles/SB1000 14240527487046085045762085831 80153672

5. Zeithaml, V., Parasuraman, A., & Berry, L. (1990). *Delivering quality service.* New York: Free Press.

6. Zeithaml, Parasuraman, & Berry, *op. cit.*

7. Entel, T. (2007). *The empathy engine: Turning customer service into a sustainable advantage.* Booz & Co. Retrieved from http://www.booz.com/ media/uploads/The_Empathy_ Engine.pdf

8. Ritz Carlton website. Gold standards page. Retrieved from http://www.ritzcarlton.com/en/ about/gold-standards

9. (a) Consumer Affairs. (n.d.). Latest in Automotive recalls page. Retrieved from http:// www.consumeraffairs.com/ recalls/arecalls_auto.htm. (b) GM: Steps to a recall nightmare. (2014). *CNN Money.* Retrieved from http://money.cnn.com/ infographic/pf/autos/gm-recall-timeline/

10. ASQ. (n.d.). Cost of quality (COQ). Retrieved from http://asq. org/learn-about-quality/cost-of-quality/overview/overview.html

11. Shingo, S., & Robinson, A. (Eds.). 1990. *Modern approaches to manufacturing improvement: The Shingo System* (pp. 214–216). Cambridge, MA: Productivity Press.

12. Antonaras, A., Memtsa, C., & Iacovidou, M. (2010, March 22–24). The challenge of measuring the cost of quality. Paper presented at the 4th annual Quality Congress Middle East. Dubai.

13. Deming, W. E. (1986). Out of the crisis (pp. 23–24). Cambridge, MA: MIT Press.

14. (a) Carman, J. M., et al. (2010). Keys to successful implementation of total quality management in hospitals. *Health Care Management Review,* 35, 283–293. (b) Short, P. J., & Rahim, R. H. (1995). Total quality management in hospitals. *Total Quality Management,* 6, 255–263. (c) Motwani, J., Sower, V. E., & Brashier, L. W. (1996). Implementing TQM in the health care sector. *Health Care Management Review,* 21, 73–80.

15. (a) Link, A. N., & Scott, J. T. (2001, October). *Economic evaluation of the Baldrige National Quality Program,* NIST Planning Report 01-3. (b) Link, A. N., & Scott, J. T.

(2001, December). *NIST Planning Report 11-2: Economic Evaluation of the Baldrige Performance Excellence Program.*

16. (a) Malcolm Baldrige National Quality Award, 2014 Award Recipient, Health Care. Retrieved from http://www.nist.gov/baldrige/award_recipients/good-samaritan_profile.cfm. (b) St. David's HealthCare, 2014 Award Recipient, Health Care Category. Retrieved from http://www.nist.gov/baldrige/award_recipients/st-davids-healthcare.cfm

17. Trusko, B., & Harrington, H. J. (2006, April 25). The prescription for healthcare excellence. *Quality Digest.* Retrieved from https://www.qualitydigest.com/inside/fda-compliance-article/prescription-health-care-excellence

18. iSixSigma. (n.d.). DMAIC versus DMADV. Retrieved from http://www.isixsigma.com/new-to-six-sigma/design-for-six-sigma-dfss/dmaic-versus-dmadv/

19. Zeithaml, Parasuraman, & Berry, *op. cit.*

20. (a) Parasuraman, A., Zeithaml, V., & Berry, L. (1985). A conceptual model of service quality and its implications for future research. *The Journal of Marketing, 49,* 41–50. (b) Zeithaml, V., & Bitner, M. J. (1996). *Services Marketing* (3rd ed.). Burr Ridge, IL: McGraw-Hill.

21. Swaid, S. I., & Wigand, R. T. (2009). Measuring the quality of e-service: Scale development and initial validation. *Journal of Electronic Commerce Research, 10*(1), p. 13.

22. (a) Alba, D. (2016, January 15). Chipotle's health crisis shows fresh food comes at a price. *Wired.* Retrieved from http://www.wired.com/2016/01/chipotles-health-crisis-shows-fresh-food-comes-at-a-price/. (b) Hollister, S. (2016, July 9). Here are the reasons so many hoverboards are catching fire. *CNet.* Retrieved from http://www.cnet.com/news/why-are-hoverboards-exploding-and-catching-fire/

23. Fish, L. A. (2011). Supply chain quality management. In D. Onkal (Ed.), *Supply chain management—pathways for research and practice.* Shanghai, China: InTech. Retrieved from http://www.intechopen.com/source/pdfs/17143/InTech-Supply_chain_quality_management.pdf

24. Monczka, R. M., Handfield, R. B., Giunipero, L. C., & Patterson, J. L. (2009). *Purchasing and supply chain management* (4th ed.). Mason, OH: South-Western Cengage Learning.

25. Sara @ Brainmates.com. (n.d.). The customer service gap model. Retrieved from http://www.brainmates.com.au/brainrants/the-customer-service-gap-model

26. MetricStream.com. (n.d.). Best practices in supplier quality management. Retrieved from http://www.metricstream.com/insights/bestPractices_supqltymgmt.htm

27. (a) Hulta, G. T. M., & Swan, K. S. (2003). A research agenda for the nexus of product development and supply chain management processes. *Journal of Product Innovation Management, 20*(6), 427–429. (b) Joglekar, N., & Rosenthal, R. (2003). Coordination of design supply chains for bundling physical and software products. *Journal of Product Innovation Management, 20*(5), 374–390. (c) Lee, H. L., & Sasser, M. M. (1995). Product universality and design for supply chain management. *Production Planning & Control, 6*(3), 270–277.

28. Simchi-Levi, D., Kaminksy, P., & Simchi-Levi, E. (2008). *Designing & managing the supply chain: Concepts, strategies and case studies* (3rd ed.). New York, NY: McGraw-Hill.

29. (a) Schneider Electric. (2015, February 26). Schneider Electric's supply chain transformation is recognized and supported by an award-winning talent strategy [Press release]. Retrieved from http://www2.schneider-electric.com/corporate/en/press/press-releases/viewer-press-releases.page?c_filepath=/templatedata/Content/Press_Release/data/en/shared/2015/02/20150226_schneider_electric_s_supply_chain_transformation_is_recognized_and_sup.xml. (b) Avery, S. (2002). Suppliers go the distance for Schneider Electric. *Purchasing, 131*(12), 53–57.

30. Penske helps Eaton leverage its global network, global logistics & supply chain strategies. (2008, July 10). Retrieved from http://www.supplychainbrain.com/content/latest-content/single-article/article/penske-helps-eaton-leverage-its-global-network/

31. Prasso, S. (2011, June 29). Why we left our factories in China. *Fortune.* Retrieved from http://fortune.com/2011/06/29/why-we-left-our-factories-in-china/

32. Pietras, A. E. (2008). Supply chain management. *Quality Digest.* https://www.qualitydigest.com/magazine/2008/dec/article/supply-chain-management.html

33. (a) LeGrone, S. (2015, July 15). Delays in Zumwalt Destroyer program hamper production of DDG-51s at Bath Iron Works. *USNI News.* Retrieved from http://news.usni.org/2015/07/15/delays-in-zumwalt-destroyer-program-hamper-production-of-ddg-51s-at-bath-iron-works. (b) O'Rourke, R. (2016, March 10). Navy DDG-51 and DDG-1000 Destroyer programs: Background and issues for Congress. Washington, DC: Congressional Research Service. Retrieved from https://www.fas.org/sgp/crs/weapons/RL32109.pdf

34. Rowley, M. J. (2016, February 8). India's digital revolution. *Cisco News.* Retrieved from http://newsroom.cisco.com/feature-content?type=webcontent&articleId=1742038

35. D'Amico, J. (2007, April 16). Six Sigma lessons from Capsugel. *Pharmaceutical Manufacturing.* Retrieved from http://www.pharmamanufacturing.com/articles/2007/070.html

36. (a) Heinz. (n.d.). Food safety and policy. Retrieved from http://www.heinz.com/sustainability/nutrition/food-safety.aspx. (b) Heinz. (n.d.). Sustainable sourcing. Retrieved from http://www.heinz.com/sustainability/supplychain/sustainable-sourcing.aspx

37. Hess, A. E. M., Calio, V., & Frohlich, T. C. (2014, May 13). America's nine most damaged brands. *24/7 Wall Street.* Retrieved from http://247wallst.com/special-report/2014/05/13/americas-nine-most-damaged-brands-3/2/

38. Irfan, U. (2014, December 18). How lithium ion batteries grounded the Dreamliner. *Scientific American.* Retrieved from http://www.scientificamerican.com/article/how-lithium-ion-batteries-grounded-the-dreamliner/

39. Feuling, B. A. (2009). Quality ≠ sustainability? Social responsibility in a world of supply chain vs. supply chain. *Business Forum China.* Retrieved from http://www.kongandallan.com/en/us_pdf/BFC-QS0903U.pdf

40. (a) KPMG. (2013, December 8). The KPMG survey of corporate responsibility reporting. Retrieved from https://home.kpmg.com/xx/en/home/insights/2013/12/kpmg-survey-corporate-responsibility-reporting-2013.html. (b) Bonini, S., Koller, T. M., & Mirvis, P. H. (2009). Valuing social responsibility programs. Retrieved from http://www.mckinsey.com/business-functions/strategy-and-corporate-finance/our-insights/valuing-social-responsibility-programs

41. (a) Manning, E., Earls, B., Bader, K., Downey, F., & Scalva, K. (2014). Application of lean Six Sigma to optimize a legacy cleaning process. *Pharmaceutical Engineering, 34,* 1–10. (b) Pfizer: Right first time, twice. (2005, April 21). *Pharmaceutical Manufacturing.* Retrieved from http://www.pharmamanufacturing.com/articles/2005/247.html

42. Pietras, *op. cit.*

43. (a) Kaptein, S. (2014, July 23). 3M: Don't let efficiency ruin your creativity. *99U.* Retrieved from http://99u.com/workbook/29593/3m-dont-let-efficiency-ruin-your-creativity. (b) Hindo, B. (2007, June 11). At 3M, a struggle between efficiency and creativity. *Bloomberg BusinessWeek.* Retrieved from http://www.bloomberg.com/news/articles/2007-06-10/at-3m-a-struggle-between-efficiency-and-creativity

44. (a) Mikkelson, D. (2014). Brown out. Retrieved from http://www.snopes.com/music/artists/vanhalen.asp. (b) Roth, D. L. (2000). *Crazy from the heat.* New York, NY: Random House.

Chapter 6

1. Pasztor, A. (2015, October 22). Largest U.S. air ambulance operator embraces satellite data, simulators. *Wall Street Journal.* Retrieved from http://www.wsj.com/articles/largest-u-s-air-ambulance-operator-embraces-satellite-data-simulators-1445555912

2. Kapadia, M. Measuring your process capability. Retrieved from http://www.symphonytech.com/articles/pdfs/processcapability.pdf

3. Phadke, M. S. (2010, February 26). Introduction to robust design (Taguchi Method). Retrieved from http://www.isixsigma.com/methodology/robust-design-taguchi-method/introduction-robust-design-taguchi-method/

4. Phadke, M. S. *op. cit.*

5. (a) Csere, C. (2011, December). The trouble with J.D. Power's initial quality study. *Car and Driver.* Retrieved from http://www.caranddriver.com/features/the-trouble-with-jd-powers-initial-quality-study-feature. (b) J.D. Power (2015, June 17). Korean brands lead industry in initial quality, while Japanese brands struggle to keep up with pace of improvement. *J.D. Power.* Retrieved from http://www.jdpower.com/press-releases/2015-us-initial-quality-study-iqs

6. Buligiu, I., Litoiu, V., & Mehedintu, A. (2008). Using Taguchi methods in information systems quality. *University of Craiova.* Retrieved from http://feaa.ucv.ro/annals/v6_2008/0036v6-016.pdf

Chapter 7

1. (a) Clifford, S. (2011, September 13). Demand at Target for fashion line crashes web site. Retrieved from http://www.nytimes.com/2011/09/14/business/demand-at-target-for-fashion-line-crashes-web-site.html. (b) CBS/AP. (2011, September 14). Missoni craze crashes Target's website. *CBSNews.com.* Retrieved from http://www.cbsnews.com/2100-500169_162-20105902.html; (c) Denley, S. (2011, September 13). Missoni for Target sparks lines, empty racks, website crash. Retrieved from http://latimesblogs.latimes.com/alltherage/2011/09/missoni-for-

target-sparks-lines-website-crash-.html. (d) Hines, A. (2011, September 14). Did Target's Missoni buzz backfire? Fashion fans crash website, storm store. *Daily Finance*. Retrieved from http://www.dailyfinance.com/2011/09/14/target-overpowered-by-missoni-buzz-fashion-fans-crash-website/

2. (a) Drug shortages due to lack of manufacturing capacity, U.S. says. (2011, October 31). Business Week. Retrieved from http://www.businessweek.com/news/2011-10-31/drug-shortages-due-to-lack-of-manufacturing-capacity-u-s-says.html. (b) Fink, S. (2016, January 29). Drug shortages forcing hard decisions on rationing treatments. *The New York Times*. Retrieved from http://www.nytimes.com/2016/01/29/us/drug-shortages-forcing-hard-decisions-on-rationing-treatments.html

3. Dorfman, P. (2015, May 20). China pushes ahead with high risk, high cost nuclear. *China Dialogue*. Retrieved from https://www.chinadialogue.net/article/show/single/en/7921-China-pushes-ahead-with-high-risk-high-cost-nuclear

4. (a) Baker, N. (2011, October 10). Qatar to build $1 billion polysilicon manufacturing plant. Retrieved from http://theenergycollective.com/nathanaelbaker/66720/qatar-build-1-billion-polysilicon-manufacturing-plant. (b) QSTec. (2016). Project update. Retrieved from http://www.qstec.com/about/project-update

5. (a) WSJ Online. (2011, January 28). DAVOS: Suntech Power chairman: To set up more manufacturing facilities overseas. *Wall Street Journal*. Retrieved from http://online.wsj.com/article/BT-CO-20110128-712430.html. (b) Bathon, M. (2015, January 12). China's Suntech Power U.S. unit seeks bankruptcy protection. *Bloomberg Business*. Retrieved from http://www.bloomberg.com/news/articles/2015-01-12/suntech-america-files-for-bankruptcy-owing-at-least-100-million

6. Sasaki, B. (2008). Capacity cushions and the airline industry. Retrieved from http://capacitycushions.blogspot.com/

7. Mitchell, K. (2014, July 23). Improving hospital-wide patient flow using real-time demand capacity management. *Institute for Health Improvement*. Retrieved from http://www.ihi.org/communities/blogs/_layouts/ihi/community/blog/itemview.aspx?List=113a95c2-dffe-41ec-abee-93b4088068ac&ID=21

8. (a) Slack, N., Chambers, S., Harland, C., Harrison, A., & Johnson, R. (2001). *Operations management* (3rd ed.). New York, NY: Pitman. (b) 123HelpMe.com. (2016, July 15). Capacity planning and control: Nestle. Retrieved from http://www.123helpme.com/view.asp?id=164052

9. Gaebler Ventures. (2011). Capacity planning for business services. Retrieved from http://www.gaebler.com/Capacity-Planning-for-Business-Services.htm

10. Wang, K., Buxton, D., Farr, R., & MacCarthy, B. (2005). Investigation of strategic capacity issues in the aerospace sector. Retrieved July 24, 2004, from http://www.vivaceproject.com/content/engine/isci_full.pdf

11. Buxbaum, P. (2016, March 21). As Panama Canal expansion nears completion, will East Coast ports benefit? *American Journal of Transportation*. Retrieved from https://www.ajot.com/premium/ajot-as-panama-canal-expansion-nears-completion-will-east-coast-ports-benef

12. Satyaveer, R. N., & Proth, J-M. (2004). Strategic capacity planning in supply chain design for a new market opportunity. *International Journal of Production Research*, *42*(11), 2197–2206.

13. Lunsford, J. L. (2007, March 27). Burned by the last boom, Boeing curbs its pace. *Wall Street Journal*. Retrieved from http://online.wsj.com/article/SB117487373132548592.16.html

14. Wang, Buxton, Farr, & MacCarthy, *op. cit.*

15. (a) Mann, T. (2016, June 7). United Technologies' Pratt struggles with supply chain for new jet engine. *Wall Street Journal*. Retrieved from http://www.nasdaq.com/article/united-technologies-pratt-struggles-with-supply-chain-for-new-jet-engine-20160607-00938. (b) Amarnath, N. (2012, July 10). World's top 3 jet engine makers exploit booming airline market. *International Business Times*. Retrieved from http://www.ibtimes.com/worlds-top-3-jet-engine-makers-exploit-booming-airline-market-722046. (c) Reuters. (2016, June 8). Under fire Pratt says aircraft engine issues resolved. *ArabianBusiness.com*. Retrieved from http://www.arabianbusiness.com/under-fire-pratt-says-aircraft-engine-issues-resolved-634685.html#.V16zueYrJBw

16. Wang, Buxton, Farr, & MacCarthy, *op. cit.*

17. Karabuk, S., & Wu, S. D. (2003). Coordinating strategic capacity planning in the semiconductor industry. *Operations Research*, *51*(6), 839–849.

18. Bullis, K. (2014, November 25). Why Apple failed to make sapphire iPhone. *MIT Technology Review*. Retrieved from https://www.technologyreview.com/s/532636/why-apple-failed-to-make-sapphire-iphones/

19. *The Economic Times*. (2015, January 30). Indian suppliers to MNCs like L'Oreal, Dell may lose out if they fail to address climate concerns. Retrieved from http://www.eco-business.com/news/indian-suppliers-mncs-loreal-dell-may-lose-out-if-they-fail-address-climate-concerns/

20. Xu, L., & Beamon, B. M. (2006). Supply chain coordination and cooperation mechanisms: an attribute-based approach. *Journal of Supply Chain Management*, *42*(1), 4–12.

21. Erkoc, M., & Wu, S. D. (2005). Managing high-tech capacity expansion via reservation contracts.

Production and Operations Management, *14*(2), 1–20.

22. (a) Kouvelis, P., & Milner, J. M. (2002). Supply chain capacity and outsourcing decisions: The dynamic interplay of demand and supply uncertainty. *IIE Transactions*, *34*(8): 717–728. (b) Jin, M., & Wu, S. D. (2007). Capacity reservation contracts for high-tech industry. *European Journal of Operational Research*, *176*(3), 1659–1677.

23. Tomlin, B. (2003). Capacity investments in supply chains: Sharing the gain rather than sharing the pain. *Manufacturing & Service Operations Management*, *5*(4), 317–333.

24. Wu, S. D., Erkoc, M., & Karabuk, S. (2005). Managing capacity in the high-tech industry: A review of literature. The Engineering Economist, 50, 125-158.

25. Koel, J. (2013, July 23). How 5 manufacturers reduce water use. *Sustainable Manufacturer Network*. Retrieved from http://sustainablemfr.com/water/5-manufacturers-reduce-water-use

26. (a) Succezz.com. (n.d.). Ethics in business. Retrieved June 24, 2015, from http://www.succezz.com/Articles/business-ethics-dilemma-reason4.html. (b) D'Silva, T. (2006). *The black box of Bhopal: A closer look at the world's deadliest industrial disaster*. Victoria, BC, Canada: Trafford. (c) Tinsley, A., & Ansell, R. (2011, October). Bhopal's never ending disaster. *The Environmentalist*, 16–20. (d) Associated Press. (2011, July 15). Nike still dogged by worker abuses. *Japan Times*, p. 4. (e) Glenn, T. (1997). Nike's cheap labor. *CRLabor.org*. Retrieved June 24, 2015, from http://www.clrlabor.org/alerts/1997/nikey001.html. (f) Reed, B. (2011, February 15). Apple nixes child labor practices at Chinese factories. Retrieved June 24, 2015, from http://www.networkworld.com/news/2011/021511-apple-child-labor.html. (g) Barry Callebaut website. About Us page. Retrieved from https://www.barry-callebaut.com/about-us. (h) Wal-Mart. (2012). Ethical sourcing. Retrieved June 24, 2015, from http://walmartstores.com/download/5133.pdf (i) Kinaxis. (2014). *An integrated approach to global capacity management*. White paper. Retrieved from http://www.kinaxis.com/Global/resources/papers/global-capacity-management-white-paper-kinaxis.pdf?elq=0a839b89c0d7495497a2f202f33da92d&elqCampaignId=

27. Kinaxis, *op. cit.*

28. Seetharaman, D. (2013, October 8). Ford targets one-third increase in global capacity within 5 years. *Automotive News*. Retrieved from http://www.autonews.com/article/20131008/OEM01/131009875/ford-targets-one-third-increase-in-global-capacity-within-5-years

29. (a) Reed, *op. cit.* (b) Barry Callebaut, *op. cit.* (c) Wal-Mart, *op. cit.*

30. Kinaxis, *op. cit.*

Chapter 8

1. (a) Muller, J. (2014, August 20). America's car capital will soon be . . . Mexico. *Forbes*. Retrieved from http://www.forbes.com/sites/joannmuller/2014/08/20/americas-car-capital-will-soon-be-mexico/. (b) Coy, P. (2013, June 27). Four reasons Mexico is becoming a global manufacturing power. *Bloomberg Business*. Retrieved from http://www.bloomberg.com/bw/articles/2013-06-27/four-reasons-mexico-is-becoming-a-global-manufacturing-power

2. Chopra, S., & Meindl, P. (2010). Network design in the supply chain. In *Supply Chain Management–Strategy, Planning and Operation* (4th ed., pp. 107–116). Upper Saddle River, NJ: Prentice-Hall.

3. Daskin, M. S., Snyder, L. V., & Berger, R. T. (2005). Facility location in supply chain design. In A. Langevin & D. Riopel (Eds.), *Logistics systems: Design and optimization* (pp. 39–65). New York, NY: Springer Science + Business Media.

4. Riley, M., & Vance, A. (2012, March 19). It's not paranoia if they steal your secrets. *Bloomsberg Businessweek*, pp. 76–84.

5. Caracas newsroom. (2012, October 7). Factbox: Venezuela's nationalizations under Chavez. *Reuters*. Retrieved from http://www.reuters.com/article/us-venezuela-election-nationalizations-idUSBRE89701X20121008

6. Industry Week Staff. (2013, November 14). Nissan celebrates phase one of $2 billion growth in Mexico. *Industry Week*. Retrieved from http://www.industryweek.com/expansion-management/nissan-celebrates-phase-one-2-billion-growth-mexico

7. (a) Shanker, A. (2011, September 20). ArcelorMittal's first Indian steel mill may beat Posco plant. Retrieved from http://www.bloomberg.com/news/articles/2011-09-19/arcelormittal-s-first-indian-steel-plant-may-beat-posco-project. (b) MeatIsplace.com. (2010, March 12). Iron ore prices to rise on China resource depletion: Fortescue. Retrieved April 24, 2010, from http://metalsplace.com/news/articles/33383/iron-ore-prices-to-rise-on-china-resource-depletion-fortescue/. (c) Parker, V. (2004). RioTinto and Madagascar—Is it Equitable? Retrieved from http://www.andrewleestrust.org/Reports/QitFer%20Minerals%20Madagascar.pdf

8. (a) Porter, M. E., & Stern, S. (2001, July 15). Innovation: Location matters. *MIT Sloan Management Review*. Retrieved from http://sloanreview.mit.edu/the-magazine/2001-summer/4242/innovation-location-matters/. (b) Feldman, M. (2011, Summer). Location, location, location: Creating innovation clusters. *Democracy*, 21. Retrieved from http://democracyjournal.org/magazine/21/location-location-location-creating-innovation-clusters/

9. (a) Philippidis, A. (2011, August 16). U.S. stem cell companies find

partners and revenues beyond the water's edge. *GEN*. Retrieved from http://www.genengnews.com/analysis-and-insight/u-s-stem-cell-companies-find-partners-and-revenues-beyond-the-water-s-edge/77899444/. (b) Kidwai, M. (n.d.). About American companies moving overseas. http://www.ehow.com/about_6403114_american-companies-moving-overseas.html#ixzz1lsgCPoDR. (c) McBride, W. (2014, February 19). Another U.S. company moves to Ireland for tax reasons. *Tax Foundation*. Retrieved from http://taxfoundation.org/blog/another-us-company-moves-ireland-tax-reasons

10. John, C. (n.d.). What issues arise when doing business globally? Retrieved from http://www.ehow.com/list_6130272_issues-arise-doing-business-globally_.html#ixzz1lvjyqBfa

11. Gao, G. (2015, March 12). How do Americans stand out from the rest of the world? *Pew Research Center*. Retrieved from http://www.pewresearch.org/fact-tank/2015/03/12/how-do-americans-stand-out-from-the-rest-of-the-world/

12. Gillespie, P. (2015, February 11). Venezuela is causing havoc on U.S. companies. *CNN Money*. Retrieved from http://money.cnn.com/2015/02/11/investing/pepsi-venezuela-hurting-us-companies/

13. IPRI. (n.d.). The International Property Rights Index 2015. Retrieved from http://internationalpropertyrightsindex.org/countries

14. Perkowski, J. (2012, April 18). Protecting intellectual property rights in China. *Forbes*. Retrieved from http://www.forbes.com/sites/jackperkowski/2012/04/18/protecting-intellectual-property-rights-in-china/#7e8ed6aa4c01

15. (a) Schmitt, B. (2012, July 27). German paper: "China steals Volkswagen patents." *The Truth About Cars*. Retrieved from http://www.thetruthaboutcars.com/2012/07/german-paper-china-steals-volkswagen-patents/. (b) Tierney, C. (2014, March 28). China, German carmakers deepen ties. *Forbes*. Retrieved from http://www.forbes.com/sites/christinentierney/2014/03/28/china-german-carmakers-deepen-ties/#68c1a22949a3

16. (a) Barnes, B. (2009, November 3). China approves Disney theme park in Shanghai. *The New York Times*. Retrieved from http://www.nytimes.com/2009/11/04/business/global/04disney.html?scp=19&sq=global%20location%20planning&st=Search. (b) Riley, C. (2016, January 13). Disney's $5 billion Chinese theme park set to open. *CNN Money*. Retrieved from http://money.cnn.com/2016/01/13/news/disney-china-shanghai-disneyland-opening/. (c) Barboza, D., & Barnes, B. (2016, June 14). How China won the keys to Disney's Magic Kingdom. *The New York Times*. Retrieved from http://www.nytimes.com/2016/06/15/business/international/china-disney.html?_r=0

17. Barnes, *op. cit.*

18. Although the breakeven analysis model is easy to understand and use, it has several shortcomings. For example, it does not take into account the time value of money like a net present value analysis does.

19. Tozzi, J. (2008, December 29). Where to locate your business. Retrieved from http://www.bloomberg.com/news/articles/2008-12-29/where-to-locate-your-businessbusinessweek-business-news-stock-market-and-financial-advice

20. Marros, R. J. (2005). Using a geographic information system (GIS) to visualize and analyze spatial location in a retail environment. Department of Resource Analysis, Saint Mary's University of Minnesota, Winona, MN 55987. Retrieved from http://www.gis.smumn.edu/GradProjects/MarrosR.pdf

21. Kalantari, A. (2013). *Facility location selection for global manufacturing*. Theses and Dissertations, Paper 233.

22. Mulvey, J. (2010, September 3). American made: Five companies bucking the outsourcing trend." *Live Science*. Retrieved from http://www.livescience.com/8570-american-companies-bucking-outsourcing-trend.html

23. Marek, J. B. (2010, September 14). How corporate location decisions are REALLY made [Blog post]. Retrieved from https://thunktank.wordpress.com/2010/09/14/how-corporate-location-decisions-are-really-made/

24. Ramsey, M. (2015, September 11). China car maker opens U.S. office. *Wall Street Journal*, p. B5.

25. Business Standard Reporter. (2015, September 10). Ikea's first India outlet not before 2017. *Business Standard*. Retrieved from http://www.business-standard.com/article/companies/ikea-s-first-india-outlet-not-before-2017-115090901025_1.html

26. Gerdeman, D. (2012, January 9). Location, location, location: The strategy of place. *Working Knowledge*. Retrieved from http://hbswk.hbs.edu/item/6916.html

27. De Andino, J. M. M. (2014, February 3). Counterfeits in the supply chain: A big problem and it's getting worse. *IndustryWeek*. Retrieved from http://www.industryweek.com/inventory-management/counterfeits-supply-chain-big-problem-and-its-getting-worse

Chapter 9

1. (a) Wrigley. (2012). Mars: Principles in action highlights 2011. White paper. Retrieved from http://www.wrigley.com/global/static/2011-principles-in-action-showcase/Wrigley-PIA-Summary-10-2012.pdf. (b) Mars., Inc. website. Our Brands page. Retrieved from http://www.mars.com/global/brands.aspx. (c) Gunther, M. (2012, May 30). Why Mars is a sustainability leader. Retrieved from http://www.marcgunther.com/why-mars-is-a-sustainability-leader/

2. Rockford Consulting Group, Ltd. (2006). Mass customization. *RCG University*. Retrieved from http://rockfordconsulting.com/mass-customization.htm

3. Menda, R., Hill, T. J., & Dilts, D. M. (1998, April 4). Using product profiling to illustrate manufacturing-marketing misalignment. *Interfaces, 28*, 47–63.

4. Slate, R. (2009). Competing with intelligence: New directions in China's quest for intangible property and implications for homeland security. *Homeland Security Affairs, V*(1), 1–27.

5. Wakefield, J. (2016, January 19). Apple, Samsung and Sony face child labor claims. *BBC News*. Retrieved from http://www.bbc.com/news/technology-35311456

6. (a) Guizzo, E. (2010, April 14). World robot population reaches 8.6 million. *IEEE Spectrum*. Retrieved from http://spectrum.ieee.org/automaton/robotics/industrial-robots/041410-world-robot-population. (b) Phillips, E. E. (2016, March 28). Massive robots keep docks shipshape. *Wall Street Journal*, pp. B1–B2.

7. Browne, E., et al. (1984). Classification of flexible manufacturing systems. *FMS Magazine, 1*, 114–117.

8. (a) Electronic Enterprise Integration Committee. (n.d.). *Standard for the Exchange of Product model data (STEP - ISO 10303)*. Arlington, VA: Aerospace Industries Association. http://www.aia-aerospace.org/assets/ebusiness/step.doc. (b) *BigCityLib*. (2012, March 25). *On replacing the F-35* [Blog post]. BigCityLib Strikes Back. Retrieved from http://bigcitylib.blogspot.com/2012/03/on-replacing-f-35.html

9. Khemani, H. (2010, January 30). Computer aided process planning or CAPP. *Bright Hub Engineering*. Retrieved from http://www.brighthubengineering.com/cad-autocad-reviews-tips/62842-computer-aided-process-planning-or-capp/

10. Roodbergen, K. J., & Vis, I. F. A. (2009). A survey of the literature on automated storage and retrieval systems. *European Journal of Operational Research, 194*, 343–362.

11. The Red Carnation Hotel Collection. (n.d.). Core Values page. Retrieved from http://www.redcarnationhotels.com/about/core-values

12. Schmenner, *op. cit.*, pp. 21–32.

13. Schmenner, *op. cit.*, pp. 21–32.

14. (a) Marchetti, S. (2010, May 30). McDonalds calls local foods campaign a success. Retrieved from http://www.globalpost.com/dispatch/italy/100521/mcdonalds-mcitaly-menu. (b) Brand Eating. (2014, December 15). McDonald's newest McItaly burger features fresh mozzarella. Retrieved from http://www.brandeating.com/2014/12/mcdonalds-newest-mcitaly-burger-features-fresh-mozzarella.html

15. Bozarth, C. C., & Handfield, R. B. (2013). *Introduction to operations and supply chain management* (3rd ed., pp. 180–181). Englewood Cliffs, NJ: Pearson Prentice-Hall.

16. Harrison, T. P., Lee, H. L., & Neale, J. J. (2005). *The practice of supply chain management*. New York, NY: Springer Science and Business Media.

17. Flores, *op. cit.*

18. Flores, *op. cit.*

19. Flores, *op. cit.*

20. West, M., & Bengtsson, J. (2007). Aggregate production process design in global manufacturing using a real options approach. *International Journal of Production Research, 45*(8), 1745–1762.

21. Dauriz, L., Remy, N., & Tochtermann, T. (2014, February). A multifaceted future: The jewelry industry in 2020. *McKinsey & Company*. Retrieved from http://www.mckinsey.com/industries/retail/our-insights/a-multifaceted-future-the-jewelry-industry-in-2020

22. Aase, G. R., Olsen, J. R., & Schneiderjans, M. J. (2004). U-shaped assembly line layouts and their impact on labor productivity: An experimental study. *European Journal of Operational Research, 156*(3), 698–711.

23. Steelcase Services. (2005, October). Boeing: Shaking things up. *Case Studies Corporate*. Retrieved from https://www.steelcase.com/insights/case-studies/the-boeing-company/. (b) Gates, D. (2015, March 21). Boeing retools Renton plant with automation for 737's big ramp-up. *The Seattle Times*. Retrieved from http://www.seattletimes.com/business/boeing-aerospace/boeing-retools-renton-plant-for-737s-big-ramp-up/

24. Weber, A. (2004, November 4). The pros and cons of cells. *Assembly Magazine*. Retrieved from http://www.assemblymag.com/articles/83136-the-pros-and-cons-of-cells

25. Booms, B. H., & Bitner, M. J. (1981). Marketing strategies and organization structures for service firms. In J. Donnelly & W. R. George (Eds.), *Marketing of services* (p. 36). Chicago, IL: American Marketing Association.

26. Aishah. (2009, January 17). Why do we need layout design? [Blog post]. *Layout Designs for Warehousing Operations*. Retrieved from http://warehouse-layoutdesigns.blogspot.com/

27. Bertorello, C. (2009, September 1). Critical steps to planning a cost-effective warehouse. *Material Handling & Logistics*. Retrieved from http://mhlnews.com/facilities-management/critical-steps-planning-cost-effective-warehouse

28. Gorodesky, R., & Madigan, E. (n.d.). Restaurant design: Elements of successful restaurant interior design. *RestaurantReport*. Retrieved from http://www.restaurantreport.com/features/ft_design.html

29. ch2m.com. (n.d.). Sustainable factory design for Nike. Retrieved from http://www.ch2m.com/corporate/services/sustainable_solutions/assets/ProjectPortfolio/Nike.pdf

30. Tyler. (2011, September 7). Keep me vertical! Sustainable factories in today's cities. *Didactic Discourse*. Retrieved from http://didacticdiscourse.wordpress.com/2011/09/07/keep-me-vertical-sustainable-factories-in-todays-cities/

31. Winter, D. (2014, October 20). Big box retail's latest bright idea: Solar power. *Bloomberg Businessweek*. Retrieved from http://www.businessweek.com/articles/2014-10-20/big-box-retails-latest-bright-idea-solar-power

32. Fletcher, O. (2012, October 15). The future of agriculture may be up. *Wall Street Journal*. Retrieved from http://online.wsj.com/article/SB10000872396390443858504576029606729855508.html

Chapter 9 Supplement

1. George Washington University School of Public Health & Health Services Center for Health Policy Research. (2011, February 4). *Charted door-to-bed process flow chart*. Princeton, NJ: Robert Wood Johnson Foundation. Retrieved from http://www.rwjf.org/en/library/research/2011/02/charted-door-to-bed-process-flow-chart.html

2. Wilson, A., Zeithaml, V. A., Bitner, M. J., & Gremler, D. D. (2008). *Services marketing: Integrating customers focus across the firm* (pp. 203–206). Glasgow, Scotland: McGraw Hill.

3. Muther, R. (1961). Simplified systematic layout planning. Boston, MA: Industrial Education Institute.

Chapter 10

1. (a) Sauers, J. (2012, December 31). Factory fires and massive protests, or, the year in fashion disasters. *Jezebel*. Retrieved from http://jezebel.com/5971735/factory-fires-and-massive-protests-or-the-year-in-fashion-disasters/gallery/1. (b) Power, C.,

& Devnath, A. (2012, December 27). Bangladesh's Tazreen fire is followed by further garment factory blazes. *Bloomberg BusinessWeek*. Retrieved from http://www.businessweek.com/articles/2012-12-27/after-the-tazreen-fire-in-bangladesh-more-fires-in-garment-factories. (c) Banjo, S. (2013, January 22). Wal-Mart toughens supplier policies. *Wall Street Journal*, pp. B1 and B7. (d) Bain, M. (2015, August 12). Bangladesh is building "garment villages" to double its already-huge clothing exports. *Quartz*. Retrieved from http://qz.com/477915/bangladesh-is-building-garment-villages-to-double-its-already-huge-clothing-exports/

2. Causey, M. (2010, February 10). Toyota woes highlight importance of supplier quality management [Blog post]. *Assurx.com*. Retrieved from http://blog.assurx.com/2010/02/10/toyota-woes-highlight-importance-of-supplier-quality-management/

3. MacKenzie, C. A., Santos, J. R., & Barker, K. (2012). Measuring changes in international production from a disruption: Case study of the Japanese earthquake and tsunami. *International Journal of Production Economics*, 138, 293–302.

4. Huang, G. (2014, March 19). Sony focuses supply chain on 250 partners to speed production. *Bloomberg*. Retrieved from http://www.bloomberg.com/news/articles/2014-03-20/sony-focuses-supply-chain-on-250-partners-to-speed-production

5. Ellram, L. M. (1993). A framework for total cost of ownership. *The International Journal of Logistics Management*, 4, 49–60.

6. Ellram, L. M. (1996). Total cost of ownership – an analysis approach for purchasing. *International Journal of Physical Distribution & Logistics*, 25(8), 4–23.

7. Tevelson, R., Zygelman, J., Farrell, P., Benett, S., Rosenfeld, P., & Alsen, A. (2013, August 21). Buyer-Supplier collaboration – a roadmap for success. *BCG Perspectives*. Retrieved from https://www.bcgperspectives.com/content/articles/sourcing_procurement_supply_chain_management_buyer_supplier_collaboration_roadmap_for_success/

8. (a) Suddath, C. (2013, February 6). Where's the Beef? Ireland hit by horse-meat scandal. *BusinessWeek*. Retrieved from http://www.businessweek.com/articles/2013-02-06/wheres-the-beef-ireland-hit-by-horse-meat-scandal. (b) Associated Press. (2013, February 7). Poland: Still no sign country source of horse meat. Retrieved from http://newsinfo.inquirer.net/354471/poland-still-no-sign-country-source-of-horsemeat. (c) BBC

News. (2013, February 14). Irish burgers recalled after new horsemeat discovery. Retrieved from http://www.bbc.co.uk/news/uk-northern-ireland-21459307

9. Matthews, C. (2013, January 16). Is Walmart's buy American/hire veterans initiative anything more than a PR stunt? Retrieved from http://business.time.com/2013/01/16/is-walmarts-buy-americanhire-veterans-initiative-anything-more-than-a-pr-stunt/

10. Robinson, D. (2007, September 1). Suppliers are the engine for innovation. *Sudbury Mining Solutions Journal*. Retrieved from http://www.sudburyminingsolutions.com/suppliers-are-the-engine-for-innovation.html

11. Charon, F. (2012, February 2). How tier 1 automotive suppliers are leading consumers toward innovation. *IndustryWeek*. Retrieved from http://www.industryweek.com/global-economy/how-tier-1-automotive-suppliers-are-leading-consumers-toward-innovation

12. (a) Ball, R. L. (2005, May 10). Strategic sourcing: A recipe for strategic excellence. *Government Product News and Government Procurement*. Retrieved October 12, 2013, from http://govpro.com/resource_center/gov_imp_27871/. (b) The Strategic Sourceror. (2012, October 12). Disney cuts ties with controversial suppliers. Retrieved from http://www.strategicsourceror.com/2012/10/disney-cuts-ties-with-controversial.html

13. Ball, R. L. (2005, May 10). *op. cit.*

14. Bartels, A., Pohlmann, T., Lo, H., & Lee, C. (2008). *Market overview 2008: Automated spend analysis*. Cambridge, MA: Forrester Research.

15. eSourcing Forum. (2010, March 16). It's what you don't know that costs you, part 2: What is the value of strong spend analysis? Retrieved from http://www.esourcingforum.com/archives/2010/03/16/it%E2%80%99s-what-you-don%E2%80%99t-know-that-cost%E2%80%99s-you-part-2-what-is-the-value-of-strong-spend-analysis/

16. Aberdeen Group. (2004, September). Best practices in spending analysis – cure for a corporate epidemic. Retrieved from https://www.unspsc.org/Portals/3/Documents/Best%20Practices%20in%20Spending%20Analysis%20--%20Cure%20for%20a%20Corporate%20Epidemic.pdf

17. Bush, D., & Strovink, E. (2006). Spend analysis and opportunity assessment. *eSourcing Wiki*. Retrieved from http://esourcingwiki.com/index.php/Spend_Analysis_and_Opportunity_Assessment

18. Aberdeen Group. *op. cit.*

19. Patterson, S. (2005). Supply base optimization and integrated

supply chain management. *Contract Management*, 45(1), 24–35.

20. Williams, M. (2012, April 10). Is dual-sourcing right for you? *Parcel*. Retrieved from http://parcelindustry.com/article-3086-is-dual-sourcing-right-for-you-.html

21. Field, A. (2014, February 25). An easy way to buy local food. *Forbes*. Retrieved from http://www.forbes.com/sites/annefield/2014/02/25/an-easy-way-to-buy-local-food/#4c549d960594

22. Blevins, J. (2011). Buyer-supplier relationships. Retrieved from http://apicstoledo.org/wp-content/uploads/2011/06/Buyer-Supplier-Relationships.pdf

23. Blevins, J. *op. cit.*

24. Warren, T. (2015, June 11). Microsoft's Oculus partnership is a very clever move. *The Verge*. Retrieved from http://www.theverge.com/2015/6/11/8768275/microsoft-oculus-partnership-is-clever

25. Ball, R. L. *op. cit.*

26. Korostelina, O. (2012, March 17). Online reverse auctions: A cost-saving inspiration for businesses. *Dartmouth Business Journal*. Retrieved from http://dartmouthbusinessjournal.com/2012/03/online-reverse-auctions-a-cost-saving-inspiration-for-businesses/

27. (a) Chopra, S., & Meindl, P. (2009). *Supply chain management: Strategy, planning, and operation* (4th ed., pp. 408–409). Upper Saddle River, NJ: Prentice-Hall. (b) Thompson, L. (2005). *The mind and heart of a negotiator*. Upper Saddle River, NJ: Prentice-Hall.

28. Zolfagharifard, E. (2011, March 28). Roll-Royce's LiftSystem for the joint strike fighter. *The Engineer*. Retrieved from http://www.theengineer.co.uk/in-depth/rolls-royces-liftsystem-for-the-joint-strike-fighter/1008008.article

29. Chopra, S., & Meindl, P. (2009). *op. cit.*, pp. 410–416.

30. Redbox. (2012, March 1). Redbox and Universal Studios Home Entertainment sign multi-year agreement. *Media Center Redbox*. Retrieved from http://www.redbox.com/release_20120301

31. Ball, R. L. *op. cit.*

32. (a) Farrell, P. V. (1982). *Aljian's Purchasing Handbook* (4th ed.). National Association of Purchasing Management. Boston, MA: McGraw-Hill. (b) Benton, W. C., & McHenry, L. (2009). *Construction purchasing and supply chain management*. Boston, MA: McGraw-Hill.

33. Sharma, B. (2009, March 18). Managing the Achilles tendon of environmental compliance. EETimes. Retrieved from http://www.eetimes.com/design/smarteenergy-design/4013563/Managing-the-Achilles-Tendon-of-Environmental-Compliance—151-Supplier-Management

34. (a) Barrett, J., & Rizza, M. N. (2008, June 6). Supplier performance management: It's more than a scorecard - it's a strategy. *AMR Research Alert.* (b) Gordon, S. (2009). Supplier performance management. *eSourcing Wiki.* Retrieved from http://www.esourcingwiki .com/index.php/Supplier_ Performance_Management

35. Gordon, S. R. (2008). *Supplier evaluation and performance excellence.* Fort Lauderdale, FL: J. Ross Publishing.

36. PYMNTS. (2015, August 19). New Target exec's supply chain challenge. *PYMNST.COM.* Retrieved from http://www .pymnts.com/in-depth/2015/ new-target-execs-supply-chain-challenge/

37. Stanford, D. D. (2013, February 4). Coke has a secret formula for orange juice, too. *Bloomberg BusinessWeek.* pp. 19–21.

38. (a) Renner, A. (2015, April 8). The five best practices for effective supplier information management. *Supply & Demand Chain Executive.* Retrieved from http://www. sdcexec.com/article/12062938/ why-is-clean-consistent-and-connected-supplier-information-important-for-effective-supplier-management. (b) Trade Interchange, (2013). What is supplier information management. *Trade Interchange, Ltd.* Retrieved from http://www.tradeinterchange. com/SIMsupplierInformation Management.aspx

39. Lawton, J. (2009, February 14). Five types of supply risk, and how to mitigate them. Retrieved from http:// blog.sourcinginnovation. com/2007/02/14/five-types-of-supply-risk-and-how-to-mitigate-them.aspx

40. Lawton, J. (2009). *op. cit.*

41. Hingorani, N. (2009, August 6). Supplier risk management. *IndustryWeek.* Retrieved from http://www.industryweek. com/articles/supplier_risk_ management_19728.aspx

42. (a) Hughes, J., & Wadd, J. (2012). Getting the most out of SRM. *Supply Chain Management Review,* 16(1), 22–29. (b) Brimacombe, A., Cotters, B. C., & Timmermans, K. (2011). Supplier relationships: Cracking the value code. Accenture. Retrieved from https://www .accenture.com/mx-es/~/media/ Accenture/Conversion-Assets/ DotCom/Documents/Local/ es-la/PDF2/Accenture-Releasing-the-Potential-from-Strategic-Supplier-Relationships.pdf

43. (a) Ludwig, C. (2013, July 1). Toyota's total supply chain vision. *Automotive Logistics.* Retrieved from http:// automotivelogistics.media/ interview/total-supply-chain-vision. (b) Choi, T. (2005, July 6). Deep supplier relationships drive automakers' success. *Arizona State University W.P. Carey School of Business.*

Retrieved from http://research. wpcarey.asu.edu/supply-chain/ deep-supplier-relationships-drive-automakers-success/

44. Albert, A. (2011, February 16). Apple audit exposes supplier malpractice. *Supply Management.* Retrieved from http://www.cips.org/supply-management/news/2011/ february/apple-audit-exposes-supplier-malpractice/

45. Busch, J. (2009, August 11). Changing suppliers is more than the cost of their parts. *Spend Matters.* Retrieved from http://www.spendmatters.com/ index.cfm/2009/8/11/Changing-Suppliers-is-More-Than-the-Cost-of-Their-Parts

46. Weiss, D. C. (2010, May 18). Deposition company ended overseas outsourcing over quality problems. *ABA Journal.* Retrieved from http://www .abajournal.com/news/article/ deposition_company_ended_ overseas_outsourcing_due_to_ quality_problems/

47. Corbett, M. (2004). *The outsourcing revolution: Why it makes sense and how to do it right.* Fort Lauderdale, FL: Kaplan Publishing.

48. Banham, R. (2010). Managing risk: Reducing disruption in the global supply chain. *Wall Street Journal.* Retrieved from http://online.wsj.com/ad/article/ managingrisk-disruption

49. Basis staff. (n.d.). How Lubrizol reduce [Sic] manual steps in their SAP change control process with Transport Expresso [Blog post]. *Basis Technologies.* Retrieved from http://www .basistechnologies.com/lubrizol-reduce-manual-sap-changes-automate-application-release-automation

50. AT Kearney. (2011). Carbon disclosure project supply chain report 2011. *AT Kearney Carbon Disclosure Project.* Retrieved from https://www.cdp.net/ cdpresults/cdp-2011-supply-chain-report.pdf

51. Reynolds, A. (2012, December 1). Zara commits to toxic-free supply chain by 2020. *Supply Management.* Retrieved from http://www.cips.org/supply-management/news/2012/ november/zara-commits-to-toxic-free-supply-chain-by-2020/

52. Strom, S. (2016, April 26). Yogurt buyers send Dannon back to the farm. *New York Times.* Retrieved from http://www.nytimes .com/2016/04/27/business/ yogurt-buyers-send-dannon-back-to-the.html?_r=1

53. Buss, D. (2013, August 29). Patagonia enjoys unique benefits of its authentic sustainability ethos. *Brandchannel.* Retrieved from http://www.brandchannel. com/home/post/2013/08/29/ Patagonia-Sustainable-Ethos-082913.aspx

54. Bredenberg, A. (2012, December 3). Businesses increasingly rationalize supply chain sustainability. *IMT Green &*

Clean Journal. Retrieved from http://news.thomasnet.com/ imt/2012/12/03/businesses-increasingly-rationalize-supply-chain-sustainability

55. (a) Leach, A. (2012, November 16). Coca-Cola trains 40,000 supply chain farmers. *Supply Management.* Retrieved from http://www.cips.org/supply-management/news/2012/ november/coca-cola-trains-40000-supply-chain-farmers/. (b) Coca-Cola. (2015). Coca-Cola's sustainability report 2013-2014. Retrieved from http://www.coca-colacompany.com/content/dam/ journey/us/en/private/fileassets/ pdf/2014/09/2013-2014-coca-cola-sustainability-report-pdf.pdf

56. (a) Walsh, B. (2014, May 21). China's food safety problems go deeper than pet treats. *Time.* Retrieved from http://time. com/107922/china-pet-food-contamination-recall-video/. (b) Associated Press. (2015, January 6). Petco pulls pet treats from China suspected of killing, sickening thousands. *CBS News.* Retrieved from http://www. cbsnews.com/news/petco-pulls-chinese-pet-treats-suspected-of-killing-sickening-thousands/

57. (a) Bullis, K. (2013, January 16). Grounded Boeing 787 Dreamliners use batteries prone to overheating. *MIT Technology Review.* Retrieved from http:// www.technologyreview.com/ news/509981/grounded-boeing-787-dreamliners-use-batteries-prone-to-overheating/. (b) Masuda, J. (2013, January 16). GS Yuasa may take months to complete Boeing 787 battery probe. *Bloomberg Technology.* Retrieved from http://www. bloomberg.com/news/2013-01-17/gs-yuasa-may-take-months-to-complete-boeing-787-battery-probe.html. (c) Norris, G. (2013, February 18). Boeing's 787 batteries "101". *Aviation Week.* Retrieved from http:// www.aviationweek.com/Blogs. aspx?plckPostId=Blog:7a78f54e-b3dd-4fa6-ae6e-dff2ffd7bdbbPost:5e8acfbf-0e5f-4354-a6f3-f19ec0ac6556

Chapter 11

1. (a) Salopek, P. (2008, October 10). Off the lawless coast of Somalia, questions of who is pirating who. *Chicago Tribune.* (b) Abdullahi, N. (2008, December 10). "Toxic waste" behind Somali piracy. *Islamweb. net.* Retrieved from http://www .islamweb.net/en/article/147073/. (c) Clayton, J. (2005, April 3). Somalia's secret dumps of toxic waste washed ashore by tsunami. *THE TIMES.* Retrieved from http://www.thetimes.co.uk/ tto/news/world/article1975917. ece. (d) Archer, V., & Pelton, R. Y. (2012). Can we ever assess the true cost of piracy? *Somalia Report.* Retrieved from http:// somaliareport.com/index. php/post/2867/Can_We_Ever_

Assess_the_True_Cost_of_Piracy. (e) Hari, J. (2011, February 18). Somalia: "Pirates" or struggling fishermen? *Voltaire Network.* Retrieved from http://www .voltairenet.org/article168525. html

2. University of Arkansas. (2005, October 6). Hurricane Katrina showed critical importance of logistics and supply-chain management. *University of Arkansas News.* Retrieved from http://news.uark.edu/ articles/10148/hurricane-katrina-showed-critical-importance-of-logistics-and-supply-chain-management

3. (a) Nansi, P. (2008). What is logistics? What does it mean to projects?" *Project Monitor,* Retrieved October 12, 2013, from http://www.projectsmonitor.com/ detailnews.asp?newsid=6968. (b) Nansi, P. (2007, March 21). Importance of logistics. *Business Logistics & SCM.* Retrieved from http://logisticsmanagement andsupplychainmanagement. wordpress.com/2007/03/21/ importance-of-logistics/

4. (a) Treacy, M., & Wiersema, F. (1993, January-February). Customer intimacy and other value disciplines. *Harvard Business Review.* Retrieved from https://hbr.org/1993/01/ customer-intimacy-and-other-value-disciplines. (b) Zabanga Marketing. (2016, April 6). Market logistics decisions. Retrieved from http://www. zabanga.us/marketing-insight/ marketlogistics-decisions.html

5. VendorSeek. (n.d.). What is the fulfillment process? Retrieved from http://www.vendorseek. com/what-is-fulfillment-process .asp

6. Association of American Railroads website. Home page. Retrieved from http://www.aar .org

7. Office of Policy and Plans, Maritime Administration. (2013, November). *2011 U.S. water transportation statistical snapshot.* Washington, DC: U.S. Department of Transportation. Retrieved from http://www. marad.dot.gov/documents/ US_Water_Transportation_ Statistical_snapshot.pdf

8. Kentucky Association of Riverports. (n.d.). Why use the river? *Water Transport Benefits page.* Retrieved from http:// kentuckyriverports.com/water_ transport_benefits/

9. Association of Oil Pipelines. (n.d.). Why pipelines? Retrieved March 21, 2015, from http://aopl. org/aboutPipelines/

10. Pienaar, W. J. (2010, November). Logistics aspects of petroleum pipeline operations. *Journal of Transport and Supply Chain Management,* 224–242. Retrieved from http://www. jtscm.co.za/index.php/jtscm/ article/viewFile/69/65

11. 3rd Party Logistics. (n.d.). Toyota milk run optimize routing JIT [Blog post]. Retrieved from http://3rdpartylogistics.blogspot

.com/2011/08/toyota-milk-run-optimize-routing-jit.html

12. Chaudhuri, A., Giffi, C., Kandaswami, K., & Singh, S. K. (2009, January 1). Necessity breeds opportunity: Constraints, innovation and competitive advantage. *Deloitte Review, 4*. Retrieved from http://dupress.com/articles/necessity-breeds-opportunity-constraints-innovation-and-competitive-advantage/

13. (a) Bix, L., Rifon, N. J., de la Fuente, J., & Lockhart, H. (2004). The packaging matrix: Linking package design criteria to the marketing mix. Retrieved from https://www.researchgate.net/publication/282313342_The_Packaging_Matrix_Linking_Package_Design_Criteria_to_the_Marketing_Mix. (b) IDS Packaging. Retrieved November 1, 2013, from http://www.idspackaging.com/Common/Paper/Paper_47/Pdflmge.pdf

14. Apple.com. (n.d.). IPhone 4 environmental report. Retrieved from http://www.apple.com/environment/reports/docs/iPhone4_Product_Environmental_Report_2011.pdf

15. Admin. (2007, January 21). Importance and scope of material handling. *Cite.Co*. Retrieved from http://www.citeman.com/1413-importance-and-scope-of-material-handling.html#ixzz2OI99VCGH

16. Admin, *op. cit.*

17. Admin, *op. cit.*

18. Gilmore, D. (2015, June 25). First thoughts. *Supply Chain Digest*. Retrieved from http://www.scdigest.com/ASSETS/FIRSTTHOUGHTS/15-06-25.php?cid=9451

19. Swedberg, C. (2012, January 26). Construction waste-management company uses RFID and GPS. *RFID Journal*. Retrieved from http://www.rfidjournal.com/articles/view?9165/3

20. JOC.com. (n.d.). NAFTA trade. Retrieved from http://www.joc.com/special-topics/nafta-trade

21. Pagadala, P. M., & Mulaik, S. (2009). Now's the time for an India strategy. *CSCMP Supply Chain Quarterly, 1*. Retrieved from http://www.supplychainquarterly.com/topics/Global/scq200901india/

22. Maritime Administration. (2008). *Glossary of shipping terms*. Washington, DC: U.S. Department of Transportation. Retrieved from http://www.marad.dot.gov/documents/Glossary_final.pdf

23. U.S. Department of Commerce. (n.d.). Methods of payment in international trade: Chapter 1. *Trade Finance Guide*. Retrieved from http://trade.gov/publications/pdfs/tfg2008ch1.pdf

24. Murphy, P. R. Jr., & Wood, D. F. (2010). International logistics. In P. R. Murphy Jr. & D. F. Wood (Ed.), *Contemporary logistics* (10th ed., ch. 14, pp. 282–283). Upper-Saddle River, NJ: Prentice-Hall.

25. Overman, C. (2012, July). Readers' choice: Top 10 3PL excellence awards 2012. *Inbound Logistics*. Retrieved from http://www.inboundlogistics.com/cms/article/readers-choice-top-10-3pl-excellence-awards-2012/

26. Kamath, R. (2006, September 30). What is 3 PL, 4 PL and 5 PL business? Why are they called so? *Times of India*. Retrieved from http://articles.timesofindia.indiatimes.com/2006-09-30/open-space/27806466_1_3pl-logistics-supply-chain

27. (a) Thomas, J. Q. (2011). Healthcare logistics: Challenges and opportunities. *Ezine Articles*. Retrieved from http://EzineArticles.com/6486152

28. Maersk Line. (2012, December 21). Maersk Line wins 'Shipping Line of the Year' award [Press release]. Retrieved from http://www.maerskline.com/link/?page=news&path=/news/news20121221

29. (a) Wu, A. (2014, July 18). Good package, bad package: top sustainable packaging mistakes. *The Guardian*. Retrieved from http://www.theguardian.com/sustainable-business/2014/jul/18/good-product-bad-package-plastic-recycle-mistakes. (b) Retail Industry Leaders Association (RILA). Packaging. Retrieved November 1, 2013, from http://www.rila.org/sustainability/sustreport/productjourney/Pages/Packaging.aspx

30. Best Buy. (n.d.). Sustainable solutions—Exclusive Brands product design and packaging. Retrieved November 1, 2013, from http://sustainability.bby.com/management-approach/sustainable-solutions/product-design-packaging/

31. Heritage Pioneer Corporate Group. (n.d.). What is PUMA's clever little shopper? Retrieved from http://www.hpcorporategroup.com/what-is-pumas-clever-little-shopper.html

32. GENCO. (n.d.). Lean and Sustainability. Retrieved from http://www.genco.com/perspectives/green-logistics.php

33. (a) Deutsche Post. (2010). Towards sustainable logistics—a review of conceptual and operational solutions. In *Delivering tomorrow: Towards sustainable* logistics (ch. 4, pp. 84–95). Bonn, Germany: Author. Retrieved from http://www.dp-dhl.com/content/dam/logistik_populaer/trends/StudieSustainableLogistics/study_towards_sustainable_logistics.pdf. (b) LBR Staff Writer. (2009, November 15). DHL extends contract with Heathrow Airport. *Logistics Business Review*. Retrieved from http://www.logistics-business-review.com/news/dhl_extends_contract_with_heathrow_airport_091116. (c) Staff Writer. (2015, March 2). Gatwick hails DHL congestion-buster. *Air Cargo News*. Retrieved from http://www.aircargonews.net/news/single-view/news/gatwick-hails-dhl-congestion-buster.html

34. Deutsche Post, *op. cit.*

35. Global Logistics. (2012, January 25). Measuring sustainability & an organizations impact on the environment [Press release]. Retrieved from http://www.globallogisticsmedia.com/articles/view/measuring-sustainability--an-organizations-impact-on-the-environment

36. Gerdes, J. (2012, February 24). How Nike, Wal-Mart and Ikea save money and slash carbon by shipping smarter. *Forbes*. Retrieved from http://www.forbes.com/sites/justingerdes/2012/02/24/how-nike-wal-mart-and-ikea-are-saving-money-and-slashing-carbon-by-shipping-smarter/

37. Wisniewski, R. (2011, June 3). Filling empty miles also fills bottom line. *Material Handling & Logistics*. Retrieved from http://mhlnews.com/distribution/filling-empty-miles-fills-bottom-line-0603

38. Makower, J. (2015, November 17). Walmart sustainability at 10: An assessment. *Green Biz*. Retrieved from https://www.greenbiz.com/article/walmart-sustainability-10-assessment

Chapter 12

1. Barrie, L. (2010, March 2). Demand-driven replenishment helps sales success. *Just-style*. Retrieved from http://www.just-style.com/analysis/demand-driven-replenishment-helps-sales-success_id106900.aspx

2. IBM Global Business Services. (2006). Demand management: The next generation of forecasting. White Paper. Retrieved from http://www-935.ibm.com/services/us/gbs/bus/pdf/g510-6014-demand-management.pdf

3. (a) Blanchard, D. (2008, October 8). Top 10 demand planning strategies. *Industry Week*. Retrieved from http://www.industryweek.com/companies-amp-executives/top-10-demand-planning-strategies. (b) Cecere, L. (2014, July 23). A practitioner's guide to demand planning," *Supply Chain 247*. Retrieved from http://www.supplychain247.com/article/a_practitioners_guide_to_demand_planning

4. Morris, B. (2013, March 26). Boom times on the tracks: Rail capacity, spending soar. *Wall Street Journal*. Retrieved from http://online.wsj.com/article/SB10001424127887324034804578348214242291132.html

5. (a) Takahashi, Y. (2013, May 31). Shortages loom for Subaru. *Wall Street Journal*, p. B1. (b) Wane Staff. (2015, September 21). Subaru adding 1,200 jobs in $140M investment in Lafayette plant. *Wane.com*. Retrieved from http://wane.com/2015/09/21/subaru-adding-1200-jobs-in-140m-investment-in-lafayette-plant/

6. (a) Kinaxis.com. Demand planning: How to reduce the risk and impact of inaccurate demand forecasts. White Paper. Retrieved August 1, 2014, from http://www.kinaxis.com/whitepapers/Demand-Planning.cfm. (b) Anderson, D. L., Britt, F. F., & Favre, D. J. (1997, April). The 7 principles of supply chain management. *Supply Chain Management Review, 3*. Retrieved from http://www.supplychain247.com/article/7_principles_of_supply_chain_management_redux

7. Kinaxis.com, *op. cit.*

8. (a) Seifert, D. (2003). *Collaborative planning, forecasting, and replenishment: How to create a supply chain advantage*. New York, NY: AMACOM. (b) Barratt, M., & Oliveira, A. (2001). Exploring the experiences of collaborative planning initiatives. *International Journal of Physical Distribution & Logistics Management, 31*, 266–289.

9. Voluntary Interindustry Commerce Standards. (2004). CPFR: An overview. Retrieved April 17, 2014, from http://www.vics.org/docs/committees/cpfr/CPFR_Overview_US-A4.pdf

10. Toiviainen, T., & Hansen, J. (2011, February 2). Collaborative planning, forecasting, and replenishment. Unpublished manuscript. Retrieved from http://www.scf.usc.edu/~jdhansen/CPFR%20Research%20Paper.pdf

11. Kinaxis.com, *op. cit.*

12. Smart Software. (n.d.). Godiva case study. Retrieved August 1, 2014, from http://www.smartcorp.com/godiva.asp

13. IBM Global Business Services, *op. cit.*

14. (a) Aberdeen Group. (2006, December). Demand management in consumer industries: Technology strategies for managing demand in today's dynamic business environment. Retrieved August 1, 2014, from http://beepdf.com/doc/2507/demand_management_in_consumer_industries.html. (b) OM Partners. (2014, March 20). Shaw Industries extends its OMP Plus footprint with Central & Collaborative Forecasting and Inventory Optimization. Retrieved from https://ompartners.com/news-events/items/2014/Shaw-Industries-extends-its-OMP-Plus-footprint

15. Gartner, F., & Klappich, C. D. (2009, March 4). Global economic crisis demands new strategies for managing global supply chains. *SupplyChainBrain*. Retrieved from http://www.supplychainbrain.com/content/technology-solutions/sc-planning-optimization/single-article-page/article/global-economic-crisis-demands-new-strategies-for-managing-global-supply-chains/

16. Bursa, K. (2006). Do you have the right prescription for global demand planning visibility? *Manufacturing & Logistics IT*. Retrieved from http://www.logisticsit.com/articles/2006/10/30/2354-do-you-have-the-right-prescription-for-global-demand-planning

17. Aimi, G. (2006). Advantages of postponement. *Forbes*. Retrieved from http://www.forbes.com/2006/12/08/amr-product-postponement-biz-logistics-cx_ga_1208postpone.html

18. (a) Pagh, J. D., & Cooper, M. C. (1998). Supply chain postponement and speculation strategies: How to choose the right strategy. *Journal of Business Logistics*, *19*, 13–33. (b) Ernst, R., & Kamrad, B. (2000). Evaluation of supply chain structures through modularization and postponement. *European Journal of Operational Research*, *124*, 495–510. (c) Gladeya01. (n.d.). Supply-chain-postponement-managing the global demand supply. *PubArticles*. Retrieved from http://articles.pubarticles.com/supply-chain-postponement-managing-the-global-demand-supply-1315995484,334093.html. (d) Aimi, *op. cit.* (e) Fernandes, N., & Wahl, M. (2014, September 2). The supply chain benefits of postponement. *OPS Rules*. Retrieved from http://www.opsrules.com/supply-chain-optimization-blog/bid/340862/The-Supply-Chain-Benefits-of-Postponement

19. Kerin, R. A., Hartley, S. W., & Rudelius, W. (2015). *Marketing* (12th ed., ch. 16). Boston, MA: McGraw Hill/Irwin.

20. Kerin et al., *op. cit.*

21. Giamanco, B. K. (n.d.). Customer service skills. *Customer Service Training Center*. Retrieved from http://www.customerservicetrainingcenter.com/customer_service_the_importance_of_quality_customer_service.htm

22. Murphy, P. J., & Wood, D. F. (2011). *Contemporary logistics* (10th ed., ch. 7, pp. 123–127). Upper Saddle River, NJ: Prentice-Hall.

23. Shopatron Staff. (2013, May 3). Five basics of omni-channel retail [Blog post]. *Shopatron*. Retrieved from http://ecommerce.shopatron.com/blog-entry/peter-sheldons-basics-omni-channel-ecommerce

24. Van Raaij, E. M., Vernooij, M. J. A., & van Triest, S. (2003). The implementation of customer profitability analysis: A case study. *Industrial Marketing Management*, *32*, 573–583.

25. (a) Spears, J. (2013, February 9). Vacation flight sits on tarmac at Pearson airport all day. *The Star*. Retrieved from http://www.thestar.com/news/gta/2013/02/09/vacation_flight_sits_on_tarmac_at_pearson_airport_all_day.html. (b) Olshan, J. (2010, March 16). A 16-hour nightmare. *New York Post*. Retrieved from http://www.nypost.com/p/news/local/starving_passengers_rationed_pringles_VMyOd8P1MCNDDT4gPgsrRP

26. (a) Murphy & Wood, *op. cit.* (b) Patel, S. (2011, December 5). 10 top-rated service companies without the service – what would happen? *Rackspace*. Retrieved from http://www.rackspace.com/blog/10-top-rated-service-companies-without-the-service-what-would-happen/. (c) Branson, R. (2012). *Like a virgin: Secrets they won't teach you at business school*. New York, NY: Penguin.

27. Lipke, M. (2013, April 9). U.S. airline complaints take off; can fliers fight back? *Reuters*, Retrieved from http://www.reuters.com/article/2013/04/09/us-airlines-complaints-idUSBRE9380JP20130409

28. (a) Griffin, J. (1999, March 21). One unhappy customer can multiply to many. *Austin Business Journal*. Retrieved from http://www.bizjournals.com/austin/stories/1999/03/22/smallb3.html?page=all. (b) Wallace, L. (2014, May 21). Why it pays to complain via Twitter. *BBC*. Retrieved from http://www.bbc.com/news/business-27381699

29. (a) Backer, *op. cit.* (b) Asaf Zentler. Retrieved from http://www.fischerjordan.com/uploads/whitepapers/the_cost_of_bad_customer_service.pdf

30. Customer Service Zone. (n.d.). What common mistakes are made when choosing customer service metrics? Retrieved from http://customerservicezone.com/faq/mistakemeasure.htm

31. Murphy & Wood, *op. cit.*, p. 127.

32. Backer, B. (n.d.). How to restore customer satisfaction after customer service failure. *CSM*. Retrieved from http://www.customerservicemanager.com/how-to-restore-customer-satisfaction-after-customer-service-failure.htm

33. Strong, J. (2011, January 1). Customer focused supply chain management. *The ACA Group*. Retrieved from http://theacagroup.com/7-25-CustomerFocusedSCM.htm

34. (a) Langdon, J. (2010, August 5). The impact of sustainability on the customer experience. Retrieved from http://jedlangdon.com/2010/08/the-impact-of-sustainability-on-the-customer-experience/. (b) Sawhney, R. (2009, July 30). Broken guitar has United playing the blues to the cost of $180 million. *Fast Company*. Retrieved from http://www.fastcompany.com/1320152/broken-guitar-has-united-playing-blues-tune-180-million

35. (a) Langdon, *op. cit.* (b) Pierson, D. (2014, September 3). Perdue farms eliminates antibiotic use in chicken hatcheries. *Los Angeles Times*. Retrieved from http://www.latimes.com/business/la-fi-perdue-antibiotics-20140903-story.html

36. (a) Krogue, K. (2013, March 10). McDonalds slaps every other fast food restaurant across the face. Forbes. Retrieved from http://www.forbes.com/sites/kenkrogue/2013/05/10/mcdonalds-slaps-every-other-fast-food-restaurant-across-the-face/. (b) Wilkey, R. (2011, November 30). San Francisco Happy Meal toy ban takes effect, sidestepped by McDonalds. *Huffington Post*. Retrieved from http://www.huffingtonpost.com/2011/11/30/san-francisco-happy-meal-ban_n_1121186.html

37. (a) Rutledge, C. (2012, Spring). Predicting the future demand of rural health care. *Effect Magazine*. Retrieved February 21, 2013, from http://www.larsonallen.com/EFFECT/Predicting_the_Future_Demand_of_Rural_Health_Care.aspx. (b) Alfero, C., Barnhart, T., Bertsch, D., Graff, S., Hill, T., Lee, D., Ross, M., Schmidt, J., Slabach, B., & Sparks, K. (2013). The future of rural health. *National Rural Health Association Policy Brief*. Retrieved from https://www.ruralhealthinfo.org/topics/rural-health-policy/publications

Chapter 13

1. (a) Laskowski, A. (2016, February 5). Can't get a pair of L.L. Bean boots? *BU Today*. Retrieved from http://www.bu.edu/today/2016/cant-get-a-pair-of-l-l-bean-boots/. (b) Lam, B. (2015, October 19). Why L.L. Bean's boots keep selling out. *The Atlantic*. Retrieved from http://www.theatlantic.com/business/archive/2015/10/llbean-duck-boot-labor-shoes-maine/410863/. Bhasin, K. (2015, September 29). Why can't L.L. Bean keep the darned duck boots in stock? *Bloomberg*. Retrieved from http://www.bloomberg.com/news/articles/2015-09-29/why-can-t-l-l-bean-keep-the-darn-duck-boots-in-stock-

2. (a) ReportLinker. (2015, August). Facial care: Global industry guide. Retrieved from http://www.reportlinker.com/p0188830-summary/Facial-Care-Global-Industry-Guide.html. (b) ReportLinker. (2013, July 3). *PRNewswire*. Retrieved from http://www.prnewswire.com/news-releases/facial-care-global-industry-guide-marketline-industry-guides-214147671.html

3. Schouten, P. (2013, October 22). Better patient forecasts and schedule optimization improve patient care and curb staffing costs. *Becker's Hospital Review*. Retrieved from http://www.beckershospitalreview.com/hospital-management-administration/better-patient-forecasts-and-schedule-optimization-improve-patient-care-and-curb-staffing-costs.html

4. Urs, R. (2008, Summer). How to use a demand planning system for best forecasting and planning results. *Journal of Business Forecasting*, *27*(2):22–23, 28–29.

5. Urs, R. (2008, Summer) *op. cit.*

6. Karolefski, J. (2015, November 15). The future of demand forecasting. *Progressive Grocer*. Retrieved from http://www.progressivegrocer.com/departments/technology/future-demand-forecasting

7. (a) Ritter, N. (2013, February 18). The role of ethics in statistical forecasting. *National Institute of Justice*. Retrieved from http://www.nij.gov/journals/271/pages/predicting-recidivism-ethics.aspx. (b) Wachs, M. (1982). Ethical dilemmas in forecasting for public policy. *Public Administration Review*, *42*:562–567. (c) Bremner, R. (2015, July 15). Ford Pinto: The eco car that was an ethical disaster. *Motoring Research*. Retrieved from http://www.motoringresearch.com/car-news/ford-pinto-the-eco-car-that-was-an-ethical-disaster

8. (a) Associated Press. (2015, February 1). 2015 Super Bowl tickets fetching high prices. *WITN*. Retrieved from http://www.witn.com/home/headlines/The-shady-story-behind-soaring-Super-Bowl-ticket-prices-290416261.html. (b) Diamond, J. (2014, January 30). The ticket to Super Bowl pricing: Mother Nature. *Wall Street Journal*. Retrieved from http://www.wsj.com/articles/SB10001424052702304428004579353351674523232

Chapter 14

1. (a) Schoettle, A. (2004, May 3). Rolls-Royce getting lean to grow plant long-term. *Indianapolis Business Journal*. Retrieved March 1, 2015, from http://www.allbusiness.com/manufacturing/transportation-equipment-mfg/10629727-1.html. (b) IBJ Staff. (2009, December 21). Rolls-Royce bags $160 million contract. *Indianapolis Business Journal*. Retrieved from http://www.ibj.com/rollsroyce-bags-160m-military-contract/PARAMS/article/15270. (c) Norris, G. (2014, August 25). Rolls-Royce details advance and Ultrafan test plan. *Aviation Week*. Retrieved from http://aviationweek.com/commercial-aviation/rolls-royce-details-advance-and-ultrafan-test-plan

2. Nash, N. C. (1996, January 20). Putting Porsche in the pink. *The New York Times*. Retrieved from http://ise.tamu.edu/people/faculty/gaukler/615/putting%20porsche%20in%20the%20pink.pdf

3. (a) Phelps, T., Hoenes, T., & Smith, M. (2003). *Developing lean supply chains: A guidebook*. Altarum

Institute, The Boeing Company and MessierDowty Inc. (b) Holmes, S. (2001, June 4). Boeing Goes Lean. *Business Week*.

4. Canis, B. (2011). The motor vehicle supply chain: Effects of the Japanese earthquake and tsunami. *Congressional Research Service*, 7-5700. Retrieved from https://www.fas.org/sgp/crs/misc/R41831.pdf

5. Jones, D., & Priolo, R. (2015, October 20). How to transform your hospital using lean. *Planet Lean*. Retrieved from http://planet-lean.com/a-great-example-of-lean-healthcare-from-a-barcelona-hospital

6. Berczuk, C. (2008, June 1). The lean hospital. *The Hospitalist*. Retrieved from http://www.the-hospitalist.org/article/the-lean-hospital

7. (a) McBride, D. (2003, August 29). The 7 wastes in manufacturing. *EMS Consulting Group*. Retrieved from http://www.emsstrategies.com/dm090203article2.html. (b) Womack, J. P., & Jones, D. T. (2003). *Lean thinking*. New York, NY: Simon & Schuster.

8. Business Dictionary. (n.d.). Definition of "value stream." Retrieved from http://www.businessdictionary.com/definition/value-stream.html

9. Developing Winners Associates. Value stream mapping for health care organizations. Retrieved April 1, 2014, from http://www.dwassoc.com/value-stream-mapping.php

10. Byrne, G., Lubowe, D., & Blitz, A. (2007). Driving operational innovation using Lean Six Sigma. *IBM Global Business Services*. Retrieved from http://www-935.ibm.com/services/us/gbs/bus/pdf/g510-6331-01-leansixsigma.pdf

11. Byrne et al., *op. cit.*

12. Romero, G. (2014, September 22). Lean innovation at Amazon. *Innovation Excellence*. Retrieved from http://www.innovationexcellence.com/blog/2014/09/22/lean-innovation-at-amazon/

13. Williams, S. (2009, September 4). Toyota quality control includes "popeye" and "greensleeves." *The New York Times*. Retrieved from http://wheels.blogs.nytimes.com/2009/09/04/toyota-quality-control-includes-greensleeves-and-popeye/

14. (a) Cutting down in WIP. *Inventory Management Review*. Retrieved June 24, 2013, from http://www.inventorymanagementreview.org/2005/10/index.html. (b) Matsui, M. (2009). *Manufacturing and service enterprise with risks: A stochastic management approach*. New York, NY: Springer.

15. MHIA. Publishing company uses automated carousel pick and return system to reduce labor by 66%. Retrieved from http://www.mhi.org/downloads/industrygroups/ofs/casestudies/remstar2.pdf

16. Womack & Jones, op. cit.

17. (a) Kumar, R. (2012, February 25). Reflections on Wipro's tryst with Lean [Blog post]. *Reflection to Transformation*. Retrieved from https://theachiever2011.wordpress.com/2012/02/21/wipros-tryst-with-lean-toyota-production-system/. (b) Premji, A. (2009, April 14). Tech-agnostic Wipro climbs the value chain. *The Australian Business Review*. Retrieved from http://www.theaustralian.com.au/australian-it/it-business/wipro-climbs-the-value-chain/story-e6frganx-1225700548328

18. Cooper, R., & Slagmulder, R. (1999). *Supply chain development for the lean enterprise*. Portland, OR: Interorganizational Cost Management, Productivity Press.

19. (a) Rovaldi, C. J., & King, P. J. (2015). The effect of an interdisciplinary QI project to reduce OR foot traffic. *AORN Journal*, 101, 666–681. (b) Martin, L. D., Rampersad, S. E., Low. D., & Reed, M. A. (2014). Process improvement in the operating room using Toyota (lean) methods. *Columbian Journal of Anesthesiology*, 42, 220–228. (c) Simons, F. E., Aij, K. H., Widdershoven, G., & Visse, M. (2014). Patient safety in the operating theater: How A3 thinking can help reduce door movements. *International Journal for Quality in Health Care*, 26, 366–371.

20. (a) ASA Research. (n.d.). Wal-Mart sets the standard for supply chain automation. *Accounting Software Research*. Retrieved from http://www.asaresearch.com/ecommerce/supplychain.htm. (b) Nash, K. (2015, May 7), Wal-Mart builds supply chain to meet e-commerce demands. *Wall Street Journal*. Retrieved from http://www.wsj.com/articles/wal-mart-builds-supply-chain-to-meet-e-commerce-demands-1431016708. (c) Bogenrief, M. (2012, January 19). Three things that Kmart needs to fix if it wants to survive. *Business Insider*. Retrieved from http://www.businessinsider.com/is-it-blue-lights-out-for-kmart-2012-1

21. Cook, R. L., Gibson, B., & MacCurdy, D. (2005, March). A lean approach to cross docking. *Supply Chain Management Review*, 54–59.

22. Baudin, M. (2004). *Lean logistics: The nuts and bolts of delivering materials and goods*. New York, NY: Productivity Press.

23. Rivera, L., Wan, H., Chen, F. F., & Lee, W. M. (2007). Beyond partnerships: The power of lean supply chains. In H. Jung, F. F. Chen, & B. Jeong (Eds.), Trends in supply chain design and management (p. 249). London, U.K.: Springer.

24. Harrison, S. (2015, March 17). Why Nissan is betting large on its new $160 million supplier park in Smyrna. *Nashville*

Bizblog. Retrieved from http://www.bizjournals.com/nashville/blog/2015/03/why-nissan-is-betting-large-on-its-new-160m.html

25. Taylor, D. (2004). *Supply chains: A manager's guide*. Boston, MA: Addison-Wesley.

26. Rivera, L., & Chen, F. F. (2006). *Cost-time profiling: Putting monetary pressures into value stream maps*. Paper presented at the annual Industrial Engineering Research Conference, Orlando, FL.

27. Phelps, T., Smith, M., & Hoenes, T. (2004, March/April). Building a lean supply chain. *Supply Chain Management Review*, 42–49.

28. Levy, D. L. (1997, Winter). Lean production in an international supply chain. *Sloan Management Review*, 94–102.

29. (a) Gonzalez, A. (2009, June 22). Crocs: From revolutionary supply chain to almost bankrupt. Retrieved from http://logisticsviewpoints.com/2009/06/22/crocs-from-revolutionary-supply-chain-to-almost-bankrupt/. (b) Holloway, C., Hoyt, D. W., Lee, H., Marks, M., & Silverman, A. (2007). Crocs: Revolutionizing an industry's supply chain model for competitive advantage. *Harvard Business Case GS57A*. Retrieved from http://www.gsb.stanford.edu/faculty-research/case-studies/crocs-revolutionizing-industrys-supply-chain-model-competitive. (c) Hirsch, C., & Anglis, J. (2014, July 24). Financial trouble for maker of Crocs sends shockwaves across the city. *New York Daily News*. Retrieved from http://www.nydailynews.com/life-style/croc-tastrophe-article-1.1879049. (d) Cheng, A. (2015, May 8). Crocs seeks to refashion itself by going back to what it's known for. *MarketWatch*. Retrieved from http://www.marketwatch.com/story/crocs-seeks-to-refashion-itself-by-going-back-to-what-its-known-for-2015-05-08

30. Langenwalter, G. (2006). "Life" is our ultimate customer: From lean to sustainability. *Target*, 22(1), 1–15

31. Kitchell, S. (2014, January 21). Lean manufacturing yields "green" results. *Environmental Leader*. Retrieved from http://www.environmentalleader.com/2014/01/21/lean-manufacturing-yields-green-results/#ixzz3KhC8DCPP

32. (a) McInnis, I. (2008). A787 supply chain nightmare. *Aerospace-Technology.com*. Retrieved from http://www.aerospace-technology.com/features/feature1690/. (b) Sanders, P., & Michaels, D. (2009). Boeing looks beyond Dreamliner's first flight. *Wall Street Journal*, B1–B2. (c) Gonzalez, A. (2009, July 13). Boeing's 787 Dreamliner: Supply chain lessons and questions. *Logistics Viewpoints*. Retrieved from http://logisticsviewpoints.

com/2009/07/13/boeings-787-dreamliner-supply-chain-lessons-and-questions/

33. (a) Hirsch, S. (2005). E-management – suppliers become closer partners. *International Trade Forum*. Retrieved from https://www.questia.com/magazine/1P3-951868291/e-management-suppliers-become-closer-partners. (b) Atkinson, W. (2006). J.C. Penney: Pioneer of supply chain efficiency. *Apparel Magazine*, 47(8), 14. Retrieved from http://connection.ebscohost.com/c/articles/20805773/j-c-penney-pioneer-supply-chain-efficiency. (c) Brown, T., Crouch, K., Findeisen, B., Habib, T., & Petry, B. (2014). Tal Apparel Limited: Stepping up the value chain. *Prezi*. Retrieved from https://prezi.com/arxia0l9njir/tal-apparel-limited-stepping-up-the-value-chain/

Chapter 15

1. Lee, T. (2013, June 22). To boost digital sales, Best Buy turns to its stores. *Star Tribune*. Retrieved from http://www.startribune.com/business/212549391.html?page=all&prepage=1&c=y#continue

2. Trendall, S. (2011, June 1). Acer takes $150m hit for mismanaging EMEA inventory. *CRN*. Retrieved from http://www.channelweb.co.uk/crn-uk/news/2075425/acer-takes-usd150m-hit-mismanaging-emea-inventory

3. Barry, J. (n.d.). Using initial customer order fill rate to measure customer service. *F. Curtis Barry & Company*. Retrieved from http://www.fcbco.com/blog/bid/156292/Using-Initial-Customer-Order-Fill-Rate-to-Measure-Customer-Service

4. Commonwealth Foundation. (2011, August 1). AG audit finds rampant PLCB waste and mismanagement. Retrieved from http://www.commonwealthfoundation.org/research/detail/ag-audit-finds-rampant-plcb-waste-and-mismanagement

5. (a) Lu, C. (2014, April 23). IKEA's inventory management strategy: how does IKEA do it? *Trade Gecko*. Retrieved from http://www.tradegecko.com/blog/ikeas-inventory-management-strategy-ikea. (b) *Forbes*. (2016, May). The world's most powerful brands. Retrieved from http://www.forbes.com/companies/ikea/

6. (a) Hamlett, K. (n.d.) Types of inventory management systems. *Demand Media*. Retrieved from http://smallbusiness.chron.com/types-inventory-management-systems-2195.html. (b) *RFID Journal* website. (n.d.). Frequently asked questions page. Retrieved from http://www.rfidjournal.com/site/faqs#Anchor-53283

7. Aeppel, T. (2010, January 27). "Bullwhip" hits firms as growth snaps back. *Wall Street Journal*. Retrieved from http://www.wsj.com/articles/SB100014240 52748704509704575019392199 662672

8. Lee, H. L., Padmanabhan, V., & Whang, S., (1997, April 15). The bullwhip effect in supply chains. *Sloan Management Review*, *38*(3). Retrieved from http://sloanreview.mit.edu/article/the-bullwhip-effect-in-supply-chains/

9. Lee et al., *op. cit.*

10. Mathers, J. (2012, April 3). Postponement: A logistics sustainability strategy worth NOT putting off. *Environmental Defense Fund*. Retrieved from http://business.edf.org/blog/2012/04/03/postponement-a-logistics-sustainability-strategy-worth-not-putting-off/#sthash.bKFGPxz9.dpuf

11. Frahm, S. (2003, April 3). Taming the bullwhip effect. *The SCRC Articles Library*. Retrieved from http://scm.ncsu.edu/scm-articles/article/taming-the-bullwhip-effect

12. Winston, A. (2011, August 8). Excess inventory wastes carbon and energy, not just money. *Harvard Business Review Post*. Retrieved from http://blogs.hbr.org/winston/2011/08/excess-inventory-wastes-carbon.html?utm_source=feedburner&utm_medium=feed&utm_campaign=Feed%3A+harvardbusiness+%28HBR.org%29

13. Conti, A. (2013, July 9). The scoop on lean inventory management techniques. *Clients First Business Solutions*. Retrieved from http://blog.clientsfirst-ax.com/blog-1/bid/314816/The-Scoop-on-Lean-Inventory-Management-Techniques

14. Jacowski, T. (2009, July 7). Lean six sigma and inventory management. *Ezine Articles*. Retrieved from http://ezinearticles.com/?Lean-Six-Sigma-and-Inventory-Management&id=2575958

15. (a) Kitchell, S. (2014, January 21). Lean manufacturing yields "green" results. *Environmental Leader*. Retrieved from http://www.environmentalleader.com/2014/01/21/lean-manufacturing-yields-green-results/. (b) Stewart, D. (2015, November 28). The lean, mean, Amazon machine. *Harvard Business School*. Retrieved from https://rctom.hbs.org/submission/the-lean-mean-amazon-machine/

16. Gerdes, J. (2012, February 24). How Nike, Wal-Mart and Ikea save money and slash carbon by shipping smarter. *Forbes*. Retrieved from http://www.forbes.com/sites/justingerdes/2012/02/24/how-nike-wal-mart-and-ikea-are-saving-money-and-slashing-carbon-by-shipping-smarter/

17. The Supply Chain Resource Cooperative. (2012, Spring).

Key sustainability issues in the electronics industry: Sustainability industry report. *The SCRC Articles Library*. Retrieved from https://scm.ncsu.edu/scm-articles/article/key-sustainability-issues-in-the-electronics-industry-sustainability-indust

18. Jackson, A. J. (2010, October 26). Ethical issues in inventory management. *Ezine Articles*. Retrieved from http://ezinearticles.com/?Ethical-Issues-In-Inventory-Management&id=5269949

19. (a) Gilpin, K. N. (2002, June 22). Ex-Rite Aid officials face U.S. charges of financial fraud. *The New York Times*. Retrieved from http://www.nytimes.com/2002/06/22/business/ex-rite-aid-officials-face-us-charges-of-financial-fraud.html. (b) Cassin, R. L. (2015, January 12). Former Rite-Aid exec and businessman admit fraud and kickbacks [Blog post]. *The FCPA Blog*. Retrieved from http://www.fcpablog.com/blog/2015/1/12/former-rite-aid-exec-and-businessman-admit-fraud-and-kickbac.html

20. Blinick, N. (2005, August 24). Global inventory management – from theory to reality/driving value from the global supply chain. Retrieved from http://globalsupplychainsolution.blogspot.com/2005/08/global-inventory-management-from.html

21. Carabelli, C. (n.d.). What types of inventory does the service industry use? *Houston Chronicle*. Retrieved from http://smallbusiness.chron.com/types-inventory-service-industry-use-33758.html

22. Neuman, S. (2013, August 3). FDA: Infected lettuce at U.S. restaurants traced to Mexico. *The Two-Way*. Retrieved from http://www.npr.org/blogs/thetwo-way/2013/08/03/208567639/fda-infected-lettuce-at-u-s-restaurants-traced-to-mexico

23. (a) Gartenstein, D. (n.d.). The inventory methods for the food industry. *eHow*. Retrieved from http://www.ehow.com/info_8095550_inventory-methods-food-industry.html#ixzz2cu7sN3DL. (b) PRWeb. (2013, August 20). Two dominant players in the hospitality industry have partnered up. Retrieved from http://bevchek.com/_docs/PressRelease_Sculpture_Bevchek.pdf

24. Gomez, V. (2013, August 15). Tuesday Morning exists digital arena. *Retailing Today*. Retrieved from http://www.retailingtoday.com/article/tuesday-morning-exits-digital-arena

25. Sisco, D. (2013, August 12). What's changing consumers' expectations? *Retailing Today*. Retrieved from http://www.retailingtoday.com/article/what%E2%80%99s-changing-consumers%E2%80%99-expectations

Chapter 16

1. (a) Algar, J. (2015, January 2). Walgreens Buys Alliance Boots, Becomes Global Pharmacy. *Tech Times*. Retrieved from http://www.techtimes.com/articles/24060/20150102/walgreens-buys-alliance-boots-becomes-global-pharmacy.htm#sthash.r4YF6K2b.dpuf. (b) Russolillo, S. (2016, April 4). Why Walgreens hasn't escaped its rut. *Wall Street Journal*. Retrieved from http://www.wsj.com/articles/why-walgreens-hasnt-escaped-its-rut-1459794846. (c) Ferrari, S. (2009, September 30). The strategic importance of optimized inventory management. *Supply Chain Matters*. Retrieved from http://www.theferrarigroup.com/supply-chain-matters/2009/09/30/the-strategic-importance-of-optimized-inventory-management/

2. (a) Shaw, H. (2015, January 15). Target Corp to exit Canada after racking up billions in losses. *Financial Post*. Retrieved from http://business.financialpost.com/news/retail-marketing/target-corp-calls-it-quits-in-canada-plans-fair-and-orderly-exit. (b) Staff. (2015). Inventory management disasters: Target Canada. *Clear Spider*. Retrieved from http://www.clearspider.com/inventory-management-disasters-target-canada/#.VzyG8PmDFBc

3. Tanel, T. (2012, June 20). How to make EOQ relevant again. *Supply Demand Chain Executive*. Retrieved from http://www.sdcexec.com/article/10732246/how-to-make-eoq-relevant-again

4. (a) Dawson, K. (2011, April 25). Wal-Mart lost billions by listening to customers. *The CMO Site*. Retrieved from http://www.thecmosite.com/author.asp?section_id=1200&doc_id=205973. (b) Gogoi, P. (2010, March 31). Wal-Mart's Project Impact craters sales, but the retailer persists. *Daily Finance*. Retrieved from http://www.dailyfinance.com/2010/03/31/walmarts-project-impact-leaves-a-crater-in-sales-but-the-ret/

Chapter 17

1. (a) Matarese, J. (2013, October 28). Black Friday 2013: Who's to blame for early start time? *ABC15*. Retrieved from http://www.abc15.com/dpp/news/national/black-friday-2013-whos-to-blame-for-early-start-time. (b) Ellis, B. (2013, November 4). Kmart to open at 6 a.m. on Thanksgiving Day. *CNN Money*. Retrieved from http://money.cnn.com/2013/11/04/pf/kmart-black-friday/index.html. (c) Tuttle, B. (2013, October 19). Hey, Thanksgiving shoppers: Macy's isn't the only one to blame for ruining the holidays. *Time*. Retrieved from http://business.

time.com/2013/10/19/hey-thanksgiving-shoppers-macys-isnt-the-only-one-to-blame-for-ruining-the-holiday/

2. APICS Dictionary. *APICS*. Retrieved from http://www.apics.org/dictionary/dictionary-information?ID=3577.

3. Hitachi Consulting. (2007). Sales and operations planning - the basics: Choosing the optimal strategy for your business. *Scribd*. https://www.scribd.com/document/185321532/WP-SalesOperationsPlanning.

4. Wells, A. M., & Schorr, J. (2009, January). Sales and operations planning: The key to continuous demand satisfaction. *SAP America and Oliver Wight Americas*. Retrieved from http://fm.sap.com/pdf/jan09/Sales_and_Operations_Planning.pdf.

5. Hawkes, H., Malhotra, A., & Mueller, C. (2009, September 16). A fresh look at sales and operations planning. *Strategy&*. Retrieved from http://www.strategyand.pwc.com/reports/fresh-look-sales-operations-planning.

6. Dougherty, J. R. (2000). Getting started with sales and operations planning. *APICS*.

7. Dougherty, J. R. (2000). *op. cit.*

8. Wells, A. M., & Schorr, J. (2009). *op. cit.*

9. Wells, A. M., & Schorr, J. (2009). *op. cit.*

10. Wells, A. M., & Schorr, J. (2009). *op. cit.*

11. Teaman, R. S&OP data management: Critical to a successful implementation. *Oliver Wight White Paper Series*. Retrieved from hhttps://www.oliverwight-americas.com/white-papers-and-articles.

12. (a) Fleischhacker, A. J., & Zhao, Y. (2011). Planning for demand failure: A dynamic lot size model for clinical trial supply chains. *European Journal of Operational Research*, 211:496–506. (b) DiMasi, J. A., Hansen, R. W., & Grabowski, H. G. (2003). The price of innovation: New estimates of drug development costs. *Journal of Health Economics*, 22:151–185.

13. Hitachi Consulting. (2007). *op. cit.*

14. Hitachi Consulting. (2007). *op. cit.*

15. Hitachi Consulting. (2007). *op. cit.*

16. Bradley, J. The impact of advertising & sales promotion in revenue. *Chron*. Retrieved from http://smallbusiness.chron.com/impact-advertising-sales-promotion-revenue-59840.html.

17. Bowman, E. H. (1963). Consistency and optimality in managerial decision making. *Management Science*, 9:310–321.

18. Partida, B. (2013, April 18). The "S" in S&OP can stand for supply chain, too. *IndustryWeek*. Retrieved from http://www.industryweek.com/planning-amp-forecasting/s-sop-can-stand-supply-chain-too.

19. Cecere, L. (2012, May 22). S&OP planning improves supply chain

agility. *Supply Chain Insights*. Retrieved from http://www .slideshare.net/loracecere/ sop-planning-improves-supply-chain-agility.

20. Lewis, N., & MacLean, J. (2009, March). Global sales and operations planning. *Capgemini*. Retrieved from http://www .capgemini.com/sites/default/ files/resource/pdf/tl_Global_ Sales_and_Operations_Planning .pdf.

21. Bursa, K. (2012, July 17). The challenges of global S&OP. *The European Business Review*. Retrieved from http://www .europeanbusinessreview.com/ the-challenges-of-global-sop/.

22. Lewis, N., & MacLean, J. (2009, March). op. cit.

23. Lewis, N., & MacLean, J. (2009, March). op. cit.

24. Lewis, N., & MacLean, J. (2009, March). op. cit.

25. Lewis, N., & MacLean, J. (2009, March). op. cit.

26. Lewis, N., & MacLean, J. (2009, March). op. cit.

27. Hung, R. (1997). Annualized hours and aggregate planning. *Production and Inventory Management Journal, 38*(4).

28. Sustainable Manufacturing Consulting. (2009). op. cit.

29. Sustainable Manufacturing Consulting. (2009). op. cit.

30. Murray, S. (2012, November 11). Cement: Matching up companies is a move to a world without waste. *Financial Times*. Retrieved from http://www. ft.com/intl/cms/s/0/1b4c777c-22a3-11e2-8edf-00144feabdc0 .html#axzz2kjUWxFeY.

31. (a) Forbes, T. (2013, November 18). Glitches aside, Sony's PS4 enjoys a winning launch. *Marketing Daily Top of the News*. Retrieved from http://www. mediapost.com/publications/ article/213651/glitches-aside-sonys-ps4-enjoys-a-winning-launch.html?edition=66982. (b) Wingfield, N. (2013, November 17). PlayStation 4 starts strong despite reports of defects. *New York Times Bits*. Retrieved from http://bits.blogs.nytimes. com/2013/11/17/playstation-4-starts-strong-despite-reports-of-defects/?_r=0. (c) Sherr, I. (2013, November 17). Sony's PlayStation 4 tops one million units in first day. Wall Street Journal Digits. Retrieved from http://blogs.wsj .com/digits/2013/11/17/sonys-playstation-4-tops-one-million-units-in-first-day/. (d) Hussain, T. (2016, May 24). Sony forecasts PS4 sales will reach 60 million by April 2017. *Gamespot*. Retrieved from http://www. gamespot.com/articles/sony-forecasts-ps4-sales-will-reach-60-million-by-/1100-6440102/

Chapter 18

1. (a) Royal Academy of Engineering. (2014, June 4). Innovation in aerospace. Retrieved from http://www.

raeng.org.uk/publications/ reports/innovation-in-aerospace. (b) Ferrari, B. (2013, July 1). Rolls-Royce continues to address extraordinary supply chain business and service life cycle management challenges. Retrieved from http://www. theferrarigroup.com/supply-chain-matters/2013/07/01/rolls-royce-continues-to-address-extrordinary-supply-chain-business-and-service-lifecycle-management-challenges/

2. APICS. (2013). *APICS dictionary*. 14th ed.

3. APICS. (2016). *APICS*. Retrieved from http://www.apics.org

4. (a) Ho, J. C., & Chang Y. L. (2001). Integrated MRP and JIT framework. *Computers & Industrial Engineering. 41*:173–185. (b) Jha, V. (2012). MRP-JIT integrated production system. *International Journal of Engineering Research and Applications. 2*(4):2377–2387.

5. Ho, J. C., & Chang Y. L. (2001) *op. cit.*

6. Ho, J. C., & Chang Y. L. (2001) *op. cit.*

7. Ho, J. C., & Chang Y. L. (2001) *op. cit.*

8. Cox, J. F., & Jesse Jr., R. R. (1981). An application of material requirements planning to higher education. *Decision Sciences. 12*(2):240–260.

9. Heksever, C., & Render, B. (2013). *Service management – An integrated approach to supply chain management and operations*. Upper Saddle River, NJ: Pearson Education. pp. 448–449.

10. (a) Ptak, C., & Smith, C. (2011, June 21). How traditional MRP takes a toll on sustainability. *Sustainable Plant*. Retrieved from http://www. sustainableplant.com/2011/06/ how-traditional-mrp-takes-a-toll-on-sustainability/. (b) Sarkis, J. (2001). Manufacturing's role in corporate environmental sustainability – Concerns for the new millennium. *International Journal of Operations & Production Management. 21*(5/6):666–686. (c) Hammarstrom, P. (2011, April 29). ERP and environmental footprint management for manufacturers. *Sustainable Plant*. Retrieved from http:// www.sustainableplant. com/2011/04/erp-and-environmental-footprint-management-for-manufacturers/

Chapter 18 Supplement

1. (a) Michel, R. (2006, March 1). Innovation accelerated. *Manufacturing Business Technology*. Retrieved from https://www.highbeam.com/ doc/1G1-143241635.html. (b) Gray, R. (2015, January 22). Gold industry looks to hit more green in '15. *Fox Business*. Retrieved from http://www.foxbusiness.

com/features/2015/01/22/golf-industry-looks-to-hit-more-green-in-15.html

2. St. John, R. E. (1998). Material and capacity requirements planning – Certification review course. Participant workbook. *Revision 4.1*. pp. 7–12.

3. Taylor, E. MRP vs. MRP II. *Chron*. Retrieved from http:// smallbusiness.chron.com/mrp-vs-mrpii-15365.html.

4. Saylor. (2011). Manufacturing resource planning. *Saylor.org*. Retrieved from http://www .saylor.org/site/wp-content/ uploads/2011/06/Manufacturing-resource-planning.pdf.

5. Saylor. (2011). *op. cit.*

6. (a) Weiss, I. (2016, January 1). HER vs. EMR. *Practice Fusion*. Retrieved from http://www. practicefusion.com/blog/ehr-vs-emr/. (b) Jamoom, E., Beatty, P., Bercovitz, A., et al. (2012). *Physician adoption of electronic health record systems: United States, 2011*. NCHS data brief, no 98. Hyattsville, MD: National Center for Health Statistics.

7. ERP Pandit. Basic ERP features. *ERP Pandit*. Retrieved from http://erppandit.com/erp-features.html.

8. Columbus, L. (2014, May 12). Gartner's ERP market share update shows the future of cloud ERP is now. *Forbes*. Retrieved from http:// www.forbes.com/sites/ louiscolumbus/2014/05/12/ gartners-erp-market-share-update-shows-the-future-of-cloud-erp-is-now/.

9. St. John, R. E. (1998). *op. cit.*

10. (a) Bosari, J. (2012, October 4). Real costs of choosing the wrong software vendor. *Forbes*. Retrieved from http:// www.forbes.com/sites/ moneywisewomen/2012/10/04/ real-costs-of-choosing-the-wrong-software-vendor/. (b) Kanaracus, C. (2010, November 5). ERP woes blamed for lumber company's bad quarter. *PC World*. Retrieved from http://www.pcworld.com/ article/209886/article.html. (c) Kanaracus, C. (2013, January 11). Marin County settles legal claims against Deloitte, SAP over software project. *Computerworld*. Retrieved from http://www.computerworld.com/ article/2494092/government-it/ marin-county-settles-legal-claims-against-deloitte-sap-over-software-project.html

11. Kelly, P. (2011, September 14). Microsoft Dynamics GP for supply chain? *Manufacturing Resource Partners*. Retrieved from http://www.mrpconsulting .com/blog/mrp-news/ ERPforSupplyChain.html.

12. Laksham, N. (2014, June 6). MRP/ERP systems failing supply chain planners. *Ultriva*. Retrieved from http://web. ultriva.com/ultriva-blog/ bid/101750/MRP-ERP-Systems-Failing-Supply-Chain-Planners.

13. Value Stream Guru. Using distribution requirements

planning. Retrieved from http://www.valuestreamguru. com/?p=329.

14. (a) Sommer, B. (2009, October 22). Sustainability: Hard for business, harder for ERP vendors. *ZDNet*. Retrieved from http://www.zdnet.com/ article/sustainability-hard-for-business-harder-for-erp-vendors/. (b) Madden, N. (2009, October 21). In manufacturing, sustainability is integrated with ERP. *TechTarget*. Retrieved from http://searchmanufacturingerp. techtarget.com/news/1372000/ In-manufacturing-sustainability-is-integrated-with-ERP. (c) Frost, R. (2015, April 21). The role of ERP in the journey toward a sustainable food supply chain. *Supply and Demand Chain Executive*. Retrieved from http://www .sdcexec.com/blog/12067086/ the-role-of-erp-in-the-journey-toward-a-sustainable-food-supply-chain. (d) Kandananond, K. (2014). A roadmap to green supply chain system through enterprise resource planning (ERP) implementation. *Procedia Engineering. 69*:377–382.

15. Bonneau, L. (2013, January 1). The recipe for standardized training at General Mills. *SAP Insider*. Retrieved from http:// sapinsider.wispubs.com/Assets/ Case-Studies/2013/January/ The-Recipe-For-Standardized-Training-At-General-Mills.

Chapter 19

1. (a) Barnes, B. (2010, December 27). Disney tackles major theme park problem: Lines. *The New York Times*. Retrieved from http:// www.nytimes.com/2010/12/28/ business/media/28disney. html?src=me&ref=business&_ r=0. (b) Kubersky, S. (2014, March 25). The wins and fails of Disney's new FastPass+. *Orlando Weekly*. Retrieved from http://www.orlandoweekly. com/orlando/the-wins-and-fails-of-disneys-new-fastpass/ Content?oid=2241047

2. Goldratt, E. (1989). *The general theory of constraints*. New Haven, CT: Avraham Y. Institute.

3. Umble, M., Umble, E., & Murakami, S. (2006). Implementing theory of constraints in a traditional Japanese manufacturing environment: The case of Hitachi Tool Engineering. *International Journal of Production Research, 44*, 1863–1880.

4. Rawe, H. (2015, August 3). SAP workforce management. *SAP Community Network*. Retrieved from http://wiki.scn.sap .com/wiki/display/Retail/ SAP+Workforce+Management

5. Manoj, U. V., Gupta, J. N. D., & Gupta, S. K. (2008). Supply Chain scheduling – just in time environments. *Annals of Operations Research, 161*, 53–86.

6. Hall, N. G., & Potts, C. N. (2000). *Supply chain scheduling: Batching and delivery.* Working Paper. Columbus, OH: Fischer College of Business, The Ohio State University.
7. Zhang, R., Chiong, R., Michalewicz, Z., & Chang, P.-C. (2015). Sustainable Scheduling of manufacturing and transportation systems. *European Journal of Operational Research, 248*(3). Retrieved from https://www.researchgate .net/publication/282769372_ Sustainable_Scheduling_ of_Manufacturing_and_ Transportation_Systems

Module A

1. Perez, D. (n.d.). How do restaurants use linear programming for menu planning? *Houston Chronicle.* Retrieved from http:// smallbusiness.chron.com/ restaurants-use-linear- programming-menu- planning-37132.html

Module B

1. Ramsey, M. (2014, April 2). Does Tesla really need a $5 billion battery? *Wall Street Journal*, B1–B2.

Module C

1. Stone, A. (2012, August 18). Why waiting is torture. *The New York Times Sunday Review.* Received from http://www .nytimes.com/2012/08/19/ opinion/sunday/why-waiting-in- line-is-torture.html?_r=0
2. Sundarapandian, V. (2009). Queueing theory. In *Probability, statistics and queueing theory* (ch. 7). New Delhi, India: PHI Learning.
3. Schlechter, K. (2009, March 2). Hershey Medical Center to open redesigned emergency room. *The Patriot-News.*
4. Peck, L. G., & Hazelwood, R. N. (1958). *Finite queuing tables.* New York: Wiley.
5. Quoted in Maister, D. (1985). The psychology of waiting lines. Retrieved from http:// davidmaister.com/articles/the- psychology-of-waiting-lines/
6. Maister, *op. cit.*

Module D

1. Saker Solutions. (n.d.). Simulation in the oil and gas sector. Retrieved from http://www.sakersolutions. com/media/wp/wp008.html
2. Banks, J., Carson, J., Nelson, B., & Nicol, D. (2001). *Discrete- event system simulation.* Upper Saddle River, NJ: Prentice Hall.

3. Maria, *op. cit.*
4. Microsoft. (n.d.). Introduction to Monte Carlo simulation. Retrieved from https://support. office.com/en-ca/article/ introduction-to-monte-carlo- simulation-64c0ba99-752a-4fa8- bbd3-4450d8db16f1

Module E

1. (a) Anthes, G. (2001, July 2). The learning curve. *Computerworld.* Retrieved from http:// www.computerworld.com/ article/2583163/the-learning- curve.html. (b) AirInsight.com. (2014, November 7). Boeing and the 787 learning curve. Retrieved from http://airinsight. com/2014/11/07/boeing-787- learning-curve/#.VVns5_IVhBd. (c) Polek, G. (2015, June 11). After record ramp-up, Boeing fine-tunes 787 production. *AINonline.* Retrieved from http:// www.ainonline.com/aviation- news/air-transport/2015-06-11/ after-record-ramp-boeing-fine- tunes-787-production
2. (a) Amor, J. P., & Teplitz, C. J. (1998). An efficient approximation for project composite learning curves. *Project Management Journal, 29,* 28–42. (b) Badiru, A. B. (1995). Incorporating learning curve effects into critical resource diagramming. *Project Management Journal, 26,* 38–46.

(c) Camm, J. D., Evans, J. R., & Womer, N. K. (1987). The unit learning curve approximation of total cost. *Computers in Industrial Engineering, 12,* 205–213. (d) Fields, M. A. (1991). Effect of the learning curve on the capital budgeting process. *Managerial Finance, 17*(2–3), 29–41. (e) Teplitz, C. J., & Amor, J. P. (1993). Improving CPM's accuracy using learning curves. *Project Management Journal, 24*(4), 15–19.
3. Wright, T. P. (1936). Factors affecting the cost of airplanes. *Journal of Aeronautical Sciences, 3*(4), 122–128.

Module F

1. Shaller Consulting. (2006). *Consumers in health care: Creating decision-support tools that work.* Prepared for California HealthCare Foundation. Retrieved from http://www.chcf.org/~/media/ MEDIA%20LIBRARY%20 Files/PDF/PDF%20C/PDF%20 CreatingDecisionSupportTools. pdf
2. Buckley, J., & Dudley, T. J. (1999). How Gerber used a decision tree in strategic decision-making. *Graziadio Business Review, 2*(3). Retrieved from http://gbr .pepperdine.edu/2010/08/how- gerber-used-a-decision-tree-in- strategic-decision-making/

Note: This index contains Company Names such as, "YouTube, LLC (San Bruno, CA)," authors cited, and names of people discussed such as, Henry Ford.